MAPPING MEANINGS

SINICA LEIDENSIA

EDITED BY

W.L. IDEMA

IN COOPERATION WITH

P.K. BOL • B.J. TER HAAR • D.R. KNECHTGES
E.S. RAWSKI • E. ZÜRCHER • H.T. ZURNDORFER

VOLUME LXIV

MAPPING MEANINGS

*The Field of New Learning
in Late Qing China*

EDITED BY

MICHAEL LACKNER

AND

NATASCHA VITTINGHOFF

BRILL
LEIDEN · BOSTON
2004

Illustration on the cover: 'mappingMEANINGS' (Ancient Chinese seal style), by Daniel Niedenführ 2004.

This book is printed on acid-free paper.

Library of Congress Cataloging-in-Publication Data

International Conference "Translating Western Knowledge into late Imperial China" (1999 : Göttingen University)
 Mapping meanings : the field of new learning in late Qing China / edited by Michael Lackner and Natascha Vittinghoff.
   p. cm. — (Sinica Leidensia, ISSN 0169-9563 ; vol. 64)
 Collection of contributions to the international conference "Translating Western Knowledge into late Imperial China," held at the … University of Gottingen University in Dec. 1999.
 Includes bibliographical references and index.
 ISBN 90-04-13919-2
 1. China—Civilization—1644-1912—Western influences. 2. Learning and scholarship—China. I. Title: Field of new learning in late Qing China. II. Lackner, Michael. III. Vittinghoff, Natascha. IV. Title. V. Series.

DS754.14.I57 1999
951'.033—dc22

2004046526

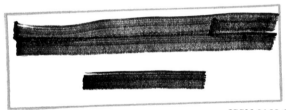

ISSN 0169-9563
ISBN 90 04 13919 2

PRINTED IN THE NETHERLANDS

CONTENTS

THE POLITICS OF GLOBAL KNOWLEDGE

DISCOURSIVE INTERFACES: LANGUAGE AND MEDIA

KNOWLEDGE BETWEEN HEART AND MIND

ACKNOWLEDGEMENTS

This volume contains a selection of papers presented at the international conference "Translating Western Knowledge into Late Imperial China", hosted by the East Asian Department of Göttingen University in December 1999 as part of the of research project *Wissenschaftssprache Chinesisch* (*WSC*) or *Studies in the Formation of Modern Chinese Terminologies* (1996-2000). Our first and special thanks go to the Volkswagen foundation, which generously sponsored this unusually large-scale conference but also supported the entire project during its years of existence through grants and various forms of financial assistance. Hiltgund Jehle, the programme director, has been of invaluable help in making possible the multifarious activities in this project, and we wish to express our special gratitude for her constant support in this endeavour.

The volume itself could, of course, not have been realized without the support of the participants of the conference, to whom we owe profound thanks for their patience and willingness to repeatedly reply to our pestering questions without jumping from board of this ship, which put out to sea much slower than originally intended. Our thanks also go to those participants whose papers have, for one reason or another, not been included into this volume or who have served as discussants and thus all have greatly enhanced the general intellectual spirit of the conference and this volume. These include Chow Kaiwing, Fang Weigui, Han Qi, Christoph Harbsmeier, Lai Chi-kong, Li Guilian, Lydia Liu, Federico Masini, Barbara Mittler, Shen Guowei, Su Xiaoqin, Uchida Keiichi, Wang Yangzong, Catherine Yeh, Xu Wenkan, Zhang Baichun, Zhou Zhenhe and Zou Zhenhuan.

Special thanks are also due to our editors at Brill, Albert Hoffstädt and Patricia Radder, who made the final preparation of this volume a delightful task.

Finally, we wish to acknowledge the invaluable help provided by friends and colleagues, who with their technical expertise and professional skills contributed to the final implementation of the manuscript. Silke Geffcken and Kirsten Pöhlker, provided indispensable support in formatting and configuring the different text versions into coherent manuscript files. We are grateful also to Matthias Niedenführ who stepped in in the last moment to complete the final crc version with dedication and a keen eye. Michael Schimmelpfennig read parts of the manuscript and provided insightful comments. Jane Chen-hsiu Chen was offered great assistance in our translations of the Chinese articles. Paul Bowman was willing to take over the nearly unachievable task of polishing the English of many contributions by non-native speakers.

Last, but not least, our particular thanks go to Iwo Amelung and Joachim Kurtz, who from the beginning were at hand whenever their technical, scholarly and emotional support was in need. All remaining mistakes, omissions and incongruences are, by all means, the sole responsibility of the editors.

Michael Lackner, Natascha Vittinghoff
Göttingen, April 2003

CONTRIBUTORS

Viviane Alleton, Centre d'études sur la Chine moderne et contemporaine, EHESS, Paris.

Iwo Amelung, European Center for Chinese Studies at Peking University, Universität Tübingen.

Arakawa Kiyohide 荒川清秀, Aichi University.

Wolfgang Behr, Fakultät für Ostasienwissenschaften, Ruhr Universität Bochum.

Benjamin Elman, East Asian Studies Department, Princeton University.

Gerlinde Gild, Ostasiatisches Seminar, Universität Göttingen.

Helena Heroldová, Department of East Asian Studies, Charles University Prague.

Andrea Janku, Sinologisches Seminar, Universität Heidelberg.

Elisabeth Kaske, Sinologisches Seminar, Universität Heidelberg.

Wolfgang Kubin, Seminar für Sinologie, Universität Bonn.

Joachim Kurtz, Department of Russian and East Asian Languages and Cultures, Emory University.

Michael Lackner, Institut für Außereuropäische Sprachen und Kulturen, Universität Erlangen-Nürnberg.

Michael C. Lazich, Department of History, Buffalo State College.

Wolfgang Lippert, Institut für Außereuropäische Sprachen und Kulturen, Universität Erlangen-Nürnberg.

Ma Jun 馬軍, Institute of History, Shanghai Academy of Social Sciences.

Angelika C. Messner, Institut für Sinologie, Universität Kiel.

Lauren Pfister, Department of Religion and Philosophy, Hong Kong Baptist University.

Yvonne Schulz Zinda, Ostasiatisches Seminar, Universität Göttingen.

Sarah E. Stevens, Indiana University, Bloomington.

Rune Svarverud, Institutt for østeuropeiske og orientalske studier, Universitetet i Oslo.

Su Rongyu 蘇榮譽, Institute for History of Natural Science, Chinese Academy of Science, Beijing.

Benjamin K. T'sou 鄒嘉彥, Language Information Sciences Research Centre, City University of Hong Kong.

Natascha Vittinghoff, Ostasiatisches Seminar, Universität Frankfurt.

Rudolf G. Wagner, Sinologisches Seminar, Universität Heidelberg.

Lawrence Wang-chi Wong 王宏志, Department of Translation, Chinese University of Hong Kong.

Timothy Man-kong Wong 黃文江, Department of History, Hong Kong Baptist University.

MICHAEL LACKNER

PREFACE

In his collection of notes and anecdotes, the Northern Song *homme de lettres* Su Shi 蘇軾 (1037–1101) relates the story of a scholar who, when for the first time visiting an official treasury, does not recognize the money which is being stored there. Asked for the reason of this incapability, he replies: "I surely knew it was money, but I just wondered why it wasn't wrapped up in paper."[1] The bookworm's non-recognition (he was only familiar with one appearance of money) is an excellent metaphor for the attitude towards Western knowledge of the overwhelming majority of Chinese literati and the emerging group of intellectuals during the second half of the nineteenth century. The imported knowledge, whose designation shifted within a few decades from "foreign knowledge" to "Western knowledge" and, finally, to "new knowledge", was surely recognizable as something dramatically different from the age-old Chinese traditions of both the contents and organization of knowledge. However, according to the Chinese *élite's* standards of perception, it could only be accepted when "wrapped up in paper." Even in the transition from reading books to studying the Book of Nature, words written on paper remained the predominant instrument. Consequently, the study of what had been written by both Chinese and Western writers about natural phenomena was often given priority over the observation of these phenomena themselves. In the same way, late Qing poets scarcely looked at the clouds over a lake, but rather studied what poets from more creative periods had written about such clouds. In this bookish universe, even the somewhat marginal attempts to prove that the Chinese canonical and classical writings had already contained the essentials of the new knowledge (and thus showing that one dealt only with an allegedly new phenomenon), were deeply rooted in the insurmountable faith in words—words whose interpretation drew heavily on more or less haphazard coincidences between ancient texts and newly coined terms that had often been created alongside the ancient terminology, thus enhancing all kinds of linguistic fetishism.

---

[1] Su Shi 蘇軾 . 1983. *Dongpo zhilin* 東坡志林 (Recollections of [Su] Dongpo), ch. 3, no. 32, Shanghai: Huadong shifan daxue, p. 108.

The intellectualistic reluctance to open one's eyes for observation was joined by an almost total abstention from practical performance in technological matters. When Zhang Zhidong 張之洞 (1837–1909), taking up older ideas about the difference between Chinese and Western knowledge, popularized the infamous formula of "Chinese knowledge as the core, Western knowledge for use" in 1898, he pointed to the performative dimension of Western knowledge, and it is significant that he cited railways as the prime example. However, people versed in performative skills did not enjoy an elevated status in late nineteenth-century China. The idea that *ingenium* or *génie* is the root of the word 'engineer', and that it was this root which conferred dignity upon the profession and made a person member of the *élite* in the West, was simply inconceivable for both scholars and intellectuals of the time. Technological performance was left to petty specialists, or at best to second-rate intellectuals (in other words, to people who could be used to produce useful things), whereas the men who saw their main task in preserving the core of Chinese knowledge contended themselves with condescendingly guiding and supervising the needed practical efforts. The literati continued to *read* and write about waht they read. Western technology may have seemed more cunning, still it was seen to belong to the same kind of second-rate business. Even the despised compradore, or the badly paid translator ("linguist") still dealt with words and figures, and were therefore more easily compatible with the standards of elitist behavior than any technician or craftsman. Much of the tragedy of Chinese modernization well into the late twentieth century can be explained by this inveterate aversion towards manual labor: neither the Westernizing "science" debates and campaigns of the Republic nor the subsequent Sovietization, where the image of soot-blackened workers and optimistic engineers was to replace the traditional self-perception of the *élite*, had any lasting success. The establishment of an academic discipline called "History of Chinese Science and Technology" was meant to remedy a national complex of inferiority, but it grew roots in the public conscience only in the last decade of the twentieth century. Even the "Great Leap Forward", destined to transform the entire population into self-made engineers, turned into a catastrophic failure. However, the often deplorable state of "physical" hardware technology in China up to the present day stands in sharp contrast to the enormous achievements in the field of "softer" technologies: here, in the realm of the "clean," as it were, deeply rooted élitist attitudes seem to have finally been reconciled with the demands of the (post-) modern period.

Theories of cross-cultural transfer, especially those which refer to intra-European transfer processes, sometimes tend to underestimate the importance of semantic ruptures which take place in the course of cultural migration. It is true that scope, speed, rhythm and results of all transfer processes are influenced by the needs and interests of the concerned social groups and the will of the political decision makers. It is also true that these processes share common chronological features, regardless of where and when they take place. However, in a civilization whose *élite* almost entirely relied more strongly on the authority of the written word than on any other kind of evidence, words become an even more crucial instrument, first, in the establishment of borders between the "new" and the "old", and, subsequently, in the amalgamation of both. No "myth of origin" needs to be established in this context, since the history of mentalities reveals sufficient behavioral continuities in the attitudes towards the abstract and the concrete; moreover, the Chinese language had some experience in dealing with concepts of foreign origin. However, the radical transformation of the entire body of knowledge and its organization cannot be narrated without taking into account its foremost medium: terms. Although it is evident that the history of the migration of terms will never come to an end, the unprecedented scope of lexical transformation in the relatively short period from late nineteenth to early twentieth century clearly speaks out in favor of the hypothesis of a formative period that continues to shape Chinese disourses.

Both Western and Chinese intellectual history have experienced several decisive breaks: for the Chinese world, we might recall the influx of Buddhism, or the rise of Song Confucianism, for the Western world, we could think of the Cartesian turn or the Enlightenment. One of the results of such breaks is that ancient texts are no longer read (and understood) as they have been read (and understood) before. A process of intra-cultural translation has taken place, and the meaning of words and their eventual mapping in more or less coherent systems have changed. In the West, the very idea of *translatio imperii*, the frequent shift of responsibility for the cultural heritage of the Ancients from one civilization (and its respective language) to another, involved continuous translation as a vital part of the culture. Concurrently, the concept of *translatio imperii*, by always referring to one and the same *imperium*, fostered the belief that all ruptures, changes and modifications came from within, and were not imported from without. The sentence "Aristotle is a Western philosopher, but he speaks different languages" reveals its full meaning only when simultaneously read vice versa: "Aristotle speaks different languages, but he is (and will always remain) a Western philosopher." At least within the realm of ideal Western self-perception, cultural continuity and discontinuity are thus kept in a comforting balance.

The absence of a similar idea in China certainly diminished a comparable inclination to translation efforts. Buddhism, definitely a faith coming "from without", took centuries before it became embedded in Chinese society, and its world-view only invited retouches to the traditional mapping of knowledge and the Chinese lexicon without completely transforming it. Moreover, only a small number of Chinese were involved in the impressive translation of the Buddhist canon. Song Confucianism, partly influenced by Buddhist forms of thought and argumentation, dramatically changed the interpretation of crucial parts of the Chinese written heritage, but there was scarcely a feeling at the time that this effort was an act of translation. From the mid-nineteenth century onwards, however, China became a member of the universal community of translators. It is difficult to assess the depth of the break with tradition brought upon by translation, in comparison with similar discontinuities in the West. Yet it seems safe to say that both the speed and the scope of translation work were unprecedented. When its climax was reached (roughly speaking in the decades before and after 1900), not only a new mental topography was acquired, but the Chinese traditions themselves began to be made "compatible" to the Western challenge. A new terminology and a new conceptual universe helped Confucius to embark on a new career, first as a specialist of natural philosophy, and, subsequently, as a moral philosopher; in the course of time, he was to become a pedagogue, an expert for the philosophy of religion, and so forth. Since the time when some Zhejiang scholars rediscovered the works of Mo Di 墨翟 (fifth century BC) in the mid- and late Qing period, the long-forgotten book bearing the philosopher's name became a main authority for "Chinese science" in the field of optics, mechanics, logic and other domains. No vital issue of the Chinese past was spared an interpretation along the lines of the new meanings and their respective mapping. Nonetheless, the fervent translation activities did not necessarily imply the perception of a Chinese *translatio imperii*. Taking up the statement about Aristotle cited above, one might therefore be enticed to say "Confucius is a Chinese thinker who always speaks Chinese." The illusory continuity of the Chinese language and the culture it represents tend to obnubilate the fact that the twentieth-century Confucius speaks a radically different kind of Chinese than all his previous traditional incarnations: and, as suchm we may say that he suffers from a complex form of linguistic alienation.

To speak of alienation in this context may still be less justified by the depth of the rupture (although it was deeper than most Westerners imagine), but even more so because of the foreign origin of the "new" knowledge and the short period of time in which it was appropriated. The fact that the break was induced from without makes an enormous difference for Chinese identity constructions up to the present day. Little wonder therefore that the alienation is sensed more strongly in fields where words matter most—in the humanities and, generally speaking, in all fields with a rich cultural matrix.

Notwithstanding the price that China had to pay for her membership in the global community of translation, the new language was a new *Chinese* language. China never entirely lost control of her political and linguistic sovereignty. And thus the story of China's loss of continuous access to the nation's past and traditions is paralleled by the story of an enormous success, which, within a few decades, enabled China to catch up with modernity, at least in terms of reading and writing. It took another century to make up ground in terms of practical performance, where words wrapped up in paper do not play a similar vital role.

The present volume is the second monograph[2] emerging from a research project studying *The Formation of Modern Chinese Terminologies* (*Wissenschaftssprache Chinesisch*, WSC), which I started, in late 1996, with Iwo Amelung and Joachim Kurtz. In the meantime, we have advanced our initially rather narrow terminological approach by establishing a preliminary database [3] containing roughly 127,000

---

[2] Cf. Michael Lackner, Iwo Amelung and Joachim Kurtz. 2001. *New Terms for New Ideas. Western Knowledge and Lexical Change in late Imperial China*, Leiden, Boston, Cologne: Brill.

[3] *WSC-Databases: An Electronic Repository of Chinese Scientific, Philosophical and Political Terms Coined in the Nineteenth and Early Twentieth Century.* Available online at http://www.wsc.uni-erlangen.de/wscdb.htm.

entries on Chinese neologisms of the nineteenth and early twentieth century. The conference organized in December 1999 was meant to enlarge the framework of the ongoing research by placing the history of migrating words and concepts into a steadily increasing context of social, political, and institutional issues. Since Natascha Vittinghoff, the co-organizer of this conference, who is also the co-editor of the present volume, has not only taken manifold pains to make this book coherent, but has also expressed, in her introduction, our acknowledgements to persons and institutions to which we are indebted, the pleasure to thank her remains entirely mine.

Michael Lackner
Erlangen, December 2003

NATASCHA VITTINGHOFF

INTRODUCTION

This volume presents a varied range of explorations which aim to open up new paths for discovering the terrain of China's encounter with Western sciences and Western knowledge in the nineteenth and early twentieth centuries.[1] It is a collection of contributions to the international conference "Translating Western Knowledge into late Imperial China" held at the Department of East Asian Studies of Göttingen University in December 1999. The collection intends to highlight areas of 'scientific' activities hitherto erased from the intellectual map of Late Qing China and to connect these findings to broader questions concerning structure and mechanisms of the production of scientific knowledge in a transcultural environment. Rather than dealing with science in its narrow sense the book covers both the academic field of scientific knowledge and popularized common knowledge from and about the West. For this reason the term 'new learning' (*xinxue* 新學) was chosen for the title. As this term was commonly used by contemporary writers, it seems more appropriate not only, because 'scientific' practice was much less standardized and professionalized in nineteenth century China than the application of the term 'science' would allow. In addition, we wish to draw attention to the fact, that a definition of 'science' as a systematized positive knowledge has largely become questionable itself.

In the last two decades, writing on the history of science in the West has undergone fundamental changes in Western historiography.[2] It is meanwhile generally acknowledged, that the history of science

---

[1] The conference was generously sponsored by the Volkswagen Foundation and the University of Göttingen and hosted 42 scholars from China, Japan, the United States and Europe. A general outline of the proceedings as well as abstracts of the papers not included in this volume can be found at the website http://www.gwdg.de/~oas/wsc/99conf.htm.

[2] William Clark, Jan Golinski and Simon Schaffer (eds.). 1999. *The Sciences in Enlightened Europe*. Chicago and London: University of Chicago Press; Hans Erich Boedecker, Peter H. Reill and Jürgen Schlumbohm (eds.). 1999. *Wissenschaft als kulturelle Praxis 1750–1900*. Göttingen: Vandenhoeck and Ruprecht. On the cultural turn in Chinese science studies see Roger Hart. 1999. "Beyond Science and Civilisation: A Post-Needham Critique", *East Asian Science, Technology Medicine* 16, pp. 88–114.

encompasses more than a chronological account of scientific results and the development of scientific disciplines, but instead reflects a complex process of negotiations about the production of new knowledge as well as its acknowledgement as such. Historians of science, therefore, are not only dealing with categories of knowledge for the supposedly known but also have to inquire into how different people coped with arcane knowledge, the unknown, anomalies and matters excluded from the scientific canon. The formation of such a canon at a certain historical juncture was the result of constant choices between competing possibilities, choices that were deliberately made or determined by contingencies of the time. This formative process is a central focus of this volume.

With the contextualisation of scientific results in social and cultural terms, scientific activities can no longer be perceived as purely intellectual endeavours nor can the history of sciences be pictured as either successful progress or linear development of disciplines. Instead, the history of sciences has become a field of multidisciplinary projects. Conceiving of sciences as cultural practice, their analysis requires methodological borrowings from sociological, anthropological, historical and literary studies, and the combination of methods and findings from such fields.

It is also generally accepted that scientific practice or the production of new ideas is determined by the specific social spaces in which these come into existence. It is therefore necessary to undertake micro-historical studies on the specific conditions of the production and reception of new knowledge, in order to chart the tensions within a new field of learning and to explore the relations of forces between science and society. Scientific practice or 'new learning' is thus meant to describe a disunified occupation with new knowledge as a local practice inseparable from the local context.

The Chinese encounter with Western sciences in the nineteenth century was preceded by various formal and informal contacts between foreign and Chinese scholars. These contacts, especially the encounter with the Jesuits in the 16th and 17th century differed fundamentally in a twofold way. On the one hand, the import of Western sciences to China in the nineteenth century was part of an imperialist expansion of the Western nations which powerfully demonstrated the global importance of sciences. It did not come along only through the writings and speeches of individuals at the court in Beijing but was accompanied by a large (and to a large part rather "convincing") armada of technology and material culture as products of the new scientific results. On the other hand, the protestant missionaries as the first ones involved in the transmission of Western sciences into China after the expulsion of the Jesuits were not aiming at a central elite, but rather seeked their audience at the margins of society. With this premise, they used a wide range of—in addition newly developed—media to spread their knowledge among the population which again occasionally determined or changed the messages. Also in contrast to the Jesuit situation, their dissemination of scientific knowledge was not as much restricted by religious premises, and in not too few cases the desire to spread enlightended knowledge even overwhelmed their committment to their respective religious schools. Moreover, the project of teaching sciences was not at all restricted to missionaries alone.[3]

The later encounter between Chinese and Western scholars dealt with in this volume foremost evolved as a *transcultural* process which neither implied a one way process of transmission and reception nor resulted in a fundamental break with an indigenous past. This perspective does not set out to undermine the significance of the Western impact on developments in China, but chooses a focus on the interplay of global relevance and local exigency which allows the abandonment of strict entitetical separations of the 'foreign' and the 'indigenous'. The focus is on the interactions between the global and the local and on questions of how putatively global or universal knowledge was put to its local uses.

New knowledge about the West and parts of the world hitherto outside Chinese attention engendered a new geographical consciousness of locality and distance, as well as new spatial hierarchies of center and periphery. China's intellectual entry into the 'family of nations' with its hierarchical structures brought about fundamental changes in the self-positioning within these hierarchies. However, it neither resulted in a forced surrender to the hierarchical eurocentric world

---

[3] There is a large field of research on the Jesuit transmission of Western sciences and it is not the aim of this introduction to provide a thorough comparison. Suffice it to note that the recognition of the complex problematique involved in the Jesuit activities in relation to religious, linguistic, political and cultural factors is accompanied by an emerging critique of former academic approaches and rather simple explanations of the Jesuits' "failure".

system as suggested by the imperialist paradigm, nor in a sublime ignorance of realities as proposed by narratives of a failed modernity. Instead, modern Western sciences entered China in a complex process of reciprocal exchanges of meaning, ideas and interpretations taking place in various institutions which opened up spaces for hitherto largely unexplored hybrid discourses. The nativisation of Western knowledge in China was influenced, restricted or engendered by such diverging factors as institutional frameworks, structures of classifying knowledge, ideological interests and indigenous exigencies. However, as many of the contributions in this volume show, a large part of these alternative ways of perceiving and actualizing the new and foreign in a familiar context, have largely been obliterated by the ideological radicalisation in the early twentieth century, which established intellectual homogenisation and did not allow for ambivalences.

The agents involved in the process of translating and disseminating Western knowledge into late Imperial China were mainly newcomers in the treaty port societies, with however strongly different social backgrounds, interests and agendas, including officials, merchants, missionaries and scientists. Instead of attempting to provide overall explanations, the studies in this volume highlight the alternatives and differences in approaches to and assessments of the historical process of the creation of a modern scientific canon.

There is clearly little doubt, that Western technology was perceived as superior and posed an irrefutable argument in the cultural and political negotiations between the global powers. The adoption of Western technological knowledge was closely connected to the imperial project to gain wealth and power and, later, to nationbuilding. There was, however, more to it than simple pragmatic transaction, for the transfer of knowledge from one person to another constitutes a specific site of power transfer. Thus its consequences touched upon questions of state authority, such as the policies of information control, educational authority and the recruitment of administrative personnel. In addition, local agency intensified through private networks undermined the officials' powers. Therefore, exploring to which effect individual agents put their possession of new knowledge within a new information order is crucially relevant and relates to wider questions of public knowledge and structures of the dominant information order. This in turn means, that it is not only important to know what was published, but also how information was collected and transmitted, and which institutional networks were at work.[4] This complex also involves the relationships between readership and public expression, in which print products are seen not only as tools for enlightenment, but also as possibilities for multiple constructions of meanings by their readers. While science played a crucial role in the public construction of a new society, at the same time the public was an important factor in shaping the specific nature of scientific practice.[5]

Looking at these new social formations based on upon new knowledge, we are lead to the still unresolved problems of the cultural status of new knowledge in Late Qing society and the social status of its possessors. The cultural negotiations we are dealing with in this encounter do not allow for a polarisation between an old tradition and a new modernity as diametrically opposed entities, but rather suggest a continuity of the past within the transformations of the present (which at times do not necessarily result in something novel). The hybrid interaction of a variety of discourses involves reinventions of indigenous traditions, hegemonic rejections of alternative models, fantasies about the marvels of the West, as well as functionalized concepts of the West as alterity. This process is fundamentally transnational in nature, as the networks of these knowledgeable actors transgressed national boundaries, as did the texts they produced and the institutions they erected.

Due to mainly ideological reasons the efficacy of this transnational cooperation was largely denied by latter historiography. The discovery of a break, success or failure in the past more often than not results from a historical narrative, that is constructed with specific statements about the present in mind. In the Chinese history of science, the Sino-Japanese War 1894/5 was long seen as such a critical turning point, which first provoked a serious intention to acknowledge and confront the Western challenge and to study the foundations of its success, the sciences. That this assumption is based on a rigid conceptualisation of

---

[4] On the 'information order' see Chris Bayly. 1996. *Empire and Information: Intelligence Gathering and Social Communication in India, 1780–1870*. Cambridge: Cambridge University Press.

[5] E.g. Constantin Goeschler. 2000. *Wissenschaft und Öffentlichkeit in Berlin. 1870–1930*. Stuttgart: Steiner; Andreas Daum. 1998. *Wissenschaftspopularisierung im 19. Jahrhundert. Bürgerliche Kultur, naturwissenschaftliche Bildung und die deutsche Öffentlichkeit, 1848–1914*. Munich: Oldenbourg.

'science' which inhibits a more profound understanding of the cultural significance of scientific activities in nineteenth century China has been argued before[6] and is testified to by the studies in this volume. Instead of reading the fundamental turn in the intellectual encounter with the West as a result of the defeat of the Chinese army, it might well be argued that a more decisive moment in the history of Chinese sciences was a nascent historiographical debate on China's sciences conducted by representatives of the New Cultural Movement in the early twentieth century, which erased all earlier activities in the field of new knowledge from the map of Chinese science history and committed them to oblivion.[7] The studies in this volume therefore follow the twofold approach of unearthing activities of knowledgeable actors prior to 1894 and of identifying historiographical and ideological layers heaped upon them. In fact, the process of a metonymic replacement of everything 'new' as Western and the 'old' as Chinese evolved only slowly as the result of a continuous self-reflection.

As knowledge is mobile, the device to allow this mobility from one linguistically different culture to another is translation. This re-territorialisation of the floating new knowledge in a new cultural context materialized in the creation of new texts, a new language and new language usages. Vice versa, the new language continuously affected and prefigured the perception, actualisation and transmission of the newly acquired knowledge.[8] Translations played a crucial role in the history of sciences, not only with regard to knowledge mobility between the East and the West, but also within the Western scientific tradition.[9]

---

[6] Cf. David C. Reynolds. 1991. "Redrawing China's Intellectual Map: Images of Science in Nineteenth Century China". *Late Imperial China* 12.1, pp. 27-61.

[7] Ibid. David Wright's study on chemistry in China is another rare example of attempts to "rehabilitate the earlier generation" of scientists in China through a meticulous historical study. David Wright. 2000. *Translating Science. The Transmission of Western Chemistry into Late Imperial China, 1840–1900*. Leiden et.al: Brill. Introduction.

[8] For a first micro-level study of this lexical change in various disciplines see Michael Lackner, Iwo Amelung and Joachim Kurtz (eds.). 2001. *New Terms for New Ideas. Western Knowledge and Lexical Change in Late Imperial China*. Leiden et.al.: Brill. On earlier linguistic studies on lexical exchange in China see their introduction. On similar processes of linguistic change in Japan during the Meiji period see the recent study by Douglas R. Howland. 2002. *Translating the West: Language and Political Reason in Nineteenth-Century Japan*. Honolulu: University of Hawaii Press.

[9] Cf. Scott L. Montgomery. 2000. *Science in Translation. Movements of knowledge through Cultures and Time*. Chicago and London: University of Chicago Press.

The translated text as manifestation of the migration of knowledge through language requires a meticulous philological research in order to map out the nativisation of concepts through linguistic devices. However, since a 'cultural turn' has taken place in translation studies as well, it is now generally acknowledged, that translation itself is a transcultural practice and that the process of translation cannot be reduced to a simple attempt of creating equivalences, but has to be seen in relation to explicit or implicit intentions of the translator. In this view, the cultural mediator-as-translator represents one culture to another, perhaps faithfully attempting to contribute to mutual understanding and accurate cross-cultural knowledge transfer, but perhaps also, strategically or not, subversively attempting to establish new meanings.

China's intellectual entry into the family of nations proceeded along many sidelines and pathways crossing hitherto undiscovered new territories. This book does not chart steps along a linear path of the accumulation of new knowledge which lead China to a modernized nation equipped with modern sciences. Instead, *Mapping Meanings* attempts to highlight what the encountered new knowledge could have meant to specific persons in a specific historical period inscribed by contingencies rather than fixed causalities.

Giving credit to these methodological presuppositions this volume maps out the field of new learning in Late Qing China from the center as well as its margins, from the nucleus of collective political power to remote artistic fields of individual self-expression. These dimensions provide the basis for the four substantial sections in the book, "The Politics of Global Knowledge", "Discoursive Interfaces: Language and Media", "The Organisation of Knowledge" and "Knowledge between Heart and Mind".

THE POLITICS OF GLOBAL KNOWLEDGE

China's encounter with Western knowledge is commonly identified with cannonboat-politics and described as a process in which foreign powers reinforced the acknowledgement and acceptance of Western superiority with imperialist threats. In this view, the Chinese reception of Western sciences was first and foremost a reaction to political crisis that forced the imperial government to introduce a new (reform) policy (*xinzheng* 新政) and new educational institutions, thus to attain

entry into the family of nations. The essays of the first section question these assumptions by addressing the relation between imperial
power politics and individual agency.

In his opening essay, Benjamin Elman situates the contested nature
of interactions between Chinese and Europeans over the meaning and
significance of natural studies in a historical perspective covering the
period from the mid–sixteenth century to the early Republican period.
He argues that unlike in India, natural studies in late Imperial China
until 1900 were part of a nativist imperial project to master and control Western views on what constituted legitimate natural knowledge.
Analyzing how the nativists and Westerners took advantage of the
mutually contested accommodation project he shows how each side
converted the other's forms of natural studies into acceptable local
conventions of knowledge. By tracing the semantic roots of the terms
for 'science'—*gezhi* 格致 and *kexue* 科學—and their subsequent
usages, he explains that until 1900, Chinese intellectuals interpreted
the scientific transition in Europe on their own terms. The subsequent
narrative of a 'failure' of the premodern 'Chinese sciences' appeared
only after 1900 as the result of the commonsensual essentialisation of
European natural studies into a universalist ideal.

Governmental institutions were the first and most visible land-
marks in the nineteenth century's intellectual landscape of the new
sciences in China. These institutions, however, were not only governed by imperial policies, but also occupied by individuals who
interpreted their cultural environment on their own terms. Shifting to
this micropolitical level of individual agency, Natascha Vittinghoff
explores the structural elements of the new field of production and
dissemination of new knowledge, including the media, the social
actors and their institutional networks. Collecting scattered biographical information of social actors involved in the field of new knowledge, she takes issue with the prevalent evaluations of the social role
and status of this nascent scientific community. Identifying the networks of these mostly highly educated and prominent actors who,
more often than not, were simultaneously involved in several projects,
she argues that their strong personal and institutional links dramatically increased their individual agency. Moreover, the rapid merging
of scientific activities and public information suggests a greater influence of the early modern educational institutions and media long

before the early twentieth century than attested by later historians of the New Culture Movement.

When the *xinzheng*-policy gradually abolished the classical educational system and made it one of their main aims to transform the educational canon, the scientific community was divided into an older generation still familiar with the classical canon and a younger one of social actors, who felt a greater distance to the classical past and were much more at ease with an overall acceptance of entirely new forms of knowledge and terminology. Wolfgang Lippert's philological study on the introduction of the term *jingji* 經濟 for 'political economy' is a case in point. It exemplifies the frequent phenomenon of a classical Chinese word being charged with new meaning in modern Japanese to render a Western model word and subsequently being borrowed back it into Chinese as a loan translation. It could well be argued that the modern Japanese lexicon, which largely consists of neologisms based on Chinese characters rather than incorporating foreign words as loanwords, was so easily accepted into the modern Chinese lexicon, because the original meanings of old classical terms, like of *jing shi ji min* 經世計民 for 'politics' or 'statemanship' were already unfamiliar to the new generation of translators of the early twentieth century.

However, as Rudolf G. Wagner's article points out, in the realm of politics in particular, new terms were not just the product and result of intellectual discourse. His explorations of the concept of 'labor/work/ Arbeit' in the Chinese world show the tactical and ideological uses of this concept in different times and spaces. Explaining the semantic dimensions of *dong* 動, movement, as part of the modern lexem for 'labor', *laodong* 勞動, he explores the transition from an understanding of movement as a mainly social and political movement in the early Republican Era to 'physical labour' (as *laozuo* 勞作) in the latter Guomindang and PRC period. As the conceptualisation of labor was devoid of any traditional Chinese elements, in this case, in contrast to the adaption of the term *jingji*, there was no adaption of an older term the meaning of which was replaced by a new Western content; instead *laodong* was imported together with the import of the foreign discourse on 'labor'.

The powerful influence of politics on the formation of a new lexicon is even more visible in Ma Jun's contribution on the shifts and changes in the creation of new military language. His investigations

of transitions of military terms in the Late Qing are especially rewarding, as they bring the ethnical and linguistic diversity of the Qing
Manchu rule into play. The Qing military system complicated the linguistic difficulties, as the national Qing army consisted of two organisations, the hereditary Chinese military men (Green Standards), and
the socio-political-military organisation of the Manchu (Eight Banners), which used different sets of military rank systems and consequently different terminologies. Investigations of the Western military
rank systems emerging after the military defeats of the Opium Wars
therefore had to tackle the linguistic complexity of the existing order,
offering a variety of choices for translations: phonetic transposition,
the mechanical application of ranks of the Qing army system, descriptive translation and finally Japanese loanwords. The new military rank
system was shaped on one hand by translations of Western military
terms, and, on the other hand, by the practical transformation of the
existing military system into a new modern army after Western and
Japanese models. Ma Jun shows how these linguistic choices reacted
towards specific military operations and exigencies, and how this lead
to a hybrid terminology combining elements of the Qing army rank
system with Japanese neologisms.

DISCOURSIVE INTERFACES: LANGUAGE AND MEDIA

The survival of the fittest terms in modern Chinese lexicon more often
than not did not occur as a natural process. Rather it was the result of
deliberate choices, that were discussed and reflected upon. The essays
of the second section each touch on such contemporary reflections on
translation, language and the role of the media in transmitting new
ideas coined in a new language.

Wolfgang Behr's historical account opens this section by tracing
the roots of the term for 'translation' in classical Chinese. Observing
the fundamental problem of a ethnical and linguistic diversity since
ancient history, he explores the earliest definitions of a Chinese ethnic
identity, which, according to his findings, was defined culturally, ethically or ecologically rather than along racial, religious or linguistic
parameters. This might have been one reason why theoretical reflections on multilingualism and translation were extremely scarce. The
lack of interest in foreign languages before the Qing period, cannot be
explained as inherent in the Chinese language, but has to be seen in

the context of shared sociological and political predispositions. After a meticulous linguistic reconstruction of different terms for 'translation', Behr argues that the consolidation of *yi* 譯 as the proper and final term arose from the massive initial encounter with Buddhism during a period of crucial linguistic transitions. This juncture was crucial, because for the first time the former assumption of translatability between languages was fundamentally unsettled.

Viviane Alleton's contribution observes a comparable lack of systematic interest in the structure of the Chinese languages, an interest which was only awakened by the encounter with Western grammatical studies. Discussing Ma Jianzhong's 馬 jian 忠 (1844–1900) first Chinese grammar and putting it in the context of the Jesuit culture, into which Ma was closely integrated, Alleton argues that the poor reception of his masterly study and grammar in general was not an intrinsic necessity based on the particularities of the Chinese language, but the result of historical circumstances. When the context of educational reform in the early twentieth century required simplified grammatical textbooks after English models, Ma Jianzhong's book was attacked for being overly influenced by Western ideas and as too traditional to be useful for a modern education. Because the new textbooks were of no theoretical linguistic value for academic discussion, the study of grammar was gradually considered as mere 'useful knowledge'. As dreary technique, it was never acknowledged as a branch of knowledge that touches upon cognitive dimensions. This phenomenon, Alleton further argues, largely persisted through the PRC history of Chinese language studies.

Increasing reflections about the nature of the Chinese language and its structures also fostered more elaborate theories about the literary act of translation. Yan Fu's 嚴復 (1853–1921) formulation of the three basic principles of translation, fidelity (*xin* 信), comprehensibility (*da* 達) and elegance (*ya* 雅) articulated in his preface to the *Tianyanlun*, is one of the most well-known attempts in this direction. Lawrence Wang-chi Wong's contribution reconsiders the significance of Yan Fu's translation by focussing his attention on the particular social, political and literary system in which his translations were produced. Wong starts his discussion by presenting the contested meanings of these concepts in contemporary discourse on translation and in Yan Fu's own writings. Testing Yan's theoretical principles against his own translations, he traces the ideological and political motives behind them that, sometimes, inhibited the application of his theoretical formulations. Moreover, the selection of works and even the literary style chosen in Yan's translations were a matter of political (and financial) patronage. As Wong shows, Yan's tremendous success was partly due to the promotion by his patron, Wu Rulun 吳汝綸 (1840–1903), who especially appreciated Yan's elegant style of writing. This encouraged Yan to continue composing his translations in this skillfull literary style, despite being well aware of the fact, that it was incomprehensible to a large part of his intended readership.

The close ties between the two realms of political leadership and private authorship are further elaborated in Elisabeth Kaske's discussion on the emerging concept of a national language. Kaske links the strains of an emerging public discourse on language reform in the periodical press with governmental education reforms in search for a unified language; identifying the separation of a written and spoken language in Chinese as the main obstacle for a nationalist reform. The two realms of language conflicted, as the propagation of a colloquialized written language was required as part of the nationbuilding project, while the concept of national authenticity was believed to require the adherence to the *wen* 文 , the classical written language as the foundations of the cultural heritage. These conflicting approaches led to two conceptionalisations of national language—*guoyu* 國語 and *guowen* 國文 . These were overcome by Hu Shi's 胡適 (1891–1962) well known proposals for literary reform, in which he identified *wen* with 'literature' (*wenxue* 文學) in the Western sense and defined *baihua* 白話 as the national language of this new literature of the new age.

Newspapers and magazines were the most widely used media which disseminated these discourses to a larger public. Their form, content and the process, by which they were produced were the result of transcultural interactions based on translation. Examining one of the first magazines of the new peridocial press, the *Dongxiyang kao meiyue tongjizhuan* 東西洋考每月統計傳 (East-West Examiner and Monthly Record) founded in 1833, Michael C. Lazich allows us a glimpse into the impressively wide range of topics covered by this supposedly religious journal. Lazich describes explanations on Western technology, discussions of natural sciences and presentations of world history and geography and explains, how this magazine epitomized the philosophy and goals of the Society for the Diffusion of

Useful Knowledge, which aimed at a transcultural interchange of knowledge and to engage Chinese readers in rational argument.

Half a century later, this exchange of rational arguments by Chinese readers and journalists had become a common phenomenon as newspapers had become more widespread in Hong Kong and Shanghai. Andrea Janku's contribution takes a closer look at how these new forms of public discourse evolved, were transformed and stabilized by observing the development of a specific journalistic genre, the leading article. The analysis of the transformation of the—originally British—'leading article' into the Chinese *shelun* 社論, addresses questions concerning the acceptance, adaptation and appropriation of a culturally defined concept in a new cultural environment. When the British newspaper gained a foothold on Chinese soil, it introduced the leading article as a genre of liberal political discourse. Translated as *lun* 論 (essay) this genre was initially integrated into the genre of *jingshiwen* 經世文 or statecraft writings, a genre that was intrinsically connected to the authoritative judgement of right and wrong in historical discourse. At this point, Janku argues, a genre that was perceived as being in the service of the state merged with a genre that was perceived as being independent from it. Different forces were at work shaping the genre vying for acceptability with the targeted readership, with both the editorial article and its readers changing dramatically over a few decades' time. In her close reading of both statecraft writings and newspaper editorials, Janku shows how the *shelun* developed into a genre that was critical towards and independent from the state; and how this led to its closer but oppositional engagement with the state, in the form of attempts to avoid censorship and state propaganda.

Benjamin T'sou's contribution situates the linguistic issues in a broader historical perspective by observing diachronic linguistic developments in the last century. His examination of concepts and words relevant to the field of mechanics, 'vehicle' in particular, is based on a comparison of entries from different editions of the *Ciyuan* from the early twentieth century with the enormous corpus of the database *Language Variation in Chinese Communities,* which draws on sources from different Chinese language communities from 1995 to 1998. This twofold approach allows for deeper insights on the origins and mechanisms of change in language in different language communities. Employing a distinctions between 'endocentric' tendencies, the use of indigenous linguistics elements, and 'exocentric' tendencies, the use of non-indigenous linguistic elements, T'sou is able to observe different linguistic preferences in specific language communities, which can be linked to specific cultural and social environments.

THE ORGANISATION OF KNOWLEDGE

The third section addresses the complex relationship between scientific works and scientific production in new institutional frameworks. The process of establishing branches of knowledges as institutionalized disciplines involved demarcation, exclusion and classification and subjected formerly diffused realms of knowledge—including liberal arts and literature—to increasing control through calculating measures and accountability. At the same time, the new established disciplines caused resistance and friction at the sites of their concrete application. The simultaneous process of producing knowledge and instituting control over its subjects is reflected in the diversity of strategies chosen to establish academic fields.

Iwo Amelung's contribution elucidates this process in his study on the strife to delineate the field of physics in China. Starting his observations with an account of the technical shifts and inventions accompanying the 'invention of physics' as a coherent subject in the first half of the nineteenth century in the West, Amelung stresses the point, that the evolution of terminology was not at all uniform in the West either. He then moves on to sketch out a history of Western physics in China by focusing on the terminological history of the subject itself and difficulties in classification that coincided with the accommodation of Western physics in China. By juxtaposing the developments of physics in the West and China, Amelung presents a vivid and detailed picture of how diverging Western national traditions—clashing over the proper understanding of modern physics as separate from natural philosophy—merged with different indigenous traditions. This resulted in different strategies to classify the field as either "new Western knowledge" or as part of the traditional *gezhi*, a term that was, as Benjamin Elman explicates in his introductory contribution, under constant redefinition at that time.

As in physics, transnational configurations in combination with increasing national consciousness were also crucial factors in establishing the field of archeology in the early twentieth century. Starting with the terminological distinction between archeology and prehistory as it developed in Western modern archeology, Su Rongyu traces the origins of an indigenous understanding of archeology from the studies of epigraphy in premodern China. Yet, as Su argues, neither classical epigraphical studies, nor the following archeological activities that were performed by foreign archeologists in the late nineteenth century mainly out of financial interests, have developed into systematic methodological or theoretical reflections on procedures in this academic field. It was, Su argues, a sense of national crisis, that set off fundamental reflections on the academic establishment of this field. At the beginning of the twentieth century, this sense of crisis stirred scholars to rewrite Chinese history as national history, using 'scientific' methods of periodisation and presentation of ancient Chinese history in the fashion of the Three Age theory. Su shows how these ideological historiographical efforts, coinciding with the famous discoveries in Anyang, merged with academic interests developed by a new generation of trained archeologists returning from Japan and the United States. The co-operation of these returned students with foreign archeologists–who by now did research for purely scientific purposes–laid the ground for the academic field of archeology in China.

The two contributions demonstrated that establishing an academic field started with negotiations about its linguistic definition. Arakawa Kiyohide's contribution extends this aspect to questions of the formation of a set of technical geographical terms. Tracing the histories of common geographical terms such as 'torrid zone', 'tropic', 'ocean current' or 'trade wind', Arakawa explores different modes of forming neologisms, and by this challenges and expands some prevalent assumptions on these linguistic processes. Emphasizing the crucial role of the Dutch-studies (*rangaku* 蘭學) scholars in Japan and the necessity to examine the Latin sources on which some of these early translations were based, he highlights, first, that part of the neologisms were received from Japan much earlier than commonly assumed, and, second, that Japanese scholars based their new creations not only on classical Chinese but also on classical Japanese expressions.

"What's in a name", is one of the fundamental questions in the philosophical field of logic. In the Chinese case logic has (mistakenly) long been connected to the School of Names (*mingjia* 名家) or translated as *mingxue* 名學 (Study of Names). Joachim Kurtz' contribution explores the evolution of the discourse on 'Chinese logic' in the early years of the twentieth century and focusses on texts written before the systematic studies by trained logicians such as Hu Shi appeared. Through the discovery and analysis of these hitherto neglected texts Kurtz is able to shed light on hybrid attempts to negotiate a 'frame of articulation' which was not yet filled by later self-assured accounts of a history of 'logical thought in China'. Kurtz shows how the fundamental questions, whether there was anything like a 'Chinese logic', in which texts it would be found, and how these texts should be understood, were differently addressed and responded to by either connecting logical elements found in *Xunzi* 荀子 (3rd c. BC) or the *Mohist Canon* to the well-developed philological discipline (*xiaoxue* 小學), or drawing on Buddhist theories of *hetuvidyā,* (knowledge of reasons). His investigation concludes by explaining how these early intracultural attempts of a specialist discourse in a brief 'age of discovery' in logic came to an early end with the intervention of Wang Guowei's stern academic rigidity in defining the field.

Rune Svarverud observes a comparable process of vivid and hybrid discourse in the field of international law, developing different vocabularies elaborated under different institutional frameworks in Beijing and Shanghai, which was abruptly ended by the monopolisation of the Chinese vocabulary through a overwhelming Japanese influx in the first years of the twentieth century. Having unearthed dozens of texts on international law from Western and Chinese authors and translators between 1864 and 1903, Svarverud is able to distinguish distinct coexisting traditions of translating international law texts in the Beijing Tongwenguan and Shanghai Arsenal, which nevertheless both failed to resist the Japanese impact. Pondering the reasons for this tremendous impact, Svarverud comes to the conclusion that it was due to the rising concerns about Chinese sovereignty, voiced largely by Chinese students in Japan, and due to the existence of an elaborate terminology of international law that had been developed in Japan since the 1870s and 1880s and which these same students encountered and readily accepted.

New scientific terminologies played a crucial role not only in the academic sciences, but in literature and the liberal arts as well, an area that has scarcely been investigated in this respect. Helena Heroldová compensates this omission by analyzing science fiction novels of the first two decades of the twentieth century. Distinguishing different types of words referring to non-empirical realities in these texts, Heroldová investigates how a remote and strange, yet still intelligible science-fiction world is created through specific linguistic devices, which familiarize its imaginary objects through descriptions of outward appearance and function. In a second step, Heroldová discusses the reception of these new linguistic formations by the readers. Both the structure of the newly coined terms and the attached descriptions helped the readers to perceive and understand the imaginary reality by actualizing it in their familiar context.

Music, as the most abstract communication system, has long been regarded as the ideal of an universal semiotic system for it could be understood without knowledge of any specific language. The contemporary promotion and ready acceptance of world-music is one example of this popular understanding. Musicologists, however, regard musical production and theory as based in specific cultural and historical context, without which the specific meaning of musical codes cannot be deciphered. As music possessed specific status in the cultural and political *imaginaire* in ancient China, it is no surprise that decisions on the introduction of a modern notation system and Western musicology were hotly contested. Gerlinde Gild's contribution deals with these questions by tracing the evolution of modern Chinese musical theory and terminology under Western influence. She shows how the cultural heritage of attributing a strong political and educational role to music was maintained in the creation of a new musicology. Developed purposefully as part of the nationbuilding project, namely in order to produce new songs that would imbue audiences with a sense of citizenship, new musicology was nevertheless accompanied by two conflicting views on whether it ought to be based on ancient tradition or lead to the overall abolishment of old notation systems. Comparable to the realm of literature, it was the rhetorical replacement of the 'classical, old Chinese' with the 'new and modern West' mainly by returned students from Japan that lead to the creation of 'new music' (*xin yinyue* 新音樂) as the dominant form of a national music, whereas the classical forms were no longer considered to be true art. From a musicologist's point of view, Gild argues, this replacement of 'old' by 'new', however, could not clarify the raising questions of what specifically constituted this new music.

KNOWLEDGE BETWEEN HEART AND MIND

The closing section of this volume addresses questions about the sensibilities of knowledge in articulations of thoughts about religion, morals and the human body with the often conflicting factors of intuition versus methods or faith versus objectivity. These areas obviously transcend the realm of precise calculation, and closely link knowledge about the unknown world to individual experience, religious truth and individual faith. Oscillating between scientific and religious truth, the emerging discourses reveal how philosophical, religious and ideological presuppositions informed and, in the end, stabilized the production of a scientific discourse in the respective areas.

Wolfgang Kubin's opening article highlights that beyond semantical importation into one's own cultural context translation also means the transformation of the translator himself. Pointing to the German meaning of the term *übersetzen* as 'to ferry across', Kubin explores the gradual transformation of the painter and poet Wu Li 吳歷 (1632-1718) when crossing not only geographical, but mental, academic and ideological borders in his travels to Macao. As Kubin shows, Wu Li's collection from Sao Paolo is an unique example of an attempt of overcoming the East West divide through dialogue. Wu Li's dialogue is founded on the premise, that understanding is never completed but always in a process of becoming. Exhausting the meaning in a constant process therefore becomes the central task not only of Wu Li but of the translator in general.

The individual, subjective aspect in the decision-making process of translation presented a salient problem in debates about the proper rendering of the Christian concept of the utmost deity in the Chinese language, commonly referred to as the 'Term Question'. Contested translations for 'God' were not only a source of division and even bitterness among different Western missionaries in China: the solution of the 'Term Question' was decisive for finding a proper standing of Christianity in Chinese culture. By extension, this question had important implications for the position of Chinese Christians in their own society. Timothy Wong takes a new look at this particular translation problem by analyzing contributions of Chinese Christians to this debates that were articulated in the missionary magazine *Wanguo gongbao*. Translating 'God' on their own terms Wong shows, that Chinese Christians did not simply follow their missionary leaders, but produced a discourse that aimed at forming new terminologies and new theories of understanding Christian doctrines. Moreover, their strategies of argumentation reveal how the Chinese Christians sided with certain foreign missionaries and opposed others and thus engendered a multivocal discourse that transcended national or cultural boundaries. Wong argues that the fact that their input did not immediately lead to an effective communication of the religious message for their Christian audience, did not undermine their role in the cultural complexities involved in the term question.

The decisive impact of the hermeneutical environment of the individual translator is illuminated in Lauren Pfister's analysis of James Legge's (1815–1897) famous translations of the *Chinese Classics*. Describing Legge's background as influenced by the then prevalent philosophical school of Scottish realism and his convictions as an evangelical Christian, Pfister takes issue with claims by historians or cultural critics, that Christian missionaries of the nineteenth century were too intimately bound up within their own backgrounds to escape the bias inherent in a fundamental Christian outlook which infused their inappropriate and distorted representations of foreign cultures. Taking a closer look at the metaphysical terms Legge discovers in the canonical literature, Pfister explains Legge's struggles with these terms as reflecting intellectual and spiritual tensions within Legge himself. He argues that Legge's choice was a self-conscious and rationally justified commitment informed by his studies in Scottish realism rather than a manifestation of 'profound ambivalence' attested to him by other authors.

The extent to which terminologies inform and reveal conditions of epistemologies is discussed in Angelika Messner's article on the 'translation' of Western psychiatry into the Chinese medical context. The introduction of new psychiatric concepts such as 'spiritual disease' (*jingshenbing* 精神病) did not change the "Chinese epistemology" of bodily function, because they did not effectively succeed in dividing bodily from mental factors, as had been done in Western psychiatry. Tracing the earliest sources of encounter between modern Western psychiatry and Chinese medicine, Messner argues that this fundamental difference between Western and Chinese psychiatry as it developed during the twentieth century, has not been overcome even a situation which is evident in the call for a 'psychiatry with Chinese characteristics' in contemporary China.

Concepts of the body relate not only to the conception of the individual self but also to its role in society. The discovery of a new and
modern body was most visibly discussed in relation to public hygiene,
reproduction and fetal education, issues which are addressed in Sarah
Steven's contribution. Discussing texts on hygiene as an important
public site for the convergence of nationalism, racial evolution and
science, Stevens shows how these texts dictated concepts of the medi-
calisation and scientification of the female body, female sexuality,
family life and parenting, transforming formerly private spaces into
sites of public contestation. This cooptism of the private in the name
of the state was the result of a merging of discourses informed by
indigenous moral views on gender roles as well as by modern social,
technical and evolutionary theories. It still prevails in the political
control over women's bodies in mainland China.

Finally, Yvonne Schulz Zinda addresses the question of how the
specific education of the citizens-to-be of this new nation-state, the
children was conceived. Basing her analysis on the textbook series for
primary students of the Shanghai Commercial Press of 1906, Schulz
Zinda examines the moral values and virtues that were selected as
appropriate. In a second step she shows, how these partly Western-
derived concepts were familiarized at the primary school level. As
patriotism was one of the key concepts to be disseminated through the
ethic primers under investigation, Schulz Zinda explores the political
strategic choices in presenting a model for the students which guaranteed a nationalist consciousness of new citizens, while at the same
time interpreting the concept as loyalty to the emperor.

The contributions to this volume display a wide-ranging variety of
concerns and occupations with science and new knowledge that flourished in many fields throughout the nineteenth and early twentieth
century. They reveal how discourses on new knowledge from and
about the West as well as on their status and meanings emerged in all
sectors of intellectual discourse. Far from covering all aspects of these
contested sites, the different approaches to the field of new knowledge
presented here can only mark the beginning of explorations which
hopefully will expand into broader investigations into full variety of
alternatives and possibilities of alterities produced during this encounter of Western and Chinese knowledges. Rather than mapping the territory of new meanings through definitions and demarcations, this
volume is intended as a first attempt at opening paths towards the

vastness and variety of as yet undiscovered topics and sources of this in many respects decisive period of modern Chinese history. The emergence of science as a central notion of public discourse is analysed as resulting from competing over new possibilities which were subject to polemics and contested historical assessments. Further explorations of historical sources and their contextual reading will foster a more profound understanding of the specific nature of these transcultural processes, an understanding which is not restricted by narrowly defined discourses on failure or success.

If we may therefore conclude with David Hume

> that there is no subject in which we must proceed with more caution than in tracing the history of the arts and sciences, lest we assign causes which never existed, and reduce what is merely contingent to stable and universal principles.Those who cultivate the sciences in any state, are always few in number: The passion, which governs them, limited: Their taste and judgment delicate and easily perverted: And their application disturbed with the smallest accident. Chance, therefore, or secret and unknown causes, must have a great influence on the rise and progress of all the refined arts.[10]

we might add that to us the only possible way out of this dilemma appears to be the continuous effort to historicize the polemics and to rediscover those alternative pathways of which the maps have been lost.

---

[10] David Hume. 1987 [1742]. "On the rise of progress of the Arts and Sciences". *Essays. Moral Political and Literary.* Eugene F. Miller (ed). Indianapolis: Liberty Fund Inc, vol. 1, ch. 14, p. 2.

REFERENCES

Bayly, Chris. 1996. *Empire and Information: Intelligence Gathering and Social Communication in India, 1780–1870*. Cambridge: Cambridge University Press.

Boedecker, Hans Erich, Peter H. Reill and Jürgen Schlumbohm (eds.). *Wissenschaft als kulturelle Praxis 1750–1900*. Göttingen: Vandenhoeck and Ruprecht.

Clark, William, Jan Golinski and Simon Schaffer (eds.). 1999. *The Sciences in Enlightened Europe*. Chicago and London: University of Chicago Press.

Daum, Andreas. 1998. *Wissenschaftspopularisierung im 19. Jahrhundert. Bürgerliche Kultur, naturwissenschaftliche Bildung und die deutsche Öffentlichkeit, 1848–1914*. Munich: Oldenbourg.

Goeschler, Constantin. 2000. *Wissenschaft und Öffentlichkeit in Berlin. 1870–1930*. Stuttgart: Steiner.

Hart, Roger. 1999. "Beyond Science and Civilisation: A Post-Needham Critique", *East Asian Science, Technology Medicine* 16, pp. 88–114.

Howland, Douglas R. 2002. *Translating the West: Language and Political Reason in Nineteenth-Century Japan*. Honolulu: University of Hawaii Press.

Hume, David. 1987 [1742]. "On the rise of progress of the Arts and Sciences". *Essays. Moral Political and Literary*. Eugene F. Miller (ed). Indianapolis: Liberty Fund Inc, vol. 1, chapter 14, p. 2.

Lackner, Michael, Iwo Amelung and Joachim Kurtz (eds.). 2001. *New Terms for New Ideas. Western Knowledge and Lexical Change in Late Imperial China*. Leiden et.al.: Brill.

Montgomery, Scott L. 2000. *Science in Translation. Movements of knowledge through Cultures and Time*. Chicago and London: University of Chicago Press.

Reynolds, David C. 1991. "Redrawing China's Intellectual Map: Images of Science in Nineteenth Century China". *Late Imperial China* 12.1, pp. 27-61.

Wright, David. 2000. *Translating Science. The Transmission of Western Chemistry into Late Imperial China, 1840–1900*. Leiden et.al: Brill.

THE POLITICS OF GLOBAL KNOWLEDGE

BENJAMIN A. ELMAN

FROM PRE-MODERN CHINESE NATURAL STUDIES 格致學 TO MODERN SCIENCE 科學 IN CHINA[1]

INTRODUCTION

This paper is about the contested nature of the interaction since 1550 between Chinese and Europeans over the meaning and significance of natural studies. Unlike the colonial environment in India, where British imperial power after 1700 could dictate the terms of social, cultural, and political interaction between natives and Westerners, natural studies in late imperial China were until 1900 part of a native imperial project to master and control Western views on what constituted legitimate natural knowledge.[2] Each side made a virtue out of the mutually contested accommodation project, and each converted the other's forms of natural studies into acceptable local conventions of knowledge. Arguably, Europe was already ahead by 1600 in producing basic machines such as clocks, screws, levers, and pulleys that would be applied increasingly to the mechanization of production. But Europeans still sought the technological secrets for silk, textile weaving, porcelain, and tea production from the Chinese.[3] Chinese literati in turn borrowed from Europe new algebraic notations (of Hindu-Arabic origins), geometry, trigonometry, and logarithms from the West. Indeed, the epistemological premises of modern Western science were not triumphant in China until the early twentieth century. Until 1900, then, the Chinese interpreted the transition in early

---

[1] Earlier versions of this paper were presented at UC, Berkeley (Center for Chinese Studies), Stanford (World History Conference), UCLA (Center for the Cultural Study of Science, Medicine, and Technology), and at the Institute for Advanced Study (Chinese Studies Program) in Princeton.

[2] On India, see Bernard Cohn. 1996. *Colonialism and Its Form of Knowledge: The British in India.* Chicago: University of Chicago Press, pp. 5–56. See also Gyan Prakash. 1999. *Another Reason: Science and the Imagination of Modern India.* Princeton: Princeton University Press, pp. 3–14, who notes that the British civilizing mission in India initiated the cultural authority of modern science in South Asia. Prakash adds that Indians also identified a body of indigenous South Asian traditions consistent with Western science.

[3] Cf. Donald F. Lach. 1977. *Asia in the Making of Europe. Volume II. A Century of Wonder, Book 3: The Scholarly Disciplines.* Chicago: University of Chicago Press, pp. 397–400.

modern Europe—from new forms of scientific knowledge to new modes of industrial power—on their own terms.[4]

Consequently, we should not underestimate Chinese efforts to master on their own terms the Western learning (known as *xixue* 西學 or *gezhi* 格致) of the Jesuits in the sixteenth, seventeenth, and eighteenth centuries.[5] Literati scholars and imperial calendrical specialists in the government interpreted early modern Western achievements in natural studies in light of native traditions of scholarship, which they used to evaluate and apply specific Jesuit techniques. This local research agenda represented neither an indigenous modernization process nor the beginnings of a modest scientific revolution, at least by Western standards.[6] And in not searching for a Western form of modernity until the late nineteenth century, late imperial Chinese and Manchus were not acting out a purely anti-Western ideological agenda either. At times, however, court politics in Beijing interceded, and the Jesuits as bearers of Western tidings were faced with the political animosities such new (*xin* 新) learning produced among those in power who were satisfied with the old (*gu* 古) learning.

To paraphrase the views of Peter Winch, we must first acknowledge that as yet we do not have appropriate categories of learning that resemble the pre-modern Chinese frames for what we call natural studies or natural history.[7] Moreover, as Donald F. Lach has pointed out, an analytical ordering of early modern European scholarship

---

    [4] See Donald Mungello. 1985. *Curious Land: Jesuit Accommodation and the Origins of Sinology.* Honolulu: University of Hawaii Press, pp. 23–43; and Lionel Jensen. 1977. *Manufacturing Confucianism: Chinese Traditions and Universal Civilization.* Durham: Duke University Press, pp. 34–75. The accommodation project carried over to natural anomalies, supernatural events, and religious faith. See Qiong Zhang. 1999. "About God, Demons, and Miracles: The Jesuit Discourse on the Supernatural in Late Ming China", *Early Science and Medicine* 4.1 (February 1999), pp. 1–36.
    [5] See Xu Guangtai 徐光台 . 1996a. "Ruxue yu kexue: yige kexueshi guandian de tantao" 儒學與科學 ：一個科學史觀點的探討 (Literati studies and science: analysis from the angle of the history of science), *Qinghua xuebao*, New Series, 26.4 (December 1996), pp. 369–92.
    [6] But see Nathan Sivin. 1995a. "Why the Scientific Revolution did not take place in China—or didn't it?". Reprinted in id. *Science in Ancient China: Researches and Reflections.* Aldershot/Brookfield: Variorum, pp. 45–66.
    [7] Cf. Peter Winch. 1970. "Understanding a Primitive Society", in: Bryon Wilson (ed.). *Rationality.* Oxford: Basil Blackwell, pp. 93–102.

within the framework of modern learning is equally problematic.[8] To understand the pre-modern Chinese frames for their knowledge systems of the natural world, as for early modern Europe, we should first try to extend our own understanding and make room for them. That will be attempted below. We will place natural studies in China within its own internal and external contexts by reconstructing in outline form its communities of interpretation.[9]

Unfortunately, one of the most common generalizations scholars make today concerning the role of science (= natural studies) in late imperial China is that after about 1300 studies of astronomy and mathematics were in steady decline there until the arrival of Jesuit missionaries in the sixteenth century.[10] When Matteo Ricci (1552–1610) described the scientific prowess of Chinese during the late Ming dynasty (1368–1644), he noted that they

> have not only made considerable progress in moral philosophy but in astronomy and in many branches of mathematics as well. At one time they were quite proficient in arithmetic and geometry, but in the study and teaching of these branches of learning they labored with more or less confusion.

Ricci concluded:

> The study of mathematics and that of medicine are held in low esteem, because they are not fostered by honors as is the study of philosophy, to which students are attracted by the hope of the glory and the rewards attached to it.[11]

Chinese mathematics and astronomy, according to this view, had reached their pinnacle during the Song (960–1280) and Yuan (1280–1368) dynasties but had declined precipitously during the Ming.[12] This longstanding perspective has been tested by recent studies that

---

[8] Cf. Lach 1977, p. 395.

[9] Cf. Stanley J. Tambiah. 1990. *Magic, Science, Religion, and the Scope of Rationality*. Cambridge: Cambridge University Press, p. 154.

[10] Cf. Keizō Hashimoto. 1988. *Hsu Kuang-ch'i and Astronomical Reform*. Osaka: Kansai University Press, p. 17.

[11] *China in the Sixteenth Century: The Journals of Matteo Ricci: 1583–1610*. 1953. Translated into Latin by Father Nichola Trigault and into English by Louis J. Gallagher, S. J. New York: Random House, pp. 31–3.

[12] For the conventional perspective, see Joseph Needham. 1959. *Science and Civilisation in China*. Cambridge: Cambridge University Press, vol. 3, pp. 173, 209; and Ho Peng Yoke. 1985. *Li, Qi, and Shu: An Introduction to Science and Civilization in China*. Hong Kong: Hong Kong University Press, p. 169.

indicate that mathematics and calendar reform remained important concerns among Ming literati before the arrival of the Jesuits in China.[13] Others have demonstrated that the Jesuits misrepresented their knowledge of contemporary European astronomy to suit their religious objectives during the late Ming and early Qing (1644–1911) dynasty. Such self-serving tactics, which produced contradictory information about new trends in European astronomy, lessened their success in transmitting the European sciences to late Ming literati.[14] From this perspective, late Ming scholars were not lifted out of their scientific 'decline' by contact via the Jesuits with European astronomy. Rather, they themselves reevaluated their astronomical legacy and its current inadequacies, successfully taking into account pertinent features of the European sciences introduced by the Jesuits.[15]

Views that late imperial literati, unlike their Song and Yuan predecessors, were participants in a strictly humanist civilization, whose elite participants were trapped in a literary ideal that eschewed interest in the natural world, have been common since the Jesuits.[16] Historians have typically appealed for corroboration to the civil examination system. Matteo Ricci wrote:

> The judges and the proctors of all examinations, whether they be in military science, in mathematics, or in medicine, and particularly so with examinations in philosophy, are always chosen from the senate of

[13] See Roger Hart. 1996. *Proof, Propaganda, and Patronage: A Cultural History of the Dissemination of Western Studies in Seventeenth-Century China*. Ph.D. diss., University of California (Los Angeles), *passim*. See also Willard Peterson. 1986. "Calendar Reform Prior to the Arrival of Missionaries at the Ming Court", *Ming Studies* 21, pp. 45–61; and Thatcher E. Deane. 1989. *The Chinese Imperial Astronomical Bureau: Form and Function of the Ming Dynasty 'Qintianjian' From 1365 to 1627*. Ph.D. diss., University of Washington (Seattle), which documents the voluminous record of calendrical reform in China from the early empire to the late Ming.

[14] Cf. Nathan Sivin. 1973. "Copernicus in China", in: *Colloquia Copernica II: Études sur l'audience de la théorie héliocentrique*. Warsaw: Union Internationale d'Historie et Philosophie des Sciences, pp. 63–114.

[15] Cf. Jacques Gernet. 1982. *China and the Christian Impact*. Cambridge: Cambridge University Press, pp. 15–24. See also Sivin's biography of Wang Hsi-shan, Nathan Sivin. 1970–78. "Wang Hsi-shan (1628–1682)", in: *Dictionary of Scientific Biography*. New York: Scribner's Sons, vol. 14, pp. 159–68; and Deane 1989, pp. 401–41.

[16] See Michael Adas. 1989. *Machines as the Measure of Men: Science, Technology, and Ideologies of Western Dominance*. Ithaca: Cornell University Press, pp. 41–68, 79–95.

philosophy, nor is ever a military expert, a mathematician, or a medical doctor added to their number.[17]

In addition, we have assumed that the classical curriculum for Ming civil examinations had refocused elite attention on a 'Dao Learning' (*Daoxue* 道學 , i.e., 'Neo-Confucian') orthodoxy stressing moral philosophy and literary values and away from earlier more specialized or technical studies. Conventional scholarship still contends that technical fields such as law, medicine, and mathematics, common in Tang and Song examinations, were not replicated in late imperial examinations.[18]

When faced with foreign rule (first under the Mongols, 1240–1368, and later under the Manchus, 1644–1911) significant numbers of literati, in addition to the usual number of candidates who failed, turned to occupations outside the civil service such as medicine. In the eighteenth and nineteenth centuries, when demographic pressure meant that even provincial and metropolitan examination graduates were not likely to receive official appointments, many literati turned to teaching, medicine, and scholarship as alternative careers.[19] Moreover, examiners used policy questions on natural events and anomalies to gainsay the widespread penetration of popular religion and the mantic

---

[17] *China in the Sixteenth Century: The Journals of Matteo Ricci: 1583–1610*, p. 41. See also George H. Dunne, S.J. 1962. *Generation of Giants: The Story of the Jesuits in China in the Last Decades of the Ming Dynasty*. Notre Dame: University of Notre Dame Press, pp. 129–30; Kiyosi Yabuuti. 1973. "Chinese Astronomy: Development and Limiting Factors", in: Shigeru Nakayama and Nathan Sivin (eds.). *Chinese Science: Explorations of an Ancient Tradition*. Cambridge, Mass.: MIT Press, pp. 98–9.

[18] See, however, Zhang Hongsheng 張鴻聲 . 1995. "Qingdai yiguan kaoshi ji tili" 清代醫官考試及題例 (Qing dynasty examinations for medical officials with examples), *Zhonghua yishi zazhi* 25.2 (April 1995), pp. 95–6, on Qing examinations to choose a limited number of medical officials, which were based on Ming precedents. See also Liang Jun 梁峻 . 1995. *Zhongguo gudai yizheng shilüe* 中國古代醫政史略 (Historical summary of medicine and government in ancient China). Huhehot: Nei Menggu renmin chubanshe. Calendrical and cosmological questions were required in Ming examinations administered for candidates applying for positions in the Astronomical Bureau. See Deane 1989, pp. 197–200.

[19] Cf. Robert Hymes. 1986. "Not Quite Gentlemen? Doctors in Song and Yuan", *Chinese Science* 7, pp. 11–85; and Joseph Levenson. 1957. "The Amateur Ideal in Ming and Early Qing Society: Evidence from Painting", in: John K. Fairbank (ed.). *Chinese Thought and Institutions*. Chicago: University of Chicago Press, pp. 320–41.

arts among examination candidates and to keep such beliefs out of politics.[20]

1. INTEREST IN NATURAL STUDIES DURING THE MING DYNASTY

Natural studies in China had at times since the Yuan dynasty been classified under the phrase *gezhi* 格致 (lit., 'inquiring into and extending knowledge', *gewu zhizhi* 格物致知). At other times, particularly in the medieval period, and often simultaneously after the Yuan, such interests were expressed in terms of *bowu* 博物 (lit., 'broad learning concerning the nature of things'). The full mapping out of the asymmetrical conceptual categories associated with these two potential candidates in Song and Ming times for natural studies and natural history respectively remains incomplete. Moreover we are still unsure how the two terms usually were deployed vis-à-vis each other.

In addition, in ancient and medieval bibliographic classifications other terms such as *shuji* 術技 (skills and techniques) were used to demarcate what we today refer to as science and technology. In the late eighteenth century *Siku quanshu* 四庫全書 (Complete collection in the Imperial Four Treasuries) scheme of disciplines, medicine and calendrical studies were included as subcategories under the Philosophy (*zibu* 子部 , lit., 'masters') category (see Table 1).

Table 1: Forty-four subdivisions of the Siku quanshu 四庫全書
(Complete collection in the Imperial Four Treasuries)

Classics (*jingbu* 經部)	History (*shibu* 史部)	Masters (*zibu* 子部)	Literature (*jibu* 集部)
Change(s)	Dynastic Histories	Literati	Elegies of Chu
Documents	Annals	Military Strategists	Individual Collections
Poetry	Topical Records	Legalists	General Anthologies
Rituals	Unofficial Histories	Agriculturalists	Literary Criticism
Spring and Autumn Annals	Miscellaneous Histories	Medicine	Songs and Drama
Filial Piety	Official Documents	Astronomy and Mathematics	

---

[20] See Benjamin A. Elman. 2000. *A Cultural History of Civil Examinations in Late Imperial China*. Berkeley: University of California Press, pp. 346–60.

Table 1: Forty-four subdivisions of the Siku quanshu 四庫全書
(Complete collection in the Imperial Four Treasuries) (cont.)

Classics (*jingbu* 經部)	History (*shibu* 史部)	Masters (*zibu* 子部)	Literature (*jibu* 集部)
General Works	Biographies	Calculating Arts	
Four Books	Historical Records	Arts	
Music	Contemporary Records	Repertories of Science	
Philology	Chronography	Miscellaneous Writers	
	Geography	Encyclopedias	
	Official Registers	Novels	
	Institutions	Buddhism	
	Bibliographies and Epigraphy	Daoism	
	Historical Criticism		

Similarly the mathematical aspects of music were subsumed under the Classics, while chronography and geography were listed under History. Hence, we cannot assume that there was a single and unified traditional field of natural studies in China before the Jesuit arrival known as *gezhixue*.[21] Nonetheless, it appears to me, tentatively, that among Song and post-Song literati elites *gezhi* was the most common epistemological frame for the accumulation of knowledge per se. *Bowu* on the other hand carried with it a more common and popular notion of curiosities.[22] For example, the *Taiping yulan* 太平御覽 (Encyclopedia of the Taiping era, 976–83), compiled under imperial auspices by Li Fang 李昉 (925–96) during the early years of the

---

[21] Cf. Xu Guangtai 徐光台 . 1996b. "Mingmo Qingchu xifang gezhixue de chongji yu fanying: yi Xiong Mingyu Gezhi cao wei li" 明末清初西方格致學的衝擊與反應：以熊明遇格致草為例 (Impact and response in late Ming and early Qing Western *scientiae*; using Gao Mingyu's draft of *Scientiae* as an example) in: Taiwan University History Department (ed.). *Shibian, qunti yu geren* 世變，群體與個人 (Epochal change, groups and history). Taibei: Taiwan National University, pp. 236–58

[22] See Robert F. Campany. 1996. *Strange Writing: Anomaly Accounts in Early Medieval China*. Albany: SUNY Press, pp. 49–52. See also Qiong Zhang. 1998. "Nature, Supernature, and Natural Studies in Sixteenth- and Seventeenth-Century China". Paper presented at the Colloquium sponsored by the Center for the Cultural Studies of Science, Medicine, and Technology, UCLA History Department, Los Angeles, November 16, 1998.

Northern Song dynasty (960–1126), included earlier texts dealing exclusively with unusual events, strange objects/things/birds/spirits, and anomalies to provide a contemporary lexicon of textual usages in antiquity and medieval times that denoted the scope of *bowu* within classical writings.[23]

On the other hand, the Southern Song (1127–1280) philosopher Zhu Xi 朱熹 (1130–1200), who became the core interpreter of the late imperial classical canon, argued that "inquiring into and extending knowledge" presupposed that all things had their principle (*wan wu zhi li* 萬物之理). Zhu therefore concluded: "one should in three or four cases out of ten seek principles in the outside realm" (*san si fen qu waimian li hui fang ke* 三四分去外面理會方可). In most cases, six to seven out of ten, however, moral principles should be sought within. Thereafter, the investigation of things became the key to opening the door of knowledge for literati versed in the Classics and Histories."[24]

Due to Zhu Xi's later scholarly eminence, *gezhi* became a popular 'Dao Learning' term borrowed from the Great Learning (*Daxue* 大學 ; one of the Four Books) in the Record of Rites (*Liji* 禮記 ; one of the Five Classics) by literati to discuss the form and content of knowledge. In fact, however, there was much classical debate surrounding Zhu Xi's single-minded prioritizing of the *gewu* 格物 passage in the Great Learning to establish the epistemological boundaries for literati learning.[25] Yü Ying-shih's 余英時 longstanding claim that the seventeenth century turn among literati elites toward precise philology in classical studies can be traced back to sixteenth century debates surrounding the Old Text version of the Great Learning (*Daxue guben* 大學古本) deserves mention here.[26]

---

[23] Cf. *Taiping yulan* 太平御覽 (Encyclopedia of the Taiping era). 1960. Reprint Taibei: Zhonghua Bookstore, vol. 612, *juan* 4a–10a (Reprint of *Sibu congkan* 四部叢刊 edition).

[24] See *Zhuzi yulei* 朱子語類 (Conversations with Master Zhu [Xi] classified topically). 1979 [1473]. Reprint Taibei: Chengwen, vol. 18, pp. 14b–15a. See also Yamada Keiji 山田慶兒 . 1978. *Shushi no shizengaku* 朱子の自然学 (Zhu Xi's natural studies). Tokyo: Iwanami, pp. 413–72.

[25] Cf. Daniel Gardner. 1986. *Zhu Xi and the Daxue: Neo-Confucian Reflection on the Confucian Canon*. Cambridge: Harvard University Council on East Asian Studies, pp. 27–59.

[26] See Yü Ying-shih. 1975. "Some Preliminary Observations on the Rise of Qing Confucian Intellectualism", *Qinghua Journal of Chinese Studies*, New Series 11.1

Wang Yangming 王陽明 (1472–1528), for instance, preferred the Old Text version of the Great Learning to gainsay Zhu Xi's 'externalist' views of the 'investigation of things' in the Four Books. Subsequently, the delicate issue of the late Ming appearance of an even more ancient "stone inscribed version of the Great Learning" (*Daxue shiben* 大學石本), which was later determined a forgery, reopened for many sixteenth and seventeenth century literati Wang Yangming's famous claim that Zhu Xi had manipulated the original text of this key passage to validate and make canonical his personal interpretation of the 'investigation of things'. In particular, Wang Yangming gainsaid Zhu Xi's emphasis on *gezhi* ahead of morality (*chengyi* 誠意 , lit. 'making one's intentions sincere'). For Wang the investigation of things and the extension of knowledge took a backseat to making one's will sincere.[27]

During the late Yuan, *gezhi* as a *Daoxue* term was already used by the medical writer Zhu Zhenheng 朱震亨 (1282–1358) to denote technical learning. In Zhu's most famous work entitled *Gezhi yulun* 格致餘論 (Views on extending medical knowledge), which was included in the *Siku quanshu* in the late eighteenth century,[28] Zhu opposed Song medical prescriptions, but he made a strong appeal to Yuan literati that they should include medical learning in their 'Learning of the Way'. In his view, medical learning was one of the key fields of study that not only complemented the moral and theoretical teachings of *Daoxue*, but it was also a key to the practical uses (*shixue* 實學) of the latter. The *Siku quanshu* editors cited Zhu's preface as arguing that medicine was one of the concrete fields that informed the "inquiry into and extension of knowledge" (*gewu zhizhi zhi yishi* 格物致知之一事).[29]

---

[26] (*cont.*) and 11.2 (December 1975), p. 125, for discussion of Wang Yangming's critique of Zhu Xi's elucidation of the *Great Learning*, which created a textual crisis in the sixteenth century.

[27] See Wang Fan-shen. 1995. "The 'Daring Fool' Feng Fang (1500–1570) and His Ink Rubbing of the Stone-inscribed Great Learning", *Ming Studies* 35 (August 1995), pp. 74–91. See also Wang Yangming 王陽明 . 1973. "Chuanxi lu" 傳習錄 (Instructions for practical living), in: *Wang Yangming quanji* 王陽明全集 (Complete works of Wang Yangming). Taibei: Kaozheng Press, p. 129.

[28] See Zhu Zhenheng 朱震亨 . 1983–86. *Gezhi yulun*格致餘論 (Views on extending medical knowledge). Reprint Taibei: Commercial Press (in the *Siku quanshu* 四庫全書 edition), vol. 746, p. 638.

[29] See the synopsis ("Tiyao" 提要) of Zhu Zhenheng's study prepared by the editors of the *Siku quanshu zongmu* 四庫全書總目 (Catalogue of the complete collection

In addition to its central epistemological place in literati classical learning since 1200, the notion of *gewu* was also applied to the collection, study, and classification of antiquities, as in Cao Zhao's 曹昭 (fl. 1387–99) *Gegu yaolun* 格古要論 ('Essential Criteria of Antiquities', lit. 'Key issues in the investigation of antiquities'), which was published in the early Ming and enlarged several times thereafter. The work originally appeared in 1387/88 with important accounts of ceramics and lacquer, as well as traditional subjects such as calligraphy, painting, zithers, stones, bronzes, and ink-slabs. The 1462 edition prepared by Wang Zuo 王佐 (*jinshi* 進士 of 1427) was enlarged considerably and included findings from the official Ming dynasty naval expeditions led by Zheng He 鄭和 (1371–1433) to Southeast Asia and the Indian Ocean from 1405 to 1433. Wang also added the subjects of imperial seals, iron tallies, official costumes, and palace architecture. In his "Preface," Wang added:

凡見一物，必遍閱圖譜，究其來歷，格其優劣，別其是否而後已
Whenever one sees an object, you must look it all over, trace its appearance, and examine its history and origins. You should investigate its strengths and weaknesses, and distinguish its accuracy.[30]

He was particularly interested in ancient bronzes, calligraphic specimens, and curiosities.[31]

The term *gezhi* was also chosen by Ming literati in the seventeenth century as one of the native categories of specialized learning (*xuewen* 學問), with the latter equivalent to early modern European *scientia*. In the late Qing, reformist Chinese officials and scholars reworked *gezhixue* to designate modern Western science between 1865 and

---

[29] (*cont.*) of the Four Treasuries). 1973. Ji Yun 記昀 et al. (comp.). Reprint Taibei: Yiwen Press, vol. 746, p. 637.

[30] See the abridged version of the *Gegu yaolun*格古要論 (Essential criteria of antiquities).1573–1619. In: Hu Wenhuan 胡文煥 (comp.). *Gezhi congshu* 格致叢書 (Collectanea of works inquiring into and extending knowledge). Microfilm: Taibei: National Central Library, Rare Books Collection (film of Ming Wanli edition) ca. 1596, vol. 25. See the preface "Xu" 序 by Wang Zuo 王佐 , pp. 1a–b. See also Sir David Percival (tr.). 1971. *Chinese Connoisseurship, the Ko Ku Yao Lun: The Essential Criteria of Antiquity*. London: Faber. The new information from other parts of Asia, however, did not challenge the existing frameworks of knowledge in Ming China, which differs from the wider impact of sixteenth century oceanic discoveries in early modern Europe. See Lach 1977, pp. 446–89.

[31] These literati practices of collecting and classifying antiquities merged into the academic discipline of archeology in the early twentieth century. On this development see Su Rongyu's contribution in this volume.

1900. Subsequently *gezhixue* was replaced in the early twentieth century by *kexue* as the Chinese equivalent for science, which suggests that native terms for Western science were contested at different times and in different ways.[32] Early Jesuit translations of Aristotle's theory of the four elements (*Kongji gezhi* 空際格致, lit., 'investigation of space', 1633) and Agricola's *De Re Metallica* (*Kunyu gezhi* 崑崳格致, lit., 'investigation of the earth', 1640) into classical Chinese, for example, had used the term *gezhi* in light of the Latin *scientia* (= 'organized or specialized knowledge', or *xuewen*, as *scientia* was translated in Chinese in the sixteenth century) in their titles.[33] 'Dao Learning' doctrine and natural studies, particularly medical and calendrical learning, were not mutually exclusive.[34]

Willard Peterson in his valuable study of Fang Yizhi 方以智 (1611–71) has noted how late-Ming views of the *Daoxue* doctrine of the 'investigation of things' (*gewu* 格物, lit., 'approaches to phenomena') had changed from a type of moral endeavor, purely, to an additional stress on external things. Fang Yizhi's opus magnum entitled *Wuli xiaozhi* 物理小識 (Notes on the principles of things) stressed material investigations to comprehend the seminal forces underlying patterns of natural change. Fang generally accepted Western explanations of natural phenomena, such as a spherical earth, limited heliocentrism, and human physiology, brought by the Jesuits, but he was critical of them for leaving behind material investigations and ending in unverified religious positions. Fang Yizhi favored, instead, descriptive knowledge of the natural world, and he inscribed the 'Dao Learning' interpretation of the 'investigation of things' with a new view of

---

[32] For discussion, see Lydia Liu. 1995. *Translingual Practice: Literature, National Culture, and Translated Modernity—China 1900–1937*. Stanford: Stanford University Press, pp. 20–42.

[33] See Pan Jixing. 1991. "The Spread of Georgius Agricola's *De Re Metallica* in Late Ming China", *T'oung Pao* 57, pp. 108–18; and James Reardon-Anderson. 1991. *The Study of Change: Chemistry in China, 1840–1949*. Cambridge: Cambridge University Press, pp. 30–6; 82–8.

[34] See Roger Hart. 1997. "Local Knowledges, Local Contexts: Mathematics in Yuan and Ming China". Paper presented at the Song-Yuan-Ming Transitions Conference, Lake Arrowhead, Cal., June 5–11, 1997. The conference volume unfortunately will not include this important paper for publication.

the accumulation of knowledge, which gainsaid both the introspective focus of Wang Yangming and the moralist focus of Zhu Xi.[35]

Similarly, the Ming scholar and Hangzhou bookseller Hu Wen-huan 胡文煥 (fl. ca. 1596) compiled and published the *Gezhi congshu* 格致叢書 (Collectanea of works inquiring into and extending knowledge) as a late-Ming repository of classical, historical, institutional, and technical works from antiquity to the present in China that presented a cumulative account of all areas of textual knowledge important to a literati audience in the seventeenth century. Although no two editions of this collectanea were the same, Hu apparently printed a total of 346 works for this and other collectanea in his print shops in Nanjing and Hangzhou, which by some accounts were divided into 37 categories (*lei* 類), such as classical instruction, philology, phonology, historical studies, rituals and regulations, legal precedents, geography, mountains and streams, medicine, Taoism, Buddhism, agriculture, stars, physiognomy, poetry and literature, painting, and epigraphy, among others. Only 181 works were apparently available to the compilers of the *Siku quanshu*, and the version of the *Gezhi congshu* that focused strictly on the 'investigation of things' contained 46 works that stressed classical philology and etymology, beginning with the *Erya* 爾雅 (Progress toward correctness) dictionary annotated by Guo Pu 郭璞 (276–324) of the Jin dynasty.[36]

The *Gegu yaolun* account of early Ming antiquities, for instance, was also included in the collection, but it was abridged by Hu Wen-huan to include only the key parts and titled *Gegu lunyao* 格古論要 (On the most important items in the investigation of antiquities). Hu noted:

> 謂古之不可不格也，古格而未有不通於今。物格而未有不通於人。格之時義大矣哉
>
> Antiquity must be investigated. When antiquity is investigated it always penetrates to the present. When things are investigated it always penetrates to humanity. Timely investigations are very meaningful.[37]

---

[35] Cf. Willard Peterson. 1975. "Fang I-chih: Western Learning and the 'Investigation of Things'", in: Wm. Theodore de Bary et al. (eds.). *The Unfolding of Neo-Confucianism.* New York: Columbia University Press, pp. 369–411.

[36] See Hu Wenhuan 1573–1619, which contains 46 works.

[37] See Hu Wenhuan's preface ("Xu" 序) to the *Gezhi congshu* edition of the *Gegu lunyao*, in *Gegu yaolun* 1573–1619, 25, pp. 1a–2a.

Overall, the *Gezhi congshu* collectanea emphasized a broad learning of phenomena (*bowu* 博物), one of the 37 categories, that encompassed natural and textual studies within a humanist and institutional agenda. Within the collection, Zhang Hua's 張華 (232–300) *Bowuzhi* 博物志 (A treatise on curiosities), and Li Shi's 李石 Song dynasty continuation, titled *Xu bowuzhi* 續博物志 (Continuation to a treatise on curiosities) were subsumed under the general category of *gezhi* here. Other works included in the *Gezhi congshu* were the *Shiwu jiyuan* 事物紀原 (Record of the origins of things and affairs) compiled by Gao Cheng 高承 (ca. 1078–85), and the *Gujin shiwu kao* 古今事物考 (Examination of ancient and contemporary things and affairs) prepared by Wang Sanpin 王三聘 in the Ming dynasty.[38]

In addition to Hu Wenhuan's Ming "*Gezhi* studies," Dong Sizhang 董斯張 completed the *Guang bowuzhi* 廣博物志 (Expansion of a treatise on curiosities), which paid more attention to 'natural history'. Such works on *bowu* 博物 as 'natural history' suggest that as a term *bowu* needs to be conceptually mapped asymmetrically with *gezhi*. Sometimes the former was included under the latter, sometimes not. In both *gezhi*-oriented and *bowu*-framed late-Ming works, the transformation of objects into artifacts, antiquities, and art objects was attempted. From heaven and earth to birds, animals, insects, fish, grasses, foodstuffs, architecture, and tools, the inventory of 'organized knowledge' from a Chinese frame of reference represented a systematic collection of data from a wide variety of native sources about China's natural resources, the arts, and manufactures. In the interaction with Western *scientia*, Chinese literati were drawn into a moderate transformation of their own traditions of natural studies.[39]

2. NATURAL STUDIES IN MING CIVIL EXAMINATIONS

Careful scrutiny of Ming dynasty examination records reveals that civil examinations also tested the candidates' knowledge of astrology (*tianwen* 天文), calendrics (*lifa* 歷法), and other aspects of the natural

---

[38] Ibid., and Campany 1996, pp. 51–2. A preface for the version of 156 works in the Library of Congress edition of the *Gezhi congshu* is entitled *Baijia mingshu xu* 百家名書序 (Preface to the *Renowned works of the Hundred schools*).

[39] Cf. *Gezhi congshu, passim*. See also Ssu-yü Teng and Knight Biggerstaff. 1971. *An Annotated Bibliography of Selected Chinese Reference Works*. Cambridge: Harvard University Press, p. 105.

world, which were referred to as 'natural studies' (*ziran zhi xue* 自然之學).[40] Ming candidates for both the provincial and metropolitan examinations, unlike their Song counterparts, were expected to grasp many of the technicalities in calendrics, astrology, anomalies (*zaiyi* 災異) and the musical pitch series (*yuelü* 樂律). The latter was the basis for official weights and measures. In the early Ming, for example, the Yongle 永樂 emperor (r. 1402–24) put calendrical and practical studies near the top of what counted for official, literati scholarship. More importantly, the emperor had legitimated 'natural studies', Thereafter such questions regularly appeared on Ming civil examinations.[41]

Table 2: Ming Dynasty Policy Questions Classified by Topic: Yingtian Prefecture, 1474–1600, 230 questions, top 15 ranks only*

Rank	Topic	Pct. of Total	Selection Probability
1	Learning/Selection (*yangcai* 養才 , *yong-ren* 用人)	9.6%	43.4%
2	Daoxue *(daoxue* 道學)	8.3%	37.5%
3	Ming rulers (*taizu* 太祖 , *chengzu* 成祖)	7.4%	33.5%
4	World ordering (*zhiguo* 治國)	7.0%	31.6%
5	Economy/Statecraft (*licai* 理財)	5.7%	25.8%
6	Ruler-official *(junchen* 君臣)	5.2%	23.5%
7	National defense (*guofang* 國防)	4.3%	19.4%
7	Classical studies (*jingxue* 經學)	4.3%	19.4%
9	Law *(faxing* 法刑)	3.5%	15.8%
9	Military matters (*bingshi* 兵事)	3.5%	15.8%
11	Literature/Poetry (*wenshi* 文詩)	3.0%	13.6%
11	Natural studies (*ziran* 自然)	3.0%	13.6%
13	History (*shixue* 史學)	2.6%	11.8%
13	Agriculture (*nongzheng* 農政)	2.6%	11.8%
13	Customs/Values *(fengsu* 風俗)	2.6%	11.8%

---

[40] See Elman 2000, pp. 461–81.

[41] See *Huang Ming sanyuan kao* 皇明三元考 (Study of the provincial, metropolitan, and palace civil examination *optimi* during the Ming dynasty). Zhang Hongdao 張弘道 and Zhang Ningdao 張凝道 (comps.). Late Ming edition, after 1618, vol. 2, p. 3b; and *Zhuangyuan ce* 狀元策 (Policy essays of *optimi*). 1997 [1733]. Jiao Hong 焦竑 and Wu Daonan 吳道南 et al. (comps.). n.p. Huaidetang edition, chapter "Zongkao" 總考 , p. 15a.

*) Source: Nanguo xianshu 南國賢書 (Record of civil examination success in the Southern Capital Region). Compiled by Zhang Chaorui 張朝瑞 (ca. 1600 edition). The probability for each policy question is calculated based on the assumption that each of the five selections is mutually independent. If the selection of five questions were mutally dependent, then the probability for each type would be slightly higher. Most topics above and below are based on actual Chinese categories. I have added a few, such as natural studies, which are based on combining categories, such as astrology, calendrical studies, and musical harmonics.

Table 2, for instance, reveals that 50 to over 75 thousand candidates empire-wide for the provincial examinations during the Ming dynasty could reasonably expect a required policy question on astrology or calendrics. In the Qing, curiously, the likelihood of such policy questions was negligible.[42] Instead, candidates increasingly had to answer questions dealing with textual issues growing out of the evidential research studies that peaked in the late eighteenth century.

We should quickly add, however, that the ability to deal with astrological, medical, mathematical calculations for calendrics, and other technical questions was an essential tool of the new classical studies emerging in the late Ming and early Qing. It just was not tested within the precincts of the Qing civil service before 1860.[43] For example, Xiong Mingyu's 熊明遇 (b. 1579) Jesuit-inspired work entitled *Gezhi cao* 格致草 (Draft for investigating things and extending knowledge) revealed how far the classical ideal of *gewu* could be extended using European criteria for determining the fundamental ground of all things in the world (*suo yi ran zhi li* 所以然之理). Published in 1648, after the fall of the Ming and in the midst of the Manchu takeover of south China, the *Gezhi cao* represented an accommodation between Jesuit natural philosophy cum theology and the classical repertoire of literati learning based on *gewu*.[44]

---

[42] See Elman 2000, pp. 720–2.

[43] See Yuan-ling Chao. 1995. *Medicine and Society in Late Imperial China: A Study of Physicians in Suzhou*. Ph.D. diss., University of California (Los Angeles); and Chu Pingyi. 1994. *Technical Knowledge, Cultural Practices and Social Boundaries: Wan-nan Scholars and the Recasting of Jesuit Astronomy, 1600–1800*. Ph.D. diss., University of California (Los Angeles). Cf. Benjamin A. Elman. 1984. *From Philosophy to Philology*. Cambridge, Mass.: Council on East Asian Studies, Harvard University, pp. 61–4, 79–85, 180–4.

[44] See Xiong's preface ("Zixu" 自敍) in Xiong Mingyu 熊明遇 . 1648. *Gezhi cao* 格致草 (Draft for investigating things and extending knowledge). n.p. (1648 edition in the Library of Congress Asian Library). For discussion see Xu Guangtai 1996b, pp. 236–58.

3. THE ELIMINATION OF NATURAL STUDIES
IN EARLY QING EXAMINATIONS

The previous discussion demonstrates that it is a mistake to read back into the Ming dynasty the view that 'Dao Learning' moral philosophy and natural studies were opposed to technical learning. Specialized knowledge about astronomy, the calendar, and musical harmonics required in the civil examinations made some difference in the cultural prestige and social status of literati-officials vis-à-vis experts employed in the Astronomy Bureau or the Office of Music. As moral generalists versed in the classical orthodoxy that granted them the highest social, political, and cultural prestige, Ming civil officials were required to know how astronomy, mathematics, calendrical studies, and musical harmonics were part of the orthodox apparatus of ritual. They were not licensed to become 'scientists', but neither were they hostile to understanding the role of natural phenomena in governance.

Moreover, the longstanding political *raison d'être* for the literatus had been his official status as a moral paragon who made his classical degree, earned by examination, relevant to his bureaucratic position. Classical statecraft had always been premised on the linkage between classical learning and political competence. That competence was not measured by the literatus' status as an expert in natural studies. Part of it, however, involved using his knowledge of the Classics to understand the role of the calendar or music in governance. In the policy questions, technical learning was not the ultimate object of the question. Rather, the examiners expected candidates to place technical learning within the classical narrative of world-ordering bequeathed by the sage-kings.

Accordingly, the policy questions on natural studies were restricted to fields relevant to bureaucratic governance and discussed in the basic Classics, or at least read into them by the early commentaries. Other fields such as medicine and alchemy were not deemed appropriate for the examination curriculum. It was important that astronomy and mathematics were discussed in the early Classics, while medicine and alchemy were not. The 'wrong' answer to such policy questions would indicate that the candidate had failed to grasp the heterodox implications of any effort to observe phenomena in the heavens or on earth in ways that challenged the dynasty in power. As a public event, the policy question and answer delivered in the precincts of an examination compound made natural studies part of the orthodox system by placing them, during the Ming, within the civil service examination curriculum. By promoting technical knowledge, the examiners successfully domesticated astrology, musical pitch, and calendrics. Literati were chosen for officialdom in this way because they knew that the moral terms of their success presupposed the subordination of expert knowledge to 'Dao Learning'.

Natural studies was justified as the proper concern of the moral generalist because it could be brought within the orthodox system. Experts, as long as they were subordinate to dynastic orthodoxy and its legal representatives, were necessary parts of the cultural, political, and social hierarchies. The literatus-official coexisted with the calendrical expert in the bureaucratic apparatus but at higher levels of political status, cultural prominence, and social prestige.[45] The Ming civil examinations, therefore, were not remarkable because they included policy questions on natural studies. They were remarkable because they successfully encapsulated natural studies within a system of political, social, and cultural reproduction that guaranteed the long-term dominance of the dynasty, its literati, and the 'Dao Learning' orthodoxy.

We have some clues, however, about why in the Qing period such policy questions on natural studies were so rare and uninformed when compared to the Ming dynasty.[46] Geography and astrological studies had been overlapping fields in earlier dynasties, but during the early Qing this linkage was broken when, as shown below, the court banned policy questions on the calendar and celestial studies. Thereafter, geography, particularly local geography, flourished as a source for provincial and metropolitan policy questions.[47] The Manchu throne sought to monopolize this potentially volatile area of expertise within the confines of the court. Contemporary calendrical debates between Jesuits and literati-officials, which challenged the Yuan-Ming calendrical system during the Ming-Qing transition gave the imperial court

---

[45] Cf. Deane 1989, pp. 353–90.

[46] See Xu Ke 徐珂 . 1920. *Qingbai leichao* 清稗類鈔 (Classified jottings on Qing dynasty unofficial history). Shanghai: Commercial Press, vol. 21, p. 65.

[47] See Shen Xinzhou 沈新周 . 1910. "Xu" 序 (Preface), in: *Dixue* 地學 (Geographical studies). Shanghai: Saoye shanfang lithograph.

pause about allowing possibly divisive questions on the calendar to appear in civil examinations.[48]

The collapse of the Ming dynasty and its Qing successor under non-Han rule created opportunities until 1685 for experts in astronomy-astrology and music to break out of their subordinate positions and to challenge a discredited Ming elite for political power under a new Manchu ruling elite. The increased cultural importance of astronomical expertise, when the new dynasty had to reformulate in expert terms its calendrical and musical *raison d'être* as quickly as possible, challenged for a time the cultural distinction accumulated by literati via mastery of classical studies. Court scholars such as Li Guangdi 李 光地 (1642–1718) actively patronized specialists in calendrical calculations (see below) and made the musical pitch series a high priority in their officially financed research.[49]

Not until the 1680s, when the Manchu dynasty had mastered its political and military enemies, did the intellectual fluidity of the early decades of the Qing begin to disappear, leaving Han literati and Manchu elites in a precarious balance at the top (and calendar specialists again in the middle) of the political and social hierarchies, which lasted into the nineteenth century. In the process, policy questions on the third session of the provincial and metropolitan examinations virtually ceased to include natural studies. By 1715, the Kangxi emperor (r. 1662–1722) successfully banned focus in the civil examinations on study of astronomical portents and the calendar because they pertained to Qing dynastic legitimacy.

The emperor could not restrict such interest among the literati community outside the civil examination bureaucracy, however. The emperor, for example, decreed in 1713 that thereafter all examiners assigned to serve in provincial and metropolitan civil examinations were forbidden to prepare policy questions on astronomical portents, musical harmonics, or calculation methods. The latest works in Qing natural studies, court projects on which the Kangxi emperor had

---

[48] See Jonathan D. Spence. 1974. *Emperor of China: Self-portrait of K'ang-hsi.* New York: Vintage Books, pp. xvii–xix, 15–6, 74–5. On the Yang Guangxian 楊光先 (1597–1669) anti-Jesuit affair in Kangxi court life in the 1660s, see Chu Pingyi. 1997. "Scientific Dispute in the Imperial Court: The 1664 Calendar Case", *Chinese Science* 14, pp. 7–34.

[49] Cf. Arthur Hummel (ed.). 1972. *Eminent Chinese of the Qing Period.* Reprint Taibei: Chengwen, pp. 473–5.

employed Jesuit experts, were put off limits to examiners and examination candidates.[50]

This evolving Qing ban on examination candidates studying astronomy, astrology, and music for the civil examinations was noted at the time in Shen Xinzhou's 沈新周 1712 preface to his study entitled *Dixue* 地學 (Studies of geography). Shen indicated that all discussions of astronomical portents (*yan tianwen* 言天文) were forbidden late in the Kangxi reign. In this public acknowledgement of Qing imperial policy, we see by way of contrast how important the Yongle emperor's early Ming decree had been in encouraging natural studies. The Yongzheng emperor 雍正 (b.1678–1735), however, changed the Kangxi emperor's policy a bit by admitting imperial students with specializations in astrology (*tianwensheng* 天文生) into the dynastic schools.[51]

4. EVIDENTIAL STUDIES AND GEZHIXUE 格致學

Such bans on natural studies, however effective in the civil examinations, did not carry over to literati learning, where a decisive sea change in classical learning was occurring. Clearly there were limits to imperial power outside the government. In contrast to their *Daoxue* predecessors, Qing 'evidential research' (*kaozheng* 考證) scholars stressed exacting research, rigorous analysis, and the collection of impartial evidence drawn from ancient artifacts and historical documents and texts. Evidential scholars made verification a central concern for the emerging empirical theory of knowledge they advocated, namely "to search truth from facts" (*shishi qiushi* 實事求是). This program involved the placing of proof and verification at the center of the organization and analysis of the classical tradition in its complete, multidimensional proportions, which now included aspects of natural studies and mathematics.

---

[50] See *Huangchao zhengdian leizuan* 黃朝政典類纂 (Classified materials on Qing dynasty government regulations). 1969. Xi Yufu 席裕福 (comp.). Reprint Taibei: Shenwu Press, vol. 191, pp. 7b–8a. For discussion of these court compilations, see Elman 1984, pp. 79–80.

[51] See Shen Xinzhou 1910. See also "Qingchao tongdian" 清朝通典 (Encyclopaedic history of institutions of the Qing dynasty). 1936. In: *Shitong* 十通 (The ten *Tong*). Shanghai: Commercial Press, vol. 18, p. 2131.

Philological studies developed and evolved during the eighteenth and nineteenth centuries because published works on the Classics were part of a dynamic classical research enterprise whose goals were not scientific or objective per se but instead were tied to a new literati commitment to use the language of the ancient Classics as an impartial means to recapture the ideas and intentions of the sage-kings of antiquity. Even if they were scholarly iconoclasts in their own time, they still were firmly conservative in their social beliefs and commitments.[52]

By the late eighteenth century, reflecting the scholarly trends of the Qianlong era (1736–95), the policy questions for civil examinations began to exhibit a common five-way division of topics, usually in the following order: 1) Classics; 2) Histories; 3) Literature; 4) Statecraft; and 5) Local geography. The primacy of classical learning in the policy questions was due to the impact of Han Learning and evidential research among literati scholars, first in the Yangzi delta, and then empire-wide via examiners from the delta provinces of Jiangsu, Zhejiang, and Anhui. What was fueling the popularity of the revival of first a poetry question on session one and then philology in the policy questions in session three of the civil examinations was the close tie between the rules for rhyming in regulated verse and the field of phonology, which became the queen of philology during the Qianlong reign. The role of phonology in evidential research studies was paying dividends by improving literati knowledge of classical sounds and rhymes.[53]

Qing dynasty evidential scholars such as Dai Zhen 戴震 (1724–77) had in mind a systematic research agenda that built on paleography and phonology to reconstruct the meaning (*yi yin qiu yi* 以音求義) of Chinese words. Later Wang Niansun 王念孫 (1744–1832), and his son Wang Yinzhi 王引之 (1766–1834), extended Dai's approach and attempted to use the meanings of Chinese words as a method to reconstruct the intentions of the sages, the farsighted authors of those words. Moreover, technical phonology when applied to the study of the history of the classical language reached unprecedented precision and exactness. To achieve this end, evidential scholars chose philo-

---

[52] See Elman 1984, *passim.*
[53] See Elman 2000, pp. 546–62.

logical means, principally the application of phonology, paleography, and etymology, to study the Classics.[54]

One byproduct of these philological trends was the full realization of how important poetry, particularly regulated verse, was for the reconstruction of antiquity via phonology, paleography, and etymology. For example, Liang Zhangju 梁章鉅 (1775–1849), who assembled one of the first cultural studies of the examination regime entitled *Collected Comments on the Crafting of 8-legged Civil Examination Essays* (*Zhiyi conghua* 制藝叢話) in the early nineteenth century, compiled another collection in which he outlined the study of poetry and the rules of regulated verse. In the conclusion, Liang traced how Qing classical scholars had finally unraveled the rhyme system of the *Poetry Classic*. They had thereby illuminated the technical rules in regulated verse and made major advances in the study of phonology.[55]

A full-blown scientific revolution as in Europe did not ensue,[56] but *kaozheng* scholars made astronomy, mathematics, and geography high priorities in their research programs, another by-product of the changes in classical studies then underway. Animated by a concern to restore native traditions in the precise sciences to their proper place of eminence, after less overt attention during the Ming dynasty, evidential scholars such as Dai Zhen, Qian Daxin 錢大昕 (1728–1804), and Ruan Yuan 阮元 (1764–1849) successfully incorporated technical aspects of Western astronomy and mathematics into the literati framework for classical learning. Qian Daxin, in particular, acknowledged this broadening of the literati tradition, which he saw as the reversal of centuries of focus on moral and philosophic problems:

> In ancient times, no one could be a literatus (*Ru* 儒) who did not know mathematical calculation. Chinese methods [now] lag behind Europe's because *Ru* do not know mathematics.[57]

The impact of evidential research made itself felt in the attention *kaozheng* scholars gave to the Western fields of mathematics and astronomy first introduced by the Jesuits in the seventeenth century.

---

[54] Cf. Hamaguchi Fujio 濱口富士雄 . 1994. *Shindai kokyogaku no shisō shi teki kenkyū* 清代考據學の思想史的研究(Research on the intellectual history of Qing dynasty evidential studies). Tokyo: Kokusho kankōkai.

[55] Elman 2000, pp. 562.

[56] See Sivin 1995a, pp. 45–66.

[57] Qian Daxin 錢大昕 . 1968. *Qianyantang wenji* 潛研堂文集 (Collected essays of the Hall of Subtle Research). Taibei: Shangwu yinshuguan, vol. 3, p. 335.

Such interest had built upon the early and mid-Qing findings of Mei Wending 梅文鼎 (1633–1721), who was sponsored by Li Guangdi and the Manchu court once his expertise in mathematical calculation (*li-suan* 歷算) and calendrical studies was recognized. Mei had contended that study of physical nature gave scholars access to the principles (*li* 理) undergirding reality. In essence, Mei saw Jesuit learning as a way to boost the numerical aspects of the *Daoxue* notion of moral and metaphysical principle.[58] At the same time, however, the imperial court and Mei Wending prepared preliminary accounts stressing the native Chinese origins (*zhongyuan* 中源) of Western natural studies. Mei (and his highly placed follower in the early Qing court Li Guangdi) sought to restore and rehabilitate the native traditions in the mathematical sciences to their former glory. Under the Kangxi emperor's imperial patronage mathematical studies were upgraded from an insignificant skill to an important domain of knowledge for literati that complemented classical studies.[59]

For example, Chen Yuanlong's 陳元龍 (1652–1736) *Gezhi jingyuan* 格致鏡原 (Mirror origins of investigating things and extending knowledge), was published in 1735, and in the 1780s it was included in the Imperial Library. A repository of detailed information divided into thirty categories culled from a wide variety of sources, the *Gezhi jingyuan* represented a post-Jesuit collection of practical knowledge by a well-placed scholar in the Kangxi and Yongzheng courts that narrowed the focus of Hu Wenhuan's late-Ming *Gezhi congshu*, much of which had already been lost, to cover almost exclusively the arts and natural studies. Special attention was given to the origins and evolution of printing and stone rubbings, in addition to topics dealing

---

[58] See John Henderson. 1980. "The Assimilation of the Exact Sciences into the Qing Confucian Tradition", *Journal of Asian Affairs* 5.1 (Spring 1980), pp. 15–31.

[59] See Limin Bai. 1995. "Mathematical Study and Intellectual Transition in the Early and Mid-Qing", *Late Imperial China* 16.2 (December 1995), pp. 23–61; and Catherine Jami. 1994. "Learning Mathematical Sciences During the Early and Mid-Qing", in: Benjamin A. Elman and Alexander Woodside (eds.). *Education and Society in Late Imperial China, 1600–1900*. Berkeley: University of California Press, pp. 223–56. On the Chinese origins theory, see Quan Hansheng 全漢昇. 1935. "Qingmo de 'xixue yuan chu Zhongguo' shuo" 清末的西學源出中國説 (Late Qing theory of the Chinese origin of Western learning), *Lingnan xuebao* 4.2 (June 1935), pp. 57–102.

[60] See Chen Yuanlong 陳元龍. 1735. *Gezhi jingyuan* 格致鏡原 (Mirror origins of investigating things and extending knowledge), in: *Siku quanshu* (Complete collection

with geography, anatomy, flora and fauna, tools, vehicles, weapons and tools for writing, as well as clothing and architecture.[60]

The seventeenth century impact of Jesuit knowledge in China was not always so easily domesticated in the eighteenth, however. Literati scholars took a range of positions concerning natural studies. A private scholar, Jiang Yong 江永 (1681–1762), for instance, combined a classical loyalty to Zhu Xi's *Daoxue* teachings with knowledge of Western Jesuit studies obtained through evidential studies. Conservative as a classical scholar, Jiang was quite radical in his critique of both Han Learning and Mei Wending in natural studies for exalting native ancient studies in all cases. Jiang Yong recognized the advantages Western astronomy had over native traditions, while at the same time he continued to uphold the cultural superiority of the *Daoxue* view of morality. Although Jiang preferred Western learning for understanding the principles of nature because they were more precise and consistent than native traditions, he maintained a clear distinction between astronomical methods and cultural values.[61]

Overall, Ruan Yuan's compilation of the *Chouren zhuan* 疇人傳 (Biographies of astronomers and mathematicians) while serving as governor of Zhejiang province in Hangzhou from 1797 to 1799, reprinted in 1849 and later enlarged, marked the climax of the celebration of natural studies within the Yangzi delta literati world of the eighteenth century, which had been increasing since the late seventeenth century. Containing biographies and summaries of the works of 280 *chouren*, including thirty-seven Europeans, this work was followed by four supplements in the nineteenth century. Limin Bai has noted how the mathematical sciences had begun to grow in importance among literati beyond the reach of the imperial court in the late eighteenth century. They were now linked to classical studies via evidential research. Because Ruan Yuan was a well-placed literati patron of natural studies in the provincial and court bureaucracy, his influential *Chouren zhuan* represented the integration of the mathematical

---

[60] (*cont.*) in the Imperial Four Treasuries), vols. 1031–2. I have also used the 1735 edition of this work available in the Library of Congress.

[61] Cf. Chu Pingyi. 1995. "Cheng-Zhu Orthodoxy, Evidential Studies and Correlative Cosmology: Chiang Yung and Western Astronomy", *Philosophy and the History of Science: A Taiwanese Journal* 4.2 (October 1995), pp. 71–108.

sciences with evidential studies. Mathematical study was no longer independent of classical studies.[62]

Literati scholars had by the late eighteenth century incorporated mathematical study into evidential research and made natural studies a part of classical studies. Their efforts provide us with another piece to the puzzle concerning the fate of natural studies and technology in late imperial China since the Jesuits first made their presence felt in the seventeenth century.

5. *GEZHIXUE* AS MODERN SCIENCE IN THE NINETEENTH CENTURY

Philology and natural studies were wedded together when Qing literati scholars such as Mei Wending and his grandson Mei Juecheng 梅 穀成 (d. 1763) evaluated early modern European findings in calendrical astronomy and searched through the classical canon for evidence that this new knowledge was likely based on ancient Chinese knowledge, which had been transmitted to the Western regions in antiquity. Mei Juecheng contended, for instance, that the Song-Yuan *Tianyuan* 天元 (heavenly origins) method for graphically representing algebraic equations was the equivalent of the algebraic formulas later introduced by the Jesuits. This more sophisticated 'Chinese origins' argument, when compared to that of the Kangxi emperor, legitimated renewed Qing literati interest in the sciences, and philology became one of the key tools later evidential research scholars employed.[63]

The mathematical studies (*shuxue* 數學) associated with evidential research in the eighteenth century was algorithmic, i.e., focusing on getting the right results, and thus was less concerned to justify methods and formulas. Wang Lai 汪萊 (1768–1813) and Jiao Xun 焦循 (1763–1820), for example, each tried to build on traditional Chinese algebraic equations, known as *Tianyuan*, rather than just automatically accept the Indic-Arabic forms of algebra that the Jesuits and later the Protestants taught when they came to China. Wang in particular derived more than one positive root for a *Tianyuan* equation, which by following Western views of positive and negative roots con-

---

[62] Cf. Hummel 1972, pp. 402. See also Limin Bai 1995, pp. 23–30.

[63] Cf. John Henderson. 1986. "Qing Scholars' Views of Western Astronomy", *Harvard Journal of Asiatic Studies* 46.1, pp. 121–48.

tributed something new to the traditional focus on a single, positive solution for any algebraic equation.[64]

Wang Lai, who was appointed to the dynastic observatory in Beijing, employed Western methods accepted in the calendrical office since the Kangxi reign, in his calculations of *Tianyuan*. As a result of his professional ties to the French Jesuit 'new studies' harbored in the observatory, Wang was criticized by more conservative *kaozheng* scholars interested in traditional mathematics for going too far in emulating Western methods. Because he was a literatus outside the court and thus tied to the Yangzi delta academic community, Li Rui 李銳 (1773–1817), who devised a theory of *Tianyuan* equations strictly in terms of Song *Tianyuan* mathematics, received more support from literati, many of whom still revered Yang Guangxian 楊光先 (1597–1669) for his prosecutions of the Jesuits in the Kangxi court in the 1660s. Before 1850, then, classical learning still took precedence over Western learning, and the antiquarian interests of evidential scholars stimulated them to study the textual history of native mathematics rather than build on the findings of Western mathematics, as Wang Lai had.

In the aftermath of the bloody defeat of the Taipings, however, a weakened Qing dynasty and its literati-officials began to face up to the new educational requirements the civil service would have to fulfill to survive in a world increasingly filled with menacing industrializing nations. The Opium War (1839–42) provoked very few important calls for introduction of Western learning into the civil service curriculum, but the situation after the fall of the Taipings in 1865 was remarkably different. Literati such as Xu Shou 徐壽 (1818–82) and Li Shanlan 李善蘭 (1810–82), who were involved in translating the Western natural sciences into Chinese at the Jiangnan Arsenal in Shanghai beginning in the 1860s, built conceptual bridges between post-industrial revolution Western learning and the traditional Chinese sciences in the middle of the nineteenth century. *Xixue* now often equalled *gezhixue*. One of the volumes that paralleled the translation project for a Science Outline Series at the Jiangnan Arsenal in Shanghai, for example, focused on British scientific knowledge compiled by

---

[64] Cf. Horng Wann-sheng. 1993. "Chinese Mathematics at the Turn of the 19th Century", in: Lin Zheng-hung and Fu Daiwie (eds.). *Philosophy and Conceptual History of Science in Taiwan*. Dordrecht: Kluwer Academic Publishers, pp. 167–208.

Henry Roscoe (Luo Sigu 羅斯古, 1833–1915) and others, which was entitled *Gezhi qimeng sizhong* 格致啟蒙四種 (Science Primer Series in four parts).[65] In the process, post-industrial revolution Western science, now called modern science, was initially introduced in the mid-nineteenth century as compatible with but no longer subordinate to native classical learning.

Both Feng Guifen 馮桂芬 (1809–74), a Hanlin academician, and Xue Fucheng 薛福成 (1838–94), who was prevented by the Taiping wars from taking civil examinations, became administrative experts and advisors to many of the chief ministers of the late Qing, including Zeng Guofan 曾國藩 (1811–72) and Li Hongzhang 李鴻章 (1823–1901), the leaders of the post-Taiping turn toward foreign studies (*yangwu yundong* 洋務運動). The classical curriculum needed to adapt more Western learning and science subjects to be viable, they claimed. Western models became a legitimate object of concern and debate to reform the civil examinations. Li Hongzhang, for example, followed Feng Guifen's recommendation and in 1863 established the *Tongwenguan* 同文館 school of Western languages and science in Shanghai, which was added to the Jiangnan Arsenal in 1869. Li also proposed establishing eight categories for civil examinations (*bake qushi* 八科取士) in 1867, which included mathematical science (*suanshu gezhi* 算數格致) and technical science (*jiqi zhizuo* 機器制作) as a single category. *Jishu* 技術, a term often used as a bibliographic term in earlier dynastic bibliographies, became the technical term for technology.[66]

Qing literati and officials became obsessed with the goal of wealth and power (*fuqiang* 富強), which in the last decades of the dynasty became the technical term for political economy, as in Joseph Edkins' (Ai Yuese 艾約瑟, 1823–1905) translation of *Political Economy* by

---

[65] The Series contained four parts, see *Gezhi qimeng si zhong* 格致啟蒙四種 (Science Primer Series in four parts). 1875. Young J. Allen and Zheng Changyan 鄭昌炎 (trsl.). Shanghai: Jiangnan zhizaoju. Henry Roscoe prepared the section for chemistry (*huaxue* 化學), Archibald Geikie (Qi Gou 祁覯, 1835–1924) for physical geography (*dilixue* 地理學), Balfour Stewart (Si Duhuo 司都薲, 1828–87) for physics (*gewuxue* 格物學), and Norman J. Lockyer (Luo Keyou 駱克優, not known) for astronomy (*tianwenxue* 天文學).

[66] See "Yangwu yundong dashiji" 洋務運動大事記 (Record of major events during the Foreign Affairs Movement). n.d. In: Xu Tailai 徐泰來 (ed.). *Yangwu yundong xinlun* 洋務運動新論 (New views of the Foreign Affairs Movement). Changsha: Hunan renmin chubanshe, pp. 349–448; and Hummel 1972, pp. 240–3, 331–3.

William Stanley Jevons (Zhe Fensi 哲分斯, 1835–1882), entitled
Fuguo yangmin ce 富國養民策 (Policies for enriching the dynasty and
nourishing the people), which was included as a volume in another
series also named *Gezhi qimeng* 格致啟蒙 (Science Primer), supported
by Sir Robert Hart (He De 赫德, 1835–1911) and edited by Joseph
Edkins.[67] While living in the treaty port of Shanghai to avoid the
Taipings, Feng Guifen prepared an essay around 1861 entitled *Gai
keju yi* 改科舉議 (Proposal for reforming the civil examinations) in
which he attempted to balance the strengths of the selection process
with the needs of the future.[68] Feng was aware that he had to sell his
recommended changes to opponents who would oppose any blatant
effort to introduce Western learning into the examination curriculum.
Accordingly, he altered the content of native traditional fields. What
Feng meant by classical studies, for instance, included evidential
research (*kaoju* 考據) and philology (*xiaoxue* 小學), subjects of
learning already included in provincial and metropolitan policy questions. In addition, he added mathematics to the field of classical studies and quietly relegated the literary essay and poetry question to the
last session.[69]

Feng also called for widening the selection process for officials to
include recommendation and the promotion of clerks who demonstrated their administrative abilities to their superiors. One way to do
this, according to Feng, was to divide the civil examination system in
two, with one group required to master machinery and physics (*zhiqi
shangxiang* 制器尚象). Based on such reforms, "our China [*Zhonghua* 中華] can begin to arise in the world." Otherwise, Feng presci-
ently predicted, she will be a victim of native militarists hiding behind
the slogan of 'self-strengthening' (*ziqiang* 自強).[70] One of the
strengths of Western learning Feng noted was its mastery of mathematics, which Feng wished to incorporate into the civil examinations.

---

[67] Cf. Joseph Edkins (tr.). 1886. "Fuguo yangmin ce" 富國養民策 (Policies for
enriching the dynasty and nourishing the people), in: Joseph Edkins (ed.). *Gezhi
Qimeng* 格致啟蒙 (Science Primer). Beijing: Zong shuiwusi, vol. 12 [Translation of
William S. Jevons, *Political Economy*, 1871].

[68] Cf. Feng Guifen 馮桂芬. 1897. *Jiaobinlu kangyi* 校邠廬抗議 (Protests from the
cottage of Feng Guifen). Reprint Taibei: Wenhai Press, pt. 2, pp. 55a–56b.

[69] Cf. Feng Guifen 1897, pt. 2, pp. 56b–57a. Zheng Guanying 鄭觀應 (1842–
1923) also was an early advocate of including Western topics in the examination
framework.

[70] Cf. ibid., pp. 57a–64a; 72b–74b.

Geography and calendrical studies, the latter banned in dynastic schools and civil examinations since the Kangxi reign, were also essential fields for literati, Feng contended. Not until 1887, however, were candidates specializing in mathematics allowed to pass the provincial examinations under a special quota, although they also had to fulfill the same classical requirements.[71]

By building on eighteenth century classicism, which had incorporated a revised version of traditional numerical studies as a part of evidential studies, literati associated with Han Learning after the Taiping Rebellion created the intellectual space needed to legitimate literati study of natural studies and mathematics. For instance, Li Shanlan first went to Shanghai in 1852 and for eight years there worked for the London Missionary Society to translate Western science works into classical Chinese. Later, Li was recommended to the newly established Beijing *Tongwenguan* translators' bureau in 1864, but he took up the appointment in 1866 only after the *Tongwenguan* was upgraded to a college and a department of mathematics and astronomy was added. There, Li Shanlan worked with W. A. P. Martin (Ding Weiliang 丁韙良, 1827–1916), who served as president of the college from 1869 to 1882, to teach mathematics and prepare scientific translations.[72]

Xu Shou initially collaborated with John Fryer (Fu Lanya 傅蘭雅, 1839–1928) at the Jiangnan Arsenal in Shanghai to translate Western scientific literature into classical Chinese, an enterprise that combined a narrow, textually based vision of science, brought by Protestant missionaries to attract Chinese converts, with the skewed *kaozheng* view of the sciences as a domain of classical studies appropriate only for literati. Xu, like Fryer, in effect remained for the most part a cultivator not a researcher of science. Together they founded the *Gezhi shuyuan* 格致書院 in Shanghai in 1874, which was curiously translated into English as the "Shanghai Polytechnic Institute."[73] From different sides, Chinese literati and Western modernizers saw in *gezhi* what they wanted to see, a native trope or Western science.

---

[71] Cf. ibid., pp. 66a–70a. See also *Guangxu zhengyao* 光緒政要 (Important issues of governance in the Guangxu reign). 1909. Shen Tongsheng 沈桐生 (comp.). Shanghai: Chongyitang, vol. 10, section 13, pp. 18a–20a.

[72] See Hummel 1972, pp. 480.

[73] This somewhat surprising translation was chosen because the model for this institution was the Polytechnical Institute on London's Regent Street.

The Institute had a reading room and library of scientific works. Xu and Fryer also created the first science journal in China entitled *Gezhi huibian* 格致彙編 , known in English as "The Chinese Scientific Magazine," which ran first monthly issues from 1876 to 1882 in Shanghai and then quarterly from 1890 to 1892. At its peak it reached some 2000 readers in the treaty ports. Such conceptual compromises were based on maintaining the post-Jesuit term for natural studies, i.e., *gezhi*, but this time using *gezhi* to refer to modern Western, not early modern, science. In this way, mathematics and the other more industrial sciences such as chemistry became acceptable, if still less popular than the civil service, activities for literati.[74]

6. THE DENIGRATION OF TRADITIONAL CHINESE NATURAL STUDIES

Despite the relative success of traditional Chinese natural studies and Western science in developing together from the seventeenth to the late nineteenth century among literati elites in China under the rubric of *gezhixue*, until 1850 there was little attention by those same elites to European science as a form of practice requiring laboratories to replicate experiments and for such experiments to confirm or reject past scientific findings. For Catholic or Protestant missionaries and literati mathematicians, natural studies was little more than a textual exercise requiring translation of technical knowledge, mastery of those technical texts, and the reproduction via memory of technical learning. Moreover, those who were drawn after the Taiping Rebellion to scholarly work in the new arsenals in Fuzhou, Shanghai, and elsewhere, or translation positions in the *Tongwenguan*, tended to be literati such as Xu Shou and Li Shanlan, men who had failed the more prestigious civil examinations several times and saw Western learning and the sciences as an alternative route to fame and fortune. Yan Fu 嚴復 (1853–1921) and Lu Xun 魯迅 (1881–1936) were also famous examples of this group of outcasts from the civil examinations that

---

[74] Cf. David Reynolds. 1991. "Re-Drawing China's Intellectual Map: 19th Century Chinese Images of Science", *Late Imperial China* 12.1 (June 1991), pp. 27–61. See also David Wright. 1996. "John Fryer and the Shanghai Polytechnic: Making Space for Science in Nineteenth-Century China", *British Journal of the History of Science* 29, pp. 1–16; and id. 1995. "Careers in Western Science in Nineteenth-Century China: Xu Shou and Xu Jianyin", *Journal of the Royal Asiatic Society*, third series, no. 5, pp. 49–90. Cf. Reardon-Anderson 1991, pp. 17–28, 45–8.

initially served as the pool of highly educated men who filled the
world of late-Qing institutions oriented toward *gezhixue*.[75]

Recent research indicates, however, that the various arsenals, shipyards, and factories in the treaty ports were important technological
venues for experimental practice where, in addition to the production
of weapons, ammunition, and navies, a union of scientific knowledge
and experimental practice among literati and artisans was first forged
in Shanghai, Nanjing, Tianjin, Wuhan, and elsewhere. Indeed, it is
likely the case that the 'techno-science'[76] of late-Qing China was an
important building block for the rise of both dynastic and private
industry in the late nineteenth century treaty ports where most of the
arsenals were established. The Jiangnan Arsenal in Shanghai and the
Fuzhou Shipyard, for instance, were generally acknowledged by
Europeans and Japanese to be more advanced than their competitor in
Meiji Japan, the Yokosuka Dockyard, until the 1880s. David Wright
has noted that the two ironclad steamships ordered by Xu Jianyin 徐建
寅 (1845–1901), Xu Shou's son, in 1879 from the Vulcan factory in
the Baltic port of Stettin for the Beiyang Fleet were more advanced
than anything the Japanese navy had at the time, although both were
sunk in the Sino-Japanese War of 1894–95. In gunpowder manufac-
ture, the machinery used in Germany was not as advanced as that in
Shanghai. Accordingly, outside the civil examination regime and its
precincts of licentiates, provincial graduates, and *jinshi* (literatus presented to the emperor for appointment), where millions competed for
few places in the bureaucracy, a notable group of doctors, nurses and
medical assistants were trained in missionary schools, and an even
larger group of engineers, military technicians, and technical specialists were instructed in the arsenals and shipyards.[77]

---

[75] Cf. David Wright. 1997. "The Great Desideratum: Chinese Chemical Nomenclature and the Transmission of Western Chemical Concepts", *Chinese Science* 14,
pp. 35–70.

[76] Bruno Latour denotes the difficulty in dividing science from technology after
the industrial revolution. Bruno Latour. 1987. *Science in Action: How to Follow Scientists and Engineers Through Society*. Cambridge, Mass.: Harvard University Press.

[77] See Meng Yue. 1999. "Hybrid Science versus Modernity: The Practice of the
Jiangnan Arsenal", *East Asian Science, Technology, and Medicine* 16, pp. 13–52. See
also Takehiko Hashimoto. 1999. "Introducing a French Technological System: The
Origin and Early History of the Yokosuka Dockyard", *East Asian Science* 16, pp. 53–
72; and David Wright 1995, p. 81.

It was not until the Sino-Japanese War, when the Japanese navy, which was tied to Yokosuka technology, decisively defeated the Qing navy, which was tied to Fuzhou and Shanghai technology, that the alleged superiority of Japan in military technology, or so it was reinterpreted, became common knowledge to Chinese and Japanese patriots. Although the Jiangnan Arsenal had appeared superior in science and technology to Yokosuka until the 1880s, after 1895 each side then read their different fates in 1895 teleologically back to the early Meiji period (later even back further to *Rangaku* 蘭學 , 'Dutch Learning'), in the case of triumphant Japan, or back to the failures of the self-strengthening movement after 1865 (later back to all classical learning), in the case of the defeated Qing.

Another sea change in elite and popular opinion in late-Qing China now determined how the Manchu-Chinese refraction of Western science and technology through the lens of *gezhixue* would be interpreted after 1895. Literati radicals such as Yan Fu declared that accommodation between Chinese ways and Western institutions had failed. The Sino-Japanese War thus altered the frame of reference for the 1860–1895 period for both Chinese and Japanese. The beginnings of the 'failure narrative' for Chinese science, i.e., why China had not produced science, paralleled the story of political decline (why no democracy) and economic deterioration (why no capitalism) during the late empire.[78]

Yan Fu, whose poor prospects in the civil examinations led him to enter the School of Navigation of the Fuzhou Shipyard in 1866, expressed long pent up bitterness toward the civil examinations, when he became a publicist and prepared articles for the reformist press that emerged after 1895. Since 1885, Yan had failed the provincial examinations four times.[79] Many like Yan Fu began in the 1890s to link the weakness of the Qing dynasty to the classical education required in civil examinations, which allegedly had wasted the minds of genera-

---

[78] Cf. Reardon-Anderson 1991, pp. 76–78. See also Nathan Sivin. 1985. "Max Weber, Joseph Needham, Benjamin Nelson: The Question of Chinese Science", in: E. Victor Walter (ed.). *Civilizations East and West: A Memorial Volume for Benjamin Nelson.* Atlantic Highlands: Humanities Press.

[79] See Yan Fu 嚴復 . 1953. "Jiuwang juelun" 救亡決論 (On what determines rescue or perishing), in: *Wuxu bianfa ziliao* 戊戌變法資料 (Sources on the 1898 reforms). Beijing: Shenzhou guoguangshe, pp. 360–71. See also Benjamin Schwartz. 1969. *In Search of Wealth and Power: Yan Fu and the West.* New York: Harper Torchbooks, pp. 22–41.

tions. Moreover, Yan and other reformist voices associated the power of the West with modern schools where students were trained in modern subjects requiring practical training in the sciences and technology.[80]

For Yan Fu and the reformers, Western schools and Westernized Japanese education were examples that the Qing dynasty should emulate. The extension of mass schooling within a standardized classroom system stressing science courses and homogeneous or equalized groupings of students seemed to promise a way out of the quagmire of the imperial education and civil examination regime, whose educational efficiency was now, in the 1890s, suspect. Uncritical presentations of Western schools and Japanese education as science-building success stories were widely accepted. Those involved with the 1898 Reform Movement contended that political reform required fundamental educational change, and educational change was possible only if the civil examinations were reformed.[81]

One of the products of the iconoclasm of the 1898 reforms that survived the Empress Dowager's coup was the Imperial University of Beijing, which was established to be at the pinnacle of an empire-wide network of schools that would expand on the Tongwenguan. The new university was designed like the Translation College to train civil degree-holders, i.e., literati, in Western subjects suitable for government service. W. A. P. Martin, who had earlier worked with Li Shan-lan, was chosen as the dean of the Western faculty. Science courses at the Imperial University, interestingly, were still referred to as *gezhi*, and the facilities included modern laboratories equipped with the latest instruments for physics, geometry, and chemistry. This promising development was short-lived, however, because rebels associated

---

[80] Cf. Marianne Bastid. 1988. *Educational Reform in Early Twentieth-Century China*. Translated by Paul J. Bailey. Ann Arbor: University of Michigan China Center, pp. 12–3; and Y. C. Wang. 1966. *Chinese Intellectuals and the West, 1872–1949*. Chapel Hill: University of North Carolina Press, pp. 52–9. Curiously, Yan Fu's own translations were criticised for their incomprehensibility because they were written in classical style. On Yan Fu's translations see Timothy Wong's contribution in this volume.

[81] See Elman 2000, pp. 585–94; and Paula Harrell. 1992. *Sowing the Seeds of Change: Chinese Students, Japanese Teachers, 1895–1905*. Stanford: Stanford University Press, pp. 11–60.

with what was called the Boxer Rebellion smashed everything in sight at the university in the summer of 1900.[82]

The delegitimation of classical learning, once complete, eventually had consequences that went beyond what the court and literati expected.[83] The race to establish new institutions of higher learning that would stress modern science accelerated after the occupation of the capital by Western and Japanese troops in 1900. The Boxer popular rebellion and the response of the Western powers and Japan to it unbalanced the power structure in the capital so much that foreigners were able to put considerable pressure on provincial and national leaders. Foreign support of reform and Western education thus strengthened the political fortunes of provincial reformers such as Yuan Shikai 袁世凱 (1859–1916) and Zhang Zhidong 張之洞 (1837–1909), who had opposed the Boxers.[84]

The story of the demise of traditional natural studies and the rise of modern science in China was more complicated than just the demise of classical learning and the rise of modern education, which would subordinate the classics to science. A social, political, and cultural nexus of classical literati values (within which natural studies were embedded), dynastic imperial power, and elite gentry status was unraveling.[85] The Qing dynasty became a party to the delegitimation of classical studies and the accompanying rethinking of the nature and scope of *gezhixue* vis-à-vis modern science. By first decanonizing the classical canon, late nineteenth century literati hoped to free them-

---

[82] See Renville Lund. 1956. *The Imperial University of Beijing*. Ph.D. diss., University of Washington (Washington), pp. 118–22; and Reardon-Anderson 1991, p. 109.

[83] Cf. Elman 2000, pp. 608–18. See also Paul Bailey. 1990. *Reform the People: Changing Attitudes Towards Popular Education in Early Twentieth Century China*. Edinburgh: Edinburgh University Press, pp. 26–7, who stresses the Boxer Rebellion as the "turning point in the court's attitude towards reform."

[84] See Stephen R. MacKinnon. 1980. *Power and Politics in Late Imperial China: Yuan Shi-kai in Beijing and Tianjin, 1901–1908*. Berkeley: University of California Press, pp. 3–4, 216–7. On the impact on the urban elite in Hunan and Hubei, see Joseph W. Esherick. 1976. *Reform and Revolution in China: The 1911 Revolution in Hunan and Hubei*. Berkeley: University of California Press, pp. 40–52. For Zhejiang province, see Mary B. Rankin. 1986. *Elite Activism and Political Transformation in China: Zhejiang Province, 1865–1911*. Stanford: Stanford University Press, pp. 172–88.

[85] For the concept of "cultural nexus", see Prasenjit Duara. 1988. *Culture, Power, and the State: Rural North China, 1900–1942*. Stanford: Stanford University Press, pp. 5–6, 38–41, 247–8.

selves from the moral and classical imperatives of the past, but they also began to distance themselves from traditional views of and approaches to natural studies, medicine, and technology.[86]

The delegitimation of classical learning after 1900 initially did not challenge the use of *gezhi* as a term from the Four Books to translate modern science into classical Chinese, however. Session one of the reformed, post-1901 civil examinations, for example, expected candidates to answer five questions dealing with Chinese institutions and politics (*Zhongguo zhengzhishi shilun* 中國政治史事論). Session two included five policy questions on Western institutions and politics (*Geguo zhengzhi yixue ce* 各國政治藝學策). The last session required three classical essays, two on quotations from the Four Books and one from the Five Classics (*Sishu yi, wujing yi* 四書義, 五經義). In theory, all three sessions were expected to count equally for the final rankings, but how this would work out in practice remained unknown. Would examiners really relegate classical essays and give priority to contemporary issues? And what role would the sciences play in this reform?

In 1902 the first civil examinations since the post-Boxer reforms took place in Kaifeng, the capital of Henan province. Because the provincial examination halls in Shuntian, where the metropolitan examinations in Beijing had also been held, had been burned down by the foreign troops sent in to relieve the Boxer siege of the international legations, the metropolitan examination could not be held in Beijing. The 1902 examination reforms failed in the short run to accomplish their goals because of the classical tenacity of the conservative examiners. Nevertheless the overall scope of the examinations became decidedly more institutional, international, and science-oriented in focus. A catalog of policy questions used in the examinations after the reforms, which was compiled in 1903, identified the thirty-two categories that were used:

---

[86] Cf. Chuzo Ichiko. 1968. "The Role of the Gentry: An Hypothesis", in: Mary Wright (ed.). *China In Revolution: The First Phase, 1900–13*. New Haven: Yale University Press, p. 299; Ernest P. Young. 1977. *The Presidency of Yuan Shih-k'ai: Liberalism and Dictatorship in Early Republican China*. Ann Arbor: University of Michigan Press, pp. 7–8; and Helen R. Chauncey. 1992. *Schoolhouse Politicians: Locality and State During the Chinese Republic*. Honolulu: University of Hawaii, pp. 10–1.

Table 3: Categories of policy questions*

1. Way of ordering (zhidao 治道)	9. Assemblies (yiyuan 議院)
2. Scholarship (*xueshu* 學術)	10. State organizations (*zhengti* 政體)
3. Domestic government (*neizheng* 內政)	11. Public laws (*gongzhi* 公治)
4. Foreign relations (*waijiao* 外交)	12. Penal laws (*xinglü* 刑律)
5. Current affairs (*shishi* 時事)	13. Education Affairs (*jiaowu* 教務)
6. Civil examinations (*keju* 科舉)	14. Astronomy (*tianxue* 天學)
7. Schools (*xuexiao* 學校)	15. Geography (*dixue* 地學)
8. Official institutions (*guanzhi* 官制)	16. Calendrical studies (*lixue* 曆學)
17. Mathematics (*suanxue* 算學)	25. Agriculture system (I) (*nongzheng* (*shang*) 農政 (上))
18. Sciences (I) (*gezhi* (*shang*) 格致 (上))	26. Agriculture system (II) (*nongzheng* (*xia*) 農政 (下))
19. Sciences (II) (*gezhi* (*xia*) 格致 (下))	27. Public works (*gongzheng* 工政)
20. State finance (*caizheng* 財政)	28. Commercial system (*shangzheng* 商政)
21. Monetary system (*bizhi* 幣制)	29. Roads and mines (*lukuang* 路礦)
22. Military system (I) (*junzheng* (shang) 軍政 (上))	30. Topography (*yudi* 輿地)
23. Military system (II) (*junzheng* (*xia*) 軍政 (下))	31. History (*shixue* 史學)
24. Defense matters (*fangwu* 防務)	32. Foreign history (*waishi* 外史)

*) Source: "Mulu" 目錄 , in: *Zhongwai shiwu cewen leibian dacheng* 中外時務策問類編大成 (Compendium of classified examination questions on current affairs in China and abroad). 1903. n.p., pp. 1a–28b.

Although the examiners' biases toward Chinese learning pervaded many of these fields, the impact of the Western sciences on the civil service curriculum was quite noticeable. For example, five of the eight questions on the natural sciences, which was still called *gezhi*, were phrased as follows:

> 1. Much of European science originates from China (*zhongguo* 中國); we need to stress what became a lost learning as the basis for wealth and power.

2. In the sciences, China and the West (*tai xi* 泰西) are different; use Chinese learning (*zhongxue* 中學) to critique Western learning (*xixue* 西學).

3. Substantiate in detail the theory that Western methods all originate from China.

6. Prove in detail that Western science studies mainly were based on the theories of China's pre-Han masters.

7. Itemize and demonstrate using scholia that theories from the Mohist Canon preceded Western theories of calendrical studies, light, and pressure.[87]

Such views revealed that in official terms, the wedding between the traditional Chinese sciences and Western science, worked out beginning in the eighteenth century, was still in effect. Publicly at least, the officials of the late-Qing dynasty maintained the fiction that

西人格致之學多來於中國諸子之説
the Western sciences for the most part derived from the teachings of the pre-Han masters.[88]

After 1905, however, when the civil examinations had been abolished, the ever increasing number of overseas Chinese students in Japan, Europe, and the United States perceived that outside of China the proper language for science included a new set of concepts and terms that superseded traditionalist literati notions of natural studies associated with *gezhi*. For example, Japanese scholars during the early Meiji period had already in the 1860s demarcated the new sciences by referring to *Wissenschaft* as *kagaku* (*kexue* 科學 , lit. 'classified learning based on technical training')[89] and natural studies as *kyūri* (*qiongli* 窮理 , lit. 'exhaustively study the principles of things'). The latter term, long associated with 'Dao Learning' in China since the Song dynasty, was reinterpreted in Japan based on the Dutch Learning tradition of the late eighteenth century, when Japanese scholars interested in Western science still used terms from Chinese

---

[87] See *Zhongwai shiwu cewen leibian dacheng*, "mulu", pp. 13a–13b.

[88] Ibid., p. 13a.

[89] Cf. Liu 1995, pp. 33; 336, presents *kexue/kagaku* as a second-hand *kanji* borrowing from classical Chinese that the Japanese used to translate science into Japanese. Her source is the Song dynasty literatus Chen Liang 陳亮 (1143–94), who uses *kexue* as a shorthand reference to mean 'civil examination studies' (*keju zhi xue* 科舉 之學 equals *kexue*). This twelfth-century usage is unique to the Song dynasty, which the Japanese borrowed.

learning (*kangaku* 漢學) to assimilate European natural studies and medicine.[90]

Chinese students and scholars initially adopted the Japanese bifurcation between technical learning and natural studies. Yan Fu, for instance, rendered the terms 'science' or 'sciences' as *kexue* in his 1900–1902 translation of John Stuart Mill's (1806–1873) *System of Logic*, while translating natural philosophy as *gewu* 格物 , or the 'investigation of things'.[91] Similarly, when regulations for modern schools were promulgated in 1903, the term *gezhi* was used to refer collectively to the sciences in general, while the sciences as individual, technical disciplines were designated as *kexue*. This two-track terminology for science lasted through the end of the Qing dynasty and was continued during the early years of the Republic of China, but Chinese students who returned from abroad increasingly saw the need to develop a single Chinese term for the Western sciences that would leave behind the earlier assimilation of traditional Chinese natural studies into modern science.[92]

Many overseas students were as radical in their political and cultural views, which carried over to their scientific iconoclasm. Traditional natural studies became part of the 'failed' history of traditional China to become 'modern', and this view now included the claim that the Chinese had never had any science. The earlier claim for the 'Chinese origins' of Western science, so prominent before 1900, was now deemed superstition (*mixin* 迷信 , lit. 'confused beliefs'). What had come before modern *kexue* was magic and the supernatural, not science. How pre-modern Chinese demarcated the natural and supernatural was lost, when both 'modernists' and 'socialists' in China accepted the West as source of all science as *kexue*, which was diametrically opposed to *gezhi*.

Linkage between political revolution and the perception by many radicals that a scientific revolution was also required influenced the

---

[90] Cf. Albert Craig. 1965. "Science and Confucianism in Tokugawa Japan", in: Marius Jansen (ed.). *Changing Japanese Attitudes Toward Modernization*. Princeton: Princeton University Press, pp. 139–42.

[91] Cf. Yan Fu嚴復 (tr.). 1902. *Mule mingxue* 穆勒名學 (Miller's *Logic*). n. p.: Jisuzhai [Translation of John Stuart Mill. 1843. *A System of Logic. Ratiocinative and Inductive*, 2 vols.]. In the nineteenth cenutry, *gewu* was also used to delimitate the new field of physics. On the establishment of this new discipline and its various designations see Iwo Amelung's contribution in this volume.

[92] Cf. Reardon-Anderson 1991, pp. 82–7.

changes that occurred after 1911. Those Chinese who thought a revolution in knowledge based on Western learning was required not only
challenged what they called 'Confucianism' (*Kongjiao* 孔教), but they
also unstitched the interwoven patterns of traditional Chinese science,
medicine, and classical learning long accepted as components of an
ideological tapestry buttressing imperial orthodoxy.[93] Those educated
abroad at Western universities such as Cornell University or sponsored by the Rockefeller Foundation after 1914 for medical study in
the United States, as well as those trained locally at higher-level missionary schools, regarded modern science as *kexue*, not *gezhixue*,
because they believed the latter term was derived from the language
of the discredited past and inappropriate for modern science. The
belief that Western science represented a revolutionary application of
scientific methods and objective learning to all modern problems was
increasingly articulated in the journals associated with the New Culture Movement. The journal *Kexue* 科學 (Science), which was published by the newly founded Science Society of China (*Zhongguo
kexueshe* 中國科學社) and first issued in 1915, assumed that an educational system based on *kexue* was the panacea for all of China's ills
because its knowledge system was superior. By 1920, the Science
Society, which had been founded by overseas Chinese students at
Cornell in 1914, had some 500 members in China and grew to 1000 in
1930.[94]

Such scientism on the part of Chinese scientists trained abroad,
many from Cornell, was iconoclastic in its implications for traditional
natural studies in China and influenced post-imperial literati such as
Chen Duxiu 陳獨秀 (1879–1942), who argued in the issues of the
journal *Xin qingnian* 新青年 (New Youth), which he helped found in
1915, that science and democracy were the twin pillars of a modern
China that must dethrone the imperial past. In the process, post-imperial scholars and novelists such as Ba Jin 巴金 (1904–2000), in his
novel *Family*, for example, initiated an assault on pre-modern natural

---

[93] See Benjamin A. Elman. 1997. "The Formation of 'Dao Learning' as Imperial
Ideology During the Early Ming Dynasty", in: T. Huters, R. Bin Wong, and P. Yu
(eds.). *Culture and the State in Chinese History*. Stanford: Stanford University Press,
pp. 58–82.

[94] See Peter Buck. 1980. *American Science and Modern China*. Cambridge: Cambridge University Press, pp. 171–85; and D. W. Y. Kwok. 1971. *Scientism in Chinese
Thought, 1900–1950*. New York: Biblo and Tannen, *passim*.

studies and medicine as a haven of superstition and backwardness. During the early Republic, the elite view of popular customs (*fengsu* 風俗) was also reconfigured in modernist terms, a trend that included Xu Ke's 徐珂 (1869–1929) *Qingbai leichao* 清稗類鈔 (Classified jottings on Qing dynasty unofficial history). In Xu's collection, popular lore was divided up and reclassified into the categories of 'magicians and shamans' (*fangji* 方伎) and 'confused beliefs', for example. Xu Ke intended his collection of lore, published in 1917, as a sequel to the Northern Song dynasty *Taiping kuangji* 太平廣記 (Expanded records of the Taiping reign, 976–83) and the later *Songbai leichao* 宋稗類鈔 (Classified jottings on Song dynasty unofficial history). However, the new cultural context ensured that such lore was publicly acceptable among modernist literati only if it could be pigeonholed as superstition.[95]

Traditional Chinese medicine, which was the strongest field of the Chinese sciences during the transition from the late Qing to the Republican era, was also subjected to such derision, although it was more successful in retaining its prestige than Chinese astrology, geomancy, and alchemy, which were dismissed by modern scholars as purely superstitious forms of knowledge.[96] When the Guomindang-sponsored Health Commission proposed to abolish Chinese medicine (*Zhongyi* 中醫) in February 1929, for example, traditional Chinese doctors responded by calling for a national convention in Shanghai on March 17, 1929, which was supported by a strike of pharmacies and surgeries nationwide. The protest succeeded in having the proposed abolition withdrawn, and the Institute for National Medicine (*Guoyiguan* 國醫館) was subsequently established. One objective, however, was to reform Chinese medicine along Western lines.[97]

Bridie Andrews has documented the remarkable odyssey of Western medicine in early Republican China. She notes that the practice of Western medicine in China was assimilated by individual Chinese doctors in a number of different ways. Some defended traditional Chi-

---

[95] Xu Ke 1920, vol. 74, p. 11, and *passim*.

[96] Cf. Eugenia Lean. 1996. "The Modern Elixer: Medicine as a Consumer Item in the Early Twentieth-Century Press". M.A. thesis paper, University of California (Los Angeles), November 1996.

[97] See Bridie Andrews. 1997a. "Tuberculosis and the Assimilation of Germ Theory in China, 1895–1937", *Journal of the History of Medicine and Allied Sciences* 52.1, 114–57; pp. 142–3.

nese medicine, but they sought to update it with Western findings. Others tried to equate Chinese practices with Western knowledge and equalized their statuses as medical learning. The sinicization of Western pharmacy by Zhang Xiqun 張錫純 (1860–1933), for example, was based on the pharmacopia in the Chinese medical tradition. Another influential group associated with the Chinese Medical Association, which stressed Western medicine, criticized traditional Chinese medical theories as erroneous because they were not scientifically based.[98]

Andrews also documents how in this cultural encounter, techniques such as acupuncture were modernized by Chinese practitioners such as Cheng Dan'an 承澹盦 (1899–1957), whose research on acupuncture enabled him to follow Japanese reforms by using Western anatomy to redefine the location of the acupuncture points. Cheng's redefinitions of acupuncture thus revived what had become from his perspective a moribund field that was rarely practiced in China and, when used, mainly served as a procedure for blood-letting. This reform of acupuncture, which included replacing traditional coarse needles with the filiform metal needles in use today, ensured that the points for inserting needles were no longer placed near major blood vessels. Instead, Cheng mapped the points according to the Western nervous system. According to Andrews, a new scientific acupuncture sponsored by Chinese research societies thus emerged.[99]

During the transition from the Qing dynasty to the Republic of China, then, new political, institutional, and cultural forms emerged that challenged the creedal system of the late empire and refracted the latter's cultural forms of knowledge, such as traditional Chinese medicine. Just as the emperor, his bureaucracy, and literati cultural forms quickly became symbols of political and intellectual backwardness, so too traditional forms of knowledge about the natural world, were

---

[98] Cf. Andrews 1997a, pp. 114–57; and Bridie Andrews. 1997b. "Medical Lives and the Odyssey of Western Medicine in Early Twentieth-Century China". Paper presented at the History of Science Society Annual Meeting, San Diego, Cal., November 8, 1997.

[99] Cf. Andrews 1997b, pp. 24–8. For other fields, see Laurence Schneider. 1988. "Genetics in Republican China", in: J. Bowers, J. Hess, and N. Sivin (eds.). *Science and Medicine in Twentieth-Century China: Research and Education*. Ann Arbor: Center for Chinese Studies, University of Michigan, pp. 3–29; and Yang Ts'ui-hua. 1993. "The Development of Geology in Republican China, 1912–1937", in: Lin Cheng-hung and Fu Daiwei (eds.). *Philosophy and Conceptual History of Science in Taiwan*. Dordrecht: Kluwer Academic Publishers, pp. 221–44.

uncritically labeled as superstition, while modern science in its European and American forms was championed by new intellectuals as the proper path to objective knowledge, enlightenment, and national power. Even those who sought to maintain Chinese traditional medicine by modernizing it according to Western standards of rigor, however, also played a part in the denigration of past medical practices.[100]

CONCLUSION

The dismantling of the traditions of *gezhixue* and *bowuxue*, among many other categories, that had linked natural studies, natural history, and medicine to classical learning from 1370 to 1905 climaxed during the cultural and intellectual changes of the New Culture Movement.[101] When their iconoclasm against classical learning and its traditions of natural studies climaxed after 1915, New Culture advocates helped replace the imperial tradition of *gezhixue* with modern science and medicine. The fall of *gezhixue* concluded a millennium of elite belief in literati values and five hundred years of an empire-wide classical orthodoxy that had encompassed the Chinese natural studies and local technologies. The legacy of destroying that cultural cum creedal system and the centering frames for human experience that it enforced should not be underestimated. What fell between 1905 and 1915 was an educational regime based on classical learning. Socially, classical credentials no longer confirmed gentry status or technical expertise, so sons of literati, and now daughters, turned to other avenues of learning and careers outside officialdom, particularly the sciences, modern medicine, and engineering. Literati increasingly travelled to Shanghai, Fuzhou, and other treaty ports to seek their fortunes in arsenals and shipyards as members of a new gentry-based post-imperial Chinese intelligentsia that would become the seeds for modern Chinese intellectuals.

As elites turned to Western studies and modern science between 1905 and 1915, fewer remained to continue the traditions of classical learning (Han Learning), moral philosophy (Song Learning), or *gezhixue* that had been the intellectual core of imperial orthodoxy and

---

[100] See Buck 1980, pp. 91–121.
[101] See Min-zhi Maynard Chou. 1974. *Science and Value in May Fourth China: The Case of Hu Shih*. Ph.D. diss., University of Michigan (Ann Arbor), pp. 23–35.

literati statuses before 1900. Thereafter, the traditional Chinese sciences, classical studies, 'Confucianism' and 'Neo-Confucianism' survived as vestigial learning in the public schools established by the Ministry of Education after 1905 and have endured as contested scholarly fields taught in the vernacular in universities since 1911. The millennial hierarchy of literati learning, based on the Four Books and Five Classics, study of the Dynastic Histories, mastery of poetry, and traditional natural studies was demolished in favor of modern science and its impact via Darwinism on social and historical studies.[102]

What then ensued after 1911 was a remarkable intellectual consensus among Chinese and Western scholars that imperial China had failed to develop science before the Western impact. Even the Chinese protagonists involved in the 1923 "Debate on Science and Philosophy of Life" accepted the West as the repository of all scientific knowledge and only sought to complement such knowledge with moral and philosophical purpose.[103] The consensus drew on heroic accounts of the rise of Western science to demonstrate that imperial China had no science worthy of the name. Both Western scholars and Westernized Chinese scholars and scientists had essentialized European natural studies into a universalist ideal. When Chinese studies of the natural world, her rich medieval traditions of alchemy, or pre-Jesuit mathematical and astronomical achievements in China were discussed, they were usually treated dismissively and tagged with such epithets as superstitious, prescientific, or irrational to contrast them with the triumphant objectivity and rationality of the modern sciences.

---

[102] See James R. Pusey. 1983. *China and Charles Darwin*. Cambridge: Harvard University Press, *passim*.

[103] See Wang Hui. 1998. "From Debates on Culture to Debates on Knowledge: Zhang Junmai and the Differentiations of Cultural Modernity in 1920's China". Paper presented at the Workshop "Reinventions of Confucianism in the Twentieth Century", sponsored by the UCLA Center for Chinese Studies under the auspices of the University of California Pacific Rim Research Program, Los Angeles, January 31, 1998. See also Charlotte Furth. 1970. *Ting Wen-chiang: Science and China's New Culture*. Cambridge, Mass.: Harvard University Press.

Many scholars were so convinced that because China had had no industrial revolution and had never produced capitalism, therefore the Chinese could never have produced science. With the exception of a reformed version of traditional Chinese medicine that has survived and is now thriving as one version of 'holistic' medicine, the traditional fields of *gezhixue* in imperial China were destroyed by the impact of modern science.[104]

---

[104] Besides Needham's *Science and Civilisation in China* series, see also the articles collected in Sivin 1995a, and Nathan Sivin. 1995b. *Medicine, Philosophy, and Religion in Ancient China: Researches and Reflections*. Aldershot, Brookfield: Variorum, and also Nathan Sivin. 1987. *Traditional Medicine in Contemporary China*. Ann Arbor: Center for Chinese Studies, University of Michigan.

REFERENCES

Adas, Michael. 1989. *Machines as the Measure of Men: Science, Technology, and Ideologies of Western Dominance*. Ithaca: Cornell University Press.

Andrews, Bridie. 1997a. "Tuberculosis and the Assimilation of Germ Theory in China, 1895–1937", *Journal of the History of Medicine and Allied Sciences* 52.1, pp. 114–57.

——. 1997b. "Medical Lives and the Odyssey of Western Medicine in Early Twentieth-Century China". Paper presented at the History of Science Society Annual Meeting, San Diego, Cal., November 8, 1997.

Bai, Limin. 1995. "Mathematical Study and Intellectual Transition in the Early and Mid-Qing", *Late Imperial China* 16.2 (December 1995), pp. 23–61.

Bailey, Paul. 1990. *Reform the People: Changing Attitudes Towards Popular Education in Early Twentieth Century China*. Edinburgh: Edinburgh University Press.

Bastid, Marianne. 1988. *Educational Reform in Early Twentieth-Century China*. Translated by Paul J. Bailey. Ann Arbor: University of Michigan China Center.

Buck, Peter. 1980. *American Science and Modern China*. Cambridge: Cambridge University Press.

Campany, Robert F. 1996. *Strange Writing: Anomaly Accounts in Early Medieval China*. Albany: SUNY Press.

Chao, Yuan-ling. 1995. *Medicine and Society in Late Imperial China: A Study of Physicians in Suzhou*. Ph.D. diss., University of California (Los Angeles).

Chauncey, Helen R. 1992. *Schoolhouse Politicians: Locality and State During the Chinese Republic*. Honolulu: University of Hawaii.

Chen Yuanlong 陳元龍. 1735. *Gezhi jingyuan* 格致鏡原 (Mirror origins of investigating things and extending knowledge), in: *Siku quanshu* (Complete collection in the Imperial Four Treasuries), vols. 1031–2.

China in the Sixteenth Century: The Journals of Matteo Ricci: 1583–1610. 1953. Translated into Latin by Father Nichola Trigault and into English by Louis J. Gallagher, S.J. New York: Random House.

Chou, Min-zhi Maynard. 1974. *Science and Value in May Fourth China: The Case of Hu Shih*. Ph.D. diss., University of Michigan (Ann Arbor).

Chu Pingyi. 1994. *Technical Knowledge, Cultural Practices and Social Boundaries: Wan-nan Scholars and the Recasting of Jesuit Astronomy, 1600–1800*. Ph.D. diss., University of California (Los Angeles).

——. 1995. "Cheng-Zhu Orthodoxy, Evidential Studies and Correlative Cosmology: Chiang Yung and Western Astronomy", *Philosophy and the History of Science: A Taiwanese Journal* 4.2 (October 1995), pp. 71–108.

——. 1997. "Scientific Dispute in the Imperial Court: The 1664 Calendar Case", *Chinese Science* 14, pp. 7–34.

Cohn, Bernard. 1996. *Colonialism and Its Form of Knowledge: The British in India*. Chicago: University of Chicago Press.

Craig, Albert. 1965. "Science and Confucianism in Tokugawa Japan", in: Marius Jansen (ed.). *Changing Japanese Attitudes Toward Modernization*. Princeton: Princeton University Press.

Deane, Thatcher E. 1989. *The Chinese Imperial Astronomical Bureau: Form and Function of the Ming Dynasty 'Qintianjian' From 1365 to 1627*. Ph.D. diss., University of Washington (Seattle).

Duara, Prasenjit. 1988. *Culture, Power, and the State: Rural North China, 1900–1942*. Stanford: Stanford University Press.

Dunne, George H., S. J. 1962. *Generation of Giants: The Story of the Jesuits in China in the Last Decades of the Ming Dynasty*. Notre Dame: University of Notre Dame Press.

Elman, Benjamin A. 1984. *From Philosophy to Philology*. Cambridge, Mass.: Council on East Asian Studies, Harvard University.

——. 1997. "The Formation of 'Dao Learning' as Imperial Ideology During the Early Ming Dynasty", in: T. Huters, R. Bin Wong, and P. Yu (eds.). *Culture and the State in Chinese History*. Stanford: Stanford University Press.

——. 2000. *A Cultural History of Civil Examinations in Late Imperial China*. Berkeley: University of California Press.

Edkins, Joseph (tr.). 1886. *Fuguo yangmin ce* 富國養民策 (Policies for enriching the dynasty and nourishing the people), in: Robert Hart and Joseph Edkins (eds.). *Gezhi Qimeng* 格致啟蒙 (Science Primer). Beijing: Zong shuiwusi, vol. 12 [Translation of William S. Jevons, *Political Economy*, 1871].

Esherick, Joseph W. 1976. *Reform and Revolution in China: The 1911 Revolution in Hunan and Hubei*. Berkeley: University of California Press.

Feng Guifen 馮桂芬. 1897. *Jiaobinlu kangyi* 校邠廬抗議 (Protests from the cottage of Feng Guifen). Reprint Taibei: Wenhai Press.

Furth, Charlotte. 1970. *Ting Wen-chiang: Science and China's New Culture*. Cambridge, Mass.: Harvard University Press.

Gegu yaolun 格古要論 (Essential criteria of antiquities). 1573–1619. In: Hu Wenhuan 胡文煥 (comp.). *Gezhi congshu* 格致叢書 (Collectanea of works inquiring into and extending knowledge). Microfilm Taibei: National Central Library, Rare Books Collection (film of Ming Wanli edition) ca. 1596, vol. 25.

Gezhi qimeng si zhong 格致啟蒙四種 (Science Primer Series in four parts). 1875. Young J. Allen and Zheng Changyan 鄭昌炎 (trsl). Shanghai: Jiangnan zhizaoju.

Gardner, Daniel. 1986. *Zhu Xi and the Daxue: Neo-Confucian Reflection on the Confucian Canon*. Cambridge: Harvard University Council on East Asian Studies.

Gernet, Jacques. 1982. *China and the Christian Impact*. Cambridge: Cambridge University Press.

Guangxu zhengyao 光緒政要 (Important issues of governance in the Guangxu reign). 1909. Shen Tongsheng 沈桐生 (comp.). Shanghai: Chongyitang.

Hamaguchi Fujio 濱口富士雄. 1994. *Shindai kokyogaku no shisō shi teki kenkyū* 清代考據學の思想史的研究 (Research on the intellectual history of Qing dynasty evidential studies). Tokyo: Kokusho kankōkai.

Harrell, Paula. 1992. *Sowing the Seeds of Change: Chinese Students, Japanese Teachers, 1895–1905*. Stanford: Stanford University Press.

Hart, Roger. 1996. *Proof, Propaganda, and Patronage: A Cultural History of the Dissemination of Western Studies in Seventeenth-Century China*. Ph.D. diss., University of California (Los Angeles).

——. 1997. "Local Knowledges, Local Contexts: Mathematics in Yuan and Ming China". Paper presented at the Song-Yuan-Ming Transitions Conference, Lake Arrowhead, Cal., June 5–11, 1997.

Hashimoto, Keizō. 1988. *Hsu Kuang-ch'i and Astronomical Reform*. Osaka: Kansai University Press.

Hashimoto, Takehiko. 1999. "Introducing a French Technological System: The Origin and Early History of the Yokosuka Dockyard", *East Asian Science, Technology, and Medicine* 16, pp. 53–72.

Henderson, John. 1980. "The Assimilation of the Exact Sciences into the Qing Confucian Tradition", *Journal of Asian Affairs* 5.1 (Spring 1980), pp. 15–31.

——. 1986. "Qing Scholars' Views of Western Astronomy", *Harvard Journal of Asiatic Studies* 46.1, pp. 121–48.

Ho Peng Yoke. 1985. *Li, Qi, and Shu: An Introduction to Science and Civilization in China*. Hong Kong: Hong Kong University Press.

Horng Wann-sheng. 1993. "Chinese Mathematics at the Turn of the 19th Century", in: Lin Zheng-hung and Fu Daiwie (eds.). *Philosophy and Conceptual History of Science in Taiwan*. Dordrecht: Kluwer Academic Publishers, pp. 167–208.

Hu Wenhuan 胡文煥 (comp.). 1573–1619. *Gezhi congshu* 格致叢書 (Collectanea of works inquiring into and extending knowledge). Microfilm Taibei: National Central Library, Rare Books Collection (film of Ming Wanli edition) ca. 1596.

Huangchao zhengdian leizuan 黃朝政典類纂 (Classified materials on Qing dynasty government regulations). 1969. Xi Yufu 席裕福 (comp.). Reprint Taibei: Shenwu Press.

Huang Ming sanyuan kao 皇明三元考 (Study of the provincial, metropolitan, and palace civil examination *optimi* during the Ming dynasty). n.d. Zhang Hongdao 張弘道 and Zhang Ningdao 張凝道 (comp). Late Ming edition, after 1618. n.p.

Hummel, Arthur (ed.). 1972. *Eminent Chinese of the Qing Period*. Reprint Taibei: Chengwen Bookstore.

Hymes, Robert. 1986. "Not Quite Gentlemen? Doctors in Song and Yuan", *Chinese Science* 7, pp. 11–85.

Ichiko Chuzo. 1968. "The Role of the Gentry: An Hypothesis", in: Mary Wright (ed.). *China In Revolution: The First Phase, 1900–1913*. New Haven: Yale University Press.

Jami, Catherine. 1994. "Learning Mathematical Sciences During the Early and Mid-Qing", in: Benjamin A. Elman and Alexander Woodside (eds.). *Education and Society in Late Imperial China, 1600–1900*. Berkeley: University of California Press, pp. 223–56.

Jensen, Lionel. 1977. *Manufacturing Confucianism: Chinese Traditions and Universal Civilization*. Durham: Duke University Press.

Lach, Donald F. 1977. *Asia in the Making of Europe. Volume II. A Century of Wonder, Book 3: The Scholarly Disciplines*. Chicago: University of Chicago Press.

Latour, Bruno. 1987. *Science in Action: How to Follow Scientists and Engineers Through Society*. Cambridge, Mass.: Harvard University Press.

Lean, Eugenia. 1996. "The Modern Elixer: Medicine as a Consumer Item in the Early Twentieth-Century Press". M.A. thesis paper, University of California (Los Angeles), November 1996.

Levenson, Joseph. 1957. "The Amateur Ideal in Ming and Early Qing Society: Evidence from Painting", in: John K. Fairbank (ed.). *Chinese Thought and Institutions*. Chicago: University of Chicago Press, pp. 320–41.

Liang Jun 梁峻. 1995. *Zhongguo gudai yizheng shilüe* 中國古代醫政史略 (Historical summary of medicine and government in ancient China). Huhehot: Nei Menggu renmin chubanshe.

Liu, Lydia. 1995. *Translingual Practice: Literature, National Culture, and Translated Modernity—China 1900–1937*. Stanford: Stanford University Press.

Lund, Renville. 1956. *The Imperial University of Beijing*. Ph.D. diss., University of Washington (Washington).

MacKinnon, Stephen R. 1980. *Power and Politics in Late Imperial China: Yuan Shikai in Beijing and Tianjin, 1901–1908*. Berkeley: University of California Press.

Meng Yue. 1999. "Hybrid Science versus Modernity: The Practice of the Jiangnan Arsenal", *East Asian Science* 16, pp. 13–52.

Mungello, Donald. 1985. *Curious Land: Jesuit Accommodation and the Origins of Sinology*. Honolulu: University of Hawaii Press.

Needham, Joseph. 1959. *Science and Civilisation in China*. Cambridge: Cambridge University Press.

Pan Jixing. 1991. "The Spread of Georgius Agricola's *De Re Metallica* in Late Ming China", *T'oung Pao* 57, pp. 108–18.

Percival, Sir David (tr.). 1971. *Chinese Connoisseurship, the Ko Ku Yao Lun: The Essential Criteria of Antiquity*. London: Faber.

Peterson, Willard. 1975. "Fang I-chih: Western Learning and the 'Investigation of Things'", in: Wm. Theodore de Bary et al. (eds.). *The Unfolding of Neo-Confucianism*. New York: Columbia University Press, pp. 369–411.

——. 1986. "Calendar Reform Prior to the Arrival of Missionaries at the Ming Court", *Ming Studies* 21, pp. 45–61.

Prakash, Gyan. 1999. *Another Reason: Science and the Imagination of Modern India*. Princeton: Princeton University Press.

Pusey, James R. 1983. *China and Charles Darwin*. Cambridge: Harvard University Press.

Qian Daxin 錢大昕. 1968. *Qianyantang wenji* 潛研堂文集 (Collected essays of the Hall of Subtle Research). Taibei: Shangwu yinshuguan.

"Qingchao tongdian" 清朝通典 (Encyclopaedic history of institutions of the Qing dynasty). 1936. In: *Shitong* 十通 (The ten *Tong*). Shanghai: Commercial Press, vol. 18, p. 2131.

Qiong Zhang. 1998. "Nature, Supernature, and Natural Studies in Sixteenth- and Seventeenth-Century China". Paper presented at the Colloquium sponsored by the Center for the Cultural Studies of Science, Medicine, and Technology, UCLA History Department, Los Angeles, November 16, 1998.

——. 1999. "About God, Demons, and Miracles: The Jesuit Discourse on the Supernatural in Late Ming China", *Early Science and Medicine* 4.1 (February 1999), pp. 1–36.

Quan Hansheng 全漢昇. 1935. "Qingmo de 'xixue yuan chu Zhongguo' shuo" 清末的西學源出中國説 (Late Qing theory of the Chinese origin of Western learning), *Lingnan xuebao* 4.2 (June 1935), pp. 57–102.

Rankin, Mary B. 1986. *Elite Activism and Political Transformation in China: Zhejiang Province, 1865–1911*. Stanford: Stanford University Press.

Reardon-Anderson, James. 1991. *The Study of Change: Chemistry in China, 1840–1949*. Cambridge: Cambridge University Press.

Reynolds, David. 1991. "Re-Drawing China's Intellectual Map: 19th Century Chinese Images of Science", *Late Imperial China* 12.1 (June 1991), pp. 27–61.

Schneider, Laurence. 1988. "Genetics in Republican China", in: J. Bowers, J. Hess, and N. Sivin (eds.). *Science and Medicine in Twentieth-Century China: Research and Education*. Ann Arbor: Center for Chinese Studies, University of Michigan, pp. 3–29.

Schwartz, Benjamin. 1969. *In Search of Wealth and Power: Yan Fu and the West*. New York: Harper Torchbooks.

Shen Xinzhou 沈新周. 1910. "Xu" 序 (Preface), in: *Dixue* 地學 (Geographical studies). Shanghai: Saoye shanfang lithograph.

Siku quanshu zongmu 四庫全書總目 (Catalogue of the complete collection of the Four Treasuries). 1973. Ji Yun 記昀 et al. (comp.). Reprint Taibei: Yiwen Press.

Sivin, Nathan. 1970–78. "Wang Hsi-shan (1628–1682)", in: *Dictionary of Scientific Biography*. New York: Scribner's Sons, vol. 14, pp. 159–68.

——. 1973. "Copernicus in China", in: *Colloquia Copernica II: Études sur l'audience de la théorie héliocentrique*. Warsaw: Union Internationale d'Historie et Philosophie des Sciences, pp. 63–114.

——. 1985. "Max Weber, Joseph Needham, Benjamin Nelson: The Question of Chinese Science", in: E. Victor Walter (ed.). *Civilizations East and West: A Memorial Volume for Benjamin Nelson*. Atlantic Highlands: Humanities Press.

——. 1987. *Traditional Medicine in Contemporary China*. Ann Arbor: Center for Chinese Studies, University of Michigan.

——. 1995a. "Why the Scientific Revolution did not take place in China—or didn't it?". Reprinted in id. *Science in Ancient China: Researches and Reflections*. Aldershot, Brookfield: Variorum, pp. 45–66.

——. 1995b *Medicine, Philosophy, and Religion in Ancient China: Researches and Reflections*. Aldershot, Brookfield: Variorum.

Spence, Jonathan D. 1974. *Emperor of China: Self-portrait of K'ang-hsi*. New York: Vintage Books.

Taiping yulan 太平御覽 (Encyclopedia of the Taiping era). 1960. Reprint Taibei: Zhonghua Bookstore (Reprint of *Sibu congkan* 四部叢刊 edition).

Tambiah, Stanley J. 1990. *Magic, Science, Religion, and the Scope of Rationality*. Cambridge: Cambridge University Press.

Teng, Ssu-yü and Knight Biggerstaff. 1971. *An Annotated Bibliography of Selected Chinese Reference Works*. Cambridge: Harvard University Press.

Wang Fan-shen. 1995. "The 'Daring Fool' Feng Fang (1500–1570) and His Ink Rubbing of the Stone-inscribed Great Learning", *Ming Studies* 35 (August 1995), pp. 74–91.

Wang Hui. 1998. "From Debates on Culture to Debates on Knowledge: Zhang Junmai and the Differentiations of Cultural Modernity in 1920's China". Paper presented at the Workshop "Reinventions of Confucianism in the Twentieth Century", sponsored by the UCLA Center for Chinese Studies under the auspices of the University of California Pacific Rim Research Program, Los Angeles, January 31, 1998.

Wang, Y. C. 1966. *Chinese Intellectuals and the West, 1872–1949*. Chapel Hill: University of North Carolina Press.

Wang Yangming 王陽明. 1973. "Chuanxi lu" 傳習錄 (Instructions for practical living), in: *Wang Yangming quanji* 王陽明全集 (Complete works of Wang Yangming). Taibei: Kaozheng Press, p. 129.

Winch, Peter. 1970. "Understanding a Primitive Society", in: Bryon Wilson (ed.). *Rationality*. Oxford: Basil Blackwell, pp. 93–102.

Wright, David. 1995. "Careers in Western Science in Nineteenth-Century China: Xu Shou and Xu Jianyin", *Journal of the Royal Asiatic Society*, Third Series, no. 5, pp. 49–90.

——. 1996. "John Fryer and the Shanghai Polytechnic: Making Space for Science in Nineteenth-Century China", *British Journal of the History of Science* 29, pp. 1–16.

——. 1997. "The Great Desideratum: Chinese Chemical Nomenclature and the Transmission of Western Chemical Concepts", *Chinese Science* 14, pp. 35–70.

Xiong Mingyu 熊明遇. 1648. *Gezhi cao* 格致草 (Draft for investigating things and extending knowledge). n.p.

Xu Guangtai 徐光台. 1996a. "Ruxue yu kexue: yige kexueshi guandian de tantao" 儒學與科學 ：一個科學史觀點的探討 (Literati studies and science: analysis from the angle of the history of science), *Qinghua xuebao*, New Series, 26.4 (December 1996), pp. 369–92.

——. 1996b. "Mingmo Qingchu xifang gezhixue de chongji yu fanying: yi Xiong Mingyu Gezhi cao wei li" 明末清初西方格致學的衝擊與反應：以熊明遇格致草為例 (Impact and response in late Ming and early Qing Western *scientiae*; using Gao Mingyu's draft of *Scientiae* as an example), in: Taiwan University History Department (ed.). *Shibian, qunti yu geren* 世變，群體與個人 (Epochal change, groups and history). Taibei: Taiwan National University, pp. 236–58.

Xu Ke 徐珂. 1920. *Qingbai leichao* 清稗類鈔 (Classified jottings on Qing dynasty unofficial history). Shanghai: Commercial Press.

Yabuuti Kiyosi. 1973. "Chinese Astronomy: Development and Limiting Factors", in: Shigeru Nakayama and Nathan Sivin (eds.). *Chinese Science: Explorations of an Ancient Tradition*. Cambridge, Mass.: MIT Press, pp. 98–9.

Yamada Keiji 山田慶兒. 1978. *Shushi no shizengaku* 朱子の自然学 (Zhu Xi's natural studies). Tokyo: Iwanami.

Yan Fu 嚴復 (tr.). 1902. *Mule mingxue* 穆勒名學 (Miller's *Logic*). n.p.: Jisuzhai [Translation of John Stuart Mill. 1843. *A System of Logic. Ratiocinative and Inductive* , 2 vols.].

——. 1953. "Jiuwang juelun" 救亡決論 (On what determines rescue or perishing), in: *Wuxu bianfa ziliao* 戊戌變法資料 (Sources on the 1898 reforms). Beijing: Shenzhou guoguangshe, pp. 360–71.

Yang Ts'ui-hua. 1993. "The Development of Geology in Republican China, 1912–1937", in: Lin Cheng-hung and Fu Daiwie (eds.). *Philosophy and Conceptual History of Science in Taiwan*. Dordrecht: Kluwer Academic Publishers.

"Yangwu yundong dashiji" 洋務運動大事記 (Record of major events during the Foreign Affairs Movement). n.d. In: Xu Tailai 徐泰來 (ed.). *Yangwu yundong xinlun* 洋務運動新論 (New views of the Foreign Affairs Movement). Changsha: Hunan renmin chubanshe, pp. 349–448.

Yü Ying-shih. 1975. "Some Preliminary Observations on the Rise of Qing Confucian Intellectualism", *Qinghua Journal of Chinese Studies*, New Series 11.1 and 11.2 (December 1975).

Young, Ernest P. 1977. *The Presidency of Yuan Shih-k'ai: Liberalism and Dictatorship in Early Republican China*. Ann Arbor: University of Michigan Press.

Zhang Hongsheng 張鴻聲. 1995. "Qingdai yiguan kaoshi ji tili" 清代醫官考試及題例 (Qing dynasty examinations for medical officials with examples), *Zhonghua yishi zazhi* 25.2 (April 1995), pp. 95–6.

Zhongwai shiwu cewen leibian dacheng 中外時務策問類編大成 (Compendium of classified examination questions on current affairs in China and abroad). 1903. n.p.

Zhu Zhenheng 朱震亨. 1983–86. *Gezhi yulun* 格致餘論 (Views on extending medical knowledge). Reprint Taibei: Commercial Press (in the *Siku quanshu* 四庫全書 edition), vol. 746, p. 638.

Zhuzi yulei 朱子語類 (Conversations with Master Zhu [Xi] classified topically). 1979 [1473]. Reprint Taibei: Chengwen.

Zhuangyuan ce 狀元策 (Policy essays of *optimi*). 1997 [1733]. Jiao Hong 焦竑 and Wu Daonan 吳道南 et al. (comps.). n.p.

NATASCHA VITTINGHOFF

SOCIAL ACTORS IN THE FIELD OF NEW LEARNING IN NINETEENTH CENTURY CHINA

INTRODUCTION

It is the purpose of this paper to sketch the features of an early 'scientific community' in late nineteenth century China. The existence of such a community before the fundamental reform of the education system in the early twentieth century is largely denied in current scholarship on the Chinese sciences. Yet, as has been argued elsewhere, a keen interest in Western sciences had already existed since the early nineteenth century, the study and practice of which was not obstructed by a traditional cultural and Confucian orthodoxy, as conventional wisdom has it. Instead the pursuit of scientific studies was convincingly integrated into the intellectual map of Late Qing literati.[1] Science therefore played a crucial role in intellectual studies of the Late Qing–yet conventional accounts repeatedly state that such studies received no acknowledgement in society. This seeming paradox has encouraged me to investigate which social actors were involved in this new intellectual endeavour and whether or how these actors were connected with each other. It thus seems necessary to start with some general deliberations about which group of social actors I am intending to deal with here.

As other science histories, also the history of modern sciences in China has, for a long time, been dominated by a focus on professional institutions, disciplines, the great achievements of single scientists in one field and a teleological narrative of a continuous rational production of scientific results. In this sense, there was, of course, no such modern professional community of scientists, institutionalized in delineated academic fields and following formalized procedures in the nineteenth century. Yet, during this period modern Western sciences entered China in a complex process and through various institutions. The creation of a modern scientific canon as the result of a transcul-

---

[1] David C. Reynolds. 1991. "Redrawing China's Intellectual Map: Images of Sciences in Nineteenth Century China", *Late Imperial China* 12.1, pp. 27–61, resp. see Benjamin Elman's contribution in this volume.

tural process was varyingly influenced, restricted or engendered by such diverging factors as institutional frameworks, structures of classifying knowledge, ideological interest and indigenous exigencies as well as linguistic factors. Therefore it seems necessary to abandon the idea of a strict division between scientific academic activities and social practice in favor of highlighting the merge of science and society.[2] The occupation with modern sciences in the Chinese nineteenth century is thus rather understood as a process of constant cultural brokerage and this understanding determines the selection of my sample group.

The study will thus follow a different approach than hitherto pursued by academic studies on Chinese sciences, treating scientific activities as a form of cultural practice that encompasses multiple forms of representations of scientific activities and new knowledge within different public sectors on both the professional academic and popular public level. Such an approach seems justified by more recent studies on the social history of sciences. These studies emphasize that the development of a scientific discipline and the growth of 'science' in general is determined by elements such as personal contacts, recruitment of new disciplines and new social structures rather than primarily the truth of scientific ideas.[3] What I am interested in here is therefore neither a scientific community engaged in one special discipline nor a specific aristocracy of science, i.e. elite members of scientific institutions. Instead, I will attempt some explorations of the scientific milieu in nineteenth century China, most developed in the treaty ports and Hong Kong, by also including the non-professionals and non-scientists on the periphery of the sciences, like their mediators and financial or political patrons, with a view to gaining some insight into the cultural and social status of the sciences and their institutions as well as their functions in Late Qing society.[4]

---

[2] We can find this cultural approach explained in more detail in recent scholarship on the history of European sciences. Cf. Hans Erich Boedeker, Peter H. Reill and Jürgen Schlumbohm (eds.). 1999. *Wissenschaft als kulturelle Praxis 1750-1900.* (Veröffentlichungen des Max-Planck Instituts für Geschichte, 154). Göttingen: Vandenhoeck and Ruprecht; Andreas W. Daum. 1998. *Wissenschaftspopularisierung im 19. Jahrhundert. Bürgerliche Kultur, naturwissenschaftliche Bildung und die deutsche Öffentlichkeit, 1848–1914.* Munich: Oldenbourg.

[3] Cf. Helge Kragh. 1987. *An Introduction to the Historiography of Science.* Cambridge: Cambridge University Press, p. 177.

[4] Reynolds, for instance, negates the existence of a scientific community because

Such a perspective allows the identification of a field of scientific activities on the popular and academic level, populated by social actors from different public sectors and with different 'professional' backgrounds.[5] We are therefore not dealing with a group of pure scientists, but with a group of actors involved in the production, dissemination and propagation of the new sciences, or better, New Learning (*xinxue* 新學), as it was generally termed at this point of time. The actors involved in this translating and transmitting of Western knowledge into Late Imperial China came from different geographical and social backgrounds, were of different age and were officials, merchants, missionaries or scientists of different nationalities. New Learning had become a private property that enabled its possessors to exert a large degree of agency. The actors dealt with here shared this common interest in the new knowledge and commonly acknowledge its importance for the future development of their country, a conviction which they propagated through various means and media. Thus it can still be maintained that they shared a scientific interest, if science is more generally identified as cognitive interests and expert knowledge.[6]

I will start this study with presenting some of the prevalent evaluations and statements about the social role of the actors under discussion and contextualizing them in a historical and transcultural

---

[4] (*cont.*) he defines scientific activities as experimental procedures that produce new knowledge. According to his view, in Late Qing China there was mainly a reception and reproduction of existing knowledge. Cf. Reynolds 1991, p. 50.

[5] As the emergence of modern professions itself is a late phenomenon of the nineteenth century it would be anachronistic to apply criteria to define a "profession" as developed by sociological studies on professions. Such criteria are: definition of the professionalization by special education or training procedures; a minimum of financial compensation; the formation of professional associations and the development of ethical standards regulating the professional practice. Cf. Howard Vollmer and Donald M. Mills. 1966. *Professionalization*. Engelwood Cliffs: Prentice Hall; Ronald M. Pavalko. 1988. *Sociology of Occupations and Professions*. Ithaca, Ill.: Peacock.

[6] Nathan Reingold suggests a distinction between 'cultivators' and 'researchers' in the field of sciences, the latter representing those who are entirely devoted to research (and the production of new scientific results), whereas the 'cultivators' are characterized by 'learned culture' rather than engagement in scientific practice. In this investigation I am not only including these 'cultivators', but they even make up the larger part of the sample group. Cf. Nathan Reingold. 1976. "Definitions and Speculations: The Professionalization of Science in America in the Nineteenth Century", in: Alexandra Oleson and Sanborn Brown (eds.). *The Pursuit of Knowledge in the Early American Republic*. Baltimore: Johns Hopkins University Press, pp. 37–9.

perspective. The following section aims at a historical reconstruction of the scientific milieu in the nineteenth century and looks at an empirical re-evaluation of these general statements. In order to decide who belongs to the group, the boundaries of which are even blurred, I have chosen an institutional approach on the one hand, and will hence open this study with an identification of the major cultural institutions which assembled these new social actors. Following the approach above I will focus not only on those institutions that were producing (or presenting translated) scientific results, but include establishments which were mediating the New Learning in society. As the modern publishing industry engendered a major change for this nascent 'scientific community', I will also include actors involved in the nascent journalistic business because they served as important 'mediators of the field of knowledge'. Moreover, as the development of the sciences in China occurred as a transcultural process, translators played an important role, too. In order to avoid the trap of identifying only those elite members, which had gained prominent positions in these institutions, I have also randomly selected some who have published, translated or co-edited works on New Learning, identified through the Bibliographical Database of the VW project *Wissenschaftssprache Chinesisch* (WSC) or *Studies in the Formation of Modern Chinese Terminologies.*[7]

The next part forms a prosopographical study which gives some information on the collective background and the biographical similarities of the sample group I have assembled, in respect of their geographical range of activities, educational background, sources of income and later careers. As academic scholarship still depicts those Chinese preoccupied with modern sciences prior to the twentieth century as insignificant misfits, who are lacking any profound education and social prestige, but has failed to present substantial and systematic studies on these social actors, such first steps on archaeological exploration of the individual histories of these actors seem necessary.

In the last section I will analyze the personal networks of these actors. I will show that early activities in the field of new knowledge were not individual and private endeavours with little public significance, but that these actors involved in the different enterprises in

---

[7] On the specific selection criteria see below. Parts of this database are available on-line now. See http://www.wsc.uni-erlangen.de/wscdb.htm.

Shanghai and Hong Kong formed a closely connected community linked together by institutional and personal co-operation. As 'organizers of the field of knowledge', these actors, if albeit small in terms of numbers, were able to multiply their individual efforts, and their mutual support, reliance and co-operation also vested them with legitimate capacities to exert effective agency.

1. CONTESTED OPINIONS ON THE STATUS OF SCIENTISTS, TRANSLATORS AND JOURNALISTS IN LATE QING CHINA

The emergence of new professions and new social groups always means a challenge to the legitimation of already existing social groups, a challenge often engendering very negative assessments about these newcomers. This is the case with the new journalists, translators and scientists who were employed in the new institutions like the *Tongwenguan* 同文館 and later the *Jingshi daxuetang* 京師大學堂 in Beijing, or the *Guangfangyanguan* 廣方言館, the Jiangnan Arsenal (*Jiangnan zhizaoju* 江南製造局), the *Gezhi shuyuan* 格致書院 in Shanghai or also the daily newspapers in Shanghai and Hong Kong, which I will introduce below. The actors attached to these new institutions are decried as incapable, unprofessional literati who could find no other way to make their living or had failed to make any successful use of their new knowledge. One rather drastic example on the position of journalists and new school teachers might suffice to illustrate this:

> It would be a long story to tell of all the journalistic ventures that have seen the light in the model settlement. There are at least two things which the man in the street can do as well or better than those whose duty it is to do them. The first thing is to conduct a school, the second to edit a newspaper. No training is required for either! Teachers and journalists are neither born nor made in the opinion of the man in the street. They grow like blackberries on the brier bush, like leaves in Vallombrosa, or like anything else that is synonym for unlimited numbers. Potential teachers and journalists are thick everywhere. The failures in life's race, the decrepit, the halt, the lame, the incapable, the unthrifty, the unsteady, and even the fool, all think that these two resources still remain open to them when all else is closed. And in a new and expanding community like that of Shanghai there were not lacking opportunities for putting the question of capacity to the test. The many failures show the result.[8]

Similar remarks on the "true nature" of the translators are evident in the following quote from Feng Guifen 馮桂芬 (1809–1874):

> Nowadays those familiar with barbarian affairs are called "linguists". These men are generally frivolous rascals and loafers in the cities and are despised in their villages and communities. They serve as interpreters only because they have no other means of making a livelihood. Their nature is boorish, their knowledge shallow, and furthermore, their moral principles are mean. They know nothing except sensual pleasures and material profit.[9]

These quotes contain the most frequently occuring and typical reproaches against the new social actors: these "dregs" are dull and mind-blind persons lacking any profound education, professional alternatives and reputation. Moreover, they conduct an unstable life and are forced to throw their literary talents on the market. Chinese sources apply the terms "dregs of the literati class" (*siwen bailei* 斯文白類),[10] or "degenerate literati" (*luotuo wenren* 落拓文人) or "shameless scholars" (*shukuang xuezi* 疏狂學子) for those early journalists.[11]

Denouncing journalists as incapable, impudent or irresponsible was a phenomenon occurring in many societies in different periods, which is probably connected to the fact that journalists very often operate in polemic contexts and in contested fields of public opinion. Also, the undefined nature of the profession itself with its irregular working hours, extensive travels and unstable life conditions, might foster such a popular assessment of the journalists. The common international trend of such assessments is obvious when we look at

---

[8] *Shanghai by night and day.* 1897. Shanghai: Shanghai Mercury, p. 164.

[9] Quoted from the translation in Ssu-yu Teng and John King Fairbank. 1965. *China's Response to the West. A Documentary Survey 1839–1923.* New York: Athenaeum, p. 51.

[10] *Siwen bailei* was first used by Cixi to denounce the journalists in her famous edict against private newspapers after her *coup d'état* in 1898 and from then on became a stock phrase used in different contexts by opponents and supporters of the old journalism. Cf. Vittinghoff. 2002a. "Unity vs. Uniformity: Liang Qichao and the Invention of a 'New Journalism' for China", *Late Imperial China* 23.1 (June), pp. 91–143, *passim.*

[11] E.g. Lei Jin 雷溍 . 1987 [1922]. "Shenbaoguan zhi guoqu zhuangkuang" 申報館之 過去狀 況 (The former conditions in the Shenbao publishing house), in: *Zuijin zhi wushi nian: 1872–1922 nian Shenbao wushi zhounian jinian* 最 近之五十年 : 1872–1922 年申報五十周年紀念 (The last fifty years: Commemorating the fiftieth anniversary of the *Shenbao*). Shanghai: Shanghai shudian, part 3, pp. 26–8; 27.

almost identical statements about early journalists in nineteenth century Europe.[12]

Moreover, in the Chinese case, most of these designations are
transmitted by newspaper historians of the early 1920s and 1930s and
reflect no more than the polemic statement of a later generation of
now "true journalists" who find it necessary to assess its predecessors
negatively in order to enhance their own status.[13] Also the quoted
statement of Feng Guifen on translators has to be seen in a polemical
context, as he is certainly not speaking against the translators per se,
but wrote this in his *Jiaobinlu kangyi* 校邠盧抗議 (Protest notes from
the *Jiaobin*-Studio) in order to highlight the urgency of his proposal to
establish schools and official translation offices for translators.

The contested nature of these evaluations becomes clear when
looking at other contemporary sources. Wang Tao 王韜 (1828–1897)
is a good example for displaying the contesting interpretations of the
psychological situation of the Chinese working in these transcultural
settings. It is maintained that they lived under miserable and depress-
ing circumstances, which explains their frustrations and subsequent
eccentric social behaviour as a way to give vent to their anger.[14] In
many accounts only the one following quote from Wang Tao's diary
serves as a proof for the psychological difficulties these literati suffered in working with the foreigners:

> I had not being intended or expected being [here] so [long]. Yet, since
> it is like this now, I have to [accept the situation] and settle down; in
> short my situation now can be described as regarding a perilous situa-
> tion as though it was a prosperous road, and treating bitter vegetables
> as though it was sweet water chestnuts. Relying on these barbarian pig-
> mies [*zhuli* 侏離] for a living is particulary offensive in its stink. ... In
> name, I am an editor, but in fact I am the one who is given orders. [My
> work] is so irrelevant and outside of true scholarship that if [the paper

---

[12] E.g. the comments of the German journalist Eduard Reich on his colleagues in
1888, quoted in Rudolf Oebsger-Roeder. 1936. *Untersuchungen über den Bildungsstand der deutschen Journalisten*. Leipzig: Universitätsverlag (Wesen und Wirkungen der Publizistik 7), p. 37.

[13] Representative for this kind of press historiography are Ge Gongzhen 戈公振.
1982 [1926]. *Zhongguo baoxue shi* 中國報學史 (A history of Chinese journalism).
Taibei: Xuesheng shuju, p. 100, or Hu Daojing 胡道靜. 1935. *Shanghai xinwen shiye
zhi shi de fazhan* 上海新聞事業之史的發展 (The historical development of Shanghai's journalism). Shanghai: Tongzhiguan [Reprint: Minguo congshu], ser. 2, vol. 49,
pp. 4–5.

[14] On their lifestyle and social habits, see below.

on which it is written] is not used for covering pickle jars or mending windows, one might as well throw it straight into the privy.[15]

As Catherine Yeh has shown, the performances of these young literati as well as their statements have to be understood as special gestures and therefore statements formed in a specific cultural environment. The often quoted abhorrence toward their work with the foreigners or low self-esteem due to their failure to pass the examinations expressed in their letters or diaries does not necessarily correspond to their actual behaviour and thinking, but may also be read as strategic devices.

In his reminiscences on his sojourn in Hong Kong, for example, Wang Tao presents a very positive picture of this Westernized modern city, its water pipes and electricity and also of his friendly intercourse with foreigners. Here he praises James Legge (1815–1897) as a respected and intimate friend:

> When Mr. Legge is not busy teaching, he sometimes invites me to spend a day in his Pokfulham home, where we while away the hours together reading or composing poems in the wafting breeze. Even immortals could hardly aspire to such pleasure. I owe it to Mr. Legge's unstinting friendship that I am allowed to share his comfort in the hot season.[16]

Similar statements about Wang Tao are made in the letters of James Legge, who wrote:

> Nor must he [Legge] fail to acknowledge gratefully the services rendered to him by Wang T'ao, a graduate from Soochow. This scholar, far exceeding in classical more than any of his countrymen whom the author had previously known, came to Hong Kong in the end of 1863, and placed at his disposal all the treasures of a large well-selected library. At the same time, entering with spirit into his labours, now explaining, now arguing, as the case might be, he has not only helped but enlivened many a day of toil.[17]

---

[15] Letter of Wang Tao, January 1858, quoted in Catherine V. Yeh. 1997. "The Life-style of Four Shanghai *wenren* in Late Qing China", *Harvard Journal of Asiatic Studies* 57.2, pp. 419–70; 430–1.

[16] Wang Tao. 1988. "My Sojourn in Hong Kong", (Translated by Yang Qinghua). *Renditions: Special Issue on Hong Kong* 29 and 30, pp. 37–41; 40.

[17] James Legge. 1985. *The Chinese Classics. Vol. I-V*. Taibei: Southern Material Center, vol. 3 (The Shoo King), preface, p. viii.

John Fryer, in a letter during his directorship of the Jiangnan Arsenal, praises his colleague, probably Xu Jianyin 徐建寅 (1845–1901), in a very similar way:

> The Chinese who are working with me are some of them really clever. There are none lower in rank than district magistrates. We get on capitally together so far. One is younger than the rest and has made quite a strong friendship with me and tells me all his affairs as if I were his brother. He is the cleverest Chinaman I ever met and I am but a child compared to him in many respects.[18]

Also the editor of the *Shenbao*, Ernest Major (Mei Cha 美查, 1841–1908) emphasized the talents of his colleague, the journalist Wu Zirang 吳子讓 (1818–1878), who had been employed in the secretarial staff of Zeng Guofan 曾國藩 (1811–1872) and had come to Shanghai after Zeng Guofan's death in 1872. A passage from Major's obituary for Wu reads as follows:

> Since Shanghai had become the center of commercial activities he [Wu] had many opportunities to observe the current situation of China and the foreign countries. He arrived just at the time when I had humbly proposed to establish the *Shenbao*. Admiring the fame of this gentleman I respectfully bade him to join our house. Most of the more general and broad discussions of the last six years [in our paper] were composed by this gentleman. Readers from near and afar admired him just like the Taishan and the Great Bear. In leading this enterprise I greatly benefitted from and relied on the support of this gentleman.[19]

Even when taking into account that these statements are about colleagues and friends and therefore perhaps flattering, they appear in printed prefaces to their works or on the public pages of big dailies like the *Shenbao;* and if Major or Legge had actually hired only poor scholars and unreliable misfits, they would most likely not have published such statements. Moreover, the statements quoted here are no exceptions but represent a general practice. The newspapers are filled with depictions of the journalists as learned, talented, famous literati, be it in job announcements, birthday congratulations or reports on vis-

---

[18] John Fryer letter to Susy Johnson, July 11, 1868, BL Bx 1, Fldr 5. Archival documents of John Fryer are quoted from Ferdinand Dagenais. 1999. "John Fryer Calendar: Correspondence, Publications and Miscellaneous Papers with Excerpts and Commentary". Unpublished manuscript, Berkeley: University of California, version 3; I wish to thank Fred Dagenais for sharing his material with me.

[19] *Shenbao*, July 4, 1878, p. 1.

its of journalists.[20] Again, it could be argued that this merely served the purpose of self-promotion, yet it seems hard to believe that such a constant promotion would be convincing if it lacked any substantial basis.

These remarks made by the colleagues and friends of these journalists and scientists stand in harsh contrast to the above-mentioned statements on their evil nature. However, as mentioned, it remains a common assumption of contemporary Western scholarship that the Chinese scientists and translators before 1895 were "those scholars whose advancement through the civil examination had stalled and who were looking for new outlets for their talents,"[21] and that the protagonists of scientific progress in the nineteenth century were "Chinese misfits and foreign missionaries" with a "narrow space to do their work" and "opposed by powerful, stubborn institutions."[22]

A major reason for such a negative picture of this group lies in the heavy influence exerted by May Fourth writers who were especially eager to denounce any development which had taken place before their own "iconoclastic", "revolutionary" movement of a new culture as "feudal", "backward", "reactionary." In order to enhance their own status and to emphasize the newness of their ideas and activities they obviously felt compelled to deny and negate all former achievements.[23] In tune, a nascent historiography of the Chinese sciences of the 1930s also played down or even neglected the achievements of the nineteenth century but emphasised the historical watershed marked by the establishment of the Chinese Science Society 中國科學社 (*Zhong-*

[20] For more examples see my dissertation, Natascha Vittinghoff. 2002. *Die Anfänge des Journalismus in China (1860–1911)* (The Rise of Journalism in China, 1860–1911). Wiesbaden: Harrassowitz (Ph.D. diss., University of Heidelberg, 1998), *passim*.

[21] James Reardon-Anderson. 1991. *The Study of Change. Chemistry in China, 1840–1949*. Cambridge: Cambridge University Press, p. 14.

[22] Ibid., p.16.

[23] For such denouncing statements about the scientists of the nineteenth century see, for instance, Hu Shih. 1934. *The Chinese Renaissance*. Chicago University Press, p. 71, quoted in David Wright. 2000. *Translating Science. The Transmission of Western Chemistry into Late Imperial China, 1840–1900*. Leiden: Brill, pp. 66–7. David Wright argues in a similar way that these statements should not be taken at face value but are to be understood in their polemical context. Another prominent example of those polemics is to be found in the writings of Liang Qichao, whose denouncements of the early Qing-press are analysed in Vittinghoff 2002a, *passim*.

guo kexue she), founded in 1914 in Cornell,[24] and pondered about the reasons for the failures of their forerunners.[25] Such denouncement found their way too easily into more recent historical accounts, yet, as I will argue below, they do not seem to quite reflect the actual situation of the new actors involved in this new business of "New Learning".

However, even if we cannot decide about the "true nature" of the status of the journalists and scientists at that time, we can at this point at least state that the status of these new social actors was very contested, and I would therefore suggest to look at some empirical data instead of repeating statements randomly picked out for certain purposes.

2. INSTITUTIONS: ARSENALS, SCHOOLS, MUSEUMS AND NEWSPAPERS IN NINETEENTH CENTURY CHINA

In 1896, Li Duanfen 李端芬 (1833–1907), a vice-president of the Board of Punishments, advocated a five point programme for educational reform in a memorial—allegedly composed by Liang Qichao 梁啟超 (1873–1928)—which dealt with the establishment of a national school system, technical laboratories, translation bureaus, newspapers and the sending of students abroad to study.[26] At this point of time, the memorial found little response. Yet, three years later, these points were taken up again during the famous Hundred Days Reform in 1898, to launch a fundamental reform of the educational system as

---

[24] Liu Xian 劉咸 . 1982 [1937]. "Kexueshi shang zhi zuijin ershi nian" 科學史上之最近二十年 (Recent twenty years in science history), in: id. *Zhonggo kexue ershinian* 中國科學二十年 (Twenty years of science in China), n.p.: Zhongguo kexue she. [Reprint *Minguo congshu*, ser. I. vol. 90], pp. 3-18, pp. 3-4.

[25] Zhang Zigao 張子高 . 1982 [1932]. *Kexue fada shilüe* 科學發達史略 (Brief History of Progress in Sciences), n.p.: Zhonghua shuju. [Reprint *Minguo congshu*, ser. I. vol. 90], p. 247; Zhang Mengwen 張孟聞 . 1982 [1947]. *Zhongguo kexueshi juyu* 中國科學史舉隅 (Aspects of the history of sciences in China), n.p.: Zhongguo wenhua fuwushe. [Reprint *Minguo congshu*, ser. I. vol. 90], p.1.

[26] Cf. Li Duanfen 李端芬 . 1961 [1896]. "Qing tuiguang xuexiao zhe" 請推廣學校摺 (A request to promoting schools). Reprint Shu Xincheng 舒新城 . *Zhongguo jindai jiaoyu shi ziliao* 中國近代教育史資料 (Material on the history of education in China). Beijing: Renmin jiaoyu chubanshe, vol. 1, p. 143; resp. Cyrus Peake. 1932. *Nationalism and Education in China*. New York: Columbia University Press, pp. 25–9. Also Li Duanfen "observes" that editors of the current newspapers were poorly educated and not to be relied upon (pp. 27–8).

one of the most important and salient tasks, which finally lead to the
establishment of the first Chinese university, the *Jingshi daxuetang* in
Beijing. Kang Youwei 康有為 (1958–1927) and Liang Qichao as the
main protagonists in this reform movement were since identified with
the introduction of these new devices and institutions of promoting
Western knowledge. As Meng Yue and Benjamin Elman have
recently shown, it was also during this period that the classical term
gezhi 格致 rendered for hybrid or universal science in general was
replaced with the Japanese return loan *kexue* 科學, now in use for
modern Western sciences.[27] Accordingly, and for many historians
until today, modern sciences in China were practically non-existent
prior to this reform movement, as there was not even a name for it,
and more importantly, not significant until the arrival of "Mr. Science" in the New Youth Journal (*Xin qingnian* 新青年) in 1915.[28]

Likewise, Li Duanfen's memorial gives the impression that all
institutions and practices he mentioned had never existed and were
yet to be established in China. It could be speculated that the motive
behind such a depiction of the field was the attempt to purposefully
play down the importance and significance of former institutions in
order to legitimize their replacement by new ones led by this new
reform group. In order to restore a more unbiased picture of the institutional landscape I will briefly introduce the major institutions
responsible for the dissemination of Western knowledge. As most of
these institutions are dealt with in secondary literature,[29] I will restrict
this section to sketching out some of those characteristics that highlight the social status and functions of these new organisations (if only
seen in the eyes of the protagonists themselves) and seem relevant for
understanding the hybrid process of this transnational cultural brokerage.

---

[27] Cf. Benjamin Elman's contribution in this volume resp. Meng Yue. 1999.
"Hybrid Science versus Modernity: The Practice of the Jiangnan Arsenal, 1864–
1897", *East Asian Science, Technology and Medicine* 16, pp. 13–52.

[28] Ibid.

[29] Most importantly Knight Biggerstaff. 1961. *The Earliest Government Schools
in China*. Ithaca, N.Y.: Cornell University Press; Su Jing 蘇精. 1978. *Qingji Tongwenguan ji qi shisheng* 清季同文官及其師生 (The *Tongwenguan*, its teachers and students in the Qing dynasty). Taibei: n.p.; Xiong Yuezhi 熊月之. 1994. *Xixue dongjian
yu wan Qing shehui* 西學東漸與晚清社會 (The dissemination of Western knowledge
and the late Qing society). Shanghai: Shanghai renmin chubanshe; Wright 2000.

1. Missionary and Government Schools

Protestant missionaries had established schools for Chinese students from the early nineteenth century on. Most prominent among them became the Anglo-Chinese College (*Yinghua shuyuan* 英華書院), founded by Robert Morrison (Ma Lixun 馬禮遜 , 1782–1834) in Batavia in 1823, which moved to Hong Kong in 1842.[30] Such missionary schools were an important training ground for the new Hong Kong elite, and several studies have shown that a large part of the new urban elite in Hong Kong had emerged from these missionary schools.[31] Some of these early Protestant missionaries were not only active in China as religious prosetylizers, but also functioned as government representatives in the Chinese Secretary's Office, as was the case of Robert Morrison (as well as his son), the German missionary Karl Gützlaff (Guo Shila 郭施拉 ,1803–1851) or Walter Henry Medhurst (Mai Dusi 麥都思 , 1796–1857).[32] Moreover, as is well known in the cases of Young J. Allen (Lin Lezhi 林樂知 ,1836–1907), Timothy Richard (Li Timotai 李提摩太 , 1845–1919) and others, they were also privately very active in political affairs and strongly engaged in current debates on China's reforms.

Missionaries were therefore also involved in the official establishment of or teaching in the new Chinese governmental schools. The erection of the *Tongwenguan* in Beijing marked the beginnings of Chinese official academic teaching of foreign knowledge or "modern sciences" and also foreign languages. Upon the initiative of Li Hongzhang 李鴻章 (1823–1901) and Feng Guifen a parallel institution was soon established in Shanghai in 1863, the *Guangfangyan guan* 廣方言館 , also called the *Shanghai tongwenguan*, and others were set up in Canton and other treaty ports.

These modern schools established upon governmental initiative were directed by foreign teachers, who instructed their students in foreign languages, mathematics, world history and other "sciences", and were under the control of the Zongli Yamen respectively the Daotais and local officials in Shanghai, who presided over the examinations.

---

[30] A list of missionary schools established between 1839–1860 is in Xiong Yuezhi 1994, pp. 288-9.

[31] Most detailed see Carl T. Smith. 1985. *Chinese Christians: Elites, Middlemen and the Church in Hong Kong*. Oxford, New York: Oxford University Press.

[32] Cf. Lydia H. Liu. 1999. *Tokens of Exchange. The Problem of Translation in Global Circulations*. Durham: Duke University Press.

Modelled after colleges in the United States and supervised like classical schools, they mainly trained interpreters and officials to serve in
foreign affairs, and technical engineers and officers of military academies, who received official degrees in order to be integrated into the
prevailing nomenclatura systems. Critical assessments of these institutions often mention the lack of laboratories and practical scientific
work in these new institutions. Yet, to expect such a modern scientific
education appears rather anachronistic, as in Europe and America as
well the large-scale development of laboratories in connection with
scientific education only set in with the increase in industrial research
laboratories in the late nineteenth century.[33]

Biggerstaff maintains that "all these schools were related to
national defense and ... were generally regarded by the Chinese as
completely outside the regular concept and system of education."[34]
Yet, given the strong cooperation under one another and the high publicity these new schools enjoyed at the time, it seems questionable
whether the regular concept and system of education was still the
decisive factor regarding career and social position.

The Beijing *Tongwenguan* employed about 60 instructors between
1862–1898, among them three to six Chinese teachers. In contrast, the
Shanghai *Guangfangyanguan* hosted about 30 teachers, mainly for
foreign languages, of which only six were of foreign origin.[35] The
Tongwenguan first recruited only students of Manchurian origin,
whereas the Shanghai *Tongwenguan* mainly had sons of wealthy merchants among their students. Governmental acknowledgement provided through governmental scholarships for the students both of the
Beijing and Shanghai *Tongwenguan* added prestige to this new educational sector, and so, too, to those participating in it.

2. Print Media

The role of the printing press market in nineteenth century has largely
been underestimated, both in the realms of newspapers as well as

---

[33] Cf. Michel Serres (ed.). 1998. *Elemente einer Geschichte der Wissenschaften.*
Frankfurt a.M.: Suhrkamp, pp. 829–867. The dictinction between "applied" and
"pure" sciences was new in late nineteenth century Europe, too. Cf. Reynolds 1991,
p. 35.

[34] Biggerstaff 1961, p. 31.

[35] Different lists are given in Xiong Yuezhi 1994, pp. 311–3; 346–7 and Su Jing
1985, pp. 43–6; 68–9; 102–3.

book productions and only recent scholarship is about to uncover the tremendous impact that the earliest modern publishing houses made long before the famous Shanghai Commercial Press was founded in 1896. Missionary publishing houses founded since the early nineteenth century included most prominently the *Mohai shuguan* 墨海書館 (Inkstone Press, 1843) in Shanghai, where Wang Tao, Li Shanlan 李善蘭 (1811–1882) and Xu Shou 徐壽 (1818–1884) had met for the first time and William Gamble's (Mei Bieli 美別利, d. 1886) *Meihua shuguan* 美華書館 (American Presbyterian Mission Press). When this publishing house moved from Ningbo to Shanghai in 1860, Gamble established the largest printing company of his time with more than 100 workers, and from then on published all the major publications of the missionaries in Shanghai, their magazines and textbooks.[36] Since the 1870s, the former publishing center of Liulichang Street in Beijing was surpassed by Shanghai's publishing houses, which was mainly due to technical innovations as lithographic printing and most successfully commercialized by the *Shenbao* publishing house (*Shenbao-guan* 申報館).[37]

Xiong Yuezhi's seminal study on the dissemination of Western knowledge in Late Imperial China has given a thorough account of a large amount of translations, collections and new writings on various aspects of New Learning, and counts 434 Western titles in Chinese only for the period between 1843–1860 (of which in the beginning, admittedly, a large part were still purely religious texts), and 555 titles for the following four decades between 1860–1900.[38]

Apart from book publishing, the newspapers and magazines prior to 1900 had an even greater impact on the dissemination of New Learning and attained a much larger readership. The most influential

---

[36] Ji Shaofu 吉少甫. 1991. *Zhongguo chuban jianshi* 中國出版簡史 (Concise history of publishing in China). Shanghai: Xuelin chubanshe, pp. 264–7. According to Xiong, the *Meihua shuguan* had a yearly output of 40,316,350 pages between 1890–1895. Cf. Xiong Yuezhi 1994, pp. 481–4.

[37] Cf. Rudolf Wagner's study on the *Shenbaoguan* and the *Dianshizhai huabao*: Rudolf G. Wagner. 2002. "Joining the Global Imaginaire: The Shanghai Illustrated Newspaper *Dianshizhai huabao*", in: id. (ed.). *Joining the Global Public. Word, Image and City in Early Chinese Newspapers 1870–1910*. Albany: SUNY Press, forthcoming. Wagner estimates that some of Shanghai's lithograph shops in the late 1880s employed more than one hundred workers and operated with steam machines.

[38] Xiong Yuezhi 1994, pp. 8–12. Compared to the dramatic increase of published titles on New Learning after 1900, these numbers seem small, nonetheless they cannot be neglected.

Shanghai *Shenbao* 申報 (founded in 1872), published by the founder of the *Shenbaoguan*, Ernest Major, quickly reached circulation figures of 8–10,000 in its early years;[39] the Hong Kong *Xunhuan ribao* 循環日報 , founded by Wang Tao in 1874, issued 1,000 copies per diem.[40] It was financed and managed by illustrious members of the Hong Kong Tung Wah Hospital and served a large community of overseas Chinese. These private activities were matched by semi-official newspapers founded by the Shanghai Daotais in the 1870s, as the *Huibao* 匯報 (1874) and *Xinbao* 新報 (1876).[41]

All these papers carried editorials on statecraft topics, *yangwu* matters, important international events and New Learning in general. Moreover, the news section, far from dealing only with trifling social scandals, contained information about new technical inventions, political events and international commercial activities, all of which were most obviously regarded as useful knowledge for a large part of the urban population in the treaty ports.[42] Furthermore job announcements in these early newspapers reveal that the journalists were required to possess broad knowledge in current affairs and sometimes even foreign language skills (because many news items were translated from foreign newpapers or telegraphs).[43]

Being the first Chinese newpaper independent from a British paper in Shanghai, the *Shenbao* employed mainly Jiangnan literati

---

[39] Cf. various announcements in the *Shenbao*, e.g. June 11, 1872 (4500); February 10, 1877 (8–9000); June 20, 1877 (10,000).

[40] Also the competitor to the *Xunhuan ribao*, the less-known *Huazi ribao* 華字日報 in Hong Kong guaranteed a circulation of about 1000 copies ("Notice", *China Mail*, February 24, 1874); the *Weixin ribao* 維新日報 (founded in 1879) sold 1900 copies per diem in 1885. See *The Hong Kong Blue Book for the Year 1885*.

[41] For a more detailed study of these earliest newspapers houses and their editors in English see Vittinghoff, 2002b. "Useful Knowledge and Proper Communication: Strategies and Models of Publishing Houses in the Formative Stage of the Chinese Press (1872–1882)", in: Rudolf G. Wagner (ed.). *Joining the Global Public. Word, Image and City in Early Chinese Newspapers 1870–1910*. Albany: SUNY Press (forthcoming), pp. 210–93.

[42] Newspaper historians estimate that about 10–15 readers shared one issue of a daily newspaper in China at that time, so the readership was therefore much larger than the mere sales figures suggest. Cf. Don Denham Patterson. 1922. "The Journalism of China", *The University of Missouri Bulletin* 23.34 (Monograph Series), p. 58; Roswell Britton. 1966 [1933]. *The Chinese Periodical Press*. Taibei: Ch'engwen, p. 129.

[43] For an analysis of these job announcements and the professional standards of the earliest modern Chinese newspapers in general see Vittinghoff 2002, ch. 8.

like Cai Erkang 蔡爾康 (1852–1920), Shen Yugui 沈毓桂 (1807/8–1907), Qian Xinbo 錢昕伯 (b. 1833) and He Guisheng 何桂笙 (1840–1894) on its editorial board, whereas the financial management of this very profitable enterprise was entirely directed by Ernest Major. Involved in the *Xunhuan ribao* were honorable personages of the new Hong Kong society like Wu Tingfang 伍廷芳 (1842–1922), He Qi 何啟 (1859–1914) and Hu Liyuan 胡禮垣 (1847–1916). The financial management was carried out by prominent compradores like Feng Mingshan 馮明珊 (d. 1898). It was closely connected to the Tung Wah Hospital, as many of the persons involved were also on its board of directors. The semi-official newspaper in Shanghai was set up by a group of officials and merchants in Shanghai, among them Ye Tingjuan 葉廷眷 , Feng Junguang 馮浚光 (1830–1877) on the official side, Tang Jingxing 唐景星 (1832–1892) and Rong Hong 容閎 (1828–1912), Zheng Guanying 鄭觀應 (1842–1922) as compradores and merchants and Yuan Zuzhi 袁祖志 (1827–ca. 1900), Kuang Qizhao 鄺其照 and others as editors. Many of these persons had strong connections to the Jiangnan Arsenal.

Apart from the newspapers, there were also a number of important and influential magazines dealing with knowledge from the West. Popular pictorial magazines, like the *Dianshizhai huabao* 點石齋畫報 covered "news" from the West in a more entertaining way—this paper is thus best known for its exotic descriptions of the West and curious technological inventions. Yet, as recent studies have shown, this magazine operated in a global imaginaire, which shared many similarities with its counterparts in the West, *The Illustrated London News*, *The Harper's* or *The Graphic*. In this context, the quest for curiosities was also part of a global trend to digest the confrontation with modern technology, and therefore not a sign for an alleged naive treatment of the new "marvels of technology", as is often assumed for the Chinese case.[44] Illustrations were also a means to introduce and explain scientific technological instruments in missionary journals like the *Xiaer guanzhen* 遐邇貫珍 (1853) of the Anglo-Chinese College in Hong Kong, the *Liuhe congtan* 六合叢談 (Shanghae Serial, 1857), published by the *Mohai shuguan* (where Wang Tao functioned

---

[44] Cf. Wagner 2002; Rania Huntington. 2003. "The Weird in the Newspaper", in: Judith Zeitlin and Lydia Liu (eds.). *Writing and Materiality in China. Essays in Honor of Patrick Hanan*. Cambridge: Harvard University Press, pp. 341–96.

as Chinese editor), the *Zhongxi wenjian lu* 中西聞見錄 (1872) or the *Wanguo gongbao* of Young J. Allen and Timothy Richard, who had hired Cai Erkang and Shen Yugui from the *Shenbao* as Chinese editors. When the *Society for the Diffusion of Knowledge* in Beijing (1872) was dissolved in 1875, its members proposed to John Fryer to transfer the subscribers from their journal to the new journal, the *Gezhi huibian* 格致彙編 (The Chinese Scientific Magazine), which he edited in collaboration with Xu Shou. This journal is regarded as one of the first truly scientific journals and became renowned for its large letter-to-the-editor section and close interaction with a nationwide readership.[45]

Scientific magazines specializing on certain topical fields first appeared in the 1890s, such as the *Nongxuebao* 農學報 which focused on agriculture and was founded by Luo Zhenyu 羅振玉 (1866–1949) in 1897, or the *Suanxuebao* 算學報 inaugurated in the same year by Huang Qingcheng 黃慶澄 (1863–1904), author of numerous books dealing with mathematics, technology and sciences in general. The *Xinxuebao* 新學報 , also from 1897, was founded by another very prolific writer of treatises on New Learning, Ye Yaoyuan 葉耀元 , and had sections devoted to specific scientific disciplines such as mathematics, medicine or politics.

Many of the authors and translators of these books are unknown today and there is hardly any biographical material on them. Biographical data on the earliest journalists in China was also scarce, if it existed at all. It might have been this lacuna that fostered the above mentioned verdicts on the actors under investigation. Evaluations of the early Chinese journalism were analogous to the low status of the sciences in China: the early newspapers and magazines were regarded as immature in terms of journalistic standards, trivial in terms of content and not accepted by readers. However, the new print media, most of all the daily papers and the periodical press, played an important role in the process of disseminating and explaining this new knowledge. Because the new discourses on sciences and new knowledge framed by these actors were now brought before a new urban public, it gained a highly important position in society.

---

[45] The letters have been studied a.o. by Li San-pao. 1974. "Letters to the Editor in John Fryer's Chinese Scientific Magazine 1876–1892: An Analysis", *Zhongyang yanjiuyuan jindaishi yanjiusuo jikan* 4, pp. 729–77.

3. Hybrid Institutions

Different from the schools and newspapers mentioned above were institutions like the *Mohai shuguan*, founded in 1843, the Jiangnan Arsenal or the Shanghai Polytechnical Institute (*Gezhi shuyuan*) founded in 1885, which were partly training Chinese in foreign languages and the sciences and partly disseminating the new knowledge via print publications or various public performances.

With the establishment of the Jiangnan Arsenal in 1865, supported by Li Hongzhang and Zeng Guofan, as well as officials from the latter's secretarial bureau, namely Ding Richang 丁日昌 (1823–1882) and Feng Junguang, the *Guangfangyanguan* merged into this institution and formed part of the translation department of the Jiangnan Arsenal inaugurated in 1868. The Jiangnan Arsenal translation department worked under the directorship of John Fryer and was one of the most productive locations in terms of publishing translations of Western books, which were ordered in several hundreds by Fryer from America.[46]

During its existence from 1868 to 1912 there were about ten foreign instructors employed in this institution, apart from Fryer these included D. J. MacGowan (Ma Gaowen 瑪高溫 , 1814–1893), C. T. Kreyer (Jin Kaili 金楷理), Young J. Allen and Alexander Wylie, who were all capable of explaining the foreign works in Chinese to the Chinese translators. There were about twenty Chinese translators in the same period, including Hua Hengfang 華蘅芳 (1830–1901), Xu Jianyin, Li Shanlan, Zhong Tianwei 鍾天緯 (1840–1900), Jia Buwei 賈步緯 (1840–1903), Qu Anglai 瞿昂來, Shu Gaodi 舒高第 and others, many of whom were also educated in some scientific areas as well.[47] The translation department also issued a yearly periodical magazine, the *Xiguo jinshi huibian* 西國近事匯編 (Collection of recent events in the West, 1872), edited by the foreign and Chinese translators. The magazine contained only translated news from the world, most of it taken from the London *Times*. It became an important reference tool for literati to become informed about important events in the world

---

[46] Cf. Adrian Bennett. 1967. *John Fryer: The Introduction of Western Science and Technology into Nineteenth Century China*. Cambridge, Mass.: Cambridge University Press, Appendix I, pp. 73–81 or the letters containing lists of orders in the Berkeley archive, edited by Dagenais 1999, *passim*.

[47] For short biographical notes on the Arsenal staff cf. Xiong Yuezhi 1994, pp. 529–37.

and was mentioned as such by readers like Kang Youwei or Liang Qichao.

Illustrious personages from elite merchant and official circles were involved in the management, financing and supervision of the Arsenal and therefore, as the *North China Herald* remarked, "the position of mandarin-superintendent of an arsenal has become a high civil appointment, and in many cases the stepping stone to the highest and most lucrative posts in the empire."[48]

Only a year after the Jiangnan Arsenal, a Navy Yard School was erected in Fuzhou upon the initiative of Zuo Zongtang 左宗棠 (1812–1885) and the French Prosper Giquel (1835–1886), also called the Fuzhou Arsenal, which is of special interest as it established an overseas student programme and sent students to France.[49]

The *Gezhi shuyuan* was established upon the private initiative of Chinese and foreign scientists, officials and merchants.[50] The model for the *Gezhi shuyuan* was the Polytechnical Institution on London's Regent Street, and the English name "Shanghai Polytechnic Institution and Reading Room" reveals that the organisation was meant to harbour a variety of institutions, classes, a library, a museum or exhibition hall and a press publishing a magazine, the *Gezhi huibian*. The building hosting the library and teaching rooms was designed in classical style by a Chinese architect in order to evoke familiarity for the Chinese visitors. Another plan was to establish a building for exhibiting industrial products to facilitate the marketing for foreign merchants, on one hand, and to introduce new technologies in form of a permanent exhibition, on the other.[51]

---

[48] "Mandarins and their Foreign Instructors", *North China Herald* [hereafter *NCH*], February 25, 1875.

[49] Cf. Biggerstaff 1961; Steven A. Leibo. 1985. *Transferring Technology to China. Prosper Giquel and the Self-Strengthening Movement*. Berkeley: Center for Chinese Studies (China Research Monograph Series, 28).

[50] The development of this enterprise is documented in the *North China Herald*, which regularly published John Fryer's reports on the status quo of the institution and the minutes of the board meetings. "The Polytechnic", *NCH*, October 14, 1875; "The Polytechnic", *NCH*, March 15, 1877; "The Chinese Polytechnic Institution and Reading Room", *NCH*, April 18, 1883.

[51] The model for such an exhibition was the London World Exhibition of 1850. Following this very successful event, the late nineteenth century had become the era of grand industrial exhibitions, and this trend, spread through writings of diplomats

The institution was directed by a board of four Westerners and four Chinese, among them Tang Jingxing, Xu Shou, Hua Hengfang, Wang Ronghe and later Xu Jianyin, Li Fengbao 李鳳苞 (1834–1887), Xu Huafeng 徐華封 , Zhang Huanlun 張煥綸 , Wang Tao, Zhao Yuanyi 趙元益 (1840–1902) and Li Pingshu 李平書 and also the Magistrate Chen, Chinese magistrate of the Mixed Court, a Mr. Wang Chun-foo, of the Chinese Hospital and a Mr. Chun Fai-ting, of the CMSN Co.[52] Most of the financial management was undertaken by Xu Shou, the well-known mathematician, who had been active in the *Mohai shuguan* already in the 1840s and became its first director. His colleague and friend, Hua Hengfang, was resident curator of the *Gezhi shuyuan* and rendered this service voluntarily and without payment by the institution. After Xu's death in 1884, Wang Tao, another former colleague at the *Mohai shuguan* who had just come back from Shanghai, took over his position.

The *Gezhi shuyuan* was financed privately and charged a tuition fee for the students. The list of financial contributors reveals a broad support of this institution among the Chinese and Western officials as well as commercial circles.[53] Still, Tang Jingxing failed to attract a large number of regular Chinese subscribers for the institution, and by 1883 only 42 Chinese, paying six Dollars per annum, were registered. Yet, gracious donations were given by many prominent provincial officials and the model of this institutions was followed in other provinces such as Jiujiang, Amoy and Canton.

The library consisted of Western translations, Chinese newspapers and recent Chinese books but, as is emphasized, also classical Chinese books. The institution was not only meant as a location for instruction, but planned as a social club, just like the foreign clubs in Shanghai, where people from different social segments of the society, the officials, literati and the merchants could meet, read and exchange

---

[51] (*cont.*) and travellers, was also noticed in China. It is often noted that the *Gezhi shuyuan*'s architecture was planned to emulate the famous Crystal Palace in London. This large building of steel and glass was such an outstanding example of modern architecture that it attracted tourists and visitors from all over Europe for many decades. Cf. Winfried Kretschmer. 1999. *Geschichte der Weltausstellungen*. Frankfurt a.M.: Campus. But such a building was only projected for an adjunct exhibition hall, which was never completed.

[52] Cf. Xiong Yuezhi 1994, p. 353; and "The Chinese Poytechnic Institution and Reading Room", *NCH*, April 18, 1883.

[53] Cf. Xiong Yuezhi 1994, p. 356–8.

their views on grounds of their common interest, the New Learning.[54]
Fryer estimated that about one hundred Chinese per month visited the
exhibition halls, where Hua Hengfang would explain the objects to
them. And it was covered with great interest in the large papers like
the *Shenbao, Wanguo gongbao* 萬國公報 (The Globe Magazine, 1874)
and *North China Herald*.[55]

An important adjunct of the *Gezhi shuyuan* was the quarterly Chinese Prize Essay Scheme, which was inaugurated after its reorganization in 1886. Its objective was to induce Chinese literati to discuss
matters of New Learning in competitive essays, a form they were
familiar with from the examination system. Themes on topics like
railways, statecraft, economy and language were set out by high officials from Shanghai, the Daotais, Magistrates and also Provincial
Governors, like Li Hongzhang and Sheng Xuanhuai 盛宣懷 (1844–
1916). It was an important new feature that this contest was a national
affair and participants from all over China sent in hundred of contributions, which made the undertaking a great success. The best pieces
were published in a series of thirteen volumes, the *Gezhi shuyuan keyi*
格致書院課藝 , and to find entry into this famous and widely read collection gurarnteed some reputation in the new cultural centres, the
treaty ports.[56]

The Prize Essays are a good example of how the new institutions
smoothly co-operated in promoting their business. Most of the topics
of these essays could be studied in books published by the Jiangnan
Arsenal or stored in the *Gezhi shuyuan*. It is clear from the books that
are quoted in these essays that the authors' major resource were the
publications of those missionaries and scientists working in the institutions described above. Such books were advertized in the *Gezhi
huibian* and the contests appear to have stimulated the sale of books to
a large degree. This example illuminates the close relationship
between these magazines and the educational institutions. The co-
operation between the different institutions intensified and multiplied

---

[54] As described in the *Shenbao*, admission to the Club was like in foreign clubs
based on recommendation of two members. A monthly fee of half a dollar was
charged.

[55] The first report of the institution was not only published in the local Chinese
papers but also distributed in pamphlet form for general attention. "The Polytechnic",
NCH, October 14, 1875.

[56] I am grateful to Zhou Zhenhe for showing his complete collection of the *Gezhi
shuyuan keyi* to the VW Project in Göttingen.

their individual efforts. Thus, although the single output of one institution might seem rather marginal, I would argue that the activities of
these new institutions, seen collectively, suggest a much larger impact
on Late Qing society than has hitherto been attested to them. This
assumption will now be tested on the individual level by taking a
closer look at the actors employed or engaged in these institutions.

3. SOCIAL ACTORS: PROSOPOGRAPHICAL DATA

As mentioned in the introduction, I combined different sources to
identify a sample group of actors in the field of New Learning, using
secondary sources as well as the WSC database.[57] By introducing the
institutions above I also intended to show which social circles were
involved in the organisation of this new field and in which milieu and
under which circumstances these actors operated. I will use two sample groups, one professionally defined, which consists of 160 journalists; the other group is one only loosely defined and assembles about
240 translators and authors of books on New Learning, selected
according to their involvement in the production or dissemination of
new knowledge from the West.[58] Among these authors and translators
also journalists are to be found, because the professions did overlap,
journalists often also being 'scientists' at the same time. As many of
the persons dealt with here are not included in standard historical
accounts of the period I have collected biographical informations
from a range of sources beginning with biographical dictionaries but

---

[57] The mixed sample group consists of members of institutions, identified in secondary sources (as the tables in Xiong Yuezhi 1994 and Su Jing 1978), and authors
identified through the database. It is a rather random selection, as there are more
authors in the database than analyzed here. The database contains about 7,000 titles
dealing with New Learning from the early nineteenth century until the 1920s and
1930s and biographical identification of my authors and translators is still in its initial
stage. For my purpose, I selected those authors, translators and editors who were still
alive in 1861, when the Zongli Yamen was erected, and who published before 1911,
in sum about 200 persons. Left out were those attached to the institutions who were
not connected to any title in the database and were not traceable in biographical dictionaries (about ten persons). Another sample group related to the journalistic field is
drawn from my dissertation (Vittinghoff 2002) in which I have investigated 160 journalists from the period between 1860–1911. The journalists were selected from the
newspapers, anniversary volumes of publishing houses, biographical sections in dictionaries on journalism or in journalism magazines like the *Xinwen yanjiu ziliao* or
Baoxue, or yearbooks of journalism such as the *Zhongguo xinwen nianjian*.

also including governmental and missionary archives, e.g. the Public Record Archive in London and Hong Kong (PO/FO), the London Missionary Society (LMS) Archive in London SOAS, and edited documents of the John Fryer Archive (JFA) in Berkeley,[59] as well as obituaries in the newspapers or random notes in letters, diaries or other forms of informal private literature.

Among the 243 persons of the mixed sample group, 77 were solely authors and 45 solely translators, which means about half of the group (121) were both. A small number of persons, 14, combined all three activities. I will treat the two sample groups differently, in order to check whether there were nevertheless any fundamental differences in terms of educational background, income or regional origin between the journalists and the authors and translators.

1. Educational background

As the main reproaches against these newcomers in new professional fields aimed at their low educational background, superficial knowledge of current affairs and their low income, which forced them to sell their literary crafts as well as their moral convictions, I will start this empirical section with an investigation of their academic training:

---

[58] The approximately 360 persons under investigation only form a minor part of the whole 'scientific milieu', but, given the fact that the few prosopographical studies on Chinese journalistic or scientific communities hitherto have dealt with groups of some 20–100 persons and with later periods (cf. Peter Buck. 1980. *American Science and Modern China, 1876–1936*. Cambridge: Cambridge University Press, pp. 92–116; Reardon-Anderson 1991, pp. 80–2; Marie-Claire Bergère et al. 1985. "Essai de prosopographie des élites Shanghaiennes à l'epoque républicaine, 1911–1949", *Annales Économies Sociétés, Civilisations,* 40.4, pp. 901–30), I feel confident to believe that the results of this prosopographical study have some representative value.

[59] Cf. Dagenais 1999.

Table 1: Educational background of early Chinese Journalists (1860–1911) [N = 128].

Classical Education		65=51%
(Ranks known)	33%	
jinshi	7%	
juren	10%	
xiucai	16%	
Individual Study		
(Ranks not known)	18%	
Private Academies/Teacher		
Foreign Education		63=49%
Mission Schools	7%	
Study/Travel abroad	44%	

Table 2: Educational background of the mixed sample group [N=243]

Classical Education		149=61%
(Ranks known)	49%	
jinshi	49%	
juren	30%	
xiucai	21%	
Individual Study		
(Ranks not known)	13%	
Private Academies/Teacher		
Foreign Education		127=53%
Mission Schools	7%	
Study/Travel abroad	46%	

It has to be noted that all these numbers are only rough estimations, as we do not have equal information on all persons under investigation. If we look, for example, at the examination rank of the second sample group, of 243 people we know only the ranks of 118. Sixteen were educated in mission schools and 31 in private academies. So in 94 cases no classical educational background is noted. Yet there were 140 officials in the mixed sample group and 71 of them are recorded without title (and are therefore not included in the 149 persons with a "classical education"). But as it is rather likely that these officials did possess a title rank, we can add these 71 to the title possessors and thus get a number of 185 candidates with an examination rank, which is about 80% of the whole group. Together with those having studied in private academies, we find 89% of these actors having received a classical education. And even among the journalists, more than half of them had received a classical education and one third had successfully taken part in the Imperial examinations. The large amount of students abroad is due to the fact that many returned students from Japan engaged in journalism after 1905. So we are dealing with a group which to a very large degree had begun a normal career in the official nomenclature system.

The tables suggest that most of these persons had received a classical education and that also most of them had reached at least the first rank in the civil examination system. Even if they did not receive a rank in the traditional examination system this did not necessarily mean that they had failed to pass it, since during the decade of the Taiping wars examinations could not take place in many areas. There are many controversial debates about the actual prestige and social status of a *xiucai* (or the *shengjian*) in the late Qing and many accounts deny such a social status for the first rank.[60] Frederic Wakeman even states that "the seedy shengyuan became something of a stock comedy character," depicted as a "down-and-out opportunist living on his uppers."[61] Yet even Wakeman gives a ratio of only 1.5% of successful candidates for the first degree in Late Qing times. The actual chances of getting this degree were thus very low, and the successful candidate was certainly an exception and therefore socially respected. Moreover, we also know of the splendid celebrations organized for the successful candidate, and in legal court cases the *xiucai* is treated as an official (and was thus clearly distinguished from the category "ordinary people" (*min* 民)). Moreover, linguistic barrier between those who could master the classical language and

---

[60] I subsume all the different and more specific designations for the different positions in the first rank, like *xuesheng, fusheng, gongsheng, linsheng, jiansheng* (scholarship student, aspirants etc.) used in the biographs under the popular label *xiucai*.

[61] Frederic Wakeman. 1975. *The Fall of Imperial China.* New York: Free Press, p. 25. For a detailed discussion of the different positions of Ho P'ing-ti, Chang Chungli or Ch'ü T'ung-tsu on this problem see Min Tu-ki. 1989. *National Polity and Local Power. The Transformation of Late Imperial China.* Cambridge, Mass.: Harvard University Press, pp. 21–49 and Benjamin Elman. 2000. *A Cultural History of Civil Examinations in Late Imperial China.* Berkeley: University of California Press, *passim*.

those, who were basically classically illiterate added another distinctive feature to separate degree-holders from those without a degree.

In any case, 49% of the identified degree-holders in the mixed sample group held a *jinshi* 進士 rank, the highest degree, and thus accumulated the highest amount of symbolic capital in the late imperial literati hierarchy.

Moreover, the table indicates that contact with the foreign world was one of the major characteristics shared by these social actors. I have subsumed these activities under the general label "study/travel abroad", which needs to be specified. The students sent abroad in nineteenth century China have not attracted much scholarly attention yet, as the common assumption prevails that these activities only began with the large scale governmental programme to send students to Japan after 1895. Single studies deal with the educational programmes of Rong Hong (between 1872 and 1881) or the Fuzhou Arsenal (between 1875 and 1911). Even if these programmes met with critiques from different sides (which again is, I think, a reason why they were regarded as marginal for late Qing intellectual developments), they nevertheless produced a considerable number of prominent personages who took leading functions in the educational, political or technological sector in late Qing.[62] Another part of this group consists of diplomats, translators and officials who went abroad for official reasons. The large amount of literature they produced, in the form of official diaries or accounts on foreign countries, was also an important source for getting acquainted with the foreign world. Moreover, these officials went to visit the publishing houses like the Anglo-Chinese College or the *Xunhuan ribao* before their departure, in order to collect informations about the foreign countries they were bound to travel to. These publishing houses therefore became important information centers for those heading abroad.[63]

Of the 111 persons identified as having been abroad in the second sample group, more than 50% (63) went for professional reasons as officials and diplomats and not for the purpose of study. Also, a smaller number went to Europe (England, France, Germany and Rus-

---

[62] Thomas E. LaFarge. 1987 [1942]. *China's First Hundred. Educational Mission Studies in the United States 1872–1881*. Washington: Washington State University Press. On the Fuzhou Arsenal see Leibo 1985.

sia, altogether 55) than to Japan (75). Moreover, many people with a classical education also went abroad, explaining why there is an overlap in terms of percentage numbers in this second table.

If we ask how many of the actors were actually educated in the West, this number is, of course, still very small. Yet there is a considerable number of persons who have been abroad before 1900, be it as diplomats, officials or individual travellers. Moreover, as I will show below, especially among those who functioned as organizers in the field of new knowledge, a great part had acquired first hand knowledge through travel experiences.

2. Income

Another shared assumption, also generated by an early historiography of the 1920s and 1930s, is that the income of these settlement literati "was so low, that no other profession could be compared with it."[64] This fact is again made responsible for their low status in society.

Many of these literati pursued a rather pompous lifestyle in Shanghai, entertaining numerous banquets in the Zhang Yuan garden and undertaking frequent visits to the theaters and teahouses or boat rides in the outskirts of Shanghai, as is handed down in various poems of them published, for instance, in the *Shenbao* a few days after such meetings or outings. Known for their excessive nightlife activities, the three colleagues at the *Mohai shuguan*, Li Shanlan, Wang Tao and Jiang Jianren 蔣劍人 (1808–1867) were coined the "three maniacs of Shanghai" (*haishang san qishi* 海上三奇士).[65] And also in Hong Kong, where Wang Tao had already gained fame as expert in things foreign and was called "Dr. Wong" in the newspapers after his return from Scotland, he still continued to pursue this excessive lifestyle in the brothels, getting drunk and bursting into tears in front of the courtesans, as is handed down in the diaries of his friend and famous

---

[63] See for instance Zhou Jiarong 周佳榮 . 2000. "Zai Xianggang yu Wang Tao huimian" 在香港與王韜會面 (Meeting with Wang Tao in Hong Kong), in: Lam Kaiyin 林啟彥 and Wong Man-kong 黃文江 (eds.). *Wang Tao yu jindai shijie* 王韜與近代世界 (Wang Tao and the modern world). Hong Kong: Xianggang jiaoyu tushu gongsi, pp. 375–94. Many of the diaries by these early travellers are collected in the series *Zou xiang shijie congshu* 走向世界叢書 (From East to West—Chinese travellers before 1911). 1984. Changsha: Yuelu shushe.

[64] This often quoted statement is again from Lei Jin 1987, p. 26.

[65] Yu Xingmin 于醒民 . 1991. *Shanghai 1862 nian* 上海 1862 年 (Shanghai 1862). Shanghai: Shanghai renmin chubanshe, p. 415.

translator Hu Liyuan 胡禮垣 .[66] Such accounts suggest a rather extravagant and costly lifestyle. Yet, on the other hand, when Ying Lianzhi 英斂之 (1867–1926), the founder of the famous *Dagongbao* 大公報 , travelled to Shanghai to prepare this project, he did not have a penny in his pocket yet went to banquets every night, went shopping to buy clothes and books, and socialized with the prestigious literati of the time, like Ma Xiangbo 馬相伯 (1840–1939) or Zhang Yuanji 張元濟 (1867–1959).[67] This raises the fundamental question—which cannot be answered in this study—whether financial capital was at all a crucial factor to evaluate the social status of a person of that time.

Yet, apart from this problem, it seems revealing to take a look at their actual income. The average income of Chinese working in foreign and/or missionary institutions in the publishing sector in the 1870s and 1880s was between 20–50 Yuan per month. The most detailed account of the costs of a newspaper house is given for the *Yuebao* 粵報 (1885) in Canton, according to which a newspaper editor would receive 50 Yuan.[68] The *Shanghai xinbao* 上海新報 (1862) paid 20–30 Dollar to their Chinese editors, whereas John Fryer received 50 Tael during his engagement in this paper.[69] Chinese teachers at the English-Chinese College in Shanghai received 12.50 Taels per month.[70]

Compared to the incomes of regular gentry teachers and even officials this seems to be a decent payment, also in comparison with actual costs for livelihood in the period under investigation.[71] Moreover, we know of instances when journalists decided that it was more

---

[66] Cf. Hu Liyuan 胡禮垣 . 1975 [1908]. "*Hu Yinan xiansheng quanji*" 胡翼南先生全集 (Complete works of Mr. Hu Yinan), in: *Jindai Zhongguo shiliao congkan, xuji* 近代中國史料叢刊續集 (Collection of historical materials on modern China, supplement). Taibei: Wenhai chubanshe, vol. 261–6; vol. 264, p. 1577.

[67] Ying describes these activities in detail in his diaries, cf. Ying Lianzhi 英斂之 . 1975 [1907]. "*Ying Lianzhi xiansheng riji yigao*" 英斂之先生日記遺稿 (Diary manuscript of Mr. Ying Lianzhi), in: *Jindai Zhongguo shiliao congkan, xuji* (Collection of historical materials on modern China, supplement). Taibei: Wenhai chubanshe, vol. 21–3, vol. 21, pp. 159ff.; 309.

[68] *Xunhuan ribao liushi zhounian tekan* 循環日報六十周年特刊 (Special edition for the sixtieth anniversary of the *Xunhuan ribao*). 1932. Hong Kong: Xunhuan ribao.

[69] FO 228/632. "Intelligence report, January 1st to May 1st 1879", by W. C. Hillier, p. 52–62; 62. Letter by John Fryer "To Stewart: About Schools and teaching in China", March 4, 1867, JFA, Box 1, Copy Book 1, pp. 4–5.

[70] "To Hearn: Attempts to resolve salary for Chinese teacher". October 3, 1867, JFA, Box 1, Copy Book 2.

paying to work in a newspaper house (where this person earned 28 Yuan a month) than to teach in a school.[72]

3. Local Origin and Recruitment

That most of the scientists, translators and journalists (in numbers more than 80%)—like many "progressive" or influential persons in Late Qing China—originate from the coastal areas and the Jiangnan provinces, seems not too surprising. Very often they come from small counties in Zhejiang, Jiangsu or Guangdong which were connected to the treaty ports and other urban centers, Shanghai, Ningbo, Tianjin or Canton and Hong Kong. This means that they certainly were exposed to new ideas and cultural practices of the treaty centers to a certain degree. Most of the persons under investigation do not only come from the same coastal provinces, but also from a rather small number of counties. Of all authors and translators from Zhejiang, 60% can be distributed to the four cities Hangzhou, Shaoxing, Wuxing and Haining. The persons from Jiangsu come to 60% from the three places Changzhou/Wuxi, Shanghai and Suzhou. Also the three cities Xinhui, Nanhai and Shunde produced 60% of the translators and authors from Guangdong.

Yet, people did not move into the publishing houses through *tong-xiang* 同鄉 (Fellow-countryman) relations, as could be concluded from this fact. Instead newspaper houses or educational institutions housed scholars from different counties. Job announcements indicate that, in principle, positions in newspaper houses were accesible also for unfamiliar applicants. But instances of formal interviews with unknown persons or application tests were scarce even in the first decade of the twentieth century. Private recollections or anniversary volumes of the institutions reveal that personal friendship or recommendation were still the main criteria for selecting the staff members.

---

[71] Chang Chung-li estimates a yearly income of 250 Taels for a teacher in an academy and about 100 Tael per annum for an average teacher. Cf. Chang Chung-li. 1962. *The Income of the Chinese Gentry.* Seattle: University of Washington Press, pp. 94; 101. Chang cites the example of Zhang Jian who received 120 Taels per annum as a secretary, which was regarded as a high salary by his father. Bao Tianxiao compares his income with his monthly costs for rent and food and finds himself very well paid. Cf. Tianxiao 包天笑. 1990. *Chuanyinglou huiyilu* 釧影樓回憶錄 (Recollections from the Bracelet Shadow Mansion). 3 vols. Taibei: Longwen chubanshe gufen you-xian gongsi. (Zhongguo xiandai zizhuan congshu 2), vol. 2, p. 381.
[72] Ibid.

As will be shown, most of these social actors did know each other before their entrance into the institutions.[73]

The most striking fact in this respect, however, is that only a very small number originated from the big commercial and Western centers like Shanghai, Hong Kong, Guangdong or Ningbo. Peter Buck has argued that this fact is to be seen in connection with the missionary conviction,

> that scientific development in China would be primarily a rural phenomenon .... Themselves products of small town and villages in mid nineteenth century America, missionary educators conceived of science as an avocation most properly cultivated by local educated elites with close ties to their communities. Familiar with that pattern at home, they anticipated that it would be replicated in China.[74]

Peter Buck, who investigated the 27 members of the *Chinese Science Society* in the 1930s, also points to the disjunction between nascent scientific activities and missionary ambitions in the countryside. Moreover, as shown above, only a minority of these actors were educated by missionaries, and those who were mostly received their education in the missionary schools of Hong Kong and Shanghai, not in the countryside. What seems more important here is that at one point in their lives these authors, translators and journalists all ended up in one of the urban centers, which means that they all arrived as newcomers in the big cities, mostly independent from their families and excluded from already existing social networks. This might be one reason why they quickly built up strong networks and maintained them over the span of their life-time, as the following analysis will show.

---

[73] Fang Hanqi describes how journalists were invited to interviews and had to deliver manuscripts before their employment, but gives no sources. Cf. Fang Hanqi 方漢奇. 1992. *Zhongguo xinwen shiye tongshi, juan yi.* 中國新聞事業通史，卷一 (A history of Chinese journalism, vol. 1). Beijing: Zhongguo renmin daxue chubanshe, p. 402. Evidences for such a practice I could only find in later sources, whereas there are numerous instances where the early journalists described their entrance via recommendation. Cf. Vittinghoff 2002, ch. 8.

[74] Buck 1980, p. 109.

4. NETWORKS

Socio-historical accounts on newspaper houses or other new institutions in Late Qing China usually treat these institutions separately, as independent institutions.[75] Even more neglected is the interaction between foreign and Chinese institutions. Yet the close relation between foreign and Chinese newspapers, for instance, is obvious in the articles of the papers, as they were constantly referring to each other. Both Chinese and foreign newspapermen, translators, missionaries and scientists operated in the same international environment and were exposed to international trends, albeit, admittedly, to different degrees).

In a first step we will look at educational, professional, friendship and family relations among the persons engaged in the three first Chinese newspapers in Shanghai and Hong Kong, the *Shenbao,* the semi-official papers *Huibao, Yibao* and *Xinbao,*[76] and the *Xunhuan ribao.*

As illustration 1 reveals, actors from the newspapers maintained a very closely knit network beyond one geographic area, but maintained personal connections also between Shanghai and Hong Kong: Wang Tao, who had spent a decade in Shanghai at the *Mohai shuguan,* had to flee to Hong Kong in 1862. There he met James Legge in the Anglo-Chinese College and translated the Chinese Classics with him. When he founded the *Xunhuan ribao,* he was sponsored by Wu Tingfang, whom some regard as having been the editor of the *Zhongwai xinbao* 中外新報 (1858) and who had also supported Chen Aiting 陳藹亭 (dates unknown) and the Hong Kong Daily *Huazi ribao* 華字日報 (1872) at that time. Moreover, Wu co-operated with He Qi in founding Wang Tao's paper and later he became a relative of He. Rong Hong, the co-founder of the semi-official newspaper *Huibao,* was already acquainted with Wang Tao during Wang Tao's first sojourn in Shanghai during the 1850s. Wang Tao supported Rong's educational scheme in his essay collection *Tao Yuan wenlu waibian* 弢園文錄外編 (Writings of Tao Yuan, second part). Also Zheng Guanying, who is

---

[75] Even Xiong Yuezhi's study does not pay much attention to the interaction of the institutions, although it is still the best study available on the topic. Xiong Yuezhi 1994.

[76] As these newspapers often only changed their names but not the staff, they are treated here as one entity.

Illustration 1: Networks of newspapermen in the first Chinese dailies (1872–1876)

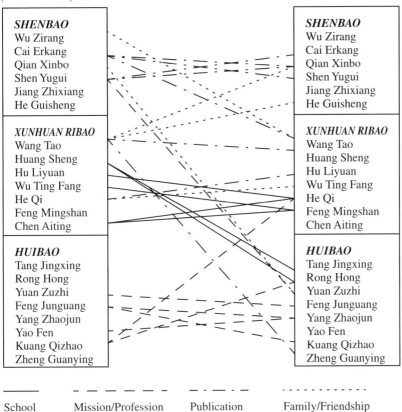

School   Mission/Profession   Publication   Family/Friendship

(*cont.*) supposed to have written the statutes of the *Huibao*, was a friend of Wang Tao, and Wang Tao had written a preface to his famous *Shengshi weiyan* 盛世危言 (Words of warning in a prosperous time). Chen Aiting, the editor of *Huazi ribao*, assisted Wang Tao in compiling his famous *Pufa zhanji* 普法戰紀 (Account of the French-Prussian War), which made Wang Tao famous in China during his exile in Hong Kong. Rong Hong was also a classmate of Huang Sheng 黃胜 (1825–1905), who was in close contact with Wang Tao during their common work at the publishing house of the LMS in Hong Kong and who had family relations with He Qi. Huang Sheng co-operated with Wang Tao in compiling an essay on cannonballs, which they sent to Li Hongzhang, and later joined the Shanghai

Guangfangyanguan for a short period. Li Hongzhang had promoted
Tang Jingxing, one of the founding members of the *Huibao*, to act as
the director of the Jiangnan Arsenal, where he was in close contact
with Zheng Guanying, who had studied in John Fryers English-Chinese College. Tang Jingxing took Yuan Zuzhi with him on his trip to
Europe. Yuan Zuzhi, who had worked as a translator and editor of the
Xiguo jinshi huibian at the Jiangnan Arsenal, was a good friend of
Qian Xinbo and later met Cai Erkang in the editorial board of the *Xinwenbao* 新聞報 (1893). Kuang Qizhao, the editor of the *Huibao*, had
studied in America and was first hired as a translator in a Bureau of
Western Affairs (*Yangwu zongju* 洋務總局) in Shanghai and sent to
the U.S. accompanying the fourth dispatch of Rong Hong's students
in 1875. In 1882 he edited an English-Chinese dictionary and later
founded the *Guangbao* 廣報 (1886) in Canton.

Such data already suggest a strong connection between the newspaper
houses and other institutions of New Learning. The following illustration further substantiates this observation:

Illustration 2: Newspaper circles and early institutions of New Learning (1872–1884)

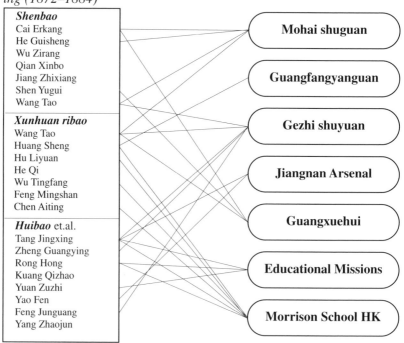

We can see from this illustration that a large part of the persons involved in the newspaper business were connected to at least one other institution of new learning, while some of them, like Wang Tao or Tang Jingxing, were even linked to three or more institutions.

In a next step we will look at the different institutions which specialized in the production of New Learning. 96 of the authors and translators in the mixed sample group were attached to at least one of the institutions selected for this analysis, i.e. the *Mohai shuguan*, the Beijing *Tongwenguan*, the Shanghai *Guangfangyanguan*, the Jiangnan Arsenal and the *Gezhi shuyuan*. This represents about 40% of the overall number.

Illustration 3: Personal connections between the early institutions of New Learning (1860–1882)

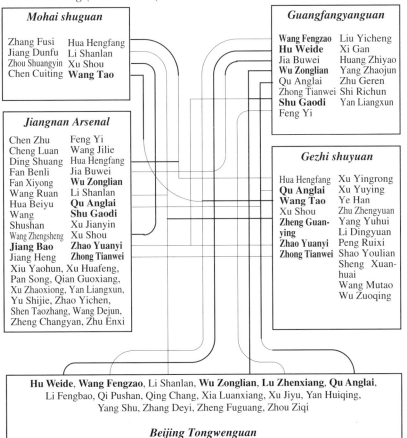

This strong inter-institutional movement suggests that members were well-informed about ongoing projects in other institutions. Institutional organisation is one criterion for judging the degree of professionalization in a certain academic milieu. It also marks the gradual transition from amateur to professional activities. Regarded as preconditions for a professional scientific milieu would be the exchange of scientific ideas, public meetings, publications, and a common agreement to approach commonly acknowledged problems with commonly acknowledged procedures and sources. The presented information of activities in these institutions from secondary sources and personal contemporary accounts indicate that dome of these factors can be traced back to the 1880s.[77]

Certain persons in the illustration seem to have functioned as kind of 'relay stations of knowledge' who could be regarded as 'organizers' of the field of knowledge, as they were engaged in nearly every institution for a certain period. The mathematician Hua Hengfang 華蘅芳 (1833–1902), a close friend of Xu Shou and Xu Jianyin, for instance, moved from the *Mohai shuguan* to the *Guangfangyanguan* and ended up in the *Gezhi shuyuan*. Also Li Shanlan, a friend of Hua Hengfang in the *Mohai shuguan*, moved from there to the Jiangnan Arsenal and was then promoted to the *Tongwenguan* in Beijing. The far less known Qu Anglai was an important translator, whose translations with Young J. Allen and others appeared in many editions. Qu was involved in the *Guangfangyanguan*, then the Jiangnan Arsenal, the *Gezhi shuyuan* and the *Tongwenguan* in Beijing. He also won the prize essay of the *Gezhi shuyuan* twice and later went abroad to become a translator in an embassy in England. Even more active was the comparatively unknown journalist and translator Cai Erkang, who translated about twenty titles, among them best-sellers such as Robert MacKenzie's *Nineteenth Century. A History*[78] and the *Zhong Dong zhanji benmo* 中東戰紀本末 (Causes and consequences of the Sino-

---

[77] However, this milieu is certainly still different from a modern scientific community characterized by an anonymity and a lack of personal acquaintance and by standardized scientific practice and recruitment procedures.

[78] Cai Erkang 蔡爾康 and Timothy Richard (Li Timotai 李提摩太) (trs.). 1895. *Taixi xinshi lanyao* 泰西新史攬要. Shanghai: Guangxuehui. [Translation of Robert Mackenzie. 1880. *Nineteenth Century. A History*, New York: Munro]. The book was one of the most sold books of the *Guangxuehui* and appeared—just like the English text—in more than a dozen reprints.

Japanese War).[79] Cai had started his career as a secretary for foreign languages in the early 1870s. Aged only 22, he joined the *Shenbao* in 1874, edited his own newspaper and an illustrated magazine in the 1880s, later became a member of and translator for the *Guangxuehui*, and was, for a short period, also on the editorial board of the *Xinwenbao*. Cai's translations of reform-oriented works at the *Guangxuehui*—which were read even by the Emperor—made him prominent in the general reform trend of the 1890's. Yet, the lucrative posts he was offered by the reformers in Hunan, were declined by him subsequently and he remained a journalist for the rest of his life.[80]

Analogous movements between institutions can be observed in the foreign circles. Most of all John Fryer, but also Young J. Allen, Alexander Wylie or D. J. MacGowan, can be found in many institutions and could also be named as field organizers. John Fryer was not only the most prolific translator and author of books on foreign knowledge, but also the most active organizer in this field, having been involved in the Beijing *Tongwenguan*, the *Guangfangyanguan*, the Jiangnan Arsenal, the *Gezhi shuyuan*, and the Chinese Text Book Committee, the *Yizhi shuhui* 益智書會 , founded in 1877.

Another interesting feature of these organizers is their shared experience abroad. In illustration 3 above, these persons are emphasised in bold. Strikingly, all those who have been abroad belong to the group I identified as "organizers", who frequently moved between the institutions. Only one person of the three big institutions in Shanghai had been abroad but was not part of the group of "movers".

A last illustration intends to show to what degree these newcomers in the field of new learning were linked to different social circles and to substantiate the assumption that they lived in a socially hybrid environment that constantly forced/enabled them to cross borders between

---

[79] Cai Erkang 蔡爾康 and Young J. Allen (Lin Lezhi 林樂知). 1900. *Zhongdong zhanji benmo sanbian* 中東戰紀本末三編 (Causes and consequences of the Sino-Japanese War in three parts). Shanghai: Guangxuehui.

[80] For more details about this very illustrious person in late Qing Shanghai see Natascha Vittinghoff. 2001. "Ein Leben am Rande des Ruhms: Cai Erkang (1852–1921) ("Living on the edge of fame: Cai Erkang (1852–1921)", in: Christina Neder, Heiner Roetz and Susanne Schilling (eds.). *China in seinen biographischen Dimensionen. Festschrift für Helmut Martin* (China and her biographical dimensions. Commemorative essays for Helmut Martin). Wiesbaden: Harrassowitz, pp. 95–105.

different professional, social and national groups. Here, this is exemplified by Li Shanlan's social contacts:[81]

Illustration 4: Social networks of Li Shanlan

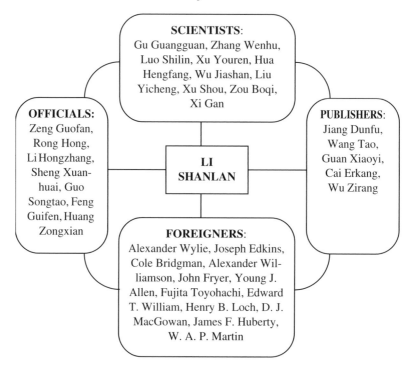

These illustrations have shown that we are not dealing with individual social actors who are interested in New Learning, but with a rather tightly organized community. This fact suggests that endeavours in the sciences and scientific procedures, the selection of objects of studies etc. were subject to institutional control from a very early stage. In the late nineteenth century scientific study in the treaty ports and the capital was no individual affair but rather quickly subjected to the powers of institutions. In its evaluation of the organisation of the *Gezhi shuyuan*, the *North China Herald* implicitly touched upon this

---

[81] This list could be greatly extended, so this illustration is more of a representative selection. The sources used were: WSC data base; Xu Xingmin 1991 and Horng Wann-sheng. 1991. *Li Shanlan: The Impact of Western Mathematics in China During the Late 19th Century*. Ann Arbor: UMI.

problem when it criticized Li Hongzhang for selecting only his allies as staff for this institution, thus making it

> part of that curious net within which the Viceroy of Chihli is striving to enfold every interest in the Empire. [... The present party in power] strives to attain to the same pre-eminence in matters intellectual, and steadily to put down any attempt at freedom of thoughts as of freedom of trade or locomotion. The manner in which it deals with the Press is one instance of this, and we may add, the Polytechnic is another.[82]

Politics thus played a crucial role in the social sciences and humanities as well as in the natural science—not only in respect to the leeway of scientific activities but also in regard to the object of study and the recruitment of scientists. Again, this was not unique in China; also in nineteenth century Europe politics very concretely determined the hierarchy of scientific disciplines.[83]

CONCLUSION

By introducing these different institutions of the production and dissemination of New Learning in nineteenth century China I intended to show that the cultural meaning of the production of scientific knowledge in Late Imperial China cannot be fully understood if we only focus on scientific results and their dissemination in printed books. As scientific activities and the public sector were closely intertwined it is instead necessary to look at the specific social, economic, political and ideological contexts of the production and dissemination of the New Learning and to perceive the production of scientific knowledge rather as a cultural practice than as a mere intellectual endeavour.

Given the manifold ways of articulations, communications and transformations of the New Learning, the sciences and popular knowledge on the foreign world, discovered through such an approach, it has become necessary to reject the 'diffusion model', which explains the transmission of a new produced knowledge dominated by Western epistemologies to a passive indigenous audience, gradually willing to receive and reproduce it.

---

[82] *NCH*, March 15, 1877.

[83] One reason for the military superiority of nineteenth century France over Germany was the focus on applied sciences in France instead of "pure mathematics", as pursued in Germany. Cf. Serres 1998, pp. 514–21.

Rather than merely looking at the textual evidence, I therefore attempted to explore cultural practices in the 'field' of scientific activities in the late nineteenth century and focused on the academic milieu rather than individual specialized scientists. The prosopographical analysis suggested that in this milieu we are dealing with a group of well-educated, well-informed individual newcomers in the treaty ports, a community, whose members were able to find rather profitable occupations in which they pursued their scientific and personal interests. This community, still small enough in number to maintain such links and to know each other by person, was not only connected through imagination, produced by newspapers and publications, but also through their practical experience, professional co-operation and personal intercourse.

When in the last decades of the nineteenth century the development of scientific activities had moved from the realm of private activities into the center of political concern, it was related to questions of the public good and the future of the nation. The scientific field then turned into a contested site deciding upon the legitimate authority in leading this new nation. Subsequently, the strong concern for current affairs led a large part of the "scientists" to political careers and governmental posts on very high levels. This phenomenon raises manifold questions to which degree their "modern scientific thinking" based upon the so-called "positive sciences" in which they had acquired specific expertise replaced the literary-historical tradition of the humanities and to what degree mythology and metaphysics had to give way to a positivistic rationality in their new explanations and novel experiences of the social body, society and politics, which hopefully await further studies.

Politics not only determined the field of New Learning, politics also decided about the historical status of these activities and their actors. The usurpation and appropriation of the field of science by the New Cultural Movement occurred at this intersection where the routes of science and revolution met at this certain historical moment. In latter historiography, the negative, polemical, ideologically motivated assessments of the merits and most of all demerits of these actors were too often and too easily taken at face value. It was one purpose of this historical contextualisation of their activities to show, that these verdicts have to be understood as strategic statements and not descriptive ones.

REFERENCES

Bao Tianxiao 包天笑 . 1990. *Chuanyinglou huiyilu* 釧影樓回憶錄 (Recollections from the Bracelet Shadow Mansion). 3 vols. Taibei: Longwen chubanshe gufen you-xian gongsi (Zhongguo xiandai zizhuan congshu 2).

Bennett, Adrian. 1967. *John Fryer: The Introduction of Western Science and Technology into Nineteenth Century China*. Cambridge, Mass.: Cambridge University Press.

Bergère, Marie-Claire et al. 1985. "Essai de prosopographie des élites Shanghaiennes à l'epoque républicaine, 1911–1949", *Annales Économies Sociétés, Civilisations*, 40.4, pp. 901–30.

Biggerstaff, Knight. 1961. *The Earliest Government Schools in China*. Ithaca, N.Y.: Cornell University Press.

Boedeker, Hans Erich, Peter H. Reill und Jürgen Schlumbohm (eds.). 1999. *Wissenschaft als kulturelle Praxis 1750-1900*. Göttingen: Vandenhoeck und Ruprecht. (Veröffentlichungen des Max-Planck Instituts für Geschichte, 154).

Britton, Roswell. 1966 [1933]. *The Chinese Periodical Press*. Taibei: Chengwen.

Buck, Peter. 1980. *American Science and Modern China, 1876–1936*. Cambridge: Cambridge University Press.

Cai Erkang 蔡爾康 and Timothy Richard (Li Timotai 李提摩太) (trs.). 1895. *Taixi xinshi lanyao* 泰西新史攬要 . Shanghai: Guangxuehui. [Translation of Robert Mackenzie. 1880. *Nineteenth Century. A History*, New York: Munro].

—— and Lin Lezhi 林樂知 (Young J. Allen). 1900. *Zhongdong zhanji benmo sanbian* 中東戰紀本末三編 (Causes and consequences of the Sino-Japanese War in three parts). Shanghai: Guangxuehui.

Chang Chung-li. 1962. *The Income of the Chinese Gentry*. Seattle: University of Washington Press.

Daum, Andreas W. 1998. *Wissenschaftspopularisierung im 19. Jahrhundert. Bürgerliche Kultur, naturwissenschaftliche Bildung und die deutsche Öffentlichkeit, 1848–1914*. Munich: Oldenbourg.

Elman, Benjamin. 2000. *A Cultural History of Civil Examinations in Late Imperial China*. Berkeley: University of California Press.

Fang Hanqi 方漢奇 . 1992. *Zhongguo xinwen shiye tongshi, juan yi*. 中國新聞事業史 , 卷一 (A history of Chinese journalism, vol. 1). Beijing: Zhongguo renmin daxue chubanshe.

LaFarge, Thomas E. 1987 [1942]. *China's First Hundred. Educational Mission Studies in the United States 1872–1881*. Washington: Washington State University Press.

FO = Foreign Office (London and Hong Kong).

Ge Gongzhen戈公振 . 1982 [1926]. *Zhongguo baoxue shi* 中國報學史(A history of Chinese journalism). Taibei: Xuesheng shuju.

Horng Wann-sheng. 1991. *Li Shanlan: The Impact of Western Mathematics in China During the Late 19th Century*. Ann Arbor: UMI.

Hu Daojing胡道靜 1935. *Shanghai xinwen shiye zhi shi de fazhan* 上海新聞事業之史的發展(The historical development of Shanghai's journalism). Shanghai: Tongzhiguan. Reprint: Minguo congshu, ser. 2, vol. 49.

Hu Liyuan 胡禮垣 . 1975 [1908]. *Hu Yinan xiansheng quanji* 胡翼南先生全集 (Complete works of Mr. Hu Yinan). Reprint *Jindai Zhongguo shiliao congkan, xuji* 近代中國史料叢刊續集 (Collection of historical materials on modern China, supplement). Taibei: Wenhai chubanshe, vol. 261–6, vol. 264.

Hu Shih. 1934. *The Chinese Renaissance.* Chicago: Chicago University Press.

Huntington, Rania. 2003. "The Weird in the Newspaper", in: Judith T. Zeitlin and Lydia H. Liu (eds.). *Writing and Materiality in China. Essay in Honor of Patrick Hanan.* Cambridge: Harvard University Press, pp. 341–96.

Ji Shaofu 吉少甫 . 1991. *Zhongguo chuban jianshi* 中國出版簡史 (Concise history of publishing in China). Shanghai: Xuelin chubanshe.

Kragh, Helge. 1987. *An Introduction to the Historiography of Science.* Cambridge: Cambridge University Press.

Kretschmer, Winfried. 1999. *Geschichte der Weltausstellungen.* Frankfurt a.M.: Campus.

Legge, James. 1985. *The Chinese Classics. Vol. I-V.* Reprint: Taibei: Southern Material Center.

Lei Jin雷瑨 . 1987 [1922]. "Shenbaoguan zhi guoqu zhuangkuang 申報館之過去狀況 (The former conditions in the Shenbao publishing house)", in: *Zuijin zhi wushi nian: 1872 nian–1922 nian. Shenbao wushi zhounian jinian* 最近之五十年: 1872–1922 年申報五十周年紀念 (The last fifty years: Commemorating the fiftieth anniversary of the Shenbao). Reprint: Shanghai: Shanghai shudian, 1987, part 3, pp. 26–8.

Leibo, Steven A. 1985. *Transferring Technology to China. Prosper Giquel and the Self-Strengthening Movement.* Berkeley: Center for Chinese Studies (China Research Monograph Series, 28).

Li Duanfen 李端芬 . 1961 [1896]. "Qing tuiguang xuexiao zhe" 請推廣學校摺 (A request to promoting schools). Reprint Shu Xincheng 舒新城 . *Zhongguo jindai jiaoyu shi ziliao* 中國近代教育史資料 (Material on the history of education in China). Beijing: Renmin jiaoyu chubanshe, vol. 1, p. 143.

Li San-pao. 1974. "Letters to the Editor in John Fryer's Chinese Scientific Magazine 1876-1892: An Analysis", *Zhongyang yanjiuyuan jindaishi yanjiusuo jikan* 4, pp. 729–77.

Liu, Lydia H. 1999. *Tokens of exchange. The problem of translation in global circulations.* Durham: Duke University Press.

Liu Xian 劉咸 . 1982 [1937]. "Kexueshi shang zhi zuijin ershi nian" 科學史上之二十年 (Recent twenty years in science history), in: id. *Zhonggo kexue ershinian* 中國科學二十年 (Twenty years of science in China), n.p.: Zhongguo kexue she. [Reprint *Minguo congshu*, ser. I. vol. 90], pp. 3-18.

Meng Yue. 1999. "Hybrid Science versus Modernity: The Practice of the Jiangnan Arsenal, 1864-1897", *East Asian Science, Technology and Medicine* 16, pp. 13-52.

Min Tu-ki. 1989. *National Polity and Local Power. The Transformation of Late Imperial China.* Cambridge, Mass.: Harvard University Press.

NCH = North China Herald (Shanghai)

——."Mandarins and their Foreign Instructors", *NCH,* February 25, 1875.

——."The Polytechnic", *NCH,* October 14, 1875.

——."The Polytechnic", *NCH,* March 15, 1877.

——."The Chinese Polytechnic Institution and Reading Room", *NCH,* April 18, 1883.

Oebsger-Roeder, Rudolf. 1936. *Untersuchungen über den Bildungsstand der deutschen Journalisten.* Leipzig: Universitätsverlag (Wesen und Wirkungen der Publizistik, 7).

Patterson, Don Denham. 1922. "The Journalism of China", *The University of Missouri Bulletin* 23.34 (Monograph Series).

Pavalko, Ronald M. 1988. *Sociology of Occupations and Professions*. Ithaca, Ill.: Peacock.

Peake, Cyrus. 1932. *Nationalism and Education in China*. New York: Columbia University Press.

PRO = Public Record Office (London).

Reardon-Anderson, James. 1991. *The Study of Change. Chemistry in China, 1840–1949*. Cambridge: Cambridge University Press.

Reingold, Nathan. 1976. "Definitions and Speculations: The Professionalization of Science in America in the Nineteenth Century", in: Alexandra Oleson and Sanborn Brown (eds.). *The Pursuit of Knowledge in the Early American Republic*. Baltimore: Johns Hopkins University Press, pp. 37–9.

Reynolds, David C. 1991. "Redrawing China's Intellectual Map: Images of Sciences in Nineteenth Century China", *Late Imperial China* 12.1, pp. 27–61.

Serres, Michel (ed.). 1998. *Elemente einer Geschichte der Wissenschaften*. Frankfurt a.M.: Suhrkamp.

Shanghai by night and day. 1897. Shanghai: Shanghai Mercury.

Shenbao (Shanghai)

Smith, Carl. T. 1985. *Chinese Christians: Elites, Middlemen and the Church in Hong Kong*. Oxford, New York: University of Oxford Press.

Su Jing 蘇精. 1978. *Qingji Tongwenguan ji qi shisheng* 清季同文官及其師生 (The *Tongwenguan*, its teachers and students in the Qing dynasty). Taibei: n.p.

Teng, Ssu-yu and John King Fairbank. 1965. *China's Response to the West. A Documentary Survey 1839–1923*. New York: Athenaeum.

Vittinghoff, Natascha. 2002. *Die Anfänge des Journalismus in China (1860-1911)* (The Rise of Journalism in China 1860-1911). Wiesbaden: Harrassowitz (Ph.D. diss., University of Heidelberg, 1998).

——. 2001. "Ein Leben am Rande des Ruhms: Cai Erkang (1852–1921)" (Living on the edge of fame: Cai Erkang (1852–1921), in: Christina Neder, Heiner Roetz and Susanne Schilling (eds.). *China in seinen biographischen Dimensionen. Festschrift für Helmut Martin* (China and her biographical dimensions. Commemorative essays for Helmut Martin). Wiesbaden: Harrassowitz, pp. 195–205.

——. 2002a. "Unity vs. Uniformity: Liang Qichao and the Invention of a 'New Journalism' for China", *Late Imperial China* 23.2, pp. 91–143.

——. 2002b. "Useful Knowledge and Proper Communication: Strategies and Models of Publishing Houses in the Formative Stage of the Chinese Press (1872–1882)", in: Rudolf G. Wagner (ed.). *Joining the Global Public. Word, Image and City in early Chinese newspapers 1870–1910*. Albany: SUNY Press, forthcoming, pp. 210–93.

Vollmer, Howard and Donald M. Mills. 1966. *Professionalization*. Engelwood Cliffs: Prentice Hall.

Wagner, Rudolf G. 2002. "Joining the Global Imaginaire: The Shanghai Illustrated Newspaper *Dianshizhai huabao*", in: id. (ed.) *Joining the Global Public. Word, Image and City in early Chinese newspapers 1870–1910*. Albany: SUNY Press, forthcoming.

Wakeman, Frederic. 1975. *The Fall of Imperial China*. New York: Free Press.

Wang Tao. 1988. "My Sojourn in Hong Kong". Translated by Yang Qinghua. *Renditions: Special Issue on Hong Kong* 29 and 30, pp. 37–41.

Wright, David. 2000. *Translating Science. The Transmission of Western Chemistry into Late Imperial China, 1840–1900*. Leiden: Brill.

Xiong Yuezhi 熊月之 . 1994. *Xixue dongjian yu wan Qing shehui* 西學東漸與晚清社
會 (The dissemination of Western knowledge and the late Qing society). Shanghai: Shanghai renmin chubanshe.

Xunhuan ribao (Hong Kong).

Xunhuan ribao liushi zhounian tekan 循環日報六十周年特刊 (Special edition for the
sixtieth Anniversary of the *Xunhuan ribao*). 1932. Hong Kong: Xunhuan ribao.

Yeh, Catherine V. 1997. "The Life-Style of Four Shanghai *Wenren* in Late Qing
China", *Harvard Journal of Asiatic Studies* 57.2, pp. 419–70.

Ying Lianzhi 英斂之 . 1975 [1907]. *"Ying Lianzhi xiansheng riji yigao"* 英斂之先生
日記遺稿 (Diary manuscript of Mr. Ying Lianzhi), in: *Jindai Zhongguo shiliao
congkan, xuji* 近代中國史料叢刊續集 (Collection of historical materials on modern China, supplement). Taibei: Wenhai chubanshe, vol. 21–3.

Yu Xingmin 于醒民. 1991. *Shanghai 1862 nian* 上海 1862 年 (Shanghai 1862).
Shanghai: Shanghai renmin chubanshe.

Zhang Mengwen 張孟聞 . 1982 [1947]. *Zhongguo kexueshi juyu* 中國科學史舉隅
(Aspects of the history of sciences in China), n.p.: Zhongguo wenhua fuwushe.
[Reprint *Minguo congshu*, ser. I. vol. 90].

Zhang Zigao 張子高 . 1982 [1932]. *Kexue fada shilüe* 科學發達史略 (Brief History of
Progress in Sciences), n.p.: Zhonghua shuju. [Reprint *Minguo congshu*, ser. I.
vol. 90].

Zhou Jiarong 周佳榮 . 2000. "Zai Xianggang yu Wang Tao huimian" 在香港與王韜
會面 (Meeting with Wang Tao in Hong Kong), in: Lam Kai-yin 林啟彥 and
Wong Man-kong 黃文江 (eds.). *Wang Tao yu jindai shijie* 王韜與近代世界
(Wang Tao and the modern world). Hong Kong: Xianggang jiaoyu tushu gongsi,
pp. 375–94.

WOLFGANG LIPPERT

THE FORMATION AND DEVELOPMENT OF THE TERM 'POLITICAL ECONOMY' IN JAPANESE AND CHINESE

The present contribution deals with the development of the term 'political economy', because it is typical for the phenomenon that an original word group in ancient Chinese was charged with a new meaning in modern times to render a Western model word.

First, let us try to make clear what 'political economy' means in the West. 'Political economy' was in use for a long time before the modern term 'economics' became the standard form. It implied some advice to the sovereign as to how economic activity should be conducted to promote 'wealth' and 'welfare'. A classification of the subject matter of political economy—which was in vogue among English writers in the century following James Mill's *Elements of Political Economy* (1821)—may serve to make more specific the content of the term. Mill's chapters deal with 1) production, 2) distribution, 3) interchange, and 4) consumption. Karl Marx in 1858 wrote his famous essay "A Critique of Political Economy", the preface of which is a text which probably was most often translated into Japanese and Chinese. It is no coincidence that the subtitle of Marx' *Capital* (1867) was *A Critique of Political Economy*. In German, *politische Ökonomie* has about the same meaning as *Nationalökonomie, Sozialökonomie* or *Volkswirtschaftslehre*. The term *politische Ökonomie* was particularly typical of Communist writings in recent times. In the *Small Political Dictionary* published in the former German Democratic Republic in 1967, *politische Ökonomie* was defined as "the science of the laws of social production and distribution of material goods on the various stages of development of human society."[1]

In Japanese the equivalent for the term 'political economy' is *keizai-gaku* 經濟學 , consisting of *keizai* 'economy' and *gaku* 'science', 'teachings'. In modern Chinese, the Western model is translated literally by inserting the modifier *zhengzhi* 政治 , 'political', to form the term *zhengzhi jingjixue* 政治經濟學 . *Jingjixue* is a loanword from Japanese; *zhengzhi* in Federico Masini's view is an autochthonous Chinese word. According to Masini, the term *zhengzhi* emerges for

---

[1] *Kleines politisches Wörterbuch.* 1967. Berlin: Dietz.

the first time in Chinese in the *Haiguo tuzhi* 海國圖志 (1844) by Wei
Yuan 魏源 (1794–1856) as an equivalent for 'politics'.[2] But this form
does not seem to have become part of the Chinese political lexicon of
the time, as it is not included in the *English and Chinese Dictionary*
by Wilhelm Lobscheid.[3] In Japan, *seiji-gaku* 政治學 as equivalent for
'politics' is found as early as 1869 in the *English-Japanese Dictionary* by Takahashi Shinkichi 高橋新吉 (1842–1918) (the so-called *Satsuma jisho*)[4] and all following English-Japanese dictionaries. So it
should perhaps rather be called a return loan from Japanese.

In Japan, the term *keizai* was already used in the Edo period by the
economist Satō Nobuhiro 佐藤信淵 (1769–1850) in his work *Keizai
yōroku* 經濟要录 (The essence of economics), published in 1827. Satō
Nobuhiro had probably learnt the Western term 'political economy' in
the course of his studies of Dutch which he pursued in Edo.

In Satō's economic thought "two things appear to have been uppermost in his mind: the economic rehabilitation of the country in order
to rescue it from poverty and starvation, and the building-up of
Japan's military power."[5] Today it cannot be determined definitely
whether the creation *keizai* to translate 'economy' was coined by him.
But it is certain that the term *keizai-gaku* had been firmly established
in the language of the late Edo period. It was entered in two dictionaries reflecting the lexicon of that time, viz. in the *Japanese and English
Dictionary* by James C. Hepburn (1867)[6] and in the *Satsuma jisho*,
mentioned above, as synonymous with 'political economy'. The latter
dictionary contains the scientific and political terminology of the *Rangaku* 蘭學 (Dutch studies) tradition.

[2] Cf. Federico Masini. 1993. *The Formation of Modern Chinese Lexicon and its
Evolution Towards a National Language: The Period from 1840 to 1898*. Berkeley:
Journal of Chinese Linguistics (Monograph Series, no. 6), p. 217.
[3] Cf. Wilhelm Lobscheid. 1866–1869. *Ying-Hua zidian* 英華字典. *English and
Chinese Dictionary with Punti and Mandarin Pronunciation*. 4 vols. Hong Kong:
Daily Press Office.
[4] Cf. Takahashi Shinkichi 高橋新吉. 1869. *Wa-yaku Ei-jisho* 和譯英辭典. *An
English-Japanese Dictionary*. Shanghai: American Presbyterian Mission Press.
[5] Ryusaku Tsunoda, Wm. Theodore De Bary and Donald Keene. 1958. *Sources of
Japanese Tradition*. 2 vols. New York, London: Columbia University Press, vol. 2, p.
56.
[6] Cf. James C. Hepburn. 1867. *Wa-Ei gorin shūsei* 和漢語林集成. *A Japanese
and English Dictionary, with an English and Japanese Index*. Shanghai: American
Presbyterian Mission Press.

The Japanese word *keizai* 'economy' can be traced back to the lexical unit *jingji* 經濟 which is to be found in works of classical Chinese literature, where it has the meaning of 'politics', 'statesmanship'. The combination *jingji* is not a primary form, but came into being by contraction of the two parallel word groups *jing shi ji min* 經世濟民 or *jing shi ji su* 經世濟俗 .

These word groups are verb-object constructions. The first one, *jing shi*, occurs in the *Zhuangzi* 莊子 , where it is used in the sense 'to put the (political) world in order', 'statesmanship', 'government'. The passage in *Zhuangzi* runs like this:

> 春秋經世先王之志
> The *Chunqiu* is the record of the former kings who governed the world.[7]

The second construction *ji min* has its source in the *Shujing* 書經 , where it is found in the passage:

> 惟爾有神尚克相予以濟兆民
> And now, ye spirits, grant me your aid, that I may relieve the millions of the people.[8]

The whole complex *jing shi ji min*, accordingly, means 'to govern the world and relieve the people'.

The word group *jing shi ji su* shows the same construction. The only difference is that the word *min* of the first complex is substituted by *su,* 'the men of the world'. This form appears in the book *Baopuzi* 抱朴子 by Ge Hong 葛洪 (ca. 250–ca. 330). There is the following passage:

> 以總明大智任經俗之器而修此事乃可必得耳
> If, by cleverness and great wisdom, one uses one's capability of governing the state and relieving the common men, then it should absolutely be possible to regulate this matter.[9]

---

[7] *Zhuangzi jishi* 莊子集釋 (Zhuangzi, with commentaries). 1978. 4 vols. Shanghai: Zhonghua shuju, vol. 1, p. 83.

[8] James Legge. 1960. *The Chinese Classics. Vol. 3: The Shoo king.* 2nd edition. Hong Kong: Hong Kong University Press, p. 314.

[9] Ge Hong 葛洪 . 1954. *Baopuzi* 抱朴子 (The Master who embraces natural simplicity), in: *Zhuzi jicheng* 諸子集成 (Collection of masters). Shanghai: Zhonghua shuju, vol. 8, ch. 18, p. 94.

The contraction of *jingji* we find in the book *Wen Zhongzi zhongshuo* 文中子中説 (Middle sayings by Wen Zhongzi) by Wang Tong 王通 (583–616):

> 是其家傳七世矣（汪家傳儒業）皆有經濟之道而位不逢（不逢明時）
> His family has passed on [the Confucian teaching] for seven genera-
> tions. All [members of the family] know the methods of statesmanship
> and of relieving the people, but in their position they have not found
> [favourable times for development].[10]

The reformer Wang Anshi 王安石 (1021–86) is praised in the *Songshi* 宋史 (History of the Song) of his sense for *jing ji*:

> 安石以文章節行高一世而尤道德經濟為己任
> [Wang] Anshi was far above his time because of his cultural refinement
> and his moderation, and, especially, he considered morals as well as
> statesmanship and [the methods of] relieving the people as his proper
> mission.[11]

In the *Yuanshi* 元史 (History of the Yuan) there already emerges the construction *jing ji zhi xue* 經濟之學, literally the 'science of *jing ji*' which is, in many respects very much like the modern form *jingjixue/keizai-gaku* 經濟學. But here it is used in its older sense, close to the modern terms 'politics', 'administration'.[12] Until the first years of the twentieth century the combination *jingji* (which became morphologized gradually) kept its original meaning. In Ming times the encyclopedia *Jingji leibian* 經濟類編 (Book of references on administration arranged according to subjects) was compiled by Feng Qi 馮琦 (1558–1603) with the intention of providing material which would be of practical value to those engaged in governing the country.[13] And in the English and Chinese Dictionary by Wilhelm Lobscheid *jingji* appears as equivalent for 'statesmanship'. In both cases *jingji* has the older meaning 'administration'.

----

[10] Wang Tong. 王通. 1893. *Wen Zhongzi zhongshuo* 文中子中説 (Middle sayings by Wen Zhongzi), in: *Ershier zi* 二十二子 (Twentytwo masters). Shanghai: Jishan shuju, vol. 6, p. 6b.

[11] Cf. *Songshi* 宋史 (History of the Song). 1977. Reprint Shanghai: Zhonghua shuju, ch. 327, p. 10553.

[12] Cf. *Yuanshi* 元史 (History of the Yuan). 1976. Reprint Shanghai: Zhonghua shuju, ch. 172, p. 4023.

[13] Cf. Ssu-yü Teng and Knight Biggerstaff. 1968. *An Annotated Bibliography of Selected Chinese Reference Works*. 3rd edition. Reprint Taibei: Shida shuyuan, pp. 122–123.

In the year 1897 examinations with new contents were proposed within the framework of the civil service examination system with the names of *jingji teke* 經濟特科 'special examination in public administration' and *jingji zhengke* 經濟政科 'regular examination in public administration', respectively (the first one was held in 1903).[14] As late as 1904, in the dictionary *Technical Terms English and Chinese*, edited by Calvin W. Mateer (Di Kaowen 狄考文),[15] the term *jingji* is not to be found under 'economy', but under 'science, governmental'.

The position of the term *keizai-gaku* as equivalent for 'economics', 'political economy' did not remain undisputed in the Japanese lexicon. Inoue Tetsujirō 井上哲次郎 (1855–1944) held the view that the extension of the concept *keizai-gaku* was wider than that of 'economics'. So he translated the latter term in his *Philosophical Dictionary* (1884) with *rizai-gaku* 理財學 ('the science of how to put property in order').[16] This technical term was in use at Tokyo University for a long time, and the Faculty of Economics at the Keiō University in Tokyo was called, until the 1930's, *rizai-gakubu* 理財學部. But the forcefulness of the term *keizai-gaku* which was favoured in the extramural sphere was greater.

Twenty years before the Chinese translation of Adam Smith's famous work *An Inquiry into the Nature and Causes of the Wealth of Nations* was completed by Yan Fu 嚴復 (1853–1921) in 1901,[17] Chinese intellectuals were able to get some basic information about the Western concept of 'political economy' in their own language for the first time. In 1881, a partial Chinese translation of the book *A Manual of Political Economy* by Henry Fawcett (first edition 1863) appeared, strangely enough, in Tokyo. The translators were Wang Fengzao 汪鳳藻 (1851–1918) and W. A. P. Martin (Ding Weiliang 丁韙良, 1827–1916), professors at the *Tongwenguan* 同文館. The same book was

---

[14] Cf. Wolfgang Franke. 1968. *The Reform and Abolition of the Traditional Chinese Examination System*. Cambridge, Mass.: Harvard University Press (Harvard East Asian Monographs 10), pp. 44–5, 68.

[15] Cf. Calvin W. Mateer (狄考文). 1904. *Technical Terms. English and Chinese*. Shanghai: Presbyterian Mission Press.

[16] Cf. Inoue Tetsujirō 井上哲次郎 and Ariga Nagao 有賀長雄. 1884. *Kaitei zōho tetsugaku jii* 改訂増補哲学字彙 (Philosophical Dictionary, revised and enlarged). Tokyo: Tōyōkan.

[17] Cf. Yan Fu 嚴復 (tr.). 1981. *Yuan fu* 原富 (On the origins of wealth). Reprint Beijing: Shangwu yinshuguan [Translation of Adam Smith, *An Inquiry into the Nature and Causes of the Wealth of Nations*].

published by the *Tongwenguan* in Beijing only two years later, in 1883. The title of the translation was *Fuguoce* 富國策 (lit., 'the policy of enriching the country'), an early Chinese attempt at rendering the Western term 'political economy'.[18]

The Japanese terms *keizai* and *keizai-gaku* were adopted as graphical loans into the Chinese language in the late nineteenth century. In the lexicographical sphere, it was as early as 1892 that the term *jingji* in its new meaning 'political economy' emerged, viz. in the *Chinese-English Dictionary* by Herbert Giles.[19] As far as the sphere of texts is concerned, the term *jingji* ('economy'), made its first appearance in Liang Qichao's writings in the year 1896, as Federico Masini points out.[20] A similar observation is made by Shen Guowei, Uchida Keiichi and others: in the *Shiwubao* 時務報 (1896) the term *jingjixue* 'economics' is used and explained by the translator as *fuguo yangmin ce* 富國養民策 ('the policy of enriching the country and of nourishing the people'). Characteristically, the new term occurs in the column "Dongwen baoyi" 東文報譯 (Translations from Japanese newspapers). The article where *jingjixue* appears is a translation from the *Tōkyō keizai zasshi* 東京經濟雜誌 (Tokyo Economics Journal).[21]

Masini gives a precise list of all the articles and books published in Chinese, dealing with the subject of 'economics' before and after the year 1900.[22] But the terms *jingji* and *jingjixue* were not easily understood by the Chinese reading public, and these terms had to supersede a variety of different forms, mostly Chinese coinages in circulation as equivalents for 'economy', 'political economy'.

---

[18] Cf. *Fuguoce* 富國策 (Policy of enriching the country). 1881. Translated by Wang Fengzao 汪鳳藻 and W. A. P. Martin. Tokyo: Rakuzendō [Translation of Henry Fawcett. 1863. *A Manual of Political Economy by Henry Fawcett*. First edition London]. I am very grateful to Dr. Iwo Amelung for bringing this book to my attention.

[19] Cf. Herbert A. Giles. 1964. *A Chinese-English Dictionary*. New York: Paragon [First edition Shanghai 1892].

[20] Cf. Masini 1993, p. 183.

[21] Cf. Shen Guowei 沈國威, Uchida Keiichi 内田慶一 et al. 1998. *Ōka kokka wo mezase: Jōhō hasshin kichi to shite no jūkyū seiki Nihon—Nihon shinbun no Chūgokugoyaku wo tōshite miru kindai Nitchū goi kōryūshi* 欧化国家を目指t:情報発信基地としての 19 世紀日本 — 日本新聞の中国語訳をとして見る近代中国語彙交流史 (Aim at becoming a Westernized country: Nineteenth-century Japan as a home base for dispatching informations—Modern Japanese-Chinese terminological exchange as seen in the light of Chinese translations of Japanese newspapers). n.p.: Kenkyū seika hōkokusho. For the original Chinese text see also *Shiwubao* 14. Reprint Taibei: Hua-wen shuju, 1967, 5 vols; vol. 2, p. 947.

[22] Cf. Masini 1993, p. 183–4.

Yan Fu almost always rendered the term 'economics' with *jixue* 計 學 ('the science of calculations') in *Tianyanlun* 天演論 , the translation of Thomas Huxley's *Evolution and Ethics and Other Essays*, published in 1898, and in *Yuan fu* 原富 , the translation of Adam Smith's *The Wealth of Nations*, published in 1901. According to Mori Toshihiko, Liang Qichao was reluctant to adopt the term *jingji* in his writings published by the turn of the century and even many years later. Evidently, he felt that its classical semantic background was too strong to charge the term with the meaning 'economy' or 'economics'.[23] So he used a large number of equivalents for the concept: *Fuguoxue* 富國學 ('the science of how to enrich the country'), *zishengxue* 資生學 ('the science of the resources and livelihood'), *licaixue* 理財學 ('the science of how to put property in order'), *shengjixue* 生計學 ('the science of the means of livelihood'), *shangxue* 商學 ('the science of business'), *shangwu* 商務 ('business affairs'), and *pingzhunxue* 平準學 ('the science of how to keep the prices on an equal level'). The last term was obviously derived from *pingzhunfa* 評 準法 'the method of equalizing' in ancient China, a system of grain purchase that enabled the government to retail it cheaply in times of scarcity. All these terms were equated by Liang in annotations with the Japanese *keizai-gaku*. In the same way, the expression *caixue* 財學 ('the science of property') as well as the phonemic loans *yekenuomi* 葉科諾米 (used by Yan Fu in *Yuan fu*), *aikangnuomi* 愛康諾米 , *yikanglaomi* 伊康老米 'economy' were in use at that time.[24]

From the treatment of the concept 'economy' in the *Xin Erya* 新爾 雅 (1903), a reference work divided according to subject categories, it can be seen that the term *jingjixue* was not the dominating one in the Chinese lexicon of that time. It states:

論生財析分交易用財之學科。謂之計學。亦謂之經濟學。俗謂之財學
The science treating production and analyzing exchange and the use of property is called *jixue* or *jingjixue*. Usually it is designated as *licaixue*.[25]

---

[23] Mori Toshihiko. 1998. "Liang Qichao and Western modernity: an analysis of his translations of the term 'political economy'". Translated by Barak Kushner and Joshua A. Fogel. Paper presented at a Conference on Liang Qichao and Japan at the University of California, Santa Barbara, September 1998.

[24] For the last two phonemic loans see Zdenka Novotná. 1967–69. "Contribution to the Study of Loan-Words and Hybrid Words in Modern Chinese", *Archiv Orientální* 35, pp. 613–48; 36, pp. 295–325; 37, pp. 48–75; p. 632.

Some years later, *jingji* and *jingjixue* were listed in general dictionaries. The *English and Chinese Standard Dictionary* (1912) has *jingji* and *licai* as equivalents for 'economy' and *licaixue, jingjixue* as equivalents for 'economics'.[26] The inclusion of *jingjixue* in the *Shehui kexue da cidian* 社會科學大辭典 (1929)[27] marks the triumph of this term over all other competitors.

In this way, for the translators of Marx, the equivalents for 'political economy' were at hand. As I already mentioned, the Chinese translation 'political economy' is *zhengzhi jingjixue* 政治經濟學 , whereas in Japanese it is simply *keizai-gaku* 經濟學 .

---

[25] Wang Rongbao 汪榮寶 and Ye Lan 葉瀾 . 1903. *Xin Erya* 新爾雅 (New *Erya*). Shanghai: Minquanshe, p. 37.

[26] Yan Huiqing. 1912. *Ying-Hua da cidian. An English and Chinese Standard Dictionary*. 2 vols. 4th edition. Shanghai: Commercial Press.

[27] Gao Xisheng 高希聖 et al. 1929. *Shehui kexue da cidian* 社會科學大辭典 (Great dictionary of social sciences). Shanghai: Shijie shuju, p. 678.

REFERENCES

Franke, Wolfgang. 1968. *The Reform and Abolition of the Traditional Chinese Examination System*. Cambridge, Mass.: Harvard University Press (Harvard East Asian Monographs 10).

Fuguoce 富國策 (Policy of enriching the country). 1881.Translated by Wang Fengzao 汪鳳藻 and W. A. P. Martin. Tokyo: Rakuzendō. [Translation of Henry Fawcett. 1863. *A Manual of Political Economy by Henry Fawcett*. First edition London.]

Gao Xisheng 高希聖 et al. 1929. *Shehui kexue da cidian* 社會科學大辭典 (Great dictionary of social sciences). Shanghai: Shijie shuju.

Ge Hong 葛洪 . 1954. *Baopuzi* 抱朴子 (The Master who embraces natural simplicity), in: *Zhuzi jicheng* 諸子集成 (Collection of masters). Shanghai: Zhonghua shuju, vol. 8, ch. 18.

Giles, Herbert A. 1964. *A Chinese-English Dictionary*. New York: Paragon. [First edition Shanghai 1892.]

Hepburn, James C. 1867. *Wa-Ei gorin shūsei* 和漢語林集成 . *A Japanese and English Dictionary, with an English and Japanese Index*. Shanghai: American Presbyterian Mission Press.

Inoue Tetsujirō 井上哲次郎 and Ariga Nagao 有賀長雄 . 1884. *Kaitei zōho tetsugaku jii* 改訂増補哲学字彙 (Philosophical Dictionary, revised and enlarged). Tokyo: Tōyōkan.

Kleines politisches Wörterbuch. 1967. Berlin: Dietz.

Legge, James. 1960. *The Chinese Classics. Vol. 3: The Shoo king*. 2nd edition. Hong Kong: Hong Kong University Press.

Lobscheid, Wilhelm. 1866–1869. *Ying-Hua zidian* 英華字典 . *English and Chinese Dictionary with Punti and Mandarin Pronunciation*. 4 vols. Hong Kong: Daily Press Office.

Masini, Federico. 1993. *The Formation of Modern Chinese Lexicon and its Evolution Towards a National Language: The Period from 1840 to 1898*. Berkeley: Journal of Chinese Linguistics (Monograph Series, no. 6).

Mateer, Calvin W. (狄考文). 1904. *Technical Terms. English and Chinese*. Shanghai: Presbyterian Mission Press.

Mori Toshihiko. 1998. "Liang Qichao and Western modernity: an analysis of his translations of the term 'political economy'". Translated by Barak Kushner and Joshua A. Fogel. Paper presented at a Conference on Liang Qichao and Japan at the University of California, Santa Barbara, September 1998.

Novotná, Zdenka. 1967–1969. "Contribution to the Study of Loan-Words and Hybrid Words in Modern Chinese", *Archiv Orientální* 35, pp. 613–48; 36, pp. 295–325; 37, pp. 48–75.

Shen Guowei 沈國威 , Uchida Keiichi 内田慶一 et al. 1998. *Ōka kokka wo mezase: Jōhō hasshin kichi to shite no jūkyū seiki Nihon—Nihon shinbun no Chūgoku-goyaku wo tōshite miru kindai Nitchū goi kōryūshi* 欧化国家を目指t：情報発信基地としての１９世紀日本 — 日本新聞の中国語訳をとして見る近代中国語彙交流史 (Aim at becoming a Westernized country: Nineteenth-century Japan as a home base for dispatching informations—Modern Japanese-Chinese terminological exchange as seen in the light of Chinese translations of Japanese newspapers). n.p.: Kenkyū seika hōkokusho.

Songshi 宋史 (History of the Song). 1977. Reprint Shanghai: Zhonghua shuju.

Takahashi Shinkichi 高橋新吉 . 1869. *Wa-yaku Ei-jisho* 和譯英辭典 . *An English-Japanese Dictionary*. Shanghai: American Presbyterian Mission Press.

Teng, Ssu-yü and Knight Biggerstaff. 1968. *An Annotated Bibliography of Selected Chinese Reference Works*. 3rd edition. Reprint Taibei: Shida shuyuan youxian gongsi.

Tsunoda, Ryusaku, Wm. Theodore De Bary and Donald Keene. 1958. *Sources of Japanese Tradition*. 2 vols. New York, London: Columbia University Press.

Wang Rongbao 汪榮寶 and Ye Lan 葉瀾 . 1903. *Xin Erya* 新爾雅 (New *Erya*). Shanghai: Minquanshe.

Wang Tong 王通 . 1893. *Wen Zhongzi zhongshuo* 文中子中説 (Middle sayings by Wen Zhongzi), in: *Ershier zi* 二十二子 (Twentytwo masters). Shanghai: Jishan shuju, vol. 6.

Yan Fu 嚴復 (tr.). 1981. *Yuan fu* 元富 (On the origins of wealth). Reprint Beijing: Shangwu yinshuguan [Translation of Adam Smith, *An Inquiry into the Nature and Causes of the Wealth of Nations*].

Yan Huiqing. 1912. *Ying-Hua da cidian. An English and Chinese Standard Dictionary*. 2 vols. 4th edition. Shanghai: Commercial Press.

Yuanshi 元史 (History of the Yuan). 1976. Reprint Shanghai: Zhonghua shuju.

Zhuangzi jishi 莊子集釋 (Zhuangzi, with commentaries). 1978. 4 vols. Shanghai: Zhonghua shuju.

RUDOLF G. WAGNER

NOTES ON THE HISTORY OF THE CHINESE TERM FOR 'LABOR'

The depiction of Chinese common folk from the careful and detailed descriptions and sketches by nineteenth century missionaries to the photo albums of our times will regularly show them at work, and at hard work at that. A note will be added that the Chinese are a very hard working people indeed, and that they are willing and able to endure the most strenuous work load. One might thus be prompted to expect a rich literature dealing with Chinese notions of labor that can draw on an equally rich body of Chinese texts throughout the ages where hard labor is being extolled and praised for its great contributions be it to one's own character and name, the fortunes of family and clan, or the welfare of the state. There is, however, very little to satisfy this expectation either in the sources, nor in modern scholarship, and, needless to say, this opens the question whether the notions and values implied in those descriptions, photographs and films are more than educated guesses that are based on the very rich European record on labor and its merits developing especially with the Reformation.[1]

In this paper, I will try to start filling the information gap by giving a sketch of the history of the modern term for labor.[2] This history, in addition, does not follow the standard sequence in the development of many parts of the modern Chinese lexicon, namely the adoption, in a translation of a Western text into Chinese or Japanese, of an older little used term with a partly overlapping meaning, the replacement of this meaning by the new Western content, and its transformation, still under a seemingly unchanging surface, into an organic part of a modern and often very specialized terminology.

---

[1] For details see the very extensive article by Werner Conze. 1997. "Arbeit", in: O. Brunner, W. Conze and R. Koselleck (eds.). *Geschichtliche Grundbegriffe. Historisches Lexikon zur politisch-sozialen Sprache in Deutschland.* Stuttgart: Klett-Cotta, vol. 1, pp. 154–215.

[2] This paper goes back to research done within a joint endeavour of the Humanities Class of the Berlin-Brandenburg Academy of Social Sciences which resulted in a more extensive article, "The concept of Work/Labor/Arbeit in the Chinese world. First Explorations" (forthcoming).

The modern Chinese lexem for 'labor' is *laodong* 勞動 . It consists of two parts, *lao* (to exert oneself, to wear oneself out) and *dong* (to move), together meaning something like 'to move with exertion'. The concept does not imply an easy go, but signals with the *lao* the sweat routinely running down the faces of actors impersonating workers and peasants laboring in Chinese films. The Party cadres leading the PRC and circumscribing the acceptable uses of the term in their correct-speak lexicon[3] as describing strenuous physical labor of the 'working classes' have not suddenly emerged from the villages. For decades before 1949 they had been part of the political contention, many of them already since the May Fourth Movement in 1919 with its student demonstrations against the Versailles Treaty and its advocacy of a 'new culture' for the masses based on a Chinese vernacular. The PRC is only the concretisation—awkwardly mediated with Chinese realities—of a construct developed previously in the imaginaire of the CCP leading cadres out of the dreams of their youth, the military organisation of the war, the Soviet institutional setup and administrative routines, and the tidbits from partial translations of Soviet handbooks and dictionaries. The leadership of the Guomindang, a party also set up along the Soviet model, shares most of this imaginaire. It might be helpful to deepen our understanding of the 'concept of labor' in the Chinese world by leaving the decidedly overcharged PRC material and explore the next layer, the Republic.

The presence of the *dong* in the compound inscribes the word into a highly-charged series of notions at the time defining (and glorifying) a life of active exertion. Since the end of Imperial China in 1911, the call for *dong* (movement) became the rallying cry for both reformers and revolutionists.[4] It appeared in the *yunDONG* 運動 or even *qunzhong yunDONG* 群眾運動 the political protest 'movements' or

---

[3] For the genesis of this lexicon and the institutional and ideological structures supporting it, see my article "Zhonggong 1940–1953 nian jianli zhengyu, zhengwen de zhengce dalüe 中共 1940–1953 年建立正語，正文的政策大略 (A Sketch of CCP policies to establish 'correctspeak' and 'correctwrite' (1940–1953))", in: Peng Xiaoyan 彭小妍 (ed.). *Wenyi lilun yu tongsu wenhua* 文藝理論與通俗文化 (Literary theory and popular culture). Taibei: Zhongyang yanjiuyuan Zhongguo wen zhe yanjiusuo zhoubeichu, 1999, pp. 11–38.

[4] The following paragraphs on the concept of *yundong* (movement) take up some of my studies on this concept in my article "The Canonization of May Fourth", in: M. Doleželová-Velingerová (eds.). 2001. *The Appropriation of Cultural Capital. China's May Fourth Project.* Cambridge and London: Harvard University Press, pp. 60–120.

'mass movements' such as the May Fourth Movement in 1919; *yundong* could also be intellectual 'movements' that push new thoughts which eventually may become the common denominator; and, finally, the *yundong* marks the movement of the active body in sports with the *yundong chang* 運動場 being the sports arena. This concept of *yundong* (movement) is in line with the glorification of constant movement and change first been elevated into the very principle of the universe by d'Alembert in his article "Movement" in the *Grande Encyclopédie* late in the eighteenth century; this thought became generally accepted during the nineteenth century in Europe and North America. An article entitled "Motion and Human Life" (*Huodong yu rensheng* 活動與人生), published 1917 in the *New Youth* (*Xin Qingnian* 新青年), one of the most influential journals at that time which was widely read among the educated youths, has to be read that way:

> Everything in space is in motion. According to Newton's law of inertia a body in movement will be continuously in movement as long as no other force had an impact on it. ... Many hundreds of millions of years ago, the universe started with motion, and after further hundreds of millions of years it will end with motion. ... As the world may be destroyed and the universe smashed but matter in space cannot go under, motion continues endlessly. Thus within time all matter is in motion. Furthermore, once there is motion, there is change, once there is change, the old and new separate and this is differentiated from the other. Without motion, the universe would stay the same without change. Staying the same, spatial differentiation would disappear, and being without change time differentiation would vanish. Thus without motion there would neither be a universe nor entities, and that means that motion is the basic characteristic of the universe and the source of entities. ... We humans with our heads round [like heaven] and our feet square [like the earth] pride ourselves to be the spiritually most nimble (*ling* 靈) among the ten thousand beings. But what makes us so? That we alone are good at being in motion.[5]

Man's motion is superior to stones who are only put in motion by other forces, to plants who while developing their own motion, have no spiritual force to guide it, and to birds who while having their own motion and a spiritual force, have no consciousness.

If the [Neoconfucian scholar] Cheng Yichuan [i.e. Cheng Yi] (1033–1107) said: 'Among all that is imbued with life between heaven and

---

5 Zhu Ruyi 1917, pp. 193–4.

earth it is man who is most richly endowed with the five elements; his root is true and tranquil',[6] I dare replace his expression 'tranquil' with 'in motion'. ... Therefore I dare make the unconditional statement that the basic character of man is but motion. Without it, he is weak and fearsome, unable to fully live out his human nature. Such a one is called a cripple. And one who goes against heaven, deviates from his nature and [thus] is not able to live out his natural endowment is called a sick body.[7]

After a few lines praising the high pitch of movement and motion in Europe which was just occupied with the First World War, the article ends with the application of this general rule to China:

In short, success or failure of an individual can be garnered from the strength or weakness of his drive ['motion power'], and, inferring from this the flourishing or demise of a state can also be garnered from the strength or weakness of the motion power of the citizens. The weakness of our state hinges just on our citizens not being good at motion. I make this statement not in order to oppose the quietism of the old philosophers. Man is not a trunk or stone, who would not enjoy some peace and happiness? I just wished that our citizens would strive for rest in the midst of progress, and would strive for peaceful happiness in the midst of motion—would it then be possible to fundamentally change this climate of rot and decay?[8]

The new imported natural science ideas found more favor with political and social reformers and revolutionists than with Chinese natural scientists. The former would mine them for metaphors giving their quest for social and political change the aura of conforming to the laws of nature. In this scenario with its strong social-darwinist overtones China is the 'Sick Man of the East', weak and fearsome because her citizens are lacking in motion and the drive for change. The teachings of their old philosophers with their emphasis on unperturbed inner calm was prompting them to go against heaven and their own nature and to end up as sickly cripples. In order to live out their endowment as men they have to join into what the aspiring new lead-

---

[6] This statement is quoted by Zhu Xi in the beginning of the second chapter of his *Jinsi lu*, see Chen Rongjie 陳榮捷 . 1992. *Jinsi lu xiangzhu jiping* 近思錄 詳注集評 (Collection of comments and explanations on *Reflections on Things at Hand*). Taibei: Xuesheng, p. 68. See also Wing-tsit Chan (tr.). 1967. *Reflections on Things at Hand. The Neo-Confucian Anthology*. New York: Columbia University Press, p. 36.

[7] Zhu Ruyi 朱如一 . 1917. "*Huodong yu rensheng*" 活動與人生 (Motion and human life), *Xin Qingnian* 新青年 (*New Youth*) 3.2, pp. 193–4.

[8] Ibid.

ers described with the neologism *yundong*, social and political movements.

There is nothing in these early texts of the glorification of the laboring masses and of the political and social talents growing out of their involuntary education in the production process. The inverse is the case. In the loud and muscular writings of the national saviors of the first two decades of the twentieth century, we rather find a general habit of cursing their countrymen for their passivity, toleration of national humiliation and petty concerns in an effort of shaming them into joining the political movement for change. The hopes that a selective import of Western technology would allow the country to become strong had been dashed for the time being in the Sino-Japanese War, and a few years later, in 1898, the hopes for a modernisation drive led by the Qing court had to be buried as well. Until the late 1920s, the focus thus was on politics and the establishment of a viable and unified nation state. Only with the success of the Northern Campaign against the warlords in 1927 conditions changed. The Guomindang, which had absorbed many of the May Fourth rebels and had received its own dose of Marxist education from its Communist allies and the Soviet Union, set up a government in Nanjing which could, to a degree, lay claim to be national in scope. Only now an ideology was developed that was to suit a state, not just a political party.

In the schools administered by this new government we find the original impulse for 'movement' and 'motion' translated into elements of a polytechnic education. The students of these schools with their school fees were a small minority of their age group, and were the recruiting pool for the elite of the country. Probably under Soviet influence, these schools had a regular subject called *laozuo* 勞作 'hard [physical] work'. The official terminological handbook of the time, the *Cihai* 辭海 of 1936, says its purpose was

> to prompt students through instruction in practical work to approach things in a practical manner, to instill into them the habit of hard work as well as an understanding that all laboring people are equal and to develop in them the mental attitude and capacity for well-planned creative action.[9]

The entry reflects the same mind-set we find in PRC dictionaries. Physical labor is to educate mental workers in work attitude, political

---

[9] *Cihai* 辭海 . 1995 [1936]. Taiyuan: Shanxi guji, p. 429.

attitude, and systematic as well as creative approaches. The object of
this *laozuo* education is the young person who is still under the impact
of the 'old philosophers'. This young person is not a doer, he thinks
himself superior and muddles along with the drift of the times instead
of imposing his will in a planned and systematic manner. The *laozuo*
program gives institutional expression to the political polemics
against the 'Confucius shop' that has been made responsible for the
weakness of China. Compared to this line, the PRC entries will contain some new elements, especially the stress on the discipline
imposed by the interaction of many participants in a high division of
labor in industry, and the subordination under the collective purpose,
both of which reflect the stronger CCP emphasis on subordination to
central party control. The handbooks of the 1930s also contain entries
on *laodong*. These entries treat it as one of the three essentials of the
economy, namely land, labor, and capital. The term gained a broad
leeway with subdivisions of mental and physical labor, directing and
executing labor as well as independent and non-independent labor all
fitting under this broad umbrella.[10] PRC definitions and uses greatly
reduced this leeway to fit the term to a use within the Soviet-type
socialist dictionary. A conceptualisation of labor as well as that of its
linguistic and argumentative environment seems to be completely
devoid of traditional Chinese elements. The creators of the modern
Chinese dictionary felt that nothing in their traditional terminology
would fit the new requirements, and thus labor, Labor Day, the laborer and the Labor Party all belong to the new world of imported con-
ceptualisations for a new order of things, all being formed with the
neologism *laodong*.

ORIGIN OF THE TERM FOR LABOR, *LAODONG*

The modern Chinese term for labor, *laodong*, is a Japanese import.[11]
Another current term, *gongzuo* 工作 , includes the term used in pre-
modern China for the craftsmen and their activity, *gong* 工 , but now
has a meaning that refers to creative and productive activity alto-

---

[10] *(Chongbian) Riyong da baike quanshu* (重編)日用大百科全書((New edition of
the) Great encyclopedia for daily use). 1934. Shanghai: Commercial Press, pp. 617–8.

[11] It is not listed as such in the handbooks of import terms such as Federico Masini. 1993. *The Formation of the Modern Chinese Lexicon and its Evolution Toward a*

gether, including that of composers or journalists. The Japanese term *rōdō* 勞動 is written with the same Chinese characters as the Chinese term, although sometimes a standard Japanese variant for the *dō/dong* 働 with the radical *ren* to the left is used, which also found its way into China.

A substantial part of the modern Chinese vocabulary in all fields of modern knowledge has been brought back to China by students returning from their studies in Japan since the beginning of the twentieth century. This includes nearly all the key terms that organize experience such as history, society, state, philosophy, literature, science, experience, practice, or theory. For a number of these terms Chinese translators of Western books between 1895 and 1905 such as Yan Fu 嚴復 (1854–1921) had made up Chinese equivalents, but few of them survived in the competition with the Japanese-educated students and the terms they brought back upon their return. The Japanese effort at creating new terms came with the Meiji restoration and its big push for catching up with the West. In creating these binomes for translation, Japanese translators used two sources. First, terms created decades earlier in the century by missionaries in China in their translations of Western works or introductions of Western technologies. In China, these texts seem to have had very little impact at the time, but once the Meiji drive started in Japan, these Chinese translations were among the first to be made available in Japan. The second source were expressions with a more or less similar meaning that occurred here and there in old Chinese texts. The old content of these expressions, however, was fully replaced by the implications of the Western term they now translated. Japanese translators and the government office in charge of new terminology also used dictionaries that had been prepared earlier, as we shall see.

The Japanese choice of Chinese characters to represent the Western concepts is surprising, coming at a time when the number of Chinese characters in Japanese texts was dramatically reduced to increase accessibility of written texts for broader audiences. At the same time,

---

11 (*cont.*) *National Language. The Period from 1840 to 1898*. Berkeley: Journal of Chinese Linguistics (Monograph Series, no. 6), because it got into the Chinese dictionary only later, and is not listed in books such as Liu Zhengtan 劉正埮 and Gao Mingkai 高名凱 (eds.). 1984. *Xiandai Hanyu wailaici cidian* 現代漢語外來詞詞典 (Dictionary of Chinese neologisms). Shanghai: Shanghai cishu chubanshe, which is characterized by its extremely restrictive understanding of imported terms.

it followed a traditional procedure because many of the terms written with Chinese characters and pronounced in the *kambun* pronunciation derived from their Chinese pronunciation had originally been imported from China as new concepts. Terms written in Chinese characters were thus marked optically and phonetically as high-register imports much like words with distinct Latin or Greek roots in German or English academic and technical language. I presume that the decision went against the use of the *katakana* nowadays normally used in Japan to phonetically transcribe foreign terms because of the inability of *katakana* to communicate the register to which these terms belonged, quite apart of the fact that the phonetic rendering does not signal to a Japanese reader the realm to which the term belongs, something the Chinese characters do. Once these Chinese characters are inserted into a Chinese text, however, they lose all markers of being translations for foreign terms. For Chinese readers growing up with these terms it is often exceedingly shocking to learn to what degree their language is made up and organized by such translation terms, and there has been substantial resistance against the very idea that the key terms of the modern Chinese vernacular have been made up abroad, in Japan, as translation terms.[12]

In the case of *rōdō* the story is still more complicated. According to the excellent handbook of Meiji terminology, the *Meiji no kotoba jiten* 明治のことば辞典 (Dictionaries of words from the Meiji Period) the term is regularly listed in Japanese dictionaries since 1872.[13] In the second edition of the first dictionary for the translation of foreign philosophical works in 1881 *rōdō* is proposed as the translation for 'labor' and has from there entered translations of compounds such as Labor Party or labor insurance.[14] The term did not suggest itself to the compiler of a dictionary to help in standardizing the translations, Hepburn, as a translation for labor in either his editions of his dictionary of 1867 or of 1886. He proposed a number of terms, among them *rō*

---

[12] See, for example, Wang Yunwu 王雲五. 1997 [1944]. "Xinmingci suyuan" 新名詞溯源 (The sources for new terms), in: id. *Jiuxue xintan* 舊學新探 (New explorations on old themes). Shanghai: Xuelin, pp. 261–75.

[13] Sogo Masaaki (惣郷正明) (ed.). 1989. *Meiji no kotoba jiten* 明治のことば辞典 (Dictionaries of words from the Meiji Period). Tokyo: Tōkyōdō shuppan, pp. 603–5.

[14] Tetsugaku jiyi 哲學字彙, quoted in Sogo Masaaki 1889, p. 604.

suru 勞する , 'to toil hard', the *rō* of which is the same as in *rōdō*.[15] This suggests that the equation between labor and *rōdō* had not now stabilized.

The term, however, is not a neologism created by Meiji translators, but an older Japanese creation. In the framework of the 'Dutch studies' (*rangaku* 蘭学), *rōdō* was created to translate the Dutch term *slooven*. According to the *Meiji no kotoba jiten*, it seems to be listed in the *Translation Key* (*Yakken* 譯鍵) of 1812.[16] I have not seen a copy of this work which is a 'corrected extract' by Fujibayashi Fuzan 藤林普山 (1781–1836) from the 1796 translation of the *Nederduits Franse Woordenboek* by F. Halma (1653–1722) done by Inamura Sanpaku 稲村三伯 (1758–1811) and others, the *Haruma wage* 波留麻和解 .[17]

Another work—this one not known to the editors of *Meiji no kotoba jiten* and surviving in the Trautz collection in the Institute of Japanese Studies at Bonn University—coming with a similar title, the *(Kaisei) Zōho yakken* 改正増補譯鍵 that was put out in 1796 in Edo and Ōsaka by Hirota Kenkan 廣田憲寛 (1718–1788) and might be independent and not based on Fujibayashi Fuzan's translation, also lists *slooven*, but instead of giving the equivalent *rōdō* 勞動 , it gives the equivalent 勞勤 which is graphically very similar, is used in this way in many Chinese texts, and would have the meaning 'exerting oneself to exhaustion'.[18]

The term *slooven* is a dialect term in Dutch that refers to heavy work at sea. In other words, the term *rōdō* originally did not translate

---

[15] J. C. Hepburn. 1867. *Wa-Ei gorin shūsei* 和英語林集成 . *A Japanese and English Dictionary, with an English and Japanese Index.* Shanghai: American Presbyterian Mission Press, sub. 'labor' in the index, p. 56 and J. C. Hepburn. 1903 [1886]. *A Japanese-English and English-Japanese Dictionary.* Tokyo: Maruya, p. 866. He does not have *rōdō* among the Japanese words in his dictionary.

[16] Sogo Masaaki 1889, p. 604c.

[17] Fujibayashi Fuzan 藤林普山 . 1812. *Yakken* 譯鍵 (Translation key). n.p.; Inamura Sanpaku 稲村三伯 (et al.). 1796. *Haruma wage* 波留麻和解 (Dutch-Japanese dictionary). n.p.

[18] Hirota Kenkan 廣田憲寛 . 1857 [1796]. *(Kaisei) zōho yakken* 改正増補譯鍵 (Corrected supplements to *Translation Key*). n.p. I am much indebted to Mr. Woldering from the Institute of Japanese Studies, University of Heidelberg, to help me get a copy of this entry from Bonn and to make available relevant bibliographical information. Other editions appeared simultaneously in 1796 in Edo: Subara Mohei publishers and in Ōsaka: Akita Taemon.

the European concepts of 'labor' or *Arbeit* with their rich theological, moral, and social implications, but a fairly marginal local Dutch term that referred to hefty labor probably connected with boats. Only during the early Meiji period it was appropriated for the uses of a completely different term on a much higher register, labor, when this had recommended itself as a modern term that referred to what was seen as a new phenomenon, industrial labor.

The term *laodong* used here by the Japanese compilers is not a newly invented binome. As can be seen from the *25 Dynastic Histories Database* it is attested, but very rarely, since early medieval times in the dynastic histories in quotations of oral utterances with the meaning of body movement or even body exertion. This might indicate a wider use in the spoken language. The *Hou Han shu* 後漢書 quotes the famous doctor Hua Tuo 華陀 , as saying to a student in a general explanation of preserving one's body for long life: "The human body does like to get exercised 欲得勞動 , but one should by no means exaggerate it!"[19] He goes on to say that mild movement keeps the joints elastic like the regular use of a door hinge will prevent it from rotting, and proposes a set of easy exercises which he has developed. There are some passages with similar uses of the term for a sport-like or military exercise. It is quite clear, however, that it did not refer in either the spoken or the written language to anything like heavy work of workmen or industrial laborers, not to mention farmers. From these uses it looks in fact like a potential candidate for translating the modern terms 'exercise' or even 'sport'. While it might have a certain terminological definiteness in parts of the medical language that have to do with light body exercises, it is not a regularly used stable term. It hardened into its modern use through its application in the Meiji translations and works.

CONCLUSION

As we have seen, the element *dō/dong* had by the early 1900s already entered different neologisms used in China, but *laodong* seems to have made its way only with the development of a modern industry in China and the massive reflux of students from Japan. I

---

[19] *Hou Han shu* 後漢書 (History of the Later Han). 1964. Beijing: Zhonghua shuju, ch. 72b, p. 2739.

have seen it first listed in A. Mateer's dictionary of new terms used in the papers in 1915 in the construction *laodongjia* 勞動家 (laborer) vs. *zibenjia* 資本家 (capitalist).[20] In this form it also was included into Hemeling's *English-Chinese Dictionary* in 1917,[21] the supplement to which also included *laodong* in the Japanese writing of *dong* as a 'neologism'.[22] By that time, however, various newly crafted and old terms were still competing. Hemeling still gives gave *lao* 勞 and *laoku* 勞苦 as translation terms for 'labor', and the traditional *qinlao* 勤勞 for 'laborious', while the Ministry of Education, for one, approved in 1912 a list of translation terms[23]—without ever publishing them—in which it settled for *gong* 工 (worker) as the core ingredient for all terms related with labor, making the Labor Party into the *Gongdang* 工黨 instead of the Japanese version that would have read *Laodong Dang* 勞動黨 in Chinese. As opposed to the various terms for labor, this creation survived the onslaught of Japanese terms and is still in use today, splitting the field right in the middle. Most importantly, the term was primarily used for industrial labor, and thus belonged to a new type of activity, a new organisation of industrial time with a labor/rest dichotomy, a new social group, the industrial worker, and a new physical setting, the industrial town.

The term, its content, its antonym and its value are thus parts of an import discourse that has its mother, logic and environment in the West and comes into the Chinese situation as a modern ready-made product to be imposed over a Chinese reality ordered in quite different ways, but to which it has given a new and now generally accepted order.

---

[20] Ada Haven Mateer. 1915. *New Terms for New Ideas. A Study of the Chinese Newspaper*. Shanghai: Methodist Publishing House.

[21] Karl E. G. Hemeling. 1917. *English-Chinese Dictionary of the Standard Chinese Spoken Language* (官話) *and Handbook for Translators, including Scientific, Technical, Modern, and Documentary Terms*. Shanghai: Statistical Department of the Inspector General of Customs, p. 761.

[22] Ibid., p. 1715.

[23] This list was put together by a committee headed by the famous translator Yan Fu, who himself had created many of the—eventually unsuccessful—new terms for Western concepts. As far as I can see, the only accessible form of this list are the terms marked *buding* (approved by the Ministry) in the Hemeling dictionary.

REFERENCES

Chan, Wing-tsit (tr.). 1967. *Reflections on Things at Hand. The Neo-Confucian Anthology*. New York: Columbia University Press.

Chen Rongjie 陳榮捷 . 1992. *Jinsi lu xiangzhu jiping* 近思錄詳注集評 (Collection of comments and explanations on *Reflections on Things at Hand*). Taibei: Xuesheng.

(Chongbian) Riyong da baike quanshu (重編)日用大百科全書 ((New edition of the) *Great encyclopedia for daily use*). 1934. Shanghai: Commercial Press.

*Cihai*辭海 . 1995 [1936]. Taiyuan: Shanxi guji.

Conze, Werner. 1997. "Arbeit", in: O. Brunner, W. Conze und R. Koselleck (eds.). *Geschichtliche Grundbegriffe. Historisches Lexikon zur politisch-sozialen Sprache in Deutschland*. Stuttgart: Klett-Cola, vol. 1, pp. 154–215.

Federico Masini. 1993. *The Formation of the Modern Chinese Lexicon and its Evolution Towards a National Language: The Period from 1840 to 1898* Berkeley: Journal of Chinese Linguistics (Monograph Series, no. 6)

Fujibayashi Fuzan 藤林普山 . 1812. *Yakken* 譯鍵 (Translation key). n.p.

Hemeling, Karl E. G. 1917. *English-Chinese Dictionary of the Standard Chinese Spoken Language* (官話) *and Handbook for Translators, including Scientific, Technical, Modern, and Documentary Terms*. Shanghai: Statistical Department of the Inspector General of Customs.

Hepburn, J. C. 1867. *Wa-Ei gorin shûsei* 和英語林集成 . *A Japanese and English Dictionary, with an English and Japanese Index*. Shanghai: American Presbyterian Mission Press.

——. 1903 [1886]. *A Japanese-English and English-Japanese Dictionary*. Tokyo: Maruya.

Hou Han shu 後漢書 (History of the Later Han). 1964. Beijing: Zhonghua shuju.

Hirota Kenkan (廣田憲寬). 1857 [1796]. *Kaisei zōho yakken* 改正增補 譯鍵(Corrected supplements to *Translation Key*). n.p.

Inamura Sanpaku 稲村三伯 et al. 1796. *Haruma wage* 波留麻和解 (Dutch-Japanese dictionary). n.p.

Liu Zhengtan 劉正埮 and Gao Mingkai 高名凱 (eds.). 1984. *Xiandai Hanyu wailaici cidian* 現代漢語外來詞詞典 (Dictionary of Chinese neologisms). Shanghai: Shanghai cishu chubanshe.

Mateer, Ada Haven. 1915. *New Terms for New Ideas. A Study of the Chinese Newspaper*. Shanghai: Methodist Publishing House.

Sogo Masaaki 物郷正明 (ed.). 1989. *Meiji no kotoba jiten* 明治のことば辞典 (Dictionaries of words from the Meiji Period). Tokyo: Tōkyōdō shuppan.

Wagner, Rudolf G. 1999. "Zhonggong 1940–1953 nian jianli zhengyu zhengwen de zhengce dalüe" 中共1940–1953年建立正語‧正文的政策大略 (A Sketch of CCP policies to establish 'correctspeak' and 'correctwrite' (1940–1953))", in: Peng Xiaoyan 彭小妍 (ed.). *Wenyi lilun yu tongsu wenhua* 文藝理論與通俗文化 (Literary theory and popular culture). Taibei: Zhongyang yanjiuyuan Zhongguo wen zhe yanjiusuo zhoubeichu, pp. 11–38

——. "The Canonization of May Fourth", in: M. Doleželová-Velingerová (eds.). 2001. *The Appropriation of Cultural Capital. China's May Fourth Project*. Cambridge and London: Harvard University Press, pp. 60–120.

Wang Yunwu 王雲五 . 1997 [1944]. "Xinmingci suyuan" 新名詞溯源 (The sources for new terms), in: id. *Jiuxue xintan* 舊學新探 (New explorations on old themes). Shanghai: Xuelin, pp. 261–75.

Zhu Ruyi 朱如一. 1917. "Huodong yu rensheng" 活動與人生 (Motion and human life), *Xin Qingnian* 3.2 (April 1917), pp. 193–4.

MA JUN 馬軍

A BRIEF STUDY ON THE TRANSLATION OF WESTERN MILITARY RANKS IN LATE QING

INTRODUCTION

In some sense, the history of Late Qing is a history of military conflicts between China and foreign countries. Apart from wars and military conflicts, there was also an intensive transfer of military know-how and technologies, after European companies had discovered China as a profitable market for gun trading. Moreover, the main purpose of the institutions which produced Western knowledge most effectively in China, the Fuzhou and Jiangnan Arsenal, was to import military knowledge and technology. Therefore, along with the transfer of Western science in the nineteenth century, knowledge about Western military culture also poured into Late Imperial China. This important aspect of technological transfer and the subsequent translation problem has not drawn much scholarly attention yet. Jiangnan Arsenal

Military Ranks are titles and signs given to soldiers according to their duties, contributions, attainments, seniority and the military unit to which they belong, which are a very important requirement to organize enlisted man, regulate cadres and fix their post. They possess important meaning for such rights as material supply, national safeguard and salaries and defining the relationship between the higher and lower ranks. Military Ranks in Western Europe originated in the fifteenth and sixteenth century and came along with the appearance of a permanent army. After the seventeenth and eighteenth century, the military rank system was further developed and specified. Used by most European and American countries, one system gradually evolved as an international standard. According to this system, soldiers can be categorized in three types: officer, noncommissioned officer and soldier. Officers can be roughly classified into three grades and every grade into three to four classes, and the noncommissioned officers and soldiers also into three to five classes or more. As all Western languages are composed of alphabetic writing systems and emerged from a similar cultural background, most of the military ranks can be traced back to the same origin. Some words even have the same spelling and are only pronounced in different ways. The translation of titles between those languages therefore did not pose a major problem. In contrast, it was not so easy to translate Western military ranks into Chinese.

Not only the linguistic situation was fundamentally different, but also the actual military organization, as the Qing dynasty had the dual system of the Eight Banners (*baqi* 八旗) and the Green Standards (*lüying* 綠營). 'Eight Banners' is the collective reference to the system of the social-political-military organization of the Manchu people in the Qing dynasty; 'Green Standards' is the collective designation for hereditary Chinese military men outside the Banner system.[1] Both of them were branches of the national Qing army, but used different sets of military rank systems and respective terminologies.

Before the Opium War, there were already some military contacts between China and the West, but they did not produce any new military terminologies in China. The Dutch army, which had fought with Zheng Chenggong 鄭成功 (1624–1662) in Taiwan in the seventeenth century, and the Russian army, which conflicted with the Qing army at the river basin of Heilongjiang, both had used the modern military rank system. The mission led by Lord George MacCartney in the late eighteenth century was also accompanied by a large group of officers, soldiers and diplomats. But such contacts did not lead to any further philological or linguistic study about the military ranks and no single thought seems to have been given to a possible transfer of foreign ranks into the indigenous military system. Instead, different kinds of documents are flooded with discriminating titles, which more or less describe the head of tribes and were used for the 'barbarian' people, mostly conveying the notion of "chief", such like *yimu* 夷目, *bingqiu* 兵酋, *bingtou* 兵頭, *yiguan* 夷官, *bingmu* 兵目, *bingbian* 兵弁, *bianmu* 弁目 etc.[2] That means, until the early period of the Opium War, the Chinese government did not have any specific knowledge

---

[1] Cf. Charles O. Hucker. 1985. *A Dictionary of Official Titles in Imperial China*. Stanford: Stanford University Press, s.v. English translations of the Chinese Qing military terms used here follow Charles O. Hucker.

[2] On the official usage of such designations and their histories see Fang Weigui. 2001. "*Yi, yang, xi, wai* and other terms: The Transition from 'Barbarian' to 'Foreigner' in Late Imperial China", in: Michael Lackner, Iwo Amelung and Joachim

about the connotation and extension of Western military ranks. Only along with the military defeats and under the strong pressure of the so-called Western 'gunboat-policy', and with a subsequent intensified exchange of foreign experts and military advisors in the Arsenals, Eastern and Western political, cultural, and military contacts increased dramatically. The question of how to translate Western military ranks thus became a crucial issue at stake.

I will therefore briefly examine the process of translating Western military knowledge into Chinese and take military ranks as an example. In general, we can distinguish four different ways to translate military ranks: phonetic transposition, mechanical application of ranks of the Green Standards and Eight Banners, descriptive translations and loanwords. In the following I will show which of these translation modes is given preference and how the translation can finally be understood as a hybrid product, influenced by three different elements: the Western, Japanese and Chinese traditional military cultures.

1. *YIYINFA* 譯音法 (PHONETIC TRANSPOSITION)

In the initial translation period, mostly the method of phonetic transposition was chosen. Western military ranks would be recorded in Chinese characters according to their pronunciations. For example, the 53rd chapter of the *Haiguo tuzhi* 海國圖志 (Illustrated treatise on the maritime countries) by Wei Yuan 魏源 (1794–1856)—"Da xiyang" 大西洋 (Atlantic ocean), "Yingjili guo" 英吉利國 (England)— contains the following two sentences:

> The head officer is called *zanniliu* 贊你留 (General), his names are *shayougeha* 沙有哥哈 (Sir Hugh Gough) and *bage* 吧噶 (Captain). In addition, the head officer naval affairs is entitled *yamilou* 押米婁 (Admiral).[3]

> Every port has a military division, [the head of which] is called *maningjie* 馬凝接 (Major General). This post is similar to the Chinese

[2] (*cont.*) Kurtz (eds.). *New Terms for New Ideas: Western Knowledge and Lexical Change in Late Imperial China.* Leiden: Brill, pp. 95–124; and Xiong Yuezhi. 2001. "Liberty, Democracy, President: The Translation and Usage of Some Political Terms in Late Qing China", in: ibid., pp. 69–93.

[3] Wei Yuan 魏源 (ed.). 1998 [1844]. *Haiguo tuzhi* 海國圖志 (Illustrated treatise on the maritime countries). 3 vols. 50 *juan*. Changsha: Yuelu shushe, p. 1468.

zongbing 總兵 (Regional Commander). In addition there is a countless amount of military officers.[4]

"General" today is translated as *lujun shangjiang* 陸軍上將 (Senior General of the Army) or *jiangjun* 將軍 (General); "Admiral" is now *haijun shangjiang* 海軍上將 (Senior General of the Navy), and "Major General" is *lujun shaojiang* 陸軍少將 (Junior General of the Army).

In the 60th chapter of the *Haiguo tuzhi*—"Waida xiyang" 外大西洋 (The Atlantic), "Milijian guoji yu'naishi dieguo zongji" 彌利堅國即育奈士迭國總記 (Comprehensive Account of the United States of America)—we find the section:

> Out of economic concerns, soldiers in this country are few. There is only one *mayuerenninaer* 馬約仁尼那爾 (Major general) and there are three *moliyadinaer ashirenni* 墨里牙底那爾阿士仁尼 (Brigadier General), 19 officers called *geluonier* 戈羅尼爾 (Colonel), 15 officers called *fugeluonier* 副戈羅尼爾 (Vice-Colonel), 28 officers called *mayue* 馬約 (Major), and 40 officers called *jidun* 急頓 (Captain).[5]

"Brigadier General" today is rendered as *lujun zhunjiang* 陸軍准將 , "Lieutenant Colonel" is translated as *lujun zhongxiao* 陸軍中將 (Ordinary General of the Army) and "Major" as *lujun shaoxiao* 陸軍少校 (Junior Grade Lieutenant of the Army). The rank of a Captain is today called *lujun shangwei* 陸軍上尉 (Senior Commandant of the Army) or *haijun shangxiao* 海軍上校 (Senior Lieutenant of the Navy).

The *Yingguo shuishikao* 英國水師考 (Examination of the English Royal Navy) published by the translation department of the Jiangnan Arsenal (*Jiangnan zhizaoju* 江南製造局) contains the following navy officer grades translated via phonetic transposition:

> Admiral as *aimeilai* 愛美賴 ,
> Commodore as *kangmoduer* 亢莫濆爾 ,
> Captain as *jiabidun* 甲必頓 ,
> Commander as *kemante* 喀曼特 ,
> Lieutenant as *lutuona* 魯脱納 , and
> Sub-Lieutenant as *xialutuona* 下魯脱納 .[6]

The advantage of phonetic transpositions lies in its easy application, while its disadvantage is more than obvious: as the translations do not transport any semantic meaning, they fail to explain the different

---

[4] Ibid., p. 1472.

[5] Ibid., p. 1655.

[6] Cf. John Fryer and Zhong Tianwei 鐘天緯 (trs.). 1886. *Yingguo shuishikao* 英國水師考 (Examination of the English Royal Navy). Shanghai: Shanghai jiqi zhizaoju.

grades, which is the most important purpose of military ranks. For this reason, phonetic transposition was just an expedient measure and would be rarely used.

2. MECHANICAL APPLICATION OF THE RANKS OF THE GREEN STANDARDS

As is well-known, in ancient China military officers in addition to their military post also had official grades. In the Zhou dynasty, the official grade was called *ming* 命 , in the Qin and Han period, it was called *shi* 石 , and in the Nanchao period *jie* 階 . In all other dynasties after the Sui it was called *pin* 品 , even if each dynasty had different ranks of *pin*. In the Qing dynasty the system of nine *pin*-ranks was in practice. Each *pin*-rank is classified into upper class (*zheng* 正 /a) and lower class (*cong* 從 /b). Both military and civil officers were classified into 18 grades (*deng* 等). Although there are differences with regard to content, purpose and meaning between this system and the Western military rank system, the Chinese system provided a similar coordinated standard which allowed to find equivalents between Western military ranks and the Chinese classifications. Translated in that sense were not the grades of *pin* but the correlative military posts of the Green Standards. Table 1 therefore shows the military posts of the Green Standards and their correlative *pin*-ranks in the Qing dynasty:

Table 1: Military posts of the Green Standards and pin-*ranks*

Luying guanzhi 綠營官職 (Green Standard posts)	*biecheng* 別稱 (alternative name)	*pinji* 品級 (rank and class)
tidu 提督 (Provincial Military Commander)	*titai* 提台 , *junmen* 軍門	*congyipin* 從一品 (1b)
zongbing 總兵 (Regional Commander)	*zongzhen* 總鎮, *zhentai* 鎮台	*zhengerpin* 正二品 (2a)
fujiang 副將 (Regional Vice Commander)	*xietai* 協台	*congerpin* 從二品 (2b)
canjian 參將 (Administrator)	*tongling* 統領	*zhengsanpin* 正三品 (3a)
youji 游擊 (Brigade Commander)	*youfu* 游府	*congsanpin* 從三品 (3b)
dusi 都司 (Brigade Vice Commander)	*guandai* 管帶	*zhengsipin* 正四品 (4a)

Table 1: Military posts of the Green Standards and pin-*ranks (cont.)*

Luying guanzhi 綠營官職 (Green Standard posts)	*biecheng* 別稱 (alternative name)	*pinji* 品級 (rank and class)
shoubei 守備 (Commandant)		*zhengwupin* 正五品 (5a)
qianzong 千總 (Company Commander)		*zhengliupin* 正六品 (6a)
baizong 百總 (Squad Leader)	*bazong* 把總	*zhengqipin* 正七品 (rank 7 upper class)
jingzhiwaiwei 經制外委 (Detached Fiscal Commissioner)	*ewaijunguan* 額外軍官	*zhengbapin* 正八品 (rank 8 upper class)

1. Diplomatic documents

To use officer ranks of the Green Standards and their alternative names mentioned above to translate Western military ranks was accepted as common practice by Chinese and foreigners and therefore the usual translation mode of diplomatic activities in the late Qing dynasty. This can be proved by the following two namelists of foreigners produced during the Chinese-English negotiations in the late period of the Opium War:

a) Yiren mingdan 夷人名單 *(Namelist of foreigners)*[7]:

> Licha 李查 , *tidu* of the Royal Navy and *fujiang* of Ordinary army;
> Batulumandun 巴圖魯滿敦 , *tidu* of English Army and *canjiang* of Ordinary Brigade;
> Batulubaozu 巴圖魯咆租 , *fujiang* of Royal Navy and the precedent *zongbing* of the Food Supply Section;
> Qili 琦理 , *fujiang* of Royal Navy;
> Batuluwenkemei 巴圖魯文珂美 , *zongbing* of the English Supply Section and third rank *canjiang* of the Firearm Brigade;
> Qibei 祁卑 , Royal Navy *fujiang*;
> Weilixun 威里訓 , *canjiang* of the Financial Bureau;
> Hajinshi 哈金士 , *canjiang* of the Grain Bureau;
> Mo 摩 , *dusi* of the Crime Section;
> Qilan 琦蘭 , *dusi* of Ordinary army of the Horse Soldiers;

---

[7] Cf. Zhang Xi 張喜 . 1957. "Fuyi riji" 撫夷日記 (Diary of appeasing the foreigners), in: *Zhongguo jindaishi ziliao congkan—yapian zhanzheng* 中國近代史資料叢刊 — 鴉片戰爭 5 (Series of source material on the history of modern China—the Opium War 5). Shanghai: Renmin chubanshe, pp. 386–8.

Antude 安突德 , *dusi* of the Firearm Brigade;
Bafuer 巴富爾 , *shoubei* of the Ordinary Army.

b) Yingguo shuishixie zongguan tepai zhu Zhonghua lingshi gong-shidachen Yilü suidaiguanyuan英國水師協總官特派駐中華領事公使大臣義律隨帶官員 *(Charles Elliot, the English Assistant Regional Commander of the Royal Navy and Appointed Consul in China and his Accompanying Officials)*:[8]

Yiershi 伊耳士 , *youji* of the Navy;
Matalun 馬他倫 , *shoubei* of the Navy;
Didun 第頓 , *shoubei* of the Navy;
Jiadun 嘉頓 , *shoubei* of the Strategy Brigade of the army at Madalasha Province of India;
Baluo 巴羅 , *shoubei* of the Firearm Brigade of the army at Monyala Province of India;
Mayi 麻伊 , *bazong* of the Navy.

Such translations were in use for decades and can be found in diplomatic documents until the downfall of the Qing dynasty. They were a common practice also during the reign of the Taiping, albeit there were special military ranks used by the Taiping government, because it stood in opposition to the Qing government and the Green Standards. For example in the title of the letter "Li Hongzhao deng zhi Yue Gang Ying Fa jun guanshu" 李鴻昭等致粵港英法軍官書 (Li Hongzhao sends a letter to the English and France military officers in Canton and Hong Kong) it was written:

To the great French Commandant of all Regiments in Guandong province and Naval military affairs;
to the Great British Appointed Supervisor of *tidu* and *junmen* of military affairs of all Regiments in Hong Kong and elsewhere;
to the Great British Appointed Representative of *tidu* and *junmen* of the Royal Navy at Quangtong.[9]

---

8 Cf. "Yapian zhanzheng" 鴉片戰爭 (The Opium War). 1957. In: *Qing Daoguangchao liuzhong mizou* 清道光朝留中密奏 (Secret memorials of the Daoguang period in the Qing dynasty, series no. 3), pp. 520–1.

9 "Li Hongzhao deng zhi Yue Gang Ying Fa jun guanshu" 李鴻昭等致粵港英法軍官書 (Li Hongzhao sends a letter to the English and France military officers in Canton and Hong Kong). 1957. In: *Zhongguo jindaishi ziliao congkan—Taiping tianguo* 中國近代史資料叢刊 — 太平天國 2 (Series of source material on the history of modern China—The Taiping 2). Shanghai: Renmin chubanshe, pp. 718–9.

2. Travel reports

In many Chinese travel reports on the West, compiled in the second half of the nineteenth century, we can also find many examples of such kind of translation of military ranks. A representative example is Guo Songtao's 郭嵩燾 (1818–1891) *Lundun yu Bali riji* 倫敦與巴黎日記 (London and Paris diary) written between 1876 and 1879, as illustrated in the following table:[10]

Table 2: Translations of military ranks in travel reports

Military Rank	English Title	Name
erdeng tidu 二等提督	2nd grade Provincial Military Commander	Lai 賴
sandeng tidu 三等提督	3rd grade *tidu*	Lan 藍
shushi zongbing 水師總兵	Regional Navy Commander	Lanboerde 藍博爾得
shuishi tidu 水師提督	Provincial Military Navy Commander	Laide 賴得
fu tidu	Provincial Vice Military Commander	Kuolunbu 閫倫布
English *fu tidu*		Guierzun 洼爾尊
zongbing		Bomei 波美
fujiang	Regional Vice Commander	Ansheng 安生
English *zongbing*		Leersi 勒爾斯
zongbing		Kelaerke 克拉爾克 (Clark)
shuishitidu		Luade 魯阿得
shuishizongbing		Gelanda 葛蘭達
zongbing		Bilo 畢婁
tidu		Nigeleida 呢格雷達
tidu		Maerkoulaida 馬爾扣來達
shuishi tidu		Erliyade 珥里雅得
shuishi tidu		Feilanei 費拉內
shuishi tidu		Daobeine 道北尼
shuishi zongbing		Mode 墨得
fujiang		Gelahamu 葛拉哈木

---

[10] Cf. Guo Songtao 郭嵩燾. 1984. *Lundun yu Bali riji* 倫敦與巴黎日記 (London and Paris diary). Changsha: Yuelu shushe (*Zouxiang shijie congshu* 走向世界叢書. *From East to West—Chinese Travellers before 1911*), pt. 1, vol. 4, *passim*.

Table 2: Translations of military ranks in travel reports (cont.)

Military Rank	English Title	Name
shuishi tidu		Mieren 密爾恩
shuishitidu		Heersi 赫爾斯
tidu		Bileshike 畢勒士克
zongbing		Lekelia 勒克黎阿
tidu		Shedeweier 舍得威爾
youji	Brigade Commander	Jingmisi 經密斯
youji in China		Youla 优拉
lujuntidu	Provincial Military Commander of the Army	Yinglan 英蘭
shuishitidu		Muxiao 穆削
tidu		Aliyong 阿立庸
yidengtidu 一等提督	1st Rank Provincial Military Commander	Gelanshang 格蘭商
tidu		Laixunsi 來遜斯

Some Chinese officials abroad and overseas students used his translations in order to introduce and describe the Western military rank system. Zhang Deyi 張德彝 (1874–1915) had, for instance, noted down in his diary *Suishi Ying'E ji* 隨使英俄記 (Records of a mission to England and Russia), written between 1876 and 1880:

> [In England] the highest rank of officer of the Navy is called *tidu*; all presidents of the Chamber of Commerce who are older than fourty-five can take this post; vice presidents can take the post *fucan* 副參 (Vice Administrator). All *waiwei* 外委 (Detached)-positions can only be taken by people younger than eighteen, who have at least two years experience on a commercial ship. The study on the Britannia (*Bulitaniya*) is confined to two years and only people between twelve or thirteen years can be selected. All Detached Squad Leaders *(weishu bazong* 委暑把 總) take examinations on their ships every year and the original examination papers must be sent to the *tidu*.[11]

The *Chushi Mei Ri Biguo riji* 出使美日秘國日記 (Diary of the embassies to USA, Japan and Peru), written in 1889–1893 by Cui Guoyin 崔國因 (*jinshi* of 1871), has the following entry:

---

[11] Zhang Deyi 張德彝 . 1984. *Suishi Ying'E ji* 隨使英俄記 (Records of a mission to England and Russia). Changsha: Yuelu shushe (*Zouxiang shijie congshu* 走向世界叢 書 . *From East to West—Chinese Travellers before 1911*), pt. 1, vol. 7, p. 603.

In the next year, the French army will have 12,278 officers and soldiers in total. Among them, 190 *zongbingguan* 總兵官 (Regional Commander), 199 *fuzong bingguan* 副總兵官 (Vice Regional Commander), 1,047 *youji*, 4,160 *qianzong* 千總 (Company Commander), 3,661 *bazong*, 3,021 *fubazong* 副把總 (Vice Squad Leader).[12]

Xu Jianyin 徐建寅 (1845–1901), when introducing the German military system, had used both methods of phonetic transposition and application of the Green Standards ranks in his *Ouyou zalu* 歐游雜錄 (Notes on a travel to Europe), written in 1879–1881:

> [In Germany] a *shaoguan* 哨官 (Company officer) is called *lefutuoneng* 勒夫脱能 (Leutnant), which can be translated to *qianzong*. An *yiguan* 翼官 (Officer of Imperial Guardsmen) is called *jiabidun* 甲必頓 (Kapitän), which can be translated to *shoubei*. An *yingguan* 營官 (Brigade Officer) called *meiyueer* 美約而 (Major), which can be translated to *dusi*.[13]

3. Military Publications

Numerous Western military publications were translated and published by the translation division of the Jiangnan Arsenal between the 1860s and 1890s under the supervision of John Fryer (Fu Lanya 傅蘭雅, 1839–1929). The main method employed here was also the mechanical application of official ranks of the Green Standards, as is seen in the above mentioned *Examination of the English Royal Navy*, in which, in addition to phonetic transposition, also the official ranks of the Green Standards were applied:

> *Qiguan* 旗官 (Flag Officers) encompass, first, the *shuishi tidu*; second, the *fu shuishi tidu* 副水師提督 (Vice Naval *tidu*), and third, the *hou shui shi tidu* 后水師提督 (Rear Naval *tidu*) as well as those responsible for management of army units, in Western language called *aimeilai* (Admiral);
> *zongbing* in Western language called *kangmoduer* (Commodore);
> *fujiang* in Western language called *jiabidun* (Captain);
> *canjiang* in Western language called *shitaiwu jiabidun* 施太勿甲必頓 (Staff Captain);
> *youji* in Western language called *kemante* (Commander);

---

[12] Cui Guoyin 崔國因. [1889–1893]. *Chushi Mei Ri Biguo riji* 出使美日秘國日記 (Diary of the embassies to USA, Japan and Peru), in: Shen Yunlong 沈雲龍 (ed.). *Jindai Zhongguo shiliao congkang* 近代中國史料叢刊 (Series of source material on the history of modern China). Shanghai: Shanghai chubanshe, vol. 28, p. 428.

[13] Xu Jianyin 徐建寅. 1984. *Ouyou zalu* 歐游雜錄 (Notes on a travel to Europe). Changsha: Yuelu shushe (*Zouxiang shijie congshu* 走向世界叢書. *From East to West—Chinese Travellers before 1911*), pt. 1, vol. 6, p. 689.

dusi in Western language called *shitaiwu kemante* 施太勿喀曼特 (Staff Commander);

shoubei in Western language called *lutuona* (Lieutenant);

xingchuan shoubei 行船守備 (Accompanying Naval Brigade Commander) in Western language called *lutuona* (Lieutenant);

qianzong in Western language called *xia lutuona* (Sub-lieutenant).[14]

In the same way, French military ranks of the army and navy were translated in the *Faguo shuishikao* 法國水師考 (Examination of the French Royal Navy):

Shuishi tidu is equivalent to the rank of the *yuanshuai* 元帥 (Commander-in-chief) of the army.

Erdeng shuishi tidu is equivalent to the rank of the *tidu* of the army.

Sandeng shuishi tidu is equivalent to the rank of the *zongbing* of the army.

Chuanzhu 船主 (Captain) is equivalent to the rank of the *fujiang* of the army.

Sanzhiwei chuanzhi 三枝桅船主 (Captain of a three-master) is equivalent to the rank of the *canjiang* of the army.

Toudeng shoubei 頭等守備 (First rank *shoubei*) is equivalent to the rank of the *youji* of the army.

Erdeng shoubei 二等守備 (Second rank *shoubei*) is equivalent to the rank of the *dusi* of the army.

Qiguan (Flag officer) is equivalent to the rank of the *shoubei* of the army.

Erdeng xuesheng 二等學生 (Second rank student) and *toudeng xuesheng* 頭等學生 (First rank student) are equivalent to the rank of the *qiangzong* of the army.[15]

Again, in the *Deguo junzhi shuyao* 德國軍制述要 (Description of the military system of Germany) the German military ranks are translated in the same way as (in hierarchical order from the highest to the lowest rank): *tidu, zongbing, erdengzongbing, fujiang, youji, dusi, erdengdusi, shoubei, qianzong, bazong, erdengbazong, shaqin* 沙芹,

---

[14] John Fryer and Zhong Tianwei, 1886.

[15] Cf. Henry B. Loch (Luo Hengli 羅亨利 and Qu Anglai 瞿昂來 (trs.). 1886. *Faguo shuishikao* 法國水師考 (Examination of the French Royal Navy). Shanghai: Shanghai jiqi zhizaoju, pp. 60–1. There are several other translations of this work done by Zhong Tianwei 鐘天緯 or John Fryer.

waiwei, *shenzhang* 什長 , *bubing* 步兵(infantry).[16] Only *shaqin* 沙芹 is a phonetic transposition for Sergeant.

4. Chinese Bilingual Dictionaries

The above cited examples show that there was no standard translation of military ranks, partly because of the different military systems and ranks in China and the Western countries, but even more so because of the different interpretations of the military systems through the translators. Different translators would sometimes produce quite different translations, which is revealed in the diversity of translations proposed in Late Qing dictionaries. In order to give evidence for this diversity, I selected four representative and very influential English-Chinese dictionaries: the English-Chinese part of Robert Morrison's (Ma Lixun 馬禮遜 , 1782–1834) *Wuche yunfu* 五車韻府 ,[17] the *Yinghan zidian* 英漢字典 by Walter Henry Medhurst (Mai Dusi 麥都思 , 1823–1885),[18] Wilhelm Lobscheid's (Luo Cunde 羅存德) *Yinghan zidian*[19] and the *Yinghan Cuilin yunfu* 英漢萃林韻府 by Justus Doolittle (Lu Gongming 盧公明 , 1824–1880).[20] Although my analysis is based on all translated names of military ranks that we can find in those lexicons, I will only present three examples to illustrate the point here:

---

[16] Cf. Shen Dunhe 沈敦和 and H. Hildebrand (Xi Leba 錫樂巴) (trs.). 1895. *Deguo junzhi shuyao* 德國軍制述要 (Important aspects of the German military system). [Translation of the narratation of Ritzenstein (Laichunshitai 來春石泰)]. Jinling edition, pp. 4–6.

[17] Robert Morrison (Ma Lixun 馬禮遜). 1815–23. *Wuche yunfu* 五車韻府 . *A Dictionary of the Chinese Language, in Three Parts. Part the first; containing Chinese and English, arranged according to the radicals, part the second, Chinese and English arranged alphabetically, and part the third, English and Chinese.* Macao: Honourable East India Company's Press.

[18] Walter Henry Medhurst (Maidusi 麥都思). 1847. *English and Chinese Dictionary.* Shanghai.

[19] Wilhelm Lobscheid (Luo Cunde 羅存德). 1866–69. *Ying-Hua zidian* 英華字典 . *English and Chinese Dictionary with Punti and Mandarin Pronunciation.* 4 vols. Hong Kong: Daily Press Office.

[20] Justus Doolittle (Lu Gongming 盧公明). 1872–73. *Ying-Hua cuilin yunfu* 英華萃林韻府 . *A Vocabulary and Hand-Book of the Chinese Language, romanized in the Mandarin dialect.* 2 vols. Fuzhou, Shanghai: Rosario, Marcal and Company.

Table 3: Diversity of translations for military ranks in Chinese bilingual dictionaries

	Morrison	Medhurst	Lobscheid	Doolittle	Modern Chinese
General	*zongbing-guan* 總兵官 (Regional Commander), *jiangjun*	*zongbing-guan, jiangjun, yuanshu, jiangshuai* 將帥, *zhu-shuai* 主帥, *tidu, yimu* 夷目	*jiangjun, zongbing-guan, yuanshuai*	*jiangjun, futong* 都統, *yuanshuai, jiangshuai, zongbing, junshuai* 軍帥	*lujun shangjiang* 陸軍上將 (Senior General of the Army), *jiangjun*
Admiral	*shuijun-detidu* 水軍的提督, *shuishitidu*	*shuishizong-bingguan* 水師總兵官, *shuishitidu*	*shuishi tidu*	*shuishi tidu, shuishi zongbing-guan*	*haijun-shangjiang* 海軍上將 (Senior General of the Navy)
Captain	*chuanzhu* 船主 (Capital), *qianzong*	*youji, baizong, qianzong, chuanzhu, shuishitong-ling* 水師統領 (Head of Brigade of the Navy)	*chuanzhu, shoubei, shofu, qianzong, qianfuzhang* 千夫長 *baifuzhang* 百夫長	*shuishitong-ling*	*lujunshangwei* 陸軍上尉 (Senior Commandant of the Army), *haijunshang-xiao* 海軍上校 (Senior Lieutenant of the Navy)

Robert Morrison and Walter Henry Medhurst were English missionaries and famous sinologists who were deeply involved in Sino-foreign contacts before the Opium War. In a certain sense, their dictionaries functioned as initiators for the translation of military ranks. They are, on the one hand, the product of their own practical experiences; on the other hand, both also exerted a strong influence on their contemporaries and their dictionaries served as guiding examples for later publications.

3. INDISCRIMINATE APPLICATION OF THE RANKS OF THE EIGHT BANNERS

Table 3 contains in addition to the official ranks of the Green Standards also a few ranks of the Eight Banners, for example *dutong* 都統 (Commander-in-chief) and *fudutong* 副都統 (Vice Commander-in-chief). Official ranks of the Eight Banners were only rarely used to translate the (Western) military ranks during late Qing dynasty, but there are some instances to be found.

The major official ranks of the Eight Banners are: *dutong* 都統 (Commander-in-chief), *fudutong* 副都統 (Vice Commander-in-chief), *xiaoqi canling* 驍騎參領 (Regimental Commander of Cavalry Brigade), *fuxiaoqi canling* 副驍騎參領 (Vice Regimental Commander of Cavalry Brigade), *zuoling* 佐領 (Company Commander), *xieling* 協領 (Assistant Commandant), *xiaoqixiao* 驍騎校 (Lieutenant of Cavalry Brigade), etc.

When Ma Jianzhong 馬建忠 (1844–1900) explained the Western navy system to Li Hongzhang 李鴻章 (1823–1901), he used both the ranks from the Green Standards as well as from the Eight Banners.

> The ranks of the foreign Navy can be classified into three grades, *duling* 督領 (Supervisor-in-chief), *guanling* 管領 (Supervisor)[21] and *zuoling* 佐領 (Company Commander). Each of these grades can be further classified into three classes *ji* 級 . Those who are alone responsible to supervise military affairs and lead military warships are called *duling* 督領 . This rank can be further specified into *tongshuai* 統帥 (Commander-in-chief), *fushuai* 副帥 (Vice Commander) and *pianshuai* 偏帥 (Commander-in-chief in a Campaigning Army).
>
> The same distinctions are made according to the number of warships they lead in the navy and this is again classified into different *pin* (rank) of *ti* 提 and *zhen* 鎮 . The officer responsible for the navigation and management of the entire ship is called *guanling* 管領 , and there are *zongling* 總領 (Wing Commander/Brigadier), *fuling* 副領 (Vice Wing Commander/Vice Brigadier), *canling* 參領 (Commandant/Colonel). Accordingly, also in the Navy the ranks are classified into different grades of official ranks as *fu* 副 (vice), *can* 參 (regimental) and *you* 游 (mobile). Each official is installed according to his qualification with regard to the size of the warships and his rank in the official service. Students, sent from the training ship to learn how to drive warships, are

---

[21] Chief clerk in the establishments of the Imperial Princes. Cf. Hucker 1985, p. 286.

called *shaocong* 少從 (Junior Assistant), which is one grade below the Three Assistants (*sanzuo* 三佐). …

Before climbing from *shaocong* to *canzuo* 參佐 (Regimental Assistant) and from *canzuo* to *fuzuo* 副佐 (Vice Assistant), a minimum service of two years on a military ship has to be performed. A *fuzuo* has to go on an ocean ship for at least two years. After that he can be promoted to a *zhengzuo* 正佐 (Upper Assistant). Officers serve as *zhengzuo* for four years, and in this period they ship the ocean once during the first two years. After that, they can be promoted to a *canling*; or stay at the same post for three years and command smaller ships in the ocean for one year; they can also stay at the same post for four years, but only after two years experience of an acting *fuling* and Commander of middle size ships they can be promoted to a *fuling*.[22]

Ma Jianzhong continues to explain each rank and each promotion procedure in that way and his account is therefore much more comprehensive than earlier descriptions, because he not only names the official ranks but also gives the details about the soldier ranks.

Xue Fucheng 薛福成 (1838–1894) and Zhang Deyi 張德彝 (1847–1915), too, have both introduced Western soldier ranks and explained their functions:

In the Navy of European countries such as Germany and France *bingding* 兵丁 (soldier) is of the same rank as *shuishou* 水手 (sailor). In the English Navy *bingding* and *shuishou* have different kinds of assignments and therefore their tasks have to be specified [by the different titles]. Therefore the English Navy is superior to the Navy of other countries.[23]

A minor offense would be punished with a one week confinement. Punishment for a serious offense may include the degrading to the second rank. Another offense may include a further degrading to the third rank. Although there are these different ranks of first, second and third among the soldiers, their pay is the same. The purpose of these distinc-

---

[22] Ma Jianzhong 馬建忠 . 1961. "Shikezhai jiyan jixing. Shang Li Boxiang fuyi He xueshi Ruzhang zoushe shuishishu" 適可齋記言記行 . 上李伯相覆議何學士如璋奏設 水師書 (Record of speeches and activities in Shikezhai. A letter to Li Boxiang regarding a memorial to establish a Navy suggested by scholar He Ruzhang), *Zhongguo jindaishi ziliaochongkang—Yangwu yundong*, series no. 1. Shanghai: Shanghai renmin chubanshe, pp. 403–51.

[23] Xue Fucheng 薛福成 . 1985. "Chushi Ying Fa Yi Bi siguo riji" 出使英法義比四 國日記 (Diary of my diplomatic mission to the four countries England, France, Italy and Belgium). Changsha: Yuelu chubanshe (*Zouxiang shijie congshu* 走向世界叢書 . *From East to West—Chinese Travellers before 1911*), pt. 1, vol. 8, p. 254.

tions lies in revealing their excellent or bad quality and to encourage them by that means.[24]

4. Descriptive terms

Descriptive terms appeared frequently in the documents about the Sino-French War between 1884 and 1885. Because rank insignia for French Army officers consisted of broad gold stripes encircling the lower sleeve of the uniform, it became common practice to count the numbers of stripes (*hua* 劃) and rings *(quan* 圈) to describe the military ranks of the French Army.

See, for instance, the *Qingying riji* 請纓日記 (Qingying diary) from Tang Jingsung 唐景崧 (*jinshi* of 1865, d. 1902):

> On April 19, between three and five o'clock, I have received a special dispatch from Yuanting 淵亭 from which I learned about the fight with the French Army at Zhiqiao 紙橋 on the thirteenth of this month and the great victory. Li Weili 李威利 , of a five stripe military rank, who was planning to occupy Vietnam, was killed during the fight, as well as thirty soldiers of four or less stripes ranks and about two hundred ordinary French soldiers. The wounded are innumerable.[25]

Also the correspondence of Xu Yanxu 徐延旭 (*Xu Yanxu laiwang handu* 徐延旭來往函牘) contains similar descriptions of French officers:

> Altogether one officer with three stripes, two officers with two stripes and three with one stripe were killed.[26]

> Moreover, a French officer with seven stripes had led four big cannon ships and one big ironclad from Saigon. On June 22 about four officers with five stripes, six officers with four stripes and more than ten officers with one to four stripes arrived at Tushan 涂山 which lies outside the coastal defense.[27]

---

[24] Zhang Deyi 1984, pt. 1, vol. 7, p. 598.

[25] Tang Jingsong 唐景崧 . 1957. "Qingying riji" 請纓日記 (Qingying Diary), in: *Zhongguo jindaishi ziliao congkan—Zhong Fa zhanzheng* 中國近代史資料叢刊 — 中法戰爭 2 (Series of source material on the history of modern China—The Sino-French War 2). Shanghai: Renmin chubanshe, p. 77.

[26] "Xu Yanxu laiwang handu" 徐延旭來往函牘 (Xu Yanxu's correspondence). 1957. In: *Zhongguo jindaishi ziliao congkan—Zhong Fa zhanzheng* 中國近代史資料叢刊 — 中法戰爭 2 (Series of source material on the history of modern China—The Sino-French War 2). Shanghai: Renmin chubanshe, pp. 249.

[27] Ibid., p. 338.

And the same can be observed in other war correspondences, like Zhang Shusheng's 張樹聲 *Zhang Shusheng laiwang handu* 張樹聲來往函牘 (Zhang Shusheng's correspondence) and the military documents of Feng Zicai 馮子材 (1818–1903) *Feng Zicai jundu jiyao* 馮子材軍牘集要 (Collection of important military correspondence of Feng Zicai):

> On the fifth of the first month a ship of *Guoluxing* came from your province along with the flood, with one officer of two rings (*quan*) and one with three rings on it. The consular communications reveal that it returned on the sixth of the first month.[28]

> These soldiers have killed more than thousand enemy soldiers and more than one hundred officers of five stripes rank and below.[29]

The officers with one to three stripes or rings mentioned above are usually junior officers of the French Army. Those with four to six stripes or rings are officers of middle class and those with seven stripes or rings and above are generals.

5. LOANWORDS (*JIEZIFA* 借字法)

For modern China, Japan is one of the countries with closest military contact although its army was not as powerful as the European or American armies. In the late Qing, Japanese military ranks were translated into Chinese as loanwords, which is still practiced today.

The Japanese system of military ranks in practice before the Meiji Restoration had stemmed from the Chinese military system of the Tang dynasty. In the course of military modernization from 1869 to 1870, the Japanese navy and army ranks were reorganized and mainly coined after the system of Western military ranks. But at the same time, they adopted ancient Chinese words connected to military and official affairs, such as *jiang, zuo, wei, shi* etc., which were also still

---

[28] "Zhang Shusheng laiwang handu" 張樹聲來往函牘 (Zhang Shusheng's Correspondence). 1957. In: *Zhongguo jindaishi ziliao congkan—Zhong Fa zhanzheng* 中國近代史資料叢刊 — 中法戰爭 2 (Series of source material on the history of modern China—The Sino-French War 2). Shanghai: Renmin chubanshe, p. 527.

[29] Feng Zicai 馮子材 . 1957. *Feng Zicai jundu jiyao* 馮子材軍牘集要 (Collection of important military correspondence of Feng Zicai), in: *Zhongguo jindaishi ziliao congkan—Zhong Fa zhanzheng* 中國近代史資料叢刊 — 中法戰爭 2 (Series of source material on the history of modern China—The Sino-French War 2). Shanghai: Renmin chubanshe, p. 96

used as standard terms for Japanese military ranks. The situation can be seen in table 4:

Table 4: Military ranks of the Japanese Army and Navy from 1895–1945

	The Army (*Lujun* 陸軍)	The Navy (*Haijun* 海軍)
jiangguan 將官 (General)	*lujun dajiang* 陸軍大將 *lujunzhongjiang* 陸軍中將 *lujun shaoiang* 陸軍少將	*haijun dajiang* 海軍大將 *haijun zhongjiang* 海軍中將 *haijun shaojiang* 海軍少將
zuoguan 佐官 *shangchangguan* 上長官	*lujun dazuo* 陸軍大佐 *lujun zhongzuo* 陸軍中佐 *lujun shaozuo* 陸軍少佐	*haijun dazuo* 海軍大佐 *haijun zhongzuo* 海軍中佐 *haijuns haozuo* 海軍少佐
weiguan 尉官 (*shiguan* 士官) (Noncommissioned Officer)	*lujun dawei* 陸軍大尉 *lujun zhongwei* 陸軍中尉 *lujun shaowei* 陸軍少尉	*haijun dawei* 海軍大尉 *haijun zhongwei* 海軍中尉 *haijun shaowei* 海軍少尉
zhunshiguan 准士官	*lujun zhunwei* 陸軍准尉 (Warrant Officer of the Army)	*haijun zhunwei* 海軍准尉
xiashiguan 下士官 (Junior Noncommissioned Officer)	*lujun caozhang* 陸軍曹長 *lujun juncao* 陸軍軍曹 *lujun wuzhang* 陸軍伍長	*haijun caozhang* 海軍曹長 *haijun juncao* 海軍軍曹 *haijun wuzhang* 海軍伍長
bing 兵 (Soldier)	*lujun shangdengbing* 陸軍上等兵 (Senior Soldier of the Army), —*yidengbing* 陸軍一等兵 (1st Rank Army Soldier), —*erdengbing* 陸軍二等兵 (2nd Rank Army Soldier)	*haijun yidengbing* 海軍一等兵 (1st Rank Navy Soldier), —*erdengbing* 海軍二等兵 (2nd Rank Navy Soldier), —*sandengbing* 海軍三等兵 (3rd Rank Navy Soldier), —*sidengbing* 海軍四等兵 (4th Rank Navy Soldier), —*wudengbing* 海軍五等兵 (5th Rank Navy Soldier)

These new Japanese military ranks did not only set the standard for the Japanese army, but also provided a convenient model for the translations of military ranks into Chinese. As the Japanese military designations were written in Chinese characters, the titles and ranks could directly be taken over. Therefore the use of official ranks of the Green Standards gradually fell into oblivion.

In most of the documents on the Sino-Japanese War from 1894 to 1895, we can find such translations. Famous Japanese officers who attended the war, as the Vice-Admirals Itō Sukeyuki 伊東祐亨 (called *haijun zhongjiang*) and Kabayama Sukenori 樺山資紀 (called *haijun zhongjiang*) or Captain Tōgō Heihachirō 東鄉平八郎 (called *haijun dazhuo)* are entitled with officer ranks that are written with the same characters both in Chinese and Japanese.

In China, Guo Songtao and Huang Zunxian 黃遵憲 (1848–1905) were among the first to describe the structure of the Japanese military organization. In his *Lundun yu Bali riji*, Guo Songtao wrote:

> On September 22 of the third year of the Guangxu … the ambassador Ueno 上野 presented the book *Guanyuan mingjian* 官員名鑒 (Mirror of official ranks) to me which contained all official ranks of his country … *Dajiang, zhongjiang, shaojiang, dazuo, zhongzuo, shaozuo, dawei, zhongwei, shaowei*, are all military officers.[30]

Huang Zunxian's *Riben guozhi* 日本國志 (Treatise on Japan) also contains a list of the Japanese army ranks.[31]

Since the 1870s it became common practice to combine the indiscriminate application of official ranks of the Green Standards for Western military ranks and Japanese loanwords to translate Japanese military ranks. These two methods would even be used together in one single document, like in the *Kaocha zhengzhi riji* 考察政治日記 (Diary of the inspection of political systems), compiled between 1905 and 1906, in which Japanese soldiers and officers are mentioned as *bubing shaozuo* 步兵少佐 like Satō Yasunosuke 佐藤安之助 , *haijun dajiang* like Tōgō Heihachirō or as *lujun dajiang* like Baron Sakuma Samata 佐久間左馬太 , just like the Japanese rank system and European and American soldiers are called *lujun canjiang* like "Loubeifuer" 樓貝佛爾 , *haijun tidu* like "Mageluofu" 馬哥羅夫 , *tidu* like "Maergai" 馬爾改 , *fujiang* like "Feifu" 斐福 or *shoubei* like "Langbeier" 朗倍爾 according to ranks of the Green Standard.[32]

---

[30] Guo Songtao 1984, pp. 340–2.

[31] Huang Gongqing 黃公慶 (i.e. Huang Zunxian). [1890]. "Riben guozhi" 日本國志 (Treatise on Japan). vol. 22: *bingzhi* 兵志 (Military), in: Shen Yunlong 沈雲龍 (ed.). *Jindai Zhongguo shiliao congkan, xuji* 近代中國史料叢刊續輯 (Collection of historical materials on Modern China, second series). Taibei: Wenhai chubanshe, vol. 96, p. 597.

[32] Cf. *Kaocha zhengzhi riji* 考察政治日記 (Diary of the inspection of political systems). 1984–1986. Changsha: Yuelu shushe (*Zouxiang shijie congshu* 走向世界叢書 . *From East to West—Chinese Travellers before 1911*), pt. 1, vol. 9, pp. 572–4; 639; 643; 645; 661.

In some official documents of the late Qing official ranks of the
Green Standards are also applied to translate Japanese military ranks.
Such translations often appeared in translations of Western documents
translated from Japanese or were the result of the cooperation of Chinese and Western translators. An example for the first case is the official *Lieguo lujunzhi* 列國陸軍制 (The military systems of various
countries) published by the translation department of the Jiangnan
Arsenal;[33] representative for the latter case is the famous *Zhongdong
zhanji benmo* 中東戰記本末 (Full account of the Sino-Japanese War)
published by the Guangxuehui 廣學會 (Society for the Diffusion of
Christian and General Knowledge Among the Chinese).[34]

6. THE FORMATION OF A FIXED TERMINOLOGY FOR THE CHINESE MILITARY SYSTEM

The Chinese defeat in the Sino-Japanese War engendered various
activities to fundamentally reform the Chinese army into a modern
army. Instead of merely changing the military practice by using new
weapons and new technology it was deemed necessary to completely
alter the military system. Therefore it was decided to emulate the
Western and Japanese military systems in order to train a new
national army. Accordingly, in June 1903 a bureau of military training
(*lianbingchu* 練兵處) was established and functioned as the new general organization for military training under the supervision of Tie
Liang 鐵良 (b. 1863) and Yuan Shikai 袁世凱 (1859–1916). Subsequently, from December 1905 to March 1911, different sets of regulations were issued by the Bureau of Military Training, Bureau of
Military Consulting and the Ministry of War. With the "Key regulations of officer and noncommissioned officer ranks and the promotion
of army staff members to officers" (*Lujun junguan junzuo renzhi
dengjiji lujun renyuan buguan tizhi zhaiyao zhangcheng* 陸軍軍官軍佐
任職等級暨陸軍人員補官體制摘要章程), "Regulations on the gradual
promotion of army staff members to officers" (*Lujun renyuan zanxing*

---

[33] Cf. Young J. Allen (Lin Lezhi 林樂知) and Qu Anglai 瞿昂來 (trs.). 1889.
Lieguo lujunzhi 列國陸軍制 (The military systems of various countries). Shanghai:
Jiangnan zhizaoju.

[34] Cf. Cai Erkang 蔡爾康 and Young J. Allen (Lin Lezhi 林樂知)(comps.). 1890.
Zhongdong zhanji benmo 中東戰記本末 (Full account of the Sino-Japanese War).
Shanghai: Guangxuehui.

buguan zhangcheng 陸軍人員暫行補官章程), and the "Imperial regulations and illustrated explanations on style and colour of army school uniforms" (*Zouding lujunjundui xuetangfuse zhangjitushuo* 奏定陸軍軍隊學堂服色章記圖説), the transfer of the Western military system was gradually accomplished. According to this new system, the officer rank was classified into three grades: *shang* (senior), *zhong* (ordinary) and *ci* 次(lower class) and each grade was further classified into three *ji* 級 (classes).[35]

The main difference between this system of ranks and the traditional rank systems lies in the fact that now the soldiers, as the most numerous staff in the army, are included into the rank system. Now the succession of ranks was regulated from the highest commander down to the lowest ordinary soldier. Moreover, the military officer grades were now classified into three grades and nine classes.

Although a new system had come into existence now, which was almost identical with the Japanese and Western military system, it would be logical to think that also the ranks and names should be identical. Yet, these military ranks were only used to designate the ranks of the own Qing government army, but not for the translation of foreign military ranks of foreign armies. In fact, the indiscriminate application of officer ranks of the Green Standards and loanword-translation from Japanese were still the dominant translation practices. This might be due to the inertia of a well-known practice or the short life of this new set of military ranks. But more importantly, the dispensing with using the old order of military ranks for coining new terms was due to the historical circumstances of the Xinhai Revolution.

When the new Chinese government was founded in Nanjing on January 1, 1912, the president Sun Yat-sen (Sun Zhongshan) 孫中山

---

[35] The first class of *shangdeng* 上等comprises *dajiangjun* 大將軍 (General-in-chief), *jiangjun*, *zhengdutong* 正都統 (Senior Commander-in-chief), the second is *fudutong* 副都統 , the third is *xiedutong* 協都統 (Junior Commander-in-chief). The first class of *zhongdeng* is *zhengcanling*, the second is *fucanling*, the third is *xiecanling*. The first class of *cideng* is *zhengjunxiao*正軍校 , the second is *fujunxiao*副軍校 , the third is *xiejunxiao*協軍校 . Below the *junguan* (Officer) is the *ewaijunguan*額外軍官 (Special Officer). Furthermore, the *junshi* 軍士 (Noncommissioned Officer) is classified to *shangshi*上士 , *zhongshi*中士 , *xiashi*下士 . Below the *junshi*軍士 his subordinates *bing* are classified to *zhengbing* 正兵 (Ordinary Soldier), *yidengbing* 一等兵 (1st Rank Soldier), *erdengbing* 二等兵 (2nd Rank Soldier). Cf. Wen Gongzhi 文公直 . 1930. *Zuijin sanshinian Zhongguo junshishi* 最近三十年中國軍事史 (The Chinese military history of the last thirty years). Shanghai: Taipingyang shudian, pp. 44–6.

(1866–1925) attempted a fundamental break with the past. Thus he issued the "Decree on army uniforms" 軍士制服令 (Junshi zhifu ling) and established a new system of military ranks.[36] Only one month later, Sun Yat-sen promulgated again *Lujun guanzuo shibing jiejibiao* 陸軍官佐士兵階級表 (Table of ranks of officers and noncommissioned officers and soldiers of the army) to revise grades and names of military ranks.[37] In the same year on August 19, Yuan Shikai, the new assigned president, issued a "Table of ranks of official and noncommissioned officers and soldiers of the army" (*Lujun guanzuo shibing dengjibiao* 陸軍官佐士兵等級表) to reformulate the military ranks again. On October 20 the government of Yuan Shikai issued also a "Table of ranks of official and noncommissioned officers and soldiers of the Navy" (*Haijun guanzuoshibing dengjibiao* 海軍官佐士兵等級表) which classified the military ranks of the navy according to the ranks of the army. The only difference is that soldiers are classified into five grades, they are *yidengbing*, *erdengbing*, *sandengbing* and two additional grades, the *yideng lianbing* 一等練兵 (1st Grade Trainee), *erdeng lianbing* 二等練兵 (2nd Grade Trainee).[38]

---

[36] Cf. Sun Yat-sen 孫中山 . 1911. "Junshi zhifulin" 軍士制服令 (Decree on army uniforms), *Dongfang zazhi* 8.10, p. 9. Already before the Xinhai Revolution, the Tongmenghui, under the leadership of Sun Yat-sen, had planned the reform of military ranks for a future the *Minguojundui* 民國軍隊 (Republican army) as laid down in the *Gemingfanglüe* 革命方略 (A general plan of revolution). It comprised the following nine successive grades: *dudu* 都督 , *fudu* 副督 , *candu* 參督 , *duwei* 督尉 , *fuwei* 副尉 , *canwei* 參尉 , *duxiao* 都校 , *fuxiao* 副校 , *canxiao* 參校 . Cf. Zou Lu 鄒魯 . 1957. "Zhongguo tongmenghui" 中國同盟會 (The Chinese alliance), in: *Zhongguo jindaishi ziliao congkan—Xinhai geming 2* 中國近代史資料叢刊 — 辛亥革命 2 (Series of source material on the history of Modern China—The Revolution of 1911 2). Shanghai: Renmin chubanshe, p. 17.

[37] Cf. Zhang Jianji 張建基 . 1989. "Minguo junxiang zhidu shulüe" 民國軍銜制度述略 (Brief account of the military rank system in Republican China), *Junshi lishi yanjiu* 3, p. 59.

[38] Cf. Yuan Shikai 袁世凱 . 1912. "Haijun guanzuo shibing dengjibiao" 海軍官佐士兵等級表 (Table of ranks of soldiers and officers of the Navy), in: *Zhonghua minguo zhengfu gongbao* 中華民國政府公報 , August 19, 1912 and October 20, 1912. Reprint Taibei: Wenhai chubanshe.

Table 5: Four alterations of the military ranks of the modern army

Green Standards	1905–1911	January 1912	February 1912	Aug.–Oct. 1912
tidu	*dajiangjun* 大將軍, *jiangjun*, *zhengdutong*	*dajiangxiao*	*dajiangjun*	*shangjiang*
zongbing	*fudutong*	*zhongjiangxiao* 中將校	*zuojiangjun* 左將軍	*zhongjiang*
fujiang	*xiedutong*	*shaojiangxiao* 少將校	*youjiangjun* 右將軍	*shaojiang*
canjiang	*zhengcanling*	*daling* 大領	*daduwei* 大都尉	*shangxiao* 上校
youji	*fucanling*	*zhongling* 中領	*zuoduwei*	*zhongxiao* 中校
dusi	*xiecanling*	*shaoling* 少領	*youduwei*	*shaoxiao* 少校
shoubei	*zhengjunxiao*	*dawei* 大尉	*dajunxiao*	*shangwei*
qingzong	*fujunxiao*	*zhongwei* 中尉	*zuojunxiao*	*zhongwei*
bazong	*xiejunxiao*	*shaowei* 少尉	*youjunxiao*	*shaowei*
jingzhiwaiwei	*ewaijunguan*	*ewaijunguan*	*siwuzhang* 司務長	*zhongwei*
	shangshi	*yidengmubing* 一等目兵	*shangshi*	*shangshi*
	zhongshi	*erdengmubing* 二等目兵	*zhongshi*	*zhongshi*
	xiashi		*xiashi*	*xiashi*
	zhengbing	*yidengbing*	*shangdengbing*	*shangdengbing* (the Army), *yidengbing* (the Navy)
	yidengbing	*erdengbing*	*yidengbing*	*yidengbing* (the Army), *erdengbing* (the Navy)
	erdengbing		*erdengbing*	*erdengbing* (the Army), *sandengbing* (the Navy)
				yidengliang-bing (the Navy)
				erdengliang-bing (the Navy)

The table reveals that although different designations were chosen in the four different rank systems, there is a general common tendency to favor traditional Chinese official ranks. The first regulations contained mainly official ranks of the Eight Banners. The highest officer is called *jiangjun*, which occurred among many designations of the imperial nobility and also as head of the garrison troops of the Eight Banners, like in *Jiangning jiangjun* 江寧將軍 and *Guangzhou jiangjun* 廣州將軍. *Dutong* is the highest commander in each Banner and the Manchurian name is *gushanezhen* 固山額真. *Canling*, which is *jialaezhen* 甲喇額真 in Manchu, is a 3a grade military official. *Junxiao* 軍校 is used in the infantry of the Eight Banners as *bujunxiao* 步軍校 and in the third Banner of the Yuanmingyuan 圓明圓 there is the *hujunxiao* 護軍校 (Summer-Palace Guard Brigade). Subsequently, even older terms were used, which originate from periods before the Qing dynasty. *Xiao* originates from the term *baxiao* 八校 (Eight Commandants) founded by Han Wudi 漢武帝 (r. 140–86 BC), *jiang* and *wei* originate from military officers of Jin 晉 of the Chunqiu-period, *shangshi*, *zhongshi* and *xiashi* were the designations for officers below the Ministers and Grand Masters (*qingdafu* 卿大夫) in the three dynasties of the Xia 夏, Shang 商 and Zhou 周.

Secondly, the four different systems also reveal a strong influence from Japan. The names appearing in the third row, such as *dawei*, *zhongwei* and *shaowei* are identical with Japanese official ranks. The fifth row, which shows the system of Yuan Shikai, is almost a copy of the Japanese military rank system: The Japanese officer rank is divided into three grades, *jiang*, *zuo*, *wei* and we find the same classifications as *jiang*, *xiao*, *wei* in the regulations issued by Yuan. Furthermore, every grade would be further classified into the three classes *da*, *zhong*, *shao* in the Japanese army and this is mirrored by Yuan's classification as *shang*, *zhong*, *shao*. Japanese soldiers have three grades in the army and five in the navy and this is also copied in the system of Yuan. Only for the noncommissioned official ranks Yuan had used traditional Chinese precedents. If we take into consideration the enormous impact of the Japanese language on the formation of a modern Chinese lexicon, the influence of Japanese military studies on the reform of the modern Chinese army and the powerful position of Yuan Shikai's Beiyang army after the Sino-Japanese War, this development is not very surprising.

It is also obvious that the fifth row, representing the changes made between August and October 1912, reveals the merging of Western, Japanese and traditional Chinese elements with regard to content and form. Because of its clarity and direct comprehensibility, this set of ranks was quickly accepted and it soon substituted the practice of applying official ranks of the Green Standards, which were, moreover, dissolved after the downfall of Qing dynasty. Subsequently it was adopted by all later translators, as it seemed suitable to translate all military systems of foreign armies, except from the Japanese army. If we look at the further history of military ranks, this system was not only adopted by the Beiyang army, but also by the latter army of the Guomindang and also the Chinese People's Liberation Army and has continuously been in use until today. In the course of time, Russian military science has deeply influenced the PLA after the 1950s, yet with regard to military terminology, especially the system of military ranks remained unchanged and was to a large part received under the influence of Japan at the beginning of this century.

Translated by Natascha Vittinghoff

REFERENCES

Allen, Young J. (Lin Lezhi 林樂知) and Qu Anglai 瞿昂來 (trs.). 1889. *Lieguo lujunzhi* 列國陸軍制 (The military systems of various countries). Shanghai: Jiangnan zhizaoju.

Cai Erkang 蔡爾康 and Young J. Allen (Lin Lezhi 林樂知) (comps.). 1890. *Zhong-dong zhanji benmo* 中東戰記本末(Full account of the Sino-Japanese War). Shanghai: Guangxuehui.

Cui Guoyin崔國因. [1889–93]. *Chushi Mei Ri Biguo riji*出使美日秘國日記(Diary of the embassies to USA, Japan and Peru), in: Shen Yunlong 沈雲龍 (ed.). *Jindai Zhongguo shiliao congkang* 近代中國史料叢刊 (Series of source material on the history of modern China). Shanghai: Shanghai chubanshe, vol. 28.

Doolittle, Justus (Lu Gongming 廬公明). 1872–73. *Ying-Hua cuilin yunfu* 英華萃林韻府. *A Vocabulary and Hand-Book of the Chinese Language, romanized in the Mandarin dialect*. 2 vols. Fuzhou, Shanghai: Rosario, Marcal and Co.

Fang Weigui. 2001. "*Yi, yang, xi, wai* and other terms: The Transition from 'Barbarian' to 'Foreigner' in Late Imperial China", in: Michael Lackner, Iwo Amelung and Joachim Kurtz (eds.). *New Terms for New Ideas: Western Knowledge and Lexical Change in Late Imperial China*. Leiden: Brill, pp. 95–124.

Feng Zicai 馮子材. 1957. *Feng Zicai jundu jiyao* 馮子材軍牘集要 (Collection of important military correspondence of Feng Zicai), in: *Zhongguo jindaishi ziliao congkan—Zhong Fa zhanzheng* 中國近代史資料叢刊 — 中法戰爭 2 (Series of source material on the history of Modern China—the Sino-French War 2). Shanghai: Renmin chubanshe.

Fryer, John and Zhong Tianwei 鐘天緯 (trs.). 1886. *Yingguo shuishikao* 英國水師考 (Examination of the English Royal Navy). Shanghai: Shanghai jiqi zhizaoju.

Guo Songtao 郭嵩燾. 1984. *Lundun yu Bali riji* 倫敦與巴黎日記 (London and Paris diary). Changsha: Yuelu shushe (*Zouxiang shijie congshu* 走向世界叢書. *From East to West—Chinese Travellers before 1911*).

Huang Gongqing 黃公慶 (i.e. Huang Zunxian). [1890]. *Riben guozhi* 日本國志 (Treatise on Japan). vol. 22: *bingzhi* 兵志 (Military), in: Shen Yunlong 沈雲龍 (ed.). *Jindai Zhongguo shiliao congkan, xuji* 近代中國史料叢刊續輯 (Collection of historical materials on Modern China, second series). Taibei: Wenhai chubanshe, vol. 96, p. 597.

Hucker, Charles O. 1985. *A Dictionary of Official Titles in Imperial China*. Stanford: Stanford University Press.

Kaocha zhengzhi riji 考察政治日記 (Diary of the inspection of political systems). 1984–86. Changsha: Yuelu shushe (*Zouxiang shijie congshu* 走向世界叢書. *From East to West—Chinese Travellers before 1911*).

"Li Hongzhao deng zhi Yue Gang Ying Fa jun guanshu" 李鴻昭等致粵港英法軍官書 (Li Hongzhao sends a letter to the English and France military officers in Canton and Hong Kong). 1957. In: *Zhongguo jindaishi ziliao congkan—Taiping tianguo* 中國近代史資料叢刊 — 太平天國 2 (Series of source material on the history of modern China—The Taiping 2). Shanghai: Renmin chubanshe, pp. 718–9.

Lobscheid, Wilhelm (Luo Cunde 羅存德). 1866–69. *Ying-Hua zidian* 英華字典. *English and Chinese Dictionary with Punti and Mandarin Pronunciation*. 4 vols. Hong Kong: Daily Press Office.

Loch, Henry B. (Luo Hengli 羅亨利 and Qu Anglai 瞿昂來 (trs.). 1886. *Faguo shuishikao* 法國水師考 (Examination of the French Royal Navy). Shanghai: Shanghai jiqi zhizaoju.

Ma Jianzhong 馬建忠. 1961. "Shikezhai jiyan jixing. Shang Li Bo xiang fuyi He xueshi Ruzhang zoushe shuishishu" 適可齋記言記行。上李伯相覆議何學士如璋奏設水師書 (Record of speeches and activities in Shikezhai. A letter to Li Bo-xiang regarding a memorial to establish a Navy suggested by scholar He Ruzhang), in: *Zhongguo jindaishi ziliao congkang—Yangwu yundong*, series no. 1. Shanghai: Shanghai renmin chubanshe, pp. 403–51.

Medhurst, Walter Henry (Maidusi 麥都思). 1847. *English and Chinese Dictionary.* Shanghai.

Morrison, Robert (Ma Lixun 馬禮遜). 1815–23. *Wuche yunfu* 五車韻府. *A Diction-ary of the Chinese Language, in Three Parts. Part the first; containing Chinese and English, arranged according to the radicals, part the second, Chinese and English arranged alphabetically, and part the third, English and Chinese.* Macao: Honourable East India Company's Press.

Shen Dunhe 沈敦和 and H. Hildebrand (Xi Leba 錫樂巴) (trs.). 1895. *Deguo junzhi shuyao* 德國軍制述要 (Important aspects of the German military system). Jinling edition.

Sun Yat-sen 孫中山. 1911. "Junshi zhifulin" 軍士制服令 (Decree on army uniforms), *Dongfang zazhi* 8.10, p. 9.

Tang Jingsong 唐景崧. 1957. "Qingying riji" 請纓日記 (Qingying Diary), in: *Zhong-guo jindaishi ziliao congkan—Zhong Fa zhanzheng* 中國近代史資料叢刊 — 中法戰爭 2 (Series of source material on the history of modern China—the Sino-French War 2). Shanghai: Renmin chubanshe.

Wei Yuan 魏源 (ed.). 1998 [1844]. *Haiguo tuzhi* 海國圖志 (Illustrated treatise on the maritime countries). 3 vols. 50 *juan*. Changsha: Yuelu shushe.

Wen Gongzhi 文公直. 1930. *Zuijin sanshinian Zhongguo junshishi* 最近三十年中國軍事史 (The Chinese military history of the last thirty years). Shanghai: Tai-pingyang shudian.

Xiong Yuezhi. 2001. "Liberty, Democracy, President: The Translation and Usage of Some Political Terms in Late Qing China", in: Michael Lackner, Iwo Amelung and Joachim Kurtz (eds). *New Terms for New Ideas: Western Knowledge and Lexical Change in Late Imperial China.* Leiden: Brill, pp. 69–93.

Xu Jianyin 徐建寅. 1984. *Ouyou zalu* 歐游雜錄 (Notes on a travel to Europe). Chang-sha: Yuelu shushe (*Zouxiang shijie congshu* 走向世界叢書. *From East to West—Chinese Travellers before 1911*).

"Xu Yanxu laiwang handu" 徐延旭來往函牘 (Xu Yanxu's correspondence). 1957. In: *Zhongguo jindaishi ziliao congkan—Zhong Fa zhanzheng* 中國近代史資料叢刊 — 中法戰爭 2 (Series of source material on the history of modern China—the Sino-French War 2). Shanghai: Renmin chubanshe.

Xue Fucheng 薛福成. 1985. "Chushi Ying Fa Yi Bi siguo riji" 出使英法義比四國日記 (Diary of my diplomatic mission to the four countries England, France, Italy and Belgium). Changsha: Yuelu chubanshe (*Zouxiang shijie congshu* 走向世界叢書. *From East to West—Chinese Travellers before 1911*), pt. 1, vol. 8.

"Yapian zhanzheng" 鴉片戰爭 (The Opium War). 1957. In: *Qing Daoguangchao liuzhong mizou* 清道光朝留中密奏 (Secret memorials of the Daoguan period in the Qing dynasty, series no. 3).

Yuan Shikai 袁世凱. 1912. "Haijun guanzuo shibing dengjibiao" 海軍官佐士兵等級表 (Table of ranks of soldiers and officers of the Navy), in: *Zhonghua minguo zhengfu gongbao* 中華民國政府公報, August 19, 1912 and October 20, 1912. Reprint Taibei: Wenhai chubanshe.

Zhang Deyi 張德彝 . 1984. *Suishi Ying'E ji* 隨使英俄記 (Records of a mission to England and Russia). Changsha: Yuelu shushe (*Zouxiang shijie congshu* 走向世界叢書 . *From East to West—Chinese Travellers before 1911*).

Zhang Jianji 張建基 . 1989. "Minguo junxiang zhidu shulüe" 民國軍銜制度述略 (Brief account of the military rank system in Republican China), *Junshi lishi yanjiu* 3, p. 59.

"Zhang Shusheng laiwang handu" 張樹聲來往函牘 (Zhang Shusheng's correspondence). 1957. In: *Zhongguo jindaishi ziliao congkan—Zhong Fa zhanzheng* 中國近代史資料叢刊 — 中法戰爭 2 (Series of source material on the history of modern China—The Sino-French War 2). Shanghai: Renmin chubanshe.

Zhang Xi 張喜 . 1957. "Fuyi riji" 撫夷日記 (Diary of appeasing the foreigners), in: *Zhongguo jindaishi ziliao congkan—yapian zhanzheng* 中國近代史資料叢刊 — 鴉片戰爭 5 (Series of source material on the history of modern China—The Opium War 5). Shanghai: Renmin chubanshe.

Zou Lu 鄒魯 . 1957. "Zhongguo tongmenghui" 中國同盟會 (The Chinese alliance), in: *Zhongguo jindaishi ziliao congkan—Xinhai geming* 中國近代史資料叢刊 — 辛亥革命 2 (Series of source material on the history of modern China—The Revolution of 1911 2). Shanghai: Renmin chubanshe.

DISCOURSIVE INTERFACES: LANGUAGE AND MEDIA

WOLFGANG BEHR

'TO TRANSLATE' IS 'TO EXCHANGE' 譯者言易也 — LINGUISTIC DIVERSITY AND THE TERMS FOR TRANSLATION IN ANCIENT CHINA[1]

It is estimated that more than 90% of the 6,000 or so languages spoken in the world today will become extinct during the next 100 years.[2] The global situation, where some 96% of these languages are spoken by only 4% of the world's population, is closely mirrored in China, where the majority of Han people (93.3% in 1993) is speaking one language only (i.e. one variety of Chinese),[3] while the members of the 55 official and of the 120 odd non-recognized minorities (6.7%) in peripheral regions are speaking a large number of non-sinitic languages. According to the thirteenth edition of the *Ethnologue*, the number of living non-sinitic languages spoken in China today is 191,[4] but more than 90% of these "minority languages" are severely endangered. Speakers of these languages are to a large extent bilinguals, occasionally even multilinguals, and the percentage of younger first-language speakers of languages with less than 5,000 speakers is so rapidly dwindling that there is little hope for revitalization.

1. LINGUISTIC DIVERSITY

Despite our exceedingly poor knowledge of the relationship between dialects, languages and the role of their respective written representa-

---

[1] I wish to thank N. Vittinghoff for a great many helpful suggestions and corrections.

[2] Cf. Ken Hale et al. 1989. "Endangered Languages", *Language* 68.1, pp. 1–42; Michael Krauss. 1995. "The Scope of Language Endangerment and Responses to it", paper presented at the International Symposium on Endangered Languages, November 1–20, Tōkyō University; Robert M. W. Dixon. 1997. *The Rise and Fall of Languages*. Cambridge: Cambridge University Press, ch. 9.

[3] Depending on the underlying theory of what constitutes a language, one might just as well talk about "a dozen of very closely related Sinitic languages." Mair's claim ("Language and Script", in: Victor H. Mair (ed.). 2001. *The Columbia History of Chinese Literature*. New York: Columbia University Press) "that there are literally hundreds of mutually unintelligible languages in China" belonging to the Sinitic group, strikes me as being grossly exaggerated.

[4] Barbara F. Grimes et al. 1996. *Ethnologue*. Dallas: Summer Institute of Linguistics, 13th ed., *s.v.* "China".

tions in early China, it is highly unlikely that the general trend
towards first language pidginization, obsolescence and subsequent
death observed today is an altogether recent phenomenon. In fact, we
know of a sizeable number of names of non-Chinese peoples and languages, mentioned in pre-modern Chinese, South-East and Central
Asian sources, which have become extinct already during medieval
and ancient periods. Unfortunately, it is usually impossible to assess
the precise number and nature of the languages in question, their functions and genealogies. They never seem to have figured as an object
of sustained interest, let alone systematic investigation, throughout
pre-Qing history, and, with very few exceptions, developed a literary
tradition only since the late nineteenth and early twentieth centuries.

During the Shang period already, oracle bone inscriptions mention
at least 69 names of *fangguo* 方國 or 'lateral countries', usually interpreted to refer to ethnicities of non-Shang extraction.[5] Many of the
216+ osteographical names of clans and lineages, not explicitly classified as *fang*, are suspect of reflecting 'foreign' peoples as well.[6] Pre-
Qin texts directly addressing the problem of tribes, kingdoms, and
statelets quote pre-Zhou kingdoms in a range between "99" and
"more than 3,000",[7] while a recent dictionary culled from a comprehensive study of pre-Qin edited sources gives a more sober impression, featuring more than 360 names of countries, many of which
were perceived as 'non-Chinese'.[8] The situation is somewhat clearer
for later periods, when for instance during the Tang dynasty all in all

[5] Shima Kunio quotes 33 (I) + 2 (II) + 13 (III) + 23 (IV) + 8 (V) = 69 names for
the different periods, but his list is far from exhaustive. See Shima Kunio 島邦男 .
1958. *Inkyo bokuji kenkyū* 殷墟卜辭研究 (Studies on the oracle inscriptions from the
ruins of Yin). Hirosaki: Hirosaki Daigaku, pp. 384–5; cf. K. C. Chang. 1980. *Shang
Civilization*. New Haven, London: Yale University Press, p. 248.
[6] Ding Shan 丁山 . 1988. *Jiaguwen suojian shizu ji qi zhidu* 甲骨文所見氏族及其
制度 (Clans and lineages reflected in the oracle bone inscriptions and their system).
Beijing: Zhonghua shuju, pp. 17–32.
[7] Lin Yun 林澐 . 1981. "Jiaguwen zhongde Shangdai fangguo lianmeng" 甲骨文
中的商代方國聯盟 (Shang dynasty lateral country alliances in the oracle bone
inscriptions), *Guwenzi Yanjiu* 6, p. 67; Wang Wenyan 王文顏 . 1984. *Fodian Hanyi
zhi yanjiu* 佛典漢譯之研究 (Studies in the Chinese translations of Buddhist documents). Taibei: Tianhua, pp. 18–9.
[8] Pan Ying 潘英 . 1985. *Zhongguo shanggu guoming diming cihui ji suoyin* 中國
上古國名地名辭彙及索引 (A vocabulary and index of archaic Chinese state and place
names). Taibei: Mingwen.

79 unambiguously 'foreign' countries are on record of conducting diplomatic interchanges with China.[9]

That 'China' (or the varying regions which eventually came to be called by that name) must certainly have been a thoroughly multiethnic territory already during the Lower Paleolithic and Neolithic is also borne out by recent genetic studies of mitochondrial DNA lineages, haplogroup and surname distributions, as well as cranio- and odontometrical data. These show that—contrary to a widespread belief, and much to the dismay of contemporary politicians—populations in China are characterized by an unusual degree of north-south heterogeneity.[10] Genetically determined population clusters quite easily transgress linguistic boundaries, especially in South China,[11] where the adjoining neighbours of a maximum parsimony dendrogram generated from genetic data will in fact so often belong to different linguistic backgrounds, that it seems to make little sense at all to uphold the notion of Neolithic Chinese unity beyond its undeniable historical and psychological significance.

It could be argued that this rich genetic diversity has its distant echo in the astonishing variety of proposals on the ancestry of the Chinese language. These currently range from the traditional concept of a Sino-Tibetan linguistic family first developed during the last quarter of the nineteenth century, over more controversial Sino (-Tibetan)-Austronesian, Sino-Tibetan-Austric, Sino-Indoeuropean, Sino-Tibetan-Indoeuropean, and Sino-Tibetan-Yeniseian-North-Caucasian proposals,[12] to the truly megalomanic Sino-Dene superphylum,[13] or even the most recent idea of the Athabaskan-Eyak-Tlingit

---

[9] *Tang huiyao* 唐會要 (94–100), cf. Li Fang 李方. 1994. "Tang Xizhou de yi-yuren" 唐西州的譯語人 (Xizhou interpreters under the Tang), *Wenwu* 2, pp. 45–51; 45.

[10] See, inter alia, the references in Luigi Luca Cavalli-Sforza. 1998. "The Chinese Human Genome Diversity Project", *Proceedings of the National Academy of Science* 95, pp. 11501–3; Du Ruofu et al. 1994. *Chinese Surnames and Genetic Difference Between North and South China*. Berkeley: Department of East Asian Studies.

[11] Cf. J. Y. Chu et al. 1998. "Genetic Relationship of Populations in China", *Proceedings of the National Academy of Sciences* 95, pp. 11763–8.

[12] For a recent overview see the conflicting contributions to William S. Y. Wang. 1995. *The Ancestry of the Chinese Language*. Berkeley: Department of East Asian Studies (Journal of Chinese Linguistics Monograph Series 8).

[13] First proposed by Edward Sapir (1884–1939). For some rather quixotic lexical equations in this same vein cf. John D. Bengtson and Václav Blažek. 1995. "Lexica Dene-Caucasica", *Central Asiatic Journal* 29, pp. 11–50.

Indian language family in the Pacific Northwest as a *branch* of Tibeto-Burman under a Sino-Tibetan supernode.[14] Whatever the merits of each of these proposals might be as far as the question of genealogical *descent* of Chinese is concerned, it is likely that most of them may to a certain degree reflect ancient loan contacts between Chinese and neighbouring languages during the late Neolithic and early bronze age.

2. FIRST ATTESTATIONS OF SOME IMPORTANT ETHNIC/LINGUISTIC TERMS

As Michael Loewe has stressed, China's "sense of unity", i.e. the ideal of an ecumenical *yitong* 一統 encompassing alien peoples beyond the pale in concentric zones of decreasing imperial authority centred around the emperor, was largely a product of Han dynasty Confucianism and expansionism.[15] The same applies to the systematization of concepts generating a dichotomy between 'the' Chinese and 'barbarians' on all levels of mythological and semiotic analysis,[16] even in cases where the underlying contrast is between ethnicities originally considered to be members of one and the same Hua-Xia 華夏 sphere.[17]

Zhongguo 中國, "the central states", is an expression first mentioned in the early Western Zhou *He zun* 夊何尊 -bronze inscription excavated in 1963 and dating to the reign of King Cheng (1042/35–1006 BC).[18] Other pre-Imperial meanings include 'capital' and 'royal domain or fiefdom', the rare use for 'medium-sized state', i.e. as a

---

[14] Jeff Leer. 1999. "Recent Advances in Athabaskan-Eyak-Tlingit Reconstruction", paper presented at the Fourteenth Athabaskan Language Conference, May 21–23, University of New Mexico, Albuquerque.

[15] Michael Loewe. 1994. "China's Sense of Unity as Seen in the Early Empires", *T'oung Pao* 80, pp. 6–26.

[16] Jurij L. Krol'. 1973. "O koncepcii 'Kitaj – Varvary'" (On the concepts 'China – The Barbarians'), in: *Obščestvo i gosudarstvo v Kitaje (Sbornik Statej)* (Society and state in China: a collection of articles). Moscow: Nauka, pp. 13–29.

[17] M. E. Kravcova. 1992. "Étnokul'turnoe raznoobrazie drevnego Kitaja" (The ethnocultural diversity of Ancient China), *Vostok* 3, pp. 56–66. On the problem of differentiating between several 'Xia' ethnicities see Tian Jizhou 田繼周. 1985. "Xiadai de minzu he minzu guanxi" 夏代的民族和民族關係 (Xia dynasty ethnic groups and inter-ethnic relationships), *Minzu Yanjiu* 4, pp. 27–34.

[18] For a good rubbing and transcription see Ma Chengyuan 馬承源 et al. (eds.). 1989–90. *Shang-Zhou qingtongqi mingwenxuan* 商周青銅器銘文選 (Selected Shang

double-antonym of *qiangguo* 強國 'strong state' and *xiaoguo* 小國 'small/weak state, statelet', recognized only recently in epigraphical materials,[19] as well as the strictly Western Zhou attestation as a prepositional phrase 'in the country'.[20] The term is likely to have originally denoted a fortified city (or *yi* 邑)[21] where the peripatetic king raised his banner or flag (*zhong* 中) as a symbol of the centrality of the royal domain.[22] *Zhongguo* slowly took over functions of the earlier term *zhongtu* 中土 'central soils', and ultimately from the 'Great City of Shang' (*dayi Shang* 大邑商) mentioned in oracle bone inscriptions.[23] It would seem, then, that the dichotomy between the increasingly extended centralized territories which came to be subsumed under the label *zhongguo* and the opposed four lateral quarters of the Barbarian 'outside world' is entirely an Eastern Zhou affair, conceptualized along the lines of the emergent cosmological duo-pentaism.[24] Until then, and possibly well beyond that period in many peripheral

---

[18] (*cont.*) and Zhou bronze inscriptions). Beijing: Wenwu, vol. 1, p. 21, vol. 3, pp. 20–2, no. 32. The relevant passage reads: "It was King Wu, having managed to conquer the great Great City of Shang, who announced in an oracle to Heaven: 'I will take residence in these *central territories* → *states* (*yu* < *[b]wək* → *guo* < *[a]k-wək*), from here I will rule the people.'"

[19] For attestations in excavated Warring States texts see Zhang Xiancheng 張顯成 . 1998. "Lun jianbo wenxian de cihuishi yanjiu jiazhi—jianlun qi Hanyushi yanjiu jiazhi" 論簡帛文獻的詞彙史研究價值 — 兼論其漢語史研究價值 (On the value of bamboo and silk documents for the history of the lexicon, including a discussion of their value for the history of the Chinese language), *Jianbo yanjiu* 3, pp. 201–2.

[20] Cf. Michael Lackner. 1998. "Anmerkungen zur historischen Semantik von 'China', 'Nation' und 'chinesischer Nation' im modernen Chinesisch", in: H. Turk, B. Schulze and R. Simanowski (eds.). *Kulturelle Grenzziehungen im Spiegel der Literaturen. Nationalismus, Regionalismus, Fundamentalismus.* Göttingen: Wallstein, pp. 323–39; p. 325, who traces the further development of the term during the Late Imperial and modern periods.

[21] I.e. the character which is used as a semantic determiner in oracle bone forms of *yu* 或 'territory' and its *k-prefixed derivation *guo* 國 'state' (OC *[a]k-wək).

[22] See Yu Xingwu 于省吾 . 1981. "Shi 'zhong guo'" 釋中國 (Deciphering 'zhongguo'), in: Zhonghua shuju chengli qishi nian jinianhui (ed.). *Zhonghua xueshu lunwenji* 中華學術論文集 (Collection of scholarly articles on China). Beijing: Zhonghua, pp. 3–10.

[23] For an excellent study of the process of state formation see Lin Yun 林澐 . 1986. "Guanyu Zhongguo zaoqi guojia xingshi de jige wenti" 關於中國早期國家形式的幾個問題 (On several problems relating to the early form of the state in China), *Jilin Daxue Shehui Kexue Xuebao* 6, pp. 1–12.

[24] Yu Rongchun 于溶春 . 1986. "'Zhongguo' yici de laiyuan, yanbian ji qi yu minzu de guanxi" ‛中國’一詞的來源·演變·及其與民族的關係 (On the derivation and development of the word 'Zhongguo', and its interrelationship with different ethnic groups), *Neimenggu shehui kexue* 2, pp. 75–80.

regions, *zhongguo* was the designation for an ethnically more or less loose political conglomeration, in which Chinese—internally diversi-fied, but not yet diverged into mutually incomprehensible 'dialects'— was but one of the many possible languages of everyday communica-tion. The perception of this state of affairs as a precarious balance and the concomitant self-redefinition through production of ethnic myths of origins or the assignment of a stereotyped locus to the 'other' was a rather late phenomenon, accelerated by the first encounter with a sophisticated foreign *oral-textual* culture after the advent of Bud-dhism.

The ethnic designation *Hanzu* 漢族 (lit. 'Han clansmen') makes its appearance in the standard dynastic histories only towards the end of the Northern Wei dynasty (386–534) in the *Bei-Qi shu* 北齊書 (His-tory of the Northern Qi, finished in 636) and in roughly contempora-neous literary works such as Li Daoyuan's 酈道元 (d. 527) *Shuijing zhu* 水經注 (Commentary on the Classic of Waterways),[25] thus indi-rectly reflecting the end of the great Inner Asian *Völkerwanderung*. The compound *Hanren* 漢人 'Han people'[26] is first attested several times already in the *Shiji* 史記 (Records of the Historian)[27] and in all subsequent dynastic histories. The claim that this term would have only appeared in a variant reading of Li Yanshou's 李延壽 *Nanshi* 南史 (History of the Southern dynasties, completed 656),[28] is, as far as I

---

[25] Li Zhimin 李志敏 . 1986. "'Hanzu' minghao qiyuan kao" '漢族' 名號起源考 (A study on the origins of the designation 'hanzu'), *Zhongguoshi yanjiu* 3, p. 49.

[26] It has been argued that *ren* 人 , from the oracle bone inscriptions (Magoshi Yasushi 馬越靖史 . 1998. "Kōkotsubun ni okeru 'jin'" 甲骨文における '人' (On 'ren' in the oracle bone inscriptions), *Tōhōgaku* 92, pp. 16–29) until at least the end of the Eastern Zhou (Robert H. Gassmann. 2000. "Auf der Suche nach der antikchine-sischen Gesellschaft. Überlegungen zu *ren* und *min*", *Minima Sinica*, 12.1, pp. 15–30.) primarily signified membership of the founding lineage of a tribe rather than the generic term 'man' or the individuation of a 'person'. For a philosophical refutation see Heiner Roetz. 1993. *Confucian Ethics of the Axial Age*. Albany: SUNY Press, pp. 123–48.

[27] Contra Li Zhimin 1986. See *Shiji* 史記 (Records of the Historian) (92.32, p. 2625; 123.63, p. 3169), *Hanshu* 漢書 (History of the Han) (45.15, p. 2164; 61.31, p. 2701; 94.64, p. 3804; 96.66, p. 3902), *Hou Hanshu* 後漢書 (History of the Later Han) (19.9, p. 721, 47.37, p. 1588; 86.76, p. 2833; 2854; 87.77, p. 2878; 2899; 88.78, p. 2925; 89.79, p. 2942; 2945; 2957–8; 90.80, p. 2991), *Sanguo zhi* 三國志 (Records of the Three Kingdoms) (1475; 1477) etc. (Here and elsewhere, all dynastic histories are quoted according to the *Zhonghua shuju*-edition).

[28] Cf. Li Zhimin 1986. EMC=Early Middle Chinese, LMC=Late Middle Chinese according to Edwin G. Pulleyblank. 1991. *Lexicon of Reconstructed Pronunciation*

can see, totally unfounded.[29] It is during this turbulent Early Medieval period as well that we first come across *Hanyu* 漢語 (Han language) as the designation for the 'Chinese language' in the *Nan-Qi shu* 南齊書 (History of the Southern Qi, finished 636)[30] and in the *Shishuo xinyu* 世說新語 (New Account of Tales of the World), while *Hanyan* 漢言 ("is expressed in the Han [language] as") starts to introduce Chinese translations and calques of Central Asian and Buddhist Hybrid Sanskrit expressions in technical definitions[31] since Yuan Hong's 袁宏 (d. 376) *Hou Han ji* 後漢記 (Records on the Later Han) of the mid-fourth century:

其精進者，號曰沙門，漢言息心，蓋息心去欲而歸無為也。

Those among them dedicated to self-improvement are called *shamen* (EMC *ṣaɨ=mən)[32] which means in Chinese [*Hanyan*] 'to set the mind at rest', i.e. by setting the mind at rest and renouncing the desires to return to non-activity.[33]

---

[28] (*cont.*) *in Early Middle Chinese, Late Middle Chinese, and Early Mandarin.* Vancouver: University of British Columbia Press.

[29] The passage is not found in the *Zhonghua shuju* (*Nanshi* 南史 70: 1699), *Bona* 百衲 (vol. 10, [696] 70: 12426b) or *Siku Quanshu* 四庫全書(70: 5b) editions, where the text has instead *Hanchao* 漢朝 (Han dynasty).

[30] *Nan-Qi Shu* 南齊書 (History of the Southern Qi) (57.38, p. 985; 59.40, p. 1023). The term appears earlier as a book title in *Hou Hanshu* (62.52, p. 2057).

[31] In this function 'X *Hanyan* 漢言 Y' gets replaced by 'X *Hanyu* 漢語 Y' in historiographical works only by the time of the *Liaoshi* 遼史 (History of the Liao) (73: 122) and *Jinshi* 金史 (History of the Jin) (1, p. 3; 4; 6; 74, p. 1693; 80, p. 1798), and, furthermore during the Yuan period by 'X *wei Hanyu* 為漢語 Y', in, e.g., *Yuanshi* 元史 (History of the Yuan) (114, p. 2882).

[32] According to Sylvain Lévi. 1910. "Études des documents tokhariens de la mission Pelliot. I.: Les bilingues", *Journal Asiatique* 10e sér. 17, p. 379; Harold Bailey. 1946. "Gāndhārī", *Bulletin of the School of Oriental and African Studies* 11.4, p. 139. But see also Ji Xianlin 季羨林. 1985. "Shuo 'chujia'" 說'出家' (On the expression 'to leave the family'), in: Guojia wenwuju guwenxian yanjiushi (ed.). *Chutu wenxian yanjiu* 出土文獻研究 (Studies of excavated documents). Beijing: Wenwu, who derives the word from a Bactrian source. *Shamen* is a loanword from Tocharian B ṣāmane, and not, as often stated, from Sanskrit śramaṇa.

[33] Ap. Li Zhimin 1986. On the reliability and date of the *Hou-Han ji* see Paul Pelliot. 1906. "[Compte rendu de] É. Chavannes, 'Les pays d'occident d'après le Wei Lio'", (*T'oung Pao* 1905.6, pp. 519–71), *Bulletin de l'École Française d'Extrême-Orient* 6, pp. 361–400. Earlier usages of *Hanyan* occur exclusively in personal names.

3. Chinese records of foreign languages
during pre-Qin and Han periods

Quite apart from these terms of ethnic and linguistic reference to the Chinese as Han, which eventually had the good fortune to survive into the modern language, direct or indirect references to the extraordinary linguistic diversity in Ancient China are surprisingly few and far between. Only four 'direct' records of foreign connected speech set in pre-Qin and Han times have come down to us so far:[34]

> a) a song of a boatman from the coastal Yue 越 (OC *^{b}wat)[35]   area, believed to represent an early form of a Kadaic language, which was transcribed by Chinese characters and 'rendered into Chu' (*Chu shuo* 楚説), i.e. transposed into the poetic form of the *Chuci* 楚辭 (Songs from Chu), by a native from Chu in 538 BC;[36]
>
> b) several lines of a military command in what is presumed to be the same language, issued by the Yue king Goujian 勾踐 (OC *^{a}k(-r-)o-s= ^{b}dzan)[37]   after his return from captivity in Wu 吳 in 484 BC;[38]

---

[34] Luo Zongtao 羅宗濤 . 1982. "Gudai fanyi shulüe" 古代翻譯述略 (A short exposition of translation in antiquity), *Hanxue yanjiu tongxun* 2, p. 38–40; Ma Zuyi 馬祖毅 . 1984. *Zhongguo fanyi jian shi—'wusi' yundong yiqian bufen* 中國翻譯簡史 — 五四運動以前部分 (A short history of translation in China—The period before the May Fourth movement). Beijing: Zhongguo duiwai fanyi, pp. 3–9; Wang Yuanxin 王遠新 . 1993. *Zhongguo Minzu yuyanxue shi* 中國民族語言學史 (History of the study of minority languages in China). Beijing: Zhongyang minzu xueyuan, p. 12.

[35] OC=Old Chinese, reconstruction according to the system of William H. Baxter. 1992. *A handbook of Old Chinese phonology*. Berlin, New York: Mouton de Gruyter, accepting some revisions detailed in Laurent Sagart. 1999. *The Roots of Old Chinese*. Amsterdam, Philadelphia: J. Benjamins; all reconstructions, if not otherwise stated, are OC. MC= Middle Chinese transcriptions according to Baxter 1992.

[36] *Shuoyuan* 説苑 (The garden of tales) (11.13, p. 89). The song is usually referred to as the *Yueren yongji ge* 越人擁楫歌 (Song of the Yue oarsmen) in modern sources. For two attempts at decipherment see Wei Qingwen 韋慶穩 . 1981. " 'Yueren ge' yu Zhuangyu de guanxi shitan" ' 越人歌' 與壯語的關係試探 (An exploration of the relationship between the 'Song of the man from Yue' and the Zhuang language), in: *Minzu yuwen lunji* 民族語文論集 (Collected studies on minority languages). Beijing: Zhongguo shehui kexueyuan; and Zheng-Zhang Shangfang. 1991. "Decipherment of Yue-Ren-Ge (Song of the Yue Boatman)", *Cahiers de Linguistique Asie-Orientale* 2, pp. 159–68.

[37] On this type of *gou*-prefixation in personal and place names from the ancient Wu and Yue areas cf. You Rujie 游汝杰 and Zhou Zhenhe 周振鶴 . 1990. "Nanfang diming fenbu de quyu tezheng yu gudai yuyan de guanxi" 南方地名分布的區域特徵與古代語言的關係 (Connections between ancient languages and regional features in the distribution of southern Chinese toponyms), in: Yin Da 尹達 (ed.). *Jinian Gu Jiegang xueshu lunwenji* 紀念顧頡剛學術論文集 (A collection of scholarly articles in memoriam Gu Jiegang). Chengdu: Ba-Shu, vol. 2, pp. 709–24; Donald B. Wagner.

c) the famous 'Xiongnu 匈奴 couplet' of the second century BC, assumed to be explainable via an ancient para-Yeniseian language;[39]

d) three songs by the king of Bailang 白狼 (OC *[a]b-r-ak=[A]C-raŋ), presented in Chinese transcription and translation during an embassy in 74 AD, and commonly assumed to represent an ancient Tibeto-Burman (probably Lolo-Burmese) language.[40]

Other indirect or later references narrate the story of an embassy from the kingdom of Yuechang 越裳 (OC *[b]wat=[b]daŋ) in the sixth year after the Zhou conquest, when three interpreters were needed to translate the greetings accompanying the gift of one white and two black pheasants to the Duke of Zhou.[41] They mention the problem of the translation of the Xiongnu chanyu's 單于 seals into Chinese,[42] or refer to interpreters of the Rong 戎 (OC *[b]nuŋ) and Di 狄 (OC *[a]lek) as

---

[37] (cont.) 1991. "The Language of the Ancient State of Wu", in: B. Arendrup et al. (eds.). The Master Said: to Study and ... Copenhagen: East Asian Institute, pp. 161–76.

[38] Yuejueshu 越絕書 (The book of Yue's records) (ACS-ed., 4: 16). For a reconstruction and tentative translation see Zheng-Zhang Shangfang 鄭張尚芳. 1999. "Goujian 'Weijia' ling zhong zhi gu Yueyu de jiedu" 勾踐 '維甲' 令中之古越語的解讀 (A decipherment of ancient Yue words in the weijia-command of Goujian), Minzu yuwen 4, pp. 1–14.

[39] Suoyin on Shiji (110.50: 2909, fn. 4). A Yeniseian affiliation of the Xiongnu was first proposed by L. Ligeti. 1950. "Mots de civilisation de Haute Asie en transcription chinoise", Acta Orientalia Hungarica 1, pp. 141–88, and was confirmed by Edwin G. Pulleyblank. 1962. "The Consonantal System of Old Chinese", Asia Major 9, pp. 58–114 and 206–65 (Appendix: "The Hsiung-nu Language", pp. 239–65); and A. Vovin. 2000. "Did the Xiongnu Speak a Yeniseian Language?", Central Asiatic Journal 54.1, pp. 87–104.

[40] Hou Hanshu (86.76: 2855), the texts of the songs have survived in Dongguan Han ji 東觀漢記 (Han records from the 'Eastern Lodge') (ACS-ed., 22.4161–163, cf. also on the backgrounds 17.5: 122). For two detailed studies of the songs see W. S. Coblin. 1974. "A New Study of the Pailang Songs", The Ts'ing-Hua Journal of Chinese Studies 12.1–2, pp. 179–211, and Zheng-Zhang Shangfang 鄭張尚芳. 1993. "Shanggu Miange—'Bailang ge' quanwen jiedu" 上古緬歌 '白狼歌' 全文解讀 (An archaic Burmese song—decipherment of the complete text of the 'Bailang song'), Minzu yuwen 1, pp. 10–21 and Minzuyuwen 2, pp. 64–70, 74.

[41] Hanshu (12.12, p. 348 and 99.69, p. 4047), Hou Hanshu (86.76, p. 2835), Hanshi waizhuan 韓詩外傳 (Inofficial traditions on the Han odes) (5.12, p. 37); see also the extended version recorded in the Cefu yuangui 冊府元龜 (Exquisite turtles from the Storehouse of Records) (663), quoted in Ma Zuyi 1984, p. 2. That this first embassy came from the south, the first direction of Zhou expansion, is usually regarded as the motivating factor behind the selection of xiang as the general term for 'interpreters' in the title xiangxu.

[42] Hanshu (94.64B: 3820–1).

sheren 舍人 or 'tongue people'.[43] Earlier, speeches by the Shang and Zhou kings, especially in investiture contexts in pre-Qin inscriptions and the *Shangshu* 尚書 (Book of Documents), were often introduced by the formula *wang ruo yue* 王若日 'the king said the following/thus spoke'(?)[44] and it has been speculated that this phrase originally introduced written renderings of the king's foreign speech or Chinese pidgin into the standard prestige (*ya* 雅) language.[45] In any case, it is clear that written communication between scriptless (*wu wen shu* 無 ~ 毋文書) people like the Xiongnu and the Chinese must have taken place *in some form* early on in the history of sino-xenic relations, since we occasionally find quotations from official letters, like in the following case: [46]

> 皇帝敬問匈奴大單于，無恙?
> The emperor respectfully asks the great *chanyu* of the Xiongnu, are you well?

Yet, with the exception of a few inscriptions and coins, especially in Kharoṣṭhī,[47] not even monolingual pre-Medieval materials in foreign languages or scripts have been excavated in the 'central states'.

4. BILINGUALISM AND SINIFICATION

In view of China's multiethnic background outlined so far, it is astonishing that we hardly ever come across any information on *how* all this translation work mentioned in the scattered references was effected, or how translators or interpreters were selected and trained. It can be safely assumed that most translators or interpreters during the pre-Qin period were bilinguals recruited from the respective states of the empire, as was clearly the case later during the Han[48] and Tang

---

[43] *Guoyu* 國語 (Discourses of the states) (Shanghai Guji ed., 2: 62 with n. 12), cf. Ma Zuyi 1984, p. 3.

[44] Cf. Yu Xingwu 于省吾. 1966. "'Wang ruo yue' shi yi" '王若日' 釋義 (An analysis of the meaning of 'wang ruo yue'), *Zhongguo yuwen* 2, pp. 147–9, 136.

[45] Chang Tsung-tung (1931–2000), personal communication, March 1996.

[46] *Hanshu* (96.94A: 3758). For the further development of written communication between China and the outside world up to the Tang cf. Hori Toshikazu. 1994. "The Exchange of Written Communications Between Japan, Sui and Tang Dynasties", *Memoirs of the Research Department of the Tōyō Bunko* 52, pp. 1–19.

[47] See John Brough. 1961. "A Kharoṣṭhī Inscription from China", *Bulletin of the School of Oriental and African Studies* 24.3, pp. 517–30.

[48] Cf. Ma Zuyi 1984, p. 4, for detailed references.

dynasties.[49] Yet again, traces of an awareness of the problem of bilingualism are almost entirely lacking. Just like in ancient Greece,[50] Egypt and Ugarit,[51] monolingualism seems to have been a characteristic of the literary elites,[52] while written information reflecting bi- or multilingualism of the lower fringes of society only rarely survives from earlier periods, as in the following *Yuefu* 樂府 poem, called *Song on Cutting the Willows* (*Zhe yangliu ge* 折楊柳歌):[53]

EMC	rhyme
遙看孟津河	*γaA
楊柳鬱婆娑	*saA
我是盧家兒	*ηi^aX
不解漢兒歌	*kaA

Looking at the [Yellow] River at Ferry of Meng from afar,
Willows are sadly rocking, drooping.
I am a boy from a slave's family,
Do not understand the Chinese boys' song.

---

[49] For a collection of Central Asian fragments relating to the work of translators and interpreters in the Western border areas under the Tang see Li Fang 1994.

[50] Cf. S. Hornblower and A. Spawnford (eds.). 1996. *The Oxford Classical Dictionary*. Oxford: Oxford University Press, *s.v.* 'bilingualism'.

[51] Cf. Alfred Hermann and Wolfram von Soden. 1959. "Dolmetscher", in: Th. Klauser (ed.). *Reallexikon für Antike und Christentum. Sachwörterbuch zur Auseinandersetzung des Christentums mit der antiken Welt*. Stuttgart: A. Hiersemann, vol. 4, col. 24–49; Fritz Freiherr Lochner von Hüttenbach. 1979. "Bemerkungen zur sprachlichen Heterogenität im Altertum", *Grazer Linguistische Studien* 9, pp. 65–78; Willy Peremans. 1983. "Les ἑρμηνεῖς dans l'Égypte gréco-romaine", in: G. Grimm, H. Heinen and E. Winter (eds.). *Das Römisch-Byzantinische Ägypten*. Mainz: P. von Zabern (Aegyptiaca Treverensia 2), pp. 11–7; Bruno Rochette. 1993. "La diversité linguistique dans l'antiquité classique", in: L. Isebaert (ed.). *Miscellanea linguistica graeco-latina*. Namur: Société des Études Classiques, pp. 219–37.

[52] References to Greeks who spoke two or more languages (like the famous Mithridates, who allegedly spoke 22!) are highly exceptional, cf. Alfred Hermann. 1956. "Dolmetschen im Altertum. Ein Beitrag zur antiken Kulturgeschichte", in: *Schriften des Auslands- und Dolmetscherinstituts der Johannes Gutenberg-Universität Mainz in Germersheim I*. Munich: Isar, pp. 25–59, pp. 43–44; Bruno Rochette. 1999a. *"Fidi interpretes*. La traduction orale à Rome", *Ancient Society* 27, pp. 75–89, p. 83.

[53] *Yuefushi ji* 樂府詩集 (Collected songs from the *Archive of Music*) (289). Rhyme words indicated in EMC.

The first theoretical attempt at explaining the problem of linguistic diversity and foreign language acquisition appears rather late as well, in a curious passage from the *Huainanzi* 淮南子 :[54]

羌，氐，僰，翟嬰兒生皆同聲。及其長也，雖重象騠狄，不能通其言，教俗殊也。

When the children of the Qiang (*[b]k-laŋ), Di (*[a]ti), Bo (*[a]p-kək), and Di (*[a]lewk) are born, they all sound the same, but when they reach adulthood, even if retransposed and -interpreted,[55] one cannot comprehend their language, because their education and customs are different.

Linguistic diversity was thus apparently thought of as a social phenomenon, which arises through the deteriorating influences of "education and customs", working on the universally communicative competence shared by all humans, shared even by the female inhabitants of the 'Dog country':[56]

… 又北，狗國，人身狗首，長毛不衣，手搏猛獸，語為犬嘷，其妻皆人，能漢語，生男為狗，女為人 …

… Further to the north [of the Qidan 契丹, EMC *k[h]it-tan], lies the Dog country, [where] men have human bodies and the head of a dog. They grow long hair and do not wear clothes, they catch wild beasts with their hands and when they speak it is like the howling of dogs. Their women are all human, and they know Chinese. If they give birth to a boy it will become a dog, if to a girl, it will become human …

Ever since the Western Zhou period, Chinese ethnic identity was, by and large, culturally, ethically or ecologically defined, rather than along racial or religious, let alone linguistic parameters. This fact, remarkable in itself, apparently rendered everyday political problems arising from widespread multilingualism a rather trivial topic in the eyes of the Chinese rulers. So trivial, indeed, that conscious construction of a linguistic identity seems to have arisen only with not yet fully sinicized 'alien' rulers. Bilingualism in ancient Chinese society, then, if it does get addressed in texts at all, appears in political discourses on foreign elite rulership in China, discussing the threat of the majority language Chinese to the linguistic and political identity of

---

[54] *Huainanzi* 淮南子 (Master Huainan) (*Zhuzi jicheng* ed., 21: 172). A passage with an almost similar wording occurs in the biography of Jia Yi 賈誼 (200–168) in *Hanshu* (48–18: 2251), there referring to Hu 胡 and Yue 粵 populations.

[55] On the technical terms *xiang* and *didi* cf. below.

[56] *Xin Wudai shi* 新五代史 (New history of the Five Dynasties) (73.B: 907).

the minority non-Chinese ruling clan or dynasty. Consider the following two quotations from the *Suishu* 隋書 (History of the Sui)[57] and the *Xin Wudai shi* 新五代史 (New history of the Five Dynasties)[58] :

> 後魏初定中原，軍容號名，皆以夷語。後染華俗，多不能通，故錄其本言，相傳教習，謂之國語。
>
> When the later Wei first pacified the Central Plains, they always used the Yi-language for orders of military discipline. Later, Chinese customs crept in, and many of them [i.e. the Wei] could not communicate [in the Wei language anymore]. Therefore the original [Wei-]language was recorded, disseminated, taught and practised among them, and they referred to it as 'the national language'.

> [G]阿保機[...] 又謂坤曰: 吾能漢語，然絕口不道於部人，懼其漢而弱怯也。
>
> [The Parhae king] Abaoji (EMC *ʔa=paw'=kij) [...] addressed Kun again, saying: 'I *am* able to speak Chinese, but I keep my mouth shut and do not speak it towards my tribesmen, for fear that once they are sinified they will become timid and weak.

Given the very few informations about ancient minority languages which eventually survived sinification, it would seem that attitudes like Abaoji's did not turn out to be very successful. Still, bilingualism must have prevailed as a geographically and socially marginalized phenomenon throughout most periods of Chinese history. It was simply not deemed worthy to spoil the carefully balanced undercurrent of unity permeating all dynastic and most private historiography since the *Shiji*.

---

[57] *Suishu* 隋書 (32.27: 947)

[58] *Xin Wudai shi* (72.A: 890); see also parallel version in the *Jiu Wudai shi* 舊五代史 (Old history of the Five Dynasties) (137, p. 1831-2).

5. THE TERMS FOR 'TO TRANSLATE, INTERPRET'/'TRANSLATOR, INTERPRETER' THROUGHOUT ANCIENT AND MEDIEVAL CHINESE HISTORY

1. Pre-Medieval period

The institutionalization of translation activities in China can be traced back to the Eastern Zhou dynasty, when so-called *xiangxu* 象胥 ('representationists-discriminators')[59] or 'interpreting functionaries', belonging to the corps of 'travelling envoys' (*xingren* 行人), were first formally integrated into the developing bureaucracy. According to the *Zhouli* 周禮 (Etiquette of the Zhou)[60]

> 象胥掌蠻夷閩貉戎狄之國。使掌傳王之言而諭説焉，以親和之。
>
> … the *xiangxu* are in charge of the countries of the Man (*^{a}m-r-on), Yi (*^{b}N-lǝj), Min (*^{b}m-r-ǝn), He (*^{a}gak), Rong (*^{b}nuŋ) and Di (*^{a}lek). They are charged to transmit (*^{b}dron) the king's words and to expound (*^{b}lo-s) and explain (*^{a}lot-s) these to them [the 'Barbarians'], in order to mollify and appease them.

It is unclear to what extent the *yashi* 邘御事使 (→ *^{a}ŋ-r-a(k)-s=^{b}s-rǝ-ʔ) or 'welcoming envoys',[61] occasionally encountered in oracle bone inscriptions, one of whose functions seems to have been to receive and look after emmissaries from neighboring tribes and states of the Shang,[62] engaged in translation work as well. The first explicit albeit

---

[59] *Xu* 胥 (OC *^{b}s-ŋa-ʔ), glossed as 'one who is talented and knowledgeable' in Zheng Xuan's 鄭玄 (127–200) commentary, is written as *xu* 諝 (*^{b}s-ŋa-ʔ) 'discrimination, knowledge', or, especially if referring to 'prosecution officers' and other bureaucratic ranks, as *xu* 偦 (*^{b}s-ŋa-ʔ). According to the *Fangyan* (Topolects) (6, p. 40.7), the underlying *xu* 胥 is a Wu 吳 -Yue 越 dialect word for *fu* 輔 (*^{b}b(-r-)a) 'assist', from which the official title could easily have been semantically derived.

[60] *Zhouli* 周禮 (Etiquette of the Zhou) (38, p. 261, SSJ 899c), cf. Édouard Biot. 1851. *Le Tcheou-Li ou rites des Tcheou*. Paris: L'Imprimerie Nationale, vol. 2, p. 435. On their relative position in the hierarchy of officials see also *Zhouli* (34: 231, SSJ 869c, translation in Biot 1851, vol. 2, p. 303), from where we also learn that there were all in all 31 posts in this office.

[61] For this meaning and reading of *ya* 御 , cf. *Shijing* (12.1): 之子于歸，百兩御 之 (this girl is going to get married, a hundred carriages meet her), where Zheng Xuan glosses *ya* 御 as *ying* 迎 'to welcome', and Lu Deming's (陸德明 , 556–627 a.d.) *Jing-dian Shiwen* 經典釋文 (Glosses on the Classics) gives the pronounciation *wu jia fan* 五嫁反 , i.e. MC *ngæH > Mandarin *ya*.

[62] Wang Guimin 王貴民 . 1982. "Shuo 'yashi'" 説 '邘事 ' (On the 'yashi'), in: Hu Houxuan 胡厚宣 (ed.). *Jiagu tanshi lu* 甲骨探史錄 (Historical explorations based on oracle bone inscriptions). Beijing: Shenghuo dushu xinzhi sanlian, pp. 303–39, pp. 322, 334.

already highly stereotyped reference to the problem of "translation" in multiethnic Zhou China comes from the chapter on "Royal Institutions" (*Wangzhi* 王制) in the *Liji* 禮記 (Records on etiquette), where it is stated that[63]

> 中國，戎夷，五方之民，皆有性也，不可推移。… 五方之民，言語不同，嗜欲不同。達其志，通其欲，東方日寄，南方日象，西方日狄鞮，北方日譯。
>
> … the people of the central states, of the Rong (*[b]nuŋ) and Yi (*[b]N-ləj) from [all of] the Five Regions, are unanimously equipped with an inherent nature, that can not be removed (*[a]thuj) or altered (*[b]lar) … The people of the Five Regions differ in words and languages, as well as in their predilections and desires. To make comprehend (*[b]lat) their will and communicate (*[a]hloŋ) their desires[64] is called 'to confide' in the eastern regions, 'to represent' in the southern regions, 'to *didi*' in the western regions, [and] 'to translate' in the northern regions.

This passage gets routinely quoted in introductions to theoretical discussions of translation in Medieval Buddhist texts,[65] as well as in Song through Qing encyclopedias[66] dealing with foreign languages. It therefore attracted the attention of Western sinologists already during the last century[67] but has, as far as I know, never been discussed from a phonological and semasiological point of view. Again, it is tempting to view the distribution of administrative areas according to the cardinal points corresponding to different government offices, so typical for the Han systematization of the center-periphery/China vs. 'the other'-dichotomy, as a continuation of Shang proto-bureaucracy, but such an assumption is rather hard to verify. It seems that all fifteen 'envoy'-titles known from the current corpus of oracle bone inscrip-

---

[63] *Liji* 禮記 (Records on etiquette) (12, p. 110, SSJ 1338b).

[64] On the relation between *da* and (its result) *tong* in the *Zhouli* see exhaustively Song Yongpei 宋永培. 1995. "*Zhouli* zhong 'tong', 'da' ciyi de xitong lianxi" 周禮中'通''達'詞義的系統聯係 (Systematic connections between the meanings of the words 'tong' and 'da' in the *Etiquette of the Zhou*), *Gu hanyu yanjiu* 29.4, pp. 41–4.

[65] See, e.g. Zanning's 贊寧 (919–1002) paraphrase in the *Song gaoseng zhuan* 宋高僧傳 (Biographies of eminent monks compiled under the Song) (*Taishō* 50.2061, 3, p. 723a), which is in turn quoted in Fayun's 法雲 preface to the *Fanyi mingyi ji* 翻譯名義集 (Semantic thesaurus of translated (Buddhist) terms) of 1157 (*Taishō* 54.2131, 1, p. 1056a).

[66] See, e.g. *Gujin tushu jicheng* 古今圖書集成 (Synthesis of illustrations and books past and present) (555, 380: 1a), *s.v. Siyiguan bu huikao* 四譯館部會考 (Collected studies on the Office of Interpreters for the Four Regions).

[67] Cf. i.e. Albert É. J. B. Terrien de Lacouperie. 1969 [1885–86]. *The Languages of China Before the Chinese*. London: D. Nutt. Reprint Osnabrück: O. Zeller, pp. 16–7.

tions do not designate fixed positions in the Shang administrative hierarchy. They were apparently conferred upon members of the ruling clans on a day to day basis, who had been selected for political and ritual embassies within and beyond the Shang territory.[68] Moreover, officials corresponding in function or title to the *xiangxu* in the Eastern Zhou are entirely lacking in Western Zhou bronze inscriptions,[69] so there is nothing like a bureaucratic supporting pier to bridge the time gap of almost a millennium.

1.1. Analysis and reconstruction

Neither the ancient commentators nor the modern Western translators of the "Wangzhi"-passage agree as to whether the series (see below: a-d) should be translated as titles of the translators[70] or as designations of their activity.[71] Both positions are defendable, but given the etymological analysis presented below, a verbal interpretation should probably be preferred. The reconstructed Old (OC) and Middle Chinese (MC) forms for the terms in question are seen in Table 1:

---

[68] Li Hu 黎虎 . 1988. "Yindai waijiao zhidu chu tan" 殷代外交制度初談 (Preliminary discussion of the system of foreign relations during the Yin period), *Lishi yanjiu* 5, pp. 36–47 (contra Wang Guimin 1982, p. 111).

[69] Cf. Zhang Yachu 張亞初 and Liu Yü 劉雨 . 1986. *Xi-Zhou jinwen guanzhi yanjiu* 西周金文官制研究 (Studies on the system of bureaucracy reflected in Western Zhou bronze inscription). Beijing: Zhonghua, p. 137.

[70] See, e.g. F. Séraphim Couvreur. 1913. *Li ki ou mémoires sur les bienséances et les cérémonies*. Ho Kien Fou: Imprimerie de la Mission Catholique, second edition, vol. 1, p. 296; James Legge. 1967. *Li Chi, Book of Rites*. New Hyde Park: University Books, vol. 1, pp. 229–30; Christoph Harbsmeier. 1998. *Language and Logic in Traditional China*, in: Joseph Needham (ed.). *Science and Civilization in China*. vol. 7. Pt. 1. Cambridge: Cambridge University Press, p. 51. Harbsmeier's Chinese text and transcription give *dishi* 狄氏 , an obvious typo for *-di* 氏 (*^{a}ti), favored by the medieval and modern homoiophonicity of the character, as well as its common attestation as a designation for several non-Chinese populations during the pre-Qin period. This variant is certainly not found in any of the ancient text editions, nor in Couvreur's modern text, from which Harbsmeier claims to quote.

[71] See Terrien de Lacouperie 1969 [1885–86], or, more recently, Robert H. Gassmann. 1997. *Antikchinesische Texte: Materialien für den Hochschulunterricht*. Bern, Frankfurt: Peter Lang, pp. 268–9.

Table 1: MC and OC for ji, xiang, didi and yi

Chinese character	*Pinyin*	MC	OC	*Guangyun/Yunjing*
a) 寄	*ji*	< *kjeH	< *[b]k(-r-)aj-s	居義切，見寘去三開
b) 象	*xiang*	< *zjangX	< *[b]zaŋ-ʔ	徐兩切，邪養上三開
c) 狄鞮	*didi*	< **dek-*dej*	< *[a]lek=*[b]de	徒歷切，定錫入四開
				部奚切，定齊平四開
d) 譯	*yi*	< *yek	< *[b]lAk	羊益切，以昔入三開

a) *ji* 寄 (var. *ji* 羈) 'to entrust, to commit to one's charge'
Ji is sometimes used as 'to entrust, to commit to one's charge',[72] but like b)–c) it is never found with the meaning 'to translate' in the edited literature or in inscriptions. In fact, *ji* < *[b]k(-r-)aj-s is quite suspect of being a mere transcription of an underlying foreign word, since the term for the East is quoted as *ji* 羈 < OC *[b]k(-r-)aj 'harness, halter, restrain' in Gao You's 高誘 (fl. 180–212) commentary to the *Lüshi chunqiu* 呂氏春秋 (Spring and Autumn Annals of Mr. Lü).[73]

b) *xiang* 象 'to outline, depict, delineate, represent, map'
Xiang is reconstructed as *[b]zaŋ-ʔ by Baxter, but Sagart has convincingly argued that Baxter's Old Chinese initial *z- should generally be rejected in favor of *s- + [-nasal]-clusters, although he does not reconstruct this particular word.[74] Even if conclusive *xiesheng*-information is lacking in this short series (GSR 728), it is clear from borrowings of the homographic word 'elephant', that we will have to posit a lateral cluster initial for *xiang*. Both semantic fields 'elephant; tusk' and 'to outline, delineate, represent, map' are found from the earliest layers of the edited literature onwards, whereas only the first meaning is amply attested in oracle bone inscriptions.[75] It occurs only once, in a late mid-Western Zhou bronze inscription, as an attributive in the gift-list

---

[72] Compare examples in *Hanyu dacidian* 漢語大詞典 , *s.v.*

[73] *Lüshi chunqiu* 呂氏春秋 (Spring and Autumn Annals of Mr. Lü) (*Zhuzi jicheng* ed., 17.5, p. 211).

[74] Sagart 1999, pp. 29–30.

[75] Cf. Zhao Cheng 1988, p. 201. Apart from the elephant as an animal hunted by the Shang, *xiang* 象 is also encountered as the name of one of Shang's enemies in *Yi* (2100.2).

expression *xiang mi* 象珥 'ivory bow ends'.[76] Schüssler considers *xiang* (< OC *s-ljaŋʔ) to be a loan from an Austroasiatic language[77] into Old Chinese and Written Tibetan glaṅ 'bull, ox; elephant', then from Old Chinese into Tai-Kadai,[78] from Tai-Kadai into Tibeto-Burman,[79] and finally from there back into Proto-Monic *ciiŋ 'elephant'![80] Peiros and Starostin straightforwardly reconstruct Sino-Tibetan *lăŋH 'a big animal (ox, elephant)' on the strength of the Old Chinese and Written Tibetan forms, as well as Jingpo *u-taŋ* 'bullock, steer'.[81]

Notice also that it is now sometimes assumed that the Common Slavic word *slonŭ, underlying Russian *slon* 'elephant', was borrowed from an unspecified Sino-Tibetan source.[82] Needless to say, that the archaeological and geographical frame for the necessary contacts between Austroasiatic and Slavic speakers during the early bronze age, remains a moot question.

Coming back to the question of the initial in *xiang* 象 'to outline, depict, delineate, represent, map' with its allograph *xiang* 像,[83] first attested in the Chu silk manuscript,[84] an argument for a lateral initial

---

[76] *Shi Tang fu ding* 師湯父鼎, see Tang Lan 唐蘭. 1986. *Xi-Zhou tongqi mingwen fendai shizheng* 西周銅器銘文分代史徵 (Western Zhou bronze inscriptions periodically arranged according to the historical evidence). Beijing: Zhonghua, p. 424, for a good transcription. Apart from that, there is a pictographic character resembling an elephant, found on the Shang *Zu Xin ding* 且辛鼎 (*Jinwenbian* 9: no. 1596.1) without any context, and a character transcribed as → 象 since Tan Qixiang 譚其驤 (1962. "E jun Qi jie mingwen shidi" 鄂君啟節銘文釋地 (Toponymical studies of the E jun tally inscription), in: *Zhonghua wenshi luncong* 2. Shanghai: Shanghai Guji, p. 169), which occurs in the *E jun Qi jie* tally inscription (II, 71) in the place name Xianghe 象禾 (near modern Biyang 泌陽, Henan province).

[77] Cf. Kharia *ɖɛʼrɛŋ*, Proto-Monic *draŋ > Literary Mon *draŋ, graŋ* 'animal horn, elephant tusk', Proto-Viet-Muong *traŋ 'tooth' etc.

[78] Proto-Tai *ɟaaŋ C 'elephant' and congeners.

[79] Cf. Proto-Lolo-Burmese *tsaŋ > Written Burmese hcaṅ 'elephant', Lepcha tyaŋ-mo 'elephant'

[80] Axel Schüssler. 1994. "Loanwords in Old Chinese", unpublished Ms., p. 23; G. Diffloth. 1984. *The Dvaravati Old Mon Language and Nyah Kur*. Bangkok: Chulalongkorn UPH, p. 63, N7, on the unexpected *-ii- for *-aa- in this root.

[81] Ilya Peiros and Sergej Starostin. 1996. *A Comparative Vocabulary of Five Sino-Tibetan Languages*. Melbourne: The University of Melbourne, Department of Linguistics, fasc. 3, p. 13, no. 44.

[82] Vjačeslav V. Ivanov. 1977. "Nazvanija slona v jazykax Evrazii. 1–3" (The designation of the elephant in the languages of Eurasia), *Ėtimologija 1975*. Moscow: Nauka, pp. 148–61.

[83] See *Zhouyi* 周易 (The Zhou 'Changes') (8, p. 74, SSJ 86a), and countless other pre-Qin examples collated for instance in Gao Heng 高亨 and Dong Zhi'an 董治安.

can also be made on the strength of *yang* 樣 < OC *^{b}laŋ-s, 'appearance, model, type'. The character, although found with this meaning only since the early medieval period, must certainly belong to the 'word-family' of *xiang* 象~像. In view of its internal and external connections, *xiang* < *s-laŋ-ʔ 'to represent' might therefore be construed as an *s-prefixed denominative derivation[85] (with *s-s > *s-ʔ long distance-dissimilation?) from an underlying nominal base, which was in turn marked as deverbal by the 'exoactive' *-s-suffix-formation, which gave rise to the Middle Chinese departing tone.[86] I will shortly return to the question if the underlying 'endoactive root' *^{b}laŋ was primary or derived through nasal suffixation from a root-finally velar root itself.

Xiang is never used in the meaning to 'translate' or 'translator' in pre-Qin literature predating the passage from the *Liji*, and in fact only starts to appear in this sense in the following passage of the twelfth of Han Gaozu's 漢高祖 (r. 206–195 BC) seventeen *Anshi Fangzhong ge* 安世房中歌 (Songs from within the chamber for the pacification of the age), recorded in the *Treatise on Etiquette and Music* (*Li-Yue zhi* 禮樂志) of the *Hanshu*:

	OC	rhyme
烏呼孝哉	*^{a}tsə	a
案撫戎國	*^{a}k-wək	A
蠻夷竭歡	*^{a}xʷar	X
象來致福	*^{b}pək	A

Oh, it is filial piety, indeed
that orders, quells the Rongish lands
The Man and Yi are in utmost delight
their translators come, blessings present.[87]

---

[83] (*cont.*) 1989. *Guzi tongjia huidian* 古字通假會典 (Handbook of phonetic loans, past and present). Jinan: Qi-Lu, p. 311.

[84] *Chu boshu* 楚帛書 (The Chu Silk Manuscript) (part 2, vol. 10, p. 26), see Noel Barnard. 1973. *The Ch'u Silk Manuscript: Translation and Commentary*. Canberra: Australian National University Press, p. 166, where it is used as a verb 'to depict'.

[85] On the functions of this prefix see Mei Tsu-lin. 1989. "The Causative and Denominative Functions of the *s-Prefix in Old Chinese", in: *Proceedings of the First International Conference on Sinology*. Taibei: Academia Sinica, pp. 33–51, and, more recently, Sagart 1999, pp. 70–3.

[86] Cf. Sagart 1999, p. 133. Note that *xiang* 橡 'oak' was freely interchangeable with *xiang* 樣 in early Chinese texts, providing another argument for the connection of the two phonophoric series.

Since *xiang* here figures in the same context of an enumeration of non-Chinese peoples, despite its being 'wrongly' assigned to both the (southern) Man and the (eastern) Yi, it is obvious that we are dealing here with an anachronistic passage, which might or might not allude to the *Liji*.

c) *didi* 狄鞮 (var. *didi* 狄騠, *diyi* 鞮譯, *yidi* 譯鞮, *yiji* 譯眡 ?)

The same is true, of course, of the quotation from the *Huainanzi* mentioned above, and the following passage found in the *Lüshi chunqiu*, where it is stressed that a 'civilized' country will not need interpreters. Lü Buwei 呂不韋 (d. 235 BC) says:

> 凡冠載之國，舟車之所通，不用象譯狄鞮，方三千里。
>
> In all countries of 'cap and sash' (=civilized countries), the area to which boats and carriages reach out, and in which one does not need 'representationists', 'translators' or '*didi*', amounts to 3,000 square miles.[88]

This consciously archaizing usage of the *Liji* set of translation terms eventually (and very sporadically) continues into the Late Imperial period, when Huang Zunxian 黃遵憲 (1848–1904) last uses the strange expression *didi* in his *Ba Meiguo liuxuesheng gan fu* 罷美國留學生感賦 (Rhapsody on my feelings about the retraction of overseas students in America) in a barely camouflaged criticism of the Qing government's lack of interest in foreign language education.[89]

Didi 狄鞮 < *^{a}lek=*^{b}de again looks like a transcription of an underlying non-Chinese word. This is hardly surprising, since borrowing of words for to 'translate, interprete' is cross-linguistically rather common in ancient languages. Notice for instance Greek ἑρμηνεύς 'interpreter', which has been borrowed from a Near Eastern language,[90] possibly from Akkadian *ta/urgumannu(m)*[91] 'dragoman', where the

---

[87] *Hanshu* (22, p. 1050), rhyme words indicated in OC. For a translation and commentary of this poem, and an excellent introduction to the cycle it forms part of, see Martin Kern. 1997. *Die Hymnen der chinesischen Staatsopfer. Literatur und Ritual in der politischen Repräsentation von der Han-Zeit bis zu den Sechs Dynastien.* Stuttgart: Steiner, p. 137 and pp. 100–73.

[88] *Lüshi chunqiu* (ZZJC 17.6: 210–1).

[89] *Renjinglu shi cao jianzhu* 人境盧詩草箋注 (Florilegium of poetry from the Hut of the Human Realm). 1981. Qian Zhonglian 錢仲聯 (ed.), Shanghai: Guji, 3 vols, vol. 1.3, p. 318: 惜哉國學舍，未及設狄鞮 (How sad that in the premises of learning of this country, / to institutionalize interpreters had not yet been achieved).

word is not native either,[92] but probably borrowed from a cuneiform Luwian-Hittite possessive base 'having an interpretation' → 'interpreter'.[93] Ancient Egyptian, on the other hand, did not even have a specific expression for 'interpreter', the word sometimes so translated[94] being in fact an onomatopoetic term for 'foreigner' corresponding to Greek βάρβαρος 'one who speaks gibberish'.[95]

The attempts of Kong Yingda 孔穎達 (574–658) to explain *di* 鞮 as a phonetic loan for causative *zhi* 知 < *[b]t-r-e 'to know',[96] and *di* 狄 as a loan for *di* 敵 < *[a]lek 'enemy', yielding a meaning 'to make the Di=enemy speech known' are certainly fanciful, but totally unconvincing, since the term occurs in several different orthographic disguises. Apart from the horse-determiner (orthographic) variant *didi* 狄 surviving in the *Huainanzi*, the same compound occurs as *yiji* 譯跽 < *[b]lAk=[b]g(-r-)ə (sic!) in the *Guanzi* 管子,[97] as *diyi* 鞮譯 in medieval dynastic histories,[98] and even as *yidi* 譯鞮 < *[b]lak=[b]de in the *History of the Liao*.[99] Moreover, the term is glossed as the 'name of a Western Rong music' by Guo Pu 郭璞 (276–324)[100] and as a northern Henei 河

---

[90] Pierre Chantraine et al. 1968–80. *Dictionnaire étymologique de la langue grecque: histoire des mots*. Paris: Klincksieck, p. 373: 'sans étymologie'. The derivation from the name of the messenger of the gods, Ἑρμῆς (cf., for instance, Hermann and von Soden 1959, col. 35) is not tenable.

[91] Ignaz J. Gelb. 1968. "The Word for Dragoman in the Ancient Near East", *Glossa* 2, pp. 93–104; Oswald Szemerényi. 1971. Review of Chantraine, *Gnomon* 43, p. 668.

[92] Wolfram von Soden. 1989. "Dolmetscher und Dolmetschen im Alten Orient", in: *Aus Sprache, Geschichte und Religion Babyloniens. Gesammelte Aufsätze*. Napels: Istituto Universitario Orientale, p. 351–7; 355.

[93] Frank Starke. 1993. "Zur Herkunft von akkad. *ta/urgumannu(m)* 'Dolmetscher', *Welt des Orients* 24, pp. 20–38; Gonzalo Rubio, "On the Alleged 'Pre-Sumerian Substratum'", *Journal of Cuneiform Studies* 51, pp. 1–16.

[94] Alan H. Gardiner. 1915. "The Egyptian Word for 'Dragoman'", *Proceedings of the Society of Biblical Archaeology* 37, pp. 117–25.

[95] Cf. Hans Goedicke. 1960. "The title [x] in the Old Kingdom", *Journal of Egyptian Archeology* 46, pp. 60–4; and ibid. 1966. "An Additional Note on [x]'Foreigner'", *Journal of Egyptian Archeology* 52, pp. 172–4.

[96] *Liji* (12, p. 110, SSJ 1338b).

[97] *Guanzi* 管子 (Master Guan) (ZZJC 14.40, p. 240).

[98] Cf. *Nanshi* (79–69: 1987), *Xin Tangshu* 新唐書 (New history of the Tang) (191, p. 5335).

[99] See for instance *Liaoshi* (81.11, p. 1286, 83.13, p. 1303).

內 place name known for its fine singers in a commentary by Wei Shao 韋邵 (204–273),[101] all pointing to a non-Chinese background.

When looking for an etymology of the word for 'to translate' or 'translator' associated with the West, one would either expect an Altaic or an Indoeuropean donor language. The most widespread word for 'interpreter' in the (Northern) Turkic languages is transparently derived from Common Turkic *tïl (younger *til) 'tongue, language' and a rare, possibly further analyzable suffix *-mac, *-macï.[102] As is well known, this very ancient cultural word turned out to become an enormously successful migratory term in- and outside the Turkic world, surviving in Modern German ('Dolmetscher'), all Slavic languages, Persian, Mongolic, several Caucasian languages, and Hungarian.[103] It would be tempting to link the second syllable of the Chinese term for 'to translate' in the West to Old Turkic tïl ~ til, but since corroborative evidence is lacking, an analysis 'to use the Di tongue' remains a non liquet so far. In the East Iranian and Tocharian B speaking Indo-European languages adjacent to the Ancient Chinese territory, there is, as far as I can see, no possible connection with didi to be found either. Tibetan, another possible source language in the region, has sgyur(-ba) for 'to translate, transform (one's body)', also for 'to alter, give up and leave', so, here again, we are facing a dead end.

---

[100] In a commentary to Sima Xiangru's 司馬相如 Shanglin fu 上林賦 (Rhapsody on the Imperial Hunting Grounds) in the Wenxuan 文選 (Anthology of literature) (Shangwu ed., vol. 1, 8: 166), repeated also in Hanshu (2569, n. 18).

[101] Shiji (117.57, p. 3039, n. 11).

[102] Cf. J. Németh. 1958. "Zur Geschichte des Wortes tolmács 'Dolmetscher'", Acta Orientalia Hungarica 8.1, pp. 1–8.

[103] See, among others, P. Jyrkänkallo. 1952. "Zur Etymologie von russ. tolmač 'Dolmetscher' und seiner türkischen Quelle", Studia Orientalia in memoriam saecularem Georg August Wallin, 1811–1852. Helsinki: Societas Orientalis Fennica, pp. 3–11; Gerhard Doerfer. 1965. Türkische und mongolische Elemente im Neupersischen: unter besonderer Berücksichtigung älterer neupersischer Geschichtsquellen, vor allem der Mongolen- und Timuridenzeit. Wiesbaden: Steiner, vol. 2, pp. 663–5, #1010, s.v. tïlmācï; Peter B. Golden. 1980. Khazar Studies. An Historico-Philological Inquiry into the Origins of the Khazars. Budapest: Akadémiai Kiadó, p. 213–4, s.v. tᶜarmačᶜ.

d) *yi* 譯 'to translate'

Let us finally take a closer look at *yi*, the only one of the *Liji*-terms which survived and eventually became to dominate the whole lexical field of 'translation' until the present day. An interesting commentarial tradition, going back at least to Kong Yingda's notes on our passage, explains *yi* < OC *blAk 'to translate' via *yi* 易 < MC *yeH < OC *blek-s 'to change':[104]

> 譯即易，謂換譯言語使相解。
> 'To translate' (*blAk) is 'to exchange (*blek-s), that is to say to alter and change the words of languages to make them mutually understandable.

Much later in the history of Buddhist translation theory, this paronomastic definition is quoted many times, most explicitly by Fayun 法雲 (1087–1158), a monk who did not know Sanskrit, but nevertheless became famous for his dictionary *cum* thesaurus—*Fanyi ming yi ji* 翻譯名義集 or *Collected Meanings of Translated Terms [in the Tripiṭaka]* of 1157. In the preface to this huge thesaurus of Buddhist terms Fayun writes:[105]

> 譯之言易也，謂以其所有，易其所無。故以此方之經，而顯彼土之法。
> To 'translate' something means to 'exchange', i.e. 'to exchange what one does have for what one does not'. That is why one replaces the teachings (*fa, dharma*) of another country using the canonical scriptures of this region here.

This connection might have been one of the rather rare cases, where a Han paronomastic gloss is not just simply a rhetorical device or a vehicle for popular etymology, but where it reflects a genuine etymological relationship. *Yi* 'to translate' and *yi* 'to change' are cognate through an ancient morphological pattern, namely an ablaut relationship, widespread in the archaic Chinese lexicon, and first noticed in several seminal papers by E. G. Pulleyblank.[106] Semantically, the shift

---

[104] Commentary on *Liji* (12: 110, SSJ 1338b–c).

[105] *Fanyi ming yiji* (*Taishō* 54.2131, 1, p. 2131a).

[106] Cf. Edwin G. Pulleyblank. 1965. "Close/Open Ablaut in Sino-Tibetan", in: G. B. Milner and E. J. A. Henderson (eds.). *Indo-Pacific Linguistic Studies*. Amsterdam: North Holland Publ., pp. 230–40; ibid. 1989. "Ablaut and Initial Voicing in Old Chinese Morphology: *a as an Infix and Prefix", in: *Proceedings of the Second International Conference on Sinology. Section on Linguistics and Paleography*. Taibei: Academia Sinica, pp. 1–21.

from 'change' to 'translate' is straightforward.[107] Moreover, just like in the case of Latin, where one of the two competing etymologies for *interpres* 'translator' explains the word via *inter-pretium*, and thereby etymologically links it to the sphere of commercial and juridical transactions in which the word is encountered in the earliest attestations,[108] *yi* 'to exchange' in Chinese is strongly associated with the domain of gift-giving, land and title bestowal, and all sorts of investiture transactions in inscriptional Archaic Chinese, via *ci* 賜 < OC *^{b}s-hlek-s.[109] This character is certainly an *s-derivation of the same root, which is quite regularly written *without* the *bei* 貝 'cowrie' determiner in pre-Qin texts. Notice also that the homographic, today even homophonic, word *yi* 易 < OC *^{b}lek 'be at ease, easy' etc.,[110] first attested epigraphically in Warring States bronze inscriptions from the state of Zhongshan 中山 , again has a direct counterpart in the ablauting phonophoric series of *yi* in the form of its homophone *yi* 懌 < OC *^{b}lak 'be relaxed, pleased, at ease'. Since both *yi* 譯 and *yi* 易 are 'introvert' under Pulleyblank's apophonic theory, one would have to look further for the 'extrovert' counterpart, for which *yi* 異 < *yiH < *^{b}lǝk-s 'be different, differ' would seem the most likely candidate. To complicate things even further, there is good evidence from the *Zhouyi* that *yi* 易 was used as a loan for *di* 狄 < *^{a}lek.[111] The same loan relationship appears again in *Baihu tong* 白虎通 (Comprehensive discussions in the White Tiger Hall), where we read:[112]

---

[107] Cf. for instance the Sumerian term for 'interpreter' *eme-bal(a)*, which means 'language changer', see von Soden 1989, p. 351.

[108] Rochette 1996a, pp. 79–80; Bruno Rochette. 1996b. "ΠΙΣΤΟΙ ΈΡΜΗΝΕΙΣ. La traduction orale en Grèce", *Révue des Études Grècques* 109, p. 328 with n. 10. The other explanation, first found in Isidorus of Seville (ca. 560–636), derives the word from *inter-partes* '[the one] standing between two sides', cf. E. Pariente. 1950. "*Partare, interpretari y pellere*", *Emerita* 18, pp. 25–37.

[109] Cf. Sagart 1999, pp. 67, 71. Peiros and Starostin 1996, vol. 3, p. 15, #52, reconstruct Sino-Tibetan *lek ~ *leŋ, where the velar final variant is posited to account for Proto-Kiranti *léŋ.

[110] Compared to Written Tibetan *legs* 'good, happy' by Peiros and Starostin 1996, vol. 3, p. 15, and reconstructed to the Sino-Tibetan level as *l[ĕ]k .

[111] Cf. Gerhard Schmitt. 1970. *Sprüche der Wandlungen auf ihrem geistesgeschichtlichen Hintergrund*. Berlin: Akademie, pp. 34, 105, who considers *di* to be a derivation from *ti* 逖 (*^{a}hlek) 'be distant; cause to be distant', or its common homophone-allograph *ti* 逷 .

[112] *Baihu tong* 白虎通 (Comprehensive discussions in the White Tiger Hall) (ACS-ed., 16.2–3), cf. Tjan Tjoe Som (Zeng Zhusen 曾珠森). 1949. *Po Hu T'ung*

戎者，強惡也，狄者，易也。

Rong means to be strong and bad, *di* to be flippant.

It is even more surprising to find *yi* as a gloss for *xiang* 象 'to represent', again in the *Zhouyi*, which opens even more doors for speculation that the items in our passage have not been selected at random, but form part of an ancient Chinese morphological pattern.[113] This would seem much more reasonable than to assume creation of this complex set of terms just in order to fulfill the quadrant scheme of the *Liji*.

Summing up, it seems likely that there was a root 'to change', which yielded *yi* in a northern dialect ablaut derivation, and which certainly must have had a morphological relationship with its nasal final counterpart 'be like, model', ultimately underlying *xiang*. Before we do not have a convincing analysis of *didi* and congeners, we cannot be sure whether the first syllable of this word belonged to the sketched root as well, while it is clear, that *ji*, the term of the East, did not.

5.2 Post-Classical period

5.2.1 fanyi 翻譯

When then did *yi* get augmented by *fan* 翻 'to turn over', to form the compound that eventually survived to the present day? The binome *fanyi* is first attested in connection with the earliest translations of Buddhist texts, and, since the *Suishu* 隋書 (History of the Sui) and *Jiu Tangshu* 舊唐書 (Old history of the Tang), found in the dynastic histories as well. The term *fan* 翻 ~ 繙 (this later variant used predominantly since the late Yuan) 'leaf through books and notes'[114] reflects the collective process of comparing written translation notes. These translation notes were taken by the audiences, sometimes numbering in the thousands, recording oral explanations by foreign monks in the so-called *yichang* 譯場 or 'translation-assemblies', which were characteristic of translation and mission procedure during phase I (148–316) and the first part of phase II (317–617) of the Buddhist transla-

---

112 *(cont.) The Comprehensive Discussions in the White Tiger Hall*. Leiden: Brill, vol. 2, p. 401. See on this passage also Krol' 1973, p. 18.

113 *Zhouyi* (46 xi B, p. 3).

114 This meaning is already attested in the *Zhuangzi* 莊子 (Harvard-Yenching ed., 13, p. 35).

tion movement in China.[115] In any case, the retrospective paronomastic pun, found in some late Medieval works, is certainly problematic, and better understood as a Buddhist popular etymology:[116]

夫翻譯者，謂翻梵天之語，轉成漢地之言。音雖似別，義則大同。〈宋高僧傳〉云：如翻綿繡，背面俱華，但左右不同耳。

To 'translate' means to 'turn over' (*fan*, EMC *p^huan) words of the 'heavens of *brahman*' (*fan*, EMC *buam^h, *brahmaloka*, i.e. Indian words) and to transform them into the language of the Han territories. Even if the sounds are seemingly different, meanings by and large correspond. In the *Biographies of eminent monks compiled under the Song* it is said: 'It is like turning over a brocade embroidery: front and back are both gorgeous, but left and right are reversed.'[117]

5.2.2 Further regional developments

Throughout the Zhou, *xiangxu* 象胥 continued to be used as the general title for governmental translation officers. During the Han dynasty the so-called 'translation officers' (*yiguan* 譯官, also *yiling* 譯令, *yishi* 譯史 'translation envoy') belonged to the newly established Great Herald's Office (*dahonglu* 大鴻臚), but during the Sui, Tang and Song dynasties, officials of the so-called *sifang guan* 四方館 ('office in charge of the four lateral regions') increasingly managed the incoming translation jobs.

Apart from *yiguan* there were at least two other regional and informal terms for 'interpreter' from Tang through Qing, which have no relationship to the governmental translation bureaucracy at all. These are *tangbo* 唐舶 (EMC *daŋ-baijk) or *tangpa* 唐帕 (EMC *daŋ-p^haij^h) 'nautical interpreter', a term assigned to the Southern Fan (*nanfan* 南番) in most sources, and the curious word *pucha* 蒲叉 (EMC *bɔ-tsai^h, usually traced to 'Western' Man 蠻 and Yao 猺 peoples, in the Chinese sources, and therefore presumably of Hmong-Mienic extrac-

---

[115] I will not deal with the history of Buddhist translations in China here, for which excellent studies abound. See, for instance, Walter Fuchs. 1930. "Zur technischen Organization der chinesischen Sanskrit-Übersetzungen", *Asia Major* 6, pp. 84–103; Ma Zuyi 1984; Tso Szu-bong (Cao Shibang) 曹仕邦. 1963. "Lun Zhongguo fojiao yichang zhi yijing fangshi yu chengxu" 論中國佛教譯場之譯經方式與程序 (On the methods and procedures of sūtra translation in the Buddhist 'translation assemblies' in China), *Xin-Ya Xuebao*, pp. 239–321; Wang Wenyan 1984; and Harbsmeier 1998, chapter (g).

[116] *Fanyi ming yi ji*, Fayun's preface of 1157.

[117] *Taishō* (50.2061, 3, p. 723a).

tion. Unfortunately, no convincing etymology has been found for these expressions so far.[118]

5.2.3 New terms relating to translation activities during the Yuan and Ming period

After the disruption of government sponsored Buddhist translation projects in 1037, a very diversified vocabulary for titles and activities relating to translation developed rapidly after the beginning of the Mongol rule. The most important titles of this period are

> *tongshi* 通事 'interpreter',
> *yishi* 譯史 'translation envoy',
> *qielimachi* 怯里馬赤 (EMC *kʰɨap=lɨ'=maɨ'=tɕʰiajk) ~ *qilimichi* 乞里覓赤 (EMC *kʰɨjʰ=lɨ'=mɛjk=tʂʰiajk) < Middle Mong. *kele(m)ec&'linguist',
> *shuxie* 書寫 copyists [of script of the various nationalities],
> *zhalichi* 扎里赤 (EMC *tʂaɨt=lɨ'=tʂʰiajk) < Mong. *jarliɣci* 'interlocutor', and
> *bishechi* 必闍赤 (EMC *pjit=dʑia=tʂʰiajk) ~ *biqieqi* 筆且齊 (EMC *pit=tsʰia'=dzɛj) < Mong. *bic[ig]eci* '[foreign] scribe'.[119]

For the most part, the officers filling these posts were under formal jurisdiction of the *Menggu Hanlinyuan* 蒙古翰林院, which had been separated form the general Hanlin-Academy in 1275. The general purpose of this academy is succinctly summarized by Ke Shaomin 柯劭忞 (1850–1933) in the treatise on bureaucracy (*Baiguan zhi* 百官志) of the *Xin Yuanshi* 新元史 (New history of the Yuan):[120]

> 蒙古翰林院拿譯寫一切文字及頌降璽書，並用蒙古文字仍各以其國字副之。
> The Mongolian Hanlin Academy is in charge of transcribing all foreign scripts, to promulgate them with the imperial seal attached, and to furthermore supplement the original characters in parallel to the Mongolian script.

Apart from the Hanlin-Academy, governmental translators were attached to the 'Chancellery of the Eight Inner Palace Offices' (*Nei ba fu zaixiang* 內八府宰相), which was originally charged with the for-

---

[118] For a collection of references cf. Han Xingzhi 韓省之 (ed.). 1991. *Chengwei da cidian* 稱謂大辭典 (Great dictionary of appellatives). Beijing: Xin shijie, p. 635.

[119] Cf. David M. Farquhar. 1990. *The Government of China Under Mongol Rule. A Reference Guide.* Stuttgart: Steiner, p. 32, p. 65n142; n143; n150; p. 128; 158n8; p. 64n139; 248; 258n33; and Charles O. Hucker. 1985. *A Dictionary of Official Titles in Imperial China.* Stanford: Stanford University Press, #7503, #5432, #4576, #4585 with references.

[120] *Xin Yuanshi* 新元史 (New history of the Yuan) (57.24, p. 646b).

mal relationships between the emperor and the princes[121] and the organization and protocol of foreign audiences,[122] and occasionally helped the *Hanlinyuan* with the translation of Mongolian edicts. Finally, interpreters were also working in the 'College of the Classics' (*jingyan* 經筵), where discussions between the emperor and his academicians were held.[123]

After the end of the Mongol period, the famous *Siyiguan* 四譯館 was established in 1407 in Nanjing. Until 1496 this translators' college was controlled by the Hanlin-Academy,[124] with which it moved to the new capital Beijing in 1420. In 1496 it became part of the *Taichangsi* 太常四 in the Ministry of Rites (*Libu* 禮部) along with the Office of the [Great] Herald (*Honglusi* 鴻臚寺).[125] Its primary occupation was to teach 'translators of documents' (*yishu* 譯書),[126] whereas the so-called *huitongguan* 會通館 'Interpreters Association Office', established already under Kubilai Khan, provided for *tongshi* 通事 or 'interpreters'. That the work of this latter institution was much more practice-oriented can be gathered from the fact that it formed part of the Ministry of War (*Bingbu* 兵部) and that it was mostly occupied with hosting and catering to foreign embassies to the court. Both offices were unified under the new title *Huitong-Siyiguan* in 1748, since, as the edict stated, the *Siyiguan* had long deteriorated into a "totally superfluous institution, characterized by rampant idleness."[127] Since the fascinating story of the *Siyiguan* has been told many times in the literature,[128] we will now conclude our little review

---

[121] See Farquhar 1990, p. 128, #17.

[122] *Xin Yuanshi* (57.24, p. 647a), *Gujin tushu jicheng* (555/380, p. 6a).

[123] *Yuanshi* (186.73b: 4270), cf. Hucker 1985, #11249.

[124] Cf. Paul Pelliot. 1948. "Le Ḥōǰa et le Sayyid Ḥusain de l'Histoire des Ming", *T'oung Pao* 38, pp. 81–292; 247; Charles O. Hucker. 1958. "Governmental Organization of the Ming Dynasty", *Harvard Journal of Asiatic Studies* 21, pp. 1–67; 34, n. 70.

[125] *Mingshi* 明史 (History of the Ming) (74.4: 1802).

[126] *Mingshi* (74.1b, p. 1797). For a translation of two longer official documents relating to the functions of this office see Walter Fuchs. 1931. "Remarks on a New 'Hua-i-i-yü'", *Bulletin of the Catholic University of Peking* 8, pp. 95–7.

[127] *Da-Qing huangdi shengxun* 大清皇帝聖訓 (The sacred edict of the Great Qing emperor) (224, p. 14), cf. Otto Franke and Berthold Laufer. 1914. *Lamaistische Klosterinschriften aus Peking, Jehol und Si-ngan, in zwei Mappen*. Berlin: Dietrich Reimer/Ernst Vohsen and Hamburg: L. Friederichsen and Co., p. 4b.

[128] See, among many others, Norman Wild. 1943–46. "Materials for a Study of the Ssu I Kuan", *Bulletin of the School of Oriental and African Studies* 11, pp. 617–

of the terms for translation and interpretation in pre-modern China a few remarks of a more general nature.

CONCLUSION

Looking at the development of translation and interpretation as reflected in non-Buddhist Ancient and Medieval Chinese texts, the most striking observation to be made is the enormous paucity of available evidence and references. It is painfully obvious that throughout most of China's pre-Qing history, there was a deeply engrained lack of interest in foreign languages, much in contrast to the rich ethnographic testimony available on foreign eating and drinking customs, hair-styles, fashions, sexual behaviours, flora and fauna, exotica, weaponry and the like. This is rather reminiscent of the situation in Ancient India, Egypt[129] and even Greece,[130] where all known references to 'translation' and 'interpretation' during the pre-Hellenic period easily fit on two letter-size pages.[131] Unlike in pre-Qin China, however, pejorative characterization of foreign tongues *did* occasionally figure in identity claims, i.e. Greek definitions of what constitutes Greekness (*to Hellenikon*).[132] Contrary to a widespread assumption it is unlikely that it was the complexity and extraordinary stability of the non-alphabetic Chinese writing system, which somehow impeded a more thoroughgoing interest in foreign ways of communication. Nor did the Old Chinese language possess any intrinsic properties that would have stood in the way of large-scale interaction with its linguis-

---

[128] (*cont.*) 40; Pelliot 1948; and the collection of primary sources in *Gujin tushu jicheng* (380, *s.v. Siyiguanbu huikao* 四譯館部會考 (Collected studies on the Office of Interpreters for the Four Regions)).

[129] See Poo Mu-chou. 1998. "Encountering the Strangers. A Comparative Study of Cultural Consciousness in Ancient Egypt, Mesopotamia, and China", in: C. J. Eyre (ed.). *Proceedings of the Seventh International Congress of Egyptologists. Cambridge, 3–9 September 1995.* Leuven: Uitgeverij Peeters (Orientalia Lovaniensia Analecta 82), pp. 885–92.

[130] See on this point Harbsmeier 1998, p. 82.

[131] Cf. Rochette 1993 and the contributions to Carl W. Müller et al. (eds.). 1992. *Zum Umgang mit fremden Sprachen in der griechisch-römischen Antike.* Stuttgart: Steiner.

[132] Cf. C. Tuplin. 1999. "Greek Racism? Observations on the Character and Limits of Greek Ethnic Prejudice", in: G. R. Tsetskhladze (ed.). *Ancient Greeks East and West.* Leiden: Brill (Mnemosyne: Bibliotheca Classica Batava, Suppl. 196), pp. 47–75.

tic neighbours, from where, as we only begin to understand recently, it absorbed considerable amounts of vocabulary and morphosyntactic structures during prolonged contact situations periodically prevailing since the late Neolithic.[133] If it still makes any sense to ask those nagging "Why did China not…" questions at all, reasons for its ignorance of translation work are unlikely to be provided by the study of the Chinese language. Rather than perpetuate the myth of an inert, isolated and isolating Chinese language, and *a fortiori*, ancient Chinese ethnos and society in general, lurking behind this type of questions, we should try to look closer into shared sociological, political, and environmental predispositions of those ancient societies, which despite constant and constantly shifting contacts with foreign languages and their speakers, managed to eschew serious theoretical interest in the problems of translation so contumaciously. Seen from this perspective, it was no accident that of the several contending expressions for 'translate/interprete' analyzed above, it was *yi*, the term associated with the north, which won out in the later lexicon. For even if the ultimate linguistic pedigree of these expressions remains somewhat elusive beneath an apparent morphological relatedness, it is clear that the definitive consolidation of *yi* arose out of the massive initial encounter of the 'Empire of writing'[134] with Buddhism—a foreign sacred tradition, with its hybrid linguistic idioms of transmission and manifold associated text and recitation cultures. All of this happened throughout the late Han and early medieval periods, i.e. during a crucial linguistic transition in China, when the written language for the first time in its attested history started to diverge radically from its underlying spoken form and a good number of sweeping typological changes in phonology, syntax and morphology firmly took root. Looking for historical parallels elsewhere, the ensuing 'diglossia' is, in a sense, comparable to the situation surrounding the incipient obsolescence of spoken Sumerian, which led to the emergence of the first extant tradition of bilingual lexicography in the form of Sumero-Eblaitic

---

[133] Cf. pp. 175–6 above and Schüssler 1994.

[134] I am borrowing this term from M. E. Lewis. 1999. *Writing and Authority in Early China*. Albany: SUNY Press (SUNY Series in Chinese Philosophy and Culture), ch. 8, pp. 337–65.

and -Akkadian word lists beginning with the twentyfourth century BC.[135]

Real-world *hic-et-nunc* linguistic diversity, it seems, has nowhere been a sufficient trigger for the development of a theoretical interest in language, languages and the ubiquitous interstices between them. Additional non-linguistic factors like the sway or decay of alien administrative or religious systems were needed. In ancient Chinese society, where the widely shared Confucian ethical vision of human transformability through self-cultivation quintessentially *included* the 'Barbarians', translatability between languages would have been taken for granted. Yet if 'to translate is to exchange', and therefore entails engagement in a kind of linguistic customer-client relationship, it is understandable why there was hardly any leeway for such an activity in the universalist Confucian anthropology of pre-Buddhist China.

---

[135] Cf. Claude Boisson et al. 1991. "Aux origines de la lexicographie: les premiers dictionnaires monolingues et bilingues", *International Journal of Lexicography* 4.4, pp. 261–315; and Giovanni Pettinato. 1981. "I vocabulari bilingui di Ebla. Problemi di traduzione e di lessicografia sumerico-eblaita", in: L. Cagni (ed.). *La lingua di Ebla*. Napels: Instituto Universitario Orientale, pp. 241–76.

References

Bailey, Harold. 1946. "Gāndhārī", *Bulletin of the School of Oriental and African Studies* 11.4, p. 139.

Barnard, Noel. 1973. *The Ch'u Silk Manuscript: Translation and Commentary.* Canberra: Australian National University Press.

Baxter, William H. 1992. *A handbook of Old Chinese phonology.* Berlin, New York: Mouton de Gruyter.

Bengtson, John D. and Václav Blažek. 1995. "Lexica Dene-Caucasica", *Central Asiatic Journal* 29, pp. 11–50.

Biot, Édouard. 1851. *Le Tcheou-Li ou rites des Tcheou.* Paris: L'Imprimerie Nationale.

Boisson, Claude et al. 1991. "Aux origines de la lexicographie: les premiers dictionnaires monolingues et bilingues", *International Journal of Lexicography* 4.4, pp. 261–315.

Brough, John. 1961. "A Kharoṣṭhī Inscription from China", *Bulletin of the School of Oriental and African Studies* 24.3, pp. 517–30.

Cavalli-Sforza, Luigi Luca. 1998. "The Chinese Human Genome Diversity Project", *Proceedings of the National Academy of Science* 95, pp. 11501–3.

Chang, K. C. 1980. *Shang Civilization.* New Haven, London: Yale University Press.

Chantraine, Pierre et al. 1968–80. *Dictionnaire étymologique de la langue grecque: histoire des mots.* Paris: Klincksieck.

Chavannes, Édouard. 1905. "Les pays d'occident d'après le Wei Lio", *T'oung Pao* 6 , pp. 519–71.

Chu, J. Y. et al. 1998. "Genetic Relationship of Populations in China", *Proceedings of the National Academy of Sciences* 95, pp. 11763–8.

Coblin, W. S. 1974. "A New Study of the Pailang Songs", *The Ts'ing-Hua Journal of Chinese Studies* 12.1–2, pp. 179–211.

Couvreur, F. Séraphim. 1913. *Li ki ou mémoires sur les bienséances et les cérémonies.* Ho Kien Fou: Imprimerie de la Mission Catholique, second edition.

Diffloth, G. 1984. *The Dvaravati Old Mon Language and Nyah Kur.* Bangkok: Chulalongkorn UPH.

Ding Shan 丁山. 1988. *Jiaguwen suojian shizu ji qi zhidu* 甲骨文所見氏族及其制度 (Clans and lineages reflected in the oracle bone inscriptions and their system). Beijing: Zhonghua shuju.

Dixon, Robert M. W. 1997. *The Rise and Fall of Languages.* Cambridge: Cambridge University Press.

Doerfer, Gerhard. 1965. *Türkische und mongolische Elemente im Neupersischen: unter besonderer Berücksichtigung älterer neupersischer Geschichtsquellen, vor allem der Mongolen- und Timuridenzeit.* Wiesbaden: Steiner.

Du, Ruofu et al. 1994. *Chinese Surnames and Genetic Difference Between North and South China.* Berkeley: Department of East Asian Studies.

Farquhar, David M. 1990. *The Government of China Under Mongol Rule. A Reference Guide.* Stuttgart: Steiner.

Franke, Otto and Berthold Laufer. 1914. *Lamaistische Klosterinschriften aus Peking, Jehol und Si-ngan, in zwei Mappen.* Berlin: Dietrich Reimer/Ernst Vohsen and Hamburg: L. Friederichsen and Co.

Fuchs, Walter. 1930. "Zur technischen Organisation der chinesischen Sanskrit-Übersetzungen", *Asia Major* 6, pp. 84–103.

——. 1931. "Remarks on a New 'Hua-i-i-yü'", *Bulletin of the Catholic University of Peking* 8, pp. 95–7.

Gao Heng 高亨 and Dong Zhi'an 董治安. 1989. *Guzi tongjia huidian* 古字通假會典 (Handbook of phonetic loans, past and present). Jinan: Qi-Lu.

Gardiner, Alan H. 1915. "The Egyptian Word for 'Dragoman'", *Proceedings of the Society of Biblical Archaeology* 37, pp. 117–25.

Gassmann, Robert H. 1997. *Antikchinesische Texte: Materialien für den Hochschulunterricht.* Bern, Frankfurt: Peter Lang.

——. 2000. "Auf der Suche nach der antikchinesischen Gesellschaft. Überlegungen zu *ren* und *min*", *Minima Sinica* 12.1, pp. 15–30.

Gelb, Ignaz J. 1968. "The Word for Dragoman in the Ancient Near East", *Glossa* 2, pp. 93–104.

Goedicke, Hans. 1960. "The title [x] in the Old Kingdom", *Journal of Egyptian Archeology* 46, pp. 60–4.

——. 1966. "An Additional Note on [x] 'Foreigner'", *Journal of Egyptian Archeology* 52, pp. 172–4.

Golden, Peter B. 1980. *Khazar Studies. An Historico-Philological Inquiry into the Origins of the Khazars.* Budapest: Akadémiai Kiadó.

Grimes, Barbara F. et al. 1996. *Ethnologue.* Dallas: Summer Institute of Linguistics, 13th ed.

Hale, Ken et al. 1989. "Endangered Languages", *Language* 68.1, pp. 1–42.

Han Xingzhi 韓省之 (ed.). 1991. *Chengwei da cidian* 稱謂大辭典 (Great dictionary of appelatives). Beijing: Xin shijie.

Harbsmeier, Christoph. 1998. *Language and Logic in Traditional China,* in: Joseph Needham (ed.). *Science and Civilization in China.* vol. 7. Pt. 1. Cambridge: Cambridge University Press.

Hermann, Alfred. 1956. "Dolmetschen im Altertum. Ein Beitrag zur antiken Kulturgeschichte", in: *Schriften des Auslands- und Dolmetscherinstituts der Johannes Gutenberg-Universität Mainz in Germersheim I.* Munich: Isar, pp. 25–59.

Hermann, Alfred and Wolfram von Soden. 1959. "Dolmetscher", in: Th. Klauser (ed.). *Reallexikon für Antike und Christentum. Sachwörterbuch zur Auseinandersetzung des Christentums mit der antiken Welt.* Stuttgart: A. Hiersemann, vol. 4, col. 24–49.

Hori Toshikazu. 1994. "The Exchange of Written Communications Between Japan, Sui and Tang Dynasties", *Memoirs of the Research Department of the Tōyō Bunko* 52, pp. 1–19.

Hornblower, S. and A. Spawnford (eds.). 1996. *The Oxford Classical Dictionary.* Oxford: Oxford University Press.

Hucker, Charles O. 1958. "Governmental Organization of the Ming Dynasty", *Harvard Journal of Asiatic Studies* 21, pp. 1–67.

——. 1985. *A Dictionary of Official Titles in Imperial China.* Stanford: Stanford University Press.

Ivanov, Vjačeslav V. 1977. "Nazvanija slona v jazykax Evrazii. 1–3" (The designation of the elephant in the languages of Eurasia), *Étimologija 1975.* Moscow: Nauka, pp. 148–61.

Ji Xianlin 季羨林. 1985. "Shuo 'chujia'" 説'出家' (On the expression 'to leave the family'), in: Guojia wenwuju guwenxian yanjiushi (ed.). *Chutu wenxian yanjiu* 出土文獻研究 (Studies of excavated documents). Beijing: Wenwu.

Jyrkänkallo, P. 1952. "Zur Etymologie von russ. *tolmač* 'Dolmetscher' und seiner türkischen Quelle", *Studia Orientalia in memoriam saecularem Georg August Wallin, 1811–1852.* Helsinki: Societas Orientalis Fennica, pp. 3–11.

Kern, Martin. 1997. *Die Hymnen der chinesischen Staatsopfer. Literatur und Ritual in der politischen Repräsentation von der Han-Zeit bis zu den Sechs Dynastien.* Stuttgart: Steiner.

Krauss, Michael. 1995. "The Scope of Language Endangerment and Responses to it", paper presented at the International Symposium on Endangered Languages, November 1–20, Tōkyō University.

Kravcova, M. E. 1992. "Étnokul'turnoe raznoobrazie drevnego Kitaja" (The ethnocultural diversity of Ancient China), *Vostok* 3, pp. 56–66.

Krol', Jurij L. 1973. "O koncepcii 'Kitaj – Varvary'" (On the concepts 'China – The Barbarians'), in: *Obščestvo i gosudarstvo v Kitaje (Sbornik Statej)* (Society and state in China: a collection of articles). Moscow: Nauka, pp. 13–29.

Lackner, Michael. 1998. "Anmerkungen zur historischen Semantik von 'China', 'Nation' und 'chinesischer Nation' im modernen Chinesisch", in: H. Turk, B. Schulze and R. Simanowski (eds.). *Kulturelle Grenzziehungen im Spiegel der Literaturen. Nationalismus, Regionalismus, Fundamentalismus.* Göttingen: Wallstein, pp. 323–39.

Leer, Jeff. 1999. "Recent Advances in Athabaskan-Eyak-Tlingit Reconstruction", paper presented at the Fourteenth Athabaskan Language Conference, May 21–23, University of New Mexico, Albuquerque.

Legge, James. 1967. *Li Chi, Book of Rites.* New Hyde Park: University Books.

Lévi, Sylvain. 1910. "Études des documents tokhariens de la mission Pelliot. I.: Les bilingues", *Journal Asiatique* 10e sér. 17, p. 379.

Lewis, M. E. 1999. *Writing and Authority in Early China.* Albany: SUNY Press (SUNY Series in Chinese Philosophy and Culture).

Li Fang 李方. 1994. "Tang Xizhou de yiyuren" 唐西州的譯語人 (Xizhou interpreters under the Tang), *Wenwu* 2, pp. 45–51.

Li Hu 黎虎. 1988. "Yindai waijiao zhidu chu tan" 殷代外交制度初談 (Preliminary discussion of the system of foreign relations during the Yin period), *Lishi yanjiu* 5, pp. 36–47.

Li Zhimin 李志敏. 1986. "'Hanzu' minghao qiyuan kao" '漢族'名號起源考 (A study on the origins of the designation 'Hanzu'), *Zhongguoshi yanjiu* 3, p. 49.

Lin Yun 林澐. 1981. "Jiaguwen zhongde Shangdai fangguo lianmeng" 甲骨文中的商代方國聯盟 (Shang dynasty lateral country alliances in the oracle bone inscriptions), *Guwenzi yanjiu* 6, p. 67.

——. 1986. "Guanyu Zhongguo zaoqi guojia xingshi de jige wenti" 關於中國早期國家形式的幾個問題 (On several problems relating to the early form of the state in China), *Jilin daxue shehui kexue xuebao* 6, pp. 1–12.

Lochner von Hüttenbach, Fritz Freiherr. 1979. "Bemerkungen zur sprachlichen Heterogenität im Altertum", *Grazer Linguistische Studien* 9, pp. 65–78.

Loewe, Michael. 1994. "China's Sense of Unity as Seen in the Early Empires", *T'oung Pao* 80, pp. 6–26.

Luo Zongtao 羅宗濤. 1982. "Gudai fanyi shulüe" 古代翻譯述略 (A short exposition of translation in antiquity), *Hanxue yanjiu tongxun* 2, p. 38–40.

Ma Chengyuan 馬承源 et al. (eds.). 1989–90. *Shang-Zhou qingtongqi mingwenxuan* 商周青銅器銘文選 (Selected Shang and Zhou bronze inscriptions). Beijing: Wenwu.

Ma Zuyi 馬祖毅. 1984. *Zhongguo fanyi jian shi—'wusi' yundong yiqian bufen* 中國翻譯簡史 — 五四運動以前部分 (A short history of translation in China—The period before the May Fourth movement). Beijing: Zhongguo duiwai fanyi.

Magoshi Yasushi 馬越靖史. 1998. "Kōkotsubun ni okeru 'jin'" 甲骨文における'人' (On 'ren' in the oracle bone inscriptions), *Tōhōgaku* 92, pp. 16–29.

Mair, Victor H. (ed.). 2001. *The Columbia History of Chinese Literature*. New York: Columbia University Press.

Mei, Tsu-lin. 1989. "The Causative and Denominative Functions of the *-s-Prefix in Old Chinese", in: *Proceedings of the First International Conference on Sinology*. Taibei: Academia Sinica, pp. 33–51.

Müller, Carl W. et al. (eds.). 1992. *Zum Umgang mit fremden Sprachen in der griechisch-römischen Antike*. Stuttgart: Steiner.

Németh, J. 1958. "Zur Geschichte des Wortes *tolmács* 'Dolmetscher'", *Acta Orientalia Hungarica* 8.1, pp. 1–8.

Pan Ying 潘英. 1985. *Zhongguo shanggu guoming diming cihui ji suoyin.* 中國上古 國名地名辭彙及索引 (A vocabulary and index of archaic Chinese state and place names). Taibei: Mingwen.

Pariente, E. 1950. "*Partare, interpretari* y *pellere*", *Emerita* 18, pp. 25–37.

Peiros, Ilya and Sergej Starostin. 1996. *A Comparative Vocabulary of Five Sino-Tibetan Languages*. Melbourne: The University of Melbourne, Department of Linguistics.

Pelliot, Paul. 1906. "[Compte rendu de] É. Chavannes, 'Les pays d'occident d'après le Wei Lio'", (*T'oung Pao* 1905.6 , pp. 519–71), *Bulletin de l'École Française d'Extrême-Orient* 6, pp. 361–400.

——. 1948. "Le H̱ōja et le Sayyid Ḥusain de l'Histoire des Ming", *T'oung Pao* 38, pp. 81–292.

Peremans, Willy. 1983. "Les ἑρμηνεῖς dans l'Égypte gréco-romaine", in: G. Grimm, H. Heinen and E. Winter (eds.). *Das Römisch-Byzantinische Ägypten*. Mainz: P. von Zabern (Aegyptiaca Treverensia 2), pp. 11–7.

Pettinato, Giovanni. 1981. "I vocabulari bilingui di Ebla. Problemi di traduzione e di lessicografia sumerico-eblaita", in: L. Cagni (ed.). *La lingua di Ebla*. Napoli: Instituto Universitario Orientale, pp. 241–76.

Poo, Mu-chou. 1998. "Encountering the Strangers. a Comparative Study of Cultural Consciousness in Ancient Egypt, Mesopotamia, and China", in: C. J. Eyre (ed.). *Proceedings of the Seventh International Congress of Egyptologists. Cambridge, 3–9 September 1995*. Leuven: Uitgiverij Peeters (Orientalia Lovaniensia Analecta 82), pp. 885–92.

Pulleyblank, Edwin G. 1962. "The Consonantal System of Old Chinese", *Asia Major* 9, pp. 58–114 and 206–65 (Appendix: "The Hsiung-nu Language", pp. 239–65).

——. 1965. "Close/Open Ablaut in Sino-Tibetan", in: G. B. Milner and E. J. A. Henderson (eds.). *Indo-Pacific Linguistic Studies*. Amsterdam: North Holland Publ., pp. 230–40.

——. 1989. "Ablaut and Initial Voicing in Old Chinese Morphology: *a as an Infix and Prefix", in: *Proceedings of the Second International Conference on Sinology. Section on Linguistics and Paleography*. Taibei: Academia Sinica, pp. 1–21.

——. 1991. *Lexicon of Reconstructed Pronunciation in Early Middle Chinese, Late Middle Chinese, and Early Mandarin*. Vancouver: University of British Columbia Press.

Renjinglu shi cao jianzhu 人境盧詩草箋注 (Florilegium of poetry from the Hut of the Human Realm). 1981. Qian Zhonglian 錢仲聯 (ed.), Shanghai: Guji, 3 vols., vol. 1.3.

Rochette, Bruno. 1993. "La diversité linguistique dans l'antiquité classique", in: L. Isebaert (ed.). *Miscellanea linguistica graeco-latina*. Namur: Société des Études Classiques, pp. 219–37.

——. 1996a. "*Fidi interpretes*. La traduction orale à Rome , *Ancient Society* 27, pp. 75–89.

——. 1996b. "ΠΙΣΤΟΙ ΄ΕΡΜΗΝΕΙΣ. La traduction orale en Grèce", *Révue des Études Grècques* 109, p. 328 with n. 10.

Roetz, Heiner. 1993. *Confucian Ethics of the Axial Age*. Albany: SUNY Press, pp. 123–48.

Rubio, Gonzalo. "On the Alleged 'Pre-Sumerian Substratum'", *Journal of Cuneiform Studies* 51, pp. 1–16.

Sagart, Laurent. 1999. *The Roots of Old Chinese*. Amsterdam, Philadelphia: J. Benjamins.

Schmitt, Gerhard. 1970. *Sprüche der Wandlungen auf ihrem geistesgeschichtlichen Hintergrund*. Berlin: Akademie.

Schüssler, Axel. 1994. "Loanwords in Old Chinese", unpublished Ms.

Shima Kunio 島邦男 . 1958. *Inkyo bokuji kenkyū* 殷墟卜辭研究 (Studies on the oracle insciptions from the ruins of Yin). Hirosaki: Hirosaki daigaku.

Som, Tjan Tjoe (Zeng Zhusen 曾珠森). 1949. *Po Hu T'ung. The Comprehensive Discussions in the White Tiger Hall*. Leiden: Brill.

Song Yongpei 宋永培 . 1995. "*Zhouli* zhong 'tong', 'da' ciyi de xitong lianxi" 周禮中 '通''達'詞義的系統聯係 (Systematic connections between the meanings of the words 'tong' and 'da' in the *Etiquette of the Zhou*), *Gu hanyu yanjiu* 29.4, pp. 41–4.

Starke, Frank. 1993. "Zur Herkunft von akkad. *ta/urgumannu(m)* 'Dolmetscher', *Welt des Orients* 24, pp. 20–38.

Szemerényi, Oswald. 1971. Review of Chantraine, *Gnomon* 43, pp. 641–75; 668.

Tan Qixiang 譚其驤 . 1962. "E jun Qi jie mingwen shidi" 鄂君啟節銘文釋地 (Toponymical studies of the E jun tally inscription), in: *Zhonghua wenshi luncong* 2. Shanghai: Shanghai guji, p. 169.

Tang Lan 唐蘭 . 1986. *Xi-Zhou tongqi mingwen fendai shizheng* 西周銅器銘文分代史徵 (Western Zhou bronze inscriptions periodically arranged according to the historical evidence). Beijing: Zhonghua.

Terrien de Lacouperie, Albert É. J. B. 1969 [1885–86]. *The Languages of China Before the Chinese*. London: D. Nutt. Reprint Osnabrück: O. Zeller.

Tian Jizhou 田繼周 . 1985. "Xiadai de minzu he minzu guanxi" 夏代的民族和民族關係 (Xia dynasty ethnic groups and inter-ethnic relationships), *Minzu yanjiu* 4, pp. 27–34.

Tso Szu-bong 曹仕邦 (Cao Shibang). 1963. "Lun Zhongguo fojiao yichang zhi yijing fangshi yu chengxu" 論中國佛教譯場之譯經方式與程序 (On the methods and procedures of sûtra translation in the Buddhist 'translation assemblies' in China), *Xin-Ya xuebao*, pp. 239–321.

Tuplin, C. 1999. "Greek Racism? Observations on the Character and Limits of Greek Ethnic Prejudice", in: G. R. Tsetskhladze (ed.). *Ancient Greeks East and West*. Leiden: Brill (Mnemosyne: Bibliotheca Classica Batava, Suppl. 196), pp. 47–75.

Wagner, Donald B. 1991. "The Language of the Ancient State of Wu", in: B. Arendrup et al. (eds.). *The Master Said: to Study and ...* Copenhagen: East Asian Institute, pp. 161–76.

Vovin, A. 2000. "Did the Xiongnu Speak a Yeniseian Language?", *Central Asiatic Journal* 54.1, pp. 87–104.

Wang Guimin 王貴民 . 1982. "Shuo 'yashi'" 説'邘事' (On the 'yashi'), in: Hu Houxuan 胡厚宣 (ed.). *Jiagu tanshi lu* 甲骨探史錄 (Historical explorations based on oracle bone inscriptions). Beijing: Shenghuo dushu xinzhi sanlian.

Wang Wenyan 王文顏 . 1984. *Fodian Hanyi zhi yanjiu* 佛典漢譯之研究 (Studies in the Chinese translations of Buddhist documents). Taibei: Tianhua.

Wang, William S. Y. 1995. *The Ancestry of the Chinese Language*. Berkeley: Department of East Asian Studies (Journal of Chinese Linguistics Monograph Series 8).

Wang Yuanxin 王遠新 . 1993. *Zhongguo Minzu yuyanxue shi* 中國民族語言學史 (History of the study of minority languages in China). Beijing: Zhongyang minzu xueyuan.

Wei Qingwen 韋慶穩 . 1981. "'Yueren ge' yu Zhuangyu de guanxi shitan" ' 越人歌 ' 與壯語的關係試探 (An exploration of the relationship between the 'Song of the man from Yue' and the Zhuang language), in: *Minzu yuwen lunji* 民族語文論集 (Collected studies on minority languages). Beijing: Zhongguo shehui kexueyuan.

Wild, Norman. 1943–46. "Materials for a Study of the Ssu I Kuan", *Bulletin of the School of Oriental and African Studies* 11, pp. 617–40.

You Rujie 游汝杰 and Zhou Zhenhe 周振鶴 . 1990. "Nanfang diming fenbu de quyu tezheng yu gudai yuyan de guanxi" 南方地名分布的區域特徵與古代語言的關係 (Connections between ancient languages and regional features in the distribution of southern Chinese toponyms), in: Yin Da 尹達 (ed.). *Jinian Gu Jiegang xueshu lunwenji* 紀念顧頡剛學術論文集 (A collection of scholarly articles in memoriam Gu Jiegang). Chengdu: Ba-Shu, vol. 2, pp. 709–24.

Yu Rongchun 于溶春 . 1986. "'Zhongguo' yici de laiyuan, yanbian ji qi yu minzu de guanxi" ' 中國 ' 一詞的來源，演變，及其與民族的關係 (On the derivation and development of the word 'Zhongguo', and its interrelationship with different ethnic groups), *Neimenggu shehui kexue* 2, pp. 75–80.

Yu Xingwu 于省吾 . 1981. "Shi 'zhong guo'" 釋中國 (Deciphering 'zhongguo'), in: Zhonghua shuju chengli qishi nian jinianhui (ed.). *Zhonghua xueshu lunwenji* 中華學術論文集 (Collection of scholarly articles on China). Beijing: Zhonghua, pp. 3–10.

Zhang Xiancheng 張顯成 . 1998. "Lun jianbo wenxian de cihuishi yanjiu jiazhi—jianlun qi Hanyushi yanjiu jiazhi" 論簡帛文獻的詞彙史研究價值 — 兼論其漢語史研究價值 (On the value of bamboo and silk documents for the history of the lexicon, including a discussion of their value for the history of the Chinese language), *Jianbo yanjiu* 3, pp. 201–2.

Zhang Yachu 張亞初 and Liu Yü 劉雨 . 1986. *Xi-Zhou jinwen guanzhi yanjiu* 西周金文官制研究 (Studies on the system of bureaucracy reflected in Western Zhou bronze inscription). Beijing: Zhonghua.

Zheng-Zhang Shangfang 鄭張尚芳 . 1991. "Decipherment of Yue-Ren-Ge (Song of the Yue Boatman)", *Cahiers de Linguistique Asie-Orientale* 2, pp. 159–68.

——. 1993. "Shanggu Miange—'Bailang ge' quanwen jiedu" 上古緬歌 ' 白狼歌 ' 全文解讀 (An archaic Burmese song—decipherment of the complete text of the 'Bailang song'), *Minzu yuwen* 1, pp. 10–21 and *Minzu yuwen* 2, pp. 64–70, 74.

——. 1999. "Goujian 'Weijia' ling zhong zhi gu Yueyu de jiedu" 勾踐 ' 維甲 ' 令中之古越語的解讀 (A decipherment of ancient Yue words in the *weijia*-command of Goujian), *Minzu yuwen* 4, pp. 1–14.

VIVIANE ALLETON

THE MIGRATION OF GRAMMARS THROUGH LANGUAGES: THE CHINESE CASE

The translation of books, from masterpieces by major authors to textbooks, is generally considered the most common way to introduce new knowledge. However, such was not the case when systematic grammar, previously neglected in China, was introduced to the Chinese educated public at the end of the nineteenth century for the first time.

Although Ma Jianzhong 馬建忠 (1844–1900), the first Chinese author to write a grammar, the *Mashi wentong* 馬氏文通 (1898), had access to a wide variety of sources, he did not 'translate' any Western grammars. This situation lasted until the end of the Qing dynasty and beyond in spite of the increasing availability of grammar sources. To my knowledge, there were no translations of texts on general linguistics texts prior to the nineteen-thirties. A significant number of foreign books have only been translated during the last two decades of the twentieth century.

Some Chinese language grammars (classical Chinese, Mandarin) were written by foreigners in different languages and for their own use. The Jesuit Joseph de Prémare wrote the only comprehensive grammar in two parts—the vernacular and the classical—in his *Notitia Linguæ Sinicæ* (1831).[1] In this book, written in Latin, the influence of Latin grammar is less significant than has often been claimed. Certain specific features of Chinese grammar are mentioned, such as the first paragraph about nouns.[2] The author was not only familiar with written Chinese but was also able to speak the Chinese vernacular fluently. A description of this spoken language precedes the longer section devoted to Classical Chinese, and at the beginning of the Second

---

[1] The manuscript, written between 1724 and 1727, was immediately sent to the French academician Fourmont and included in the "Bibliothèque du Roi" in 1730. It was only published one hundred years later in Malacca. Cf. Joseph Henri de Prémare. 1831. *Notitia Linguæ Sinicæ*. Malacca: Cura-Academia Anglo-Sinensis. Republished in Hong Kong: Société des Missions Etrangères, 1894.

[2] Cf. ibid., p. 37: *Sinæ non inflectunt nomina per casus et numeros, sed habent certas notas quibus haec omnia clare distinguunt.* "Chinese do not use inflections for cases and number, but they have some signs to clearly distinguish all these [values]."

Part, Prémare refers explicitly to the syntax of the vernacular.[3] We do not find any reference to this book in Chinese texts. However, following its re-publication in Hong Kong in 1894, it may have become better known by the few educated Chinese able to read Latin. Distribution in China was certainly not wider for the two most important European grammars of Chinese written in the nineteenth century, the *Eléments de Grammaire chinoise*, by Jean-Pierre Abel-Rémusat,[4] who admitted that he was inspired by Prémare, and the *Chinesische Grammatik* by Georg von der Gabelentz.[5]

We should also mention that, after 1845, Protestant missionaries wrote a number of descriptive works to help them teach and learn, most of these dealing with spoken dialects. Some textbooks on foreign languages included brief indications written in Chinese.[6]

1. THE SITUATION IN CHINA BEFORE THE END OF THE NINETEENTH CENTURY

The word 'grammar' is polysemic. It may refer to a book as a concrete object, but may also designate the content of the book, that is, the systematic analysis of the functions and meanings of linguistic forms and the construction of texts in a given language. A third meaning of the word 'grammar' is the system at work in the language under consideration—a system that we can know through observation of actual usage. It is reasonable to suppose that this system is, at some level, universal.

What was the situation in China in the second part of the nineteenth century?

---

[3] Cf. ibid., p. 125: *Quœ ad grammaticam et syntaxim sinicam pertinent, satis fuse jam exposui in prima hujus operis parte*. "What is relevant for Chinese grammar and syntax had been already presented in the first part of this book."

[4] Cf. Jean-Pierre Abel-Rémusat. 1822. *Éléments de la grammaire chinoise*. Paris: Imprimerie Royale. Reprint Paris: Ala Productions, 1987.

[5] Cf. Georg von der Gabelentz. 1881. *Chinesische Grammatik*. Leipzig: Weigel.

[6] One of the most systematic textbooks that includes all the grammatical explanations in Chinese is a German textbook (Wang Zan-Tzeng. 1911. *Lehrbuch der Deutschen Grammatik*. Shanghai: Commercial Press). The series entitled *English and Chinese Readers*, published by the Commercial Press (1900–1901) with no author's name, was probably the translation of a textbook used by missionaries in India that includes only a few grammatical terms in Chinese, and seems more typical of this category of books.

In the sense of 'books about grammar', the answer is simple. No such publication existed during that period. As for the second meaning of the word 'grammar', that is, 'systematic analysis', we do find a widespread philosophical interest in the subject throughout China, inasmuch as language has been a central concern among Chinese thinkers since antiquity. One may even say that the views of Xunzi on the relationship between words and objects were relatively sophisticated.[7] Philological studies have a complex history in China, and during certain periods they were among the requirements of the highest levels of education. We also know that language was the main focus for an important group of scholars during the eighteenth century, and, thanks to Benjamin Elman, we have a precise description of this milieu.[8] However the essential tools remain those of the great Chinese tradition—dictionaries, lexical analysis, and phonology.

It has long been known that the poetics and rhetoric of Chinese imply certain classifications that may be connected with grammatical concepts (oppositions between 'empty' and 'full', 'dead' and 'living'). The meaning and usage of these terms were explicitly described, but only from a lexical point of view, and we can find no sign of a system of rules.

Alain Peyraube recently brought to light an important point. He claims that some Ming and Qing authors used methods of analysis and terms identical to those found in the *Mashi wentong*, considered to be the first Chinese grammar written by a Chinese scholar.[9] However, these texts were included in treatises on rhetoric. The set may be considered a corpus, but originally it was not seen as such, and it was the reading of classical texts that was at stake, not the system itself. Such a situation is quite common in the first stages of the perception

---

[7] Cf. Redouane Djamouri. 1993. "Théorie de la 'rectification des dénominations' et réflexion linguistique chez Xunzi", *Extrême-Orient Extrême-Occident* 15: *Le Juste Nom*, pp. 55–74.

[8] Benjamin A. Elman. 1984. *From Philosophy to Philology: Intellectual and Social Aspects of Change in Late Imperial China*. Cambridge, Mass.: Harvard University Council on East Asian Studies.

[9] Alain Peyraube. 1999. "Qingdai '*Mashi wentong*' yiqian de yufa zhishi" 清代馬氏文通以前的語法知識 (Knowledge on grammar in the Qing dynasty prior to the *Mashi wentong*). Paper presented at the Second International symposium on the Qing Philology, Gaoxiong, pp. 66, 72. The examples are taken from the *Zhuzi bianlue* 助字辨略 (1711) by Liu Qi 劉淇 and the *Xuzi shuo* 虛字説 (1710) by Yuan Renlin 袁仁林. The author insists on the grammatical value of the *Gushu yiyi juli* 古書疑義舉例, by Yu Yue 俞樾 (1821–1906), the teacher of Zhang Bingling 章炳麟 (1868–1936).

of the grammaticality of a language. The first grammatical indications found in Alexandria include exegetic remarks about the Homeric texts. At the outset, concerns about grammar often encourage a philological interpretation of texts.

However, we may observe that the birth of systematic grammar in the Mediterranean world was also related to translation of literary, philosophical, and technical texts as well as texts used to teach foreign languages, primarily from Greek to Latin. In China, although translation was an important activity during certain periods (translations of Buddhist texts), it was a technical activity alien to the world of the Chinese literati. A few possible exceptions do not constitute a 'milieu'. As Wolfgang Behr clearly shows, interest in Buddhist texts, even during periods when that religion was widely accepted, never generated an interest in translation *per se*.[10]

As for the third meaning of the word 'grammar'—the grammaticality of the language under consideration—what is involved here is no less than the universality of linguistic competence.[11] The earliest missionaries did not raise this question because their religious faith implied universality. However, given the absence of inflexion in the Chinese language, and especially the fact that time is not indicated by tenses, there was a tendency among foreigners to believe that Chinese was devoid of grammar.[12] Wilhelm von Humboldt and Jean-Pierre Abel-Rémusat were the outstanding exceptions during the first part of the nineteenth century. Both men recognised the grammaticality of the Chinese language—with a high degree of specificity for Humboldt and a less considerable gap between Chinese and European languages for Abel-Rémusat.[13] However their scholarly opinions had no

---

[10] Cf. Wolfgang Behr's contribution in this volume.

[11] This problem must not be reduced to a confrontation between Chinese and Indo-European languages. The many controversies on the grammars of the Amerindian languages have a long history. More generally, if we consider a universal framework, it necessarily includes all the written and unwritten languages in the world.

[12] Cf. Viviane Alleton. 1994. "L'oubli de la langue et l''invention' de l'écriture chinoise en Europe", *Études Chinoises* 13.1–2, pp. 259–82. [Chinese translation: Ai Letong 艾樂桐 . "Ouzhou wangji le hanyu que 'faxian' le hanzi" 歐洲忘記了漢語卻 發現了漢字 , in: Denys Lombard (Long Baer 龍巴爾) and Li Xueqin 李學勤 (eds.). *Faguo hanxue* 法國漢學 (French Sinology). Beijing: Qinghua daxue, vol. 1, pp. 182–98].

[13] Jean Rousseau and Denis Thouard (eds). 1999. *Lettres édifiantes et curieuses sur la langue chinoise; Humboldt/Abel-Rémusat (1821–1831)*. Villeneuve-d'Asc: Presses Universitaires du Septentrion.

impact on the European public, where preconceptions about the lack of grammar in the Chinese language were already well established.

Chinese in contact with foreign countries, such as scholars sent abroad on diplomatic missions, were interested primarily in institutions as well as economic and technical achievements. Their few remarks about language were incidental jottings and did not refer to the Western method of analysing languages. More generally, even if the most enlightened among them attempted to promote translation activities, the Chinese were not interested in grammar, a branch of knowledge they considered to be simply a device to learn foreign languages.

The Chinese lack of interest in grammar is strikingly illustrated by its non-inclusion in the long list of sciences and techniques that the Chinese claimed to have originated in China's distant past—but which did include the alphabetic system. Benjamin Elman noted that the famous scholar Dai Zhen 戴震 (1723–1777)

> not only argued that various astronomical and mathematical concepts were of native origin, but after Ricci's alphabet system was introduced, he contended that it was originally plagiarized from the Chinese syllabic transcription system.[14]

To my knowledge there is no mention of this type of claim for grammar at any time.[15]

During the last decades of the empire, the study of language was still purely an internal affair. When Wang Guowei 王國維 (1877–1927) published his translation of the "Elementary Lessons in Logic" by William Stanley Jevons (Suiwen 隨文 , 1835–1882) under the title *Bianxue* 辨學 , it would have been a complete translation if he had not skipped an entire lesson (XI: "The sentence"), where the relationship between the logical forms and the grammar of the English language

---

[14] Elman 1984, p. 217.

[15] It is only in the recent years, in connection with the rise of nationalism and the so-called *Zhongguo wenhua yuyanxue* 中國文化語言學 "School of cultural linguistics", that some professors (most of them teaching foreign languages) began to consider grammar as a field worth some discussion. They want to prove that the existing grammar imported from the West has no validity beyond Indo-European languages. I shall not discuss this position here, as it implies a certain ignorance of the diversity of the many human languages. Cf. Gao Yihong. 1997. *Collected Essays of Shen Xiaolong on Chinese Cultural Linguistics.* Changchun: Northeast Normal University Press.

are discussed.[16] Conversely, Zhang Binglin 章炳麟(1868–1936) wrote
a long text entitled *Lun yuyan wenzi zhi xue* 論語言文字之學 (On the
study of language and writing).[17] His object was the Chinese language
as it had been studied for centuries under the heading *xiaoxue* 小學,
including phonology, semantics and graphic etymology. There is
nothing about grammar anywhere in this text.

2. THE FIRST NATIVE GRAMMAR: THE *MASHI WENTONG*

The *Mashi wentong* was indisputably the first Chinese systematic
grammar written by a Chinese scholar.

1. Publication and authorship

This book was first published in 1898 by the Commercial Press,
founded two years earlier. The author died in 1900, and a second edition was published in 1904, again by the Commercial Press. The first
edition was far less widely circulated than the second, and as a result
certain authors suspected that the book was posthumous. In the same
vein, it was suggested that the Ma Grammar was at least partly written
by the elder brother of Ma Jianzhong, Ma Jianchang 馬建常 (*zi*:
Xiangbo 相伯, 1840–1939), whose intellectual and social reputation at
the time was far superior to that of his younger brother.[18] This hypothesis was presented in a recent dissertation.[19] In the chronology of the
life of Ma Xiangbo,[20] his part in the authorship of the *Mashi wentong*
(*MSWT* hereafter) is presented as a fact:

---

[16] Wang Guowei 王國維. 1908. *Bianxue* 辨學 (Logic). Beijing: Jingshi wudaomiao shoushuchu. Transation of William Stanley Jevons. *Elementary Lessons in
Logic*, 1870. I would like to thank Joachim Kurtz for this information.

[17] Zhang Binglin 章炳麟. 1907. "Lun yuyan wenzi zhi xue" 論語言文字之學 (On
the study of language and writing), *Guocui xuebao* 2.12 & 2.13. Frédéric Devienne
translated this text in French in his Ph.D. dissertation. Cf. Frédéric Devienne. 2001.
*Considérations théoriques sur l'écriture par deux lettrés chinois au début du 20e siè-
cle. Analyse de l'œuvre linguistique de Zhang Binglin (1869–1936) et de son disciple
Huang Kan (1886–1935)*. Paris: École Pratique des Hautes Études.

[18] We may note that Ma Xiangbo survived his younger brother by almost a half
century.

[19] Peter Peverelli. 1986. *The History of Modern Chinese Grammar Studies*. Ph.D.
diss., Leiden University.

[20] Zhu Weizheng 朱維錚 (ed.). 1996. *Ma Xiangbo ji* 馬相伯集 (Collection of Ma
Xiangbo). Shanghai: Fudan daxue, p. 1350.

– 1898, [he is] fifty nine years old.

– 1898, 59 years old. … He completes the manuscript of the *Mashi wentong* in co-operation with his younger brother Jianzhong.

– 1904, [he is] 65 years old. Publication of the *Mashi wentong* at the Commercial Press in Shanghai.

The actual situation appears to be more complex. In the first edition of the *MSWT* (1898), which includes only the first two parts out of four (six chapters out of ten), the last sentences claim authorship of Ma Jianzhong and the existence of the entire text as already written.

In the presentation of their reference edition, the *Mashi wentong duben* 馬氏文通讀本,[21] Lü Shuxiang 呂叔湘 and Wang Haifen 王海棻 quote these lines at the beginning of the book, before the table of contents, under the title *Shang ce fu yin tiji* 上冊付印題記 (Note on the printing of the first volume).

From their analyses of certain testimonies from that period, they conclude that Ma Jianzhong was beyond all doubt the author of the *MSWT* and that his elder brother probably gave him some assistance.[22]

We compared certain texts firmly attributed to Ma Jianzhong with the two prefaces and some passages of the *MSWT*, and we are convinced that the same person has not only 'written', but also 'conceived' these different texts. In contrast, the style of the short preface by Ma Xiangbo to his Latin grammar seems quite different. Of course, one cannot rely on simple 'reading' of texts to decide their relationship. To achieve any certainty it would be necessary to complete a systematic comparison of the vocabulary, syntax and stylistic qualities. Such an effort would seem excessive given the issue at stake.

The focus of Ma Jianzhong's interest was the linguistic education as a whole that enabled young Europeans to successfully master the written language without the painstaking efforts required from young Chinese. He resented as an absurdity the fact that the Chinese language (Classical Chinese), "the simplest language in the world," was at his time "the most difficult to learn" (西文本難也而易學如彼，華文本易也而難學如此著。).[23]

---

[21] Lü Shuxiang 呂叔湘 and Wang Haifen 王海棻 (eds.). 1986. *Mashi wentong duben* 馬氏文通讀本 (*Mashi wentong* reader). Reprint Shanghai: Shanghai jiaoyu.

[22] *MSWT*, pp. 2–3, *Daoyan* 導言 (Presentation by the editor).

[23] *MSWT*, *Hou xu*.

2. *The book and its prefaces*

In the (First) Preface *Xu* 序 the author recalls the great linguistic tradition of China, discussing the science of graphic forms (*tizhi* 體制), the commentaries (*xungu* 訓詁) and phonology (*yinyun* 音韻). In spite of the great accomplishments of these three sciences, uncertainties in the interpretation of the Classics remain. This is one of the reasons why he decided to base his research on texts from antiquity and quotes them as references. This systematic enquiry concerns words and sentences. We quote:

> 為之字楷句比，繁稱博引，比例而同之，觸類而長之，窮古今之簡篇，字裡行間，渙然冰釋，皆有一得其會通，輯為一書，名曰文通。
> I compared a number of quotations. When I found analogies, I organized them into one category; I connected the categories and constructed them. I dug into ancient and modern documents for each word, each column. It is as clear as crystal. Everything may have its own explanation, its own category. (Translation by the author)

After this manifesto in support of the inductive method, Ma Jianzhong presents the four parts of his book. In the first chapter, called *zheng ming* 正名 (rectify the appellations), he insists on distinguishing terms in relation to various sciences, each science having its own set of terms. The second and third chapters deal with full words and empty words respectively. The function of these empty words is not only to segment the text but also to "categorize words according to their functions." The topic of the last chapter is *ju dou* 句讀 (punctuation). This is an ancient term, and its origin may be attributed to Han Yu 韓愈 (768–824). In the *MSWT* it designates propositions and sentences, that is, syntax. This is the shortest part of the book and its interpretation is somewhat controversial.

The conclusion of this Preface reminds us of the Prefaces of two of the masterpieces that laid the foundations for linguistic science in China: the *Shuowen jiezi* 說文解字 (Explain the patterns and interpret the characters) in the field of lexicography and the *Qieyun* 切韻 (Rhyme classification of characters) in phonology. Xu Shen 許慎 (58–147), at the end of the first century AD, Lu Fayan 陸法言 (fl. ca. 601 AD) in the seventh century, and later Ma Jianzhong all manifest a similar feeling of pride. They present themselves as being responsible for China's cultural heritage, and they state their conviction that they are providing their contemporaries with the best possible tool for coping with the difficulties of their period.[24]

The Second Preface, *Hou xu* 後序 is placed immediately after the *Xu* in the original edition, and they are dated at a short interval of six months. Sinological tradition suggests a literal translation of *hou xu* by "postface", although in our languages, this word has very different connotations.

In this Second Preface—we prefer this translation—which is shorter than the first one, Ma Jianzhong affirms that all languages are different but that good translations are always possible because certain basic principles are constant throughout the evolution of languages. We note that his perception of linguistic diversity is not only interlingual (space) but also diachronic (time). Ma Jianzhong states that the rules of construction in the Classics are implicit but that it is possible to extract them. He finishes with a reference to the present situation in China, arguing that the Chinese will be unable to resist foreign powers if they do not acquire their fundamental tools.

Some commentators see proof that Ma Jianzhong was directly inspired by the model of Western grammars in the "introductory remarks" *liyan* 例言 that follow the two Prefaces. Alain Peyraube focuses on the sentence *ci shu xi fang gelangma er zuo* 此書係仿葛郎瑪而作 (This book was written on the model of a Western grammar), to assert the plausibility of a specific translation. However he does cautiously admit that this sentence is ambiguous, with *xifang gelama* meaning either "the grammar" (generic meaning) or "the grammar (of Port Royal)" (specific meaning). Given that we have no further evidence on this point, the question remains open.

We suggest that these texts must be examined at a higher level. Just as Ma Jianzhong refers to the foundations of the Chinese civilization, he refers to rationality when speaking about Europe. He applies the principles of this rationality to language, but he does not take the achievements of linguistics in the West in this field as specific models. The focus is on methodology.

3. The terminological data

We have seen that one of the topics of "*MSWT* studies" is research into the book(s) that may have inspired the author. This quest begins

---

[24] Curiously enough, all these enterprises were 'private initiatives of officials', more precisely of 'officials on the margins'—with the reservation that the *Qieyun* of Lu Fayan may have been partly a collective achievement.

with the idea that Ma Jianzhong necessarily used specific model(s), and that certain sentences in the Preface confirm this hypothesis. One of the tests used is concordance of terms.

In a field such as grammar with a long history, terms with approximately the same form or cognate forms have a range of values that depend on the language under analysis and the philosophical background of the authors. Most of the basic grammatical words now used for European languages received their first grammatical definitions during the Hellenistic period. In the *Tékhne Grammatiké*, attributed to Dionysius Thrax (second and first century BC), we find some 150 technical terms, most of them still in use today.[25] As time went on, these words were used in a number of different contexts, and thus we cannot claim that their content remains the same.[26] The parallelism of two lists of terms in different texts does not prove a direct relation, unless each term of a pair of corresponding terms has the same value in comparable paradigms.

In this perspective we believe that there is a close connection between the terminology of Ma Jianzhong and that generally used in the West at the end of the nineteenth century. The exact relation to the *Grammaire de Port-Royal*,[27] apparently one of the best potential candidates, seems somewhat hypothetical. The *Grammaire* was closely related to the *Logique de Port Royal*, whose purpose was also to illustrate the theological theories of the Jansenists. Thus Ma's Jesuit teachers would probably not have used that book. Moreover, Ma was absorbed in many different subjects during his relatively short stay in Europe. The few essays he wrote during his visit to France primarily concern educational and political institutions, and none deals with grammar. Ma approached the study of grammar only towards the end of his public life, motivated by a desire to be useful to the Chinese State, whose failures had become evident in the last years of that cen-

---

[25] Pierre Swiggers. 1997. *Histoire de la pensée linguistique. Analyse du langage et réflexion linguistique dans la culture occidentale de l'Antiquité au XIXe siècle*. Paris: Presses Universitaires de France, p. 50; Gustav Uhlig. 1883. *Grammatici Graeci, I-1: Dionysii Thracis Ars Grammatica*. Leipzig: Teubner.

[26] As an example, we find the notion of pronominal category in the most ancient grammatical texts, but over time the number of species included in the genre 'pronoun' did not remain constant.

[27] This is the most common designation for the *Grammaire Générale et Raisonnée* Cf. Antoine Arnauld and Claude Lancelot. 1660. *Grammaire Générale et Raisonnée*. Paris: Pierre le Petit. (Reprinted Paris: Editions Allia, 1997.)

tury. His aim was to restore the learning potential to younger generations and to provide to them better access to the Classics—whose relevance he did not question.

We shall now examine the biography of Ma in its entirety.

4. The author

Ma Jianzhong (*zi*: Meishu 眉叔 , Christian name: Mathias) was born in Dantu (Jiangsu) to a family noted for its scholarly accomplishments. They provided him with the foundations of a complete Chinese education. Moreover, this family had been converted to Catholicism in the time of Matteo Ricci. We know that Ma Xiangbo, his elder brother, left his family to go to Shanghai in 1851 at the age of eleven. He soon entered at the Jesuit College of Saint Ignatius in Shanghai. At that time, Ma Jianzhong was only seven. As during the first part of their life the two brothers were never separated, it is thus very probable that they entered the Jesuit school at the same time albeit at different levels.

It soon becomes quite clear that they sought to acquire a dual education that embraced both Chinese and Western curricula.

During its first years, the College of St. Ignatius devoted a major portion of its efforts to the teaching of Chinese Classics. This was considered indispensable in China since at the time the highest ambition was to successfully pass the official examinations, especially as there was no other way to reach the higher echelons of the government bureaucracy, and this also corresponded to the wishes of the students' families. In addition, interest in Chinese studies was an integral part of Jesuit politics in China, defined three centuries before by Matteo Ricci. When the Company returned to China in 1842, some seventy years after their eviction in 1773, it is hardly surprising that some members attempted to renew the tradition. Thus, the traditional Chinese education the Ma brothers had first received in their family was reinforced.

The linguistic component was a major part of the Western program of study, and we know that when Ma Jianzhong left Zi Jia Wei (徐家匯), the Jesuit compound, as an adult, he had mastered Latin, French, and English, and had some knowledge of Ancient Greek and Russian.

Latin was the dominant language during his years of education. We must not underestimate the fact that religious instruction held place of pride in the College of St. Ignatius, this being for the Jesuits the real justification of their activities. Soon a number of pupils expressed the wish to become priests, and when a noviciate was opened in 1862 the Ma brothers were among the first to enter. In the catalogue of Fathers and Brothers in China since the time of Matteo Ricci, it is recorded that the elder brother, Ma Xiangbo, entered in the noviciate in 1862 (no. 542) and Ma Jianzhong in 1867 (no. 590).[28] Entering Jesuit order as a novice implied intensive intellectual training based on exercises of mutual criticism, mastery of oral and written expression and, in the field of languages, considerable familiarity with Latin.

In 1853 Angelo Zottoli, a young Italian Jesuit, was named principal of the school and in 1862 he was given the responsibility of the noviciate. He showed a degree of interest in Chinese culture that was quite unusual at a time when the 'sinophilia' of previous centuries was evolving into a degree of 'sinophobia'.[29] He was the author of a large collection of Chinese texts[30] written to introduce Chinese culture to foreigners. In addition, he was the author of a Latin textbook to be used by his Chinese pupils based on the *Institutio Grammatica* by Emmanuel Alvarez,[31] an adaptation of the grammar used in most of the Jesuit colleges around the world since the sixteenth century. The fate of the *Institutio Grammatica*, well respected by grammarians at the time of publication although this is no longer the case, is very intriguing. It had been used for many years in Portuguese-speaking South American countries[32] and in Jesuit colleges in most parts of Europe (for example in Poland where it was taught until 1773, and

---

[28] A copy of this list is kept in the archives of the Province of France, in Vanves.

[29] Michel Cartier (ed.). 1998. *La Chine entre amour et haine. Actes du VIIIe colloque de sinologie de Chantilly.* Paris: Desclée de Brouwer (Variétés sinologiques 87).

[30] Angelo Zottoli. 1879–82. *Cursus Literatura Sinicae.* 5 vols. Shanghai: Typographia Missionis Catholice. This book contains a selection of classical and vernacular Chinese texts, with literal translation in Latin as well as philological and historical notes.

[31] Angelo Zottoli. 1859. *Emmanuelis Alvarez institutio Grammatica ad sinenses alumnos accomodata.* Shanghai: A. V. de Carvalho. After the first edition in Latin, published in Portugal (1772), the textbook of Alvarez was republished a number of times, either in the original form, or translated in different European languages, sometimes abbreviated. The edition used by Zottoli was probably the *Grammatica di Emmanuel Àlvaro della S.d.G. volgarizzata*, edited in 1842 at Naples, where he was studying at that time.

[32] Cf. Swiggers 1997, pp. 149–50.

discontinued only when certain objections were raised by Polish scholars on the lack of the notion of aspect, an essential component of the Polish language). It was also used in Asia. When it once again became possible to study Latin in Japan during the Meiji period, the Portuguese Jesuit's book, written three centuries before, was used once again and was republished when the Jesuits received permission to return to Japan in 1868. This work was certainly familiar to Ma Jianzhong, thanks to the translation by Zottoli published in 1859. In examining Zottoli's text we can see that although he reduced the size of the original book, he clearly made no effort to straddle the apparent gap between Latin and Chinese. We may suppose that the focus of his linguistic teaching was not so much on content, but rather on methodology and the art of analysis. By using the Alvarez grammar, he remained faithful to a specific pedagogical tradition.

Ma Jianzhong, however, did not become a priest. After a series of disagreements with the French superiors who replaced Angelo Zottoli, and longing to serve his country, he left the Society of Jesus in 1873 at age 26 after some twenty years in Zi Jia Wei. He then entered a government career as interpreter, diplomat and adviser, but as he did not pass the Chinese examinations, he was unable to obtain any official position of importance.[33]

In 1877, he joined the group of young diplomats and scholars that accompanied Guo Songtao's 郭嵩燾 (1818–1891) mission as the first Chinese ambassador to Paris. As this part of his life is well documented, the biographical indications given in dictionaries as well as historical or linguistics commentaries primarily cover this period. During his travels Ma studied diplomacy, institutions, economics, and international law. He was awarded a *licence de droit* (at that time equivalent to a M.A. in law) and a special diploma from the École Libre des Sciences Politiques. Incidentally, we know that his position also gave him opportunities for more mundane activities and travelling. Li Shuchang 黎庶昌 (1837–1897), who was in Europe during the same period, mentions him as being present during such occasions as a night at the Opera, a visit to a textile factory, a military parade, travel from the Riviera to Rome and then Naples to see Guo Songtao

---

[33] Cf. Li Tiangang. 1996. "Christianity and Cultural Conflict in the Life of Ma Xiangbo", in: Ruth Hayhoe (ed.). *Ma Xiangbo and the Mind of Modern China 1840–1939.* Armonk: Sharpe, pp. 89–149.

off on a ship, a private voyage through the south of France and Venice, and an official voyage to Berlin.[34] Ma Jianzhong left Europe in 1880 and returned to a position under Li Hongzhang 李鴻章 (1823–1901), responsible for various tasks in the fields of interpretation, diplomacy, and organization of a navy. It was only during the last ten years of his life that he retired to Shanghai and wrote the *Mashi wentong*.

This short biographical sketch shows that even though we cannot claim that the *MSWT* was a Jesuit achievement, since the author had left the Society of Jesus seventeen years before writing it, it is still undeniably a product of the Jesuit culture.

We would like to emphasise two other facts about this author. Ma Jianzhong was a polyglot, and knew several foreign languages in their written form and at least two in their spoken form (French and English). We may add that as a native of Jiangsu province he also probably spoke the local Wu dialect. This implies that his concept of universality may have been grounded on the notion of the diversity of human languages. Very few of the Chinese linguists that followed had such broad experience. They usually knew only English or, alternatively, only French, German, Russian, or Japanese. After Ma Jianzhong, most of the Chinese people with multi-lingual expertise were not found among linguists. This is a paradoxical situation. We may note that the introduction of grammar into Japan occurred in a multilingual context, which may explain its relative success. As early as the last decades of the Tokugawa period, the Japanese translated or transposed grammars of Dutch and English into their own language. It was the vocabulary created at that time that was used to describe the Japanese language during the Meiji period. Japanese scholars were able to adapt the conceptual framework borrowed from the West to the specific aspects of the Japanese language while also including ele-

---

[34] Cf. Li Shuchang 黎庶昌 . 1981. *Xiyang zazhi* 西洋雜誌 (Travel notes on a journey to the West). Reprint Changsha: Renmin chubanshe. See also Li Shuchang. 1988. *Carnet de notes sur l'Occident. Translated by Shi Kangqiang.* Paris: Éditions de la Maison des sciences de l'homme.

ments of their philological tradition.[35] The result was a grammatical analysis that was well accepted at the time and is still in use.

Ma Jianzhong was not specialized in a single field. He had a broad cultural background and multiple interests, as was the case for many Chinese literati during the last centuries of the empire and for many scholars in Europe of the past. This quality enhanced his ability to mediate between the two civilizations. However, it also helps us understand why he was considered a man of the past once the need for scientific specialization that triumphed in the West during the nineteenth century had reached China.

3. THE CHINESE PERCEPTION OF GRAMMAR IN THE TWENTIETH CENTURY

1. Criticism of the Mashi wentong

The *Mashi wentong* had soon been recognized as a 'cornerstone text' that opens a number of ways forward. At the same time, it raised strong oppositions. One argument was the difficulty of the text. This characteristic, quite common among the authors of that time, is not specific to the *MSWT*. During the first decades of the twentieth century, criticism of this book was an important topic, culminating in 1929 with the publication of Yang Shuda's 楊樹達 (1885–1956) *'Mashi wentong' kanwu* (Errors in the *Mashi wentong*), a systematic criticism of Ma's interpretations of the ancient texts he quotes.[36] Most of the points raised by Yang are considered relevant, as it is clear that the *MSWT* is not a model of philological excellence. This is unsurprising since Ma Jianzhong, although considered brilliant, was never in a position to devote himself to Chinese philology with the same intensity as a 'pure' literati. Basically, this grammar has been criticized for contradictory reasons—as a copy of Western models that were not appropriate for use with the Chinese language, and as based on a corpus of classical Chinese texts when this form of Chinese was rejected for the *guoyu* 國語 or 'national language'. In other words, it suffered

---

[35] Cf. Hubert Maës 1975. "La terminologie linguistique japonaise", *Travaux du Groupe de Linguistique Japonaise. Université Paris VII*, vol. 1, pp. 45–55.

[36] Cf. Yang Shuda 楊樹達 . 1983 [1929, 1962]. *'Ma shi wen tong' kanwu* 馬氏文通 刊誤 (Errors in the *Mashi wentong*). Beijing: Zhonghua shuju. The basic meaning of the term *kanwu* 刊誤 is "misprint".

from being associated both with Western ways of thinking and Classical Chinese.

The rapid rejection of the *MSWT* considerably limited its perception as an intellectual achievement. However there are some exceptions, such as Hu Shi 胡適 (1891–1962), who was one of the most influential and active advocates of *guoyu*, the 'national language' that was replacing Classical Chinese as the written style, the very Classical Chinese that was the subject of the *MSWT*. There are a number of remarks by Hu Shi about the importance of grammar scattered through his works. One example from a "Project for the reform of literature" (Chapter 3: *Xu jiangqiu wenfa* 須講求文法 (It is necessary to respect the rules of grammar)) states:

> Today writers of poetry and prose do not care about grammar …. However, those who do not respect grammar are in danger of becoming incomprehensible. This is so clear that it is not even necessary to demonstrate it.[37]

The most explicit text of Hu Shi on that topic, as far as we know, is an undated article, not published at that time. It is included in a collection of his works. We know that it was probably written in 1919 because Liu Zhongkai 留仲愷 mentioned in a letter that he was waiting for this article in order to publish it in the journal *Jianshe*.[38]

It is not a grammatical text but a reflection on the relationship between the *guoyu* and the *guowen* as well as on methods for building a grammar. Hu Shi states the foundations of this method: induction, comparison, and history. He illustrates these principles with some points in *guoyu* as well as in *guowen*. (Examples: position of pronouns in negative sentences, inventory of the personal pronouns). He stresses the qualities of the *Mashi wentong*: care, rationality, rigor, principle of induction (*guina* 歸納). He has some critics, who primarily attack Ma Jianzhong's lack of historical perspective in that he did not understand that contemporary Chinese languages (*guoyu* and dia-

---

[37] Hu Shi 胡適 . 1994 [1917]. "Wenxue gailiang chuyi" 文學改良芻議 (Some modest proposals for the reform of literature), in: Wang Rongwen 王榮文 (ed.). *Hu Shi zuopinji* 胡適作品集 (Collected works of Hu Shi). Taibei: Yuanliu chubanshe, vol. 3, p. 7.

[38] Cf. id. 1988. "Guoyu wenfa gailun" 國語文法概論 (Project for the reform of literature), in: Wang Rongwen 王榮文 (ed.). *Hu Shi zuopinji* 胡適作品集 (Collected works of Hu Shi). Taipei: Yuanliu chubanshe, pp. 443–99.

lects) are a result of a thousand years of changes in the Chinese language as revealed in *guwen* 古文 (Old Text School) texts.[39]

2. *Followers of the* Mashi Wentong *and the utilitarian bias*

Very few Chinese grammars were published immediately after the *MSWT*. His Chinese followers continued to use the categorization approach and some of the terms, but ignored the method and most of the details of analysis. Before 1911, we can quote only two important works, written by Lai Yuxun 來裕恂 (1873–1962)[40] and Zhang Shizhao 章士釗 (1881–1973).[41] Zhang Shizhao is considered to have introduced the term *ci* with the meaning of 'word'. He has great respect for the *MSWT* and roughly follows the same presentation, the main difference being the elimination of the last chapter.

The needs of pedagogy have motivated the systematic study of language everywhere, and from the start all the important texts in grammar take this aspect into consideration. The *Mashi wentong* itself is an example. However, exclusive emphasis on easy ways to learn languages, as if everything were clear and not subject to further questioning, leads to sterility.

The most popular grammar in the first half of the twentieth century was the *Xinzhu guoyu wenfa* 新著國語文法 (New grammar of Chinese) by Li Jinxi 李錦熙 (1890–1978) the first comprehensive Chinese grammar.[42] In the Preface, the author demonstrates an obsession with the effectiveness of his teaching. As for methods, he lays greater emphasis on technical procedures ("write ideas on bits of paper and paste them…") rather than the intellectual processes implicated in the study of language. The result is a textbook that is not too difficult to read and where the facts are presented as pre-established norms. The first chapters are about syntax, and the importance placed on the construction of the text is Li Jinxi's most significant innovation: this explains why he is considered among the pioneers in the field of Chi-

---

[39] On the developments of different notions for a new national language, see Elisabeth Kaske's contribution in this volume.

[40] Cf. Lai Yuxun 來裕恂 . 1906. *Han wen dian* 漢文典 (A manual of Chinese grammar). Shanghai: Shangwu yinshuguan. Republished in 1924, 8th edition.

[41] Cf. Zhang Shizao 章士釗 . 1926 [1907]. *Zhongdeng guo wen dian* 中等國文典 (A manual of Chinese grammar for middle school). Shanghai: Shangwu yinshuguan.

[42] It was printed in twenty editions before 1956. Li Jinxi 李錦熙 . 1957 [1924]. *Xinzhu guoyu wenfa* 新著國語文法 (New grammar of Chinese). Shanghai: Shangwu yinshuguan.

nese grammar, although he was inspired by English textbooks, particularly Nesfield's series.[43] To adapt this model to the Chinese language he simply suppressed some of the specific features of the English language. Moreover, he systematically added tables and diagrams.[44]

It is not hard to understand that such a dry account of their language would not greatly appeal to Chinese people.

3. The position of grammar in China today

In 1998, the centennary of the *MSWT* was the occasion of large gatherings of linguists and many publications about the *MSWT*. As a result of research over the last decades of the twentieth century, a number of Chinese linguists now perceives the originality and outstanding qualities of the *MSWT*.[45] A broad range of opinions was presented, but these evaluations, although indeed fascinating, do not affect either current grammatical research or the reception of grammar in China. It has become a topic of historical interest.

If you mention "Chinese grammar" in China, not only to the man in the street but also to educated people with no special connection to the field of linguistics, the most frequent response will be 漢語語法沒有 *Hanyu yufa meiyou* (Chinese, grammar, it does not exist). However, the discipline does exist, and there are excellent linguists in most of the Chinese Language and Literature Departments in the universities (*zhongwenxi* 中文系). A number of journals and monographs are published each year, and the field covers the grammar of all varieties of Chinese, including ancient Classical language, ancient vernacular, contemporary common language, dialects, and others. It seems that the success of these academic activities has no influence on the image of Chinese grammar in the eyes of the public, however. Indeed, the number of Chinese linguists is not very large in proportion to the size of China's population, and it is very possible that there are as many

---

[43] Cf. J. C. Nesfield. 1913. *English Grammar Series*. Book I. London: Macmillan.

[44] Li Jinxi had previously given a short presentation of his system in the form of tables. Cf. Li Jinxi 李錦熙 . 1920. "Guoyu wenfa biaojie caoan" 國語文法表解草案 (Draft for an explanatory diagram of the Chinese grammar), *Min yi* 2.2, pp. 2–10.

[45] Cf. Guo Xiliang 郭錫良 . 1998. "Zai tan Ma Jianzhong he 'Mashi wentong'" 再談馬建忠和馬氏文通 (Once again on Ma Jianzhong and the *Mashi wentong*), *Zhongguo yuwen* 267, pp. 432–4.

foreigners as Chinese linguists working on the richness of Chinese grammar—assuming that we may refer to the large group of American linguists of Chinese origin as 'foreigners'.

Considered from a European perspective, this situation seems paradoxical, as in our culture educated people are conscious of the significance of grammar even though it may not be their cup of tea. It would be interesting to study the representation of grammar among the general public in other countries.

In ancient civilizations, written language was learned by reciting, reading aloud, memorising, and quoting remarkable texts that had been 'canonized'. This was certainly the case for the Greeks and Homer as well as the Chinese with the Classics, and the same holds true for a number of other civilizations. Thus, the Chinese situation is not at all unusual in this respect. Two factors may lead to the development of grammatical analyses of a given language: practical necessity and contact with other civilizations with grammars. The need for grammatical analysis does not arise in a closed world, but only when contacts with other languages impose teaching of foreign languages and translation.[46] In China at the end of the nineteenth century both these conditions were met due to the unprecedented development of international relations and access to Western grammars.

If you ask a number of Chinese of various ages and activities "Under what circumstances do you read aloud when you are alone?", among those who do so, some will answer "ancient poetry," a few will answer "texts that are difficult to understand," but the majority will answer "texts in foreign languages." These answers correspond to the three main functions of reading aloud: pleasure, cognition, and memorization. If we look at memorization of texts as the best way to learn a language in the written medium, the Chinese would memorize great texts from their own tradition in the past. Now they apply this method to foreign texts. In other words, they learn written English through the traditional device of memorization, in addition to the more or less simple grammatical analyses they find in innumerable English textbooks. We are not sure that such efforts are still devoted to the assimilation of texts from their own written traditions. When the need for contacts with foreign languages appears in a society, one

---

[46] Neither China nor Greece were really 'closed' worlds. A better adjective would be 'believed by themselves to be the center of the civilized world'.

question will be: "Which language should we focus on, the one from outside or our own language?" For Chinese in our century, it is clear that the focus is on the language of outsiders, represented almost exclusively by English. However we must not forget that for almost thirty years the dominant language was Russian.[47] Although a number of intellectuals between the ages of fifty and sixty are definitely more fluent in Russian than in English, other traces of that period remain tenuous.

The application of a number of Western sciences and techniques to Chinese realities has been contested, but grammar is the only one to have been almost completely ignored.

4. THE POOR RECEPTION OF GRAMMAR: ACCIDENT OR NECESSITY?

We may clearly state that the opinion held by most Chinese of the irrelevance of the grammatical science to their own language cannot be explained by the particularities of the Chinese language, which is just as liable to grammatical analysis as any other language.

Language may be seen as the system of operations activated by human beings to build up spoken or written discourses and, when listening or reading, to develop hypotheses about the meanings of oral or written texts. This faculty is used for all languages, albeit in different ways, and in the description of a particular language we may find devices that are not present in others. The Western grammatical tradition was not built through accumulation into a homogenous body of knowledge, but developed rather as a field for elaborate intellectual analysis. This was certainly the case for the study of Latin between the sixteenth and the twentieth century, and was long thought to be one of the best possible 'intellectual training fields', on a par with mathematics.[48] Throughout history, a number of very different languages were successfully included. Every time a language with no explicit grammar was studied, it introduced a change of perspective, of focus. The great revolutions include that from Greek to Latin and later to Arabic, from Latin to some European vernaculars, later to all

---

[47] 1949–79. Although the Russian influence declined sharply after 1966, linguistic education was not changed before the end of the seventies since during the Cultural Revolution there was no education.

[48] Cf. Françoise Waquet 1998. *Le latin ou l'empire d'un signe, 16e au 20e siècles.* Paris: Albin Michel.

the different modern European languages, shortly after to the languages spoken in South and North America, and finally the East Asian languages.[49]

In describing Latin, the focus remained on morphology because of the eminent role played by inflexions in this language. The basic semantic oppositions were crystallized within the word itself. But with the introduction of modern European languages such as Spanish, English and French, word order had to be taken into consideration. In other words, syntax, the analysis of the internal structure of a text that was far less important than morphology in ancient times, now became a priority.[50] If we then look at the Chinese language, it requires a change of focus in the same direction, but does not imply a more revolutionary approach—we may even say it is 'less revolutionary'. Grammatical science in its present state tends to integrate data from all the languages of the world. This integration is possible because the same cognitive and pragmatic operations are present in all languages. The differences lie in the relative importance of what is necessarily explicit and what is optional in each language and the practical ways they are implemented. It is often noted that Chinese has no gender distinctions, but among the languages that have this category some have three terms with a neutral, while others have only two. As for the demonstrative, Chinese and English are among the languages with an alternative, *zhei/nei*, this/that whereas French has a neutral third term, *ce*. For every grammatical feature, the actual mapping may be different for each language.

Although the convergence between Chinese and Indo-European languages is seldom discussed, we shall give two examples.

Chinese presents the problem of isomorphism between phrases and compound words. For example, the determinative/determined succession is the rule that governs construction of the nominal phrase, and it is also one of the most productive modes of word composition.[51] Linguists do not agree about the extension of this isomorphism, that is, on

---

[49] India was not included in this game since the great grammarian Panini built a special system independently prior to the others.

[50] Cf. Marc Baratin. 1989. *La naissance de la syntaxe à Rome*. Paris: Éditions de Minuit, p. 491.

[51] Regarding the morphology, composition and features of the 'word' in Chinese, cf. Jerome L. Packard (ed.). 1998. *New Approaches to the Chinese Word Formation. Morphology, Phonology and the Lexicon in Modern and Ancient Chinese*. Berlin, New York: de Gruyter.

the tests used to distinguish syntactic and morphological processes. Such a phenomenon has also been shown to be a very common feature of languages, as stated by Émile Benveniste:

> It is necessary, according to our views, to stop considering compound words as morphological types, and look at them as syntactic. Nominal composition is a 'micro-syntax'. Every type of compound must be studied as the transformation of a free syntactic text .... Thus, it is impossible to explain the creation of compound words as simply the immediate junction of two anterior signs.[52]

Although the examples used by Benveniste are primarily taken from Indo-European languages (Sanskrit and a number of modern languages), his remarks are very similar to certain formulations of Chao Yuen Ren:

> In Chinese most compounds are syntactic, and only the relatively few cases of an obscure relationship between the parts in compounds may be considered asyntactic.[53]

Unexpected echoes may be found in many aspects of different languages.

Another example is the rhetorical interrogation (*fanwenju* 反問句) present in all languages. Aside from intonation, which appears to be universal, each language has its own devices to mark this type of pseudo interrogation: adverbs, unusual tense, etc. Among other devices, Modern Chinese 'grammaticizes' it by the inversion of the negation and the adverb or by the inversion of the negation and the verb of possibility.[54] This interesting fact is never mentioned in the current grammars available in China. We could give a number of examples of this type. Many constructions cannot be analysed without

---

[52] "Il faut, à notre avis, envisager les composés non plus comme des espèces morphologiques, mais comme des organizations syntaxiques. La composition nominale est une mico-syntaxe. Chaque type de composé est à étudier comme la transformation d'un type d'énoncé syntaxique libre" (1974, pp. 145–6). "On ne peut donc plus expliquer la création des composés par la simple jonction immédiate de deux signes antérieurs" (1974, p. 160). Émile Benveniste. 1967. "Fondements syntaxiques de la composition nominale", *Bulletin de la Société de Linguistique de Paris* 12.1, pp. 15–31. Re-edited in: id. (ed.). 1974. *Problèmes de linguistique générale* 2. Paris: Gallimard, pp. 145–62.

[53] Chao Yuan Ren. 1968 [1948]. *Mandarin Primer*. Cambridge, Mass.: Harvard University Press, p. 366. We may suppose that in this context the term 'asyntactic' means 'cannot be analysed according the rules of syntax'.

[54] Viviane Alleton 1970. *L'écriture chinoise*. Paris: Presses Universitaires de France (Coll. *Que sais-je?* no. 1374); 6th edition 2002.

a semantic and formal confrontation of texts, and even when they have been described—which is not always the case—they are to be found only in specialized journals, often written in English and having absolutely no impact whatever on the general public. Of course, we refer to spoken as well as written texts. This is unsurprising given that the scientific study of Chinese grammar is less than a century old.

My point with this overly long excursus is to stress that the poor acclimatization of grammar in China is not an intrinsic necessity but a kind of historical accident.

This does not exclude another historical change. The study of the Chinese dialects, previously limited to phonology and lexicography, is now extending to grammar. And, although the general public still tends to perceive other foreign languages as mere variants of English, a number of Chinese linguists in China are now becoming aware of the diversity of languages.

CONCLUSION

We shall conclude with some reflections on the objectives of grammatical studies. These may be used in learning and teaching, as the basis of standardization, and to reinforce intellectual abilities.

As we have noted, to learn a language in both its written and spoken form, grammatical analysis is not a necessary condition, but it is helpful in organising pedagogical material. This function is more important in learning foreign languages than for the acquisition of a native language, even in the written form. This is a somewhat artificial way to distinguish the pedagogical and the cognitive dimensions, and here we are primarily considering the aims of people who promote grammar.

Standardization of language is a universal concern of governments as well as a number of social groups or classes. In ancient China, this was accomplished through control of the writing system, memorization of the canonical texts and through examinations. Today the Chinese State still controls the writing system, the schools, and, we may add, the media. Some notions of grammar have been introduced into the middle school program (中學 *zhongxue*), however. This inclusion at a homeopathic dose has the same end in view as the use of another 'Western' device, *pinyin* 拼音 , or alphabetic transcription, now mandatory during the first year of elementary school. In both cases, what is at stake is the unity of the common language, spoken as well as written, throughout China. The common language taught at school is a second language for a large number of Chinese. As such, it is influenced by dialectal usage, as has been shown in comparisons between Mandarin Chinese as spoken in Beijing, Shanghai and Taibei, where the morphology, syntax and semantics of a number of adverbs reveal noticeable differences, for example. It is understandable that the State seeks to inject some grammar in the school programs to combat these trends. However, the normative style and the elementary level of the program generates some scepticism as to its effectiveness.

We may say that the real and essential justification of grammar is knowledge. It explains why some people feel pleasure when they discover the grammatical rules of a language that they know or learn either on their own or through a teacher. We all seek to understand the mechanisms of the languages we use ('*les langues*'), while linguists seek to understand the principles of this human activity ('*le langage*'). More importantly, however, it may be considered as one of the primary tools for developing intellectual abilities.

My last remarks will discuss the position of grammar within the typology of the "Translation of Western Knowledge at the turn of the nineteenth Century". At best, grammar was considered as 'practical knowledge', a technical device useful in learning foreign languages. But fundamentally the cognitive dimension of grammar was overlooked. The Chinese accepted logic for the benefits of this 'science of sciences', as Joachim Kurtz reminds us,[55] but saw no such advantage in linguistic. They did not realize that the perception of the mental operations involved in language can generate considerable benefits.

To those who try to understand and formalize it—the linguists—grammar provides the pleasure and intellectual benefits of a sophisticated branch of knowledge. It combines the need for universal rules with the contingent nature of practical applications, depending on the language and for use in an infinite number of contexts. More importantly, grammar may help develop a higher degree of self-knowledge in any user of language, both as a member of a linguistic community (not necessarily a nation) and as a human being who constructs him or herself through dialogue. Having overlooked this dimension of grammar, it is no surprise that the Chinese were not greatly attracted by

---

[55] Cf. Joachim Kurtz' contribution in this volume.

what simply appeared to be only an uninteresting and dreary technique.

In present-day China the question of grammar no longer involves the 'transmission' issue or a discussion of the foreign origin of grammar, but rather the diffusion of this method among the population at large. Until now, knowledge and understanding of grammar has remained the sole privilege of a small group of renowned scholars.

REFERENCES

Abel-Rémusat, Jean-Pierre. 1822. *Éléments de la grammaire chinoise*. Paris: Imprimerie Royale. Reprint Paris: Ala Productions, 1987.

Ai Letong 艾樂桐 . "Ouzhou wangji le hanyu que 'faxian' le hanzi" 歐洲忘記了漢語 卻發現了漢字 (L'oubli de la langue et l''invention' de l'écriture chinoise en Europe), in: Denys Lombard (Long Ba'er 龍巴爾) and Li Xueqin 李學勤 (eds.). *Faguo hanxue* 法國漢學 (French sinology). Beijing: Qinghua daxue, vol. 1, pp. 182–98 (Translation of Alleton 1994).

Alleton, Viviane. 1970. *L'écriture chinoise*. Paris: Presses Universitaires de France (Coll. *Que sais-je?* no. 1374); 6th edition 2002.

——. 1988. "The so-called 'Rhetorical Interrogation' in Mandarin Chinese", *Journal of Chinese Linguistics* 16. 2, pp. 278–96.

——. 1994. "L'oubli de la langue et l''invention' de l'écriture chinoise en Europe", *Études Chinoises* 13.1–2, pp. 259–82.

Alvarez, Emmanuel. 1842. *Grammatica di Emmanuel Àlvaro della S.d.G. volgarizzata*. Naples.

——. 1974. *De institutione grammatica libre tres; conjugationibus accessit interpretation Japponica*. Tokyo: Tenri Central Library.

Arnauld, Antoine and Claude Lancelot. 1660. *Grammaire Générale et Raisonnée*. Paris: Pierre le Petit. (Reprinted Paris: Editions Allia, 1997.)

Baratin, Marc. 1989. *La naissance de la syntaxe à Rome*. Paris: Éditions de Minuit.

Benveniste, Émile. 1967. "Fondements syntaxiques de la composition nominale", *Bulletin de la Société de Linguistique de Paris* 12.1, pp. 15–31. Re-edited in: id. (ed.). 1974. *Problèmes de linguistique générale* 2. Paris: Gallimard, pp. 145–62.

Cartier, Michel (ed.). 1998. *La Chine entre amour et haine. Actes du VIIIe colloque de sinologie de Chantilly*. Paris: Desclée de Brouwer (Variétés sinologiques no. 87).

Chao Yuan Ren. 1968 [1948]. *Mandarin Primer*. Cambridge, Mass.: Harvard University Press.

Devienne, Frédéric. 2001. *Considérations théoriques sur l'écriture par deux lettrés chinois au début du 20e siècle. Analyse de l'œuvre linguistique de Zhang Binglin (1869–1936) et de son disciple Huang Kan (1886–1935)*. Paris: École Pratique des Hautes Études.

Djamouri, Redouane. 1993. "Théorie de la 'rectification des dénominations' et réflexions linguistiques chez Xunzi", *Extrême-Orient Extrême-Occident* 15, pp. 55–74.

Elman, Benjamin A. 1984. *From Philosophy to Philology: Intellectual and Social Aspects of Change in Late Imperial China*. Cambridge, Mass.: Harvard University Council on East Asian Studies.

Gao Yihong. 1997. *Collected Essays of Shen Xiaolong on Chinese Cultural Linguistics*. Changchun: Northeast Normal University Press.

Gabelentz, Georg von der. 1881. *Chinesische Grammatik*. Leipzig: Weigel.

Guo Xiliang 郭錫良 . 1998. "Zai tan Ma Jianzhong he 'Mashi wentong'" 再談馬建忠 和馬氏文通 (Once again on Ma Jianzhong and the *Mashi wentong*), *Zhongguo yuwen* 267, pp. 432–4.

Hu Shi 胡適 . 1994 [1917]. "Wenxue gailiang chuyi" 文學改良芻議 (Some modest proposals for the reform of literature), in: Wang Rongwen 王榮文 (ed.). *Hu Shi zuopinji* 胡適作品集 (Collected works of Hu Shi). Taibei: Yuanliu chubanshe, vol. 3, p. 7.

——. 1988. "Guoyu wenfa gailun" 國語文法概論 (Project for the reform of literature), in: Wang Rongwen 王榮文 (ed.). *Hu Shi zuopinji* 胡適作品集 (Collected
works of Hu Shi). Taipei: Yuanliu chubanshe, pp. 443–99.

Lai Yuxun 來裕恂. 1906. *Han wen dian* 漢文典 (A manual of Chinese grammar).
Shanghai: Shangwu yinshuguan. Republished in 1924, 8th edition.

Li Jinxi 李錦熙. 1920. "Guoyu wenfa biaojie caoan" 國語文法表解草案 (Draft for an
explanatory diagram of the Chinese grammar), *Min yi* 2.2, pp. 2–10.

——. 1957 [1924]. *Xinzhu guoyu wenfa* 新著國語文法 (New grammar of Chinese).
Shanghai: Shangwu yinshuguan.

Li Shuchang 黎庶昌. 1981. *Xiyang zazhi* 西洋雜誌 (Travel notes on a journey to the
West). Reprint Changsha: Renmin chubanshe.

——. 1988. *Carnet de notes sur l'Occident*. Translated by Shi Kangqiang. Paris: Editions de la Maison des Sciences de l'Homme. (Translation of Li Shuchang
1981).

Li Tiangang. 1996. "Christianity and Cultural Conflict in the Life of Ma Xiangbo",
in: Ruth Hayhoe (ed.). *Ma Xiangbo and the Mind of Modern China 1840–1939*.
Armonk: Sharpe, pp. 89–149.

Lü Shuxiang 呂叔湘 and Wang Haifen 王海棻 (eds.). 1986. *Mashi wentong duben* 馬
氏文通讀本 (Mashi wentong reader). Reprint Shanghai: Shanghai jiaoyu.

Ma Jianzhong 馬建忠. 1983 [1898, 1904]. *Mashi wentong* 馬氏文通 (Mr. Ma's
grammar). Shanghai: Shangwu yinshuguan.

Maës, Hubert. 1975. "La terminologie grammaticale japonaise", *Travaux du Groupe
de Linguistique Japonaise. Université Paris VII*, vol. 1, pp. 45–55.

Nesfield, J. C. 1913. *English Grammar Series*. Book I. London: Macmillan.

Packard, Jerome L. (ed.). 1998. *New Approaches to the Chinese Word Formation.
Morphology, Phonology and the Lexicon in Modern and Ancient Chinese*. Berlin, New York: de Gruyter.

Peverelli, Peter. 1986. *The History of Modern Chinese Grammar studies*. Ph.D. diss.,
Leiden University.

Peyraube, Alain. 1999. "Qingdai '*Mashi wentong*' yiqian de yufa zhishi" 清代馬氏文
通以前的語法知識 (Knowledge on grammar in the Qing dynasty prior to the
Mashi wentong). Paper presented at the Second International symposium on the
Qing Philology, Gaoxiong.

Prémare, Joseph Henri de. 1831. *Notitia Linguæ Sinicæ*. Malacca: Cura-Academia
Anglo-Sinensis. Republished in Hong Kong: Société des Missions Etrangères,
1894.

Rousseau, Jean and Denis Thouard (eds). 1999. *Lettres édifiantes et curieuses sur la
langue chinoise; Humboldt/Abel-Rémusat (1821–1831)*. Villeneuve-d'Asc:
Presses Universitaires du Septentrion.

Swiggers, Pierre. 1997. *Histoire de la pensée linguistique. Analyse du langage et
réflexion linguistique dans la culture occidentale de l'Antiquité au XIXe siècle*.
Paris: Presses Universitaires de France.

Uhlig, Gustav. 1883. *Grammatici Graeci, I-1: Dionysii Thracis Ars Grammatica*.
Leipzig: Teubner.

Wang Guowei 王國維. 1908. *Bianxue* 辨學 (Logic). Beijing: Jingshi wudaomiao
shoushuchu.

Wang Zan-Tzeng. 1911. *Lehrbuch der Deutschen Grammatik*. Shanghai: Commercial Press.

Waquet, Françoise. 1998. *Le latin ou l'empire d'un signe, 16e au 20e siècles*. Paris:
Albin Michel.

Yang Shuda 楊樹達 . 1983 [1929, 1962]. *'Ma shi wen tong' kanwu* 馬氏文通刊誤 (Errors in the *Mashi wentong*). Beijing: Zhonghua shuju.

Zhang Binglin 章炳麟 . 1907. "Lun yuyan wenzi zhixue" 論語言文字之學 (On the study of language and writing), *Guocui Xuebao* 12–13.

Zhang Shizao 章士釗 . 1926 [1907]. *Zhongdeng guo wen dian* 中等國文典 (A manual of Chinese grammar for middle school). Shanghai: Shangwu yinshuguan.

Zhu Weizheng 朱維錚 (ed.). 1996. *Ma Xiangbo ji* 馬相伯集 (Collection of Ma Xiangbo). Shanghai: Fudan daxue.

Zottoli, Angelo. 1859. *Emmanuelis Alvarez institutio Grammatica ad sinenses alumnos accomodata*. Shanghai: A. V. de Carvalho.

——. 1879–1882. *Cursus Literatura Sinicae*. 5 vols. Shanghai: Typographia Missionis Catholice.

LAWRENCE WANG-CHI WONG 王宏志

BEYOND *XIN DA YA* 信達雅 : TRANSLATION PROBLEMS IN THE LATE QING[1]

INTRODUCTION

The present paper is an attempt to identify the major problems faced by translators of Western works in the Late Qing and to analyze their approaches to tackling the problems they encountered. Instead of making textual comparisons between originals and the translations and pinpointing 'technical' problems, greater emphasis will be placed on the social and political context of the time. There are two reasons for this. For one, recent translation theories show unmistakeably that translation is not done in a vacuum.[2] Numerous factors affect the decisions made by translators in their choice of works, methods adopted for translation and means of promoting the works. For another, the motives for translating Western works at that time were basically political. By introducing Western knowledge into China, the Chinese hoped to modernize and strengthen the country in order that it would be able to resist foreign invasion. With such a specific objective in mind, late Qing translators encountered specific problems.

In the following, frequent reference will be made to translations of literary works. This will not be too great a digression from the main theme of the conference, as literary translations in the late Qing served the same political purpose as technical translations. People believed that, since literary works would help to enlighten the minds of the people, especially the general masses, literary translation was also a necessary step in introducing Western strength into China, especially when the mere importation of military and technological knowledge could not save the country from further defeats.

---

[1] The paper is a product of a research project entitled "Translation and Politics: A Comprehensive Study of the Translation Activities of the Late Qing", funded by the Hong Kong Research Grant Council Earmarked Research Grant.

[2] Cf. Andre Lefevere. 1992. *Translation, Rewriting and the Manipulation of Literary Frame*. London, New York: Routledge, p. 14.

1. THE CONDITIONS OF TRANSLATORS IN THE
LATE NINETEENTH CENTURY

The first major statement on the problems involved in translating Western knowledge into China during the Late Qing was made by probably the most important translator of the time Yan Fu 嚴復 (1854–1921). Yan, in his famous "Notes to the Translation of *Tianyanlun*" (Thomas H. Huxley's *Evolution and Ethics),* attempted to explain the difficulties in translation in three terms, *xin da ya* 信達雅 ,[3] which have since then been taken as the gospel of translation in China.

Most people translate *xin da ya* as "fidelity, comprehensibility and elegance". Apparently the three constitute technical, or practical, problems in translation: in what ways can one translate the contents of an original piece of work faithfully, comprehensibly and clearly? Very often, the three elements are viewed as oppositional forces: because of the huge gap between the source language and target language and between their cultures, any attempt to translate faithfully would have to sacrifice comprehensibility and elegance; or vice versa, translating in comprehensible and elegant target language would certainly involve a distortion of the meaning. Whether these problems can be dealt with satisfactorily depend largely on the capability of the translators. A capable translator should be able to strike a good balance between the three.

Unfortunately the major and fundamental problem in the Late Qing translation was the lack of competent translators. During the initial encounters of the West and China from the beginning of the nineteenth century until its last couple of decades, those who had a command of Chinese and a Western language were almost entirely the Westerners. Missionaries and diplomats like Robert Morrison (1782–1834), William Milne (1785–1822), John Fryer (1839–1928), Elijah C. Bridgman (1801–1861), Karl Gützlaff (1803–1851), Walter H. Medhurst (1823–1885), Thomas F. Wade (1818–1895) or William A. P. Martin (1827–1916) constituted the first group of translators in China. Most of them acquired the Chinese language after they had arrived China or in South East Asia. In this early stage, with a few exceptions, most of them could not master classical written Chinese

---

[3] Yan Fu 嚴復 . 1986b. "*Tianyanlun* yiliyan" 天演論譯例言 (Notes to the translation of *Tianyanlun*), in: Yan Fu 嚴復 . 1986a. *Yan Fu ji* 嚴復集 (Collected works of Yan Fu [Hereafter *YFJ*]). 5 vols. Beijing: Zhonghua shuju, vol. 5, p. 1321.

very satisfactorily. They had to rely on their Chinese collaborators to polish the translations.

A brief look at the Chinese side, however, shows that their team of translators was even weaker. Expectedly, there were few Chinese who possessed reasonable foreign language proficiency at that time. The Chinese, having a strong pride in their language and cultural heritage, looked down upon the 'foreign devils' and hence rarely contemplated learning their languages. More importantly, learning a foreign language would not bring them any further on the trail of officialdom. Such a situation adversely affected the standard of translation and the status of the translators. We will come to this again when we discuss the case of Yan Fu.

The first group of Chinese translators was the collaborators. Unfortunately, the foreigners had not been able to recruit the best Chinese in helping them to translate and those who assisted Westerners in translation, at the early stage, were those who had no opportunity to sit for the imperial examinations or those who had failed in the examinations. The sole reason for their joining the translation profession was an economic one; they had to make a living, albeit reluctantly, by working with the foreigners. The social status as well as the self-image of this group of people was extremely low. One notable example was Wang Tao 王韜 (1828–1897) in Shanghai. In private letters to his close relatives, he expressed a strong dislike for the job in which he had to "serve the barbarians."[4] With very few exceptions, Wang Tao being one of them, no Chinese collaborators were worthy of notice in the history of translation.[5] There is little wonder that the standard of works was not satisfactory.

However, after repeated military defeats, China saw an urgent need to learn from the West. The *Tongwenguan* 同文館 (College of Foreign Languages) was formally established in Beijing in 1862 for the training of translators. As the general feeling towards foreigners and foreign ideas was still skeptical, the institute, at the initial stage, faced serious problems in attracting students. Even if some were recruited, most of them were of mediocre caliber and did not take the programs

---

[4] Wang Tao 王韜 . 1959. *Taoyuan chidu* 弢園尺牘 (Letters of Wang Tao). Beijing: Zhonghua shuju, pp. 22–3.

[5] For Wang Tao's position and contributions in pre-modern China, see Paul Cohen. 1974. *Between Tradition and Modernity: Wang Tao and Reform in Late Ching China*. Cambridge, Mass.: Harvard University Press.

seriously.[6] It was the *Shanghai Tongwenguan*, which was established in 1863 and renamed as the *Guangfangyanguan* 廣方言館 in 1867, that achieved better results, for two reasons. First, the students were not confined to the Manchu as was the case in Beijing. Second, there were more opportunities to have encounters with the Westerners in Shanghai.[7] Although the two institutes had eventually trained the first group of Chinese who had a good mastery of foreign languages, not all of their graduates turned translators. Since proficiency in foreign languages was such an asset, many became senior officers in the Foreign Office.[8]

In the initial stage, most of these language and translation institutes employed Westerners as instructors and translators. Again, this was due to the fact that Westerners took the initiative to learn Chinese and became the first group of people who could handle both languages. Naturally, the mode of translation in the institutes followed the one adopted by the early Western translators in Shanghai. The Western translator would interpret the works and explain them to a Chinese collaborator who would record them in beautiful classical Chinese. This mode of translation had been accepted as a most legitimate method of translation for several decades.[9] But to us, the problem is obvious enough. The Western translator's ability in Chinese was not good enough to judge whether the translation was a true representation of the originals. On the other hand, Chinese collaborators had no way to decide if they had fully and correctly understood the originals. Hence although a considerable number of works had been trans-

---

[6] Xiong Yuezhi 熊月之. 1994. *Xixue dongjian yu wanqing shehui* 西學東漸與晚清社會 (The dissemination of Western learning and the Late Qing society). Shanghai: Shanghai renmin chubanshe, p. 304.

[7] Ibid., p. 342.

[8] For a discussion of the graduates of the *Guangfanyanguan* and their career, cf. Xiong Yuezhi 熊月之. 1989. "Shanghai guang fanyanguan shilue" 上海廣方言館史略 (A brief history of the *Shanghai Guangfangyanguan*), in: Tang Zhenchang 唐振常 and Shen Hengchun 沈恆春 (eds.). Shanghai shi yanjiu 上海史研究 (A study of the history of Shanghai). Shanghai: Xuelin chubanshe, pp. 176–211. For a discussion of the biographical background and social status of the members of these new institutions see also Natascha Vittighoff's contribution in this volume.

[9] John Fryer. 1984. "Jiangnan zhizaoju fanyi xishu shilue" 江南製造局翻譯西書史略 (A brief account of the translation of Western works by the Jiangnan Arsenal), in: Luo Xinzhang 羅新璋 (ed.). *Fanyi lunji* 翻譯論集 (Collection of essays on translation). Beijing: Commercial Press, pp. 211–26.

lated,[10] most people were not satisfied. In 1894, Ma Jianzhong 馬建忠 (1844–1900) in his appeal for the establishment of a translation academy, severely criticized the unsatisfactory team of translators available at the time:

> Those who know a Western language do not know Chinese and those who know Chinese do not know any foreign language. There is little wonder that the translations are so unsatisfactory and messy, inviting criticism and scorn.[11]

Hence, in his proposal, he urged the recruitment of a chief instructor, who should have a good command of both Chinese and some other foreign languages, followed by a team of four to five who excelled in classical Chinese to polish the translations and act as Chinese language instructors. Such a structure, he hoped, would serve to improve the standard of translation. Obviously, this was also not a satisfactory arrangement; there was no great difference in nature to the previous translation practice. Unfortunately even this proposal was not put into practice and, for some time, China lacked good translators.

2. YAN FU'S CONCEPTION OF FAITHFUL TRANSLATION

Before the turn of the century, however, a trained distinguished translator emerged: Yan Fu. Many would agree that Yan was probably the most highly qualified translator during the Late Qing. Possessing an excellent command of both English and classical Chinese, he should have had little problem in translating faithfully, comprehensibly and elegantly. Yet, critics have accused Yan Fu of not translating faithfully, and a cursory comparison of the originals and his translations clearly shows that Yan adopted a far too liberal manner of translation. But on the other hand, Yan himself refused to acknowledge the charge that he was not faithful to the original. On the contrary, he apologized for the bad style in his translation, saying that it resulted from priori-

---

[10] For example, the Jiangnan Arsenal translated and published 160 titles of works between 1871 and 1909. Cf. Xiong Yuezhi 1994, p. 499.

[11] Ma Jianzhong 馬建忠 . 1996. "Nishe fanyi shuyuanyi" 擬設翻譯書院議 (A proposal for the establishment of a translation academy), in: Li Nanqiu 黎難秋 (ed.). *Zhongguo kexue fanyi shiliao* 中國科學翻譯史料 (Historical materials of Chinese scientific translation). Hefei: Zhongguo kexue jishu daxue chubanshe, pp. 313–7; 314–6.

tizing the meaning.[12] These different views of Yan's translations show that there must be a discrepancy in the understanding of the meaning of, or even the relationship between the terms *xin da ya*.

In his "Notes to the translation of *Tianyanlun*", Yan told his readers that he was not translating, he was only "giving the gist" (*dazhi* 達旨). This gave him great liberty in the process of translation; and of course, the price he had to pay was that he was accused of not having translated faithfully. Yet when he came to explain the word *da*, Yan remarked that, because of the great differences between Chinese and English, one had to make some changes to the word order and sentence structure. As far as translation method was concerned, he suggested that the translator should first have a thorough understanding of the original, and then rewrite the text in a somewhat spontaneous manner. Changes might be made; and additions and deletions might be necessary. According to Yan, all such changes were means of achieving *da*, or, in other words, of making the translation comprehensible to the readers. However, no matter what changes were to be made, the most important thing was that the meaning should not be sacrificed, because the purpose of making such changes was to show or reveal the meanings of the originals more clearly. When he explained his method of *dazhi*, he emphasized that "the meanings should not be different from those of the original." It is from this that we have his important assertion that "to have *da* is to have *xin*." Obviously, the *xin*, faithfulness to the original, in Yan Fu's mind, does not refer to faithfulness with regard to the external elements such as word order or sentence structure. It is faithfulness in meaning that matters. If changes to the external elements can help to reveal the meaning more effectively, then the translator should go ahead with such changes. For this reason, textual comparisons that pay attention to formal similarities would show that Yan made many changes to the original.

What about the third problem, *ya*? Of the three, *ya* has been the most controversial. Yan Fu advocated the use of pre-Han syntax and expressions to translate and to attain *ya*. This invited severe criticism. We will explain later why he would have suggested using pre-Han style in order to attain *ya*, but one important point needs to be clarified

---

[12] Yan Fu 1986c. "*Tianyanlun zixu*" 天演論自序 (Preface to *Tianyanlun*), in: *YFJ*, vol. 5. p. 1322.

first: for Yan, *ya* was not a force that obstructed *xin* and *da*. Instead, "by using pre-Han syntax and expressions, it is easy to attain *da*." Again, we will account for this belief below, but it is clear that, to Yan's mind, *ya*, *da* and *xin*, instead of being contradictory, are complementary to each other. By achieving *ya* through the use of pre-Han syntax and expressions, one can easily attain *da*; and since "to have *da* is to have *xin*," then *ya* would also be a means to achieve *xin* as well. In short, *xin*, faithfulness to the meanings of the original, is the most fundamental component.

While it seems just natural for a translator to be faithful in meaning, there are numerous examples of how translators deliberately change or distort the meanings of the originals, especially in the Late Qing. An interesting example is Su Manshu's 蘇曼殊 (1884–1918) rendition of Victor Hugo's masterpiece *Les Misérables* (*Can shijie* 慘世界). Translating faithfully was probably the last thing on the translator's mind. He went as far as creating a new character, Nande 男德 , and by putting his own words into this invented French protagonist's mouth, he condemned the backwardness of Chinese society.[13] This was the sole purpose of "translating" a French novel.

As more recent translation studies theories suggest, translation is a purposeful activity. When translators decide to pick up a certain piece of work to translate, they wish the translation to serve a certain purpose, be it political, economic, educational or aesthetic.[14] When Yan Fu translated the *Tianyanlun*, he had a special purpose to fulfill. He started to translate the work shortly after China's disastrous defeat in

---

[13] For instance, in the translation, there is a 'speech' made by this French protagonist: "Only the despicable Chinese would take the slavery Confucian education as the golden rule. Should we, the noble French citizens, listen to all this bullshit?" In another paragraph, a female protagonist said the following words: "Yes, I have heard about a place in the East, in Asia, called China. The customs of the Chinese are barbaric. They spend a lot of money in burning incense and paper to worship the clay or wooden Buddha. More ridiculous still, their women use a piece of white cloth to bind up their own feet. They cannot really walk because their feet become as pointed as the hoofs of pigs. Don't you think that is ridiculous?" (Su Manshu 蘇曼殊 (tr.). 1991. "Can shijie" 慘世界 (Les Misérables), in: *Su Manshu wenji* 蘇曼殊文集 (Collected works of Su Manshu). Guangzhou: Huacheng chubanshe, pp. 671–753; 696, 718).

[14] Cf. Christiane Nord. 1997. *Translating As a Purposeful Activity: Functionalist Approaches Explained*. Manchester: St. Jerome; Roman Alvarez and Carmen-Africa Vidal (eds.). 1996. *Translation, Power, Subversion*. Clevedon: Multilingual Matters.

the Sino-Japanese War.[15] By translating *Tianyanlun*, he hoped to introduce the theory of social evolution into China. The chief message he wanted to convey to the Chinese was that in human society, as much as in nature, the principle of natural evolution applied. Only the fittest would survive the competition while the weak would be liable to extermination. He therefore hoped to alert the Chinese to the possibility of racial extermination and wanted them to face up to challenges in a modern world and make the requisite changes and adjustments.

Hence, the political mission of translating *Tianyanlun* is most obvious. Yan's other translations serve similar purposes. On translating Adam Smith's *An Inquiry into the Nature and Causes of the Wealth of Nations*, he told the readers that the book revealed the weaknesses and shortcomings of China's concepts of wealth and economy.[16] In his recommendation of John Stuart Mill's *A System of Logic*, another important work he translated, he said the ideas in the book would clarify the muddles of many old Chinese sayings and beliefs.[17] Yan Fu was not a productive translator, but his rich command of Western knowledge marked him apart from many other translators. He was able to pick the kinds of works that, in his opinion, would best serve China's interest.

Apparently there was not the need for him to adapt the originals, if the works were carefully chosen to suit China's need. However, critics have pointed out that, even in terms of the contents, Yan's *Tianyanlun* is far from being a faithful translation.[18] It is not the purpose of this paper to determine whether Yan Fu was faithful to the original or not. But what should be stressed is that, at the time, there was not the issue as to whether Yan had been translating faithfully or not. The purpose of Yan Fu's claim to translate faithfully was to "invoke the

---

[15] Yan Qu 嚴璩 . 1986. "Houguan Yan xiansheng nianpu" 侯官嚴先生年譜 (A chronology of Mr. Yan Fu), in: *YFJ*, vol. 5, pp. 1545–52; 1548.

[16] Yan Fu (tr.). 1931a. *Yuanfu* 原富 (The Origins of Wealth). Shanghai: Commercial Press, pp. 2–3. [Translation of Adam Smith. *An Inquiry into the Nature and Causes of the Wealth of Nations,* 1776].

[17] Yan Fu's letter to Zhang Yuanji 張元濟 in September 1901, in: *YFJ*, vol. 3, p. 546.

[18] Cf. Elizabeth Sinn. 1995. "Yan Fu", in: Chan Sin-wai and David Pollard (eds.). *An Encyclopaedia of Translation.* Hong Kong: Chinese University Press, pp. 432–6; Mau-sang Ng 吳茂生 . 1991. "Reading Yan Fu's Tian Yan Lun", in: Roger Ames et al. (eds.). *Interpreting Culture Through Translation.* Hong Kong: Chinese University Press, pp. 167–84; 167–8.

authority" of the Western work in order to have a stronger impact on China.[19]

One could rightly question why there could not be faithfulness in the formal features such as the sentence structure or word order as well. We have seen that Yan Fu explained that changes in sentence structure and word order were necessary as Chinese and English were so different. This was by no means a groundless excuse, and all Chinese/English translators would have to find the means to bridge the differences between the two languages. Changes made as a result of grammatical or structural needs should be minimal, but the changes in Yan's translations were certainly more than necessary. For example, Yan Fu has changed the narrator in *Tianyanlun* from a first person "I" to a third person "Huxley". While this made no significant differences to the content, this was certainly not done out for grammatical reasons. Rather, it was in line with the practices in fiction translation of the period. One literary historian has pointed out that in the three earliest important translated novels during the Qing dynasty, the narrator was changed from a first person to a third person. This practice was adopted because traditional Chinese fiction relied almost entirely on third-person narrative; and the translator worried that the readers accustomed to reading traditional fiction might mistake the "I" of the narrator for the translator himself.[20] Yan Fu, like the fiction translators, had to pay attention to contemporary reading habits.

3. PATRONAGE AND YAN FU'S ELEGANT STYLE OF WRITING

The reader was certainly an influential factor in the translation of Western works in the Late Qing. In late imperial China where, firstly, education was confined to a privileged minority and, secondly, most

---

[19] Lefevere once asked an important question in translation: "Why produce texts that 'refer to' other texts? Why not simply produce originals in the first place?" And his answer is: "If you produce a text that 'refers to' another text, rather than producing your own, you are most likely to do so because you think the other text enjoys a prestige far greater than the prestige your own text might possibly aspire to. In other words, you invoke the authority of the text you represent." (Andre Lefevere. 1992b. *Translation, Rewriting and The Manipulation of Literary Fame*. London, New York: Routledge, pp. 2–3).

[20] Chen Pingyuan 陳平原 . 1988. *Zhongguo xiaoshuo xushi moshi de zhuanbian* 中國小說敍事模式的轉變 (The transformation of narrative modes in Chinese fiction). Shanghai: Shanghai renmin chubanshe, p. 76.

people were not interested in Western learning, translations were read
by a limited group of people. This group of people, who very often
occupied senior positions in officialdom, also played the role of
patrons.

Patronage has become an important issue in recent translation studies. According to Lefevere, patronage can be understood to mean
"something like the powers (persons, institutions) that can further or
hinder the reading, writing, and rewriting of literature." It can be
exerted by persons, or groups of persons, a religious body, a political
party, a social class, a royal court, and in the modern world, by publishers and even mass media like newspapers, magazines and televi-
sion corporations. Moreover it consists of three elements: ideological
component, economic component and status component; and there are
two distinct categories of patronage: differentiated patronage and
undifferentiated patronage.

> Patronage is undifferentiated when its three components, the ideologi-
> cal, the economic, and the status components, are all dispensed by one
> and the same patron, [such as an absolute ruler in the past.] Patronage is
> differentiated, on the other hand, when economic success is relatively
> independent of ideological factors, and does not necessarily bring sta-
> tus with it.[21]

This concept of patronage is helpful in understanding the translation activities in the Late Qing since, in a country like imperial China,
no translation of Western works would have been allowed without the
ultimate blessings of the ruler.[22] Hence in the early stage, translation
of Western knowledge, except those done by foreign missionaries at
the treaty ports, was not done by voluntary translators but initiated by
political leaders.

The first group of patrons were the leaders of the Self-strengthening Movement.[23] Seeing the repeated defeats of China at the hands of
the foreign powers, they urged an importation of Western knowledge

---

[21] The discussion of patronage is largely taken from Lefevere 1992, pp. 15–7.

[22] In fact in the early Qing, some Jesuit missionaries were allowed to stay in China
and they translated some books of science and technology. Emperor Yongzhen 雍正
put a ban on Christianity and drove out the Jesuit missionaries in 1723. Translation
was abruptly put to an end.

[23] Some regard Lin Zexu 林則徐 as "the first one who encouraged and sponsored
the activities of translating materials of new knowledge from the West." Lin, before
the Opium War, as a means to gather information of his enemies, ordered the translation of the news and reviews from European-run newspapers in Canton and South

in order to modernize and strengthen China. The first person to petition to the Emperor for the establishment of a foreign language institute, in early 1859, was Guo Songtao 郭嵩燾 (1818–1927) who was to
become the first Chinese ambassador to Britain and France from 1876
to 1878. But it was not until 1862 when the *Tongwenguan* was established at the petition of Prince Gong (Gong qinwang Yi Xin 恭親王奕
訢 , 1833–1898) and other Manchu nobles that China had its first foreign language and translation institute.

Comparatively speaking, these reformers were liberal and open.
Among them, Prince Gong played an important role, as he was then in
charge of foreign affairs. Although he himself was not the emperor,
he basically acted as an undifferentiated patron, as he, with the backing of the Empress Dowager, was responsible for setting up a governmental translation institute that provided ideological and economic
control as well as status to the translators. But unfortunately the translation activities he supported were not successful, as they did not
make much impact. Since their objective in translating Western
knowledge was simple and straightforward, the scope of works translated was limited. Books produced by these institutes fell into one of
the several major categories such as science and technology, international law, geography and histories of foreign countries. The readership was confined to the small group of reformers. People in general
were either indifferent or skeptical towards the new learning. There
were also the conservatives who could not accept that the Chinese
should learn from the barbarians. Very often these patrons had to fight
hard wars in order to push for some new moves.[24] Furthermore, as
mentioned above, although the patrons were responsible for providing
the translators with economic support and social status, the terms

---

[23] (*cont.*) East Asia, such as Canton Press, Canton Register and Singapore Free
Press. Cf. Ma Zuyi 馬祖毅 . 1984. *Zhongguo fanyi jianshi: Wusi yiqian bufen* 中國翻
譯簡史：五四以前部分 (A brief history of Chinese translation: before the May
Fourth). Beijing: Zhongguo duiwai fanyi chuban gongsi, pp. 225–7. But I do not consider this the beginning of translating Western knowledge in China as Lin's activity
was extremely confined and did not have any impact on China at all.

[24] One move by Prince Gong that offended the conservatives immensely was that
he imposed a regulation that senior officials should be recruited to be students in the
Tongwenguan. For a brief account of the struggle between Prince Gong and the conservatives, see Xiong Yuezhi, 1994, pp. 324–33; also Immanuel C. Y. Hsü. 1970. *The
Rise of Modern China*. Hong Kong: Oxford University Press, pp. 348–50.

offered were far from attractive.[25] Most important of all, translators of Western learning could not climb up high on the ladder of official-dom. Translation failed to attract talented people and the translation products were inferior in quality. Hence, despite powerful patronage, translation and translators were regarded as peripheral.

We should at this point come back to Yan Fu. After a brief early tradi-tional education, he studied at the Majiang Naval Academy of the Fuzhou Shipyard, which was one of the earliest institutes set up as a part of the reform programme. After graduation, he was sent to Eng-land and studied at the Greenwich Naval College. Upon return, he taught for a year at the Fuzhou Naval Academy and then became dean of the newly founded Beiyang Naval Academy in Tianjin. His imme-diate boss was Li Hongzhang 李鴻章 (1823–1901) who was in charge of all naval affairs of China.[26] However, it did not seem that Li held him in high regard. Although he was recognized by many as the most knowledgeable person in Western and Chinese learning, because he had not passed the imperial examination, he was not respected and was not able to take up any senior position in officialdom.[27] In the previous section, we have seen that early translators had a low self-image. It is no exaggeration that some of them might have had an

---

[25] According to a petition made by Prince Gong to the Emperor on December 22, 1865, those who graduated from *Tongwenguan*, with good results, might be award-edthe eighth or ninth grade of officialdom. (Cf. Li Nanqiu 1996, p. 57). This is a jun-ior post. Even the remuneration for a translator in the ambassadorial delegation was not attractive. Wu Tingfang 伍廷芳 (1842–1922), a solicitor trained in Hong Kong, was offered the post of a translator by Guo Songtao, the ambassador sent to the United Kingdoms. But he declined because what he could earn from being a transla-tor/interpreter was 200 dollars a month, while being a solicitor, he could easily make 1,000 dollars per month. Ibid., p. 304.

[26] For the role of Li Hongzhang in China's modernization process, see Samuel Chu and Kwang-ching Liu (eds.). 1994. *Li Hung-chang and China's Early Moderni-zation*. New York: M. E. Sharpe.

[27] The most senior position that Yan took up was being the Chief Instructor of the Imperial University. Chen Baochen, when he wrote Yan's epitaph, said, "he only took up an empty title and could not participate in important matters." Chen Baochen 陳寶琛. 1986. "Qing gu zizheng dafu haijun xiedutong Yanjun muzhiming" 清故資政大夫海軍協都統嚴君墓志銘 (The epitaph of Yan Fu), in: *YFJ*, vol. 5, pp. 1541–5; 1541. It is important to note that Yan had not for a time given up the idea of climbing up the ladder of officialdom through the 'proper channel'. Between 1885 and 1894, he sat for the imperial examination for four times. Each time he failed.

inferiority complex or other psychological problems.[28] Yan Fu, unfortunately, shared this kind of feeling. In a poem he expressed his regret at having learned English, since it had resulted in being looked down upon as a barbarian.[29]

However, even if he had had the favour of Li Hongzhang and even if he had occupied a more senior position in officialdom, Yan would not have been able to earn the reputation he enjoys today in contemporary Chinese history. Yan is now remembered as the most important translator who brought the theory of social evolution into China and thus had an immeasurable impact on the thinking of the Chinese for a long time. Such a position would not have been brought about with a patron like Li Hongzhang. If he had chosen Li as his patron for translation, he would not have been very much different from other earlier translators in *Tongwenguan* or Jiangnan Arsenal; and his translation would be regarded as one of those insignificant reformist textbooks. But what gave him personal success and marked him as different from other translators, especially the earlier ones, was that he carefully picked for himself a patron that would help him immensely in winning general support. With the backing of this patron, plus the special translation strategy he adopted, Yan successfully won for himself a big group of readers.

The person Yan chose as his patron was Wu Rulun 吳汝綸 (1840–1903). In the bureaucracy hierarchy, Wu was far below Li Hongzhang. Yet he enjoyed a reputation as one of the greatest masters of the Tongcheng Essay School (*Tongchengpai* 桐城派), the most prominent literary school in the Qing. On the other hand, being a patriot, he was supportive of modernization. He was highly sympathetic towards Yan Fu, saying that it was most unfair that Yan's talent and ability had not been fully appreciated.[30] The backing he lent to Yan tremendously helped the latter to publicize his translations and won him support even among the conservatives.

Wu Rulun was the first reader of *Tianyanlun* and Yan's other translations—Yan sent Wu the manuscripts for comments before they

---

[28] One of the Chinese translators of the London Missionary Society Press in Shanghai, Li Shanlan 李善蘭, a colleague of Wang Tao, was reported to have to resort to shouting aloud frequently to vent the discomfort. This shows that they were subjected to high social pressure. Xiong Yuezhi 1994, p. 269.

[29] *YFJ*, vol. 1, p. 361

[30] Wu Rulun 1986b. (Letter to Yan Fu), in: *YFJ*, vol. 5, p. 1560.

went to print.[31] Wu loved *Tianyanlun* to the extent that he copied the whole book and put it under his bed so that he could read it as frequently as he wished.[32] Most significant of all, he wrote a preface to Yan's *Tianyanlun*, which was described by one critic as "a masterpiece of Tongcheng essay that would enjoy a fame for over five hundred years."[33] A closer look into the preface is highly justified.

In the preface, Wu opened with a commendation of Huxley's theory, saying that it was unheard of and groundbreaking in China, but he very quickly shifted to Yan Fu. Wu wrote that he was able to understand Huxley's ideas because of Yan's translation. The important thing to note here is that his emphasis was on Yan's style of writing, not the content of the work: Huxley's ideas could not have been brought into light without Yan's elegant pen. Interestingly enough, in the preface, Wu dealt with some length with the essay tradition of China, starting from the Zhou Dynasty. The central point was that, without elegant writing, ideas could not communicate themselves. Similarly, Huxley's important theory would not have been accepted if it had not been expressed by the beautiful writing of Yan Fu. Wu touched upon the translations done by others during his time. While he agreed that Western learning could help to enlighten the people, he criticized the fact that most of the translations had not been able to achieve this goal because they were written in bad Chinese. But Yan's essays were comparable to those written in the Eastern Zhou. This judgement of Yan's essay led to the following key line in the preface: "One can talk about translating books if one can write essays as good as Yan Fu's."[34] With the recommendation from such a celebrated figure in the classical world of letters, Yan's status rose tremendously among the conservatives.

From this, we can also understand the reasons behind Yan's insistence on *ya* and the use of pre-Han style of writing in his translations. Since the Tongcheng essay school argued that the best essays ever written in China could be found in the Spring and Autumn Period

---

[31] Yan Fu 1986d. "Qunxue yiyan yiyu zhuiyu" 群學肄言譯余贅語 (Afterword of *The Study of Sociology*), in: *YFJ*, vol. 1, pp. 126–7.

[32] Xiong Yuezhi 1994, p. 683.

[33] Xu Liting 徐立亭 . 1996. *Wanqing jurenzhuan: Yan Fu* 晚清巨人傳：嚴復 (A biography of a Late Qing giant: Yan Fu), Harbin: Ha'erbin chubanshe, p. 261.

[34] Wu Rulun 吳汝綸 . 1986a. "*Tianyanlun* Wu xu" 天演論吳序 (Wu's preface to *Tianyanlun*), in: *YFJ*, vol. 5, pp. 1317–9; 1317.

(Chunqiu 春秋 , 770–476 BC), that was, the pre-Han period, Yan's *ya* was but a means to win the support of, or at least, an attempt to associate himself with, this largest school of Qing essays. With the assistance of a powerful patron, Yan succeeded in winning a large readership for his translation. Lu Xun in the thirties provided a convincing explanation of Yan's use of beautiful classical Chinese:

> At that time, returned students did not enjoy such a high status as our returned students now. People thought that Westerners could only make machines, especially clocks. As returned students could only use the language of the barbarians, they were not considered as a member of the gentry. So he [Yan Fu] had to use beautiful essays, so beautiful that he successfully moved the old Wu Rulun to write him a preface. With this preface, other business came.[35]

If we interpret the word "business" not as money making ventures but as a higher status in society, or more specifically among the gentry, we can then see the role played by the patron and the importance of using pre-Han style of writing.

A similar case is that of Lin Shu 林紓 (1852–1924), the so-called greatest fiction translator of the time. It is a well-known fact that Lin did not know any foreign language; and he had to depend entirely on a collaborator, who would explain the story to him in Chinese. From the present point of view, the ones who were actually translating were his collaborators—they were doing what we now call 'at-sight translation'. This, as we have seen, was not uncommon. But unfairly, most, if not all, of the credits went to Lin. This was because Lin was treasured for his elegant Tongcheng essays. Beyond doubt, beautiful essays made a much stronger impression on the readers than the contents of the works.

4. COMPREHENSIBILITY AND YAN FU'S PROSPECTED READERSHIP

Yan's choice of Wu Rulun as his patron matched very well with the readership he projected. Liang Qichao once criticized Yan for using too difficult a language for translation. In his reply to this accusation, Yan spelt out the kind of readership he expected for his translation:

---

[35] Lu Xun 魯迅 . 1981. "Guanyu fanyi de tongxin" 關於翻譯的通信 (Correspondences on translation), in: *Lu Xun quanji* 魯迅全集 (Complete works of Lu Xun), Beijing: Renmin wenxue chubanshe, vol. 4, pp. 370–88; 380–1.

What I have translated are books of great learning. I do not expect that they are to be read by school boys and that these schoolboys can be benefited. My translations are for those who have read a lot of Chinese classical writings. If the readers have not read any Chinese classical writings and want to read my translation, the blame should be theirs and not the translator's.[36]

The readers he expected—"those who have read a lot of Chinese classical writings"—were clearly also those who exerted an influence on the politics of China, and, most likely, on Yan's career. Liang Qichao, however, had identified a quite different group of readers:

One thing I feel regret about is that his [Yan's] writing is too difficult and elegant, attempting to imitate the pre-Qin style. Unless someone has read a lot of classical writings, it is not possible to understand the translations. We should have had a literary revolution long ago. Further, as these books contain great learning, unless they are translated in fluent and plain writing, how can they benefit schoolboys? Translation is a means of spreading civilization ideas to the people. It is not something to be hidden away in deep forests to earn an immortal reputation for the translators.[37]

Unfortunately, China at that time did not have a mass population of schoolboys (*xuetong* 學僮). The readership, even for translated novels, not to mention works like *Tianyanlun*, was made up of traditional men-of-letters.[38] A misconception of the prospective readers caused difficulties for Liang's approach to modernization through translation of foreign novels; while Yan's full awareness of the nature of his

---

[36] Yan Fu. 1986e. "Yu *Xinmin congbao* lun suoyi *Qunxue yiyan*" 與新民叢報論所譯群學肄言 (Discussing *The Study of Sociology* with *Xinmin congbao*), in: *YFJ*, vol. 3, p. 516.

[37] Liang Qichao 梁啟超 . 1990. "Shaojie xinzhu yuanfu" 紹介新著原富 (Introducing *An Inquiry into the Nature and Causes of the Wealth of Nations*), in: Niu Yangshan 牛仰山 and Sun Hongni 孫鴻霓 (eds.). *Yan Fu yanjiu ziliao* 嚴復研究資料 (Research materials of Yan Fu). Fuzhou: Haixia wenyi chubanshe, pp. 266–8; 267.

[38] Xu Nianci, a translator of Western fiction once reported that ninety per cent of those who bought and read modern fiction were from the traditional sector. Xu Nianci 徐念慈 . 1989. "Yuzhi xiaoshuo guan" 余之小説觀 (My views of fiction), in: Chen Pingyuan 陳平原 and Xia Xiaohong 夏曉虹 (eds.). 1984. *Ershi shiji Zhongguo xiaoshuo lilun ziliao* 二十世紀中國小説理論資料 (Materials on twentieth century Chinese fiction theory). Beijing: Beijing daxue chubanshe, pp. 310–6; 314. Another critic also said that those who had long spent their time on the traditional classics turned to buy and read new novels. Lao Li 老隸 . 1989. "Wenfeng zhi bianqian yu xiaoshuo jianglai zhi weizhi" 文風之變遷與小説將來之位置 (The change in literary style and the future position of fiction), in: Chen Pingyuan and Xia Xiaohong (eds.), pp. 204–7; 206.

readers made his translations a success in the sense that they were widely read and highly respected.

The question remains as to what actually constituted the readership at the time. No doubt, at the time when Yan Fu translated his *Tianyanlun* and Liang Qichao urged the translation of foreign novels to modernize the people at the turn of the century,[39] the opposition to modernization was not as strong as that in the mid-nineteenth century, when Prince Gong petitioned for the establishment of the *Tongwenguan*. However, most people still believed that the Western powers were superior only in military strength; and it was very difficult to convince them that, even on the intellectual side, there were things to learn from the West. This was especially true for Yan's projected readers: those who had read a large number of classical Chinese writings. Of course, they may have had some sympathy towards Western learning, since otherwise they would not have attempted to read the translations at all. What had to be done was to convince them that the contents of the translation works were worthy of serious attention.

As we have just seen, Yan adopted the Tongcheng style of writing to attract readers to his translations; and this was his controversial *ya* strategy. But this was not enough, because conservative ideas could also be written in elegant styles and be appealing to the traditional readers. Thus a further problem that Yan and other translators had to solve was how to get conservatives to swallow the pride and accept Western learning. Here the *da* came in again. It has been demonstrated that Yan, in his explanation of *da*, urged the use of pre-Han syntax and expressions. In his words, "for conveying profound ideas and sublime words, it is easy to attain *da* by using pre-Han syntax and expressions." Again, it looks odd to the present-day readers why Yan should have said that pre-Han syntax and expressions helped to convey Western learning. But if we look into a practice frequently adopted by Yan Fu to translate foreign concepts and ideas, it can be seen that this was an effective means to win over conservatives.

In the first place, beyond doubt, Yan was very careful and meticulous about translating terms. One famous saying of his was "it took days and even months of consideration to formulate one single

---

[39] Liang Qichao 梁啟超 . 1989. "Lun xiaoshuo yu qunzhi zhi guanxi" 論小說興群治之關係 (On the relationship between fiction and the government of the people), in: Ibid., pp. 33–7.

term."[40] Yan successfully coined many new terms that have been widely used for a long period of time and have made an immense impact on China. A notable and readily available example would be *tianyan* for 'evolution'.

However, one strategy he adopted deserves even greater attention: to employ and adapt terms from classical works to denote a concept from the West. For example, when he translated John Stuart Mill's *A System of Logic*, he adapted two terms from the Yijing 易經 , *neizhou* 內籀 and *waizhou* 外籀 to represent 'induction' and 'deduction' respectively.[41] These two terms were subsequently dropped, and we all now use the expressions *guina* 歸納 and *yanyi* 演繹 . But the significance of using *neizhou* and *waizhou* then was to impress two things upon those who were conversant with classical Chinese writings: first, that Yan Fu himself was well versed in classical learning; second, that these foreign ideas were not that 'foreign'. While the former aspect was related to the personal status of Yan, the latter was concerned with the general acceptance of Western learning as a whole. By using terms from classical Chinese writings to translate Western concepts, he gave the impression that such Western concepts might had their origins in China, or at least, such concepts "had long existed" in China (*gu yi you zhi* 古已有之). Since traditional readers took great pride in Chinese culture, by convincing them of the possible link between traditional Chinese learning and barbarian Western learning, Yan was able to reduce or even eliminate opposition to Westernization. It is for this reason that Yan told his readers that by using pre-Han expressions, one could translate profound Western works more easily. One critic suggests that this was the candy coating of some bitter medicine. Accepting that only Western learning could save the nation was too bitter a pill to swallow for the conservatives an something sweet had to be given to them to help it go down.[42]

---

[40] Yan Fu 1986b, p. 1322.

[41] Yan Fu 1986c, pp. 1319–20.

[42] Wang Zuoliang 王佐良 . 1982. "Yan Fu de yongxin" 嚴復的用心 (The minds of Yan Fu), in: Editorial Section of the Commercial Press (ed.). *Lun Yan Fu yu Yanyi mingzhu* 論嚴復與嚴譯名著 (On Yan Fu and Yan Fu's translations). Beijing: Commercial Press, pp. 22–7.

Similar practices can be found in fiction translation. As the readers of translated fiction[43] at that time were those who had been reading traditional writings, they were basically the same group of people who read Yan Fu's *Tianyanlun*. For many of them, while they might have wanted to know something about Western literature, they could not accept things too 'unconventional', especially on the ideological side. Very often translators, to avoid trouble, had to omit those parts that would offend the readers. One example was religious references in the novels. Translators had to be very careful when they dealt with religious matters, either deleting them altogether or disclaiming any association with them.[44] Another example we could cite was the full translation of *Joan Haste* by Lin Shu, which invited severe criticism from the conservatives as it revealed the heroine Joan Haste gave birth to an illegitimate child, while a shorter version, which had deleted this part, was much more popular.[45] Obviously many readers, when they came to read translated fiction, did so with the same expectations as they had towards traditional novels. In order to please them, the translators had to adopt a number of strategies.

Among the various strategies, the most commonly practised one is related to the *gu yi you zhi* issue. Lin Shu once commended H. Rider Haggard's *Allan Quatermain* saying that "how a Westerner's style of writing resembles that of Sima Qian."[46] Similar words can be found in

---

[43] For a discussion of the problems and strategies in fiction translation in the Late Qing, cf. Wang-chi Lawrence Wong. 1999. "An Act of Violence: Translation of Western Fiction in the late Qing and early Republican Period", in: Michel Hockx (ed.). *The Literary Field of Twentieth Century China*. Surrey: Curzon, pp. 21–39.

[44] The same translator, Lin Shu, employed both ways to deal with religious matters in Western fiction. In translating *Uncle Tom's Cabin*, he deleted most of the religious matters, on the pretext that "it was for the convenience of the readers." Lin Shu 林紓. 1989a. "*Heinu yutianlu* liyan" 黑奴籲天錄例言 (Notes on translating *Uncle Tom's Cabin*), in: Chen Pingyuan and Xia Xiaohong (eds.), pp. 27–8. On the other hand, when he came to translate *Robinson Crusoe*, he retained the religious matter, explaining that he, as a translator, had to respect the original. Lin Shu. 1989e. "*Lu-binxun piaoliuji* xu" 魯濱遜漂流記 (Preface to *Robinson Crusoe*), in: Chen Pingyuan and Xia Xiaohong (eds.), pp. 145–7.

[45] Cf. Lin Shu. 1989c. "*Jia'an xiaozhuan* xiaoyin" 迦茵小傳小引 (A short introduction to *Joan Haste*), in: Chen Pingyuan and Xia Xiaohong (eds.), p. 138. For the criticism on Lin's translation of *Joan Haste*, see Yin Bansheng. 1989. "Du *Jiayin xiaozhuan* liangyiben shuhou" 讀迦因小傳兩譯本書後 (Writing after reading the two translations of *Joan Haste*), in: Chen Pingyuan and Xia Xiaohong (eds.), pp. 228–30.

[46] Lin Shu. 1989d. "*Feizhou yanshui chouchenglu* xu" 斐洲煙水愁城錄 (Preface to *Allan Quatermain*), in: Chen Pingyuan and Xia Xiaohong (eds.), pp. 141–2.

the prefaces of his other translations. These were certainly the same tactics adopted by Yan Fu in translating: any credits in the Western works would go to traditional Chinese heritage. Another example that may be of interest can be found in the preface to Lin Shu's translation of another of Haggard's novels, *Montezuma's Daughter*. Although Lin understood very well that this was a story about the subjugation of Mexico, he deliberately shifted the emphasis and stressed the revenge of the protagonist Thomas for his father. The title of the book was changed into *Revenge of a Filial British Boy*. This is significant not because Lin Shu upheld filial piety, but because Lin wanted to demonstrate that it was wrong to think Westerners paid no attention to filial piety. With this he is saying that wrong conceptions about Westerners were harmful to the promotion of Western learning. By translating this book, he could let fathers and elder brothers in China know that Westerners were also filial and hence Western learning could be promoted in China.[47]

From this, it is obvious that no matter whether it was Yan Fu's theory of translation or the actual strategies adopted by translators, the decisive factors rested not on translation per se, but have been formulated out of consideration for a variety of factors.

Returning to the question of patrons and readers, we have seen that at the early stage, when translation of Western learning was mainly a state enterprise, the patrons were of the undifferentiated kind. In other words, the translators had to rely entirely on patrons for financial security and social status; and hence control over ideology and aesthetics would be very strong and powerful. However, in the history of Late Qing translation, one important issue was the change in the nature of patronage brought about by the abolition of the imperial examination system in 1905. This event has a very far-reaching impact on modern Chinese history. For the educated, it put an abrupt end to their path to officialdom, hence to power and wealth. They had to look for other ways of making a living. In other words, they would have to look for other patrons, especially for financial reasons. On the other hand, following the opening of the treaty ports, the most important one being Shanghai, there was a rapid growth in urban population

---

[47] Lin Shu. 1983b. "*Yingxiaozi huoshan baochoulu* xu" 英孝子火山報仇錄序 (Preface to *Montezuma's Daughter*), in: Xue Suizhi and Zhang Juncai (eds.). *Lin Shu yanjiu ziliao* 林紓之研究資料 (Materials on the study of Lin Shu). Fuzhou: Fujian renmin chubanshe, pp. 108–9.

and a popular demand for entertainment. Magazines and newspapers began to appear in large numbers. Some people began to pick up translation and writing as a means to earn a living. China had its first group of 'professional' writers and translators. Apparently the authors and translators were relatively well-paid[48] and their copyrights were protected by law.[49] With this change, translators would now look more to the readers as a supporting force of their translation activities. This was especially true for fiction translation, while translation of Western technical learning, for a time, remained very much a state enterprise.

CONCLUSION

As the paper attempts to discuss the problems that Late Qing translators faced, we may quote two paragraphs from Yan Fu on the difficulties they had in translating Western learning:

> The most important writings of Confucius were the Yijing and the Spring and Autumn. If Westerners now want to understand the meaning of these works, can they achieve this through translation? The essays of the Qin and Han periods, the Li Sao 離騷 of Qu Yuan 屈原 , or the Historical Records of Sima Qian 司馬遷 , are they not distinguished works? If Westerners now want to appreciate the complex contents and the elegant style, can they achieve this through translation? How big the differences are between the West and the East! The difficulties in translating Western learning are even greater than this.[50]

The second reads:

> For academic matters, I know that it is necessary to go to the place of origin in order to get the truth. If one works hard there and can see the real picture, it would be the best method. Alternatively and less satisfactorily, one can depend on books or learn from teachers and friends.

---

[48] We do not have information of the standard pay of translators at that time. But according to Bao Tianxiao, after translating two books of altogether 40,000–50,000 words, he made a hundred dollars, which was good enough for several months expenses. Bao Tianxiao 包天笑 . 1971. *Chuanyinglou huiyilu* 釧影樓回憶錄 (Recollections from the Bracelet Shadow Mansion). Hong Kong: Dahua chubanshe, p. 174.

[49] Fan Boqun 范伯群 and Zhu Donglin 朱棟霖 . 1993. *Zhongwai wenxue bijiaoshi (1898–1949)* 中外文學比較史 (A history of Chinese and Foreign comparative literature, 1898–1949). Nanjing: Jiangsu jiaoyu chubanshe, p. 195.

[50] Yan Fu 1986f. "*Yingwen hangu* zhiyan" 英文漢詁卮言 (An introduction to *A Chinese explanation of English*), in: *YFJ*, vol. 1, p. 153.

Nevertheless for both, it is no doubt necessary to make use of the original language. The worst of all is to rely on translations. How wide the gap is, and what a big difference it is from the truth![51]

How demoralizing it is to hear these words from the mouth of the most important translator of the time!

---

[51] Yan Fu 1986g. "Yu *Waijiaobao* zhuren shu" 與外交報主人書 (Letter to the manager of *Waijiao Bao*), in: *YFJ*, vol. 3, p. 561

References

Alvarez, Roman and Carmen-Africa Vidal (eds.). 1996. *Translation, Power, Subversion*. Clevedon: Multilingual Matters Ltd.

Bao Tianxiao 包天笑. 1971. *Chuanyinglou huiyilu* 釧影樓回憶錄 (Recollections from the Bracelet Shadow Mansion). Hong Kong: Dahua chubanshe.

Chen Baochen 陳寶琛. 1986. "Qing gu zizheng dafu haijun xiedutong Yanjun muzhiming" 清故資政大夫海軍協都統嚴君墓志銘 (The epitaph of Yan Fu), in: Yan Fu 嚴復. *Yan Fu ji* 嚴復集 (Collected works of Yan Fu). 5 vols. Beijing: Zhonghua shuju, vol. 5, pp. 1541–5.

Chen Pingyuan 陳平原. 1988. *Zhongguo xiaoshuo xushi moshi de zhuanbian* 中國小說敘事模式的轉變 (The transformation of narrative modes in Chinese fiction). Shanghai: Shanghai renmin chubanshe.

—— and Xia Xiaohong 夏曉虹 (eds.). 1989. *Ershi shiji Zhongguo xiaoshuo lilun ziliao* 二十世紀中國小說理論資料 (Materials on twentieth century Chinese fiction theory). Beijing: Beijing daxue chubanshe.

Chu, Samuel C. and Kwang-ching Liu (eds.). 1994. *Li Hung-chang and China's Early Modernization*. New York: M. E. Sharpe.

Cohen, Paul. 1974. *Between Tradition and Modernity: Wang Tao and Reform in Late Ching China*. Cambridge, Mass.: Harvard University Press.

Fan Boqun 范伯群 and Zhu Donglin 朱棟霖. 1993. *Zhongwai wenxue bijiaoshi (1898–1949)* 中外文學比較史 (A history of Chinese and Foreign comparative literature, 1898–1949). Nanjing: Jiangsu jiaoyu chubanshe.

Fryer, John. 1984. "Jiangnan zhizaoju fanyi xishu shilue" 江南製造局翻譯西書史略 (A brief account of the translation of Western works by the Jiangnan Arsenal), in: Luo Xinzhang 羅新璋 (ed.). *Fanyi lunji* 翻譯論集 (Collection of essays on translation). Beijing: Commercial Press, pp. 211–26.

He Lin 賀麟. 1925. "Yan Fu de fanyi" 嚴復的翻譯 (The translation of Yan Fu), *Dongfang zazhi* (The Eastern Miscellany) 22. 21, pp. 75–87.

Hsü, Immanuel C. Y. 1970. *The Rise of Modern China*. Hong Kong: Oxford University Press.

Lao Li 老隸. 1989. "Wenfeng zhi bianqian yu xiaoshuo jianglai zhi weizhi" 文風之變遷與小說將來之位置 (The change in literary style and the future position of fiction), in: Chen Pingyuan 陳平原 and Xia Xiaohong 夏曉虹 (eds.). 1989. *Ershi shiji Zhongguo xiaoshuo lilun ziliao* 二十世紀中國小說理論資料 (Materials on twentieth century Chinese fiction theory). Beijing: Beijing daxue chubanshe, pp. 204–7.

Lefevere, Andre. 1992a. *Translation/History/Culture: A Sourcebook*. London, New York: Routledge.

——. 1992b. *Translation, Rewriting and The Manipulation of Literary Fame*. London, New York: Routledge.

Li Nanqiu 黎難秋 (ed.). 1996. *Zhongguo kexue fanyi shiliao* 中國科學翻譯史料 (Historical materials of Chinese scientific translation). Hefei: Zhongguo kexue jishu daxue chubanshe.

Liang Qichao 梁啟超. 1989. "Lun xiaoshuo yu qunzhi zhi guanxi" 論小說與群治之關係 (On the relationship between fiction and the government of the people), in: Chen Pingyuan 陳平原 and Xia Xiaohong 夏曉虹 (eds.). 1989. *Ershi shiji Zhongguo xiaoshuo lilun ziliao* 二十世紀中國小說理論資料 (Materials on twentieth century Chinese fiction theory). Beijing: Beijing daxue chubanshe, pp. 33–7.

——. 1990. "Shaojie *Xinzhu yuanfu*" 紹介新著原富(Introducing *An Inquiry into the Nature and Causes of the Wealth of Nations*), in: Niu Yangshan 牛仰山 and Sun Hongni 孫鴻霓 (eds.). *Yan Fu yanjiu ziliao* 嚴復研究資料 (Research materials of Yan Fu). Fuzhou: Haixia wenyi chubanshe, pp. 266–8.

Lin Shu 林紓. 1989a. "*Heinu yutianlu* liyan" 黑奴籲天錄例言 (Notes on translating *Uncle Tom's Cabin*), in: Chen Pingyuan 陳平原 and Xia Xiaohong 夏曉虹(eds.). 1989. *Ershi shiji Zhongguo xiaoshuo lilun ziliao* 二十世紀中國小説理論資料 (Materials on twentieth century Chinese fiction theory). Beijing: Beijing daxue chubanshe, pp. 27–8.

——. 1989b. "*Yingxiaozi huoshan baochoulu* xu" 英孝子火山報仇錄序 (Preface to *Montezuma's Daughter*), in: Xue Suizhi and Zhang Juncai (eds.). *Lin Shu yanjiu ziliao* 林紓之研究資料 (Materials on the study of Lin Shu). Fuzhou: Fujian renmin chubanshe, pp. 108–9.

——. 1989c. "*Jia'an xiaozhuan* xiaoyin" 迦茵小傳小引 (A short introduction to *Joan Haste*), in: Chen Pingyuan 陳平原 and Xia Xiaohong 夏曉虹 (eds.). 1989. *Ershi shiji Zhongguo xiaoshuo lilun ziliao* 二十世紀中國小説理論資料 (Materials on twentieth century Chinese fiction theory). Beijing: Beijing daxue chubanshe, p. 138.

——. 1989d. "*Feizhou yanshui chouchenglu* xu" 斐洲煙水愁城泉 (Preface to *Allan Quatermain*), in: Chen Pingyuan 陳平原 and Xia Xiaohong 夏曉虹 (eds.). 1989. *Ershi shiji Zhongguo xiaoshuo lilun ziliao* 二十世紀中國小説理論資料 (Materials on twentieth century Chinese fiction theory). Beijing: Beijing daxue chubanshe, pp. 141–2.

——. 1989e. "*Lubinxun piaoliuji* xu" 魯濱遜漂流記 (Preface to *Robinson Crusoe*), in: Chen Pingyuan 陳平原 and Xia Xiaohong 夏曉虹 (eds.). 1989. *Ershi shiji Zhongguo xiaoshuo lilun ziliao* 二十世紀中國小説理論資料 (Materials on twentieth century Chinese fiction theory). Beijing: Beijing daxue chubanshe, pp. 145–7.

Lu Xun 魯迅. 1981. "Guanyu fanyi de tongxin" 關於翻譯的通信 (Correspondences on translation), in: *Lu Xun quanji* 魯迅全集 (Complete works of Lu Xun). Beijing: Renmin wenxue chubanshe, vol. 4, pp. 370–88.

Luo Xizhang 羅新璋 (ed.). 1984. *Fanyi lunji* 翻譯論集 (Collection of essays on translation). Beijing: Commercial Press.

Ma Jianzhong 馬建忠. 1996. "Nishe fanyi shuyuanyi" 擬設翻譯書院議 (A proposal for the establishment of a translation academy), in: Li Nanqiu 黎難秋 (ed.). *Zhongguo kexue fanyi shiliao* 中國科學翻譯史料 (Historical materials of Chinese scientific translation). Hefei: Zhongguo kexue jishu daxue chubanshe, pp. 313–7.

Ma Zuyi 馬祖毅. 1984. *Zhongguo fanyi jianshi: Wusi yiqian bufen* 中國翻譯簡史：五四以前部分 (A brief history of Chinese translation: before the May Fourth). Beijing: Zhongguo duiwai fanyi chuban gongsi.

Ng, Mau-sang 吳茂生. 1991. "Reading Yan Fu's Tian Yan Lun", in: Roger Ames et al. (eds.). *Interpreting Culture Through Translation*. Hong Kong: Chinese University Press, pp. 167–84.

Niu Yangshan 牛仰山 and Sun Hongni 孫鴻霓 (eds.). 1990. *Yan Fu yanjiu ziliao* 嚴復研究資料 (Research materials of Yan Fu). Fuzhou: Haixia wenyi chubanshe.

Nord, Christiane. 1997. *Translating As a Purposeful Activity: Functionalist Approaches Explained*. Manchester: St. Jerome.

Schwartz, Benjamin. 1964. *In Search of Wealth and Power: Yen Fu and the West*. Cambridge, Mass.: Harvard University Press.

Sinn, Elizabeth. 1991. "Yan Fu as Translator: A Textual Criticism of the *Tianyan lun*", in: Liu, C. C. (ed.). *Fanyi xinlunji* 翻譯新論集 (A new collection of essays on translation). Hong Kong: Commercial Press, pp. 359–66.

——. 1995. "Yan Fu", in: Chan Sin-wai and David Pollard (eds.). *An Encyclopaedia of Translation*. Hong Kong: Chinese University Press, pp. 432–6.

Su Manshu 蘇曼殊 (tr.). 1991. "Can shijie" 慘世界 (Les Misérables), in: *Su Manshu wenji* 蘇曼殊文集 (Collected works of Su Manshu). Guangzhou: Huacheng chubanshe, pp. 671–753.

Tang Zhenchang 唐振常 and Shen Hengchun 沈恆春 (eds.). Shanghai shi yanjiu 上海史研究 (A study of the history of Shanghai). Shanghai: Xuelin chubanshe, pp. 176–211.

Wang Tao 王韜. 1959. *Taoyuan chidu* 弢園尺牘 (Letters of Wang Tao). Beijing: Zhonghua shuju.

Wang, Zuoliang 王佐良. 1982. "Yan Fu de yongxin" 嚴復的用心 (The minds of Yan Fu), in: Editorial Section of the Commercial Press (ed.). *Lun Yan Fu yu Yanyi mingzhu* 論嚴復與嚴譯名著 (On Yan Fu and Yan Fu's translations). Beijing: Commercial Press, pp. 22–7.

Wong, Wang-chi Lawrence. 1999. "An Act of Violence: Translation of Western Fiction in the late Qing and early Republican Period", in: Michel Hockx (ed.). *The Literary Field of Twentieth Century China*. Surrey: Curzon, pp. 21–39.

Wu Rulun 吳汝綸. 1986a. "*Tianyanlun* Wu xu" 天演論吳序 (Wu's preface to *Tianyanlun*), in: Yan Fu 嚴復. *Yan Fu ji* 嚴復集 (Collected works of Yan Fu). 5 vols. Beijing: Zhonghua shuju, vol. 5, pp. 1317–9.

——. 1986b. (Letter to Yan Fu), in: Yan Fu 嚴復. *Yan Fu ji* 嚴復集 (Collected works of Yan Fu). 5 vols. Beijing: Zhonghua shuju, vol. 5, p. 1560.

Xiong Yuezhi 熊月之. 1989. "Shanghai Guangfanyan guan shilue" 上海廣方言館史略 (A brief history of the *Shanghai Guangfangyan guan*), in: Tang Zhenchang 唐振常 and Shen Hengchun 沈恆春 (eds.). Shanghai shi yanjiu 上海史研究 (A study of the history of Shanghai). Shanghai: Xuelin chubanshe, pp. 176–211.

——. 1994. *Xixue dongjian yu wanqing shehui* 西學東漸與晚清社會 (The dissemination of Western learning and the Late Qing society). Shanghai: Shanghai renmin chubanshe.

Xu Nianci 徐念慈. 1989. "Yuzhi xiaoshuo guan" 余之小説觀 (My views of fiction), in: Chen Pingyuan 陳平原 and Xia Xiaohong 夏曉虹 (eds.). 1989. *Ershi shiji Zhongguo xiaoshuo lilun ziliao* 二十世紀中國小説理論資料 (Materials on twentieth century Chinese fiction theory). Beijing: Beijing daxue chubanshe, pp. 310–6.

Xu Liting 徐立亭. 1996. *Wanqing jurenzhuan: Yan Fu* 晚清巨人傳：嚴復 (A biography of a Late Qing giant: Yan Fu), Harbin: Ha'erbin chubanshe.

Xue Suizhi 薛綏之 and Zhang Juncai 張俊才 (eds.). 1983. *Lin Shu yanjiu ziliao* 林紓之研究資料 (Materials on the study of Lin Shu). Fuzhou: Fujian renmin chubanshe.

Yan Fu 嚴復 (tr.). 1931a. *Yuanfu* 原富 (The origins of wealth). [Translation of Adam Smith, *An Inquiry into the Nature and Causes of the Wealth of Nations*]. Shanghai: Commercial Press.

——. (tr.). 1931b. *Mingxue qianshuo* 名學淺説 (The primer of logic). Shanghai: Commercial Press.

——. 1986a. *Yan Fu ji* 嚴復集 (Collected works of Yan Fu [*YFJ*]). 5 vols. Beijing: Zhonghua shuju.

——. 1986b. "*Tianyanlun* yiliyan" 天演論譯例言 (Notes to the translation of *Tianyanlun*), in: *YFJ*, vol. 5, p. 1321.

——. 1986c. "*Tianyanlun* zixu" 天演論自序 (Preface to *Tianyanlun*), in: *YFJ*, vol. 5, p. 1322.

——. 1986d. "*Qunxue yiyan* yiyu zhuiyu" 群學肄言譯餘贅語 (Afterword of *The Study of Sociology*), in: *YFJ*, vol. 1, pp. 126–7.

——. 1986e."Yu *Xinmin congbao* lun suoyi *Qunxue yiyan*" 與新民叢報論所譯群學肄言 (Discussing *The Study of Sociology* with *Xinmin congbao*), in: *YFJ*, vol. 3, p. 516.

——. 1986f. "*Yingwen hangu* zhiyan" 英文漢詁卮言 (An introduction to *A Chinese explanation of English*), in: *YFJ,* vol. 1, p. 153.

——. 1986g. "Yu *Waijiaobao* zhuren shu" 與外交報主人書 (Letter to the manager of *Waijiao Bao*), in: *YFJ,* vol. 3, p. 561.

Yan Qu 嚴璩 . 1986. "Houguan Yan xiansheng nianpu" 侯官嚴先生年譜 (A chronology of Mr. Yan Fu), in: Yan Fu 嚴復 . *Yan Fu ji* 嚴復集 (Collected works of Yan Fu). 5 vols. Beijing: Zhonghua shuju, vol. 5, pp. 1545–52.

Yin Bansheng. 1989. "Du *Jiayin xiaozhuan* liangyiben shuhou" 讀迦因小傳兩譯本書後 (Writing after reading the two translations of *Joan Haste*), in: Chen Ping-yuan 陳平原 and Xia Xiaohong 夏曉虹 (eds.). 1989. *Ershi shiji Zhongguo xiaoshuo lilun ziliao* 二十世紀中國小説理論資料 (Materials on twentieth century Chinese fiction theory). Beijing: Beijing daxue chubanshe, pp. 228–30.

ELISABETH KASKE

MANDARIN, VERNACULAR AND NATIONAL LANGUAGE— CHINA'S EMERGING CONCEPT OF A NATIONAL LANGUAGE IN THE EARLY TWENTIETH CENTURY

INTRODUCTION

Three terms have been important in the modern Chinese discourses about language during the first two decades of the twentieth century: *guanhua* 官話 'Mandarin', *baihua* 白話 'vernacular' and *guoyu* 國語 'National Language'. All three terms had played a certain role in China before the nineteenth century. In the process of negotiating a unified language for China their contents changed and with them the reality they described—the linguistic situation of China and the role certain languages played in society.

As is well known, the so-called 'Literary Revolution', which started shortly before the beginning of the May Fourth Movement, replaced literature written in a language called *wenyan* 文言 ('classical language') by literature in another language called *baihua* ('vernacular'). This movement is rightly seen as a milestone in the process of creating a Chinese modern national language which was to be called *guoyu* in the 1920s.

Like many other modern discourses, also the new discourse about language started in the 1890s. As in other parts of the world, the appearance of the 'language question' in China was also closely tied to the introduction of nationalism. The ideological foundation of new conceptions of language was a new understanding of the functioning of a modern nation and the role of its people. The search for a new medium to spread modern ideas to the popular national masses and the recognition of spoken language as a part of national identity lead to a reorganization of the functions and roles which were assigned to certain languages in traditional Chinese society. Thus *guanhua* (or Mandarin) gained in status and was reshaped from a *lingua franca* into the national language of China.

This paper tries to show how the modern demand for a national language became absorbed into the context of the Chinese linguistic situation and how it then started to change this situation, a process lasting until the end of Qing dynasty. I wish to identify the two driving forces in the process of nationalization of language: the emergence of a national press which renamed *guanhua* into *baihua*, thus reshaping it at the same time into a national tool of mass communication; and the modernization and nationalization of the school system which called for the teaching of a nationally unified spoken language, soon called *guoyu*.

1. LITERARY THEORY AND LINGUISTIC PRACTICE IN QING CHINA

In his famous essay on diglossia, the linguist Charles Ferguson, taking Arabic as an example, describes a linguistic situation in which a language has two varieties—a High Variety and a Low Variety—differing in function and prestige, in the literary heritage connected with them, as well as in the degree of standardization and stability and in the methods of acquisition. To have or have not, in such a society, command over the High Variety of language will decide over the social status of a person.[1] In Imperial China such a linguistic situation was beautifully manifested in literary theory.

Doleželová-Velingerová observes in her study of the Chinese novel at the turn of the century, that in the realm of literature orthodox Confucian aesthetics had advocated an 'ahistorical' approach to Chinese literature. She writes:

> For centuries this rigidly normative aesthetics stubbornly adhered to the concept of two mutually exclusive literatures in China. On the one hand, there were those texts which satisfied its normative ideals and which were defined by the double function, of conveying the moral principles of Confucian sages and of Assisting the ruler to govern the nation (*jing ji*) .... On the other hand, there were fiction and drama, excluded from the Confucian concept of literature, whether written in *wenyan*, *koine*, or dialect, because they were considered pure entertainment with no didactic value.[2]

As the Confucian concept of *wenxue* 文學 ('literature', probably better translated as 'literary studies' or German *Schriftgelehrsamkeit*) included only texts that were written in one of the ancient styles

---

[1] Charles Ferguson. 1959. "Diglossia", *Word* 15, pp. 325–40.
[2] Milena Doleželová-Velingerová (ed.). 1980. *The Chinese Novel at the Turn of the Century*. Toronto: University of Toronto Press, p. 5.

referred to as *wen* as well as the process of writing itself, the same postulate is also true for the theory of language.

In the minds of the Confucian intellectuals of the Qing dynasty, the unity of culture and civilization and of the empire was inseparably linked to writing. Nivison, for example, explains this Confucian concept of *wen* in the writings of the historian and philosopher Zhang Xuecheng 章學誠 (1738–1801):

> One of the most vexing words in Chang's vocabulary (and in the writing of many Chinese literary theorists) is the word *wen*—'writing' or 'literary expression'. The whole point ... depends on this word having two meanings: 'writing' in the ordinary sense, and 'writing' in an esoteric sense as the visible expression of the *tao*. *Wen* is culture itself ("Chou declined and culture decayed").[3]

The main function of *wen* in society was to secure cultural continuity, i.e. to convey cultural meaning (*dao* 道) by linking the present to the past, the knowledge of *wen* 文 (*neng wen* 能文) thus giving legitimacy to those who governed the country. On a more practical level, the function of writing was to unite the large country with its numerous provinces which produced a great linguistic diversity.[4] Accordingly, only the different styles (*wenyan* 文言 , *wenli* 文理 , *wenzhang* 文章 — being a certain literary style—etc.) of the classical language were able to fulfil the double function of horizontal and vertical unification. Only the classical language was taught in the reading and writing classes in school.[5] Other forms of writing which had developed in China, especially the vernacular forms, were not considered as writing (*wen*), they remained what in German linguistics is called *Schreibdialekt*, written dialect.[6] In Chinese these were considered as *hua* (話), called 'local parlance' (*fangyan* 方言), 'vulgar language' (*suhua* 俗

---

[3] David S. Nivison. 1966. *The Life and Thought of Chang Hsüeh-ch'eng (1738–1801)*. Stanford: Stanford University Press, p. 117.

[4] The linguistic effects of this diversity are dealt with in a historical perspective by Wolfgang Behr in this volume.

[5] Cf. Evelyn Sakakida Rawski. 1979. *Education and Popular Literacy in Ch'ing China*. Ann Arbor: University of Michigan Press; Zhang Zhigong 張志公 . 1962. *Chuantong yuwen jiaoyu chutan* 傳統語文教育初探 (Preliminary investigations of traditional language and literature teaching). Shanghai: Jiaoyu chubanshe.

[6] The emancipation of the German language from the Latin is described in Werner Besch. 1983. "Dialekt, Schreibdialekt, Schriftsprache, Standardsprache: Exemplarische Skizze ihrer historischen Ausprägung im Deutschen", in: Werner Besch et al. (eds.). *Dialektologie: Ein Handbuch zur deutschen und allgemeinen Dialektforschung*. Berlin: Walter de Gruyter, pp. 961–90.

話), 'village talk' (*xiangtan* 鄉談) etc., not *wen*. There was not even a word for 'language' including both the written and spoken variety, the former appearing as *wenzi* 文字 , the latter as *yuyan* 語言 in late Qing texts on language (thus the study of foreign languages always included *waiguo yuyan wenzi* 外國語言文字 —"foreign spoken and written language").

With the simultaneous expansion of vernacular literature occurring at the same time, such a theory came more and more into contradiction with the developing linguistic situation. Until the beginning of the nineteenth century several of the regional *koine* in China had developed their own written forms. Especially *guanhua* (Mandarin), *koine* of Northern China, had—thanks to the relatively early and extended development of novels in Northern Chinese and the frequent travel of the officials to the capital Beijing—emerged as the dialect which was best developed and understood in most parts of China in its spoken as well as in its written form.

Guanhua as a spoken dialect even enjoyed a certain degree of governmental support as the *lingua franca* of the state apparatus. As dialects were considered to be merely a matter of phonetics, authoritative dictionaries of the eighteenth century, like the *Kangxi zidian* 康熙字典 (Dictionary of Kangxi, 1716) and later the *Yinyun chanwei* 音韻闡微 (Subtle explanation of phonology, 1726) of Yongzheng's times, also defined a standard Mandarin pronunciation of the Chinese characters together with the literary pronunciation. The Yongzheng emperor, annoyed by officials from Fujian and Guangdong speaking unintelligible dialects, even prescribed the study of *guanhua* pronunciation for them. A number of phrase books for learners of Mandarin in Zhejiang, Fujian and Guangzhou were published in the eighteenth and nineteenth centuries.[7] But except for practical administrative considerations, *guanhua* did not enjoy a higher status than other dialects. Spoken dialects did not pose any threat to the imperial unity of *wen*. That is why, on an informal level, they were held in high esteem and remained the most important means of oral conversation even among the intellectual class.

---

[7] Collected in Nagazawa Kikuya 長沢規矩也 . 1974. *Min Shin zokugo jisho shūsei* 明清俗語辭書集成 (Collected vernacular dictionaries of the Ming- and Qing-dynasties). Tokyo: Kyūko Shoin; see also Paola Paderni. 1988. "The Problem of Kuan-hua in Eighteenth Century China: the Yung-cheng Decree for Fukien and Kwangtung", *Annali di Istituto di Napoli* 48.4, pp. 258–68.

Written *guanhua*, on the other hand, was the language which constituted the main body of the vernacular literature, therefore this language just like the vernacular literature were denounced by Confucian intellectuals. While Song and Ming philosophers such as Zhu Xi 朱熹 (1130–1200) and Lü Kun 呂坤 (1536–1618) had found no fault in using a simple written language close to the spoken one,[8] intellectual currents of the Qing dynasty, be it the *Kaozhengpai* 考證派 (Evidential Research School) or especially the *Tongchengpai* 桐城派 (Tongcheng School), tended to oppose the natural tendency of colloquialism to undermine the proper written language. Literature in the vernacular or even in mixed styles was held in low esteem and considered incapable of conveying morality and higher principles.[9] Only when the need for education of the masses prevailed over considerations of proper literary expression, exceptions from this rule were tolerated. The most famous examples are the exhortations to the people issued by Ming and Qing emperors, such as the "Six Maxims" (*Liuyu* 六諭) ascribed to the Ming emperor Taizu 太祖 (1368–1398), the "Sacred Edict" (*Shengyu* 聖諭) of the Qing Kangxi 康熙 emperor (1670) and the "Amplified Instructions of the Sacred Edict" (*Shengyu guangxun* 聖語 廣訓) issued by the Yongzheng 雍正 emperor in 1724. During the Qing dynasty all of them circulated in various vernacular (*guanhua*) editions to convey Confucian ethics to the uneducated folks.[10] The same was thought about at least one of the historical novels, the "Elaborated History of the Three Kingdoms" (*Sanguo yanyi* 三國演 義). Although novels in general were despised, in 1886 this novel was thought to be suitable literature for the cadets at the newly established Tianjin Military Academy (*Tianjin wubei xuetang* 天津武備學

---

[8] See for instance Joanna Handlin. 1983. *Action in Late Ming Thought: The Reorientation of Lü K'un and Other Scholar-Officials*. Berkeley: University of California Press, pp. 143–60.

[9] Cf. Doleželová-Velingerová 1980, p. 5; Theodore Huters. 1987. "From Writing to Literature: The Development of Late Qing Theories of Prose", *Harvard Journal of Asiatic Studies* 47.1, pp. 51–96; Chow Tse-tsung. 1960. *The May Fourth Movement: Intellectual Revolution in Modern China*. Cambridge, Mass.: Harvard University Press, pp. 269–70.

[10] Cf. Victor Mair. 1985. "Language and Ideology in the Written Popularization of the Sacred Edict", in: David Johnson et al. (eds.). *Popular Culture in Late Imperial Culture*. Berkeley: University of California Press, pp. 325–59.

堂).[11] The process of bringing elite ideals to the uneducated people was called *yan* 演 or *yanyi* 演義 , meaning 'to elaborate, to explain', or 'to render' (always into the vernacular language), an expression found in the titles of historical novels and also some of the vernacular versions of the Imperial exhortations. Although the materials are written, this was assumed to be an oral process of explanation, and very often it was one in reality, because the Sacred Edict was customarily lectured to the people and the novels constituted the repertoire of the storytellers.[12]

In modern times Western missionaries, pouring into China from the 1860s on, were among the first to be dissatisfied with the complicated linguistic situation. Whatever they did to bring evangelism to the Chinese they could reach only a small portion of the population. In Europe, where most of the missionaries came from, national languages were well developed and standardized at this time. Nevertheless, most missionaries did not tackle the language issue from a national perspective—one exception being perhaps Timothy Richard (Li Timotai 李提摩太 , 1845–1919)—and underestimated the role *guanhua* written in Chinese characters already had in Chinese society. Instead of attempting to change the situation, they tried to adapt to varieties of high and low languages. In the 1890s the different Protestant missions started to co-operate with a plan to create four different kinds of Bible translation for one country: one in High Wenli, one in Low (Simple) Wenli, one in Mandarin (these three were known as the Union Version), and several in romanized dialects of the South. When the three committees for the three language editions of the Union Version were formed, most of the participants in the translation considered it a great honour to serve in the High Wenli Committee, showing the high esteem in which the classical style was still held.[13] On the other hand, missionaries working with the lower classes of the Chi-

[11] Cf. Gao Shiliang高時良 (ed.). 1992. *Zhongguo jindai jiaoyushi ziliao huibian: Yangwu yundong shiqi jiaoyu* 中國近代教育史資料匯編 : 洋務運動時期教育 (A collection of source materials for the history of modern education in China: Education during the Yangwu Movement). Shanghai: Shanghai jiaoyu chubanshe, p. 502.

[12] For the *Sanguo yanyi* the process of transmitting official history is described in Boris L'vovic Riftin. 1970. *Istoriceskaja epopeja i fol'klornaja tradicia v kitae*. Moscow: Nauka.

[13] Cf. Jost Zetzsche. 1999. "The Work of Lifetimes: Why the Union Version Took Nearly Three Decades to Complete", in: Irene Eber (ed.). *Bible in China: The Literary and Intellectual Impact*. Nettetal: Steyler, pp. 77–100; 83.

nese population outrightly denied the usefulness of Mandarin to pros-
elytize the Chinese heathen, and preferred instead the local dialect.[14]
And quite a number of missionaries even despised the Chinese characters and favoured newly created alphabetic scripts transcribing local
dialects. However, soon after the beginning of the translation work,
the missionaries' plans were outmoded by a rapidly changing social
and linguistic reality. Finally, of the original plans, only the Mandarin
Version suvived. For this reason the direct influence of the missionary
enterprise on the development of a Chinese national language
remained small.[15]

Nevertheless, in a time of ideological crisis, contacts with Western
countries and Japan through missionary and other sources produced
new and influential ideas on language. New questions about the language issue had been raised since the 1880s. During the 1890s
demands for the abolishment of one of the most difficult classical
styles—the Eight-Legged Essay (an essay in strict form and metrical
language, called *baguwen* 八股文 or simply *wenzhang* 文章)—were
growing in number. Such proposals aimed at enlarging access to the
examinations for young men talented in practical knowledge, not
merely in high literature. The final abolishment of this essay form in
state-examinations in 1901 was the beginning of further changes in
the linguistic situation of China.[16]

---

[14] E.g. Y. K. Yen. 1892. "The Shanghai Vernacular", *The Chinese Recorder* 22.8,
pp. 386–8.

[15] Cf. Zetzsche 1999, pp. 77–100; John De Francis. 1948. "A Missionary Contribution to Chinese Nationalism", *Journal of the North China Branch of the Royal Asiatic Society* 83, pp. 1–34. De Francis states a certain influence of the missionaries on
Chinese schemes of phonetical writing (which are not discussed here), but concerning
the impact of the Bible translation, he also found out that the translators were rather
astonished when they discovered that in 1902 Mandarin versions of the Bible sold
best of all Bibles ever produced in China. The Mandarin Union Version started in
1890 was published only in 1919 and is said to have been used later in government
schools as part of a standardized national language curriculum. Cf. Lihi Yariv-Laor.
1999. "Linguistic Aspects of translating the Bible into Chinese", in: Irene Eber (ed.).
Bible in China: the Literary and Intellectual Impact. Nettetal: Steyler, pp. 101–122;
102.

[16] Cf. Wolfgang Franke. 1963. *The Reform and Abolition of the Traditional Chinese Examination System*. Cambridge, Mass.: Harvard University Press, pp. 52–4.

2. FROM *GUANHUA* TO *BAIHUA*—
NEW FUNCTIONS FOR AN OLD STYLE

Inspired by the Western and Japanese success with public education, reformers soon began to demand not only an adaptation of classical style to modern needs, but a so-called "unification of the written and spoken languages". The Confucian obsession for antiquity was eroded by a new esteem for progress. In 1887, Huang Zunxian 黃遵憲 (1848–1905) wrote in his famous "Treatise on Japan" (*Riben guozhi* 日本國志 , published only in 1895):[17]

> From the times of the Zhou and the Qin, style (*wenti* 文體) has often changed. Today's memorials, commands, proclamations and judgements are [written] clearly and comprehensibly, their objective being only to transmit a message. The ancients certainly did not have such a style. If now the novelists directly use dialect (*fangyan* 方言) to write it down in their books, then language and writing are almost again unified. Who knows whether in the future there will not be a new style which is suitable for today and broadly used among the common people?[18]

The new slogan was a direct borrowing from the Japanese language scene. The Japanese written and spoken language of the time was also very different. Since the 1860s there existed a so-called *genbunitchi* 言文一致 (meaning exactly "unification of the written and spoken language") movement which resulted in the publication of the first modern novel in a colloquial Japanese language based on Tokyo speech, Futabatei Shimei's 二葉亭四迷 (1864–1909) *Ukigumo* 浮雲 (Floating clouds, 1887–1889).[19] From this time on for the rest of the Qing dynasty, changing conceptions of language in China owe much to the Japanese example.

---

[17] Cf. Noriko Kamachi. 1981. *Reform in China: Huang Zunxian and the Japanese Model*. Cambridge, Mass.: Harvard University Press, pp. 53–4.

[18] Huang Zunxian 黃遵憲 . 1963. "Riben guozhi: Wenxuezhi" 日本國志：文學 (Treatise on Japan: Literature), *Jindaishi ziliao* 2, p. 116.

[19] Cf. Nanette Twine. 1978. "The Genbunitchi movement: Its Origin, Development and Conclusion", *Monumenta Nipponica* 33.3, pp. 333–56; Yamamoto Masahide 山本正秀 . 1981. *Genbunitchi no rekishi ronkō* 言文一致の歴史論考 (A historical discussion of the movement for the unification of the spoken und written languages). Tokyo: Ōfūsha, pp. 30–51; Nannette Twine. 1988. "Standardizing Written Japanese: a Factor in Modernization", *Monumenta Nipponica* 43.4, pp. 425–54; 443; see also Marleigh G. Ryan (tr. and comm.). 1967. *Japan's First Modern Novel: Ukigumo of Futabatei Shimei*. New York: Columbia University Press.

One outcome of the new demands for the "unification of the written and spoken language" (in Chinese: *yuyan wenzi heyi* 語言文字合一) was the creation of a vernacular style which came to be called *baihua*.[20] The new style was used for translations of books from *wenyan*, political essays and news reporting in a special kind of newspaper or journal which was created with the objective to serve as a tool for disseminating modern ideas to a presumably uneducated readership or to "enlighten the people" (*kaitong minzhi* 開通民智).[21] In 1897 and 1898 the group of reformers close to Liang Qichao 梁啟超 (1873–1929) and Wang Kangnian 汪康年 (1860–1911) and the publishers of the *Shiwubao* 時務報 (this group also including Huang Zunxian) in Shanghai founded a number of such enlightenment journals and newspapers using the new newspaper style *baihua*: the *Yanyi baihuabao* 演義白話報 ([Popular] Renditions Vernacular Newspaper, in 1897); the *Mengxue bao* 蒙學報 (Primary Education Journal, founded by Wang Kangnian in the same year); the *Wuxi baihuabao* 無錫白話報 (Wuxi Vernacular Journal, founded in 1898 by Qiu Tingliang 裘廷梁 (1857–1943) in Wuxi) and the *Nüxue bao* 女學報 (Women's Education Journal, founded by a daughter of Kang Youwei 康有為 (1858–1927) and a niece of Qiu Tingliang in 1898 in Shanghai).[22]

---

[20] Another outcome was the more radical attempt of 'unification' made by the script reformers, who planned to free the education for the poor from the burden of the Chinese characters (not to abolish the Chinese characters at all) and teach basic knowledge using phonetic scripts for the dialects, see John De Francis. 1950. *Nationalism and Language Reform in China*. Princeton: Princeton University Press. Such a double understanding of the same slogan was again connected to the ambiguity of Chinese conceptions of language. The word *wenzi* 文字 in *yuyan wenzi heyi* 語言文字合一 could be understood as 'written language' (synonymous to *wenyan* 文言) or as 'writing' (*Schrift*) (i.e. the Chinese characters).

[21] As stated above, of course, literature in vernaculars, especially in *guanhua*, already existed, however, this was a style of the novel and other forms of vernacular literature, not of political essays or introductions of modern science. For such a purpose, the style as well as its name was really 'invented'. When the Qing government opened *Quanxuesuo* 勸學所 (Associations for the Fostering of Public Education) to exhort people to follow its reform program, the materials used for lecturing in these institutions were devided in 'novel style' and '*baihua* style'. Cf. *Xuebu guanbao* 4 (September 28, 1906), vol. 1, pp. 95–6.

[22] For the *Yanyi baihuabao* 演義白話報 and *Mengxue bao* 蒙學報 see A Ying 阿英 . 1958. *Wan Qing wenyi baokan shulüe* 晚清文義報刊述略 (Short account of literary periodicals of the Late Qing dynasty). Shanghai: Gudian wenxue chubanshe,

The *Wuxi baihuabao* was probably the most influential of them, thanks especially to a famous polemical essay "*Baihua* is the foundation of reform" (*Baihua wei weixin zhi ben* 白話為維新之本) which Qiu Tingliang published in 1898—in the classical language. There he stated:

> With writing (*wenzi*), a state is wise, without writing (*wenzi*) it is ignorant; a literate people is a wise people, an illiterate people is an ignorant people. This is the same all over the world. Only our China has writing, but cannot become a wise country. Our people knows the characters (*zi*) but cannot become a wise people. How can that be? Qiu Tingliang says: This is the evil of *wenyan*!

And he continues:

> When *wenyan* prospers, then practical studies are abandoned. When *baihua* becomes popular, then practical studies prosper. If practical studies do not prosper, then this means that there is no people.[23]

The terms *baihua* for the new style and *baihuabao* for the journals written in the new style seem to have been newly coined by their inventors in the late 1890s.[24] Although the term *baihua* itself was not

---

[22] (*cont.*) pp. 63–4; Liang Qichao 梁啟超 . 1953. "Mengxue bao, Yanyi bao hexu" 蒙學報演義報合序(Joint preface for the *Mengxue bao* and *Yanyi bao*) in: Zhongguo shixuehui 中國史學會 (ed.). *Wuxu bianfa* 戊戌變法 (The reform in 1898). 4 vols. Shanghai: Shenzhou Guoguangshe, vol. 4, pp. 539–40; Wang Kangnian 汪康念 et al. "Mengxue huibao jianzhang" 蒙學會報簡章 (Short regulations for the *Mengxue huibao* and the *Mengxue bao*), in: ibid., pp. 540–2. For the *Wuxi baihuabao* 無錫白話報 see Fan Fang 范方 . 1963. "Zhongguo guanyin Baihuabao" 中國官音白話報 (The Chinese vernacular journal in the Mandarin pronunciation), *Jindaishi ziliao* 2, pp. 110–13; Zhu Chuanyu 朱傳譽 . 1985. *Baoren, baoshi, baoxue* 報人,報史,報學 (Journalists, history of journalism, journalism). Taibei: Taiwan shangwu yinshuguan, pp. 7–11; Liu Jialin 劉家林 . 1989. "Baihuabao yu baihuawen de zuizao chuangzaozhe—Qiu Kefu" 白話報與白話文的最早創造者 — 裘可桴 (The earliest creator of a *baihua* Journal and of texts in *baihua*—Qiu Kefu), *Xinwen yanjiu ziliao* 47, pp. 32–9; Qiu Tingliang 裘廷梁 . 1953. "Wuxi baihuabao xu" 無錫白話報序 (Preface to the *Wuxi baihuabao*), in: *Wuxu bianfa*, pp. 542–5. For the *Nüxuebao* 女學報 see Cai Lesu 蔡樂蘇 . 1987. "Qingmo minchu de yibaiqishi yu zhong baihua baokan" 清末民初的一百七十餘種白話報刊 (More than 107 vernacular papers of the Late Qing and early Republican Period), in: Ding Shouhe 丁守和 (ed.). 1982–88. *Xinhai geming shiqi qikan jieshao* 辛亥革命時期期刊介紹(Introduction to the periodicals around the Xinghai Revolution). Beijing: Renmin chubanshe, vol. 5, pp. 493–546; 498; Fang Hanqi 方漢奇 . 1991. *Baoshi yu baoren* 報史與報人 (The history of journalism and the journalists). Beijing: Xinhua chubanshe, pp. 295–6.

[23] Qiu Tingliang 裘廷梁 . 1963. "Lun Baihua wei weixin zhi ben" 論白話為維新之本 (On the vernacular as the basis for reform), *Jindaishi ziliao* 2, pp. 120, 123.

[24] The earlier usage of the term *baihua* is discussed below.

from Japan, its introduction as a newspaper style for a less educated readership was owed much to the Japanese example. Under the slogans *bunmei kaika* 文明開化 ("civilization and enlightenment", Chinese: *wenming kaihua*) and *jiyu minken* 自由民權 ("freedom and democracy", Chinese: *ziyou minquan*) in the early 1870s and again in the 1880s larger newspapers introduced columns in the colloquial. The political parties published so-called small papers (*shōshimbun* 小新聞) in the colloquial language. Furthermore, many reading materials were published in the colloquial to educate the people.[25] In 1876 the Shanghai *Shenbao* was the first to try to found a kind of *shōshimbun* called *Minbao* 民報 (People's Gazette, the same name as the later journal of Zhang Binglin in Japan, but with a completely different definition of *min*, i.e. people) in a simple language for the "women and children and the small merchants and craftsmen"[26] who did not know the *wenli* very well. The language of this paper was intended to be so simple and easy to understand that only a few years of education would be required to be able to read the text. It was not called *baihua*, and it is not clear whether even *guanhua* was used or rather the Shanghai dialect, or simple *wenyan*. What is more important, however, is that this paper was not successful and ceased publication very soon.[27]

To call the new style *baihua* and the journals *baihuabao* was certainly a lucky choice with respect to the acceptability of the new style. The term was chosen as a euphemism for *suhua* 俗話 , the 'common language' with the connotation of 'low' or 'vulgar'. It now became the 'clear' and 'direct' language.[28] However, in the beginning, the term posed some problems for definition. *Baihua* was a word which came from the South Chinese dialects designating the local *koine*

[25] Cf. Nanette Twine 1978, pp. 333–56, Yamamoto Masahide 1981, pp. 30–51.

[26] *Shenbao* May 5, 1876.

[27] The new paper is mentioned for the first time in the *Shenbao* issue of March 29, 1876. In an article about a public charity school ("Lun Yixue" 論義學) appearing on June 6, 1876, the editors had to admit that only very few people bought the *Minbao* 民報 . Later, in an article about the sales of the *Shenbao* (February 2, 1977), the *Minbao* is not even mentioned. I have not seen the paper itself.

[28] Compare the enthusiastic definition by Hu Shi some 20 years later, Hu Shi 胡適 . 1994a. "Da Qian Xuantong" 答錢玄同 (An answer to Qian Xuantong), in: Wang Rongwen 王榮文 (ed.). *Hu Shi zuopin ji* 胡適作品集 (Collected works of Hu Shi). 37 vols. Taibei: Yuanliu chuban gon gsi, vol. 3, p. 44.

which was different from both the *wenyan* and the *guanhua*.[29] The political ambitions of the reformers, on the other hand, were national ones. From the very beginning they recognized the important role which *guanhua* already had in Chinese society and its potential to become a language of a national scope. Thus they made *guanhua* a tool to disseminate their ideas with the hope of reaching a nationwide readership. Both journals mentioned above, the *Yanyi baihuabao* and the *Wuxi baihuabao,* used *guanhua* and not the local dialect, although they were both founded in a region (Jiangsu-Shanghai) where *guanhua* was not the spoken language of the people supposed to be the readership of these journals. Thus, from the very beginning, the new newspaper style *baihua* became closely associated with *guanhua*. Nevertheless, in the first decade after the creation of the new term, a journal calling itself *baihuabao* was compelled to always define which language style it was going to use, especially in South China. The *Nüxuebao*, for instance, gave this definition:

> Because a dialect (*tuhua* 土話) can only be understood in one district or one prefecture, and cannot be understood throughout a province or a country, we decided in our statutes to use *guanhua*, this is done with the intention to make it public in the whole empire.[30]

In the case of the *Wuxi baihuabao*, where such definition was omitted, misunderstandings resulted. The journal had to be renamed *Zhongguo guanyin baihuabao* 中國官音白話報 (Chinese Vernacular Journal in the Mandarin Pronunciation), because people believed the paper was written in the Wuxi dialect.[31]

There were, to be sure, also a number of journals written in the local dialect. Some of them used their dialect name in their title, as

---

[29] Cf. Frederico Masini. 1993. *The Formation of Modern Chinese Lexicon and its Evolution Toward a National Language: The Period from 1840 to 1898.* Berkeley: Journal of Chinese Linguistics (Monograph Series, no. 6), p. 54. *Guanhua* readers written for South Zhejiangese, Fujianese or Cantonese learners annotated the *guanhua* pronunciation (*guanyin*) as opposed to the local pronunciation (*baiyin*) of the Chinese characters (e.g. Cai Shi 蔡奭. 1974. "Guanyin Huijie bianlan" 官音彙解便覽 (Explanations on the *guanhua* pronounciation), in: Nagazawa Kikuya 長澤規矩也 (ed.). *Min Shin zokugo jisho shusei* 明清俗語辭書集成 (Collected vernacular dictionaries of the Ming- and Qing-dynasties). Tokyo: Kyūko Shoin, vol. 3, p. 399).

[30] "Shanghai *Nüxuebao* yuanqi: lun yong guanhua" 上海女學報源起：論用官話 (The origins of the Shanghai *Nüxuebao*: on the usage of Mandarin), cited from: Cai Lesu 1987, p. 498.

[31] Fan Fang 1963, pp. 110–3.

several journals and newspapers in Beijing did, for instance the *Jing-hua bao* 京話報 (Journal in Beijing dialect) of 1901 or the *Jinghua ribao* 京話日報 (Daily Journal in Beijing dialect) of 1904. But these also were counted as a kind of *baihua*-journal. In Canton *guanhua* was not very popular and the influence of popular novels in the north Chinese dialects was felt less. Several journals in this province used the word *baihua* in their titles, but were actually written in the Canton dialect—for instance the *Lingnan baihuabao* 嶺南白話報 (Lingnan Vernacular Journal) of 1908. There was even a bilingual *Xizang baihuabao* 西藏白話報 (Tibet Vernacular Journal) in Chinese and Tibetan.[32] Other journals experimented with language styles. A Shanghai *Fangyan bao* 方言報 (Dialect Journal) of 1902 wrote articles, besides in *guanhua*, in the dialects of Beijing, Ningbo, Guangdong and Suzhou. The nationalist paper *Eshi jingwen* 俄事警聞 (Alarming News about Russia) in 1903 experimented with using different types of *baihua* for a different readership, for instance *Hunan bai* 湖南白 for Hunanese, *Guangdong bai* 廣東白 for Cantonese and so on, *guanhua* being left to the Manchus, Tibetan, Mongolians and the inhabitants of the three northeastern provinces.[33] But only less than a year later the former journal is said to have gone bankrupt because none of its readers knew all these dialects,[34] while the nationalist editors of the latter journal (among them Cai Yuanpei 蔡元培, 1868-1940) also adopted *guanhua* alone as the medium of their Chinese nationalism.

---

[32] Cf. Bai Runsheng 白閏生. 1989. "Woguo zuizao de zangwen baozhi—'Xizang baihuabao'" 我國最早的藏文報紙 — 西藏白話報 (China's earliest newspaper in Tibetan—'Tibet Vernacular Newspaper'), *Xinwen yanjiu ziliao* 46, pp. 124–7.

[33] Cf. *Eshi jingwen* 1 (December 25, 1903). In its first number the newspaper published its regulations for language use. Following readers were to be adressed in *wen-yan*: journalists, officials, foreign representatives, the government, Chinese students abroad, the China Education Organization (i.e. the editors themselves!), high military commanders, the students community, the different political groups (constitutionalists, revolutionaries, conservatives etc.) and the gentry, traditional teachers, people active in the examination system and so on. People to be addressed in *baihua* (without specification) were overseas merchants, people who had purchased their official title, workers, merchants, peasants, Christians, Buddhist monks, beggars, prostitutes, mounted highway robbers and so on. The system makes sense as most of the articles were in the form "To…" ("*Gao* 告…") directly adressing the people concerned to stir up their national feelings.

[34] Cf. Shi He 史和 et al. (eds.). 1991. *Zhongguo jindai baokan minglu* 中國近代報刊名錄 (A title list of China's modern periodicals). Fuzhou: Fujian remin chubanshe, p. 101.

The year of the Manchurian crisis, 1903, saw a new wave of nationalism in China, and especially in the Yangzi region. Aside from many other activities, several *baihua* journals were founded which were all more or less connected with the China Education Organization (*Zhongguo jiaoyu hui* 中國教育會) under the leadership of Cai Yuanpei, among them the *Zhongguo baihuabao* 中國白話報 (China Vernacular Journal) founded in December 1903 by Lin Xie 林獬 (1873–1926) and Liu Shipei 劉師培 (1884–1919)[35] in Shanghai. The *Zhongguo baihuabao* was the *baihua* 'sister journal' of the *wenyan* daily *Eshi jingwen* (later renamed into *Jingzhong ribao* 警鐘日報 (The Alarming Bell Daily News)), both of which were founded immediately after the shutdown of the radical *Subao* 蘇報 and the detention of Zhang Binglin 章炳麟(1869–1936) and Zou Rong 鄒榮(1885–1905).[36] Shortlived as most of the *baihua*-journals but quite influential,[37] the *Zhongguo baihuabao* may serve as a good example of the nationalist attitude concerning the use and content of *baihua*.

Lin Xie, the editor of the *Zhongguo baihuabao,* was one of the foremost *baihua* writers of his time. He had been previously successful as a contributor to the *Hangzhou baihuabao* 杭州白話報[38] and styled himself the "*Baihua* Monk" (*Baihua Daoren*). In the "Zhong-

---

[35] Cf. Ding Shouhe 1982–88, vol 1, pp. 441–60; Lin Weijun 林慰君 . 1969. "Lin Baishui xiansheng zhuan" 林白水先生傳 (Biography of Mr. Lin Baishui), *Zhuanji wenxue* 14.1, pp. 43–50; 14.2, pp. 45–50; 14.3, pp. 41–7.

[36] Another *baihua*-journal was the *Ningbo baihuabao* founded in November 1903 by Ma Yuzao 馬裕藻 (1880–1945), a pupil of Zhang Taiyan 章太炎 (1869–1936), who later played an important role in the creation of the phonetical script *Zhuyin Zimu* 注音字母 . Cf. Ding Shouhe 1982–88, vol. 1, pp. 431–40; Li Jinxi 黎錦熙 . 1990. *Guoyu yundong shigang* 國語運動史綱 (Historical outline of the National Language Movement). Shanghai: Shanghai shudian, pp. 51, 56. Chen Duxiu 陳獨秀 (1879–1942) had opened a *Guomin ribao* 國民日報 (National Daily, in *wenyan*) together with Zhang Shizhao 章士釗 (1881–1973) and others in Shanghai after the "Subao-Case", but he soon returned to his hometown Wuhu to found the *Anhui suhuabao* in March 1904. Cf. Ding Shouhe 1982–88, vol. 2, pp. 163–89. For the *Subao* Case see J. Lust. 1964. "The Su Bao Case: An Episode in the Early Chinese Nationalist Movement", *Bulletin of the School of Oriental and African Studies* 27.2, pp. 408–29.

[37] The journal was not only sold all over the Yangzi area, but it was also read in Beijing. An article with the title "To our brothers in the army" ("Gao dangbing de xiongdimen" 告當兵的兄弟們), *Zhongguo baihuabao* 18 (August 10, 1904) was serialized shortly thereafter in the daily *Jinghua ribao* 9–12 (August 24–27, 1904).

[38] The *Hangzhou baihuabao* was founded in 1901 and continued to exist until the end of the Qing dynasty, even after Lin Xie had left the paper. Cf. Xu Yunjia 徐運嘉 and Yang Pingping 楊萍萍 . 1989. "Qingmo Hangzhou de san zhong baozhi—'Jing-

guo baihuabao fakanci" 中國白話報發刊辭 (Inaugural statement of the *Zhongguo baihuabao*), Lin described his main intention for using *baihua* as to recruit new groups of the population for his ideas:

> In our China the most useless people are the educated people (*du-shuren* 讀書人). This is not to say that they do not have principles or that they lack talent. But even if they have high principles, good talent and deep knowledge, they only use it to speak some empty words (*kong hua* 空話) or to write some empty texts (*kongwen* 空文). Is there any other great enterprise they are able to undertake except from these two occupations? Today's monthly journals and daily newspapers are all made for the educated readers. However, no matter how full of emotion and tears you speak to them, it is like playing the zither for the oxen. It's of no use at all. … For today's educated people in China, there is left no hope anymore. Thus all hope is resting on those of our people who cultivate the land, carry on a craft, go in trade or serve in the army as well as on our teenaged boys and girls.[39]

Thus *baihua* was thought of as a tool to speak to the uneducated people, i.e. not just to educate them as intended by the reformers, but to move them to act. As to the content of *baihua*, Lin also favours *guanhua* in the hope to make his words understood by a Chinese rather than by a local readership:

> Suppose we would open a huge public speaker's hall in Shanghai and invite men and women from all 18 provinces, and I, the *Baihua* Monk, would climb the stage and hold a speech in my Fujianese, then I am afraid you would not understand what I say. Oh! The difficult writing (*wenfa* 文法), you cannot read, and if we speak to you to listen, you would again not understand. Moreover, by holding one public speech in Shanghai, I can never hope to make all the people of the eighteen provinces listen to my words, for my voice will not be loud enough to be heard all over the country. To solve this problem, I discussed with my friends for some days, nobody found a better solution than to make a *baihua*-journal! In this journal we use the great and famous *guanhua*, to make every sentence clear and plain.[40]

---

[38] (cont.) shi bao', 'Hangbao', 'Hangzhou baihuabao'" 清末杭州的三種報紙 — 經世報，杭報，杭州白話報 (Three Hangzhou newspapers in Late Qing–*Jingshibao, Hangbao* and the *Hangzhou baihuabao*), *Xinwen yanjiu ziliao* 47, pp. 132–9.

[39] Lin Xie 林獬 . 1970. "Zhongguo baihuabao fakanci" 中國白話報法刊辭 (Inaugural statement of the *Zhongguo baihuabao*), in: Chang Yü-fa et al. *The Revolutionary Movement during the Late Ch'ing. A Guide to Chinese Periodicals.* Washington D.C.: Center for Chinese Research Materials, p. 55.

[40] Ibid.

Whether the journal really reached its objective to move the "people who cultivate the land, carry on a craft, go in trade or serve in the army" deserves some further research. It seems to have been read in North China. In Beijing the Public Newspaper Reading Room of the Western City (*Xicheng yuebaoshe* 西城閱報社), established in April 1905, offered almost all editions of the *Zhongguo baihuabao* to the readers, although the journal had already been discontinued at this time. This, however, says nothing about the readers of the journal, as this reading room, managed by Hunanese people, also served a somewhat elevated public, and, in September 1905, even planned to establish first-, second-, and third-class reading rooms.[41] For South China, where *guanhua* was not the spoken language of most of the population, some doubts may be raised as to the success of such a claim. However, the journal certainly did achieve its aim of reaching the "teenaged boys and girls" studying in the modern or semi-modern schools. This fact is revealed in an advertisement of the *Zhongguo baihuabao* of 1904:

> Most of our readers belong to the student community. Yet, the students appreciate the paper [not only for their own sake, but], also for the sake of the women and children as well as for the uneducated people of their homeplaces. It is true that the explanations in our journal are easy to understand, but our concepts are quite difficult. If we cannot reach the eyes and ears of the common people through the mediation of our comrades, then we must fear that our words will not be heard.[42]

The boom of *baihua*-journals after 1903 might thus have been connected not only to the upsurge of nationalism after the Manchurian crisis but also to the establishment of a modern school system in 1902.

Thus, in effect, the stress on *baihua* in the nationalist journals and newspapers, at least in South China, served a different purpose than the professed winning of new readers among the peasants, workers, and soldiers. In the first instance, it made venerable *guanhua*, formerly restricted to entertainment and some moral tractates, into a language of politics and science. The first *baihua*-journals until about

---

[41] *Dagongbao* (5.5.1905); cited from Li Xiaoti 李孝悌. 1992. *Qingmo de xiaceng shehui qimeng yundong, 1901–1911* 清末的下層社會啟蒙運動 (Lower class enlightenment in the Late Qing, 1901–1911). Taibei: Zhongyang yanjiuyuan jindaishi yanjiusuo, p. 54; See also *Jinghua ribao* 228 (April 8, 1905); 265 (May 15, 1905); 364 (September 23, 1906).

[42] *Jingzhong ribao* 37 (April 2, 1904).

1901 contained mainly articles and news, which had been originally written in *wenyan* and were now translated into the vernacular language. Many of the translations were from works of the Westerners John Fryer (Fu Lanya 傅蘭雅 , 1838–1928), Timothy Richard and others, which were themselves translations from Western languages into classical Chinese. Another type of material published in the *baihua*-journals were vernacular histories and other forms of didactical novels of the *yanyi* 演義 type.[43] The process of translation from the *wenyan* works on modern topics was also called *yan* or *yanyi*, meaning 'to explain' or 'to render', showing the intention of the 'translators' to stress the close relationship of their work to that of moral educators of former times. Furthermore, *yan* stresses the orality of *baihua* as different from the literality of *wen*. The above mentioned *Hangzhou baihuabao* introduced the leading article (*lunshuo* 論説) in 1901.[44] This was imitated by other *baihua*-journals. However, in the beginning, the contents of these editorials still very much recall moral sermons.[45] Only after 1903, and especially in the nationalistic papers of the Yangzi region, political editorials in *baihua* appeared. Furthermore, with a view to the needs of the student readership special columns for science and education topics were established.[46] Owing to the nationalists' wish to bring revolutionary ideas about social change, scientific progress and national strength to their readers, 'difficult concepts' in the form of new words like *guomin* 國民 (citizen),

---

[43] The earliest *baihua*-newspaper, the *Yanyi baihuabao*, consisted mainly of novels, like the "History of [China's] opening up for trade rendered [into the vernacular]" (*Tongshang yuanwei yanyi* 通商原委演義 , later known as "Poppy flower", *yingsuhua* 罌粟花), and news. The *Wuxi baihuabao* had many translations. Both periodicals had no leading articles containing authentic political statements in *baihua*. Cf. A Ying 1958, pp. 63–4 (Heidelberg University also obtained some copies of the newspaper); see also the table of content of "Wuxi baihuabao, Zhongguo guanyin baihuabao" 無錫 白話報，中國官音白話報 . 1980–84. In: *Zhongguo jindai qikan bianmu huilu* 中國近 代 期刊編目彙錄 (Index to Chinese journals of the modern times). 5 vols. edited by Shanghai tushuguan 上海圖書館 . Shanghai: Shanghai renmin chubanshe, vol. 1, pp. 922–5.

[44] For the development of the leading article in the *wenyan* press see Andrea Janku's contribution in this volume.

[45] Cf. "Hangzhou baihuabao" 杭州白話報 , in: *Zhongguo jindai qikan bianmu huilu* 1980–84, vol. 2, pp. 178–95; "Jinghua bao" 京華報 , ibid., pp. 196–7; "Suzhou baihuabao" 蘇州白話報 , ibid., pp. 221–2.

[46] The *Zhongguo baihuabao* contained the columns 'leading article' (*lunshuo* 論 説), 'history' (*lishi* 歴 史), 'geography' (*dili* 地理), 'biographies' (*zhuanji* 傳記), 'education' (*jiaoyu* 教育), 'industry' (*shiye* 實業), 'science' (*kexue* 科學) etc. As is

geming 革命 (revolution), or *jiaoyu* 教育 (education), which had
enriched the modernized *wenyan* style of the regular newspapers and
journals, now poured into *baihua* in large numbers.

On the other hand, *baihua*-journals accustomed a whole generation
of students to the use of *baihua* and trained them in its use. Thus it
laid the foundation for the Literary Revolution. A very important step
forward in this direction was the foundation of the famous China
National Institute (*Zhongguo gongxue* 中國公學) in Shanghai in
1905. This school was founded by students who had returned from
Japan in protest against the "Rules Governing Chinese Students in
Japan" promulgated by the Japanese ministry of education on the initiative of the Qing government. Conceived as an all-Chinese university the school had students and teachers from all over the country.
One of its students was Hu Shi 胡適 (1891–1962). According to his
reminiscences, this was the first school in China to employ only
teachers who spoke *guanhua*.[47] Students of this school published the
baihua-journal *Jingye xunbao* 兢業旬報 (Striving for Accomplishe-
ment Journal). The journal did not have the word *baihua* in its title,
which usually marked a paper as one to "enlighten the people".
Indeed it was not intended to "enlighten the people" but, according to
Hu, to publish "propaganda for the young citizens in the elementary
school",[48] who would be, as Hu Shi himself, the future intellectual
leaders of the country. Its first number of October 1906 also contained
an article about *guanhua*:

> If we want to save China, we must first unite the minds of the Chinese
> people. If we want to unite the minds of the Chinese people, we must
> first unify the Chinese dialects .... But today, considering the countless
> numbers of Chinese dialects, how can we tell them to unite around
> one? ... There is no other way than to use Mandarin .... If all of China

---

[46] (*cont.*) already easily seen from the titles of these colums, modern Japanese
loanwords are used instead of older Chinese terms or loans (*dili* 地理 instead of *yudi*
興地 , *lishi* instead of *shixue* 史學 , *kexue* instead of *gezhi* 格致). The *Ningbo baihuabao* adapted its columns to the formate of the *Zhongguo baihuabao* in its "New
Series" in 1904. "Zhongguo baihuabao", in: *Zhongguo jindai qikan bianmu huilu*
1980–84, vol. 2, pp. 1128–36; "Ningbo baihuabao", ibid., pp. 1124–7.

[47] The students called their language "common speech" (*putonghua* 普通話),
which was a loan from the Japanese term *futsugo* 普通語 . But the discussion of this
term leads to the question of the contents of *guanhua*, which cannot be dealt with
here.

[48] Hu Shi 胡適 . 1978–79. "An Autobiographical Account at Forty", *Chinese Studies in History* 12.2, p. 30.

is to adopt Mandarin, we should copy Peking Mandarin as the common national dialect.[49]

The journal continued to exist until 1909 and was one of the longest-lasting *baihua*-journals. Thus at this early stage *baihua* already showed the tendency to become a modern written language and a communication tool for the educated classes.

And finally, *baihua*-journals linked the question of language to nationalism and made *baihua* a tool of nationwide propaganda, thus beginning to rob *wenyan* step by step of its monopolizing status to unite China.

Baihua-journals proved to be quite successful. Shortly after the turn of the century *baihua* had already become a widely accepted term for a tool used to enlighten the people. And the nationalists were by far not the only group to use *baihua* to disseminate their ideas to the people. Although statistics about this kind of material are rather incomplete, one can safely assume that until the end of the Qing dynasty more than one hundred *baihua*-journals had existed through-out China.[50] The pressure of public opinion was such that the Qing government was forced to extend its use of *guanhua* in communicating with its subjects, and, from about 1903 on, even used the term *baihua* for *guanhua* materials published to educate the people. This movement started in 1903 when the governor-general of Sichuan, Cen Chunxuan 岑春萱 (1861–1933), had an Imperial edict against foot binding of women translated into *baihua* and distributed among the people. The text was thought to be lectured to the people, but was also published in different *baihua* newspapers and journals. Other provincial governments followed, as did also the Zhili government of Yuan Shikai 袁世凱 (1859–1916), which issued the famous pamphlet *Guomin bidu* 國民必讀 (Citizen's Essential Reader) and others.[51] Some *baihua* journals were even financed by officials, like the *Shanxi baihua yanshuobao* 山西白話演說報 (Shanxi Journal for Lectures in Baihua) of 1905, or the *Jilin baihuabao* 吉林白話報 (The Jilin Baihua-Journal) founded in 1907.[52] All of these materials were writ-

---

[49] Ibid., p. 31, cited from the English translation.

[50] Cai Lesu counted 170 *baihua*-journals until 1915. However, neither this account nor the largest list of early modern periodicals edited by Shi He and others is complete or fully reliable; Cai Lesu 1987, pp. 493–546; Shi He 1991, s.v.

[51] Cf. Li Xiaoti 1992, pp. 31–4.

[52] Cf. Cai Lesu 1987, pp. 517–8; Ding Shouhe 1982–88, vol. 2, pp. 548–62.

ten in *guanhua*. The use of *guanhua* in such lecture activity had a long tradition in China. Thus, to rename this kind of material into *baihua*, was another step in fixing the relationship between the two terms.

However, in spite of this success there were still certain limitations in the use of *baihua*. On the one hand, *baihua*-journals still posed in professed orality. The language of the *baihua*-journals in general, including the nationalist ones, almost exaggerated its relation to oral speech, such that, to give an example, the passage cited above from the *Zhongguo baihuabao* contains phrases like *ni kankan ba* 你看看吧 ("Look!") or even *tianqi leng a!* 天氣冷啊 ("It's cold [today]!") as an introduction,[53] making it to seem suitable for interactive communication with an audience. Early *baihua* texts use spaces instead of punctuation to facilitate reading aloud to an audience. The official use of *baihua* confined its role completely to oral lecturing in the tradition of the sermons of the Sacred Edict in the past. Especially after the movement for a constitutional government had begun in 1906 and *Quanxuesuo* 勸學所 (Offices for exhorting [the people] to study) for out-of-school education of the people were founded all over the country, *baihua* materials constituted a part of the lecturing program.[54]

On the other hand, contrary to the famous statement of Qiu Tingliang, the status of *wenyan* was rarely openly challenged. And even if it was, in reality the status of *baihua* remained lower than that of *wen*, since all the journalists at the *baihua*-journals wrote *wenyan* articles, *wenyan*-letters and so on when adressing their equals. The modern intellectuals pretending now to speak to their fellow intellectuals *as well as* to the "people who cultivate the land, carry on a craft, go in trade or serve in the army as well as on our teenaged boys and girls" also maintained the difference between high and low. They did not speak in one tongue to the whole nation but in two—*wenyan* and *baihua* (mostly *guanhua*), which means that the national press operated with two divergent discoursive strategies in this period. Many *wenyan* newspapers and journals had their little sister in *baihua*, starting with the *Shanghai wanbao* in 1898, the sibling of the *Zhongwai ribao*. In Shanghai the *Jingzhong ribao* was accompanied by the *Zhongguo baihuabao*, in Beijing the vernacular *Jinghua ribao* came out together with the *Zhonghua bao* in *wenyan*, in Shanxi the *Shanxi*

---

[53] Cf. Lin Xie 1970, p. 54.
[54] Cf. *Xuebu guanbao* 4 (28. 9. 1906), vol. 1, pp. 95–6.

baihua yanshuobao was a supplementary of the *Jin Bao* 晉報 (Shanxi News). Several of the big commercial newspapers had *baihua* columns, as for example the *Tianjin Dagongbao* 天津大公報 (*L'impartial*).[55]

3. *GUOYU* VS. *GUOWEN*—IN SEARCH FOR A NATIONAL LANGUAGE

However, to say that the process of developing *guanhua* into the national language of China was, as Hu Shi later called it, a completely "unconscious"[56] process, misses the point. The creation of *baihua*-journals went hand in hand with an extensive debate on the question of language. The demands for the "unification of the written and spoken language" where followed closely by demands for a nationally unified spoken language. Liang Qichao addressed the issue first in 1896 in the pages of the *Shiwubao*:

> Considering the reasons for the strength or weakness of a country, then it's always the degree of openness or seclusion [...; in China] roads are not built, that's why [people of] Shaanxi and Zhejiang are indifferent to the wellbeing or problems of the other province; the languages (*yuyan*) are different, that's why Fujian and Guangdong, on one side, and the Central Plain on the other are like two different countries.[57]

The necessity of a national language became especially pressing when a national school system was established and decisions had to be made as to which language to teach the children of China and what this language was to be called. Cai Yuanpei published his essay "On School Education" (*Xuetang jiaokelun* 學堂教科論) in 1901. There he tried to solve the problem of a unified spoken language by proposing to teach spoken *guanhua* with the help of a phonetical script (without Chinese characters!) during the first two years (age 6–8) of school.[58]

Only one year later, in 1902, Japanese influence contributed a new term to designate that unified spoken language. In this year Japanese

---

[55] Cf. Shi He, 1991. s.v.

[56] Cf. Hu Shi 胡適. 1994b. "Jianshe de wenxue geming lun" 建設的文學革命論 (A constructive theory of literary revolution), in: Wang Rongwen (ed.). *Hu Shi zuopinji* 胡適作品集 (Collected works of Hu Shi). 37 vols. Taibei: Yuanliu chubanshe vol. 3, p. 63.

[57] Liang Qichao 梁啟超. 1936. "Lun baoguan youyi yu guoshi" 論報館有益于國事 (On the benefit of newspapers for national affairs), in: id. *Yinbingshi wenji* 飲冰室文集 (Collected works from the Ice-Drinker's Studio). Edited by Lin Zhijun 林志鈞. 16 vols. Shanghai: Zhonghua shuju, vol. 1, p. 100.

language debates reached their height with the establishment of the National Language Research Council (*Kokugo chōsa iinkai* 國語調查 委員會), which marked the beginning of conscious language planning. In Japan, the term *kokugo* in its modern meaning as 'national language' was derived from its older meaning as "a language of our own state", which meant only colloquial Japanese in contrast to Chinese. The term had acquired the meaning "language of a country" only during the last half of the nineteenth century through contacts with foreign countries. In 1894 Ueda Kazutoshi 上田萬年 (1867–1937) published his book *Kokugo to kokka to* 中國と國家と (The national language and the nation), imbuing the term *kokugo* with a very nationalistic flavour. Following Japan's new self-confidence after its victory over China, *kokugo* became a term delineating a single language representing Japan.[59]

In the year of the establishment of Japan's National Language Research Council, Wu Rulun 吳汝綸 (1840–1903), then dean of the Imperial University at Beijing, went to Japan to investigate the Japanese educational system. He was a well-known essayist of the *Tongchengpai* school of literary composition and an educationalist who had compiled several anthologies of classical Chinese literature. With a view to the education of the lower classes he supported a scheme for a phonetical script for the Beijing dialect (similar to the Japanese Kana) which had been devised by Wang Zhao 王照 (1859–1933) when he was exiled in Japan after the Hundred-Days Reform of 1898.[60] Now Wu Rulun wrote to the Chancellor of the Beijing Imperial University, Zhang Baixi 張百熙 (1847–1909):

> Today many important educators believe that we cannot leave the people in the state of speaking different mutually incomprehensible languages. In Japanese schools there are always textbooks for the national language (*guoyu*). If we follow the Japanese example we will also have to adopt a simple script.[61]

---

[58] Cf. Cai Yuanpei 蔡元培. 1984. "Xuetang Jiaoke Lun" 學堂教科論 (On school education), in: id. *Cai Yuanpei quanji* 蔡元培全集 (Complete works of Cai Yuanpei). Edited by Gao Pingshu 高平叔. 4 vols. Beijing: Zhonghua shuju, vol. 1, pp. 147–9.

[59] Cf. Robert Ramsey. 1991. "The Polysemy of the Term *Kokugo*", *Sino-Platonic Papers* 27 (August 31, 1991), p. 37–47; Twine 1988, pp. 425–54.

[60] Cf. Li Jinxi 1990, pp. 33–40.

[61] *Qingmo wenzi gaige wenji* 清末文字改革文集 ([Documentary] Collections of the reform of writing during Late Qing dynasty).1958. Beijing: Wenzi gaige chubanshe, p. 29.

Zhang Baixi, however, did not follow the Japanese example, neither in terminology nor in substance. The school regulations of 1902 contain nothing about the problem of a national language or a phonetical script at all.

As in Japan prior to the Meiji era, in nineteenth century China *guoyu* meant the Manchu language in contrast to Chinese. It was still used in this sense in Zhang Binglin's famous polemical letter against Kang Youwei addressed to the Chinese overseas merchants (1903) and in an official document of the Ministry of Education in 1906.[62] Wu Rulun's letter seems to be the earliest mention of a new meaning for the term *guoyu* in China, obviously used as a proper name for the Japanese national language. At the same time, the term *kokugo* travelled from Japan to China by another route, in the luggage of patriotic students returning from their studies in Japan. It was taken up in the newspapers of the coastal cities. In 1904 the slogan "Unify the national language" (*guoyu tongyi* 國語統一) appeared in Chinese journals and newspapers. In these articles *guoyu* became a term designating a spoken national language of any country, implicating the wish that China also should have one. Remarkably, it was Chen Duxiu, who in April 1904, published an article about "National language education" in his vernacular journal *Anhui suhuabao* 安徽俗話報. There he wrote in a simple vernacular *baihua* style:

> Nowadays, in the elementary schools of all countries, a very important subject is the subject called 'National language education'. What is 'National language education'? It means to teach the speaking of one's own country (*benguo de hua* 本國的話) …. There are two reasons why we have to value national language education. The first is that the small children do not yet understand difficult literary texts and profound principles. Thus we should make text books for them where ancient and modern things and some matters of human intercourse and material principles are described in a common language that is understood all over our country. Later, when they have gradually acquired some knowledge, we still can give them books in the literary language (*wenli* 文理) to read. The second reason is that our country is very large. If everyone speaks only the language of his own place, and one who

---

[62] Cf. Zhang Binglin 章炳麟. 1985. "Bo Kang Youwei lun geming shu" 駁康有為論革命書 (A rejection of Kang Youwei's letter on revolution), in: id. *Zhang Taiyan quanji* 張太炎全集 (Complete works of Zhang Taiyan [i.e. Zhang Binglin]). 6 vols. Shanghai: Renmin chubanshe, vol. 4, pp. 173–84; "Xuebu zi waiwubu wen" 學部咨外務部文 (Letter of the Ministry of Education to the Foreign Ministry), in: *Qingmo wenzi gaige wenji* 1958, p. 68.

meets a compatriot does not understand his language, as if he would meet a foreigner, how then will it be possible for there to be something like affection between the compatriots? That is why we need national language education. Then the people of the whole country can speak the same language.

For the content of his national language education he proposed the following:

> Even if we are not able to produce such perfect national language text books as they have in foreign countries, we should nevertheless ask a teacher who knows *guanhua* to teach one lesson of *guanhua* every day … thus, after studying for three years, the student will probably be able to use *guanhua*. If they later go to another province or prefecture, this will save them the inconvenience of feeling as if they were in a foreign country, simply because they do not understand *guanhua*.[63]

This shows that *guanhua* was intended to become the national language of China and that *guoyu* was not yet used as a proper name.

An even more nationalistic argument is to be found in an article from October 1904 in the reform-oriented Tianjin newspaper *Dagongbao* which had been founded in 1902 by the Manchu Ying Hua 英華 (1867–1926). The author, using a pseudonym, writes in classical *wenyan*:

> How can a people with a common race and a common history be so full of contradictions? The reasons may be too complicated to list them all here. But the worst thing is that the national language is not unified.

The author does not equate China's national language with *guanhua*, but he states that China's national language does not yet exist, but has to be created on the basis of *guanhua*:

> To create a national language is a difficult question, but among the languages of China none is more generally used than *guanhua*. Moreover Beijing is the capital and the officials of all provinces on their [regular] tour [to the capital] learn the language of this place. Therefore it has a greater potential to be successfully popularized than the languages of the other provinces. On the other hand, many ambitious men are currently busy creating books and journals in *baihua* to enlighten the lower classes, because the Chinese written language is too difficult.

---

[63] San Ai 三愛 (Chen Duxiu 陳獨秀). 1904. "Guoyu jiaoyu" 國語教育 (Education in the national language), *Anhui suhuabao* 3 (March 15, 1904).

This also shows that *guanhua* is in general use today and known to everyone.[64]

With revised school regulations promulgated at the end of the year 1903, the Qing government also became aware of its national task of guaranteeing the linguistic unity of China. Whereas in the educational regulations of 1902 the language courses in school were simply to cover "characters", "reading of the classics" and "essay writing", the courses stipulated in the new regulations of 1904 were now called "Chinese Characters" (*Zhongguo wenzi* 中國文字) in lower primary school (*chudeng xiaoxuetang* 初等小學堂) and "Chinese Literary Studies" (*Zhongguo wenxue* 中國文學) in upper primary school (*gaodeng xiaoxuetang* 高等小學堂).[65] The government's standard of linguistic unity was, naturally, a traditional one, it was mainly a unity of writing. Only the unity of classical *wenyan* could guarantee the twofold unity of both the horizontal (regional) and vertical (historical) dimensions:

> In the schools the Chinese literary styles (*wenci* 文辭) cannot be dropped ... If literary studies are dropped, no-one would be able to read the classical works anymore. In the schools of foreign countries, the highest value is also placed on the preservation of the national essence, and this is an important element of the national essence.[66]

The Qing regulations do not at this time adopt the term *guoyu* (national language). However, a subject *guanhua* was to be added as part of the *Zhongguo wenxue* lesson. The regulations stipulated that "all schools are to teach the pronunciation of *guanhua*" and explained:

---

[64] Guan Sheng 觀生 . 1904. "Lun Guoyu tongyi zhi guanxi he tongyi zhi fa" 論國語統一之關係和統一之法 (The importance of unifying the national language and its methods), *Dagongbao* 28 (October 30, 1904).

[65] Cf. "Qinding xiaoxuetang zhangcheng" 欽定小學堂章程 (Imperial regulations for modern primary schools). 1985 [1902]. In: Shu Xincheng 舒新城 . *Zhongguo jindai jiaoyushi ziliao* 中國近代教育史資料 (Source material on the history of education in China). 3 vols. Beijing: Renmin jiaoyu chubanshe, vol. 2, pp. 404–10; "Zouding chudeng xiaoxue zhangcheng" 奏定初等小學章程 (Regulations for modern lower level primary schools) 1985 [1903], ibid., p. 420; "Zouding gaodeng xiaoxue zhangcheng" 奏定高等小學章程 (Regulations for modern higher level primary schools) 1985 [1903], ibid., p. 435.

[66] "Xuewu gangyao" 學務綱要 (Outline of the educational tasks), in: Shu Xincheng 1985, vol. 1, p. 202.

In all states there is a uniform spoken language (*yuyan*) for the whole country, thus the feelings of the people of the same country are easily harmonized. This begins already with the teaching of the alphabet in primary school. In China the folks all use their local pronunciation (*tuyin* 土音), so much that even the people of one province cannot talk to each other and many problems occur in handling affairs. We plan to unify the spoken language of the Empire with the help of *guanhua* pronunciation (*guanyin* 官音), therefore we will, beginning from normal school and upper primary school, install the subject *guanhua* as part of the 'Chinese letters' lesson. The practice of *guanhua* will be based on the standard of the book "Direct Explanations of the Amplified Instructions of the Sacred Edict" (*Shengyu guangxun zhijie* 聖諭廣訓直解). In the future the teachers in the schools of all provinces will use *guanhua* pronunciation in their teaching of all subjects. Even if they cannot reach the proficiency of one who has grown up in Beijing, they have to acquire a clear and correct reading pronunciation of the characters and fluent and bright rhyming.[67]

The government's approach to the issue of a unified national language was a traditional one. Looking for precedents in Chinese administrative history, it stuck very close to the Yongzheng policies of the eighteenth century. *Guanhua* is only recognized in its spoken form, the unification of language being understood simply as a matter of pronunciation. Thus it is thought to be sufficient to teach the future teachers of China's national school system (graduates of normal and upper primary schools) correct *guanhua* pronunciation with the help of reciting the most famous of the vernacular versions of the Yongzheng Emperor's exhortation edited by Wang Youpu 王又樸 (1680–1761). No regulations concerning standardization of grammar and vocabulary of *guanhua* were made, and every step which would give *guanhua* the status of an independent language including both spoken *and* written language was carefully avoided. To adopt the term *guoyu*, however, regardless of the fact that it still meant the Manchu language, would have been too great a step in this direction.

Thus the term *guoyu* in the Chinese context already had a fixed meaning which could not easily be replaced, at least as long as the Manchus ruled the country. On the other hand, even many of the nationalists shared a contempt for the vernacular and preferred to see its function restricted to the education of the uneducated masses outside school. Interestingly, in its rigid position to make a clear hierar-

---

[67] Ibid., p. 210

chical difference between *wen* and *hua*, the Qing government came closest to the opinions of its worst enemies, the group around the *Min-bao* and Zhang Binglin. Zhang, together with Tao Chengzhang 陶成章 (1878–1912), founded a political journal in *baihua* in 1910 called *Jiaoyu jinyu zazhi* 教育今語雜誌 (Magazine for Teaching Contemporary Language) which was designed to spread propaganda among the overseas Chinese community. To the radical nationalists the role of *baihua* had to be confined to the sphere of public speeches (*yanshuo* 演說) as a means of nationalist propaganda. All of Zhang's contributions to his journal are actually speech drafts. The preface of this journal sounds very much like the words of the government document cited above:

> One who throws away the national writing (*guowen* 國文) and eradicates national history ... will destroy his own country.[68]

For the language curriculum inside the schools, a modernized and simplified classical style was preferred, which came to be referred to by the term *guowen* (national written language) derived from the Japanese *kokubun*.

In Japanese educational circles the term *kokubun* (National Style) had not played any prominent role, it designated the written style or the written styles of the national language, as such being a part of national language lessons in school, especially in the higher grades. However, the name of the school subject was always *kokugo* (National Language), not *kokubun* (National Style).[69] In China, the new term also appeared for the first time around the year 1902. In this year, Cai Yuanpei renamed the Chinese classes of the Patriotic Study Society (*Aiguo xueshe* 愛國學社), newly founded by the China Education Organization, into *Guowen*.[70] In the nationalist circles the new term was given quite different definitions. Cai Yuanpei did not define

---

[68] Cited from Cai Lesu 蔡樂蘇 . 1983. "Jiaoyu jinyu zazhi" 教育今語雜誌 (Magazine for teaching contemporary language), in: Ding Shouhe 1982–88, vol. 3, pp. 630–38; 631; Tang Zhijun 湯志鈞 . 1990. "Zhang Taiyan yu baihuawen" 章太炎與白話文 (Zhang Taiyan and vernacular writing), *Jindai shi yanjiu* 2, pp. 112–9; 119.

[69] Cf. Nishio Minoru 西尾實 et al. (eds.). 1957. *Kokugo kyōiku jiten* 國語教育辭典 (Dictionary of national vernacular education). Tokyo: Asakura shoten, p. 280; Kaigo Tokiomi 海後宗臣 und Arata Naka 仲新 . 1979. *Kyōkasho de mite kindai Nihon no kyōiku* 教科書でみる近代日本教育 (Modern Japanese education as expressed in the school textbooks). Tokyo: Tōkyō Shoseki, pp. 89–120.

[70] Cf. "Aiguo xueshe zhangcheng" 愛國學社章程 (Regulations of the Patriotic Study Society), in: Gao Pingshu 1984, vol. 1, pp. 166–7.

the contents of his language classes, but it is certain that classical Chinese language and literature was taught. Lin Xie, in his above mentioned *Zhongguo baihuabao*, stated that

> the foreigners divide writing (*wenzi*) into two different categories: one is ancient writing (*guwen* 古文), this is Greek and Latin literature (*wen*); one is national writing (*guowen*), this is the written language of their own country (*benguo de wenzi* 本國的文字). There is nobody who has not complete command of the written language of his own country, because this written language is the same like speaking (*shuohua* 説話).[71]

He thus uses *guowen* in the same meaning as *guoyu* in its broadest sense—as the written and spoken national language of a country. At the same time, he admits that such a division between ancient writing and national written language does not exist in China. To make such a differentiation also in China is demanded by an anonymous author (possibly Lin Xie himself) a little later in an article on "The importance of *baihua*-journals for the future of China" in the daily *Jingzhong ribao*.[72] However, another author in his article on "The methods of teaching *guowen*" published in the same journal understands *guowen* in a narrow sense only as the Chinese characters.[73]

However defined, it is clear that the term *guowen* was the Chinese answer to the Japanese *kokugu*. The most important reason for this was that the word *yu* only referred to spoken language. If the language classes in school were to teach writing, the term *guoyu* would appear inappropriate. The other reason might have been that the term *guowen* was more readily accepted than the term *guoyu*, as it had a traditional meaning which came close to the new national one, delineating something that might be translated as "the literary cultural heritage of the state" ("literary" including the notions of both literary language and literature).

---

[71] Lin Xie 1970, p. 55.

[72] Cf. "Lun baihuabao yu Zhongguo qiantu zhi guanxi" 論白話報與中國前途之關係 (The relation between *baihua*-journals and the future of China), *Jingzhong ribao* (April 25, 1904).

[73] Cf. "Lun guowen zhi jiaoshoufa" 論國文之教授法 (On the methods of teaching *guowen*), *Jingzhong ribao* (November 7, 1904).

The school regulations of late 1903 used *guowen* in this sense, stipulating that

> the use of substanceless foreign nouns has to be avoided, in order to preserve the literary heritage of the state (*guowen*) and to hold up the morals of the literati (*duan shifeng* 端士風).[74]

Actually, the creation of *Zhongguo wenzi* resp. *Zhongguo wenxue* lessons in primary school as a subject separated from the readings of the classical canon, was already a step in the direction of the teaching of a modernized classical style. For the *Zhongguo wenxue* lesson of upper primary school it was stated that

> it aims at teaching the pupils to know the written language (*wenli* 文理) and the poetry (*ciju* 詞句) in everyday use among the four classes [literati, peasants, workers, merchants].[75]

This step shows itself to be half-hearted, if we consider that when it comes to the details the ancient literary style (*guwen* 古文)—rather than a practical modernized style—is defined as an important part of the lessons. Furthermore, the time assigned to the *Zhongguo wenzi* resp. *Zhongguo wenxue* lessons in the curriculum sets these courses very much in a disadvantageous position in relation to the study of the classics: it is taught only four hours in lower primary school, as compared to twelve hours reserved for the classical canon. In upper primary school the proportion is still eight to twelve hours, although the ancient style (*guwen*) and *guanhua* are added in the *Zhongguo wenxue* lesson.[76]

---

[74] "Xuewu gangyao" 學務綱要 (Outline of the educational tasks), in: Shu Xincheng 1985, vol. 1, p. 205. So-called substanceless nouns were all terms derived from Japanese which could not prove a proper ancestry in ancient Chinese texts, as *tuanti* 團體 (organization), *guohun* 國魂 (national soul/spirit), *wutai* 舞台 (stage), *daibiao* 代表 (representative) etc. Still in 1911, an encyclopedia defined *guoyu* as "the spoken language, that is unique for one country. In our country it means the Manchu language." *Guowen* is defined as "the literary studies of one country, usually it means the literary studies of our own country." Cf. Huang Mohai 黃摩海 (ed.). 1911. *Putong baike xin da cidian* 普通百科新大辭典 (New general encyclopedic dictionary). Shanghai: Shanghai tushu tulunshe, s.v.

[75] "Zouding gaodeng xiaoxue zhangcheng" 奏定高等小學章程 (Regulations for modern higher level primary schools), in: Shu Xincheng 1985, vol. 2, p. 435.

[76] "Zouding chudeng xiaoxue zhangcheng", in: Shu Xincheng 1985, vol. 2, p. 423; "Zouding gaodeng xiaoxue zhangcheng", ibid., vol. 2, p. 437.

4. THE POWER OF THE INSTITUTIONS: THE TRIUMPH OF *GUOYU*

However, the Qing government was not able to avoid the modernizing trend. One of the practical reasons for this was that in its school policies it was almost totally dependent on the Shanghai publisher Commercial Press for delivering the textbooks used in the new curriculum. Commercial Press at this time was the largest and most advanced textbook publisher in China. This publishing company co-operated closely with Japan's large textbook publisher Kinkōdō and published between 1904 and 1906 its famous textbook series "Most Modern National Language Readers" (*Zuixin guowen jiaokeshu* 最新國文教科書), which in 1906 was officially recognized by the newly established Ministry of Education (*xuebu* 學部) for use in government-sponsored primary schools.[77]

Thus Shanghai nationalists together with their Japanese colleagues gained a direct influence on the government's educational policies. A year later, the Ministry tried to free itself from its dependency on the Shanghai textbook publisher and published volumes one and two of its own language textbook series for primary schools. They were also called "National Language Readers" (*Guowen jiaokeshu* 國文教科書), thus using the term *guowen* for the first time officially as a proper name for China's 'National Language'. However, being a somewhat rude copy of the Commercial Press text books with a more traditional outlook, they were sharply criticized by the South Chinese educationalists. The Commercial Press textbook series continued to sell much better.[78]

---

[77] Cf. Manying Ip. 1985. *The Life and Times of Zhang Yuanji 1867–1959*. Beijing: Shangwu yinshuguan, pp. 117–28. See also "Jiaokeshu zhi fazhan gaikuang 1868–1918" 教科書之發展概況 1868–1918 (Outline of the development of school textbooks, 1868–1918). 1953. In: Zhang Jinglu 張靜盧 (ed.). *Zhongguo jindai chuban shiliao chubian* 中國近代出版史料初編 (Source material on the historyon the history of modern publishing in China, vol. 1). Shanghai: Qunlian shushe, pp. 219–53; Manying Ip 1985, pp. 128–30. The "Zuixin" series for lower primary school was taught in the first year of the lower primary school. Of course, this is too early an age to introduce science and technology to the pupils. Cf. *Chudeng xiaoxue yong Zuixin Guowen jiaokeshu* 初等小學用最新國文教科書 (Most modern national language reader for lower primary school). 1910. Shanghai: Shangwu yinshuguan (60th edition). For further informations on the textbook series see also Yvonne Schulz Zinda's contribution in this volume.

[78] Cf. Jiang Mengmei 江夢梅 . 1953. "Qian xuebu bian shu zhuangkuang" 前學部編書狀況 (The situation of textbook editing in the former Ministry of Education),

For a time now classical *wenyan* had become the National Written Language of China. But the demands for a nationally unified spoken language (named *guoyu*) became more pressing. In 1906 the Association of Students from all Provinces in Shanghai (*Ge sheng liu Hu xuesheng zonghui* 各省留滬學生總會), founded by students returning from Japan, demanded the publishing of *baihua*-journals and newspapers in all provinces and the teaching of *guoyu* (now used as a proper name for the National Language of China) in all schools. In the end this policy was to lead to the abolition of the dialects.[79] In 1907 Commercial Press published the first and only *guoyu* Reader (*Guoyu jiaokeshu* 國語教科書) during the Qing dynasty.[80] This book was published on the initiative of the publisher alone, again in anticipation of a corresponding government policy. The government took up language policy anew only in connection with its preparations for a constitutional government. A step by step programme for the nation-wide teaching of Mandarin (*guanhua*) started in 1909, and the Ministry accordingly ordered the production of textbooks for Mandarin.[81] But the more opportunity for political participation was given to educators in the provinces, the louder grew the demands to introduce the national language. In 1910 Jiang Qian 江謙 of the Jiangsu Educational Association rallied thirty-two members of the National Assembly to petition the Ministry of Education to create a Committee for the Investigation of the National Language (*Guoyu diaocha hui* 國語調查總會) on the Japanese model. They also demanded that *guanhua* (Mandarin) be renamed as *guoyu*:

> Every creative activity starts with the rectification of names. The name 'Mandarin' is not appropriate in its meaning. If you let the language belong to the officials, then the peasants, craftsmen, merchants and soldiers do not need to learn it. The name does not give a signal that you really intend to popularise and unify this language. When in the future

---

[78] (*cont.*) in: Zhang Jinglu 張靜廬 (ed.). *Zhongguo jindai chuban shiliao chubian* 中國近代出版史料初編 (Source material on the history of modern publishing in China, vol. 1). Shanghai: Qunlian shushe, pp. 210–4.

[79] Cf. Chow Tse-tsung 1960, p. 34.

[80] Cf. *Minguo shiqi zong shumu (1911–1949): Zhong xiao xue jiaocai* 民國時期總書目：中小學教材 (Bibliography of the Chinese republic: Middle school and primary school teaching materials). Edited by Beijing tushuguan 北京圖書館. Beijing: Shumu wenxian chubanshe, p. 328.

[81] Cf. *Xuebu guanbao* 85 (April 30, 1911), vol. 3, pp. 341–3.

these text books are send to the throne to be officially promulgated, must not their name be changed into "National Language Readers"?[82]

In the same year in October, the *guoyu* text book of the Commercial Press was officially licensed to be used in the schools, stating:

> The National Language Reader was edited with the intention to make the National Language the foundation of unifying the country, attention is paid to grammar (*yufa*), and the pronunciation is standardized according to a middle way between the southern and northern pronunciations of the whole country. The reader starts with simple matter proceeding to the complicated, its language, although different from the written language (*wenli*), is not low dialect, the contents of the lessons is well-balanced and able to arouse the interest of the children. Thus it can serve as a first step to further pursue of literary studies [i.e. study of the literary language], and should be admitted for use as textbook of the lower primary school.[83]

This was the first time that the term *guoyu* appeared in an official document of the Qing dynasty (except in the sense of Manchu language). Now the term *guoyu* had changed its meaning to be a proper name for the Chinese national language. It replaced the term *guanhua* which later was rarely used except in English language publications ('Mandarin'). The statement cited above shows how much the government had deviated from its original standpoint under the pressure of the South Chinese educationalists. The national language had now become more than a matter of pronunciation. It was a full-fledged language, spoken and written, with a distinct grammar of its own. Introduced already in lower primary school (rather than in upper primary and normal school as stipulated in the original regulations of 1904), it was to serve as a basis for proceeding to the higher literary styles. Thus teaching *guoyu* (rather than *guanhua*) became a part of the *guowen* lessons. A further concession is made to the Southerners by giving up the monopoly of Beijing pronunciation in favour of a mixed standard.

In March 1911 the establishment of the Committee for the Investigation of the National Language (*Guoyu diaocha hui* 國語調查會) demanded by the Jiangsu educationalists, and the promulgation of officially sanctioned National Language Readers were announced in

---

[82] *Qingmo wenzi gaige wenji* 1958, p. 117.
[83] *Xuebu guanbao* 136 (October 23, 1910), vol. 4, p. 472.

connection with revised plans for constitutional government.[84] In July 1911 the Qing Ministry of Education finally yielded to the South Chinese expertise in educational matters and convened the Central Education Conference (*Zhongyang jiaoyu huiyi* 中央教育會議) with Zhang Jian 張謇 (1853–1926), head of the above mentioned Jiangsu Educational Association, as chairman and Zhang Yuanji 張元濟 (1867–1959), head of the Commercial Press' Compilation and Translation Center, as vice-chairman. The conference passed a plan for the foundation of a Central Committee for the Investigation of the National Language (*Guoyu diaocha zonghui* 國語調查總會), which was to initiate a process of phonetical, lexical and grammatical standardization of *guoyu*.[85] But the end of the dynasty, for the time being, was also the end of further language planning.

When the Qing government was just about to rethink its attitudes toward language and initiated a real standardization of *guoyu*, the Ministry of Education of the new Republic took one step back and only convened a Conference for the Standardization of Character Readings in 1913, thus returning to a rather conservative stance, seeing the unification of the spoken language as a matter of standardized readings of the Chinese characters. At least, in this conference, the phonetical script *Zhuyin Zimu* 注音字母 was created, serving later as a basis for the compilation of new dictionaries. Only in 1916, after the breakdown of the Yuan Shikai 袁世凱 (1859–1916) regime, the National Language Study Commission of the Republic of China (*Zhonghua Minguo guoyu yanjiuhui* 中華民國國語研究會) was established and full-scale language planning could begin.[86]

CONCLUSION

Colloquialization of the language (i.e. to make the medium of communication more easily accessible to the mass of people) was an important factor for all who wished to broaden their communications with the less educated strata of Chinese society. However, nationalism did not automatically serve as a motor of colloquialization. In a

---

[84] Cf. *Xuebu guanbao* 146 (March 11, 1911), vol. 4, pp. 625–6.

[85] Cf. Ni Haishu 倪海暑 . 1959. *Qingmo hanyu pinyin yundong biannian shi* 清末漢語拼音運動編年史 (Chronological history of the Late Qing movement for a phonetical writing). Shanghai: Shanghai renmin chubanshe, pp. 235–6.

[86] Cf. Li Jinxi 1990, pp. 50–67.

country where writing and literature were such an important part of cultural identification, *wen* could not easily be given up without conflicting with another goal of nationalism, authenticity.[87] China of the late Qing was in a transitional stage in this respect. As shown above, a broad nationalist movement for the education of the popular masses was the motor to initiate a process which would reshuffle language functions and roles in Chinese society. Even the Qing government was forced by public opinion and its own wish not to lose leadership in the nation building process to acknowledge the need for a spoken national language and to take the first steps toward its standardization. The process to reshape *guanhua* into a full-fledged national language (*guoyu*), however, was hampered by a deep conceptual gap between the written and the spoken realm of language and by the belief that only the classical written language was able to be the guarantee of both: national authenticity and national unity. This belief united *all* agents in the national language discourse. Thus, in their theories on national language, we can now find two national languages—the written *guowen* and the spoken *guoyu*.

Hu Shi and his comrades in the so-called Literary Revolution closed the conceptual gap between *wen* and *hua*. In order to do so two basic conceptual changes were needed: 1. the development of a holistic concept of language as one inseparable entity of the written and the spoken; 2. the development of a horizontal concept of the nation, that is to give the territorial unity of the present priority over the cultural authenticity of the past. This was achieved by a new concept of literature found in Hu Shi's "Modest proposals for a Literary Reform". *Wenxue* was no longer the whole of the Chinese historical knowledge of *wen* but simply 'literature' in a modern Western sense. Thus Hu Shi could claim that "one time has the literature of one time"[88] and identify *baihua* as a language of literature, which was to serve as the foundation for the creation of the literature and the language of the

---

[87] Similar developments have been desribed in literature for different countries. Cf. Joshua Fishman. 1972. *Language and Nationalism: Two Integrative Essays.* Rowley, Mass.: Newbury House; Joshua Fishman et al. (eds.). 1968. *Language Problems of Developing Nations.* New York: Wiley.

[88] Hu Shi 胡適 . 1994c [1917]. "Wenxue gailiang chuyi" 文學改良芻議 (Preliminary suggestions for a literary reform), in: Wang Rongwen 王榮文 (ed.). *Hu Shi zuopinji* 胡適作品集 (Collected works of Hu Shi). 37 vols. Taibei: Yuanliu chubanshe, vol. 3, p. 7.

present time, a "Literature in the national language and a literary national language."[89]

However, after *guoyu* had become a literary language, *guowen* continued to exist (in administration, in the higher classes at school etc.). China still conceived of two national (and literary) languages, the classical *guowen* and the modern *guoyu*. Thus, actually the Literary Revolution was not as revolutionary as it professed to be. It was only a bigger step in a series of many small steps on the way of *guoyu*, winning ground against the dominance of *guowen*. And while the communists' total break with tradition brought about a thorough colloquialization of language in the Peoples Republic, in Taiwan the struggle for the right balance between *guowen* and *guoyu* was carried on well into the second half of the twentieth century.[90]

---

[89] Hu Shi 1994b, p. 57.

[90] *'Guoyu' yu 'guowen' zhengming wenti* ' 國語' 與 ' 國文 ' 正名問題 (The problem of rectifying the names for the terms 'guoyu' and 'guwen'). 1967. Taibei: Guoyu ribaoshe.

REFERENCES

A Ying 阿英 . 1958. *Wan Qing wenyi baokan shulüe* 晚清文義報刊述略 (Short account of literary periodicals of the late Qing Dynasty). Shanghai: Gudian wenxue chubansche, pp. 63–4.

Bai Runsheng 白閏生 . 1989. "Woguo zuizao de zangwen baozhi – 'Xizang Baihuabao'" 我國最早的藏文報紙 — 西藏白話報 (China's earliest newspaper in Tibetan—'Tibet Vernacular Newspaper'), *Xinwen yanjiu ziliao* 46, pp. 124–7.

Besch, Werner. 1983. "Dialekt, Schreibdialekt, Schriftsprache, Standardsprache: Exemplarische Skizze ihrer historischen Ausprägung im Deutschen", in: Werner Besch et al. (eds.). *Dialektologie: Ein Handbuch zur deutschen und allgemeinen Dialektforschung.* Berlin: Walter de Gruyter, pp. 961–90.

Cai Lesu 蔡樂蘇 . 1983. "Jiaoyu jinyu zazhi" 教育今語雜誌 , in: Ding Shouhe 丁守和 (ed.). 1982–88. *Xinhai geming shiqi qikan jieshao* 辛亥革命時期期刊介紹 (Introduction to the periodicals around the Xinghai Revolution). Beijing: Renmin chubanshe, vol. 3, pp. 630–8.

——. 1987. "Qingmo minchu de yibaiqishi yu zhong baihua baokan" 清末民初的一百七十餘種白話報刊 (More than 170 vernacular papers of the Late Qing and Early Republican Period), in: Ding Shouhe 丁守和 (ed.). 1982–88. *Xinhai geming shiqi qikan jieshao* 辛亥革命時期期刊介紹 (Introduction to the periodicals around the Xinghai Revolution). Beijing: Renmin chubanshe, vol. 5, pp. 493–546.

Cai Shi 蔡奭 . 1974 [n.d.]. "Guanyin huijie bianlan" 官音彙解便覽 (Explanations on the *guanhua* pronunciation), in: Nagazawa Kikuya 長澤規矩也 (ed.). *Min Shin zokugo jisho shūsei* 明清俗語辭書集成 (Collected vernacular dictionaries of the Ming- and Qing-dynasties). Tokyo: Kyūko Shoin, vol. 3, p. 399.

Cai Yuanpei 蔡元培. 1984. "Xuetang Jiaoke Lun" 學堂教科論 (On school education), in: id. *Cai Yuanpei quanji* 蔡元培全集 (Complete works of Cai Yuanpei). Edited by Gao Pingshu 高平叔 . 4 vols. Beijing: Zhonghua shuju, vol. 1, pp. 147–9.

Chow, Tse-tsung. 1960. *The May Fourth Movement: Intellectual Revolution in Modern China.* Cambridge, Mass.: Harvard University Press.

Chudeng xiaoxue yong Zuixin Guowen jiaokeshu 初等小學用最新國文教科書 (Most modern national language reader for lower primary school). 1910. Shanghai: Shangwu yinshuguan (60th edition).

De Francis, John. 1948. "A Missionary Contribution to Chinese Nationalism", *Journal of the North China Branch of the Royal Asiatic Society* 83, pp. 1–34.

——. 1950. *Nationalism and Language Reform in China.* Princeton: Princeton University Press.

Ding Shouhe 丁守和 (ed.). 1982–88. *Xinhai geming shiqi qikan jieshao* 辛亥革命時期期刊介紹 (Introduction to the periodicals around the Xinghai Revolution). 5 vols. Beijing: Renmin chubanshe.

Doleželová-Velingerová, Milena (ed.). 1980. *The Chinese Novel at the Turn of the Century.* Toronto: University of Toronto Press.

Fan Fang 范方 . 1963. "Zhongguo guanyin Baihuabao" 中國官音白話報(The Chinese vernacular journal in the Mandarin pronunciation), *Jindaishi ziliao* 2, pp. 110–13.

Fang Hanqi 方漢奇 . 1991. *Baoshi yu Baoren* 報史與報人 (The history of journalism and the journalists). Beijing: Xinhua chubanshe.

Ferguson, Charles. 1959. "Diglossia", *Word* 15, pp. 325–40.

Fishman, Joshua. 1972. *Language and Nationalism: Two Integrative Essays*. Rowley, Mass.: Newbury House.

Fishman, Joshua et al. (eds.). 1968. *Language Problems of Developing Nations*. New York: Wiley.

Franke, Wolfgang. 1963. *The Reform and Abolition of the Traditional Chinese Examination System*. Cambridge, Mass.: Harvard University Press.

Gao Shiliang 高時良 (ed.). 1992. *Zhongguo jindai jiaoyushi ziliao huibian: Yangwu yundong shiqi jiaoyu* 中國近代教育史資料匯編：洋務運動時期教育 (A collection of source materials for the history of modern education in China: education during the Yangwu Movement). Shanghai: Shanghai jiaoyu chubanshe.

Guan Sheng 觀生. 1904. "Lun Guoyu tongyi zhi guanxi he tongyi zhi fa" 論國語統一之關係和統一之法 (The importance of unifying the national language and its methods), *Dagongbao* 28 (October 30, 1904).

'Guoyu' yu 'guowen' zhengming wenti '國語' 與 '國文' 正名問題 (The problem of rectifying the names for the terms 'guoyu' and 'guwen'"). 1967. Taibei: Guoyu ribaoshe.

Joanna Handlin. 1983. *Action in Late Ming thought: The Reorientation of Lü K'un and Other Scholar-Officials*. Berkeley: University of California Press.

Hu Shi 胡適. 1978–79. "An Autobiographical Account at Forty", *Chinese Studies in History* 12.2, p. 30.

——. 1994a. "Da Qian Xuantong" 答錢玄同 (An answer to Qian Xuantong), in: Wang Rongwen 王榮文 (ed.). *Hu Shi zuopin ji* 胡適作品集 (Collected works of Hu Shi). 37 vols. Taibei: Yuanliu chuban gongsi, vol. 3, p. 44.

——. 1994b. "Jianshe de wenxue geming lun" 建設的文學革命論 (A constructive theory of literary revolution), in: Wang Rongwen (ed.). *Hu Shi zuopinji* 胡適作品集 (Collected works of Hu Shi). 37 vols. Taibei: Yuanliu chubanshe vol. 3, p. 63.

——. 1994c [1917]. "Wenxue gailiang chuyi" 文學改良芻議 (Preliminary suggestions for a literary reform), in: Wang Rongwen 王榮文 (ed.). *Hu Shi zuopinji* 胡適作品集 (Collected works of Hu Shi). 37 vols. Taibei: Yuanliu chubanshe, vol. 3, p. 7.

Huang Mohai 黃摩海 (ed.). 1911. *Putong baike xin da cidian* 普通百科新大辭典 (New general encyclopedic dictionary). Shanghai: Shanghai tushu tulunshe.

Huang Zunxian 黃遵憲. 1963. "Riben Guozhi: Wenxuezhi" 日本國志：文學 (Treatise on Japan: Literature), *Jindaishi ziliao* 2, p. 116.

Huters, Theodore. 1987. "From Writing to Literature: The Development of Late Qing Theories of Prose", *Harvard Journal of Asiatic Studies* 47.1, pp. 51–96.

Ip, Manying. 1985. *The Life and Times of Zhang Yuanji 1867–1959*. Beijing: Shangwu yinshuguan.

Jiang Mengmei 江夢梅. 1953. "Qian xuebu bian shu zhuangkuang" 前學部編書狀況 (The situation of textbook editing in the former Ministry of Education). In: Zhang Jinglu 張靜廬 (ed.). *Zhongguo jindai chuban shiliao chubian* 中國近代出版史料初編 (Source material on the history of modern publishing in China, vol. 1). Shanghai: Qunlian shushe, pp. 210–4.

Kaigo Tokiomi 海後宗臣 und Arata Naka 仲新. 1979. *Kyokasho de mite kindai Nihon no kyōiku* 教科書でみる近代日本教育 (Modern Japanese education as expressed in the school textbooks). Tokyo: Tōkyō Shoseki.

Kamachi, Noriko. 1981. *Reform in China: Huang Zunxian and the Japanese Model*. Cambridge, Mass.: Harvard University Press.

Li Jinxi 黎錦熙. 1990. *Guoyu yundong shigang* 國語運動史綱 (Historical outline of the national language movement). Shanghai: Shanghai shudian.

Li Xiaoti 李孝悌 . 1992. *Qingmo de xiaceng shehui qimeng yundong, 1901–1911* 清末的下層社會啟蒙運動 (Lower class enlightenment in the Late Qing, 1901–1911). Taibei: Zhongyang yanjiuyuan jindaishi yanjiusuo.

Liang Qichao 梁啟超 . 1936. "Lun baoguan youyi yu guoshi" 論報館有益于國事 (On the benefit of newspapers for national affairs), in: id. *Yinbingshi wenji*飲冰室文集 (Collected works from the Ice-Drinker's Studio). 16 vols. Edited by Lin Zhijun 林志鈞 Shanghai: Zhonghua shuju, vol. 1, p. 100.

———. 1953. "Mengxue bao, Yanyi bao hexu" 蒙學報演義報合序(Joint preface for the *Mengxue bao* and *Yanyi bao*), in: Zhongguo shixuehui 中國史學會 (ed.). *Wuxu bianfa* 戊戌變法 (The reform in 1898). 4 vols. Shanghai: Shenzhou guoguangshe, vol. 4, pp. 539–40.

Lin Weijun 林慰君 . 1969. "Lin Baishui xiansheng zhuan" 林白水先生傳 (Biography of Mr. Lin Baishui), *Zhuanji wenxue* 14.1, pp. 43–50; 14.2, pp. 45–50; 14.3, pp. 41–7.

Lin Xie 林獬 . 1970. "Zhongguo baihuabao Fakanci" 中國白話報發刊辭 (Inaugural statement of the *Zhongguo baihuabao*), in: Chang Yü-fa et al. *The Revolutionary Movement during the Late Ch'ing. A Guide to Chinese Periodicals*. Washington D.C.: Center for Chinese Research Materials, p. 55.

Liu Jialin 劉家林 . 1989. "Baihuabao yu baihuawen de zuizao chuangzaozhe—Qiu Kefu" 白話報與白話文的最早創造者 — 裴可桴 (The earliest creator of a *baihua* journal and of texts in *baihua*—Qiu Kefu), *Xinwen yanjiu ziliao* 47, pp. 32–9.

Lust, J. 1964. "The Su Bao Case: an Episode in the Early Chinese Nationalist Movement", *Bulletin of the School of Oriental and African Studies* 27.2, pp. 408–29.

Mair, Victor. 1985. "Language and Ideology in the Written Popularization of the Sacred Edict", in: David Johnson et al. (eds.). *Popular Culture in Late Imperial Culture*. Berkeley: University of California Press, pp. 325–59.

Masini, Frederico. 1993. *The Formation of Modern Chinese Lexicon and its Evolution Toward a National Language: The Period from 1840 to 1898*. Berkeley: Journal of Chinese Linguistics (Mongraph Series, no. 6).

Minguo shiqi zong shumu (1911–1949): Zhong xiao xue jiaocai 民國時期總書目：中小學教材 (Bibliography of the Chinese republic: Middle school and primary school teaching materials). Edited by Beijing tushuguan 北京圖書館 . Beijing: Shumu wenxian chubanshe.

Nagazawa Kikuya 長澤規矩也 . 1974. *Min Shin zokugo jisho shūsei* 明清俗語辭書集成 (Collected vernacular dictionaries of the Ming- and Qing-dynasties). Tokyo: Kyūko Shoin.

Ni Haishu 倪海暑 . 1959. *Qingmo hanyu pinyin yundong biannian shi* 清末漢語拼音運動編年史 (Chronological history of the Late Qing movement for a phonetical writing). Shanghai: Shanghai renmin chubanshe.

Nishio Minoru 西尾實 et al. (eds.). 1957. *Kokugo kyōiku jiten* 國語教育辭典 (Dictionary of national vernacular education). Tokyo: Asakura shoten.

Nivison, David S. 1966. *The Life and Thought of Chang Hsüeh-ch'eng (1738–1801)*. Stanford: Stanford University Press.

Paderni, Paola. 1988. "The Problem of Kuan-hua in Eighteenth Century China: The Yung-cheng Decree for Fukien and Kwangtung", *Annali di Istituto di Napoli* 48.4, pp. 258–68.

Qingmo wenzi gaige wenji 清末文字改革文集 ([Documentary] Collections of the reform of writing during Late Qing dynasty). 1958. Beijing: Wenzi gaige chubanshe.

Qiu Tingliang 裴廷梁 . 1953. "Wuxi baihuabao xu" 無錫白話報序 (Preface to the *Wuxi baihuabao*), in: Zhongguo shixuehui 中國史學會 (ed.). *Wuxu bianfa* 戊戌

變法 (The reform in 1898). 4 vols. Shanghai: Shenzhou guoguangshe, vol. 4, pp. 542–5.

——. 1963. "Lun Baihua wei weixin zhi ben" 論白話為維新之本 (On the vernacular as the basis for reform), *Jindaishi ziliao* 2, pp. 120, 123.

Ramsey, Robert. 1991. "The Polysemy of the Term *Kokugo*", *Sino-Platonic Papers* 27 (August 31, 1991), p. 37–47.

Rawski, Evelyn Sakakida. 1979. *Education and Popular Literacy in Ch'ing China.* Ann Arbor: University of Michigan Press.

Riftin, Boris L'vovic. 1970. *Istoriceskaja epopeja i fol'klornaja tradicia v kitae.* Moscow: Nauka.

Ryan, Marleigh G. (tr. and comm.). 1967. *Japan's First Modern Novel: Ukigumo of Futabatei Shimei.* New York: Columbia University Press.

San Ai 三愛 (Chen Duxiu 陳獨秀). 1904. "Guoyu jiaoyu" 國語教育 (Education in the national language), *Anhui suhuabao* 3 (March 15, 1904).

Shi He 史和 et al. (eds.). 1991. *Zhongguo jindai baokan minglu* 中國近代報刊名錄 (A title list of China's modern periodicals). Fuzhou: Fujian remin chubanshe.

Shu Xincheng 舒新城. 1985. *Zhongguo jindai jiaoyushi ziliao* 中國近代教育史資料 (Source material on the history of education in China). 3 vols. Beijing: Renmin jiaoyu chubanshe.

Tang Zhijun 湯志鈞. 1990. "Zhang Taiyan yu baihuawen" 章太炎與白話文 (Zhang Taiyan and vernacular writing), *Jindai shi yanjiu* 2, pp. 112–9.

Twine, Nanette. 1978. "The Genbunitchi Movement: Its Origin, Development and Conclusion", *Monumenta Nipponica* 33.3, pp. 333–56.

——. 1988. "Standardizing Written Japanese: a Factor in Modernization", *Monumenta Nipponica* 43.4, pp. 425–54.

Wang Kangnian 汪康年 et al. 1953. "Mengxue Huibao jianzhang" 蒙學會報簡章 (Short regulations for the Mengxue hui and the Mengxue bao), in: Zhongguo shixuehui 中國史學會 (ed.). *Wuxu bianfa* 戊戌變法 (The reform in 1898). 4 vols. Shanghai: Shenzhou Guoguangshe, vol. 4, pp. 540–42.

Wang Rongwen 王榮文 (ed.). 1994. *Hu Shi zuopin ji* 胡適作品集 (Collected works of Hu Shi). 37 vols. Taibei: Yuanliu chuban gongsi.

Xu Yunjia 徐運嘉 and Yang Pingping 楊萍萍. 1989. "Qingmo Hangzhou de san zhong baozhi—'Jingshi bao', 'Hangbao'. 'Hangzhou baihuabao'"清末杭州的三種報紙捃 — 經世報，杭報，杭州白話報 (Three Hangzhou newspapers in Late Qing–*Jingshibao, Hangbao* and the *Hangzhou baihuabao*), *Xinwen yanjiu ziliao* 47, pp. 132–9.

Yamamoto Masahide 山本正秀. 1981. *Genbunitchi no rekishi ronkō* 言文一致の歷史論考 (A historical discussion of the movement for the unification of the spoken und written languages). Tokyo: Ōfūsha.

Yariv-Laor, Lihi. 1999. "Linguistic Aspects of Translating the Bible into Chinese", in: Irene Eber (ed.). *Bible in China: The Literary and Intellectual Impact.* Nettetal: Steyler, pp. 101–122.

Yen, Y. K. 1892. "The Shanghai Vernacular", *The Chinese Recorder* 22.8, pp. 386–88.

Zetzsche, Jost. 1999. "The Work of Lifetimes: Why the Union Version Took Nearly Three Decades to Complete", in: Irene Eber (ed.). *Bible in China: The Literary and Intellectual Impact.* Nettetal: Steyler Verlag, pp. 77–100.

Zhang Binglin 章炳麟. 1985. "Bo Kang Youwei lun geming shu" 駁康有為論革命書 (A rejection of Kang Youwei's letter on revolution), in: id. *Zhang Taiyan quanji* 張太炎全集 (Complete works of Zhang Taiyan [i.e. Zhang Binglin]). 6 vols. Shanghai: Renmin chubanshe, vol. 4, pp. 173–84.

ELISABETH KASKE

Zhang Jinglu 張靜盧 (ed.). 1953. *Zhongguo jindai chuban shiliao chubian* 中國近代出版史料初編 (Source material on the history of modern publishing in China, vol. 1). Shanghai: Qunlian shushe.

Zhang Zhigong 張志公 . 1962. *Chuantong yuwen jiaoyu chutan* 傳統語文教育初探 (Preliminary investigations of traditional language and literature teaching). Shanghai: Jiaoyu chubanshe.

Zhongguo jindai qikan bianmu huilu 中國近代期刊編目彙錄 (Index to Chinese journals of the modern times). 1980–1984. Edited by Shanghai Tushuguan 上海圖書館 . 5 vols. Shanghai: Shanghai renmin chubanshe.

Zhu Chuanyu 朱傳譽 . 1985. *Baoren, baoshi, baoxue* 報人，報史，報學 (Journalists, history of journalism, journalism). Taibei: Taiwan shangwu yinshuguan.

MICHAEL C. LAZICH

THE DIFFUSION OF USEFUL KNOWLEDGE IN CHINA: THE CANTON ERA INFORMATION STRATEGY

In the years preceding the Opium War, relations between Westerners and Chinese deteriorated rapidly as tensions escalated over the opium trade and as Westerners grew increasingly frustrated with the 'Canton system' of trade. Wary of the growing possibility of military confrontation, a small group of prominent missionaries and merchants sought to devise a new strategy to break down the cultural barriers that they believed were obstructing more honorable and effective communications. They seized upon the idea of transmitting Western scientific, technological, and cultural information to the Chinese in the hope that it would impress them sufficiently with the achievements of the West to induce them to open more positive and productive exchanges with the foreign 'barbarians.' To achieve this end, the men formally established the "Society for the Diffusion of Useful Knowledge in China" (SDUKC) in November 1834.

According to its founders, the objective of the SDUKC was

> by all means in its power, to prepare and publish, in a cheap form, plain and easy treatises in the Chinese language, on such branches of useful knowledge as are suited to the existing state and condition of the Chinese empire.[1]

During the few years of its brief existence, the SDUKC did its best to live up to this promise, publishing a variety of works in Chinese that presented an impressive range of topics and information. Included among these was the *Dongxi yangkao meiyue tongjizhuan* 東西洋考每月統計傳 (East-West Examiner and Monthly Recorder), a periodical that contained articles on subjects such as Western technology, natural science, and world history and geography. Modeled upon a similarly entitled periodical published several years earlier by the Prussian missionary Karl Gützlaff (1803–1851), this work epitomized the philosophy and goals of the SDUKC.

---

[1] "Minutes of the SDUKC", published in the *Chinese Repository* [hereafter *CR*], vol. 3 (Dec. 1834), p. 380. The *CR* was a well-known journal of sinology that Bridgman had begun publishing in Canton in 1832.

While the information strategy of the SDUKC did not succeed in fore-stalling the violence of the Opium War, it did provide a valuable introduction for many Chinese to the history and accomplishments of the Western foreigners they were increasingly forced to contend with. This paper traces the events and analyzes the thinking that led to the adoption of an information strategy by the SDUKC. It also examines the style and contents of the *Dongxi yangkao meiyue tongjizhuan*, the society's most interesting and representative publication.

1. THE LORD NAPIER INCIDENT AND PRINTING IN CHINESE BY WESTERNERS

Following the suspension of the British East India Company's monopoly of English trade in China in 1833, Westerners doing busi-ness in Canton held high hopes for a favorable readjustment of Sino-foreign relations. Since the mid-eighteenth century, Western trade with the Chinese had been tightly regulated under the Canton system which, among other things, channeled all commercial activity and official communications through the Cohong appointees of the Qing government in the port of Canton. While this system of 'managing the barbarians' served the imperatives of the imperial government ade-quately enough, foreign traders had grown increasingly frustrated with the constraints and corruption of the system and had long demanded an expansion of commercial and diplomatic relations. Therefore, in the summer of 1834, shortly after the revocation of the Company monopoly by the British government, Lord William John Napier (1786–1834) was sent to Canton as the newly designated Chief Superintendent of British Trade to attempt to negotiate a more satisfactory set of arrangements with Chinese officials.

Merchants were not the only Westerners residing in China in 1834 that desired major reforms in the Canton system. Since 1807, Robert Morrison (1782–1834) of the London Missionary Society had also been attempting to pry open the doors of the 'Middle Kingdom' for the sake of winning the Chinese masses to the ranks of Christianity. In 1830, he was joined in his efforts by E. C. Bridgman (1801–1861) of the American Board of Commissioners for Foreign Missions. Over the next couple of years, the budding Protestant mission was further reinforced by the arrival of the renowned Prussian missionary Karl Gützlaff (1803–1849) and another representative of the American

Board, Samuel Wells Williams (1812–1884). And while by 1834 the number of Protestant missionaries in Canton had still only grown to about a half dozen souls, they exercised a great influence over the opinions and affairs of the residents of the foreign factories and were among the most vocal proponents of major reform in the existing system of Sino-foreign relations.

Unfortunately, Lord Napier's mission was an unmitigated failure. Soon after arriving in Canton he made a brash attempt to contact the governor of Canton, Lu Kun 盧坤, by delivering a letter directly to the city gates. This was an explicit violation of Chinese regulations regarding official communications, and Lu Kun reacted angrily by expelling Napier from Canton and suspending British trading rights. As tensions escalated, Napier took his argument to the Chinese people by posting a public statement in Chinese that blamed the "ignorance and obstinacy" of the Chinese governor for the current disturbance and insisted that the British intended "to trade with China on principles of mutual benefit" and would continue to pursue this end until they gained this "point of equal importance to both countries."[2] To demonstrate his resolve, Napier ordered the British frigates Andromache and Imogene up the Canton River as far as Whampoa. If the Chinese failed to respond more positively to his demands, he was prepared to press the issue with military force.

But Lord Napier would not live long enough to carry out his threat, for he became desperately ill with fever and passed away in Macao on October 11, 1834. Tragically, Robert Morrison, who had befriended Napier and had offered to serve as his translator, also died earlier that summer after a rainy, night-time journey upriver from his home in Macao to join the British Superintendent in Canton. Thus, in the end, Napier's mission had not only failed to achieve its original objective of readjusting relations with the Chinese, but had robbed the missionaries of their most experienced member and had intensified the suspicion and hostility of Chinese officials towards the Western residents of Canton.

---

[2] Cited by Samuel Wells Williams. 1965 [1847]. *The Middle Kingdom. A Survey of Geography, Government, Education, Social Life, Arts, Religion, etc., of the Chinese Empire and Its Inhabitants*. 2 vols. Taibei: Ch'engwen, p. 473.

2. ORIGINS OF THE INFORMATION STRATEGY

With the authorities now on the alert for what they considered heterodox or seditious publications by the foreigners, Bridgman and the others could no longer print religious tracts in Chinese as they had been
doing in the shop operated by their devoted convert Liang Ahfa 梁阿
發 (1789–1855), nor could they as openly or easily distribute such
materials among the residents of Canton. In fact, a public decree
issued by the "Chief Magistrate of Nanhae" ordered the seizure and
destruction of all the "evil and obscene books of the foreign barbarians," threatening that any Chinese printers found assisting the missionaries would be "immediately seized and punished with severity."[3]

The new restrictions imposed by the Chinese forced the missionaries to search for alternatives to their former evangelical strategy. Prior
to this unfortunate episode, the emphasis had been on the printing and
distribution of materials such as Liang Ahfa's famed *Good Words to
Admonish the Age* (勸世良言 *Quanshi liangyan*).[4] This activity had
been generously supported by the various Bible and tract societies in
England and America.[5] And although there were regulations of the
Chinese government that prohibited this, they were laxly enforced.
Distributing these materials to the examination candidates who peri-
odically gathered in Canton proved an effective way of conveying
their message to the most literate segment of Chinese society, who
would then take the materials to their homes in the Chinese interior. In
April 1834, E. C. Bridgman had proudly informed the American Tract
Society of the success of Gützlaff and Liang Ahfa in handing out
Christian publications in the area around Canton.[6] But after the Lord
Napier incident, Bridgman was constrained to report that "it is proba-

---

[3] This edict was translated by Bridgman and J. R. Morrison (son of Robert) and
distributed in a circular letter dated Jan. 20, 1835, *Papers of the American Board of
Commissioners for Foreign Missions* [hereafter *ABCFM*], reel 256. The edict issued
by "Chief Magistrate Hwang" was announced August 30, 1834.

[4] Liang Ahfa 梁阿發 . 1832. *Quanshi liangyan* 勸世良言 (Good words to admonish the age). Canton: Christian Union in China.

[5] These included the American Bible Society, the British and Foreign Bible Society, and the American Tract Society.

[6] Bridgman to the American Tract Society, Canton, April 14, 1834, *ABCFM*, reel
256.

ble that a year or two will lapse, before Afah, or any one else, will be able to resume the distribution of books in this place."[7]

To Bridgman, who following Morrison's death became the senior member of the Protestant mission in China, the Lord Napier incident proved how the lack of mutual understanding and communication continued to blight relations between Westerners and the Chinese. The Chinese, of course, were seen to harbor most of the blame for this, for their lack of knowledge of the world outside of China had led them to view foreigners with contempt and to refuse to accept them on equal terms. In Bridgman's view, it was this Chinese pride, born of ignorance, that prevented them from reforming their system of relations with the Western nations and kept them deprived of the wonders and benefits of the new age.

Bridgman, along with most evangelical Protestants of the early nineteenth century, was convinced that the world was on the eve of the great Christian Millennium of universal peace and prosperity as prophesied in the Bible. The unprecedented expansion of knowledge around the world and the rapid improvement in the human condition witnessed in the West seemed to herald the imminent arrival of this 'postmillennial' new world order.[8] This faith in the power of human knowledge—including technical and scientific knowledge—led Bridgman to believe that China's troubling backwardness was due to the reluctance of the Chinese to look beyond the sphere of their traditional cultural and political boundaries. As Bridgman had written a year earlier in the *Chinese Repository*:

> This whole nation is in a profound sleep, and while she is dreaming of greatness and glory, she is borne backward by a strong and rapid tide of influence; and if the nation be not speedily roused, who can tell where her retrogression will end? ... The gradual decline of this empire is owing, in no small degree, to its retrogression in knowledge. The Chinese have schools and high literary titles in great numbers, and there are many inducements to learn. Still, though many do learn, knowledge is not increased.[9]

---

[7] Bridgman to Anderson, Canton, Jan. 20, 1935, ibid.

[8] This postmillennial interpretation of biblical prophecy suggested that Christ would return to judge the world after a thousand year era of universal peace. This vision differed dramatically with the 'premillennialist' interpretation of the late nineteenth century popularized by fundamentalists in which Christ would return and judge the world prior to inaugurating the Millennium of peace and prosperity.

[9] E. C. Bridgman. 1833. "Introductory Remarks", *CR*, vol. 2 (May 1833), p. 4.

On the basis of this assumption, Bridgman concluded that the most
effective way to transform the Chinese and thus improve Sino-foreign
relations was to "learn as accurately as possible their true condition;
to exhibit it to themselves; and then to put within their reach the
means of improvement."[10] This meant, first of all, to study the Chinese language in order to initiate a badly needed "interchange of
knowledge" and engage the Chinese in rational argument. Bridgman
argued that in order to convince the Chinese of the benefits to be
gained from Western science and religion, it would be necessary to
become thoroughly familiar with their various modes of thought and
expression and better acquainted with their literary and philosophical
heritage. Only then could the Western merchant, diplomat, and missionary hope to "couch his thoughts in such language as may not only
be easily and clearly understood, but as shall gain for him a patient
and attentive hearing."[11] Stressing the importance of transmitting new
ideas in a pleasing and familiar idiom, Bridgman wrote:

> If new and interesting thoughts, pure and elevated sentiments, and
> above all the sublime truths of divine revelation are rightly exhibited in
> a native costume, then they may have a charm and a power which will
> rouse the mind, sway the passions, correct the judgment, and eventu-
> ally work a mental and moral revolution throughout the empire.[12]

In short, Bridgman believed that a "diffusion of knowledge", initiated
by Westerners in China would have the power to

> effectively reach the morals and the religion of the nation; and purify
> the sources of authority, ... would save the empire from destruction,
> and place it in its proper rank among the nations.[13]

Far preferable to a military conquest, which would inevitably result in
the vast destruction of life and property, the advantage obtained from
a diffusion of knowledge would represent

> a conquest of principles, the triumph of right reason, the victory of
> truth, ... will be glorious in its results, and carry the blessings of peace,
> and the bright hopes of immortality to the multitudes of this nation.[14]

---

[10] Ibid.
[11] Ibid.
[12] E. C. Bridgman. 1834. "The Chinese Language", *CR*, vol. 3 (May 1934), p. 3.
[13] Ibid., p. 10.
[14] Ibid.

According to Bridgman, those things worthy of communicating to the Chinese included that whole range of knowledge that he saw as conducive to the progress of human civilization, such as those principles of science, art, technology, and government that had been disseminated throughout Europe since the advent of the printing press and were key to the "march of improvement"[15] witnessed in those nations.

Actually, Bridgman's views were not entirely unprecedented, for William Milne, acting upon similar assumptions, had earlier transmitted some Western scientific, geographical, and historical knowledge to the Chinese in his *Cha shisu meiyue tongjizhuan* 察世俗每月統計傳 or *Chinese Monthly Magazine* as it was known to the missionaries.[16] Although primarily religious in content, Milne's periodical had occasionally included articles that provided his readers with some basic information about the nations of the West and their achievements.[17] Some of these were contributed by Robert Morrison and another representative of the London Missionary Society, W. H. Medhurst (1796–1857), who, along with Milne, constituted the tiny number of English-speaking Westerners able to compose such articles at that time.[18]

3. KARL GÜTZLAFF'S *DONGXI YANGKAO MEIYUE TONGJIZHUAN*

Beginning in the summer of 1833, Karl Gützlaff, who had just taken up residence in Canton, expanded upon Milne's pioneering effort with his publication of the *Dongxi yangkao meiyue tongjizhuan* 東西洋考每月統計傳 (East-West Examiner and Monthly Recorder). Gützlaff had

---

[15] Ibid.

[16] William Milne was a representative of the London Missionary Society sent to join Morrison in Canton in 1813. Milne spent only six months with Morrison however, after which he toured the immigrant Chinese communities of Batavia, Malacca, and Penang searching for a more secure and promising base for missionary operations. He finally established a mission at Malacca where he published his *Chinese Monthly Magazine*, sporadically, from 1815–1821.

[17] Cf. Alexander Wylie. 1967 [1867]. *Memorials of Protestant Missionaries: Giving a List of Their Publications, and Obituary Notices of the Deceased, with Copious Indexes*. Shanghai: American Presbyterian Mission Press. Reprint: Taibei: Ch'eng-wen, p. 20.

[18] W. H. Medhurst was yet another among the earliest missionaries to the Chinese appointed by the London Missionary Society. Arriving in Malacca in June 1817, he resided in various Chinese settlements throughout Southeast Asia until relocating to Canton in 1835.

intended to use this periodical to convey an awareness of the power
and achievements of the Western nations to Chinese readers, hoping
thereby to dispel what he saw as their delusions of cultural superiority. Proclaiming his intentions in an article written for the *Chinese
Repository*, Gützlaff wrote:

> While civilization is making rapid progress over ignorance and error in
> almost all other portions of the globe .... The Chinese alone remain sta-
> tionary, as they have been for ages past. Notwithstanding our long
> intercourse with them, they still profess to be first among the nations of
> the earth, and regard all others as "barbarians". ... This monthly peri-
> odical ... is published with a view to counteract these high and exclu-
> sive notions, by making the Chinese acquainted with our arts, sciences,
> and principles. It will not treat of politics, nor tend to exasperate their
> minds by harsh language upon any subject. There is a more excellent
> way to show we are not indeed "barbarians"; and the Editor prefers the
> method of exhibiting the facts, to convince the Chinese that they still
> have much to learn.[19]

Gützlaff attempted to attract readers to his new publication by embel-
lishing its cover with a provocative maxim that mimicked the wording
and style of the Confucian classics. These would normally emphasize
the value of comprehensive learning or encourage a more accommodating attitude towards foreigners. The cover of one issue declared,
for example, that

> 儒者博學而不窮。篤行而不倦
> the [true] scholar studies widely with inexhaustible diligence and ear-
> nestly perseveres without tiring.[20]

Yet another included the pronouncement that

> 四海為家萬姓為子
> all within the four seas [the world] are one family, and the ten thousand
> surnames [all the people of the world] are the children.[21]

Gützlaff also listed the contents of each issue on the front cover, providing additional inducement to those Chinese inquisitive enough to

---

[19] Karl Gützlaff. 1833. "Prospectus for a Chinese Magazine", *CR*, vol. 2 (1833), p.
187.
[20] *Dongxi yangkao meiyue tongjizhuan* 東西洋考每月統計傳 [hereafter *DXYK*],
11: cover (1833).
[21] *DXYK*, 3: cover (1834).

wish to see a map of Russia or examine a chart of the northern con-
stellations conceived of by Westerners.[22]

Although Gützlaff's periodical focused primarily on non-religious
topics, some articles and essays were designed to convey Christian
principles as well, particularly those that might have the effect of
broadening the Chinese world view. The introduction to the first
issue, for example, explained how the peoples of the earth shared a
common ancestor, "the nations of the earth being as the limbs of one
body sharing the same lifeblood."[23] Such declarations were said to
correspond with the teachings of the sages of old, who said that
"within the four seas all men are brothers."[24] Thus linking his ideas
with the concepts and terminology of the ancient Confucian classics,
Gützlaff affirmed that the entire world of humanity was ruled over by
God (*Shangdi* 上帝), "whose radiance was shed on all men and all
things and who was the source of all that was good, despite the fact
that he could not be heard or seen."[25]

Gützlaff encouraged his readers to open their minds to foreign
knowledge by reminding them of Confucius' injunction to "listen
widely, select what is good and abide by it."[26] After all, Gützlaff
insisted, did not Confucius emphasize the value of learning from others? Did he not say: "when I walk along with two others, they may
serve me as my teachers. I will select their good qualities and follow
them, their bad qualities and avoid them."[27] The Chinese, Gützlaff
thus implied, should strive to be more patient and respectful when
dealing with foreigners. As Confucius responded to Fan Chi 樊遲
when asked about benevolence (*ren* 仁):

> It is, in retirement, to be sedately grave; in the management of business,
> to be reverently attentive; in intercourse with others, to be strictly sin-
> cere. Though a man go among rude, uncultivated tribes, these qualities
> may not be neglected.[28]

Throughout the course of its publication, from mid-1833 through mid-
1834, Gützlaff's periodical indeed introduced Chinese readers to a

---

[22] *DXYK*, 11: cover (1833); 12: cover (1833).
[23] *DXYK*, 6: 2b (1833).
[24] Ibid.
[25] Ibid.
[26] *DXYK*, 6: 1b (1833)
[27] Ibid.
[28] Ibid. Original quotation from *Analects* 20:19.

broad range of knowledge about the history and achievements of the Western world. Among the regular features of his publication was a column entitled "Comparative Chronology of East and West" (*Dongxi shiji hehe* 東西世紀和合). This series appears to have been based upon articles that W. H. Medhurst had written in Chinese while serving in Batavia and Malacca. In general, this series highlighted the richness and antiquity of the Western civilization by correlating the history of China with that of the West, beginning with the biblical story of creation. Describing his intentions in an article published in the *Missionary Herald*, Medhurst explained:

> I have been led to draw up this work from the consideration of the practice of the Chinese, in boasting, so often as they do, of their high antiquity, looking with contempt on the comparatively modern dates of Europeans, and throwing out the hint, that we have no records of a date older than the Christian era. I have, therefore, endeavored, by a regular exhibition of dates, and by the production of incidents connected with every remarkable period, to show them that we have a system of chronology that can be depended on, more authentic and ancient than their own ....[29]

Medhurst's labors in this regard were similar to those undertaken by the Catholic "figurists" of the late sixteenth and early seventeenth centuries who took the historical chronologies of the Chinese and compared them to Biblical chronologies in order to illustrate the essential unity of Scriptural and world history.[30] One portion of Medhurst's series, entitled "The Aftermath of the Great Flood" (*Hongshui houji* 洪水後記), attempted to illustrate how the legend of China's ancient sage-kings—who had also contended with the effects of a great flood— paralleled the story of Noah in the Old Testament.[31] By thus correlating the legend of Yao, Shun, and Yu told in the Confucian classics with the stories contained in the Book of Genesis, the author hoped to demonstrate that the founders of Chinese civilization were actually the direct descendants of Noah.

Another section of Gützlaff's periodical was regularly devoted to geography (*dili* 地理), which covered not only the lands and peoples

---

[29] Letter of Medhurst, July 1828, *Missionary Herald* (January 1829), p. 193.

[30] See Zhuo Xinping 卓心平 . 1996. *"Suoyinpai yu zhongxi wenhua rentong"* 索隱派與中西文化認同 (The Figurists and the acknowledgement of similarities in Chinese and Western cultures). Unpublished paper presented at "International Symposium on the History of Christianity in China", Hong Kong (October 1996).

[31] *DXYK*, 7: 16a–19b (1833).

of Europe, but also Africa, the Middle East, and even those regions adjacent to the Qing empire that the Chinese still only vaguely understood. One issue, for example, included a map of Southeast Asia and the Southern Sea, with designations in Chinese of the various geographic features, kingdoms, and cities of that region.[32] Yet another issue contained a map of Russia, an area that the Chinese would likewise have had a strong interest in learning more about.[33]

Articles on natural science printed in Gützlaff's *Dongxi yangkao* provided scientific explanations of phenomena such as solar and lunar eclipses and the changing of the seasons.[34] Essays on Western technology included, for example, a diagram and an explanation of the principles behind the operation of a steam engine.[35] Gützlaff's periodical also featured a brief column on current events (*xinwen* 新聞), which provided information on recent developments both inside and outside of China. Occasionally, he would also print a table of commodity prices which listed the current value of silk, tea, foodstuffs and other goods traded in the markets of Canton. In short, Gützlaff's periodical provided his Chinese readers with broad insights into Western civilization while furnishing them with a range of valuable information.

4. THE SOCIETY FOR THE DIFFUSION OF USEFUL KNOWLEDGE IN CHINA

Unfortunately, following the Lord Napier incident, Gützlaff's periodical was forced to discontinue as the Chinese authorities enforced their prohibitions against foreign publications more rigorously. The *Chinese Repository* nevertheless continued to advocate the need for a publication such as Gützlaff's magazine as the missionaries sought desperately for means to convey their message of modern progress and religious salvation to the Chinese. In fact, by November 1834, the aim of conveying scientific and practical knowledge to the Chinese found new life as the missionaries residing in Canton joined with a

---

[32] "Dong nanyang ya nanyang tu" 東南洋亞南洋圖 (Map of the East Asian South Sea), *DXYK*, 6: foldout (1833).

[33] *DXYK*, 11: foldout (1833).

[34] *DXYK*, 8: 22b–23a (1833); 3: 35a–36a (1834).

[35] *DXYK*, 5: 8a–9a (1835).

few interested merchants for the purpose of forming a "Society for the Diffusion of Useful Knowledge in China".[36]

The committee appointed to oversee the formation of the new Society consisted of James Matheson, D. W. C. Olyphant (d. 1851), William S. Wetmore, James Innes, and Thomas Fox, with Bridgman and Gützlaff acting as the "Chinese secretaries" and J. R. Morrison the English secretary.[37] Stating their objectives in the *Chinese Repository*, the members declared:

> In our days, many nations have begun the race for improvement; and are now moving onward in swift career, their course being constantly made more luminous by the light of science, and more rapid by the force of truth. This has resulted from the *diffusion of useful knowledge* among them. But no influence of this kind has yet reached the 'central nation', and China still stands stationary, shielding herself from the contaminating influence of barbarians. While, therefore, we must ascribe it chiefly to the apathy, the national pride, and the ignorance of the Chinese, that they have not joined the other nations in the march of intellect; we are by no means prepared to excuse ourselves from the guilt of indifference and inactivity in not having placed within their reach the means of improvement, and roused their sleeping energies to inquiries after knowledge.[38]

The undertaking was seen as a favorable alternative to military engagement where, instead of real weaponry, the "intellectual artillery" of knowledge would smash to pieces those cultural barriers that prevented China from being brought "into an alliance with the civilized nations of the earth."[39] To promote this end, the SDUKC intended

> by all means in its power, to prepare and publish, in a cheap form, plain and easy treatises in the Chinese language, on such branches of useful knowledge as are suited to the existing state and condition of the Chinese empire.[40]

---

[36] The name and concept for this organization came from the "Society for the Diffusion of Useful Knowledge" in existence at that time in England. Its effort to vastly increase the availability of useful information by lowering the cost of printed works was heartily approved of by the foreign community in Canton. See *CR* (October 1833), p. 329.

[37] From the minutes of the organizational meeting of the "Society for the Diffusion of Useful Knowledge" in China published in the *CR* (December 1834), p. 380.

[38] Ibid., p. 379.

[39] Ibid., p. 380.

[40] Ibid., p. 383.

By thus shifting their conflict with the Chinese to the cultural and intellectual front, the group hoped that the ensuing warfare would be of such a nature that "the victors and the vanquished will meet only to exult and rejoice together."[41]

While the objectives of the SDUKC enjoyed wide support, there were very few Westerners who were sufficiently skilled in writing Chinese to produce the kind of works that the group had in mind. Bridgman and Gützlaff were, nevertheless, more capable in this respect than anyone else on the committee—with the notable exception of J. R. Morrison—so they were assigned the responsibility of compiling the necessary materials. Both men were heavily preoccupied with other duties, however, and with the recent disturbance in Canton still fresh in the minds of the Chinese authorities, it was difficult to employ Chinese assistants. Therefore, the work of the new society was limited to reprinting a few revised editions of Gützlaff's *Dongxi yangkao* on a newly acquired lithographic press operated by the American Board missionaries.

Unfortunately, even this project had to be discontinued after Gützlaff and Edwin Stevens (1802–1837), a newly arrived American missionary, were discovered illegally journeying up the Min River (Fujian Province) in April 1835 distributing Christian books and tracts. Coming so soon after the Lord Napier incident, this venture was particularly foolhardy and, as should have been expected, stirred Chinese officials to new heights of vigilance. It was not, therefore, until the end of 1836, by which time the American Board had successfully established a facility for printing in Singapore under the management of Ira Tracy, that the SDUKC could once again risk printing materials to be distributed in the region around Canton.[42]

5. THE SDUKC'S *DONGXI YANGKAO MEIYUE TONGJIZHUAN*

The first project undertaken by the SDUKC in 1836 was the resumption of the *Dongxi yangkao meiyue tongjizhuan*. The new version of the periodical was issued the first month of 1837 and followed the same general format as that used by Gützlaff when he published it in 1833 and 1834. And while the magazine preserved its original goal of

---

[41] Ibid., p. 380.
[42] Cf. Bridgman to Anderson, Canton, September 7, 1836, *ABCFM*, reel 256.

introducing the Chinese to the history, geography, and science of the West, it now drew upon the budding linguistic talents of its contributors to give added emphasis as well to the arts and humanities with newly written articles on Western poetry, literature, and philosophy.

The cover page of each issue was similar to that used in the earlier editions and included a brief table of contents and a thought provoking maxim drawn from some widely familiar Chinese source. These maxims were intended to highlight Christian-like principles within China's own traditions, or promote the value of broad learning, or to advance the principles of benevolent government. On of the cover of one issue, for example, was printed:

> 道也者不可須臾離也
> He who possesses the Way (Dao) cannot bear to part with it for even a moment.[43]

On another was printed:

> 詩云民之所好，好之。民之所惡，惡之
> In the Odes it is said: Cherish that which the people cherish, and despise that which the people despise.[44]

In their introduction to the first issue, the editors welcomed their Chinese readers by saying:

> May God (*Shangdi* 上帝) look down upon China and upon the Han people and grant them the utmost felicity and enjoyment of goodness. May He bestow upon their hearts an awareness of the favorable blessings of the Lord of all things, ... for to God who grants us all our food and drink, we must extend out unlimited gratitude.[45]

The editors then declared that while their "feeble talents" are enough to make them "blush with shame," they hoped their readers would overlook the shortcomings of this newly produced *Dongxi yangkao*. In such characteristically Chinese fashion, the editors humbly declared that while their knowledge of history and their personal experience is not that broad, they hoped

---

[43] *DXYK*, 8: cover (1838).

[44] *DXYK*, 7: cover (1838).

[45] *DXYK*, 1: 1a (1837). None of the articles featured in the periodical included the name of the specific author, so it is difficult to determine who contributed to this or other articles included in the *DXYK*. Nevertheless, this introduction very clearly reflects the style and content of other work composed in Chinese by E. C. Bridgman.

to demonstrate the parallel development of the history of the Middle Kingdom and the outside states by fully illustrating the beauty of the historical records of ancient and recent times of both China and the outside, and thereby bring people to look up to the sages and worthies of all countries.[46]

"After all", they affirmed, "it is in learning of the history of China and the world that we are able to see that the rewarding of good and punishment of evil is the universal way of Heaven."[47]

The editors promised that the *Dongxi yangkao* would serve as a valuable source of reference on a variety of topics, containing "essays illustrating the countries of both sides of the world" and even "entering into a basic discussion of astronomy."[48] There will also be articles concerning "birds and animals, plant life, and minerals—the knowledge of which will bring great benefit." Westerners, so the editors claimed, are "clever and ingenious people who unceasingly devise new methods for doing things, and their arts and crafts are beheld in great astonishment." The people of Europe (*Ouluoba* 歐羅巴) were said to be "very rich in literature and informational periodicals which are circulated widely in innumerable quantities." The editors vowed that those things of most interest or importance from these works will be selected for translation into Chinese. The only fear is that in "the passing of such facts, the promotion of virtue may lose place to an overemphasis on the things of this world"; therefore, the editors also promised to encourage much discussion of moral issues (*shanyan* 善言), urging people to accept the "teachings of heaven" (*Tianzhijiao* 天之教) and thus "safeguard their wills and take pleasure in the Way."[49]

The editors assured their readers that the subjects selected for the *Dongxi yangkao* would be of great benefit to the people, and they asked them to "labor energetically to disseminate this knowledge widely."[50] Again using phrases designed to evoke a favorable response from their Chinese readers, the editors encouraged them to value the cultural achievements of the world outside of China, affirming that the literature of the world is "as vast as the ocean, and setting out on its surface may cause one to forget both food and sleep in the

---

[46] Ibid.
[47] Ibid.
[48] Ibid., p. 1b.
[49] Ibid.
[50] Ibid., p. 2a.

quest to cultivate one's intelligence and complete one's virtue." Cleverly combining Christian and Confucian themes, the editors wrote:

> When God created man, He endowed him with innate talents and abilities, and commanded him to nurture them; if people do not study, they will not be able to complete their virtue.[51]

The first issue of the *Dongxi yangkao* included a re-edited version of Medhurst's article entitled "The Aftermath of the Great Flood." In addition to making a connection between Noah's flood and the inundation of China during the time of the ancient sage-kings, this article related how people had once all spoken the same language until they displeased God by "building the tower of Babel that reached into the clouds."[52] For this, readers are told, their common language was confused and the various races were scattered; and "it was from this scattering of people to East Asia that the Han people owed their origins."[53] According to the author, this story demonstrated the essential kinship of the various peoples of the world which

> as water divides into separate streams, and trees divide into their various branches, although the distances separating are great, and size and density differ, in regard to their origin are all one. The races of men are, like the four limbs of the body, of the same trunk; all interconnected by the same vessels of blood; and if any suffer illness, all are mutually affected.[54]

On the basis of this article, a column entitled "Historical Records" (*Shiji* 史記) would become a regular feature of subsequent issues. Over the course of its publication, this column would present a variety of articles on the history of the world outside of China, providing many Chinese readers with their first glimpse at the richness and antiquity of the civilizations of Europe and the Middle East. Among these were discussions of Western classical civilization in articles with titles such as "The Ancient History of the West" (*Xiguo gushi* 西國古史) and "A Brief History of Greece" (*Xilaguo shilüe* 希臘國史略).[55] Other articles highlighted some of the more recent historical achievements of Westerners, such as "The Search for New Lands by

---

[51] Ibid.

[52] Walter Medhurst. 1837. "Hongshui houji" 洪水後紀 (The aftermath of the Great Flood), *DXYK*, 1: 4b.

[53] Ibid.

[54] Ibid.

[55] *DXYK*, 9: 7a–9b (1838); 1: 3a–7a (1838).

the Nations of Europe" (*Ouluoba lieguo zhi min xun xindi lun* 歐羅巴
列國之民尋新地論).[56] Yet others attempted to bring Chinese readers
up to date with the historical developments of their own age, as in the
presentation entitled "Affairs of the Countries of the World During
the Era of the Great Qing" (*Da Qing nianjian geguo shi* 大清年間各國
事).[57]

Naturally, this feature placed great emphasis on the biblical history
of Israel (*Yiselie* 以色烈). Indeed, most Chinese readers would have
been led to assume that the kingdom of Israel was the greatest and
most influential state of the ancient West. Articles on this subject
included such titles as "Israel Under the Rule of the Judges" (*Zhushi
zhili yiselie* 主師治理以色烈), "A Record of King Solomon"
(*Suoluomen wangji* 瑣羅門王紀), "A Record of the Jewish Kings"
(*Youtaiguo wangji* 猶太國王紀), and "The Israeli Migration to the
Nations of the West" (*Yiseliemin chulai xiguo* 以色烈民出來西國).[58]
In all of these accounts, special emphasis was given to the preeminent
role of God in both preserving and punishing the Jews. The chronology of these accounts was carefully correlated with the reigns of
ancient Chinese rulers, thereby highlighting the great antiquity of
Jewish civilization and, hence, the Judeo-Christian cultural heritage.

While many articles in the *Dongxi yangkao* attempted in this fashion to convey the religious themes that were of importance to the missionaries, the publication also included, as its editors had promised, a
wide variety of articles on science, technology, economics, politics,
and literature. Sections devoted to geography, for example, provided
an abundance of information on the various countries and peoples of
the world outside of China. Naturally, particular emphasis was
accorded to Europe, with separate articles devoted to the various
countries such as Sweden (*Ruidian* 瑞典), Portugal (*Putaoyaguo* 葡萄
牙國), Russia (*Eluosiguo* 峨羅斯國), and Ireland (*Erlandi* 耳蘭地).[59]
These articles provided basic information on the history, rulers, capital cities, and products of each country along with important details

---

[56] *DXYK*, 5: 8a–9a (1837).

[57] Ibid.; 7: 89a–92a (1837).

[58] *DXYK*, 10: 123a–126a (1838); 5: 83b–85b (1838); 8: 3b–6a (1838); 5: 4a–6a
(1837).

[59] *DXYK*, 4: 71a–74b (1838); 8: 3b–6a (1837); 9: 120a–124a (1837); 9: 127a–b
(1837).

regarding their domestic politics and present role in the international community.

The *Dongxi yangkao* also included separate articles on some of the more progressive social and political institutions of the West, particularly those that could furnish an enlightening model for the Chinese. One such presentation, for example, provided a glowing account of "England's Joint Assembly" (*Yingjiliguo zhenggonghui* 英吉利國政共會), or Parliament.[60] Yet another described the public management and services of Western hospitals (*Yiyuan* 醫院).[61] The editors also printed essays that attacked political despotism, such as one entitled "The Difference Between Kingship and Despotism" (*Wangba yidao* 王霸異道), or denounced the torture of criminals, as in the article "Excessively Cruel Punishments Should Not be Used in Prisons" (*Lun jiannei buying guoyu kuxing* 論監內不應過於苦刑).[62] These presentations were obviously intended to promote social and political reform in China by introducing humanitarian alternatives to some of the crueler customs and practices of the Chinese.

Articles on science and technology printed in the *Dongxi yangkao* frequently explained natural phenomena that would have been largely a mystery to Chinese readers. A regularly featured column on astronomy (*tianwen* 天文), for example, included such titles as "An Astronomical Account of [Seasonal] Changes in the Length of the Day" (*Tianwen richangduan* 天文日長短), "The Physical Geography of the Moon" (*Yuemian* 月面), and "The Universe [Solar System]" (*Yuzhou* 宇宙).[63] Climatic and geological phenomenon were also common topics of discussion, with brief scientific explanations of such things as "Dew, Hail, Frost, and Snow" (*Lu bao xiang xue* 露雹霜雪), "Earthquakes" (*Dizhen* 地震), and "Volcanos" (*Huoshan* 火山).[64] There were also naturalist descriptions of exotic animals that many Chinese readers would have found intriguing, such as lions (*shizi* 獅子), whales (*jingyu* 鯨魚), ostriches (*tuoniao* 鴕鳥), and jackals (*chai* 豺).[65] Human anatomy was yet another subject addressed by the editors, with one issue, for example, presenting an article entitled "A

---

[60] *DXYK*, 4: 63a–65b (1838).

[61] *DXYK*, 8: 8b–9b (1838).

[62] *DXYK*, 8: 103a–105b (1837); 5: 94b–96b (1838).

[63] *DXYK*, 1: 8a–b (1837); 8: 110a–112a (1837); 4: 8a–9a (1837).

[64] *DXYK*, 10: 140a–141b (1837); 3: 57a–b (1838); 6: 9a–b (1837).

[65] *DXYK*, 3: 7b–8a (1837); 11: 156a–b (1837); 8: 109a (1837); 8: 109a–b (1837).

Look at the Study of Bones and Joints [Orthopedics]" (*Chashi gujiezhixue* 察視骨節之學).[66] Intending to spark a greater appreciation for Western technology, the editors also included articles on such things as underwater diving gear (*shuinei jianglong* 水內匠籠) and steam locomotion (*huozhengche* 火蒸車).[67]

Some of the more interesting and nicely written presentations in the *Dongxi yangkao* focused on literature and philosophy. Like the articles on science and technology, these were designed to instill an appreciation for the refinement and accomplishments of Western civilization by appealing to the cultural sentiments and natural curiosity of the Chinese. In the beginning of one essay on the history of poetry in the West, for example, the author noted that "all people embody soul and spirit, and if one is not nourished by literature and poetry, even though one has food and clothing, the soul suffers deprivation."[68]

In this same article, the author explained how the countries of Europe have an ancient and flourishing poetic tradition, "verses from which are recited around the world." The Han people, however, were said to

> recite only the great poets of their own heritage, and do not chant verses of European poetry; this because they imagine that foreigners have no literature or poetry, and thus see no value in translating their works.[69]

Intent to dispel this notion, the author explained how there is, in fact, a wide variety of poetic forms in the West, and that the art has a long tradition extending back to ancient times. Pointing to Homer (*Hema* 和馬) and Milton (*Militun* 米里屯) as two outstanding poets of the West, the author remarked how "in terms of profundity their works are as broad and deep as the Way, and widely encompassing in their meaning."[70]

Very few issues of the *Dongxi yangkao* failed to include some criticism of China's reluctance to appreciate the remarkable achievements of the West. In an article entitled "The Classics" (*Jingshu* 經書), the author remarked that "although the classical works of China have

---

[66] *DXYK*, 7: 12b–13a (1838).

[67] *DXYK*, 6: 7b–8a (1837); 3: 10b–11b (1837).

[68] *DXYK*, 1: 9a (1837).

[69] Ibid., p. 10a.

[70] Ibid..

been translated into Western languages for all to read, China has not yet translated any of the Western classics."[71] This was attributed to the fact that China has always looked down upon the literary works of foreigners; this despite the fact that "each of the various countries has its own books and poetry capable of exciting respect and admiration for their intelligence and talent."[72]

The classical tradition of the West, the reader was told, began in ancient Greece, as early as the Zhou dynasty reign of King Gong (946–943 BC) and King Yi (943–909 BC). After Greek civilization declined, the tradition was carried on by the eminent poets of Rome, such as Vergil (*Wei'erzhi* 味耳治) and Horace (*Helashi* 和喇士), and by the great historians such as Livy (*Liwei* 利味) and Tacitus (*Daxiduo* 大西多).[73] Readers were also informed that, in addition to these great literary classics, the Sacred Scriptures (*Shengshu* 聖書), which represented the teachings of God and are regarded as the "expressions of His sacred will for all creatures," have been esteemed by Westerners throughout the ages.[74]

Articles devoted to trade and economics were also featured regularly in the *Dongxi yangkao*. A column entitled "Trade" (*Maoyi* 貿易),[75] for example, reported recent changes and developments in the commercial activities of the foreign merchants operating in Canton. This column would frequently lament the shortcomings of the Canton system or criticize the lawlessness and corruption that was beginning to create serious tensions between the Chinese and their foreign trading partners. The editors' promotion of *laissez faire* commerce was also evident in articles such as "Money" (*Yinqian* 銀錢),[76] which offered an explanation of the Western banking system and business practices.

The final section of the *Dongxi yangkao* was normally devoted to news of recent events. This feature consisted of a series of short reports on subjects ranging from recent typhoons along the China

---

[71] *DXYK*, 2: 8b (1837). Jesuit translations of Chinese literature into Latin began to enter Europe in the late sixteenth century. By the eighteenth century French Catholic missionaries had also translated many Chinese works into French.

[72] Ibid. This view, of course, overlooks China's historical admiration for and translation of Buddhist sūtras obtained from India.

[73] Ibid., p. 9a.

[74] Ibid.

[75] This column appears first in *DXYK*, vol. 1 (1838).

[76] *DXYK*, 7: 14a–15a (1838).

coast to European politics. These reports emphasized the interrelationship of events around the globe in a manner that revealed the mil-
lenarian thinking of Protestant Evangelicals in the mid-nineteenth
century. The first issue of 1837, for example, described how the previous year had been marked by deadly thunderstorms and torrential
rains in both China and England, demonstrating the omnipotence and
wrath of God in punishing the evil and the unbelieving.[77] The next
two reports explained the recent political turmoils in France (*Falanxi*
法蘭西) and Spain (*Xibanya* 西班牙) and how the lawlessness and
disorder created by the struggle for political power in these predominantly Catholic states was undermining their societies.[78] Yet another
report described the recent jailing and humiliation of an English
envoy by the prime minister of Turkey (*Tuerji* 土耳基).[79] According
to this report, such an insult was sure to incite the animosity of the
British government if it were not properly redressed. Here, the editors
of the *Dongxi yangkao* obviously intended to convey an implicit
warning to the Chinese.

CONCLUSION

The *Dongxi yangkao* attempted boldly to foster a positive intercultural dialogue by transmitting basic information about the Western
world to Chinese readers. In this respect, it was a commendable contribution to the development of modern Sino-Western relations—
regardless of the religious agenda and cultural prejudices of its publishers. Although it is impossible to determine the exact extent of the
publication's circulation, there is much evidence that it was read by
many Chinese who appeared to have been greatly impressed with its
contents.[80] Indeed it served as one of the few sources of information
about the outside world at a time when Chinese officials were suddenly faced with the need to learn as much as they could about the
ways of the Western foreigners.

Suzanne Barnett has noted, for example, how Wei Yuan's 魏源
(1794–1856/57) famous geographical work, *Illustrated treatise on the*

---

[77] *DXYK*, 1: 14a (1837).

[78] Ibid., p. 14b.

[79] Ibid., p. 15a.

[80] See Fred Drake's comments on the circulation of the earlier version produced
by Gützlaff in Drake 1985, p. 100.

maritime countries (*Haiguo tuzhi* 海國圖志) was based in part on excerpts from the *Dongxi yangkao*.[81] Issues of the periodical were also among those materials presented to Xu Jiyu 徐繼畬 (1795–1873) by the American missionary David Abeel (1804–1846) prior to the compilation of that Chinese official's equally famous work, *Brief account of the maritime circuit* (*Yinghuan zhilue* 瀛環志略), printed in 1848.[82]

These works by Wei Yuan and Xu Jiyu greatly influenced the attitudes of their countrymen towards the world at large and their place within it, not to mention providing them with a vast amount of new knowledge and information. Fred Drake is not alone in noting that Chinese research into world geography, facilitated by missionary publications such as the *Dongxi yangkao*, not only belied the myth of China's supremacy in the world but also introduced ideas that ultimately helped to undermine the Confucian order.[83] As Bridgman himself noted in a review of Xu Jiyu's book published in the *Chinese Repository*:

> It will, we think, do much to destroy the conceit, and dissipate the ignorance of the rulers and scholars of China, proving to them that they do not belong to the only nation on the globe.[84]

At the very least, the *Dongxi yangkao* represented a new form of journalism to its readers, which at least one modern Chinese scholar has described as the first modern Chinese-language periodical published in China.[85]

---

[81] Suzanne Barnett. 1970. "Wei Yuan and Westerners: Notes on the Sources of the Hai-Kuo T'u-Chih", *Ch'ing-shih wen-t'i* 2.4 (November 1970), p. 8.

[82] Fred Drake provides an excellent study of this work in Fred Drake. 1975. *China Charts the World: Hsu Chi-yu and His Geography of 1848*. Cambridge, Mass.: Harvard University Press.

[83] Ibid., p. 3.

[84] E. C. Bridgman. 1851. "Universal Geography of Su Ki-yu", *CR* (April 1851), p. 193.

[85] Cai Wu 蔡武 . 1969. "Tantan Dongxi yangkao meiyue tongjizhuan: Zhongguo jingnei diyizhong xiandai zhongwen qikan" 談談東西洋考每月統記傳：中國境內第一種現代中文期刊 (*The East-West Examiner and Monthly Recorder*: the first modern Chinese periodical), *National Central Library Bulletin* (April 1969), pp. 23–46.

REFERENCES

American Board of Commissioners for Foreign Missions, Papers. Missions to China (*ABC* 16.3). Yale Divinity School Library Archives.

Barnett, Suzanne W. and John K. Fairbank (eds.). 1985. *Christianity in China: Early Protestant Missionary Writings.* Cambridge, Mass.: Harvard University Press.

Barnett, Suzanne. 1970. "Wei Yuan and Westerners: Notes on the Sources of the Hai-Kuo T'u-Chih", *Ch'ing shih wen-t'i* 2.4 (November 1970), pp. 1–20.

Broomhall, Marshall. 1927. *Robert Morrison: a Master Builder.* London: Student Christian Movement.

Cai Wu 蔡武 .1969. "Tantan Dongxi yangkao meiyue tongjizhuan: Zhongguo jingnei diyizhong xiandai zhongwen qikan" 談談東西洋考每月統記傳：中國境內第一種現代中文期刊 (*The East-West Examiner and Monthly Recorder*: the first Modern Chinese periodical), *National Central Library Bulletin* (April 1969), pp. 23–46.

Drake, Fred W. 1975. *China Charts the World: Hsu Chi-yu and His Geography of 1848.* Cambridge, Mass.: Harvard University Press.

——. 1985. "Protestant Geography in China: E. C. Bridgman's Portrayal of the West", in: Suzanne Wilson Barnett and John K. Fairbank (eds.). *Christianity in China: Early Protestant Missionary Writings.* Cambridge, Mass.: Harvard University Press, pp. 89–106.

Williams, Samuel Wells. 1965 [1847]. *The Middle Kingdom: A Survey of the Geography, Government, Education, Social Life, Arts, Religion, etc., of the Chinese Empire and Its Inhabitants.* 2 vols. Taibei: Ch'engwen.

Wylie, Alexander. 1967 [1867]. *Memorials of Protestant Missionaries to the Chinese: Giving a List of Their Publications, and Obituary Notices of the Deceased, with Copious Indexes.* Shanghai: American Presbyterian Mission Press. Reprint: Taibei: Ch'eng-wen.

——. 1964. *Notes on Chinese Literature: with Introductory Remarks on the Progressive Advancement of the Art; and a List of Translations from the Chinese into Various European Languages.* New York: Paragon Book Reprint.

Zhuo Xinping 卓新平 . 1996. "Suoyinpai yu zhongwen xihua rentong" 索隱派與中西文化認同 (The figurists and the acknowledgement of similarities in Chinese and Western Cultures). Unpublished paper presented at "International Symposium on the History of Christianity in China", Hong Kong (October 1996).

ANDREA JANKU

TRANSLATING GENRE: HOW THE 'LEADING ARTICLE' BECAME THE *SHELUN*[1]

The idea to translate a textual genre raises some irritating questions concerning the nature of translation, different conceptual levels of translation and the TransFormations certain concepts undergo in the process of translation. In this paper I will focus on the case of a newspaper genre that was very prominent in nineteenth century journalistic writing, and its uses in the Chinese environment to explore these TransFormations on the terminological and on the cultural level.[2] This genre, in England known as 'editorial' since the early nineteenth century (and a little later as the 'leading article'),[3] was first introduced to China through the missionary press during the nineteenth century, followed very soon by commercial undertakings. But, as the case of the 'leading article' will show, this introduction and the ensuing process of translation was not a one-sided transaction. Translation almost always implies adaptation and change, the degree of which depends on the nature of the interplay between the different cultural environments involved and—in our case—on the respective social uses of genre in these cultural environments.[4]

---

[1] This paper is based on parts of my dissertation "Nur leere Reden: Das Genre 'Leitartikel' in der chinesischsprachigen Tagespresse Shanghai (1884–1907) und die Revolutionierung des 'Weges der Rede'" (Heidelberg 1999). I am grateful to Wolfgang Kubin for his critique, to Mary B. Rankin, who was so kind to comment carefully on an earlier version of this paper, and to Natascha Vittinghoff for her painstaking editorial work.

[2] For a recent study focussing on the question of cultural translation, but with a rather different approach see Lydia H. Liu. 1995. *Translingual Practice. Literature, National Culture, and Translated Modernity—China, 1900–1937*. Stanford: Stanford University Press. For a collection of essays on different theoretical and philosophical aspects of translation see also Rolf Elberfeld et al. (eds.). 1999. *Translation und Interpretation*. Munich: Wilhelm Fink.

[3] Cf. *The Oxford English Dictionary*. 1989. Oxford: Clarendon, vol. 5, p. 72; vol. 8, p. 751. I use the two terms synonymously, as the 'leading articles' e.g. in the London *Times* at that time are invariably editorial articles in the sense that they represent the opinion of the newspaper editors.

[4] For this sociological concept of genre see e.g. Carolyn R. Miller. 1985. "Genre as Social Action", *Quarterly Journal of Speech* 70, pp. 151–67 and John Swales. 1993. "Genre and Engagement", *Revue Belge de Philologie et d'Histoire* 71, pp. 687–98.

In England during the Victorian era writing leading articles enjoyed great prestige and—in the hands of a bourgeois elite—it came to be a powerful instrument of politics, closely interwoven with the parliamentary system and its protagonists. Newspaper editors were considered central figures in the evolution of an 'urban nation' and a 'stable society', (outstanding) journalists were crucial figures in the formation of the 'bourgeois world'.[5] Thus, the social uses of the newspaper—epitomized in the leading articles of prestige papers such as the London *Times*—implied a strong 'state-building agenda' which must have been very appealing to the politically marginalized literati-elite of late imperial China. Actually, Ernest Major (1841–1908), editor of one of the earliest Chinese-language Shanghai papers, the *Shenbao* 申報 (1872–1949), drew heavily on this appeal for his marketing strategies. He, among others, adapted this Western concept of the newspaper to the new Chinese market emerging and expanding from the Shanghai treaty port and was very successful with it.

The story of how the 'leading' or 'editorial' article became the Chinese *shelun* 社論 sheds some light on some crucial issues of cultural translation insofar as it addresses questions concerning the acceptance, adaptation and appropriation of a concept that is defined culturally. How could a genre that is connected to a certain mode of social action, to a certain discourse, find its place within a Chinese cultural environment? Was the leading article just transferred into a new environment to fill a former vacuum or—more likely—did it encounter a Chinese counterpart, with which it came into conflict, although this encounter was transformed into something new? How could it be accepted and which detours did it have to make in the process of cultural appropriation? With the *shelun* do we finally get a Chinese equivalent to the 'leading article' after all and what does the use of this new term mean?

---

5   Joel H. Wiener (ed.). 1985. *Innovators and Preachers. The Role of the Editor in Victorian England*. Westport: Greenwood, p. xiii. Cf. also Derek Frazer. 1985. "The Editor as Activist: Editors and Urban Politics in Early Victorian England", in: Joel H. Wiener (ed.). *Innovators and Preachers. The Role of the Editor in Victorian England*. Westport: Greenwood, pp. 121–43. What I describe here is an ideal-type representation of the liberal press as it was held in high esteem by its protagonists. It should be clear that this is not necessarily an accurate image of 'reality'. Cf. e.g. Aled Jones. 1990. "Local Journalism in Victorian Political Culture", in: Laurel Brake (ed.). 1990. *Investigating Victorian Journalism*. Houndsmills: MacMillan, pp. 63–70.

I will tackle these questions on the basis of the leading articles in the early Chinese press, mainly of the Shanghai paper *Shenbao (*due to its early and steady publication), including some of its commercial and missionary precursors, and the engaged writings of the socio-political elite, namely the writings found in the compilations of *jingshiwen* 經世文 (statecraft writings) by the literati, i.e. 'men of culture' (文人 *wenren*). In a first step I will describe the content and purpose of these texts and which conventions the respective authors followed in their writing; in a second step I will reconnect these findings to the questions of cultural translation as formulated above.

On the basis of these two levels of analysis I will make two arguments. The first refers to the cultural level: the 'leading article' as a Western import would have been without consequences if it were not for a successful merger between journalistic writings shaped on the Western model with the above-mentioned forms of engaged literati writings, through the nineteenth century. The 'leading article' was translated by the early editors—be they Western or Chinese, missionary or commercial—into the conceptual frame of statecraft writings. Thus it was through a gradual convergence that Chinese literati could appropriate a modified journalistic genre then most commonly called *lunshuo* 論説 , modelled on a classical type of essay writing that could be found in the *jingshi*-compilations, most prominently in the forms of *lun* 論 and *shuo* 説 —critical essay, persuasive discussion. Although the vehicle was—in terms of publicity and the actuality and topical broadness of debates it allowed—absolutely innovative, it carried a discourse that largely confined itself to the familiar conceptual level of the *fuqiang* 富強 ('enrich the country and strengthen the army') discourse, which had become all-pervasive due to the political and social disruptions caused by the Nanjing treaty and the Taiping rebellion during the mid-nineteenth century, and which itself was based on the statecraft discourse that had gained prominence since the early nineteenth century. But notwithstanding this confinement, in the long run these formal features—topical broadness, actuality and, most importantly, publicity—furthered the transformation of engaged literati writing in guise of 'leading articles' into something substantially new, insofar as it placed the familiar statecraft discourse in an entirely different sociopolitical environment and thus involved 'society' into political discussions from which it was hitherto excluded. In short, political discussions were opened to the public. Therefrom evolved

the terminological argument. Actually, a new genre was in use decades before there was a new term for it. Initially, the familiar genres
seemed apt enough to comprise the new social uses, or—to say it the
other way round—the new social uses could still be confined to the
old generical frame. Only decades later, when a newly emerging intellectual elite, heavily inspired by the experience of abortive reform
from above and the ensuing Japanese exile, felt the need to give their
political manifestations a new frame of reference, was the modern
term *shelun* coined. This new term was not an innovation brought by
foreigners. It was the young Chinese themselves—now intellectuals—who consciously picked up the foreign term 'editorial' via the
Japanese translation to give expression to their own new concept of
social and political engagement. It might not be too bold to point to
the concept of 'society' (社會 *shehui)* implied in the new term, very
much en vogue in the first decade of the twentieth century.[6] Interestingly enough, the term *shelun* was obviously perceived as a distinct
political statement, used by the 'new' intellectuals to differentiate
themselves from the 'old' literati. In their perception, their articles
reflected the position of society 社會 (*shehui*) at large, which was not
restricted to the newspaper 報社 (*baoshe*) per se. As distinct from the
English term 'editorial' the Chinese term *shelun* could imply both
meanings.

Even though the case of the leading article is but one very special
case, with its own rather peculiar features, it is a paradigmatic one
nonetheless, insofar as it explores the changing cultural uses of a specific genre during a crucial period in Chinese history, a period in
which the old elite was destroyed and which led to the birth of a modern Chinese nation-state. It allows us to observe the emergence of a
different pattern of political participation and the replacement of the
old time-honoured literary elite. The new medium and the new genre
used for the articulation of engaged (political) opinion urged on fundamental social and political changes that finally led to the collapse of
the old system.

---

[6] Ada Haven Mateer comments on the term *shelun* in her study on the newspaper
language: "usually sociological in its character, hence the name" (Ada Haven Mateer.
1915. *New Terms for New Ideas. A Study of the Chinese Newspaper*. Shanghai: Methodist Publishing House, p. 62). This possibly implies a similar interpretation.

1. THE INTRODUCTION OF THE 'LEADING ARTICLE' TO CHINA

If we first have a look at the formation of the modern term we can find a striking difference between the Chinese and the Japanese case. Like in China, the first modern-style Japanese-language papers were founded in the 1860s. More substantial and enduring newspapers came in the 1870s, beginning with the *Tōkyō nichinichi shimbun* 東京日日新聞 founded in 1872—the same year the *Shenbao* was established in Shanghai. From then on, in Japan as well as in the Chinese treaty port, the editorial article occupied a very prominent place. After returning from a trip to Europe in 1874, the writer Fukuchi Gen'ichirō 福地源一郎 (1841–1906) made the editorial article the most important feature of the *Nichinichi shimbun*. He became most famous for the institution of a daily editorial column and developed a new precedent-setting editorial style. From the Western model he adopted the 'editorial We', using the term *gosō* 五曹 of Chinese origin, which was so peculiar that it earned him the nickname Gosō Sensei 五曹先生. Before that one could find only occasional essays or opinion pieces, called *ronsetsu* 論説 (treatise, discussion), often in the correspondence columns and with no editorial consistency.[7] It was in this early phase of Japanese journalism that the neologism *shasetsu* 社説 was coined: a dictionary of 1878 explained it as "essay (or opinion piece) by the editor of a newspaper, which was obviously an adaptation of the English 'editorial article' and stressed the authoritative attitude of the newspaper.[8] Thus in Japan there was an alternative term for the leading article, stressing the editorial role of the journalist. There was a new term for a new concept at the very beginnings of modern journalism. Not so in China.

But that does not mean that there was not in the early Chinese press an equivalent for the editorial. The first appearance of editorials was in the early 1830s in the missionary press, then playing a short interlude on mainland Chinese soil. The eminent missionary Karl Gützlaff (1793–1851) in his *Dongxi yangkao meiyue tongjizhuan* 東西洋考每月統記傳 (*Chinese Magazine*, 1833.8–1834.5) would laconically entitle his short editorial pieces—mostly on religious but also on diplo-

---

[7] James L. Huffmann. 1980. *Politics of the Meiji Press. The Life of Fukuchi Gen'ichirō*. Honolulu: University of Hawaii Press, pp. 84–90.

[8] *Meiji no kotoba jiten* 明治のことば辞典 (Dictionary of words from the Meiji period). 1989. Tokyo: Tōkyōdō shuppan, p. 213.

matic issues—*lun*, by which he made use of an ancient and venerable genre in Chinese literature. But his publication was soon banned from Chinese territory.

More than three decades later, when the missionary press began to appear in the newly opened treaty ports, the term *lun* was again used and rendered as 'editorial'. Young J. Allen's (1836–1907) *Jiaohui xinbao* 教會新報 (Church News, 1868–1874) had English versions of the table of contents, which attributed the label 'editorial', for example, to an article with the title "Xiaobian mingjiao lun" 消變明教論 (On the elimination of the evils of the Confucian teaching), which he rendered as "Christian Morality and the Confucian Moral Code".[9] And yet, the *Church News* was a paper that definitely did not exert much influence on a general Chinese public. In 1874 Allen transformed it into the—later on very influential—*Wanguo gongbao* 萬國公報 (The Globe Magazine, 1874–1883, 1889–1907), leaving behind the strong proselytizing smell of the earlier missionary publications.

The first commercial Chinese language paper, published in Shanghai by the *North China Herald* Company and edited by missionaries, the *Shanghai xinbao* 上海新報 (1860–1872), had no leading articles as an important feature. It was prominent for its reporting on the Taiping movement, but its efforts to become a forum for public discussion met with hardly any considerable response. For sure, in view of the very unstable political situation, the Christian background of the editors and the fear of being connected with the rebels could have scared off potential Chinese contributors.

It was Major with his *Shenbao*, an explicitly commercial paper, who more or less from one day to the next made the leading article a most important genre in the Chinese periodical press[10] (comparable perhaps to the role Fukuchi Gen'ichirō played for the Japanese press). Major assigned a very prominent role to his leading article by the simple fact of having them invariably printed on the first, the title page of his paper. This was in a marked contrast to the practice of e.g. the

---

[9] "Xiaobian mingjiao lun" 消變明教論 (On the elimination of the evils of the Confucian teaching), *Jiaohui xinbao,* January 8, 1870.

[10] Cf. the judgement in "*Shenbao* zhiyi" 申報質疑 (Problems in the *Shenbao*), *Yongbao,* March, 1881, and in Huang Xiexun 黃協壎. 1987 [1922]. "Ben bao zuichu shidai zhi jingguo" 本報最初時代之經過 (Experiences from the earlier period of this newspaper), in: *Zuijin zhi wushi nian: 1872–1922 nian. Shenbao wushi zhounian jinian* 最近之五十年：1872–1922 年申報五十周年紀念 (The last fifty years: Commemorating the fiftieth anniversary of the *Shenbao*). Shanghai: Shanghai shudian.

London *Times*, which at that time, printed usually three 'leading arti-cles' under that heading in the middle pages of the paper.[11] But there was no conscious attempt to translate the English term into Chinese—at least we do not have any evidence for such an effort. Another dis-tinct feature of the *Shenbao*'s leading articles was the fact that, espe-cially in the early years, many of them were readers' contributions. Major's call for contributions met with an overwhelming response, and, not least, the commercial success of the *Shenbao* is to be attrib-uted to a large extent to its success in attracting a considerable part of the literati of the treaty port and the whole Jiangnan area. Very soon the *Shenbao* became a lively forum for public discussion, whereby Major was very careful to differentiate between editorial and readers' opinion.

Articles not written by the editors themselves (i.e. Major, or the Chinese literati he had employed) were signed, usually with pen-names. But both, and this was different from the *Times*, were pub-lished as leaders on the first page of the newspaper.[12]

One of the first debates was on the issue of the 'public bridge' in Shanghai (1872), and one of the most stirring early debates was on the destruction of the Shanghai-Wusong railway (1874). A variety of terms were used to classify this kind of articles, the most common being *lun* (discursive essay on what is right and what is wrong), *shuo* (persuasive speech), *ni* 擬 *.../niqing* 擬請 *... yi* 議 (proposal), *shuhou* 書 後 (comment on), *bian* 辨 (refutation), *yin* 引 (introduction), *yuanqi* 緣 起 (on the origins of). Among these terms *lun*, and to a lesser extent *shuo*, were the most frequently used. 'To write a *lun*' (作論 *zuo lun*)

---

[11] Wang Tao 王韜 (1828–1897), with his Hong Kong based *Xunhuan ribao* 循環 日報 followed the model of the *Times* when he placed his leaders, usually two or three per issue, on page three.

[12] This feature is perhaps suggestive of the notion of *qingyi* 清議 (disinterested lit-erati opinion), which was the legitimate form of *individual* articulation of critique. For the press to establish itself as a new authority in the public sphere in its own rights would have been perceived as an illegitimate move. Thus, by implicitly suggesting to use the paper as a forum for the articulation of some kind of *qingyi*, the *Shenbao* attempted to situate itself somewhere within the established societal structures. For a general discussion of *qingyi* in the nineteenth century cf. Mary B. Rankin. 1982. "Public Opinion and Political Power: Qingyi in Late Nineteenth Century China", *Journal of Asian Studies* 41.3, pp. 453–84; for a discussion of journalistic writings perceived as an articulation of *qingyi* critique see my unpublished manuscript "Pre-paring the Ground for Revolutionary Discourse: From the Statecraft Anthologies to the Periodical Press in Nineteenth Century China."

was soon translated as 'to write a leader'[13] and we can find the composite term *lunshuo* in its ancient meaning 'to discuss' as well as in its new meaning 'a leading article' (e.g. *Shenbao,* October 31, 1895, very probably also earlier). But in the Shanghai papers we cannot find a column entitled *lunshuo* until the first pioneer of a modernized layout, Wang Kangnian's 汪康年 (1860–1911) *Zhongwai ribao* 中外日報 (The Universal Gazette, 1898–1908) in 1898.[14]

The abortive reform efforts of 1898 were a major turning point and completely changed the Shanghai/Chinese newspaper scene. The reformer and revolutionary refugees in Japan adopted the term *shasetsu/sheshuo* 社説 from the Japanese press and used it widely, first in their publications in Japan, then also in the journals published in Shanghai. It was a specific feature of the revolutionary press with a very strong political agenda.[15] At the same time, the established papers felt themselves forced to undertake some reform efforts, not least due to the success of the reform paper *Shibao* 時報 (The Eastern Times, 1904–1936), which very quickly grew to become a serious rival. One effect of these internal reforms was the introduction of separate columns, each with its own heading (what Wang Kangnian had ventured to do already in 1898 without success), one of them being the *lunshuo*, now definitely and consciously the 'leading article'. For the case that the author did not belong to the editorial board of the paper, the heading was changed to *dailun* 代論 ('in place of the *lun*'). The modern term *shelun* appeared for the first time on January 5, 1907 on the pages of the *Shibao* (that until then had also used the term *lunshuo*). It was obviously coined after the Japanese *shasetsu* and rendered more refined and more 'Chinese' by the ending *lun*. Still it was

---

[13] Herbert A. Giles. 1892. *Chinese-English Dictionary.* London: Quaritch.

[14] Beginning with the first issue (August 17, 1898) the *Zhongwai ribao* has a column *lunshuo*, which is preceded by imperial edicts and the news conveyed via telegram. Cf. also Wang Yinian 汪詒年 (ed.). n.d. [1938]. *Wang Rangqing (Kangnian) xiansheng zhuanji yiwen* 汪穰卿 (康年)先生傳記遺文 (Biography of and posthumous writings on Mr. Wang Kangnian). Taibei: Wenhai chubanshe, p. 106. Here reference is made to the innovative layout of Wang's paper, stating that these were premature efforts that could not yet be accepted by the Chinese readers.

[15] Chinese papers used the term *sheshuo* since 1903 (these articles tended to be long serialized political treatises). Those were the *Guomin riribao* 國民日日報 (1903.6–10), the *Jingzhong ribao* 警鐘日報 (The Alarming Bell Daily News, 1904.2– 1905.3), the *Minhu ribao* 民呼日報 (1909.5–8) and the *Minxu ribao* 民吁日報 (The People's Wail, 1909.10–11), and finally the *Guomin gongbao* 國民公報 (Beijing, 1910.7–1919).

considered a Japanese import by an early Chinese chronicler of the history of the press.[16] Next to use the new term was the newly founded *Shenzhou ribao* 神州日報 (The National Herald, 1907.4–1927), associated with Sun Yatsen's revolutionary party.

The conscious adoption of the new term thus stood conspicuously for an innovative force coming from the own ranks of the new Chinese intelligentsia,[17] while the 'conservative' papers still stuck to the term *lunshuo* for a considerable period of time, despite their efforts to adapt layout and style to the new conventions.[18] What I intended to show is that the initial translation of the leading article (or editorial) took place in the early 1870s at its latest, but that the translation process, the cognition of the fundamental difference of the social uses of the new genre and the genuine adoption of this new concept in the Chinese mindset was only concluded during the first decade of the twentieth century, when Chinese reformers themselves introduced a new term (*shelun*) into China. The Western concept 'editorial' was translated at an early point in time, using an existing Chinese concept (*lun*), which then under the influence of the new uses underwent a process of transformation, ending up with the coining of a new term which the Chinese authors considered more apt to express the genuine social uses of the genre.

The new Chinese term *shelun* appeared at a time that was witnessing a new consciousness of political participation and activism among the whole populace, especially in the Jiangnan-area. Not least due to the end of the ban on political expression and association, this was the period of the self-government movement and the first exercises in distinctly modern forms of joint public protest, like the rights recovery movement.[19] The people, guided by a gentry-merchant-elite, began to become aware of the potential weight of their public voice, be it immediately effective or not. At least the bureaucrats had to take it into consideration.

---

[16] Cf. Yao Gonghe 姚公鶴 . 1989 [1917]. *Shanghai xianhua* 上海閑話 (Idle chats on Shanghai). Shanghai: Shanghai guji chubanshe, p. 126.

[17] Besides the leading article, there were numerous other terms used for the new forms of opinion articles emerging by that time, the most famous being the *Shibao's shiping* 時評 .

[18] The Shanghai paper *Xinwenbao* 新聞報 (1893–1949) first used the term *shelun* in the late 1930s, *Shenbao* followed only in the late 1940s.

2. CONCEPTUALIZING THE LEADING ARTICLES AS STATECRAFT ESSAYS

As shown above, it was the missionary and, most effectively, the commercial press in the treaty ports who had established the leading article as a regular feature in newspapers since the early 1870s. Thereby, the conceptualization of the newspaper article in terms of statecraft essay played a crucial role. From the beginnings of his journalistic activities Allen, the editor of the *Jiaohui xinbao*, had shown an editorial attitude that fitted into the statecraft pattern of literati discourse. Adrian Bennett, in his study on Allen's magazines, stated that

> not content with advocating controversial issues within missionary circles, Allen expanded his horizons for the paper within eight months of starting it (i.e. since 1871) by addressing the Ch'ing court. Here he showed an ability to think in terms of what the state would do to benefit the people.[20]

This formulation, describing the attitude of a missionary journalist, which is also reminiscent of the parliamentary function of the elite press in Victorian England, is also suggestive of the idealized role of the Chinese literati within the polity. Thus, there was a basis on which the two structurally rather different concepts of political engagement could meet.[21]

---

[19] Cf. John H. Fincher. 1981. *Chinese Democracy. The Self-Government Movement in Local, Provincial and National Politics, 1905–1914*. London: Australian National University Press; Min Tu-ki. 1989. "The Soochow-Hangchow-Ningpo Railway Dispute", in: id. *National Polity and Local Power. The Transformation of Late Imperial China*. Cambridge, Mass.: Harvard University Press, pp. 181–218; Madeleine Chi. 1973. "Shanghai-Hangchow-Ningpo Railway Loan. A Case Study of the Rights Recovery Movement", *Modern Asian Studies* 7.1, pp. 85–106. For more details on the performance of the Shanghai press in this case in 1907 see Andrea Janku. 1999a. "Der Leitartikel in der frühen chinesischen Presse. Aspekte kultureller Interaktion auf der Ebene des Genres", in: Dietmar Rothermund (ed.). *Aneignung und Selbstbehauptung. Antworten auf die europäische Expansion*. Munich: Oldenbourg, pp. 111–36.

[20] Adrian A. Bennett. 1983. *Missionary Journalist in China. Young J. Allen and His Magazines, 1860–1883*. Athens: University of Georgia Press, pp. 133–4.

[21] Despite its crucial role for the later development of the periodical press, the missionary press preceding the very successful *Wanguo gongbao* (founded in 1874, two years after the *Shenbao*) can only be considered as a marginal player within the Chinese public sphere (at least in its elite segment). With the *Wanguo gongbao* the missionary press gained an intellectually very influential minority of avid readers, and obviously the Chinese editors and journalists of the commercial papers drew heavily from the knowledge published and disseminated through this missionary magazine, giving it an even broader audience.

Ernest Major, *Shenbao*'s British editor, doubtlessly built on this ideal of disinterested literati engagement for the well-being of the polity when he drafted the regulations for his newspaper. Albeit he stressed the popularization effect of the new medium in his inaugural statement ("knowledge should no longer be a privilege of the educated elite"),[22] this emphasis, however, shifted to the great potential the new press bore for matters of government in the more concrete regulations and in later proclamations. In his call for contributions to the paper he had to address the interests and the abilities of the potential contributors and readers—the educated elite, which was considerably numerous in the Jiangnan area. What the readers were asked to contribute was—besides advertisements that had to be paid for—poetry on the one hand and the essays we are interested in on the other. In this announcement we can read (in an early translation):

> If anyone has notable addresses or essays (*danglun* 讜論) which truly relate to the national economy (*guoji* 國計), the people's livelihood (*minsheng* 民生), the cultivation of the land, and irrigation, conservancy, and the like, whether appertaining to the economic duties (*jingji zhi xu* 經濟之需) of the imperial government or revealing the trials of the toiling common folk, these may be published in the paper. Such contributions will not be paid for.[23]

The reminiscences to the classical topics of statecraft writing in the announcement were obvious. The management of government, the care for the welfare of the people, agriculture and water conservancy belonged to the main concerns in memorials and petitions to the throne, the most outstanding of which were included in the *jingshiwen* compilations. After only a short while, this announcement met with a strong response from among the Shanghai and Jiangnan *wenren*—and again, the discourses dominating the political landscape manifested themselves unmistakeably. Among the readers' contributions we find the classical statecraft essays (on taxation, official corruption, natural calamities, secret societies, popular unrest, banditry, civil examinations, administration, military and border issues, public morals, etc.) as well as articles on the 'Western affairs' (*yangwu* 洋務) topics (such

---

[22] "Benguan gaobai" 本館告白 (Editorial announcement), *Shenbao*, April 30, 1872. Translated in Roswell Britton. 1966 [1933]. *The Chinese Periodical Press, 1800–1912*. Taibei: Ch'engwen, pp. 64–5.

[23] "Benguan tiaoli" 本館條例 (Editorial regulations), *Shenbao*, April 30, 1872; also translated in Britton 1966, p. 66, which is quoted here.

as steamship navigation, railways, mining, natural sciences, modern education, opium trade and consumption, international trade, diplomacy, Christianity, missionaries, etc.). Moreover, discussions on local issues like court cases, gambling, prostitution, coolie trade etc. more often were related to the question of how to govern the country and how to achieve wealth and power.

To justify their existence the newspaper editors emphasized over and over again the usefulness of newspapers for the government. *Tong shang xia zhi qing* 通上下之情 (to establish the flow of information between above and below) was the catchword of the day that articulated this claim—in line with ancient structures of communication. The new press was designed as a remedy for the notoriously blockaded old 'avenues of opinion' (*yanlu* 言路), if not in the first place as an alternative to them. The English language press in Shanghai even conferred the epithet 'censorate' to the new Chinese press,[24] thereby placing it within the existing bureaucratic structures.

Natascha Vittinghoff has shown this by analysing the self positionings of the major Shanghai and Hong Kong papers, including Wang Tao's Hong Kong-based *Xunhuan ribao* 循環日報 (The Universal Circulating Herald, 1874–1937). When the old 'avenues of opinion', crucial for the government of the country, were blocked, the newspaper was introduced as a medium to re-establish this ancient institution, to '[re-] connect above and below' (*tong shang xia* 通上下). This being the case, she argues, the new daily press not only claimed to continue the established institutions, but actually stood in competition to them.[25] The usefulness of newspapers for the affairs of government lay in their being an instrument

> 廣見聞, 通上下, 俾利弊灼然, 無或壅蔽
>
> to broaden the knowledge [of the people, or—as another possible reading—about the people], to connect above and below, in order to bring to light good and evil, that nothing might obstruct [the flow of communication].[26]

Thus the socio-political role ascribed to the editors and early journalists was clearly formulated in terms that served the self-esteem of the

---

[24] "The Censorate at Shanghai", *North China Herald,* September 11, 1880.

[25] Natascha Vittinghoff. 2002. *Die Anfänge des Journalismus in China (1860–1911)*. Wiesbaden: Harrassowitz., pp. 278–89.

[26] "Changshe ribao xiaoyin" 倡設日報小引 (Short introduction to the establishment of our daily paper), *Xunhuan ribao*, February 12, 1874.

literati involved in the newspaper business and thereby furthered the cultural acceptance of the new medium. From the very beginning, newspapers were perceived as a potential political instrument (by the articulation of critique of political affairs and officials, a perception derived from the English press, in Japan as well as in China) by a handful of rather progressive intellectuals with more or less profound knowledge of the West (like Fukuchi Gen'ichirō, Wang Tao and others). But at the same time in both China and Japan culturally accepted and successful journalism was, in its early days, perceived as being in the service of the state.[27] While this was the form most likely to be tolerated by the state, the publication of political criticism thus made possible aimed at an initially small but rapidly increasing audience, thus preparing the ground for less restrained articulations in the last decade of the Qing reign. That the reinforced concern for the advancement of the nation would finally lead to the demise of the existing state and dynasty was not self-evident from the beginning for the protagonists themselves.

The most immediate evidence for this policy-centered vision of the function of the press are *Shenbao*'s early editorials, which discussed topics such as the construction of railroads, waterworks, mining, Western medicine, flood control, shipping, innovations in communications, Western institutions like insurances, auctions, business corporations, etc. Many of the frequently discussed topics reflect the major concerns of the more open-minded members of officialdom, urging for the modernization of the Chinese state, esp. its military and economy. This kind of discussion, up to that date more or less restricted to the intra- and para-bureaucratic channels of communication, was now publicized and—concerning the style of writing—to some degree vulgarized. By this the press had very soon become an indispensable medium for all those who had an interest in this kind of discussion, including the gentry-merchants involved in such enterprises, and officialdom. From the beginning it was this kind of engagement and competent participation in policy-issues in guise of ideologically sanctioned statecraft proposal that very soon made the *Shenbao* one of the most important cultural resources of the Jiangnan

---

[27] Speaking about the 'patronage-paper' (goyō 御用) status of the *Tōkyō nichi-nichi shimbun*, James L. Huffman called this "a peculiar Meiji, non-Western definition" of the press. Cf. Huffmann 1980, pp. 93–4.

literary elite. The leading article had been translated into the Chinese language press in form of the *lun, shuo, yi* etc.—essays on the national economy and the people's livelihood—synthesized in the term *lun-shuo*.

3. THE *LUN* IN LATE QING POLITICAL DISCOURSE

For early Chinese journalistic writing it seemed to be a rather obvious choice to use the labels *lun, shuo*, etc. These were the discursive genres that were at its disposal. Besides this, some of the conventions of editorial writing, like the 'editorial We' or the authoritative and critical attitude, were nothing new to Chinese writers. The great innovation was the new print medium, the vulgarization of the written language, and, at the same time, the popularization of a more profound literacy and thus of a political discourse that once was the exclusive domain of a relatively small—though continuously growing —educated elite. But that came gradually. In terms of literary prestige, the *lun* was not a bad choice. It was the most eminent genre of the literati. As a classical genre used for interpretation and comments on the classics and history, its author assumed the authority to judge over right and wrong (*lun shifei* 論是非). Therefore the *lun* was an established genre for the articulation of political critique, usually from outside the bureaucracy, but closely connected to potential or actual office-holders and thus had some authoritative power. As a journalistic genre it allowed its author to conceptualize his role in terms quite similar to the role of the literati-gentry. At the same time, through the transplantation of the elite political discourse to the much more open newspaper press, this discourse was liberated to a certain degree from the fixed hierarchies, and a process of experimenting with new structures of social organization had become possible.

The political discussions carried on in the commercial papers led straight to the reform discourse at the end of the century, with Liang Qichao 梁啟超 (1873–1929) and his essays published in the *Shiwubao* 時務報 (The Chinese Progress, 1896–1898) as the paragon. But the ethos on which the discursive action of the journalists was built, their intellectual self-conception, can be traced further back in history. It was the elite discourse that found its most influential outlet in the *jingshiwen* compilations that was continued in and transformed by the leading article of the newspaper press.

Renewed literati engagement in the form of elite political discussions can be traced back to the late eighteenth century. From then on we can witness a revival of a more critical scholarly attitude, one reconnecting with the late Ming legacy of moralistic critique. The philological debates between the different schools of learning were now subordinated to a new zeal for intellectual engagement in government affairs.[28] This resulted in the *Huangchao jingshi wenbian* 皇朝經世文編 (1828), compiled by He Changling 賀長齡 (1785–1848) and Wei Yuan 魏源 (1794–1856). This "Compilation of Writings on the Statecraft of Our August Dynasty" became extremely popular in the second half of the century, and numerous editions and sequels of it appeared.[29] The first two sections of the *Huangchao jingshi wenbian*, entitled *xueshu* 學術 —(theories of statecraft) and *zhiti* 治體 (essence of governance; I follow Benjamin Elman's translation)—, treated the ideological fundament of the Confucian state. The remaining six sections related to the six boards included documents and essays reflecting the collected knowledge about the implementation of these fundamentals in daily administration. The aim was to create a compendium that "could be used as a source of ideas and methods to reform the sagging imperial bureaucracy."[30] This new concern for

---

[28] Cf. James M. Polachek. 1992. *The Inner Opium War*. Cambridge, Mass.: Harvard University Press; Susan Mann Jones. 1975. "Scholasticism and Politics in Late Eighteenth Century China" *Ch'ing-shih wen-t'i* 3.4 (December), pp. 28–49; Frederic Wakeman. 1972. "The Price of Autonomy: Intellectuals in Ming and Ch'ing Politics", *Daedalus* 101.2, pp. 35–70; and Benjamin A. Elman. 1990. *Classicism, Politics, and Kinship. The Ch'ang-chou School of New Text Confucianism in Late Imperial China*. Berkeley: University of California Press.

[29] He Changling 賀長齡 and Wei Yuan 魏源 (eds.). 1992 [1886]. *Qing jingshi wenbian* 清經世文編 (Collection of writings on statecraft from the Qing dynasty). 3 vols. Beijing: Zhonghua shuju [reprint of the *Huangchao jingshi wenbian* Sibulou 思補樓 edition]. Other editions include: Fuzhou Rao Yucheng keben (Wenhai reprint), 1873; Sibulou chongjiaoben, 1886 (Reprint by Zhonghua shuju, 1992; among others a lithographic edition appeared in 1901. Cf. *Qing jingshi wenbian* 清經世文編 . 1992. Beijing: Zhonghua shuju, "Preface"). There were numerous sequels to this edition, for instance: Zhang Pengfei *Huangchao jingshi wenbian bu* (1851, 58 *juan*); Rao Yucheng *Huangchao jingshiwen xubian* (1882, 120 *juan*); Ge Shijun *Huangchao jingshiwen xubian* (1888, reprint Shanghai, 1901); Sheng Kang *Huangchao jingshiwen xubian* (1897, 120 *juan*); Chen Liangyi *Huangchao jingshi wen sanbian* (1902, 80 *juan*); He Liangdong *Huangchao jingshiwen si bian* (1902, 52 *juan*); Qiushizhai *Huangchao jingshi wenbian wu ji* (Shanghai: Yijinshi shiyin, 1902, 32 *juan*).

[30] Benjamin Elman. 1988. "The Relevance of Sung Learning in the Late Ch'ing: Wei Yuan and the Huang-ch'ao ching-shih wen-pien", *Late Imperial China* 9.2, pp. 56–85; p. 58. Cf. also Frederic Wakeman. 1969. "The Huang-ch'ao ching-shih

statecraft reform (that replaced the former statecraft system mainte-
nance) led in the course of the nineteenth century to a re-evaluation of
the Donglin 東林 movement of the late Ming.[31] In the early years of
the Qing the Donglin partisans were made responsible for the demise
of the Ming dynasty and were therefore used as a pretext for the ban
on any form of literati-associations. After the death of the Qianlong
emperor, the imperial favourite Heshen was criticized, just as Wei
Zhongxian 魏忠賢 (1568–1627) had been criticized by the Donglin-
partisans. This led to the establishment of new associations, and the
articulation of upright critique was to be a new *raison d'être* for the
literati-elite.[32] From this movement resulted what Elman called "a
more activist ancient-style-prose rhetoric by literati associations."[33]

The anthologies of ancient prose that were published at about the
same time supplied the literary patterns for the appropriate form of
articulation of such critique, first Yao Nai's 姚鼐 (1731–1815)
Guwenci leizuan 古文詞類纂 (preface dated 1779, but first printed
around 1820),[34] then Zeng Guofan's 曾國藩 (1811–1872) *Jingshi baijia zachao* 經史白家雜鈔 (1860). These anthologies were extremely
influential and became the most basic textbooks for the education of
generations of students, including the generation of Liang Qichao.[35]
In these anthologies the *lun*-genre occupied the most prominent place,
and basically they were the stylistic model for all the other genres. In
the *jingshiwen*-compilations the *lun* is the most frequent genre after
the memorial, which is more or less a *lun* casted in the form of an official document.

The inclusion of Ouyang Xiu's 歐陽修 (1007–1072) essay "On fac-
tions" 朋黨論 ("Pengdang lun") in the *Guwenci leizuan* was perhaps

---

[30] (*cont.*) wen-pien", *Ch'ing-shih wen-t'i* 1.10, pp. 8–22; and Feng Tianyu 馮天瑜 .
1987. "Daoguang Xianfeng nianjian de jingshi shixue" 道光咸豐年間經世實學 (The
school of practical statecraft during the Daoguang and Xianfeng reigns), *Lishi yanjiu*
4, pp. 138–51.

[31] Elman 1990, pp. 299–300.

[32] For a study of these literati groups see James M. Polachek. 1976. "Literati
Groups and Literati Politics in Early Nineteenth Century China." Ph.D. diss., University of California, Berkeley.

[33] Elman 1990, p. 296.

[34] Yao Nai 姚鼐 . [Guangzhu] Guwenci leizuan [廣注] 古文詞類纂 (Classified
anthology of classical prose, amply annotated). Hefei: Huangshan shushe.

[35] Cf. Satō Ichirō 佐藤一郎 . 1996. *Zhongguo wenzhang lun* 中國文章論 (On literary composition in China). Shanghai: Shanghai guji chubanshe, p. 19.

the most remarkable evidence for the new spirit of the time.[36] In this essay Ouyang Xiu argued that there could be noble motives for forming associations, denying that there inevitably, quasi per definition, had to be selfish motives involved. The Yongzheng emperor himself wrote an essay harshly condemning this view and had it distributed to the schools all over the country, together with his predecessor's, the Kangxi emperor's Sacred Edict (*Shengyu guangxun* 聖諭廣訓).[37] Zeng Guofan included in his anthology texts from the classical canon in which the unrestrained discussion of matters of government was emphasized. From among these, the "Hong fan" 洪範 chapter from the *Shangshu* 尚書 —the first piece in Zeng's anthology—would be cited again and again in the reform writings after 1895.

The gradual convergence of these compilations with the *lunshuo* printed in the new daily press can be shown by looking at the thematic content of later *jingshiwen* compilations. The sequel published by Ge Shijun 葛士濬 in the late 1880s included an additional *yangwu* section, obviously a response to the new challenges that had arisen since the 1850s and reflecting the modernization policies of people like Zeng Guofan and Li Hongzhang 李鴻章 (1823–1901).[38] Similar topics were also treated in the daily press. Still later sequels included almost exclusively texts by reformers or politicians inclined to reform. Moreover, they reprinted numerous translations and articles that had first been published in the periodical press.[39] Towards the end of the century, the *jingshi*-compilations also called themselves 'new' in their

---

[36] Cf. Yao Nai, pp. 44–5. But only the second sequel *Xu guwenci leizuan* compiled by Wang Xianqian 王先謙 (1842–1917) and published in 1889 dared to include writings by the outspoken early Qing critic Dai Mingshi 戴名世 (1653–1713). Cf. Satō 1996, p. 95.

[37] David S. Nivison. 1959. "Ho-shen and His Accusers: Ideology and Political Behaviour in the Eighteenth Century", in: David Nivison and Arthur F. Wright (eds.). *Confucianism in Action*. Stanford: Stanford University Press, pp. 209–43; 225–7.

[38] Ge Shijun 葛士濬 (ed.). 1972. *Huangchao jingshiwen xubian* 黃朝經世文續編 (Supplement edition to the writings on statecraft from our august dynasty). Taibei: Wenhai chubanshe.

[39] E.g. the Huangchao *jingshi wenbian wu ji* (1902) included numerous writings by Liang Qichao—though not mentioning his name (such as the "Xixue shumu biao" 西學書目表 (Bibliography of books on Western learning) and broad sections of "Bianfa tongyi" 變法通議 (General discussion of reform) that had first been published in the *Shiwubao*—and other reform protagonists, and translations from the Western and Japanese press. Cf. Qiushizhai 求是齋 (ed.) 1972 [1902]. *Huangchao jingshi wenbian wu ji* 皇朝經世文編五集 (Fifth collection of writings on statecraft of our august dynasty). Taibei: Wenhai chubanshe.

titles, most important the *Huangchao jingshiwen xinbian* by Mai Zhonghua 麥仲華 (1876–1956), with the preface by Liang Qichao dated 1898. These were edited under the aegis of reform activists who at the same time were doing 'public relations work' by means of the press.[40]

Even the genres included allow a comparison with the press. The most important labels used for the leading articles—as already mentioned—were *lun* and *shuo*, followed by various kinds of commentary like *shu*, *shuhou*, *zhu* or *du* 讀 ... *hou* 後 ...and proposals like *ni/niqing* ...*yi* or *ce* 策. This coincides to a considerable extent with the labels occurring in the *jingshiwen*-compilations. There are only two exceptions: the official memorial 疏 (*shu*) and the private letter 書 (*shu*), both genres which were exceedingly prominent in the latter, but only played a minor role as a form of the leading article.[41] This again is indicative of the changes in the structure of public communications implied in the use of newspapers.

Turning again to the *guwen* 古文 -anthologies, we find Zeng Guofan classifying different sub-genres belonging to the category *lunzhu* 論著 (argumentative writing) in his prefatory remarks. Besides three

---

[40] Mai Zhonghua—one of Kang Youwei's 康有為 students and married to Kang's daughter Kang Tongwei 康同薇 —was the first to abandon He Changling's organizational structure. The chapters of his *Huangchao jingshiwen xinbian*, headed by chapters on 'general theoretical issues' (*tonglun* 通論) and 'the moral character of the ruler' (*junde* 君德), were 'bureaucratic administration' (*guanzhi* 官制), 'law' (*falü* 法律), 'schools' (*xuexiao* 學校), 'national economy' (*guoyong* 國用), 'agriculture' (*nongzheng* 農政), 'mining' (*kuangzheng* 礦政), 'technology' (*gongyi* 工藝), trade' (*shangzheng* 商政), 'monetary system' (*bizhi* 幣制), 'taxation' (*shuize* 稅則), 'postal transportation' (*youyun* 郵運), 'military policy' (*bingzheng* 兵政), 'diplomacy' (*jiaoshe* 交涉), 'history of foreign countries' (*waishi* 外史), 'associations' (*huidang* 會黨), 'civil administration' (*minzheng* 民政), 'descendancy of the [Confucian] teaching' (*jiaozong* 教宗), 'learning' (*xueshu* 學術) and 'miscellaneous' (*zazuan* 雜纂). Gan Han's *Qingchao jingshiwen xinbian xuji* and the *Qiushizhai* compilation mentioned above, both published in 1902, followed Mai Zhonghuas chapter divisions. Cf. Mai Zhonghua 麥仲華 (ed.). 1972. *Huangchao jingshiwen xinbian* 皇朝經世文新編 (New collection of writings on statecraft from our august dynasty). Taibei: Wenhai chubanshe.

[41] Occasionally there might be a memorial reprinted as a lead article or a letter to the editor appearing as such as a leading article. But I would not regard them as typical examples of the genre. Instead, a critical comment on a memorial, often including the text of the memorial, or a reader's essay addressed directly to "the people in charge" (*dangzhouzhe* 當軸者) would be a formally typical expression of the leading article. Apart from that, countless memorials and letters to the editor were reprinted in other sections of the paper.

text labels that are attributed to the philosophers, he identifies six labels, namely the *lun, bian, yi, shuo, jie* 解 (explanation) and *yuan* 原 (on the origin of), that are to be associated to the masters of 'ancient prose' (*guwenjia* 古文家).[42] It were the latter which were to be considered for editorial writing, according to a programmatic *lunshuo* in the *Shenbao*:

> Concerning the titles of the *lunshuo*, they could be called *lun* or *shuo*, *yi* 議 or *ji* 紀 (record), *zhu* 注 (commentary) or *shuhou*, *wenda* 問答 (questions and answers) or *ce* 策 (strategy), *kao* 考 (investigation) or *bian*, there are a lot of [sub-] genres. It is also common to use two or three characters that grasp the general meaning of the text for a title, like in the writings of the philosophers and the compositions of [the ancient prose masters] Han [Yu] and Su [Shi].[43]

Engaged political discourse could only be imagined in the style of ancient prose by the classically educated literati,[44] and it was through the new Western medium of public expression that innovative ways of communication were opened through which reform discourse itself finally could lead to genuine innovation. By the use of the *lun* in the new press and its transformation into the Chinese leading article these concerns could be served. Moreover, concerning the statecraft agenda of the early journalist writings, the reform press explicitly made the connection to the *jingshi*-discourse, one of its magazines being entitled *Jingshibao* 經世報.[45]

In the heated intellectual climate created by the defeat by Japan in 1895 and the ensuing influx of social darwinist ideas of evolution the germs of the desire for active political participation hidden under the surface of the statecraft editorial since the early 1870s began to break through this rather smooth surface. The people (*min* 民)—at least in political rhetoric—began to replace the old elite (*shi* 士), social evils caused by an all pervading selfishness (*si* 私) were to be cured by

---

[42] Zeng Guofan 曾國藩 (ed.). *Jingshi baijia zachao* 經史百家雜鈔 (Miscellaneous writings copied from the classics, historical writings and the one hundred philosophical schools). *Sibu beiyao* edition. "Xuli", 1b.

[43] Zhengdun baowu yuyan" 整頓報務餘言 (Remaining words on the adjustment of our newspaper), *Shenbao*, August 24, 1898.

[44] Satō Ichirō considers this to be the most sublime form of literati expression, inseparable from political engagement and the quintessential *raison d'être* of the *wenren*. (Cf. Satō 1996, pp. 1–7).

[45] The paper was founded by a.o. Zhang Taiyan 章太炎 (1868–1936) in Hangzhou and Shanghai in August 1897.

public-mindedness (*gong* 公), the social fragmentation (*san* 散) causing the weakness of the Chinese state should be overcome by building
an integrated society (*hequn* 合群), and the old idea of a passive people in peaceful rest (*jing* 靜) was to be replaced by that of an active
people that would be in move (*dong* 動).[46] All these new ideas put
forth through Liang Qichao's powerful rhetoric had, by 1898, found
their way into mainstream statecraft writing, and the realization of
their import would have had far-reaching consequences, reaching well
beyond the institutional reforms which the ruling house of the Qing
was willing to perform at that point in time.

Into a discourse that still was very much defined in terms of official and para-official statecraft thought, reflecting the hierarchical
structures of political communication, ideas were integrated, which
were in a basic conflict with this structure of communication, ideas,
which would demand a substantial reorganization of state-society
relationships. And at the very moment as this kind of contents gained
broader ground in the journalistic writings, as it began to intrude the
general statecraft agenda, the press was relegated to its former confines, the reformers were exiled, progressive papers were shut down,
and the 'conservative' papers retreated from their engagement for
reform to conformism or cynicism. 1898 was the turning point insofar
as the exiled reformers now could step over the threshold of state
orthodoxy and continue their experiments with the periodical press
from that point from where it had been impossible to go any further
within the sphere of influence of the Qing state. With the physical
separation from the system radically reformist thought had long since
left behind, the ideological confines of statecraft reform could be dis-
carded. Now the political exiles felt the need to adopt a new term for
what they were doing, they translated the 'leading article' into
sheshuo—'talking on behalf of society'—and transferred it, through
their papers printed in Yokohama and Tokyo, to the Chinese mainland.

---

[46] These ideas, largely derived from Liang Qichao's writings, are used in a *Shenbao* editorial as arguments for the establishment of modern schools, seen as crucial
for the re-building of a strong Chinese nation-state (*guojia* 國家). Cf. "Lun Zhongguo
zhi ruo youyu minzhi bu kai" 論中國之弱由於民智不開 (The reason for China's
weakness is the ignorance of the people), *Shenbao*, September 28, 1898. This article
is analysed in detail in my "Preparing the Ground...."

Conclusion

Translation is a dynamic process of constant exchange. The example of translating the genre 'leading article' has illustrated this, and further observation of the genre's development in the years to come would only corroborate this view. There are a variety of forces that influence the uses of a genre brought to a new environment, and to get a grasp of these complex processes I will present a simplified image of the ensemble of these forces.

After the 'leading article' was transferred with the modern press to China from the West, there were cultural forces at work both from the Western and the Chinese side, that tried to give it a shape familiar to the targeted Chinese readership. The impact of the attitudes and self-perception of the writers on the process of translation became evident in the result. The journalists—while striving for social prestige—still held to their inherited exalted role as the foremost class of the people—the 'men of culture' (*wenren*)—, carrying the burden of responsibility for the moral integrity and material welfare of the country on their shoulders. The *lunshuo*-leading article was perceived by the *wenren*-journalists as an instrument to save their country (that was on the way to becoming the 'nation') for it educated the people and informed the government, and was hence very much in accord with established forms of social and political literati engagement. To a certain extent this was even true for the *sheshuo*-leading article of the revolutionary press and its engagement for nation-building. 'The people' was little more than a rhetorical figure emerging from a new intellectual and political environment, serving the old cause in a new guise, the newness of which was highlighted by the conspicuous use of a new term.

But there were other forces different from cultural ones that tried to impede a thorough, 'genuine' translation of certain concepts. The social uses of the genre to some degree depended on official acceptance or non-acceptance—and on the power with which this non-acceptance was reinforced. The *shelun*-leading article gained considerable power at the local level, as the uses of the genre during the period of local self-government and the rights recovery movement show. 'The people', as far as they were represented by local gentry-merchant interests, had attained a voice that had to be taken into consideration. But that seems to have been only a short period of bloom-

ing and contending. The political authorities took over again and tried
to confine editorial discourse to the frame defined by themselves.
Demanding and dissenting views again had to find their expression in
alternative genres. The authoritative editorial voice was very soon
once again exclusively reserved for official governmental discourse.
Under the Nationalist government, party organs and the state-control-
led press most naturally used the *shelun* as a means of propagation of
their view of things, which had to be taken as the true and only one.
This is the case—in the People's Republic at least—until today, in the
authoritative editorials of the *People's Daily*, editorials that have a
function distinctly different from the articles we can find on the editorial or opinion pages in the modern liberal press.

REFERENCES

"Benguan gaobai" 本館告白 (Editorial announcement) *Shenbao*, April 30, 1872.

"Benguan tiaoli" 本館條例 (Editorial regulations), *Shenbao*, April 30, 1872.

Bennet, Adrian A, 1983. *Missionary Journalist in China. Young J. Allen and His Magazines, 1860–1883*. Athens: University of Georgia Press.

Brake, Laurel. 1990. *Investigating Victorian Journalism*. Houndsmills: MacMillan.

Britton, Roswell. 1966 [1933]. *The Chinese Periodical Press, 1800–1912*. Taibei: Ch'engwen.

"The Censorate at Shanghai", *North China Herald*, September 11, 1880.

"Changshe ribao xiaoyin" 倡設日報小引 (Short introduction to the establishment of our daily paper), *Xunhuan ribao*, February 12, 1874.

Chi, Madeleine. 1973. "Shanghai-Hangchow-Ningpo Railway Loan. A Case Study of the Rights Recovery Movement", *Modern Asian Studies* 7.1, pp. 85–106.

Elberfeld, Rolf et al. (eds.). 1999. *Translation und Interpretation*. Munich: Wilhelm Fink.

Elman, Benjamin A. 1990. *Classicism, Politics, and Kinship. The Ch'ang-chou School of New Text Confucianism in Late Imperial China*. Berkeley: University of California Press.

——. 1988. "The Relevance of Sung Learning in the Late Ch'ing: Wei Yuan and the Huang-ch'ao ching-shih wen-pien", *Late Imperial China* 9.2, pp. 56–85.

Feng Tianyu 馮天瑜. 1987. "Daoguang Xianfeng nianjian de jingshi shixue" 道光咸豐年間經世實學 (The school of practical statecraft during the Daoguang and Xianfeng reigns), *Lishi yanjiu* 4, pp. 138–51.

Fincher, John H. 1981. *Chinese Democracy. The Self-Government Movement in Local, Provincial and National Politics, 1905–1914*. London: Australian National University Press.

Frazer, Derek. 1985. "The Editor as Activist: Editors and Urban Politics in Early Victorian England", in: Joel H. Wiener (ed.). *Innovators and Preachers. The Role of the Editor in Victorian England*. Westport: Greenwood, pp. 121–43.

Ge Shijun 葛士濬 (ed.). 1972. *Huangchao jingshiwen xubian* 皇朝經世文續編 (Supplement edition to the writings on statecraft from our august dynasty). Taibei: Wenhai chubanshe.

Giles, Herbert A. 1892. *Chinese-English Dictionary*. London: Quaritch.

He Changling 賀長齡 and Wei Yuan 魏源 (eds.) 1992 [1886]. *Qing jingshi wenbian* 清經世文編 (Collection of writings on statecraft from the Qing dynasty). 3 vols. Beijing: Zhonghua shuju [reprint of the *Huangchao jingshi wenbian* Sibulou 思補樓 edition].

Huang Xiexun 黃協塤. 1987 [1922]. "Ben bao zuichu shidai zhi jingguo" 本報最初時代之經過 (Experiences from the earlier period of this newspaper), in: *Zuijin zhi wushi nian: 1872–1922 nian. Shenbao wushi zhounian jinian* 最近五十年：1872–1922年申報五十周年紀念 (The last fifty years: Commemorating the fiftieth anniversary of the *Shenbao*). Shanghai: Shanghai shudian.

Huffmann, James L. 1980. *Politics of the Meiji Press. The Life of Fukuchi Gen'ichirō*. Honolulu: University of Hawaii Press.

Janku, Andrea. 1999a. "Der Leitartikel in der frühen chinesischen Presse. Aspekte kultureller Interaktion auf der Ebene des Genres", in: Dietmar Rothermund (ed.) *Aneignung und Selbstbehauptung. Antworten auf die europäische Expansion*. Munich: Oldenbourg, pp. 111–36.

——. 1999b. *Nur leere Reden. Das Genre 'Leitartikel' in der chinesischsprachigen Tagespresse Shanghais (1884–1907) und die Revolutionierung des Weges der Rede*. Ph.D. diss., University of Heidelberg.

Jones, Aled. 1990. "Local Journalism in Victorian Political Culture", in: Laurel Brake (ed.). *Investigating Victorian Journalism*. Houndsmills: MacMillan, pp. 63–70.

Liu, Lydia H. 1995. *Translingual Practice. Literature, National Culture, and Translated Modernity—China, 1900–1937*. Stanford: Stanford University Press.

"Lun Zhongguo zhi ruo youyu minzhi bu kai 論中國之弱由於民智不開 (The reason for China' s weakness is the ignorance of the people)", *Shenbao*, September 28, 1898.

Mai Zhonghua 麥仲華 (ed.). 1972. *Huangchao jingshiwen xinbian* 皇朝經世文新編 (New collection of writings on statecraft from our August dynasty). Taibei: Wenhai chubanshe.

Mann Jones, Susan, 1975. "Scholasticism and Politics in Late Eighteenth Century China", *Ch'ing-shih wen-t'i* 3.4 (December), pp. 28–49.

Mateer, Ada Haven. 1915. *New Terms for New Ideas. A Study of the Chinese Newspaper*. Shanghai: Methodist Publishing House.

Meiji no kotoba jiten 明治のことば辭典 (Dictionary of words from the Meiji period). 1989. Tokyo: Tōkyōdō shuppan.

Miller, Carolyn R. 1985. "Genre as Social Action", *Quarterly Journal of Speech* 70, pp. 151–67.

Min Tu-ki. 1989. "The Soochow-Hangchow-Ningpo Railway Dispute", in: id. *National Polity and Local Power. The Transformation of Late Imperial China*. Cambridge, Mass.: Harvard University Press, pp. 181–218.

Nivison, David S. 1959. "Ho-shen and His Accusers: Ideology and Political Behaviour in the Eighteenth Century", in: David Nivison and Arthur F. Wright (eds.). *Confucianism in Action*. Stanford: Stanford University Press, pp. 209–43.

The Oxford English Dictionary. 1989. Oxford: Clarendon.

Polachek, James M. 1992. *The Inner Opium War*. Cambridge, Mass.: Harvard University Press.

——. 1976. "Literati Groups and Literati Politics in Early Nineteenth Century China." Ph.D. diss., University of California, Berkeley.

Qiushizhai 求是齋 (ed.). 1972 [1902]. *Huangchao jingshi wenbian wu ji* 皇朝經世文編五集 (Fifth collection of writings on statecraft of our August dynasty). Taibei: Wenhai chubanshe.

Satō Ichirō 佐藤一郎 . 1996. *Zhongguo wenzhang lun* 中國文章論 (On literary composition in China). Shanghai: Shanghai guji chubanshe.

"*Shenbao* zhiyi" 申報質疑 (Problems in the *Shenbao*), *Yongbao,* March, 1881.

Swales, John. 1993. "Genre and Engagement", *Revue Belge de Philologie et d'Histoire* 71, pp. 687–98.

Vittinghoff, Natascha. 2002. *Die Anfänge des Journalismus in China (1860–1911)*. Wiesbaden: Harrassowitz.

Wakeman, Frederic. 1969. "The Huang-ch'ao ching-shih wen-pien", *Ch'ing-shih wen-t'i* 1.10, pp. 8–22.

——. 1972. "The Price of Autonomy: Intellectuals in Ming and Ch'ing Politics." *Daedalus* 101.2, pp. 35–70.

Wang Yinian 汪詒年 (ed.). n.d. [1938]. *Wang Rangqing (Kangnian) xiansheng zhuanji yiwen* 汪穰卿 (康年)先生傳記遺文 (Biography of and posthumous writings on Mr. Wang Kangnian). Reprint Taibei: Wenhai chubanshe.

Wiener, Joel H. (ed.). 1985. *Innovators and Preachers. The Role of the Editor in Victorian England*. Westport: Greenwood.

"Xiaobian mingjiao lun", 消變明教論 (On the elimination of the evils of the Confucian teaching), *Jiaohui xinbao,* January 8, 1870.

Yao Gonghe 姚公鶴 . 1989 [1917]. *Shanghai xianhua* 上海閑話 (Idle chats on Shanghai). Shanghai: Shanghai guji chubanshe.

Yao Nai 姚鼐 . [Guangzhu] Guwenci leizuan [廣注]古文詞類纂 (Classified anthology of classical prose, amply annotated). Hefei: Huangshan shushe.

Zeng Guofan 曾國藩 (ed.). *Jingshi baijia zachao* 經史百家雜鈔 (Miscellaneous writings copied from the classics, historical writings and the one hundred philosophical schools). *Sibu beiyao* edition.

"Zhengdun baowu yuyan" 整頓報務餘言 (Remaining words on the adjustment of our newspaper), *Shenbao*, August 24, 1898.

BENJAMIN K. T'SOU

TOWARDS A COMPARATIVE STUDY OF DIACHRONIC AND SYNCHRONIC LEXICAL VARIATION IN CHINESE[1]

This paper examines how concepts and words relevant to the domain of *vehicular devices*, have developed in Chinese within the last century. By comparing relevant entries from the different editions of the *Ciyuan* 辭源 , first published in the early 1900s, and the latest *Cihai* 辭海 , published almost a century later, some general diachronic lexical developments can be traced and analyzed. Further comparison within the 25 million character synchronous corpus of Chinese (LIVAC) based on newspapers from five different Chinese speech communities from 1995 to 1998 provides an unusual window on the differential spread of lexical innovations from a synchronic perspective. It also yields insights on the origin and mechanism of change in language and culture, and the dichotomy between *endocentric* and *exocentric* predispositions towards external cultural stimulus as well as its manifestation and resolution.

1. INTRODUCTION

Language is an integral part of human culture and reflects man's accumulative experience, both cultural and social. Thus as human society and culture evolve over time, the saliency of some artifacts would undergo rise or fall, or both, depending on the period in time, and leading to the appearance of new words as well as the disappearance of others. In the latter case, the disappearance of words may not be total in literate societies which could have chronicled their use in the language, either through texts, or through dictionaries. The latter

---

[1] The research report here is supported by a Competitive Earmarked Research Grant (CERG) of the Research Grant Council of Hong Kong (No. 1202/98H) as well as by the CCK Foundation in Taiwan (RG021-91). Some parts of this paper have previously appeared in Chinese as Benjamin K. T'sou (Zou Jiachan) 鄒嘉產 and Feng Liangzhen馮良珍 . 2000. "Hanyu (wu di) yu riyu xin gainian ciyu duibi yanjiu—cong xin wenshi kan cihui yansheng yu zhongzheng" 漢語(五地)與日語新慨念詞語對比研究 — 從新聞視窗看詞匯 衍生與重整 (Comparative research on terms for new concepts in Chinese (of five cities) and Japanese— Deriving and reassembling of vocabulary as seen from the media angle), *Yuyan yanjiu*, 2000.3, pp. 51–70. I am grateful for comments by Federico Masini, Elisabeth Kaske, W. F. Tsoi and N. Fuminobu.

can also have the function of filter and codification because of inevitable selectivity. In some instances, words whose saliency might have ebbed might not disappear altogether. They could be embedded in a literary or high register which only the learned or educated class would use, sometimes in their characteristic display of verbal flair, and other times as a marker of social class status. In other instances, and in non-literate societies, some words may be retained only selectively in certain dialects but not others. Dialects which retain such words in significant numbers are sometimes seen to be more conservative than others which do not retain them, and often the literary language draws on archaic words. The new words could replace some existing words (i.e. *lexical substitution*) or they could represent newly lexicalized cultural artifacts (i.e. *lexical importation*). The lexical form *(signifie* à la de Saussure) of such a new word may be the *phonetic replica* of a *model* from another language, whose culture has provided the source of the lexical importation. Or it may be the *semantic replica* (*calgue*) of a non-indigenous model, or simply the semantic extension of morphemes already in the indigenous language.[2] In the first instance of phonetic replication, we see it as *exocentric* because the adaptation is modelled after a non-indigenous language when an alternative exists. But in the latter case of semantic replication we see it as *endocentric* because the adaptation is based on the use of indigenous linguistic material. This dichotomy and the significance of the underlying conceptual framework are not commonly recognised and discussed, and even less adequately understood.[3]

2. A BASIS FOR DIACHRONIC COMPARISON

In the case of the Chinese language, a comparison among lexical repertoires based on modern principles reveal some interesting global trends. The compilation of the *Ciyuan* 辭源 began in 1908 and it was first published in 1915. But following rapid global societal changes,

---

[2] For a more detailed discussion of these concepts, see Benjamin K. T'sou. 2001. "Language Contact and Lexical Innovation", in: Michael Lackner, Iwo Amelung and Joachim Kurtz (eds.). 2001. *New Terms for New Ideas. Western Knowledge and Lexical Change in Late Imperial China*. Leiden: Brill, pp. 35–53.

[3] For exocentric and endocentric tendencies, I use the Chinese terms *cixinli* 辭心雕 and *xiangxinli* 向心力 respectively. See T'sou and Feng 2000.

an extended edition of the *Ciyuan* was published in 1931 for the following reason:

十餘年中，世界之演進，政局之變革，在科學上自有不少之新名辭發生。
Within more than a decade and following progressive developments in the world and changes within the political scene, it is natural that in science many new words have emerged.[4]

A new combined edition was thus published in 1939. A comparison of these two editions of the *Ciyuan* (1931 and 1939) provides a good overview on lexical changes which in most cases began before the decade between 1931 and 1939, to cover the turn of century and extending into the early part of the twentieth century when the epoch making May Fourth Movement took place. For ease of reference the two editions will be designated as *Ciyuan* 31 and *Ciyuan* 39. They are primarily concerned with lexical items whose etymologies have historical value and are therefore accumulative. They do not, for example, include pronouns in current usage, nor function words in the contemporary language. There is also the *Cihai* 辭海 , published since the 1940s, which is concerned with the comprehensive coverage of words in current use. Thus, the *Cihai* contains some items from the *Ciyuan* which are still of current usage but would for this reason have a larger repertoire than the *Ciyuan*. The *Xiandai hanyu cidian* 現代漢語詞典 or *Xianhan*[5] is an authoritative publication much more focused on words currently and commonly used in Modern Standard Chinese (MSC), which, though similar in timeframe, would thus form a subset of those in the *Cihai*.

Since 1995, the Language Information Sciences Research Centre at the City University of Hong Kong has undertaken a project to synchronously and systematically collect Chinese newspapers texts published in different Chinese speaking communities (LIVAC—Linguistic Variation in Chinese Communities). Its database for the period 1995–1998 has about 25 million characters from Hong Kong, Macao, Shanghai, Singapore and Taibei. From this database we can extract a very large collection of words in use in the different Chinese speech communities. We refer to this as the LIVAC Lexicon of Contemporary

---

    4 Explanatory notes from the 1931 extended edition of the *Ciyuan*, by Fang Yi.
    5 *Xiandai Hanyu cidian* 現代漢語詞典 (Modern Chinese dictionary). 1996. Beijing: Shangwu yinshuguan. It is often abbreviated as *Xianhan* 現漢 .

Chinese, LIVACL, which contains more than 300,000 lexical entries culled from the textual database.[6]

Table 1 below provides a quantitative summary of the entries in the above collections.

Table 1: Numbers of entries in major Chinese lexicons

Lexicon	Year	Number of entries
Ciyuan	1931	65,555
Ciyuan	1939	88,074
Xianhan	1996	50,333
Cihai	1999	127,841
LIVACL (1.0)	1995–98	300,000++

A comparison of *Ciyuan* 31 with *Ciyuan* 39 indicates that there was nearly a 35% net increase in words recognized and incorporated into the 1939 edition. However, when compared with the *Ciyuan*, both the *Cihai* and the LIVACL are produced on the basis of different principles and with different purposes in mind, as noted above. It would be useful to undertake some quantitative and qualitative comparisons.

If we examine the class of concrete objects or nouns related to *vehicle*, we would see that this sub-class of *mechanisms/machinery*, has undergone significant growth since the industrial revolution, especially within the last century. For the purpose of comparison a closer examination of the related lexical items under this rubric has yielded the figures in Table 2.

Table 2: Total number of entries relevant to vehicle *in major Chinese lexicons*

Lexicon	Year	Number of Entries
Ciyuan	1931	178
Ciyuan	1939	240
Xianhan	1996	135

---

[6] see Benjamin K. T'sou 鄒嘉產 1998a. *Zhongwen gediqu gongshi ciyu yanjiu baogao* 中文各地區共時詞語研究報告 (Linguistic Variation in Chinese Communities—LIVAC 1.0). Hong Kong City University Language Information Sciences Research Centre. LIVAC has grown by 2003 to more than 500,000 words from the expanded database of 1 billion characters (http://www.rcl.cityu.edu.hk/livac/).

Table 2: Total number of entries relevant to vehicle *in major Chinese lexicons (cont.)*

Lexicon	Year	Number of Entries
Cihai	1999	239
LIVACL	1995-98	1,406 (784)

It is interesting to note from Table 2 that the two editions of the *Ciyuan* show an increase of about 30% for entries relating to *vehicle,* which is basically in keeping with the overall net increase in the lexicon within the decade. Moreover, one entry from *Ciyuan* 31 was dropped in favor of the addition of 65 news entries.

The only dropped lexical item: *linche* 臨車 represents a relatively obscure historical artifact which had become outdated. In its place, a number of vehicular words have remained common to both the 1931 and 1939 editions of the *Ciyuan*—as can be seen in Table 3.

Table 3: Some vehicular words in both Ciyuan 1931 and 1939

1. *dongyangche* 東洋車	7. *kuaiche* 快車	13. *renliche* 人力車
2. *huoche* 火車	8. *leiche* 雷車	14. *ruanlunche* 軟輪車
3. *huolunche* 火輪車	9. *leihuoche* 雷火車	15. *yiche* 衣車
4. *jiguanche* 機關車	10. *lieche* 列車	16. *zhinanche* 指南車
5. *jiaotache* 腳踏車	11. *luche* 路車	17. *zidongche* 自動車
6. *jiaoche* 轎車	12. *qiche* 氣車	18. *zizhuanche* 自轉車

The above list indicates that by the third decade of the twentieth century many new machineries or vehicular objects have found their way into Chinese society and were given new and special lexical designations. These include "rickshaw" (No. 1 東洋車, No. 13 人力車), "locomotive" (No. 2 火車, No. 4 機關車), "express train" (No. 7 快車), "bicycle" (No. 17 自動車, No. 5 腳踏車), and "motorized bicycle" (No. 12 氣車, No. 18 自轉車).

It is also noteworthy that there were exceptionally old entries which have undergone change in meaning. For example, No. 6 轎車 initially meant a sedan carried between two mules or horses, but in MSC it has come to mean a sedan car. No. 15 衣車 meant a vehicle for transporting clothing or a cart with shades, but in present day Chinese it means sewing machine ([個] 衣車). Moreover, No. 14 軟輪車 does not mean vehicles with pneumatic tires. These are examples of *semantic shift*.

There are also instances of *relexification*.[7] For example, No. 3 火輪車 ('汽車之俗稱' a common term for (steam) gaseous vehicle) was a descriptive term for the early steam engine, No. 4 機關車, "locomotive" (now 火車); No. 12 氣車 and No. 17 自動車 ("即摩托車") "motorcycle"; and No. 18 自轉車 ("或稱腳踏車") "bicycle".

But by *Ciyuan* 39, quite a few additional new vehicular items had also appeared: "train" (*dianche* 電車), "gun carriage" (*paoche* 砲車), "motorcycle" (*motuoche* 摩托車), "autocar" (*qiche* 汽車), which are different from the "(steam) gaseous vehicle" (*huolunche* 火輪車), "Western car" (*yangche* 洋車), and "tank" (*tanke zhanche* 坦克戰車) of the past.

The lexical entry *tank* deserves special attention because we can trace its pattern of chronological adaptation:

坦克戰車 → 坦克車 → 坦克

It began as a compound *hybrid form*: 坦克戰車 [tank-combat-vehicle], underwent *simplification* twice before being *relexified* as a disyllabic *phonetic adaptation* 坦克 [*tanke*]. This is only a broad view of the diachronic development. A synchronic comparison yields yet more interesting findings below.

3. A SYNCHRONIC COMPARISON

Table 4: Re-lexification and lexical innovation by location—tank, jeep *and* taxi *(1995-1998)*

		Hong Kong	Shanghai	Singapore	Taiwan
		(%)	(%)	(%)	(%)
1.	*tankeche* 坦克車	10	0	0	30
2.	*tanke* 坦克	90	100	100	70
	Total (%)	100	100	100	100
3.	*jipuche* 吉普車	100	75	0	100
4.	*jipu* 吉普	0	25	0	0
	Total (%)	100	100	0	100
5.	*dishiche* 的士車	0	1	0	0

----

[7] see T'sou 2001.

Table 4: Re-lexification and lexical innovation by location—tank, jeep *and* taxi *(1995-1998) (cont.)*

		Hong Kong	Shanghai	Singapore	Taiwan
		(%)	(%)	(%)	(%)
6.	*dishi* 的士	95	1	0	6
7.	*chuzuche* 出租車	4	90	0	0
8.	*chuzuqiche* 出租汽車	0	6	1	0
9.	*jichengche* 計程車	1	0	2	94
10.	*deshi* 德士	0	0	97	0
11.	*dadi* 打的	0	3	0	0
	Total (%)	100	100	100	100

Table 5: Re-lexification and lexical innovation by word—tank, jeep *and* taxi

		Hong Kong	Shanghai	Singapore	Taiwan	Total
		(%)	(%)	(%)	(%)	(%)
1.	*tankeche* 坦克車	50	0	0	50	100
2.	*tanke* 坦克	36	26	28	10	100
3.	*jipuche* 吉普車	54	23	0	23	100
4.	*jipu* 吉普	0	100	0	0	100
5.	*dishi* 的士	94	0	0	6	100
6.	*dishiche* 的士車	0	100	0	0	100
7.	*chuzuche* 出租車	5	95	0	0	100
8.	*chuzuqiche* 出租汽車	0	90	10	0	100
9.	*jichengche* 計程車	1	0	1	98	100
10.	*deshi* 德士	0	0	100	0	100
11.	*dadi* 打的	0	100	0	0	100

From Tables 4 and 5, which contain data taken from LIVACL (1.0), we could see further global trends in the mechanism of relexification for *tank* and a number of other vehicular words.

For *tank*, Shanghai and Singapore have gone from the hybrid form *tankeche* 坦克車 to *tanke* 坦克 , whereas Taiwan is the most conservative, followed by Hong Kong, in retaining the hybrid form *tankeche* 坦克車 to varying degrees.

By comparison, *jeep* shows that the transition from the hybrid form *jipuche* 吉普車 to the purely phonetic form *jipu* 吉普 has only begun. It is worthy of note that Shanghai again leads in this process, as is the case with *tank*.

In the case of *taxi*, each community has a preferred designation: Hong Kong *dishi* 的士, Shanghai *chuzuche* 出租車, Singapore *deshi* 德士, and Taiwan *jichengche* 計程車. However, there is also incipient spread of the lexical items amongst the communities, with Shanghai showing the highest degree of flexibility.

Table 5 shows that in the case of *tank* and *jeep*, there is the overall predominance of the disyllabic relexified form 坦克 over the earlier trisyllabic hybrid form 坦克車 and also indication of the incipient relexification of 吉普車 to 吉普. This direction of relexification is in fact a common trend, because 坦克 and 吉普 by themselves do not carry semantic content, but with the head word 車 which they modify, they become new and regular words. With time, when the vehicles they represent become sufficiently familiar to the particular society, the simpler and often preferred disyllabic phonetic representation becomes a welcome abbreviation.

4. VEHICULAR WORDS IN DIFFERENT CHINESE COMMUNITIES

As an alternative to the static dictionary approach, an attempt is made to compare lexical variation from a sociolinguistic perspective of actual language use. This would allow a more realistic appreciation of the extent and impact of lexical variation. This window approach is taken for a period of 30 days between December 1996 to January 1997, in which extensive newspaper material from Hong Kong, Macao, Shanghai, Singapore and Taibei were synchronously sampled, along with the *Asahi Shimbun* in Japan.

All lexical items associated with *vehicle* were culled from the corpus for quantitative and qualitative analysis. Given the window approach we have taken, 353 words related to vehicles were uncovered.[8] Of these, only 144 words or about 40% of the words were found in common amongst all communities. There were 209 items

---

[8] see Annex 1.

(Hong Kong: 45, Macao: 30, Shanghai: 73, Taibei: 22, Singapore: 39) which appeared only in one community within the designated window. These unique lexical items, with some exceptions, tend to reflect salient traits of local culture and language features:

1. Hong Kong

The 45 words in the Hong Kong window provide the following observations:

xiaoba 小巴 "mini-bus", *bashixian* 巴士線 "bus line", *chengba* 城巴 "city bus", *lüyouba* 旅遊巴 "tourist bus", *xiaoba* 校巴 "school bus" and *lüba* 綠巴 "green bus" show that *bashi* 巴士 "bus" has been taken as a single lexical item and that the simplified form *ba* 巴 has been used as a head word to derive other new words. They show the rich development of one mode of public transportation in Hong Kong, as well as the impact of the English language from which Hong Kong has phonetically adopted *bus*.

Weibanche 尾班車 "tail-end vehicle", *shangluoche* 上落車 "enter/exit vehicle", etc. reflect indigenous Cantonese dialectal structure in Hong Kong: *wei* 尾 in Cantonese has the extended meaning of "last" (i.e. tail-end) and *luo* 落 in Cantonese can take a noun object just as *shang* 上 does in MSC, and it replaces *xia* 下 in MSC *xia che* 下車 "to alight from vehicle".

2. Macao

The 30 words in the Macao corpus: *fangchesai* 房車賽 "sedan car race", *saichechang* 賽車場 "grand prix course", *cheshou* 車手 "racing car driver", *saichehui* 賽車會 "racing (car) cub" etc., reflect a unique aspect of Macanese car-racing Grand Prix culture within the window being observed. In the case of *kongba* 空巴 "airbus", a simplification of *kongzhong bashi* 空中巴士 , it reflects an analogic extension of the Hong Kong trend in simplification, similar to the derivation of *xiaoba* 小巴 "mini-bus" from *xiaoxing bashi* 小型巴士 "small scale bus".

3. Shanghai

There are 73 unique entries for Shanghai within the window, representing the highest number among the five communities. They also reflect certain cultural traits:

(a) *sanlunche* 三輪車 "trishaw", *jixingche peng* 自行車棚 "bicycle shed", *shoupiaoche* 售票車 "ticketing car", *gongjiao chepiao* 公交車票 "omnibus ticket", *songshuiche* 送水車 "water vehicle", *gongjiaoche* 公交車 "public bus", *bianminche* 便民車 "leisure class car" etc. reflect the saliency of some basic necessities of daily life.

(b) *kongtiaoche* 空調車 "air-conditioned car" reflects the relative saliency of air-conditioned vehicles which stood out and were noticeable until recently, whereas such vehicles have been perhaps more common in the other communities and thus required no special marking.

(c) *dadi* 打的 "hail taxi" represents a relatively recent and increasingly popular activity relevant to mode of transportation, in contrast to the more traditional *jiao chuzuche* 叫出租車 "hail rental car". It is also a manifestation of a newly derived head word *di* 的 from *dishi* 的士, in parallel to *ba* 巴 from *bashi* 巴士 .

4. Taiwan

Taiwan has only 22 unique entries, the smallest among the 5 communities:

(a) *zhuzhanche* 主戰車 "main combat vehicle", *qingzhanche* 輕戰車 light combat vehicle", *dizhanche* 敵戰車 "enemy combat vehicle" etc. reflect a particular concern about cross-Straits hostilities and armed conflict within the time period of the window through which observations are made.

(b) *binshi* 賓士 "Mercedes-Benz" represents a prestigious consumer product appreciated but not usually attainable by the masses. This rendition in Taiwan has connotations of gentry and social class, which is a comparatively better rendition than all other communities.

5. Singapore

There are 39 unique words for Singapore:

(a) *bashiche* 巴士車 "bus-vehicle", *xinba* 新巴 "Singapore Bus (Co.)" etc. reflect a similar trend as Hong Kong.

(b) *niuche* 牛車 "bullock cart", *chelu* 車路 "vehicular road", *baoche* 包車 "chartered vehicle", *jiaoche* 腳車 "bicycle" ("foot cart") etc. reflect Singapore's links with neighboring developing countries.

(c) *deshi* 德士 "taxi", *luoli* 羅里 "lorry" reflect a different trend in phonetic adaptation because of the predominance of South Min speakers in the population. 德士 in southern Min is *teksi* which is phonetically quite close to the English "taxi" [t'eksi], even though 德士 already exists in the older Chinese language to designate a special priest.

The singular lexical items had come about as a result of individual, perhaps idiosyncratic, development within a specific community. Clearly many of the words found only in a single speech community may be readily understood by members from one or more speech communities. But there are others which might baffle members from other speech communities.

5. MUTUAL INTELLIGIBILITY

The different and sometimes divergent trends in historical development among different speech communities can lead to substantive lexical, phonological, and other linguistic variations, and can even result in the emergence of separate dialects or languages. The significance of these developments may be gauged by the extent of mutual intelligibility. Previous studies have been based on phonological and phonetic variation.[9] One common assumption is that the basic vocabulary provides the best basis for comparison. But this kind of comparison provides only a theoretical measure of possible mutual intelligibility in a hypothetical context. This is because there is no certainty that the words unique to one community may be encountered by speakers in another community in actual use. Thus the possibility for an alternate measure exists, based on actual language use, sampled through a window approach, rather than hypothetical comparison.

Taking our 30-day window, we attempt a different approach described below:

---

[9] see, for example, You Rujie 游汝杰 and Yang Bei 楊蓓 . 1998. "Guangzhouhua, Shanghaihua he putonghua cihui jiejinlü de jiliang yanjiu" 廣州話，上海話和普通話詞匯接近率的計量研究 (Quantitative research on the closeness of Cantonese, Shanghainese and Mandarin vocabulary), in: Benjamin K. T'sou 鄒嘉產 et al. (eds.). *Hanyu jiliang yu jisuan yanjiu* 漢語計量於計算研究 (Quantitative and Computational Studies on the Chinese Language). Hong Kong: City University of Hong Kong, Language Information Sciences Research Center, pp. 57–77; Zheng Jinquan 鄭錦全 . 1994. "Hanyu fangyan goutongdu de jisuan" 漢語方言溝通度和方音計算 (Computation of understandability of Chinese dialects), *Zhongguo yuwen* 94.1, pp. 35–43.

—we focus on the actual words related to *vehicles* which are found in actual use within the synchronous corpus LIVAC,

—we do not look at phonological mutual intelligibility, but focus on the printed word, coded through the unique logographic writing system, and therefore the written language. Hence we take a wider and drastically different perspective than before, but it reflects the situation when the average member of a Chinese speech community attempts to read and understand textual material from another community,

—we focus on a common category of lexical items, taking vehicle as a theme, so as to attempt more in-depth and systematic analysis, and

—we also wish to find a meaningful way to consider whether mutual intelligibility is bi-directional or reciprocal, which is often assumed.

The following results are obtained from a comparison of Hong Kong and Shanghai.

1. Hong Kong and Shanghai

The two lists of vehicular words from the 30-day window for both communities are analyzed as follows:

(a) Words found in both communities.

(b) Words appearing only in one community but understandable to the other.

(c) Words appearing only in one community but which are not understood by members from the other community.

The full Hong Kong list yielded 146 items, and Shanghai 166. Of these 55 are common to both communities, i.e. about one-third of the words are found to be common within the window. Of the other 91 words found only in Hong Kong and 111 words found only in Shanghai, many can be readily understood by members from the other community, but there are some which are not. A summary of the cases is given as follows:

(a) Words from one community whose meaning can be correctly guessed by residents from the other speech community: Hong Kong's *bashixian* 巴士線, *weibanche* 尾班車, *liushuiche* 泵水車, *jiushangche* 救傷車 can be readily understood by Shanghainese. Shanghai's *chongxiche* 沖洗車, *zixingche* 自行車 likewise can be readily understood by Hong Kong residents.

(b) Hong Kong words not readily understood by Shanghainese e.g.: *shangluoche* 上落車, *mutouche* 木頭車, *diaobiche* 吊臂車, *diaojiche*

吊雞車 , *rongjia* 溶架 , *pochezai* 泊車仔 , *zhulongche* 豬籠車 , *danche-jing* 單車徑 , *jiuba* 九巴 .

(c) Shanghai words not readily understood by Hong Kong residents: *dadi* 打的 , *chatou* 差頭 , *mianbaoche* 麵包車 , *candi* 殘的 , *huangyuche* 黃魚車 , *chefeng* 車風 .

On this basis, the following may be noted:
Words from Hong Kong understandable in Shanghai:
   77 out of 144—53.35%.
Adding to this 38.19% words common to both communities, we can arrive at an index on Hong Kong Intelligibility of Shanghai words: I H-S:
   I H-S: 53.45 + 38.19 = 91.64%
Words from Shanghai understandable in Hong Kong:
   79 out of 166—47.59%.
Adding to this 33.13% words common to both communities, we can arrive at an index for Shanghai intelligibility of Hong Kong words: I S-H:
   I S-H: 47.59 + 33.13 = 80.32%
Conversely this means non-intelligibility would be:
   Hong Kong words by Shanghai residents: 8.4%.
   Shanghai words by Hong Kong residents: 19.6%.
This indicates that intelligibility is not reciprocal, and that Shanghai residents can understand more Hong Kong words than Hong Kong residents can understand Shanghai words.

Why is this the case? There can be a number of causes. Foremost among these may be cultural orientation and favourable (pre-)disposition of one community with respect to the other, which may not be evenly matched.

If the same comparison between written Japanese and Chinese is made, the corresponding figures on intelligibility are as follows:[10]

   Japanese vehicular words (in *kanji* 漢字) by Chinese 77.96%.
   Chinese vehicular words (in *hanzi* 漢字) by Japanese 51.27%.
This also reflects in matters relating to vehicles a greater orientation of Chinese to Japanese culture than the opposite case. This is not surprising, given the greater prominence of the automobile culture in Japan and the leading position of the Japanese car industry in the

---

[10] T'sou and Feng 2000 (op. cit.)

world. Thus in the case in Hong Kong automobile culture, there has been a much longer history of mature consumerism than in Shanghai. It is therefore not surprising that Shanghai might have looked towards Hong Kong more in the cultural adaptation.

6. COMPARISON OF MODES OF LEXICAL DERIVATION

The data also reveal different means by which new lexical items are formed:

(A) descriptive term or *calgue,* e.g. *jiuhuche* 救護車 "ambulance", *zhuangjiache* 裝甲車 "armoured car".

(B) phonetic adaptation, e.g. *luoli* 羅里 "lorry", *dishi* 的士 "taxi", *bashi* 巴士 "bus".

(C) derivation based on hybrid semantic and phonetic adaptation, e.g. *bashizhan* 巴士站 "bus station", *dishizhan* 的士站 "taxi stand".

(D) phonetic designator, e.g. *kache* 卡車 "truck-car", *motuoche* 摩托車 "motorcycle".

The following provides a breakdown of the distribution of the different means:

Table 6: Distribution of different means of forming new lexical items

Place	Entry	A		B		C		D	
Hong Kong	83	60	72.29%	15	18.07%	3	3.61%	5	6.02%
Macao	69	58	84.05%	3	4.35%	4	5.79%	4	5.79%
Shanghai	85	72	84.70%	3	3.53%	4	5.88%	5	5.88%
Taiwan	49	40	81.63%	3	6.12%	3	6.12%	3	6.12%
Singapore	57	47	82.46%	4	7.02%	3	5.26%	3	6.12%
Japan	90	42	46.60%	27	30%	19	21.11%	2	2.22%

From the above, it can be seen that the derivation of new words involve two primarily opposite processes: on the one hand, using indigenous linguistic elements as in descriptive designation or *calgues* (裝甲車 , 救護車) [A] and, on the other, using non-indigenous linguistic elements, as in phonetic adaptation [B] (e.g. 巴士 , 的士).

Between these two extremes there is the intermediate model of combining both [C and D], as in 卡車 , 摩托車 .

We have seen in Section 2 how a *tank* provides an example of a typical progression in diachronic lexical development:

坦克戰車 (*Ciyuan* 39) → 坦克車 (*Cihai*) → 坦克 (*Xianhan*)

Within this proposed framework we have referred to the use of indigenous linguistic elements as an *endocentric tendency* in word formation, and the use of non-indigenous linguistic elements as *exocentric tendency*. Let us first take the exclusive use of indigenous linguistic elements as a basis for comparison with respect to Table 6. This is justified because the truly naive native speaker may not be familiar with non-indigenous phonetically adapted morphemes.

The comparison yields the following ranking of *endocentrism* in descending order:

Shanghai→Macao→Singapore→Taibei→Hong Kong→Japan

The difference between the first four communities, ranging between 81% to 85%, is quite minimal. But Hong Kong shows only a 72.29% usage of exclusively indigenous linguistic elements, the lowest among the Chinese speech communities. By further comparison, Japan shows only 46.67%, i.e. less than half, in terms of the usage of exclusive indigenous linguistic elements.

We could also take the opposite extreme of comparing the use of exclusively non-indigenous language elements (i.e. B) on the basis of Table 5. The ranking order of *exocentrism* would be as follows:

Japan→Hong Kong→Singapore→Taibei→Macao→Shanghai

This is almost the exact reverse of the ranking order in terms of *endocentrism* (except for the two communities: Singapore and Taibei)

The two opposite approaches validate each other and confirm the overall continuum. It also provides an index on *endocentrism* (*xiangxinxing* 向心性) versus *exocentrism* (*lixinxing* 離心性) in the reception and resolution of foreign cultural stimuli for the different Chinese speech communities, with at one end, Shanghai/Macao leading in *endocentric* disposition and, at the other end, with Hong Kong leading in *exocentric* disposition, developing in a way similar to, but not matching, Japan.

These findings are not surprising. The opening of Japan since the Meiji Era and the subsequent American occupation of Japan after World War II have brought about on a massive scale a switch towards the adaptation and assimilation of things Western. One and a half centuries of sustained British presence in Hong Kong, in contrast to the Bamboo curtain which hung over the Mainland for several decades, has also induced a similar social, cultural and psychological opening in Hong Kong. It is also noteworthy that Japan and Hong Kong during the period under the window were known for their exceptional freedom of the press.

Shanghai's earlier opening to the West was arrested if not reversed during the Bamboo curtain period. The case of Macao appears surprising on first glance because of its even longer colonial history than Hong Kong's. However it should be noted that the colonial administration in Macao had little impact on the broad cultural front because of the simple co-existence between the small but elite Portuguese community and the majority Chinese (Cantonese) speaking population which had always looked toward Hong Kong and China in matters Chinese and which had considered English much more important than Portuguese as a second language.[11]

50 years of Japanese colonial administration in Taiwan in the first half of the twentieth century introduced traits similar to those in Japan but the resumption of Chinese rule over Taiwan in the last half century has arrested some of the developments.[12] The Singapore situation should have been more like Hong Kong, given a similar colonial history. However, it should be noted that in the window framework we have adopted in this paper only written language from the Chinese media was used and that there has been organised societal concern about the recognition and use of Modern Standard Chinese (MSC), especially in the high register language in Singapore. Thus the relative conservative ranking of Singapore in the line-up on *endocentric* disposition is not unexpected, but would show considerable difference in comparable spoken language situations.

Perhaps more significantly, this study has demonstrated that lexical innovation, either through "loan" words or other newly coined words, are not just of piecemeal interest as has been commonly shown, but

---

[11] see T'sou 1997. *Multilingual Matters*. "Aspects of the Two Language System and Three Language Problem in the Changing Society of Hong Kong" in *One Country, Two Systems, Three Languages: A Survey of Changing Language Use in Hong Kong*, Clevendon: Multilingual Matters, ed. Sue Wright and Helen Kelly-Holmes, pp. 22–33.

[12] see Huang Shuan-fan (Huang Xuanfan) 黃宣籓 . 1994. *Yuyan, Shehui yu zuqun yishi* 語言，社會與族群意識 (Language, society and ethnicity). Taibei: Wenhe chuben.

that the phenomenon deserves systematic investigation which could yield new theoretical significance. The findings also allow us to have a better understanding of how the development of lexical variation may be traced to causes outside language itself, to the more holistic societal context and collective cognitive disposition of the larger community.

ANNEX

Annex 1: Chinese words related to "vehicle" found in a 30 day window (December 1996 to January 2000) from Hong Kong, Macao, Taiwan, Shanghai and Singapore newspapers

1 九巴	35 火車站	69 自行車棚	103 車巡
2 十字車	36 火車票	70 行車	104 車房
3 三輪車	37 火車頭	71 行車証	105 車況
4 三輪車夫	38 牛車	72 行車線	106 車型
5 三輪車主	39 主戰車	73 衣車	107 車客度
6 下車	40 出車	74 作案車	108 車架
7 下車處	41 出租車	75 助動車	109 車流
8 上下車	42 出租隊	76 尾班車	110 車流量
9 上車	43 包車	77 快車	111 車胎
10 上落車	44 卡車	78 快車隊	112 車風
11 土方車	45 囚車	79 快車道	113 車展
12 大巴	46 失車	80 沖洗車	114 車庫
13 大車	47 巨龍車	81 汽車	115 車座
14 大篷車	48 平板車	82 汽車司	116 車租
15 小巴	49 平治車	83 汽車組	117 車站
16 小巴車	50 打的	84 汽車業	118 車迷
17 小汽車	51 民車	85 汽車廠	119 車商
18 小車	52 瓦斯車	86 汽機車	120 車票
19 小型車	53 用車	87 私車	121 車船
20 工程車	54 田螺車	88 私家車	122 車速
21 中巴	55 白搭車	89 車	123 車頂
22 公交車	56 列車	90 車子	124 車場
23 公交車票	57 列車長	91 車手	125 車廂
24 公共汽車	58 列車員	92 車斗	126 車牌
25 公車	59 列車站	93 車主	127 車程
26 太空車	60 吉普車	94 車卡	128 車費
27 巴士	61 吊車	95 車扒	129 車軸
28 巴士車	62 吊秤車	96 車名	130 車間
29 巴士站	63 吊臂車	97 車次	131 車隊
30 巴士線	64 吊雞車	98 車行	132 車隊長
31 手推車	65 名車	99 車位	133 車號
32 木頭車	66 地車	100 車尾	134 車資
33 水車	67 老爺車	101 車系	135 車資卡
34 火車	68 自行車	102 車身	136 車路

Annex 1: Chinese words related to "vehicle" found in a 30 day window (December 1996 to January 2000) from Hong Kong, Macao, Taiwan, Shanghai and Singapore newspapers (cont.)

137 車道	172 的士業	207 候車	242 彩車
138 車禍	173 直通車	208 候車停	243 掃車
139 車禍率	174 空中巴士	209 候車室	244 掃路車
140 車種	175 空巴	210 修車	245 掛車
141 車價	176 空調車	211 座車	246 推土車
142 車廠	177 臥鋪士	212 座駕車	247 推車
143 車潮	178 花車	213 旅巴	248 採訪車
144 車輛	179 長途車	214 旅遊巴	249 救火車
145 車輛組	180 便民車	215 旅遊車	250 救傷車
146 車輪	181 便車	216 校巴	251 救護車
147 車輪牌	182 剎車	217 校車	252 棄車
148 車錢	183 剎車器	218 消防車	253 貨車
149 車險	184 剎車燈	219 班車	254 貨櫃車
150 車頭	185 前導車	220 起步車	255 貨櫃車架
151 車縫	186 城巴	221 起重車	256 通車
152 車籍	187 宜傳車	222 送水車	257 單車
153 車齡	188 客車	223 送貨車	258 單車徑
154 車軟盤	189 客車化	224 送款車	259 單機車
155 巡邏車	190 客貨車	225 馬車	260 廂型車
156 坦克	191 客運車	226 高檔車	261 殘的
157 坦克車	192 架子車	227 停車	262 渣土車
158 定位車	193 洗車房	228 停車位	263 買車者
159 房車	194 泵水車	229 停車處	264 越野車
160 房車賽	195 看車	230 停車場	265 超車
161 拉煤車	196 砂石車	231 停車費	266 超載車
162 拉臂車	197 計程車	232 停車點	267 跑車
163 拖車	198 計程車業	233 偵察車	268 郵政車
164 拖架車	199 軍車	234 偷車	269 郵遞車
165 服務車	200 風車	235 偷車賊	270 開車
166 泥頭車	201 飛車	236 售車量	271 開倒車
167 泊車	202 飛虎車	237 售票車	272 開道車
168 泊車仔	203 乘車	238 堵車	273 雲梯車
169 泊車員	204 乘車人	239 執勤車	274 黃魚車
170 的士	205 乘車証	240 宿營車	275 基車
171 的士牌	206 倒車	241 專車	276 搬場車

Annex 1: Chinese words related to "vehicle" found in a 30 day window (December 1996 to January 2000) from Hong Kong, Macao, Taiwan, Shanghai and Singapore newspapers (cont.)

277 新巴	298 電單車	315 槽罐車	336 翻車
278 滑車	299 慢車到	316 豬籠車	337 轉車
279 腳車	300 綠巴	317 輪椅車	338 轉車站
280 腳踏車	301 肇事車	318 駕車	339 醫療車
281 裝甲車	302 豪華車	319 駕車者	340 雙向車
282 解款車	303 賓士	320 學車者	341 騎車人
283 試車	304 輕單車	321 戰車	342 羅車人
284 賊車	305 廢土車	322 擁車	343 轎車
285 跟車	306 廢棄車	323 擁車証	344 鏟車
286 跟車員	307 德士	324 機車	345 驚車
287 運兵車	308 摩托	325 機動車	346 麵包車
288 運金車	309 摩托車	326 燒車	347 贓車
289 運草車	310 摩托車尾箱	327 獨輪車	348 鐵箱車
290 運貨車	311 摩托車廠	328 輸送車	349 驅車
291 運鈔車	312 撞車	329 壓縮車	350 飆車
292 運輸車	309 摩托車	330 擠車	351 飆車隊
293 遊覽車	310 摩托車尾箱	331 賽車	352 靈車
294 過山車	311 摩托車廠	332 賽車場	353 藍車站
295 電車	312 撞車	333 賽車會	
296 電車站	313 敵戰車	334 櫃車	Total Frequency:
297 電動車	314 樣車	335 翻斗車	4,712

Annex 2: Japanese words related to "vehicle" found in a 30 day window (Dec. 1996 to Jan. 2000) from Japanese newspapers

1 車（クルマ）	10 違法駐車	19 停車	28 消防車
2 自動車	11 車線	20 車いす（ヴイス）	29 車検
3 自動車道	12 外国車	21 電気自動車	30 新車
4 軽自動車	13 車内	22 輸入車	31 乗車率
5 乗用車	14 車両	23 国産車	32 盗難車
6 高級乗用車	15 自転車	24 機関車	33 公用車
7 小型乗用車	16 車種	25 中古車	34 愛車
8 駐車	17 列車	26 駐車中	35 車外
9 駐車場	18 電車	27 駐車禁止	36 乗車場

Annex 2: Japanese words related to "vehicle" found in a 30 day window (Dec. 1996 to Jan. 2000) from Japanese newspapers (cont.)

37 駐車違反	67 英国車	97 大衆車	127 エアバッグ製備車
38 国際戦略車	68 満車	98 最新式作車	128 巡回サービス車
39 救急車	69 逆諭入車	99 飛車	129 ガソリン車
40 対向車	70 発車	100 車間距離	130 ドイツ車
41 車台	71 営業車	101 緊急車	131 トヨタ車
42 図書館車	72 同車	102 対向車線	132 ホンダ車
43 蒸気機関車	73 小型車	103 単車	133 ヨーロッパ車
44 爆弾	74 無保険車	104 三輪車	134 イタリア車
45 車体	75 高級車	105 保冷車	135 モデル車
46 改造車	76 収集車	106 貨車	136 カー用品
47 駐亭車	77 洗車場	107 搭載車	137 宣伝カー
48 後続車	78 持帰車	108 型商用車	138 選挙カー
49 犯行車両	79 車輪	109 車座	139 バス
50 四輪駆動車	80 歯車	110 震災工作車	140 バス停
51 自家用車	81 未来車	111 関係車両	141 タクシー
52 廃車	82 土足厳禁車	112 人車人体	142 トラック
53 送迎車	83 集金車	113 車	143 バイク
54 国民車	84 馬車	114 車列	144 ミニバイク
55 事故車	85 積載車	115 米国車	145 カーナビ
56 外車	86 車道	116 片側一車	146 オートバイ
57 新型車	87 二輪車	117 直進車線	147 リヤカー
58 送迎車	88 降車口	118 車寄せ	148 パトカー
59 大型車	89 車庫	119 ワゴン車	149 カーナビゲーション
60 停車中	90 下車	120 プレスパッカー車	150 ソーラーカー
61 海外生産車	91 指導車	121 レジャー用車（RV）	151 マイカー
62 除雪車	92 台車	122 コンクリート打設車	152 ソーラーカーレース
63 車規制	93 降車場	123 ミクサー車	153 ソーラーカーコンペ
64 車裂（中国刑法）	94 先導車	124 ポンプ車	154 タンク
65 右折車	95 警護車	125 フォード車	155 タンクローリ
66 直進中	96 左折車	126 プロトン車	156 ダンプカー

Annex 2: Japanese words related to "vehicle" found in a 30 day window (Dec. 1996 to Jan. 2000) from Japanese newspapers (cont.)

157 アジアカー	160 カーナビシステム	163 モノレール	
158 スポーツカー	161 レンタカー	164 ワンボックスカー	Total Frequency:
159 カーフェリー	162 レーシングカー	165 カーナビゲーションシステム	2,094

REFERENCES

Cihai 辭海 . 1999. Shanghai: Shanghai cishu chubanshe.

Ciyuan 辭源 . 1931.

Ciyuan 辭源 . 1939.

Huang Shuan-fan (Huang Xuanfan) 黃宣範 . 1994. Yuyan, Shehui yu zuqun yishi 語言，社會與族群意識 (Language, society and ethnicity). Taibei: Wenhe Chuben.

Masini, Federico. 1993. *The Formation of Modern Chinese Lexicon and its Evolution Toward a National Language: The Period from 1840-1898.* Berkeley: Journal of Chinese Linguistics (Monograph Series, no. 6).

T'sou, Benjamin K. 1975. "On the Linguistic Covariants of Cultural Assimilation", *Anthropological Linguistics* 17, pp. 445–65.

——. 1995. "Some Methodological Remarks on Lexical Innovation in Chinese", paper presented at the conference "Prisma Sprache: Chinesische Versuche der Bewältigung Westlichen Gedankenguts", Bad Homburg, Germany.

——. 1997. *Multilingual Matters.* "Aspects of the Two Language System and Three Language Problem in the Changing Society of Hong Kong" in *One Country, Two Systems, Three Languages: A Survey of Changing Language Use in Hong Kong*, Clevendon: Multilingual Matters, ed. Sue Wright and Helen Kelly-Holmes, pp. 22-33.

——. 1998a. *Zhongwen gediqu gongshi ciyu yanjiu baogao*中文各地區共時詞語研究報告 (Linguistic Variation in Chinese Communities—LIVAC 1.0). Hong Kong: Hong Kong City University Language Information Sciences Research Centre (http://www.rcl.cityu.edu.hk/livac/).

——. 1998b. "A Window on Re-lexification in Chinese", paper presented at "Linguistic Change and the Chinese Dialects: An International Symposium dedicated to the Memory of the late Professor Li Fang-kuei", University of Washington, Seattle.

——. 2001. "Language Contact and Lexical Innovation", in: Michael Lackner, Iwo Amelung and Joachim Kurtz (eds.). *New Terms for New Ideas. Western Knowledge and Lexical Change in Late Imperial China.* Leiden: Brill, pp. 35–53.

—— and Feng Liangzhen 馮良珍 . 2000. "Hanyu (wu di) yu riyu xin gainian ciyu duibi yanjiu—cong xin wenshi kan cihui yansheng yu zhongzheng" 漢語（五地）與日語新概念詞語對比研究— 從新聞視窗看詞匯衍生與重整 (Comparative research on terms for new concepts in Chinese (of five cities) and Japanese— Deriving and reassembling of vocabulary as seen from the media angle), *Yuyan yanjiu*, 2000.3, pp. 51–70.

Xiandai Hanyu cidian 現代漢語詞典 (Modern Chinese dictionary). 1996. Beijing: Shangwu yinshuguan.

You Rujie 游汝杰 and Yang Bei 楊蓓 . 1998. "Guangzhouhua, Shanghaihua he putong-hua cihui jiejinlü de jiliang yanjiu" 廣州話，上海話和普通話詞匯接近率的計量研究 (Quantitative research on the closeness of Cantonese, Shanghainese and Mandarin vocabulary), in: Benjamin K. T'sou 鄒嘉產 et al. (eds.). *Hanyu jiliang yu jisuan yanjiu* 漢語計量於計算研究 (Quantitative and Computational Studies on the Chinese Language). Hong Kong: City University of Hong Kong, Language Information Sciences Research Centre, pp. 57–77.

Zheng Jinquan鄭錦全 . 1994. "Hanyu fangyan goutongdu de jisuan" 漢語方言溝通度和方音計算 (Computation of understandability of Chinese dialects), *Zhongguo yuwen* 94.1, pp. 35–43.

THE ORGANIZATION OF KNOWLEDGE

IWO AMELUNG

NAMING PHYSICS: THE STRIFE TO DELINEATE A FIELD OF MODERN SCIENCE IN LATE IMPERIAL CHINA

INTRODUCTION

The aim of this paper is to give a short overview of the process by which physics was accommodated as a field of knowledge in late Qing China.[1] Specifically I will focus on the question of how physics was named and how its boundaries were delineated during the period under review. It is not my intention to suggest that the terminological problems I will describe here are to be made responsible for the difficulties that physics encountered when it was first introduced in China. Rather I want to suggest that a close look at terminological issues can be fruitfully employed as a methodological device to get a clearer picture of the problems which had to be overcome when China tried to accommodate Western sciences. As a matter of fact during its early phase of reception physics was often mingled with the different designations for 'sciences' available in nineteenth century China. At the same time the different subbranches of physics were promoted as quasi independent sciences. Only during the last years of the nineteenth century the terminological and classificatory ambiguity brought about by the developments of the decades before it became clear to translators and the 'scientific public' at large. A first response to this dilemma was to revive a term first coined by the Jesuit mission in the seventeenth century. Eventually, however, a completely new and uncompromised term for physics was adopted which became the standard term when physics was established as a field of scientific inquiry and academic education in China.

1. THE EMERGENCE OF PHYSICS IN THE WEST

If one examines attempts to define the contents of physics as a subject of scientific inquiry one will find vastly differing situations in differ-

---

[1] I would like to thank Rui Magone for many helpful comments on earlier drafts of this paper.

ent countries and at different times. Research during the last decades has shown, however, that the first half of the nineteenth century was a decisive time for delineating the boundaries of physics as an academic subject and establishing it as a distinct academic discipline taught at institutions of higher learning. This process, which has been called "the invention of physics"[2] started in the eighteenth century when physics, then used synonymously with 'natural philosophy' broke away from the realm of 'natural history' (due especially to the prominence accorded to the classification efforts of Linné and others) and entered its decisive stage at the beginning of the nineteenth century when chemistry was established as an independent science. Beginning with Fresnel the subjects of 'particular' or 'experimental' physics such as the study of sound, heat, light, electricity, and magnetism and 'general' physics (i.e. Newtonian mechanics) were subsequently unified[3] and finally drawn together under the roof of a new definition of 'energy physics'.[4]

In the context of this paper, it is useful to stress that the process of the "invention of physics" in the West was accompanied by numerous terminological shifts and inventions. New terms were used to initiate and underline conceptual departures from tradition. Well-known examples are Faraday's newly-coined terms 'anode' and 'cathode', which were devised in collaboration with William Whewell in the 1830s.[5] At the same time, it became clear that the re-classification and professionalization of the sciences as well as curricular changes required the coinage of new terms such as the word 'scientist' itself, which was created by Whewell as well. In fact, terms like 'scientist' and the later 'physicist' helped reinforce the distinction between the "decaying" metaphysical and moral sciences and the natural sciences

---

[2] Cf. Susan Faye Cannon. 1978. *Science in Culture*. New York: Science History Publications, p. 111.

[3] Cf. Robert H. Silliman. 1975. "Fresnel and the Emergence of Physics as a Discipline", *Historical Studies in the Physical Sciences* 4, pp. 137–62.

[4] Cf. Peter Michael Harman. 1982. *Energy, Force and Matter. The Conceptual Development of Nineteenth Century Physics*. Cambridge: Cambridge University Press (Cambridge History of Science).

[5] Cf. William Whewell. 1847. *Philosophy of the Inductive Sciences. Founded upon Their History*. London: John W. Parker, 2nd edition, vol. 1, p. 51.

and physics, which rapidly gained importance during the first half of the nineteenth century.[6]

It is important to note that the terminological evolution was anything but uniform in the West. Whereas *Physik* in Germany and *physique* in France[7] were widely used already early on, the term 'physics' was not readily recepted in Britain, where 'natural philosophy' remained much more popular.[8] Many chairs at British universities which since the 1840s or 1850s exclusively dealt with physics, were still called 'chairs of natural philosophy'—now understood in a much narrower sense. A number of works on physics translated into English from French in the 1860s still were rendered as dealing with 'natural philosophy' although at the same time books which employed 'physics' in the title were published as well. Significantly, educational practice at British universities was quite different from the continent. At Cambridge, the leading university in the field, the teaching of physics was provided mainly within the framework of the 'Mathematical Tripos' (The 'Natural Sciences Tripos' founded in 1851 did not enjoy much popularity at the beginning, and the Cavendish Laboratory and the chair for experimental physics were only established in 1871–74).[9] Notwithstanding its high quality, the curriculum did not employ a term for a 'unified' physics, focussing instead on the single sub-divisions of physics which enjoyed a certain degree of independence. The link was not provided by an overarching concept of 'physics' but rather by the fact that important axioms could be understood by applying methods used in advanced mathematics.[10]

---

[6] Cf. Sydney Ross. 1962. "Scientist: The Story of a Word", *Annals of Science* 18, pp. 65–85.

[7] Cf. Rudolf Stichweh. 1984. *Zur Entstehung des modernen Systems wissenschaftlicher Disziplinen. Physik in Deutschland 1740 bis 1890*. Frankfurt: Suhrkamp; Maurice Crosland and Crosbie Smith. 1978. "The Transmission of Physics from France to Britain: 1800–1840", *Historical Studies in the Physical Sciences* 9, pp. 1–62.

[8] The *British Cyclopedia* of 1835–1838 distinguished between 'chemistry' and 'natural philosophy' "to which the term physics is applied". For more examples from contemporary encyclopedias cf. Richard Yeo 1991. "Reading Encyclopedias. Science and the Organization of Knowledge in British Dictionaries of Arts and Sciences, 1730–1850", *Isis* 82, pp. 24–49.

[9] Romuldas Sviedrys. 1976. "The Rise of Physics Laboratories in Britain", *Historical Studies in the Physical Sciences* 7, pp. 405–36.

[10] David B. Wilson. 1982. "Experimentalists among the Mathematicians: Physics in the Cambridge Natural Sciences Tripos, 1851–1900", *Historical Studies in the Physical Sciences* 12:2 (1981/82), pp. 253–84.

2. THE DIFFUSION OF WESTERN PHYSICS IN CHINA BETWEEN THE 1850S AND THE 1890S

The modern Chinese term for 'physics' is *wulixue* 物理學 . As other terms, used to denote subjects of the sciences as for example *jingjixue* 經濟學 and *zhexue* 哲學 for 'economics' and 'philosophy' respectively, the term originated from Japan where it is pronounced *butsurigaku*. After its first appearance as the title of a book it made a stunningly fast career. Within two years it became the most frequent and in due time the only Chinese translation for physics.

It has been established that one of the main reasons for the late arrival and the rapid standardization of terms of Japanese origin in the realm of social sciences was that up to the turn of the century when more and more Chinese students went to Japan for study, these fields had been largely absent from the Chinese scientific discourse so that there was little need for an appropriate terminology.[11] After the Sino-Japanese War in 1894/95 the Chinese finally turned to Japanese terms (written in *Kanji*) which proved easy to adopt and showed a high level of consistency. This consistency was the result of a long process, which had begun soon after the Meiji-reform, during which Japanese scholars were able to develop a highly sophisticated language of science—albeit not without difficulties.[12]

However, it is important to be aware of the fact, that in the field of the natural and especially the applied sciences the situation was markedly different. Western knowledge had begun to pour into China already in the seventeenth century by way of translations and books written by Jesuit missionaries and Chinese converts. In fact Aleni's *Xixue fan* 西學凡 (General outline of Western learning) and other Jesuit books provide a transliteration of the term 'physics'—'physics' of

---

[11] For example prior to 1895 only four Western monographs dealing with 'Economics' had been translated into Chinese, cf. Ye Shichang 葉世昌 . 1998. *Jindai Zhongguo jingji sixiang shi* 近代中國經濟思想史 (A history of modern Chinese economic thinking), Shanghai: Shanghai renmin chubanshe, p. 83.

[12] For a brief discussion of some of these problems in the field of physics cf. Kenkichiro Koizumi. 1975. "The Emergence of Japan's First Physicists: 1868–1900", *Historical Studies in the Physical Sciences* 6, pp. 3–108, especially pp. 46–7. For a more exhaustive analysis cf. Nihon butsurigaku kai 日本物理学会 (ed.). 1978. *Nihon no butsurigaku shi* 日本の物理学史 (History of physics in Japan). 2 vols. Tokyo: Tokai daigaku, vol. 1, pp. 77–88.

course in an Aristotelian sense[13] —even though the term *feixijia* 費西
加 did not leave any marks in Chinese history. The second phase of
the introduction of Western physical knowledge, which began only
after the First Opium War of 1840 was closely connected to the scientific enterprises of protestant missionaries. As it is well known, these
activities had a far-reaching impact on some of the more open-minded
Chinese intellectuals. Moreover the widely perceived need for modernization led to the establishment of a number of institutions of
higher learning in which Western knowledge and Western sciences
were taught. According to incomplete calculations between 1851 and
1890 39 works relating on physics only (i.e. excluding astronomy and
chemistry) were translated into Chinese. In the period between 1891
and 1910 at least another 47 works followed.[14] Although this quantitative assessment is revealing to some extent—showing for example
that during the late imperial era physical knowledge was being introduced at a considerably faster pace, it does not say much about the
process of how physical knowledge was actually diffused nor can it
provide a full picture of the way in which Western physics was introduced to and received in China.[15]

From 1851 to 1868, the first phase of disseminating physical
knowledge to China after the First Opium War, the situation was surprisingly confusing as far as the Chinese terms for 'physics' were
concerned. To some extent this phase was decisive for the later developments because in this period missionaries and translators failed to
introduce a universally accepted term for physics yet succeeded in
establishing the branches of physics as quasi independent 'sciences'.
In this context the first important work was a small book compiled by
the medical missionary Benjamin Hobson (Hexin 合信 , 1816–73)

---

[13] Cf. Giulio Aleni (Ai Rulüe 艾儒略) and Yang Tingyun 楊廷筠 . 1623. *Xixue fan*
西學凡 (General outline of Western learning). Hangzhou, p. 4b.

[14] Cf. Wang Bing 王冰 . 1986. "Ming Qing shiqi (1610–1910) wulixue yizhu
shumu kao" 明清時期物理學譯著書目考 (A bibliographical study on translations of
Western books on physics during the Ming and Qing (1610–1910)), *Zhongguo keji
shiliao* 7.5, pp. 3–20.

[15] We know little about the number of copies that these books actually sold. As to
the question of bootlegged copies, no research has been done on this important topic
yet.

which was published in 1855 carrying the suggestive title *Bowu xin-bian* 博物新編 .[16] It was received favorably in China and only three years later reprinted in Japan.[17] Unfortunately we don't know which sources Hobson drew upon or why he chose this particular title for his book. As it happens *bowu* 博物 was a term widely used in traditional China which can be translated as "broad learning of the phenomena". It became the title of several works such as Zhang Hua's *Bowu zhi* 博物志 (3rd century AD.) commonly translated as 'Treatise on curiosities'. A closer examination of the book makes quite clear that Hobson had the intention to introduce Western scientific and technological knowledge to China. Perhaps Hobson used the term *bowu* as a translation of the term 'natural philosophy'[18]—however not in its more restricted sense as 'physics' but rather going back semantically to the eighteenth century where 'natural philosophy' encompassed almost all categories of 'learning about the nature'.[19] Although there was probably some potential to narrow down the term to something like 'physics' as it had happened in the West since the middle of the eighteenth century,[20] this did not occur in China.[21] In fact, Hobson's rather unsystematic treatment of the different scientific fields and his emphasis on quite 'exotic' technological and scientific discoveries of the West, like for example the diving bell, suggests that Chinese read-

---

[16] Cf. Benjamin Hobson (Hexin合信). 1855. *Bowu xinbian* 博物新編(Natural philosophy). Shanghai: Mohai shuguan. Already in 1851 Daniel MacGowan (Ma Gaowen瑪高溫) had published a book with the title *Bowu tongshu* 博物通書 (Almanac of the sciences), which, however, had a very limited impact. The *xin* in Hobson's work may have been an allusion to this book, cf. id. 1851. *Bowu tongshu* 博物通書 (Almanac of the sciences). Ningbo: Aihuatang.

[17] Cf. Benjamin Hobson (Hexin合信). 1858. *Bowu xinbian* 博物新編(Natural philosophy). Edo: Rokosan.

[18] As such it was referred to by later missionaries.

[19] Cf. the appendix.

[20] Lobscheid for example suggested *bowu* as translation for 'natural philosophy', cf. Wilhelm Lobscheid. 1866–1869. *Ying-Hua zidian* 英華字典 . *English and Chinese Dictionary with Punti and Mandarin Pronunciation*. 4 vols. Hong Kong: Daily Press Office.

[21] Interestingly *bowu* in the early twentieth century became the term that was used for 'natural history', e.g. the subjects (zoology, botany and mineralogy) which had been separated from natural philosophy in eighteenth-century Europe, cf. for example Zeng Pu 曾樸 and Xu Nianci 徐念慈 . 1907. *Bowu da cidian* 博物大辭典 (Great dictionary of natural history). Shanghai: Hongwenguan.

ers may have regarded the book as yet another work on 'curiosities' as ambiguous title seemed to imply. The next major effort to introduce Western scientific knowledge to China was undertaken by a group of missionaries. A member of this group was Alexander Wylie (1815–1887) who published in 1857/58 a "scientific serial" titled *Liuhe congtan* 六合叢談 at the Inkstone Press (*Mohai shuguan* 墨海書館) in Shanghai. This publication constituted a rather systematic effort to convey Western knowledge of the sciences to China.[22] In our context it gains its importance mainly through the fact that it was a deliberate effort to delineate Western sciences—including the branches of physics—as *xue* 學 , 'learning' or 'science'.[23] Despite the lack of conclusive evidence, it seems likely that this effort was based on the model first put forward in Jesuit translations as the *Yuanxi qiqi tushuo* 遠西奇器圖説 , compiled by Johann Schreck (Deng Yuhan 鄧玉函 , 1576–1630) and Wang Zheng 王徵 (1571–1644) towards the end of the Ming dynasty. The *tushuo* stated that *zhongxue* 重學 , which was the term employed for Western (naturally pre-Newtonian) mechanics, should be considered to be a kind of 'learning' (*xue*) on par with other 'sciences' (like for example *wenxue* 文學).[24] The terms used for the different branches of learning in the *Liuhe congtan* still differ from the terms employed later. However it is highly probable that it was in the context of the *Mohai shuguan* that the terms for a number of physical sciences were coined, some of them being in use until today.[25] Within the 'scientific discourse' of late Imperial China the sub-branches of physics thus were established on equal status with other

[22] Cf. Wang Yangzong 王揚宗 . 1999. "'Liuhe congtan' zhong de jindai kexue zhishi ji qi zai Qing mo de yingxiang" 《六合叢談》中的近代科學知識及其在清末的影響 (Knowledge of science in Alexander Wylie's *Shanghae Serial* and its impact in nineteenth century China), *Zhongguo keji shiliao* 20.3, pp. 211–26.

[23] Cf. Alexander Wylie (Weilie Yali 偉烈亞力). 1857. "Liuhe congtan xiaoyin" 六合叢談小引 (Introduction to the *Shanghae Serial*), in: *Liuhe congtan* 六合叢談 1.1, pp. 1a–2a.

[24] Johann Terrenz Schreck (Deng Yuhan 鄧玉函) and Wang Zheng 王徵 . 1993 [1627]. *Yuanxi qiqi tushuo luzui* 遠西奇器圖説錄最 (Diagrams and explanations of the wonderful machines of the Far West), in: Ren Jiyu 任繼愈 (ed.). *Zhongguo kexue jishu dianji tonghui: jishu juan* 中國科學技術典籍通彙・技術卷 (Anthology of classical works of Chinese science and technology: Technology). Zhengzhou: Henan jiaoyu chubanshe, vol. 1, pp. 599–693; 610. The reprint is based on the *Shoushange* edition of 1844.

[25] Feng Guifen, who probably was one of the very first Chinese using the modern term for optics *guangxue,* was in close contact to at least some of the persons working at the Inkstone Press. One of the earliest translations on optics done after the

sciences. Still lacking however was a more general term for physics. As I will outline in greater detail below, this had "levelling" effect which it made it harder to reclassify the different subjects under new, more embracing terms. In 1868 W. A. P. Martin (Ding Weiliang 丁韙良, 1827–1916) published the *Gewu rumen* 格物入門, a textbook, which soon was used at the newly founded Tongwenguan 同文館 (College of Foreign Languages) in Beijing.[26] Although of poor quality it proved tremendously influential and saw several reprints even in Japan. It is unknown which sources Martin drew upon for its compilation. We know however, that he himself referred to the book as his "Introduction of Natural Philosophy".[27] Obviously Martin had a rather broad concept of 'natural philosophy'. Mainly the book deals with physical knowledge and no mention is made of botany or zoology. The inclusion of a part on chemistry (*huaxue rumen* 化學入門) however, shows that Martin's use of *gewu* 格物 was not synonymous with physics in a stricter sense. By using *gewu* in the title of his book Martin certainly wanted to appeal to his Chinese readers, who associated the term with the phrase *gewu zhizhi* 格物致知 ('the extension of knowledge by investigating the things') from the *Daxue* 大學. In fact *gewu* served as one of the foundations of Zhu Xi's 朱熹 (1130–1200) Neo-Confucian synthesis of Chinese thought. *Gewu* stood in a somehow ambiguous relationship to another abbreviation of the same passage *gezhi* 格致. While *gewu* was probably more 'fact'-centered—or better 'thing'-centered as seen for example in Fang Yizhi's 方以智 (1611–1671) *Wuli xiaoshi* 物理小識 from the seventeenth century[28]—*gezhi* was the more general term and during late Ming and early Qing-times had been often used as a translation for Western *scientia* which

---

[25] *(cont.)* Opium War, was compiled as a collaborative effort between Edkins and Zhang Fuxi 張福僖. Significantly the title of this compilation, which was probably completed in 1851 (but only published in 1896), was still titled *Guang lun* 光論 ("On light" or "Theories on light"). There seems to have been another work on acoustics titled in the same fashion. Cf. Wang Yangzong 王揚宗. 1994. "Wan Qing kexue yizhu zakao" 晚清科學譯著雜考 (On some Chinese translations of Western scientific books during the late nineteenth century), *Zhongguo keji shiliao* 15.4, pp. 32–40; 34–5.

[26] W. A. P. Martin (Ding Weiliang 丁韙良). 1868a. *Gewu rumen* 格物入門 (Introduction to the sciences). Beijing: Tongwenguan,

[27] Cf. W. A. P. Martin. 1966. *A Cycle of Cathay or China, South and North. With Personal Reminiscences*. New York: Paragon, pp. 235–6.

[28] Willard J. Peterson. 1976. "From interest to indifference: Fang I-chih and Western Learning", *Ch'ing-shih wen-t'i*, vol. 3. pp. 60–80.

was as its Chinese translation laden both with empirical and moral concerns.[29] In such a perspective then, *gewu* was a reasonable candidate as a term for physics. Indeed when in 1880 Young J. Allen (Lin Lezhi 林樂知 , 1836–1907) translated the *Science primer series'* volume on physics by Balfour Stewart into Chinese and thus published the first real textbook which drew together all the branches of Western physics (and unlike Martin's *Gewu rumen* did not include chemistry), he titled it *Gezhi qimeng gewuxue* 格致啟蒙格物學 .[30] Although the translation was of high quality the book did not gain much attention.[31] Nor did the possibilities of the term *gewu* or *gewuxue* for that matter. Quite the opposite, by and large the distinctions between *gezhi* and *gewu* tended to vanish.[32] The emergence of the term *gexue* 格學 , which of course in Chinese was understood as an abbreviation for both *gezhi* or *gewu*, and which apparently was first used by William Muirhead (Mu Weilian 慕維廉 , 1822–1900) as translation for 'science' (or using the terminology of the time, probably rather 'inductive science') in his introduction to the first part of Bacon's *Novum Organum*[33] and against the end of the nineteenth century became quite popular,[34] certainly did not help clarify the situation but was rather efficient in levelling all distinctions if there were any left.

[29] Cf. David C. Reynolds. 1991. "Redrawing China's Intellectual Map: Images of Science in Nineteenth Century China", *Late Imperial China* 12.1, pp. 27–61; 40.

[30] Cf. Balfour Stewart. 1880. *Gezhi qimeng gewuxue* 格致啟蒙格物學(Science primers: Physics). Translated by Young J. Allen (Lin Lezhi 林樂知). Shanghai: Jiangnan zhizaoju. The book was based on Balfour Stewart. 1872. *Physics* (Science Primers). London: Macmillan.

[31] In his *Xinlingxue* published in 1889 Yan Yongjing used the term *gewuxue* for physics and *gewu houxue* 格物後學 for metaphysics. This book was published by the School and Textbook Series Committee in Shanghai, of which Young J. Allen was a member. Cf. Joseph Haven (Haiwen 海文). 1889. *Xinlingxue* 心靈學 (Mental philosophy). Translated by Yan Yongjing 顏永京 . Shanghai: Yizhi shuhui.

[32] This has been recently noted by Xi Zezong 席澤宗 . 1999. *Zhongguo chuantong wenhua li de kexue fangfa* 中國傳統文化里的科學方法 (The scientific method in China's traditional culture). Shanghai: Shanghai keji jiaoyu chubanshe, pp. 39; see also Wang Yangzong 王揚宗 . 1994. "Cong 'gezhi' dao 'kexue'" 從「格致」到「科學」 (From *gezhi* to *kexue*), *Lishi daguanyuan* 10, pp. 56–7.

[33] Cf. William Muirhead (Mu Weilian 慕維廉). 1876. "Gezhi xinfa" 格致新法 (New methods of the sciences), *Yizhi xinlu*, July 1876. This text was republished in the *Gezhi huibian* in 1877 and a revised version was published as *Gezhi xinji* 格致新機 as a book in 1888.

[34] Cf. for example Timothy Richard (Li Timotai 李提摩太). 1894a. "Xu lun gexue", 續論格學 (Sequel to the discussion on 'science') in Timothy Richard and Zhong Ying 仲英 , *Yangwu xinlun* 洋務新論 , 2, 8a.

Physical knowledge continued to pour into China, mostly by way
of the very productive translation bureau of the Jiangnan Arsenal
(*Jiangnan zhizaoju fanyiguan* 江南製造局翻譯館), which published a
large amount of books related to physics. Almost exclusively these
publications addressed specific fields within the realm of physics like
optics (*guangxue* 光學), acoustics (*shengxue* 聲學), heat (*rexue* 熱學)
and electrics (*dianxue* 電學). A similar pattern of piecemeal introduction of physical knowledge (yet at the same time rather comprehensive) is visible in the writings of most missionaries.

3. THE RECEPTION OF 'PHYSICS' IN CHINA

How then was this knowledge received in China? To provide an
answer to this rather complex question it might be useful to focus on
those texts which made a conscious effort to delineate physics as a
branch of learning. One of the central features of these texts was the
use of the *xue*-suffix in order to name individual sciences and
branches of sciences. This feature is already present in Feng Guifen's
馮桂芬 (1809–1874) famous *Jiaobinlu kangyi* 校邠盧抗議 (Protest
notes from the *Jiaobin*-studio) which was completed during the late
Xianfeng-era.[35] Most likely the Chinese recipients of Western knowledge were capable of a more subtle distinction between *gezhi* and
gewu than the Western missionaries and translators. This would have
offered, as just mentioned, at least a possibility to distinguish between
'sciences in general' and 'physical sciences' or an even more
restricted 'physics' (the *gewuxue* suggested in the title of Young J.
Allen's translation). In practice, however, this theoretical possibility
was not used. In 1895, for example, the physics-school of the Tongwenguan which for some time (it is not clear since when) had been
called *gewu guan* 格物館 changed its name to *gezhi guan* 格致館 "in
order to fit together name and reality" (*yi fu ming shi* 以符名實).
Although Fan Hongye 樊洪業 has suggested that this development
was a step towards some form of standardization,[36] I would claim that

---

[35] Cf. for example Feng Guifen 馮桂芬 . 1998. *Jiaobinlu kangyi* 校邠盧抗議 (Protest notes from the *Jiaobin*-Studio). Zhengzhou: Zhongzhou guiji chubanshe, pp.
209–13.

[36] Cf. Fan Hongye 樊洪業 . 1988. "Cong gezhi dao kexue" 從格致到科學 (From
gezhi to *kexue*), *Ziran bianzhengfa tongxun* 10.3, pp. 39–50; 44. Wang Hui 汪暉 has
suggested that the change of names is related to the 'Theory of the Chinese Origin of

it was just the opposite, since it actually obscured the distinction between the sciences in general and their branches.[37] Although the terms *gewu* and *gezhi* continued to be used until the end of the Imperial era, the two most common designations for the new knowledge were *xixue* 西學 ('Western knowledge') and later on *xinxue* 新學 ('modern learning') which was ideologically somehow more digstible.[38] These designations seemed to elevate Western knowledge to the same level as the native traditional learning. There was one important consequence, however, which probably should be viewed in connection with the Chinese tradition of classification, which Nakayama Shigeru has characterized as follows: "If a phenomenon appeared that proved hard to file in one of the existing compartments, a new box could always be made for it." According to Nakayama's analysis this "documentary tradition" was able to forestall the emergence of a crisis which would have eventually occurred, as did in the West, as soon as the inconsistencies between different subjects put into one larger

---

[36] (*cont.*) the Western Sciences', cf. Wang Hui 汪暉. 1997. "Kexue de guannian yu Zhongguo de xiandai rentong" 科學的觀念與中國的現代認同 (The concept of science and China's modern identity), in: id. *Wang Hui zixuanji* 汪暉自選集 (Selected works of Wang Hui). Guilin: Guangxi shifan daxue chubanshe, pp. 208–305; 220. If *gezhi* ever was a "hybrid science" as claimed by Meng Yue, this in my opinion was due only to the fact that the *Xixue zhongyuan* theory called for a re-classification of the Chinese literary canon along the Western lines of classification. Discovering the Chinese scientific and technological tradition, however, does not mean that this tradition could and would be successfully employed in 'scientific practice', cf. Meng Yue. 1999. "Hybrid Science versus Modernity: The Practice of the Jiangnan Arsenal 1864–1897", *East Asian Science, Technology and Medicine* 16, pp. 13–52.

[37] The degree of confusion between *gezhi* and *gewu* can be seen from the diploma held by the first student who ever graduated from a Chinese university (the Beiyang xuetang 北洋學堂). According to this document he had studied *gezhixue*, which however did not include *huaxue* (chemistry) and *tianwenxue* (astronomy), and hence was not meant to denote 'science'. The curriculum included the subjects of *gewuxue, zhongxue, huaxue, dixue* (geography/geology). This seems to suggest that *gezhixue* referred to 'physics' while *gewuxue* might have meant 'physics without mechanics'. Cf. Beiyang daxue Tianjin daxue xiaoshi bianjishi (comp.) 北洋大學天津大學校史編輯室 (編) . 1990. *Beiyang daxue-Tianjin daxue xiaoshi* 北洋大學天津大學校史 . 2 vols. Tianjin: Tianjin daxue chubanshe, vol. 1, plate before the text and p. 30 (cf. appendix). In the preface to Edkins' *Xixue lüeshu*, Li Hongzhang mistakenly referred to Martin's *Gewu rumen* as *Gezhi rumen* 格致入門 , cf. Joseph Edkins (Ai Yuese 艾約瑟). 1886. "Xixue lüeshu" 西學略述 (A brief description of Western learning), in: *Gezhi qimeng* 格致啟蒙 , Beijing: Zong shuiwusishu, vol. 1, *xu*, 4a.

[38] Cf. Xiong Yuezhi 熊月之 . 1994. *Xixue dongjian yu wan Qing shehui* 西學東漸與晚清社會 (The dissemination of Western learning and late Qing society). Shanghai: Shanghai renmin chubanshe, pp. 729 –30.

nomological became too numerous.[39] As far as Western knowledge in late Imperial China is concerned, it seems possible to go one step further and to suggest that there was not only one box of "Western knowledge". Rather there was within this box a plethora of smaller boxes for the branches and subbranches of modern sciences. If a new or supposedly new branch was introduced, another small box was made to accommodate it. As mentioned above this had a levelling or equalizing result with the side-effect, however, that branches of knowledge which were either incompatible or identical in content coexisted in the same big box. In this context the most striking case is the field of mechanics, which in China originally had been called *zhongxue* ('the study of weight'), a term introduced by Jesuit missionaries in the seventeenth century. In 1868, however, W. A. P. Martin introduced the competing term *lixue* 力學 ('the study of force') which was more in accordance with the basic intend of Newtonian mechanics.[40] However, it came to be viewed by many Chinese as a new branch of knowledge demanding the construction of a new box, which ended up coexisting with the *zhongxue*-box. As a matter of fact, numerous late Qing writers tended to include both *zhongxue* and *lixue* while referring to Western knowledge or the subjects taught at Western universities.[41] This prevailing confusion and incapability to arrive at a better classification can also be perceived in those cases in which

---

[39] Nakayama Shigeru. 1984. *Academic and Scientific Traditions in China, Japan, and the West*. Tokyo: University of Tokyo Press, p. 58.

[40] Cf. W. A. P. Martin, *Lixue rumen* 力學入門 , part of his *Gewu rumen* published at the Tongwenguan in 1868. On the problem cf. Iwo Amelung. 2001. "Weights and Forces: The Reception of Western Mechanics in Late Imperial China", in: Michael Lackner, Iwo Amelung, Joachim Kurtz (eds.). *New Terms for New Ideas. Western Knowledge and Lexical Change in Late Imperial China*. Leiden: Brill, pp. 197–232.

[41] Cf. For example, Yu Yue's 俞樾 preface to Wang Renjun 王仁俊 . 1993 [1896]. *Gezhi guwei* 格致古微 (Ancient subtleties on science), in: Ren Jiyu 任繼愈 (ed.). *Zhongguo kexue jishu dianji tonghui: jishu juan* 中國科學技術典籍通彙 · 技術卷 (Anthology of classical works of Chinese science and technology: Technology). vol. 7. pp. 791–886, 792, Zhengzhou: Henan jiaoyu chubanshe; Liang Qichao 梁啟超 . 1896a. "Lun xuexiao shisan" 論學校十三 (On schools, 13), *Shiwu bao* GX22/10/1, p. 2a. As late as 1906 Yan Wenbing, in his preface to a standard textbook on mechanics, complained about this terminological confusion. He even proposed to introduce a completely new terminology for mechanics and its subbranches but in the end refrained from using it, see Philip Magnus (Magena Feili 馬格訥斐立). 1906. *Lixue kebian* 力學課編 (Lessons on mechanics). Translated by Yan Wenbing 嚴文炳 and Chang Fuyuan 常福元 . Beijing: Xuebu bianyi tushuju.

terms which were used for describing sciences as a whole were put on the same level of classification as its subbranches.[42]

The tendency to accept the designation of a certain branch or subbranch of Western sciences as sufficient for classifying it had another consequence, namely that all knowledge which actually or supposedly belonged to one branch would be put into the respective compartment. Accordingly some of the branches of knowledge, including those of physics, acquired a meaning which they did not possess in the West. The most striking examples for this development are the terms *shuixue* 水學 and *qixue* 氣學, which were probably both first introduced by W. A. P. Martin in his *Gewu rumen*. As these branches were considered as subbranches of mechanics according to the Western canon, they occupied a rather unsystematic position in Martin's opus. Already Martin overstretched the boundaries of these fields by including descriptions of phenomena and inventions that do not have to do much with the natural sciences (or 'Natural Philosophy' as he called it). In the *shuixue* section, for example, we find on the one hand, the basics of hydromechanical knowledge. On the other hand, however, there are many descriptions of different water-powered devices, which in a strict sense belong to the technology domain. Even more striking is Martin's introduction of *qixue* which covered nearly everything related to gas or steam (including locomotives and steamships of course). Obviously this approach was by no means compatible with any definitions of physics. This pragmatic treatment of physics, however, seems to be related to the fact that the new knowledge as it was being introduced to China should above all focus on "application".[43] As a matter of fact, this focus on application can be even detected in the Qing-statutes (*huidian* 會典). In the 1899 edition of this compilation we find a description of the subjects to be taught as *gezhi* at the Tongwenguan in Beijing—specifically mechanics, hydraulics, acoustics, pneumatics/steam, heat, optics, and electricity—emphasizing

---

[42] See, for example, Zhang Deyi 張德彝. 1986. *Suishi Ying E ji* 隨使英俄記 (Records of a companion of a mission to England and to Russia). Changsha: Yuelu shushe (*Zou xiang shijie congshu* 走向世界叢書. *From East to West—Chinese Travellers before 1911*), p. 605 (refers to 1876).

[43] This is probably one of the reasons why chemistry was accorded a relative prominent status within the canon of Western sciences. We should note in passing that contrarily to the situation in the realm of physics the term for chemistry *huaxue* was very early stabilized and is still in use today.

their "advantageousness for application" (*li yu yong* 利於用).[44] The
tendency to extend the semantic field of individual terms of some of
the subbranches of physics is clearly visible in a number of publications up to the turn of the century and makes retranslations sometimes
difficult.[45]

On the whole the situation concerning the delineation and classification of physics in the second half of the nineteenth century in China
is characterized by the lack of a common designation on the one hand,
and the exaggerated emphasis on the single branches of the field on
the other hand. Not surprisingly professional designations also suffered from the same ambivalences. Terms like *gezhijia* 格致家 , *gewu-
jia* 格物家 or *gexuejia* 格學家 blurred the distinction between
'scientists' in general and 'physicists' in particular rather than offering guidance or help for classification of the ever increasing amount
of incoming new knowledge from the West. At the same time we can
observe the emergence of specific terms for persons professionals in
the sub-branches of physics. Words like *dianxuejia* 電學家 for example,[46] bear a certain resemblance to the German designation *Elektris-
ierer*, which in the eighteenth century was often used for those people
who demonstrated electrical experiments on fairs, but was gradually
phased out when *Physik* became a legitimate field of scientific
inquiry.[47] It seems to me that this 'independence' of the subbranches
of physics may have had a facilitating effect on the application of the
theory of the Chinese origin of the Western sciences (*Xixue zhong-*

---

[44] Cf. *Qinding da Qing huidian* 欽定大清會典 . Taibei: Zhongwen shuju (Reprint
of 1899 edition), *juan* 100, pp. 10–11.

[45] See, for example, "Taixi shuixue" 泰西水學 , in: Gu Qiyi 顧其義 and Wu
Wenzao 吳文藻 (eds.). 1898. *Xi Fa cexue huiyuan er ji* 西法策學匯源二集 (Digest of
Western knowledge for policy questions. Second collection). Shanghai: Hongbao
shuju. In fact, the rendering of *shuixue* as given in the *Gewu rumen* as 'hydraulics' is
misleading.

[46] Cf. e.g. Timothy Richard (Li Timotai 李提摩太). 1894b. "Gezhi shumu
shuolüe" 格致書目說略 (Notes on a bibliography of the sciences), in: Timothy Richard and Zhong Ying 仲英 . *Yangwu xinlun* 洋務新論 (A new treatise on Western
affairs). n.p., 2, 9a. For references to these kind specialized scientists in texts written
by Chinese see for example the examination essay by Peng Ruixi 彭瑞熙 . 1887.
"Gezhi zhi xue Zhong Xi yitonglun" 格致之學中西異同論 (On the differences and
similarities of *gezhi* in China and the West), in: Wang Tao 王韜 (comp.). *Gezhi xueyuan keyi* 格致書院課藝 (Examination essays from the Shanghai Polytechnic), p. 1b.

[47] Cf. Stichweh 1984, pp. 257–60.

yuan 西學中源), which was ubiquitous during the late Qing.[48] Of great importance was the discovery that propositions from the *Mojing* 墨經 (Mohist canon), a text that back then was still corrupt, could be linked to subjects of Western physics. This connection was first made by Zou Boqi 鄒伯奇 (1819–1869) during the Daoguang-period. According to Zou there were obvious parallels between certain passages of the Mohist *Canon* and Western mechanics as well as optics/perspective (*shixue* 視學).[49] Since up to now not much research has been done this fascinating topic it seems useful to provide one example how this theory was applied. In Huang Zunxian's 黃遵憲 (1848–1905) *Riben zashi shi* 日本雜事詩 (Poems on the various things and affairs in Japan), which was completed in 1879 and first published in 1880, Huang discusses the Chinese origins of different sciences. In respect to the origins of optics (*guangxue*) he states:

臨鑑立景 二光夾一光 足被下光故成景於上首被下光故成景於下
鑑者近中則所鑑大景亦大遠中則所鑑小景亦小 此光學之祖也 [50]

This passage was shortly afterwards repeated verbatim in Zhang Zimu's 張自牧 (1833–1886) *Yinghai lun* 瀛海論 (Discourse of the Seapowers)[51] and soon showed up in numerous essays and examination questions of the very late Qing.[52] The only attempt to explain it in terms of optical content I found in an examination-essay for the *Gezhi shuyuan* 格致書院 by Peng Ruixi 彭瑞熙 who states that it matches the theories of "reflection, refraction, the transmission and the emis-

---

[48] Cf. Quan Hansheng 全漢昇 . 1935. "Qingmo de Xixue yuanchu Zhongguo shuo" 清末的西學源出中國說 (The late Qing theory of the Chinese origin of Western knowledge), *Lingnan xuebao* 4.2, pp. 57–102.

[49] Cf. Zou Boqi 鄒伯奇 . 1845. "Lun Xi fa jie gu suoyou" 論西法皆古所有 in: id. *Xue ji yi de* 學計一得 , *juan* 2, 20a–23b. Of course the strategy of relating Western mathematics and astronomy to the Chinese tradition had been already applied in the seventeenth century and was eventually endorsed by the Kangxi-emperor.

[50] Huang Zunxian 黃遵憲 . 1981 [1879]. Riben zashi shi *guangzhu* 日本雜事詩廣 註 (Annotated edition of the *Poems on miscellaneous subjects from Japan*). Changsha: Hunan renmin chubanshe (*Zou xiang shijie congshu* 走向世界叢書 . *From East to West—Chinese Travellers before 1911*), p. 97.

[51] Cf. Zhang Zimu 張自牧 . 1877–1897. "Yinghai lun" 瀛海論 (Discourse on the maritime powers), in: Wang Xiqi 王錫祺 (ed.). *Xiaofanghuzhai yudi congchao* 小方 壺齋輿地叢鈔 (Collected country surveys from the *Xiaofanghuzhai*-Studio). Shanghai: Zhuyitang, vol. 11, pp. 483–95; 488.

[52] Cf. for example Zheng Guanying 鄭觀應 . 1998. "Xixue" 西學 (Western knowledge), in: id. *Shengshi weiyan*, pp. 73–8; see also Liu Guanghan 劉光漢 (i.e. Liu Shipei 劉師培), "Zhoumo xueshu shi zongxu" 周末學術史總序 (General preface on learning at the end of the Zhou period), *Guocui xuebao* 1;1, 2, 3, 4, 5; 3.

sion of light 回光折光傳光射光 " of the "opticians" (*guangxuejia* 光學家).[53] All these passages from the *Mojing* of course have to do with optics, as has been established by modern research.[54] The interesting point is that to my knowledge they do not correspond with any of the versions of the Mohist *canon* available then,[55] a fact obviously not noted by the men who did not see any problems in quoting it as it was. A translation of these passages could read the following way:

> If one approaches a mirror a shadow [image?] will appear.
> Two light [-rays?] grip to one light [-point].[56]
> The bottom receives light from below, for this reason the shadow [image] is above, the top receives light from above for this reason the shadow [image] is below.[57]
> If the man looking at himself approaches the center [focal point?] [of a concave mirror?] that what is being mirrored is large and the shadow is large as well. If [the man looking at himself] is far away [from the focal point of a concave mirror?] that what is being mirrored is small and the image is small as well.

This reading contains a considerable amount of interpretation from my side[58] and of course does not intend to give an explanation of what the *Mojing* may have meant. Rather my purpose is to show that it was possible to establish correspondences with the literature on optics available at that time. Actually, this had already been done by Zou

---

[53] Cf. Peng Ruixi 1887.

[54] Cf. especially Qian Linzhao 錢臨照 . 1942. "Shi Mojing zhong guangxue lixue zhu tiao" 釋墨經中光學力學諸條 (Explanations on the passages on optics and mechanics in the Mojing), in: *Li Shizeng xiansheng liushi sui jinian wenji* 李石曾先生六十歲紀念文集 (Essays commemorating the sixtieth birthday of Mr. Li Shizeng). Kunming: Guoli Beiping yanjiuyuan, pp. 135–62.

[55] The first passage without doubt must read 臨鑑而立景到 (A. C. Graham. 1978. *Later Mohist Logic, Ethics and Science*. Hong Kong, London: The Chinese University Press, B 22), the second passage is correct although shortened (Graham 1978, B 18 explanation), the third passage originally reads 足蔽下光故成景於上首蔽上光故成景於下 (Graham 1978, B 19 explanation). The last passage originally reads 鑑者近中則所鑑大景亦大遠中則所鑑小景亦小而必正 (or 必易 depending on whether one quotes from the explanation identified as 中之內 or 中之外)(Graham 1978, B 23 explanation).

[56] It may be possible to explain this by imagining two parallel light-rays passing through a convex lens.

[57] Such an understanding would establish a relationship to the *camera obscura*.

[58] Actually even a reading of a passage of the *Mojing* which is not corrupted or changed as the ones I deal with here contains a very large amount of interpretation. This can be easily seen from the very different interpretations of, e.g., Needham, Graham and Qian Linzhao, cf. Joseph Needham. 1962. *Science and Civilisation in*

Boqi, who indeed tried to establish direct correspondences between passages from the *Mojing* and propositions found in the available literature on Western optics. However, Zou's correspondences remained rather crude since his main source of information on Western optics was Adam Schall von Bell's (Tang Ruowang 湯若望, 1591–1666) *Yuanjing shuo* 遠鏡說 (On the telescope) published two hundred years earlier. In 1894 Feng Cheng 馮澂 published a whole book on the same subject. While not necessarily more correct than Zou Boqi, he used most of the literature on optics which had been translated into Chinese from Western texts.[59] Incidentally he provided 'evidence' that the passage 二光夾一光 from the Mohist *canon* attests to the existence of the telescope in pre-imperial China.[60]

The fact that Huang Zunxian, whose text certainly was particular influential, tried not to establish such correspondences makes me suspect that Huang and many others, who did not have a scientific education, at least partially may have been influenced by the suggestiveness of a term like *guangxue* ('the science of light'), a phenomenon we can observe in respect to the integration of mechanics (*zhongxue* 'the science of weights') into the *Xixue zhongyuan* discourse as well.[61] By contrast even the most simple definition of physics did not allow the easy establishment of such suggestive relations,[62] let alone a more sophisticated understanding of physics as a highly abstract and mathematized science.

---

[58] (*cont.*) *China. Vol. IV: Physics and Physical Technology. Part 1: Physics.* Cambridge: Cambridge University Press, pp. 81–6, Graham 1978 and Qian Linzhao 1942. Even today, new and supposedly more exact explanations are forwarded almost on a regular basis, cf. for example, Sun Zhongyuan 孫中原. 1993. *Moxue tonglun* 墨學通論 (A discussion of Mohist studies). Shenyang: Liaoning chubanshe, pp. 227–41.

[59] Including *Guangxue* (Optics) translated by Carl Kreyer and Zhao Yuanyi 趙元益, *Guangxue tushuo* 光學圖說 (Charts and explanations on optics) translated by John Fryer, *Guangxue jieyao* 光學揭要 (Essentials on optics) as well as the relevant parts of W. A. P. Martin's *Gewu rumen* and *Gewu cesuan* 格物測算 (Scientific measuring and calculating).

[60] Cf. Feng Cheng 馮澂. 1900. *Guangxue shumo* 光學述墨 (Using optics to describe Mozi). Nanjing: Nanjing shuju (preface dates from 1894).

[61] Cf. Amelung 2001.

[62] The two translations of Balfour Stewart's *Physics* actually begin with a 'negative' definition of physics, stating that it deals with phenomena not covered by 'chemistry' *huaxue* 化學.

4. CLASSIFICATION OF THE SCIENCES AND THE EMERGENCE
OF NEW TERMS FOR 'PHYSICS'

As mentioned above, the first textbook drawing together all the sub-branches of physics had been published under the title *Gewuxue* in 1880. Already during the 1870s, however, the English missionary Joseph Edkins (Ai Yuese艾約瑟, 1823–1905) had attempted to acquaint his Chinese readers with the unity of the physical sciences. In a long but rather incomprehensible article published in the *Zhongxi wenjianlu* 中西聞見錄(Peking Magazine) in 1874/5 he introduced Faraday's theories on electrolysis and especially Faraday's theory on the unity of forces (and thus harking back to dynamistic concepts without naming them). However, Edkins failed to provide a name for the science in the context of which such theories could be applied.[63] This was done in some of the early bilingual dictionaries offering some terms which denoted physics, for most part descriptive.[64] In 1886 Edkins re-translated Balfour Stewart's *Physics* and used the term *zhixue* 質學,[65] which together with *tixue* 體學 went back to the original meaning of physics. When in 1898 A. Parker (Pan Shenwen 潘慎文) published a translation of Steele's *Popular Physics* under the title *Gewu zhixue* 格物質學, he noted in the "reading instructions" that in the past 'physics' had been translated as *gewu*. This he considered as incorrect since *gewu* actually "means all kinds of studies in the universe". Eventually, however, he retained the *gewu* in the title as a concession to earlier translations.[66] But both *tixue* and *zhixue* were not without problems since *tixue* was often employed as a term for denoting 'anatomy'[67] while *zhixue* occasionally was used as a Chinese ren-

---

[63] Cf. Joseph Edkins (Ai Yuese) 艾約瑟. 1874/75. "Guang re dian xi xinxue kao" 光熱電吸新學考 (Research into the new science of light, heat, electricity and attraction, *Zhong Xi Wenjianlu* 28 and 29. We should note here that his article had a Christian message as well.

[64] Lobscheid for example suggested *xingli* 性理 or *xingxue* 性學, cf. Lobscheid. 1866–69.

[65] Cf. Balfour Stewart. 1886. *Gezhi zhixue qimeng* 格致質學啟蒙 (A Primer of Physics). Translated by Joseph Edkins (Ai Yuese 艾約瑟). Beijing: Zong shuiwusi, (*Gezhi qimeng* 10).

[66] Cf. J. D. Steele (Shi Dier 史砥爾). 1898. *Gewu zhixue* 格物質學. Translated by A. P. Parker (Pan Shenwen 潘慎文) and Xie Honglai 謝洪賚. Shanghai: Meihua shuguan, p. 4.

[67] Cf. Karl E. G. Hemeling (He Meiling 赫美玲). 1916. *English-Chinese Dictionary of the Standard Chinese Spoken Language* (Guanhua 官話) *and Handbook for*

dition for 'chemistry'[68] and in some cases even for the sciences as a whole.[69] Even if these terms were not employed on a large scale, their emergence seems to indicate that there was a growing uneasiness about earlier attempts to come to terms with physics as a scientific discipline. When more and more Chinese became interested in Western knowledge in the 1890s—a development closely related to the increasingly urgent issues of how to modernize army and state and how to establish a "better" (i.e. more modern) education system[70]—it became necessary to reclassify the existing knowledge. This was partly done by publishing bibliographies. The inadequacy of the existing classification system was noted for example by Liang Qichao 梁啟超 (1873–1929), who in the foreword to his *Xixue shumubiao* 西學書目表 (Bibliography of Western knowledge) stated that "the classification of Western books is most difficult". Interestingly, he was especially concerned with the question of how to classify some of the aspects of applied sciences. For example he suggested to reclassify photography, which hitherto had been treated as part of *guangxue* ('optics'), and steam engines, which up to that date had been considered as *qixue*. According to Liang, both fields should be relocated to the 'industry' (*gongyi* 工藝) category.[71] Around the turn of the century the Shanghai serial *Huibao* 匯報, which was dedicated to the propagation of Western science (and the catholic faith, as it was partly financed by French Jesuits) published a question put forth by one of its readers who styled himself "principal of the studio for reading translated books" (*du yishu zhai zhuren* 讀譯書齋主人): "How is

---

[67] (*cont.*) *Translators, including Scientific, Technical, Modern and Documentary Terms.* Shanghai: Statistical Department of the Inspectorate General of Customs.

[68] Cf. for example Yan Fu 嚴復. 1931. *Mule mingxue* 穆勒名學 (Mill's *Logic*). 3 vols. Shanghai: Shangwu yinshuguan, p. 1.

[69] Cf. "Zhendan xueyuan zhangcheng" 震旦學員章程 (Statutes of the Zhendan [Aurora] College). 1903. *Zhejiangchao* 6.

[70] That there was a growing awareness of Western sciences in ever larger circles of the population has been shown by Xiong Yuezhi in his analysis of the letters to the editor published in the *Gezhi huibian* 格致彙編 and the *Gezhi xinbao* 格致新報. According to Xiong the letters to the *Gezhi xinbao*, which was printed in 1898, reveal a much better understanding and a more systematic treatment of the Western sciences than the *Gezhi huibian*'s letters, which were published 20 years earlier. Cf. Xiong Yuezhi 1994, pp. 457–8.

[71] Cf. Liang Qichao 梁啟超. 1896b. "Xixue shumubiao xuli" 西學書目序例 (Preface and reading instructions to a bibliography of Western knowledge), *Shiwubao* GX22/9/11, pp. 3b–6a.

Western learning classified and ordered"? The answer he received
from the editors reads as follows:

> Western Learning is divided into the two branches of heavenly and
> human learning. Heavenly learning deals with the miracle of creation,
> with that which is embedded in the disposition. It deals with that which
> is beyond the ordinary carnal desires and that which is known and put
> into practice without labor and effort. Human learning is divided into
> two branches: One inquires into the facts of the past—this is history.
> The other examines the persevering principles of things and is divided
> into five branches. One is called mathematics (*jihe* 幾何), one is called
> physics (*xingxing* 形性), one is called astronomy, one is called chemis-
> try, one is called "natural history" (*bowu*). Mathematics (*jihe*) com-
> prises arithmetics (*suanxue* 算學), algebra, geometry, trigonometry and
> other methods. Physics (*xingxing*) comprises mechanics, acoustics,
> optics, heat, magnetics, electrics. If one wishes to engage in astronomy
> he first needs to know about arithmetics and geometry.[72]

If we leave aside the terminological curiosities,[73] this short text, as
many others, shows quite clearly that the growing awareness of the
classification of Western knowledge was to some extent coupled with
the emergence of a modern notion of physics. Incidentally, as can be
seen from the passage above the term *xingxing* or *xingxingxue* 形性學
first used by Jesuit missionaries in the seventeenth century became a
strong contender for naming physics in Chinese.[74] Apparently this
term owed its sudden resurrection to Catholic missionaries and Chinese converts who in 1898 decided to publish the *Gezhi xinbao* 格致
新報 (*Revue Scientifique*), a newspaper dedicated to the dissemination
of Western sciences. In a series entitled "Guiding thread through the
sciences" (*Gezhi chuguang* 格致初桄), already in its first issue a classification of the sciences was provided listing the fields of zoology,
botany, mineralogy, chemistry, physics (*xingxingxue*) and neurol-

---

[72] *Huibao* No. 109 (1901).

[73] There for example is no explanation for the fact that the term *jihe*, which had
been employed for geometry since the Jesuit mission and was widely accepted in
China, suddenly came to be used as a designation for mathematics as a whole. Engelfriet has shown that *jihe* was no transliteration for geometry but he admits that it was
closely associated with geometry, cf. Peter Engelfriet. 1998. *Euclid in China. The
Genesis of the First Translation of Euclid's* Elements *in 1607 and its Reception up to
1723*. Leiden: Brill, pp. 138–9. We should note as well that social sciences were
totally excluded from the explanation.

[74] Cf. e.g. Francisco Furtado (Fu Fanji 傅汎際) and Li Zhizao 李之藻. 1965
[1631]. *Mingli tan* 名理探 (Logica). Taibei: Taiwan Shangwu yinshuguan, p. 315.

ogy.[75] While not being the only term for physics used in this newspaper, *xingxingxue* soon acquired some prominence. As a matter of fact, *Xingxingxue yao* 形性學要 was the title given by a publishing house, which was closely related with Jesuit activities, to a translation of Ganot's *Cours de Physique Purement Experimentale. A l'usage des Gens du Monde*, which happened to be one of the most popular physics textbooks of the nineteenth century.[76] *Xingxingxue* certainly was not a bad choice as a translation for physics and was moreover based on the Jesuit's tradition. However, it was not without its risks either. This becomes clear from the question put forth by an interested reader to the successor journal of the *Gezhi xinbao,* the *Huibao.* The question reads:

> 'Living things' (*shengwu* 生物) also have form (*xing* 形) and nature (*xing* 性), why is it that physics (*xingxingxue)* does not cover them as well?

The editors' reply was:

> That what in Chinese is called *xingxingxue* is called 'physique' [in French in the original text] in Western languages. It is also called *xingxue.* Although living things (*shengwu*) have a form as well, Westerners have the special discipline of *bowuxue* 博物學 'Histoire naturelle' to teach and explore it in the finest way. Indeed, the intellectual capacity of one person has limits. If he delves into different fields he cannot avoid loving the universal without hitting the essence. For this reason [the sciences] were differentiated into various fields.[77]

Obviously, these de-abstractions of terms employed to describe the Western sciences could happen in other fields as well and there is no evidence that it was the danger of de-abstraction which is to be made responsible for the 'victory' of *wulixue* as ultimate Chinese term for 'physics'. Early references to this term and its short form *wuli* 物理, which are clearly meant as translations of Western 'physics' instead of being quotations from Japanese texts as Guo Songtao's 郭嵩燾

---

[75] Cf. Jiang Zhuan 姜顗. 1898. "Gezhi chuguang xu" 格致初桄序 (Preface to "A guiding thread through the sciences"), *Gezhi xinbao* 1 (January 13, 1898).

[76] Cf. Adolphe Ganot (Jia Nuo 迦諾). 1898. *Xingxingxue yao* 形性學要 (Essentials of physics). Translated by Li Di 李杕 and Louis Vanhée (He Shishen 赫師慎). Shanghai: Gezhi yiwen baoguan.

[77] *Huibao* No. 101 (1901).

(1818 –1891) reference to it in 1878[78] and Huang Zunxian's reference in 1890,[79] show up in a 1890 book by Wang Tao 王韜 (1828–1897),[80] in Song Yuren's 宋育仁 (1858–1931) 1895 *Caifeng ji* 采風記 (Notes on customs)[81] and in the 1897 statutes for the Nanyang College (*Nanyang gongxue* 南洋公學) in Shanghai.[82] In the *Gezhi xinbao* from 1898 one can find several references to this term, sometimes in the same issues in which the adoption of the term *xingxingxue* was promoted, thus certainly not making comprehension easier for the readers. In all likelihood, however, the decisive event was the 1900 publication by the Jiangnan arsenal of a book carrying the title *Wulixue*.[83]

Although some of the older terms continued to be used for some time, there were to my knowledge no controversies about the suitability of the new term,[84] which rapidly made its way into school-regulations,[85] was used as title for textbooks[86] as well as in 1908 even as a

---

[78] Cf. Guo Songtao 郭嵩燾 . 1984. *Lundun yu Bali riji* 倫敦與巴黎日記 (London and Paris diary). Changsha: Yuelu chubanshe (*Zou xiang shijie congshu* 走向世界叢書 . *From East to West—Chinese Travellers before 1911*), p. 462.

[79] Cf. Huang Zunxian 黃遵憲 . 1968. *Riben guozhi* 日本國志 (Treatise on Japan). Taibei: Wenhai chubanshe, p. 804

[80] Cf. Wang Tao 王韜 . 1890. *Chongding Faguo zhilüe* 重訂法國志略 (Revised edition of *Brief description of France*), p. 15.

[81] Song Yuren 宋育仁 . 1895. *Caifeng ji* 采風記 (Notes on observed customs). n.p.: Xiuhai shanfang, *juan* 2, p. 9b.

[82] Cf. "Nanyang gongxue zhangcheng" 南洋公學章程 (Statute of the Nanyang college). 1897. *Jicheng bao* 7, p. 25.

[83] Cf. Iimori Teizō 飯盛挺造 . 1900. *Wulixue* 物理學 (Physics). Translated by Fujita Toyohachi 藤田豊八 and Wang Jilie 王季烈 . Shanghai: Jiangnan jiqi zhizao zongju.

[84] Even the dictionary *Technical Terms. English and Chinese*, which was finished in 1902 and result of the standardization efforts made by the Educational Association of China, which had been founded by missionaries and which in respect to emerging new terminologies was rather conservative since most of the persons involved preferred the terms they had coined themselves, included *wulixue* as one possible, but not preferable translation for physics, cf. Educational Association of China (comp.). 1902. *Technical Terms. English and Chinese*.

[85] For example *Qinding xuetang zhangcheng* 欽定學堂章程 (Statute of the Imperial university), 1902. p. 5a.

[86] See, for example, Isaac Taylor Headland (He Delai 何德賚). 1902. *Zuixin jianming zhongxue yong wulixue* 最新簡明中學用物理學 (New [textbook of] physics for the use at middle schools). Translated by Xie Honglai 謝洪賚 .

title of one of the first specialized multilingual dictionaries in China.[87] Even discussions on possible origins and the misleading construction of supposed traditions were largely avoided,[88] so that the term was widely understood as that what it was: a technical term whose purpose it was to delineate a homogenous field of scientific inquiry.[89] Arguably, the adoption of *wulixue* as a term used for physics in China signifies the beginning of a new era as far as the introduction of knowledge is concerned. This time, however, the epistemological impact would come from Japan on a wholesale scale. But the 1900 translation of *Wulixue* although based on a Japanese book, was deeply rooted in the terminological tradition that had unfolded since the 1850s in China. This tradition, however, had not been standardized and it did not include the term *wulixue* for that matter.[90]

---

[87] Cf. Xuebu shending ke 學部審定科 (comp.). 1908. *Wulixue yuhui* 物理學語彙 (Vocabulary of physics). Shanghai: Shangwu yinshuguan.

[88] We should note, however, that already in 1905 Mozi was designated as a 'physicist' (*wulixuejia* 物理學家)—a development which of course was of great importance for the development of the historiography of science in China, cf. Jue Zhen 覺晨. 1905. "Zhongguo wulixuejia Mozi" 中國物理學家墨子 (The Chinese physicist Mozi), *Lixue zazhi* 1905.4, pp. 63–70 and 1906.6, pp. 75–87.

[89] In its classical meaning *Wuli* signified 'the principle of things'. As such it had a long history in China. After the turn of the century Chinese scholars became aware of the fact that *wulixue* was something decidedly different from *wuli*, see for example Yan Fu 嚴復. 1986. "Lun jinri jiaoyu yinggai yi wuli kexue wei dangwu zhi ji" 論近日教育應該以物理科學為當務之極 (Modern education should stress physics), in Wang Shi (ed.). *Yan Fu ji* 嚴復集. Beijing: Zhonghua shuju, vol. 2, pp. 278–86. In this speech, which was probably held in or shortly after 1901, Yan Fu carefully distinguishes between *wuli kexue* and *wuli,* which would extend to chemistry, astronomy and other sciences as well. The suggestion that already Wang Fuzhi may have used the term *wuli* as translation for 'physics' (and actually also the term *huaxue* as translation for 'chemistry') has already been convincingly refuted by Shen Guowei, cf. Zhang Binglun 張秉倫 and Hu Huakai 胡化凱. 1998. "Zhongguo gudai 'wuli' yi ci de youlai yu ciyi yanbian" 中國古代物理一詞的由來與詞意演變 (The origins and the shift of meaning of the ancient Chinese word *wuli*), *Ziran kexueshi yanjiu* 17.1, pp. 55–60; Shen Guowei 沈國威. 1999. "Wang Fuzhi yongguo *wuli, huaxue* ma?" 王夫之用過物理化學馬？ (Did Wang Fuzhi employ the terms *wuli* and *huaxue*?), *Ciku jianshe tongxun* 1999.3, pp. 29–30.

[90] To give just a few examples: While the Japanese original for all kinds of undulatory motions employed the term *bo* 波 (jap. *ha)*, the Chinese translation referred to *lang* 浪, which had been in use since the 1860s. For refraction the translation employed the term *zheguang* 折光 rather than the Japanese *qushe* 屈射 (jap. *kussetsu)*.

CONCLUSION

In this paper I have focussed on the terminological and classificatory difficulties encountered during the process by which Western physics were accommodated in late Imperial China. While it is certain that the reception of Western sciences met with numerous political, institutional and intellectual obstacles, it is at the same time also true that strains within the field of physics itself which were created by the process of reception had a definite impact on the process of reception and adoption. I do not want to suggest that this factor was decisive for the process of reception. What seems clear, however, is the fact that no comprehensive treatment of the way the Western sciences were translated into Chinese can afford not to take the impact of these internal strains into account. These strains were to a large extent created by the piecemeal fashion in which physics was disseminated in China. More often than not, the transmitted knowledge lacked a clear delineation, which may be partially blamed on the transmitter's insufficient, in some cases ideologically tainted, understanding of the scientific knowledge involved. The persistence of the notion 'natural philosophy' in England and the United States, even in the nineteenth century when this term became eventually restricted to continental 'physics', may have influenced the process by which China adopted physical knowledge. We might speculate that missionaries from France or Germany, where the notion of 'natural philosophy' was less prominent, would have conveyed a more convincing and more consistent picture of physics than the British and American missionaries and translators who actually got to do the job. The Chinese, on the other hand, were poorly equipped for the task of accommodating and appropriating this knowledge handed over by British and American transmitters. Consequently, they filed such knowledge as 'Western' or 'modern', which were both obscure terms offering no guidance through the multitude of knowledge coming into China at that time; or the classified this knowledge—partly in accordance with the intention of the transmitters—into the categories of *gewu* or *gezhi*, two notions which were both rather vague and therefore in a constant process of semantical renegotiation.[91] The Japanese example—a comprehensive, consistent

---

[91] In 1903 Zhang Binglin 章炳麟 (1869–1936) chastized China's "dumb scholars" who used the term *gezhi* for that what in Japan was called *wulixue* since this would obscure the real meaning of the term *gezhi* as well as obscure the understanding of

and successful "modernization from above"—shows that a successful delineation and classification of new knowledge was possible. Although there was some terminological confusion, practical considerations enforced on Japanese physicists (the fact that there *were* physicists actually constitutes a big difference to China) the need to develop a consistent terminology which could be used for scientific and educational purposes. Additionally the Japanese tradition of lecturing in foreign languages may have been an important factor as to why Japan succeeded in developing a consistent scientific language. By contrast, the system by which the Chinese classified physics fell apart under the pressure of the internal strains created by the process of reception which became clearly visible when the need to establish a "modern" system of education arose—a system in which physics as a well delineated field of scientific inquiry was to play an important role.

---

[91] (*cont.*) physics. Zhang obviously did not think that the use of the term *wulixue* would bring about the same dire results, cf. Zhang Binglin 章炳麟. 1977 [1903]. "Lun chengyong weixin er zi zhi huangmiu" 論乘用維新二字之荒謬 (On the incorrectness of the application of the two characters *weixin*), in: Tang Zhijun 湯志鈞 (ed.). *Zhang Taiyan zhenglun xuanji* 章太言政論選集 (Collection of Zhang Binglin's political essays). Beijing: Zhonghua shuju, pp. 242–4; 242.

APPENDIX

Table 1: Definitions and 'delineations' of physics in translated texts and texts written by Western missionaries

year	description	Chinese text	translation
1855	contents of Hobson's *Bowu xinbian*	地氣論，熱論，水質論，光論，電氣論，天文略論，鳥獸略	On the atmosphere, on heat, on the properties of water, on light, on electricity, on astronomy, on animals.[a]
1857	introduction to the *Liuhe congtan* describing "Western Learning"	精益求精超前軼古啟名哲未言之奧闢造化未洩之奇請略舉其綱一為化學。。。一為察地之學。。。一為鳥獸草木之學。。。一為測天之學。。。一為電氣之學。。。別有重學流質數端，以及聽視諸學，皆窮極毫芒，精研物理	Ever seeking refinement, it surpasses the ancient and solves the mysteries about which the wise men did not speak. It develops the hidden wonders of creation. Please allow me to briefly introduce its principles: One is chemistry … one is the learning of exploring the Earth … one is the learning of birds, beasts and plants … one is the learning of measuring the heavens … one is the learning of electricity … there are also mechanics and the principles of fluids as well as acoustics, optics which are all exhaustive to the extreme and refined in exploring the principles of things.[b]
1868	contents of Martin's *Gewu rumen*	水學，氣學，火學，電學，力學，化學，算學	Hydraulics, pneumatics, heat, electrics, mechanics, chemistry, measurement and calculating.[c]
1874	"Learning from the West" as defined in an article by J. Edkins	近來泰西新學分為二門一為格致學一為化學計天下萬物除神魂而外再無有能出於斯二者即如天學地學格致之士已考得在下之地球與在上之日月星	The new learning from the West is divided into two branches: One is physics, the other is chemistry. If one wants to calculate the ten thousand things with the

Table 1: Definitions and 'delineations' of physics in translated texts and texts written by Western missionaries (cont.)

year	description	Chinese text	translation
1874 (*cont.*)		日月星辰咸有互相吸引之力又用算法三角形圓形方形八線之學考知地球上諸物各點如何運動之理凡造大砲火輪車船及鐵路等項咸出於格致之學	exception of the supernatural beings there is nothing which could excel these two. Astronomers and geologists for example already have found out that on the earth below and in the sun, the moon and the stars above there is the force of mutual attraction. They use mathematics, the learning of the triangle, of the circle of the square and trigonometry in order to determine the principle of the movement of all points of every body on earth. The manufacture of big cannons, locomotives, steam-ships, railways etc. are all based on physics.[d]
1886	contents of *juan* 7 (sciences) of Edkins' *Xixue lüeshu*	天文，質學，地學，動物學，金石學，電學，化學，天氣學，光學，重學，流質重學，氣質重學，身體學，較動物體學，身理學，植物學，醫學，幾何原本學，算學，代數學，曆學，稽古學，風俗學	Astronomy, physics, geology, zoology, mineralogy, electricity, chemistry, atmospheric sciences, optics, mechanics, hydromechanics, gas mechanics, anatomy, comparative anatomy (?), hygiene (?), botany, medicine, geometry, arithmetics, algebra, calendric system, archaeology, ethnology (?).[e]
1886	definition of physics in Edkins' Xixue lüeshu	質學乃論物之質與性為格致中最要之一學如論力有攝引力黏合力以及性異之物合而為一之力又有助力諸器如天平與舉重杆皆是也	Physics treats the matter and nature of objects. It is one of the most important branches of the sciences. It for example discusses forces. There is the force of attraction,

Table 1: Definitions and 'delineations' of physics in translated texts and texts written by Western missionaries (cont.)

year	description	Chinese text	translation
1886 (*cont.*)			molecular force and the force which draws together objects of different nature. There are a number of simple machines as for example the balance and the lever which all belong to it.[f]
1898	table of contents of Steele's *Gewu zhixue*	動與力，吸力，機器本原，流氣二質，壓力，聲學，光學，熱學，磁學，電學	Movement and force, attraction, the origins of machines, the pressure of fluids and gases, acoustics, optics, heat, magnetics, electrics.[g]
1899	subject of *xingxingxue* as defined in *Xingxingxue yao*	形性一學所包尤廣曰重學曰水學曰氣學曰聲學曰熱學曰光學曰磁學曰電學凡八門分之各為一學合之總稱形性學	[The subjects] treated by physics are very broad. They are called mechanics, hydraulics, pneumatics, acoustics, heat, optics, magnetics and electrics. All these eight subjects are single sciences when they are divided. When they are taken together they are called physics.[h]
1900	physics as defined in Iimori's *Wulixue*	物理學分為二大科一物體運動之學（即重學）一質點運動之學而物體運動學更分三派一定質重學一流質重學一氣質重學。。。至質點運動學亦分為六科如左浪動通論，聲學，光學，熱學，磁氣學，電學	Physics is divided into two branches: The study of the moving bodies (i.e. mechanics) and the study of the movement of molecules. The study of the movement of bodies is divided into three groups: solid body mechanics, fluid mechanics, gas mechanics. The study of the movement of molecules is divided into the six branches listed below: general laws of undulatory motion, acoustics,

Table 1: Definitions and 'delineations' of physics in translated texts and texts written by Western missionaries (cont.)

year	description	Chinese text	translation
1900 (*cont.*)			optics, heat,undulatory motion, acoustics, optics, heat, magnetism, electricity.[i]

Notes: (a) Hobson 1855. (b) Wylie 1857. (c) Martin 1868. Optics (*guangxue*) was included into the part on Heat. (d) Edkins 1874. (e) Edkins 1886, p. 70–86. (f) Edkins 1886, p. 71. (g) Steele 1898, table of contents. (h) Ganot 1899, preface by Li Di 李杕 , p. 1b. (i) Iimori Teizō 1900.

Table 2: Definitions and 'delineations' of physics found in Chinese sources

year	description	Chinese text	translation
1861	Feng Guifen about books introducing 'Western Knowledge'	算學重學視學光學化學皆得格物至理	Mathematics, mechanics, perspective, optics and chemistry all profit from the highest principles of *gewu*.[a]
1868	Wang Tao on 'practical learning' in England	英國以天文地理電學火學氣學光學化學重學為實學	In England astronomy, geography, electricity, heat, pneumatics, optics, chemistry and mechanics are considered as 'practical learning'.[b]
1876	Zhang Deyi describing subjects taught at the universities of Oxford and Cambridge	通國以英格蘭之敖克斯佛與堪卜立址之二大學院首。。。二學所教者系英文華文英薩森文亞喇伯文賽拉的文希伯來文希臘文拉丁文印度文日本文天竺古文日斯巴尼亞文法文德文俄文義文天文地理教學化學道學醫學算學光學性學音學化學詩學力學歌學壯學氣學測學重學格物學寫字學藥性學金石學草木學禽獸學古教學治理學教訓學減筆學機器學泥瓦學	All over the world the two universities of Oxford and Cambridge in England are considered to be the best. At these two schools the [following subjects] are taught: English, Chinese, Medieval English, Arabian, Celtic, Hebrew, Greek, Hindi, Japanese, Sanskrit, Spanish, French, German, Russian, Italian, astronomy, geography, religion, chemistry, philosophy (?), medicine,

Table 2: Definitions and 'delineations' of physics found in Chinese sources (cont.)

year	description	Chinese text	translation
1876 (*cont.*)		律例學今例古例印度律萬國律羅馬例猶太例今史古史萬國公法及行軺指掌等	mathematics, optics, physiology (?), acoustics, arts, poetry, mechanics (dynamics?), music, (?), pneumatics, measuring (surveying?), mechanics (statics?), physics (?), writing, pharmacology, mineralogy, botany, zoology, history of religions (?), administration, education, stenography, mechanical engineering, architecture, law, modern law, ancient law, Indian law, international law (?), Roman law, Jewish law, modern history, ancient history, international law and diplomacy.[c]
1890s	'Western learning' in a section on "Nourishing talent" from a book on policy questions	西學以歷算為基格致為宗一切光學化學汽學電學皆從此出	Western learning takes calendar-studies and mathematics as basis and 'sciences' as guiding principle. All optical, chemical, mechanical, acoustical, pneumatical and electrical learning comes from this.[d]
1895	Describing the system of French universities	譯其科名目義亦曰學問統光電汽熱音重算諸學合天文地理為一科	If one translates the names of the subject of studies, which are also called 'learning', then optics, electricity, heat, sound, mechanics and arithmetics are combined with astronomy and geography and form one department.[e]
1896		西人所言化學光學重學力學蓋由格物而至於盡物之性者也	That which the Westerners call chemistry, optics, mechanics

Table 2: Definitions and 'delineations' of physics found in Chinese sources (cont.)

year	description	Chinese text	translation
1896 (*cont.*)			(dynamics?), all starts from the investigation of things and arrives at the nature of things.[f]
1896		間嘗涉獵西書探其大旨算學為經重學化學為緯天學機學隸重學地學礦學隸化學水學氣學熱學電學及火器水師等學又兼隸重學化學外此若聲學光學乃氣學熱學之分支似非重學化學所可隸者	In the past I intermittently browsed through Western books and was able to find out their guiding principle. They all take mathematics as warp and mechanics and chemistry as woof. Astronomy and machinery belong to mechanics while earth sciences and mining belong to chemistry. Hydraulics, pneumatics, heat, electricity and fire-arms and navy belong to both mechanics and chemistry. The others as acoustics and optics are branches of pneumatics and heat and it seems that they cannot be [classified] as belonging to mechanics and/or chemistry.[g]
1896	Describing scientific associations in the West	西人為學也有一學即有一會故有農學會有礦學會有商學會有工藝會有法學會有天學會有地學會有算學會有化學會有電學會有聲學會有光學會有重學會有力學會有水學會有熱學會有醫學會有動植兩學會有教務會	For everything that the Westerners take as 'learning' exists an association. Thus there is an agricultural association, a mining association, an economic association, an industrial association, a law association, an astronomical association, a geographical (?) association, a mathematical association, a chemical association, an electrical association, an acoustics association, an

Table 2: Definitions and 'delineations' of physics found in Chinese sources (cont.)

year	description	Chinese text	translation
1896 (*cont.*)			optical association, a mechanical (?) association, an association of dynamics (?), a hydraulic association, an association for the study of heat, a medical association, a zoological association, a botanical association and an educational association.[h]
1898	Describing a part of the classification of Western learning	其學別類分門有條不紊曰天文學曰地理學曰金石學曰電學曰化學曰氣學曰光學曰火學曰水學曰重學曰動物學曰植物學曰幾何學茲數者為西學之要即中學所謂格致也	This learning is classified into numerous subjects as astronomy, geography, mineralogy, electricity, chemistry, pneumatics, optics, heat, hydraulics, mechanics, zoology, botany and geometry. These few are the most important ones of Western learning and they correspond to that what in Chinese learning is called *gezhi*.[i]
1898	Classification of 'science' in Liang Qichao's *Xixue shumubiao*	算學，重學，電學，化學，聲學，光學，汽學，天學，地學，全體學，動植物學，醫學，圖學	Mathematics, mechanics, electrics, chemistry, acoustics, optics, pneumatics, astronomy, geological sciences, anatomy, biology, medicine, cartography.[j]
1900	Subjects studied by the first university graduate in China	英文，幾何學，八線學，化學，格致學，身理學，天文學，富國策，通商約章，律法總論，羅馬律例，英國合同律，英國罪犯律，萬國公法，商務律例，民間詞訟律，英國憲章，田產易主律例，船政律例，聽訟法則	English, geometry, trigonometry, chemistry, physics, physiology, astronomy, economics, international trade, law in general, Roman law, English contract law, English penal law, international law, business law, private law, English constitutional law, property law,

Table 2: Definitions and 'delineations' of physics found in Chinese sources (cont.)

year	description	Chinese text	translation
1900 (*cont.*)			shipping law and court regulation[k]
1900	Subjects taught at Bei-yang da-xuetang in the second year	駕駛並量地學，重學，微分學，格物學，化學，筆繪圖並機器繪圖，作英文論，翻譯英文	Navigation and surveying, mechanics, calculus, physics, chemistry, map-drawing and engineering drawing, writing of English articles, English translation.
1901	Describing the classification of 'Western learning'	問西學分派之次序如何西學分天人二種天學論造化之奇性情之蘊超乎俗見塵心之上非庸碌之所能知能行人學分二種一考已往事端即史學也一考恆有之物理分五種曰幾何曰形性曰天文曰化學曰博物幾何包算學代數形學三角等法形性包重聲光熱磁電等學天文須先知算學形學方能從事化學即分合物之元粒博物包無生有生二種無生博物即地理地質曠工氣候流水等學有生博物即植物動物全體增長知覺等學另有學之總剛講究萬物之本末終始西人名為格物學	Question: How is Western learning classified and ordered? Answer: Western Learning is divided into the two branches of heavenly and human learning. Heavenly learning deals with the miracle of creation, with that which is embedded in the disposition. It deals with that which is beyond the ordinary carnal desires and that which is known and put into practice without labor and effort. Human learning is divided into two branches: One inquires into the facts of the past - this is history. The other examines the persevering principles of things and is divided into five branches. One is called mathematics, one is called physics, one is called astronomy, one is called chemistry, one is called 'natural history'. Mathematics comprises arithmetics, algebra, geometry, trigonometry and other methods.

Table 2: Definitions and 'delineations' of physics found in Chinese sources (cont.)

year	description	Chinese text	translation
1901 (*cont.*)			Physics comprises mechanics, acoustics, optics, heat, magnetics, electrics. If one wishes to engage in astronomy one first needs to know about arithmetics and geometry. Chemistry deals with the separation into and the combination of molecules. Natural history comprises the two branches of the inorganic and the organic. Inorganic natural history deals with geography, geology, mineralogy, meteorology and hydrology. Organic natural history comprises the studies of botany, zoology, anatomy, reproduction (?) and neurology. Except for this there are the fundamental principles of learning which inquire into the essential and non-essential and the beginning and the end of the ten thousand affairs and the ten thousand things. The Westerners call it philosophy.[m]
1901	Proposal of courses to be taught at Shandong University	藝學一門分為八科一算學二天文學三地質學四測量學五格物學內分水學力學汽學熱學聲學光學磁學電學八目六化學七生物學內分植物學動物學兩目八譯學泰西方言附	The school of sciences is divided into eight departments: Mathematics, astronomy, geology, surveying, physics (divided into eight subjects: hydromechanics, mechanics, pneumatics, heat, acoustics, optics,

Table 2: Definitions and 'delineations' of physics found in Chinese sources (cont.)

year	description	Chinese text	translation
1901 (*cont.*)			magnetics and electricity), chemistry, biology (divided into botany and zoology) and translation with foreign languages as an addition.[n]
1902	Statutes of Imperial University	格致科之目六一曰天文學二曰地質學三曰高等算學四曰化學五曰物理學六曰植物學	The science department is divided into six subjects: Astronomy, geology, higher mathematics, chemistry, physics, biology.[o]
1903	Defining physics	物理學者研究物象而操天工人代之權也或謂為形性學若光水重熱聲電諸科並隸焉	Physics researches objects and the natural power which act for man. It sometimes is called *xingxingxue* and it comprises the fields of optics, hydraulics, mechanics, heat, acoustics and electricity.[p]
1903	Defining *gezhi*	釋格致：重學。。。聲學。。。光學。。。熱學。。。磁氣學。。。電學。。。氣象學	An explanation of *gezhi*: Mechanics, acoustics, optics, heat, magnetics, electricity, meteorology.[q]

Notes:
(a) Feng Guifen 1998, pp. 209–13.
(b) Wang Tao 王韜. 1982. *Manyou suilu* 漫遊隨錄 (Memories of my peregrinations). Changsha: Hunan renmin chubanshe (*Zou xiang shijie congshu* 走向世界叢書. *From East to West—Chinese Travellers before 1911*), p. 116.
(c) Zhang Deyi 1986, p. 605.
(d) *Zhong Xi jingji celun tongkao, juan* 5, 3a.
(e) Song Yuren 1895 2, 12.
(f) Yu Yue's preface to Wang Renjun 1896.
(g) Lin Yishan's preface to Wang Renjun 1896.
(h) Liang Qichao 1896.
(i) "Xixue wei fuqiang zhi ben lun" 西學為富強之本論 (Western learning as the foundation of wealth and power), *Gezhi yiwen huibao* 1.1898.
(j) Liang Qichao 1898.
(k) *Beiyang daxue-Tianjin daxue jiaoshi, diyijuan,* plate prior to the text).
(l) *Beiyang daxue-Tianjin daxue jiaoshi, diyijuan* p. 30.
(m) *Huibao* No. 109.

(n) Yuan Shikai 袁世凱 . 1991. "Zou ban Shandong daxuetang zhe" 奏辦山東大學堂摺 (Memorial on the management of Shandong university), in: Qu Xingui 璩鑫圭 and Tang Liangyan 唐良炎 (eds.). *Zhongguo jindai jiaoyu ziliao huibian—xuezhi yanbian* 中國近代教育資料匯編 — 學制演變 (Sources on modern education in China—Changes in the educational system). Shanghai: Shanghai jiaoyu chubanshe, p. 54.

(o) *Qinding xuetang changcheng* (Classes taught at *Jingshi daxue tang*).

(p) Wang Jingyi 王景沂 (ed.). 1903. *Kexue shumu tiyao chubian* 科學書目提要初編 (First collection of an annotated bibliography of books related to science). Beijing: Guanbaoju, p. 15a.

(q) Wang Rongbao 汪榮寶 and Ye Lan 葉瀾 . 1903. *Xin Erya* 新爾雅 (The new *Erya*). Shanghai: Minquanshe, pp. 121–31.

References

Aleni, Giulio (Ai Rulüe 艾儒略) and Yang Tingyun 楊廷筠 . 1623. *Xixue fan* 西學凡 (General outline of Western learning). Hangzhou.

Amelung, Iwo. 2001. "Weights and Forces: The Reception of Western Mechanics in Late Imperial China", in: Michael Lackner, Iwo Amelung, Joachim Kurtz (eds.). *New Terms for New Ideas. Western Knowledge and Lexical Change in Late Imperial China.* Leiden: Brill, pp. 197–232.

Beiyang daxue Tianjin daxue xiaoshi bianjishi (comp.) 北洋大學天津大學校史編輯室 (編). 1990. Beiyang daxue-Tianjin daxue xiaoshi 北洋大學天津大學校史 . 2 vols. Tianjin: Tianjin daxue chubanshe.

Cannon, Susan Faye. 1978. *Science in Culture.* New York: Science History Publications.

Crosland, Maurice and Crosbie Smith. 1978. "The Transmission of Physics from France to Britain: 1800–1840", *Historical Studies in the Physical Sciences* 9, pp. 1–62.

Edkins, Joseph (Ai Yuese) 艾約瑟 . 1874/75. "Guang re dian xi xinxue kao" 光熱電吸新學考 (Research into the new science of light, heat, electricity and attraction), *Zhong Xi Wenjianlu* 28 and 29.

——. 1886. "Xixue lüeshu" 西學略述 (A brief description of Western learning), in: *Gezhi qimeng* 格致啟蒙 , Beijing: Zong shuiwusishu, vol. 1, *xu*, 4a.

Educational Association of China (comp.). 1902. *Technical Terms. English and Chinese.*

Engelfriet, Peter. 1998. *Euclid in China. The Genesis of the First Translation of Euclid's* Elements *in 1607 and its Reception up to 1723.* Leiden: Brill.

Fan Hongye 樊洪業 . 1988. "Cong gezhi dao kexue" 從格致到科學 (From *gezhi* to *kexue*), *Ziran bianzhengfa tongxun* 10.3, pp. 39–50; 44

Feng Cheng 馮澂 . 1900. *Guangxue shumo* 光學述墨 (Using optics to describe Mozi). Nanjing: Nanjing shuju (preface dates from 1894).

Feng Guifen 馮桂芬 . 1998. *Jiaobinlu kangyi* 校邠廬抗議 (Protest notes from the *Jiaobin*-Studio). Zhengzhou: Zhongzhou guiji chubanshe.

Fryer, John (Fu Lanya 傅蘭雅) (tr.), *Guangxue tushuo* 光學圖説 (Charts and explanations on optics).

Furtado, Francisco (Fu Fanji 傅汎際) and Li Zhizao 李之藻 . 1965 [1631]. *Mingli tan* 名理探 (Logica). Taibei: Taiwan Shangwu yinshuguan.

Ganot, Adolphe (Jia Nuo 迦諾). 1898. *Xingxingxue yao* 形性學要 (Essentials of physics). Translated by Li Di 李杕 and Louis Vanhée (He Shishen 赫師慎). Shanghai: Gezhi yiwen baoguan.

Graham, A. C. 1978. *Later Mohist Logic, Ethics and Science.* Hong Kong, London: The Chinese University Press.

Guangxue jieyao 光學揭要 (Essentials on optics) 1898 [1893]. Translated by W. M. Hayes (He Shi 赫士) and Zhu Baochen 朱葆琛 . Shanghai: Yiwen Shanghui.

Guo Songtao 郭嵩燾 . 1984. *Lundun yu Bali riji* 倫敦與巴黎日記 (London and Paris diary). Changsha: Yuelu chubanshe (*Zou xiang shijie congshu* 走向世界叢書 . *From East to West—Chinese Travellers before 1911*).

Harman, Peter Michael. 1982. *Energy, Force and Matter. The Conceptual Development of Nineteenth Century Physics.* Cambridge: Cambridge University Press (Cambridge History of Science).

Haven, Joseph (Haiwen 海文). 1889. *Xinlingxue* 心靈學 (Mental philosophy). Translated by Yan Yongjing 顏永京 . Shanghai: Yizhi shuhui.

Headland, Isaac Taylor (He Delai 何德賚). 1902. *Zuixin jianming zhongxue yong wulixue* 最新簡明中學用物理學(New [textbook of] physics for the use at middle schools). Translated by Xie Honglai 謝洪賚.

Hemeling, Karl E. G. (He Meiling 赫美玲). 1916. *English-Chinese Dictionary of the Standard Chinese Spoken Language (*Guanhua 官話*) and Handbook for Translators, including Scientific, Technical, Modern and Documentary Terms.* Shanghai: Statistical Department of the Inspectorate General of Customs.

Benjamin Hobson (Hexin 合信). 1855. *Bowu xinbian* 博物新編 (Natural philosophy). Shanghai: Mohai shuguan

——. 1858. *Bowu xinbian* 博物新編 (Natural philosophy). Edo: Rokosan.

Huang Zunxian 黃遵憲. 1968. *Riben guozhi* 日本國志 (Treatise on Japan). Taibei: Wenhai chubanshe.

——. 1981 [1879]. *Riben zashi shi guangzhu* 日本雜事詩廣註 (Annotated edition of the Poems on miscellaneous subjects from Japan). Changsha: Hunan renmin chubanshe (*Zou xiang shijie congshu* 走向世界叢書. *From East to West—Chinese Travellers before 1911*).

Huibao 匯報. No. 109 (1901).

Iimori Teizō 飯盛挺造. 1900. *Wulixue* 物理學 (Physics). Translated by Fujita Toyohachi 藤田豐八 and Wang Jilie 王季烈. Shanghai: Jiangnan jiqi zhizao zongju.

Jiang Zhuan 姜顟. 1898. "Gezhi chuguang xu" 格致初桄序 (Preface to "A guiding thread through the sciences"), *Gezhi xinbao* 1 (January 13, 1898).

Jue Zhen 覺晨. 1905. "Zhongguo wulixuejia Mozi" 中國物理學家墨子 (The Chinese physicist Mozi), *Lixue zazhi* 1905.4, pp. 63–70 and 1906.6, pp. 75–87.

Koizumi, Kenkichiro. 1975. "The Emergence of Japan's First Physicists: 1868–1900", *Historical Studies in the Physical Sciences* 6, pp. 3–108.

Kreyer, Carl T. (Jin Kaili 金楷理) and Zhao Yuanyi 趙元益 (trs.). 1876. *Guangxue* 光學 (Optics). Shanghai: Jiangnan zhizaoju.

Liang Qichao 梁啟超. 1896a. "Lun xuexiao shisan" 論學校十三 (On schools, 13), *Shiwu bao* GX22/10/1, p. 2a.

——. 1896b. "Xixue shumubiao xuli" 西學書目序例 (Preface and reading instructions to a bibliography of Western knowledge), *Shiwubao* GX22/9/11, pp. 3b–6a.

Liu Guanghan 劉光漢 (i.e. Liu Shipei 劉師培), "Zhoumo xueshu shi zongxu" 周末學術史總序 (General preface on learning at the end of the Zhou period), *Guocui xuebao* 1;1, 2, 3, 4, 5; 3.

Lobscheid, Wilhelm. 1866–1869. *Ying-Hua zidian* 英華字典. *English and Chinese Dictionary with Punti and Mandarin Pronunciation.* 4 vols. Hong Kong: Daily Press Office.

MacGowan, Daniel (Ma Gaowen 瑪高溫). 1851. *Bowu tongshu* 博物通書 (Almanac of the sciences). Ningbo: Aihuatang

Magnus, Philip (Magena Feili 馬格訥斐立). 1906. *Lixue kebian* 力學課編 (Lessons on mechanics). Translated by Yan Wenbing 嚴文炳 and Chang Fuyuan 常福元. Beijing: Xuebu bianyi tushuju

Martin, W. A. P. (Ding Weiliang 丁韙良). 1868a. *Gewu rumen* 格物入門 (Introduction to the sciences). Beijing: Tongwenguan.

——. 1883. *Gewu cesuan* 格物測算 (Scientific measurements and calculations). Beijing: Jingshi tongwenguan.

——. 1966. *A Cycle of Cathay or China, South and North. With Personal Reminiscences.* New York: Paragon, pp. 235–6.

Meng Yue. 1999. "Hybrid Science versus Modernity: The Practice of the Jiangnan Arsenal 1864–1897", *East Asian Science, Technology and Medicine* 16, pp. 13–52.

Muirhead, William (Mu Weilian 慕維廉). 1876. "Gezhi xinfa" 格致新法 (New methods of the sciences), *Yizhi xinlu*, July 1876.

Nakayama Shigeru. 1984. *Academic and Scientific Traditions in China, Japan, and the West*. Tokyo: University of Tokyo Press.

"Nanyang gongxue zhangcheng" 南洋公學章程 (Statute of the Nanyang college). 1897. *Jicheng bao* 7, p. 25.

Needham, Joseph. 1962. *Science and Civilisation in China. Vol. IV: Physics and Physical Technology. Part 1: Physics*. Cambridge: Cambridge University Press, pp. 81–6.

Nihon butsurigaku kai 日本物理学会 (ed.). 1978. *Nihon no butsurigaku shi* 日本の物理学史 (History of physics in Japan). 2 vols. Tokyo: Tokai daigaku.

Peng Ruixi 彭瑞熙. 1887. "Gezhi zhi xue Zhong Xi yitonglun" 格致之學中西異同論 (On the differences and similarities of *gezhi* in China and the West), in: Wang Tao 王韜 (comp.). *Gezhi xueyuan keyi* 格致書院課藝 (Examination essays from the Shanghai Polytechnic), p. 1b.

Peterson, Willard J. 1976. "From interest to indifference: Fang I-chih and Western Learning", *Ch'ing-shih wen-t'i*, pp. 60–80.

Qian Linzhao 錢臨照. 1942. "Shi Mojing zhong guangxue lixue zhu tiao" 釋墨經中光學力學諸條 (Explanations on the passages on optics and mechanics in the Mojing), in: *Li Shizeng xiansheng liushi sui jinian wenji* 李石曾先生六十歲紀念文集 (Essays commemorating the sixtieth birthday of Mr. Li Shizeng). Kunming: Guoli Beiping yanjiuyuan, pp. 135–62.

Qinding da Qing huidian 欽定大清會典. Taibei: Zhongwen shuju (Reprint of 1899 edition), *juan* 100, pp. 10–11.

Qinding daxuetang zhangcheng 欽定大學堂章程 (Statute of the Imperial university), 1902, table, p. 5a.

Quan Hansheng 全漢昇. 1935. "Qingmo de Xixue yuanchu Zhongguo shuo" 清末的西學源出中國説 (The late Qing theory of the Chinese origin of Western knowledge), *Lingnan xuebao* 4.2, pp. 57–102.

Reynolds, David C. 1991. "Redrawing China's Intellectual Map: Images of Science in Nineteenth Century China", *Late Imperial China* 12.1, pp. 27–61.

Richard, Timothy (Li Timotai 李提摩太). 1894a. "Xu lun gexue", 續論格學 (Sequel to the discussion on 'science') in: Id., Zhong Ying 仲英, *Yangwu xinlun* 洋務新論, n.p., 2, 8a.

——. 1894b. "Gezhi shumu shuolüe" 格致書目説略 (Notes on a bibliography of the sciences), in: Ibid., Zhong Ying 仲英. *Yangwu xinlun* 洋務新論 (A new treatise on Western affairs). n.p., 2, 9a.

Ross, Sydney. 1962. "Scientist: The Story of a Word", *Annals of Science* 18, pp. 65–85.

Schreck, Johann Terrenz (Deng Yuhan 鄧玉函) and Wang Zheng 王徵. 1993 [1627]. *Yuanxi qiqi tushuo luzui* 遠西奇器圖説錄最 (Diagrams and explanations of the wonderful machines of the Far West), in: Ren Jiyu 任繼愈 (ed.). *Zhongguo kexue jishu dianji tonghui: jishu juan* 中國科學技術典籍通彙・技術卷 (Anthology of classical works of Chinese science and technology: Technology). Zhengzhou: Henan jiaoyu chubanshe, vol. 1, pp. 599–693.

Shen Guowei 沈國威. 1999. "Wang Fuzhi yongguo *wuli*, *huaxue* ma?" 王夫之用過物理化學馬？ (Did Wang Fuzhi employ the terms *wuli* and *huaxue*?), *Ciku jianshe tongxun* 1999.3, pp. 29–30.

Shiwubao 時務報 . 1967 [1896.8–1898.8]. Edited by Wang Kangnian 汪康年 . Shanghai. Reprinted Taibei: Huawen shuju.

Silliman, Robert H. 1975. "Fresnel and the Emergence of Physics as a Discipline", *Historical Studies in the Physical Sciences* 4, pp. 137–62.

Steele, J. D. (Shi Dier 史砥爾). 1898. *Gewu zhixue* 格物質學 . Translated by A. P. Parker (Pan Shenwen 潘慎文) and Xie Honglai謝洪賚 . Shanghai: Meihua shuguan.

Stewart, Balfour. 1880. *Gezhi qimeng gewuxue* 格致啟蒙格物學 (Science primers: Physics). Translated by Young J. Allen (Lin Lezhi 林樂知). Shanghai: Jiangnan zhizaoju.

——. 1886. *Gezhi zhixue qimeng* 格致質學啟蒙 (A Primer of physics). Translated by Joseph Edkins (Ai Yuese 艾約瑟). Beijing: Zong shuiwusi, (*Gezhi qimeng* 10).

Stichweh, Rudolf. 1984. *Zur Entstehung des modernen Systems wissenschaftlicher Disziplinen. Physik in Deutschland 1740 bis 1890*. Frankfurt: Suhrkamp.

Song Yuren宋育仁 . 1895. *Caifeng ji* 采風記 (Notes on observed customs). n.p.: Xiuhai shanfang, *juan* 2, p. 9b

Sun Zhongyuan 孫中原 . 1993. *Moxue tonglun* 墨學通論 (A discussion of Mohist studies). Shenyang: Liaoning chubanshe, pp. 227–41.

Sviedrys, Romuldas. 1976. "The Rise of Physics Laboratories in Britain", *Historical Studies in the Physical Sciences* 7, pp. 405–36.

"Taixi shuixue" 泰西水學 , in: Gu Qiyi 顧其義 and Wu Wenzao 吳文藻 (eds.). 1898. *Xi Fa cexue huiyuan er ji* 西法策學匯源二集 (Digest of Western knowledge for policy questions. Second collection). Shanghai: Hongbao shuju.

Wang Bing 王冰 . 1986. "Ming Qing shiqi (1610–1910) wulixue yizhu shumu kao" 明清時期物理學譯著書目考 (A bibliographical study on translations of Western books on physics during the Ming and Qing (1610–1910)), *Zhongguo keji shiliao* 7.5, pp. 3–20.

Wang Hui 汪暉 . 1997. "Kexue de guannian yu Zhongguo de xiandai rentong" 科學的觀念與中國的現代認同 (The concept of science and China's identity), in: id. *Wang Hui zixuanji* 汪暉自選集 (Selected works of Wang Hui). Guilin: Guangxi shifan daxue chubanshe, pp. 208–305.

Wang Jingyi 王景沂 (ed.). 1903. *Kexue shumu tiyao chubian* 科學書目提要初編 (First collection of an annotated bibliography of books related to science). Beijing: Guanbaoju.

Wang Renjun王仁俊 . 1993 [1896]. *Gezhi guwei* 格致古微 (Ancient subtleties on science), in: Ren Jiyu 任繼愈 (ed.). *Zhongguo kexue jishu dianji tonghui: jishu juan* 中國科學技術典籍通彙・技術卷 (Anthology of classical works of Chinese science and technology: Technology). Zhengzhou: Henan jiaoyu chubanshe, vol. 7, p. 791–886.

Wang Rongbao 汪榮寶 and Ye Lan 葉瀾 . 1903. *Xin* Erya 新爾雅 (The new *Erya*). Shanghai: Minquanshe, pp. 121–31.

Wang Tao 王韜 . 1890. *Chongding Faguo zhilüe*重訂法國志略 (Revised edition of *Brief description of France*), p. 15.

——. 1982. *Manyou suilu*漫遊隨錄 (Memories of my peregrinations). Changsha: Hunan renmin chubanshe (*Zou xiang shijie congshu* 走向世界叢書 . *From East to West—Chinese Travellers before 1911*).

Wang Yangzong 王揚宗 . 1994a. "Wan Qing kexue yizhu zakao" 晚清科學譯著雜考 (On some Chinese translations of Western scientific books during the late nineteenth century), *Zhongguo keji shiliao* 15.4, pp. 32–40.

——. 1994b. "Cong 'gezhi' dao 'kexue'" 從 「格致」 到 「科學」 (From *gezhi* to *kexue*), *Lishi daguanyuan* 10, pp. 56–7.

——. 1999. "'Liuhe congtan' zhong de jindai kexue zhishi ji qi zai Qing mo de yingxiang" 《六合叢談》中的近代科學知識及其在清末的影響 (Knowledge of science in Alexander Wylie's *Shanghae Serial* and its impact in nineteenth century China), *Zhongguo keji shiliao* 20.3, pp. 211–26.

Whewell, William. 1847. *Philosophy of the Inductive Sciences. Founded upon Their History.* 2 vols. London: John W. Parker (2nd edition).

Wilson, David B. 1982. "Experimentalists among the Mathematicians: Physics in the Cambridge Natural Sciences Tripos, 1851–1900", *Historical Studies in the Physical Sciences* 12:2 (1981/82), pp. 253–84.

Wylie, Alexander (Weilie Yali 偉烈亞力). 1857. "Liuhe congtan xiaoyin" 六合叢談小引 (Introduction to the *Shanghae Serial*), in: *Liuhe congtan* 六合叢談 1.1, pp. 1a–2a.

"Xixue wei fuqiang zhi ben lun" 西學為富強之本論 (Western learning as the foundation of wealth and power), *Gezhi yiwen huibao* 1.1898.

Xi Zezong 席澤宗. 1999. *Zhongguo chuantong wenhua li de kexue fangfa* 中國傳統文化里的科學方法 (The scientific method in China's traditional culture). Shanghai: Shanghai keji jiaoyu chubanshe.

Xiong Yuezhi 熊月之. 1994. *Xixue dongjian yu wan Qing shehui* 西學東漸與晚清社會 (The dissemination of Western learning and late Qing society). Shanghai: Shanghai renmin chubanshe.

Xuebu shending ke 學部審定科 (comp.). 1908. *Wulixue yuhui* 物理學語彙 (Vocabulary of physics). Shanghai: Shangwu yinshuguan.

Yan Fu 嚴復. 1931. *Mule mingxue* 穆勒名學 (Mill's *Logic*). 3 vols. Shanghai: Shangwu yinshuguan.

——. 1986. "Lun jinri jiaoyu yinggai yi wuli kexue wei dangwu zhi ji" 論近日教育應該以物理科學為當務之極 (Modern education should stress physics), in Wang Shi (ed.). *Yan Fu ji* 嚴復集. Beijing: Zhonghua shuju, vol. 2, pp. 278–86.

Ye Shichang 葉世昌. 1998. *Jindai Zhongguo jingji sixiang shi* 近代中國經濟思想史 (A history of modern Chinese economic thinking), Shanghai: Shanghai Renmin chubanshe.

Yeo, Richard. 1991. "Reading Encyclopedias. Science and the Organization of Knowledge in British Dictionaries of Arts and Sciences, 1730–1850", *Isis* 82, pp. 24–49.

Yuan Shikai 袁世凱. 1991. "Zou ban Shandong daxuetang zhe" 奏辦山東大學堂摺 (Memorial on the management of Shandong university), in: Qu Xingui 璩鑫圭 and Tang Liangyan 唐良炎 (eds.). *Zhongguo jindai jiaoyu ziliao huibian—xuezhi yanbian* 中國近代教育資料匯編 — 學制演變 (Sources on modern education in China—changes in the educational system). Shanghai: Shanghai jiaoyu chubanshe, p. 54.

Zeng Pu 曾樸 and Xu Nianci 徐念慈. 1907. *Bowu da cidian* 博物大辭典 (Great dictionary of natural history). Shanghai: Hongwenguan.

Zhang Binglin 章炳麟. 1977 [1903]. "Lun chengyong weixin er zi zhi huangmiu" 論乘用維新二字之荒謬 (On the incorrectness of the application of the two characters *weixin*), in: Tang Zhijun 湯志鈞 (ed.). *Zhang Taiyan zhenglun xuanji* 章太言政論選集 (Collection of Zhang Binglin's political essays). Beijing: Zhonghua shuju, pp. 242–4.

Zhang Binglun 張秉倫 and Hu Huakai 胡化凱. 1998. "Zhongguo gudai 'wuli' yi ci de youlai yu ciyi yanbian" 中國古代物理一詞的由來與詞一演變 (The origins and the shift of meaning of the ancient Chinese word *wuli*), *Ziran kexueshi yanjiu* 17.1, pp. 55–60.

Zhang Deyi 張德彝 . 1986. *Suishi Ying E ji* 隨使英俄記 (Records of a companion of a mission to England and to Russia). Changsha: Yuelu shushe (*Zou xiang shijie congshu* 走向世界叢書 . *From East to West—Chinese Travellers before 1911*).

Zhang Zimu 張自牧 . 1877–1897. "Yinghai lun" 瀛海論 (Discourse on the maritime powers), in: Wang Xiqi 王錫祺 (ed.). *Xiaofanghuzhai yudi congchao* 小方壺齋輿地叢 鈔 (Collected country surveys from the *Xiaofanghuzhai*-Studio). Shanghai: Zhuyitang, vol. 11, pp. 483–95.

Zheng Guanying 鄭觀應 . 1998. "Xixue" 西學 (Western knowledge), in: id. *Shengshi weiyan*, pp. 73–8.

Zhong Xi jingji celun tongkao 震中西經濟策論通考 (Comprehensive compendium for answering policy questions concerning China and the West). 1902. Shanghai, *juan* 6, 22a.

"Zhendan xueyuan zhangcheng" 震旦學員章程 (Statutes of the Zhendan [Aurora] College). 1903. *Zhejiangchao* 6.

Zou Boqi 鄒伯奇 . 1845. "Lun Xi fa jie gu suoyou" 論西法皆古所有 in: id. *Xue ji yi de* 學計一得 , *juan* 2, 20a–23b.

SU RONGYU 蘇榮譽

THE RECEPTION OF 'ARCHAEOLOGY' AND 'PREHISTORY' AND THE FOUNDING OF ARCHAEOLOGY IN LATE IMPERIAL CHINA[1]

INTRODUCTION

Antiquarian collecting and the study of antique objects was pursued for centuries in China just as in Europe and hence Chinese scholars had quite a clear understanding of a prehistoric Chinese past already before the arrival of Western 'archaeology'. Yet this interest neither developed, as was the case in nineteenth century Europe, into the establishment of 'archaeology'—understood as an academic discipline dealing with the technique of excavations—nor of 'prehistorical studies' understood as a discipline dealing with methods of interpreting earliest historical sources, be it textual or artifactual evidence.

In the following study I will trace different developments that led to the establishment of the academic discipline of archaeology and its professionalization in China. I will argue that archaeological studies and expeditions undertaken by Western and Japanese scholars or individuals took place in China long before the idea of archaeology emerged there, and therefore did not exercise a profound impact on the development of the academic field of archaeology. Only decades later, at the beginning of the twentieth century, were archaeology and prehistorical studies to be introduced to China, mainly from two sources: firstly, as part of the general trend of translating books from Japanese and, secondly, with the introduction of the social sciences to China after the Sino-Japanese War and especially after the Boxer Revolt.

Archaeology is not an exception among the social and natural sciences in its political involvement; hence in China, just as in Europe, the evolution of the scientific discipline was closely interconnected

[1] The author wishes to thank Dr. Natascha Vittinghoff for this translation and her editorial work, which greatly benefited this paper. Thanks also go to Dr. Chen Xing-gan, whose 1997 book was a valuable source of material for this study.

with the rise of nationalist sentiments.[2] First approaches to the academic field of archaeology were accordingly undertaken in the context of historiographic efforts to rewrite a History of China. Coincidentally, such endeavours were fostered by the great archaeological discoveries of the early twentieth century, whose findings forced historians to take a new look at the native historical scholarship.[3] As part of the project of rewriting China's history, scholars like Zhang Taiyan 章太炎 (1868–1936), Liang Qichao 梁啟超 (1873–1929) or Jiang Zhiyou 蔣智由 (1865?–1929) began to reflect on Chinese traditional historiography and new historiographical methods of the West.

But 'archaeology' as the academic discipline *kaoguxue* 考古學 ("studies in investigations of the old") was not established before the 1920's in China, the result of cooperation between Chinese scholars who had received archaeological education abroad and foreign archaeologists who had researched in China.[4]

1. THE DEVELOPMENT OF MODERN ARCHAEOLOGY IN EUROPE

Yet archaeology as a scientific discipline was a new field in Western academic studies of the nineteenth century too. The Western term—in English 'archaeology/archeology', in French *archaeologie*, in Ger

---

[2] For the European context see Margarita Diaz-Andreu and Timothy Champion (eds.). 1996. *Nationalism and Archeology in Europe*. Boulder and San Francisco: Westview Press.

[3] The profound impact new excavations have on the scholarship of ancient China can still be observed today, and findings like the recently discovered Guodian texts have fundamentally challenged the paradigms of the established scholarship. On the tremendous impact of twentieth century archaeology on our knowledge of ancient China cf. Michael Loewe and Edward L. Shaughnessy. 1999. *The Cambridge History of Ancient China. From the Origins of Civilization to 221 B.C.* Cambridge: Cambridge University Press, *passim*.

[4] The Chinese term *kaoguxue* was most likely a re-imported term from Japan. Nevertheless, one of the early appearances of the term 'archaeology' is in the Japanese lexicon by Inoue Tetsujirō 井上哲次郎 and Ariga Nagao 有賀長雄 (1884. *Kaitei zōho tetsugaku jii* 改訂增補哲學字彙 (Philosophical dictionary, revised and enlarged). Tokyo: Tōyōkan), where it is still rendered as *guwuxue* 古物學. The historian Inoue himself was part of the conservative historiographical trend in Japan to write a new "History of the East" *tōyōshi* 東洋史, which represented a "return to Japan" from the Meiji world histories in Japanese historiography. Cf. Tang Xiaobing. 1996. *Global Space and the Nationalist Discourse of Modernity. The Historical Thinking of Liang Qichao*. Stanford: Stanford University Press, pp. 30ff; 71f.

man *Archäologie*, in Italian *archaeologia* and in Spanish *arqueologia*—originates from the Greek words *arche* and *logos* and means the 'science of (cultural) origins', i.e. the study of ancient times. In the seventeenth century the meaning of the term was reduced to studies of antique objects and relics. As these were all artistic objects, until the eighteenth century the field of study was conceived as part of art history. Only in the nineteenth century did 'archaeology' began to imply researches into all aspects of material culture, as it does today. As recent studies on the interrelationship between archaeology and political ideologies suggest, the scientific discipline of archaeology as the study of the past might never have advanced beyond the status of a hobby or a pastime without the strong motor of nationalism. In nineteenth century France and Britain, for instance, the professionalization of archaeology was accelerated by governmental and academic activities, such as the creation of national museums, or the erection of the Disney Chair of Archaeology in Cambridge in 1852.[5]

Modern archaeology developed from studies of antique objects. In Europe, the Renaissance fostered research on both ancient scripts and letters as well as art, and people began to collect classical Greek and Roman inscriptions and sculptures. Such an interest was extended to the collection of objects from Palestine, the Christian Holy Land, and even Egypt and Babylon in the Near East. The French revolution gave a new impulse to archaeological activities: Napoleon sent scholars to search for antique relics and objects in Egypt, and antiquarian objects in Italy and Spain were plundered during war expeditions and brought to France, where they were housed in the new Louvre museum, found in 1793. Napoleon also sent scholars to Pompeii to perform large-scale excavations. Developments in the field of geology and biology in the nineteenth century, particularly Charles Darwin's theories of biological evolution and Herbert Spencer's theories on social evolution, fundamentally challenged views from the past, especially the belief that God had created man. Hence prehistoric archaeology was fostered by a growing interest in the origins of human beings.

The historian of archaeology, Daniel Glyn, holds that archaeology as a science was prepared jointly by scientists investigating antique objects and natural scientists, from the sixteenth to the eighteenth cen-

---

[5] Cf. Margarita Diaz-Andreu and Timothy Champion (ed.). 1996. Introduction and *passim*.

tury. In the initial stage, prehistory and archaeology were often treated together, because prehistoric studies completely relied on archaeological findings. In 1819, the director of the Danish Royal Museum, Christian Juergensen Thomsen (1788–1865), formulated the theory of the "Three Ages" on the basis of his studies of the collections in the museum. According to his theory, ancient Denmark had experienced three ages, the Stone Age, the Bronze Age and the Iron Age. In 1838 the French archaeologist Jacques Boucher de Perthes (1788–1868) discovered flint samples in the Somme Gravels which he interpreted as tools of prehistoric men. His theory was verified in 1859, when an English archaeologist and geologist re-examined his discoveries. In 1865, in his *Prehistoric Times,* Lord John Lubbock Avebury (1834–1913) divided the Stone Age into two periods: the Chipped Stone Age and the Polished Stone Age. The former is termed the Old Stone Age, characterized by "the excavated stone implements at the Somme gravel, when man shared the possession of Europe with the mammoth, the cave bear, the woolly-haired rhinoceros, and other extinct animals."[6] The later is termed the New Stone Age, "a period characterized by beautiful weapons and instruments of flint and other kinds of stone."[7] This growing capacity to differentiate prehistorical phases is, in the opinion of Daniel Glyn, the reason why 1859 may be taken as the founding year of archaeology in Europe.

2. STUDIES OF EPIGRAPHY IN PREMODERN CHINA

In China, historical interest in the past had since ancient times fostered the study of epigraphy, the Bronze and Stone Inscriptions. Already at the time of Confucius (551–479 BC), ancient people had to rely on grave excavations to form an idea about their past, because the original meaning of the ceremonies and music systems in Shang 商 and Zhou 周 dynasties had been lost. Following the ancient saying "when the [meaning of the] rites are lost, search for it at the periphery [of the Empire]",[8] scholars in Han times had begun to study folk customs at

---

[6] Daniel Glyn. 1976. *A Hundred and Fifty Years of Archaeology.* Cambridge Mass.: Harvard University Press, p. 85.

[7] Ibid.

the periphery of the empire and to investigate the customs of the so-called Four Barbarian Tribes (siyi 四夷). Sima Qian 司馬遷 (145–86 BC) wrote in his autobiographical postface in the *Shiji* 史記 (Records of the Historian) that he

> climbed the *Huiji* mountain and investigated the cave of Emperor Yu; he visited the nine hills; he sailed on the rivers Yuan and Xiang and went northwards to the rivers Wen and Si; he became familiar with the scholarship in the capitals of Qi and Lu and learned respectfully about the customs and institutions taught by Confucius; he took part in the ceremony of shooting arrows at the summit of Mt. Yi; … He was employed by the government of Lanzhong and took part in a mission to the South to *Ba* and *Shu*; he went southwards to attack and occupy the city *Kunming*. When he returned he reported everything.[9]

Furthermore, when the Old Texts (*guwen* 古文) were discovered during the Han dynasty, Xu Shen 許慎 (190–220 AD) commented on them:

> In the mountains and rivers in the prefectures and fiefs are often found tripod vessels and vases. The inscriptions on them are ku-wen of earlier times, and all bear resemblances to each other. Although it is not possible to construct their remote development, the details can be explained in broad outline.[10]

Such early investigations on Bronze and Stone inscriptions form the initial phase of epigraphical studies in China, as they reveal a serious effort to base historical studies on objective sources.

More profound studies of Bronze and Stone inscriptions emerged during the Sung dynasty. In the reign of Song Emperor Renzong 仁宗 (1023–1063), Liu Chang 劉敞 (1019–1068) had eleven ancient objects of his own collections engraved, printed and also drawn, and edited these in his collection *Xianqin guqi tubei* 先秦古器圖碑 (Illustrations of pre-Qin stone tables), now unfortunately lost. He stated his inten-

---

[8] This sentence by Confucius is quoted in the *Hanshu*, Chapter "Yiwenzhi di shi" 藝文志第十 (Bibliography section ten). Cf. Ban Gu 班固 . 1964. *Hanshu* 漢書 (History of the Han Dynasty). Beijing: Zhonghua shuju, vol. 30, p. 1736.

[9] Sima Qian 司馬遷 . "Taishigong zixu"太史公自序 (Autobiographical postface of Taishigong), in: *Shiji* 史記 (Records of the Historian), vol. 10. Beijing: Zhonghua shuju, p. 3293

[10] Xu Shen 許慎 . *Shuowen jiezi* 説文解字 . Postface. Quoted from K. L. Thern. 1966. *Postface of the Shuo-wen Chieh-tzu. The First Comprehensive Chinese Dictionary*. Madison, Wis.: University of Wisconsin (Wisconsin China Series, no. 1), p. 15.

tion as: "in order that those studying rites would learn about the ritual system, [I] carefully restored the characters and hand them down to later generations."[11]

In 1061, Ouyang Xiu 歐陽修 (1007–1072) copied inscriptions from bronzes and stones he had personally discovered and collected. Together with some historical investigations on the objects, he published them in his *Jigulu* 集古錄 (Record of collected antiques), also lost today.[12] The earliest illustrated records concerning antique objects which we have today are compiled in the *Kaogutu* 考古圖 (Charts of investigations of antiquities), published in 1092.[13] It contains not just illustrations of ancient bronzes, but also explanations regarding the sizes, measurements and weights of these objects as well as the names of their collectors. Later, the *Xuanhe bogutu* 宣和博古圖 (Charts on investigations of antiquities of the Xuanhe period) by Wang Fu 王黼 (1079–1126) was published in 1123.[14] This work contains 880 collected antique objects and surpasses the *Kaogutu* by additionally recording the places of discovery and indicating the proportional relation between illustrations and the real objects. Wang Fu's collection therefore represents a rather complete presentation of antique objects. In general, these publications mark the birth of epigraphical studies in China.

Neither the Yuan nor the Ming dynasties saw larger contributions to the development of epigraphy. Yet, as Benjamin Elman has shown, the study of antiquities rose together with an increasing interest in natural studies during the Ming. Ming literati included the collection, study and classification of antiquities into the field of the classical *gewu* 格物 (inquiring knowledge) studies and formulated strict rules on how to handle the objects:

---

[11] Liu Chang 劉敞 . 1981. "*Xianqin guqi ji* zhong tichu guqi de yanjiu fangfa" 先秦古器集中提出古器的研究方法 (Methods to study ancient objects proposed in the *Collection of Ancient Objects of the Pre-Qin period*), in: Zhu Jianxin 朱劍心 . *Jin shi xue* 金石學 (Epigraphy). Shanghai: Wenwu chubanshe, p. 21.

[12] Ouyang Xiu 歐陽修 (comp.). 1984 [1646]. *Jigulu* 集古錄 (Record of collected antiques), in: *Wenyuange Siku quanshu* 文淵閣四庫全書 (Wenyuan Pavilion edition of the *Siku quanshu*). Reprint: Taibei: Shangwu yinshuguan.

[13] Lü Dalin 呂大臨 . 1983 [1092]. *Kaogutu* 考古圖(Charts of investigations of antiquities). Reprint: Taiwan: Taiwan shangwu shuju, 10 vols.

[14] Wang Fu 王黼 . 1991 [1123]. *Xuanhe bogutu* 宣和博古圖 (Charts on investigations of antiquities of the Xuanhe period), vol. 30. Yangzhou: Jiangsu Guangling guji yinkeshe.

Whenever one sees an object, you must look it all over, trace its appearance, and examine its history and origins. You should investigate its strenghts and weaknesses, and distinguish its accuracy.[15]

However, epigraphical studies began to flourish again during the Qing dynasty. The *Sijian* 四鑒 (Four mirrors), edited under Emperor Qianlong 乾隆 (1736–1796) and containing more than 4,000 bronze pieces with descriptions, greatly fostered the renaissance of epigraphical studies which, subsequently, became a major object of study of the so-called *Qianjia* 乾嘉 school. Statistics reveal 67 publications on Bronze and Stone Inscriptions between the Northern Song Dynasty (960–1126) and the Qianlong period and 906 titles from the Qianlong period until the end of Qing dynasty in 1911.[16] This shows the enormous growth in interest in epigraphy during the Qing dynasty. There are not only dynastic epigraphical publications, for example, the *Liang Han jinshiji* 兩漢金石記 (Epigraphy in the Han dynasties),[17] but also regional ones, for example, the *Liangzhe jinshiji* 兩浙金石記 (Epigraphy in two Zhe provinces).[18] The scope of the collections is also very broad. In addition to traditional inscriptions in bronzes and stones, we now find statues, stone reliefs, autographs, tomb steles, weights and measures, coins, jade articles, stamps, bricks, pottery figurines, and even relics from the Ming as new objects of study described in these epigraphic publications by scholars in epigraphy such as Wu Dacheng 吳大澂 (1836–1902) and Sun Yirang 孫詒讓 (1848–1908).[19]

Although this original interest in epigraphy had in fact developed into to studies of antique artifacts, I would argue that the Qing dynasty was witness neither to a theoretical nor a methodological break-

---

[15] Elman quotes the preface of Wang Zuo 王佐 (*jinshi* 進士 of 1427) to the abridged version of the *Gegu yaolun* 格古要論 (Essential criteria of antiquities). Cf. Benjamin Elman's contribution in this volume.

[16] Rong Yuan 容媛 . 1930. "Chaodai renming tongjian 朝代人名通檢 (Comprehensive survey of personal names through the dynasties), in: *Jinshishu mulu* 金石書目錄 (General catalogue of epigraphical literature). Beijing. Shangwu yinshuguan, pp. 1–24.

[17] *Liang Han jinshiji* 兩漢金石記 (Epigraphy in the Han dynasties). 1967 [1786]. Reprint: Taibei: Wenhai chubanshe.

[18] Ruan Yuan 阮元 (ed.). 1890. *Liangzhe jinshilji* 兩浙金石記 (Epigraphy in two Zhe provinces), vol. 16. Hangzhou: Zhejiang shuju.

[19] Zhang Qizhi 張豈之 (ed.). 1996. *Zhongguo jindai shixue xueshushi* 中國近代史學學術史 (History of historiographical scholarship in modern China). Beijing: Zhongguo shehui kexue chubanshe, pp. 384–8.

through in this academic field. The study of artifacts was only a simple inheritance from and the further development of the epigraphy in the Sung dynasty. Although epigraphy has a long history in China, it did not develop into archaeology. Compared to Europe, China saw neither a Romantic movement, nor a systematic approach to collecting and describing excavated artifacts.

3. ARCHAEOLOGICAL ACTIVITIES OF FOREIGN SCHOLARS IN CHINA

As in Egypt, Greek and Mesopotamia, Chinese archaeological practice was also initiated by Western explorers. As early as 1860 the Englishman Sir John Anderson (1833–1900), director of the Calcutta Museum in India, had collected a group of polished stone implements from Yunnan, including stone adzes and stone cauldrons.[20]

The Western region of China had always been a very attractive region for the Western imperialist countries in the nineteenth century. At the same time, foreign scholars and explorers did archaeological research with various purposes in mind. Between 1863 and 1864 the Indian Mohamad el Hameed was ordered by the English government to inspect the Xinjiang region. It was in his report that the ancient buried city of Hetian 和闐 was mentioned for the first time. In 1865 the English explorer W. Johnson travelled to the Taklamakan desert and confirmed that there were many ancient cities buried in the sands of the desert. Eight years later, the Englishman Sir Douglas Forsyth again toured through Xinjiang and confirmed the existence of ancient cities buried under the desert. For the first time he also sent people to inspect one buried city to the east of Hetian. The small Buddha statues and coins found there were taken out of China and some research on these objects appeared in Europe.[21] After that many groups from England, Russia, France, Germany and Sweden undertook archaeological expeditions in Xinjiang, Ningxia, Gansu, Inner Mongolia and Tibet and exported the ancient objects found to their home countries.

---

[20] John Anderson. 1871. *A Report on the Expedition to Western Yunan via Bhamo.* Calcutta: Office of the Superintendent of Government Printing.

[21] Yang Hanzhang 楊漢璋 (tr.). 1983. *Sichou zhilushangde waiguo mogui* 絲綢之路上的外國魔鬼 (Foreign Devils on the Silk Road). [Translation of Peter Hopkirk. 1980. *Foreign Devils on the Silk Road: the Search for the Lost Cities and Treasures of Chinese Central Asia.* London. Murray]. Lanzhou: Gansu renmin chubanshe, pp. 29–36.

Among the most well-known individuals were the Swede Sven Hedin (1865–1952), the Hungarian archaeologist Marc Aurel Stein (1862–1943), the Russian Dimitri Klements (1848–1914) and the Frenchman Paul Pelliot (1878–1945).[22]

Sven Hedin was a geographer from Sweden who toured the western region of China four times, in 1890–1896, 1899–1902, 1904–1909 and 1927–1935. He is famous for his discoveries and excavations of the ancient city of Loulan 樓蘭 (Miran) and, during his second expedition, for the discovery of books written in Tibetan scripts.[23] In 1898 Dimitri Klements organized the first archaeological expedition sent by the St. Petersburg Academy. In Turfan they searched for ancient cities and cut off mural paintings from ancient temples, which they subsequently sent home to Europe.[24]

Between 1900 and 1905 Marc Aurel Stein not only discovered a large number of ancient cities in northwest China, but also performed the first small-scale excavations in Dandan wulike 丹丹烏利克 , which he recorded in detail in descriptions and photographs.[25] Between 1906 and 1914 Stein went to Xinjiang several times, where he searched for ancient relics, took down wall-paintings from Miran, collected a large amount of relics from Dunhuang 敦煌 , and even found and excavated some relics from the Stone Age.[26]

In 1906 Paul Pelliot visited Keshen 喀什 in Xinjiang and discovered an ancient Buddhist temple, a Buddha statue and a large amount of written material in Tumuxiuke 吐木休克 . He is, however, most famous for his discovery of large amounts of Buddhist scriptures and cultural relics in Dunhuang in the following year. The Italian E. H. Giglioti (1845–1909) described too how he collected historical relics

---

[22] Chen Xingcan 陳星燦 . 1997. *Zhongguo shiqian kaoguoxueshi yanjiu* 中國史前考古學史研究, *1885–1949* (The research of Chinese prehistory and archaeology between 1885 and 1949). Beijing: Shenhuo dushu xinzhi sanlian shudian.

[23] Li Shuli 李述禮 (tr.). 1984. *Yazhou fudi lüxingji* 亞洲腹地旅行記 (Travel to the Asian hinterland). [Translation of Sven Hedin. 1925. *My Life as an Explorer*. New York]. Shanghai: Shanghai shudian.

[24] Yang Hanzhang 1983.

[25] Xiang Da 向達 (tr.). 1936. *Sitanyin xiyu kaoguji* 斯坦因西域考古記 (The archaeological activities of Stein in the western regions). [Translation of Marc Aurel Stein. 1933. *On Ancient Central Asia Tracks: Brief Narrative of Three Expeditions in Innermost Asia and North-Western China*. London: Macmillan]. Shanghai: Zhonghua shuju.

[26] See Marc Aurel Stein. 1928. *Innermost Asia: Detailed Report of Explorations in Central Asia, Kan-su and Eastern Iran*. Oxford: Clarendon Press, p. 85.

in China, such as jade cauldrons in Fuzhou and stone knives in holes in Yan'an in 1898.[27] Numerous other foreign scholars went on archaeological expeditions to China, such as S. Couling (1852–1922), J. C. Brown, E. C. David and others. These scholars collected stone implements in different regions, including Shandong, Yunnan, Sichuan and Inner Mongolia. Apart from their archaeological research, these scholars sometimes also published absurd descriptions in Western newspapers, for example of dragon skeletons in Chinese drugstores. But such reports exerted little influence on Western academic circles.[28]

After the Sino-Japanese War in 1894/95 Japanese archaeologists became active in China. Torii Ryūzō 鳥居龍藏 (1870–1953), sent by the Tokyo Imperial University, travelled to Liaodong from August to December 1895 to do anthropological and archaeological research. In places like Lüshun 旅順, Dalian 大連, Xiongyuecheng 熊岳城, Gaiping 蓋平, Haicheng 海城, Dashiqiao 大石橋 and Liaoyang 遼陽 he investigated prehistoric relics and relics from the Han dynasty. In Gaiping, Jinxian 金縣 and Piziwo 貔子窝 he found stone cauldrons and in Ximucheng 析木城 the relics of stone shacks. Between 1905 and 1908 Torii went twice more to the Liaodong peninsula. He finally published his results in 1910 as *Minami Manshu chōsa hōkoku* 南滿州調查報告 (Survey report of Southern Manzhou), an example of excellent research from the first generation of Japanese anthropologists and archaeologists.[29] After 1906 Torii and his wife extended the range of their archaeological activity to the Inner Mongolian grassland: they researched in Kelaqinqi 喀喇沁旗 (Xaracin), Chifeng 赤峰, Linxi 林西, Dasai nuoer 達賽諾爾 (Talainor), Duolun naoer 多倫淖爾 (Dolonghor), Zhangjiakou 張家口 and Mongolia, and also found prehistoric relics in Hongshanhou 紅山后 and other places. In 1911 they published their experiences in *Mengu jixing* 蒙古記行 (Mongolian travel report);[30] in 1914 a report of their travels appeared in French,[31]

---

[27] See Gu Jiegang 顧頡剛. 1980. "Qian Xuantong 錢玄同 (Qian Xuantong)". *Gushi bian* 古史辯, 1. Reprint: Shanghai: Shanghai guji chubanshe.

[28] Pei Wenzhong 裴文中. 1983. "Shiqian kaoguxue jichu" 史前考古學基礎 (The foundations of prehistoric archaeology), *Shiqian yanjiu* 1, pp. 172–4.

[29] Torii Ryūzō 鳥居龍藏. 1910. *Minami Manshu chōsa hōkoku* 南滿州調查報告 (Survey report of Southern Manzhou). Tokyo: Shūeisha.

[30] Ibid. 1911. *Man Mō no tansa* 満蒙の探查 (Inquiries in Manzhou and Mongolia). Tokyo: Banrikaku shuhō.

followed by another research report in French about the southern areas of Liaodong in the following year.[32]

When Tanaka Shōtarō 田中正太郎 found stone implements in Taipei in 1896, he was soon followed by Awano Dennojō 粟野傳之丞 and Inō Kanori 伊能嘉矩 (1867–1925), who collected stone implements in Gangshan 岡山 and found relics of molluscs in 1907. Torii also subsequently discovered some stone implements during his surveys in Gangshan and confirmed that the relics of the Stone Age in Taiwan belonged to the prehistoric period.[33] Under the Japanese regime in Taiwan archaeological activities increased enormously. Statistical surveys reveal that before October 30, 1902 relics had been found in 93 places, while by 1910, 169 sites of archaeological research had already been established.[34]

The archaeological activities of foreigners before 1920 in China had been summarized by Chen Xingcan 陳星燦 in terms of the following five characteristics: 1) priority was given to survey, whereas excavations were only performed randomly; 2) historical periods were given priority over prehistoric periods; 3) most of the surveyors were scholars, some of them were even professional archaeologists, such as the Japanese Hamada Kōsaku 濱田耕作 (1881–1938) and Torii Ryūzō. But there were also some amateurs, intelligence agents and cultural plunderers such as the Japanese Tachibana Zuichō 橘瑞超 (1890–1968); 4) most archaeological surveys and excavations were recorded both in written descriptions as well as in photographs and were therefore in accord with academic standards; and 5) most of the archaeological activities took place without the permission of the Chinese government and with no Chinese participation. Accordingly, most reports were published in foreign languages and the cultural objects were mostly taken out of China.[35]

---

[31] Ibid and K. Torii. 1914. "Populations primitives de la Mongolie Oriental", *Journal of Science* 36 (March), pp. 1–100.

[32] Ibid. 1915. *Populations primitives prehistoriques de Mondchourie Meridionale.* Tokyo: Tokyo University.

[33] Kanaseki Takeo 金關丈夫 and Kokubu Naoichi 國分直一. 1979. "Taiwan kōkogaku kenkyūshi" 臺灣考古學研究史 (Short history of archaeological researches in Taiwan), in: ibid. *Taiwan kōkoshi* 臺灣考古志 (Treatise on archaeology in Taiwan). N.p.: Hōsei daigaku shuppan kyoku, pp. 1–20.

[34] Ibid.

[35] Chen Xingcan 1997, p. 49.

Due to their archaeological activities and research in China foreign researchers and their successors received great honours in many countries and enriched both public and private collections of ancient objects of the world. Yet, they had little influence on the development of Chinese archaeological scholarship, and fostered instead an increase of illegal excavations in China. Since the cultural objects were not accessible to Chinese scholars and the reports about them were published in foreign languages and outside of China, all this intensive archaeological activity of Western scholars in northwest China and of Japanese scholars in northeast China and Taiwan, with its array of ideas, theories and methods of archaeology could not be conveyed to Chinese academic circles.

4. The import of the concepts of 'archaeology' and 'prehistory' to China

The above-mentioned rising interest in epigraphical studies in Late Qing China coincided with the famous discoveries of oracle bones and bamboo strips at the end of the Qing dynasty. This marked a great watershed in the development of Chinese historiography and formed the basis of the initial stage of archaeology in China.

When the first tortoise shells were discovered and sold by farmers to antique sellers in 1910 at the city of Xiaotun 小屯 near Anyang 安陽, the site of one capital of the Shang dynasty, the scholar Luo Zhenyu 羅振玉 (1866–1940) immediately wanted to purchase them. Within a single year about ten thousand pieces were found. The following year Luo sent his young brother Luo Zhenchang 羅振常 (1875–1942) and young brother-in-law Fan Zhaochang 范兆昌 to buy the bone fragments and to record everything about the places and details of excavation. Luo Zhenyu was the first person to also buy tortoise shells without characters on them.[36] In 1915 Luo Zhenyu himself travelled to Anyang to inspect the situation of the unearthing of tortoise shells.[37] He not only collected tortoise shells but also stone

---

[36] Luo Zhenchang 羅振常 . 1936 [1911]. *Huan Luo fanggu youji* 桓洛訪古游記 (Travels in search for antiquities at the Huan and Luo rivers). Reprint: n.p.: Tanyinlu

[37] Luo Zhenyu 羅振玉 . [between 1912–1936]. *Wushiri menghenlu* 五十日夢痕錄 (Records of dreamlike traces of fifty days). Shangyu: no publisher.

implements, such as stone knives and cauldrons, jade implements, such as *bi* 璧 (bi-discs), ivories and implements made of ivory. In 1916 he published *Yinxu guqiwu tulu* 殷墟古器物圖錄 (Illustrations of antique objects of the Yin ruins).[38] His replacement of the traditional name 'Bronze and Stone' *jinshi* 金石 by 'antique implements' (*guqiwu* 古器物) in the title of the book might reflect his idea of the necessity of breaking through the rigid framework of traditional epigraphy. Taking up the tradition of natural studies, he proposed that research in epigraphy should not be confined to the study room, but should include expeditions and the study of natural phenomena.

During his second journey to the western regions of China between 1906 and 1908 Marc Aurel Stein had obtained bamboo strips; these were published by the French scholar Éduard Chavannes (1865–1918) in his *Les documents Chinois discouverts par Aurel Stein dans les sables du Turkestan Oriental* in 1913.[39] The book presented 991 bamboo strip texts. Only a year later, Luo Zhenyu and Wang Guowei 王國維 (1877–1927) presented their textual research on 588 of these pieces, publishing their results in *Liusha zhuijian* 流沙墜簡 (Fallen strips from drifting sands).[40] This was the first time that Chinese scholars had used material from modern excavations for their researches. Luo and Wang had already started their research before Chavannes published his book. Since they read Chavannes' publication before they finished their own book, they added the following comment:

> We know that in Chavannes' book designations added on top of every bamboo strip indicate the places of excavation. The order of arrangement is from West to East, from number 1 to number 30, probably according to Mr. Stein's illustrations. When we attempted to do philological studies on [these objects we discovered that] already half of the items had been studied [by Chavannes]. Therefore we have only listed the order of illustrations as well as all unearthed strips at the end of our book, and will point out only the most important strips.[41]

---

[38] Ibid. 1916. *Yinxu guqiwu tulu* 殷墟古器物圖錄 (Illustrations of antique objects of the Yin ruins). Published by the author.

[39] Eduard Chavannes. 1913. *Les documents Chinois discouverts par Aurel Stein dans les sables du Turkestan Oriental.* Oxford: Oxford University Press

[40] Chen Xingcan 1997, pp. 30–5.

[41] Cf. Wang Guowei 王國維. "Houxu" 後序 (postface), in: Luo Zhenyu and Wang Guowei. 1993 [1934]. *Liusha zhuijian* 流沙墜簡 (Fallen strips from drifting sands).

The subsequent development of archaeological studies by scholars such as Luo Zhenyu and Wang Guowei was accompanied by the belief that only a profound revision of China's historical past would allow a modern Chinese identity. The great discoveries at Anyang and other sites provided a most welcome opportunity to test the cherished beliefs of the past. Archaeology entered China at a specific historical moment, as the apparent military weakness of the country compelled Chinese scholars to reflect upon the essence of their culture. This lead them to pose questions about the origins of Chinese culture. Western scholars had discussed this problem as early as the seventeenth century, when the German Jesuit Athanasius Kircher (1601–1680), in his *Cedipi Aegyptiaci* written in 1654, established the theory that Chinese culture originated from Egypt. From then on, numerous theories existed about the origin of the Chinese, ranging from places like Babylon, India, the Orient and even Europe.[42]

In China, discussions on the origins of the Chinese and ideas of prehistory were disseminated at the beginning of the twentieth century. Zhang Taiyan's *Zhongguo tongshi lueli* 中國通史略例 (Concise history of China), published in 1900, already shows a familiarity with Western archaeology.[43] Zhang Taiyan also investigated the relationship between archaeological discoveries and historical research. Two years later in 1902, in a letter to Wu Junsui, Zhang discussed the problems of historiography stressing that unearthed textural material and objects were the essential sources for historical research.[44]

Liang Qichao's rising interest in historiography, as represented in his extensive readings of foreign histories, documented in the *Xixue shumu biao* 西學書目表 (Bibliography of Western knowledge), and in

---

[41] (*cont.*) Shangyu: Luoshi Chenhanlou. Reprint: Beijing: Zhonghua shuju, 3 vols. In 1914 the first edition appeared in three volumes in Japan; in 1916 and 1934 revised versions were published in Shanghai.

[42] Chen Xingcan 1997, pp. 30–5.

[43] Zhang Taiyan 章太炎. 1984 [1900]. *Zhongguo tongshi lüeli* 中國通史略例 (Concise history of China), in: ibid. *Qiushu chongdingben. Ai Qing shi* 訄書重訂本. 哀清史 (A revised edition of the *Qiushu.* Painful history of the Qing). *Zhang Taiyuan quanji*. 章太炎全集 (Complete works of Zhang Taiyuan). Shanghai: Shanghai renmin chubanshe, vol. 3, p. 331.

[44] Ibid. 1977 [1902]. "Zhi Wu Junsui shu" 致吳君遂書 (A letter to Mr. Wu Junsui), in: Tang Zhijun 湯志鈞 (ed.). *Zhang Taiyuan zhenglun xuanji* 章太炎政論選集 (Selection of Zhang Taiyuans writings on politics). Beijing: Zhonghua shuju, p. 172.

his numerous writings on New Historiography (*xin shixue* 新史學), has been well documented in the recent study by Tang Xiaobing.[45] In 1901, Liang Qichao began preparations for writing a book about Chinese history, in the course of which he elaborated extensively on the idea of prehistory and archaeology. Liang revealed a rather clear understanding of prehistory which, based on archaeological evidence, should be separated from mythical periods of Chinese history. In his "Zhongguoshi xulun" 中國史紋論 (Preliminary discussion of Chinese history), he made clear distinctions concerning the theory, ideas, systems and periodizations of Chinese history, which he planned to elaborate later in the larger study.[46] In the chapter "Youshi yiqian zhi shidai" 有史以前之時代 (The prehistoric age) he introduces Thomsen's doctrine of the three prehistoric periods:

> Since 1847 the Society of European Archaeology has sent people to unearth relics and therefore developed prehistoric studies as a discipline. Meanwhile, the so-called theory of the three prehistoric periods is established wisdom: the first is the Stone-Sword Age, the second is the Bronze-Sword Age, the third is the Iron-Sword Age; among these, the Stone-Sword Age can be divided into the New and the Old Stone Age in order to separate particular periods. The ages appeared at different times in different places with different lengths of time, but the order of the sequence is always the same. ... Since academic research is not developed in China, underground stratified stones have still not been found. But according to the general rules of material, the same process should take place everywhere. Therefore we take this theory as an example to show that prehistoric studies in China are also necessary. According to the descriptions of these scholars, the two Stone Ages, the Old and the New, were the longest periods. During that time there were no domestic animals, potteries or agriculture. In China, Shennong 神農 had invented farm tools and Chiyou 蚩尤 bows and arrows long before the time of Huangdi 黃帝 , which must have been, as many indications show, already after the Stone Age and during the Bronze Age. The origin of human beings dates far back, certainly long before the Great Flood.[47]

---

[45] Liang Qichao 1896. *Xixue shumu biao* 西學書目表 (Bibliography of Western knowledge). Shanghai: Shiwu baoguan. Liang lists about 50 different history works and over 100 volumes in total. Cf. Tang Xiaobing 1996, pp. 31ff. and passim.

[46] Ibid. 1989 [1901]. "Zhongguo shi xulun" 中國史紋論 (Preliminary discussion of Chinese history), in: *Yinbingshi heji* 飲冰室合集 (Collected works from the *Ice-Drinker's Studio*). Edited by Lin Zhijun 林志鈞 . Shanghai: Zhonghua shuju 1936. Reprint: Beijing 1989, 12 vols., vol. 1.

[47] See the chapter "Youshi yiqian zhi shidai" 有史以前之時代 (The prehistoric age), in ibid., pp. 8–10.

It is obvious that Liang's conceptualization of prehistory was already relatively mature. It is interesting to note that Liang had also discussed the traditional concept of "Three Ages" (*sanshi* 三時) in his "Xin shixue" 新史學 (New historiography) and attempted to integrate it into a theory of historical evolution.[48]

Wang Rongbao 汪榮寶 (1878–1933), a graduate from Nanyang gongxue and student at the Waseda University in Tokyo, translated and edited the *Shigaku hōhōron* 史學方法論 (Theory of historiographical methods) of the Japanese historian Tsuboi Kumezō 坪井九馬三 (1858–1936) in 1903.[49] In 1902, under the pseudonym Gun Fu衮甫 , he had published his review of current Japanese historiography as "Shixue gailun" 史學概論 (An introduction to historiography) in *Yishu huibian* 譯書匯編 (A collection of translated books). Wang pointed out that archaeologists would often divide history:

> ... into two periods, before and after the invention of books. For the natural anthropologist the period before the invention of books is more important, whereas in the eyes of the historian the period before the invention of books is less important and doesn't need too much research to be done. [He holds] that archaeological history refers only to archaeology after the invention of books.[50]

Wang simply defined 'prehistory' as the period before the invention of books'; such a distinct division between the definition of prehistory and history had never been made before.

One year later, in 1903, another Chinese student in Japan, Li Haosheng 李浩生 , translated the *Shigaku genron* 史學原論 (Discussion of the origins of historiography), the lecture notes of the Japanese historian Ukita Kazutami 浮田和民 (1959–1946), as *Shixue tonglun* 史

---

[48] According to the "three ages" theory, history moves progressively from through the ages from Chaos to Approaching Peace to the age of Great Peace. Tang Xiaobing 1996, p. 65 and p. 249, fn. 55.

[49] Tsuboi Kumezō 坪井九馬三 .1903. *Shigaku hōhōron* 史學方法論 (Theory of historiographical methods). Tokyo: Waseda Daigaku.

[50] Gun Fu 衮甫 (Wang Rongbao 汪榮寶). 1902. "Shixue gailun" 史學概論 (An introduction to historiography) in: *Yishu huibian* 9 (December 12, 1902) and 10 (December 27, 1902). Wang Rongbao's "Introduction to historiography" was published one year before his translation of Tsuboi's book on historiographical methods. Yu Danchu assumes that Wang has translated and edited the class lectures of Tsuboi. Yu Danchu 俞旦初 . 1983. "Ershi shiji chunian xifang jindai kaoguxue sixiang zai Zhongguo de jieshao he yinxiang" 二十世紀初年西方近代考古學思想在中國的介紹和影響 (What was the influence of the introduction of early twentieth century Western thoughts on modern archaeology to China?), *Kaogu yu wenwu* 4, p. 111, fn. 16.

學通論 (General discussion of historiography). He explains how to write history:

> Historians in ancient time had no other material than records of public praises. They only could assemble, compare or correct this material, reproduce it and then take it as correct history. In recent times, historians have taken relics and souvenirs as historical materials. Therefore history begins to step on real ground and will move on progressively.

The book also describes the value of relics and their correct methodological treatment:

> Although relics are important documents for archaeology, they nevertheless are broken, scattered and lost, and are so-called accidental findings. That is why one should not focus on one of the three materials at the expense of the others. The historical research method lies in flexibly combining these historical materials in order to enlarge its framework.[51]

In 1903, Henry Thomas Buckle's (Bo Kelu 勃克魯, 1821–1862) *History of Civilisation in England (Yingguo wenmingshi* 英國文明史), written in 1857–61 and left half finished, was translated and published by the translation department of the Nanyang College (Nanyang gongxue yishuyuan 南洋公學譯書院). Here the progress of writing history in Europe is described as follows:

> So-called good history in our Europe is nothing but a rather complete history. For example, if one finds ancient coins during the excavation of an ancient city, the text of the coin is investigated first, and the form of the letters and pictures of the seal on the surface of coins all serve as material for historical research. Even if research on languages now long lost is done, one has to understand their principles and describe them in detail. There are definite patterns to prove how human languages change or get lost and people in recent times have numerous methods to prove these.[52]

---

[51] Li Haosheng 李浩生 (tr.). 1903. *Shixue tonglun* 史學通論 (General discussion of historiography). [Translation of Ukita Kazutami 浮田和民. *Shigaku genron* 史學原論 (Discussion of the origins of historiography), Lectures at Waseda University]. Hangzhou: Hezong yishu ju, quoted from Yu Danchu 俞旦初. 1982. "Ershi shiji chunian Zhongguo de xin shixue sichao chukao 二十世紀初年中國的新史學思潮初考 (Preliminary investigations on the current trend of new historiography in the early years of the twentieth century), *Shixueshi yanjiu* 3, pp. 54–8. In 1903 six translations of these lecture notes appeared in China.

[52] Yu Danchu 1983, pp. 107–11. The book is said to have had a tremendous influence on the new historiography, not only because it fell in line with the appreciated

The poet, journalist and colleague of Liang Qichao, Jiang Zhiyou, began to distinguish between traditional studies of antique artifacts in premodern China and archaeology in the West. In 1903, under the pen-name Guan Yunzhi 觀雲智, he published "Shijie zui gu zhi fadian" 世界最古之法典 (The oldest code of the world) in the serial *Xinmin congbao* 新民叢報. The test describes the French expedition to Persiain 1901, where the Babylonian Codex of Hammurabi was discovered. This not only proves that Chinese academics had already begun to pay serious attention to the activities of the foreign academic circle; the article also reveals Jiang Zhiyou's profound comprehension of the science and archaeology of his time.

> Nowadays, the foreign scholars have not only developed a new discipline, but with their employment of empirical methods they also find out many new things which happened at earlier times. They are quite different from the scholars in our country who only argue with each other on paper. Our countrymen are proud of the 'archaeology' (*kaogu* 考古) they have developed, but if they really want to know how to do archaeological research, it is unavoidable for them to use the new methods (*xinfa* 新法) in order to do real *kaogu*. If they only study the thirteen Confucian classics in their rooms and still think that the ancient times were not different from the present, they really reveal a self-satisfied attitude. … Everything that happens in a later generation has its cause in earlier times. Even if things look quite different from each other, we can find all the connections [between them] if we carefully explore the traces of the process [by which they came into being]. More often than not we are then able to resolve problems better. Therefore, archaeology is not only interesting but also has practical benefit for people today. Although they should know sociology (*qunxue* 群學) first, before they study archaeology, it would change their views completely [if they were familiar with both]. If one is only doing archaeological research, the framework is too narrow, such an archaeology is not worth a single glance.[53]

Jiang distinguished for the first time between a 'Chinese archaeology' (*Zhongguo de kaogu* 中國的考古) and 'true archaeology' (*zhenzheng de kaogu* 真正的考古).

---

[52] (*cont.*) *bunmei shi* 文明史 (History of civilisation) historiography of Meiji Japan (cf. Tang Xiaobing 1996, pp. 30ff; 70ff), but also because it presented a history of England as well as elaborated in detail on Buckle's positivistic historiographical theory. Zhang Qizhi 1996, p. 82.

[53] Guan Yun 觀雲. 1903. "Shijie zuigu zhi fadian 世界之法典 (The oldest code in the world)", *Xinming congbao* 33, pp. 19–22; 34, pp. 31–9.

In the same year, Liu Chengyu 劉成禺 (ca. 1873–1952) published "Lishi guangyi neipian" 歷史廣義內篇 (General meaning of history, first part) in the journal *Hubei xueshengjie* 湖北學生界 . In the section "Youshi yiqian zhi renzhong" 有史以前之人種 (Prehistoric races) he not only introduced the idea of the three prehistoric periods, but also expressly mentioned the "theory of discovering ancient objects" (*guwu faxian xueshuo* 古物發現學説) in the West.

> By knowing the instruments used by human beings [at a certain period] the archaeologist is able to examine the level of intelligence and evolution. When a big drought in Europe dried the middle of a Swiss Lake, workers found more than two hundred corpses, stoves, stone, timber, carbon, axes and hooks. Examinations of the houses revealed that they were surrounded by water in all four directions, which proves that these people lived near the water in ancient times. Many wall pictures show that people in ancient Egypt were hunting bears, elephants and deers as food. From this we can know that ancient people bit and chewed.[54]

In 1907 another historiographical treatise was translated and edited by Wu Yuanming 吳淵民 as *Shixue tongyi* 史學通義 (General discussion of historiography) and published in the journal *Xuebao* 學報 . The article contained a section "Youshi yiqian zhi gaikuang" 有史以前之概況 (Outline of prehistory) which established that the science of prehistory began about fifty years previously. The article gives a short overview on the history of archaeology, explains the origin of the theory of the three ages and points out the unequal development of history. This shows knowledge that was far more profound than that of Liang Qichao.[55]

The Japanese text *Taixi shiwu qiyuan* 泰西事物起源 (The origins of European objects), which was translated by editors in the Guangzhi shuju 廣智書局 in 1903, clearly explains the Three Ages:

> The evolution of human beings in the ancient, sciptless period can be divided into three Ages, first, the Stone Age, second, the Bronze Age, and third, the Iron Age.

He also elaborates in detail on the specific characteristics of every age:

---

[54] Liu Chengyu 劉成禺 . 1903. "Lishi guangyi neipian 歷史廣義內篇 (General meaning of history, first part), *Hubei xueshengjie* 3, quoted from Yu Danchu, 1983, p. 10.

[55] Wu Yuanmin 吳淵民 (tr.). 1907. "Shixue tongyi" 史學通義 (General discussion of historiography) *Xuebao* 1, quoted from Yu Danchu, 1983, pp. 58, 60.

> In the Stone Age the people used stone, bone, wood and horn to make instruments and it is the oldest Age in ancient times. As people did not know how to use metal at that time, they mostly used chipped stone. At the beginning they only knew how to cut stones, but later, they were also able to polish stones. The Stone Age can further be divided into two periods, the former is called the Old Stone Age, the later one is the New Stone Age.[56]

These sources show clearly how the idea of archaeology and prehistory emerged at the beginning of the twentieth century in Chinese academic circles. Although we do not know which sources originally had informed Liang Qichao's ideas about archaeology and prehistory, the fact that most of the publications quoted were translations from Japanese scholars and that most of the authors were Chinese students in Japan clearly suggests, that these ideas of modern archaeology and prehistory in China were imported from Japan.

6. CHINESE OVERSEAS STUDENTS AND THE INSTITUTIONAL ESTABLISHMENT OF ARCHAEOLOGY IN CHINA

The new cultural movement symbolized by the May Fourth was an iconoclastic and revolutionary attempt to attack and even remove the old tradition and to construct a new rationality. The core of the new rationality was conveyed through the concepts of democracy and science. In the fields of historical sciences, this was represented by the "Movement to discuss ancient history" (*Gushibian yundong* 古史辯運動). Gu Jiegang 顧頡剛 (1893–1980), the pioneer of this movement, proposed "creating a fundamentally new Chinese ancient history." He totally denied the traditional doctrine of the existence of the Three Emperors and the Five Lords, and suggested that nature should establish the new ancient history.

> The theory about the Three Emperors and the Five Lords has naturally collapsed. An ancient Chinese history based on archaeological research has just begun to be discovered and we cannot draw any simplistic conclusions from it.[57]

---

[56] Se Jiangbao 澀江保 (ed.). 1926. *Taixi shiwu qiyuan*. 泰西事物起源 (On the origins of Western things). Shanghai: Wenming shuju, p. 23.

[57] Gu Jiegang 顧頡剛 . 1926. "Zixu" 自序 (Own preface), *Gushibian* 1, Reprint: Beijing: Bushe, pp. 51ff.

In tune with the iconoclastic agenda of the May Fourth Movement, Gu Jiegang attempted to uncover the textual layers of China's historiographical past in order to arrive back at the pristine origins of the historical sources. To Gu Jiegang and his followers, the excavated artifacts and new findings on ancient China's history served to testify that the Chinese tradition was far less grandiose than the cherished beliefs of the past had suggested. His critical examination of historical evidence and sceptical attitude (*yigu* 疑古) was inherited from the empirical scholarship of early Qing scholars', the *kaozheng* tradition, which he had been taught by his grandfather and which had also influenced the new rise of epigraphical scholarship.

Moreover, the archaeological discoveries of the early twentieth century had fundamentally challenged the previous methods of pure textual studies and fostered the development of objective methods to evaluate the historical sources. In 1923, Gu had even planned to study ancient implements himself, yet he felt he was already too old for such studies.[58] When Hu Shi 胡適 (1891–1962) returned from the U.S. in 1917, he formed a scholarly circle together with Gu Jiegang at Peking University to discuss issues of history and the Chinese classics. Furthermore, Hu Shi, who profoundly influenced the development of a modern historiographical methodology, propagated the establishment of archaeology as a discipline, commenting on Chinese archaeological activities as follows:

> When in the future we have established methods of epigraphy and archaeology and in addition use unearthed historical materials we can slowly approach the ancient history before the Eastern Zhou dynasty.[59]

Finally, Li Xuanbo 李玄伯 (1895–1974) remarked: "The only method to solve questions of ancient history is archaeology."[60] Such strict academic requirements laid a good foundation for the development of archaeology in China.

---

[58] Ibid. 1923. "Yu Qian Xuantong xiansheng lun gushi shu" 与錢玄同先生論古史書 (Discussions on books on ancient history with Qian Xuantong). *Gushibian* 1, Reprint: Beijing: Bushe, pp. 59–66.

[59] Hu Shi 胡適 . 1926 [1921]. "Zi shu gushi guan shu" 自述古史觀書 (A letter [to Gu Jiegang] describing my views about ancient history), *Gushibian* 1, Reprint: Beijing: Bushe, pp. 22–3.

[60] Li Xuanbo 李玄伯 . 1926 [1924]. "Gushi wenti de weiyi jiejue fangfa 古史問題的唯一解決方法 (The only way to solve problems of ancient history), *Gushibian* 1, Reprint: Beijing: Bushe, p. 270.

The discovery of a large number of prehistoric relics from the Stone Age, such as those collected by E. Edgar in the basin of the Min River between 1914 and 1915, further fostered the development of palaeolithic studies in China. Edgar published his report about this expedition in 1917.[61] In 1913 the French Jesuit Emile Licent (Sang Zhihua 桑志華,1876–1952) had established that northern China was the major area for finding prehistoric relics, publishing his results ten years later.[62] The Swedish geologist Johan Gunnar Andersson (An Tesheng 安特生, 1874–1960) was the first person to do palaeontological surveys at Zhoukoudian 周口店,in 1918, and discovered the first neolithic sites known in China. In his opinion, a large amount of palaeolithic vertebral fossils was buried there.[63] In contrast to the archaeological activities of previous researchers, Andersson had already cooperated closely with Chinese colleagues of geological studies, which lead to the establishment of science museums in China: the geologist Ding Wenjiang 丁文江 (1877–1936), another close intellectual associate of Gu Jiegang, had visited the laboratories of Emile Licent in Tianjin and then collaborated with Andersson in establishing a museum of natural sciences in Beijing in 1916.

At around the same time as the debates about a new Chinese history were taking place in the intellectual circles of the *Gushibian* journal, Li Ji 李濟 (1896–1979) had finished his dissertation in anthropology at Harvard University and returned to China. Li Ji was able to unearth *Yangshao* 仰韶 cultural relics in Xiyin 西陰 village in 1926, which marks the beginning of archaeological practice done by Chinese. Together with Li Ji came other overseas students who took major positions in new archaeological institutes, such as Xu Xusheng 徐旭生 (1888–1976), a student of philosophy in France, who joined a research team of Sven Hedin; Liang Siyong 梁思永 (1904–1954), who had graduated from the same Department of Anthropology at Harvard as Li Ji, and the latter Harvard student Feng Hanji 馮漢驥 (1899–1977); as well as Lin Huixiang 林惠祥 (1901–1958), Pei Wenzhong

---

[61] E. Edgar. 1917. "Stone Implements on the Upper Yangtze and Min River". *Journal of North China Branch of the R. A. S.*, XILIII. Chen Xingcan holds this to be one of very few archaeological reports on pre-history of that period. Chen Xingcan, 1997, p. 48.

[62] E. Licent and Teilhard de Chardin. 1928. "Le palaeolithique de la Chine", *Anthropologie* 35, pp. 201–34.

[63] J. G. Andersson. 1934. *The Children of the Yellow Earth*. London: K. Paul Trench.

裴文中 (1904–1982) and others.[64] Li Ji also lead the first Chinese large scale excavations in Anyang undertaken by the newly established Academia Sinica, founded in 1928. The archaeological branch of the Institute of History and Philology was the earliest and most important scientific institution for archaeology in China.

CONCLUSION

Chinese scholars had held an interest in antique objects since the early Han times and frequently made them their object of study; yet, until the early twentieth century, they never attempted to develop these studies into a systematic academic discipline. In the Song dynasty the object of study was mainly art objects and such studies were conducted by art connoisseurs. In the Qing dynasty scholarly interest in epigraphy increased with the rise of critical text studies. The breakthrough for Chinese scholarship and a systematic interest in archaeological methods, however, came with the famous discoveries of tortoise shells in Anyang in the early twentieth century. From then on, Chinese scholars took notice of Western works done in this field and developed an academic discussion.

Although foreigners had performed archaeological surveys and explorations in China since the middle of the nineteenth century, they did not import archaeology to China at this early stage—but instead exported a large amount of cultural relics out of China. The idea of archaeology and prehistory came to China via Japan, again not in the form of results from surveys and excavations by Japanese archaeologists working in China, but mediated by Chinese students in Japan. Their interest in archaeology was motivated by a strong inclination to rewrite China's history according to modern, scientific historiographical standards. New theories of the Three Ages were therefore favourably received, and archaeological methods served as means to criticise the textual research tradition of classical Chinese historiography.

When foreign archaeologists began to do archaeological research for purely scientific purposes at the beginning of the twentieth century, and so to cooperate with Chinese scholars in these activities, the ground for the development of archaeology in China was laid. Never-

---

[64] Cf. Zhang Qizhi, 1996, pp. 460–8.

theless, archaeology as a scientific discipline was only formally established by Chinese students returning to China after having received Western training in anthropology or archaeology abroad.

Their famous discoveries, such as that of the Shang capital at Yinxu with its major findings of the Bronze Age and the oracle bones also found in that area, established the new discipline as an important academic field. Yet, they also opened up a new discussion concerning the essence of Chinese culture and the reliability of its transmission, one which had been engendered by the *gushibian* group. Archaeology thus remained closely linked to the project of legitimizing a "national spirit".

Translated by Natascha Vittinghoff

REFERENCES

Anderson, John. 1871. *A Report on the Expedition to Western Yunan via Bhamo*. Calcutta: Office of the Superintendent of Government Printing.

Andersson, J. G. 1934. *The Children of the Yellow Earth*. London: K. Paul Trench.

Ban Gu 班固. 1964. *Hanshu* 漢書 (History of Han dynasty). Beijing: Zhonghua shuju.

Chavannes, Eduard. 1913. *Les documents Chinois discouverts par Aurel Stein dans les sables du Turkestan Oriental*. Oxford: Oxford University Press

Chen Xingcan 陳星燦. 1997. *Zhongguo shiqian kaoguoxueshi yanjiu*中國史前考古研究, *1885–1949* (The research of Chinese prehistory and archaeology between 1885 and 1949). Beijing: Shenhuo dushu xinzhi sanlian shudian.

Diaz-Andreu, Margarita and Champion, Timothy (eds.). 1996. *Nationalism and Archeology in Europe*. Boulder and San Francisco: Westview Press.

Edgar, E. 1917. "Stone Implements on the Upper Yangtze and Min River". *Journal of North China Branch of the R. A. S.*, XILIII.

Glyn, Daniel. 1976. *A Hundred and Fifty Years of Archaeology*. Cambridge Mass.: Harvard University Press.

Gu Jiegang 顧頡剛. 1923. "Yu Qian Xuantong xiansheng lun gushi shu" 与錢玄同先生論古史書 (Discussions on books on ancient history with Qian Xuantong). *Gushibian* 1, Reprint: Beijing: Bushe, pp. 59–66.

——. 1926. "Zixu" 自序 (Own preface), *Gushibian* 1, Reprint: Beijing: Bushe, pp. 51ff.

——. 1980. "Qian Xuantong 錢玄同(Qian Xuantong)". *Gushibian*古史辯, 1. Reprint: Shanghai: Shanghai guji chubanshe.

Guan Yun 觀雲. 1903. "Shijie zuigu zhi fadian 世界最古之法典 (The oldest code in the world)", *Xinming congbao* 33, pp. 19–22; 34, pp. 31–9.

Gun Fu 衮甫 (Wang Rongbao 汪榮寶). 1902. "Shixue gailun" 史學概論 (An introduction to historiography) in: *Yishu huibian* 9 (December 12, 1902) and 10 (December 27, 1902).

Hu Shi 胡適. 1926 [1921]. "Zi shu gushi guan shu" 自述古史觀書 (A letter [to Gu Jiegang] describing my views about ancient history), *Gushibian* 1, Reprint: Beijing: Bushe, pp. 22–3.

Kanaseki Takeo 金關丈夫 and Kokubu Naoichi 國分直一. 1979. "Taiwan kōkogaku kenkyūshi"臺灣考古學研究史 (Short history of archaeological researches in Taiwan), in: ibid.*Taiwan kōkoshi* 臺灣考古志 (Treatise on archaeology in Taiwan). N.p.: Hōsei daigaku shuppan kyoku, pp. 1–20.

Li Haosheng李浩生 (tr.). 1903. *Shixue tonglun* 史學通論 (General discussion of historiography). [Translation of Ukita Kazutami 浮田和民. *Shigaku genron* 史學原論 (Discussion of the origins of historiography), Lectures at Waseda University]. Hangzhou: Hezong yishu ju.

Li Shuli 李述禮 (tr.). 1984. *Yazhou fudi lüxingji* 亞洲腹地旅行記 (Travel to the Asian hinterland). [Translation of Sven Hedin. 1925. *My Life as an Explorer*. New York]. Shanghai: Shanghai shudian.

Li Xuanbo 李玄伯. 1926 [1924]. "Gushi wenti de weiyi jiejue fangfa 古史問題的唯一解決方法 (The only way to solve problems of ancient history), *Gushibian* 1, Reprint: Beijing: Bushe, p. 270.

Liang Qichao 1896. *Xixue shumu biao* 西學書目表 (Bibliography of Western knowledge). Shanghai: Shiwu baoguan.

——. 1989 [1901]. "Zhongguo shi xulun" 中國史敘論 (Preliminary discussion of Chinese history), in: *Yinbingshi heji* 飲冰室合集 (Collected works from the *Ice-Drinker's Studio*). Edited by Lin Zhijun 林志鈞. Shanghai: Zhonghua shuju 1936. Reprint: Beijing 1989, 12 vols., vol. 1.

Liang Han jinshiji 兩漢金石記 (Epigraphy in the Han dynasties). 1967 [1786]. Reprint: Taibei: Wenhai chubanshe.

Licent, E. and Chardin, de Teilhard. 1928. "Le palaeolithique de la Chine", *Anthropologie* 35, pp. 201–34.

Liu Chang 劉敞. 1981. "*Xianqin guqi ji* zhong tichu guqi de yanjiu fangfa" 先秦古器集中提出古器的研方法 (Methods to study ancient objects proposed in the *Collection of Ancient Objects of the Pre-Qin period*), in: Zhu Jianxin 朱劍心. *Jin shi xue* 金石學 (Epigraphy). Shanghai: Wenwu chubanshe.

Lü Dalin 呂大臨. 1983 [1092]. *Kaogutu* 考古圖 (Charts of investigations of antiquities). Reprint: Taiwan: Taiwan shangwu shuju, 10 vols.

Luo Zhenchang 羅振常. 1936 [1911. *Huan Luo fanggu youji* 洹洛訪古游記 (Travels in search for antiquities at the Huan and Luo rivers). Reprint: n.p.: Tanyinlu.

Luo Zhenyu 羅振玉. [between 1912–1936]. *Wushiri menghenlu* 五十日夢痕錄 (Records of dreamlike traces of fifty days). Shangyu: no publisher.

——. 1916. *Yinxu guqiwu tulu* 殷墟古器物圖錄 (Illustrations of antique objects of the Yin ruins). Published by the author.

——. and Wang Guowei 王國維. 1993 [1934]. *Liusha zhuijian* 流沙墜簡 (Fallen strips from drifting sands). Shangyu: Luoshi Chenhanlou. Reprint: Beijing: Zhonghua shuju, 3 vols.

Loewe, Michael and Shaughnessy, Edward L. 1999. *The Cambridge History of Ancient China. From the Origins of Civilization to 221 B.C.* Cambridge: Cambridge University Press.

Ouyang Xiu 歐陽修 (comp.). 1984 [1646]. *Jigulu* 集古錄 (Record of collected antiques), in: *Wenyuange Siku quanshu* 文淵閣四庫全書 (Wenyuan Pavilion edition of the *Siku quanshu*). Reprint: Taibei: Shangwu yinshuguan.

Pei Wenzhong 斐文中. 1983. "Shiqian kaoguxue jichu 史前考古學基礎" (The Foundations of prehistoric archaeology), *Shiqian yanjiu* 1, pp. 172–4.

Rong Yuan 容媛. 1930. "Chaodai renming tongjian 朝代人名通檢 (Comprehensive survey of personal names through the dynasties), in: *Jinshishu mulu* 金石書目錄 (General catalogue of epigraphical literature). Beijing. Shangwu yinshuguan.

Ruan Yuan 阮元 (ed.). 1890. *Liangzhe jinshilu* 兩浙金石記 (Epigraphy in two Zhe provinces), vol. 16. Hangzhou: Zhejiang shuju.

Se Jiangbao 澀江保 (ed.). 1926. *Taixi shiwu qiyuan.* 泰西事物起源 (On the origins of Western things). Shanghai: Wenming shuju.

Sima Qian 司馬遷. "Taishigong zixu" 太史公自序 (Autobiographical postface of Taishigong), in: *Shiji* 史記 (Records of the Historian), vol. 10. Beijing: Zhonghua shuju.

Stein, Marc Aurel. 1928. *Innermost Asia: Detailed Report of Explorations in Central Asia, Kan-su and Eastern Iran.* Oxford: Clarendon Press.

Tang Xiaobing. 1996. *Global Space and the Nationalist Discourse of Modernity. The Historical Thinking of Liang Qichao.* Stanford: Stanford University Press.

Inoue Tetsujirō 井上哲次郎 and Ariga Nagao 有賀長雄 (1884. *Kaitei zōho tetsugaku ji-i* 改訂增補哲學字彙 (Philosophical dictionary, revised and enlarged). Tokyo: Tōyōkan)

Thern, K. L. 1966. *Postface of the Shuo-wen Chieh-tzu. The First Comprehensive Chinese Dictionary.* Madison, Wis.: University of Wisconsin (Wisconsin China Series, no. 1).

Torii Ryūzō 鳥居龍藏 . 1910. *Minami Manshu chōsa hōkoku* 南滿州調查報告 (Survey report of Southern Manzhou). Tokyo: Shūeisha.

——. 1911. *Man Mō no tansa* 滿蒙の探査 (Inquiries in Manzhou and Mongolia). Tokyo: Banrikaku shuhō.

—— and K. Torii. 1914. "Populations primitives de la Mongolie Oriental", *Journal of Science* 36 (March), pp. 1–100.

——. 1915. *Populations primitives prehistoriques de Mondchourie Meridionale*. Tokyo: Tokyo University.

Tsuboi Kumezō 坪井九馬三 . 1903. *Shigaku hōhōron* 史學方法論 (Theory of historiographical methods). Tokyo: Waseda Daigaku.

Wang Fu 王黼 . 1991 [1123]. *Xuanhe bogutu* 宣和博古圖 (Charts on investigations of antiquities of the Xuanhe period), vol. 30. Yangzhou: Jiangsu Guangling guji yinkeshe.

Xiang Da 向達 (tr.). 1936. *Sitanyin xiyu kaoguji* 斯坦因西域考古記 (The archaeological activities of Stein in the western regions). [Translation of Marc Aurel Stein. 1933. *On Ancient Central Asia Tracks: Brief Narrative of Three Expeditions in Innermost Asia and North-Western China*. London: Macmillan]. Shanghai: Zhonghua shuju.

Yang Hanzhang 楊漢璋 (tr.). 1983. *Sichou zhilushangde waiguo mogui* 絲綢之路上的外國魔鬼 (Foreign Devils on the Silk Road). [Translation of Peter Hopkirk. 1980. *Foreign Devils on the Silk Road: the Search for the Lost Cities and Treasures of Chinese Central Asia*. London. Murray]. Lanzhou: Gansu renmin chubanshe.

Yu Danchu 俞旦初 . 1982. "Ershi shiji chunian Zhongguo de xin shixue sichao chukao 二十世紀初年中國的新史學思潮初考 (Preliminary investigations on the current trend of new historiography in the early years of the twentieth century), *Shixueshi yanjiu* 3.

——. 1983. "Ershi shiji chunian xifang jindai kaoguxue sixiang zai Zhongguo de jieshao he yinxiang" 二十世紀初年西方近代考古學思想在中國的介紹和影響 (What was the influence of the introduction of early twentieth century Western thought on modern archaeology to China?), *Kaogu yu wenwu* 4.

Zhang Qizhi 張豈之 (ed.). 1996. *Zhongguo jindai shixue xuexhushi* 中國近代史學學術史 (History of historiographical scholarship in modern China). Beijing: Zhongguo shehui kexue chubanshe.

Zhang Taiyan 章太炎 . 1977 [1902]. "Zhi Wu Junsui shu" 致吳君遂書 (A letter to Mr. Wu Junsui), in: Tang Zhijun 湯志鈞 (ed.). *Zhang Taiyuan zhenglun xuanji* 章太炎政論選集 (Selection of Zhang Taiyuans writings on politics). Beijing: Zhonghua shuju.

——. 1984 [1900]. *Zhongguo tongshi lüeli* 中國通史略例 (Concise history of China), in: ibid. *Qiushu chongdingben. Ai Qing shi* 訄書重訂本哀清史 (A revised edition of the *Qiushu*. Painful history of the Qing). *Zhang Taiyuan quanji*. 章太炎全集 (Complete works of Zhang Taiyuan). Shanghai: Shanghai renmin chubanshe, vol. 3.

ARAKAWA KIYOHIDE 荒川清秀

FORMATION AND DISSIMINATION OF JAPANESE GEOGRAPHICAL TERMINOLOGIES

I started my research on the formation of geographical terms about ten years ago during my analyis of synpictographical terms (*Ri Zhong tongxing ci* 日中同形詞 , Japanese and Chinese terms with common morphems) when I became suspicious about the origin of the term *redai* 熱帶 (torrid zone). Taking *redai* as a start, I have continued to examine and analyse the origin and dissemination of common geographical terms, such as *huiguixian* 回歸線 (tropics), *hailiu* 海流 (ocean current), *maoyifeng* 貿易風 (trade wind). My purpose was not only to trace the origin of single terms, but to find regularities in the formation and dissemination of the translated terms imported into both Chinese and Japanese. This article will present different ways of forming neologisms in the geographical vocabulary.

1. GEOGRAPHICAL TERMS FROM EUROPEAN LANGUAGES

1. Terms from Latin: redai 熱帶 , wendai 溫帶 *(temperate zone),* handai 寒帶 *(frigid zone)*

The *Hanyu wailaici cidian* 漢語外來詞詞典[1] (Dictionary of Chinese neologisms) lists *redai* as a Japanese loan-term, but in Japanese *shu* 暑 and not *re* 熱 would normally be used for the weather expressions, so the proper term in Japanese should be *shotai* 暑帶 . Since *re* is used in Chinese instead of *shu* I considered *redai* to possibly be a new term formed in China. In order to establish the origin of this term I consulted English-Chinese dictionaries published in China around the time of the Meiji Reformation as reference. The *Ying-Hua zidian* 英華字典 (*English and Chinese dictionary*, 1866–69), edited by Wilhelm Lobscheid (Luo Cunde 羅存德), is especially helpful in this respect, because it is generally assumed that Lobscheid did not use any mate-

---

[1] Liu Zhengtan 劉正 ..and Gao Mingkai 高名凱 (eds.). 1982. *Hanyu wailaici cidian* 漢語外來詞詞典 (Dictionary of Chinese neologisms). Shanghai: Shanghai cishu chubanshe.

rial from Japan for the compilation of his dictionary.[2] *Redai* appears in this dictionary as 'the tropics' and the 'torrid zone', and therefore most likely was not formed in Japan but in China. As Lobscheid coined many terms in the dictionary himself, it is possible that he was the creator of *redai*. But the many translations conducted in the long tradition of Western learning (*xixue* 西學) in China could also have been a reference source for Lobscheid. The Japanese linguist Satō Tōru 佐藤亨 has pointed out that the term *redai* appeared in the *Zhifang waiji* 職方外紀 (Record of the places outside the jurisdiction of the Office of Geography) written by the Jesuit Giulio Aleni (Ai Rulüe 艾儒略 , 1582–1649) in the seventeenth century.[3] Aleni gives the following explanation:

> The globe is divided into five zones; in the area around the equator and between the two tropics of cancer and of capricorn (*er zhigui* 二至規) the sun is mostly in the perpendicular; this is called the 'tropical zone' (*redai*). The zones between the tropic of cancer and the north pole and between the tropic of capricorn and the south pole, where the sun is neither far nor near the earth, are called 'temperate zone' (*wendai*). Those two zones around the north and south pole, where the sun appears only half-yearly, are called 'frigid zone' (冷帶 *lengdai*).[4]

Apart from *redai*, the two terms *wendai* and *lengdai* also appear already in this text. Yet the record of the history of geography recommends us to further consult earlier texts such as Matteo Ricci's (Li Madou 利瑪竇 , 1552–1610) *Kunyu wanguo quantu* 坤輿萬國全圖 (Charts of all countries in the world), in which he writes:

> According to its geological condition the globe can be divided into mountains and the seas; from the north to the south it is divided into five zones; one is between the longitude at the northern hemisphere (*zhouchang* 晝長 [which here means the tropic of cancer]) and the longitude of the southern hemisphere (*zhouduan* 晝短[which here means the tropic of capricorn]). The weather in this zone is very hot, because the sun is close to the earth; the second lies inside the arctic circle; the

---

    [2] Cf. Wilhelm Lobscheid (Luo Cunde 羅存德). 1866–69. *Ying-Hua zidian* 英華字典 *English and Chinese Dictionary with Punti and Mandarin Pronunciation*. Hong Kong: Daily Press Office.
    [3] Satō Tōru 佐藤亨 . 1983. *Kinseigoi no kenkyū* 近世語彙的研究 (Research of modern vocabularies). Tokyo: Ōfūsha.
    [4] Giulio Aleni (Ai Rulüe 艾儒略). 1623. *Zhifang waiji* 職方外紀 (Record of the places outside the jurisdiction of the Office of Geography). Hangzhou. Reprint in: *Tianxue chuhan* 天學初函 (Early letters on nature studies). 1972. Taibei: Xuesheng shuju, *juan* 1, pp. 1313–4.

third is inside the antarctic circle. The weather in those two zones is
very cold, because the sun is far away from the earth; the fourth lies
between the two longitudes of the northern hemisphere [which here
mean the tropic of cancer and the arctic circle]; the fifth is between the
two longitudes of the southern hemisphere [which here mean the tropic
of capricorn and the antarctic circle]; those two zones would be called
the 'temperate zone' (*zhengdai* 正帶), the weather here is neither cold
nor hot, because the sun in those areas is neither close nor far away
from the earth.[5]

Obviously only one compound term, *zhengdai,* is to be found here,
whereas the other two zones have no names yet. But there is a lead to
see how the term *redai* was formed. Aleni has formed the term *redai*
according to the sentence:

其地甚熱帶近日輪故也
The weather in this zone is very hot, because the sun is close to the
earth.

and formed the term *lengdai* 冷帶 according to the sentence:

此二處地居甚冷帶遠日輪故也
The weather in those two zones is very cold, because the sun is far
away from the earth.

Why is now *handai,* not *lengdai,* used in scientific geography? We
can assume that Aleni would have formed *handai,* had he not been
following the explanations in Ricci's *Kunyu wanguo quantu.* But why
did Ricci not write *qi di shen han* 其地甚寒 for "the weather is very
cold", but *ci er shu di ju shen leng?* In Chinese classical sources we
always find the term *han* meaning 'cold'. Although *leng* 冷 was listed
in the etymological dictionary of the Han dynasty, the *Shuowen jiezi*
説文解字 ,[6] as "*leng* means *han*", *han* was the term to be used for
'cold' in the period before the Six Dynasties. Only then did *leng*
appear in the same meaning as *han.*

If it had been Ricci's intention to create names for the five zones,
he would probably have used *handai.* But because he wanted to
explain the frigid zone to common readers he unconsciously used a

---

5 Matteo Ricci (Li Madou 利瑪竇). 1602. *Kunyu wanguo quantu* 坤輿萬國全圖
(Charts of all countries in the world). 3 maps reprinted by Miyagiken bunkazai hogo
kyōkai.
6 Xu Shen 許慎 . 1977. *Shuowen jiezi zhu* 説文解字注 (The *Shuowen jiezi* with
commentary [by Duan Yucai]). Beijing: Zhonghua shuju, s.v.

colloquial term, *leng,* and Aleni had—faithful to Ricci's explana-tions—formed the term *lengdai.*

Federico Masini has remarked concerning the reception of *redai* that "in Ricci the compound appears to still be free, while in Aleni it is clearly a bound compound."[7] Except for *zhengdai,* Ricci had in fact not formed any new term in his *Kunyu wanguo quantu,* but only explained what tropic zone and frigid zone meant, without giving a specific term for these parts of the world. But Ricci had used the term earlier in his *Qiankun tiyi* 乾坤體義 (The Meaning of the system of the universe):

> The zone where the weather is very hot, is called *redai,* because the sun is close to the earth. The two zones where the weather is very cold are called *handai,* because the sun is far away from the earth.[8]

Qiankun tiyi was published in 1605, three years after the *Kunyu wan-guo quantu.* And yet, the comparison of these two works reveals that *Qiankun tiyi* was edited earlier than *Kunyu wanguo quantu,* because the explanations on the theory of the five zones in *Qiankun tiyi* are more elaborate, whereas the *Kunyu wanguo quantu* only gives a short and general explanation of it.

When Aleni read about the five zones in Ricci's account, he only saw the term *zhengdai* (the temperate zone) and no terms describing zones according to their temperature. Then he substituted *zheng* by *wen* and formed the term *wendai.*

But why did *zhengdai* appear in Ricci's *Kunyu wanguo quantu?* The key to this question lies in the European languages. At that time, the formal language used in Europe was Latin. The Latin word analo-gous in meaning to *wendai* (temperate zone) was *temperatus,* but *tem-peratus* did not necessarily have anything to do with heat or temperature. The *Oxford English-Latin Dictionary* explains *tempera-tus* as 'temperate, moderate, mild', connotating the meaning 'under control, not exceeded, appropriate'. As Ricci formed *zhengdai,* he must have had the Latin term *zona temperata* in mind.

---

[7] Federico Masini. 1998. *Xiandai hanyu cihui de xingcheng — shijiu shiji hanyu wailaici yanjiu* 現代漢語詞匯的形成 — 十九世紀漢語外來詞研究 (The Formation of Modern Chinese Lexicon and its Evolution Toward a National Language: The Period from 1840 to 1898). Translated by Huang Keqing 黃河清. Shanghai: Hanyu dacidian chubanshe, p. 193.

[8] Matteo Ricci (Li Madou 利瑪竇). 1605. *Qiankun tiyi* 乾坤體義 (Meaning of the system of the universe). *Siku quanshu* edition.

Similar phenomena regarding the term for temperate zone can be observed in Japanese sources. For example in the *Nigi ryakusetsu* 二儀略説 (Outline of two instruments) the term *kaikisen* 回歸線 (tropic) appears and, analogous to the term *wendai, hedai* 和帶 is used.[9] Yama-mura Saisuke 山村才助 (1770–1807), the finest geographer of the Edo period, had used Dutch to explain *wendai* in his *Teisei zōyaku sairan igen* 訂正增譯采覽異言 (A new edited translation of *Collection of unorthodox words*) and said "*wendai* 溫帶 is called *gematigd lijn* and *gematigd* means neutral [temperature] (*zhonghe* 中和)."[10]

Similarly, *redai* is also not a proper translation, because the analogous term in Latin is *zona torrida*, which means high-tempered rather than hot and even has the meaning of *zao* 燥 (hot-tempered). The *English and Chinese Dictionary* by Lobscheid has accordingly the following entry: "torrid *re, zao, zaore* 燥熱 ."[11]

2. Terms from English: hailiu 海流 (ocean current) and maoyifeng 貿易風 (trade wind)

Another pattern of forming geographical neologisms was to base the translations on English sources, as in the examples of 'ocean current', 'trade wind' or 'basin' (*pendi* 盆地).

The existence of ocean currents had probably been known to sailors in the world for a long time already, and since the term looks like a direct translation, it would seem quite likely that the term *hailiu* would have existed for a long time as well. However, it did not appear in print until 1890, and was formed by Japanese and not a direct Chinese translation. *Hailiu* can not be found in the earlier literature, in which 'ocean current' is translated as follows:

> *Dili beikao* 地理備考 (References on geography):[12] *liu* 流 (stream, flow)
> *Dili quanzhi* 地理全志 (Comprehensive treatise on geography):[13] *pingliu* 平流 (calm flow)

[9] Kobayashi Kentei 小林謙貞 . *Nigi ryakusetsu* 二儀略説 (Outline of two instruments). Manuscript, Kokuritsu kobun shokan naikaku bunko 國立公文書館內閣文庫 .

[10] Yamamura Saisuke 山村才助 . 1979 [1802]. *Teisei zōyaku sairan igen* 訂正增譯采覽異言 (A new edited translation of *Collection of unorthodox words*). 4 vols. Tokyo: Seishisha, vol. 1, p. 79.

[11] Lobscheid 1866–69. s.v.

[12] Jose Martins-Marquez (Ma Jishi 瑪吉士). 1847. *Xinshi dili beikao quanshu* 新釋地理備考全書 (Reference of geography). Reprint in Haishan xianguan congshu 海山仙館叢書 (Encyclopedia from the Haishanxian guan), vol. 2, chapter "Shuiliu lun (On Water)".

Gewu tanyuan 格物探原 (Explorative principles of science):[14] *heliu* 河流 (flow, river)

Dizhi qimeng 地志啟蒙 (Elementary knowledge of topology):[15] *shuiliu* 水溜 (water current)

The reason for this can be traced back to the usage of this term in English. According to the *Oxford English Dictionary* the term 'ocean current' did not occur until 1863, and before 'stream', or words with a meaning similar to 'stream', were used. Such a usage of 'stream' can be traced back to 1375, when the term appeared in the word *Gulf stream*.

Another interesting example is the term *maoyifeng* 貿易風. Although *maoyifeng* is indeed a direct translation of the English term *trade wind*, in the past, there had also existed other terms formed to translate it. For example, Benjamin Hobson (He Xin 合信, 1816–1873), in his famous *Bowu xinbian* 博物新編 (Natural philosophy), says "*hengxinfeng* 恆信風 is commonly called *maoyifeng*,"[16] while in Lobscheid's *English and Chinese Dictionary* we can find the entry: "*redai changfeng* 熱帶常風 (wind frequently occurring in the tropic zone)."[17] Also in translations of scholars of the so-called Dutch studies (*rangaku* 蘭學) of the Edo period we find translations such as the 'wind with specific direction', as in *dingfeng* 定風 and *dingxiangfeng* 定向風.

These different terms arose because of the complex history of the term 'trade wind'. Originally, the term did indeed mean 'wind with specific direction' and had nothing to do with commerce. According to the *Oxford English Dictionary*, the first example that 'trade wind' had something to do with commerce appeared only in 1699. The term *maoyifeng* was formed according to this new meaning. The explanation of the *Bowu xinbian,* in which it is said that *hengxinfeng* could commonly also be called *maoyifeng*, shows that both the new and old translations existed at the same time.

---

[13] William Muirhead (Mu Weilian 慕維廉). 1853–54. *Dili quanzhi* 地理全志 (Comprehensive treatise on geography). Shanghai: Mohai shuguan.

[14] Alexander Williamson (Wei Lianchen 韋廉臣). 1878. *Gewu tanyuan* 格物探原 (Explorative principles of science). Beijing: Zong shuiwusi.

[15] Joseph Edkins (Ai Yuese 艾約瑟). 1886. *Dizhi qimeng* 地志啟蒙 (Elementary knowledge of topology). Beijing: Zong shuiwusi.

[16] Benjamin Hobson (He Xin 合信). 1855. *Bowu xinbian* 博物新編 (Natural philosophy). Shanghai: Mohai shuguan, vol. 1, p. 9.

[17] Lobscheid 1866–69. s.v.

So, originally *maoyifeng* was only the popular name. That Lobscheid instead used the term *redai changfeng* is related to the German translation. *Passat*, the creation of which is based on Latin, is very similar in its meaning to 'wind with specific direction' (*hengxinfeng)*, and not to commerce. After *maoyifeng* had been used for a period of time in China, 'trade wind' was later substituted by *xinfeng* 信風 , a term we can find in classical texts already and which had the same meaning as *jifeng* 季風 (seasonal wind). Now in China, *maoyifeng* is again the colloquial name for trade wind and *xinfeng* is the official scientific term. As far as I know, English and Japanese are the only two languages in which the term is still connected to trade and commerce.

3. Terms from German and French: bingshan 冰山 (iceberg) and binghe 冰河 (glacier)

Bingshan is a geographical term representative for those originating from German. Although it had already appeared in the *Zhifang waiji* of the Italian Jesuit Aleni, it is a direct translation of *Eisberg*.

Binghe (glacier) originates from the French *glace*. Lobscheid already gives *bingtian* 冰田 or *shanshang bingtian* 山上冰田 in his dictionary. For him *binghe* is not a kind of river but a field. Today in China, both *bingchuan* 冰川 and *binghe* are used, but more often *bingchuan* appears. Since c*huan* 川 also means 'plain' (*pingyuan* 平原) I assume the meaning of *chuan* in *bingchuan* is 'plain', like in *bingtian*.

2. TERMS CREATED BY JAPANESE SCHOLARS

1. From kunjōmini 訓讀 (Japanese reading) to onjōmini 音讀 (Chinese reading): huiguixian 回歸線 (tropic, Japanese: kaikisen)

Although a large part of geographical terms originally appeared in the *Kunyu wanguo quantu* by Matteo Ricci, *huiguixian* does not appear in this text. The Japanese term *shotai* 暑帶 appeared in the astrological book *Nigi ryakusetsu* edited in the seventeenth century in Japan and seems very much like a Japanese term. Since also the term *kaikisen* appears in the *Nigi ryakusetsu*, it is possibly a typical Japanese term.

A special characteristic of the Japanese language is the existence of two pronunciation systems—the *kunjōmini*, i.e. the Japanese reading, and the *onjōmini*, i.e. the Chinese reading. The Japanese reading is employed for Chinese characters that have a similar meaning in Japanese and Chinese. For example the *kunjōmini* of *hai* 海 (sea) is *umi*. Japanese immediately think of the Japanese term *umi* when seeing this character. The *onjōmini* of the same character is *kai,* i.e. the Japanese pronunciation of the Chinese *hai.* The explanation of the term 'tropic' in the *Raponichi taiyaku jisho* 羅葡日對譯辭書 (Roman-Portuguese-Japanese dictionary) edited by a Jesuit missionary in Japan is an apt example: it is "the northern and southern boundary, in between which the sun moves back and forth (*meguri-kaeru* 巡回去)."[18]

I assume that the Japanese Jesuit formed the term *kaiki* 回歸 according to the explanation of *meguri-kaeru*. In modern Chinese *huigui* 回歸 is a compound term with two characters having similar meanings, and here also *hui* 回 means the same as *gui* 歸 .

2. *Terms created from Dutch:* bandao 半島 *(peninsula, Japanese:* hantō*)*

Japanese scholars of Dutch studies in the Edo period translated from Dutch to Japanese by translating the meanings of single elements of the Dutch compound words, as for example:

> Power of attraction: *Aantrekkings* (引 , pull) *Kracht* (力 , power) = *inryoku* 引力
> Duodenum: *Twaalf* (十二 , twelve) *Vingerigen* (指 , finger) *Darm* (腸 , intestine) = *jūnishichō* 十二指腸
> Tranquil sea: *Still* (靜) *Zee* (海) = *seikai* 靜海
> Peninsula: *Half* (半 , half) *Eiland* (島 , island) = *hantō* 半島

Let us take a closer look at the problems of the formation and dissemination of the term 'peninsula' (Chinese: *bandao* 半島). In Dutch *bandao* is called *schiereiland*, for which the term *jitō* 似島 (similar to – island) would be the direct translation, as is explained in *Edo haruma* 江戶波留麻 (Japanese-Dutch dictionary in the Edo period),[19] one of the Japanese-Dutch dictionaries published in the Edo period. Still the term *hantō* is a typical example for direct translations from Dutch, and is also found in the *English and Chinese Dictionary* by Lobscheid.

---

[18] *Raponichi taiyaku jisho* 羅葡日對譯辭書 (Roman-Portuguese-Japanese dictionary). 1595. (Reprinted Tokyo: Benseisha.).
[19] Inamura Sanpaku 稲村三伯 . 1796a. *Edo haruma* 江戶波留麻 (Japanese-Dutch dictionary of the Edo period). Edo.

With regard to Japanese loans Zhou Zhenhe 周振鶴 has said:

> In the past there were some misunderstandings that modern Chinese neologisms (*wailaici* 外來詞) would mainly come to China via Japan. This is only partially true. In fact, in the earlier period before the Meiji Reformation, the direction of contact between Chinese, Japanese and the European languages and their neologisms was vice versa from Europe to China to Japan. Only in the later period at the beginning of this [i.e. twentieth] century, did the direction change and [terms would travel from] Europe to Japan [and then arrive in] China. In the time between these two periods, between the Meiji Reformation [1868] in Japan and the Wuxu Reform [1898] in China, [words were exchanged in] both directions.[20]

I would add that the next misunderstanding is the general assumption that loan-terms originating from Japanese were only received in China after the Sino-Japanese War of 1894/95. I have mentioned above that the *English and Chinese Dictionary* by Lobscheid can be taken as an indication for terms originating from Chinese. But, turning back to our example of peninsula, we might have to reconsider these earlier statements.

The term *peninsula* was not included in the English-Chinese dictionaries by Robert Morrison[21] or Samuel Wells Williams[22] in the nineteenth century. In Walter H. Medhurst's dictionary 'peninsula' was explained as follows:

> An island connected to the continent (*lian di zhi dao* 連地之島), continent with a neck (*you jing zhi zhou* 有頸之洲), an island which is not entirely surrounded by water (*shuiliu wei zhou zhi yu* 水流未周之嶼).[23]

Lobscheid took over parts of the translations by Medhurst but also added the term *bandao*:

---

[20] Zhou Zhenhe 周振鶴 . 1998. "Chudu *Xiandai hanyu cihui de xincheng* zhongyiben" 初讀現代漢語詞匯的形成中譯本 (Preliminary reading of the Chinese translation of *The Formation of Modern Chinese Lexicon and its Evolution Toward a National Language: The Period from 1840 to 1898*), *Ciku jianshe tongxun* 15, p. 6.

[21] Cf. Robert Morrison. 1815–23. *A Dictionary of the Chinese Language*. 3 parts, 6 vols. Macao: East India Company's Press.

[22] Cf. Samuel Wells Williams. 1844. *English and Chinese Vocabulary, in the Court Dialect*. Macao: Office of the Chinese Repository.

[23] Walter Henry Medhurst. 1847–48. *English and Chinese Dictionary*. Shanghai: Missionary Press.

> A piece of earth connected to a continent (*lian zhou zhi di* 連洲之地);
> an island connected to a continent (*lian zhou zhi dao* 連洲之島); penin-
> sula (*bandao* 半島); an island which is not entirely surrounded by water
> (*shui bu quan zhi dao* 水不全之島).[24]

The term *bandao* did not appear in Chinese translations of Western
books before the publication of Lobscheid's dictionary, but it was
included in the *Eiwa taiyaku shūchin jisho* 英和對譯袖珍辭書 (Concise
English-Japanese dictionary) from Hori Tatsunosuke 崛達之助
(1823–1894).[25] Morioka Kenji 森岡健二 has pointed out that approximately sixty percent of the terms collected in this dictionary originated from Dutch-Japanese dictionaries of the Edo period.[26] Indeed,
the following dictionaries and geographical books contained the term
hantō 半島 :

> *Teiseizōyaku sairai igen* (A new edited translation of *Collection of
> unorthodox words*)
> *Yochishi* 輿地志 (Treatise on geography)[27]
> *Shinshaku yochizusetsu* 新釋輿地圖説 (New edition of *Illustrated geog-
> raphy*)[28]
> *Oranda jii* 和蘭字匯 (Japanese-Dutch dictionary)[29]

This shows that *hantō* is a genuine Japanese term. How, then, should
we evaluate the appearance of the term *bandao* in the dictionary by
Lobscheid? One possible explanation would be that Lobscheid and
Hori had formed the same term separately, since in German, Lob-
scheid's mother language, *bandao* is *Halbinsel* (semi-round island).
The other possibility is that Lobscheid had seen Japanese material.
According to the researches of Endō Tomoo 遠藤智夫[30] and Nasu

---

[24] Lobscheid 1866–69. s.v.

[25] Cf. Hori Tatsunosuke 堀達之助 .1862. *Eiwa taiyaku shūchin jisho* 英和對譯袖
珍辭書 (Concise English-Japanese dictionary). Edo: Yōsho shirabesho.

[26] Cf. Morioka Kenji 森岡健二 . 1969. *Kindaigo no seiritsu: meigiki goihen* 近代
語の成立 : 明治期詞匯編 (The formation of modern language—vocabularies in the
Meiji period). Tokyo: Meiji Shoin.

[27] Cf. Aochi Rinsō 青地林宗 . 1827. *Yochishi* 輿地志 (Treatise on geography).
Manuscript.

[28] Cf. Watanabe Kazan 渡邊崋山 . 1836. *Shinshaku yochizusetsu* 新釋輿地圖説
(New edition of *Illustrated geography*). Manuscript.

[29] Cf. Katsuragawa Hoshū 桂川甫周 . 1855–58. *Oranda jii* 和蘭字匯 (Japanese-
Dutch dictionary). Edo: Yamashiroshi.

[30] Cf. Endō Tomoo 遠藤智夫 . 1996. "*Eiwa taiyaku shūchin jisho* to Medhurst no
Yinghan zidian" 英和對譯袖珍辭書與 Medhurst 的英漢字典 (The *Concise English-
Japanese dictionary* and the *English-Chinese Dictionary* by Medhurst), *Eigakushi
kenkyū* 29, pp. 47–59.

Masayuki 那須雅之 ,[31] Lobscheid had worked as translator of Chinese and Dutch and had come to Japan together with Henry Adams (d. 1869), the adjutant of Matthew C. Perry (1794–1879). During his negotiations with the Japanese government Lobscheid met Hori Tatsunosuke, and sent him the English-Chinese and Chinese-English dictionary edited by Medhurst. Later, in 1862, during his second visit of Japan, he perhaps bought a dictionary edited by Hori Tatsunosuke.

Therefore I assume that it is possible that Lobscheid had seen the dictionary from Hori. Lobscheid had to make choices when he composed his own dictionary. A rough comparison of the geographical terms in both dictionaries shows that only the words *bandao* 半島 , *xuebeng* 雪崩 (avalanche, Japanese: *nadare*) and *zhouye pingfenxian* 晝夜平分線 (equinox) seem to have been taken over from Hori's dictionary.

This example may serve as evidence that neologism also disseminated from Japan to China prior to the Sino-Japanese War. In general, any research about the interchange of terms between Japanese and Chinese in modern times should start with an investigation of the dictionaries by Hori Tatsunosuke and Lobscheid.

And yet, by no means all the terms created by Lobscheid were accepted into other dictionaries published later. This is especially true for dictionaries edited by missionaries, as we can see from the following examples:

> *Yinghua cuilin yunfu* 英華萃林韻府 : Part I: not included, Part III: *tugu* 土股 (earth thigh).[32]
> *Technical Terms English and Chinese*: *tugu*.[33]
> *English-Chinese Dictionary of the Standard Chinese Spoken Language*: *tugu, bandao*.[34]

---

[31] Cf. Nasu Masayuki 那須雅之 . 1996. "W. Lobscheid shōdenhoi—Lobscheid teki hōnichi yo Hori Tatsunosuke" W. Lobscheid 小傳補遺 —Lobscheid 的訪日與堀達助 (Addition to the short biography of W. Lobscheid—Lobscheid's visit to Japan and Hori Tatsunosuke), paper prepared for the Conference of the Society of Modern Chinese Research, Toyohashi, Japan.

[32] Cf. Justus Doolittle (Lu Gongming 盧公明). 1872. *Yinghua cuilin yunfu* 英華萃林韻府 . *A Vocabulary and Hand-Book of the Chinese Language, Romanized in the Mandarin Dialect*. 2 vols. Fuzhou: Rozario, Marcal and Company.

[33] Cf. Calvin W. Mateer. 1904. *Technical Terms English and Chinese. Prepared by the Committee of the Educational Association of China*. Shanghai: Presbyterian Press.

[34] Cf. Karl E. G. Hemeling (He Meiling 赫美玲). 1916. *English-Chinese Dictionary of the Standard Spoken Language (Guanhua* 官話 *) and Handbook for Transla-*

The problem of how the missionaries in China understood Japanese translated terms still requires further investigation. At any rate, the term *bandao* would be used for the first time by a missionary in the *Guanhua* dictionary by Karl Hemeling (He Meiling 赫美玲).

3. *Borrowings from classical sources*—shanmai 山脈 *(mountain range)*

Before the Meiji Reformation, the Japanese always borrowed terms from classical Chinese to translate European and American neologisms as, for example, *yanyifa* 演譯法 (deduction), *xing er shang xue* 形而上學(metaphysics), *xiangdui* 相對(relativity), *juedui* 絕對(absolute), *lunlixue* 倫理學(ethics), etc. But there are also examples of borrowings from classical Japanese in the process of creating neologisms.

Shanmai was originally a term used to describe geomantics (*fengshui* 風水). Watanabe Kazan 渡邊華山 (1796–1841), a *rangaku* scholar, formed the terms *sansa* 山鎖 and also *sanmyaku* 山脈 to translate *bergketen* (mountain range) from Dutch, both of which are direct translations. *Sanmyaku* later supplanted *sansa* and became the commonly used term. For example, in *Konyo zushikiho* 坤輿圖識補 (Supplements to *Illustrated knowledge about the world*) by Mitsukuri Shōgo 箕作省吾 (1821–1847) there appears *andesu daisanmyaku* 暗得大山脈 (the big mountain range of the Andes);[35] and Sugita Seikei's 杉田成卿 (1817–1859) *Chigaku shōsō* 地學正宗 (Orthodox schools of geography) contains *sanmyaku* and also *renzan* 連山 (mountain chain).[36] Udagawa Yōsei 宇田川榕精 explains *sanmyaku* in his *Bankoku chigaku wage* 萬國地學和解 (Japanese comments on geographical studies of the world).[37] This might serve as evidence that the geographical term *shanmai* is a Chinese term originating from the Japanese. In *Dili quanzhi* 地理全志 by William Muirhead (Mu Weilian 慕維廉, 1822–1900) we find the following record: "There are

---

[34] (*cont.*) *tors, including Scientific, Technical, Modern, and Documentary Terms.* Shanghai: Shanghai Statistical Department of the Inspectorate General of Customs.

[35] Cf. Mitsukuri Shōgo 箕作省吾. 1846. *Konyo zushikiho* 坤輿圖識補 (Supplements to *Illustrated knowledge about the world*). Edo.

[36] Cf. Sugita Seikei 杉田成卿. 1851. *Chigaku shōsō* 地學正宗(Orthodox schools of geography). Edo: Tenshirō.

[37] Cf. Udagawa Yōsei 宇田川榕精. 1868. *Bankoku chigaku wage* 萬國地學和解 (Japanese comments on geographical studies of the world). Manuscript.

four forms of the earth's surface; there are five directions of mountain ranges (*shanmai*)."[38]

The term used here is in my opinion probably a traditional geomantic term and not a term from geography, because Muirhead did not use *shanmai* in the passage about the theory of the origins of mountains (*shanyuan lun* 山原論) in the *Dili quanzhi*; furthermore, terms used by missionaries at the turn of the twentieth century include *ling* 岭 (ridge of a hill) or *shanling* 山岭 (mountain ridge) for 'mountain range', but not *shanmai*. This can be seen from the following examples:

> *Yinghua cuilin yunfu*: Part I, *ling*; Part III, *shanling*.
> *Technical Terms English and Chinese*: *shanling*, *gangling* 岗陵 (ridge of a hill).
> Hemeling's *Guanhua*: *lianshan* 連山 (connected mountains), *shanling*.

This means that *shanmai* used as a term in geography originally stemmed from Japan and disseminated to China.

4. Misunderstandings: huashi 化石 (fossil, Japanese: kaseki)

The *Hanyu wailaici cidian* writes "the term *huashi* originates from Japanese",[39] but Masini has raised doubts concerning this point of view.[40] In fact, the process of forming the term *huashi* is very complicated.

Huashi is the abbreviation of *huaweishi* 化為石 (to turn into stone), which is a word group but not a compound term. Masini holds it to be a compound term consisting of a modifier and the word it modifies. This is a possible explanation for modern Chinese. But still it was originally a word group consisting of a verb and an object. In my opinion, *huashi* was a word group, not a compound term. This word group appeared for the first time in *Wuli xiaoshi* 物理小識 (Simple knowledge about physics)[41] by Fang Yizhi 方以智 (d. 1671) of the Kangxi period. *Wuli xiaoshi* was disseminated to Japan during the Edo period and influenced many Japanese scholars, especially scholars of natural sciences. For Chinese, *huashi* is definitely a word group,

---

[38] Muirhead 1853–54, *juan* 1–5.
[39] Liu and Gao 1982. s.v.
[40] Cf. Masini 1993, p. 177.
[41] Cf. Fang Yizhi 方以智 . 1664. *Wulixiaoshi* 物理小識 (Simple knowledge of physics). n.p.

but for Japanese scholars of natural sciences, like Hiraga Gennai 平賀源內 (1728–1779), Shiba Kōkan 司馬江漢 (1747–1818), Kiuchi Sekitei 木內石亭 etc. it is a compound term and used as such in their publications like *Butsurui hinshitsu* 物類品質 (Classification of things),[42] *Tenchiritan* 天地理譚 (On cosmology),[43] and *Unkonshi* 雲根志 (Treatise on the origins of clouds).[44] Although the term *jiangshi* 礓石 (mortar) formed by the missionaries, as in *Chigaku senshaku* 地學淺釋 (Brief comments on geography),[45] was used for a period of time in Japan, *kaseki* 化石 later became the correct geological term. After its establishment as geological term the structure of this term was not debated anymore and it was easily accepted by the academic circles in China.

Just as Masini assumes, the term *huashi* today would be taken as a compound term consisting of a modifier and the word it modifies. But what do we do with formulations like *songhuashi* 松化石, which appear in the *Wuli xiaoshi*? If we take the term *songhuashi* as a compound term, we have to understand it as *songhua de shi* 松化的石 (pine turned to stone) and not as a compound term consisting of a modifier and the word it modifies. In fact there are very few compound terms of this sort in Chinese. Ren Xueliang 任學良 has collected some in his study on modes of forming Chinese words from medical vocabulary and I have identified them as loan-terms from Japanese.[46]

5. Deformation: jiankang 健康 *(health, Japanese:* kenkō)

Jiankang is formed by reversing the term *kangjian* 康健. The term *kangjian* appeared in earlier texts like the *Mengxi bitan* 夢溪筆談 (Notes from the Meng River)[47] from Shen Kuo 沈括 (1031–1095) of

---

[42] Cf. Hiraga Gennai平賀源內. 1763. *Butsurui hinshitsu* 物類品質 (Classification of things). Edo, Osaka: Shōraikan.

[43] Cf. Shiba Kōkan 司馬江漢. 1816. *Tenchiritan* 天地理譚 (On cosmology). Manuscript.

[44] Cf. Kiuchi Sekitei 木內石亭. 1994 [1764]. *Unkonshi* 雲根志 (On the origins of clouds). Tokyo.

[45] Cf. *Chigaku senshaku* 地學淺釋 (Brief comments on geography). 1873. Shanghai: Jiangnan zhizaoju.

[46] Cf. Ren Xueliang 任學良. 1981. *Hanyu zaocifa* 漢語造詞法 (Modes of forming Chinese words). Beijing: Shanghai shehui kexueyuan.

[47] Cf. Shen Kuo 沈括.1975. *Mengxi bitan* 夢溪筆談 (Notes from the Meng River). Beijing: Wenwu chubanshe, *juan* 24.

the Song dynasty, and in vernacular novels like *Rulin waishi* 儒林外史 (The Scholars)[48] or *Hongloumeng* 紅樓夢 (Dream of the Red Chamber).[49] The earliest examples of the term *kenkō* in Japanese are to be found in the following series of terms in some Dutch-Japanese dictionaries edited by *rangaku* scholars:

Haruma wage 波留麻和解 (Japanese-Dutch dictionary): welstand welvaarende welzyn.[50]
Yakken 譯鍵 (Translation key): wekstand pluis.[51]
Orandajii 和蘭字匯 (Dutch-Japanese dictionary): opkoomen.[52]
(Kaisei) Zōho yakken 改正増補譯鍵 (Corrected supplements of *Translation key)*: pluis opkoomen.[53]

In the Dutch-Japanese dictionaries, the only words to be listed under the term *gezondheid* (health) would be those like *kōken* 康健 or *jōnari* 狀也 , etc. Only after the effort of the *ranganku* scholar Ogata Kōan 緒方洪庵 (1810–1863) and the first health minister Nagayo Sensai 長與専齋 (1838–1902), would *kenkō* be gradually accepted as the correct medical term. After that, the term *kenkō* disseminated to China and supplanted the term *kangjian* 康健 , which originally meant health.[54]

Why did the Japanese reverse the term *kōken* to *kenkō* ? The first reason is: At that time there already existed a large number of disyllabic terms with reverse order in Chinese. For example, *liaozhi* 療治 / *zhiliao* 治療 (treatment), *jingzheng* 竟爭 */zhengjing* 爭竟 (competition), *zhanzheng* 戰爭 */zhengzhan* 爭戰 (war), etc. Chinese linguistic studies revealed that about eighty percent of compound disyllabic terms are

---

[48] Cf. Wu Jingzi 吳敬梓 . 1985. *Rulin waishi* 儒林外史 (The Scholars). Beijing: Renmin wenxue chubanshe.

[49] Cf. Cao Xueqin 曹雪芹 . 1958. *Hongloumeng* 紅樓夢 (Dream of the Red Chamber). Beijing: Renmin wenxue chubanshe.

[50] Cf. Inamura Sanpaku 稲村三伯 . 1796b. *Haruma wage* 波留麻和解 (Dutch-Japanese dictionary). Edo.

[51] Fujibayashi Fuzan 藤林普山 . 1811. *Yakken* 譯鍵 (Translation key). (Reprinted Tokyo: Seishisha, 1981).

[52] Cf. Katsuragawa 1855–58.

[53] Cf. Hirota Kenkan 廣田憲寬 . 1864. *(Kaisei) Zōho yakken* 改正増補譯鍵 (Corrected supplements of *Translation key*). n.p.

[54] Cf. Ada Haven Mateer. 1913. *New Terms for New Ideas. A Study of the Chinese Newspaper*. Shanghai: Presbyterian Mission Press, p. 139: "Chienkang 健康 , robust, strong, vigorous; formerly the order was reversed, and the term was used with reference to superiors, as son speaking of father. In this present form its use is unrestricted as to age, but is not used of inanimate objects."

arranged according to the sequence of tones.[55] Because the Japanese were usually not aware of this rule, they believed they could form a new term by reversing the sequence of the syllables.

The second reason is that the Japanese were in need of a large number of new terms because they were translating so many books from the West. For the sake of making the novelty of particular terms noticeable, it is a convenient method to use terms that already existed and to change them into new words. For example, terms like *ichō* 胃腸 (intestine, Chinese: *weichang*) and *umpan* 運搬 (move, Chinese: *ban-yun*) are formed as the reversed versions of *changwei* 腸胃 and *ban-yun* 搬運 . The term *kenkō* for 'health' has substituted the term *kangjian* in Chinese, but *ichō* and *umpan* have not supplanted *chang-wei* and *banyun*.

CONCLUSION

My elaborations on the formation of geographical terms served the purpose of displaying the variety of options open to the Chinese or Japanese scholar in forming new terms. Translators could employ methods of translating terms directly from the original languages, as shown in the examples of terms from English, German or French. In some instances, the terms in the original languages were neologisms themselves and therefore mostly based on Latin origins. In order to trace back these original meanings one has to consult the Latin origins and meanings of these terms as well.

Moreover, I intended to show that the common assumption about the route of reception of Chinese neologisms, namely Europe-China-Japan before the Meiji Restauration and Europe-Japan-China after the Sino-Japanese War, is not correct in all instances. Instead we also find many terms which had been formed in Japan and received in China long before the turn of the twentieth century. In Japan, *rangaku* schol-ars played a crucial role in forming new terminologies. From the examples cited above we can also see that apart from adaptations from Western foreign languages, Japanese scholars did in fact base the largest part of neologisms on classical Chinese expressions, but

---

[55] Cf. Chen Aiwen 陳愛文 and Yu Ping 于平 . 1979. *Binlieshi shuangyinci de zixu* 並列式雙音詞的字序 (The word sequence of compound disyllabic terms). Beijing: Zhongguo yuwen chubanshe.

there existed also new creations that were based on classical Japanese expressions.

As shown in the case of Lobscheid, his contact with Japanese and travels to Japan were certainly influential in his choices for coining new terms in geography. Therefore the formation of new terms must be understood as a complex process which also involved the individual experiences of the single translators.

Translated by Natascha Vittinghoff

References

Aleni, Giulio (Ai Rulüe 艾儒略). 1623. *Zhifang waiji* 職方外紀 (Record of the places outside the jurisdiction of the Office of Geography). Hangzhou. Reprint in: *Tianxue chuhan* 天學初函 (Early letters on nature studies). 1972. Taibei: Xuesheng shuju.

Aochi Rinsō 青地林宗. 1827. *Yochishi* 輿地志 (Treatise on geography). Manuscript.

Cao Xueqin 曹雪芹. 1958. *Hongloumeng* 紅樓夢 (Dream of the Red Chamber). Beijing: Renmin wenxue chubanshe.

Chen Aiwen 陳愛文 and Yu Ping 于平. 1979. *Binlieshi shuangyinci de zixu* 並列式雙音詞的字序 (The word sequence of compound disyllabic terms). Beijing: Zhongguo yuwen chubanshe.

Chigaku senshaku 地學淺釋 (Brief comments on geography). 1873. Shanghai: Jiangnan zhizaoju.

Doolittle, Justus (Lu Gongming 盧公明). 1872. *Yinghua cuilin yunfu* 英華萃林韻府. *A Vocabulary and Hand-Book of the Chinese Language, Romanized in the Mandarin Dialect*. 2 vols. Fuzhou: Rozario, Marcal and Company.

Edkins, Joseph (Ai Yuese 艾約瑟). 1886. *Dizhi qimeng* 地志啟蒙 (Elementary knowledge of topology). Beijing: Zong shuiwusi.

Endō Tomoo 遠藤智夫. 1996. "*Eiwa taiyaku shūchin jisho* to Medhurst no *Yinghan zidian*" 英和對譯袖珍辭書與 Medhurst 的英漢字典 (The *Concise English-Japanese dictionary* and the *English-Chinese Dictionary* by Medhurst), *Eigakushi kenkyū* 29, pp. 47–59.

Fang Yizhi 方以智. 1664. *Wulixiaoshi* 物理小識 (Simple knowledge of physics). n.p.

Fujibayashi Fuzan 藤林普山. 1811. *Yakken* 譯鍵 (Translation key). (Reprinted Tokyo: Seishisha, 1981.)

Hemeling, Karl E. G. (He Meiling 赫美玲). 1916. *English-Chinese Dictionary of the Standard Spoken Language (Guanhua* 官話*) and Handbook for Translators, including Scientific, Technical, Modern, and Documentary Terms*. Shanghai: Shanghai Statistical Department of the Inspectorate General of Customs.

Hiraga Gennai 平賀源内. 1763. *Butsurui hinshitsu* 物類品質 (Classification of things). Edo, Osaka: Shōraikan.

Hirota Kenkan 廣田憲寬. 1864. *(Kaisei) Zōho yakken* 改正增補譯鍵 (Corrected supplements of *Translation key*). n.p.

Hobson, Benjamin (He Xin 合信). 1855. *Bowu xinbian* 博物新編 (Natural philosophy). Shanghai: Mohai shuguan.

Hori Tatsunosuke 堀達之助. 1862. *Eiwa taiyaku shūchin jisho* 英和對譯袖珍辭書 (Concise English-Japanese dictionary). Edo: Yōsho shirabesho.

Inamura Sanpaku 稻村三伯. 1796a. *Edo haruma* 江戶波留麻 (Japanese-Dutch dictionary of the Edo period). Edo.

——. 1796b. *Haruma wage* 波留麻和解 (Dutch-Japanese dictionary). Edo.

Katsuragawa Hoshū 桂川甫周. 1855–58. *Oranda jii* 和蘭字匯 (Japanese-Dutch dictionary). Edo: Yamashiroshi.

Kiuchi Sekitei 木內石亭. 1764. *Unkonshi* 雲根志 (On the origins of clouds). (Reprinted Tokyo, 1994).

Kobayashi Kentei 小林謙貞. *Nigi ryakusetsu* 二儀略説 (Outline of two instruments). Manuscript, Kokuritsu kobun shokan naikaku bunko 國立公文書館內閣文庫.

Liu Zhengtan 劉正 .and Gao Mingkai 高名凱 (eds.). 1982. *Hanyu wailaici cidian* 漢語外來詞詞典 (Dictionary of Chinese neologisms). Shanghai: Shanghai cishu chubanshe.

Lobscheid, Wilhelm (Luo Cunde 羅存德). 1866–69. *Ying-Hua zidian* 英華字典 *English and Chinese Dictionary with Punti and Mandarin Pronunciation*. Hong Kong: Daily Press Office.

Martins-Marquez, Jose (Ma Jishi 瑪吉士). 1847. *Xinshi dili beikao quanshu* 新釋地理備考全書 (Reference of geography). Reprint in Haishan xianguan congshu 海山仙館叢書 (Encyclopedia from the Haishanxian guan).

Masini, Federico. 1998. *Xiandai hanyu cihui de xingcheng — shijiu shiji hanyu wailaici yanjiu* 現代漢語詞匯的形成 — 十九世紀漢語外來詞研究 (The Formation of Modern Chinese Lexicon and its Evolution Toward a National Language: The Period from 1840 to 1898). Translated by Huang Keqing 黃河清. Shanghai: Hanyu dacidian chubanshe.

Mateer, Ada Haven. 1915. *New Terms for New Ideas. A Study of the Chinese Newspaper*. Shanghai: Presbyterian Mission Press.

Mateer, Calvin W. 1904. *Technical Terms English and Chinese. Prepared by the Committee of the Educational Association of China*. Shanghai: Presbyterian Press.

Medhurst, Walter Henry. 1847–48. *English and Chinese Dictionary*. Shanghai: Missionary Press.

Mitsukuri Shōgo 箕作省吾. 1846. *Konyo zushikiho* 坤輿圖識補 (Supplements to *Illustrated knowledge about the world*). Edo.

Morioka Kenji 森岡健二. 1969. *Kindaigo no seiritsu: meigiki goihen* 近代語の的成立：明治期詞匯編 (The formation of modern language—vocabularies in the Meiji period). Tokyo: Meiji Shoin.

Morrison, Robert. 1815–23. *A Dictionary of the Chinese Language*. 3 parts, 6 vols. Macao: East India Company's Press.

Muirhead, William (Mu Weilian 慕威廉). 1853–54. *Dili quanzhi* 地理全志 (Comprehensive treatise on geography). Shanghai: Mohai shuguan.

Nasu Masayuki 那須雅之. 1996. "W. Lobscheid shōdenhoi—Lobscheid teki hōnichi yo Hori Tatsunosuke" W. Lobscheid 小傳補遺 —Lobscheid 的訪日與堀達助 (Addition to the short biography of W. Lobscheid—Lobscheid's visit to Japan and Hori Tatsunosuke), paper prepared for the Conference of the Society of Modern Chinese Research, Toyohashi, Japan.

Raponichi taiyaku jisho 羅葡日對譯辭書 (Roman-Portuguese-Japanese dictionary). 1595. Reprint Tokyo: Benseisha.

Ren Xueliang 任學良. 1981. *Hanyu zaocifa* 漢語造詞法 (Modes of forming Chinese words). Beijing: Shanghai shehui kexueyuan.

Ricci, Matteo (Li Madou 利瑪竇). 1602. *Kunyu wanguo quantu* 坤輿萬國全圖 (Charts of all countries in the world). 3 maps reprinted by Miyagiken bunkazai hogo kyōkai.

——. 1605. *Qiankun tiyi* 乾坤體義 (Meaning of the system of the universe). *Siku quanshu* edition.

Satō Tōru 佐藤亨. 1983. *Kinseigoi no kenkyū* 近世語匯的研究 (Research of modern vocabularies). Tokyo: Ōfūsha.

Shen Kuo 沈括. 1975. *Mengxi bitan* 夢溪筆談 (Notes from the Meng River). Beijing: Wenwu chubanshe, *juan* 24.

Shiba Kōkan 司馬江漢. 1816. *Tenchiritan* 天地理譚 (On cosmology). Manuscript.

Sugita Seikei 杉田成卿. 1851. *Chigaku shōsō* 地學正宗 (Orthodox schools of geography). Edo: Tenshirō.

Udagawa Yōsei 宇田川榕精. 1868. *Bankoku chigaku wage* 萬國地學和解 (Japanese comments on geographical studies of the world). Manuscript.

Watanabe Kazan 渡邊崋山. 1836. *Shinshaku yochizusetsu* 新釋輿地圖説 (New edition of *Illustrated geography*). Manuscript.

Williams, Samuel Wells. 1844. *English and Chinese Vocabulary, in the Court Dialect.* Macao: Office of the Chinese Repository.

Williamson, Alexander (Wei Lianchen 韋廉臣). 1878. *Gewu tanyuan* 格物探原 (Exploring principles of science). Beijing: Zong shuiwusi.

Wu Jingzi 吳敬梓. 1985. *Rulin waishi* 儒林外史 (The Scholars). Beijing: Renmin wenxue chubanshe.

Xu Shen 許慎. 1977. *Shuowen jiezi zhu* 説文解字注 (The *Shuowen jiezi* with commentary [by Duan Yucai]). Beijing: Zhonghua shuju, s.v.

Yamamura Saisuke 山村才助. 1979 [1802]. *Teisei zōyaku sairan igen* 訂正增譯采覽異言 (A new edited translation of *Collection of unorthodox words*). 4 vols. Tokyo: Seishisha.

Zhou Zhenhe 周振鶴. 1998. "Chudu *Xiandai hanyu cihui de xincheng* zhongyiben" 初讀現代漢語詞匯的形成中譯本 (Preliminary reading of the Chinese translation of *The Formation of Modern Chinese Lexicon and its Evolution Toward a National Language: The Period from 1840 to 1898*), *Ciku jianshe tongxun* 15, p. 6.

JOACHIM KURTZ

MATCHING NAMES AND ACTUALITIES:
TRANSLATION AND THE DISCOVERY OF 'CHINESE LOGIC'

INTRODUCTION

It was Wang Guowei 王國維 (1877–1927) who first characterized the decades surrounding the turn of the twentieth century as an 'age of discovery' (*faxian shidai* 發現時代) unparalleled in China's history.[1] His emphatic assessment is justified in more than one sense. Wang himself referred to the disclosure of written and material evidence from China's distant past that had become available through the unearthing of oracle bones in Henan 河南, bamboo and silk manuscripts around Dunhuang 敦煌 , as well as long-lost documents and historical artefacts found at various other places, often at the fringes of the empire. But one could also cite less tangible discoveries to corroborate his appraisal. The renewed encounter with occidental knowledge, introduced through translations from European languages or via Japanese, had incited a massive expansion of the Chinese terminological repertoire and eventually fomented a radical reordering of China's discursive space. The adaptation of Western-derived terms and notions led not only to the gradual displacement of the terminological and conceptual schemes that had framed scholarly discourses in China for centuries; it also fuelled the discovery, or rediscovery, of neglected aspects of China's intellectual heritage which were subsequently translated into new historical narratives and utilized for the construction of alternative or presumably forgotten traditions.

The emergence of a discourse on 'Chinese logic' in the early years of the twentieth century is a paradigmatic case of an intellectual discovery of this second kind. Nevertheless, it has attracted only scant attention. Chinese historians of logic and philosophy usually brush over the tentative efforts of the earliest discoverers of explicit indige-

---

[1] Wang Guowei 王國維 . 1925. "Zuijin ersanshi nian zhong Zhongguo xin faxian zhi xuewen" 最近二三十年中中國新發現之學問 (Studies of new discoveries in China during the past twenty or thirty years), *Qinghua zhoukan* 350. Reprinted in: id. 1997. *Wang Guowei wenji* 王國維文集 (The works of Wang Guowei). Edited by Yao Ganming 姚淦銘 and Wang Yan 王燕 . 4 vols. Beijing: Zhongguo wenshi chubanshe, vol. 4, pp. 33–8; 33.

nous theorizing on logical problems[2] and focus their analyses instead on the first systematic studies, written at least a decade later, by trained logicians such as Hu Shi 胡適 (1891–1962), Zhang Shizhao 章士釗 (1881–1973), Guo Zhanbo 郭湛波 or Yu Yu 虞愚 (1909–1989).[3] Outside of China, very few articles have touched upon the problematique at all.[4]

In this essay, I shall try to show that this neglect is an unfortunate omission. A close look at the first texts that interpret ancient Chinese writings in logical terms offers rare insights into what was at stake in

---

[2] The only monographs dealing with these developments in any detail are: Li Kuangwu 李匡武 (ed.). 1989. *Zhongguo luojishi* 中國邏輯史 (A history of Chinese logic). 5 vols. Lanzhou: Gansu renmin chubanshe, vol. 4, pp. 126–80; Peng Yilian 彭漪漣. 1991. *Zhongguo jindai luoji sixiang shilun* 中國近代邏輯思想史論 (Essays in the history of logical thought in Modern China). Shanghai: Shanghai renmin chubanshe; Zeng Xiangyun 曾祥云. 1992. *Zhongguo jindai bijiao luoji sixiang yanjiu* 中國近代比較邏輯思想研究 (Studies in comparative logical thought in Modern China). Harbin: Heilongjiang jiaoyu chubanshe; and Zhao Zongkuan 趙總寬 (ed.). 1999. *Luojixue bainian* 邏輯學百年 (A century of studies in logic). Beijing: Beijing chubanshe, pp. 5–131. Relevant materials are collected in: Zhou Yunzhi 周云之 et al. (eds.). 1991. *Zhongguo luojishi ziliao xuan* 中國邏輯史資料選 (Selected materials on the history of Chinese logic). 6 vols. Lanzhou: Gansu renmin chubanshe, vol. 4, pp. 240–357.—Most histories of Chinese logical thought devote no more than a few pages to the subject. Cf., e.g., Wang Dianji 王奠基. 1961. *Zhongguo luoji sixiangshi fenxi* 中國邏輯思想史分析 (Analysis of the history of logical thought in China). Beijing: Zhonghua shuju; id. 1979. *Zhongguo luoji sixiangshi* 中國邏輯思想史 (A history of logical thought in China). Shanghai: Shanghai renmin chubanshe; Zhou Wenying. 1979. *Zhongguo luoji sixiang shigao* 中國邏輯思想史搞 (A draft history of logical thought in China). Beijing: Renmin chubanshe; Yang Peisun 楊沛蓀 (ed.). 1988. *Zhongguo luoji sixiangshi jiaocheng* 中國邏輯思想史教程 (A course in the history of logical thought in China). Lanzhou: Gansu renmin chubanshe; and Wen Gongyi 溫公頤 and Cui Qingtian 崔清田 (eds.). 2001. *Zhongguo luoji sixiangshi jiaocheng (Xiudingben)* 中國邏輯思想史教程（修訂本）(A course in the history of logical thought in China. Revised edition). Tianjin: Nankai daxue chubanshe.

[3] Hu Shih (Hu Shi 胡適). 1922. *The Development of the Logical Method in Ancient China* (Ph.D. diss., Columbia University 1917). Shanghai: Yadong tushuguan; id. 1919. *Zhongguo zhexueshi dagang* 中國哲學史大綱 (Outline history of Chinese philosophy). Shanghai: Shangwu yinshuguan; Zhang Shizhao 章士釗. 1943. *Luoji zhiyao* 邏輯指要 (Essentials of logic). Chongqing: Shidai jingshenshe (manuscript completed in 1917); Guo Zhanbo 郭湛波. 1932. *Zhongguo bianxueshi* 中國辯學史 (A history of Chinese logic). Shanghai: Zhonghua shuju; and Yu Yu 虞愚. 1937. *Zhongguo mingxue* 中國名學 (Chinese logic). Nanjing: Zhenghong shuju.

[4] Cf. Takada Atsushi 高田淳. 1967. "Chūgoku kindai no 'ronri' kenkyū" 中国近代の「論理」研究 (Studies in 'logic' in modern China), *Kōza Tōyō shisō* 講座東洋思想 4, Series 2: *Chūgoku shisō* 中国思想 3, pp. 215–27; and Uwe Frankenhauser. 1996a. "Logik und nationales Selbstverständnis in China zu Beginn des 20. Jahrhunderts", in: Christiane Hammer and Bernhard Führer (eds.). *Chinesisches Selbstverständnis und kulturelle Identität: 'Wenhua Zhongguo'*. Dortmund: Projekt, pp. 69–80.

the twofold process of translation—first *intercultural* and then *intra-cultural*—that has shaped modern discourses on China's intellectual past, first in China herself and then, as a result of renewed translation, also in the West. Despite their impressionistic character, the texts I will discuss—essays by Liu Shipei 劉師培 (1884–1919), Zhang Bing-lin 章炳麟 (1869–1936), Liang Qichao 梁啟超 (1873–1929) and Wang Guowei—highlight not only the ingenuity of the authors who ventured to map an uncharted territory with untested conceptual tools; they also reveal that the early interpreters had already set up and negotiated the 'frame of articulation'[5] which later writers were to fill with their self-assured accounts of the history of 'logical thought in China'. My paper is thus intended as a first step towards a genealogy of a discourse whose emergence, as I would like to argue, was all but inconceivable until the end of the nineteenth century.

1. EUROPEAN LOGIC IN LATE MING AND EARLY QING CHINA

In order to substantiate this latter claim, it is necessary to recall the utter indifference with which occidental logic was received in China when it was first introduced in the seventeenth and then once again in the nineteenth century. As far as we know, the first trifles of European logic were translated into Chinese by the Jesuit missionaries Michele Ruggieri (Luo Mingjian 羅明堅, 1543–1607) and Matteo Ricci (Li Madou 利瑪竇, 1552–1610) who touched in their catechistic writings upon the Aristotelian notions of the 'four causes' and other concepts related to the practice of inferential reasoning.[6] In addition, forms of deductive proof were introduced, however imperfectly, in translations

---

5 Cf. Frithjof Rodi. 1988. "Historical Philosophy in Search of Frames of Articulation", in: Peter H. Hare (ed.). *Doing Philosophy Historically*. Buffalo, N.Y.: Prometheus Books, pp. 329–40. Although I use the term not entirely in Rodi's sense, I would subscribe to his definition that such a frame "is a complex network of influences, orientations, and mediations focused on the development of an individual theory or system" and that it "is composed of elements of common language as well as technical terms; notions and definitions by individual authors; their integration and interpretation by subsequent philosophers; reflections on such mediations that in turn become new theories and systematic positions; and also determining factors from outside philosophy, such as general issues of the time, political and social trends, cross-cultural relations with literature, arts and sciences, etc., etc." Ibid., p. 334.

6 Cf. Michele Ruggieri (Luo Mingjian 羅明堅). 1584. *Tianzhu shengjiao shilu* 天主聖教實錄 (A true account of the Lord of Heaven and the Holy Doctrine). Beijing, pp. 4a–b; Matteo Ricci S. J. 1985 [1601]. *The True Meaning of the Lord of*

of mathematical works, most notably of Euclid's *Elements*.[7] None of these texts, however, informed their readers that the notions they presented belonged to an independent branch of Western science named 'logic' (or 'dialectic'). The earliest explicit reference to logic as such is made by Giulio Aleni (Ai Rulüe 艾儒略, 1582–1649) in 1623. In his *Xixue fan* 西學凡 (General outline of Western knowledge) and the more widely read *Zhifang waiji* 職方外記 (Record of the places outside the jurisdiction of the Office of Geography), Aleni presented 'logic' (*luorijia* 落日加) as one of the subjects taught during the preparatory year in European universities.[8] While defining the discipline more or less neutrally as a "method to discriminate right from wrong" and to discern "substantial knowledge from guessing and error," Aleni left no doubt that *luorijia*, like philosophy as a whole, was in fact no more than a 'handmaiden of theology' or *ancilla theologiae*.[9]

The remarkable capacities of this handmaiden were first illustrated in the *Mingli tan* 名理探 (*De Logica*, literally: 'The exploration of names and principles'), a partial rendition of a Latin textbook based on Aristotle's *Categories* and Porphyry's *Eisagogue*, which was published in two parts in 1631 and 1639 by Francisco Furtado (Fu Fanji 傅汎際, 1587–1653).[10] The *Mingli tan* was the result of more than five years of painstaking labors by Furtado himself, who claimed to have

---

[6] (*cont.*) *Heaven (T'ien-chu Shih-i)*. Translated by Douglas Lancashire and Peter Hu Kuo-chen S. J. St. Louis: The Institute of Jesuit Sources, p. 84. Cf. Giorgio Melis. 1984. "Temi e tesi della filosofia europea nel 'Tianzhu Shiyi' di Matteo Ricci", in: *Atti del convegno internazionale di studi Ricciani*. Macerata: Centro studi Ricciani, pp. 65–92.

[7] Cf. Peter M. Engelfriet. 1998. *Euclid in China. The Genesis of the First Translation of Euclid's* Elements *Book I–VI* (Jihe yuanben. *Beijing, 1607*) *and its Reception up to 1723*. Leiden: Brill.

[8] Giulio Aleni (Ai Rulüe 艾儒略). 1623a. *Xixue fan* 西學凡 (General outline of Western knowledge). Hangzhou. Reprinted in: *Tianxue chuhan* 天學初函 (First collection of heavenly studies). 1965 [1628]. Edited by Li Zhizao 李之藻 . 6 vols. Taibei: Taiwan xuesheng shuju, vol. 1, pp. 1–60; 31–3; id. 1623b. *Zhifang waiji* 職方外記 (Record of the places outside the jurisdiction of the Office of Geography). Hangzhou. Reprinted in: *Tianxue chuhan*, vol. 3, pp. 1269–496; 1360–1.

[9] *Xixue fan*, p. 31. Cf. also Bernard Hung-Kay Luk. 1997. "Aleni Introduces the Western Academic Tradition to Seventeenth Century China. A Study of the *Xixue Fan*", in: Tiziana Lippiello and Roman Malek (eds.). *Scholar from the West. Giulio Aleni S.J. (1582–1649) and the Dialogue between Christianity and China*. Nettetal: Steyler, pp. 479–518; 493–5.

[10] Francisco Furtado (Fu Fanji 傅汎際) and Li Zhizao 李之藻 . 1965 [1631–1639]. *Mingli tan* 名理探 (*De Logica*). Hangzhou. Reprinted in 2 vols. Taibei: Taiwan

'translated the meaning' (*yiyi* 譯意), and the convert Li Zhizao 李之藻 (1565–1630), who had done his best to put this meaning into 'comprehensible words' (*daci* 達辭).[11] From our point of view, the most interesting aspect of this truly admirable effort is the fact that even Li and Furtado were unable to think of a suitable Chinese context in which to situate Western logic. Literally none of the dozens of technical terms Li Zhizao invented in the course of their translation was derived from a text or context that is today considered as a constituent part of China's logical heritage.[12] Moreover, because the work "bristled with a purpose-built, forbiddingly technical vocabulary,"[13] it is unlikely that any reader, no matter how well versed in Chinese literature and previous Jesuit writings, would have been able to grasp its meaning without the continued help of a capable instructor. The same is true of an expanded version of the text included by Ferdinand Verbiest (Nan Huairen 南懷仁 , 1623–1688) in his *Qionglixue* 窮理學 (*Philosophia*, literally: 'The science of fathoming principles') of 1683, a comprehensive anthology of Western science and philosophy compiled in the

---

[10] (*cont.*) Shangwu yinshuguan. The Latin original of the *Mingli tan* had been compiled by Sebastian da Couto at the University of Coïmbra and printed in Cologne in 1611 (first edition 1607) as *Commentarii Collegii Conimbricences e Societas Iesu in Universam Dialecticam Aristotelis Stagiritæ, nunc primum in Germania in lucem editi*. Cf. H. Verhaeren. 1935. "Aristote en Chine", *Bulletin Catholique de Pékin* 264 (Août 1935), pp. 417–29; 425–7; and Fukazawa Sukeo 深沢助雄 . 1986. "'Meiri tan' no yakugyō ni tsuite" 「名理探」の訳業について (On the translation of the *Mingli tan*), *Chūgoku—Shakai to bunka* 1, pp. 20–38.

[11] Furtado and Li 1965, vol. 1, p. 1.

[12] Cf. the "Glossary of Technical Terms" in Robert Wardy. 2000. *Aristotle in China. Language, Categories, and Translation*. Cambridge: Cambridge University Press, pp. 153–60. A similar observation with regard to the "Dialectical Chapters" (*Mobian* 墨辯) of the *Mozi* 墨子 is stated in Bao Zunxin 包遵信 . 1986. "'Mobian' de chenlun he 'Mingli tan' de fanyi" 《墨辯》的沉淪和《名理探》的翻譯 (The decline of the *Mobian* and the translation of the *Mingli tan*), *Dushu* 1, pp. 63–71. In contrast, Christoph Harbsmeier claims that "[t]here is evidence in [Li's] translations that he had prepared himself for the task by looking at some texts on Buddhist logic", but he does not substantiate his assessment. Cf. id. 1998. *Language and Logic in Traditional China*, in: Joseph Needham (ed.). *Science and Civilisation in China. Vol. VII, Pt. 1*. Cambridge: Cambridge University Press, p. 165. The only obvious exception is Li Zhizao's term for 'logic', *mingli* 名理 , which did of course play a significant role in the scholarly debates of the third and fourth centuries and had been used as a vague general name for matters related to argumentation since the early Han. Cf. ibid., p. 354.

[13] Wardy 2000, p. 86.

vain hope of attracting imperial support for a Christianized educational curriculum.[14] It is therefore hardly surprising that the work, and
scholastic logic as a whole, never exerted any noticeable influence
outside Christian communities and soon fell into oblivion.[15]

2. LOGIC IN THE LATE QING

The radical alterity that characterized the first erratic appearance of
Western logic in a Chinese discursive context continued to make itself
felt when the subject was once again intermittently introduced in the
second half of the nineteenth century. In contrast to other sciences,
references to logic remained scattered until the turn of the twentieth
century—not least because the Protestant missionaries who were now
offering and selling knowledge to China attributed much less importance to the subject than their Jesuit precursors. One exception was
Joseph Edkins (Ai Yuese 艾約瑟 , 1823–1905), who wrote the first
new account of logic in his "Yalisiduodeli zhuan" 亞里斯多得里傳
(Biography of Aristotle) of 1875.[16] Yet, unaware of the sophisticated
terminology invented by the Jesuits, or perhaps unwilling to adopt it,
Edkins had difficulties in explaining how Aristotle's 'principles of
argumentation' (*bianlun zhi li* 辯論之理 , i.e., logic) or, more specifically, his 'complete principle of the three steps beginning, middle and
end' (*chuzhongzhong sanji wanbei zhi li* 初中終三級完備之理 , i.e., the
syllogism) could be used by people from all walks of life, as he
claimed, to arrive at eternal truths and convince others in disputation.[17]

   A more substantial contribution was his *Bianxue qimeng* 辨學啟蒙
(Logic primer), a rendition of William Stanley Jevons' popular high-

---

[14] Cf. Ad Dudink and Nicolas Standaert. 1999. "Ferdinand Verbiest's *Qionglixue* 窮理學(1683)", in: Noël Golvers (ed.). *The Christian Mission in China in the Verbiest Era: Some Aspects of the Missionary Approach*. Leuven: Leuven University Press, pp. 11–31.
   [15] Even for an influence within Christian communities, evidence is scarce. Cf. Cao Jiesheng 曹杰生 . 1982. "Lüelun *Mingli tan* de fanyi ji qi yingxiang" 略論《名利探》 的 翻譯及 其影響 (A brief discussion of the translation and influence of the *Mingli tan*), in: *Zhongguo luojishi yanjiu* 中國邏輯史研究 (Studies in the history of Chinese logic). Beijing: Zhongguo shehui kexue chubanshe, pp. 285–302; 294.
   [16] Joseph Edkins (Ai Yuese 艾約瑟). 1875. "Yalisiduodeli zhuan" 亞里斯多得里 傳 (Biography of Aristotle), *Zhong-Xi wenjian lu* 32, pp. 7a–13b.
   [17] Ibid., p. 11a.

school textbook *Logic* that Edkins completed in 1886.[18] Although he often turned to paraphrases instead of coining a proper technical vocabulary, and was hence unable to achieve a degree of accuracy comparable to that of the *Mingli tan*, his translation was certainly not incomprehensible to an audience accustomed to the hybrid scientific literature of the times.[19] Even if readers could not rely unreservedly on his text to study valid forms of inferences, they were introduced to a discipline that had little in common with the logic taught and practiced by Aristotle or the Jesuits. No longer the mere handmaiden of the Christian faith or renaissance science, the logic of the *Bianxue qimeng* appeared as a powerful tool of 'progress'. Still, there are no indications of positive responses from Chinese readers. The same applies to a summary of Francis Bacon's *Novum Organum* that was serialized in three missionary magazines under the titles *Gezhi xinli* 格致新理 (New principles of science) or *Gezhi xinfa* 格致新法 (New methods of science), and of a partial rendition of the same text published as a monograph as *Gezhi xinji* 格致新機 (New tools for science) in 1888.[20]

A number of further observations may illustrate how far removed logic remained from mainstream as well as reformist discourse until

---

[18] William Stanley Jevons (Zhefensi 哲分斯). 1886. *Bianxue qimeng* 辨學啟蒙 (Logic primer). Translated by Joseph Edkins, in: Joseph Edkins (ed.). *Gezhi qimeng* 格致啟蒙 (Science primers). 16 vols. Beijing: Zong shuiwusi. Original by William Stanley Jevons. 1876. *Logic* (*Science Primers*). London: Macmillan.

[19] In this respect, I disagree with Li Kuangwu 1989, pp. 127–32, and Yang Peisun 1988, pp. 291–2. For a detailed analysis of Edkins' terminological choices, cf. my "Translating the Science of Sciences: European and Japanese Models in the Formation of Modern Chinese Logical Terminology, 1886–1912", in: James C. Baxter and Joshua A. Fogel (eds.). 2002. *Historiography and Japanese Consciousness of Values and Norms*. Kyoto: International Research Institute for Japanese Studies, pp. 53–76.

[20] Summaries of the *Novum Organum* were published as: William Muirhead (Mu Weilian 慕維廉). 1876. "Gezhi xinli" 格致新理 (New principles of science), *Yizhi xinlu* 益知新錄 (*Miscellany of Useful Knowledge*), 1.1-1.5 (1876.7-1876.11); id. 1877. "Gezhi xinfa" 格致新法 (New methods of science), *Gezhi huibian* 格致匯編 (*The Chinese Scientific Magazine*), 2.2 (1877.3); 2.3 (1877.4); 2.7 (1877.8); 2.8 (1877.9); and 2.9 (1877.10); and id. 1878. "Gezhi xinfa" 格致新法 (New methods of science), *Wanguo gongbao* 萬國公報 (*The Globe Magazine*), 1.506-1.513 (1878.9-1878.11). A translation of Book One of the *Novum Organum* appeared as: Francis Bacon (Beigeng 貝庚). 1888. *Gezhi xinji* 格致新機 (New tools for science). Translated by William Muirhead and Shen Yugui 沈毓桂 . Beijing: Tongwen shuhui and Shanghai: Gezhi shushi. On the latter, cf. Zou Zhenhuan 鄒振環 . 2000. *Yilin jiuzong* 譯林舊蹤 (Old tracks in the forest of translation). Nanchang: Jiangxi jiaoyu chubanshe, pp. 55–7.

the end of the century. First, we may note that lexicographers were unable to record established Chinese equivalents even for the term 'logic' itself until 1902 and, for want of alternatives, felt compelled to invent ever more new words or paraphrases that were probably never used outside their works.[21] Secondly, logic was prominently absent from the wide-spread theories about the "Chinese origins of Western science" (*Xixue Zhongyuan* 西學中源) that did so much to popularize other branches of occidental knowledge.[22] Not even the *summa* of this discourse, the voluminous *Gezhi guwei* 格致古微 (Ancient subtleties on science), which was explicitly designed to prove that all branches of the supposedly 'new' knowledge had roots in China, contained a single line on logic.[23] Finally and perhaps most strikingly, as late as 1896 an otherwise well-informed bibliography on Western knowledge listed Edkins' *Logic Primer* in the category of 'unclassifiable titles'— alongside travelogues, museum guides and cookbooks.[24]

3. YAN FU AND THE ORGANON OF MODERNITY

The abrupt appearance of Western logic in Chinese discourse around 1900 seems all the more remarkable. Barely six years after the only available textbook on logic had left bibliographers perplexed, the discipline was being taught at the country's most prestigious institutions of higher learning, and the Translation Office at the Imperial University specifically mentioned the task of translating textbooks on logic

---

[21] See Joachim Kurtz. 2001. "Coming to Terms with Logic. The Naturalization of an Occidental Notion in China", in: Michael Lackner, Iwo Amelung and Joachim Kurtz (eds.). *New Terms for New Ideas. Western Knowledge and Lexical Change in Late Imperial China*. Leiden et al.: Brill, pp. 147–76; 156–7.

[22] Cf. Quan Hansheng 全漢昇 . 1935. "Qingmo de Xixue yuanchu Zhongguo shuo" 清末的西學源出中國説 (The late-Qing theory of the Chinese origin of Western science), *Lingnan xuebao* 4.2, pp. 57–102.

[23] Cf. Wang Renjun 王仁俊 . 1993 [1896]. *Gezhi guwei* 格致古微 (Ancient subleties on science). Reprinted in: *Zhongguo kexue jishu dianji tonghui* 中國科學技術典籍通彙 (Anthology of classical works of Chinese science and technology). Edited by Ren Jiyu 任繼愈 . vol. 1, pt. 7. Zhengzhou: Henan jiaoyu chubanshe. For exceptions see Kurtz 2001, p. 156.

[24] Liang Qichao 梁啟超 (ed.). 1896. *Xixue shumu biao* 西學書目表 (Bibliography of Western knowledge). Shanghai: Shenshiji zhai, 3.20a–b.

in its statutes.[25] Many widely-read journals carried articles on the subject, mostly translated from the Japanese,[26] and private publishers struggled to supply readable introductions in order to meet the growing demand from educational institutions and curious readers.[27]

The sudden wave of logical interest was, of course, closely related to the general opening towards all kinds of 'modern' knowledge in the aftermath of the Sino-Japanese War and the abortive reforms of 1898, as well to the influx of new ideas from Japan, where logic had been a subject of university education since the 1880s.[28] Yet, as many commentators have argued, the peculiar image of logic in early twentieth-century China was shaped above all by Yan Fu 嚴復 (1851–1921), the first scholar of renown to develop a sustained passion for the science.[29]

Yan's part in modern China's intellectual history certainly tends to be exaggerated, but in the narrow context with which I am concerned here his interventions were indeed decisive. Not only did he finally detach logic from religion (that 'deviant faith' [*yijiao* 異教] which still aroused so much suspicion in China); he also introduced many of the concepts, albeit not the terms, that were to determine logical discourse well into the 1920s. Among Yan's lasting achievements was a partial

---

[25] Cf. "Jingshi daxuetang yishuju zhangcheng" 京師大學堂譯書局章程 (Statutes for the Translation Office at the Imperial University). 1903. Reprinted in: Li Nanqiu 黎難秋 (ed.). 1996. *Zhongguo kexue fanyi shiliao* 中國科學翻譯史料 (Materials for a history of scientific translation in China). Hefei: Zhongguo kexue jishu daxue chubanshe, pp. 493–7; 494.

[26] Cf. Zhou Yunzhi 1991, vol. 5.1, pp. 503–43; *1900–1949 nian quanguo zhuyao baokan zhexue lunwen ziliao suoyin* 1900–1949 年全國主要報刊論文資料索引 (Index of articles on philosophy in major Chinese periodicals). 1989. Edited by Fudan daxue zhexuexi ziliaoshi 复旦大學哲學系資料室 and Sichuan daxue zhexuexi ziliaoshi 四川大學哲學系資料室. Beijing: Shangwu yinshuguan, pp. 215–22.

[27] Cf. Wang Yunwu 王云五. 1973. *Shangwu yinshuguan yu xin jiaoyu nianpu* 商務印書館與新教育年譜 (A chronicle of the Commercial Press and educational reform). Taibei: Taiwan Shangwu yinshuguan, p. 16.

[28] Cf. Funayama Shin'ichi 船山信一. *Meiji ronrigakushi kenkyū* 明治論理学史研究 (Studies in the history of logic during the Meiji period). Tokyo: Risōsha, pp. 19–44.

[29] Cf. in particular Benjamin Schwartz. 1964. *In Search of Wealth and Power. Yen Fu and the West*. Cambridge, Mass.: Harvard University Press, pp. 186–96; Zhang Zhijian 張志建 and Dong Zhitie 董志鐵. 1982. "Shilun Yan Fu dui Woguo luojixue yanjiu de gongxian" 試論嚴復對我國邏輯學研究的貢獻 (A tentative account of Yan Fu's contribution to Chinese research on logic), in: *Zhongguo luojishi yanjiu* 中國邏輯史研究 (Studies in the history of Chinese logic). Beijing: Zhongguo shehui kexue chubanshe, pp. 303–20; Sun Zhongyuan 孫中原. 1992. "Lun Yan Fu de luoji chengjiu" 論嚴復的邏輯成就 (Yan Fu's logical achievements), *Wenshizhe* 3, pp. 80–5.

rendition of John Stuart Mill's monumental *System of Logic*, for which he created an entirely new terminology in his antiquarian style allusive of, or rather imitating, pre-Qin prose.[30] Although hardly any of his lexical inventions survived,[31] the text was widely read and cited, if only, as some critics argued, due to Yan's public clout.[32] Moreover, Yan propagated the new science through a short-lived Logical Society (*Mingxuehui* 名學會) as well as many public lectures.[33] And his persistent lobbying was also instrumental in paving the way for the swift inclusion of logic in the curricula of secondary schools and universities.

For Yan, logic was certainly more than a purely academic concern. Deeply entrenched in Mill's 'fanatical inductionism,' for which he had fallen while studying at the Royal Naval College in Greenwich,[34] Yan conceived of logic as an all-pervading 'art' that, when applied consistently, promised unlimited scientific and socio-political progress. The foundation of Western 'strength' was the Baconian spirit of scientific inquiry, but this spirit had found its practical application only through the use of logic. Thus, logic alone had enabled Europeans to establish the 'new principles' (*xinli* 新理) that had made their continent wealthy and powerful in the modern era. China, on the contrary, had not been able to proceed on the universal road to progress because her classics lacked logical rigour and imagination

---

[30] Yan Fu 嚴復 (tr.). 1931 [1905]. *Mule mingxue* 穆勒名學 (Mill's *Logic*). 3 vols. Shanghai: Shangwu yinshuguan. The manuscript was circulated among Yan's peers from 1902. The original was John Stuart Mill. 1843. *A System of Logic. Inductive and Ratiocinative*. London: Parker. Some years later, Yan published a new translation of Jevons' *Logic*: id. (tr.) 1981 [1909]. *Mingxue qianshuo* 名學淺説 (Logic primer). Beijing: Shangwu yinshuguan. By then, however, numerous books on logic were available which were much easier to read than his eccentric prose, so that the work had only a very limited impact.

[31] Of the more than 200 technical terms of logic introduced in Yan's works, no more than a handful are still in use. Cf. Michael Lackner, Iwo Amelung and Joachim Kurtz. 2001. *WSC-Databases: An Electronic Repository of Chinese Scientific, Philosophical and Political Terms Coined in the Nineteenth and Early Twentieth Century*. Retrieved from http://www.wsc.uni-erlangen.de/wscdb.htm.

[32] For this claim cf. Zhu Zhixin 朱執信 . 1905. "Jiu lunlixue bo Xinmin congbao lun geming zhi miu" 就論理學駁新民叢報論革命之謬 (Applying logic to refute the errors in a discussion of revolution in the *Xinmin congbao*), *Minbao* 6, pp. 65–78; 65.

[33] Cf. Wang Quchang 王蘧常 . 1936. *Yan Jidao nianpu* 嚴幾道年譜 (Annalistic biography of Yan Fu). Shanghai: Shangwu yinshuguan, p. 55.

[34] Cf. Schwartz 1964, pp. 189–90.

and, due to a total disregard for proper definitions, had become soaked with ambiguity.[35]

From 1895 onward, Yan instructed his growing readership over and again that the potentially miraculous art of logic consisted of just two basic methods: 'induction' (which he rendered alternately as *neidao* 內導 or *neizhou* 內籀) and 'deduction' (*waidao* 外導 or *waizhou* 外籀). In 'induction', he wrote in an early essay, one "unites different things and looks at what they have in common in order to arrive at general rules," while in 'deduction' one "already has a general rule in mind" which is put to test by means of "experimentally gathered evidence," and, therefore, "the more evidence one has, the more certain will be one's principles."[36] Induction was hence the royal road along which the natural sciences that China so urgently needed had to proceed, but Yan also shared Mill's belief that deduction offered a way to infer and confirm *a priori* principles, be it mathematical laws or political and philosophical beliefs, on the basis of brute facts alone. Taken together, then, the 'two ends' of occidental logic, as portrayed by Yan Fu, appeared as the indispensable organon of modernity and thus as the perfect cure for China's many ills. The speed with which interest in the new science spread throughout the learned public in the first years of the twentieth century attests to the extent to which Yan succeeded in convincing his audience to share this exceedingly optimistic faith.

4. FROM INTERCULTURAL TO INTRACULTURAL TRANSLATION

Almost immediately after 'Western' logic had thus been naturalized in the Chinese discursive universe, scholars of diverse intellectual and political persuasions embarked on a second, *intracultural* process of translation that eventually led to the formation of a separate discourse concerned with what we have since come to call 'Chinese logic'. It should be clear from the above that the rapid emergence of this discourse was far from self-evident. In contrast to other branches of European knowledge that could be related, rightly or wrongly, to a

---

[35] Cf. Peng Yilian 1991, pp. 62–5.

[36] Yan Fu 嚴復 . 1898. "Xixue menjing gongyong" 西學門徑功用 (Means and applications of Western knowledge). Reprinted in: id. 1986. *Yan Fu ji* 嚴復集 (The works of Yan Fu). Edited by Wang Shi 王栻. 5 vols. Beijing: Zhonghua shuju, pp. 92–5; 94.

wide range of sources with comparative ease (as confirmed by the vast *Xixue Zhongyuan*-literature), materials containing explicit logical reflections were much harder to find.

Or at least this was the opinion of the first Westerners who set out to look for relevant passages in the classical Chinese canons. Matteo Ricci himself stated repeatedly that Chinese scholarship, despite all its sophistication, had produced "no conception of the rules of logic" and knew nothing of "dialectic."[37] Echoes of this blunt but influential judgement reverberated into the twentieth century. In 1902, Alfred Forke, one of the first Europeans to study the extant writings of the School of Names (*mingjia* 名家), wrote that the "dialectic" of these "Chinese Sophists" is

> of the most rudimentary kind. … The Chinese mind has never risen above these rudiments and developed a complete system of logic, per-haps because it is altogether too illogical in itself.[38]

Although not quite as condescending in their formulations, the first Japanese scholars introducing European logic into Meiji thought were equally convinced that neither China nor Japan had ever known, or desired, a comparable branch of knowledge.[39]

The eventual discovery of 'Chinese logic'—again, in the sense of explicit logical theorizing expressed in ancient Chinese texts—is often attributed to the philologist Sun Yirang 孫詒讓 (1848–1908). In a posthumously published letter to Liang Qichao dated 1897, i.e., shortly after the revised version of his invaluable reconstruction of the *Mozi* first appeared in print, Sun purportedly wrote:

> I said earlier that the *Mohist Canons* (*Mojing* 墨經) contain many fine principles, and I mentioned, but did not develop, that they are the ancestors of the words of the School of Names in the Zhou period. I suspect that they must contain subtle insights similar to the European logician Aristotle's deductive method (*yanyifa* 演繹法), Bacon's induc-

---

[37] *Fonti Ricciane. Documenti originale concernenti Matteo Ricci e la storia delle prime relazioni tra l'Europa e la Cina (1579–1615).* 1942–1949. 3 vols. Edited by Pasquale D'Elia. Rome: Libreria dello stato, vol. 1, p. 39; vol. 2, p. 77. Cf. also *China in the 16th Century. The Journals of Matthew Ricci 1583–1610.* 1953. Translated by Louis J. Gallagher. New York: Random House, pp. 30; 325; 341.

[38] Alfred Forke. 1902. "The Chinese Sophists", *Journal of the China Branch of the Royal Asiatic Society* 34, pp. 1–100; 5.

[39] Cf. Sakade Yoshinobu 坂出祥伸. 1968. "Meiji tetsugaku ni okeru Chūgoku kodai ronrigaku no rikai" 明治哲学に於ける中国古代論理学の理解 (Views of ancient Chinese logic in Meiji philosophy), in: Funayama 1968, pp. 242–68, pp. 242–8.

tive method (*guinafa* 歸納法) and the Buddhist theories of *yinming* 因明 [from Sanskrit: *hetuvidyā*, 'knowledge of reasons'].[40]

Unfortunately, however, Sun never substantiated his 'suspicion'. No less vague was a suggestion made by Yan Fu in the following year in the preface to his *Tianyanlun* 天演論 (On evolution):

> Sima Qian wrote [in the *Shiji* 史記 (Records of the Historian)]: 'The *Yi* 易 (Book of Changes) makes manifest what is originally hidden, and the *Chunqiu* 春秋 (Spring and Autumn Annals) infer the hidden from the visible.' These are the most exquisite words ever uttered in our realm. Initially, I thought that 'making manifest what is originally hidden' referred merely to reading the *Images* (*xiang* 象) and the *Attached Verbalizations* (*Xici* 繫辭) [in the *Changes*] in order to determine good or bad fortune, and that 'inferring the hidden from the visible' meant no more than judging and criticizing human intentions. However, when I became aware of Western logic, I realized that these [phrases] were in fact related to the investigation of things and the extension of knowledge: they refer to induction and deduction. Induction means examining the part in order to know the whole, gathering details in order to understand what things have in common. Deduction means judging all matters on the basis of general laws, setting definite examples in order to predict future events. When I first looked into books [on logic], I stood up and said: 'Can it be? This is none other than the knowledge of our *Changes* and *Spring and Autumn Annals*!' What [Sima] Qian called 'making manifest what is originally hidden' is deduction, and what he termed 'inferring the hidden from the visible' is induction. His words as much as confirm it. The two [arts] are the most important methods in fathoming the principles of things. Yet, later scholars failed to expand upon and use them, and because they never applied them properly, they hardly ever mentioned them in their works.[41]

Even in the extensive notes that he added to his translations of Mill and Jevons, Yan Fu never moved beyond the mere assertion that "the art of logic must have existed in pre-Qin China."[42] If he made any significant contribution to the emerging discourse on Chinese logic, it was his insistence on *mingxue* 名學 ('the science of names') as the

---

[40] Sun Yirang 孫詒讓 . 1897. "Yu Liang Zhuoru lun Mozi shu" 與梁桌如論墨子書 (A letter to Liang Qichao discussing the *Mozi*). Reprinted in: id. 1963. *Sun Zhouqing xiansheng ji* 孫籒廎 先生 集 (The works of Mr. Sun Yirang). 15 vols. Taibei: Wenyi chubanshe, vol. 2, pp. 581–5; 582.

[41] Yan Fu 嚴復 . 1897. "Yi 'Tianyanlun' zixu" 譯天演論自序 (Translator's preface to the *Tianyanlun*). Reprinted in: id. 1986. *Yan Fu ji*, pp. 1319–21; 1319–20.

[42] Yan Fu 1981, p. 46.

most appropriate rendition of the term 'logic', despite criticisms that this choice implied unwarranted parallels between an entirely foreign science and the concerns of the School of Names.[43] Thus, the claim that either Sun Yirang or Yan should be revered as the discoverers of a 'tradition' that had been forgotten for more than two thousand years is based on rather weak evidence. In fact, if spelling out the mere suspicion that one or another passage of a classical text may contain insights related to European logic suffices to earn this honorific title, then it ought to be attributed to the grammarian Georg von der Gabelentz, who wrote the following in a brief introduction to the *Mozi*, published in 1888:

> Book X—chaps. 40 to 43—is particularly difficult. It appears to consist mainly of definitions; the style is exceedingly concise and abstract, and in many places the text seems intentionally unclear. The whole [book] has an esoteric flavour. At times we are led to suspect that a synthetic judgment or an affirmative proposition may be hidden behind a definition, then again it seems as though formal logic and dialectic were to be taught by example. It is one of the most opaque texts I have ever seen.[44]

In any case, none of these pioneering 'discoverers' did much for the construction of the actual frame of articulation in which discourses on Chinese logic came to be expressed in the course of the twentieth century. Instead, the constituent elements of this frame were identified and negotiated in a handful of essays written between 1903 and 1909 by Liu Shipei, Zhang Binglin, Liang Qichao and Wang Guowei, each of whom made an original contribution to its future shape despite their very different approaches to the subject.

5. THE CLASSICIST: LIU SHIPEI

Liu Shipei's role in this context is often underestimated. The precocious offspring of a distinguished scholarly lineage from Yangzhou 揚州 , a center of Han-learning since the seventeenth century, he is best

---

[43] Cf. id. 1931, vol. 1, pp. 2–3. For critiques, cf., e.g., Zhu Zhixin 1905, p. 65.

[44] Georg von der Gabelentz. 1888. "Über den chinesischen Philosophen Mek Tik", *Berichte über die Verhandlungen der Königlich Sächsischen Gesellschaft der Wissenschaften zu Leipzig. Philologisch-Historische Klasse* 40, pp. 62–70; 68. (Translation from German is mine, J.K.)

known for his chameleonesque political radicalism.[45] In the first years of the twentieth century, however, he was also considered one of China's intellectual hopefuls, due to the sound philological training he had received in his Yangzhou home, his quick and audacious pen, and his versatility in absorbing foreign ideas and blending them with endemic concepts. His first book, the *Zhongguo minyue jingyi* 中國民約精義 (The refined meaning of the Chinese social contract), published in 1903, is a stunning example of this ability.[46] In order to propagate notions borrowed from Jean-Jacques Rousseau's *Contrat social*, which had become known in China through a translation from Japanese, Liu deliberately cut the text into pieces, paraphrased useful passages, and corroborated his interpretations by attaching quotations from authoritative Chinese texts.[47] Certainly, Liu was by no means the first to apply this technique—which resembled the argumentative strategy of many texts expounding the 'Chinese origins of Western science'—but he employed this exegetical device with greater persuasive efficiency than had previous writers. In particular, he freely reversed the order of *explanans* and *explanandum* according to his interpretive needs. Thus, in his *Rangshu* 攘書 (Book of expulsion), a radical anti-Manchu treatise that contained some chapters with a scholarly focus, Liu used Yan Fu's rendition of Mill's *Logic* to corroborate Xunzi's 荀子 (c. 325–238 BC) deliberations "On the Correct Use of Names" (*Zhengming pian* 正名篇) and, wherever necessary, vice versa.[48]

In his understanding of logic, Liu Shipei depended almost entirely on Yan Fu—in the *Rangshu* as much as in his later writings. Like Yan, he regarded 'induction' and 'deduction' as the central concerns of the logical trade, and he also cited a passage from Yan's translation of Mill stressing that logic should not be conceived of as a purely formal 'study of thinking' (*si zhi xue* 思之學) but rather as a 'quest for

---

[45] Cf. Hao Chang. 1987. *Chinese Intellectuals in Crisis. Search for Order and Meaning, 1890–1911*. Berkeley: University of California Press, pp. 146–79.

[46] Liu Guanghan 劉光漢 [Liu Shipei 劉師培]. 1903a. *Zhongguo minyue jingyi* 中國民約精義 (The refined meaning of the Chinese social contract). Reprinted in: Liu Shipei. 1997. *Liu Shipei quanji* 劉師培全集 (The complete works of Liu Shipei). 4 vols. Beijing: Zhonggong zhongyang dangxiao chubanshe, vol. 1, pp. 560–97.

[47] Cf. Wang Xiaoling. 1998. "Liu Shipei et son *contrat social chinois*", *Études chinoises* 17.1–2, pp. 155–90.

[48] Liu Guanghan 劉光漢 [Liu Shipei 劉師培]. 1903b. *Rangshu* 攘書 (Book of expulsion). Reprinted in: Liu Shipei. 1997. *Liu Shipei quanji*, vol. 2, pp. 1–17; 15–7.

authenticity' (*qiucheng zhi xue* 求成之學) entailing moral and spiritual aspects.[49] Yan's influence was also apparent in Liu's attempt to find a place for logic within the boundaries of traditional Chinese scholarship. Drawing on Yan's rendition of Western logic as a 'science of names', Liu tried to situate logic within the framework of philology and textual criticism (or 'lesser learning', *xiaoxue* 小學). Obviously, this was no easy task. Liu approached it by synthesizing a broad range of opinions on the properties and functions of 'names' from classical Chinese sources into a theory of conceptualization that was mainly inspired by Xunzi.[50] In this effort, Liu repeatedly drew on logic to corroborate Xunzi's remarks on the methods of classification. A novel element in his effort was the identification of specific equivalents to key terms of Western logic in classical Chinese texts. Thus, he glossed Xunzi's *gongming* 共名 (general name) and *bieming* 別名 (specific name) as 'general term' (*gongming* 公名) and 'particular term' (*zhuanming* 專名), and matched the terms *da gong* 大共 (greatest generality) and *da bie* 大別 (greatest specificity) with 'induction' (*guina* 歸納) and 'deduction' (*yanyi* 演繹).[51] In addition, he presented a number of *yinming* terms as functional equivalents of European notions, thus substantiating Sun Yirang's earlier hint at similarities between Western logic and Chinese Buddhist reasoning (which was itself only just beginning to be rediscovered in China).[52] However, even though he ventured further in his search for possible equivalencies than his predecessors, Liu Shipei insisted that both Western logic and *yinming* were only suited to complement, but not replace, Chinese

---

[49] Ibid., vol. 2, p. 15.

[50] In addition to his remarks in the *Rangshu*, Liu developed this theory in Liu Guanghan. 1905a. "Xiaoxue fawei bu" 小學發微補 (Additions to the essentials of philology). Reprinted in: Liu Shipei. 1997. *Liu Shipei quanji*, vol. 1, pp. 422–42; id. 1905b. "Guoxue fawei" 國學發微 (Essentials of national studies), ibid., vol. 1, pp. 474–99; id. 1905c. "Zhoumo xueshu shi xu" 周末學術史序 (Prefaces to an intellectual history of the late Zhou), ibid., vol. 1, pp. 500–25; and id. 1907. "Xunzi mingxue fawei" 荀子名學發微 (Essentials of Xunzi's logic), ibid., vol. 3, pp. 316–8.

[51] Liu Guanghan 1903b, pp. 16–7. English translations of the terms used in *Xunzi* 22.2f adapted from John Knoblock. 1994. *Xunzi. A Translation and Study of the Complete Works*. 3 vols. Stanford: Stanford University Press, vol. 3, p. 130.

[52] Liu Guanghan 1903b, pp. 16–7. For the rediscovery of Buddhist logic in late Qing and Republican China, cf. Uwe Frankenhauser. 1996b. *Die Einführung der buddhistischen Logik nach China*. Wiesbaden: Harrassowitz, pp. 205–17; and Yao Nanqiang 姚南強. 2000. *Yinming xueshuoshi gangyao* 因明學説史綱要 (Outline history of *yinming* theories). Shanghai: Sanlian shudian, pp. 328–39.

philology, since they had not evolved on the basis of the unique Chinese language and script.

Liu's professed belief in the superiority of traditional Chinese scholarship also fuelled his involvement in the movement to preserve China's 'National Essence' (*guocui* 國粹) from 1905 onward. In the context of this movement, he made another, more lasting contribution to the emerging discourse on Chinese logic. One aim of the National Essence group was to bring about a revival of China's intellectual heritage comparable to the rediscovery of Greek thought in the European renaissance.[53] For the first issues of the group's journal, Liu drew up a detailed plan for such a revival under the title "Zhoumo xueshushi xu" 周末學術史序 (Prefaces to an intellectual history of the late Zhou).[54] What he suggested in this outline was nothing less than a complete revision of ancient Chinese intellectual history along the lines of the modern academic disciplines (among which he tacitly embedded two chapters on traditional Chinese philology).[55] Chapter 3 of this hybrid history *nova methodo*, following 'psychology' and 'ethics', was to be dedicated to a 'history of logic' (*lunlixue shi* 論理學史).

The proposed contents of this chapter read less revolutionary than its title. After glossing *lunlixue* 論理學 ('the science of reasoning', a common Japanese loan for 'logic'[56]) again with Yan Fu's *mingxue*, Liu basically offered a revised version of his remarks in the *Rangshu*. However, his rearrangement of the quoted passages brought a question to the fore that he had to answer for all chapters of his projected new history: which texts, schools or individuals should be discussed in the context of a certain discipline? In his *Rangshu*, Liu had pointed

---

[53] Cf. Zheng Shiqu 鄭師渠 . 1997. *Wan Qing guocuipai: wenhua sixiang yanjiu* 晚清國粹派—文化思想研究 (The National Essence Group in the Late Qing: Studies in cultural thought). Beijing: Beijing Shifan daxue chubanshe, pp. 132–9; Martin Bernal. 1976. "Liu Shih-p'ei and National Essence", in: Charlotte Furth (ed.). *The Limits of Change. Essays on Conservative Alternatives in Republican China*. Cambridge, Mass.: Harvard University Press, pp. 90–112; 106.

[54] Liu Guanghan 1905c. Since Liu never planned to write the book for which these "Prefaces" seemed to be intended, the title should perhaps rather be translated as "Prolegomena to ...". Cf. Li Jinxi 黎錦熙 . 1936. "Xu" 序 (Preface). Reprinted in: *Liu Shipei quanji*, vol. 1, p. 26.

[55] Cf. Wu Guangxing 吳光興 . 1995. "Liu Shipei dui Zhongguo xueshushi de yanjiu" 劉師培對中國學術史的研究 (Liu Shipei's researches in Chinese intellectual history), *Xueren* 7, pp. 163–86; 172–6.

[56] For a survey of early Japanese translations of the term 'logic', cf. Funayama 1968, pp. 19–28.

out similarities between logic and a broad range of classical texts, including seemingly less likely candidates such as the *Liji* 禮記 (Book of rites), early dictionaries like the *Erya* 爾雅 (Approaching elegance) or the *Shiming* 釋名 (Explication of names), and Dong Zhongshu's 董仲舒 (c. 195–105 BC) *Chunqiu fanlu* 春秋繁露 (Luxuriant gems of the *Spring and Autumn Annals*). Now, however, he had come to the conclusion that a history of early Chinese logic should exclusively focus on Xunzi's "On the Correct Use of Names." Other schools and texts, including those that are customarily raised in discussions of Chinese logic today—notably the School of Names and the *Mohist Canons*, but also the *Yinwenzi* 尹文子 and parts of the *Zhuangzi* 莊子 —were explicitly excluded from the envisioned canon on the ground that their authors only "split hairs and messed with words in order to elevate themselves," hence: that they were 'sophists' (*guibianjia* 詭辯家) and not 'logicians', i.e., true "scientists of names."[57]

6. THE BUDDHIST: ZHANG BINGLIN

Zhang Binglin, Liu's long-time scholarly associate, shared many of his student's political and intellectual inclinations and was even more firmly rooted in 'Old Text' (*guwen* 古文) philology. Old Text learning played a decisive part in the revival of studies in 'non-canonical philosophers' (*zhuzi* 諸子) during the late Qing.[58] For our purpose, this peculiar brand of scholarship is of interest for two reasons: on the one hand, many texts that have found their way into twentieth-century canons of Chinese logic, namely the *Mojing*, would not be intelligible without the meticulous textual criticism conducted by proponents of this school from the eighteenth century onward. Without the efforts of Sun Yirang and his precursors, it would have been much harder, if not

---

[57] Liu Guanghan 1905c, p. 503.

[58] Cf. Wang Fansen 王汎森 . 1985. *Zhang Taiyan de sixiang. Jianlun qi dui ruxue chuantong de chongji* 章太炎的思想—兼論其對儒學傳統的衝擊 (Zhang Taiyan's thought. With a discussion of his attacks against the Confucian tradition). Taibei: Shibao wenhua chuban gongsi, pp. 26–33. For a general introduction to the revival of *zhuzixue* in the late Qing, cf. Luo Jianqiu 羅檢秋 . 1997. *Jindai zhuzixue yu wenhua sichao* 近代諸子學與文化思潮 (Studies of non-canonical philosophers and trends of cultural thought in modern China). Beijing: Zhongguo shehui kexue chubanshe, pp. 50–200.

altogether impossible, to discover their logical import.[59] On the other hand, by the end of the nineteenth century, the continued effort to prove the diversity of China's intellectual heritage had led to a serious erosion of the paramount position of Confucius' teachings as upheld by orthodox doctrine. It was only this erosion that enabled Liu Shipei to declare in his "Prefaces" that "Confucians are but one among the nine schools"[60] and to propose a design for a new master narrative of China's intellectual history that ignored the time-honoured boundaries between studies of canonical and non-canonical texts (or *jingxue* 經學 and *zixue* 子學).

Zhang Binglin did not go quite so far as this in his deliberations. Rejecting Liu Shipei's proposal to reorganize China's intellectual heritage along disciplinary lines, he suggested adapting the classification of the *Hanshu yiwenzhi* 漢書藝文志 (Bibliographical records in the *Book of Han*) to the contemporary intellectual environment. One adaptation concerned the School of Names, which in Zhang's opinion needed to be redefined in order to make more space for logic. In his "Zhuzixue lüeshuo" 諸子學略説 (Brief account of studies of non-canonical philosophers) of 1906, he outlined this new understanding in due clarity:

> The rectification of names was not an art of any single school. Confucians, Daoists, Mohists and Legalists all relied on this science (*xue* 學), for without it they would not have been able to establish their own theories and refute those of others. Thus, the Confucians have Xunzi's discourse 'On the Correct Use of Names', and the Mohists have the two 'Canons' and their 'Explanations'—both contain truths (*zhendi* 真諦) from the School of Names which were scattered among the thinkers of the time. On the contrary, the art of Hui Shi 惠施 [c. 370–310 BC], Gongsun Long 公孫龍 [c. 325–250 BC] and others, whose writings and deeds were exclusively centered on *mingjia*-matters, must be likened to the Sophists because they made far-fetched and useless distinctions.[61]

In this passage, Zhang implicitly replaced the familiar sense of the term *mingjia* as the name of one of the nine philosophical schools of the pre-Qin period with a new meaning very much akin to 'European'

---

[59] Cf. Angus C. Graham. 1978. *Later Mohist Logic, Ethics and Science*. Hong Kong et al.: The Chinese University Press, pp. 64–72.

[60] Liu Guanghan 1905*c*, p. 500.

[61] Zhang Binglin 章炳麟 . 1906. "Zhuzixue lüeshuo" 諸子學略説 (Brief account of studies of non-canonical philosophers). Reprinted in: *Zhongguo xiandai xueshu jing-dian. Zhang Taiyan juan* 中國現代學術經典—章太炎卷 (Modern Chinese classics:

logic. While acknowledging that traces of this knowledge could be found among all schools, Zhang left no doubt that he regarded Xunzi's "Zhengming pian" and the *Mohist Canons* as the richest sources in this regard. Similarly to Liu Shipei, he praised Xunzi for his insights into the relations between names, perception, the intellect and the outside world of facts, and dismissed the extravagant art of the 'Sophists' Hui Shi 惠施 and Gongsun Long 公孫龍. Contrary to Liu, however, he moved beyond the understanding of logic as a mere 'science of names', i.e., a primarily term-based enterprise. For Zhang, logic was indeed an 'art of reasoning' (*lunlixue* 論理學) with a verifiable value for the practice of argumentation, and he therefore paid greatest respect to the *Mojing* which—in Sun Yirang's reconstructed version—seemed to provide at least a rudimentary theory of the forms and conditions of valid inference.[62]

Zhang elaborated this claim, which entailed the discovery of yet another crucial element of logical theory in ancient China, through a highly complex exercise of translation, re-translation and interpretation. In this effort, he identified the Mohist term 'reason' (*gu* 故, 'something that is inherently so')[63] with the 'logical reason' (*yin* 因) put forth in the 'tripartite inference' (*sanzhi biliang* 三支比量) of Chinese Buddhist reasoning, and then proceeded to relate both to the 'minor premise' (*xiao qianti* 小前提) of the Aristotelian 'syllogism' (*sanduanfa* 三段法).[64] Besides the unusual degree of sophistication required for this operation, readers used to believing in the *a priori* superiority of 'modern' theory may feel bewildered because Zhang, notwithstanding his apparent familiarity with European thought, explained all notions he introduced in *yinming* and thus endemic terms—an interpretive strategy rarely applied at the time, even by cultural 'conservatives'.

Zhang Binglin's choice of endemic terms for his frame of reference reflected his conviction that *yinming* provided a more effective 'art of reasoning' than either the *Mohist Canons* or European logic were able

---

[61] (*cont.*) Zhang Taiyan). 1996. Edited by Liu Mengxi 劉夢溪. Shijiazhuang: Hebei jiaoyu chubanshe, pp. 479–97; 493. For the significance of this text in modern Chinese intellectual history, cf. Shimada Kenji. 1990. *Pioneer of the Chinese Revolution. Zhang Binglin and Confucianism*. Translated by Joshua A. Fogel. Stanford: Stanford University Press, pp. 116–22.

[62] Zhang Binglin 1906, pp. 494–6. Cf. also Luo Jianqiu 1997, p. 157.

[63] Cf. Graham 1978, pp. 189–90.

[64] Cf. Zhang Binglin 1906, pp. 495–6.

to provide. In his essay "Yuan Ming" 原名 (On [the School of] Names) of 1909, Zhang stated this belief even more firmly:

> The way of argumentation is this: start with the purpose, then elucidate the foundation, then put forth an example to complement it and a material reason that may illustrate it; in *yinming* these [steps] are called 'thesis' (*zong* 宗), 'reason' (*yin* 因) and 'examples' (*yu* 喻) (comprising both the 'substantial example' [*yuti* 喻體] and the 'concrete examples' [*yuyi* 喻依]). In India, the order of argument is: first the thesis, then the reason, and then the examples. In the West, the order is: first the substantial example, then the reason, then the thesis. As tripartite inferences these two are identical. In the *Mohist Canons* the reason is called *gu*; the order in which proofs are established is: first the reason, then the substantial example, then the thesis. … The inferences of the Westerners and of the *Mozi* place the substantial example before the thesis. But those who put the substantial example first cannot allow for concrete examples. In this respect, both are inferior to *yinming*.[65]

Zhang Binglin's attempt at intracultural translation thus took on an unusual shape. In his ingenious synthesis he demonstrated that it was possible, at least on a very elementary level, to assert the precedence of a 'traditional', viz., Chinese Buddhist frame of articulation while simultaneously redefining individual notions, such as the boundaries of the logical realm, in accordance with a Western-derived understanding. Nevertheless, with few but notable exceptions, the success of his effort remained confined to Buddhist circles.

7. THE PALAEONTOLOGIST: LIANG QICHAO

While the proponents of Old Text learning thus answered the question of 'Chinese logic' consistently in the affirmative, Liang Qichao, who had studied with Kang Youwei 康有為 (1858–1927), one of the champions of the 'New Text' (*jinwen* 今文) school, initially responded with scepticism. In several essays he criticized Yan Fu's translation of the term 'logic' by *mingxue* precisely because this rendering linked the discipline too closely with "the theories about the 'hard and white' and 'similarity and difference' (*jianbai tongyi* 堅白同異) in the Warring States period," while "in effect this science has nothing to do

---

[65] Zhang Binglin 章炳麟 . 1909. "Yuan Ming" 原名 (On [the School of] Names). Reprinted in: *Zhongguo xiandai xueshu jingdian. Zhang Taiyan juan* 1996, pp. 111–8; 115–6.

with the words of the ancient Chinese Sophists."[66] In his "Lun Zhongguo xueshu sixiang bianqian zhi dashi" 論中國學術思想變遷之大勢
(General tendencies in the development of Chinese thought), which is
often seen as the first 'modern' history of Chinese thought written in
Chinese, Liang came to an even more critical assessment. In this text,
he identified "the lack of logical thinking" as the first and most conse-
quential deficit of Chinese philosophy, especially as compared with
ancient India and Greece, where logic had been established as an 'academic discipline' (*ke* 科) of its own right at a very early stage. In
China, Deng Xi 鄧析 (d. 501 BC), Hui Shi and Gongsun Long had
only "dallied with sophisms" (*bonong guibian* 播弄詭辯) and had
therefore been unable to open up the secure path of logical inquiry.[67]
Liang identified three reasons for the absence of logical theory in
China: first, Chinese scholars had always been overtly concerned with
practical application and had never found it necessary "to pay attention to the discussion of true and false"; secondly, China had never
worked out a 'grammar' (*wendian* 文典 or *yudian* 語典) for her language and, thus, the "methods of syntactic analysis" (*cuoci sheju zhi
fa* 措辭設句之法) were never understood; and, thirdly, exaggerated
respect for dogma and teachers had prevented open debate and argumentation.[68]

Yet, as in so many other matters, Liang soon changed his mind,
and as usual with a vengeance. After a trip to the United States in
1903, which significantly altered his political and intellectual outlook,[69] he too became fascinated with the idea of a Chinese renaissance. Just like his opponents in the National Essence camp, Liang
now felt that the revival of Chinese scholarship depended on the re-
invention of its ancient heritage. In 1904 he wrote that

---

[66] Cf. Liang Qichao 梁啟超. 1902a. "Jinshi wenming chuzu er da jia zhi xueshuo"
今世文明初祖二大家之學説 (The theories of two great precursors of modern civilization). Reprinted in: id. 1990a [1936]. *Yinbingshi wenji* 飲冰室文集 (Collected essays
from the Ice Drinker's Studio). Edited by Lin Zhijun 林志鈞. Beijing: Zhonghua
shuju, 13.1–12; 13.2.

[67] Liang Qichao. 1902b. "Lun Zhongguo xueshu sixiang bianqian zhi dashi" 論中
國學術思想變遷之大勢 (General tendencies in the development of Chinese thought).
Reprinted in: id. 1990a. *Yinbingshi wenji*, 7.1–104; 7.33.

[68] Ibid., 7.34.

[69] Cf. Joseph R. Levenson. 1953. *Liang Ch'i-ch'ao and the Mind of Modern
China*. Cambridge, Mass.: Harvard University Press, pp. 103–20.

The civilization of the modern West has its roots in the revitalization of ancient knowledge (*guxue fuxing* 古學復興). We should follow this example. It will therefore be a worthwhile undertaking to employ the new principles from Europe and append them to ancient Chinese knowledge.[70]

One of the first texts to embark on this enterprise was Liang's essay "Mozi zhi lunlixue" 墨子之論理學 (Mozi's logic), which was to become an important point of reference for later historians of China's logical past.

In accordance with his declared intention, Liang Qichao built the frame of reference for this essay exclusively from terms of Western origin, which he freely selected from the works of Yan Fu and some texts translated from Japanese. For someone who not long before had denied the existence of anything similar to Western logic in Chinese antiquity, Liang applied these terms with astonishing ease and certainty. The opening section of his essay under the heading "Shi ming" 釋名 (Explicating terms) was a breathtaking exercise in a modernized version of the 'matching of meanings' (*geyi* 格義). Without taking pains to offer much evidence, Liang linked a number of terms from the *Mojing* to a set of basic logical notions comprising: 'term' (*mingci* 名詞), 'proposition' (*mingti* 命題), 'premise' (*qianti* 前提), 'conclusion' (*duan'an* 斷案), 'middle term' (*meici* 媒詞), 'particular proposition' (*techeng mingti* 特稱命題), 'hypothetical proposition' (*jiayan mingti* 假言命題), 'form' (*fashi* 法式), 'verification' (*lizheng* 立證), 'comparison' (*bijiao* 比較), 'sorites' (*jidieshi* 積疊式), and 'inference' (*tuilun* 推論).[71] Examples of his interpretive strategy read as follows:

> Name (*ming* 名). Chapter "Xiaoqu" 小取 ('The lesser pick'): 'One uses names to refer to actualities'. Note: What Mozi calls name is called 'Term' [English in the original, J.K.] (*mingci* 名詞) in logic. When we say 'Mozi is Chinese', then 'Mozi' and 'Chinese' are two terms.
>
> Sentence (*ci* 辭). Chapter "Xiaoqu": 'One uses sentences to transmit intentions'. Note: What Mozi calls sentence is called 'Proposition' [English in the original, J.K.] (*mingti* 命題) in logic. When we say 'Mozi is Chinese', then this entire phrase is a proposition.

---

[70] Liang Qichao 梁啟超. 1904. "Mozi zhi lunlixue" 墨子之論理學 (Mozi's logic). Reprinted in: id. 1990b [1936]. *Yinbingshi zhuanji* 飲冰室專集 (Collected monographs from the Ice Drinker's-Studio). Edited by Lin Zhijun 林志鈞. Beijing: Zhonghua shuju, 37.55–72; 37.55.

[71] Ibid., 37.56–8.

    <u>Explanation</u> (*shuo* 説). Chapter "Xiaoqu": 'One uses explanations to bring out reasons'. Note: What Mozi calls explanation is called 'Premise' [English in the original, J.K.] (*qianti* 前提) in logic. Logic must of necessity always rely on the syllogism. The first section [of the syllogism] is called the major premise, the second is called the minor premise. When we say 'He who has the Way and can save others through his actions is a Holy Man,' then this is a major premise; and when we say 'Mozi has the Way and can save others through his actions,' then this is a minor premise. Further note: It would be wrong to say that Mozi's explanation refers exclusively to minor premises.[72]

Two points are worth noting. First, in these and all ensuing examples Liang paid greater attention to explaining the meaning of the Western terms into which he translated the presumed equivalents from the *Mozi* than to justifying his choice of a particular match. Secondly, on the basis of the evidence provided by Liang alone, readers were hard put to form a reasoned judgment as to whether or not the 'translation' he proposed was valid. Some of his matches, like the rather obvious one between *ming* and 'term', were adopted or at least considered by later scholars; most were instantly dismissed. At least for the remaining sections of his essay, however, Liang succeeded in establishing a set of key terms with a professedly confirmed textual backing, and this palæontological evidence, as it were, enabled him to try and rebuild the long-lost logical 'system' that presumably lay fossilized in the *Mojing*.

    In the manner Liang Qichao portrayed it, this forgotten 'system' looked strikingly similar to a basic form of traditional European textbook syllogistics. In addition to the matches of logical notions he had found in the first part of his essay, he now uncovered implicit or hitherto unrecognized knowledge of the principles of 'distribution' (*puji* 普及) as well as the eight 'rules' (*gongli* 公例) of the syllogism which "logicians regard as holy and inviolable."[73] Finally, even more boldly, he asserted that Mozi's doctrine of the 'three standards' (*san biao* 三 表 or *san fa* 三法) had anticipated Bacon's insights into the nature and value of inductive logic by more than two millennia, and that Mozi should therefore be celebrated as "our Bacon of the East."[74]

---

[72] Ibid., 37.56. Translations of the passages from "Xiaoqu", no. 11, adapted from Graham 1978, pp. 432–3.

[73] Cf. Liang Qichao 1904, 37.58–63.

[74] Cf. ibid., 37.70–1.

Although most of the claims he made in his essay were hardly convincing, Liang must be credited with two significant discoveries: on the one hand, he was the first author to suggest that a fully developed system of logic lay hidden in the logical fragments of ancient Chinese literature and that this system might be recovered through a combination of textual analysis and what we would call today 'rational reconstruction'—a suggestion that was to spur an extremely productive interest in the *Mozi* and other texts during the 1920s and 1930s. On the other hand, by relating his 'systematic' findings to Mozi's actual practice of argumentation,[75] Liang showed that research in 'Chinese logic' must not exclusively focus on explicit logical theory but has at least as much to gain from examining the logic implicit in discursive practices.

8. THE ARCHIVIST: WANG GUOWEI

Wang Guowei shared Liang Qichao's initial scepticism regarding the question of whether ancient China had known logical theory. In contrast to Europe and India, he wrote in 1905, China had "disputation, but no logic," because the Chinese generally lacked theoretical interest and imagination.[76] Yet, only two months after this negative judgment, Wang published a short essay entitled "Zhou-Qin zhuzi zhi mingxue" 周秦諸子之名學 (The logic of the non-canonical philosophers of the Zhou and Qin [periods]).[77] The text was probably a delayed echo of an article on "Xunzi's Logical Theory" by the Japanese philosopher Kuwaki Gen'yoku 桑木嚴翼 (1874–1946), which Wang had translated into Chinese in 1904.[78]

---

[75] Cf. ibid., 37.63–8.

[76] Wang Guowei 王國維. 1905*a*. "Lun xin xueyu zhi shuru" 論新學語之輸入 (On the importation of new scholarly terms). *Jiaoyu shijie* 96. Reprinted in: id. 1997. *Wang Guowei wenji*, vol. 3, pp. 40–3; 40.

[77] Wang Guowei 王國維. 1905*b*. "Zhou-Qin zhuzi zhi mingxue" 周秦諸子之名學 (The logic of the non-canonical philosophers of the Zhou and Qin). *Jiaoyu shijie* 98, 100. Reprinted in: id. 1997. *Wang Guowei wenji*, vol. 3, pp. 219–27.

[78] Kuwaki Gen'yoku 桑木嚴翼. 1904. "Xunzi zhi lunli xueshuo" 荀子之論理學説 (Xunzi's logical theory), *Jiaoyu shijie* 74. The original was id. 1898. "Junshi no ronri setsu" 荀子の論理説 (Xunzi's theory of logic), *Waseda gakuhō* 14. Reprinted in: id. 1900. *Tetsugaku gairon* 哲学概論 (Outline of philosophy). Tokyo: Hakubunsha, pp. 449–63.

Whatever his motives, Wang was certainly qualified for the task at hand. Among the scholars discussed in this paper, he had received by far the soundest training in 'European' logic. Already in 1902 he had begun to study Jevons' *Logic* with his Japanese teachers Fujita Toyo-hachi 藤田豐八 (1870–1929) and Taoka Sayoji 田岡佐代治 (1870–1912) at the Nanyang Gongxue 南洋公學 in Shanghai, and he had never lost interest in the subject.[79] In addition, he had acquired a solid grasp of logical terminology in the course of his translations of philo-sophical texts from Japanese and English, which, as a rule, displayed a degree of lexical consistency unparalleled in China at the time.[80]

Perhaps it was this firm background that gave him the confidence to open his essay with a resolute statement on the necessary condi-tions for the flourishing of logical theory. History proves, he wrote, that logic is the result of abstraction from arguments exchanged in scholarly debate. In Greece, dialectic was developed in order to meet the challenge of Zeno's paradoxes; later Aristotle synthesized the available logical knowledge in response to criticisms from the Soph-ists. A similar process had led to the discovery of *yinming* schemes in India, and had also incited the beginning of logical reflection in China. The founding-father of Chinese logic, according to Wang, was Mozi, who had to defend his ethical and political doctrines against Confucian scorn. In the same manner, Xunzi had to protect the Confu-cian heritage against the irresponsible sophisms of Deng Xi, Hui Shi and their followers. With Xunzi's treatise "On the Correct Use of Names" Chinese logic had reached its early climax.[81] The ideological stratification under the Han-Emperor Wu 漢武帝 (140–87 BC) had effectively brought all scholarly debate to an end by "suppressing any opinion but one," and had thus cut off the tradition of logical thought in China—for good, as Wang emphasized. With this last remark, he

---

[79] Cf. Liu Xuan 劉烜. 1996. *Wang Guowei pingzhuan* 王國維評傳 (Critical biog-raphy of Wang Guowei). Nanchang: Baihuazhou wenyi chubanshe, pp. 14–5. One occasion where he could apply this knowledge was his reading of Schopenhauer's treatise on the principle of sufficient reason. Cf. Hermann Kogelschatz. 1986. *Wang Kuo-wei und Schopenhauer. Eine philosophische Begegnung*. Stuttgart: Franz Steiner, pp. 86–8.

[80] For an account of Wang Guowei's achievements as a translator, cf. Cecile Chu-chin Sun. 1998. "Wang Guowei as Translator of Values", in: David Pollard (ed.). *Creation and Translation. Readings of Western Literature in Early Modern China, 1840–1918*. Amsterdam, Philadelphia: John Benjamins, pp. 253–82.

[81] Cf. Wang Guowei 1905b, pp. 219, 224–7.

unveiled a truth that no author had as yet explicitly stated: in contrast to discourses on 'Western' or rather contemporary logic, which seemingly promised potentially endless social, scientific and intellectual progress, discussions of 'Chinese logic', no matter how broadly defined, were and would continue to be of archival interest only.

Still, the question remained how these archives should be accessed, arranged and kept in order. Wang's solution was to start with an honest assessment of what they actually contained. In his view, China's logical heritage consisted of no more than three elements: a discussion of 'definitions' (*dingyi* 定義), developed in the "Explanations" to the *Mohist Canons*, an incomplete inventory of 'fallacies of reasoning' (*tuilun zhi miuwang* 推論之謬妄) that could be extracted from the *Mozi* chapters "Daqu" 大取 (The greater pick) and "Xiaoqu" 小取 (The lesser pick), and a theory of 'conception' (*gainian* 概念) as presented by Xunzi.[82] Unfortunately, however, only two of these elements could be reconstructed, since in the *Mozi* only the relevant passages of the "Xiaoqu" were fully intelligible.

Wang's treatment of this chapter illustrates the way in which his approach to China's forgotten logical heritage differed from Liang Qichao's. Both relied in their interpretations entirely on Western-derived frames of articulation. But because he was not interested in the reconstruction of hidden 'systems' or 'theories', Wang was able to select much more refined analytical tools from within this frame for his explorations. While Liang had to find equivalents of central logical terms in order to complete the 'system' which was to contribute to China's renaissance, Wang could content himself with whatever his material indicated, even if this meant that he was only able to discover faint hints pointing toward possible notions of a 'fallacy of equivocation' (*nuanmei zhi miuwang* 暧昧之謬妄) or a 'fallacy of accident' (*ouranxing zhi miuwang* 偶然性之謬妄).[83] This much more cautious approach was reflected in Wang's assessment of the respective merits of 'Chinese logic' as compared with the logic of ancient Greece. Since, unlike Aristotle, neither Mozi nor Xunzi had discovered

---

[82] Ibid., pp. 219.
[83] Ibid., pp. 220–1.

abstract rules of reasoning, he wrote, their logical insights were as powerless as "the defenders of Lu against the invaders from Qin."[84]

CONCLUSION

With Wang Guowei the 'age of discovery' in the history of 'Chinese logic' came to an early end. Within less than a decade after a specialist discourse on logic had been established in China, the authors I have discussed here sketched the outlines of a complementary field of inquiry that eventually was to assert itself as a distinct discourse on 'Chinese logical thought'. Within the same brief period, the excitement as well as the uncertainties which were apparent in Liu Shipei's eclectic exuberance had given way to Wang Guowei's sobering academic rigidity.

In the course of this rapid development, the early discoverers of Chinese logic singled out and negotiated three questions that came to dominate discourses on Chinese logical thought until today: i) is there indeed anything like 'Chinese logic'?; ii) if so, which texts or fragments are to be considered constituent parts of its supposed 'tradition'?; and, finally, iii) in which terms or frame of articulation are these texts best understood?

With regard to the first question, all authors soon agreed that traditional Chinese thought did indeed entail explicit logical theories or at least fragments of such theories, especially if logic was defined as a 'science of names'. Opinions on the second question were hardly more varied. Xunzi's "On the Correct Use of Names" and the *Mohist Canons* were almost unanimously accepted and there was similar agreement on the need to exclude the thinkers of the School of Names, who were relegated to the ranks of frivolous and potentially dangerous 'Sophists'. The third question was the most contested issue in the period under consideration and beyond. Liu Shipei half-heartedly suggested a synthesis of logic and *xiaoxue* within the context of traditional Chinese philology, but he failed to construct a convincing frame of articulation that would effectively link the two disciplines. Zhang Binglin succeeded in his attempt to extract the rudiments of

---

[84] Wang Guowei 王國維. 1906. "Mozi zhi xueshuo" 墨子之學說 (Mozi's theories), *Jiaoyu shijie* 121. Reprinted in: id. 1997. *Wang Guowei wenji*, vol. 3, pp. 159–74; 173.

such a frame from the *yinming*-lexicon but his effort never attracted much interest outside Buddhist circles. Liang Qichao adopted a rough and ready-made version of a Western-derived frame of reference that obviously fitted the needs of his non-specialist audience better than Wang Guowei's sophisticated, but highly selective, terminological arsenal. It was a combination of these last two frames that was to be refined and consolidated in writings on Chinese logical thought in the course of the twentieth century, sometimes extended to include terms from symbolic logic which began to be studied in China during the 1920s.[85]

Finally, what, if any, were the lasting contributions of our authors? Liu Shipei supplied the idea of rewriting Chinese intellectual history along Western lines, i.e., to regroup or redress the textual legacy of ancient Chinese thought into the now familiar compartments of contemporary science and philosophy. This challenge was soon taken up by scholars such as Cai Yuanpei 蔡元培 (1868–1940), Hu Shi and Zhang Shizhao, but it was only fully developed by Feng Youlan 馮友蘭 (1895–1990), Liu's student at Beijing University. Zhang Binglin drew attention to tacit resonances between the different logical traditions known in China, and can thus be regarded as the first author to have transposed the culturalist idea of a 'tripod' of world civilizations—counting only Europe, India and China herself—to the realm of logic. Liang Qichao was an inspiration to too many writers to list them individually. His influence is probably most obvious in Hu Shi, who in his famous dissertation applied Liang's idea of an implicit logical or methodological 'system' to the entire bulk of ancient Chinese philosophical literature. Only Wang Guowei failed to find any devoted followers, perhaps because his rigid assessment sounded already like a last word on a discourse that was just about to come into existence.

---

[85] Cf. Lin Xiashui 林夏水 and Zhang Shangshui 張尚水. 1983. "Shuli luoji zai Zhongguo" 數理邏輯在中國 (Mathematical logic in China), *Ziran kexueshi yanjiu* 2.2, pp. 175–82.

REFERENCES

1900–1949 nian quanguo zhuyao baokan zhexue lunwen ziliao suoyin 1900–1949 年全國主要報刊論文資料索引 (Index of articles on philosophy in major Chinese periodicals, 1900–1949). 1989. Edited by Fudan daxue zhexuexi ziliaoshi 复旦大學哲學系資料室 and Sichuan daxue zhexuexi ziliaoshi 四川大學哲學系資料室. Beijing: Shangwu yinshuguan.

Aleni, Giulio (Ai Rulüe 艾儒略). 1623a. *Xixue fan* 西學凡 (General outline of Western knowledge). Hangzhou. Reprinted in: *Tianxue chuhan* 1965, vol. 1, pp. 1–60.

——. 1623b. *Zhifang waiji* 職方外記 (Record of the places outside the jurisdiction of the Office of Geography). Hangzhou. Reprinted in: *Tianxue chuhan* 1965, vol. 3, pp. 1269–1496.

Bacon, Francis (Beigeng 貝庚). 1888. *Gezhi xinji* 格致新機 (New tools for science). Translated by William Muirhead (Mu Weilian 慕維廉) and Shen Yugui 沈毓桂. Beijing: Tongwen shuhui and Shanghai: Gezhi shushi.

Bao Zunxin 包遵信. 1986. "'Mobian' de chenlun he 'Mingli tan' de fanyi" 《墨辯》的沉淪和《名理探》的翻譯 (The decline of the *Mobian* and the translation of the *Mingli tan*), *Dushu* 1, pp. 63–71.

Bernal, Martin. 1976. "Liu Shih-p'ei and National Essence", in: Charlotte Furth (ed.). *The Limits of Change. Essays on Conservative Alternatives in Republican China*. Cambridge, Mass.: Harvard University Press, pp. 90–112.

Cao Jiesheng 曹杰生. 1982. "Lüelun *Mingli tan* de fanyi ji qi yingxiang" 略論《名利探》的翻譯及其影響 (A brief discussion of the translation and influence of the *Mingli tan*), in: *Zhongguo luojishi yanjiu* 中國邏輯史研究 (Studies in the history of Chinese logic). Beijing: Zhongguo shehui kexue chubanshe, pp. 285–302.

Chang, Hao. 1987. *Chinese Intellectuals in Crisis. Search for Order and Meaning, 1890–1911*. Berkeley: University of California Press.

China in the 16th Century. The Journals of Matthew Ricci 1583–1610. 1953. Translated by Louis J. Gallagher. New York: Random House.

Dudink, Ad and Nicolas Standaert. 1999. "Ferdinand Verbiest's *Qionglixue* 窮理學 (1683)", in: Noël Golvers (ed.). *The Christian Mission in China in the Verbiest Era: Some Aspects of the Missionary Approach*. Leuven: Leuven University Press, pp. 11–31.

Edkins, Joseph (Ai Yuese 艾約瑟). 1875. "Yalisiduodeli zhuan" 亞里斯多得里傳 (Biography of Aristotle), *Zhong-Xi wenjian lu* 32, pp. 7a–13b.

—— (ed.). 1886. *Gezhi qimeng* 格致啟蒙 (Science primers). 16 vols. Beijing: Zong shuiwusi.

——. See also: Jevons 1886.

Engelfriet, Peter M. 1998. *Euclid in China. The Genesis of the First Translation of Euclid's* Elements Book I–VI (Jihe yuanben. *Beijing, 1607) and its Reception up to 1723*. Leiden: Brill.

Fonti Ricciane. Documenti originale concernenti Matteo Ricci e la storia delle prime relazioni tra l'Europa e la Cina (1579–1615). 1942–1949. 3 vols. Edited by Pasquale D'Elia. Rome: Libreria dello stato.

Forke, Alfred. 1902. "The Chinese Sophists", *Journal of the China Branch of the Royal Asiatic Society* 34, pp. 1–100.

Frankenhauser, Uwe. 1996a. "Logik und nationales Selbstverständnis in China zu Beginn des 20. Jahrhunderts", in: Christiane Hammer and Bernhard Führer (eds.). *Chinesisches Selbstverständnis und kulturelle Identität: 'Wenhua Zhong-guo'*. Dortmund: Projekt, pp. 69–80.

——. 1996b. *Die Einführung der buddhistischen Logik nach China*. Wiesbaden: Harrassowitz.

Fukazawa Sukeo 深沢助雄. 1986. "'Meiri tan' no yakugyō ni tsuite" 「名理探」の訳業について (On the translation of the *Mingli tan*), *Chūgoku—Shakai to bunka* 1, pp. 20–38.

Funayama Shin'ichi 船山信一. *Meiji ronrigakushi kenkyū* 明治論理学史研究 (Studies in the history of logic during the Meiji period). Tokyo: Risōsha.

Furtado, Francisco (Fu Fanji 傅汎際) and Li Zhizao 李之藻. 1965 [1631–1639]. *Mingli tan* 名理探 (*De Logica*). Hangzhou. Reprinted in 2 vols. Taibei: Taiwan Shangwu yinshuguan.

Gabelentz, Georg von der. 1888. "Über den chinesischen Philosophen Mek Tik", *Berichte über die Verhandlungen der Königlich Sächsischen Gesellschaft der Wissenschaften zu Leipzig. Philologisch-Historische Klasse* 40, pp. 62–70.

Graham, Angus C. 1978. *Later Mohist Logic, Ethics and Science*. Hong Kong et al.: The Chinese University Press.

Guo Zhanbo 郭湛波. 1932. *Zhongguo bianxueshi* 中國辯學史 (A history of Chinese logic). Shanghai: Zhonghua shuju.

Harbsmeier, Christoph. 1998. *Language and Logic in Traditional China*, in: Joseph Needham (ed.). *Science and Civilisation in China. Vol. VII, Pt. 1*. Cambridge: Cambridge University Press.

Hu Shih (Hu Shi 胡適). 1919. *Zhongguo zhexueshi dagang* 中國哲學史大綱 (Outline history of Chinese philosophy). Shanghai: Shangwu yinshuguan.

——. 1922. *The Development of the Logical Method in Ancient China* (Ph.D. diss., Columbia University 1917). Shanghai: Yadong tushuguan.

Jevons, William Stanley. 1876. *Logic* (*Science Primers*). London: Macmillan.

—— (Zhefensi 哲分斯). 1886. *Bianxue qimeng* 辨學啟蒙 (Logic primer). Translated by Joseph Edkins, in: Joseph Edkins (ed.). *Gezhi qimeng* 格致啟蒙 (Science primers). 16 vols. Beijing: Zong shuiwusi.

——. See also: Yan Fu 1981 [1909].

"Jingshi daxuetang yishuju zhangcheng" 京師大學堂譯書局章程 (Statutes for the Translation Office at the Imperial University). 1903. Reprinted in: Li Nanqiu 黎難秋 (ed.). 1996. *Zhongguo kexue fanyi shiliao* 中國科學翻譯史料 (Materials for a history of scientific translation in China). Hefei: Zhongguo kexue jishu daxue chubanshe, pp. 493–7.

Knoblock, John. 1994. *Xunzi. A Translation and Study of the Complete Works*. 3 vols. Stanford: Stanford University Press.

Kogelschatz, Hermann. 1986. *Wang Kuo-wei und Schopenhauer. Eine philosophische Begegnung. Wandlung des Selbstverständnisses der chinesischen Literatur unter dem Einfluß der klassischen deutschen Ästhetik*. Stuttgart: Franz Steiner.

Kurtz, Joachim. 2001. "Coming to Terms with Logic. The Naturalization of an Occidental Notion in China", in: Michael Lackner, Iwo Amelung and Joachim Kurtz (eds.). *New Terms for New Ideas. Western Knowledge and Lexical Change in Late Imperial China*. Leiden et al.: Brill, pp. 147–76.

——. 2002. "Translating the Science of Sciences. European and Japanese Models in the Formation of Modern Chinese Logical Terminology, 1886–1912", in: James C. Baxter and Joshua A. Fogel (eds.). *Historiography and Japanese Consciousness of Values and Norms*. Kyoto: International Research Institute for Japanese Studies, pp. 53–76.

Kuwaki Gen'yoku 桑木厳翼 . 1898. "Junshi no ronri setsu" 荀子の論理説 (Xunzi's theory of logic), *Waseda gakuhō* 14. Reprinted in: id. 1900. *Tetsugaku gairon* 哲学概論 (Outline of philosophy). Tokyo: Hakubunsha, pp. 449–63.

——. 1904. "Xunzi zhi lunli xueshuo" 荀子之論理學説 (Xunzi's logical theory). Translated by Wang Guowei 王國維 , *Jiaoyu shijie* 74.

Lackner, Michael, Iwo Amelung and Joachim Kurtz. 2001. *WSC-Databases: An Electronic Repository of Chinese Scientific, Philosophical and Political Terms Coined in the Nineteenth and Early Twentieth Century.* Retrieved from http://www.wsc.uni-erlangen.de/wscdb.htm.

Levenson, Joseph R. 1953. *Liang Ch'i-ch'ao and the Mind of Modern China.* Cambridge, Mass.: Harvard University Press.

Li Jinxi 黎錦熙 . 1936. "Xu" 序 (Preface). Reprinted in: Liu Shipei 1997. *Liu Shipei quanji*, vol. 1, p. 26.

Li Kuangwu 李匡武 (ed.). 1989. *Zhongguo luojishi* 中國邏輯史 (A history of Chinese logic). 5 vols. Lanzhou: Gansu renmin chubanshe, vol. 4, pp. 126–80.

Li Zhizao 李之藻 , see Furtado 1965 and *Tianxue chuhan* 1965.

Liang Qichao 梁啟超 . 1896. *Xixue shumu biao* 西學書目表 (Bibliography of Western knowledge). Shanghai: Shenshiji zhai.

——. 1902a. "Jinshi wenming chuzu er da jia zhi xueshuo" 今世文明初祖二大家之學説 (The theories of two great precursors of modern civilization). Reprinted in: id. 1990a. *Yinbingshi wenji*, 13.1–12.

——. 1902b. "Lun Zhongguo xueshu sixiang bianqian zhi dashi" 論中國學術思想變遷之大勢 (General tendencies in the development of Chinese thought). Reprinted in: id. 1990a. *Yinbingshi wenji*, 7.1–104.

——. 1904. "Mozi zhi lunlixue" 墨子之論理學 (Mozi's logic). Reprinted in: id. 1990b. *Yinbingshi zhuanji*, 37.55–72.

——. 1990a [1936]. *Yinbingshi wenji* 飲冰室文集 (Collected works from the Ice Drinker's-Studio). Edited by Lin Zhijun 林志鈞 . Beijing: Zhonghua shuju.

——. 1990b [1936]. *Yinbingshi zhuanji* 飲冰室專集 (Collected monographs from the Ice Drinker's-Studio). Edited by Lin Zhijun 林志鈞 . Beijing: Zhonghua shuju.

Lin Xiashui 林夏水 and Zhang Shangshui 張尚水 . 1983. "Shuli luoji zai Zhongguo" 數理邏輯在中國 (Mathematical logic in China), *Ziran kexueshi yanjiu* 2.2, pp. 175–82.

Liu Guanghan 劉光漢 [Liu Shipei 劉師培]. 1903a. *Zhongguo minyue jingyi* 中國民約精義 (The refined meaning of the Chinese social contract). Reprinted in: Liu Shipei. 1997. *Liu Shipei quanji*, vol. 1, pp. 560–97.

——. 1903b. *Rangshu* 攘書 (Book of expulsion). Reprinted in: Liu Shipei 1997. *Liu Shipei quanji*, vol. 2, pp. 1–17.

——. 1905a. "Xiaoxue fawei bu" 小學發微補 (Additions to the essentials of philology). Reprinted in: Liu Shipei. 1997. *Liu Shipei quanji*, vol. 1, pp. 422–42.

——. 1905b. "Guoxue fawei" 國學發微 (Essentials of national studies). Reprinted in: Liu Shipei. 1997. *Liu Shipei quanji*, vol. 1, pp. 474–99.

——. 1905c. "Zhoumo xueshu shi xu" 周末學術史序 (Prefaces to an intellectual history of the late Zhou). Reprinted in: Liu Shipei. 1997. *Liu Shipei quanji*, vol. 1, pp. 500–25.

——. 1907. "Xunzi mingxue fawei" 荀子名學發微 (Essentials of Xunzi's logic). Reprinted in: Liu Shipei 1997. *Liu Shipei quanji*, vol. 3, pp. 316–8.

Liu Shipei 劉師培 . 1997. *Liu Shipei quanji* 劉師培全集 (The complete works of Liu Shipei). 4 vols. Beijing: Zhonggong zhongyang dangxiao chubanshe.

Liu Xuan 劉烜 . 1996. *Wang Guowei pingzhuan* 王國維評傳 (Critical biography of Wang Guowei). Nanchang: Baihuazhou wenyi chubanshe.

Luk, Bernard Hung-Kay. 1997. "Aleni Introduces the Western Academic Tradition to Seventeenth Century China. A Study of the *Xixue Fan*", in: Tiziana Lippiello and Roman Malek (eds.). *Scholar from the West. Giulio Aleni S.J. (1582–1649) and the Dialogue between Christianity and China*. Nettetal: Steyler, pp. 479–518.

Luo Jianqiu 羅檢秋. 1997. *Jindai zhuzixue yu wenhua sichao* 近代諸子學與文化思潮 (Studies of non-canonical philosophers and trends of cultural thought in modern China). Beijing: Zhongguo shehui kexue chubanshe.

Melis, Giorgio. 1984. "Temi e tesi della filosofia europea nel 'Tianzhu Shiyi' di Matteo Ricci", in: *Atti del convegno internazionale di studi Ricciani*. Macerata: Centro studi Ricciani, pp. 65–92.

Mill, John Stuart. 1843. *A System of Logic. Inductive and Ratiocinative*. London: Parker.

Muirhead, William (Mu Weilian 慕維廉). 1876. "Gezhi xinli" 格致新理 (New principles of science), *Yizhi xinlu* 益知新錄 (*Miscellany of Useful Knowledge*), 1.1-1.5 (1876.7-1876.11).

——. 1877. "Gezhi xinfa" 格致新法 (New methods of science), *Gezhi huibian* 格致匯編 (*The Chinese Scientific Magazine*), 2.2 (1877.3); 2.3 (1877.4); 2.7 (1877.8); 2.8 (1877.9); and 2.9 (1877.10).

——. 1878. "Gezhi xinfa" 格致新法 (New methods of science), *Wanguo gongbao* 萬國公報 (*The Globe Magazine*), 1.506-1.513 (1878.9-1878.11).

——. See also: Bacon 1888.

Peng Yilian 彭漪漣. 1991. *Zhongguo jindai luoji sixiang shilun* 中國近代邏輯思想史論 (Essays in the history of logical thought in Modern China). Shanghai: Shanghai renmin chubanshe.

Quan Hansheng 全漢昇. 1935. "Qingmo de Xixue yuanchu Zhongguo shuo" 清末的西學源出中國說 (The late-Qing theory of the Chinese origin of Western science), *Lingnan xuebao* 4.2, pp. 57–102.

Ricci, Matteo, S. J. 1985 [1601]. *The True Meaning of the Lord of Heaven (T'ien-chu Shih-i)*. Translated by Douglas Lancashire and Peter Hu Kuo-chen S.J. St. Louis: The Institute of Jesuit Sources.

Rodi, Frithjof. 1988. "Historical Philosophy in Search of Frames of Articulation", in: Peter H. Hare (ed.). *Doing Philosophy Historically*. Buffalo, N.Y.: Prometheus Books, pp. 329–40.

Ruggieri, Michele (Luo Mingjian 羅明堅). 1584. *Tianzhu shengjiao shilu* 天主聖教實錄 (A true account of the Lord of Heaven and the Holy Doctrine). Beijing.

Sakade Yoshinobu 坂出祥伸. 1968. "Meiji tetsugaku ni okeru Chūgoku kodai ronrigaku no rikai" 明治哲学に於ける中国古代論理学の理解 (Views of ancient Chinese logic in Meiji philosophy), in: Funayama 1968, pp. 242–68.

Schwartz, Benjamin. 1964. *In Search of Wealth and Power. Yen Fu and the West*. Cambridge, Mass.: Harvard University Press.

Shimada Kenji. 1990. *Pioneer of the Chinese Revolution. Zhang Binglin and Confucianism*. Translated by Joshua A. Fogel. Stanford: Stanford University Press.

Sun, Cecile Chu-chin. 1998. "Wang Guowei as Translator of Values", in: David Pollard (ed.). *Creation and Translation. Readings of Western Literature in Early Modern China, 1840–1918*. Amsterdam, Philadelphia: John Benjamins, pp. 253–82.

Sun Yirang 孫詒讓. 1897. "Yu Liang Zhuoru lun Mozi shu" 與梁卓如論墨子書 (A letter to Liang Qichao discussing the *Mozi*). Reprinted in: id. 1963. *Sun Zhouqing xiansheng ji* 孫籀廎先生集 (The works of Mr. Sun Yirang). 15 vols. Taibei: Wenyi chubanshe, vol. 2, pp. 581–585.

Sun Zhongyuan 孫中原. 1992. "Lun Yan Fu de luoji chengjiu" 論嚴復的邏輯成就 (Yan Fu's logical achievements), *Wenshizhe* 3, pp. 80–5.

Takada Atsushi 高田淳. 1967. "Chūgoku kindai no 'ronri' kenkyū" 中国近代の「論理」研究 (Studies in 'logic' in modern China), *Kōza Tōyō shisō* 講座東洋思想 4, Series 2: *Chūgoku shisō* 中国思想 3, pp. 215–27.

Tianxue chuhan 天學初函 (First collection of heavenly studies).1965 [1628]. Edited by Li Zhizao 李之藻. 6 vols. Taibei: Taiwan xuesheng shuju.

Verhaeren, H. 1935. "Aristote en Chine", *Bulletin Catholique de Pékin* 264 (Août 1935), pp. 417–29.

Wang Dianji 王奠基. 1961. *Zhongguo luoji sixiangshi fenxi* 中國邏輯思想史分析 (Analysis of the history of logical thought in China). Beijing: Zhonghua shuju.

——. 1979. *Zhongguo luoji sixiangshi* 中國邏輯思想史 (A history of logical thought in China). Shanghai: Shanghai renmin chubanshe.

Wang Fansen 王汎森. 1985. *Zhang Taiyan de sixiang. Jianlun qi dui ruxue chuantong de chongji* 章太炎的思想—兼論其對儒學傳統的衝擊 (Zhang Taiyan's thought. With a discussion of his attacks against the Confucian tradition). Taibei: Shibao wenhua chuban gongsi.

Wang Guowei 王國維. 1905*a*. "Lun xin xueyu zhi shuru" 論新學語之輸入 (On the importation of new scholarly terms). *Jiaoyu shijie* 96. Reprinted in: *Wang Guowei wenji*, vol. 3, pp. 40–3.

——. 1905*b*. "Zhou-Qin zhuzi zhi mingxue" 周秦諸子之名學 (The logic of the non-canonical philosophers of the Zhou and Qin periods). *Jiaoyu shijie* 98, 100. Reprinted in: *Wang Guowei wenji*, vol. 3, pp. 219–27.

——. 1906. "Mozi zhi xueshuo" 墨子之學說 (Mozi's theories), *Jiaoyu shijie* 121. Reprinted in: *Wang Guowei wenji*, vol. 3, pp. 159–74.

——. 1925. "Zuijin ersanshi nian zhong Zhongguo xin faxian zhi xuewen" 最近二三十年中中國新發現之學問 (Studies of new discoveries in China during the past twenty or thirty years), *Qinghua zhoukan* 350. Reprinted in: *Wang Guowei wenji*, vol. 4, pp. 33–8.

——. 1997. *Wang Guowei wenji* 王國維文集 (The works of Wang Guowei). Edited by Yao Ganming 姚淦銘 and Wang Yan 王燕. 4 vols. Beijing: Zhongguo wenshi chubanshe.

Wang Quchang 王蘧常. 1936. *Yan Jidao nianpu* 嚴幾道年譜 (Annalistic biography of Yan Fu). Shanghai: Shangwu yinshuguan.

Wang Renjun 王仁俊. 1993 [1896]. *Gezhi guwei* 格致古微 (Ancient subleties on science). Reprinted in: *Zhongguo kexue jishu dianji tonghui* 中國科學技術典籍通彙 (Anthology of classical works of Chinese science and technology). Edited by Ren Jiyu 任繼愈. vol. 1, pt. 7. Zhengzhou: Henan jiaoyu chubanshe.

Wang Xiaoling. 1998. "Liu Shipei et son *contrat social chinois*", *Études chinoises* 17.1–2, pp. 155–90.

Wang Yunwu 王云五. 1973. *Shangwu yinshuguan yu xin jiaoyu nianpu* 商務印書館與新教育年譜 (A chronicle of the Commercial Press and educational reform). Taibei: Taiwan Shangwu yinshuguan.

Wardy, Robert. 2000. *Aristotle in China. Language, Categories, and Translation.* Cambridge: Cambridge University Press.

Wen Gongyi 溫公頤 and Cui Qingtian 崔清田 (eds.). 2001. *Zhongguo luoji sixiangshi jiaocheng (Xiudingben)* 中國邏輯思想史教程（修訂本）(A course in the history of logical thought in China. Revised edition). Tianjin: Nankai daxue chubanshe.

Wu Guangxing 吳光興. 1995. "Liu Shipei dui Zhongguo xueshushi de yanjiu" 劉師培對中國學術史的研究 (Liu Shipei's researches in Chinese intellectual history), *Xueren* 7, pp. 163–86.

Yan Fu 嚴復. 1897. "Yi 'Tianyan lun' zixu" 譯天演論自序 (Translator's preface to the *Tianyan lun*). Reprinted in: id. 1986. *Yan Fu ji*, pp. 1319–21.

——. 1898. "Xixue menjing gongyong" 西學門徑功用 (Means and applications of Western knowledge). Reprinted in: id. 1986. *Yan Fu ji*, pp. 92–5.

——. 1931 [1905]. *Mule mingxue* 穆勒名學 (Mill's *Logic*). 3 vols. Shanghai: Shangwu yinshuguan.

——. 1981 [1909]. *Mingxue qianshuo* 名學淺説 (Logic primer). Beijing: Shangwu yinshuguan.

——. 1986. *Yan Fu ji* 嚴復集 (The works of Yan Fu). Edited by Wang Shi 王 栻. 5 vols. Beijing: Zhonghua shuju.

Yang Peisun 楊沛蓀 (ed.). 1988. *Zhongguo luoji sixiangshi jiaocheng* 中國邏輯思想史教程 (A course in the history of logical thought in China). Lanzhou: Gansu renmin chubanshe.

Yao Nanqiang 姚南強. 2000. *Yinming xueshuoshi gangyao* 因明學説史綱要 (Outline history of *yinming* theories). Shanghai: Sanlian shudian.

Yu Yu 虞愚. 1937. *Zhongguo mingxue* 中國名學 (Chinese logic). Nanjing: Zheng-zhong shuju.

Zeng Xiangyun 曾祥云. 1992. *Zhongguo jindai bijiao luoji sixiang yanjiu* 中國近代比較邏輯思想研究 (Studies in comparative logical thought in modern China). Harbin: Heilongjiang jiaoyu chubanshe.

Zhang Binglin 章炳麟. 1906. "Zhuzixue lüeshuo" 諸子學略説 (Brief account of studies of non-canonical philosophers). Reprinted in: *Zhongguo xiandai xueshu jingdian. Zhang Taiyan juan* 1996, pp. 479–97.

——. 1909. "Yuan Ming" 原名 (On [the School of] Names). Reprinted in: *Zhongguo xiandai xueshu jingdian. Zhang Taiyan juan* 1996, pp. 111–8.

Zhang Shizhao 章士釗. 1943. *Luoji zhiyao* 邏輯指要 (Essentials of logic). Chong-qing: Shidai jingshenshe.

Zhang Zhijian 張志建 and Dong Zhitie 董志鐵. 1982. "Shilun Yan Fu dui Woguo luojixue yanjiu de gongxian" 試論嚴復對我國邏輯學研究的貢獻 (A tentative account of Yan Fu's contribution to Chinese research on logic), in: *Zhongguo luojishi yanjiu* 中國邏輯史研究 (Studies in the history of Chinese logic). Bei-jing: Zhongguo shehui kexue chubanshe, pp. 303–20.

Zhao Zongkuan 趙總寬 (ed.). 1999. *Luojixue bainian* 邏輯學百年 (A century of stud-ies in logic). Beijing: Beijing chubanshe.

Zheng Shiqu 鄭師渠. 1997. *Wan Qing guocuipai: wenhua sixiang yanjiu* 晚清國粹派—文化思想研究 (The National Essence Group in the Late Qing: Studies in cul-tural thought). Beijing: Beijing Shifan daxue chubanshe.

Zhongguo xiandai xueshu jingdian. Zhang Taiyan juan 中國現代學術經典 — 章太炎卷 (Modern Chinese classics: Zhang Taiyan). 1996. Edited by Liu Mengxi 劉夢溪. Shijiazhuang: Hebei jiaoyu chubanshe.

Zhou Wenying. 1979. *Zhongguo luoji sixiang shigao* 中國邏輯思想史搞 (A draft his-tory of logical thought in China). Beijing: Renmin chubanshe.

Zhou Yunzhi 周云之 et al. (eds.). 1991. *Zhongguo luojishi ziliao xuan* 中國邏輯史資料選 (Selected materials on the history of Chinese logic). 6 vols. Lanzhou: Gansu renmin chubanshe.

Zhu Zhixin 朱執信. 1905. "Jiu lunlixue bo Xinmin congbao lun geming zhi miu" 就論理學駁新民叢報論革命之謬 (Applying logic to refute the errors in a discus-sion of revolution in the *Xinmin congbao*), *Minbao* 6, pp. 65–78.

Zou Zhenhuan 鄒振環. 2000. *Yilin jiuzong* 譯林舊蹤 (Old tracks in the forest of trans-lation). Nanchang: Jiangxi jiaoyu chubanshe.

RUNE SVARVERUD

THE FORMATION OF A CHINESE LEXICON OF INTERNATIONAL LAW 1847–1903

INTRODUCTION

The Chinese literary language (*wenyanwen* 文言文) had for all practical purposes been firmly established through the extensive Chinese literary corpus from pre-Qin to late Qing times, and served as literary medium for the Chinese administration, for political and philosophical prose, for certain modes of fiction as well as for poetry throughout the imperial period. The grammar of this standard was poorly described in terms of modern linguistic scholarship, yet the principles for literary composition and interpretation of the Chinese literary heritage were well defined through the literary corpus and its commentaries. The lexicon of this standard is recorded in a long lexicographic tradition with its origins in Han times. When this traditional literary medium was subjected to new impulses, new notions, or frameworks and sets of new knowledge, it gradually subsumed these conceptual innovations into its lexical structure; this was the case for instance when Buddhism, and the Western knowledge brought by the Jesuits, were introduced into the framework of traditional Chinese culture.

The standardization of the Chinese language as a part of political surge in nationalism which was effected during just the first decades of the Republic, is often referred to as one of the cultural effects of the primarily political May Fourth Movement; however, while many of the innovations and 'modernizations' in terms of its lexicon had in fact already been integrated into the literary language of imperial China before the political and nationalistic movements of the 1910s and 1920s. Lexical innovations and loans are in most cases integrated into a language by its users rather that by its political elite. The standardization of a language and the import of new lexical elements is not primarily a process of political negotiation but a question of social acceptance by its users,—to what extent these new forms and constituents are incorporated into the language by its users.

This is also the case for the introduction of new lexicons of technical terms for the new branches of Western learning in late imperial

China. Many new spheres of knowledge were introduced into China in the decades following the Opium War, in most cases by Western missionaries, in cooperation with Chinese scholars, translating texts from European languages into Chinese. Through these translations new sets of technical terms were established, either as foreign loans in one form or another, or as neologisms coined specifically for the purpose. Whenever the new knowledge introduced by these sets of new terms was of acute significance in the immediate technological, social or political process these sets of terms quickly settled as elements of the linguistic orthodoxy. When this knowledge and its relevant terminology remained distant from the immediate current sociopolitical processes in China, however, we may see a long process of standardization and integration, occasionally also with competing schools of translation and terminology, before the social process allowed for a general absorption of this new reality into its orthodoxy.

In the case of China between the Opium War and the establishment of the Republic, the general tendency is that the lexicons of technical innovations and the natural sciences imported from the West were quickly absorbed and accepted into the standard language, while the social sciences and their relevant vocabularies went through a much longer and more elaborate process of negotiation before they were integrated into the standard *wenyanwen* vocabulary of late imperial China. The intention of this article is to discuss the process and the historical context for the earliest branch of the social sciences to be introduced into China, namely international law, as a Western political philosophy and as a scheme of conduct in international relations and intercourse. I wish to show that contending traditions of translating the principles and major works of Western international law into Chinese failed to gain general recognition of their technical terminology and their language of translation for a long period of time. In fact, none of the Chinese encounters with the Western 'barbarians', the 'unequal treaties', the tariff-system or extraterritorial rights occasioned the Chinese to fully integrate the theories of international law and its vocabulary into their standard language. Only after the humiliating experiences with their Eastern neighbour Japan in 1894–95 did Western international law appear as a useful and even indispensable tool in China's international relations in the eyes of official China. I shall argue that the establishment of a new lexicon within a new branch of learning in a language may be a task undertaken by a group of people, scientists, missionaries or politicians, guided by scientific, political or religious motivations, while the integration of that same lexicon into the recognized literary standard language is a result of a historical and social process mainly directed by external factors independent from political and intentional processes. In the case of international law, these factors were only to a limited extent the primarily economic consequences of the Western encroachment on China, and to a much larger extent the results of a growing national crisis of identity after the humiliating Chinese encounters with the modern Japanese military machine in 1894–95.

The decline and eventual demise of the Chinese imperial political order between the first Opium War and the establishment of the Republic was indeed a slowly evolving Chinese national crisis of identity. Time-honored sets of beliefs and traditional social and political institutions were challenged by the 'barbarian' sociopolitical order forced on China. Traditional notions were discredited and a new national identity was negotiated, both internally and externally, in a reciprocal interchange of ideas with the West.

In terms of the domestic political order a national transformation of identity may be distinguished in the shift from authoritarianism to popular sovereignty, first formulated in attempts at establishing a constitutional monarchy and shortly after in a republican system, both as Western imports. In international relations the challenges posed to China by her new relationship with the Western treaty powers were expressed in her identity being transformed from a traditional, non-negotiable, self-contained and all-encompassing Chinese cultural identity to one where China was continuously negotiating her cultural 'self' in juxtaposition to the Western 'other'. By the end of the nineteenth century full Chinese sovereignty may have seemed to be the only viable hope for the afflicted Chinese cultural 'self'. Yet China negotiated full national sovereignty in her international relations relatively late after her first contacts with the West, compared for instance to Japan. The response to this external pressure was belated, presumably because the potential establishment of Chinese sovereignty eventually also forced China into embracing the entire conceptual and legal framework of international law, which, I shall argue, was not perceived as imperative to the Chinese nation before the Sino-Japanese War. In the following I shall attempt to show that the crisis of China's international identity was mainly brought into being by the

challenge from the East rather than from the West, and that the crisis
of national identity inflicted upon the Chinese nation by Japan as a
result of the Sino-Japanese War of 1894–95 was exceedingly more
disturbing in terms of national identity than extraterritorial rights,
"unequal treaties" and the opium trade had been in the period between
the Treaty of Nanjing in 1842 and the war in 1894–95.

Western international law was introduced during the same period
of time from the 1860s in both Japan and China without extensive linguistic contact between the two. We find, however, a close terminological correspondence between the modern Chinese and the Japanese
vocabulary on international law. The purpose of this article is also to
probe into the question of how and why a nearly 40-year old tradition
of translating international law texts and encountering international
legal questions in China was entirely 'Japanized' during a very short
time span in the early twentieth century, shortly after the Sino-Japanese War. Hence, why was the lexicon of international law in China,
after four decades of an indigenous tradition of translating international law texts, so unstable and open to foreign influence that even
most of its core vocabulary was susceptible to Japanese influence
around 1903?

International law was the first branch of the Western social sciences to be introduced into China in the second half of the nineteenth
century. We may readily apprehend how the latecomers among the
social sciences were open to influence from the Japanese Kanji-
vocabulary when these branches of the Western sciences were introduced for the first time into China via Japan, and hence how there
came to be a correspondence in vocabulary for 'society' (*shehui* 社
會), 'science' (*kexue* 科學), 'social science' (*shehui kexue* 社會科
學), 'sociology' (*shehuixue* 社會學) etc. in the Chinese and Japanese
languages of the twentieth century. But how is it that there is also a
correspondence between the twentieth century Japanese and Chinese
terms for 'international law' (*guojifa* 國際法), 'neutrality' (*zhongli* 中
立), 'independent state' (*duliguo* 獨立國), 'natural law' (*ziranfa* 自然
法) etc., when these terms had their Chinese indigenous translations
different from the Japanese prior to 1903?[1] These twentieth century
international law terms would have appeared contextually idiosyn-

---

[1] For general discussions of terminological influence from the West on late imperial China, see Lydia H. Liu. 1995. *Translingual Practice: Literature, National Culture, and Translated Modernity—China, 1900–1937*. Stanford: Stanford University

cratic in the language of late nineteenth century China. In the following I shall analyze some aspects of the history of the Chinese dissemination of international law prior to the Japanese influence, in order to apprehend its readiness to be Japanized within a few months in 1902–03.

1. TWO 'BARBARIAN' INTERNATIONAL LAW TRADITIONS IN CHINA

In the European context international law has its roots in the regulation of the relationship between the different regions of the Roman empire, often referred to as *Jus gentium*—or Law of Nations. When Europe during the Middle ages was divided into a number of independent states no longer under the political supremacy of the Vatican, alliances, wars, treaties and the balance of power in Europe came to constitute the foundation of the theoretical discipline of international law—or Law between Nations. The dawn of the theoretical discipline of international law is commonly ascribed to the authorship of Hugo Grotius (1583–1645) and his work *De Jure Belli ac Pacis* (On the Law of War and Peace), first published in 1625, and the commencement of the practice of the new European international order is attributed to the treaty between European nations after the Peace of Westphalia in 1648.

During imperialism and the European expansion, international law played an instrumental role in distinguishing between the uncivilized states of the non-European world and the Christian culture, with its rights and duties to civilize barbarian and semi-barbarian states. In the eyes of the European civilizers it was evidently unfavorable if the semi- or non-civilized states were to become fully civilized, that is, recognized as full members of the international family of nations with perfect international rights and duties as sovereign and independent states. For the trading Western nations the role of the civilizer was indeed a very convenient character to play, as they were invariably in a position to confer on their counterpart whatever rights and duties they found suitable. This was also the situation in China in the aftermath of the First Opium War. The British and later most of the trading

---

[1] (*cont.*) Press; Federico Masini. 1993. *The Formation of Modern Chinese Lexicon and Its Evolution Toward a National Language: The Period from 1840 to 1898.* Berkeley: Journal of Chinese Linguistics (Monograph Series, no. 6.)

nations of Europe present in China after the Opium War were mainly concerned that China would conform to the established treaties, and not primarily interested in civilizing China to integrate her into the international community of civilized states. The European nations were content with China adhering to her traditional world order of the Chinese empire in East-Asia. When China began to access writings on the theoretical aspects of international law it was therefore not sanctioned by the European nations present in China. It was, rather, a Chinese initiative with the assistance of a number of European individuals, and received not without a certain reservation from many contemporary Europeans in China.

The only attempt to interpret international law in a Chinese context before the Second Opium War and the Dagu crisis in 1858–60 is to be found in Lin Zexu 林則徐 (1785–1850) and Wei Yuan's 魏源 (1794–1857) anthology on overseas nations, the *Haiguo tuzhi* 海國圖志 (Maps and Documents on Maritime Countries), which was first published as a 50-volume text in 1842. In 1847 the text was enlarged into a 60-volume edition, where two different translations, one by the American medical missionary Peter Parker (1804–1888) and one by the Chinese interpreter Yuan Dehui 袁德輝 (b. ca. 1800), from three chapters of Emmerich de Vattel's (1714–1767) *Law of Nations* were included. As a result, a number of new terms and expressions were coined to convey the ideas of international law to its Chinese readership in 1847.[2] The translation does not seem, however, to have had any substantial influence on the systematic introduction of international law in China which commenced two decades later. It was only

---

[2] Cf. Rune Svarverud. 2000. "Jus Gentium Sinense: The Earliest Chinese Translation of International Law with some Considerations Regarding the Compilation of Haiguo tuzhi", *Acta Orientalia* 61, pp. 203–237. See also Hsi-t'ung Chang. 1950. "The Earliest Phase of the Introduction of Western Political Science into China", *Yenching Journal of Social Studies* 5, pp. 1–29; Immanuel Hsü. 1960. *China's Entrance into the Family of Nations: The Diplomatic Phase 1858–1880*. Cambridge, Mass.: Harvard University Press, pp. 121–5; Li Zhaojie. 1999. "How international law was introduced into China", in: *Guoji falü wenti yanjiu* 國際法律問題研究 (A study of international legal questions). Beijing: Zhongguo zhengfa daxue chubanshe, pp. 53–135; 82–96; Wang Weijian 王維儉. 1985. "Lin Zexu fanyi Xifang guojifa zhuzuo kaolüe" 林則徐翻譯西方國際法著作考略 (Some remarks on Lin Zexu's translation of a work on Western international law), *Zhongshan daxue xuebao* 1, pp. 58–67; Xiong Yuezhi 熊月之. 1996. "Haiguo tuzhi zhengyin xinshu kaoshi" 海國圖志徵引西書考釋 (A study of the western sources for the *Haiguo tuzhi*), in: *Zhonghua*

after the Second Opium War, the establishment of the Zongli Yamen 總理衙門 in 1861 and, on a larger scale, only after China established diplomatic relations with Europe from 1876, that the systematic introduction of the theoretical discipline of international law became a Chinese enterprise.

The American William A. P. Martin (Ding Weiliang 丁韙良, 1827–1916) arrived in China as a missionary in 1850. Martin's interest in diplomatic relations and the Chinese language inspired him to take up the translation of Vattel's entire text into Chinese. There are no indications that in this task Martin was in any way influenced by the earlier *Haiguo tuzhi* translations. Shortly afterwards, Martin was encouraged by John E. Ward (1814–1902), the US minister to China during the 1860 Dagu crisis, to set aside the Vattel project and start working on a translation of *Elements of International Law* by the American Henry Wheaton (1785–1848). Robert Hart (1835–1911), at that time chief assistant to the inspector-general of the Chinese Maritime Customs, had earlier translated 24 sections on the rights of legations in Wheaton's text for the Zongli Yamen. When the Yamen in the spring of 1863 approached the American minister in Beijing, Anson Burlingame (1820–1870), for advice regarding a suitable text on international law for translation, Burlingame also suggested Wheaton. The differences in national bias and interest between individual Western publicists and writers is an evident feature of nineteenth century international law publications. Hence, when it became clear that the officials of the Zongli Yamen were determined to introduce international law in Chinese, we may implicitly sense a national American motivation in promoting an American text on international law. It became known that Martin was already working on the translation of Wheaton in Shanghai. Martin's unfinished translation was consequently brought before Prince Gong (Gong qinwang Yi Xin 恭親王奕訢, 1833–1898), and the Zongli Yamen. Four officials were appointed to assist him in the translation and a sum of 500 taels was granted for printing and publication. Nevertheless, because of opposi-

---

2 *(cont.)* wenshi luncong 中華文史論叢 (Collection of essays on Chinese literature and history). Shanghai: Shanghai guji chubanshe, vol. 55, pp. 235–59; Zhang Jingcao. 1992. "How Western International Law Was Introduced into China and Its Influence upon China", in: Bernhard H. K. Luk (ed.). *Contacts Between Cultures. Vol. 4: Eastern Asia: History and Social Sciences*. Lewiston: Mellen, pp. 264–70.

tion within the Yamen itself, the manuscript was initially not sanctioned for publication.[3]

In spring 1864, because of Bismarck's war with Denmark in Europe, Prussia had captured three Danish ships off Dagu port outside Tianjin as prizes of war. Based on a reading of passages in the Chinese translation of Wheaton, Prince Gong maintained that Prussia had no right to capture Danish ships within Chinese maritime jurisdiction. The case was successfully resolved, Prince Gong won acceptance at the Yamen for the publication of Martin's translation, and the text entitled *Wanguo gongfa* 萬國公法 was published that same year.

Martin was offered a post as teacher of English at the newly established imperial translation bureau Tongwenguan 同文館 in Beijing in 1865. He became a paid employee of the Qing government and left his missionary work. In 1867 Martin became professor of international law and went back to America to study international law at the University of Indiana. Two years later when he returned to China he was appointed president of the Tongwenguan.[4]

During his time at the Tongwenguan Martin worked on a number of texts on international law and diplomacy. Two Chinese colleagues

---

[3] Cf. Hungdah Chiu. 1967. "The Development of Chinese International Law Terms and the Problem of Their Translation into English", *Journal of Asian Studies* 27, pp. 485–501; 486–91; Hsü 1960, pp. 125–38; E. R. Hughes. 1968. *The Invasion of China by the Western World.* London: Adam and Charles Black, pp. 104–9; Li Guilian 李貴連. 1998. "Ershi shiji chuqi de Zhongguo faxue" 二十世紀初期的中國法學 (Chinese law in the early twentieth century), in: id. (ed.) *Ershi shiji de Zhongguo faxue* 二十世紀的中國法學 (Chinese law in the twentieth century). Beijing: Beijing Daxue chubanshe, pp. 1–65; Lydia H. Liu. 1999. "Legislating the Universal: The Circulation of International Law in the Nineteenth Century", in: id. (ed.). *Tokens of Exchange: The Problem of Translation in Global Circulation.* Durham, London: Duke University Press, p. 127–64; Wang Lixin 王立新. 1997. *Meiguo chuanjiaoshi yu wan Qing Zhongguo xiandaihua* 美國傳教士與晚清中國現代化 (American missionaries and modernization in late imperial China). Tianjin: Tianjin renmin chubanshe, pp. 261–5; 271–6; 365–77; Xiong Yuezhi 熊月之. 1994. *Xixue dongjian yu wanqing shehui* 西學東漸與晚清社會 (The Eastern transmission of Western learning and the society of late imperial China). Shanghai: Shanghai renmin chubanshe, 301–33; Zhang Jingcai 1992, pp. 264–70; Zou Zhenhuan 鄒振環. 1996. *Yingxiang Zhongguo jindai shehui de yibai zhong yizuo* 影響中國近代社會的一百種譯作 (One-hundred translated works which have influenced modern Chinese society). Beijing: Zhongguo duiwai fanyi chuban gongsi, pp. 82–7.
[4] Cf. Jonathan Spence. 1969. *The China Helpers.* London: The Bodley Head; Wang Weijian 王維儉. 1987. "Dingzheng ruogan Zhong Wai cishu zhong 'Ding Weiliang' cimu sheji de shishi" 訂正若干中外詞書中'丁韙良'涉及的史實 (The rectification of some historical facts regarding W. A. P. Martin in Chinese and foreign encyclopaedia), *Zhongshan daxue xuebao* 2, pp. 68–76; 68–70.

in the French section of the Tongwenguan, Lian Fang 聯芳 (dates unknown) and Qing Chang 慶常 (b. 1899), translated a French guide on diplomacy by Charles de Martens (1790–1861) entitled *Guide diplomatique*. Martin supervised the translation and had it published with the title *Xingyao zhizhang* (星軺指掌) at the Tongwenguan in 1876; the text was frequently consulted by the new Chinese corps of diplomats sent on missions abroad from that same year. The second theoretical international law text to be translated into Chinese, by W. A. P. Martin, Wang Fengzao 汪鳳藻 and others, was *Introduction to the Study of International Law* by the American Theodore Dwight Woolsey (1801–1889). Martin had made acquaintance with Woolsey at Yale University during his studies in America and found his book suitable for teaching purposes at the College, Tongwenguan, in Beijing. The text was subsequently published under the title *Gongfa bianlan* (公法便覽) at the Tongwenguan in 1877. In terms of theoretical deliberations on international law, not taking into account Martens' French practical guide to diplomacy, there had so far been a manifest American national bias at the College. This inclination was partly rectified by the translation of the Swiss publicist Johann Caspar Bluntschli's (1808–1881) text *Das moderne Völkerrecht der civilisierten Staaten als Rechtbuch dargestellt* and its publication under the title *Gongfa huitong* (公法會通)[5] at the Tongwenguan in 1880. As there were no translators trained in translating German texts at the College, Bluntschli's book was translated from the French version by Lian Fang, Qing Chang and Martin himself at the French section of the Tongwenguan. A manual of the rules for warfare on land was issued and sanctioned by the Institute of International Law (Institut de Droit International) entitled *Les Lois de la Guerre sur Terre* and published in Brussels and Geneva in 1880. The French section of the Tongwenguan, supervised by Martin, also translated this short text and had it published at the Tongwenguan under the title *Ludi zhanli xinxuan* (陸地戰例新選) in 1883.

In the preface to the *Wanguo gongfa* in 1864 Martin promoted the Chinese notion that an origin of an international legal order was also to be found in China during the Zhou period, supporting the Chinese

---

[5] The working title of the translation was *Gongfa qianzhang* 公法千章 and it was referred to by this title in lists of scheduled publications prior to this publication in 1880.

assumption that the origins of Western learning in fact were to be
found in the East *(xixue dongyuan* 西學東源):

> International law in its present form, is the mature fruit of Christian
> civilization. It springs, however, spontaneously from the intercourse of
> nations; and a rudimentary code was even recognized by the states of
> Greece at an early date.
>
> About the same time, analogous rules were observed by the feudal
> kingdoms into which the Chinese empire was then divided. Acknowl-
> edging a nominal allegiance to the house of Chow, they were really
> independent, and the varying relations which they sustained to each
> other in the intercourse of peace and war through a succession of centu-
> ries, gave rise to numerous usages, a collection of which would be at
> once curious and instructive.[6]

Martin visited Europe in 1881 promoting these assumptions of an
indigenous Chinese international order akin to the European tradition.
His lecture at the Congress of Orientalists in Berlin on September 13
that year entitled "Traces of International Law in Ancient China" was
published in *Congrès des Orientalists* the subsequent year and in
International Review and *Chinese Recorder* in 1883. Because of the
great Chinese interest in these deliberations, Wang Fengzao translated
the text into Chinese and published it at the Tongwenguan in 1884
under the title *Zhongguo gushi gongfa lunlüe* (中國古世公法論略).[7]

The young Englishman John Fryer (1839–1928) was employed as
headmaster of an English College in Hong Kong in 1861 and worked
there for 2 years while simultaneously learning the Cantonese language. In 1863 he was offered a position teaching English at the
Tongwenguan in Beijing, where he stayed for only two years. He left
for Shanghai in 1865 and in 1868 took up a position as translator of
scientific books at the translation department of the Jiangnan Arsenal
(*Jiangnan zhizaoju fanyiguan* 江南製造局翻譯館), where he worked
until 1896. Fryer was exceptionally productive during his time at the
Arsenal. Between 1870 and 1880 he published at least 34 translations
on natural science and technological subjects. Between 1880 and
1896 he translated another 74 texts and also added texts on law and

---

[6] W. A. P. Martin (Ding Weiliang 丁韙良) (tr). 1864. *Wanguo gongfa* 萬國公法
(International law). Beijing: Chongshiguan, preface p. 1.

[7] Occasionally this text was also referred to by the titles *Gushi gongfa lunlüe* 古世
公法論略 or *Zhongguo gushi gongfa* 中國古世公法 .

political economy to his long list of publications.[8] Fryer translated two texts on international law during his time at the Arsenal, apparently working on both texts simultaneously. The first to be completed was the shorter of the two, a translation of Edmund Robertson's article on international law in *Encyclopedia Britannica*. The translation was performed in cooperation with Wang Zhensheng 汪振聲 (1883–1945) and published with the title *Gongfa zonglun* 公法總論[9] at the Arsenal some time between 1886 and 1894.[10] Supplying further material for sustaining a British counterweight to Martin's Tongwenguan translations, Fryer was simultaneously working on the translation of a monumental 4-volume work by Sir Robert Joseph Phillimore (1810–1885) entitled *Commentaries upon International Law*. The translation of the first 3 volumes on public international law was in part completed already in 1878[11] but was not published until 1894. The 1894 publication of these three volumes carries the title *Geguo jiaoshe gongfalun* （各國交涉公法論）and is the fruit of a cooperation between Fryer, Wang Zhensheng, Yu Shijue 俞世爵 and Qian Guoxiang 錢國祥. The fourth and last volume of Phillimore's work on private international law was printed as a separate publication at the Arsenal some time between 1898 and 1902.[12] It carries the title *Geguo jiaoshe bianfalun* 各國交涉便法論,[13] and is ascribed to the work of Fryer and Qian Guoxiang.

---

[8] Cf. Spence 1969, pp. 140–54; See also Adrian Arthur Bennett. 1967. *John Fryer: The Introduction of Western Science and Technology into Nineteenth-Century China*. Cambridge, Mass.: Harvard University Press; and Wang Yangzong 王揚宗. 2000. *Fulanya yu jindai Zhongguo de kexue qimeng* 傅蘭雅與近代中國的啟蒙 (Fryer and the enlightenment in Modern China). Beijing: Kexue chubanshe.

[9] Later it was also entitled *Wanguo gongfa zonglun* 萬國公法總論.

[10] The Jiangnan edition does not reveal its date of publication, which may only be deduced as from Fryer's own bibliographical listssome time between 1886 and 1894. Cf. Wang Yangzong王揚宗. 1995. "Jiangnan zhizaoju fanyi shumu xinkao" 江南製造局翻譯書目新考 (A new investigation of books translated at the Jiangnan Arsenal). *Zhongguo keji shiliao* 2, pp. 3–18, 6.

[11] Cf. Guo Songtao 郭嵩燾. 1984 [1891]. *Lundun yu Bali riji* 倫敦與巴黎日記 (London and Paris diary). Changsha: Yuelu shushe (*Zouxiang shijie congshu* 走向世界叢書. From East to West—Chinese Travellers before 1911), pp. 746–7. The preliminary title of the text as it was presented to Guo Songtao in London in 1878 was *Wanguo jiaoshe gongfalun* 萬國交涉公法論.

[12] Again, no date is given on the Jiangnan Arsenal edition and the date of publication may only be deduced from bibliographical lists. Cf. Wang Yangzong 1995, p. 6.

[13] Occasionally also referred to as *Jiaoshe bianfalun* 交涉便法論.

John Fryer left China to take up a chair as professor of Oriental Language and Literature at the University of California in 1896. Prior to that he had started working on the translation of a more practically-sized work on international law to be published in the Jiangnan Arsenal tradition in cooperation with Cheng Zhanluo 程瞻洛. The Dutch ambassador to China between 1872 and 1894, Jan Helenus Ferguson (1881–1923), wrote extensively on international questions, including questions pertaining to Chinese international relations. In 1884 his major general work entitled *Manual of International Law: For the Use of Navies, Colonies and Consulates* was published in The Hague and London and found suitable for Fryer's purpose. The translation had not been completed for publication in 1896 when Fryer left China. Cheng continued working on the text with the assistance of Le Zhirang 樂志讓, and the translation entitled *Bangjiao gongfa xinlun* 邦交公法新論 appeared as a publication at the Chinese Scientific Book Depot (*Gezhi shushi* 格致書室) in Shanghai in 1901.

William A. P. Martin did not translate any international law texts during the latter half of the 1880s and the 1890s. Only in 1903 did his last translation of an international law text appear, this time *A Treatise on International Law* by the Englishman William Edward Hall (1836–1894). When Martin was appointed president of the Imperial University (*Jingshi daxuetang* 京師大學堂) in 1898 he started working on the translation of Hall's work with the assistance of Qi Ce'ao 綦策鰲, but their work was interrupted by the Boxer rebellion. Martin managed to save the manuscript from the rebels and completed the translation, entitled *Gongfa xinbian* 公法新編, in late 1902. The Chinese translation was published with prefaces by both Li Hongzhang 李鴻章 (1823–1901) and Duan Fang 端方 (1861–1911) by the Society for the Diffusion of Christian and General Knowledge among the Chinese (*Guangxuehui* 廣學會) in 1903. Martin and Qi Ce'ao were also responsible for a collection of lectures on the history of international relations in the West, published by the Guangxuehui in 1904. These lectures had been given by Martin to Zhang Zhidong's 張之洞 (1833–1909) officials at the Hubei Mandarin Institute (*Hubei Shixueyuan* 湖北仕學院) between 1902 and 1904. The title of the book, *Outlines of History with Special Reference to International Law* or *Bangjiao tiyao* 邦交提要, indicates that this is in fact a book introducing Western history rather than international law.

Young J. Allen (Lin Lezhi 林樂知, 1836–1907) had been appointed teacher of English at the *Guangfangyanguan* 廣方言館 in Shanghai in 1864, and transferred with that institution to the Jiangnan Arsenal in 1870. From 1871 Allen was serving in both these two institutions teaching and translating books. During his period in service as translator at the Arsenal from 1871 to 1881 he translated 8 works on 'diplomatic relations' (*jiaoshe* 交涉) and Western 'national histories' (*guozhi* 國志).[14] During the last 20 years of his life in the service of the Society for the Diffusion of Christian and General Knowledge among the Chinese, from 1887 until his death in 1907, he worked on a number of books on international relations and education, and translated one book on international law. In cooperation with Cai Erkang 蔡爾康 (1852–1920) he took up the translation of Thomas Joseph Lawrence's (1849–1919) *A Handbook of Public International Law,* and published it at the Society for the Diffusion of Christian and General Knowledge among the Chinese in Shanghai in 1903 with the title *Wanguo gongfa yaolüe* 萬國公法要略 . Martin's translations were their main source of vocabulary, but a certain Japanese influence may already be discerned in their language and lexicon of international law.

National interests were of salient importance for the two major contending traditions of translating international law texts from Western languages into Chinese between the first publication in 1847 and Martin's last publication on international law in Shanghai in 1903. These two traditions thrived under the personal fervor of two 'barbarians' in China, together with the enthusiastic support of a group of able and reform-minded Chinese scholars and students, within the relatively liberal and West-receptive political framework of post-Second Opium War China. Nationally, on both the Western and the Chinese sides, there was no official sanction or support for the translation and introduction of international law as such in China. Translators and their institutions, however, found support for continuing their work within the circle of Chinese reformers and enlightened gentry-officials. Until the middle of the 1890s hardly any Chinese debate on international law grew out of these translations and the theoretical deliberations on international rights and duties now made available to the Chinese

---

[14] Cf. Xiong Yuezhi. 1994, pp. 614–37.

intellectuals. Members of the Chinese literati did question China's acceptance of exterritorial rights conferred upon the foreign nations; these Chinese objections were, however, raised even without a technical term for 'exterritorial rights' in the current Chinese language. Yet, European legal philosophy and practice were available to the concerned readership in these two different traditions of translations. It is therefore significant that indigenous theoretical writings, translations and debates on Chinese sovereignty and China's international position only surfaced after the Sino-Japanese War and the treaty of Shimonoseki in 1895.

2. INDIGENOUS CHINESE ATTENTION TO INTERNATIONAL LAW

The Treaty of Shimonoseki appeared to put an end to the hopes for the Chinese self-strengthening program, and the new relationship with neighbouring Korea and Japan undermined China's position in the traditional international order of the East. The establishment of full Chinese sovereignty in international relations must have appeared as the only assurance for the humiliated Chinese national 'self', and as such fundamentally different from the challenges within the framework of the traditional imperial order posed to China by the European nations between 1842 and 1894. Reforms were initiated in Hunan modeled on what appeared to the Chinese to be successful educational and political reforms in Meiji-Japan. Modern educational institutions were set up, and international law was for the first time included in the curriculum of Chinese educational institutions, at the *Shiwu xuetang* (時務學堂) in Hunan. In the wake of the Treaty, Bi Yongnian 畢永年 established a Society for the Study of International Law (*Gongfaxue xuehui* 公法學學會) in Changsha, Hunan. But his confidence in the use of international law to restore China's international position in the East crumbled with the crackdown of the 1898 Wuxu reform, and the society was disbanded.[15]

---

[15] Cf. Cai E 蔡鍔 . 1902. *Guoji gongfa zhi* 國際公法志 (Treatise of international law). Shanghai: Guangzhi shuju, preface p. 1a; Ding Pingyi 丁平一 . 2000. *Hunan-weixin yundong shi 1895 zhi 1898 nian* 湖南維新運動史 1895 至 1898 年 (The history of the Hunan reform movement 1895 to 1898). Taibei: Han-Chung, p. 91.

Simultaneously, in the year 1898, Ding Zuyin 丁祖蔭 compiled a volume on international law and had it published in Changshu.[16] He based his work on passages from the Martin translation of Wheaton, but also supported his arguments with passages from the other Martin translations as well as Fryer texts. As a Confucian scholar, he argues that whereas international law may regulate the balance between equal members of an international society, only the Confucian Way of Benevolence (*rendao* 仁道) may establish permanent harmony among nations—and presumably also restore China's position as the 'ruler of nations' in the East. Ding Zuyin does not seem to have left much of an impact on the introduction of international law in China.

Tang Caichang 唐才常 (1867–1900) and Cai E 蔡鍔 (1882–1916), however, by compiling a number of texts on international law, sovereignty and diplomacy between 1898 and 1902, seem to have exerted a certain influence on the indigenous introduction of international legal theory. They were both associated with the Hunan group of reformers and wrote extensively on international law questions and their application in China during the years of the Hunanese reforms. Tang Caichang acted as chief editor of the influential Hunan reform periodical *Xiangxue xinbao* 湘學新報 from 1897, and published a number of articles on international legal questions and China's international relations in *Xiangxuebao* 湘學報 and the daily newspaper *Xiangbao* 湘報 in 1897–98.[17] Tang derived his knowledge and theoretical deliberations on international law mainly from Fryer's translation of Phillimore, but also shows that he had access to and applied material from Martin's translations as well. Cai E was a native Hunanese, associated with Bi Yongnian, Tang Caichang and the Hunan reformers, and later a very influential politician and military leader in early republican years. His writings on international law published in 1902 appear to be among the earliest individual general treatises on international law written by a Chinese national to be published in China.[18]

---

[16] Ding Zuyin 丁祖蔭 . 1898. *Wanguo gongfa shili* 萬國公法釋例 (Explanations on international law), in: id. *Changshu Dingshi congshu* 常熟丁氏叢書 (Encyclopedia of Mr Ding from Changshu). Changshu: n.p.

[17] Reprinted in: Tang Caichang 唐才常 . n.d. *Gongfa tongyi* 公法通義 (General explanations on international law). n.p. (1898-1902); and id. 1903 [1898]. *Juedian mingzhai neiyan* 覺顛冥齊內言 . *Xinxue da congshu* 新學大叢書 (Great encyclopedia on new learning). Shanghai: Jishan qiaoji shuju.

[18] Cf. Cai E. 1902.

Cai's writings appeared, however, at a time when the Chinese
sources and the two Chinese traditions were already in disfavour, and
Cai chose to extensively apply Japanese sources and vocabulary. His
association with Tang and the Hunanese reformers indicates that he
most certainly was familiar with both Martin's, Fryer's and Tang's
texts representing the indigenous Chinese traditions. His text was also
included in the *Xinxue da congshu* 新學大叢書 published in Shanghai
1903 together with Tang's texts. The fact that he makes no reference
to these sources is already a strong indication of the monumental Japanese impact around the turn of the century.

The realization that international law was in fact a useful and even
indispensable tool for China in international affairs when dealing with
the Western powers and Japan was growing among intellectuals and
officials in China towards the end of the century. There had been Chinese scholars studying international law in the West already in the
1870s, such as Ma Jianzhong 馬建忠 (1844–1900), but they did not in
any discernible way influence or contribute to the public discourse on
China's international position within the framework of international
law. There were two potential 'barbarian' sources that could serve as
foundation for the development of this debate in China in the latter
half of the 1890s; Martin's Tongwenguan tradition and Fryer's Jiangnan Arsenal tradition. A merging of these two traditions was a third
possibility that gained influence through some of the late nineteenth
century publications. But none of these conventional forms were
established firmly in the Chinese discourse before the monumental
Japanese influence in 1902–03.

From that time on, hardly any texts in international law were translated directly from Western languages, and the traditions established
by the institutions supervised by the Western missionaries were discontinued. Japanese texts on international law dominated the discourse, and Western texts were translated and retrieved via Japanese,
all using the already well-established Japanese Kanji-vocabulary on
international law. Cai E's early Japanese influence may be traced to
his military training in Japan. Shortly after the Treaty of Shimonoseki
China had started sending students to Japan in their hundreds.[19] There
are no accurate records of how many of these received training in

---

[19] Cf. Paula Harrel. 1992. *Sowing the Seeds of Change: Chinese Students, Japanese Teachers, 1895–1905*. Stanford: Stanford University Press.

international law. There must, however, have been a considerable group of students studying law in general and international law in particular in Japan, and their influence on the writings on international law for a Chinese audience is very conspicuous in the writings and translations from Cai E onwards.

Yang Tingdong 楊廷棟 (1861–1950) was a Jiangsu native and a member of the Jiangsu Provincial Assembly. Yang belonged to a group of Jiangnan constitutionalists and is the author of two works on constitutionalism and the provincial assemblies. He translated Rousseau's *Social Contract* and had it published in the journal *Yishu huibian* 譯書彙編 in 1901. Yang Tingdong also organized a constitutional preparation society, *Xianzheng yubeihui* 憲政豫備會 , and published the journal *Xianzheng zazhi* 憲政雜誌 . He studied at the Waseda University 早稻田大學 in Tokyo.[20] His publication *Gongfa lungang*公法論綱 (Outline discussion of international law)[21] is based on Japanese material presumably gathered at university lectures in Japan. In the preface he compares the experience of the Meiji restoration in Japan with the last 30 years development in China and is deeply troubled by China's position "outside the scope of international law," as he formulates it.

Yang and Cai's texts are the first independent Chinese comprehensive treatises on international law not based on translations from foreign texts. They are also the first deliberations on international law published in China to be based entirely on a Japanese experience. From this time on, the concurrence of these two circumstances has greatly contributed to the formation of an entirely new Chinese vocabulary on international law to replace the existing terminological traditions.

The only two translations of Western texts on international law after these events and before the establishment of the Republic, except for the 1903/1904 publications by Allen and Martin mentioned above,[22] are two texts translated from French and German and published in 1902–03. The French lawyer Arthur Desjardins (1835–1901)

---

[20] Cf. Joan Judge. 1996. *Print and Politics: 'Shibao' and the Culture of Reform in Late Imperial China*. Stanford: Stanford University Press.

[21] Cf. Yang Tingdong楊廷棟 . 1902. *Gongfa lungang*公法論綱 (Outline discussion of international law). Shanghai: Putong xueshushi and Kaimingshe.

[22] Another exception is a 1910 translation of Thomas Joseph Lawrence's *The Principles of International Law*. Dan Tao 但濤 (tr.). 1910. *Guoji gongfa tigang* 國際公法提綱 (A general outline of international law). Shanghai: Changming gongsi and Biaoming gongsi.

had been very much engaged in the international legal questions of the East. He became acquainted with the Japanese international law specialist Ariga Nagao 有賀長雄 (1860–1921), who was working in Paris for some time, and later wrote an article on China and international law entitled "La Chine et le Droit des Gens" which was published in *Revue des Deux Mondes* December 1900. The article depicts China very much from the perspective of contemporary Japan, as an unreliable partner in international affairs, unlike Japan, which is described as an international co-partner on equal footing with the European nations. Wu Qisun 吳啟孫 translated the article into Chinese and published it with a full Japanese technical vocabulary of international law under the title *Zhina guojilun* 支那國際論 in Shanghai/Tokyo in 1902. The second of these texts is the 1903 Shanghai Commercial Press 商務印書館 publication of a translation of Franz von Liszt's (1851–1919) *Das Völkerrecht: Systematisch dargestellt.* Liszt's book was translated from the German by the Commercial Press and published with the title *Guoji gongfa dagang* 國際公法大綱. By this time the vocabulary was now entirely Japanized, and Japanese was accepted in China as the language and vocabulary of international law translations.

Otherwise, all texts published in China and Japan for a Chinese readership between 1903 and 1911 are either translations from Japanese, or texts written by Chinese students in Japan and entirely based on their Japanese experiences. The single most important influence from Japan may be ascribed to Nakamura Shingo 中村進午 (1870–1939), professor of law and author of a number of important texts on international law in Japan. The texts introducing the Japanese interpretation of international law between 1903 and 1911 made available to a Chinese readership were:

Fan Diji 范迪吉 et. al. (trs.). 1903. *Guoji gongfa* 國際公法. Translations of texts by Hōjō Motoatsu 北條元篤 and Kumagai Naota 熊谷直太.
—— et. al. (trs.). 1903. *Guoji gongfa* 國際私法. Translations of texts by Nakamura Tarō 中村太郎.
Lin Qi 林棨 (tr.). 1903. *Guoji gongfa jingyi* 國際公法精義. Translations of various Japanese texts on international law.
Yuan Fei 袁飛 (tr.). 1903. *Wanguo gongfa yaoling* 萬國公法要領. Translation of text by Numazaki Jinzō 沼崎甚三.
Wang Hongnian 王鴻年 (tr.). 1904. *Guoji zhongli faze tigang* 國際中立法則提綱. Translations of international rules and regulations on neutrality.
—— (tr.). 1904. *Zhanshi xianxing guoji fagui* 戰時現行國際法規. Translations of international rules and regulations on warfare.

Ye Kaiqiong 葉開瓊(tr.). 1905. *Pingshi guoji gongfa* 平時國際公法 . Translations of lectures by Nakamura Shingo 中村進午 .

Zhang Fuxian 張福先 (tr.). 1905. *Zhanshi guoji gongfa* 戰時國際公法 . Translations of lectures mainly by Nakamura Shingo 中村進午 .

Guo Bin 郭斌 (tr.). 1905. *Guoji sifa* 國際私法 . Translations of lectures by Mita Hiroshi 三田博士 .

Liao Weixun 廖維勳(tr.). 1905. *Pingshi guoji gongfa* 平時國際公法 . Translations of lectures by Nakamura Shingo 中村進午 .

Chen Jiahui陳嘉會(tr.). 1905. *Zhanshi guoji gongfa* 戰時國際公法 . Translation of Japanese lectures on international law in time of war.

Cao Lüzhen曹履貞(tr.). 1905. *Guoji sifa* 國際私法 . Translations of lectures and publications by Yamada Saburō 山田三良 .

Jiang Yong 江庸 (tr.). 1905. *Zhanshi guoji tiaogui jilan* 戰時國際條規輯覽 . Japanese translations of international rules in time of war.

Wanguo gongfa tiyao 萬國公法提要 . 1905. Translations of texts by Takahashi Sakuei 高橋作衛by an anonymous translator.

Xiong Kaixian 熊開先(tr.). 1906. *Pingshi guoji gongfa* 平時國際公法 . Translations of lectures by Ogata Iichi 緒方維一 .

Zhao Xiangqian 趙象謙 (tr.). 1906. *Zhanshi guoji gongfa* 戰時國際公法 . Translations of lectures by Ogata Iichi 緒方維一 .

Feng Yinmo馮誾模 (tr.). 1906. *Guoji sifa tujie* 國際私法圖解 . Translations of texts by Ishimitsu Saburō 石光三郎 and Mori Sōnosuke 森惣之祐 .

Jin Baokang 金保康 (tr.). 1907a. *Pingshi guoji gongfa* 平時國際公法 . Translations of lectures by Nakamura Shingo 中村進午 .

——. 1907b. *Zhanshi guoji gongfa ji juwai zhongli* 戰時國際公法及局外中立 . Translations of lectures by Nakamura Shingo 中村進午 .

Fu Qiang 傅彊 (tr.). 1907. *Guoji sifa* 國際私法 . Translations of lectures and a university teaching compendium by Yamada Saburō 山田三良 .

Yuan Xilian 袁希濂 (tr.). 1907. *Xinyi guoji sifa* 新譯國際私法 . Translations of lectures by Nakamura Shingo 中村進午 .

Yan Xianzhang 嚴獻章(tr.). 1908. *Zhanshi guoji gongfa* 戰時國際公法 .Translation of a text by Ariga Nagao有賀長雄 .

Xu E 徐鍔 and Guo Enze 郭恩澤 (trs.). 1908. *Zhanshi guojifa yaolun* 戰時國際法要論 . Translations of three texts by Takahashi Sakuei 高橋作衛 .

Li Zhuo 李倬 (tr.). 1911. *Guoji sifa* 國際私法 . Translation of a text by Yamada Saburō 山田三良 .

Chen Shixia陳時夏 (tr.). 1911a. *Pingshi guoji gongfa* 平時國際公法 . Translation of a text by Nakamura Shingo 中村進午 .

——. 1911b. *Zhanshi guoji gongfa* 戰時國際公法 . Translation of a text by Nakamura Shingo 中村進午 .

The indigenous Chinese attention to international law coincides with the experiences from the Sino-Japanese War and the reforms initiated in Hunan in 1897. As a result, the first theoretical deliberations on international legal questions in China branched off from the two traditions of translating international law texts in China. But it appears that before long the Chinese students returning from Japan disregarded these traditions, and established a basis for a debate on China's international position and role from their experiences from Japan. In the following I shall investigate some features of the formation of a vocabulary and lexicon of international law in Chinese between the first translations into Chinese commencing in 1864 until the beginning of Japanese influence in 1902–03, in order to examine whether or not the traits of the changes in institutional, historical and interpretative agents in the Chinese discourse on international law described above may also be identified in the early modernization of the Chinese lexicon of international law.

3. VOCABULARIES OF INTERNATIONAL LAW

China had established the Zongli Yamen in 1861 and permanent legations abroad in 1876. China was also invited to participate in the sixth meeting of the Conference for the Reform and Codification of International Law in Brussels in 1878, and China's envoy to London, Guo Songtao 郭嵩燾 (1818–1891), attended the meeting. Guo expressed high hopes for the work done by the association for the benefit of all governments and peoples. He also excused China for not having entirely subscribed to the rules of international law, this being because of the differences in cultural and political background between the West and China. But he also expressed hope that China would soon embrace the science of international law, and that it certainly would be beneficial to China to do so. In return, Guo Songtao was elected honorary vice-president of the Association, a position he retained even 35 years after his death. Since Guo himself did not know any English, the references to foreign terms in his diary are transliterations and not his attempts at creating translations of terms. He refers, for instance, to the above-mentioned Conference for the Reform and Codification of International Law as *keng-fu-lin-si fa-er qi li-fa-er-mu an-de ke-di-fei-ge-lin-sheng a-fu ying-de-na-sheng-er na* 鏗弗林斯法爾齊立法爾姆安得科諦費格林升阿甫英得納升爾那 .[23]

One would thus assume that the translated texts by Martin and Fryer would be vital to official China when securing its position as a member of the international family of nations and in asserting its rights and duties as an equal partner in international affairs. China's traditional world order was crumbling, and to avoid being "divided up

---

[23] Cf. Guo Songtao. 1984, p. 302; see also Hsü 1960, pp. 206–7.

as a melon," China would need to seek acceptance as an international equal and sovereign partner. In order to assess the development and the influence between the schools and traditions of international law translations in the formation of a lexicon of international law I have selected a number of the most prominent cases of contested terms and terminological flux during the period in question (See Table 1).[24]

Martin coined a relatively small number of neologisms for his international legal translations from the 1860s onwards. In most cases of conveying new ideas within the theoretical discipline of international law he drew on the current Chinese lexicon of terms and phrases. The most prominent case of a term coined for his translations is his use of the binome *quanli* 權利 for 'rights', also encountered in early Chinese literature but adopted as a neologism for 'rights' by Martin already in his 1864 translation, and explained as a neologism in the Chinese language in the preface to the Woolsey translation.[25] In other cases, such as the term *wanguo gongfa* 萬國公法 for 'international law' and the cluster of terms related to 'sovereignty' and 'independence', Martin also contributed to the early formation of technical terms drawing on the current language. In the case of *Wanguo gongfa*, this term only reflects the early Roman notion of *Jus gentium*, Law of nations, and not the semantics of the later term 'international law' coined by Jeremy Bentham (1748–1832) in the early nineteenth century, and hence did not outlive the later Japanization and the Japanese innovation *kokusai/guoji* 國際 .

Martin's translation of Wheaton was exported to Japan already the year after its publication in China, and his vocabulary and formulations constituted the early foundation of the Japanese vocabulary on international law. After the Meiji-reforms, however, Japan soon developed her independent vocabulary based on Kanji innovations and extensions of the Chinese literary tradition. The only terms to be retained from Martin's vocabulary were 'rights' and 'sovereignty',

---

[24] As there are also resemblances between Yuan Dehui and Peter Parker's 1847 translations printed in *Haiguo tuzhi* and later translations, their vocabularies are omitted in this comparative analysis.

[25] W. A. P. Martin (tr.). 1877. *Gongfa bianlan* 公法便覽 (Introduction to international law). Beijing: Tongwenguan, *fanli* 2b–3a. See also Rune Svarverud. 2001. "The Notions of 'Power' and 'Rights' in Chinese Political Discourse", in: Michael Lackner, Iwo Amelung and Joachim Kurtz (eds.). *New Terms for New Ideas: Western Knowledge & Lexical Change in Late Imperial China*. Leiden: Brill, pp. 125–43.

Table 1: Contested terms in international law (1864–1903)

	MARTIN TONGWENGUAN 1864–1903	FRYER JIANGNAN ARSENAL 1886–1901	JAPANESE INFLUENCE 1902–
sovereignty	*zhuquan* 主權	*zhuquan* 主權	*zhuquan* 主權
FRYER 'BORROWING' FROM MARTIN			
independent state	*zizhu zhi guo* 自主之國	*zizhu zhi guo* 自主之國	*duliguo* 獨立國
neutral	*juwai* 局外	*juwai* 局外, *zhongli* 中立	*zhongli* 中立
high seas	*dahai* 大海	*dahai* 大海	*gonghai* 公海
JAPAN 'BORROWING' FROM MARTIN			
rights	*quanli* 權利	*fen suo dang de* 分所當得	*quanli* 權利
jurisdiction	*guanxia* 管轄	*guanli* 管理	*guanxiaquan* 管轄權
balance of power	*junshi zhi fa* 均勢之法	*pingquan zhi li* 平權之理	*junshizhuyi* 均勢主義
JAPANESE NEOLOGISMS, NO 'BORROWING'			
duties	———	*fen suo dang wei* 分所當為	*yiwu* 義務
(public) international law	*wanguo gongfa* 萬國公法	*jiaoshe gongfa* 交涉公法	*guojifa* 國際法
private international law	*gongfa zhi sitiao* 公法之私條	*jiaoshe bianfa* 交涉便法	*guoji sifa* 國際私法
natural law	*xingfa* 性法	*tianran zhi fa* 天然之法	*ziranfa* 自然法
positive law	———	*shizai lüfa* 實在律法, *teshe zhi lü* 特設之律	*zhidingfa* 制定法, *shidingfa* 實定法, *shitifa* 實體法
exterritorial rights	*bu gui difang guanxia* 不歸地方管轄	———	*zhiwai faquan* 治外法權
right of self-protection	zihu zhi quan 自護之權	zixing baowei 自行保衛	ziweiquan 自衛權

(*cont.*) and extensions of the Chinese literary tradition. The only terms to be retained from Martin's vocabulary were 'rights' and 'sovereignty', and for the terms 'jurisdiction' and 'balance of power' an influence may possibly be discerned.

The *Wanguo gongfa* obtained a prominent status in both official and non-official contexts soon after its publication, both because of its proven applicative value and because for a long time it was the only text of its kind in the Chinese language. When Martin published his later international law translations, in many cases with a slightly altered technical vocabulary, it seems that these texts only gained influence within relatively narrow circles. When theoretical deliberations of Western international law were discussed by late nineteenth century Chinese scholars,[26] we find that they refer to and discuss the theories and doctrines of Wheaton in Chinese translation and not other texts, indicating that the other Martin translations as well as other translations in late nineteenth century China were not widely distributed or well-known among the intellectuals.

With regard to Fryer's Jiangnan Arsenal translations, hardly any resemblance to the Tongwenguan tradition may be discerned in terms of technical vocabulary. Fryer did make use of Martin's terms for 'sovereignty' and 'independence', and his application of terms for 'neutral' and 'high seas' coincide with Martin's terms, drawing on the current vocabulary. Otherwise, Fryer established an altogether independent Jiangnan tradition. The vocabulary of the voluminous Fryer translations on international law between 1886 and 1901 suggests that his translations met a fate similar to Martin's later translations. The only time Fryer's translations of international law texts are known to have exercised practical influence was when Guo Songtao acquired a copy of Fryer's unfinished Chinese translation of Phillimore's text in London in 1878, 16 years before its publication at the Arsenal.[27] At that time only Martin's translations of the theoretical works of the two American publicists were available in China, but as the first Chinese

---

[26] Cf. Zheng Guanying 鄭觀應 . 1998 [1894]. *Shengshi weiyan* 盛世危言 (Words of warning in prosperous times). Zhengzhou: Zhongzhou guji chubanshe; Wang Tao 王韜 . 1998. *Tao Yuan wenlu waibian* 弢園文錄外編(Essays by Wang Tao, part 2). Zhengzhou: Zhongzhou guji chubanshe.

[27] Fryer's manuscript was then referred to as *Wanguo jiaoshe gongfa lun* 萬國交涉 公法論 , and not with the title of the translation *Geguo jiaoshe gongfa lun* 各國交涉公 法論 as published later.

envoy to Europe and as delegate to the Conference for the Reform and
Codification of International Law that same year Guo presumably
found it inappropriate to refer to these American philosophers of
international law. In spite of his voluminous production, Fryer's terminological apparatus was not taken up in the Chinese language and
did not enter contemporary dictionaries.

Since no indigenous debate on these issues surfaced in China
before 1895, these two institutions were operating independently from
each other and no urge to establish a national standard for these
notions is discernible. When the first debates on these theoretical
issues did surface shortly after the treaty of Shimonoseki, a temporary
confusion of terms and ideas was caused by Martin's and Fryer's very
different use of terminologies.[28] Those debates could potentially have
led to the merging of these two terminological traditions, had not the
influence from Japan been so profound. The Chinese students, however, first publishing texts in Chinese in Japan and later returning
from Japan after years of Western-style university education, brought
back the entire international legal vocabulary from the Japanese language. Because these students had very little or no experience of the
two Chinese traditions and the early translations of international law,
and most of them were young and receptive to the modern Japanese
educational system and Western scientific disciplines in Japanese dis-
guise, they brought an entirely new set of terms for this new reality
back to China. The entire Chinese discourse on international questions was Japanized in terms of vocabulary and the Tongwenguan and
Jiangnan Arsenal traditions were rejected within a matter of months.
The only remnants of the early Chinese terminological traditions in
the modern Japanese and Chinese vocabularies may be found in the
terms 'rights' and 'sovereignty', which were Martin innovations
transferred to Japan as early as the 1860s. Otherwise, the Japanese
Meiji influence on China was persuasive enough and brought sufficient confidence in Chinese sovereignty and hope for the humiliated
national identity to sweep away the entire tradition and embrace that
of the Japanese, which had been the occasion for the wretched sense
of Chinese national 'self' in the first place. Among examples of contested terms in Chinese which were open to the Japanese influx on
Chinese international law texts and translations from 1902, we find

---

[28] This was the case in Ding Zuyin's and Tang Caichang's publications.

indispensable international law terms such as: 'duties', '(public) international law', 'private international law', 'natural law', 'positive law',
'exterritorial rights' and 'right of self-protection'.

Japan had been sending students to Europe to study international law
as early as 1862, and already by the early 1880s a vocabulary of international law, based on Kanji, was firmly established in Japan.[29] At the
same time, a number of Western texts on international law were translated and published in Japan. In 1902 the Japanese Association of
International Law was established and in the same year the Journal of
International Law (*Kokusaihō zasshi* 國際法雜誌) was published for
the first time. It has earlier been suggested that the Japanese influence
on the terminology in China took place during the early decades of the
twentieth century.[30] This list of terms and the relevant bibliographical
evidence indicates, however, that this transition to a vocabulary influenced by Japan in fact took place during a short period of time
between 1902 and 1903 simultaneously with the first Chinese students returning from Japan. This terminological change may be discerned in the Chinese translations from Western languages as well as
in the translations from Japanese texts on international law.

CONCLUSION

In 1901 Li Hongzhang noted in the preface to Martin's translations of
Hall that international law was becoming a part of the Chinese political reality:

> International Law belongs to all the nations of the globe. If they
> observe it, they may dwell in quiet; if they neglect it, they are sure to
> have trouble. A year ago, the Boxer bandits arose, murdered a Foreign
> Minister and laid siege to the Legations. This unheard-of proceeding
> was due to a clique of narrow-minded ministers who, not knowing the
> lessons of history, could not be expected to know International Law. ...
> As we in the first instance had failed to observe International Law, (the
> Allied Forces) set aside International Law in dealing with us—as a sort

---

[29] This is confirmed through the dictionary *Tetsugaku jii* 哲學字彙, published in
Tokyo in 1884 (Inoue Tetsujirō 井上哲次郎 and Ariga Nagao 有賀長雄. 1884. *Kaitei
zōho tetsugaku jii* 改訂増補哲学字彙 (Philosophical dictionary, revised and enlarged).
Tokyo: Tōyōkan).
[30] Chiu 1967, p. 489.

of retribution. Yet when the North was in commotion, the South-East remained quiet. That it remained undisturbed in such a crisis was due to the fact that we observed International Law, and the foreigners also observed it.[31]

At the outset of this paper I raised the question of how it is possible that a nearly 40-year old indigenous tradition of translating international law texts in China was to such an extent open and subject to the precipitous Japanese influx around 1902–03. My assumption is that this could take place because neither of the two contending traditions of translating international law texts from Western languages, the Tongwenguan and the Jiangnan Arsenal tradition, which had coexisted between 1864 and 1903, had managed to establish itself with a firm basis in the standard literary language and technical vocabulary of late imperial China. There was hardly any terminological interchange between the two, except for a tendency around the turn of the century to merge the two terminological traditions. This merging of terminology appeared too late, however, to contest the rapid Japanese influx. Japan had initially been influenced by the 1864 Martin translation, but in the 1870s and 1880s established an indigenous Japanese lexicon of international law based on Kanji terms. Only a very small part of that lexicon was originally Chinese. When Chinese students brought this lexicon back from Japan around 1902–03, it very rapidly monopolized the Chinese vocabulary, and dominated the later development of an understanding of international law in China at a period when China for the first time was embracing international law, as indicated by Li Hongzhang in 1901. The fact that the Chinese students leaving for Japan to participate in the Japanese 'modern'-style Western education were not scholars already trained in scientific disciplines, but primarily inexperienced and young students unfamiliar with the existing Chinese traditions within Western studies, made them particularly receptive to the language, lexicon and scientific environment they experienced in Japan. The fact that Japan had already established a firm tradition both in terms of vocabulary, in extensive publications, and in terms of modern institutions for training and for the study of the Western sciences, including international law, made the Japanese experience very influential on these young

---

[31] W. A. P. Martin (tr.). 1903. *Gongfa xinbian* 公法新編 (New edition of international law). Shanghai: Guangxuehui, preface 1a.

students when they came to Japan. When these students in turn graduated from the Japanese educational institutions, they brought the new reality and the new Japanese instruments for describing that reality back to the famished Chinese national 'self'. Precisely because this terminological influx coincided with a growing demand for knowledge on international law, international rights and awareness of sovereignty as an instrument to save China's identity, particularly in her relationship to her former tributary states, the new terminological apparatus was readily accepted into the literary standard. Had the rights and duties of states been acknowledged as necessary instruments in China's international relations prior to the Sino-Japanese War, the linguistic process would certainly have commenced earlier and with a basis in one of the earlier existing terminological traditions, as may be observed within most of the branches of the natural sciences. The terminological shift taking place within the language of international law in China 1902–03 is a strong confirmation of the gravity of the international crisis inflicted on China by Japan in 1894–95.

REFERENCES

Bennet, Adrian Arthur. 1967. *John Fryer: The Introduction of Western Science and Technology into Nineteenth-Century China*. Cambridge, Mass.: Harvard University Press.

Cai E 蔡鍔 . 1902. *Guoji gongfa zhi* 國際公法志 (Treatise of international law). Shanghai: Guangzhi shuju.

Chang, Hsi-t'ung. 1950. "The Earliest Phase of the Introduction of Western Political Science into China", *Yenching Journal of Social Studies* 5, pp. 1–29.

Chiu, Hungdah. 1967. "The Development of Chinese International Law Terms and the Problem of Their Translation into English", *Journal of Asian Studies* 27, pp. 485–501.

Dan Tao 但濤 (tr.). 1910. *Guoji gongfa tigang* 國際公法提綱 (A general outline of international law). Shanghai: Changming gongsi and Biaoming gongsi. [Translation of Thomas Joseph Lawrence, *The Principles of International Law*].

Ding Pingyi 丁平一 . 2000. *Hunan weixin yundong shi 1895 zhi 1898 nian* 湖南維新運動史 1895 至 1898 年 (The history of the Hunan reform movement 1895 to 1898). Taibei: Han-Chung.

Ding Zuyin 丁祖蔭 . 1898. *Wanguo gongfa shili* 萬國公法釋例 (Explanations on international law), in: id. *Changshu Dingshi congshu* 常熟丁氏叢書(Encyclopedia of Mr Ding from Changshu). Changshu: n.p.

Guo Songtao 郭嵩燾 .1984 [1891]. *Lundun yu Bali riji* 倫敦與巴黎日記 (London and Paris diary). Changsha: Yuelu shushe (*Zouxiang shijie congshu* 走向世界叢書 . from East to West—Chinese Travellers before 1911).

Harrel, Paula. 1992. *Sowing the Seeds of Change: Chinese Students, Japanese Teachers, 1895–1905*. Stanford: Stanford University Press.

Hsü, Immanuel. 1960. *China's Entrance into the Family of Nations: The Diplomatic Phase 1858–1880*. Cambridge, Mass.: Harvard University Press.

Hughes, E. R. 1968. *The Invasion of China by the Western World*. London: Adam and Charles Black.

Inoue Tetsujirō 井上哲次郎 and Ariga Nagao 有賀長雄 . 1884. *Kaitei zōho tetsugaku jii* 改訂增補哲学字彙 (Philosophical dictionary, revised and enlarged). Tokyo: Tōyōkan.

Judge, Joan. 1996. *Print and Politics: 'Shibao' and the Culture of Reform in Late Imperial China*. Stanford: Stanford University Press.

Li Guilian李貴連 . 1998. "Ershi shiji chuqi de Zhongguo faxue"二十世紀初期的中國法學 (Chinese law in the early twentieth century), in: id. (ed.) *Ershi shiji de Zhongguo faxue* 二十世紀的中國法學 (Chinese law in the twentieth century). Beijing: Beijing Daxue chubanshe, pp. 1–65.

Li Zhaojie. 1999. "How international law was introduced into China", in: *Guoji falü wenti yanjiu* 國際法律問題研究 (A study of international legal questions). Beijing: Zhongguo zhengfa daxue chubanshe, pp. 53–135.

Liu, Lydia H. 1995. *Translingual Practice: Literature, National Culture, and Translated Modernity—China, 1900–1937*. Stanford: Stanford University Press.

——. 1999. "Legislating the Universal: The Circulation of International Law in the Nineteenth Century", in: id. (ed.). *Tokens of Exchange: The Problem of Translation in Global Circulation*. Durham, London: Duke University Press

Martin, W. A. P. (Ding Weiliang 丁韙良) (tr.). 1864. *Wanguo gongfa* 萬國公法 (International law). Beijing: Chongshiguan.

——— (tr.). 1877. *Gongfa bianlan* 公法便覽 (Introduction to international law). Beijing: Tongwenguan.

——— (tr.). 1903. *Gongfa xinbian* 公法新編 (New edition of international law). Shanghai: Guangxuehui.

Masini, Federico. 1993. *The Formation of Modern Chinese Lexicon and Its Evolution Toward a National Language: The Period from 1840 to 1898*. Berkeley: Journal of Chinese Linguistics (Monograph Series, no. 6).

Spence, Jonathan. 1969. *The China Helpers*. London: The Bodley Head.

Svarverud, Rune. 2000. "Jus Gentium Sinense: The Earliest Chinese Translation of International Law with some Considerations Regarding the Compilation of *Haiguo tuzhi*", *Acta Orientalia* 61, pp. 203–37.

———. 2001. "The Notions of 'Power' and 'Rights' in Chinese Political Discourse", in: Michael Lackner, Iwo Amelung and Joachim Kurtz (eds.). *New Terms for New Ideas: Western Knowledge & Lexical Change in Late Imperial China*. Leiden: Brill, pp. 125–43.

Tang Caichang 唐才常 . n.d. *Gongfa tongyi* 公法通義 (General Explanations on International Law). n.p.

———. 1903 [1898]. *Juedian mingzhai neiyan* 覺顛冥齊內言 (Intimate words from the Juedian Mingzhai), in: *Xinxue da congshu* 新學大叢書 (Great encyclopedia on new learning). Shanghai: Jishan qiaoji shuju.

Tian Tao 田濤 and Li Zhuhuan 李祝環 . 2000. "Qingmo fanyi waiguo faxue shuji pingshu" 清末翻譯外國法學書籍評述 (A critical account of translations of foreign works on Law in Late Qing times), *Zhongwai faxue* 3, pp. 355–71.

Wang Lixin 王立新 . 1997. *Meiguo chuanjiaoshi yu wan Qing Zhongguo xiandaihua* 美國傳教士與晚清中國現代化 (American missionaries and modernization in late imperial China). Tianjin: Tianjin renmin chubanshe.

Wang Tao 王韜 . 1998. *Tao Yuan wenlu waibian* 弢園文錄外編(Essays by Wang Tao, part 2). Zhengzhou: Zhongzhou guji chubanshe.

Wang Weijian 王維儉 . 1985. "Lin Zexu fanyi Xifang guojifa zhuzuo kaolüe" 林則徐翻譯西方國際法著作考略 (Some remarks on Lin Zexu's translation of a work on Western international law), *Zhongshan daxue xuebao* 1, pp. 58–67.

———. 1987. "Dingzheng ruogan Zhong Wai cishu zhong 'Ding Weiliang' cimu sheji de shishi"訂正若干中外詞書中'丁韙良'涉及的史實 (The rectification of some historical facts regarding W. A. P. Martin in Chinese and foreign encyclopaedia), *Zhongshan daxue xuebao* 2, pp. 68–76.

Wang Yangzong 王揚宗 . 1995. "Jiangnan zhizaoju fanyi shumu xinkao" 江南製造局翻譯書目新考 (A new investigation of books translated at the Jiangnan Arsenal), *Zhongguo keji shiliao* 2, pp. 3–18.

———. 2000. *Fulanya yu jindai Zhongguo de kexue qimeng* 傅蘭雅與近代中國的啟蒙 (Fryer and the enlightenment in modern China). Beijing: Kexue chubanshe.

Xiong Yuezhi 熊月之 .1994. *Xixue dongjian yu wanqing shehui* 西學東漸與晚清社會 (The Eastern transmission of Western learning and the society of late imperial China). Shanghai: Shanghai renmin chubanshe.

———. 1996. "Haiguo tuzhi zhengyin xishu kaoshi" 海國圖志徵引西書考釋 (A Study of the Western sources for the *Haiguo tuzhi*), in: *Zhonghua wenshi luncong* 中華文史論叢 (Collection of essays on Chinese literature and history). Shanghai: Shanghai guji chubanshe, vol. 55, pp. 235–59.

Yang Tingdong 楊廷棟 . 1902. *Gongfa lungang*公法論綱 (Outline discussion of international law). Shanghai: Putong xueshushi and Kaimingshe.

Zhang Haipeng 張海鵬 . 1998. *Zhuiqiuji: Jindai Zhongguo lishi jincheng de tansuo* 追
    求集：近代中國歷史進程的探索 (Pursuit: An investigation into the progress of
    modern Chinese history). Beijing: Shehui kexue wenxian chubanshe.
Zhang, Jingcao. 1992. "How Western International Law Was Introduced into China
    and Its Influence upon China", in: Bernhard H. K. Luk (ed.). *Contacts Between
    Cultures. Vol. 4: Eastern Asia: History and Social Sciences.* Lewiston: Mellen,
    pp. 264–70.
Zheng Guanying 鄭觀應 . 1998 (1894). *Shengshi weiyan* 盛世危言 (Words of warn-
    ing in prosperous times). Zhengzhou: Zhongzhou guji chubanshe.
Zou Zhenhuan 鄒振環 . 1996. *Yingxiang Zhongguo jindai shehui de yibai zhong yizuo*
    影響中國近代社會的一百種譯作 (One-hundred translated works which have
    influenced modern Chinese society). Beijing: Zhongguo duiwai fanyi chuban
    gongsi.

HELENA HEROLDOVÁ

GLASS SUBMARINES AND ELECTRIC BALLOONS: CREATING SCIENTIFIC AND TECHNICAL VOCABULARY IN CHINESE SCIENCE FICTION

In science fiction, objects which do not exist in common reality outside the text constitute an important part of its fictional worlds. However, although a reader of science fiction will never actually see the imaginary objects he reads about, s/he is able to imagine them in her/his mind. This paper aims to explain how the reader is led down the path of her/his imagination. In principle, I will argue that in the Chinese language, the imaginary non-empirical objects are mediated to the reader through complex linguistic signs whose structure and choice of elements are patterned along certain models that help the reader to visualize the objects.

In this paper, I analyze the scientific and technical vocabulary denoting the imaginary objects in science fiction novels and short stories written in China during the first two decades of the twentieth century. First, I define the principles by which linguistic signs with imaginary non-empirical referents are constructed, and secondly, I point out the relationship between those signs and non-empirical reality. The analysis of construction of newly-created terms denoting imaginary objects is based on previous studies by Zdenka Heřmanová and Federico Masini, both of whom deal with the coinage of new words in modern Chinese language.[1] Their remarks on the descriptive character of newly coined words have served as a basis for my attempt to analyze the relationship between linguistic signs with non-empirical referent and imaginary reality.

The concept of imaginary non-empirical reality in science fiction is based upon the study by Marc Angenot on fictional worlds in science fiction. According to him, fictional worlds in science fiction are composed of signs which do not refer to objects known in our common empirical world, as do those found in so-called 'realistic' fiction. As

---

[1] Cf. Zdenka Novotná. 1967–1969. "Contributions to the Study of Loan-words and Hybrid words in Modern Chinese", in: *Archív orientální* 35, pp. 613–48; 36, pp. 295–325; 37, pp. 48–75. Zdenka Heřmanová-Novotná. 1974. "Coinage and Structure of Economic Terms in Modern Chinese", *Asian and African Languages in Social Context*. Prague: Oriental Institute in Academia, pp. 45–77.

pointed out by Angenot, the aesthetic goal of science fiction "consists in creating a remote, estranged, and yet intelligible 'world'."[2]

1. TEXTS UNDER SCRUTINY

The analysis is based on the examination of approximately fifty terms found in Chinese novels and short stories written between 1904 and 1918. The bulk of the works under scrutiny is dated from the period 1905–1912, the richest epoch in the early development of Chinese science fiction.

I have found information on approximately eighty science fiction works from the first two decades of the twentieth century, including original novels and short stories by Chinese authors as well as their adaptations of Western works. A relatively small number of the works currently known have been studied, while the rest of them remain fertile ground for research. Some works are little-known or known only under their titles.[3] In this article, I have chosen some works already analyzed by other authors, as well as lesser-known works. The criterion for selection is the frequent use of newly created scientific and technical vocabulary.

During 1904–1905, the incomplete novel *Yueqiu zhimindi* 月球殖民地 (Colony on the Moon) by an author known under the pen-name Huangjiang diaosou 荒江釣叟 (Old fisherman on a desolate river) was serialized in the journal *Xiuxiang xiaoshuo* 繡象小説 (Fiction Illustrated).[4] In thirty-five chapters the adventures of a group of Chinese and Japanese men and women who plan to travel to the Moon in a bal-

---

² Marc Angenot. 1979. "The Absent Paradigm: An Introduction to the Semiotics of Science Fiction", *Science Fiction Studies* 6, pp. 9–19; p. 10.

³ Cf. Wu Dingbo and Patrick D. Murphy. 1989. *Science Fiction from China.* New York: Praeger; David Der-wei Wang. 1997. *Fin-de-Siècle Splendor. Repressed Modernities of Late Qing Fiction, 1849–1911.* Stanford: Stanford University Press; Chen Pingyuan. 1998. "From Popular Science to Science Fiction: An Investigation of 'Flying Machines'", in: David Pollard (ed.). *Translation and Creation.* Amsterdam, Philadelphia: John Benjamins, pp. 209–39; David Pollard. 1998. "Jules Verne, Science Fiction and Related Matters", in: David Pollard (ed.). *Translation and Creation.* Amsterdam, Philadelphia: John Benjamins, pp. 177–207; and Guo Zhen 郭蓁. 1999. "Lun wan Qing zhengzhi wutuobang xiaoshuo" 論晚清政治烏托邦小説 (On Late Qing political utopian fiction), *Qingmo xiaoshuo* 22, pp. 53–86.

⁴ Cf. Huangjiang diaosou 荒江釣叟. 1904–1905. "Yueqiu zhimindi" 月球殖民地 (Colony on the Moon), *Xiuxiang xiaoshuo* 31.2–62.11. (Reprinted Hong Kong: Shangwu yinshuguan, 1980.)

loon are described. According to David Der-wei Wang, the novel is a mediocre piece of work with many clichés drawn from traditional Chinese fiction.[5] The novel, however, deserves a closer look for its complex symbolism connecting Moon, balloon and science with expatriation, and the search for exile or for personal fulfillment and perfection.

In the short story "Xin Faluo xiansheng tan" 新法螺先生譚 (New story of Mr. Loudhailer) written by Xu Nianci 徐念慈 (1874–1908) under the pen-name Donghai juewo 東海覺我 and published in *Xiao-shuo lin* 小説林 (Forest of Fiction),[6] the protagonist practises spiritual and intellectual training that cause his body and mind to split. His body enters the subterranean world deep inside the Earth, while his mind wanders around the planets and stars. Xu Nianci was in turn inspired by a Japanese short story by Iwaya Sazanami 巖谷小波 (1870–1933) translated into Chinese by Bao Tianxiao 包天笑 (1876–1973).[7] The Japanese story was itself an adaptation of German stories about Baron von Münchhausen (1720–1797). David Der-wei Wang maintains that the novel expressed a twofold archetype of late Qing intellectuals —their quest for knowledge as well as their willingness to sacrifice themselves for the sake of mankind.[8]

The novel *Xin shitou ji* 新石頭記 (New Story of the Stone) by Wu Jianren 吳趼人 (1866–1910), published in the journal *Nangong bao* 南公報 (Southern Journal), depicts the adventures of Jia Baoyu 賈寶玉, the hero of Cao Xueqin's 曹雪芹 (1715–1763) novel *Shitou ji* 石頭記 (Story of the Stone), later better known as *Honglou meng* 紅樓夢 (Dream of the Red Chamber, 1792), in early twentieth-century China.[9] In the original novel, Jia Baoyu, a heir of an aristocratic family, was not interested in studying, whereas in Wu's novel, he has

---

[5] Cf. Wang 1997, p. 288.

[6] Cf. Xu Nianci 徐念慈. 1997 [1905]. "Xin Faluo xiansheng tan" 新法螺先生譚 (New story of Mr. Loudhailer), in: Yu Runqi 于潤琦(ed.). *Qingmo minchu xiaoshuo shuxi. Kexue juan* 清末民初小説書系。科學卷 (Fiction from the Late Qing and Early Republic. Science). Beijing: Zhongguo wenlian chuban gongsi, pp. 1–20 [Originally published in *Xiaoshuo lin* 6 (1905)].

[7] Cf. Wang 1997, pp. 295–301, 383.

[8] Cf. Wang 1997, p. 296.

[9] Cf. Wu Jianren 吳趼人. 1986 [1905]. *Xin shitou ji* 新石頭記 (New Story of the Stone). Zhengzhou: Zhengzhou guji chubanshe. [Originally published in *Nangong bao* 8–11 (1905)].

turned into an ardent admirer of modern science and technology, once he had been transplaced into modernizing Shanghai.

In the incomplete novel *Wutuobang youji* 烏托邦游記 (Travel to Utopia) by Xiaoran Yusheng 簫然郁生, published in the journal *Yueyue xiaoshuo* 月月小説 (All-Fiction Monthly), the narrator sets off on a journey to Utopia Island; however, after this promising beginning, the novel finishes abruptly at chapter five.[10]

The short story "Kongzhong zhanzheng weilai ji" 空中戰爭未來記 (Future Wars in the Sky) by Bao Tianxiao, also published in the journal *Yueyue xiaoshuo*, presents a vivid portrayal of a world war between Germany, Britain and Russia between the years 1900 and 1930.[11]

In "The Doomsday" (*Shijie mori ji* 世界末日記) by Bao Tianxiao, a first person narrator describes the last days of mankind. The Earth is about to be destroyed due to the collapse of the solar system. Famous scientists discuss the possibility of rescuing mankind. Engineers envision several possibilities, such as the construction of an artificial planet or a flight into space. Philosophers maintain that the human soul is immortal and can therefore survive any material catastrophe.[12]

The novel *Dian shijie* 電世界 (Electric World) by the author known under the pen-name Gao Yang shi bu caizi 高陽氏不才子 (Gao Yang, a beclouded scholar),[13] published in the journal *Xiaoshuo shibao* 小説

[10] Cf. Xiaoran Yusheng 簫然郁生. 1997 [1906]. "Wutuobang youji" 烏托邦游記 (Travel to Utopia), in: Yu Runqi 于潤琦 (ed.). *Qingmo minchu xiaoshuo shuxi. Kexue juan* 清末民初小説書系。科學卷 (Fiction from the Late Qing and Early Republic. Science). Beijing: Zhongguo wenlian chuban gongsi, pp. 73–86. [Originally published in *Yueyue xiaoshuo* 1–2 (1906)].

[11] Cf. Bao Tianxiao 包天笑. 1997a [1908]. "Kongzhong zhanzheng weilai ji" 空中戰爭未來記 (Future wars in the sky), in: Yu Runqi 于潤琦 (ed.). *Qingmo minchu xiaoshuo shuxi. Kexue juan* 清末民初小説書系。科學卷 (Fiction from the Late Qing and Early Republic. Science). Beijing: Zhongguo wenlian chuban gongsi, pp. 94–9. [Originally published in *Yueyue xiaoshuo* 21 (October 1908)].

[12] Cf. Bao Tianxiao 包天笑. 1997b [1908]. "Shijie mori ji" 世界末日記 (The Doomsday), in: Yu Runqi 于潤琦 (ed.). *Qingmo minchu xiaoshuo shuxi. Kexue juan* 清末民初小説書系。科學卷 (Fiction from the Late Qing and Early Republic. Science). Beijing: Zhongguo wenlian chuban gongsi, pp. 87–93. [Originally published in *Yueyue xiaoshuo* 19 (August 1908)].

[13] Probably Xu Zhiyan 許指岩 (also 嚴), pen-name of Xu Guoying 許國英 (1875–1923).

時報 (Fiction News), depicts the modernization and technical as well as social and development of China during the years 2009 to 2209.[14]

In the short story "Shuidi qianxingting" 水底潛行艇 (Submarine) by Mei Meng 梅夢, published in the journal *Xiaoshuo yuebao* 小説月報 (Fiction Monthly), the narrator, a sailor, is gravely hurt during the attack of an enemy submarine during a war. In a hospital, he sees in his dreams new types of war-submarines.[15]

2. PRINCIPLES OF CREATING NEOLOGISMS

A common trait of newly-created words is their descriptive character.[16] The choice and combinations of the constituents used in compounds and naming units correspond to the construction of imaginary objects. The determined constituent of a term designates the imaginary object in general, and the determining member expresses its basic characteristic. In the case of scientific and technical terminology in science fiction, we ask which constituents are chosen, and how they are combined in order to create terms denoting non-empirical reality.

The analyzed terms are divided into two categories. In the first category, traditional or newly-coined words with extended meaning are discussed. The second category presents newly-created words and naming units.[17]

1. Words with extended meaning

As demonstrated by Federico Masini in his excellent study on the formation of the modern Chinese lexicon, one method of creating new

---

[14] Cf. Gao Yang shi bu caizi 高陽氏不才子 1909. "Dian shijie" 電世界 (Electric world), *Xiaoshuo shibao* 1, pp. 1–58.

[15] Cf. Mei Meng 梅夢. 1997 [1918]. "Shuidi qianxing ting" 水底潛行艇 (Submarine), Yu Runqi 于潤琦 (ed.). *Qingmo minchu xiaoshuo shuxi. Kexue juan* 清末民初小説書系。科學卷 (Fiction from the Late Qing and Early Republic. Science). Beijing: Zhongguo wenlian chuban gongsi, pp. 209–17. [Originally published in *Xiaoshuo yuebao* 9.8 (1918)].

[16] Cf. Novotná 1967–1969, p 620, Heřmanová-Novotná 1974, p. 63

[17] The words are given in *pinyin* transcription followed by Chinese characters. The constituting elements of the bisyllabic and multisyllabic words are given in square brackets. The constituting elements in brackets are presented only when they are necessary for the analysis of word construction. The constituents that form a semantic unit in the multisyllabic compounds are given in angle brackets. The translation of the term is in parentheses.

vocabulary resides in the extension or change of the semantic field of
existing lexical items.[18] According to my study of Chinese science
fiction, two types of existing vocabulary are used: first, words of the
'common' lexical system, and second, newly-coined scientific and
technical terms used to designate objects known in common reality. I
found only one example of the extension of meaning among existing
'common' words: in the novel *Dian shijie*, chapter 3, the word
chibang 翅膀 (bird's wings) is used for a small flying machine constructed for one person. The employment of scientific and technical
terms coined at the end of the nineteenth century or earlier is more
frequent.[19] In particular, words with the semantic morpheme *dian* 電
(electric, electricity), such as *dianbao* 電報 (telegram), *diandeng* 電燈
(electric light), *dianguang* 電光 (electric rays) or *dianche* 電車 (tram-
car, car), are often used. Chinese science fiction of the period uses
words denoting various kinds of vehicles known in empirical reality
in order to refer to imaginary means of transport. For example, in the
novel *Electric World*, the trains on elevated rails (*gonggong dianche*
公共電車) are constructed as a means of public transport for hundreds
of passengers.[20] The balloons *qiqiu* 汽球 with furnace are anchored in
the sky in order to produce an artificial climate.[21] The balloon *qiqiu* is
capable of flying to the Moon.[22] The flying machines *feiji* 飛機 have
the capacity to hold hundreds of passengers.[23]

2. *Bisyllabic and trisyllabic compounds*

New creations constitute the major part of new terms. According to
Zdenka Heřmanová, neologisms in Chinese are newly-coined words
created according to the usual word-formation patterns.[24] New creations are coined either without the influence of foreign models or, during the process of coinage, foreign words can inspire the neologism.[25]

---

[18] Cf. Federico Masini. 1993. *The Formation of Modern Chinese Lexicon and its
Evolution Towards a National Language: The Period From 1840 to 1898*. Berkeley:
Journal of Chinese Linguistics (Monograph Series, no. 6), p. 152.
    [19] Cf. Masini 1993, p. 127
    [20] Cf. Gao Yang shi bu caizi 1909, ch. 8.
    [21] Cf. Wu Jianren 1986 [1905], *passim*.
    [22] Cf. Huangjiang diaosou 1980 [1904], *passim*.
    [23] Cf. Gao Yang shi bu caizi 1909, *passim*.
    [24] Cf. Heřmanová 1967, p. 614
    [25] Cf. Masini 1993, p.152; Heřmanová 1967, p. 614.

I place the neologisms into two distinct categories according to their construction patterns: bisyllabic and trisyllabic compounds on the one hand, and multisyllabic naming units on the other hand.

The category of bisyllabic neologisms is represented by the pattern found in the word *feiting* 飛艇 [fly + boat] (flying machine). The constituents are arranged into determining—determined structure. The determined constituent has a characteristic of an object designated by an attribute. The attribute is chosen in order to describe the designated object. The following examples represent the bisyllabic pattern:

Table 1: Bisyllabic patterns

dianqiang 電搶	electricity + gun	electric gun[a]
dianzhen 電針	electricity + shot	electric rays emitted by the electric gun[b]
dianguang 電光	electricity + light, ray	electric rays[c]
shuixue 水靴	water + boots	water boots = a machine that enables persons to move on a water surface[d]
feiting 飛艇	fly + boat	flying machine[e]
feiche 飛車	fly + car	flying machine[f]

a. Gao Yang shi bu caizi 1909, ch. 2 and 5.
b. Ibid., ch. 5.
c. Ibid., ch. 2.
d. Wu Jianren 1986 [1905], ch. 34.
e. Gao Yang shi bu caizi 1909, *passim*.
f. Wu Jianren 1986 [1905], ch. 34.

The trisyllabic compounds are represented by a type of composita like *liuxiangjing* 留象鏡 [<leave + image> + mirror, lens, glass]. In the pattern *liuxiangjing*, the monosyllabic nominal head formed by a morpheme or a word is determined by a bisyllabic verb-object attribute. The examples of this pattern are numerous.

Table 2: Trisyllabic patterns I

rushuiyi 入水衣	<enter + water> + suit	diving suits[a]
wanghaijing 望海鏡	<observe + sea> + mirror, lens, glass	telescope[b]

Table 2: Trisyllabic patterns I (cont.)

toushuijing 透水鏡	\<penetrate + water\> + mirror, lens	telescope[c]
wangyuanjing 望遠鏡	\<observe + distance\> + mirror, lens	telescope[d]
zhumingjing 助明鏡	\<help, promote + distance\> + mirror, lens	telescope[e]
ceyuanjing 測遠鏡	\<survey + distance\> + mirror, lens	telescope[f]
feikongting 飛空艇	\<fly + sky\> + boat	flying machine[g]

a. Ibid., ch. 28.
b. Gao Yang shi bu caizi 1909, *passim*.
c. Wu Jianren 1986 [1905], ch. 29.
d. Xiaoran Yusheng 1997 [1906], p. 80.
e. Wu Jianren 1986 [1905], ch. 25.
f. Ibid.
g. Xiaoran Yusheng 1997 [1906], *passim*.

As the attribute, verbal or nominal constructions are also used:

Table 3: Trisyllabic patterns II

shengjiangji 昇降機	\<rise + lower\> + machine	flying machine engine[a]
jintuiji 進退機	\<advance + retreat\> + machine	flying machine engine[b]
qianlijing 千里鏡	\<thousand + mile\> + mirror, lens, glass	telescope[c]
bolichuan 玻璃船	glass + boat	glass submarine[d]
feixing zhi qi 飛行之器	fly + particle + appliance	flying machine[e]

a. Wu Jianren 1986 [1905], ch. 26.
b. Ibid.
c. Ibid., ch. 25.
d. Gao Yang shi bu caizi 1909, ch. 14.
e. Bao Tianxiao 1997a [1908], p.90.

In the last example, a structural particle connects both the modifier and the word being modified. In a few cases, the trisyllabic compounds are constructed on a different basis. As the nominal head, the bisyllabic word appears, and the attribute is monosyllabic, for example: *dianshouqiang* 電手鎗 [electricity + gun] (electric gun)[26] or *dian-feiliao* 電肥料 [electricity + fertilizer] (electric fertilizer).[27]

3. Multisyllabic naming units

The multisyllabic naming units represent the majority of neologisms with imaginary referents. The four-syllable naming units are organized on the determining attribute—determined object pattern. Both the determined head and the determining attribute are bisyllabic words. Consider the following examples:

Table 4: Multisyllabic patterns

feixing jiandui 飛行艦隊	\<fly\> + \<fleet, vessel\>	flying warship[a]
zhizao tianqi 製造天氣	\<make, create\> + \<weather\>	artificial Earth atmosphere[b]
zhizao rongqi 製造容器	\<make, create\> + \<hold, contain + air, atmosphere\>	artificial climate in a submarine[c]
zhaoxiang qiju 照相器具	\<to photograph\> + \<utensil\>	photographic camera[d]
jiasu feiche 加速飛車	\<accelerate\> + \<flying machine\>	ultraspeed flying machine[e]
kongzhong feiting 空中飛艇	\<atmosphere + postposition\> + \<flying boat\>	flying machine[f]
ziran dianche 自然電車	\<auto\> + \<electric car\>	automobile[g]
kongqi dianqiu 空氣電球	\<atmosphere, air\> + \<electric balloon\>	spaceship[h]

a. Ibid., ch. 5.
b. Wu Jianren 1986 [1905], ch. 22.
c. Ibid., *passim*.
d. Xiaoran Yusheng 1997 [1906], p. 80.
e. Wu Jianren 1986 [1905], *passim*.
f. Gao Yang shi bu caizi 1909, *passim*.
g. Ibid.
h. Ibid.

Trisyllabic compounds often serve as determined constituents in five- and six-syllabic naming units. Here, the trisyllabic compounds with nominal head and verbal or verb-object attributes are employed as

[26] Gao Yang shi bu caizi 1909, chapters 2 and 5.
[27] Ibid., ch. 9.

determined constituents. The determining constituent consists of two nouns or a noun with postposition. For example:

Table 5: Trisyllabic compounds in multisyllabic patterns

haidi toushuijing 海底透水鏡	\<deep sea, seabed\> + \<tele-scope\>	(telescope used for under-sea observation)[a]
shuidi qianxingting 水底潛行艇	\<deep sea\> + \<submarine\>	(deep-sea submarine)[b]
diantong fayinji 電筒發音機	\<electric + tube\> + \<emit + sound + machine \>	(personal wireless tele-phone)[c]
kongzhong feixingchuan 空中飛行船	\<air, atmosphere + postpo-sition\> + \<flying machine\>	(flying machine)[d]
kongzhong diandiqi 空中電遞器	\<air, atmosphere + postpo-sition\> + \<electricity + deliver, send + machine\>	(wireless telegraph used on a board of a flying machine)[e]
kongzhong shusong lieche 空中輸送列車	\<air, atmosphere + postpo-sition\> + \< \<transport\> + \<train\> \>	(flying transport machine)[f]
zhangxing ruanboli 障形軟玻璃	\<block, barrier + form\> + \< \<soft + \<glass\> \>	(protective modulated soft glass)[g]

a. Wu Jianren 1986 [1905], *passim*.
b. Mei Meng 1997 [1918], *passim*.
c. Gao Yang shi bu caizi 1909, ch. 7.
d. Bao Tianxiao 1997 [1908], *passim*.
e. Xiaoran Yusheng 1997 [1906], p. 82.
f. Gao Yang shi bu caizi, 1909, *passim*.
g. Wu Jianren 1986 [1905], ch. 26.

In the last example, the trisyllabic head as determined constituent con-sists of a noun determined by an adjective. The nominal head consti-tuting the determined member is occasionally determined by the attribute *da* 大 'great' or *xiao* 小 'small', for example in a naming unit *haidi qianshui dachuan* 海底潛水大船 [\<deep sea\> + \<to dive + water\> + \<great + boat\>] (deep-sea great submarine)[28].

---

[28] Cf. Gao Yang shi bu caizi, 1909, ch. 15.

3. THE READER'S CONSTRUCTION OF IMAGINARY REALITY

The reader who reads fiction relates the elements of a fictional world to empirical reality.[29] He ideates in her/his mind the fictional world according to his previous literary and non-literary experience.[30] While reading science fiction, the reader has to actualize fictional worlds which do not exist in common reality outside the text. In order to make the science fictional world intelligible and imaginable, the structure of the text and the structure of its elements have to lead the reader down a certain path. At first, the constituents of terms denoting imaginary objects are chosen in order to make the imaginary objects possible to imagine. Although the terms refer to imaginary reality, they are necessarily formed by constituents that refer to our common empirical world, as we can see from the examples given above. It is the choice and combination of these constituents that makes the words denoting imaginary objects intelligible. Therefore, the imaginary objects have to be placed in a familiar context which helps the reader to actualize them.[31]

As a medium of actualization of imaginary objects, descriptions are often employed. The analysis of descriptions teaches us about what the imaginary objects meant for Chinese readers of the period. The descriptions tell us about the features of imaginary worlds that interested Chinese readers. In general, the imaginary objects were described as new, recently invented or newly designed. This was usually followed by a description of their shape, form, function and use. A good example of the role of description is that of flying machines, which appear most frequently in the science fiction of the period. Chen Pingyuan 陳平原 considers flying machines to be symbols of progress and journey to the future.[32] Descriptions of flying machines focused on their speed, range of flight and extraordinary dimensions. Flying machines could fly to the Sun and return to the Earth in a sin-

---

[29] Cf. Carl Darryl Malmgren. 1985. *Fictional Space in the Modernist and Post-modernist American Novel.* Lewisburg: Associated University Presses, p. 53.

[30] Cf. Wolfgang Iser. 1987. *The Act of Reading. A Theory of Aesthetic Response.* Baltimore, London: Johns Hopkins University Press, p. 35.

[31] Cf. Iser 1987, p. 35.

[32] Cf. Chen Pingyuan. 1998. "From Popular Science to Science Fiction: An Investigation of Flying Machines'", in: David Pollard (ed.). *Translation and Creation.* Amsterdam, Philadelphia: John Benjamins, pp. 209–39. p. 236.

gle day.[33] A huge flying machine on its way to Utopia Island had five boards with rooms, a library, a theater, factories, a museum and a chemical laboratory.[34] Transport flying ships were immense balloons with a diameter of three kilometers and a capacity of more than one hundred thousand cubic meters of gas. They were capable of flying at a height of seven kilometers.[35] The flight from Europe to New York in a small balloon with three hundred cabins for one thousand passengers lasted twelve hours.[36] The journey from Shanghai to North America and back to China in a small one-person flying machine lasted three hours and fifty minutes.[37] Beside flying machines limited to the Earth's atmosphere, we also find examples of flying machines capable of flying in space, such as the spaceship 'electric balloon' in the novel *Electric World*. It is revealing that in descriptions of flying machines, they always appear as immense vehicles capable of extraordinary speed and range of flight. Their characteristics makes them an ideal means of long-distance communication. In general, flying machines are symbols of communication, and consequently of impact and control. These symbols were at the center of fictional worlds in Chinese science fiction shortly after the turn of the century, when new technological inventions shaped the image of the future.

CONCLUSION

The fictional worlds in science fiction consist of imaginary objects that do not exist in the reader's empirical world. In order to create these non-empirical objects in her/his mind, the reader is guided along her/his path of imagination by clues provided by the text, including vocabulary that refers to non-empirical reality.

In Chinese science fiction, words referring to non-empirical reality are of different types. Traditional words with extended meanings form a minority of words with non-empirical referent. The majority of terms denoting non-empirical reality is formed by bisyllabic and tri-syllabic words and multisyllabic naming units. The constituents of newly-coined words are organized into a determining—determined

---

[33] Cf. Wu Jianren 1986 [1905], ch. 34.
[34] Cf. Xiaoran Yusheng 1997 [1906], *passim*.
[35] Cf. Bao Tianxiao 1997, *passim*.
[36] Cf. Bao Tianxiao 1997, p. 94.
[37] Cf. Gao Yang shi bu caizi 1909, ch. 3.

pattern. The choice and combination of the constituents of words denoting imaginary reality reflect the characteristic features of the imaginary objects perceived by readers. The determined elements represented the imaginary objects in general, and the determining constituents designates its basic characteristic. In order to make the imaginary object familiar, descriptions of their appearance and function are attached. Both the structure of newly-coined terms and attached descriptions help readers to perceive and understand the imaginary reality.

The question remains, however, who the reader of early twentieth-century Chinese science fiction was. Who was the addressee, whose empirical world, knowledge and previous literary and non-literary experiences formed the perception of science fiction as distinct from non-empirical reality? The evidence as to who read science fiction is incomplete, but includes remarks on science fiction made by the authors and advertisements in newspapers, as well as the texts themselves, which provide us with the model reader of Chinese science fiction.

Judging from the number of the published works during the first two decades of the twentieth century that I mentioned in the introduction, science fiction was a popular genre; furthermore, the stories were published in leading journals. Some science fiction novels were serialized for several months or years, such as *Colony on the Moon*, which appeared during 1904 and 1905. Some works were published at least twice, first in a newspaper, and later in book form, such as *New Story of the Stone*, which was first serialized in the *Southern Journal* in 1905. In 1908, the novel was published by Gailiang xiaoshuoshe in Shanghai.[38]

Advertisements, as well as remarks on science fiction by its authors and editors, are unfortunately sparse. In six volumes of a journal *Fiction Monthly*, I found four advertisements for science fiction stories during the period between the years 1910 and 1915. The short advertisement of two unknown pieces of works entitled "Yixing qishu" 易形奇術 (The Strange Skill of Shape-shifting) and "Boming-hua" 薄命花 (Flower of Ill Fate) appeared in the fourth number of the 1911 volume of *Fiction Monthly*. The other advertisement for two

---

[38] Other examples see Wu and Murphy 1989, p. xiv; Wang 1997, pp. 178, 381; Pollard 1998, pp. 179, 190, 204; Guo Zhen 1999, p. 85.

works adapted from Western languages provides a more detailed description of the works. Both appeared in the seventh number of the 1911 volume of *Fiction Monthly*. The advertisements for "Mimi dian-guang-ting" 秘密電光艇 (Secret Electric Rays Boat) praise the danger-ous adventures experienced by the staff of an electrically powered ship. The advertisement for *Huitou kan* 回頭看 (Looking Backward), the adaption of Edward Bellamy's (1850–1889) novel *Looking Back-ward: 2000–1887* (1888), invites the reader to a splendid future world.[39]

The authors' remarks on science fiction focused upon the existence of science fiction in the Western literature, as well as on the need for it in Chinese fiction for didactic reasons. The examples of this opinion can be found in Lu Xun's 魯迅 (1881–1936) preface to his adaption of Jules Verne's novel *De la terre à la Lune trajet en 97 heures et 20 minutes* (Ninety-seven hours and twenty minutes from the earth to the Moon, 1865), and later in comments and remarks on science fiction made by Xia Ren 俠人 (1905), Xu Nianci (1907) and Mei Meng (1918).[40]

The advertisements and authors' remarks on science fiction do not deal with the addressed reader of science fiction works. Indirect evi-dence concerning them is found in the narrative strategies, including the model reader, the text's vocabulary and certain intertextual mark-ers that offer clues as to what kind of people read science fiction. But,

---

[39] Cf. *Huitou kan* 回頭看 (Looking Backward). 1987 [1904]. *Libai liu*, pp. 25–36. (Reprinted Jiangsu Guanling guji keyin she.) [Translation of Edward Bellamy. *Look-ing Backward: 2000–1887*, (1888)].

[40] Lu Xun's adaptation was published in 1903 under the title *Yuejie lüxing* 月界旅行 (Travel to the Moon), in: *Xin yue xiaoshuo* 新月小説 (New fiction monthly). Cf. Chen Pingyuan 陳平原. 1989. "*20 shiji Zhongguo xiaoshuo shi (1897–1916)*" 20世紀中國小説史 (History of the twentieth century Chinese fiction (1897–1916)). Beijing: Beijing daxue chubanshe, vol. 1, p. 49; Wang 1997, pp. 252, 378; Pollard 1998, p. 190. The preface of *Travel to the Moon* is customarily discussed in every work on Chinese science fiction. See Robert Matthew. 1978. *The Origins of Japanese Science Fiction*. Brisbane: Department of Japanese, University of Queensland (Occasional Papers 4), p. 2; Wu and Murphy 1989, p. xiii; Wang 1997, p. 252; Pollard 1998, p. 186; Mikael Huss. 2000. "Hesitant Journey to the West: SF's Changing Fortunes in Mainland China", in: *Science Fiction Studies* 27.1, p. 92. New editions in *Lu Xun quanji* 魯迅全集 (Complete works of Lu Xun). 1973. Beijing: Renmin wenxue chu-banshe, vol. 11, pp. 9–11, and *Lu Xun quanji* 魯迅全集 (Complete works of Lu Xun). 1981. Beijing: Renmin wenxue chubanshe, vol. 10, pp. 151–2.
For the remarks by Xia Ren and Xu Nianci, see Yu 1997, p. 13; for the remarks by Mei Meng, see Yu 1997, p. 219.

despite the fact that the model reader of early Chinese science fiction is thought to be an urban, middle-class male with both traditional Chinese and Westernized background who is concerned with the future of the Chinese state, there is still no direct proof to support this assumption. The popularity of the genre and its spread are demonstrated by the relatively high number of published works, as well as their repeated publishing during the period scrutinized, from 1905 to 1912, which also shows science fiction to have been an important part of the early twentieth century Chinese literary scene.

REFERENCES

Angenot, Marc. 1979. "The Absent Paradigm: An Introduction to the Semiotics of Science Fiction", *Science Fiction Studies* 6, pp. 9–19.

Bao Tianxiao 包天笑. 1997a [1908]. "Kongzhong zhanzheng weilai ji" 空中戰爭未來記 (Future wars in the sky), in: Yu Runqi 于潤琦 (ed.). *Qingmo minchu xiaoshuo shuxi. Kexue juan* 清末民初小說書系。科學卷 (Fiction from the Late Qing and Early Republic. Science). Beijing: Zhongguo wenlian chuban gongsi, pp. 94–9. [Originally published in *Yueyue xiaoshuo* 21 (October 1908)].

——. 1997b [1908]. "Shijie mori ji" 世界末日記 (The Doomsday), in: Yu Runqi 于潤琦 (ed.). *Qingmo minchu xiaoshuo shuxi. Kexue juan* 清末民初小說書系。科學卷 (Fiction from the Late Qing and Early Republic. Science). Beijing: Zhongguo wenlian chuban gongsi, pp. 87–93. [Originally published in *Yueyue xiaoshuo* 19 (August 1908)].

Chen Pingyuan 陳平原. 1989. *"20 shiji Zhongguo xiaoshuo shi (1897–1916)"* 20 世紀中國小說史 (1897–1916) (History of the twentieth century Chinese fiction (1897–1916)). Beijing: Beijing daxue chubanshe.

——. 1998. "From Popular Science to Science Fiction: An Investigation of 'Flying Machines'", in: David Pollard (ed.). *Translation and Creation*. Amsterdam, Philadelphia: John Benjamins, pp. 209–39.

Gao Yang shi bu caizi 高陽氏不才子. 1909. "Dian shijie" 電世界 (Electric world), *Xiaoshuo shibao* 1, pp. 1–58.

Guo Zhen 郭蓁. 1999. "Lun wan Qing zhengzhi wutuobang xiaoshuo" 論晚清政治烏托邦小說 (On Late Qing political utopian fiction), *Qingmo xiaoshuo* 22, pp. 53–86.

Huangjiang diaosou 荒江釣叟. 1904–1905. "Yueqiu zhimindi" 月球殖民地 (Colony on the Moon), *Xiuxiang xiaoshuo* 31.2–62.11. (Reprinted Hong Kong: Shangwu yinshuguan, 1980.)

Huitou kan 回頭看 (Looking Backward). 1987 [1904]. *Libai liu*, pp. 25–36 (1904). (Reprinted Jiangsu Guanling guji keyin she, 1987.) [Translation of Edward Bellamy. *Looking Backward: 2000–1887*, (1888)].

Huss, Mikael. 2000. "Hesitant Journey to the West: SF's Changing Fortunes in Mainland China", *Science Fiction Studies* 27.1, pp. 92–104.

Iser, Wolfgang. 1987. *The Act of Reading. A Theory of Aesthetic Response*. Baltimore, London: Johns Hopkins University Press.

Malmgren, Carl Darryl. 1985. *Fictional Space in the Modernist and Postmodernist American Novel*. Lewisburg: Associated University Presses.

Masini, Federico. 1993. *The Formation of Modern Chinese Lexicon and its Evolution Towards a National Language: The Period From 1840 to 1898*. Berkeley: Journal of Chinese Linguistics (Monograph Series, no. 6).

Matthew, Robert. 1978. *The Origins of Japanese Science Fiction*. Brisbane: Department of Japanese, University of Queensland (Occasional Papers 4).

Mei Meng 梅夢. 1997 [1918]. "Shuidi qianxingting" 水底潛行艇 (Submarine), in: Yu Runqi 于潤琦 (ed.). *Qingmo minchu xiaoshuo shuxi. Kexue juan* 清末民初小說書系。科學卷 (Fiction from the Late Qing and Early Republic. Science). Beijing: Zhongguo wenlian chuban gongsi, pp. 209–17. [Originally published in *Xiaoshuo yuebao* 9.8 (1918)].

Novotná, Zdenka. 1967–1969. "Contributions to the Study of Loan-words and Hybrid words in Modern Chinese", in: *Archív orientální* 35, pp. 613–48; 36, pp. 295–325; 37, pp. 48–75.

—— [Heřmanová-]. 1974. "Coinage and Structure of Economic Terms in Modern Chinese", *Asian and African Languages in Social Context*. Prague: Oriental Institute in Academia, pp. 45–77.

Pollard, David. 1998. "Jules Verne, Science Fiction and Related Matters", in: id. (ed.). *Translation and Creation*. Amsterdam, Philadelphia: John Benjamins, pp. 177–207.

Wang, David Der-wei. 1997. *Fin-de-Siècle Splendor. Repressed Modernities of Late Qing Fiction, 1849–1911*. Stanford: Stanford University Press.

Wu, Dingbo and Patrick D. Murphy. 1989. *Science Fiction from China*. New York: Praeger.

Wu Jianren吳趼人 . 1986 [1905]. *Xin shitou ji* 石頭記 (New Story of the Stone). Zhengzhou: Zhengzhou guji chubanshe. [Originally published in *Nangong bao* 8–11 (1905)].

Xiaoran Yusheng 簫然郁生 . 1997 [1906]. "Wutuobang youji" 烏托邦游記 (Travel to Utopia), in: Yu Runqi 于潤琦 (ed.). *Qingmo minchu xiaoshuo shuxi. Kexue juan* 清末民初小説書系。科學卷 (Fiction from the Late Qing and Early Republic. Science). Beijing: Zhongguo wenlian chuban gongsi, pp. 73–86. [Originally published in *Yueyue xiaoshuo* 1–2 (1906)].

Xu Nianci 徐念慈 . 1997 [1905]. "Xin Faluo xiansheng tan" 新法螺先生譚 (New story of Mr. Loudhailer), in: Yu Runqi 于潤琦 (ed.). *Qingmo minchu xiaoshuo shuxi. Kexue juan* 清末民初小説書系。科學卷 (Fiction from the Late Qing and Early Republic. Science). Beijing: Zhongguo wenlian chuban gongsi, pp. 1–20. [Originally published in *Xiaoshuo lin* 6 (1905)].

Yu Runqi 于潤琦 (ed.). *Qingmo minchu xiaoshuo shuxi. Kexue juan* 清末民初小説書系。科學卷 (Fiction from the Late Qing and Early Republic. Science). Beijing: Zhongguo wenlian chuban gongsi.

GERLINDE GILD

THE EVOLUTION OF MODERN CHINESE MUSICAL THEORY AND TERMINOLOGY UNDER WESTERN IMPACT

INTRODUCTION

The important task ascribed to music in China during the first decades of the twentieth century was to stimulate change and act as a stabilising factor in the new society. This redefined role can only be understood against the background of traditional Chinese music and culture, which also helps to account for later lexical changes. The first texts consisted exclusively of musical notation. The significance of this aspect becomes obvious when we recall the difference between the European and the Chinese systems of musical notation. European notation consisted of a system with fixed rhythmical units, whereas Chinese notation did not serve a prescriptive function but was rather aimed at a documentary or descriptive preservation of the old tunes.

Despite the strong influence of central Asia, especially during the Tang period, the Chinese system of musical notation and its terminology remained relatively unchanged throughout history. This is evident in the cyclical form of historiographic musical theory, the homology of which was rooted in Confucianism and which strove towards the perfection of the music of the ancestors. These retrogressive ways of thinking that are embedded in Confucian historiography led to a musical theory based on learned treatises which mainly relied on lengthy explanatory quotations for their didactic purposes. In this way, the terminology of Chinese musical theory remained remarkably stable from the time of the early Zhou until the late Qing dynasty. Throughout this period, musical terminology was embedded in the general formation of Chinese culture.

In this paper I am going to investigate the works of three important Chinese musicologists of the early twentieth century who presented different approaches for introducing Western music and notation to China: Shen Xingong 沈心工 (1869–1947), as the first teacher of singing in Chinese schools, Li Shutong 李叔同 (1880–1942), as an advocate for moderate westernization and an integration of classical Chinese poetry set to music, and Zeng Zhimin 曾志忞 (1879–1929),

as the 'father' of Chinese music pedagogy. I will briefly discuss their encounter with Western musical theory, which in all cases took place in Japan; in a second step, I will investigate the lexical changes in musical terminology as a result of this contact with modern Japanese musicology.

1. MUSICAL THEORY IN CHINA PRIOR TO 1900:
A BRIEF HISTORICAL INTRODUCTION

Since the first contacts between China and the West, music and musical instruments have played a prominent role. Both sides considered music as the essence of their respective cultures and as an expression of human 'innermostness'. In 1601, Matteo Ricci wrote the *Xiqin quyi* 西琴曲意 (Eight songs for the cembalo),[1] which presented eight Christian songs; these, however, were written down without any musical notation. Although we find only four musical terms (*xiqin* 西琴 'harpsichord' or 'cembalo', *yaqin* 雅琴, the Chinese 'zither with seven strings', *qu* 曲 'song' and *yin* 音 'tone') in Ricci's short introduction, this treatise can be taken as the first Chinese text on European music. More specifically, Ricci introduced the 'Western harpsichord' (*xiyang yaqin* 西洋雅琴), which was among the Jesuit gifts to the Wanli emperor.

The first text to extensively deal with European musical terminology is the *Lülü zhengyi xubian* 律呂正義續編 (The correct meaning of the pitchpipes), written by Tomaso Pereira and Theodorico Pedrini, and published in 1713.[2] But it was to take another 190 years (from 1713 to 1903) until a theoretical text on European notation was written by a Chinese author.

During the Jesuit era, the reach of music and musical theory, just like that of the European sciences, was limited to the uppermost strata of Chinese society, the palace officials and the imperial family. When the Jesuits fell into disfavour and had to leave the imperial court, European music also fell into oblivion. Interest in Western music was

---

[1] Ricci edited the text with the editorial assistance of Li Zhizao 李之藻. See Li Zhizao. 1965. "Jiren Shipian" 畸人十篇 (Ten chapters by an unconventionalist), *Xiqin Quyi* 西琴曲意 (Eight songs for the cembalo), *Tianxue chuhan congshu* 天學初函叢書. Taibei: Taiwan xuesheng shuju.

[2] *Lülü Zhengyi Xubian* 律呂正義續編 (The correct meaning of the *Lülü*). 1713. Reprinted in: *Qinding siku quanshu* 欽定四庫全書, *Jingbu* 經部 9, pp. 1–221.

only aroused again through the activities of Protestant missionaries in the late nineteenth century. Although the missionaries wrote a multitude of hymn-books, hardly any of these touched upon the theory or terminology of music. The only three surviving hymn-books that deal with elements of musical theory are the *Xiaoshipu* 小詩譜 (Tune-book in Chinese notation) by Mrs. Timothy Richard,[3] the *Shengshipu:Yuefa qimeng* 聖詩譜：樂法啟蒙(Christian hymns: Introduction to musical notation) by Julia B. Mateer,[4] and the *Laba chuifa* 喇叭吹法 (Technique of trumpet-playing) by Carl T. Kreyer.[5]

In 1903, when Zeng Zhimin composed his *Yueli Dayi* 樂理大意 (Introduction to musical theory), the first Chinese modern musical theory, there was a lack of teaching material. And because of the lack of suitable teachers there was no text uniformity in China . This situation was characterised by Zeng as follows: "In the whole country there were only two or three books, out of which one or two were badly or superficially written."[6] Through my research work at the Beijing Library and the Music Research Institute I came to the conclusion that these "two or three" texts alluded to by Zeng were the abovementioned written by European missionaries.[7] These texts contain an introduction to Western notation and singing:

1. The *Lülü zhengyi xubian*, which marks the beginning of the evolution of a systematic Chinese music terminology.[8]

2. The *Xiaoshipu* by Mrs. Timothy Richard. Timothy Richard had used the tonic-sol-fa-system for teaching singing in the missionary

---

[3] Timothy Richard (Li Timotai 李提摩太). 1883. *Xiaoshipu* 小詩譜 (Tune-book in Chinese notation). Shanghai: Society for the diffusion of Christian and general knowledge. (Reprint 1901).

[4] Julia Brown Mateer (Di Jiulie 狄就烈). 1892. *Shengshipu - Yuefa Qimeng* 聖詩譜：樂法啟蒙 (Christian hymns: Introduction to musical notation). Shanghai: Meihua shuguan. (First edition 1872, supplement 1879, second edition 1892, third edition 1907.) (I had the edition of 1892 in my hands).

[5] Karl Kreyer (Jin Kaili 金楷理). n.d. *Laba Chuifa* 喇叭吹法 (Introduction to trumpet-playing). (Without place or time of publication, not in the booklist of the Jiangnan-Arsenal). See Adrian A. Bennett and John Fryer. 1967. *The Introduction of Western Science and Technology into Nineteenth Century China*. Cambridge, Mass.: Harvard University Press, pp. 21f.

[6] Zeng Zhimin 曾志忞 . 1903b. "Yinyue Jiaoyulun (1)" 音樂教育論 (1) (On music pedagogy), *Xinmin congbao* 3.14, pp. 55–60.

[7] I draw this conclusion from the fact no other sources are mentioned at all, and all sources to be found were those written by European missionaries.

[8] See Gerlinde Gild-Bohne. 1991. *Das Lülü Zhengyi Xubian. Ein Jesuitentraktat über die europäische Notation in China von 1713*. Göttingen: Edition Re.

school until he realized that China had her own solmization technique, the *gongchipu*-System (工尺譜). The *Xiaoshipu*, written by his wife, represents the development of a Chinese notational system, by adding the expressive signs of Western notation to the pitches of the *gongchi*-system (for instance the graphical representation of the crescendo and decrescendo).

3. The *Shengshipu - Yuefa Qimeng*, which is the first work in Chinese history for the laity in the mission schools; it conveys basic musical theoretical knowledge and concerns itself with the European musical system and its terminology. In the Chinese preface of Mateer (there is a short one in English as well) she mentions the *Lülü zhengyi xubian*, but brings forth the difficulty in understanding the text, which originated during the transition period from church modes to the major/ minor system.

The fourth text, compiled by Karl Kreyer, the *Laba Chuifa*, was most probably used as teaching material for the first Chinese brass band directed by Sir Robert Hart,[9] and makes use mainly of the same terms as Mateer.

2. THE EVOLUTION OF MODERN CHINESE MUSICAL THEORY

The renewal of Chinese music goes back to the reform period at the end of the nineteenth century. Following the call for a reform of the educational system by Liang Qichao 梁啟超 (1873–1928), Kang You-wei 康有為 (1858–1928) and others, the musical system was thoroughly transformed. The transformation began almost immediately after the two reformers had fled to Japan. The medium in which the changes of the musical system manifested themselves were journals edited in Japan, such as *Xinmin congbao* 新民叢報 , *Jiangsu* 江蘇 and *Xingshi* 醒獅 .[10] From that period on, and especially after the May Fourth Movement of 1919, the Chinese musical system as well as its terminology were anchored in the basic notions of Western musical theory, which were brought into China via Japan.

---

[9] John King Fairbank et al. (eds.). 1975. *The I.G. in Peking. Letters of Robert Hart. Chinese Maritime Customs, 1868–1907*. Cambridge, Mass.: Belknap Press, vol. 2, p. 1330.
[10] Unfortunately I did not have access to *Xingshi*.

When the first Chinese students arrived in Japan at the end of the nineteenth century, there already existed a highly developed system of musical pedagogy, including regular singing in kindergarten, school and university. The most important person for the introduction of modern musical theory and terminology in Japan was Izawa Shūji 伊沢修二 (1851–1917).[11] One of his most renowned works is *Yōgaku kotohajime* 洋樂事始 (Fundamentals in Western music).[12] Inspired by Izawa's activities, Shen Xingong, one of the early Chinese students in Japan, developed an enthusiastic interest in modern music. In 1902 he founded the "Society for the Study of Music" (*yinyue jiangxihui* 音樂講習會), later renamed "Society for Refined Asian Music" (*yaya yinyuehui* 亞雅音樂會). In the statutes of this society, which were published in the *Xinmin congbao*, probably by Liang Qichao himself, who supported the society, Article One defining the aims of the society calls for the development of music in schools and public life "in order to awaken the 'national spirit' (*guomin jingshen* 國民精神)."[13] The statutes paved the way which Chinese music was to follow. The founders of the statutes of the music-study society were the leading music educationalists of this period, Zeng Zhimin, Shen Xingong and Li Shutong. Tamura Torazō 田村虎藏 and Izawa Shūji also belonged to the music society.

The first Chinese student who studied music in Japan was Zeng Zhimin.[14] He went to Japan in 1901. In 1902 he joined the music-study society (*yinyue jiangxihui* 音樂講習會). 1903 he switched from the study of law to that of music, at the Music Institute in Tokyo (*Tōkyō ongaku gakkō* 東京音樂學校), which was founded in 1879.[15]

Shen Xingong, who as a licentiate (*xiucai* 秀才) bore the fruits of a classical education, went to Japan in 1902. As the founder of the

---

[11] William P. Malm. 1971. "The Modern Music of Meiji Japan", in: Donald H. Shively (ed.). *Tradition and Modernisation in Japanese Culture*. Princeton: Princeton University Press, pp. 257–300; 265.

[12] Izawa Shūji 伊沢修二 . 1884. *Yōgaku kotohajime* 洋樂事始 (Fundamentals in Western music). Tokyo: Heibonsha. (Reprint 1971).

[13] "Yaya yinyue hui zhi lishi" 亞雅音樂會之歷史 (History of the Asian Refined Music Society). 1903. *Xinmin Congbao* 3.9, pp. 101–4.

[14] See Chen Lingjun 陳聆群 . 1983. "Bu ying bei yiwang de yiwei xianbei yinyuejia Zeng Zhimin" 不應被遺忘的一位先輩音樂家曾志忞 (Never forget a musicologist of the first generation. Zeng Zhimin), *Zhongyang yinyue xueyuan xuebao* 3, pp. 44–8.

[15] Zeng's work will be introduced below.

music-study society he was entitled to engage Suzuki Yonejirō 鈴木米
次郎 (1868–1940), the well-known Japanese music pedagogue, as a
teacher. In public life, schools and political propaganda there, he
became conscious of the importance of singing. In February 1903 he
returned to China and took a position as a teacher in one of the
schools next to the Nanyang College. This was the beginning of modern music teaching in Shanghai.

The second early composer of school songs, Li Shutong,[16] went to
Japan and studied oil-painting at the Tokyo Art Academy. Simultaneously, he took to piano instrumentation at the Music Institute.[17] From
my own research, Li Shutong and Shen Xingong produced very few
theoretical writings. Nevertheless, the few writings of both scholars
are important for the understanding of the different approaches to the
meaning of composition of modern music and school songs.

1. Shen Xingong and the introduction of singing in Chinese schools

Shen established in several schools the subject of singing, and simultaneously undertook the education of music teachers. After the founding of the "Society for the Study of Music" in Tokyo, the
establishment of the teaching of singing (*changge ke* 唱歌課) in the
schools in 1903 was the second milestone in the introduction of modern music teaching to China. Owing to the shortness of his stay in
Japan, Shen failed to round off his theoretical notions. He left no
musical theoretical publications of importance, but did leave a collection of songs.[18] In this *Xuexiao changgeji* 學校唱歌集 (Anthology of
school songs), the first volume also consists of a short introduction to
singing, the *Yueli cuoyao* 樂理撮要, and a short introduction to playing the organ. The second section of the preface contains the following observations:

> On my way to learning the writing of songs (*zuo geshi* 作歌試) I
> selected mainly Japanese melodies. But nowadays I am not fond any-

---

[16] Li Shutong had studied traditional painting and in 1901 he, like his predecessors, joined the pedagogical Institute in Shanghai, the Nanyang Gongxue.

[17] In his song collection *Guoxue Changgeji* 國學唱歌集 (Anthology of songs for
public schools) already published in 1906, a very small part consisted of his own
compositions, which are based on Japanese and Western melodies appended with
Chinese poetry.

[18] Shen Qia 沈洽. 1983. "Shen Xingong zhuan" 沈心工傳 (A biography of Shen
Xingong), *Yinyue yanjiu* 4, p. 60.

more of those songs, instead I mostly choose European melodies, because of the small tonal range of Japanese tunes, which makes them good on the ear, but characterized by meanness. On the other hand, the tonal range of Western melodies is more complete and clear. They give the impression of something like a high-minded phenomenon. The general psychology of the Chinese tends to a preference for Japanese tunes. They are not very fond of Western tunes. Surprisingly, some teachers during song teaching append something extra (*jiahua* 加花), which makes them very proud. (Such an amendment) in the field of music is disastrous.[19]

This short passage reflects Shen's pedagogical intention in choosing school songs. On the one hand, the author conveys to the reader the high-minded supremacy of Western melodies, more pedagogically adaptable than Japanese melodies, while on the other, the transitional stage becomes evident, in the sense that the Chinese learned how to keep exactly to an original version without the introduction of rhythmical ornaments within the frame of traditional Chinese folksong, which is a prerequisite for their vivacity and originality.

2. Li Shutong and the integration of classical Chinese poetry into modern music

It is remarkable to note that after such a short time of study in 1906 Li Shutong managed to publish the first Chinese musical journal, the *Yinyue xiao zazhi* 音樂小雜志 , in which he wrote the preface under the name of Xi Shuang (息霜). In this journal, below the caption "Musical Theory" (*yuedian* 樂典), an introduction to modern musical theory is given by Tamura Torazō. It is the centerpiece of the journal and the longest article in it (see below). Under "Miscellaneous" (*zazuan* 雜纂) there follows another article by Li Shutong, the *Zuofeilu* (past errors written down). This short article, together with the following, "*Wuhu, cizhang!*" 嗚呼詞章 (Oh, polished phraseology)[20] point to Li Shutong's moderate reforming spirit. After the initial

---

[19] Shen Xingong 沈心工 . 1915. *Xuexiao Changgeji* 學校唱歌集 (Anthology of school songs). Shanghai: Wenming shuju, preface p. 3.

[20] Matthews gives "polished phraseology" in translating *cizhang* (R. H. Matthews. 1974. *Chinese-English dictionary*. Cambridge, Mass.: Harvard University Press, p. 1031). *Cizhang* is not mentioned as a category in William H. Nienhauser's *Indiana Companion to Traditional Chinese Literature* (1986. Bloomington: Indiana University Press).

enthusiasm for the new Western music in Japan there followed deep reflection:

> In the song-books published during recent times in China there has been no notation for voice volume and time (*qiangruo huanji deng jihao* 強弱緩急等記號). Teachers have usually either treated corresponding parts carelessly, or they have simplified the matter as they think fit. Consequently the vitality and the charm of the songs are lost completely.[21]

In the last part of the article, after he had considered the significance of intensive study and practising of the songs, and singing them with harmonium (*feng qin* 風琴) accompaniment, Li Shutong gives air to his frustrations:

> Last year a friend asked me to compile a Chinese song-book, a matter which I undertook at once. When nowadays I reflect on this matter I feel grossly disturbed. I have already written a letter to this friend in which I have requested him to suspend the sale of the books and to destroy them.

His failure—but also and more importantly the failure of his preceding colleagues—was rooted in dilettantism, which becomes evident in the following article:

> From the time I came to live in Japan I have occupied myself very superficially with Japanese songs. About 95% of the texts derive the meaning of their words from ancient Chinese poems (the most famous Japanese songtext-writers are versed in Classical Chinese poetry). Since the Qing dynasty Chinese literati have made painstaking efforts to write in the schematic *cizhang* 詞章 (polished phraseology) style. Hence classical poetry and prose have gone into oblivion. Later, Western sciences were introduced and became fashionable. The word *cizhang* is hardly mentioned. For this type of literati, who had no grasp of classical texts and were incapable of understanding them, the only options were to falsify or to misinterpret the texts. Classical knowledge is dishonoured or discarded. Thus, when such people deal with Japanese song texts they greatly admire the fascinating thoughts. They consider as arch-Japanese what the Japanese take from our classical poetry. In such a situation all those concerned become ridiculous, to the Japanese as well as to the Chinese.[22]

---

[21] Xi Shuang 息霜 (Li Shutong). 1906a. "Zuofeilu" 昨非录 (Record of our mistakes in the past), *Yinyue xiao zazhi* 1, p. 19.

[22] Xi Shuang 息霜 (Li Shutong). 1906b. "Wuhu, Cizhang!" 嗚呼詞章 (Oh, polished phraseology), *Yinyue xiao zazhi* 1, p. 20.

Thus Li Shutong argues for a sound classical education instead of following the fashionable stylistic trends of the day. His bond with tradition became evident as he set poems from the *Shijing* 詩經 and the *Chuci* 楚辭 to Japanese and Western tunes. Li thus combined the early reception of European music through the introduction of school songs with classical education. The transmission of Western music theory and terminology was due to Zeng Zhimin.

3. Zeng Zhimin and the beginnings of Chinese musical science

In comparison with his predecessors, the theoretical work of Zeng Zhimin is wide-ranging[23] and forms the basis of modern music pedagogy. Zeng wrote the first theoretical texts and translations and so introduced modern terminology from Japan into China. As quoted above, Zeng did not see any substantial musical theory available at his time. Moreover, another statement explains why he felt the need to establish a radically new theory: "If civilization is [only] imported and not self-constructed, [any attempts] to establish it are doomed to failure."[24] Owing to the fact that Zeng Zhimin classified the above mentioned theoretical texts prior to 1900 as inferior and superficial, he neither mentions any of their titles, nor does he use any of the coined termini, but bases his work upon the Japanese texts of musical theory only. In addition, he is eager to integrate musical research into the framework of the sciences. In the second part of his treatise "Yinyue jiaoyu lun" 音樂教育論 (On musical education) he insists on the necessity of a wide-ranging modern terminology as a basis for instruction, in order to provide a scientific basis for musical research:

> Everything existing implies a definition (*dingyi* 定義). Quality implies a function and function implies meaning. ... Music is considered today as one of the sciences, but if it is a science, this implies that it has to be treated as all sciences, and then as such it must be investigated. Likewise, its definitions must be known.[25]

Zeng Zhimin was the first Chinese to introduce Western musical notation to China in a systematic treatise. It was published in the journal of

---

[23] See Liu Jingzhi 劉靖之 . 1986. *Zhongguo xinyinyue shi lunji* 中國新音樂史論集 (Collection of treatises on the history of Chinese New Music). Hong Kong: Xianggang Daxue yazhou yanjiu zhongxin, p. 28.

[24] Zeng, 1903b, p. 55.

[25] Zeng Zhimin. 1903c. "Yinyue Jiaoyulun (2)" 音樂教育論 (2) (On music pedagogy), *Xinmin congbao* 3.20, pp. 61–74; p. 61.

the Union of Jiangsu-Chinese, *Jiangsu*.[26] In the short introduction Zeng presents the newly awakened interest in music pedagogy from the perspective of traditional ethics.

> The musical development of our country attained high standard in ear-liest times. It developed during the *sandai*-epoch to full bloom, and music was counted as one of the six arts.[27] From ancient times peda-gogues considered music to be of great importance. From the Han dynasty on ritual music (*yayue* 雅樂) lost its importance and profane music (*suyue* 俗樂) became licentious and degenerate, so from that time on music was unworthy of men of letters.[28]

In classical diction, Zeng carries on Confucian argumentation: Start-ing from Han dynasty folk music was gathered and permeated the upper social strata. This resulted in a blending, a situation quite unac-ceptable to the Confucians, who rejected the non-literati tradition of folkmusic (*suyue*) and its emotive qualities. These considerations of Zeng Zhimin give the impression to the reader that Chinese music has been in a period of stagnation ever since the Han dynasty. He then proceeds to the meaning of modern educational song teaching as he had learned it in Japan. In his concept of music pedagogy Zeng did not have recourse to his own musical tradition, neither to the instru-mentarium nor to music-ethics. For instance, for the transitional period he considered the recruiting of Japanese and European teachers who were not acquainted with Chinese music. Zeng took the organ as his main musical instrument for teaching, utilising Chinese poems as songtexts, and Chinese folksong melodies in order to preserve tradi-tion.

From the rules which Zeng established in his last chapter of the *Yinyue jiaoyulun*, it appears that he demanded a new way of thinking and the departure from Chinese culture with respect to school music:

> 1. An original composition should not be altered.
> 2. The stanzas of a song should not be shortened.
> 3. To a song, committed to memory, no new words should be added.
> 4. Ignorance of musical theory permits neither the writing of songs, nor the transcription of notation.[29]

---

[26] Zeng Zhimin. 1903a. "Yueli dayi" 樂理大意 (Fundamentals of musical theory), *Jiangsu zazhi* 6, pp. 63–70.

[27] *Liuyi* 六藝 : propriety, music, archery, charioteering, writing and mathematics, according to R. H. Matthews. 1974. *Chinese-English dictionary*. Cambridge, Mass.: Harvard University Press, p. 597.

[28] Zeng 1903a, p. 63.

To maintain authenticity in music the introduction of the five-line system in China was necessary. The invention of the five-line-system in European music was regarded by the Chinese as the main reason for Western musical progress and for the backwardness of Chinese music.

In the first issue of the *Yinyue zazhi* 音樂雜誌 (Music Journal)[30] Xiao Youmei 蕭友梅 (1884–1940)[31] described music education in China in the Zhou time as having been mostly in the hands of blind musicians. The same phenomenon of blind musicians also occurred in Europe, but there they had never been educationalists, but simply musicians. For this reason the notational system of the West was improved every year, and ever since the fifteenth century music could be transmitted and older music could be performed. Certainly, in China there had been many good musical pieces and techniques, but whenever there was neither a friend nor a disciple with a good ear, melodies and techniques were irrevocably lost. "For this reason Boya played no more and broke his qin after the death of Zhong Ziqi. Otherwise could we not listen to that music today?"[32]

Certainly a very clever argument, but the author makes no mention of the highly developed Qin music notation of this refined Chinese classical music. The reasons for the backwardness of Chinese music which we observe in Zeng's writings were analysed by Xiao Youmei. In the light of the development of Western music Xiao saw the following differences:

1. Keyboard instruments, seen by Xiao as the origin of polyphony (erroneously).

2. As well, the invention of the mensural and staff notation on which counterpoint was based.

3. The respected profession of organist and cantor.

4. The mastersingers, that is the art of singing in the guilds, and their predecessors the *minnesingers*.

---

[29] Zeng 1903c, pp. 72–3.

[30] Chen Lingjun 陳聆群 et al. 1990. *Xiao Youmei yinyue wenji* 蕭友梅音樂文集 (Collected essays on music by Xiao Youmei). Shanghai: Shanghai yinyue chubanshe, p. 166.

[31] Xiao Youmei studied in Tokyo and Leipzig. In 1927 he became director of the newly established conservatory of music. See Chen 1990, p. 555.

[32] Xiao Youmei, cited in Chen 1990, p. 555.

5. The establishment of music schools in Europe in the sixteenth century.

The consequences of these considerations were that teachers and musicians of the old style had to learn Western notation, harmony, counterpoint, instrumentation and composition, and that only under this proviso could there be said to be a reform of Chinese music.[33]

In China the available literature on musical texts were not reference texts, because these texts were as varied in their termini as in their structure. The first ten chapters of the *Lülü zhengyi xubian*, for instance, deal with the notation of melody and the following chapters with notation of rhythm. But, as already mentioned, later authors were reluctant in utilising these texts, probably because of their emergence during the transitional period from the heptachord to the minor/major system and the ensuing difficulties. In the *Yuefa qimeng*, which was presented in the form of a dialogue between teacher and pupil, Mateer adopted some of the termini of the *Lülü zhengyi xubian*, but the sole element which these early texts have in common is that they consist of a section describing the notation of melody followed by a section on the notation of rhythm.

3. THE EVOLUTION OF MODERN CHINESE MUSICAL TERMS

For the analysis of musical terms in order to distinguish their specific origins, I have chosen six categories of coining word structures in Chinese, derived from the authoritative studies of Wolfgang Lippert and Federico Masini:[34]

1. Phonemic loans, i.e. foreign words rendered into Chinese by means of phonemic borrowing, for instance the solmization syllables

---

[33] Chen 1990, p. 414.

[34] For methodological purposes I refer to linguistic studies by Wolfgang Lippert, who classifies foreign words in Chinese into the four categories phonemic loans, semantic loans, hybrids and graphical loans; and by Federico Masini, who appended the category of return loans and neologisms proper (or loan creations, German: *Lehnschöpfungen*). Wolfgang Lippert. 1979. *Entstehung und Funktion einiger chinesischer marxistischer Termini. Der lexikalisch-begriffliche Aspekt der Rezeption des Marxismus in Japan und China.* Wiesbaden: Steiner; Federico Masini. 1993. *The Formation of Modern Chinese Lexicon and Its Evolution Toward a National Language: The period from 1840 to 1898.* Berkeley: Journal of Chinese Linguistics (Monograph Series no. 6).

do re mi fa sol la si, which is *wu, le, ming, fa, shuo, la, xi*, 烏勒鳴乏朔
拉犀), or Piccolo flute, *bigeluo* (比各洛).

2. Semantic loans, i.e. words or morphemes which do exist in the
traditional lexicon, but are endowed with an hitherto unknown meaning, for instance "musical note, *jihao* 記號 ", which in the traditional
lexicon denotes a sign or a mark.

3. Graphic loans, words which take their meaning and written form
from a language with a Chinese writing system, for instance "national
anthem, *kokka* 國歌 " from Japan.

4. Return loans, i.e. words which existed in the traditional lexicon,
were borrowed into Japanese, later went out of use in China and came
back to China via Japan; for instance 'harmony' *hesheng* 和聲 which
in the traditional lexicon denotes 'harmonious music', was adopted in
the Japanese lexicon as *wasei*, and now means 'harmony'.

5. Hybrids, words in which a phonemic loan is combined with an
autochthonous element, for instance the instrument 'kettledrum'
(Kesselpauke) 扣得爾鼓 (*koudeergu*), where '*koudeer*' is the phonemic and '*gu*' (drum) the autochthonous element.

6. Neologisms proper. These are, according to Masini, "new formations stimulated by a foreign word but not based on any foreign
model,[35] for instance 'accordion' rendered as *shoufengqin* 手風琴 .

I will compare the early terminology on Western music as it
appears in the *Lülü zhengyi xubian*, the *Yuefa qimeng* by Julia B.
Mateer, the *Yōgaku kotohajime* 洋樂事始 by Izawa Shūji, the *Yuedian
Dayi* 樂典大意 by Tamura Torazō, the teacher of Zeng Zhimin, and
the works by Zeng Zhimin.[36] Pars pro toto I have chosen the terms for
notation, composition and note, and will discuss the genetic structure
of their various Chinese equivalents. This analysis will lend further
credit to the argument stated above, that Japanese musicology was
crucial for the formation of Chinese musicology, including in terms of
lexical change.

1. Notation:

Traditionally, 'notation' was rendered as *pu* 譜 or *qupu* 曲譜 and, in a
musical context, meant to fix a melody on paper with the help of
abbreviated characters (in Qin-notation), with the characters for the
twelve Lü (*Lülü pu* 律呂譜), or with graphical emblems combined

---

[35] Masini 1993, pp. 128f.
[36] See *Yueli Dayi* 樂理大意 and *Yinyue jiaoyulun* 音樂教育論 , ibid.

with shortened characters (*gongchipu*) and the like. As yet it was not uniform, but differed with the various Instruments and epochs. Since rhythm and measure had no particular aspect but, rather, many different ones, depending on their respective composers/players, there were no fixed units for time.

Lülü zhengyi xubian: *zipu* 字譜 appears for 'notation' in the preface, whereas in the actual text the term *yuetu* 樂圖 is used. *Tu* denotes an illustration, a map, a picture or a diagram. The combination with *yue* is a neologism (or loan creation).

Yuefa qimeng: the combination *yuebiao* 樂表 used for 'notation' in this text is not found in the traditional lexicon. *Biao* denotes an index, a chart, a watch etc. The translation of this neologism would be 'musical chart'.

Yōgaku kotohajime: Izawa Shūji gives *gakufu* 樂譜 as equivalent to 'notation' which was used in China from the Song dynasty, but later went out of use. In later Chinese works this is a reimported term.

Yuedian dayi: *pubiao* 譜表

Zeng: *pubiao* 譜表 is evidently a graphical loan from Japan.

2. Composition

In the European musical tradition 'composition' has the sense of individual creation, which satisfies the criterion of originality and is represented in a written form of tone semiotics. In this sense there is no equivalent for tis term in classical Chinese, as the idea of composition as a sound pictogram to the requirements of originality did not exist in China. The composer was the performer at the same time:

> The compositional process was very often a recreational process and included the recomposing, arranging and editing of existing musical works. The recreator might use such material almost in its entirety, adding his own personal stylizations (mannerisms), or partially selecting certain musical phrases and reworking them with additional material. As a result many different versions exist for certain common pieces, which may be found in different musical genres.[37]

Hence, instead of a concept of 'composition' there were recreational processes and new arrangements of existing tunes. This was *dapu* 打譜 in *qin* 琴 art, a kind of recreating composition, where only the pitch structure (German: *Tonhöhenverlauf*) was written down, and the exact rhythm was neglected.

---

[37] Liang Mingyue. 1985. *Music of the Billion. An Introduction to Chinese Musical Culture*. New York: Heinrichshofen, pp. 174–5.

Lülü zhengyi xubian: *Duqu* 度曲 denotes 'singing a written tune'.[38] In the *Lülü zhengyi xubian* it has the connotation of 'musical notation'. We can count it as a semantic loan.

Yuefa qimeng: no mention of the term

Yōgaku kotohajime: *gakkyoku* 樂曲, in the sense of a 'musical opus'; *senpō* 旋法 in the sense of the 'compositional process'.

Yuedian dayi: no mention of the term

Zeng: *zuoqu* 作曲 does not exist in traditional sources. It is a graphical loan from the Japanese lexicon.

3. Note

In the European notation system a note means a symbol representing the pitch and duration of a musical sound. Such notes are not found in traditional Chinese music.

Lülü zhengyi xubian: *xinghao* 形號 neological word structure

Yuefa qimeng: *hao* 號, *yuehao* 樂號. *Hao* is a semantic loan and *yuehao* is a neological word structure.

Yōgaku kotohajime: *onpu* 音符

Yuedian dayi: *yinfu* 音符

Zeng: *yinfu* 音符 is not found in traditional Chinese sources and is a graphical loan.

The new terminology of the early phase of modernization corresponds exactly to that of the Japanese, with nearly all new terms adopted as graphical loans. Compared to earlier Chinese musical treatises it becomes evident that the reception of European terminology—as demonstrated in three typical examples above—started with the sojourn of Chinese students in Japan.

In the next developmental phase, during the May Fourth Movement, Chinese students went to Europe and collected large quantities of technical terms, mainly neologisms and hybrids, which they brought back to China. The high quantity of graphical loans, neologisms and hybrids in comparison to the very few semantical loans shows that little time was left for reflection, however necessary, on the differences or similarities between East Asian and Western musi-

---

[38] See *Hanyu Dacidian* 漢語大詞典 (Great Chinese dictionary). 1990. "An qupu changge" 按曲譜唱歌 (Singing a written tune). Shanghai: Hanyu da cidian chubanshe, vol. 3, p. 1225.

cal cultures. Instead Chinese music was degraded—in tune with the general iconoclasm of the May Fourth agenda.

The complete adoption of the Western system consisting of polyphony and harmony led to the repression of traditional music, even long before the Europeanization of traditional instruments at the beginning of the Communist era, when autochthonous instruments were reconstructed in such a way that the form was preserved, but the pitch and strength of volume was increased.[39]

4. CONCLUSION: THE PROBLEMS OF DEFINING MODERN CHINESE MUSIC

The unsolved problems concerning the evolution of Chinese music are reflected in the discussions outlined above, on school songs and academic studies on music, on the dichotomy of art- and folk music, and on the differences between Chinese indigenous music, Western music or the New Music of the twentieth century. From the beginning, these reflections on modern Chinese music were undertaken in comparison to the development of Western classical music, and thereby the connection of musical questions with the question of traditional heritage and national culture was quickly established.

At first it was Liang Qichao himself who gave incentives for a school curriculum in music, and to compose new melodies for old and new poems. When Liang postulated a musical form which supported the transformational processes in China,[40] this implies that Liang took a definite nationalistic attitude,[41] one which already pointed to the future of a new musical culture; its requirements were:

> From now on new songs have to be composed which can be used for teaching purposes. This is not easy, because poems like those (the *yankongge* 演孔歌 and the *aiguoge* 愛國歌 are very refined (*ya* 雅) and very learned, and consequently are not fit for the occasion.[42] On the other hand, if they are too simple (*su* 俗) they are too tasteless (*wuwei*

---

[39] See Alan Thrasher. 1980. *Foundations of Chinese Music. A Study of Ethics and Aesthetics*. Ann Arbor: U.M.I, pp. 167 f.

[40] Liang Qichao 梁啟超 (Yin Bingshi 飲冰室). 1905. "Yin Bingshi shihua" 飲冰室詩話(Yin Bingshi on poetry), *Xinmin congbao* 3.9, pp. 87–94: p. 87.

[41] Joseph R. Levenson. 1968. *Confucian China and its Modern Fate*. Berkeley: University of California Press, p. 97.

[42] *Yankongge*, the song in honour to Confucius, was written by Kang Youwei; the *Aiguoge*, "Patriotic song", was written by Liang Qichao. Both songs have been efforts in the direction of national anthems. See Liang Qichao 1905, p. 91.

無味). It had to be something in between the two [categories]. What children intend to sing should not miss the pregnancy of substance of the literature of our country.[43]

Liang explicitely equates the function of the New Music with the new role of modern literature, a role that was mainly—at least most prominently—formulated by Liang himself. In the process of evaluating traditional and new Chinese music, Chinese scientists had accordingly adopted the Western criteria of evaluation, which means that they did not consider traditional Chinese music as art-music. Instead, they adopted the prevalent view, that Chinese music had not developed since the classical period but only stagnated, and therefore the particularity of Chinese music was not acknowledged, at least not in a terminological sense.

Whereas the modern meaning of folk music is *minjian yinyue* 民間 音樂 (music within the people) we find no adequate meaning for the refined music, the former *yayue* 雅樂 . Instead, New Music or Contemporary Music *(xinyinyue* 新音樂 or *xiandai yinyue* 現代音樂), is used as an equivalent to the former *yayue* 雅樂 (refined music) which is the counterpart of *minjian yinyue*, and which is made subject to the high demands of Western art music. *Xinyinyue* denotes composition in European style, that is, the application of harmony, counterpoint, form and the playing techniques of Western instruments, but nevertheless with Chinese melodies and rhythms, and the occasional use of one or more Chinese instruments.

As far as music is concerned, Liang Qichao was a layman, but he proved himself a guide with respect to the new musical culture and music pedagogy. It is therefore very important to lay stress upon the first stage of Westernization of Chinese Music.

The leading figures of this newly established New Music were Zeng Zhimin and Xiao Youmei. The term *yayue* 雅樂 , when meaning refined music, was left over from the historical phenomenon of court ritual music. Xiao Youmei, who also had studied in Japan and Germany, was consequently an opponent of the restoration of old Chinese

---

[43] Liang Qichao 1905, p. 91. Here Liang does not take into consideration the rules of word-orientation in traditional Chinese singing. The conception of composing (*pu* 譜) has for the first time—as in Western composition—taken the shape of written music. See Wang Mei-chu. 1987. "Chinesische Notenschriften", *Zeitschrift für Semiotik* 9.3–4, pp. 301–15.

music and supported the reform of Chinese music. All the aforesaid
can be summarized in the following quotation by Xiao Youmei:

> We should not so much speak of restoration of ancient music 复興中國
> 音樂, but rather direct much more interest to the reform of Chinese
> music, 改造中國音樂. The restoration of ancient music would only be,
> after all, the renewed continuation of the old methods. Speaking of
> reform, however, means keeping its essence, but clearing it from
> unnecessary garbage. Furthermore, new forms of expression should be
> found for music. And for this reason certain techniques and tools of the
> West must be applied. Nevertheless, its own essence has to be kept and
> the national character should not be lost.[44]

Xiao clearly set his argument in the established dichotomy of *ti* 體
(essence) and *yong* 用 (practice) that had prevailed among some
reformers since the late nineteenth century. He had concrete plans as
to the development of Chinese music and proposed the following:

> Collection of folksong, clearing it of vulgar phrases and subsequent
> substitution of the obscure by easily understandable phrases and simple
> melodies; folksongs should be systematized and endowed with equiva-
> lent harmonies.[45]

The same applied to folk melodies, *minqu* 民曲, and old operas, *jiuju*
舊劇. The necessity of stimulating the writing and notation of folk
songs should become an imperative task for government and the
music institutions. The distribution of prizes had been considered as
an incentive for the new generation.

And yet, despite these efforts to introduce modern music to China,
the specific meaning of New Music remains obscure even today. Significantly, the Chinese lexicon gives definitions of *yayue* 雅樂, of
suyue 俗樂, of *gudian yinyue* 古典音樂 (Western classical music) and
of *xianfengpai* 先鋒派 (Avant-garde music, which is defined in terms
of the European Avant-garde, whereas the Chinese Avant-garde,
which has already been introduced into Europe is not mentioned with
one word).[46] Also included are the terms for serious music and light
music, *yansu yinyue* 嚴肅音樂 and *qing yinyue* 輕音樂. But when
looking up the definitions of *xin yinyue* 新音樂, since it is often men-

---

[44] Xiao Youmei, cited in Chen 1990, p. 465.

[45] Ibid., p. 466.

[46] See Frank Kouwenhoven. 1990. "Mainland China's New Music. The Age of
Pluralism", *Chime. Journal of the European Foundation for Chinese Music Research*
5, p. 76–134.

tioned in newspaper articles and musicological discussions,[47] for instance in the Encyclopedia of Music and Dance,[48] or the *Zhongguo yinyue cidian* 中國音樂辭典 , the only entry to be found refers to a newspaper with the title *Xinyinyue*, founded in 1940. We also find a Society of New Music (*xin yinyue she*) and the Movement of New Music (*Xin yinyue yundong*). However, we are not able to form an idea about what constitutes this New Music in terms of musical theory. Instead, the label 'new' is attached to these trends of Westernizing Chinese music at the beginning of the twentieth century, rather as a catchword with ideological ramifications than as a theoretical musical term.

---

[47] See Liu Qingzhi, ibid.; Gao Qiu 高秋 . 1982. "Xin Yinyue she shulüe" 新音樂社述略 (A short description of the Society for [Chinese] New Music), *Yinyue yanjiu* 2, pp. 95–9; Mao Yurun 茅于潤 , "Yige xinqigri de wuhou" 一個星期日的午后 (One Sunday afternoon), *Yinyue yishu* 2, pp. 16–22; Chen Lingjun. 1993. "Xiao Youmei de yinyue lilun gongxian" 蕭友梅的音樂理論貢獻 (Xiao Youmei's contribution to music theory), *Zhongguo yinyuexue* 2, p. 20.

[48] *Zhongguo dabaike quanshu* 中國大百科全書 (The great Chinese encyclopaedia). *Yinyue wudao* 音樂舞蹈 (Music and dance). 1989. Beijing, Shanghai: Zhongguo dabaike quanshu chubanshe.

REFERENCES

Bennett, Adrian A. and John Fryer. 1967. *The Introduction of Western Science and Technology into Nineteenth Century China*. Cambridge, Mass.: Harvard University Press.

Brown Mateer, Julia (Di Jiulie 狄就烈). 1892. *Shengshipu - Yuefa Qimeng* 聖詩譜：樂法啟蒙 (Christian hymns: Introduction to musical notation). Shanghai: Meihua shuguan.

Chen Lingjun 陳聆群 . 1983. "Bu ying bei yiwang de yiwei xianbei yinyuejia Zeng Zhimin" 不應被遺忘的一位先輩音樂家曾志忞 (Never forget a musicologist of the first generation. Zeng Zhimin), *Zhongyang yinyue xueyuan xuebao* 3, pp. 44–8.

—— et al. 1990. *Xiao Youmei yinyue wenji* 蕭友梅音樂文集 (Collected essays on music by Xiao Youmei). Shanghai: Shanghai yinyue chubanshe.

——. 1993. "Xiao Youmei de yinyue lilun gongxian" 蕭友梅的音樂理論貢獻 (Xiao Youmei's contribution to music theory), *Zhongguo yinyuexue* 2, p.20.

Fairbank, John King et al. (eds.). 1975. *The I.G. in Peking. Letters of Robert Hart. Chinese Maritime Customs, 1868–1907*. Cambridge, Mass.: Belknap Press, vol. 2, p. 1330.

Gao Qiu 高秋 . 1982. "Xin Yinyue she shulüe" 新音樂社述略 (A short description of the Society for [Chinese] New Music), *Yinyue yanjiu* 2, pp. 95–9.

Gild-Bohne, Gerlinde. 1991. *Das Lülü Zhengyi Xubian. Ein Jesuitentraktat über die europäische Notation in China von 1713*. Göttingen: Edition Re.

Hanyu Dacidian 漢語大詞典 (Great Chinese dictionary). 1990. "An qupu changge" 按曲譜唱歌 (Singing a written tune). Shanghai: Hanyu da cidian chubanshe.

Izawa Shūji 伊沢修二 . 1971 [1884]. *Yōgaku kotohajime* 洋樂事始 (Fundamentals in Western music). Tokyo: Heibonsha.

Kouwenhoven, Frank. 1990. "Mainland China's New Music. The Age of Pluralism", *Chime. Journal of the European Foundation for Chinese Music Research* 5, pp. 76–134.

Kreyer, Karl (Jin Kaili 金楷理). n.d. *Laba Chuifa* 喇叭吹法 (Introduction to trumpet-playing).

Levenson, Joseph R. 1968. *Confucian China and its Modern Fate*. Berkeley: University of California Press.

Li Zhizao 李之藻 . 1965. "Jiren Shipian" 畸人十篇 (Ten chapters by an unconventionalist), *Xiqin Quyi* 西琴曲意 (Eight songs for the cembalo), *Tianxue chuhan congshu* 天學初函叢書 . Taibei: Taiwan xuesheng shuju.

Liang Mingyue. 1985. *Music of the Billion. An Introduction to Chinese Musical Culture*. New York: Heinrichshofen.

Liang Qichao 梁啟超 (Yin Bingshi 飲冰室). 1905. "Yin Bingshi shihua" 飲冰室詩話 (Yin Bingshi on poetry), *Xinmin congbao* 3.9, pp. 87–94.

Lippert, Wolfgang. 1979. *Entstehung und Funktion einiger chinesischer marxistischer Termini. Der lexikalisch-begriffliche Aspekt der Rezeption des Marxismus in Japan und China*. Wiesbaden: Steiner.

Liu Qingzhi 劉靖之 . 1986. *Zhongguo xinyinyue shi lunji* 中國新音樂史論集 (Collection of treatises on the history of Chinese New Music). Hong Kong: Xianggang Daxue yazhou yanjiu zhongxin.

Lülü Zhengyi Xubian 律呂正義續編 (The correct meaning of the *Lülü*). 1713. Reprinted in: *Qinding siku quanshu* 欽定四庫全書 , *Jingbu* 經部 9, pp. 1–221.

Malm, William P. 1971. "The Modern Music of Meiji Japan", in: Donald H. Shively (ed.). *Tradition and Modernisation in Japanese Culture*. Princeton: Princeton University Press, pp. 257–300.

Mao Yurun 茅于潤 , "Yige xinqigri de wuhou" 一個星期日的午后 (One Sunday afternoon), *Yinyue yishu* 2, pp. 16–22.

Masini, Federico. 1993. *The Formation of Modern Chinese Lexicon and Its Evolution Toward a National Language: The period from 1840 to 1898*. Berkeley: Journal of Chinese Linguistics (Monograph Series no. 6).

Matthews, R. H. 1974. *Chinese-English dictionary*. Cambridge, Mass.: Harvard University Press.

Nienhauser, William H. 1986. *Indiana Companion to Traditional Chinese Literature*. Bloomington: Indiana University Press.

Richard, Timothy (Li Timotai 李提摩太). 1901 [1883]. *Xiaoshipu* 小詩譜 (Tunebook in Chinese notation). Shanghai: Society for the diffusion of Christian and general knowledge.

Shen Qia 沈洽 . 1983. "Shen Xingong zhuan" 沈心工傳 (A biography of Shen Xingong), *Yinyue yanjiu* 4, p. 60.

Shen Xingong 沈心工 . 1915. *Xuexiao Changgeji* 學校唱歌集 (Anthology of school songs). Shanghai: Wenming shuju.

Thrasher, Alan. 1980. *Foundations of Chinese Music. A Study of Ethics and Aesthetics*. Ann Arbor: U.M.I.

Wang Mei-chu. 1987. "Chinesische Notenschriften", *Zeitschrift für Semiotik* 9.3–4, pp. 301–15.

Xi Shuang 息霜 (Li Shutong 李叔同). 1906a. "Zuofeilu" 昨非彔 (Record of our mistakes in the past), *Yinyue xiao zazhi* 1, p. 1.

——. 1906b. "Wuhu, Cizhang!" 嗚呼詞章 (Oh, polished phraseology), *Yinyue xiao zazhi* 1, p. 20.

"Yaya yinyue hui zhi lishi" 亞雅音樂會之歷史 (History of the Asian Refined Music Society). 1905. *Xinmin Congbao* 3.9, pp.101–4.

Zeng Zhimin 曾志忞 . 1903a. "Yueli dayi" 樂理大意 (Fundamentals of musical theory), *Jiangsu zazhi* 6, pp. 63–70.

——. 1903b. "Yinyue Jiaoyulun (1)" 音樂教育論 (1) (On music pedagogy), *Xinmin congbao* 3.14, pp. 55–60.

——. 1903c. "Yinyue Jiaoyulun (2)" 音樂教育論 (2) (On music pedagogy), *Xinmin congbao* 3.20, pp. 61–74.

Zhongguo dabaike quanshu 中國大百科全書 (The great Chinese encyclopaedia). *Yinyue wudao* 音樂舞蹈 (Music and dance). 1989. Beijing, Shanghai: Zhongguo dabaike quanshu chubanshe.

KNOWLEDGE BETWEEN HEART AND MIND

WOLFGANG KUBIN

TO TRANSLATE IS TO FERRY ACROSS:
WU LI'S 吳歷 (1632–1718) *COLLECTION FROM SAO PAOLO*

INTRODUCTION

Though the academic discipline of Sinology began with the translation activities of the Jesuits, neither the origin of Sinology nor the role of translation at that early time are well understood, not even among those who are professionally engaged in the transmission of knowledge about China to the West. On the whole, translating is still considered of minor importance. While those with Chinese skills are advised to read the original text, those whose language efficiency does not allow them to do so might read an English, Japanese or German translation which gives them only a shadowy glimpse of the original. Moreover, the best thing that can happen to a translator of Chinese is that he or she[1] gets off lightly in the criticism of colleagues. One will either be accused of having overseen a particular implication in a phrase, or be attacked for insufficient knowledge of one's native language. In most cases the critics are people who themselves do not translate and have only a vague comprehension of the translator's enterprise. They, of course, enhance their status by means of their caustic jibes, whereas the translator's professional reputation is often painfully scarred.

But translation is not just the mechanical act of matching words and sentences between languages. Translation is interpretation, in the sense that a translation should be regarded only as *one possible* interpretation. In this respect, a translation, as long as it deserves the name translation, can never be outright "wrong", but can only reflect variant understandings. Thus, fault-finding should not be the chief business of a sinologue. Rather, he or she should direct his or her efforts at trying to determine what role a certain translation played or plays in a certain culture.

Translation and cultural development are inextricably linked, like the two sides of a coin. Without translation culture is, in a sense,

---

[1] It is only out of political correctness that I make a distinction between he and she. In my eyes it would be necessary to add a third entity: it.

impossible. Consider, for example, the revolutions and reform movements that have swept across China since the Opium War. The Chinese revolution is unthinkable without the translations of Marx, and
the reform movements were deeply influenced by the Chinese renderings of Adam Smith (1723–1790) and Charles Darwin (1809–1882),
among others. Insofar as important translations push a society forward
in its development, translation is a vital agent in any social, mental
and academic change. Of course, for the first time when it encountered European civilization, China did not experience this kind of
change. With the transmission of Buddhism to China beginning
almost two thousand years ago, Sanskrit changed the Chinese language in a similar way as English, Japanese or German have been
doing since the beginnings of China's reform and opening process.

Translation is always a semantical importation into one's own cultural context. Thereby it is impossible to maintain exactly the entire
content and rich meaning of an original text, just as it is impossible to
avoid adding new shades of meaning. Translation is a decision-making process: during the translation the translator must decide what to
keep and what to discard. For this reason translations are different
from the original work, and by being very different they demonstrate
the depth and richness of the original. A text that could be translated
word for word is shallow and of ephemeral worth. Why are we still
translating the socratic dialogues of Plato, the Bible and the *Zhuangzi*
莊子 to this day? They are treasures of multifaceted meaning that can
never be exhausted.

In German "to translate" is *übersetzen*, a term with a double meaning. In its second meaning, to "ferry across", we could regard a translator as a ferryman who takes something or someone from one shore
to another, from the known to the unknown. Not only the passengers
and the freight, but also the ferryman himself is involved in the
change. In this sense, I spoke of translating in a former essay as
dying.[2] Translation also means "self-transformation": in the creative
act of turning the unknown in the elements of a foreign language into
a new linguistic medium my old self passes away.

---

[2] Wolfgang Kubin. 1999. "Die Bücher werden dich töten! Übersetzen und Thanatos oder: Ein Übersetzer wider Willen", in: Rolf Elberfeld et al. (eds.). *Translation
und Interpretation*. Munich: Wilhelm Fink (Schriften der Académie du Midi, no. 5),
pp. 133–42.

1. CROSSING THE BORDER

When the painter and poet Wu Li 1681 crossed the border to Macao, he had already been baptized.[3] Why then did he go? Upon his arrival he started to compose a cycle of thirty poems he called "Songs of Macao" (*Ao zhong zayong* 澳中雜詠). The first poem in this series provides an answer to this question:[4]

Kaum an der Grenzstation vorbei, geht's schon hinab zum Sandstrand,
Die Hügel von Macao sind nach Art der Blumen.
Einwohner aus der Fremde, erschreckt nicht,
ich habe mich nicht verirrt,
Ich komme von weit, um Theologie zu studieren in den Mauern von Sao Paulo.

關頭閱盡下平沙
濠境山形可類花
居客不驚非誤入
遠從學道到三巴

I pass the border and go down to the beach,
The hills of Macao are flowerlike.
People from afar, don't be scared, I didn't get lost,
I've come here to study the Truth in the church of Sao Paolo.

This is, in many respects, an astonishing text, and the same can be said of the whole cycle of poems/stanzas. Let us start with the most obvious matter: 'Dao' 道 in the last line does not mean Daoist, Confucian or Buddhist Dao, but Christian Truth or (Catholic) Theology. How can this view be justified? First, Wu Li mentions the name of the place he is visiting, namely San Ba 三巴 . He writes: "San Ba, that is

---

[3] Cf. Jonathan Chaves. 1993. *Singing of the Source. Nature and God in the Poetry of the Chinese Painter Wu Li*. Honolulu: University of Hawaii Press, p. 52. Wu Li was born in Changshu (Jiangsu), one of the centers of missionary activities in the early Qing period. He was baptized under the name Simon-Xavier in 1679–80. In 1681 Wu passed Macao on a planned journey to Rome and stayed there for eight years. His experiences are described in his poetry collection San Ba ji 三巴集 (Collection from Sao Paolo). Although few of his paintings are extant, he is regarded as one of the great artists of the Qing period.

[4] Unfortunately, I have to present my own English translation and thus break the rule of translation theory, only to translate into one's own mother language. My interpretations differ too much from those of Jonathan Chaves (p. 140–54). His translation might be based on a source to which I have no access. My translations follow Wu Li 吳歷 . 1681. "San Ba ji" 三巴集 (Collection from Sao Paolo), in: *Tushu jicheng* 圖書集成 (*TSCC*) 3.203, pp. 1–6. Subsequently, I shall always give my German translation before my English translation.

the name of a church/university (*tang* 堂), run by Jesuits". Sao Paolo, the ruins of which can still be seen in Macao and which have become a famous landmark, was at that time not only the name of a Catholic cathedral, but also of a theological seminar. For some scholars it is even regarded as the first Asian university. Second, Wu Li knows that he is crossing more than a simple border (*guan* 關) station that divides a tiny Portuguese territory from China, but also a mental, academic and ideological border. Otherwise he would be telling the people coming from abroad (*juke* 居客) that they need not be astonished to see a visitor of non-Portuguese provenance. Wu Li knows that travelling to Macao means entering a different world, becoming a stranger and being scrutinized as a stranger. He therefore feels compelled to explain that he did not lose his way, but instead willfully entered a place where Chinese were generally not expected to enter, except to conduct commercial transactions. With its implicit sense of taking leave of one's old identity and assuming a new one, the notion of "crossing the border" is expressed by the Chinese binome *yuejin* 閱 盡 , which has the double meaning of 'passing the very end' and 'watching to the very end'. The poem could be understood in the following way: "I, Wu Li, have seen everything in China. I am now leaving it and passing into a world that is completely new and is going to make me new." "Leaving the border station" means leaving the hills, going down to the sea, reaching the sand beach, from where all the hills "could be compared to purple flowers—to purple flower buds." "Purple flower buds" must have a metaphorical meaning: I see in them a possible suggestion of the robes of Catholic priests,[5] and then an indication of the fact that buds naturally symbolize a new start, both for the landscape and its onlooker. That which will be new to the poet and will be changing him totally can, however, only be translated into the forms of one's culture: Dao is the Christian Truth, and Christian Truth is Dao. Only with the passing of time will Wu Li be able to find new expressions in Chinese for Christian doctrines of faith, among them *shizi* 十子 for 'cross'.[6]

---

[5] This is, of course, open for discussion.

[6] For an elaborate discussion of how the missionary James Legge rendered the term 'Dao' in English see also Lauren Pfister's contribution in this volume.

2. THE TRANSFORMATIVE FORCE OF CULTURAL DIFFERENCE

Someone who studies the Dao or possesses the Dao becomes a representative of the Dao (*daoren* 道人). In a Daoist sense, being a *daoren* and pursuing art do not stand in contradiction to each other. Why then does Wu Li think of giving up the arts after his Christian awakening as a man of Christian Truth (*daoren* 道人), as in poem no. 20? He touches upon this problem in poem no. 28.

> Alt und gebrechlich holt keiner den Vers der Jugend zurück,
> Ich befleißige mich täglich, vielleicht nicht mehr fix genug.
> Ich halte mich an alten Brauch: Zuerst weg mit dem Tuschstein,
> Und dann ein Ende mit den Zeichen, keine Gedichte mehr.

> 老去誰能補狀時
> 工夫日用恐遲遲
> 思將舊習先焚硯
> 且斷塗鴉并發時

> When old and weak no one can rejuvenate their poetry,
> I put in my efforts every day, perhaps too slowly.
> I stick to an old custom: first to do away with the inkstone,
> Then to stop writing and composing poetry.

We can understand the intention of Wu Li here only if we take into consideration his own comments on this poem: he is going to devote himself "to the study of the Dao" (*xue dao* 學道). Dao, with the underlying sense of theology, viz. Christian Faith, must here connote a complete transformation of one's personality. Wu Li does not mention this transformation explicitly, but does hint at it obliquely. We know from *The Dream of the Red Chamber* (1792) that European pendulum clocks or chiming clocks (*ziming zhong* 自鳴鍾) were a common accoutrement of an affluent Chinese household in the eighteenth century. As far as I know, their value was only in their mechanical and not their symbolic character. Wu Li, who meticulously describes the Western world he encounters in Macao, turns the above-mentioned clock into a symbol. He wants to give a name to the difference that he observes between the East and the West, between China and Europe. This name stems from differing concepts of time. Let us examine poem no. 19:

> Rote Lichee, Mond im Westen,
> Ich schaue den Tau unter dem Wind,
> nach dem Schlaf die Augen noch schläfrig.
> Hier unter der Lampe ist nicht des Scholaren Kammer:

Das Ohr erfüllt vom Schlag der Pendeluhr,
nicht vom Krähen des Hahns.

紅荔枝頭月又西
起看風露眼猶迷
燈前此地非書館
但聽鍾聲不聽雞

Red Lichee, moon in the West,
I watch the dew under the wind, my eyes still sleepy.
This is not a Confucian academy, under the lamp,
My ears just hear a chiming clock, not the rooster.

Wu Li seems to have more than just the geographical meaning of the 'West' in mind. He is in Southern China, surrounded by Catholic churches and living in a Portuguese house. He probably has to get up very early in the morning to take part in the morning prayers. The world about his new home does not rely on 'natural' time. If one depended upon the crow of the rooster, one might not arrive punctually for the oratories. The change in life and faith means a new ordering of time: now it is regulated, the mechanical time that organizes daily affairs, not the vague sense of time represented by a rooster. In this respect Wu Li writes: "Dawn and dusk are arranged by the sound of the chiming clock [in Macao] only." Thus "this place cannot be a Confucian academy (*shuguan* 書館)."

In this new world there are mainly two kinds of sounds: the clock and the bell, that is the sound of time and that of the Sacred. The first sound means: "get prepared", the second: "change yourself". The last two lines of poem no. 20 tell of the change brought about by the hearkening to church bells:

Das Geläut der Glocken inmitten der Hügel
Weckt den Gläubigen aus eitlem Traum.

前山後嶺一聲聽
醒欲道人閒夢斷

The sound of bells among the hills
Awakes the man of faith out of his vain dreams.

What I translate here as "man of faith" (*daoren*) could also, of course, be understood as "a man bound by traditional Chinese values". No matter how we interpret *daoren*, the message is clear: it involves an enlightenment (*xing* 醒) by means of Christian Faith.

At this point we have to come back to the initial question: Why did Wu Li want to give up painting and poetry? Here we can do little more than speculate. Painting and poetry in China quite naturally have a Chinese background, which can be found in this cycle, too. Giving up painting and poetry would mean giving up the Chinese way of painting and poetry after awakening to Christian Truth, and turning to a Christian art, as he did after finishing his cycle in Macao.

3. TRANSLATION AS DIALOGUE

Wu Li describes a world astonishingly free of xenophobia. Instead of becoming hostile to things foreign, he seems to enjoy the new (in-) sights the Macao Portuguese have to offer. He is well aware of the differences between East and West, but he tries to overcome the gap through dialogue. One of the differences he notices is that of language and script. In poem no. 26 Wu Li depicts the difficulties China and Europe have in their communication.

> Draußen vor der Tür die Sprachen der Welt, mal Ost, mal West,
> Verstehen wir uns nicht, öffnen Pinsel und Stift die Kommunikation.
> Ich male Fliegenköpfe, du schreibst Vogelkrallen,
> Ob horizontal oder vertikal, das Auge erschöpft's nicht.

> 門前鄉語各西東
> 未解遲教筆可通
> 我寫蠅頭君鳥爪
> 橫看直視更難窮

> In front of the door one hears languages of all kinds,
> some Eastern, some Western,
> If we don't understand another,
> we trust our brush or pen for communication.
> I paint the heads of flies, you describe birds' legs,
> Whether read horizontally or vertically,
> our eyes have even a harder time.

This is a splendid way to expound differences: communication between East and West, whether spoken or written, is a difficult matter for both sides. Even today, after centuries of exchange between China and Europe, we can still hear voices claiming that the West does not understand the East and vice versa. Unfortunately there is no perfect means of communication between two interlocutors. At best each side makes strong efforts to understand the other. Our understanding is never completed, but always in a process of becoming. This is why Wu Li makes use of the character *qiong* 窮 (to exhaust) and puts it at the end of the poem: the eyes engaged in reading can

hardly exhaust the meaning of the Chinese characters and foreign letters they perceive.

4. GOING HOME

We know that in Chinese culture since the middle ages the cult of
friendship might come close to the worship of a higher spiritual being.
According to traditional Occidental understanding it is God who
makes the world a home for man and makes life meaningful. Vice
versa, it is a *zhiyin* 知音 or *zhiji* 知己 , someone who knows me, that is,
a friend, who turns the earth into a place of mutual understanding,
longing and communication. Thus the space between me and the
other, between here and there, between near and far is not empty, but
filled by the spirit of two men. But what happens if one is a Catholic
convert and the other a non-Chinese? Is a Chinese-style friendship
still possible? Wu Li, who had the opportunity of going with Philippe
Couplet, S.J. (1623–1693) to Rome, yet in the end stayed in Macao,
extends the cult of friendship to include Westerners. In this respect he
is enlarging the compass of his perceived spiritual space as far as
Rome. In his mind he is accompanying Philippe Couplet (as can be
seen from poem no. 10) and probably Balthasar-Didacus de Rocha
(poem no. 16) on their way to the Far West (*daxi* 大西). His imagination includes not only the spatial, but also the mental: the last line of
poem no. 16 reads:

> Wenn wieder daheim, mit wem wird er [d.i. de Rocha] erörtern das
> Leben und den Tod?
>
> 歸向何人説死生
>
> When home again, with whom is he [i.e. de Rocha] going to talk about
> life and death?

'Going home' (*gui* 歸) in Chinese also means 'to die', to go back to
where one comes from, to be buried. It is well-known that Chinese
usually avoid the topic of death because of their prediction for the living. Death, however, is of vital importance in Christianity; dying and
suffering play central roles not only in Western arts, but have also
been determining elements of public space: the figure of Jesus Christ
on the cross could—and, of course, can still be—found within and
outside Christian churches. Thus the question Wu Li is raising is in
some respects astonishing. It might be for reasons of rhyme that he

changes *sheng si* 生死 (life and death) into *si sheng* 死生 (death and life), but not only the Chinese tradition, the Christian Faith as well allows this reversal: After death there will be resurrection and eternal life. If I see it correctly, in poem no. 16 the poet is making use of Western rhyming couplets: *qi-qu*, *heng-sheng*. This is, of course, open for discussion. *Qu* 去 could be understood in the sense of 'to go' or 'to die' and *qi* 起 in the sense of 'to rise', 'to come to life (again)' or 'to be resurrected'. The pondering upon the foreign friend's journey to the West would thus end in a theological question, and relegate the Chinese tradition to a matter of secondary importance.

CONCLUSION

Wu Li's contribution to an East-West encounter is unique, not only in his time, but also from today's perspective. What I always very much regret is that many visitors from China do not seem to be able to perceive the Westerness of the West. They are always talking about their homeland (*zuguo* 祖國) and 'our China' (*zanmen Zhongguo* 咱們中國), even in the streets of Bonn. But Wu Li does not mention the Great Qing Dynasty or anything of the sort. He does apprehend the differences between East and West, and he does go about describing them. He observes Portuguese men and women wearing exotic costumes, Africans working in the households of the Caucasian foreigners, Hakka and Tonka engaging in commercial transactions, Catholics performing street processions and making preparations for Christmas. He has an eye for the staging of the sacred, whether in the churches, at home or in the streets. He refers to this as *sheng* 聖 , i.e. he is translating something into *his* culture, the character of which is quite foreign to it. *Sheng* in Confucianism or Daoism means something totally different from *Holy* in Christian Faith. It is the underlying experience that makes the difference. But how do we as scholars or translators know that Dao is not Dao, but theology, and that *sheng* is not *sheng*, but the *Holy*, the *Sacred*? We need someone who can tell us. In our case we are lucky enough to find in Wu Li a person who is aware of possible difficulties for the readers. That is the reason why he glosses his own writings and tells us what he is actually sinifying (theology: Dao), and which neologisms he is inventing (Sao Paulo: San Ba). Thus Wu Li stands at the beginning of a tradition that is still being practised today.

References

Chaves, Jonathan. 1993. *Singing of the Source. Nature and God in the Poetry of the Chinese Painter Wu Li*. Honolulu: University of Hawaii Press.

Kubin, Wolfgang. 1999. "Die Bücher werden dich töten! Übersetzen und Thanatos oder: Ein Übersetzer wider Willen", in: Rolf Elberfeld et al. (eds.). *Translation and Interpretation*. Munich: Wilhelm Fink (Schriften der Académie du Midi, no. 5), S. 133–42.

Wu Li 吳歷. 1681. "San Ba ji" 三巴集 (Collection from Sao Paolo), in: *Tushu jicheng* 圖書集成 TSCC 3.203, pp. 1–6.

TIMOTHY MAN-KONG WONG 黃文江[1]

THE RENDERING OF GOD IN CHINESE BY THE CHINESE: CHINESE RESPONSES TO THE TERM QUESTION IN THE *WANGUO GONGBAO*

The most challenging assignment faced by the Reformation interpreters of the Bible was not exegesis but translation, as it would in turn become their most enduring monument. Biblical exegetes could, and often did, elide their way around obscure or difficult passages, but biblical translators could not get away with that: they were expected to do it all, word by word and phrase by phrase. A translator faithful to the principles of the Reformation had to be an exegete first, using the tools of sacred philology in Hebrew and Greek to discover the correct reading of the text and then its correct meaning.[1]

Jaroslav Pelikan (b. 1923)

1. INTRODUCTION: IDENTIFYING THE ISSUES

Further to the above insights on the unavoidable difficulty in translating the Bible, Pelikan offers another useful comment from his study of the history of Bible translation. He singles out translating vocabulary as the "most obvious problem," for which he comes up with three possible options. He remarks,

When missionaries were translating the Bible into a new language, were they to employ the ready-made religious terms that were familiar to their prospective converts on the basis of their pagan tradition, ... thus risking confusion between the old and the new faith? Or were they to transpose, or even transliterate, the technical terms of the original or of an older version into the new version ...? Or were they to invent a brand-new set of words and phrases for their new churches? ... The history of biblical translation has been marked by each of these several solutions, and by various combinations of them.[3]

---

[1] This paper is an output of a research project funded by the Hong Kong Baptist University (FRG/ 97–98/ I–32). I wish to thank the university for its generous sponsorship. The author wishes to sincerely acknowledge the comments and assistance offered by Lauren F. Pfister of the Hong Kong Baptist University and Su Ching 蘇精 (Su Jing) of Tamkang University, Taiwan.

[2] Jaroslav Pelikan. 1996. *The Reformation of the Bible; The Bible of the Reformation*. New Haven: Yale University Press, p. 41.

[3] Ibid., p. 43.

To decide to follow any one of these three options (use an old term, transliterate it, or invent a new term) is certainly a long and difficult process. Furthermore, when we mean translating as communicating, Eugene Albert Nida (b. 1914) pointedly suggests that the receptor-sources, including the sets of presupposition from the receptors' cultures, are essential.[4]

When Protestant missionaries approached late Imperial China, unlike their Catholic counterparts one of the urgent items on their mission agenda was to translate the Bible into Chinese. Of all the issues related to Bible translation, the question of how to render God in Chinese was essential. Moreover, Protestant missionaries strongly advocated the "uniformity in terms used for God," while also they did not want to confuse their Chinese audience, in that they might "seem to be talking about different deities."[5]

According to Pelikan, the three options for Protestant missionaries in China over the Term Question were: 1) to use an old term (finding a Chinese equivalent), 2) to transliterate it, or 3) to invent a new one. While nineteenth century missionaries would hold firmly to the very core conception of 'God' in Christian faith as sharing the connotation of its being universal and omnipotent, the first choice was generally thought to be imperative. To take into the account the receptor-source, we need to realise that the situation China missionaries faced was very complicated in their search for the "exact Chinese rendering" for the biblical terms referring to 'God' in the Christian context, including the terms such as, *Tian* 天, *Tianzhu* 天主, *Shangdi* 上帝, and *Shen* 神. The complicated and lengthy set of controversies on the terms for God in Chinese is called the "Term Question".

The volume of writings on the Term Question is substantial. However, only a few give a serious study of its history. As far as I know, a complete coverage of the whole issue has not yet been accomplished. So far, the historical pieces written by Lee Ka-kiu and Irene Eber are the most comprehensive accounts.[6] Two features are common to their

---

[4] Eugene A. Nida and William D. Reburn. 1987. *Meaning Across Cultures*. New York: Orbis Books, pp. 20–32.

[5] Kenneth Scott Latourette. 1929. *A History of Christian Missions in China*. London: Society for Promoting Christian Knowledge, p. 261.

[6] Lee Ka-kiu 李家駒 (Li Jiaju). 1991. "Yichang 'shen' huo 'shangdi' da zhenglun: zaoqi laihua xinjiao jiaoshi duiyu 'God' yici de fanyi yu jieshi (1807–1877)" 一場神或上帝大爭論：早期來華新教教師對於 'God' 一詞的翻譯與解釋 (1807–1877)

works, namely, their ending in the late 1870s, and their giving only a passing mention to Chinese voices on this matter. The year 1877 was significant in that the first general conference of all Protestant missionaries took place in which it was agreed not to touch upon the Term Question. That the Chinese voices did not receive due attention probably had two reasons. In the first place, the general picture of the Chinese Christians in China only began to be painted not long ago in the field of modern Chinese history in general and the history of Christianity in China in particular. Today, one may still find relevant what John King Fairbank (1907–1991) wrote more than a decade ago; he complained that "We are totally uninformed about the Chinese Christian community, its membership, and influence."[7] Secondly, not much background knowledge of those Chinese Christians who were involved in the Term Question has been uncovered.

Having benefited from the recent studies on the Term Question and Chinese Christians, I am prepared to look into the Chinese participants in the Term Question. However, as a preliminary study of this extensive issue, I will limit the scope of this paper to the Chinese voices recorded in the *Wanguo gongbao* 萬國公報 (The Globe Magazine).[8]

2. THE TERM QUESTION: THE VOICES FROM MISSIONARIES

While Protestant missionaries were the ones who translated the Bible into Chinese and initiated the debates on the Term Question, it would seem useful to begin with basic viewpoints and positions of a few well-known missionaries involving in debates related to the Term

---

[6] (*cont.*) (Controversies over the term *Shen* or *Shangdi*: early Protestant missionaries' translations and interpretations of the term 'God' (1807–1877)). M. Phil. thesis. Hong Kong: Chinese University of Hong Kong; Irene Eber. 1999. "The Interminable Term Question, in: Irene Eber, Wan Sze-kar and Knut Walf (eds.). *Bible in Modern China: The Literary and Intellectual Impact*. St. Augustin: Institut Monumenta Serica, pp. 135–61.

[7] John King Fairbank. 1984. "Introduction: The Place of Protestant Writings in China's Cultural History", in: John King Fairbank and Suzanne Wilson Barnett (eds.). *Christianity in China: Early Protestant Missionary Writings*. Cambridge, Mass.: Harvard University Press, p. 3.

[8] I use the reprint edition *Wanguo gongbao* 萬國公報 . 1969 [1876–1877]. Taibei: Huawen Bookstore [hereafter quoted as *WGGB*] and follow its page numbers accordingly.

Question in late Imperial China. In 1814, a Chinese translation of the New Testament was completed and printed by Robert Morrison (Ma Lisun 馬禮遜, 1782–1834). It was entitled *Yesu Jilishidu Wozhu Jiuzhe xinyi zhaoshu* 耶穌基利士督我主救者新遺詔書. It is very likely that only the latter part of the title, *Wozhu Jiuzhe xinyi zhaoshu*, might have sounded sensible to its contemporary Chinese readers, meaning "a newly inherited (or posthumous) imperial edict from my Lord, the saviour." In 1823, a Chinese translation of the Old and New Testaments was completed and printed, with the title *Shentian shengshu* 神天聖書. Compared with the 1814 edition, the title of this 1823 edition which means "the holy book from the heavenly deity," conveyed the sacredness much clearly to its contemporary Chinese readers. Although Morrison sometimes used the word *Shen* as the Chinese equivalent of God, he did not single out one particular term for all his references to God in his writings and translation. As revealed in the title of 1823 edition, he used both *Shen* and *Tian*. Morrison did leave us some clues as to how he saw his work as a translator of the Bible. He wrote:

> In my translations, I have studied fidelity, perspicuity, and simplicity; I have preferred common words to rare and classical ones; I have avoided technical terms, which occur in the pagan philosophy and religion. I would rather be deemed inelegant, than hard to be understood. In difficult passages I have taken the sense given by the general consent of the gravest, most pious, and least eccentric divines, to whom I had access.[9]

In addition, he suggested that a joint effort by both missionaries and Chinese Christians would be a way out from the difficulties encountered in the translation of the Bible. He wrote:

> It is my opinion, that a union of European Christian translators, and of native students, who have some years attended to European literature, in conjunction with the study of the Christian religion, is most likely to produce the best translation [of the Bible] into Chinese; and on this ground, I beg to recommend to the patronage of the friends of the Bible, the Anglo-Chinese College now building at Malacca, intended expressly for the reciprocal cultivation of Chinese and European literature, and the general diffusion of Christian knowledge.[10]

---

[9] Eliza Morrison (ed.). 1839. *Memoirs of the Life and Labours of Robert Morrison, D. D. Compiled by His Widow, with Critical Notices of His Chinese Works by Samuel Kidd and an Appendix Containing Original Documents.* 2 vols. London: Longman, vol. 2, p. 9.

From the 1830s onwards, a need to re-translate Morrison's Bible was generally felt by China missionaries. On August 22, 1843, a meeting of 12 American and British missionaries was held in Hong Kong to discuss the re-translation project. While Robert Morrison's Bible was rejected, his recommendation of putting together both missionaries and the learned Chinese Christians in the translation project was also cast aside. As revealed in the different stages of the production of the so-called Delegates' Version, the need for assistance from the Chinese was only felt when missionaries were struggling with how to polish the language. Wang Tao 王韜 (1828–1897), for instance, was highly praised for his assistance in polishing the translation of Job and Psalms.[11] One may be tempted to think that the reason for not having any Chinese in the translation team was that no Chinese had received sufficient training for the translation task, as Morrison had anticipated. But a recent study reveals that there was at least one choice, Ho Tsun-sheen 何進善 (He Jinshan, 1817–1871), who was a dependable colleague of James Legge (Li Yage 理雅各, 1815–1897) and well-qualified to take part in the Bible translation project, as he had been a "native evangelist" since 1843.[12] Ho proved himself a capable translator of the Christian message when he managed to write a commentary to the gospel according to Matthew.

In the 1843 Hong Kong meeting, the arrangement for the joint effort of missionaries from different nations in producing a re-translation of the Bible was finalised. However, due to the Term Question, the joint effort of the Anglo-American missionaries turned out to be in vain. A Chinese Bible was completed by British missionaries, notably under the leadership of Walter Henry Medhurst (Mai Dusi 麥都思, 1796–1861), in 1852. The version by American missionaries, which was under the leadership of Elijah Coleman Bridgman (Bi Zhiwen 裨治文, 1801–1861), was completed in 1858. Medhurst and James

---

[10] Ibid., p. 10.

[11] Su Ching 蘇精 (Su Jing). 2000. "Wang Tao de Jidujiao xili" 王韜的基督教洗禮 (On the Christian baptism of Wang Tao), in: Lam Kai Yin 林啟彥 (Lin Qiyan) and Wong Man Kong 黃文江 (Huang Wenjiang) (eds.). 2000. *Wang Tao yu jindai shijie* 王韜與近代世界 (Wang Tao and the Modern World). Hong Kong: Hong Kong Educational Publishing Company, pp. 435–52; 440–1.

[12] Lauren F. Pfister. 1999. "A Transmitter But Not a Creator; Ho Tsun-sheen (1817–1871), The First Modern Chinese Protestant Theologian", in: Irene Eber, Wan Sze-kar and Knut Walf (eds.). *Bible in Modern China: The Literary and Intellectual Impact*. St. Augustin: Institut Monumenta Serica, pp. 165–98; 177.

Legge were major spokesmen advocating the use of the term
Shangdi,[13] while William Boone (Wen Huilian 文惠廉, 1811–1864)
and Elijah Coleman Bridgman were the representatives of the side
defending the use of *Shen*.[14] In brief, the basic issues around the Term
Question that concerned many missionaries are neatly summarised as
follows,

> To define what was meant by the "True God", Protestants wished at the
> outset to differentiate between an absolute or generic term and a rela-
> tive name. If the Tetragrammaton was considered an absolute term,
> Elohim would be a relative name. But which terms in Chinese were
> absolute, and which relative? ... Together with the question of absolute
> and relative terms, the missionaries also asked whether the Chinese had
> the idea of God and what the nature and practice of Chinese religion
> was. Was there an ancient monotheism, or were the Chinese always
> polytheists?[15]

Furthermore, the Term Question touched upon fundamental differences in the mind-set and even the religious belief system of each

---

[13] The two works by Medhurst that are of particular relevance for the Term Question are: *An Inquiry into the Proper Mode of Rendering the Word God in Translating
the Sacred Scriptures into the Chinese Language*. 1847a. Shanghai: Mission Press; *A
Dissertation on the Theology of the Chinese with a View to the Elucidation of the
Most Appropriate Term for Expressing the Deity in the Chinese Language*. 1847b.
Shanghai: Mission Press. The two works that precisely reflect Legge's position in this
matter are: James Legge. 1877. *Confucianism in Relation to Christianity: A Paper
Read Before the Missionary Conference in Shanghai on May 11th 1877*. 1877. Shanghai, London: Kelly and Welsh; and ibid. 1880. *A Letter to Professor F. Max Müller,
chiefly on the Translation into English of the Chinese Terms Ti and Shang Ti in Reply
to a Letter by 'Inquirer' in the Chinese Recorder and Missionary Journal for May–
June 1880*. London: Trübner and Co.

[14] William Boone. 1848. *An Essay on the Proper Rendering of the Words Elohim
and Theos into the Chinese Language*. Canton: Chinese Repository. James Legge did
not take a long time to make a forceful response, see *The Notion of the Chinese Concerning God and Spirits with an Examination of the Defense of an Essay, on Proper
Rendering of the Words Elohim and Theos into the Chinese Language, by William
Boone D. D. Missionary Bishop of the Protestant Episcopal Church of the United
States to China*. 1852. Hong Kong: Hong Kong Register Office. In addition to many
articles published in the Chinese Recorder, it is also important to note the following
representative publications: John Chalmers. 1876. *The Question of Terms Simplified,
or the Meanings of Shan, Ling and Ti in Chinese Made Plain by Induction*. Canton:
E-Shing; William Armstrong Russell. 1877. *Term Question: An Enquiry as to the
Term in the Chinese Language which Most Nearly Represents Elohim and Theos as
They Are Used in the Holy Scriptures*. Shanghai: American Presbyterian Mission
Press; Henry Blodget and Ernest John Eitel. 1877. *The Chinese Term for God: State-
ment and Reply*. London: T. Williams.

[15] Eber 1999, p. 138.

missionary. Taking Legge as an example, the Term Question constituted a part of his search for the compatibility of Confucianism with
Christianity.[16] Moreover, the Term Question was partly a result of the
differences in missionaries' backgrounds, namely, "rival nineteenth-
century understandings—British imperial and American democratic
(or 'young republican')—of the nature of God Himself." Irwin Hyatt
has further remarked:

> Was God, that is, simply the eternally all-powerful being—which was
> the idea that *shang-ti* basically conveyed—or was He, as *shen* implied
> to many missionaries, rather the proven true one of a multitude of his-
> torical spirits, and perhaps identical with the individual human
> soul?[17]

When the first general conference of Protestant missionaries in China
took place in 1877, to eschew any further discord from the Term
Question it was agreed that "the question of the proper term for God
should not be discussed."[18] However, the controversies over the Term
Question did not end in 1877. The debate over the Term Question
"gradually died down" while entering the twentieth century as the
Boxer Uprising "unexpectedly ushered in a new era of co-operation
among missionaries."[19]

3. THE VOICES OF THE OVERLOOKED: THE VIEWS OF CHINESE CHRISTIANS IN THE *WANGUO GONGBAO*

Thanks to recent studies on Liang Fa 梁發 (1789–1855), Hong Xiuquan 洪秀全 (1814–1864), Ho Tsun-sheen, Wang Tao, and a group of
eight Hakka Christians in nineteenth century China, we are now better
informed about the conversion experiences of some Chinese Christians in nineteenth century China. Almost without exception, they had

---

[16] Timothy Man-Kong Wong. 1996. *James Legge: A Pioneer at Crossroads of East and West*. Hong Kong: Hong Kong Educational Publishing Company, pp. 99–113.

[17] Irwin T. Hyatt, Jr. 1976. *Our ordered Lives Confess: Three Nineteenth-Century American Missionaries in East Shantung*. Cambridge, Mass.: Harvard University Press, pp. 231–2.

[18] *Records of the General Conference of the Protestant Missionaries of China, held at Shanghai, May 10–24, 1877*. 1877. Shanghai: Presbyterian Mission Press, p. 20.

[19] Pui-lan Kwok 郭佩蘭 (Guo Peilan). 1992. *Chinese Women and Christianity 1860–1927*. Atlanta: Scholars Press, p. 32.

gone through deep reflection upon their personal and religious problems. Their conversion and reflection certainly affected the way that
they looked at Christianity and its relations to Chinese traditions, and
so accordingly formulated their views on Christianity. Whether or not
their understanding of Christianity can be regarded as theology, and
whether or not their theology suffices them to be called theologians
are the two essential questions that demand a broader historical perspective, which is indeed a subject of another study. Nonetheless, it is
evident that people like Liang Fa, Hong Xiuquan, and Ho Tsun-sheen
became Christians and preached Christianity not simply because of
what missionaries told (or taught) them to do. Clearly, therefore it is
important to study their voices in their own terms.[20]

In regard to the Chinese voices on the Term Question, some pieces
were written by Chinese Christians in the *Jiaohui xinbao* 教會新報
(Church News).[21] However, the *Wanguo gongbao* deserves special
attention because it served as a platform for altogether 48 articles
which appeared within a relatively short time span of less than 2
years, from 1877 to 1878. John S. Roberts (Lu Pei 陸佩 or Lu Peishu
陸佩書), a missionary from the Board of Foreign Missions of the

---

[20] On Liang Fa, see P. Richard Bohr. 1984. "Liang Fa's Quest for Moral Power",
in: John King Fairbank and Suzanne Wilson Barnett (eds.). *Christianity in China:
Early Protestant Missionary Writings,* Cambridge, Mass.: Harvard University Press,
pp. 35–46. On Hong Xiuquan, see Rudolf Wagner. 1982. *Reenacting the Heavenly
Vision: The Role of Religion in the Taiping Rebellion.* Berkeley: Institute of East
Asian Studies; Jonathan D. Spence. 1996. *God's Chinese Son: The Taiping Heavenly
Kingdom of Hong Xiuquan.* New York: W. W. Norton & Company, and P. Richard
Bohr. 1998. "The Theologian as Revolutionary: Hung Hsiu-chuan's Religious Vision
of the Taiping Heavenly Kingdom", in: Hao Yen-p'ing and Wei Hsiu-mei (eds.). *Tra-
dition and Metamorphosis in Modern Chinese History: Essays in Honor of Professor
Kwang-ching Liu's Seventy-fifth Birthday.* Taibei: Institute of Modern History,
Academia Sincia, vol. 2, pp. 907–54. On Wang Tao, see Lam Kai Yin 林啟彦 (Lin
Qiyan) and Wong Man Kong 黃文江 (Huang Wenjiang) (eds.). 2000. *Wang Tao yu
jindai shijie* 王韜與近代世界 (Wang Tao and the Modern World). Hong Kong: Hong
Kong Educational Publishing Company, pp. 435–52. On Hakka Christians, see Jessie
G. Lutz and Rolland Ray Lutz. 1998. *Hakka Chinese Confront Protestant Christian-
ity, 1850–1900, with the Autobiographies of Eight Hakka Christians, and Commen-
tary.* New York: M. E. Sharpe. On Chinese Christians in early Hong Kong, see Carl
T. Smith. 1985. *Chinese Christians: Elites, Middlemen, and the Church in Hong
Kong.* Hong Kong: Oxford University Press.
[21] Adrian A. Bennett. 1983. *Missionary Journalist in China: Young J. Allen and
His Magazines, 1860–1883.* Athens: University of Georgia Press, pp. 114–9; Ying
Fuk-tsang 邢福增 (Xing Fuzeng). 1995. *Wenhua shiying yu Zhongguo Jidutu, 1860–
1911* 文化適應與中國基督土, 1860–1911 (Cultural accommodation and Chinese
Christians, 1860–1911). Hong Kong: Alliance Bible Seminary, pp. 123–4.

Presbyterian Church in the United States, was interested in the Term Question. After reading an article by Huang Pinsan 黃品三 (1823–1890), who proposed a new term as an alternative, he called for papers from Chinese Christians to discuss the Term Question in the *Wanguo gongbao*.[22] The 48 articles published in the *Wanguo gongbao* were the result. Instead of recapitulating all the details, some notable representatives from these 48 pieces are selected here to illuminate the dynamics of Chinese voices on the Term Question.

Huang Pinsan was the first participant in this series of debates. Huang was from an affluent family in Jiangsu province. He had received a good education in the Chinese classics and, in addition, had been deeply involved in Daoism while he was young. His connection with Christianity was reinforced after he was hired in a girls' school under the management of Martha Crawford (1830–1909), and later also served there as Crawford's Chinese language tutor. In 1855, Huang was baptised; two years later, in 1857, he was ordained to be a deacon to assist Matthew Yates (Yan Matai 晏馬太, 1819–1888). During the American Civil War between 1861 and 1865, when his missionary society was unable to pay him full salary, Yates had to work as an interpreter of Chinese in the American consulate in Shanghai. Huang therefore took on more duties in the church. In 1870 Huang was ordained as a pastor. He enjoyed a high reputation as a preacher whose useful insights and guidance for Chinese Christians were generally appreciated. Also worthy of notice are his numerous literary contributions: 14 articles in the *Jiaohui xinbao* and 24 in the *Wanguo gongbao*.[23] Christian living and ethics constituted the major parts of his writings, such as the problem of evil and free will, opium smoking, and polygamy.[24] He also wrote of his conversion experience, which inspired Young J. Allen (Lin Lezhi 林樂知, 1836–1907) to initiate a series of articles by Chinese Christians on their conversion experience to be published in the *Wanguo gongbao*.[25] In brief,

---

[22] John S. Roberts. 1876. "Some General Principles for Guidance in Translating the S. S. Terms for 'God'", *Chinese Recorder* 7.2 (March-April 1876), pp. 136–41, and 7.3 (May-June 1876), pp. 213–6. See also, John S. Roberts. 1877. "Principles of Translation into Chinese", in: *Records of the General Conference of the Protestant Missionaries of China*, pp. 418–29.

[23] Zha Shijie 查時傑. 1983. *Zhongguo jidujiao renwu xiaochuan* 中國基督教人物小傳 (Concise biographies of important Chinese Christians). Taibei: China Evangelical Seminary Press, pp. 15–20.

[24] Bennett 1983, pp. 113; 138–9; 142–4.

Huang was a well-educated Chinese with more than twenty years of connection with Christianity before he initiated a discussion of the *Shenghao lun* 聖號論 ("On the Sacred Appellation").

In the *Shenghao lun*, Huang criticised the current options (*Shen* and *Shangdi*), regarding these two terms as too inaccurate to be the term for the Christian conception of God in Chinese. Instead, he was more in favour of an innovative term—*Zaohua zhu* 造化主 ("the Lord of Creation")—to render God in Chinese. The basic idea behind this was the expression *Tian wei Zaohua* 天為造化 meaning "the Heaven equated *Zaohua*". Furthermore, the term *Zaohua zhu* was not used in Buddhist and Daoist texts; neither had it ever been used to imply or denote what Christians would consider to be a false god in Chinese traditions. Similarly, Huang rejected the use of transliteration, and thought the best option would be a term slightly deviating from existing vocabularies. The term he promoted carried a sensible denotation which at the same time did not suggest or would not be confused with ideas in the religious traditions of either Buddhism or Daoism.[26]

Roberts disagreed with Huang's innovative alternative. He therefore invited contributions from other Chinese Christians to discuss the Term Question. As far as I know, this was the first time when missionaries opened up the Term Question for public and published debate among Chinese Christians. But at the same time, the discussion was limited to the following stated guiding points:

> Whether or not *Shangdi*, the Creator of all beings, worshipped in the ancient times was like what Huang described and discussed.
>
> What were the meanings of *di* 帝 and *Shangdi*?
>
> Whether the term *Shangdi* was used for referring to one deity or a group of deities. [i.e. Was *Shangdi* a generic or absolute term?]
>
> What was the meaning of *Shen*?
>
> Whether the term *Shen* was used for referring to one deity or a group of deities. [i.e. Was *Shen* a generic or absolute term?]
>
> Could *Shangdi* be classified as a kind of *Shen*?
>
> Whether or not being intangible and immortal of a human being was equal to *Shen*. If so, why?

---

[25] Ibid., p. 167.

[26] Huang Pinsan 黃品三 . 1969a [1877]. "Shenghao Lun" 聖號論 (On the Sacred Appellation), *WGGB* (July 21, 1877), pp. 3880–1.

What was the meaning of *Ling*? Did it mean an immortal human body? Was it necessary to add one word to *Ling* in order to use it to represent God?[27]

The first published response was also from Huang Pinsan. Excited that his article had inspired Roberts to open up a forum for Chinese voices to discuss the Term Question, he pointed out that he had gleaned no prior knowledge of the current and past debates over the Term Question within missionary circles. Furthermore, he pointed out that he had not been asked to stand for any side or support any person: it was his original contribution. He acknowledged the fact that there was not a single Chinese term which would convey the meaning of God as the creator of the whole universe, despite the fact that Chinese people had a lot of terms for deities. He stressed once again that he considered the term *Zaohua Zhu* to be the best option to render God. He also disagreed with Roberts' way of handling the issue by setting up a eight-point discussion format to restrict contribution of new options from the Chinese voices.[28]

In his reply, Roberts first pointed out that he did not intend to examine if Huang's option was correct. Apparently, Roberts was pre-occupied with the eight points that he had raised: he was still inviting Chinese voices to search for the absolute and generic terms for deities and for Christian conceptions of God. He also mentioned that the essence of the debates among the missionaries was how to find a Chinese term for generic use and particular use.[29]

In his third article, Huang changed the key word of its title from *Shenghao* 聖號 (sacred appellation) to *Shouyao chengming* 首要稱名 (primary compellation). In this article, he tried to answer Roberts' concerns. He considered that the term *Shen* shared a generic connotation for which he gave the following examples *Shendao* 神道 (the spiritual way), *Shenming* 神明 (the spiritual lightness), *Shenling* 神靈 (the spiritual soul), *Shenfo* 神佛 (the spiritual Buddha), and *Shenxian* 神賢

---

[27] John S. Roberts (Lu Pei 陸佩). 1969a [1877]. "Shenghao lun lieyan" 聖號論列言 (Guidelines for the discussion of the Term Question), *WGGB* (July, 21, 1877), pp. 3881–2.

[28] Huang Pinsan 黃品三. 1969b [1877]. "Zuo Shenghao lun yuanyi" 作聖號論原意 (The original intentions of writing *Shenghao lun*), *WGGB* (August 11, 1877), p. 3955.

[29] John S. Roberts. 1969b [1877]. "Shenghao lun lieyan yuanyi" 聖號論列言原意 (The original intentions of writing the *Guidelines for the discussion of the Term Question*), *WGGB* (August 11, 1877), pp. 3955–6.

(the spiritual sage). He also explained that it was only the emperor of imperial China who was entitled to worship *Shangdi*; consequently he felt that it was impossible for common Chinese people to use *Shangdi* as a generic term. More importantly, he was opposed to simply adopting a dichotomy of either *Shen* or *Shangdi* in the rendering of God. He acknowledged the importance of observing and retaining the historic circumstances conveyed in the text. He gave an example of what to consider in translating of Acts 2:15. He thought the best translation was to use *si* 巳 (actually in some English translations "the third hour of the day" was used) instead of "nine o'clock in the morning", which was the modern measurement of time. Through this example, he wanted to show Roberts that the translation of the Bible in general, and the rendering of God in particular, was much more subtle matter than determining which terms for the highest sacred being or other beings in the Chinese language shared generic or absolute denotations.[30] In his very short reply to Huang, Roberts thanked him for his contribution, agreeing that his article dealt more with "primary compellation" than "sacred appellation", and called for further contributions from other Chinese voices.[31]

After more than one year, Huang wrote a much shorter piece on the Term Question, in which he showed his flexible attitude as to how to render the Hebrew term *Elohim*. He pointed out that it was good to have a suitable translation. But even if there were diverse views on it, to maintain harmony and peace was essential while Christianity was a religion of peace. In other words, Huang hinted that he did not want to see so many rebuttals and criticisms centering on the Term Question.[32] Perhaps it was a surprise for Huang to see that the debates over the Term Question between Roberts and Chinese Christians, and sometimes among the Chinese Christians themselves, went on ceaselessly. What follows are some further examples.

---

[30] Huang Pinsan 黃品三. 1969c [1877]. "Shouyao chengming" 首要稱名 (Primary compellation), *WGGB* (August 18, 1877), p. 3985.

[31] John S. Roberts. 1969c [1877]. "Meiguo jiaoshi Lupeishu shouyao chengming lun hou" 美國教士陸佩書首要稱名論後 (American missionary Roberts on the *Primary compellation*, with an epilogue), *WGGB* (August 18, 1877), p. 4000.

[32] Huang Pinsan 黃品三. 1969d [1878]. "Zhi heping lun" 致和平論 (In quest of peace), *WGGB* (March 9, 1878), p. 4725.

The next response was written by Luluzi 碌碌子 , a pseudo-name of Yao Chengquan 姚成全 from Wuchang. Luluzi claimed that the answers to Roberts' questions were obtained after discussion with numerous people. In other words, it can be regarded as a collective piece. Unlike Huang, Luluzi followed Roberts' eight-point format closely, and offered their views accordingly.

Their reading of the Chinese classics, notably the *Yijing* 易經 , did not lead them to conclude that *Shangdi* was the creator of all beings.

Di meant the king or ruler, while *Shangdi* was a term for god, but not the creator of all beings.

They did not have any answer as to whether or not the term *Shangdi* was a generic term. They pointed out that there were different *Di* 帝 as deities, such as *Yudi* 玉帝 (Jade god, a god with a higher status in the Daoist tradition); but at the same time Chinese would not use *Di* in names which would become *Yu Shangdi* 雨上帝 (rain god) or *Cai Shangdi* 財上帝 (wealth god).

They thought the word *Shen* was used widely in religious (such as *Shengming*) and general terms (such as *Xinshen* 心神).

They considered *Shen* to be a generic term.

They regarded *Shangdi* a kind of *Shen*, but not vice versa.

They did not agree that what was intangible and immortal in a human being was equal to *Shen*.

They found the meanings of *Ling* were very diversified. It could mean an immortal human body, one's intellectual aptitude (such as *Lingmin* 靈敏), or the presentation of a deity's power (such as *Lingyan* 靈驗).[33]

Another contribution on the Term Question came from Pan Xunru 潘恂如 of the London Missionary Society in Shanghai. A word about Pan's background is useful. In 1854, he came to Shanghai to see Wang Tao, and later served as a Chinese teacher to William Muirhead (Mu Weilian 慕維廉 , 1822–1900), a missionary of the London Missionary Society. In 1855, he was baptised and later ordained as a pastor. In 1858, he returned to his native county for the civil service examination, in which he did very well. Afterwards, he returned to Shanghai and continued to serve as a pastor at the London Missionary

---

[33] Luluzi 碌碌子 (i.e. Yao Chengquan 姚成全). 1969 [1877]. "Da Lupei xiansheng shenghao lielun" 答陸佩先生聖號列論 (A response to Roberts' call for papers on the Term Question), *WGGB* (September 15, 1877), pp. 4064–5.

Society. Evidently, he acquired a high level of literacy skills and of knowledge in the Chinese classics. He was a scholar-pastor, with a respectable status in Shanghai.

Pan traced the original meanings of the term *Shangdi*. In his study of *Yudian* 虞典 he concluded that the term *Shangdi* shared the meaning of the only and greatest deity. Furthermore, he pointed out that the Daoists had imbued the term *Di* with a religious sense, especially after the rise of Daoism in the Han dynasty. *Yudi* was the example he gave. Pan also warned against the use of the term *Shen*, for it carried a strongly polytheist connotation. After *Feng Shenbang* 封神榜 , a popular fairy tale connected to the founding of the dynasty of Zhou (ca. eleventh century BC–256 BC) the term *Shen* could be used in many various contexts. So missionaries were wise to use the word *Zhen* 真 before the word *Shen* in order to avoid making the Christian idea of God simply one among many kinds of deities. Moreover, Pan agreed that Huang Pinsan's choice, *Zaohua zhu*, was only sensible to the educated. Pan's personal preference was the word *Tian*, which was sensible to both the educated and the general public.[34]

Soon after Pan's article was published, a contribution from Ho Yuk-tsun 何玉泉 (He Yuquan, 1806–1903) stirred the strongest feedback from Roberts. It seems useful to begin with Ho's background in order to understand his views. Ho was well educated in the Chinese classics. He earned his living as a teacher in a village school in Hong Kong. Because of his commitment to translating the Chinese classics, Legge was probably keen to know any Chinese scholars in Hong Kong. Legge had known Ho quite well before he converted to Christianity. Legge recommended him for the post as a teacher in a government-aided school in Wong-Nei-Chung in 1857. Wilhelm Lobscheid (Luo Cunde 羅存德 , b. 1822), the Inspector of Schools who was an ex-missionary of the Rhenish Missionary Society (*Rheinische Missions-Gesellschaft*), inspected the Wong-Nei-Chung school and had debates with Ho over ancestral worship. Finally, Hong Rengan 洪仁玕 (1822–1864), who later became the Shield King of the Taiping Rebellion, joined Legge and successfully persuaded Ho to convert to Christianity. Ho was baptised on October 25, 1857.[35] Perhaps it is useful to quote a remark by John Chalmers (Zhan Yuehan 湛約翰 , 1825–1899)

---

[34] Pan Xunru 潘恂如 . 1969 [1877]. "Shenghao Lun" 聖號論 (The Sacred Appellation), *WGGB* (September 22, 1877), pp. 4092–3.

through which we can see Ho more clearly after he became a Christian. Chalmers remarked:

> Ho Yuk-tsun has been a steady and faithful evangelist and has no doubt
> been the means of much good ... He has had a notion since the death of
> the Rev. Ho Tsun-shin in 1871 that he was his legitimate successor in
> the office of pastor, and though never called to that office, he has been
> disposed to exercise its function and assume its dignity rather more
> than was desirable; and I suspect that he would place himself strongly
> in opposition to their calling any one else to be their pastor ... and Ho
> Yuk-tsun has his special friends who would stand by him.[36]

Ho was a deacon in the church and, more importantly, after Ho Tsun-sheen passed away in 1871 he regarded himself the pastor-to-be. His role as a leader was reinforced by his higher social status as a teacher for many years. His self-assumed role as a leader might have sufficed to motivate him to provide his answer to the Term Question— *Tiandao hecan* 天道合參 .

Ho's theory of *Tiandao hecan* originated from his persisting contemplation upon Confucianism and Christianity. He had become a Christian at age 51, and he saw his conversion experience in a Confucian way—knowing the Heaven's way at age 50. He had felt puzzled for a long time about the meaning of *Shangdi* in the *Liujing* 六經 (Six Classics). After his conversion to Christianity, he found his answer. The more he studied, the more he inclined to think that the *Tiandao*, Heaven's Way, could be obtained by studying both Christian and Chinese scriptures, because they were supplementary to each other. He went on to claim that ancient Chinese persons had also received revelation from God. The fact that there were sacrifices as religious services in both Jewish and Chinese ancient traditions was taken by Ho as evidence for this claim. He thought that the God of the Bible was *Shangdi* as proclaimed in the Six Classics. Moreover, he considered

---

[35] William Lobscheid. 1859. *A Few Notices on the Extent of Chinese Education and the Government Schools of Hong Kong, with Remarks on the History and Religious Notions of the Inhabitants of This Island*. Hong Kong: China Mail Press, pp. 34–5. See also Hong Kong Station of the London Missionary Society. 1939 [Repr.]. "Register and Record of the Chinese Church; and of Events Connected with the Mission". Unpublished document, reproduced on October 2, 1939, now kept in the Chung Chi College library, the Chinese University of Hong Kong.

[36] John Chalmers. 1880. "The History of the Hong Kong District, 1870–1880". Unpublished manuscript. Deposited at the Archives of the London Missionary Society, now known as Council for World Missions. South China/ Report/ Box 1, pp. 7–8.

using the Confucian notion of *Shangdi* the best means to preach Christianity. To him, the rendering of God was *Shangdi*.[37]

Roberts was very critical of Ho's theory of the compatibility of Confucianism with Christianity, and thus wrote a seven-point refutation. Firstly, he rejected Ho's notion that *Tiandao* could be obtained from studying Confucian scriptures, since he asserted that only the Bible contained divine revelation from God. Secondly, he opposed Ho's uncritical use of the term *Shangdi*, which Ho took to convey a generic connotation. Thirdly, he stressed again that Jesus was the only source of salvation. Fourthly, he pointed out that there were many differences in the meanings of the sacrifices as religious services in Jewish and Chinese traditions. Fifthly, he was opposed to the use of the word *Tian* to render *Theos*. Sixthly, the Bible was unique, so that it alone told the message of the salvation in Christ. Finally, the major obstacle for the spread of Christianity was one's pride, believing in one's personal efforts in making salvation possible. Accordingly, Roberts criticised Ho's intention of proving *Shangdi* in the Six classics to be equal to the Christian ideal of God, since it encouraged pride in Chinese, so driving them away from the core teaching of Christian salvation. Thus he damned Ho's suggestion, even though it may have sounded sensible to the Chinese audience to begin with a Confucian notion of *Shangdi*.[38]

Ho responded vigorously to Roberts' criticism. He stressed that his positive evaluation of Confucianism had been inspired by Legge. Moreover, he firmly believed in his theory of *Tiandao hecan*, which he put it in six points. First, in response to Roberts' contention that only the Bible contained divine revelation from God, Ho clarified that he was referring to the truth in a conceptual sense (*dao* 道 , meaning 'truth'), and not the writing (*shu* 書 , meaning 'writing' or 'scripture') in and of itself. Ho also believed that God would appreciate those who feared Him, regardless of the nations they belonged to. Second, concerning Roberts' criticism of Ho's uncritical use of the term *Shangdi*, Ho emphasised that he was following Medhurst's translation of the Old Testament. He went on to stress that he had no intention of lower-

---

[37] He Yuquan 何玉泉 (Ho Yuk-tsun). 1969a [1877]."Tiandao hecan" 天道合參 (Compatibility of heavenly ways), *WGGB* (September 29, 1877), pp. 4122–4.

[38] John S. Roberts. 1969d [1877]. "Lupei xiansheng shu He Yuquan xiansheng Tiandao hecan hou" 陸佩先生書何玉泉先生天道合參後 (Roberts' response to Ho's Tiandao hecan). *WGGB* (September 29, 1877), pp. 4125–6.

ing the position of Jesus, the only source of salvation; rather, he was just following the Bible. The passage in the Bible that he hinted at was the following:

> to the Jews I became as a Jew, that I might win Jews, to those who are under the law, as under the law, that I might win those who are under the law.[39]

Third, in refutation of Roberts' claim that there were many differences in the meanings of the sacrifices in religious services in Jewish and Chinese traditions, he restated that *Shangdi* in the Chinese classics was the God in Christianity. His frame of reference was based on the diffusion theory of the ancient history, in that he suggested that Fuxi 伏羲 appeared at the time around that of Noah after the great flood, as expounded in Genesis chapter 7. In other words, he thought it was likely that the very ancient Chinese would have known about God. Fourth, he pointed out that he was following Medhurst's use of *Tian* in the translation of the word *Theos*. Fifth, in response to Robert's statement that the Bible was unique in relation to other books, he stressed that *Tiandao* could be known and be conveyed in many different texts. Sixth, he agreed that the major obstacle for the spread of Christianity was one's pride, that is to say, believing in one's personal efforts leading to salvation. However, he disagreed with Roberts' claim that the approach of proving *Shangdi* in the Chinese classics was equivalent to the Christian idea of God involved an unacceptable pride. Instead, he strongly believed his doing so could more effectively carry the message of salvation to the Chinese audience.[40]

Roberts did not find Ho's arguments convincing; in response he made fourteen points. The first nine remarks were phrased in question format to forcefully query the grounds of Ho's argument. The latter five were aimed at reiterating his position. 1) From which source did he see *Shangdi* as *Yahweh*? 2) How could he be so certain about *Yahweh* as *Shangdi*? 3) Could he render God in Chinese? 4) Under his theory of *Tiandao hecan*, would he call himself a prophet? 5) As he believed that *Tian* was equivalent to *Shangdi*, would he render God as *Tian*? 6) As he asserted that *Tiandao* was universal, what were the positions of the Chinese sages if they could contemplate and under-

---

[39] Bible. 1 Corinthians 9: 29.

[40] He Yuquan 何玉泉 . 1969b [1877]. "Xu Tiandao hecan" 續天道合參 (Compatibility of heavenly ways, part 2). *WGGB* (December 8. 1877), pp. 4400–6.

stand *Tiandao*? Were they equal to Jesus? 7) Since he regarded ancient characters such as Wen Wang 文王 and Confucius as righteous people, what were his standards for being righteous? 8) While he regarded *Shangdi* as God (*Shen*), why did he reject the word *Shen* as the absolute term? 9) Would he not agree that Paul asked one to follow some regulation or custom that did not contradict the essential teaching of the Christian belief? 10) According to Genesis chapter 7, only the family of Noah feared and worshipped God. It was impossible that the Chinese worshipped the same God as Noah did. 11) Sacrifices as practised by ancient kings in China did not share a connotation of ransoming their people from sin. 12) Sacrifices in the Old Testament signified the crucifixion of Christ to save human souls. 13) The Bible represented the "only way", *yidao* 一道, saving the human beings across nations. 14) These views were expressed in order to show the true way and to glorify Jesus.[41]

After the above fourteen-point remark, Ho did not contribute any more articles to the forum. Instead, Wang Xianyu 王獻吁 made an interesting response. Not much concerning his background is known, except that he was from Guangdong. Of his numerous points, two are particularly worthy of notice. First, he thought that Roberts had over-reacted in the way he attacked Ho's articles, while both of them shared divine knowledge in their hearts (*xincun shengdao* 心存聖道). Second, he advocated a broad-minded attitude to the definition of *Tiandao*—any insight that accorded with the Bible should be acceptable. Here Roberts had stressed the supreme authority of the Bible from which only *Tiandao* could be found. Wang would however acknowledge the *Dao* in the Chinese classics as *Zhendao* 真道 ("true way"), instead of *Tiandao*.[42]

In the midst of the heated debates between Ho and Roberts, there was an interlude. Ying Shaogu 英紹古, a pastor from the London Missionary Society in Beijing, also participated in this debate. His approach was more pragmatic, suggesting getting rid of scholarly

[41] John S. Roberts. 1969f [1877]. "Lupei xiansheng shuxu Tiandao hecan hou" 陸佩先生書續天道合參後 (Roberts' response to Ho's Tiandao hecan, part 2). *WGGB* (December 8, 1877), pp. 4406–9.

[42] Wang Xianyu 王獻吁. [1878]. "Niyu He Yuquan Tiandao hecan bing Lupei houlun" 擬閱何玉泉天道合參並陸佩後論 (An attempt to understand Ho Yuk-tsun's Tiandao hecan and Roberts' response to Ho's ideas), *WGGB* (January 12, 1878), pp. 4539–42.

debates on the Term Question. He thought it was important to identify a sensible term from existing vocabulary. To him, the term *Shangdi* stood out clearly as the sensible rendering of God in Chinese, while at the same time it was also the highest deity worshipped in China.[43] But Roberts still thought it was impossible that the term *Shangdi* could convey the Christian connotation of God, as he had already expressed in his rebuttal of Ho. Furthermore, Roberts did not agree with giving up the debate over the Term Question before a definite answer was found. He did not want a harmony that was at the expense of the truth.[44]

In addition to those who had received a solid education in the Chinese classics, a few graduates from mission schools also took part in the debate. The cases to be cited here are Wang Bingkun 王炳堃 (also known as Wang Qianru 王謙如, 1846–1907) and Wang Bingyao 王炳耀 (also known as Wang Yuchu 王煜初, 1843–1902). A word about their backgrounds is certainly useful. Wang Bingkun and Wang Bingyao were brothers, and their father was Wang Yuanshen 王元沈 (1818–1914). Wang Yuanshen had come to Hong Kong in 1847 where he became a committed Christian and assisted the missionary work of Karl Gützlaff (Guo Shila 郭施拉, 1803–1851). Bingkun and Bingyao were sent to study under Ferdinand Genähr (Ye Naqing 葉納清, d. 1864) of the Rhenish Mission, to prepare them to be pastors. After graduation, Bingyao joined the Rhenish Mission while Bingkun joined the Berlin Missionary Society ("Gesellschaft zur Beförderung der Evangelischen Missionen unter den Heiden"). Both of them were active preachers travelling in Guangdong province. Their educational background did not lead them away from identifying with Chinese culture. In their numerous articles and religious tracts, they put together the Christian teachings with Chinese thoughts.[45]

Wang Bingkun wrote a careful piece examining the original meaning of the terms *Shangdi*, *Shen*, and *Tianzhu*. In doing so, he looked into the Chinese classics (such as *Zhouli* 周禮 and *Xiao Ya* 小雅) and

[43] Ying Shaogu 英紹古. 1969 [1877]. "Shenghao dingcheng shuo" 聖號定稱説 (The final answer to the Term Question), *WGGB* (December 1, 1877), pp. 4374–5.

[44] John S. Roberts (Lu Peishu 陸佩書). 1969e [1877]. "Lupei xiansheng shuxu shenghao dingcheng hou" 陸佩先生書續聖號定稱後 (Roberts' response to Ying's *The final answer to the Term Question*), *WGGB* (December 1, 1877), pp. 4436–8.

[45] Luo Xianglin 羅香林. 1969. "Zhongguo zupu suoji Jidujiao zhi chuanbo yu jindai Zhongguo zhi guanxi" 中國族譜所記基督教之傳播與近代中國之關係 (The

Chinese history. Interestingly enough, as far as I know Wang Bingkun was the first Chinese voice on the Term Question who took into account the historical experience of the Jesuits in late Ming and early Qing China. He concluded that the term *Shangdi* was the best choice to render God.[46] After about a year, Wang Bingyao saw another aspect of the Term Question debate. He became quite discontented at seeing so many debates centering around the Term Question, which had gradually led to diverse views and even hostile division, instead of promoting unity. He intended calling off the debate.[47] Not long after Wang Bingyao's request, the *Wanguo gongbao* put an end to the debate on the Term Question. However, this was not because of Wang's influence, but because a new editor for religious articles wanted to avoid any further bitterness or division in the missionary and church circles.[48]

CONCLUSION

A closer look into the Chinese voices on the Term Question as recorded in the *Wanguo gongbao* enables us to see that Chinese Christians had their own views over the cultural translation of the core of the Christian idea—the highest deity. It is consistent with the findings of the previous studies on nineteenth century Chinese Christians that they did not simply follow what the missionaries told or taught them. The impression that the missionaries played a more dominant role in the history of Christian missions was as pointed out by Daniel Bays, a consequence of the fact that Chinese Christians were placed in an inferior position. Chinese Christians simply did not gain recognition of their contributions. Bays points out that

---

[45] (*cont.*) spread of the Christian faith and its influence on the course of the history of Modern China, as seen in the Chinese genealogical records), *Journal of Oriental Studies* 7.1 (January 1969), pp. 1–22. Zha Shijie 1983, pp. 39–43, and Liu Yuesheng 劉粵聲. 1941. *Xianggang Jidujiaohui shi* 香港基督教會史 (A history of Christianity in Hong Kong). Hong Kong: Hong Kong Chinese Christian Churches Union, pp. 254–8.

[46] Wang Bingkun 王炳 堃 . 1969 [1878]. "Huihao lun" 徽號論 (On titles), *WGGB* (January 26, 1878), pp. 4573–9.

[47] Wang Bingyao王炳耀 . 1969 [1878]. "Shang Lupei mushi diyi shu" 上陸佩牧師第一書 (The first letter to Rev. Roberts), *WGGB* (May 11, 1878), pp. 4940–1.

[48] "Qing wu fubian" 請勿復辯 (No more debates [on the Term Question]). 1969 [1878]. *WGGB*, (June 29, 1878), p. 5147.

No mission society was uninvited to, or refused to attend, any of these meetings [general missionary meetings in 1877, 1890, and 1907]. About 1,100 attended the 1907 meeting, over 25% of all Protestant missionaries in China. Only six or seven Chinese Christians were invited. This is very revealing, of course.

Moreover, the Chinese voices were not recorded. He commented that

Mission records seriously understate the Chinese role, and often don't even have the names of Chinese participants, but they were there.[49]

In this vein, given that their views were not made available in many other sources, these voices as recorded in the *Wanguo gongbao* are of particular historical significance.

Conspicuously, there was a sharp difference of views over the Term Question between John S. Roberts and these Chinese Christians. One may be therefore tempted to go along with

Jacques Gernet's contention that the basic concepts and values of Confucianism and Christianity are incompatible and that the Jesuits had in the long run little chance of success.[50]

However, it should also be remarked that "many mission historians took exception to Gernet's thesis."[51] Taking these views into perspectives, how do we examine the rift between Roberts and Chinese Christians? If we just focus on Roberts and his views, it is very easy for one to follow Gernet's thesis that the cleavage between Christianity and Chinese culture was hardly to be bridged. But having looked into the Chinese responses, another picture emerges. We can see that a number of them plainly expressed their deprecation of Roberts' inflexible handling of the debates. Perhaps it is useful here to quote an observation on the Chinese participants in the Term Question debate:

When we turn to the debates among the Chinese Christians, we can see that some were more free to adopt the symbol of God into their tradition because they did not share some of the missionaries' assumptions.

---

[49] Daniel H. Bays. 1994. "Missions and Christians in Modern China, 1850–1950". Manuscript of a keynote speech paper presented at the "American Missionaries and Social Change in China: Collision and Confluence," Linfield College, Oregon, 1994, pp. 6–7.

[50] Jessie Lutz. 1998. "Chinese Christianity and Chinese Missions, Western Literature: The State of the Field", *Journal of the History of Christianity in Modern China*, 1, p. 36.

[51] Ibid.

Furthermore,

> Chinese Christians played an important role in the Term Question by helping to make the alien symbol of a monotheistic God more accessible. They opted for an indigenous and respectable term for God, and they incorporated the doctrine of God into their wholistic [sic] and cosmological religiosity.[52]

Apparently, Chinese Christians were innovative in their views, ranging from new terminology to theories of understanding Christian doctrines. In the longer run, their inputs certainly did prove useful in the process of translating Christianity for the Chinese. Despite the fact that their inputs did not immediately lead to an effective communication of the Christian message for their Chinese audience, they were at least early attempts at achieving this. To better understand the cultural complexities involved in the Term Question in particular, or the historical experience of Christianity in China in general, a thorough study of the voices of Chinese Christians is imperative.

---

[52] Kwok Pui-lan 1992, pp. 36–7.

REFERENCES

Bays, Daniel H. 1994. "Missions and Christians in Modern China, 1850–1950". Manuscript of a keynote speech paper presented at the "American Missionaries and Social Change in China: Collision and Confluence", Linfield College, Oregon, 1994.

Bennett, Adrian A. 1983. *Missionary Journalist in China: Young J. Allen and His Magazines, 1860–1883*. Athens: University of Georgia Press.

Blodget, Henry and Ernest John Eitel. 1877. *The Chinese Term for God: Statement and Reply*. London: T. Williams.

Bohr, P. Richard. 1984. "Liang Fa's Quest for Moral Power", in: John King Fairbank and Suzanne Wilson Barnett (eds.). *Christianity in China: Early Protestant Missionary Writings*. Cambridge, Mass.: Harvard University Press, pp. 35–46.

———. 1998. "The Theologian as Revolutionary: Hung Hsiu-chuan's Religious Vision of the Taiping Heavenly Kingdom", in: Hao Yen-p'ing and Wei Hsiu-mei (eds.). *Tradition and Metamorphosis in Modern Chinese History: Essays in Honor of Professor Kwang-ching Liu's Seventy-fifth Birthday*. Taibei: Institute of Modern History, Academia Sincia, vol. 2, pp. 907–54.

Boone, William. 1848. *An Essay on the Proper Rendering of the Words Elohim and Theos into the Chinese Language*. Canton: Chinese Repository.

Chalmers, John. 1876. *The Question of Terms Simplified, or the Meanings of Shan, Ling and Ti in Chinese Made Plain by Induction*. Canton: E-Shing.

———. 1880. "The History of the Hong Kong District, 1870–1880". Unpublished manuscript. Deposited at the Archives of the London Missionary Society, now known as Council for World Missions.

Eber, Irene. 1999. "The Interminable Term Question", in: Irene Eber, Wan Sze-kar and Knut Walf (eds.). *Bible in Modern China: The Literary and Intellectual Impact*. Sankt Augustin: Institut Monumenta Serica.

Fairbank, John King. 1984. "Introduction: The Place of Protestant Writings in China's Cultural History", in: John King Fairbank and Suzanne Wilson Barnett (eds.). *Christianity in China: Early Protestant Missionary Writings*. Cambridge, Mass.: Harvard University Press.

He Yuquan 何玉泉 (Ho Yuk-tsun). 1969a [1877]."Tiandao hecan" 天道合參 (Compatibility of heavenly ways), *WGGB* (September 29, 1877), pp. 4122–4.

———. 1969b [1877]. "Xu Tiandao hecan" 續天道合參 (Compatibility of heavenly ways, part 2). *WGGB* (December 8, 1877), pp. 4400–6.

Hong Kong Station of the London Missionary Society. 1939 [Repr.]. "Register and Record of the Chinese Church; and of Events Connected with the Mission". Unpublished document, reproduced on 2 October 1939, now kept in the Chung Chi College library, the Chinese University of Hong Kong.

Huang Pinsan 黃品三. 1969a [1877]. "Shenghao lun" 聖號論 (On the Sacred Appellation), *WGGB* (July 21, 1877), pp. 3880–1.

———. 1969b [1877]. "Zuo Shenghao lun yuanyi" 作聖號論原意 (The original intention of writing *Shenghao Lun*), *WGGB* (August 11, 1877), p. 3955.

———. 1969c [1877]. "Shouyao chengming" 首要稱名 (Primary compellation), *WGGB* (August 18, 1877), p. 3985.

———. 1969d [1878]. "Zhi heping lun" 致和平論 (In quest of peace), *WGGB* (March 9, 1878), p. 4725.

Hyatt, Irwin T. Jr. 1976. *Our Ordered Lives Confess: Three Nineteenth-Century American Missionaries in East Shantung.* Cambridge, Mass.: Harvard University Press.

Kwok, Pui-lan. 1992. *Chinese Women and Christianity 1860–1927.* Atlanta: Scholars Press.

Lam Kai Yin 林啟彥 (Lin Qiyan) and Wong Man Kong 黃文江 (Huang Wenjiang) (eds.). 2000. *Wang Tao yu jindai shijie* 王韜與近代世界 (Wang Tao and the Modern World). Hong Kong: Hong Kong Educational Publishing company.

Latourette, Kenneth Scott. 1929. *A History of Christian Missions in China.* London: Society for Promoting Christian Knowledge.

Lee Ka-kiu 李家駒 (Li Jiaju). 1991. "Yichang 'shen' huo 'shangdi' da zhenglun: zaoqi laihua xinjiao jiaoshi duiyu 'God' yici da fanyi yu jieshi (1807–1877)" 一場神或上帝大爭論：早期來華新教教師對於 'God' 一次大翻譯與解釋 (1807–1877) (Controversies over the term *Shen* or *Shangdi*: early Protestant missionaries' translations and interpretations of the term 'God' (1807–1877)). M. Phil. thesis. Hong Kong: Chinese University of Hong Kong.

Legge, James. 1852. *The Notion of the Chinese Concerning God and Spirits with an Examination of the Defense of an Essay, on Proper Rendering of the Words Elohim and Theos into the Chinese Language, by William Boone D. D. Missionary Bishop of the Protestant Episcopal Church of the United States to China.* Hong Kong: Hong Kong Register Office.

——. 1877. *Confucianism in Relation to Christianity: A Paper Read Before the Missionary Conference in Shanghai on May 11ᵗʰ 1877.* Shanghai and London: Kelly and Welsh.

——. 1880. *A Letter to Professor F. Max Müller, chiefly on the Translation into English of the Chinese Terms Ti and Shang Ti in Rely to a Letter by 'Inquirer' in the Chinese Recorder and Missionary Journal for May-June 1880.* London: Trubner and Co.

Liu Yuesheng 劉粵聲 . 1941. *Xianggang Jidujiaohui shi* 香港基督教會史 (A history of Christianity in Hong Kong). Hong Kong: Hong Kong Chinese Christian Churches Union.

Lobscheid, William. 1859. *A Few Notices on the Extent of Chinese Education and the Government Schools of Hong Kong, with Remarks on the History and Religious Notions of the Inhabitants of This Island.* Hong Kong: China Mail Press.

Luluzi 碌碌子 (i.e. Yao Chengquan 姚成全). 1969 [1877]. "Da Lupei xiansheng shenghao lielun" 答陸佩先生聖號列論 (A response to Roberts' call for papers on the Term Question), *WGGB* (September 15, 1877), pp. 4064–5.

Luo Xianglin 羅香林 . 1969. "Zhongguo zupu suoji jidujiao zhi chuanbo yu jindai Zhongguo zhi guanxi" 中國族譜所記基督教之傳播與近代中國之關係 (The spread of the Christian faith and its influence on the course of the history of Modern China, as seen in the Chinese genealogical records), *Journal of Oriental Studies* 7.1 (January 1969), pp. 1–22.

Lutz, Jessie. 1998. "Chinese Christianity and Chinese Missions, Western Literature: The State of the Field", *Journal of the History of Christianity in Modern China*, 1.

—— and Rolland Ray Lutz. 1998. *Hakka Chinese Confront Protestant Christianity, 1850–1900, with the Autobiographies of Eight Hakka Christians, and Commentary.* New York: M. E. Sharpe.

Medhurst, Walter Henry. 1847a. *An Inquiry into the Proper Mode of Rendering the Word God in Translating the Sacred Scriptures into the Chinese Language.* Shanghai: Mission Press.

——1847b. *A Dissertation on the Theology of the Chinese with a View to the Eluci-dation of the Most Appropriate Term for Expressing the Deity in the Chinese Language*. Shanghai: Mission Press.

Morrison, Eliza (ed.). 1839. *Memoirs of the Life and Labours of Robert Morrison, D. D. Compiled by His Widow, with Critical Notices of His Chinese Works by Sam-uel Kidd and an Appendix Containing Original Documents*. 2 vols. London: Longman.

Nida, Eugene A. and William D. Reburn. 1987. *Meaning Across Cultures*. New York: Orbis Books.

Pan Xunru 潘恂如 . 1969 [1877]. "Shenghao Lun" 聖號論 (The Sacred Appellation), *WGGB* (September 9, 1877), pp. 4092–3.

Pelikan, Jaroslav. 1996. *The Reformation of the Bible; The Bible of the Reformation*. New Haven: Yale University Press.

Pfister, Lauren F. 1999. "A Transmitter But Not a Creator; Ho Tsun-sheen (1817–1871), The First Modern Chinese Protestant Theologian", in: Irene Eber, Wan Sze-kar and Knut Walf (eds.) 1999. pp. 165–98.

"Qing wu fubian" 請勿復辯 (No more debates [on the Term Question]). 1969 [1878]. *WGGB*, (June 29, 1878), p. 5147.

Records of the General Conference of the Protestant Missionaries of China, held at Shanghai, May 10–24, 1877. 1877. Shanghai: Presbyterian Mission Press.

Roberts, John S. 1876. "Some General Principles for Guidance in Translating the S. S. Terms for 'God'", *Chinese Recorder* 7.2 (March-April 1876), pp. 136–41, and 7.3 (May-June 1876), pp. 213–6.

——. 1877. "Principles of Translation into Chinese", in: *Records of the General Con-ference of the Protestant Missionaries of China*, pp. 418–29.

——(Lu Pei 陸佩). 1969a [1877]. "Shenghao lun lieyan" 聖號論列言 (Guidelines for the discussion of the Term Question), *WGGB* (July 21, 1877), pp. 3881–2.

——. 1969b [1877]. "Shenghao lun lieyan yuanyi" 聖號論列言原意 (The original intentions of writing the *Guidelines for the discussion of the Term Question*), *WGGB* (August 11, 1877), pp. 3955–6.

——. 1969c [1877]. "Meiguo jiaoshi Lupeishu shouyao chengming lun hou" 美國教士陸佩書首要稱名論後 (American Missionary Roberts on the Primary compel-lation, with an epilogue), *WGGB* (August 18, 1877), p. 4000.

——. 1969d [1877]. "Lupei xiansheng shu He Yuquan xiansheng Tiandao Hecan hou" 陸佩先生書何玉泉先生天道合參後 (Roberts' response to Ho's *Tiandao Hecan*). *WGGB* (September 29, 1877), pp. 4125–6.

——(Lu Peishu 陸佩書). 1969e [1877]. "Lupei xiansheng shuxu shenghao ding-cheng hou" 陸佩先生書續聖號定稱後 (Roberts' response to Ying's *The final answer to the Term Question*), *WGGB* (December 1, 1877), pp. 4436–8.

——. 1969f [1877]. "Lupei xiansheng shuxu Tiandao Hecan hou" 陸佩先生書續天道合參後 (Roberts' response to Ho's *Tiandao Hecan*, part 2). *WGGB* (December 8, 1877), pp. 4406–9.

Russell, William Armstrong. 1877. *Term Question: An Enquiry as to the Term in the Chinese Language which Most Nearly Represents Elohim and Theos as They Are Used in the Holy Scriptures*. Shanghai: American Presbyterian Mission Press.

Smith, Carl T. 1985. *Chinese Christians: Elites, Middlemen, and the Church in Hong Kong*. Hong Kong: Oxford University Press.

Spence, Jonathan D. 1996. *God's Chinese Son: The Taiping Heavenly Kingdom of Hong Xiuquan*. New York: W. W. Norton and Company.

Su Jing 蘇精 . 2000. "Wang Tao di Jidujiao xili" 王韜的基督教洗禮 (On the Christian baptism of Wang Tao), in: Lam Kai Yin (Lin Qiyan 林啟彥) and Wong Man Kong (Huang Wenjian 黃文江) (eds.). *Wang Tao yu jindai shijie* 王韜與近代世界 (Wang Tao and the Modern World). Hong Kong: Hong Kong Education Publishing Company, pp. 435–52.

Wagner, Rudolf G. 1982. *Reenacting the Heavenly Vision: The Role of Religion in the Taiping Rebellion*. Berkeley: Institute of East Asian Studies.

Wanguo Gongbao 萬國公報 (The Globe Magazine). 1969 [1876–1877]. Taibei: Huawen Bookstore [quoted as *WGGB*].

Wang Bingkun 王炳 坤. 1969 [1878]. "Huihao lun" 徽號論 (On titles), *WGGB* (January 26, 1878), pp. 4573–9.

Wang Bingyao 王炳耀 . 1969 [1878]. "Shang Lupei mushi diyi shu" 上陸佩牧師第一書(The first letter to Rev. Roberts), *WGGB* (May 11, 1878), pp. 4940–1.

Wong Timothy Man Kong. 1996. *James Legge: A Pioneer at the Crossroads of East and West*. Hong Kong: Hong Kong Education Publishing Co.

Ying Fuk-tsang 邢 幅增 (Xing Fuzeng). 1995. *Wenhua Shiying yu Zhongguo Jidutu, 1860–1911* 文化適應與中國基督土, 1860–1911 (Cultural Accommodation and Chinese Christians, 1860–1911). Hong Kong: Alliance Bible Seminary, pp. 123–4.

Ying Shaogu 英紹 古. 1969 [1877]. "Shenghao dingcheng shuo" 聖 號定稱説 (The final answer to the Term Question), *WGGB* (December 1, 1877), pp. 4374–5.

Zha Shijie 查時傑. 1983. *Zhongguo jidujiao renwu xiaochuan* 中國基督教人物小傳 (Concise biographies of important Chinese Christians). Taibei: China Evangelical Seminary Press.

LAUREN PFISTER

NINETEENTH CENTURY RUIST METAPHYSICAL TERMINOLOGY AND THE SINO-SCOTTISH CONNECTION IN JAMES LEGGE'S *CHINESE CLASSICS*

1. Legge's hermeneutic environment: Scottish realism

What James Legge (1815–1897) brought with him to the southeast China coastline in 1843, when he moved the Anglo-Chinese College (*Yinghua shuyuan* 英華書院, 1818–1856, 1920–) from Malacca into the newly created colony of Hong Kong, was more than an educational institution. His mind was infused with an evangelical Christian conviction self-consciously taken up as his own way to live dutifully in the world, one fully adopted only after he had graduated at the age of 20 with a Master's degree from King's College in Aberdeen. In fact, Legge had grown up in a pious Congregational home in northeastern Scotland and had absorbed many influences from his eldest brother's theological reflections as well as the prevailing Scottish philosophy of his day.[1] In the latter case, philosophical reflections among Scottish intellectuals, many being ministers in the state-supported Presbyterian church of Scotland, had provided an articulate response to the radical empiricism and scepticism of David Hume (1711–1776), by means of a reconsideration of the "fundamental laws of human belief" and the "primary elements of human reason". Though highly rational and imbued with methodological thoroughness inherited from Aristotelian ways of thinking, the basic tenets of this Scottish school set out to reconceive the way in which human beings come to know the world.

---

[1] Details regarding the philosophical, theological and intellectual influences on Legge and his eldest brother, George, were first discussed in my articles, see Lauren Pfister. 1990b. "Some New Dimensions in the Study of the Works of James Legge (1815–1897): Part I", *Sino-Western Cultural Relations Journal* 12, pp. 29–50; id. 1991. "Some New Dimensions in the Study of the Works of James Legge (1815–1897): Part II", *Sino-Western Cultural Relations Journal* 13, pp. 33–46. An intellectual biography of Legge's missionary career is being considered for publication through the Scottish Studies centre of the University of Mainz. If it is feasible to publish, the work will be entitled *Pursuing the Whole Duty of Man. James Legge (1815–1897) and the Scottish Encounter with China.*

In ways that were very much like the epistemological accounts later extrapolated in the early twentieth century by Gabriel Marcel (1889–1973), Thomas Reid (1710–1796) and his nineteenth century followers claimed that sensations were not mediated by "innate ideas" as assumed and presented in the English philosophies of John Locke (1632–1704) and George Berkeley (1684–1753) and the Scottish empiricism of Hume; rather, they were spontaneous events of embodiment which led to inherent judgments about the basic nature of the way things are. Sensitivities to causal relationships, the fact that there is an external world, and the generality of certain basic human values and relational duties all come through this complex and pre-rational engagement of people in their social and natural environments. Not assuming an analytical stance as the most fundamental position of a person in the world, even though logical analysis of mental phenomena may help philosophers to bring out new understandings to the nature of mental powers, these Scottish realists argued that there was a basic orientation in commonly held beliefs that was generally acceptable if not actually true, recognizably related to certain basic experiences of persons within their lifeworlds. The judgments relying on this orientation to one's lifeworld are graded into various degrees of truth values, some being "certain, others such as are probable, in various degrees, from the highest probability to the lowest." Beliefs derived from spontaneous sensate experience then could carry weight as "contingent truths" or be identified in a few very significant cases as related to "necessary truths".[2] Here, then, was an account of human ways in the world that appealed to "common sense" as a justifiable orienting factor in human experiences, and one that could also account for differences in beliefs and beliefs systems in various places among different people. This was done without appeal to a faculty psychology which Immanuel Kant (1724–1804) had already worked out in continental Europe in the late eighteenth century, but which Scottish philosophers did not know well until the 1850s, when Kant's

---

[2] Quotations here come from William Hamilton (ed.) and Harry M. Bracken (comm.). 1967. *Thomas Reid—Philosophical Works*. vol. 1. Hildesheim: Georg Olms Verlagsbuchhandlung, pp. 209–11.

[3] There was an attempt in the mid-nineteenth century by the Scottish philosopher and commentator of the "Commonsense School", William Hamilton, to bridge the differences between Kant's faculty psychology and the Scottish realists' arguments for actively informing sensations against "innate ideas", but in the end this only hastened the domination of Kant's transcendentalism in the later part of the nineteenth

system and transcendental method began to overshadow their own alternative approach to the nature of the mind, sensations and beliefs.[3]

So, for example, the pain of gout in a big toe not only "informs" me in a passive manner that there is pain, but also simultaneously presents to consciousness the concomitant and positive "belief" that "my toe" exists in the world as part of "my body". This is a general state of my being-in-the-world, and though sensations of this sort may occasionally be untrue due to unusual circumstances (a post-amputation relapse into feeling what is a no-longer-existent limb, for example), these false impressions can be analyzed, corrected, and made understandable to 'common sense'.

This was of particular significance to the young Legge's own orientation to a complex nineteenth century world with its diverse beliefs, giving him a means to unravel a number of major problems which restrained him from embracing Christian faith until the year following his graduation from King's College in 1835. As he also learned from these Scottish realists, there were 'first principles' of necessary truths which provided a basic orientation to the nature of grammar, logic, mathematics, aesthetic taste, morality and metaphysics. So, Legge's will to search for hermeneutic principles within the Chinese texts he investigated was certainly motivated by this preunderstanding that these were basic principles of understanding which would lead to reasonable and justifiable interpretations of any text. Consequently, his highlighting of a hermeneutic principle located in the *Mencius* by placing it on the flyleaf of each volume of the *Chinese Classics* was itself a self-conscious affirmation that evidence of the recognition of these first principles in logic and interpretation did exist in the Ruist scholarly world.[4] In the moral realm, relational 'duties' involved a very strong assertion of the inherent rightness of filial affection between brothers and parental care for children,

---

[3] (*cont.*) century. Only in the later decades of the twentieth century in North American discussions of "reformed epistemology" (Alvin Plantinga and Nicolas Wolterstorff being some of the more prominent figures in this growing discussion), does one see a new international appeal to arguments originally raised by these Scottish philosophers, particularly as they are presented in Reid's works.

[4] The text came from the *Mencius* 5A:4, in: James Legge (tr. and comm.). 1893 [1861]. *The Chinese Classics with a translation, critical and exegetical notes, prolegomena, and copious indexes* [hereafter *CC*]. Oxford: Clarendon Press, vol. 2, p. 353, and stated "[Interpreters] may not insist on one term so as to do violence to a sentence, nor on a sentence so as to do violence to the general scope. They must try

reflecting sentiments justified by Scottish realist arguments that were remarkably parallel to very similar values in Ruist-informed world-views in the late Qing dynasty.[5] In the metaphysical realm, there were explicit arguments related to the existence of deity in the highest sense (among a number of other issues), providing extensive arguments relating to the distinction between natural and special revelation. These were worked out in great detail by Dugald Stewart, (1753–1828) making possible under the rubric of "natural theology" a very articulate account of various conceptualizations of spiritual and divine categories reached or dictated by unaided human reason.[6] It was this account that had been particularly helpful to Legge in extending theological discussions into the realms of comparative religious investigations, and apparently had a role in leading him to convictions about the reality of divine 'special revelation' which he embraced as a Christian.

As a consequence, Legge brought with him to the Chinese continent a set of philosophical and theological orientations that provided a particularly flexible and utilizable method for seeking out common understandings and for sensing areas where there were conflicts in general beliefs supported by Christian and Ruist worldviews. It is this orientation which guided Legge in his studies of the Ruist canon, investigations initiated in earnest in the early 1840s; he employed it as he studied the texts and their commentaries, all used to prepare his lectures to students at the Anglo-Chinese College in Hong Kong from 1844 to 1856. Only after this amount of thorough immersion in the

---

[4] (cont.) with their thoughts to meet that scope and then shall apprehend it." A fuller discussion of the significance and problematic of the citing of this passage as a hermeneutic principle has been offered in my article, "Mediating Word, Sentence and Scope without Violence: James Legge's (1815–1897) Understanding of 'Classical Confucian' Hermeneutics" in: Ching-I Tu (ed.). 2000. *Classical Interpretations. The Hermeneutic Traditions in Chinese Culture.* New Brunswick, New Jersey: Transaction Press, pp. 370–82.

[5] This was so much the case that McCosh, in his account of Thomas Brown's (1778–1820) meteoric career as a member of the Scottish Commonsense School, was upheld as a paragon of filial virtue due to his close relationship with his parents and siblings. Cf. James McCosh. 1875. *The Scottish Philosophy: Biographical, Expository, Critical, From Hutcheson to Hamilton.* London: MacMillan and Company.

[6] There is a very extensive passage in Stewart's work dealing with these matters, explicitly developed because of the anti-theistic tendencies he recognized in the ideologies of the French Revolution. See these discussions and arguments in William Hamilton (ed.). 1854. *The Collected Works of Dugald Stewart.* 11 vols. Edinburgh: Thomas Constable and Company, vol. 7, pp. 12–227.

Ruist scriptures and their commentarial traditions did Legge initiate the translations which would lead to the publication of the first of eight tomes of the *Chinese Classics* in 1861.

2. FUSION AND CONFUSION? LEGGE'S RENDERINGS OF RUIST METAPHYSICAL TERMS

Having understood the hermeneutic pre-understandings influencing Legge's approach to the massive and life-long project of translating the whole of the Ruist canonical literature, we can now move directly into discussing a few major instances of his renderings of Ruist metaphysical terminology. The focus of our subsequent discussions will be placed on:

(a) Legge's handling of elements and dimensions of the Ruist spiritual world;

(b) The apparent troubles he faced in seeking to make sense of the organismic cosmology inherent in and undergirding Ruist accounts of human beings; and

(c) His multiform rendering of the term, *dao* 道 , which manifests numerous points where Scottish realist principles informed translations and so reshaped a 'daological' universe into a Neo-Aristotelian conceptual framework.

In pursuing these particular areas of metaphysical terminology, we are consciously attempting to reveal how Legge's Scottish realism and Non-conformist theology informed and influenced his search for conceptual equivalents between Ruist and Christian worldviews. In addition, we will show how these ways of thinking guided him in locating, explaining, and evaluating the nature of general beliefs held among scholarly Chinese commentators which were drawn from their interpretations of the Ruist scriptures. Furthermore, we will seek to show how Legge employed the potentials of different dimensions of his published texts—the translations themselves, his prolegomena, the commentarial notes beneath the translations, and his inchoate classical dictionaries at the back of each volume—to explore alternative renderings, indicate his Scottish realist judgments on certain issues, point out ambiguities in various Chinese passages, and express his own evaluations and emotions in facing some of the more difficult metaphysical conceptions which taxed his Scottish Christian view of reality in general and his understanding of Chinese beliefs in particular. We will argue that while Legge was a remarkably sensitive translator and interpreter in numerous areas, he failed to provide an adequate account of the organismic cosmology inherent in both Ruist and Daoist worldviews. So, while opening a door for Christian apologetics in the realm of natural theological discoveries within the Ruist canonical literature, in other areas his translations actually limited the access to readers of one of the major ways Ruist scholarship interpreted their ancient scriptures.

1. God, Ruist Pneumatology, and Legge's Account of Levels of Ruist Spirituality

It is clear that by 1852 Legge had already become convinced by his own study of Ruist scriptures and their commentators (including some Roman Catholic secondary sources) that *shangdi* 上帝 was the best way to translate the words *theos* and *'elohim* in the biblical texts. The debate and its long term importance has been worked out elsewhere, and so will not be repeated here.[7]

Subordinate to the "Lord on High" (*shangdi*) were a number of spiritual beings, all generally categorized as *shen* 神 or *guishen* 鬼神 . Their presence in the texts of the Ruist scriptures in general were undeniable, even in spite of the serious problem that in one important passage in the *Analects* Master Kong[8] (551 BC–479 BC) was described as not having discussed matters related to these *shen*.[9] In his notes to this passage, Legge indicates how Zhu Xi 朱熹 (1130–1200) and

---

[7] Legge made this explicit in his extensive writings related to the Term Controversy (the debates over how to translate "God", "spirit" and other biblical terms into Chinese written language) between 1850 and 1852, the culmination of his efforts being inscribed in his lengthy essay, *The Notions of the Chinese concerning God and Spirits: with an Examination of the Defense of an Essay, on the proper rendering of the words Elohim and Theos, into the Chinese Language.* 1852. Hong Kong: Hong Kong Register Office. His position was restated in 1877 by means of a much briefer argument and less extensive reference to original Chinese texts in a controversial work of 12 pages, *Confucianism in Relation to Christianity*, where he set forth in cogent form the basic positions which would become associated with "Leggist" accommodation strategies in Christian missiology for the last decades of the nineteenth century (James Legge. 1877. *Confucianism in Relation to Christianity.* London: Trübner and Sons). Extensions of this controversy are seen in the context of Chinese debates in 1877 in the article included here by Wong Man-kong, and in the sixth chapter of Irene Eber's recent book (Irene Eber. 1999. *The Jewish Bishop & the Chinese Bible: S. I. J. Schereschewsky (1831–1906).* Leiden: Brill, pp. 199–233).

[8] Kongzi, "Confucius".

[9] *Analects* 7:20 (*CC*1, p. 201).

Wang Su 王肅 (195–256) both identify *shen* with activities of a mysterious sort which were comprehensively and collectively associated with "ghosts and spirits" (*guishen*).[10] So, whether or not Master Kong actually lectured on them or not, the question would be to understand what was portrayed in any 'activities of a mysterious sort' that were regularly associated with spiritual beings in other places within the Ruist scriptures.

In the *Zhongyong* 中庸 there is a place where the Chinese Sage is recorded as having taught the following lessons about spiritual beings:

> How abundantly do spiritual beings [*guishen*] display the powers that belong to them! We look for them, but do not see them; we listen to [locate them], but do not hear them; yet they enter into all things, and there is nothing without them. They cause all the people in the kingdom to fast and purify themselves, and array themselves in their richest dresses, in order to attend at their sacrifices. Then, like overflowing water, they seem to be over the heads [*ru zai qi shang* 如在其上], and on the right and left [*ru zai qi zuoyou* 如在其左右] *of their worshippers.*[11]

Such a straightforward explanation provides a firm foundation for Ruist pneumatology. Here we not only have this particular account of how spirits act and influence human behavior, it also includes specific details that go far beyond a shamanist invitation of spirits into a medium for the sake of divination. Rather, it suggests that these spirits promote human rituals appropriate to the recognition of their existence, their powers of blessing, and the roles which specific humans must assume in various kinds of ritual contexts. Spirits were part of the harmonious universe in which humans could take a specific ritual position of respectful propriety, interacting with them by means of physical symbols just as the spirits engaged them on spiritual planes.

Far more significant in this context is the interpretive malaise Legge experienced in deciding how to translate the phrase *guishen*. In

---

[10] For Legge the information gleaned from these interpretive glosses support was particularly significant, because since the late 1840s he had opposed another group of missionaries who insisted on using the term *shen* to translate the idea of the biblical 'God'. These glosses obviously suggested Legge's claims were correct: the meaning of the term *shen* was too broad to be useful in designating a unique and ultimate being.

[11] *Zhongyong* 16 (*CC*1, pp. 397–8). Parenthetical comments and Chinese characters are added here by this author, but the italicized phrase is as in the original text.

his notes to the first passage mentioned in the *Zhongyong* above, Legge discusses at length the meaning of the phrase and decides at the very end that "in the text [here] they blend together, and are not to be separately translated. They are together equivalent to 神 [shen]."[12] Yet when he reveals the metaphysical discussions related to this phrase in the Song Ruist traditions, citing passages from Zhu Xi, the Cheng 程 brothers,[13] and Zhang Zai 張載 (1020–1077), Legge finds himself unable to accept their attempts at unifying images of the *yin-yang* forces and a universe united by means of "the two breaths of nature" with the *guishen*. He concludes with an air of frustration: "It is difficult—not to say impossible—to conceive in one's self exactly what is meant by such descriptions." In explanations prepared by the Qing scholar Mao Qiling 毛奇齡 (1623–1716), Legge found more understandable beliefs where the *guishen* were equated with the *dao*: they "are the 道 [dao], embodied in Heaven (*ti tian* 體天) for the nourishment of things."[14] While adding no critical remark to this statement, Legge is apparently not fully convinced by Mao Qiling's interpretation of these metaphysical issues. What Mao is essentially presenting is an organismic universe, one in which different dimensions of the spiritual world interact with material realms for the sake of their "nourishment". If this is the case, then from the Ruist point of view human beings would have a heightened potential to engage and interact with these spiritual beings, perhaps even to the point of taking on qualities normally associated with them.

2. Ruist Anthropology: Tracing the Transformative Possibilities of Humans

This function of spirits—the nourishment of human beings by means of spiritual embodiment—is in fact a part of the scriptural teachings of the Ruist canon Legge did know, but it was here that his own Christian world view began to feel very uncomfortable. Where it is stated in the *Zhongyong* that the "most entirely sincere" person (*zhi cheng* 至誠) may come to the point of "assisting the transforming and nourishing powers of Heaven and Earth" so that he may "form a ternion"

---

[12] See *CC*1, p. 398.
[13] Cheng Hao 程顥 (1030–1085) and Cheng Yi 程頤 (1033–1107).
[14] See *CC*1, p. 398.

with these two powers, Legge demurs. It is an "extravagance" not truly descriptive of a more limited human nature.[15] When the same kind of person is described in a subsequent passage as one "like a spirit" (*ru shen* 如神), Legge lets loose a blast of Scottish "common-sense", revealing his own comparative religious hierarchy of spiritual experiences, and so resisting any attempt to place the image into a more reasonable light:

> The whole chapter is eminently absurd, and gives a character of ridicu-lousness to all the magniloquent teaching about 'entire sincerity.' The foreknowledge attributed to the Sage,—the mate of Heaven,—is only a guessing by means of augury, sorcery, and other follies.[16]

Though this could be read as a point where Legge temporarily lost his patience with Chinese Ru scholarship, this response would be too superficial. For Legge, the metaphysical stakes at this point were high: If humans can in some sense become divine or "like spirits", then there would be no need for a Christian salvation; yet his own convictions about the nature of human beings is that they were far from this kind of perfection, easily deterred into immoral and unjust behavior, and rarely if ever so gifted as to be "like a spirit". In other places Master Meng[17] had also made an even stronger claim, one which once more touched this sensitivity in Legge's beliefs, conse-quently prompting a rather awkward coining in English in order to avoid the obvious connection. In the *Mencius* 7B:25, there is an explicit hierarchy of cultivated human beings, starting with the "good man" and developing through stages of being "faithful", "beautiful", and "great" to the point where they are recognized as "sages" or "sagely" (*sheng* 聖). But this is not the last stage: one further transfor-mation is possible. Legge offers the following rendering: "When the sage is beyond our knowledge, he is what is called a spirit-man."[18] The final term, however, is *shen*, "a spirit" or "spiritual". In an organ-ismic cosmology such as the one promoted here, this kind of trans-formative development would be feasible because the basic nature of all things is the same.[19] Legge, however, could not conceive of this

---

[15] *Zhongyong* 22 (*CC*1, p. 416).

[16] See comments to *Zhongyong* 24 (*CC*1, p. 418, notes, left column).

[17] Mengzi, "Mencius" (ca. 372 BC–ca. 289 BC).

[18] *CC*2, p. 490.

[19] I have developed more thoroughly this comparative cosmological suggestion in a paper presented to the workshop on Mencius at the National University of Singa-

cosmology as being true, and so addressed the problem directly and thoroughly in his attached comments:

> 聖而不可知之之謂神, ["what is sagely and we cannot know it, this is called divine"]—with this we may compare what is said in the Doctrine of the Mean [*Zhongyong*], 至誠如神, 'the individual possessed of the most complete sincerity is like a spirit.' In the critical remarks in the 四書合講 [*Sishu hejiang*, Combined Commentaries and Paraphrases to the Four Books], it is said, indeed, that the expression in the text is stronger than that there, but the two are substantially to the same effect. Some would translate 神 [shen] by 'divine,' a rendering which it never can admit of, and yet, in applying to man the term appropriate to the actings and influence of Him whose way is in the sea, and His judgments a great deep, Chinese writers derogate from the prerogatives of God.[20]

While recognizing the error of interpreting *shen* in too high a manner, Legge here nevertheless is unable to accept any possibility that a human being may take on the characteristics these Ruist scriptures claim for them. By means of the oblique gloss from the Psalms and Proverbs, where the sea remained a symbol of the unfathomable, something clearly beyond rational comprehension, Legge argues that human beings are necessarily limited in their abilities to achieve these kind of things. In fact, Legge's sensitivities also could have cited other passages within the Ruist scriptures to indicate a point of tension within various texts of their own canonical literature. He had previously translated in the *Zhongyong* another passage which clearly stated:

> Common men and women, however ignorant, may intermeddle with the knowledge of [the way of the superior man]; yet in its utmost reaches, there is that which even the sage does not know. Common men and women, however much below the ordinary standard of character, can carry it into practice; yet in its utmost reaches, there is that which even the sage is not able to carry into practice.[21]

Legge's note to this passage, once more struggling to find an overall coherence for the Ruist placement of human beings in the midst of

---

[19] (*cont.*) pore in January 1999. See my "Why the Demophilic cannot be Democratic and what might make it so: Reconstructing 'Moral Humans' in Master Meng's Philosophy", in: Alan Chan and Jiuan Heng (eds.). 2002. *Mencius: Context and Interpretation*. Honolulu: University of Hawaii Press.

[20] *CC*2, p. 490–91.

[21] *Zhongyong* 12 (*CC*1, p. 392).

Heaven and Earth, illustrates again his battle with the implications of an organismic cosmology in which humans can reach heights equivalent to spirits.

> ... I confess to be all at sea in the study of this paragraph. Chu [Zhu Xi] quotes from the scholar Hau (侯氏), that what the superior man fails to know was exemplified in Confucius's having to ask about ceremonies and offices, and what he fails to practise was exemplified in Confucius not being on the throne, and in Yao and Shun's being dissatisfied that they could not make every individual enjoy the benefits of their rule. He adds his own opinion, that what men complained of in Heaven and Earth, was the partiality of their operations in overshadowing and supporting, producing and completing, the heat of summer, the cold of winter, etc. If such things were intended by the writer, we can only regret the vagueness of his language, and the want of coherence in his arguments.[22]

In this response, Legge is criticizing Zhu Xi's interpretation of the passage, suggesting that Zhu Xi had missed the real point which is in Legge's mind more obvious and practical. Certainly, as in the case of the other person's comments Zhu cited, there would be historical and institutional matters that any person would not necessarily know, and so they would have to be learned by inquiry; in addition, one could be disappointed in not being able to fulfill what one felt destined to accomplish. But these specific examples miss what for Legge would seem to be more generalizeable: humans, even at their greatest heights of understanding and strength, still cannot do all that is ideally placed before them. Interpretations which avoid this implication, a matter bound up with the ontic and daological nature of humans in and of themselves, would appear in Legge's mind to have missed the point.

But if this is in fact the case, Legge continues to inquire, why would such "extravagant" sayings be made about Master Kong as the "universal Sage" at the end of the *Zhongyong*? In Legge's sight these involved contradictions of the first principles of understanding about the human mind and human actions, and so he could only point out the inconsistencies which he felt obliged to indicate, and persist in arguing that even in some of the texts of the ancient Ruist traditions themselves it could be suggested that humans were less powerful and potentially transformable than the highest Ruist ideals would permit.

---

[22] *CC*1, p. 393, notes.

3. Revealing Dimensions of the Dao by means of Scottish Realist Principles

One of the most challenging terms to render into English is the *dao*, partly because of its diverse meanings, but mostly because of the metaphysical fecundity of its employment in all the major Chinese traditions. In his dictionary entry for the term *dao* at the end of the first volume of the Chinese Classics, Legge summarized the renderings of the term under two major categories: (1) a road, a path; (2) doctrines, principles, teachings.[23] In fact, however, within this first volume of the Chinese Classics there are many more tropes for *dao*, some of which are full of significance for us after having investigated Legge's handling of some other major metaphysical terms in the Ruist canonical vocabulary.

Illustrating the thoroughness of a fine scholar and considerate translator, we can follow Legge in all the places where the term *dao* portrayed some rather mundane meanings: *dao* can be a physical "road"[24] and a general "course"[25] of life; it can mean simply to "speak"[26] or can refer to the act of "leading" or "ruling" over others.[27] Only in a few cases was it used with other meanings not always clearly explained.[28] In the *Zhongyong* it appears many times as the "path", but this is a metaphorical figure of speech with another meaning which we will clarify further on.[29]

---

[23] *CC*1, p. 497, right column. He admittedly adds a subcategory to the first definition, pointing out that it "very often" appears with a "moral application." In addition, he adds without further comment, it may be "the course or courses, the ways proper to," and even sometimes "the right way, what is right and true." In these latter renderings we begin to feel the impact of his Scottish commonsense account of the term. Under the second category he also mentions a pair of tropes which appear fairly often: *you dao* 有道 and *wu dao* 無道 , which he points out can be applied to persons as being "principled" or "unprincipled" or to political kingdoms which are "well-governed" or "ill-governed". Once more, in the former rendering the presence of Scottish realist terminology is undeniable.

[24] *Analects* 6:10; 9:11; 17:14 (*CC*1, pp. 189, 221, 324).

[25] *Analects* 8:7; 15:39 (*CC*1, pp. 210, 305); *Great Learning (Daxue)* 10 as the "great course" of the "sovereign" (*CC*1, pp. 378–9; *Zhongyong* 30:3 as the "courses of the seasons and of the sun and moon" (*CC*1, p. 427) .

[26] *Analects* 11:30 and 16:5 (*CC*1, pp. 286, 311–2); *Great Learning* 3 (*CC*1, p. 363).

[27] *Analects* 1:5; 2:3; 12:23; 19:25 (*CC*1, pp. 189, 221, 324).

[28] e. g. see *Great Learning* 10 (*CC*1, pp. 375–6).

[29] *Zhongyong* 1, 2, 4, 5, 13, 27:1 (*CC*1, pp. 383–5, 387–8, 393–4, 422).

Though there is at least one occasion when Legge renders the term as "practical courses",[30] and so reflects other times when he recognizes that it determines what is "characteristic" of a certain way of acting and living,[31] the more significant tropes to reveal the imprint of Scottish realism on Legge's translation vocabulary occur in passages dealing with Ruist politics, moral and ethical situations, and places where an ultimate concern are expressed by this term.

With regard to the political realm, when the general phrases *you dao* 有道 and *wu dao* 無道 appear, Legge often renders these as "when good government prevails" or "when the kingdom is well-governed" in parallel with "when bad government prevails" or "when the kingdom is ill-governed".[32] But in other contexts he shifts his rendering to reflect the Neo-Aristotelian terminology: "when right principles prevail", "when right principles are prostrated" as well as simply "principled" versus "unprincipled" conditions.[33] Because these passages often occur in tandem within the same saying, it is clear at this point that Legge used reference to "principles" as a briefer way to specify actions that displayed proper political judgment. Here the metonymic power of the symbol, *dao*, is lost; Legge chooses to replace it with a more direct and more narrowed reference to the rules and regulations by which these actions can be assessed.

Although there are other metaphorical ways in which the *dao* is used to describe the patterns of life of a father, of the ancient kings, and of archery,[34] among the most prominent phrases in this category is the "way of the superior man".[35] There are a few times in these texts where there are more general references to the "way of Heaven" (*tiandao* 天道 or *tian zhi dao* 天之道), the "way of men" (*ren zhi dao* 人之道), and the "way of Heaven and Earth" (*tiandi dao* 天地道).[36] Here the translation carries over the metonymy and applies it as in the

---

[30] *Analects* 1:2 (*CC*1, p. 138–9).

[31] Legge actually uses the phrase "it is characteristic of…" in a number of contexts describing the "superior man" (*junzi* 君子) and the "good man" (*shan ren* 善人) in *Analects* 5:12, 11:19 (*CC*1, pp. 178, 243–4).

[32] *Analects* 5:2; 8:13; 14:1; 15:6; 16:2 (*CC*1, pp. 172–3, 212, 275, 296, 310); *Zhongyong* 27:7 (*CC*1, p. 423).

[33] *Analects* 8:13; 12:9; 16:2 (*CC*1, pp. 212, 258, 310); *Zhongyong* 10 (*CC*1, pp. 389–90).

[34] *Analects* 1:11, 1:12, 3:16 (*CC*1, pp. 142, 143, 160).

[35] *Analects* 14:30, 19:12 (*CC*1, pp. 286, 343); *Zhongyong* 12, 13, 15, 33:1 (*CC*1, pp. 391, 394, 396, 431).

[36] *Analects* 5:12 (*CC*1, pp. 177–8); *Zhongyong* 20:18, 26:7/8 (*CC*1, pp. 413, 420).

Chinese original to the person, being, or activity which it describes: this "way" has a normative force, suggesting that it not only typifies a particular role but becomes prescriptive for those who would follow it. In this sense, we can begin to see why Legge might be willing to use normative terms to augment the meaning of the single Chinese character *dao* in other contexts.

One of the ways which norms are transferred is by means of teachings, and so in the context of the Ruist emphasis on teacher and student relationships, augmented by the concern for equipping people to learn well, it is appropriate at times to see Legge render *dao* as the "doctrines", "principles" or even "institutions" of great people such as Master Kong and the ancient sage-kings.[37] With this in mind Legge stretches our sensitivities for appropriate translation when he takes the beginning phrase of the *Great Learning* and offers it as "What the Great Learning teaches is…" when it would read more literally "The way of the Great Learning is…".[38]

While these turns of language are generally expected or acceptable, it is in the contexts where Legge feels obliged to reveal the moral, ethical, and axiological dimensions of the *dao* that his philosophical heritage becomes intimately bound up in a more complex hermeneutic act of translation. Sometimes Legge portrayed the *dao* as the "proper way" or the "upright way", other times as "their duties" when the possessive pronoun was present (*qi dao* 其道).[39] A stronger feeling is produced when the dao is called the "right way", simply "what is right", or pluralized as "true principles".[40] The height of this moralized or ethicized *dao* is expressed in Legge's phrase, the "path of duty" or "the rule", but also much more emphatically in the *Zhongyong* as "THE PATH", the "universal path" (*tianxia zhi da dao* 天下之達道) or, for the same phrase, "the duties of universal obliga-

---

[37] *Analects* 4:15 rendered as "my teachings" (*CC*1, p. 169); *Analects* 5:6 personalized without pronoun in text (*CC*1, p. 174); *Analects* 6:10; 14:38; 19:22 and *Zhongyong* 29:3 as "institutions" (*CC*1, pp. 188, 346, 425).

[38] *Great Learning* "Text of Confucius" and ch. 3 (*CC*1, pp. 356–357, 363), where Legge continues to render the term as "what is taught" and *daoxue* 道學 as "the work of learning".

[39] *Analects* 4:5; 18:2; 19:19; *Zhongyong* 27:1 as found in *CC*1, pp. 166, 331–2, 345, 422 respectively.

[40] *Analects* 4:8, 6:22, 11:23 (*CC*1, pp. 189, 221, 324); *Zhongyong* 20:18 (*CC*1, p. 413).

tion".[41] Though context has a large impact on Legge's choices for these translation tropes, it is obvious that in these renderings he is relying on his own moral understandings and offering translation equivalents that do not attempt to portray in a simple or single metonymy the family of meanings inherent in the concept of *dao*.

At a few moments in these texts Legge is driven to use other axiological terms in order to portray what he senses in the ultimate concern of the Ruist scriptures. So when Master Kong describes his basic orientation toward life as being "set on *dao*" or his "object" being *dao*, Legge transforms it to being "set on truth" and simply seeking "truth".[42] In at least one place it appears as "excellence", revealing a superlative plane of interests and concerns.[43]

What is ponderous about these moralizing and axiological tropes in Legge's portrayal of the metaphysical *dao* is that the richness of the original metanymy is lost in the precision of the translation. The Scottish realist concern for "principles" and "duties" becomes his major mental scaffolding for portraying what may also include a more dynamic cosmological background. While his renderings tend to privilege the rational qualities of a person's self-conscious awareness of their obligations and rules for working out these duties in a particular role, it does not come close to offering a sense of the "course", "path", "road" or "way" which characterizes their being-in-the-world as well as their mode of existence.

Apparently this factor in his way of translating the *dao* did continue to test and tax Legge's mind, so that years later, when he was preparing a translation of the *Daodejing*, Legge returned to the problem of translating *dao*. Having been caught up in a controversy with the vituperative Herbert Giles (1845–1935), Legge carefully rethought his own approach to the *dao* within the Daoist universe of symbols, and finally suggested, in a context quite unexpected for Daoist translations, that the "Tao" is really not a "positive being" at

---

[41] *Analects* 7:6, 15:28, rendered in the notes as "Principles of duty" (*CC*1, pp. 196, 302); *Analects* 15:41 as "the rule for..." (*CC*1, p. 306); *Zhongyong* 1 as "path of duty" (*CC*1, p. 383?); *Zhongyong* 3, 13 as "THE PATH" (*CC*1, pp. 383–5, 393); *Zhongyong* 20:8, 13 as "the duties", "the duties of universal obligation" (*CC*1, pp. 407, 409).

[42] *Analects* 4:9, 15:31 (*CC*1, pp. 168, 303).

[43] *Analects* 9:26 (*CC*1, p. 225).

all, but a "mode of being" a "phenomenon".[44] While most Daoist philosophers and religious adherents would probably find this questionable, since they are much more willing to emphasize the transcendent and 'depth' dimensions of the *dao* in their own tradition, Legge obviously was struggling with a serious metaphysical matter. The *dao* of the *Daodejing* expresses itself through the invisible presence of subtle activity, while the *dao* of the Ruist scriptures is embodied in the person who "expands the *dao*", since the *dao* in and of itself does not expand the man. But it was here already in 1861 that Legge had faced a major quandary, missing the potential cosmological significance of this saying. He rendered the passage as follows: "A man can enlarge the principles *which he follows*; those principles do not enlarge the man." In his notes Legge was spurred to elaborate this passage. Unexpressed and yet influencing his comments was the sense that this *dao* identified with "principles" seemed so passive, a *dao* which, for him as a Christian (where the incarnate *logos* had also been perceptively rendered as the *dao* in John 1:1), should have an active life of its own. So he elaborated:

> PRINCIPLES OF DUTY AN INSTRUMENT IN THE HAND OF MAN. This sentence is quite mystical in its sententiousness. The 翼 says:[45] — 道 [dao] here is the path of duty, which all men, in their various relations, have to pursue, and man has the three virtues of knowledge, benevolence and fortitude, wherewith to pursue that path, and so he enlarges it. That virtue remote, occupying an empty place, cannot enlarge man, needs not to be said.' That writer's account of 道 here is probably correct, and 'duty unapprehended,' 'in an empty place,' can have no effect on any man; but this is a mere truism. Duty apprehended is constantly enlarging, elevating, and energizing multitudes, who had previously been uncognizant of it. The first clause of the chapter may be granted, but the second is not in accordance with truth. Generally, however, man may be considered as the measure of the truth in morals

---

[44] Consult James Legge. 1885. "Book of rites", in: F. Max Müller (ed.). *Sacred Books of the East*. Oxford: Clarendon Press, vol. 39, p. 15.

[45] This text is the *Sishu yizhu lunwen* 四書翼註論文 , a collection of essays by a Hanlin scholar named Zhang Zhentao 張甄陶 , who produced this work during the Qianlong 乾隆 period (1736–1796). Legge translates its title as "A Supplementary Commentary, and Literary Discussions, on the Four Books". Like a few of the works cited by Legge, this is not a well known piece of work, and the person's name does not appear in any of the standard biographical and bibliographical works in English or Chinese. Nevertheless, Legge's gloss on the text (*CC*1, p. 129) is helpful: The author was a Zhu Xi follower, and wrote essays for "advanced" students. Legge studied it "with interest and advantage."

and metaphysics which he holds; but after all, systems of men are for the most part beneath the highest capacities of the model men, the Chun-tsze [junzi 君子].[46]

It is somewhat ironic that Legge at this juncture, having moralized the concept of *dao* by making it into "principles" and the "principles of duty", would feel that the "superior man" would ultimately go beyond this. What is it that completes the superior man's life? According to Master Kong, through the translation of Legge, we learn, "If a man in the morning hears the *dao*, he may die in the evening without regret."[47] Legge had the man hear "the right way", and so came very close to capturing the sense of that unseen power which could, in fact, become the defining way of shaping a Ruist's life.[48]

3. THE SIGNIFICANCE OF THE SINO-SCOTTISH CONNECTION IN JAMES LEGGE'S TRANSLATION OF THE *CHINESE CLASSICS*

As an informed Scottish and committed Christian translator of the ancient Ruist scriptures, James Legge understandably carried many aspects of his intellectual upbringing with him into his office when he worked out his translations. This is both hermeneutically expected

---

[46] *Analects* 15:28 (*CC*1, p. 302 in the notes).

[47] *Analects* 4:8 (*CC*1, p. 168).

[48] Nearly 80 years after Legge published his first edition of the *Chinese Classics*, the influential modern Chinese philosopher, Feng Youlan 馮友蘭 (1895–1990) published in his own philosophical work a synopsis of the meanings of the term *dao*. In general, Feng claimed, *dao* carried six meanings. These include (1) road, which is extended in meaning to include "the way one should act", and so entails the basic meaning of "the truth" (*zhenli* 真理). (2) In Ruist traditions it can mean "the highest truth" or "truth in totality" (*zhenli quanti* 真理全體). This denotation Feng explicitly associates with the passage mentioned above, where Legge renders it as "the right way." (3) In Daoist traditions, it can mean the "true and original vital energy" (*zhenyuan zhi qi* 真原之氣). (4) the "moving universe". (5) the linkage between the Supreme Ultimate (*taiji* 太極) and the Ultimateless (*wuji* 無極). (6) the Heavenly Way (*tiandao* 天道), which for Feng was akin to the second meaning, but carried a special attachment to what he took to be the highest level of conscious human attainment in thought. The diversity of these meanings and their breadth of denotations, though not always overlapping with Legge's accounts due to their much broader range of sources employed in Feng's synopsis, provides a remarkably positive affirmation of Legge's diverse renderings for the term, including its metaphysical translations. See Feng Youlan 馮友蘭 . 1996. *Zhen yuan liu shu* 真元六書 (Six books on the True and Original). Shanghai: Huadong Normal University Press, pp. 72–3.

and should be carefully assessed. A number of historians, translatologists, and culture critics—some of the most articulate being Raymond Dawson, Eugene Chen Eoyang, and Edward Said—have claimed from their various professional viewpoints that nineteenth Christian missionaries were too intimately bound up within their own backgrounds. By this they meant that the broader interests of the missionary and cultural projects which these Christian missionaries adhered to made their publications and translations nothing more than a distorted picture of the texts and cultures they studied. Eoyang directs his poignant criticisms, spiced with a generally tasteful and sometimes bitter sarcasm, directly at Legge. His focus is primarily on passages related to the concept of "Heaven/heavens" (*tian* 天), where in some of Legge's translation there are errors, and in others a number of intellectual and spiritual tensions. Unlike the approach we have taken above in relating how Legge struggled with understanding and portraying an alternative form of cosmology, Eoyang criticizes the underlying Christian commitments which arise in Legge's renderings and commentaries in various portions of the *Analects* or *Lunyu* and the *State of Harmony and Equilibrium* or *Zhongyong*:[49]

> [T]here is a profound ambivalence in Legge's attitude toward the Confucian tradition: to the texts themselves, so commonsensical and rational, Legge is passionately impatient; to the commentaries, so often intuitive and mystical, Legge is positivistic and skeptical. ... Legge shows his largesse and views Confucius with the same indulgence and pity that Dante felt for the denizens of limbo. ... Legge's compassion for Confucius reflects the magnanimity of nineteenth-century Christianity to the less fortunate, to the unbaptized. ... Yet, as benighted as Legge saw Confucius to be, he was no more receptive to Neo-Confucian commentaries which did "meddle- ... with metaphysics". He quotes Zhu Xi's exegesis of Confucius, and rather than being inspired by it, or finding that it satisfied his penchant for "revelation", or being impressed by its efforts to answer questions relating to "the human condition and destiny", Legge is derisive. ... If the commentator were Mat-

---

[49] Eugene Chen Eoyang. 1993. *The Transparent Eye: Reflections on Translation, Chinese Literature, and Comparative Poetics.* Honolulu: University of Hawaii Press, pp. 175–6 *in passim*. The second Ruist scripture mentioned here is often called the *Doctrine of the Mean*, a title Legge himself had conceived as a possible but unsatisfying translation in 1861, but decided to change in 1893 to the English rendering above. Unfortunately, his editor in Oxford apparently preferred the former, more Aristotelian-sounding title, and so Legge could only add his protest in a footnote to the introductory notes to that particular text.

thew and not Zhu Xi, and if instead of such phrases as "equilibrium and harmony" Legge had read "the peace that passeth all understanding", one wonders whether he would have been quite so unsympathetic.

Having made insightful criticisms of mistranslations and misdirections in some of Legge's specific renderings, Eoyang summarizes his criticisms at a higher level of ideological critique:[50]

> It is not Legge's own bias, but the bias inherent in a fundamentally Christian outlook which he could not escape, nor see objectively, that infuses his intemperate and inconsistent critiques of the Confucian canon. He saw Confucius as a false prophet, a Messiah *manqué*, whose practical wisdom was useful in developing moral character but whose thought would be forever mired in unbaptized and unredeemed benightedness.

While Eoyang's piercing rhetoric suggests that Legge's translation is inherently skewed, interpretatively blinded by a biased "Christian outlook" which can understand neither its own "bias" nor the "commonsensical and rational" vision of Ruist "secularism", Eoyang's own bold expression of ideological resentment carries its own ironies. Does Eoyang's monolithic characterization of "the Confucian tradition" as a "commonsensical" and "secular" present a fair and balanced account of the Ruist metaphysics involving 'heaven', 'ghosts and spirits', a transcendent 'Way' and a spiritually informed 'sageliness'? Can it adequately explain the ritual and spiritual significance of the imperial sacrifices offered in Beijing by the emperor at every equinox and solstice, dictated by the ritual scriptures of the Ruist canon, and constantly practiced during Legge's lifetime?[51] Were there no alternative Ruist interpretations of these canonical texts and of Zhu Xi's dualistic metaphysics which struggled over the meaning of the original scriptures and decried Zhu Xi's dualism, even though it was the 'orthodox standard' for canonical interpretations, as incoherent? Are the 'passionately impatient' criticisms of anti-Zhu Xi scholars during the Qing dynasty such as Wang Fuzhi 王夫之(1619–1692), Huang Zongxi 黃宗羲 (1610–1695), Yan Yuan 顏元(1635–1704), and Dai Zhen 戴震 (1723–1777) "inherently biased" because their own Ruist

---

[50] Eoyang 1993, p. 177.

[51] For a comprehensive summary of these issues, offering a number of advances on Legge's own account of these matters as presented in his work, *The Religions of China* (1880), consult Jeffrey Meyer. 1991. *The Dragons of Tiananmen: Beijing as a Sacred City*. Columbia: University of South Carolina Press.

monistic cosmology finds Zhu Xi's dualism philosophically incoherent?[52] Rather than projecting a singular and inflexible 'Confucian tradition' as the counterpoint to Legge's putatively vitiated method of translation, we should take the multiformity of the Ruist traditions which Legge himself addressed much more seriously. For example, would Eoyang reconsider his ideological critique of Legge's "interpretive blindness" if he knew, as Legge did in his own day, of a systematic monotheistic interpretation of the Ruist canon by a nineteenth century Cantonese scholar-official? Legge had actually met this person, Luo Zhongfan 羅仲藩 (d. 1850), and possessed copies of his works in his own personal library.[53] Would it increase the feasibility of Legge's monotheistic preferences in translating certain passages in the Ruist scriptures if Eoyang knew that there were also major eighteenth century Korean Ruists whose monotheistic interpretations were a source for a reformist vision within that national expression of the 'Confucian tradition'?[54]

These are examples of why we have tried here to understand in a more hermeneutically comprehensive manner the Scottish realism which informed Legge's translation judgments. Certainly Legge did have self-conscious commitments, ones he brought to bear on both texts and commentators. One would not expect, if Eoyang's account of Legge's "intemperate and inconsistent critiques" of Ruism is correct, that Legge, having so unselfconsciously distorted the meanings of the Ruist scriptures, would have anything insightful or positive to say at all about these texts and their traditions. On Eoyang's interpre-

---

[52] A general account of the positions of most of these Qing dynasty scholars appears in the second volume of Feng Yulan's *A History of Chinese Philosophy*, but more mature and lengthy reflections on these matters appear in the fifth and sixth volumes of Feng's larger and Marxist-oriented work in this same realm, *Zhongguo zhexueshi xinbian* (Feng Yulan. 1953. *A History of Chinese Philosophy*. Translated by Derk Bodde. Princeton: Princeton University Press; id. 1985–87. *Zhongguo zhexueshi xinbian* 中國哲學史新編 (A new edition of *A History of Chinese Philosophy*). Beijing: Great People's Press).

[53] See my interpretation of one of these texts by Luo, Lauren Pfister. 1999. "Discovering Monotheistic Metaphysics: The Exegetical Reflections of James Legge (1815–1897) and Lo Chung-fan (d. circa 1850)", in: Ng On-cho et al. (eds.). *Imagining Boundaries: Changing Confucian Doctrines, Texts and Hermeneutics*. Albany: State University of New York Press, pp. 213–54.

[54] This historical influence in Korean Ruism is discussed briefly in Mark Setton. 1997. *Chong Yagyong: Korea's Challenge to Orthodox Neo-Confucianism*. Albany: State University of New York.

tation of Legge can we understand, then, how Legge could refer to Mencius as a "Chinese philosopher" of equal status to one of his own country's eighteenth century Christian statesmen and philosopher, Joseph Butler?[55] Would it be possible to understand why Legge rejected as many times as he accepted the monotheistic Ruist interpretation of the *Great Learning* by Luo Zhongfan?[56] Could this position explain why Legge preferred Zhu Xi's interpretations of other texts more often than not?[57] Our approach through the Sino-Scottish connection crafted by Legge on the basis of his Scottish realist commitments makes these positive and nuanced assessments by Legge more understandable. In addition, it provides a broader hermeneutic basis for grasping why, at times, he would also reject certain concepts and commentaries within particular Ruist traditions.

We have shown in our study that metaphysical terms and concepts were in fact present within the Ruist canonical literature, and that Legge struggled with some of them because he did feel within himself an intellectual and spiritual tension. At times, as Eoyang rightly points out, Legge found those terms and concepts unacceptable, but did this disqualify him completely as a translator? From a hermeneutically informed position, it would be more balanced to consider Legge's own context in Qing dynasty China, the interpretive options available to him, and a fuller range of translations he actually employed within these texts. In addition, we have sought to explain why, on the basis of Scottish realist philosophical principles, Legge would make judgments which strike Eoyang as "intemperate". While one can understand how Eoyang, taking up a secularist account of early Ruist philosophical traditions, would feel this way, we have strong reasons on the basis of our hermeneutic approach to challenge his claim that Legge was "inconsistent" and blindly or unselfconsciously "biased". He was committed, but it was a self-conscious and rationally justified commitment which he gleaned from his studies in Scottish realism.

---

[55] Legge describes Mencius in these terms in his prolegomena to *CC*2, pp. 54 ff.

[56] Legge's comments on Luo's commentary and his reasons for rejecting it are given in the commentarial notes at the bottom of the page beneath his translation of the *Great Learning*. This is found in *CC*1, pp. 358, 367–9, 371, 376, and 378–9.

[57] Because Legge referred to Zhu Xi's commentaries not only in relationship to the Four Books but also in his studies of the Book of Poetry, this is a very rich area of study. Some details of Legge's various responses to Zhu Xi's commentaries in relationship to three of the Four Books has already been documented in my articles (Pfister 1991).

His nuanced account of Ruist traditions, which Eoyang counts as a "profound ambivalence", reveals the seriousness and self-conscious effort Legge took to deal with as much of these texts and their commentaries as he could. Under these conditions, the fact that Legge changed his very negative overall assessment of "Confucius" in 1861 to a more positive critical appreciation of him in 1893 illustrates how Scottish realism also provided some of the principles he employed to reassess his justifications and guided him toward new convictions.[58]

What we have shown here is that the Sino-Scottish connection reveals both the strengths and the weaknesses of Legge's renderings. It would be fairer to both the multiform Ruist traditions and Legge's numerous translations of their canonical literature to have both the weaknesses and strengths of his renderings and evaluations kept before us in a balanced perspective. He did experience these interpretive limitations, general interpretive limitations we should recognize from a hermeneutical standpoint as affecting anyone who does translating. In doing so, we may learn more about how and why Legge's translations did occasionally run into difficulties and conundrums. In addition, we might learn how he managed to avoid a number of refractory pitfalls in translation which some of his predecessors in the French Academy (especially Guilliame Pauthier) and earlier missionary translations (especially that of David Collie) did not successfully overcome.[59]

---

[58] Eoyang actually mentions this transition in Legge's ideas in a footnote (Eoyang 1993, p. 177), but leaves the impression that this change in Legge's attitude was nevertheless somehow ingenuine or, at the very least, part of the "profound ambivalence" which he senses in the portions of Legge's work which he has investigated. I have offered another interpretation of that transition in Pfister 1991, and would prefer a hermeneutically guided assessment of Legge's transition as one that moved from a profound rejection of a "Confucius of Ruist traitions" in 1861 to a critical appreciation of a more accutately portrayed image of the historical person of Confucius in 1893. An article which will reveal these assessments in greater detail is being written for an issue of the *Bochumer Jahrbuch fuer Ostasienkunde* on Chinese hermeneutics to be edited by Heiner Roetz.

[59] The translations of these earlier nineteenth century figures have been put into contrast with Legge's renderings in my article, cf. Lauren Pfister. 1990a. "Serving or Suffocating the Sage? Reviewing the Efforts of Three Nineteenth Century Translators of The Four Books, with Special Emphasis on James Legge (AD 1815–1897)", *The Hong Kong Linguist* 7, pp. 25–56.

REFERENCES

Eber, Irene. 1999. *The Jewish Bishop & the Chinese Bible: S. I. J. Schereschewsky (1831–1906)*. Leiden: Brill.

Eoyang, Eugene Chen. 1993. *The Transparent Eye: Reflections on Translation, Chinese Literature, and Comparative Poetics.* Honolulu: University of Hawaii Press.

Feng, Youlan 馮友闌 (Feng Yulan). 1953. *A History of Chinese Philosophy.* Translated by Derk Bodde. Princeton: Princeton University Press

——. 1985–87. *Zhongguo zhexueshi xinbian* 中國哲學史新編 (A new edition of *A History of Chinese Philosophy*). Beijing: Great People's Press.

——. 1996. *Zhen yuan liu shu* 真元六書 (Six books on the True and Original). Shanghai: Huadong shifan daxue.

Hamilton, William (ed.) and Harry M. Bracken (comm.). 1967. *Thomas Reid—Philosophical Works.* 2 vols. Hildesheim: Georg Olms Verlagsbuchhandlung.

Hamilton, William (ed.). 1854. *Collected Works of Dugald Stewart.* 11 vols. Edinburgh: Thomas Constable and Company.

Legge, James (tr. and comm.). 1852. *The Notion of the Chinese Concerning God and Spirits: with an Examination of the Defense of an Essay, on the proper rendering of the words Elohim and Theos, into the Chinese Language.* Hong Kong: Hong Kong Register Office.

——. 1877. *Confucianism in Relation to Christianity.* London: Trübner and Sons.

——. 1885. "Book of rites", in: F. Max Müller (ed.). *Sacred Books of the East.* Oxford: Clarendon Press.

——. 1891. *Sacred books of China: The Texts of Taoism. Part V. The Tao Teh King, The Writings of Kwang-Sze, Books I–XVII.* Oxford: Oxford University Press.

——. 1893 [1861]. *The Chinese Classics with a translation, critical and exegetical notes, prolegomena, and copious indexes.* Oxford: Clarendon Press.

McCosh, James. 1875. *The Scottish Philosophy: Biographical, Expository, Critical, From Hutcheson to Hamilton.* London: MacMillan and Company.

Meyer, Jeffrey. 1991. *The Dragons of Tiananmen: Beijing as a Sacred City.* Columbia: University of South Carolina Press.

Pfister, Lauren. 1990a. "Serving or Suffocating the Sage? Reviewing the Efforts of Three Nineteenth Century Translators of The Four Books, with Special Emphasis on James Legge (AD 1815–1897)", *The Hong Kong Linguist* 7, pp. 25–56.

——. 1990b. "Some New Dimensions in the Study of the Works of James Legge (1815–1897): Part I", *Sino-Western Cultural Relations Journal* 12, pp. 29–50.

——. 1991. "Some New Dimensions in the Study of the Works of James Legge (1815–1897): Part II", *Sino-Western Cultural Relations Journal* 13, pp. 33–46.

——. 1999. "Discovering Monotheistic Metaphysics: The Exegetical Reflections of James Legge (1815–1897) and Lo Chung-fan (d. circa 1850)", in: Ng On-cho et al. (eds.). *Imagining Boundaries: Changing Confucian Doctrines, Texts and Hermeneutics.* Albany: State University of New York Press, pp. 213–54.

——. 2000. "Mediating Word, Sentence and Scope without violence: James Legge's (1815–1897) Understanding of 'Classical Confucian' Hermeneutics", in: Ching-I Tu (ed.). *Classical Interpretations. The Hermeneutic Traditions in Chinese Culture.* New Brunswick, New Jersey: Transaction Press, pp. 371–82.

——. 2002. "Why the Demophilic cannot be Democratic and what might make it so: Reconstructing 'Moral Humans' in Master Meng's Philosophy", in: Alan Chan and Jiuan Heng (eds.). *Mencius: Context and Interpretation*. Honolulu: University of Hawaii Press.

Setton, Mark. 1997. *Chong Yagyong: Korea's Challenge to Orthodox Neo-Confucianism*. Albany: State University of New York.

ANGELIKA C. MESSNER

ON 'TRANSLATING' WESTERN PSYCHIATRY INTO THE CHINESE CONTEXT IN REPUBLICAN CHINA

INTRODUCTION

As medical missionaries, beginning in the late nineteenth century, attempted to introduce Western science and technology (including medicine),[1] they did not initially focus much on madness, for they were convinced that due to the comparatively quiet life in China madness would not often occur.[2] John Glasgow Kerr (Jia Yuehan 嘉約翰, 1821–1901)[3] had spent more than two decades of his life founding the first 'Refuge for the Insane' (1898 in Canton). It was to be the first in Chinese history. Undoubtedly his thinking was full of philanthropic values; nevertheless, his actual activities for the 'Chinese insane' were strongly determined by his North American background, i.e. the new and still consolidating psychiatric profession in the nineteenth century, which was tightly connected to the economic, political and social transformations occurring at that time. Madness became a central cultural problem during the Enlightenment. Inquiries into the functions of the nervous system led to the formation of the concept of mental illness. Medicalization of madness was based on the 'qualita-

---

[1] The expansion of the medical mission work throughout China can be observed in general: in 1881 there were 34 mission doctors in China; by 1887 there were 16 hospitals and 24 dispensaries; by 1890 there were 61 hospitals and 44 dispensaries. See Sara Waitstill Tucker. 1983. "The Canton Hospital and Medicine in Nineteenth Century China 1835–1900". Ph.D. diss., Harvard University. Reprint Ann Arbor: UMI, p. 232.

[2] With regard to insanity, Benjamin Hobson (He Xin 合信, 1816–1873) reports that within his eight year stay in China, he only observed two cases of insanity. Cf. Benjamin Hobson. 1850. "Medical Missions. I. General Report of the Hospital of Kam-li-fau in Canton, from April 1848 to Nov. 1849", *Chinese Repository* 19.5, p. 303. Dr. Wenyon, the senior British medical officer in the province of Canton, also reported that insanity occurred relatively seldom in China. Cf. Wenyon. 1891. "Letter to the Editor", *The China Medical Missionary Journal* 5, p. 1.

[3] Born in Duncansville, Ohio, November 30, 1824, he graduated in March 1847 from the Jefferson Medical College in Philadelphia. He was accepted by the Presbyterian Board of Foreign Missions in 1854. On May 5, 1855 he took charge of the Canton Hospital, which had begun as the Ophtalmic Hospital (at Factory No. 3, at Canton) in 1835 under the guidance of Dr. Peter Parker (Bo Jia 伯駕, 1804–1889), the first medical missionary in China. Cf. Tucker 1983, pp. 126ff.

tive' conception of the "Diseases of the Mind" newly developed in Britain in the late eighteenth century.[4] The mental hospital replaced the former madhouse and asylum; the mental patient replaced the former madman or madwoman. The building of the mental hospital itself became as "important as any drugs or other remedies in the alienist's armamentarium."[5] The medical superintendent in North-America defined both medical *and* moral treatment,[6] his optimism based on the "cult of curability" of insanity. From this background, Kerr's conviction that Chinese society had never cared for its mad members and his demand that at least three hundred insane hospitals for one thousand inmates each be built in China at least seems understandable.[7]

Regardless of which point of view we adopt for our analysis, whether we feel passionately committed to the view of psychiatry as an important tool of repression and exclusion and thus are committed to interpreting sources solely as a form of domination through medicalization,[8] or whether we are convinced that the history of psychiatry is essentially the history of humanism,[9] a few facts concerning the context of traditional Chinese medicine need to be considered which are quite independent from such considerations. Firstly, within traditional Chinese medical discourse madness had been recognized and dealt with as a medical phenomenon since early times (second century

---

[4] Cf. Michael Donnelly. 1984. *Managing the Mind: A Study of Medical Psychology in Early Nineteenth-Century Britain*. London, New York: Tavistock, p. viii. For the shift from 'quantitative' to 'qualitative' concepts concerning the perception of 'normal' and 'anormal' in nineteenth century Europe, see Georges Canguilhelm. 1972. "Das Normale und das Pathologische", in: Wolf Lepenies and Henning Ritter (eds.). *Hanser Anthropologie*. Munich: Hanser, pp. 81; and Wolf Lepenies. 1977. "Probleme einer Historischen Anthropologie", in: Reinhard Rürup (ed.). *Historische Sozialwissenschaften. Beiträge zur Hinführung in die Forschungspraxis*. Göttingen: Vandenhoeck and Ruprecht, pp. 126–60; p. 141.

[5] Andrew T. Scull. 1981. "The Social History of Psychiatry in the Victorian Era", in: id. (ed.). *Madhouses, Mad-Doctors, and Madman. The Social History of Psychiatry in the Victorian Era*. London: Athlone Press, p. 10.

[6] Ibid., p. 12.

[7] Cf. J. G. Kerr. 1898. "The 'Refuge for the Insane', Canton", *The China Medical Missionary Journal* 12.4, pp. 177–8; p. 178.

[8] Michel Foucault. 1961. *Histoire de la folie*. Paris: Libraire Plon.

[9] This definition is given by Gregory Zilboorg. 1967. *A History of Medical Psychology*. New York: The Norton Library, p. 524.

BC),[10] but no specialized institution exclusively dealing with mad people ever emerged. Secondly, since early times, madness was recognized within the judicial discourse as a state of weakness.[11]

I shall focus in the following on textual evidence regarding the sensitive problem of why the introduction of Western psychiatric concepts and practices did not work within the Chinese context, because of different conceptualizations of "normal" and "abnormal", which in turn reflected different conceptualizations of the "body".

1. ON TRADITIONAL MEDICAL PERCEPTIONS OF MADNESS

Dian 癲 derives its meaning from the character *dianfu* 癲覆 'to fall down'; *dianwei* 癲危 'to collapse, decline'; *dianpei* 癲沛 'to fall down, overturn, to die'; *diandao* 癲倒 'to fall down, confusion, to put something top down'. Each character bears the meaning of misfortune and catastrophe. … Different character compounds exist for the term *kuang* 狂, such as *kuangxiao* 狂笑 'to laugh excessively'; *kuangdang* 狂蕩 'unrestrained', *kuangyan* 狂言 'to talk nonsensically'; *kuangtong* 狂童 'crazy fellow'. These character principles have different meanings. Explaining these [diseases] as being simply caused by fire would mean a simplification. … For instance, some physicians (*yiliu* 醫流) wrongly take *dian* 癲 for *xian* 癇 'epilepsy' and [sometimes] they even confuse it with *feng* 瘋 'frenzy'.[12]

This passage is taken from a medical textbook published in 1834. It deals with the most significant terms indicating madness in late imperial China. Besides *dian*, *kuang*, *xian* and *feng*, many other terms indi-

---

[10] Cf. *Mawangdui Hanmu boshu* 馬王堆漢墓帛書 (Silk manuscripts of the Han tomb in Mawangdui). 1985. Edited by Mawangdui Hanmu boshu zhenglixiaozu 馬王堆漢墓帛書整理小組. Beijing: Wenwu chubanshe; Zhou Yimou 周一謀 and Xiao Zuotao 蕭佐桃. 1988. *Mawangdui yishu kaozhu* 馬王堆醫書考注 (Commentaries on the medical texts from Mawangdui). Tianjin: Tianjin kexue jishu chubanshe, pp. 78, 105–7.

[11] Cf. Karl Hunger. 1950. "The Punishment of Lunatics and Negligents According to Classical Chinese Law", *Studia Serica* 9.2, pp. 1–16; Martha Li Chiu. 1981. "Insanity in Imperial China: A Legal Case Study", in: Arthur Kleinman and Tsung-Yi Lin (eds.). *Normal and Abnormal Behavior in Chinese Culture*. Dordrecht: D. Reidel, pp. 75–94; Vivien Ng. 1990. *Madness in Late Imperial China: From Illness to Deviance*. Norman: University of Oklahoma Press.

[12] Zhang Bilu 張必祿. 1990 [1834]. "Yifang biannan dacheng" 醫方辨難大成 (Great compendium of medical remedies and differentiation of difficult issues). Sichuan Bazhou: Hefei kanben. Reprinted in: *Diankuangxian* 癲狂癇 (Falling sickness, madness and epilepsy). 1990. Edited by Hua Beiling 華蓓苓, Zhou Zhangfa 周長發 and Zhu Xinghai 朱興海. Beijing: Zhongyi guji chubanshe, p. 193.

cating madness and related phenomena circulated in late imperial medical discourse, such as *xiandian* 癇癲 'epilepsy', *dianchi* 癲癡 'imbecility', *diandai* 癲呆 'imbecility', *yangxian* 羊癇 'epilepsy' etc. Some authors, as for instance Wang Qingren 王清任 (1768–1831), preferred the term *diankuang* 癲狂 as one category, without differentiating between the two terms from which it is formed, whereas others emphasized the difference. The difference between *dian* and *kuang* was explained already in the *Nanjing* 難經 (The Classic of Difficult Issues, AD 100):[13]

> A doubling of the *yang* 陽 [influences results in] madness (*kuang* 狂); a doubling of the *yin* 陰 [influences results in] falling sickness (*dian* 癲). When the *yang* [influences] are lost, however, one sees demons; when the *yin* [influences] are lost, one's eyes turn blind.[14]

Besides this systematic differentiation between two kinds of madness and the indications for their cause, another passage in the *Nanjing* focuses on different manifestations of the "two faces of madness".

> By what [criteria] can the illnesses of madness and falling sickness be distinguished? It is like this: During the initial development of madness, one rests only rarely and does not feel hungry. One will [speak of] oneself as occupying a lofty, exemplary position. One will point out one's special wisdom, and one will behave in an arrogant and haughty way. One will laugh—and find joy in singing and making music—without reason, and one will walk around heedlessly without break. During the initial development of falling sickness, however, one's thoughts (*yi* 意) are unhappy. One lies down and stares straight ahead...[15]

The sharp difference between the "two faces" of madness manifests itself on two levels. First, the difference is characterized by the opposite direction of bodily movement: *kuang* is manifested by the direction to the top and outward movement and by restlessness; *dian* is manifested by the direction to the bottom, collapsing and sinking down. The same directions appear on the second, 'social' level: a *kuang* person will feel superior to other people; a person suffering

---

[13] The authorship of this book is not clear. Cf. Paul Unschuld (tr. and comm.). 1986. *Nan-ching: The Classic of Difficult Issues—With Commentaries by Chinese and Japanese Authors From the Third Through the Twentieth Century.* Berkeley, Los Angeles, London: University of California Press.

[14] Cf. Unschuld 1986, p. 268.

[15] Cf. ibid., p. 527.

from *dian* will withdraw from the outside world, lacking any joy and ambition. Hence, the two "faces" of madness can be interpreted in terms of the loss of "bodily economy",[16] which would normally maintain the "middle between too much extension—*kuang*—and too much of narrowing—*dian*." The physician has to differentiate between the two "faces" and to act appropriately, i.e. to re-establish the harmony between *yin* and *yang*.

Besides the aforementioned cause for madness (the doubling of *yin* or *yang*) within the *Huangdi neijing* 黃帝內經 (Inner Classic of the Yellow Emperor, around 100 BC) (not in the *Nanjing*), the following factors also appeared to cause madness, factors which are inherent to late imperial medical discourse on madness: the reversion of *qi* 氣 - flow at the *yangming* 陽明 meridian of the foot; *yinyang* 陰陽 disharmony; a state of depletion or repletion (*xushi* 虛實) of *qi*; and a disharmony of emotions.[17]

Within the late imperial medical discourse on madness, two dominant patterns can be discerned: on the one hand, the possession by demons and, on the other hand, the medicine of correspondences.

---

[16] For a philosophical discussion of these two antagonistic bodily states, see Hermann Schmitz. 1990. *Der unerschöpfliche Gegenstand: Grundzüge der Philosphie*. Bonn: Bouvier, pp. 122–4.

[17] Within the *Huangdi neijing*, different forms of madness figure within different contextual frameworks: *Kuang* appears mostly in connection with talking and laughing as 'crazy talking' (*kuangyan* 狂言) (cf. *Huangdi neijing. Suwen: Suwen zhushi huicui* 素問注釋匯粹 (The Inner Classic of the Yellow Emperor. Basic questions with selected commentaries). 1982. Edited by Cheng Shide 程士德 et al. 2 vols. Beijing: Renmin weisheng chubanshe, 9.33, p. 470) and 'crazy laughing' (*kuangxiao* 狂笑), (cf. *Lingshujing jiaoshi* 靈樞經校釋 (Critical Edition of the Divine Pivot). 1982. Edited by Hebei yixueyuan 河北醫學院 . 2 vols. Beijing: Renmin weisheng chubanshe, 1.4, p. 93). In these cases *kuang* seems to be interchangeable with *wang* 妄 'absurd' [For *wangzou* 妄走 'absurd walking' cf. *Huangdi neijing. Suwen* 8.30, p. 434 and for *wangdong* 妄動 'absurd moving' cf. *Huangdi neijing. Lingshu* 4.22, p. 399], and seems to indicate a temporary state. Other passages indicate *kuang* as 'madness', which never appears isolated, but always as a constituent part of a wide, variable and flexible disease picture: once *kuang* appears in connection with the shrinking of the genitals, forgetfulness and dry skin (cf. *Huangdi neijing Lingshu* 2.8, pp. 174–83). See Martha Li Chiu. 1986. "Mind, Body, and Illness in a Chinese Medical Tradition". Ph.D. diss., Harvard University. Reprint Ann Arbor: UMI; and Christian Schütz. 1991. "Psychiatrische und psychosomatische Ansätze in den Heiltraditionen bis zur Zeit der Yuan-Dynastie". Ph.D. diss., LMU Munich.

Although the majority of late imperial texts strongly base their explications on the "medicine of correspondences", they simultaneously clearly indicate that demons and ghosts have by no means fully disappeared.[18] They therefore require that the physician first find out whether the state of madness was due to possession or due to a disharmony of *yinyang* and other bodily imbalances.[19] Others explicitly argue against the 'belief' in demons and ghosts in cases of madness.[20]

---

[18] This is especially evident in the writings of Zhang Jiebin 張介賓 (ca. 1563–1640) in his *Zhangshi leijing* 張氏類經 (The classified canon of Zhang Jiebin) (1624), where he demands healing by incantation (*zhuyou* 祝由) in the official medical canon. His arguments are based on his conviction that some diseases can only be healed through incantations. Cf. Zhang Jiebin 張介賓. 1983 [1624]. *Zhangshi leijing* 張氏類經 (The Classified Canon of Zhang Jiebin). Taibei: Wenguang tushu youxian gongsi, *juan* 20, p. 247. He argues that demons actually originate in the heart (*gui sheng yu xin* 鬼生於心), that they would not attack the human being from the outside but were produced by extreme emotions, cf. ibid., *juan* 20, p. 246a. Zhang describes a case where he himself cured a woman suffering from madness (*kuang* 狂), frightening (*jing* 驚), heat in the stomach and demons and ghosts 'in her tow-line' by incantations and a "white tiger decoction", cf. ibid., *juan* 12, p. 247. It is not the place here to speculate in how far Zhang Jiebin himself 'believed' in demons or rather only assumed this 'belief' in the patients. Another physician living at the same time, however, clearly explains that he was able to drive out the demons through acupuncture. See Yang Jizhou 楊繼洲. 1994 [1601]. "Zhenjiu dacheng" 針灸大成 (Great compendium of acupuncture and moxibustion), in: *Lidai ming qi'an ji* 歷代名奇案集 (Famous and strange medical case studies through the ages). Edited by Da Meijun 達美君. Shanghai: Sanlian shudian Shanghai fendian, p. 86. An explanation is found in the *Chuanya neibian*, whose author Zhao Xuemin 趙學敏 (ca. 1719–1805), a *ruyi* 儒醫 scholar physician, is assumed to have recorded the recipes of a *lingyi* 鈴藝 travelling physician. He describes the case of a woman suffering from madness (*diankuang*), where after being cured, something (*wu* 物) disappeared from her chest. Cf. *Chuanya neibian xuanzhu* 串雅內編選注 (Internal treatise on folk medicine with selected commentaries). 1980 [1851]. Edited by Changchun zhongyi xueyuan 長春中醫學院. Beijing: Renmin weisheng chubanshe, p. 37. See also Paul Unschuld. 1978. "Das Ch'uan-ya und die Praxis chinesischer Landärzte im 18. Jahrhundert", *Sudhoffs Archiv* 62.4, pp. 378–407.

[19] As for instance Li Guanxian 李冠仙, a native from Dantu (present Jiangsu province), living in the early nineteenth century, in his *Shangyu yicao* (1835, printed in 1887) explicitly does. Cf. Li Guanxian 李冠仙. 1990b [1835]. *Shangyu yicao* 傷寓意草 (An imitation of significance of herbs). Reprinted in *Lidai zhongyi zhenben jicheng* 歷代中醫珍本集成 (Collection of precious works on Chinese medicine through the ages). Edited by Shanghai Zhongyi xueyuan wenxian yanjiusuo 上海中醫學院文獻研究所. Shanghai: Shanghai sanlian shudian, vol. 34.

[20] Cf. Xie Xinghuan 謝星煥. 1986 [1861]. "Dexin ji yi'an" 得心集醫案 (Collection of medical records as desired), in: Wang Yurun 王玉潤 et al. (eds.). *Zhenben yishu jicheng* 珍本藝書集成 (A collection of precious books on medicine). Shanghai: Kexue jishu chubanshe, vol. 12.

The explanation of madness as caused by a disharmony of *yinyang* or by an imbalance within the sequences of the five phases (*wuxing* 五行), or by an imbalance of the relationship between depletion and repletion of *qi* led to the simple fact that madness was not perceived as a disease that was essentially and 'qualitatively' different from other diseases. This is also shown by the language used in explaining madness.[21]

It is true that health manuals in Ming and Qing times invoked similar theories, since they heavily quoted identical passages from texts such as the *Huangdi neijing Suwen* (The Inner Classic of the Yellow Emperor: Basic Questions) and *Huangdi neijing Lingshu* (The Inner Classic of the Yellow Emperor: Divine Pivot) and the *Nanjing*. Nevertheless, they put forward highly individual insights and explanations specific to different regions and to the period of late imperial China.[22] For instance, the "warm-restoring-school" (*wenbu xue* 溫補學) which appeared in Southern China in late Ming times was based on the assumption that heat deficiency was the main pathogenic factor in most cases.[23] Hence, many Qing textbooks explained different forms of madness as an accompanying symptom of heat-diseases.[24] In con-

---

[21] This is also stated by Vivien Ng. 1990.

[22] Cf. Frank Dikötter. 1997. *Imperfect Conceptions: Medical Knowledge, Birth Defects and Eugenics in China*. London: Hurst, p. 24.

[23] The so-called 'warm disease school' (*wenre xue* 溫熱學)—focussing on the pattern of the four stages—which developed from the late Ming dynasty through the Qing dynasty, was first conceived as complementary and increasingly in opposition to the cold-damage conception. The big epidemics afflicting the whole of China in the early seventeenth century could have been the cause for the systematization of this school. Cf. Helen Dunstan. 1975. "The Late Ming Epidemics: A Preliminary Survey", *Ch'ing-shih wen-t'i* 3.3, pp. 1–59; Lu Dong, Ma Xi and François Thann. 1995. *Les maux épidémiques dans l'empire chinois*. Paris: Harmattan; Ouyang Bing 歐陽兵 . 1995. "Mingdai shanghanlun yanjiu dui houshide yingxiang" 明代傷寒論研究對後時的影響 (The influence of the 'Treatise on cold damage'—Studies carried out by Ming-scholars on later times), *Zhonghua yixue zazhi* 25.2, pp. 92–4; Qiu Peiran 裘沛然 et al. (eds.). 1984. *Zhongyi lidai gejia xueshuo* 中醫歷代各家學說 (Different Academic schools of Chinese medicine through the ages). Shanghai: Shanghai kexue jishu chubanshe, pp. 123–8 and 185–91; *Zhongguo renwu cidian* 中國人物辭典 (Chinese biographical dictionary). 1988. Edited by Li Jingwei 李經緯 et al. Shanghai: Cishu chubanshe, pp. 350–1; Paul Unschuld. 1980. *Medizin in China. Eine Ideengeschichte*. Munich: Beck, pp. 160–1. See also the discussion in Martha Hanson. 1998. "Robust Northeners and Delicate Southerners: The Nineteenth-Century Invention of a Southern Medical Tradition", *positions—east asia cultures critique* 6.3, pp. 515–50.

[24] Cf. i.e. Ye Tianshi 葉天士 . 1984 [1746]. *Linzheng zhinan yi an* 臨証指南醫案 (A guide to clinical practice with medical records). Taibei: Guoli gugong bowuyuan

trast to this, however, prominent Qing physicians returned to the earlier view prevalent in Song-Yuan times, which emphasized the importance of heat purgatives in maintaining good health.[25] Within these different schools, madness too was subject to different explanations.

And this is in fact the intention expressed by Zhang Bilu 張必祿 (1843) in the text quoted above. In the West, at the very same time as the textbook quoted above appeared, i.e. at the beginning of the nineteenth century, the brain, as the only location and cause for the outbreak of madness, became the crucial organ, and hence madness was now termed a "mental disease". Zhang Bilu criticized the current trend of defining all different phenomena of madness simply as a disease of fire as being reductionist.

Others interpreted different manifestations of madness as being caused by a cold stroke (*zhong* 中). Others again focussed on fire at the *yangming* meridian (corresponding to the stomach).[26] Still others emphasized wind in the heart as the main cause for *kuang*, and mucus/phlegm in the chest as the main cause for *dian*.[27] Some focussed on the spleen—as part of the *yin*-organ system corresponding to the

---

[24] (*cont.*) *juan* 10.7; Wang Shixiong 王士雄. 1990 [1929]. *Wang Mengying yihua jinghua* 王孟英醫話精華 (Selected medical records of Wang Mengying), in: Qin Bowei 秦伯未(ed.). *Qingdai mingyi yihua jinghua* 清代名醫醫話精華(Selected medical records of famous Qing-physicians). 4 vols. Reprinted in: *Lidai zhongyi zhenben jicheng* 歷代中醫珍本集成 (Collection of precious works on Chinese medicine through the ages). Edited by Shanghai Zhongyi xueyuan wenxian yanjiusuo 上海中醫學院文獻研究所. Shanghai: Shanghai sanlian shudian, vol. 40, *juan* 7, pp. 1–150; 116–7; Wu Tang 吳塘. 1990 [1916]. *Diankuang* 癲狂 (Falling sickness), in: *Wu Jutong yi an* 吳鞠通醫案 (Wu Jutong's medical cases), *juan* 5. Reprinted in *Diankuangxian*, pp. 228–30.

[25] Although Zhang Zhongjing 張仲景 (ca. 150 AD– ca. 219) in his *Shanghan zabing lun* 傷寒雜病論 (On different diseases caused by cold damages), did not mention any form of madness caused by cold damage, Chen Shiduo 陳士鐸 (late seventeenth century) identifies a form of *kuang* madness as due to exogenic cold damage. Cf. Chen Shiduo 陳士鐸. 1991 [1687]. *Shishi milu* 石室秘錄 (Secret records from the stone room). Beijing: Zhongguo zhongyiyao chubanshe [Reprint of Xuanyongtang edition], pp. 295–6. Guo Chuanling 郭傳鈴, the author of the first medical textbook within the Chinese context to deal exclusively with madness, the *Diankuang tiaobian*, applied the pattern of the Six Warps (*liujing bianzheng* 六經辨症) for the outbreak of different kinds of madness. Guo Chuanling 郭傳鈴. 1909. *Diankuang tiaobian* 癲狂條辯 (Systematized identification of madness). Reprinted in: *Diankuangxian* 1990, pp. 170–5.

[26] Cf. i.e. Xie Xinghuan 1986 [1861], p. 135.

[27] Cf. Li Guanxian 1990a [1929]. "Li Guanxian yihua jinghua" 李冠仙醫話精華 (Selected medical records of Li Guanxian), in: Qin Bowei 1990, vol. 40, *juan* 8.

stomach and to the earth (within the five phases paradigm).[28] Physicians focussed equally on the liver and the bladder or on the heart and the heart envelope, which could be penetrated by phlegm (*tan* 痰) or by wind.

Especially those who chiefly refered to the five phases paradigm argued on the basis of many different forms and phenomena of madness. According to this paradigm, all related elements (such as emotions, climatic influences, etc.) to the five *yin*-organ systems could cause different forms of madness, depending on the location within the viscera where the imbalance took place. Hence, at least more than ten different phenomena of madness could be diagnosed. Thus madness, in the discourse of traditional Chinese medicine, was regarded as being caused by certain disharmonies and imbalances—like any other disease. Therefore, a single exclusive factor causing madness was never identified. The strictly systemic pattern of thinking prevented physicians from viewing mental factors as independent from bodily processes. This can be underlined by the fact that within Chinese medical discourse, there has never been a necessity to write books which exclusively deal with "madness", and concomitantly, people suffering from 'madness' have never been confined to special places called 'insane hospitals'.

Therefore, it seems natural that any concept alien to this explication had to be incorporated into one of the concepts already existing within the framework of the Chinese medical knowledge system, because the systemic approach does not allow the assignment of a function to a single organ but only to a working unit consisting of more than one element. Consequently, one could account for 'thinking' within the brain only when brain function was considered in combination with other elements.

2. INCORPORATING WESTERN CONCEPTS OF MADNESS INTO THE CHINESE CONTEXT

Since the late nineteenth century, Chinese intellectuals had strongly demanded a fundamental reform of China. Within their arguments,

---

[28] Cf. i.e. Kang Yingchen 康應辰 . 1902. "Dianbing" 癲病 (Falling sickness), in: *Yixue tanli quanji* 醫學探驪全集 (Complete collection of investigations in medicine). Reprinted in: *Diankuangxian* 1990, p. 209.

the topic of 'mental illness' became a more and more central concern. Already in 1897 Kang Youwei 康有為 (1858–1927) formulated his vision of a new society totally free from the insane.[29] His special concern for the medical profession as the key for the development of the new society matches well with different discourses emerging in the Western hemisphere since the late eighteenth century.

But Kang did not focus on the patterns of explanation of insanity. The linking of the social implications of madness with its (Western) medical explanation which took place in the Chinese context is evidenced by a few articles appearing around the May Fourth Movement of 1919. Wang Wanbai 王完白 ,[30] in 1919, explains that Chinese (traditional) physicians do not know of 'psychological' (*xinli* 心理) causes of insanity on the one hand, of the 'physiological' (*shengli* 生 理) causes of insanity on the other. The differentiation between bodily and psychic factors appears here as implicit 'pre-knowledge', in the sense of a premise of the splitting of 'mental and/or psychic' processes from the bodily processes. One of the more important translations in the 'science of the psychic life' appeared in 1907.[31] Wang speaks of *jingshenbing* 精神病 , indicating 'insanity', meaning 'men-

---

[29] Cf. Wolfgang Bauer. 1974. "Introduction", in: K'ang, Yu-wei. 1974. *Ta T'ung Shu: Das Buch von der Großen Gemeinschaft.* Translated and commentated by Laurence G. Thompson. Edited by Wolfgang Bauer. Düsseldorf, Cologne: Diederichs, pp.16–7; Chang Hao. 1980. "Intellectual Change and the Reform Movement, 1890– 8", in: *Cambridge History of China. Vol. 11: Late Ch'ing, 1800–1911*, part 2, pp. 274–339; See also Nancy N. Chen. "Translating Psychiatry and Mental Health: Twentieth Century Clue", in: Lydia Liu (ed.). *Tokens of Exchange. The Problem of Translation in Global Circulations.* Durham, London: Duke University Press, pp. 305–30.

[30] As a Christian physician, Wang also worked as a missionary. He was a member of the Chinese Medical Association (*Zhonghua yixuehui* 中華醫學會) and of the Association for the Translation of Scientific Terms (*Zhongguo kexue mingci shenchahui daibiao* 中國科學名詞審查會代表). He was engaged in the public recognition of Western medicine in China. In the 1920s, he founded a hospital in his home town Changzhou where he dedicated himself to the distribution of the smallpox vaccination. Later on at Suzhou he founded a small Insane Hospital (*fengrenyuan* 瘋人院). Cf. Wang Wanbai 王完白 . 1919. "Fengrenyuan zhi zhongyao yu biyi" 瘋人院之重要 與裨益 (On the importance and benefit of lunatic asylums), *Zhonghua yixue zazhi* 3.5, pp. 127–31; 127.

[31] Wang Guowei 王國維 (1877–1927) translated Höffding's *Psychologie in Umrissen auf der Grundlage der Erfahrung* under the title *Xinlixue gailun* 心理學概 論 (Outline of Psychology). Cf. Gao Juefu 告覺敷 et al. (eds.). 1986. *Zhongguo xinlixue shi* 中國心理學史 (A history of Chinese psychology). Beijing: Renmin jiaoyu chubanshe, p. 21.

tal disease'. He explains that Chinese people were not aware that ex-prisoners and bandits stirring up trouble everywhere (*raoluan difang zhi feitu* 擾亂地方之匪徒) and idiots (*chunyu* 蠢愚) are actually in general a disguised kind of mad people (*fengren* 瘋人) who have to be cured in special hospitals. His demand for the nationwide building of such hospitals is based on the argument that these institutions would protect society from the handicapped (*canzei* 參 賊), dumb (*yu* 愚) and weak (*ruo* 弱) in as much the reproduction of all these could be prevented there.[32]

The scientific medical knowledge that insanity ultimately would always be a disease of the brain (*naobing* 腦病) should replace the 'absurd' concept of a "sputum which blocks the heart holes" adopted by traditional Chinese physicians, or the concept of 'demons and ghosts' believed by the 'dumb' people (*wuzhi yumin* 無知愚民).[33]

The notion that all intellectual, mental and psychic activities would take place exclusively in the brain was alien to the traditional medical discourse in China.[34] But this was one of the concepts crucial to the specific Western psychiatric discourse at that time. The idea of the "definition of the human being as brain", i.e. the determination of the qualities of the human being through the brain, can indeed be seen as one of the most "effective terms of modernity for the definition of the human being."[35]

---

[32] Wang Wanbai, p. 130.

[33] Ibid., p. 127.

[34] Although Wang Qingren 王清任 (1768–1831) mentioned the idea of the brain as the location for the outbreak of epilepsy (*xian* 癇) (whether influenced by Western thought or not), this viewpoint did not achieve any significance within general medical discourse on madness until the 1930s. Cf. Wang Qingren 王清任 . 1937 [1831]. *Yilin gaicuo* 醫林改錯 (Corrections of errors in the forest of medicine [i.e. among physicians]). Shanghai: Dadong shuju, vol. 1, p. 1. On Wang Qingren's challenge, see Zhao Hongjun 張洪鈞 . 1989. *Jindai Zhongyi lun zhengyi* 近代中醫論爭議 (History of the modern controversies over Chinese vs. Western medicine). Anhui: Kexue jishu chubanshe, p. 46; Ma Kanwen 馬堪溫 . 1963. "Zuguo Qingdai jiechude yixuejia Wang Qingren" 祖國清代傑出的醫學家王清任 (On the outstanding Qing-physician Wang Qingren), *Kexueshi jikan* 6, pp. 66–74; Bridie Andrews. 1994. "Tailoring Tradition: The Impact of Modern Medicine on Traditional Chinese Medicine, 1887–1937", in: Viviane Alleton and Alexei Volkov (eds.). *Notions et Perceptions du Changement en Chine: Textes Présentés au IXe Congrès de L'Association Européenne d'Études Chinoises*. Collège de France: Institut des Hautes Études Chinoises, pp. 59–165.

[35] Cf. Michael Hagner. 1997. *Homo cerebralis: Der Wandel vom Seelenorgan zum Gehirn*. Berlin: Berlin Verlag, p. 293.

3. Zhang Xichun's explanation of madness

Whereas Wang Wanbai merely adopted the Western conception of insanity, which he deemed to be the only objective and scientific solution, others, like Zhang Xichun 張錫純 (1860–1933),[36] one of the leading Chinese physicians of his time, questioned this "objectivity". For example, in the *Yixue zhongzhong canxi lu* 醫學衷中參西錄 (The assimilation of Western and Chinese medicine),[37] it is the heart as well as the spleen which are said to be the communicating partners of the brain and of no less importance than the brain itself. Zhang Xichun argued that the principles of traditional and modern medicine are the same; and that Western medicine could be used to clarify enigmatic classical texts:

> The head is the place of the brilliance of the essence (*jingming* 精明). The center of the head is the brain.[38] Since [the *Suwen*] calls it brilliance of the essence, why should it not have [the ability/ function] of thinking? The brain cannot think by itself. Looking at the old character 思 (*si*), we see that it is identical with 蒽 (*cong*); 囪 (*cong*)[39] means brain. The [character] *xin* 心 [beneath] means heart. Hence, we know that the character 思 has the meaning of 'thinking'. Actually, heart and brain complement each other. In addition [they] need the spleen-earth in order to get the function of calmness.[40]

---

[36] He served as military physician at the end of the Qing dynasty, and from 1918 was head of a hospital in Liaoning. From 1928, he lived in Tianjin running 'correspondence courses' for traditional medicine.

[37] His text book appeared between 1918 and 1934, published in 7 parts (in 30 *juan*). It was completed by an eighth part (posthumous) in 1957, which contains writings for his students. The edition of 1974, despite omissions, contains many changed passages. The edition of 1985 (the edition of 1995 is a reprint of 1985) is based on the original edition (including the eighth part of 1957). Zhang Xichun 張錫純 . 1995 [1918–1934]. *Yixue zhongzhong canxi lu* 醫學衷中參西錄 (The assimilation of Western and Chinese medicine). Hebei: Kexue jishu chubanshe.

[38] This passage clearly refers to the brilliance of the essence, which is located in the head. Some commentators (from the late Qing dynasty) interpret this by referring to the essence *qi* deriving from the five viscera which goes up to the head. According to Herrmann Tessenow (personal communication), the original meaning of *jingming* clearly refers to a substance (essence) which has been assumed to be located by necessity in the eyes in order that one could see. Cf. *Huangdi neijing. Suwen* 5.17, p. 235.

[39] The point of the head. Cf. *Shuowen jiezi zhu* 説文解字注 (Commented edition of the *Shuowen jiezi*). 1988. Edited and commentated by Duan Yucai 段玉裁 . Shanghai: Shanghai guji chubanshe, p. 501.

[40] Zhang Xichun 1995, vol. 1, part 3, *juan* 1, p. 3.

The author here is referring to a passage in chapter 17 of the *Suwen*. He seems eager to give evidence for autochthonous knowledge of the brain as the *locus* for thinking.

Nowadays, scholars interpret the meaning of *jingming*精明 in this very passage as a substance within the eyes which is assumed to be essential for seeing. It is not very clear however, whether Zhang also had this meaning of *jingming* in mind when he was referring to this term. He could also have meant the essence *qi* arising out of the five viscera into the head —as it was for instance interpreted by Zhang Jie-bin 張介賓 , which can be 'seen' there (on the head) as particular brilliance. Whatever he may have thought, he did argue that "essence brilliance" has the function of thinking. This interpretation led him to the analysis of the related characters. By referring to the *Shuowen jiezi* 說文解字 (Explanations of single component graphs and analyses of compound characters) he equates *tian* 田 'field' with *cong* 囟 'fontanelle', or in the words of Zhang 'brain', thus supplying proof for his assumption. He does not reveal, however, that the explanation in the *Shuowen* actually stems from the Qing commentary by Duan Yucai 段 玉裁 (1735–1815)—and not from ancient times as he suggests.

Zhang Xichun's main concern seems to be the "fact" that the brain cannot think by itself. It essentially needs the heart. In his opinion, there is an endless connection of a silk thread between heart and brain. The Western insight of 'the brain receiving one seventh of the whole blood by heart function' serves as another confirmation for his connection-paradigm. Additionally, he mentions a third necessary element for thinking: the spleen. In saying so, he does not depart from the traditional pattern of medical thinking at all.

In the first chapter, dealing with *yin*-depletion (*yinxu* 陰虛), heat and disharmonies within the stomach organ system, Zhang explains the following:

> Some people asked me: The *Neijing* says that the spleen controls thinking; people in the West say, that thinking arises in the brain (*naobu* 腦 部). What do you say [on the view], that thinking takes place in the heart? [My] answer is: When the *Neijing* says that the spleen controls thinking, it does not mean that the spleen can think by itself. The spleen corresponds to the earth. The earth controls calmness. Only if men are silent, can they think.[41]

---

[41] Ibid.

Here again, there are three *loci classici* of thinking. Two can be traced back to the traditional medical discourse: first, the spleen with its specific *shen* 神 —namely *yi* 意 'intention, imagination'—and secondly, the heart with the *shen* in all its emotional and cognitive functions. The third is the Western conception of the brain. Zhang connects them all in a functional way. This makes it impossible for him to look upon one single *locus* within the human body as having the power to control everything.

> What the Chinese refer to as *diankuang* is what Western people call disease of the nerves (*shenjingbing*).[42]

So what did he perceive as madness? Does he refer to madness (*diankuang*) as a multiple disharmony? Does he thus refer to the constantly changing concept of a "Chinese body", which manifests madness when *qi* and/or phlegm is sticking somewhere, or heat and/or fire and wind are expanding, etc.? Or does he refer to the brain-controlled body which suffers from a brain-nerve-disease (*naosui shenjing bing* 腦髓神經病), because the brain has lost control? He seems to refer to *none* of them. He more or less speaks about a new body, which is however grounded deeply in the Chinese tradition, only enriched by another element (the brain) within this bodily system.

This is clearly shown in his explanations referring to madness (*diankuang*), which arises, according to him, when the connection between brain and heart is blocked by persistent phlegm/sputum, and hence the *shenming* (the *shen* brilliance) can no longer move fluently within the connection-thread between heart and brain. Hence, when explaining causes and manifestations of madness, he "switches" between two different terms, indicating different conceptions of the body and so of madness: on the one hand, brain-and-nerve-disease (*shenjingbing*), and *diankuang* on the other. He clearly recognizes the brain and the nerves as important elements within the body, but he does not use these terms according to the meaning they had in Western discourse at that time. In other words, he invests them with a completely new meaning when referring to the Chinese body. Treating *diankuang* still meant to administer medicine which leads to a discharging of blocks of *qi* and phlegm, to draining fire etc. Nowhere does Zhang Xichun give an explanation of the nerves: it seems quite

---

[42] Cf. ibid., p. 152.

reasonable that by the "connection" between heart and brain he also meant the nerve-path (through the spinal cord) where *shen* continuously moves. *Shen* (indicating spirit, cognition and emotions) was never thought of as being independent from *jing* (essence), *xue* (blood) and *qi*, and as such indicated 'vital force'. Zhang "deprives" the brain of its rights as the autocratic ruler of all bodily and mental functions and processes. He "dethrones" the brain from its powerful position. Hence, through Zhang's interpretation, the brain became an equal member among all other bodily functions.

CONCLUSION

In sum, the newly introduced significant terms, which were to transfer "psychiatric concepts" like *jingshenbing* 精神病 (Zhang speaks of *shenjingbing* 神經病), did not change the "Chinese epistemology" of the bodily function, and so did not succeed in dividing purely bodily from purely mental factors. This term had and has to be perceived certainly not in the sense of mental or psychological diseases, but in the sense of "vital-force-disease" implicating all bodily functions consisting of the finest *qi* moving with and along the vital-spiritual-emotional processes: *shen* itself is a manifestation of *qi*.

It may be because of these essential difficulties at the epistemological level that all disease records relating to "mental illness" at the Peking Union Medical College (PUMC), which was founded in 1921 as an American transplant, i.e., all classifications and prescriptions for "mental disease" (used within this hospital), were exclusively "communicated" and recorded in the English language.[43] Looking for equivalents to psychiatric terms in the Chinese language is a process which cannot be solved by linguists, and has yet to be concluded. This may be the reason for the urgent requirement of the development of a "psychiatry with Chinese characteristics"[44] by contemporary Chinese medical scholars—about 100 years after psychiatry was first introduced into China.

---

[43] Cf. Hugh Shapiro. 1995. "The View from a Chinese Asylum: Defining Madness in 1930s Peking". Ph.D. diss., Harvard University.

[44] Veronica Pearson. 1995. *Mental Health Care in China: State Policies, Professional Services and Family Responsibilities*. London: Gaskell, p. 5.

REFERENCES

Andrews, Bridie. 1994. "Tailoring Tradition: The Impact of Modern Medicine on Traditional Chinese Medicine, 1887–1937", in: Viviane Alleton and Alexei Volkov (eds.). *Notions et Perceptions du Changement en Chine: Textes Présentés au IXe Congrès de l'Association Européenne d'Études Chinoises.* Collège de France: Institut des Hautes Études Chinoises (Mémoires de l'Institut des Hautes Études Chinoises, vol. 36), pp. 59–165.

Bauer, Wolfgang. 1974. "Introduction", in: K'ang, Yu-wei. *Ta T'ung Shu: Das Buch von der Großen Gemeinschaft.* Translated and commentated by Laurence G. Thompson. Edited by Wolfgang Bauer. Düsseldorf, Cologne: Diederichs.

Bünger, Karl. 1950. "The Punishment of Lunatics and Negligents According to Classical Chinese Law", *Studia Serica* 9.2, pp. 1–16.

Chang Hao. 1980. "Intellectual Change and the Reform Movement, 1890–8", in: *Cambridge History of China. Vol. 11: Late Ch'ing, 1800–1911*, part 2, pp. 274–339.

Chen, N. Nancy. 1999. "Translating Psychiatry and Mental Health: Twentieth Century China", in: Lydia H. Liu (ed.). *Tokens of Exchange. The Problem of Translation in Global Circulations.* Durham, London: Duke University Press, pp. 305–30.

Chen Shiduo 陳士鐸. 1991 [1687]. *Shishi milu lu* 石室秘路錄 (Secret records from the stone room). Beijing: Zhongguo Zhongyiyao chubanshe. [Reprint of the Xuanyongtang 萱永堂 ed.].

Chiu, Martha Li. 1981. "Insanity in Imperial China: A Legal Case Study", in: Arthur Kleinman and Tsung-Yi Lin (eds.). *Normal and Abnormal Behavior in Chinese Culture.* Dordrecht: D. Reidel, pp. 75–94.

——. 1986. "Mind, Body, and Illness in a Chinese Medical Tradition". Ph.D. diss., Harvard University. Reprint Ann Arbor: UMI.

Chuanya neibian xuanzhu 串雅內編選注 (Internal treatise on folk medicine with selected commentaries). 1980 [1851]. Edited by Changchun zhongyi xueyuan 長春中醫學院. Beijing: Renmin weisheng chubanshe.

Canguilhelm, Georges. 1972. "Das Normale und das Pathologische", in: Wolf Lepenies and Henning Ritter (eds.). *Hanser Anthropologie.* Munich: Hanser, pp. 81.

Croizier, Ralph C. 1968. *Traditional Medicine in Modern China: Science, Nationalism and the Tensions of Cultural Change.* Cambridge, Mass.: Harvard University Press.

Diankuangxian 癲狂癇 (Falling sickness, madness and epilepsy). 1990. Edited by Hua Beiling 華蓓苓, Zhou Zhangfa 周長發 and Zhu Xinghai 朱興海. Beijing: Zhongyi guji chubanshe.

Dikötter, Frank. 1997. *Imperfect Conceptions: Medical Knowledge, Birth Defects and Eugenics in China.* London: Hurst.

Donnelly, Michael. 1984. *Managing the Mind: A Study of Medical Psychology in early Nineteenth-Century Britain.* London, New York: Tavistock.

Dunstan, Helen. 1975. "The Late Ming Epidemics: A Preliminary Survey", *Ch'ing-shih wen-t'i* 3.3, pp. 1–59.

Foucault, Michel. 1961. *Histoire de la folie.* Paris: Libraire Plon.

Gao Juefu 告覺敷 et al. (eds.). 1986. *Zhongguo xinlixue shi* 中國心理學史 (A history of Chinese psychology). Beijing: Renmin jiaoyu chubanshe.

Guo Chuanling 郭傳鈴. 1909. *Diankuang tiaobian* 癲狂條辯 (Systematized identification of madness). Reprinted in: *Diankuangxian* 癲狂癇. 1990. Edited by Hua

Beiling 華蓓苓, Zhou Zhangfa 周長發 and Zhu Xinghai 朱興海. Beijing: Zhongyi guji chubanshe, pp. 170-5.

Hagner, Michael. 1997. *Homo cerebralis: Der Wandel vom Seelenorgan zum Gehirn.* Berlin: Berlin Verlag.

Hanson, Martha. 1998. "Robust Northeners and Delicate Southerners: The Nineteenth-Century Invention of a Southern Medical Tradition", *positions—east asia cultures critique* 6. 3, pp. 515–50.

Hobson, Benjamin. 1850. "Medical Missions. I. General Report of the Hospital at Kam-li-fau in Canton, from April 1848 to Nov. 1849", *Chinese Repository* 19.5, pp. 300–11.

Huangdi neijing Suwen: *Suwen zhushi huicui* 素問注釋匯粹 (The Inner Classic of the Yellow Emperor. Basic questions with selected commentaries). 1982. Edited by Cheng Shide 程士德 et al. 2 vols. Beijing: Renmin weisheng chubanshe.

Kang Yingchen 康應辰. 1990 [1902]. "Dianbing" 癲病 (Falling sickness), in: *Yixue tanli quanji* 醫學探驪全集 (Complete collection of investigations in medicine). Reprinted in *Diankuangxian* 癲狂癇. 1990, p. 209.

K'ang, Yu-wei. 1974. *Ta T'ung Shu: Das Buch von der Großen Gemeinschaft.* Translated and commentated by Laurence G. Thompson. Edited by Wolfgang Bauer. Düsseldorf, Köln: Diederichs.

Kerr, John Glasgow. 1898. "The 'Refuge for the Insane', Canton", *The China Medical Missionary Journal* 12.4, pp. 177–8.

Lepenies, Wolf. 1977. "Probleme einer Historischen Anthropologie", in: Reinhard Rürup (ed.). *Historische Sozialwissenschaften. Beiträge zur Hinführung in die Forschungspraxis.* Göttingen: Vandenhoeck and Ruprecht, pp. 126–60.

Lepenies, Wolf and Henning Ritter (eds.). 1972. *Hanser Anthropologie.* Munich: Hanser.

Li Guanxian 李冠仙. 1990a [1929]. "Li Guanxian Yihuajinghua" 李冠仙醫話精華 (Selected medical records of Li Guanxian), in: *Qingdai mingyi yihua jinghua* 清代名醫醫話精華 (Selected medical records of famous Qing physicians). Edited by Qin Bowei 秦伯未. 4 vols. Reprinted in: *Lidai zhongyi zhenben jicheng* 歷代中醫珍本集成 (Collection of precious works on Chinese medicine through the ages). Edited by Shanghai Zhongyi xueyuan wenxian yanjiusuo 上海中醫學院文獻研究所. Shanghai: Shanghai sanlian shudian, vol. 40, *juan* 8.

——. 1990b [1835]. *Shangyu yicao* 傷寓意草 (An imitation of significance of herbs), Reprinted in *Lidai zhongyi zhenben jicheng* 歷代中醫珍本集成 (Collection of precious works on Chinese medicine through the ages). 1990. Edited by Shanghai Zhongyi xueyuan wenxian yanjiusuo 上海中醫學院文獻研究所. Shanghai: Shanghai sanlian shudian, vol. 34.

Li Jingwei 李經緯 and Li Zhidong 李志東. 1990. *Zhongguo gudai yixue shilüe* 中國古代醫學史略 (Brief history of Chinese old medicine). Hebei: Hebei kexue jishu chubanshe.

Lingshujing jiaoshi 靈樞經校釋 (Critical edition of the *Divine Pivot*). 1982. Edited by Hebei yixueyuan 河北醫學院. 2 vols. Beijing: Renmin weisheng chubanshe.

Liu, Lydia H. (ed.). 1999. *Tokens of Exchange. The Problem of Translation in Global Circulations.* Durham, London: Duke University Press

Lu Dong, Ma Xi and François Thann. 1995. *Les maux épidémiques dans l'empire Chinois.* Paris: Harmattan.

Ma Kanwen 馬堪溫. 1963. "Zuguo Qingdai jiechude yixuejia Wang Qingren" 祖國清代傑出的醫學家王清任 (On the outstanding Qing-physician Wang Qingren), *Kexueshi jikan* 6, pp. 66–74.

Mawangdui Hanmu boshu 馬王堆漢墓帛書 (Silk manuscripts of the Han tomb in Mawangdui). 1985. Edited by Mawangdui Hanmu boshu zhenglixiaozu 馬王堆漢墓帛書整理小組. Beijing: Wenwu chubanshe.

Ng, Vivien. 1990. *Madness in Late Imperial China: From Illness to Deviance*. Norman: University of Oklahoma Press.

Ouyang Bing 歐陽兵. 1995. "Mingdai Shanghanlun yanjiu dui houshide yingxiang" 明代傷寒論研究對後時的影響 (The influence of the 'Treatise on Cold Damage'—Studies carried out by Ming-Scholars on later times), *Zhonghua yixue zazhi* 25.2, pp. 92–4.

Pearson, Veronica. 1995. *Mental Health Care in China: State Policies, Professional Services and Family Responsibilities*. London: Gaskell.

Qin Bowei 秦伯未 (ed.). 1990 [1929]. *Qingdai mingyi yihua jinghua* 清代名醫醫話精華 (Selected medical records of famous Qing-physicians). 4 vols. Reprinted in: *Lidai zhongyi zhenben jicheng* 歷代中醫珍本集成 (Collection of precious works on Chinese medicine through the ages). Edited by Shanghai Zhongyi xueyuan wenxian yanjiusuo 上海中醫學院文獻研究所. Shanghai: Shanghai sanlian shudian, vol. 40.

Qiu Peiran 裘沛然. 1984. *Zhongyi lidai gejia xueshuo* 中醫歷代各家學說 (Different academic schools of Chinese medicine through the ages). Shanghai: Shanghai kexue jishu chubanshe.

Scull, Andrew T. 1981. "The Social History of Psychiatry in the Victorian Era", in: id. (ed.). *Madhouses, Mad-Doctors, and Madman. The Social History of Psychiatry in the Victorian Era*. London: Athlone Press, pp. 5–32.

Schmitz, Hermann. 1990. *Der unerschöpfliche Gegenstand: Grundzüge der Philosphie*. Bonn: Bouvier.

Schütz, Christian. 1991. "Psychiatrische und psychosomatische Ansätze in den Heiltraditionen bis zur Zeit der Yuan-Dynastie". Ph.D. diss., LMU Munich.

Shapiro, Hugh. 1995. "The View from a Chinese Asylum: Defining Madness in 1930s Peking". Ph.D. diss., Harvard University.

Shuowen jiezi zhu 説文解子注 (Commented edition of the *Shuowen jiezi*). 1988. Edited and commentated by Duan Yucai 段玉裁. Shanghai: Shanghai guji chunbanshe.

Sivin, Nathan. 1995. "Emotionals Counter-Therapy", in: id. *Medicine, Philosophy and Religion in Ancient China: Researches and Reflections*. Great Yarmouth, Norfolk: Galliard, part 2, pp. 1–19.

——. 1998. "The History of Chinese Medicine: Now and Anon", *positions—east asia cultures critique* 6.3, pp. 731–62.

Spence, Jonathan. 1975. "Commentary on Historical Perspectives and Ch'ing Medical Systems", in: Arthur Kleinman et al. (eds.). *Medicine in Chinese Cultures: Comparative Studies of Health Care in Chinese and Other Societies*. Washington: U.S. Government Printing Office, pp. 77–83.

Suwen zhushi huicui 素問注釋匯粹 (The basic questions with selected commentaries). 1982. Edited by Cheng Shide 程士德. 2 vols. Beijing: Renmin weisheng chubanshe.

Tucker, Sara Waitstill. 1983. "The Canton Hospital and Medicine in Nineteenth Century China 1835–1900". Ph.D. diss., Harvard University. Reprint Ann Arbor: UMI.

Unschuld, Paul. 1978. "Das Ch'uan-ya und die Praxis chinesischer Landärzte im 18. Jahrhundert", *Sudhoffs Archiv* 62.4, pp. 378–407.

——. 1980. *Medizin in China. Eine Ideengeschichte*. Munich: Beck.

—— (tr. and comm.). 1986. *Nan-ching: The Classic of Difficult Issues—With Commentaries by Chinese and Japanese Authors From the Third Through the Twentieth Century*. Berkeley, Los Angeles, London: University of California Press.

Wang Qingren 王清任 . 1937 [1831]. *Yilin gaicuo* 醫林改錯 (Corrections of errors in the forest of medicine). Shanghai: Dadong shuju.

Wang Shixiong 王士雄 . 1990 [1929]. *Wang Mengying yihua jinghua* 王孟英醫話精華 (Selected medical records of Wang Mengying), in: Qin Bowei 秦伯未 (ed.). *Qingdai mingyi yihua jinghua* 清代名醫話精華 (Selected medical records of famous Qing-physicians). 4 vols. Reprinted in: *Lidai zhongyi zhenben jicheng* 歷代中醫珍本集成 (Collection of precious works on Chinese medicine through the ages). Edited by Shanghai Zhongyi xueyuan wenxian yanjiusuo 上海中醫學院文獻研究所 . Shanghai: Shanghai sanlian shudian, vol. 40, *juan* 7, pp. 1–150.

Wang Wanbai 王完白 . 1919. "Fengrenyuan zhi zhongyao yu biyi" 瘋人院之重要與裨益 (On the importance and benefit of lunatic asylums), *Zhonghua yixue zazhi* 3.5, pp. 127–31.

Wenyon. 1891. "Letter to the Editor", *The China Medical Missionary Journal* 5, p.1.

Wu Tang 吳塘 . 1990 [1916]. *Diankuang* 癲狂 (Falling sickness), in: *Wu Jutong yi an* 吳鞠通醫案 (Wu Jutong's medical cases), *juan* 5. Reprinted in *Diankuangxian* 癲狂癇 , pp. 228–30.

Xie Xinghuan 謝星煥 . 1986 [1861]. "Dexin ji yi an" 得心集醫案 (Collection of medical records as desired), in: *Zhenben yishu jicheng* 珍本藝書集成 (A Collection of precious books on medicine). Edited by Wang Yurun 王玉潤 et al. Shanghai: Kexue jishu chubanshe, vol. 12.

Yang Jizhou 楊繼洲 . 1994 [1601]. "Zhenjiu dacheng" 針灸大成 (Great compendium of acupuncture and moxibustion), in: *Lidai ming qi'an ji* 歷代名奇案集 (Famous and strange medical case studies through the ages). Edited by Da Meijun 達美君 . Shanghai: Sanlian shudian Shanghai fendian chuban.

Ye Tianshi 葉天士 . 1984 [1746]. *Linzheng zhinan yi an* 臨証指南醫案 (A guide to clinical practice with medical records). Taibei: Guoli gugong bowuyuan.

Zhang Bilu 張必祿 . 1990 [1834]. "Yifang biannan dacheng" 醫方辨難大成 (Great compendium of medical remedies and differentiation of difficult issues). Sichuan Bazhou: Hefei kanben. Reprinted in: *Diankuangxian* 癲狂癇 , p. 193.

Zhang Jiebin 張介賓 . 1983 [1624]. *Zhangshi leijing* 張氏類經 (The classified canon of Zhang Jiebin). Taibei: Wenguang tushu youxian gongsi.

Zhang Xichun 張錫純 . 1995 [1918–34]. *Yixue zhongzhong canxi lu* 醫學衷中參西錄 (The assimilation of Western and Chinese medicine). Hebei: Kexue jishu chubanshe.

Zhao Hongjun 張洪鈞 . 1989. *Jindai Zhongyi lun zhengyi* 近代中醫論爭議 (History of modern controversies over Chinese vs. Western medicine). Anhui: Kexue jishu chubanshe.

Zilboorg, Gregory. 1967. *A History of Medical Psychology*. New York: Norton.

Zhongguo renwu cidian 中國人物辭典 (Chinese Biographical Dictionary). 1988. Edited by Li Jingwei 李經緯 et al. Shanghai: Cishu chubanshe.

Zhou Yimou 周一謀 and Xiao Zuotao 蕭佐桃 . 1988. *Mawangdui yishu kaozhu* 馬王堆醫書考注 (Commentaries on the medical texts from Mawangdui). Tianjin: Tianjin kexue jishu chubanshe.

SARAH E. STEVENS

HYGIENIC BODIES AND PUBLIC MOTHERS: THE RHETORIC OF REPRODUCTION, FETAL EDUCATION, AND CHILDHOOD IN REPUBLICAN CHINA[1]

INTRODUCTION

In my examination of the discourse of hygiene and the way in which hygienic texts constructed women's bodies, I am not dismissing the real health concerns which preoccupied hygienists. I take seriously Nancy Tomes's criticism that "social historians have tended to treat the expressed concern about disease prevention as a rationalization for some other, more genuine, objective such as reinforcing gender roles, class difference, or ethnic prejudices."[2] I am quite willing to believe that the primary goal of hygienists in Republican China was to safeguard public and personal health, sanitize household life, and improve the well-being of the Chinese populace. Nevertheless, a reading of hygienic texts also reveals that the rhetoric, vocabulary, and ideology of hygiene have serious repercussions for the understanding of women's bodies and female sexuality. In particular, hygiene functioned as a method of social control, subordinating individual women to the reproductive power of Woman, and strictly harnessing such reproductive roles to the sled of the nation-state. The technical language and scientific authority of hygiene replaced traditional moral discourse on motherhood and the nation, revealing a new and modern rationale that justified conservative views of gender and reproduction.

To begin my investigation, it is critical to locate hygienic discourse within the historical and social context of the Republican decades. Intellectuals participating in hygienic discourse were situated within a

---

[1] I am grateful to the organizers and participants of the international conference "Translating Western Knowledge into Late Imperial China". In particular, this paper has benefited from the comments of Catherine Yeh and my panel-mates Chow Kai-wing and Angelika Messner. Barbara Mittler, Jean Robinson, Lynn Struve, Jeff Wasserstrom, and Yingjin Zhang have also provided me with valuable insights during this work. Finally, my thanks go to Natascha Vittinghoff for her thoughtful comments, her keen critical eye, and her tireless editing of this paper.

[2] Nancy Tomes. 1990. "The Private Side of Public Health: Sanitary Science, Domestic Hygiene, and the Germ Theory, 1870–1900", *Bulletin of the History of Medicine* 64, p. 512.

web of various influences, including traditional Chinese medicine, traditional conceptions of the body, the family and reproduction, contemporary biological models, and popular concepts of nationalism, evolution, eugenics, and progress. In the late nineteenth century and the early decades of the twentieth century, intellectuals who were eager to reform China and modernize society saw Western science as a savior. Science was equated with absolute truth and intellectuals believed that abiding by scientific principles would lead the Chinese nation to modernity, thus redressing Chinese humiliations at the hands of foreign powers.

Hygienic discourse served as an important site for the convergence of ideas on nationalism, science, and racial evolution. During the Republican decades, evolutionary theory was widely acclaimed and played a crucial role in shaping ideas of sex, race, nation, and reproduction. Frank Dikötter has convincingly demonstrated that the popular Chinese understanding of evolution was non-Darwinian until the mid-1900s. Instead of understanding evolution to be an open-ended process of random change, adaptation, and natural selection, the predominant picture of evolution in China was Neo-Lamarckian.[3] Evolution was pictured to be a linear progress through a hierarchy of stages, visible in the notions of progress versus degeneration (*jinhua* 進化 and *tuihua* 退化). These views of evolution also treated the adult male as the highest rung on the evolutionary ladder. Women and children were considered to be less evolved, thus needing protection and guidance.[4] In addition, Spencerian ideas of group evolution influenced the development of eugenic theories which dominated discussions of reproduction. Racial evolution was conceptualized as a crucial element of national strengthening.[5] Discussions of evolution-based

---

[3] Frank Dikötter. 1992. *The Discourse of Race in Modern China*. Stanford: Stanford University Press, pp. 99–102.

[4] Ibid., pp. 99–102; see also Charlotte Furth. 1999. *A Flourishing Yin: Gender in China's Medical History, 960–1665*. Berkeley: University of California Press.

[5] Although Chinese notions of racial evolution were based on Spencerian ideas of group evolution, there are some similarities between this drive to improve the Chinese race and the pre-1933 racial hygiene movement in Germany, which was based on social Darwinism. For instance, both campaigns focussed on instilling a sense of reproductive duty in their citizens, by calling on the need to safeguard the collective health of the nation. Cf. Frank Dikötter. 1998. *Imperfect Conceptions: Medical Knowledge, Birth Defects and Eugenics in China*. New York: Columbia University Press, and Sheila Francis Weiss. 1987. "The Race Hygiene Movement in Germany", *Osiris* second series 3, pp. 193–236.

eugenics (*youshengxue* 優生學 , literally "the study of superior births") were included in many hygienic texts, particularly those dealing with pregnancy and reproduction.

The discipline of hygiene (*weisheng* 衛生) in China encompasses the areas of public health, personal hygiene, domestic science, and home economics. The term *weisheng* first appeared in the Song dynasty, but came into its current usage in the late Qing, when it was adopted back from the Japanese and used to translate the English word "hygiene". Ruth Rogaski, in her work on hygiene in Tianjin, translates *weisheng* as "hygienic modernity", in an attempt to capture the "complex allusions to science, order, and government authority" which the term evoked.[6] The term saw a great increase in usage and status in the 1900s. During the Republican decades, the field of hygiene was subdivided and labeled with various terms like personal hygiene (*geren weisheng* 個人衛生), public hygiene (*gonggong weisheng* 公共衛生) or "mass hygiene" (*dazhong weisheng* 大眾衛生), social hygiene (*shehui weisheng* 社會衛生), racial hygiene (*zhongzu weisheng* 種族衛生), family hygiene (*jiating weisheng* 家庭衛生) or "household-affairs hygiene" (*jiashi weisheng* 家事衛生), and women's hygiene (*funü weisheng* 婦女衛生). These terms frequently appeared in journal articles and invoked the rhetoric of strengthening the Chinese nation.

In this paper, I will examine hygienic texts found in popular journals, such as *The Ladies' Journal* (*Funü zazhi* 婦女雜志), *Mass Hygiene* (*Dazhong weisheng* 大眾衛生), *Hygiene Journal* (*Weishengbao* 衛生報), and the *Far Eastern Miscellany* (*Dongfang zazhi* 東方雜志).[7] I argue that these texts use the rhetoric of nationalism and racial survival to appropriate formerly private spaces (namely the home and the womb), turning them into public spaces. First, I will discuss my theoretical understandings of the terms public and private within the Chinese context. The second section of this paper will examine metaphors of weakness and sacrifice that were used to represent the female reproductive body. These metaphors form a core thread of feto-centric

---

[6] Ruth Rogaski. 2000. "Hygienic Modernity in Tianjin", in: Joseph W. Esherick (ed.). *Remaking the Chinese City: Modernity and National Identity, 1900–1950.* Honolulu: University of Hawaii Press, p. 30.

[7] For a discussion of the implied audience of these various journals, see Sarah Stevens, 2001. *Making Female Sexuality: Women's Bodies in the Discourses of Hygiene, Literature, and Education.* Ph.D. diss. Indiana University, Chapters 1–2.

discourse. The third section of this paper will focus on texts on fetal education, an area of hygiene that entirely privileges the nation's interest in a healthy fetus and a future citizen. Fourth, I will look at depictions of children and child-rearing in hygienic texts as a continuation of this nationalistic appropriation of reproductive acts. In my conclusion, I theorize that the terminology and textual conventions of hygienic discourse indicate a shift in the patriarchal construction of female sexuality and reproductive acts. During the course of the twentieth century, control over reproduction, which was once ceded to the private arena and the (male) head of the household, is appropriated by the nation-society.[8] This shift began in the transitional and Republican decades and became further articulated in the later half of the twentieth century, during the People's Republic of China (PRC). During this time period, the scientific rationale of evolution and eugenics replaced earlier moral language in policing women's bodies.

1. THEORIZING THE PUBLIC AND PRIVATE IN CHINA

I do not use the term 'public space' with the positive connotations that Jürgen Habermas or Hannah Arendt set forth in their views of the "public sphere". Both Habermas and Arendt variously theorize the public sphere to be an arena of free discourse and political participation through communication, distinct from any state apparatus.[9] The early Republican era saw a flourishing of some aspects of a Habermasian public sphere, with the proliferation of periodicals, literary

---

[8] I am using the term 'nation-society' in this context, instead of 'nation-state' or 'society'. The term 'nation-state' would imply that a particular government or state-run organization was policing or creating hygienic dialogue. The term 'society' would oversimplify the situation and would not foreshadow the future nation-state interference that is so present in the People's Republic of China. What I hope to capture in using the term 'nation-society' is the overwhelming presence of nationalism that permeated every aspect of Chinese society during these decades. The call to "save the nation" (*jiuguo* 救國) echoed in all aspects of Chinese life. The level of state involvement by the Guomindang government varied over time and across social movements. The Guomindang, Leftists, the Chinese Communist Party, foreign missionaries—all these groups at some point in time used hygiene and physical culture as rallying points for the nation.

[9] Hannah Arendt. 1998. *The Human Condition*. Chicago: University of Chicago Press, and Jürgen Habermas. 1989. *The Structural Transformation of the Public Sphere: An Inquiry into a Category of Bourgeois Society*. Translated by Thomas Burger. Cambridge, Mass.: The MIT Press.

groups, coffeehouses and other arenas for free discourse. However, at the same time, hygienic discourse is one site that shows the ways in which the public sphere in China was contaminated by the presence of the nation-state, or the nation-society. In addition, Habermas's theory has been rightly criticized on the grounds of gender, class, and a misleading universalism, all of which make his theories problematic for this study. Arendt's theory—while more useful to me in this context due to her emphasis on physical spaces and her desire for a pluralistic public sphere—is equally suspect in the Chinese context, where the Chinese nation-state tends to play a large role in most public spheres.[10]

My use of the terms 'public' and 'private' more loosely accords with the general guidelines set out by Nancy Fraser. Fraser breaks the word "public" into four general definitions: 1) accessible by all (like a public park or a public library), 2) for the common good of all (like public health), 3) related to the state (like public taxes), 4) of concern to everyone (like a public issue of debate). All four of these arenas of public-ness have an opposite, which is understood to be part of the private domain. In addition, "private" has two additional meanings: 5) related to private property, 6) "pertaining to intimate, domestic or personal life, including sexual life".[11] This last definition of private is the one I would like to highlight. In hygienic discourse, private matters "pertaining to intimate, domestic, or personal life, including sexual life" are made into public matters—for the common good of all, of concern to everyone, and related to the nation.

My use of the term 'private' in the Chinese context is decidedly more related to the domestic, or familial, sphere than to a realm of individual control. Arguably, throughout history, women in China have never had control over their own reproduction. In premodern times, women's childbearing was largely controlled by the family and

---

[10] Virginia Cornue. 1999. "Practicing NGOness and Relating Women's Space Publicly: The Women's Hotline and the State", in: Mayfair Mei-hui Yang (ed.). *Spaces of Their Own: Women's Public Sphere in Transnational China*. Minneapolis: University of Minnesota Press, p. 86; Mayfair Mei-hui Yang. 1999. "Introduction", *Spaces of Their Own: Women's Public Sphere in Transnational China*. Minneapolis: University of Minnesota Press, pp. 9–11.

[11] Nancy Fraser. 1990. "Rethinking the Public Sphere: A Contribution to the Critique of Actually Existing Democracy", *Social Text* 25/26, pp. 70–1.

the (male) head of the household.[12] Beginning in the late 1800s, this locus of power over reproduction shifted away from the family towards the idea of Chinese nation-society. This change is signified by a change in the rhetoric surrounding matters of reproduction. Language shifts from moral to scientific, as the focus of reproduction shifts from the family to the nation.

A rigid distinction between the public and the private is often used by the ideology of male supremacy as a means to exclude important matters from political debate, and this type of exclusion almost always works to the advantage of dominant groups and individuals.[13] However, the act of blurring the boundaries between public and private is equally fraught with danger.[14] Fixing the boundaries of public and private is "always a matter of balancing the potential political uses of publicity against the dangers of loss of privacy."[15] Gail Kligman, in her discussion of reproductive politics in Romania, calls such a blurring of the distinction between public and private a dangerous "transgression of embodied boundaries."[16] It is this potential danger of transgression, this "loss of privacy" which I wish to explore further.

From my vantage point in *fin-de-siècle* twentieth century America, where a mere click of the remote allows me to surf past reality TV, and other such shows ad nauseam, it is easy to see how a conflation of public and private leads to the construction of the "citizen consumer"[17] or even the "citizen voyeur". In the Chinese context of the

---

[12] Francesca Bray's work looks at how some women may have negotiated within the institution of motherhood, using the categories of biological and social motherhood in order to gain power over their reproduction. Cf. Francesca Bray. 1997. *Technology and Gender: Fabrics of Power in Late Imperial China*. Berkeley: University of California Press.

[13] Fraser 1990, p. 73, and Nancy Fraser. 1992. "Sex, Lies, and the Public Sphere: Some Reflections on the Confirmation of Clarence Thomas", *Critical Inquiry* 18, pp. 595–612; 609.

[14] Seyla Benhabib. 1993. "Feminist Theory and Hannah Arendt's Concept of Public Space", *History of the Human Science* 6.2, pp. 97–114.

[15] Fraser 1992, p. 610.

[16] Gail Kligman. 1998. *The Politics of Duplicity: Controlling Reproduction in Ceausescu's Romania*. Berkeley: University of California Press, p. 5. Kligman's account provides a chilling look at the politics of reproduction and the dangers inherent in nation-state domination of the domestic sphere. Many of her observations about Romania can be aptly applied to my argument, as hygiene can be seen as one discourse in which "the state as personified being spoke incessantly about itself and exercised power in its own interests, presented as those of its subjects" (p. 4).

early twentieth century, clearly the idea of blurring the public and the private did not lead to the production of a "citizen-consumer" or a "citizen-voyeur" in quite the same manner. Rather, I would argue that public appropriation of some private spaces, such as the physical spaces of the womb and the household and the temporal space of childhood, led to the development of a "citizen-subject". I use this term "citizen-subject" drawing upon both the notion of being a serf, under the control of the nation-society, and the notion of being subjected by the nation-society, with individual desires made subject to larger national goals. In particular, hygienic discourse uses the modern rubric of science and technology to strengthen traditional virtues found in classic texts. In so doing, authority shifts from morality to scientific truth, as the balance of power is shifted from the family to the nation-society.

2. MENSTRUATION, PREGNANCY, AND THE SACRIFICIAL WOMAN

Through their use of nationalistic and eugenic rhetoric, hygienic texts were imbued with the social function of saving the nation and preserving the race. The common train of logic is quite evident in one early text "The hygiene of household affairs", published in 1916 in *The Ladies' Journal*. The rhetoric can be paraphrased thusly: Each person is a part of the citizenry and these citizens constitute the nation-family (*guojia* 國家). The strength of the nation therefore depends on whether or not people are healthy and whether the nation flourishes or fails depends on the people's individual hygiene.[18] This article goes on to connect the nation-family (the *guojia*) to the individual family and gives instructions on everyday matters like proper light and ventilation. These simple matters of household cleanliness are thus ideologically linked to the good of the whole nation. Hygiene played a key role in colonial discourse, as the foreigners/colonizers often labelled the native/colonized unhygienic—dirty, unclean, unmodern, and visibly inferior. Hence, a discussion of hygiene is

---

[17] Benhabib 1993, p. 109.
[18] He Fei 合肥. 1916. "Jiashi weisheng" 家事衛生 (The hygiene of household affairs), *Funü zazhi* 2.5, pp. 1–5.

inextricably linked to colonial discourse, visible in the nationalistic drive to "make foreigners stop mocking us as 'Sick men of Asia'."[19]

This attitude which equated hygiene with national salvation was prevalent throughout the Republican decades. A 1943 article that is responding to the pressures of World War II and the Japanese invasion illustrates the unchanging nature of this focus on hygiene. The author states:

> We can say that the day hygiene education is common will be the day the health care movement will succeed. The day the health care movement succeeds will be the day that the Chinese race will revive. I hope that everyone will use their mass force and strength to make the realization of this nation their first priority.[20]

The lines connecting hygiene, health, racial survival, and a prospering nation are thus drawn quite clearly. But how does hygienic discourse specifically depict women and their role in the hygiene movement?

Hygienic discourse asserted a view of women that prioritized their biological role in reproduction and centralized their role as mothers. As stated in a 1922 article entitled "The Psychological Life of Women" and written by Li Rongdi 李榮第 (under the pen-name Y.D.):

> The goal of men is self-preservation, so they are physically strong. They are predisposed to various skills and are progress-oriented. They have the ability to be logical and analyze many things and can face danger. The goal of women is the preservation of the race. They are predisposed to art. Regarding their abilities, one cannot say that they can't do things, but when considering their ability to protect the race, they all have an innate inclination towards it.[21]

An interesting duality is set up in this text. The goal of men is self-preservation, while the goal of women is the preservation of the race. In other words, the abilities of men are targeted towards the individ-

---

[19] "Ertongnian de qiwang" 兒童年的期望 (Hopes for Children's Year). 1935. *Dazhong weisheng* (*Mass Hygiene*) 1.2, pp. 1–2. This dichotomy of masculine-hygienic-colonizer versus feminine-dirty-colonized must be seen in the context of contemporary evolutionary thought wherein the female (and the feminized nation) is seen to be less evolved, and in the context of a scientized society, where the modern medicine represented progress and cleanliness.

[20] Zhou Shang 周尚 . 1943. "Weisheng jiaoyu yu guomin jiankang" 衛生教育與國民健康 (Hygiene education and the people's health), *Dongfang zazhi* 39.19, p. 39.

[21] Y. D. (Li Rongdi李榮第). 1922. "Funü de jingshen shenghuo" 婦女的精神生活 (The psychological life of women), *Funü zazhi* 8.1, p. 67.

ual, while women's skills are focused on the public good. Women "preserve the race" through their reproductive roles, by producing the best possible offspring and mothering them in the proper manner.

Charlotte Furth has shown that Late Imperial medical constructions of women's bodies involved a shift from metaphors of pollution to metaphors of weakness and inferiority.[22] This new model naturalized women's subordinate status by referring to Chinese biological concepts, such as the idea that blood was the central force influencing female health and that menstruation resulted in weakness. During the Republican era, hygienic texts continue to describe a weak and vulnerable female body. On one hand, the association between menstruation, pregnancy and weakness clearly shows that this naturalized weakness is related to the Late Imperial model of the female body, in which menstruation was depicted as a cycle of loss and motherhood was represented as a sacrifice. On the other hand, these Late Imperial views are joined by modern views of naturalized weakness, namely, ideas which refer to Western biology and evolutionary theory. Models of argumentation show that science had become the most convincing source of authority, rather than referring to classical knowledge. Both women and children were viewed as inherently, biologically inferior to the adult male. Women, in particular, were believed to be over-emotional—a long standing view which was given a modern, biological basis. Emotionality was therefore one trait which hygienic texts worked hard to control. This tenet forms the central thread of articles like "Responses of the psyche during pregnancy".[23]

Republican hygienic literature describes the reproductive female body as a vulnerable body which must be protected from the outside world. One female-authored hygienic text addresses an audience of "We generally delicate and weak women" who experience things like menstrual problems and pregnancy and "therefore, much more than men, we women need to place special emphasis on the area of

---

[22] Charlotte Furth. 1986. "Blood, Body and Gender: Medical Images of the Female Condition in China, 1600–1850", *Chinese Science* 7 (1986), pp. 43–66, and ibid. 1999. *A Flourishing Yin: Gender in China's Medical History, 960–1665*. Berkeley: University of California Press, pp. 130–3; 178–86 and 305–12.

[23] Xi Shen 西神. 1916. "Renshen zhong zhi jingshen ganying" 妊娠中之精神感應 (Responses of the psyche during pregnancy), *Funü zazhi* 2.10, no pagination. This article is actually a translation of a portion of a Japanese text, "The World of Japanese Women"—a book which the translator must have thought to have universal applications.

hygiene."[24] During menstruation, during pregnancy, and after birth, women are advised to be very careful in order to avoid disastrous physical consequences. For instance, some instructions to menstruating women include telling them to stay calm and not exercise, but not to stay in bed all day, not to eat things that are too hot or too cold, but to carefully monitor their nutrition, to wash gently, but not to wash the vagina, and to avoid emotional stimulation. If women do not follow these hygienic instructions, texts warn of dire consequences, including menstrual irregularities, infections of the uterus, an inability to reproduce in the future, and poor physical health. In particular, women are warned that during menstruation, the "mouth" of the uterus is open, leaving the uterus at a very high risk for disease. During this time, women must be very careful to make sure that the menstrual blood flows easily and does not collect in the womb, as too much blood in the womb furthers the risk of infection. Hygienic texts written during the transitional decade of the 1910s are often particularly concerned with giving a biological rational to these instructions. Twice, Zhen He's 真和 1918 article mentions the possibility of an inflammation of the lining of uterus. Zhen He also warns not to wash the vagina, lest infection enter through the "mouth of the womb", or cervix.[25]

Pregnancy is another moment that is thought to weaken the female body. Fan Xuqin 樊須欽 begins the article "The hygiene of pregnancy" by stating that, because the body and the spirit both change so much during pregnancy, it is very easy for illness to occur.[26] The article goes on to say that if the mother's body is healthy, then the fetus is healthy. But, if the mother's body has some sort of problem, it will affect the fetus. A text in the *The Ladies' Journal* also makes clear the associations between pregnancy and weakness. Women are warned not to become angry, scared, sad, or overly happy, in order to avoid having an early birth, a still birth, or a deformed baby.[27] The text also warns against sexual contact during certain periods of pregnancy.

---

[24] Zhu Xiujuan 朱秀娟 . 1927. "Bianji zhi yan" 編輯之言 (Words from the editor), *Weishengbao* 1.6, no pagination.

[25] Zhen He 真和 . 1918. "Yuejing zhi weisheng" 月經之衛生 (Menstrual hygiene), *Funü zazhi* 4.12, pp. 4–6; 4–5.

[26] Fan Xuqin 樊須欽 . 1927. "Renshenzhi weisheng" 妊娠之衛生 (The hygiene of pregnancy), *Weishengbao* 1.13, no pagination.

[27] Chen Yaozhiping 陳姚雉屏 . 1916. "Renshen yixitan" 妊娠一夕談 (An evening chat about pregnancy), *Funü zazhi* 2.5, pp. 5–11; 7.

Pregnancy is generally treated as a potentially dangerous time, when the woman's body is permeable and vulnerable to invasion by outside forces.

Along with language that indicates that pregnancy is dangerous, other texts praise the sacrificial nature of motherhood. A close investigation of a text by Zhu Wenyin 朱文印, "Fetal education and eugenics", reveals the following passage about reproduction:

> As a result of the sexual union of the male and female sex, from the male sex, the necessary materials for creating a person are transported over and use the woman's womb as a workshop. In its interior, because of myriad mysterious cellular activities, the right amount of time passes, and various work is completed. This then is what biology terms pregnancy. From this you can see, although we say creating living beings is the result of both the male and female sexes working together diligently, the man's side is no more than providing the necessary material to create a person. In addition to this, there must be additional work in the woman's womb, before [the fetus] can be fully created. Also, as for that exquisite and complex human body [of the fetus], on the part of the female sex, it is not just in the womb for nine months and completed without effort. Within the period of pregnancy, in order to complete the work of human creating human, [the woman] cuts up her own flesh and spirit to give the fetus. Day and night, for nine months, [she] continues to take [her] blood and pass it gradually to the fetus. Embracing strong maternal expectations finally makes the sexual union of male and female become the complete soul and flesh of a human child raising the first cry of life. In all the world, the female sex that can accomplish the work of creating a living being, isn't that [woman] the greatest artist in the world?[28]

The industrial metaphors at work here are unmistakable. In the first few sentences, the process of conception and the development of the fetus are described using the words *cailiao* 材料, *gongchang* 工廠, and *gongzuo* 工作. *Cailiao* means "materials" in a broad sense and often specifically refers to raw materials used in production. In this context, *cailiao* refers to the raw building materials used to construct a fetus. The man donates these "materials", transporting them to the woman's womb that becomes a workshop. The word used here is *gongchang*, meaning a workshop, a work-site, or even a factory. In this workshop-womb, the work—the *gongzuo*—of creating the fetus occurs. The word *gongzuo* is repeated throughout the paragraph in discussing the

---

[28] Zhu Wenyin 朱文印. 1931. "Taijiao yu youshengxue" 胎教與優生學 (Fetal education and eugenics), *Funü zazhi* 17.8, pp. 11–19; 2.

work of creating human beings and the root half of the word also occurs in the phrase "to add work" (*jiagong* 加工), or, as I have translated it for convenience in English, "additional work".

Both the production metaphor and the implied power structure are clear. The passage paints a picture of a scene where the supervising male provides crucial materials for the worker female. This worker female is then responsible for the drawn-out toil. The woman's work in creating the fetus is not merely described as difficult, dangerous or painstaking. Instead, her work is described as the ultimate self-sacrifice. Within her workshop womb, the worker-woman divides up her own flesh and spirit, literally "cuts" herself up and gives portions of herself to the fetus. The passage highlights the new employment of technical metaphors in discussions of motherhood.

In addition to positing woman-as-worker, the passage equates the woman with the physical workshop. The woman is both the site of production—the workshop—and the menial laborer in the workshop.[29] The agency of the woman is thus doubly effaced. She is a place, a background against which the work of reproduction takes place. And she is the worker, who toils at the manual labor of reproduction, while the male figure is imagined as a supervisor, providing the all-important raw materials while being physically removed from the scene. The phrasing of the passage, with its care to give credit to the woman for all her work, seems patronizing. The attitude is much the same as that of a higher-up praising a lower-level employee.

In this text, as in those discussed above, the underlying concern is clearly for the fetus. Most literature on pregnancy reveals this emphasis on the well-being of the child. Texts on female weakness emphasize the importance of female health for the well-being of the future children. The equation of motherhood and sacrifice also prioritizes the fetus, praising women for offering their own selves in order to create a new generation. These same feto-centric (and eugenic-based) views of the female body are clearly revealed in texts on fetal education.

---

[29] My use of the term 'labor' here is intentional and points to the associations between childbirth and work in English. As shown by Rudolf G. Wagner in this volume, in the Republican period, the concept of physical 'labor' had become a tool for educating the weak and degenerate young person and was used polemically as the remedy for the general weakness of China. The woman-worker depicted here is endowed with the same agenda of strengthening China, by giving birth to children.

3. FETAL EDUCATION AND THE PUBLIC WOMB

The concept of *taijiao* 胎教 (fetal education) is different from 'prenatal education'. The current Western notion of prenatal education encompasses ideas of proper nutrition and health for the pregnant woman, and hence the fetus. The concept of *taijiao* also includes the idea that the mind, body, and spirit of the fetus can be molded by the outside world while it is still in the womb. The concept of *taijiao* is an old one, prevalent in traditional texts. An oft-quoted early definition is found in the *Stories of Virtuous Women* (*Lienüzhuan* 列女傳): "The eyes shall hear no evil colors, the ears shall hear no evil sounds, the mouth shall speak no evil words. This is the meaning of *taijiao*." To use a more modern metaphor found in a 1915 issue of the *The Ladies' Journal*: "When taking photographs, if there is a smile, then after developing the image, there is the same smile. If there is anger, then after developing, there is the same anger."[30] This rephrasing of the definition of *taijiao* provides an excellent example of the prevalent use of technical metaphors in describing physical processes.

Both of these quotations emphasize that the impressionable fetus can be influenced by the signs and sounds experienced by the pregnant woman, as well as the woman's own emotional state during pregnancy—her smiles or anger. What is new in the Republican period is the nationalistic rationale behind the rubric of *taijiao*. In the Late Imperial era, women who paid attention to the principles of fetal education were praised as good mothers and their own social status might have been raised by their child's later success.[31] Beginning in the late Qing, the concept of *taijiao* began to be associated with racial evolution and eugenics, as fetal education was depicted as a way to influence the strength and intelligence of the race-as-nation.[32] Women were now instructed to be careful about fetal education so that the race would prosper.

---

[30] He Xishen 何錫琛 . 1915. "Shenxin yu sixu zhi guanxishuo" 身心與飼畜之關系說 (About the relationship between body, mind, and descendent), *Funü zazhi* 1.7, pp. 1–4; 1.

[31] Francesca Bray. 1997. *Technology and Gender: Fabrics of Power in Late Imperial China*. Berkeley: University of California Press, passim.

[32] Frank Dikötter. 1992. *The Discourse of Race in Modern China*. Stanford: Stanford University Press, pp. 166–7.

Taijiao did not enjoy universal support during the 1920s and 30s. In 1931, Huang Shi 黃石 published a critical article titled "What is 'fetal education'" in the *The Ladies' Journal*. Here, the author explains the superstitious roots of *taijiao* and shows that there is absolutely no "medical" base to the idea that the intelligence, strength, or character of the fetus can be influenced before birth.[33] This argument reveals the ways in which debates on fetal education became politicized and participated discussions of the Chinese nation. Since *taijiao* is related to feudal times and superstitions, its proponents used scientific and medical language to create a new, modern rational behind fetal education. Huang's attacks on *taijiao* serve to reify the supremacy of science. Articles that appealed to the scientific rationale behind *taijiao* were being routinely published. Even articles that do not mention the term *taijiao* appeal to its basic tenets, instructing pregnant women to live an upright lifestyle, in order to protect the baby.[34] In addition to discussions of nutrition, cleanliness, and exercise, pregnant women were instructed not to read popular fiction, not to go to the cinema, and not to engage in any activity which might cause emotional stimulation.[35] All these instructions were given medical reasons.

These instructions are clearly linked to the eugenic mission of improving the Chinese race. As one text advises: "As for the matter of fetal education, its purpose is not just to make sure that the fetus receives good influences: it also has an extremely important significance for the evolution of the human races."[36] In hygienic discourse, motherhood was a woman's path to involvement in the nation. This rhetoric contains a curious mixture of empowerment and subordination. On the one hand, an argument can be made that the inclusion of women in work for the nation increases their social status and imbues

---

[33] Huang Shi 黃石 . 1931. "Shenmo shi '*taijiao*'" 甚麼是胎教 (What is 'fetal education'), *Funü zazhi* 17.11, pp. 19–28.

[34] Ai Zhu 藹諸 . 1935. "Yuying changshi" 育嬰常識 (Common knowledge about bringing up infants), *Dazhong weisheng* 1.2, pp. 13-6.

[35] Such instructions are widespread. Good examples can be found in Xi Shen. 1916, n.p., and Zhu Wenyin. 1931, p. 15. This type of warning was also prevalent in educational discourse on sexual education. For more information, see Stevens 2001, chapter three and four.

[36] Zhu Wenyin 1931, p. 13.

them with social responsibility.[37] On the other hand, as I would argue, that women were subjugated to the paternalistic power of the state. I would further argue that neither of these extremes—neither the idea that *taijiao* empowers women nor the idea that it functions strictly as a means of subordination—is sufficient in and of itself to give a clear picture of how hygienic discourse may have functioned. In fact, when we examine hygienic rhetoric, we need to also allow for the possibility that authors of various texts might have used the socially acceptable rhetoric of nationalism and race in order to make empowering arguments, even if the rhetoric itself is not empowering.

One example of this textual possibility is a 1937 article entitled "Hygiene during pregnancy and fetal education" by Yun Qin 韻琴. The text begins with the statement:

> Regardless of whether we're discussing the preservation of the race or the strengthening of the people's health, the hygiene of pregnant women and fetal education are both very significant and have a value that is not easy to ignore.[38]

Starting with this endorsement of the common view of women as servants of the race-nation, the author then moves on to imbue the argument with empowering overtones. She argues that women therefore need more control over their bodies and their sexuality, pointing out that if a married woman does not have a "harmonious" sex life, it will hurt her body, psyche, her future children, and thus the race.

Yun Qin's article also contains a section that proscribes a proper course of action for men, in particular, for husbands. Using the common conception that equates female emotional upheaval with danger to the fetus, the author says that husbands must treat their pregnant wives with an increased level of respect. She states:

> If the husband treats his wife the same as always and does not give her special psychological comfort and tender care, or if he goes to the extent of feeling as if the home is unpleasant and seeks pleasures elsewhere because his wife is sick in pregnancy, or if he is not happy with

---

[37] Frank Dikötter argues for this empowering function in his *Sex, Culture and Modernity in China: Medical Science and the Construction of Female Identities in the Early Republican Period*. Honolulu: University of Hawaii Press. 1995, pp. 94–5.

[38] Yun Qin 韻琴. 1937. "Renshen zhong de weisheng yu taijiao" 妊娠中的衛生與胎教 (Hygiene during pregnancy and fetal education), *Dongfang zazhi* 34.7, p. 257.

his wife and gets mad at her, this [behavior] is enough to make the pregnancy agitated or troublesome, directly influencing the fetus.[39]

This passage can even be read as an argument for male fidelity, as the author warns men against "seek[ing] pleasures elsewhere." Another text warns against husbands returning home late and "smelling of alcohol."[40]

Read between the lines, portions of these texts can be seen as one example of the ways in which women may have been able to maneuver within the rhetoric of racial and national survival, in order to gain greater control over their own bodies. Such texts may even create a space for personal expression and fulfillment within the larger structure of hygiene, which viewed female sexuality and reproductive capacities in strict terms of social good, nationalism, and racial improvement. At the same time, however, Yun's text paints a picture of a weak and vulnerable pregnant woman, who must control her sexual urges and her emotions.

The rough picture I have sketched out above is one in which the hygienic discourse exerts a paternalistic control over women's reproductive capacities through the use of scientific logic and terminology. Regardless of the gender of their authors, hygienic texts largely act for the (male) nation-state, advising the (female) citizen-subject how to act, how to feel, and how to reproduce. Using the language of race, nation and science, women's wombs are reconfigured as a space that must be used only for the public good. Hygienic texts that deal with children and the household continue this rhetoric of national appropriation, using metaphors which indicate that children are mutable and must be carefully groomed into proper citizens.

4. CHILDHOOD: A NATIONAL PLAYGROUND

Many hygienic texts that addressed women also focused on the idea of family hygiene, especially as it related to childrearing. Through these texts, the physical space of the household and the temporal space of childhood were made into public spaces where the needs and dictates of the nation took first precedence. Texts dealing with household or family hygiene often assumed that care of the household was

---

[39] Ibid., p. 260.
[40] Zhu Wenyin 1931, p. 15.

an arena of female concern. Proper ordering of the household was associated with proper ordering of the nation. Texts on child rearing assumed that children were a national resource that needed to be carefully trained and preserved for the good of the nation-state. This connection is semantically exemplified by the term *guojia* 國家, or "nation-family".

Most texts on family hygiene were specifically targeted towards women, as evidenced by the inclusion of a special section entitled "Family hygiene" in *The Ladies' Journal* for several years. Women were given detailed instructions on proper housekeeping and told that deviation from these norms could lead to unhealthy families and an unhealthy China. In terms of the physical ordering of the household, everything from proper ventilation to proper cleaning techniques was carefully specified. The article "Common illnesses of the woman's world" illustrates that women were still conceptually linked to domestic life, even with the advances made in education.[41] In this text, the "woman's world" is clearly the household, even though the author starts by mentioning that the health of young girls has been improved by their pursuit of education and their experiences in the wider world. The author devotes the majority of the article to addressing women as housewives and details common illnesses that can be remedied by proper hygiene in the home. In addition, the rationale behind proper hygiene is clearly paternalistic, aiming to protect children and the family unit. In addressing the problem of tuberculosis—a fatal disease—the author emphasizes the necessity for women to protect children:

> If you have tuberculosis and then you have children, you will transmit it to them. Therefore, because of this serious problem, you must pay attention to preventing this illness.[42]

In other words, women's health needs to be protected from a fatal illness not because of fear for the women's lives, but out of fear for the children, who are the real resources of the nation-state.

The notion of children as a state resource goes hand in hand with the long-standing tendency to subordinate children's interests to those of the social unit, visible in premodern China and continuing into the

---

41 Hu Dingan 胡定安 . 1922. "Funüjie de putongbing" 婦女界的普通病 (Common illnesses of the woman's world), *Funü Zazhi* 8.8, pp. 81–2.

42 Ibid., p. 81.

modern era.[43] The definition of this all-important "social unit", however, has changed with time, variously emphasizing the individual
natal family unit, the chain of continuity from ancestors to descendants, the community at large, and the nation-state.[44] Angela Ki Che
Leung argues that the late Qing decades saw a shift to a world-view
which envisioned children as important members of society, with the
potential to be either useful or dangerous social beings.[45] She sees this
view as a change from earlier periods that located children within the
family, and asserts that "the late-nineteenth-century society now perceived the child as a complex social being with specific needs."[46] The
social importance of children began to be stressed, with consonant
improvements to relief institutions for children. This increasing
emphasis on social responsibility for destitute children is directly connected to the type of discourse found in hygienic texts. This discourse
reflects the paternalistic role of state and society, where the nation-
state acts as a parental figure and children are claimed within the *guojia*, the nation-family.

In China, notions of childhood and child development have primarily been influenced by two conflicting schools of thought, popular
with different people and at different times. According to the first
school of thought, children hold natural wisdom and can in fact reach
a level of spiritual perfection surpassing that of adults. This school of
thought has been popular in the Daoist tradition and with various
other groups of intellectuals.[47] This same view of childhood is also
visible in modern China, particularly in some of the May Fourth

---

[43] Anne Behnke Kinney. 1995b. "Introduction", in: Id. (ed.). *Chinese Views of
Childhood.* Honolulu: University of Hawaii Press, p. 2.

[44] For more information on the connectedness of children and the family unit, see
Wu Hung. 1995. "Private Love and Public Duty: Images of Children in Early Chinese
Art", in: Anne Behnke Kinney (ed.). *Chinese Views of Childhood.* Honolulu: Univer-
sity of Hawaii Press, pp. 79-110, and Ann Waltner. 1995. "Infanticide and Dowry in
Ming and Early Qing China", in: Anne Behnke Kinney (ed.). *Chinese Views of Child-
hood.* Honolulu: University of Hawaii Press, pp. 193–218.

[45] Angela Ki Che Leung. 1995. "Relief Institutions for Children in Nineteenth-
Century China", in: Anne Behnke Kinney (ed.). *Chinese Views of Childhood.* Honolulu: University of Hawaii Press, pp. 251–78.

[46] Ibid., p. 254.

[47] Wu Pei-yi discusses the prevalence of this view in the Wang Yangming school.
Cf. Wu Pei-yi. 1995. "Childhood Remembered: Parents and Children in China, 800 to
1700", in: Anne Behnke Kinney (ed.). *Chinese Views of Childhood.* Honolulu: University of Hawaii Press, 129–56.

thinkers who were influenced by John Dewey and his child-centered philosophy. Some writers of this period wrote literature adopting the child's perspective, revealing nostalgia for the fresh and natural state of youth and privileging childish wisdom.[48]

The other school of thought emphasized the child as a potential. This perspective saw childhood as a phase of human development, respected for its intellectual and moral potential, but not valued in and of itself.[49] This view stressed the necessity of education and the proper training of children and was associated with fetal education.[50] As one example of this view, Anne Behnke Kinney examines views of childhood in the Han dynasty, claiming the child was construed as a "base of potentialities that require development through instruction."[51] According to this view, the child is malleable at birth (and before birth) and needs guidance. This educational process was usually referred to as *jianhua* 漸化, or gradual transformation. Kinney proceeds to semantically investigate this term and show how the word *jian* 漸 is related to the process of dying cloth. She concludes that

> … the slow process whereby textiles are steeped in dye and absorb color is an appropriate metaphor for the Han concept of how personalities are formed.[52]

This view of children as malleable, blank texts is very close to the view of childhood asserted in hygienic texts. The notion of dyeing cloth is echoed in the common hygienic metaphor that children are "blank paper". In one article discussing the meaning of Children's Day, the author states that "Children's minds are like blank paper. They originate without any knowledge."[53] The argument proceeds to aver that children must be given the right kind of knowledge and their

---

[48] Catherine E. Pease. 1995. "Remembering the Taste of Melons: Modern Chinese Stories of Childhood", in: Anne Behnke Kinney (ed.). *Chinese Views of Childhood.* Honolulu: University of Hawaii Press, pp. 279–320.

[49] Kinney 1995b, p. 12.

[50] Some aspects of Bray's argument on motherhood also reflect on this issue, as she discusses the traditional Chinese view that nurture is stronger than nature. Cf. Bray 1997, passim.

[51] Anne Behnke Kinney. 1995a. "Dyed Silk: Han Notions of the Moral Development of Children", in: Id. (ed.). *Chinese Views of Childhood.* Honolulu: University of Hawaii Press, p. 18.

[52] Ibid., p. 30.

[53] Liu Jiushi 劉九始. 1935. "Tan ertongjie yu ertong de jiankang jiaoyu" 談兒童 節與兒童的健康教育 (Discussing Children's Day and children's health education), *Dazhong weisheng* 1.4, p. 10.

health must be protected. The logic ends on a nationalistic note, urging society to devote this "Children's Year" to carrying out the words of Sun Yat-sen (Sun Zhongshan 孫中山, 1866–1925): "Make developing children the foundation!"[54] The importance of proper training cannot be overestimated:

> If in youth [a child] has proper training and obtains good education, this will lead to [it] conducting its later life like a person, and moreover, being able to bring benefit to society![55]

To look at the negative of this statement, a child with improper training and a bad education may harm society and destroy the nation. Such sentiments are commonly spoken by proponents of new education, including education in the science of hygiene.

Other articles echo the metaphor of "blank paper", and advise "If [you] write with black ink, [they] turn black; if [you] write with red ink, [they] turn red."[56] In another version:

> Children are originally like a sheet of blank paper, if they are dyed in green, they are green; if they are dyed in yellow, they are yellow.[57]

Parents must therefore be very careful to color their children's experience in certain ways, to benefit the public. This attitude is akin to that found in the text I cited earlier, during the discussion of *taijiao*. That particular passage used the metaphor of photography to discuss fetal education, which can be extended to refer to childhood potential.

> When taking photographs, if there is a smile, then after developing the image, there is the same smile. If there is anger, then after developing, there is the same anger.[58]

In its original context, this quotation means that the woman's emotional state during conception and pregnancy will determine the future emotional well being of the child. Taken one step further, the child is equated to a passive roll of film. The final picture (baby) reflects the initial stimuli of gestation. In much the same way, the final product—the adult—is dependent on the developing process of childhood. This

---

[54] Ibid., p. 11.
[55] Ai Zhu 1935, p. 16.
[56] "Ertong nian de qiwang", loc. cit., p. 1.
[57] Huang Huaixin 黃懷信 . 1935. "Bensuo fuying weisheng gongzuo gailüe" 本所婦嬰衛生工作概略 (Generally speaking about this institution of women's and children's hygiene), *Dazhong weisheng* 1.8 (mislabelled 7), pp. 20–4; 23.
[58] He Xishen 1915, p.1.

metaphor also reveals the increasing reliance on technological language in presenting the rationale behind proper reproduction and child-rearing.

Children are blank paper and undeveloped negatives. While the care-giver, in particular the mother, is granted the responsibility of writing on the paper—or developing the negatives—hygienic texts assert the right of the nation to mandate what type of ink should be used, or what type of developing fluid is needed to create the final, ideal citizen. This view is intrinsically opposed to that of some May Fourth literature, which advocates childhood freedom, child-centered education, and youthful wisdom. On the contrary, this hygienic view asserts the nation-state's interest in children as a resource—a national resource—that must be groomed in certain ways to benefit the public.

CONCLUSION

I have shown how women's wombs were co-opted into the national agenda, through the use of feto-centric texts that described women's weakness, the sacrificial nature of motherhood, and fetal education. Hygienic literature thus functioned as a method of social control, supporting a narrow view of female sexuality and prioritizing the fetus, rather than the individual woman. Women's wombs are configured as breeding grounds for future citizens and the nation-state interest is heavily prioritized. As for children, they were envisioned to be vast resources of national potential, blank paper that needed to be properly filled in order to improve the nation-state. These conclusions lead to a picture of a paternalistic state, guarding its vested interests in future citizens. In this sense, men are part of the state, while women and children are protected by and must serve the state. These ideas are backed by scientific logic and a new reliance on technological vocabulary, which replace former moral discussions of reproduction and child-rearing.

During the Republican decades, many competing discourses struggled with issues of female sexuality and women's roles as mothers and citizens. Hygienic discourse is but one thread of this tapestry. Competing images are shown in many places, including educational discourse, pictorial magazines, film, and literature. Images of the strong "new woman" (*xin nüxing* 新女性) and the decadent "modern girl" (*modeng gu'er* 摩登孤兒) conflict with the eugenic ideal of the reproductive, "flawless" (*jianquan* 健全) woman found in hygienic materials.

Although hygienic discourse represents but one vision of reproduction, this vision of public wombs and public mothers is a link in the evolution of political control over women's bodies in twentieth century China. Put in the perspective of current PRC reproductive policies, hygienic discourse can be identified as one possible starting point for the onset of nation-state interference with women's bodies. The one-child family policy implemented in 1978–9 can be seen as merely one link in a long chain of patriarchal control over motherhood. During the Republican period, the locus of this power over reproduction began to shift away from the family towards the nation.[59] This shift was related to the rise of eugenics and the current view of evolution in China. The rhetorical blurring of the public/ private boundary and the assertion of nation-state supremacy over familial allegiances continued throughout the twentieth century. The implementation of population policies during the 1950s, the destruction of the family bond during the Cultural Revolution in the 1960s–70s, and the strict enforcement of the one-child family policy in the 1980s can all be seen in this light. Republican era hygienic rhetoric drew on the strong discourses of nationalism and racial survival and, in so doing, subordinated the role of the individual woman to the will of the nation-state. Current PRC rhetoric on population continues to invoke a slippage between the ideas of family and nation, woman and country, reproduction of children and production of the people.[60]

---

[59] As Delia David states, "It is the misfortune of women that it is their reproductive power and their bodies which are being fought over in this struggle between the State and the still patriarchal family." Cf. Delia Davin. 1987. "Gender and Population in the People's Republic of China", in: Haleh Afshar (ed.). *Women, State, and Ideology: Studies from Africa and Asia.* Albany: State University of New York Press, p. 126.

[60] For more information about the continuities in the institution of motherhood and reproductive politics in Twentieth century China, see my article "Motherhood, Reproductive Politics, and the Chinese Nation-State", in: Andrea O'Reilly (ed.). *The Legacy of Adrienne Rich's Of Woman Born.* Albany: SUNY Press (forthcoming).

References

Ai Zhu 藹諸 . 1935. "Yuying changshi" 育嬰常識 (Common knowledge about bringing up infants), *Dazhong weisheng* (Mass Hygiene) 1.2, pp. 13–6.

Arendt, Hannah. 1998. *The Human Condition*. Chicago: University of Chicago Press.

Benhabib, Seyla. 1993. "Feminist Theory and Hannah Arendt's Concept of Public Space", *History of the Human Science* 6.2, pp. 97–114.

Bray, Francesca. 1997. *Technology and Gender: Fabrics of Power in Late Imperial China*. Berkeley: University of California Press.

Chen Yaozhiping 陳姚雉屏 . 1916. "Renshen yixitan" 妊娠一夕談 (An evening chat about pregnancy), *Funü zazhi* (The Ladies' Journal) 2.5, pp. 5–11.

Cornue, Virginia. 1999. "Practicing NGOness and Relating Women's Space Publicly: The Women's Hotline and the State", in: Mayfair Mei-hui Yang (ed.). *Spaces of Their Own: Women's Public Sphere in Transnational China*. Minneapolis: University of Minnesota Press, pp. 68–94.

Davin, Delia. 1987. "Gender and Population in the People's Republic of China", in: Haleh Afshar (ed.). *Women, State, and Ideology: Studies from Africa and Asia*. Albany: State University of New York Press, pp. 111–29.

Dikötter, Frank. 1992. *The Discourse of Race in Modern China*. Stanford: Stanford University Press.

——. 1995. *Sex, Culture, and Modernity in China: Medical Science and the Construction of Sexual Identities in the Early Republican Period*. Honolulu: University of Hawaii Press.

——. 1998. *Imperfect Conceptions: Medical Knowledge, Birth Defects and Eugenics in China*. New York: Columbia University Press.

Duden, Barbara. 1991. *The Woman Beneath the Skin: A Doctor's Patients in Eighteenth-Century Germany*. Translated by Thomas Dunlap. Cambridge, Mass.: Harvard University Press.

"Ertong nian de qiwang" 兒童年的期望 (Hopes for children's year). 1935. *Dazhong weisheng* (Mass Hygiene) 1.2, pp. 1–2.

Fan Xuqin 樊須欽 . 1927. "Renshen zhi weisheng" 妊娠之衛生 (The hygiene of pregnancy), *Weishengbao* (Hygiene Journal) 1.13, no pagination.

Fraser, Nancy. 1990. "Rethinking the Public Sphere: A Contribution to the Critique of Actually Existing Democracy", *Social Text* 25/26, pp. 56–80.

——. 1992. "Sex, Lies, and the Public Sphere: Some Reflections on the Confirmation of Clarence Thomas", *Critical Inquiry* 18, pp. 595–612.

Furth, Charlotte. 1986. "Blood, Body and Gender: Medical Images of the Female Condition in China, 1600–1850", *Chinese Science* 7, pp. 43–66.

——. 1999. *A Flourishing Yin: Gender in China's Medical History, 960–1665*. Berkeley: University of California Press.

Habermas, Jürgen. 1989. *The Structural Transformation of the Public Sphere: An Inquiry into a Category of Bourgeois Society*. Translated by Thomas Burger. Cambridge, Mass.: The MIT Press.

He Fei 合肥 . 1916. "Jiashi weisheng" 家事衛生 (The hygiene of household affairs), *Funü zazhi* (The Ladies' Journal) 2.5, pp. 1–5.

He Xishen 何錫琛 . 1915. "Shenxin yu sixu zhi guanxishuo" 身心與飼畜之關系説 (About the relationship between body, mind, and descendent), *Funü zazhi* (The Ladies' Journal) 1.7, pp. 1–4.

Hu Dingan 胡定安 . 1922. "Funüjie de putong bing" 婦女界的普通病 (Common illnesses of the woman's world), *Funü zazhi* (The Ladies' Journal) 8.8, pp. 81–2.

Huang Huaixin 黃懷信 . 1935. "Bensuo fuying weisheng gongzuo gailüe" 本所婦嬰 衛生工作概略 (Generally speaking about this institution of women's and children's hygiene), *Dazhong weisheng* (Mass Hygiene) 1.8 (mislabelled 7), pp. 20–4.

Huang Shi 黃石 . 1931. "Shenmo shi 'taijiao'" 甚麼是胎教 (What is 'fetal education'), *Funü zazhi* (The Ladies' Journal) 17.11, pp. 19–28.

Kinney, Anne Behnke. 1995a. "Dyed Silk: Han Notions of the Moral Development of Children, in: Id. (ed.). *Chinese Views of Childhood*. Honolulu: University of Hawaii Press, pp. 17–56.

——. 1995b. "Introduction", in: Id. (ed.). *Chinese Views of Childhood*. Honolulu: University of Hawaii Press, pp. 1–16.

Kligman, Gail. 1998. *The Politics of Duplicity: Controlling Reproduction in Ceausescu's Romania*. Berkeley: University of California Press.

Leung, Angela Ki Che. 1995. "Relief Institutions for Children in Nineteenth-Century China", in: Anne Behnke Kinney (ed.). *Chinese Views of Childhood*. Honolulu: University of Hawaii Press, pp. 251–78.

Liu Jiushi 劉九始 . 1935. "Tan ertongjie yu ertongde jiankang jiaoyu" 談兒童節與兒 童的健康教育 (Discussing Children's Day and children's health education), *Dazhong weisheng* (Mass Hygiene) 1.4, pp. 10–1.

Pease, Catherine E. 1995. "Remembering the Taste of Melons: Modern Chinese Stories of Childhood", in: Anne Behnke Kinney (ed.). *Chinese Views of Childhood*. Honolulu: University of Hawaii Press, pp. 279–320.

Rogaski, Ruth. 2000. "Hygienic Modernity in Tianjin", in: Joseph W. Esherick (ed.). *Remaking the Chinese City: Modernity and National Identity, 1900–1950*. Honolulu: University of Hawaii Press, pp. 30–46.

Stevens, Sarah E. 2001. "Making Female Sexuality in Republican China: Women's Bodies in the Discourses of Hygiene, Literature and Education". Ph.D. diss. Indiana University.

——. "Motherhood, Reproductive Politics, and the Chinese Nation-State", in: Andrea O'Reilly (ed.). *The Legacy of Adrienne Rich's Of Woman Born*. Albany: SUNY Press. (forthcoming).

Tomes, Nancy. 1990. "The Private Side of Public Health: Sanitary Science, Domestic Hygiene, and the Germ Theory, 1870–1900", *Bulletin of the History of Medicine* 64, pp. 509–39.

Waltner, Ann. 1995. "Infanticide and Dowry in Ming and Early Qing China", in: Anne Behnke Kinney (ed.). *Chinese Views of Childhood*. Honolulu: University of Hawaii Press, pp. 193–218.

Weiss, Sheila Francis. 1987. "The Race Hygiene Movement in Germany", *Osiris* 3 (second series), pp. 193–236.

Wu, Hung. 1995. "Private Love and Public Duty: Images of Children in Early Chinese Art", in: Anne Behnke Kinney (ed.). *Chinese Views of Childhood*. Honolulu: University of Hawaii Press, pp. 79–110.

Wu, Pei-yi. 1995. "Childhood Remembered: Parents and Children in China, 800 to 1700", in: Anne Behnke Kinney (ed.). *Chinese Views of Childhood*. Honolulu: University of Hawaii Press, pp. 129–56.

Xi Shen 西神 . 1916. "Renshen zhong zhi jingshen ganying" 妊娠中之精神感應 (Responses of the psyche during pregnancy), *Funü zazhi* (The Ladies' Journal) 2.10, no pagination.

Y. D., (Li Rongdi 李榮第). 1922. "Funüde jingshen shenghuo" 婦女的精神生活 (The psychological life of women), *Funü zazhi* (The Ladies' Journal) 8.1, pp. 63–9.

Yang, Mayfair Mei-hui. 1999. "Introduction", In: Mayfair Mei-hui Yang (ed.). *Spaces of Their Own: Women's Public Sphere in Transnational China*. Minneapolis: University of Minnesota Press, pp. 1–34.

Yun Qin 韻琴 . 1937. "Renshen zhong de weisheng yu taijiao" 妊娠中的衛生與胎教 (Hygiene during pregnancy and fetal education), *Dongfang zazhi* (Far Eastern Miscellany) 34.7, pp. 257–60.

Zhen He 真和 . 1918. "Yuejingzhi weisheng" 月經之衛生 (Menstrual hygiene), *Funü zazhi* (The Ladies' Journal) 4.12, pp. 4–6.

Zhou Shang 周尚 . 1943. "Weisheng jiaoyu yu guomin jiankang" 衛生教育與國民健康 (Hygiene education and the people's health), *Dongfang zazhi* (Far Eastern Miscellany) 39.19, pp. 34–9.

Zhu Wenyin 朱文印 . 1931. "Taijiao yu youshengxue" 胎教與優生學 (Fetal education and eugenics), *Funü zazhi* (The Ladies' Journal) 17.8, pp. 11–9.

Zhu Xiujuan 朱秀娟 . 1927. "Bianjizhi yan" 編輯之言 (Words from the editor), *Weishengbao* (Hygiene Journal) 1.6, no pagination.

YVONNE SCHULZ ZINDA

PROPAGATING NEW 'VIRTUES' —'PATRIOTISM' IN LATE
QING TEXTBOOKS FOR THE MORAL EDUCATION OF
PRIMARY STUDENTS

INTRODUCTION

The idea of moral training (*xiushen* 修身) in schools was introduced
by way of Japan in the Late Qing period and added to the curriculum
in the plans and regulations for modern schools (*xuetang*學堂) in 1902
and 1904.[1] It was meant to preserve, on the one hand, traditional virtues such as filial piety and fraternal duty (*xiaoti* 孝悌).[2] On the other
hand, in a new international environment of threatening interference
from without—politically as well as in terms of new knowledge and a
growing national consciousness, those values no longer seemed sufficient for the demands of moral education. Western values and ideas
such as the idea of citizenship (*guomin* 國民), patriotism (*aiguo*愛國)
or hygiene (*weisheng* 衛生) were introduced.[3] The examination of
modern textbooks for moral education in the Late Qing period provides a direct way to analyse how these Western-derived values and
ideas, which were controversially discussed among Chinese intellectuals, were first translated into practice. This seems to be even more
intriguing since the establishment of the modern school-system also
marked the beginning of mass education in China. Thus the definition
of those new 'virtues' as a guideline for moral behaviour had far-
reaching political consequences.[4] The ethics textbooks for education

[1] I especially want to thank Joachim Kurtz, Barbara Mittler, and Zhang Baichun
for their remarks on this paper, as well as Natascha Vittinghoff for additional advice.

[2] That connection is suggested in: Paul Bailey. 1990. *Reform the People. Changing Attitudes towards Popular Education in Early Twentieth-Century China*. Edinburgh: Edinburgh University Press, p. 32.

[3] On the reception of the idea of citizenship and patriotism see e.g. Joshua A.
Fogel. 1997. *Imagining the People. Chinese Intellectuals and the Concept of Citizenship*. Armonk, N.Y.: M. E. Sharpe and Jonathan Unger (ed.). 1996. *Chinese Nationalism*. Armonk, N.Y.: M. E. Sharpe; On hygiene see the paper by Sarah E. Stevens.

[4] Bastid describes the two diverging attitudes towards the role of nationalism
ineducation. According to the official view, nationalism was an instrument to restore

at the lower primary level are especially suitable for an investigation, since they had to explain the new 'virtues' in an easily accessible way, suitable for pupils at the age of seven to eleven. They were also the most influential in shaping the way in which those new values were understood among the masses, because most students of poor origin would leave school after the primary level.

Patriotism is a good case in point. Whereas it is sometimes difficult to establish whether ideas or values were influenced by Western thought, with respect to the term patriotism, the reference is quite clear. In addition, patriotism was the general educational aim stated in the regulations in 1904—though not further defined. The case of patriotism shows how the new 'virtues', here in the sense of right conduct, were introduced, and to what extent they were transformed through the interpretative explanations in particular but also in general through the different frameworks of the textbooks.

1. PRELIMINARY CONDITIONS FOR THE COMPILATION OF MODERN ETHICS TEXTBOOKS

As part of the new regulations, only two hours a week were provided for moral training in the curriculum of primary students, as opposed to 12 hours for reading the classics (*dujing* 讀經). In 1904, as stated in the preamble to the regulations for schools of the lower primary level, it was considered important that the students should be made to understand the ethical principles of the patriots. The love of community, meaning the 'people' to whom one belonged, would be the basis of later patriotism. In reading and reciting old songs, the children's character would be formed. In the case of too few instructors or facili-

---

⁴ (*cont.*) stability and to create unity around the emperor, based on the loyalty of his subjects. Thus the emperor, equipped with modern economic and military means, was to remain responsible to his people. According to Bailey, patriotism was equated with the support of the Qing, which did not allow for any political interference by individuals (Bailey 1990, p. 34). In contrast, the reformists, such as Zhang Jian, Luo Zhenyu or Liang Qichao, believed that the idea of nation was formed in response to the danger of interference from the West and national shame arising from previous encounters. Nationalistic education was to make China into a strong nation around the emperor by strengthening the people and giving them the independence to understand and fulfil the needs of their nation (Marianne Bastid. 1971. *Aspects de la Réforme de l'Enseignement en Chine au Début du 20e Siècle. D'après les Ecrits de Zhang Jian.* Paris: Mouton, pp. 58–9).

ties, the moral lessons, which are listed first, can be combined with the reading of the classics. It seems that the moral training was seen within a traditional framework.[5] At the same time, the reading of the classics can be classified as a form of moral education, since traditionally the aim of reading the classics was to instruct children in the proper conduct and the wisdom of *dao* 道 . This shows that state officials put a clear emphasis on moral education in modern schools by stipulating that 14 out of 30 hours a week was to be spent on reading the classics and moral training.

Not only the content of the textbooks and the aim of education seemed to have changed, but the method of instruction was also given special attention. In the regulations relating to the method of education in 1904, it is stated that lessons have to be conducted in an orderly fashion. It points out the importance of explaining the lessons, and in order to make it more accessible for less intelligent pupils the instructor is admonished to combine his explanations with suitable examples from his own experience. It even warns that (traditional) rote memorising is bad for the intellect.[6]

Historically, there were no primers devoted exclusively to the purpose of moral education. In general, primers were designed to teach a combination of literacy and knowledge of words and names, and to provide various historical anecdotes—with a growing emphasis on morality becoming dominant under the Neo-Confucian school of the Song, especially with Zhu Xi 朱熹 (1130–1200). Aside from poetry textbooks, the compilation of Chinese elementary textbooks reached

---

[5] Zouding chudeng xiaoxuetang zhangcheng 1903" 奏定初等小學堂章程 1903 (Regulations for lower primary modern schools 1903), in: Shu Xincheng 舒新城 (ed.). 1985. *Zhongguo jindai jiaoyu ziliao* 中國近代教育資料 (Source material on the history of Chinese education). Beijing: Renmin chubanshe, 1985, vol. 2, pp. 411–27; 411. In the collection by Taga Shūgorō the date is stated as 1904 since it is in the 11th month in the 29th year of reign Guangxu (Taga Shūgorō 多賀秋五郎 (ed.). 1972–1976. *Kindai Chūgoku kyōiku shi shiryō. Shimmatsu hen.* 近代中國教育史資料 清末編 (Source material on the history of education in China. Late Qing). Tokyo: Nihon gaku jitsu shinkōkai, vol. 3, p. 7)

[6] "'Zouding xuetang zhangcheng' guanyu xiaoxuetang xueji bianzhi he jiaoshou fangfa de guiding" ' 奏定學堂章程 ' 關於小學堂學級編制和教授方法的規定 13.1.1904 (The 'regulations for modern schools' in reference to the rules for the organization of class levels and teaching methods), in: Chen Xuexun 陳學恂 (ed.). 1986. *Zhongguo jindai jiaoyushi jiaoxue cankao ziliao* 中國近代教育史教學參考資料 (Reference material on pedagogy and the history of education in China). Beijing: Renmin chubanshe, vol. 1, pp. 665–6.

its peak by the thirteenth century. By Ming times the *Thousand Character Essay* (*Qianzi wen* 千字文), the *Hundred Surnames* (*Baijia xing* 百家姓) and the *Three-Character Classic* (*Sanzi jing* 三字經) were the most widely used textbooks. However, the *Thousand Character Essay*, written around the sixth century, only taught characters, which were arranged in four-character sentences rhymed for reciting with special emphasis on not repeating a single word. The *Hundred Surnames*, compiled in the early Song, contained exclusively the names of the different families in China. The *Three-Character Classic*, a Song primer, was to teach in three-character phrases knowledge of daily life, Chinese history as well as the classics. Putting a greater emphasis on the classics and sharing the Neo-Confucian concern for moral cultivation, the book indicates a shift towards moral education. It also did not disallow the repetition of words. Even though it might have served as a basis for modern ethics primers, it still lacked the didactic traits of modern educational methods.[7]

This shows that there was no strong tradition that could have served as a basis for instruction in a modern school-system and no substantial foundation for the compilation of modern primers, not mention for addressing the new ethical requirements. Most of the Chinese teaching material for modern schools was translated from Japanese. This was especially true in the case of science books, most of which were of Japanese origin.[8] In 1898 the influential educator Luo Zhenyu 羅振玉 (1866–1940), who had begun to train Chinese translators for Japanese in his Japanese Language School (*Dongwen xueshe* 東文學社), recommended adopting the main ideas of Japanese education and even called for the translation of Japanese textbooks. He judged them to be suitable since they were translated from Western books and had already been adapted to the customs of the Japanese. His opinion also reflected the widely accepted idea of a common cul-

---

[7] For an introduction to Chinese elementary textbooks see Thomas H. C. Lee. 2000. *Education in Traditional China. A History*. Leiden: Brill. (Handbook of Oriental Studies, IV China, 13), pp. 435–68. Despite the fact that the *Thousand Character Classic* did not seem didactically effective, not even for teaching Chinese, since it denounced any repetition of words, it was officially chosen by the English government to teach their diplomatic corps. Lobscheid amended it by writing a commentary in modern Chinese (Lee 2000, p. 461). All three textbooks also served as the basis of preparation for exams in traditional schools in the Qing (Bastid 1971, p. 35).

[8] Douglas R. Reynolds. 1993. *China, 1898–1912. The Xinzheng Revolution and Japan*. Cambridge, Mass.: Harvard University Press, p. 117.

ture (*tongwen* 同文) shared by the Japanese and Chinese, held until the fall of the Qing dynasty. In the case of textbooks on history, geography etc., however, Luo wanted them to be amended and adapted to Chinese conditions. Natural sciences or mathematiccs, by contrast, could be taken over in total.[9] Thus, it is of further interest to look at the ethics textbooks, since they can also be listed under the textbooks that had to be asapted to Chinese circumstances.

2. ELEMENTARY ETHICS AND ETHICS PRIMER

The following discussion focuses on the *Zuixin chudeng xiaoxue xiushen jiaokeshu* 最新初等小學修身教科書, translated as *Elementary Ethics*, published in 1906 by the *Shangwu yinshuguan* 商務印書館 (Commercial Press) in Shanghai. The text is of particular interest for two reasons. First, it belonged to a textbook series called *Zuixin chugao xiaoxue jiaokeshu* 最新初高小學教科書, in English translated as the "Commercial Press's New Primary School Text Books", including other subjects such as national studies, geography, history or mathematics[10] for all school levels. The preparations for the series were started around 1902[11] when plans and regulations for the modern school-system were officially issued. It was the first textbook that was

---

⁹ Luo Zhenyu 羅振玉. 1903. "Riben jiaoyu dazhi" 日本教育大旨 (Principles of education in Japan), in: *Xinxue dacongshu* 新學大叢書 (Great compendium to new knowledge). Shanghai: Jishan qiaoji shuju, vol. 81, pp. 14b–17b; 16b–17a.

¹⁰ Jiang Weiqiao 蔣維喬. 1987 [1935]. "Bianji xiaoxue jiaokeshu de huiyi (1897–1905 nian)" 編輯小學教科書的回憶 (1897–1905 年) (Recollections of the compilation of primary textbooks (1897–1905)), in: *Shangwu yinshuguan jiushi nian. Wo he Shangwu yinshuguan* 商務印書館九十年。我和商務印書館 (Ninety years of the Commercial Press. The Commercial Press and I). Beijing: Shangwu yinshuguan, pp. 54–61; 59.

¹¹ Xiong Yuezhi states the first issue to be in 1904 (Xiong Yuezhi 熊月之. 1994. *Xixue dongjian yu wan Qing shehui* 西學東漸與晚清社會 (The dissemination of Western learning and the Late Qing society). Shanghai: Shangwu yinshuguan, p. 667). Jiang Weiqiao also states the beginning of the series to be marked by the first issue of the *Guowen jiaokeshu* 國文教科書 (*National reader*) in 1904 (Jiang Weiqiao 1987, p. 59). Whereas Zhuang Yu identifies 1902 as the beginning of the series (Zhuang Yu 莊俞. 1987. "Tantan wo guan bianji jiaokeshu de bianqian" 談談我館編輯教科書的變遷 (Talking about the evolution in the compilation of textbooks in my publishing house), in: *Shangwu yinshuguan jiushi nian*, pp. 62–72; 68). Given that Zhuang Yu, as well as Jiang Weiqiao, were concerned with the publication of the series at that time and neither of them were mistaken, it might be presumed that the start of the preparation for the series was begun in 1902, and 1904 was the date of the first actual publication.

exclusively written in Chinese[12] according to the new regulations and influenced by Western pedagogical methods, though not directly based on Western textbooks.[13] Second, the "New Textbook" series served as a model for generations of textbooks to follow.[14] The *Elementary Ethics* of that series had at least eleven editions in 1906, the first year of its publication.

In addition, I shall compare the *Elementary Ethics* with the primary textbook *Mengxue xiushen jiaokeshu* 蒙學修身教科書 (hereafter translated as *Ethics Primer*) published by *Wenming shuju* 文明書局 in 1905.[15] another important publishing house for schoolbooks. Before 1904 it had been, alongside the Nanyang College (*Nanyang gongxue* 南洋公學), an influential publisher of textbooks.[16] After the publication of the "New Textbook" series, its influence declined and the Shanghai Commercial Press became the most powerful publishing house for modern schoolbooks in the Late Qing period. By 1906 the Ministry of Education (*Xuebu* 學部), had authorized 102 textbooks

---

[12] Xiong Yuezhi mentions three other modern textbooks written by the Chinese before the plans and issues of regulations for modern schools were issued: the *Liji jiaojing* 利濟教經 (Liji school classic) written by Chen Qiu 陳虬 (1851–1904) for the Liji Medical School (Liji yixuetang 利濟學堂) in 1895, the *Mengxue keben* 蒙學課本 (Primary textbook) published by the Nanyang College (Nanyang gongxue 南洋公學) in 1897 and the *Dushu le* 讀書樂 (Pleasures of studying) edited by Zhong Tianwei 鐘天緯 (1840–1900) in 1898 (Xiong Yuezhi 1994, pp. 664–6).

[13] According to Peake they were influenced through the missionary textbooks (Cyrus H. Peake. 1970. *Nationalism and Education in Modern China*. New York: Howard Fertig, p. 169).

[14] Jiang Weiqiao 1987, p. 56. Only slight amendments were made for the following series *Jianming jiaokeshu* 簡明教科書, partly in response to the new regulation of 1906 which limited the lower primary level to four instead of five years (Jiang Weiqiao 1987, p. 60; Zhuang Yu 1987, pp. 62–3)

[15] Li Jiagu 利嘉鼓 (ed.). 1905. *Mengxue xiushen jiaokeshu* 蒙學修身教科書 (Ethics Primer). Shanghai: Wenming shuju.

[16] Though established comparatively late in 1902, the Wenming Publishing House was leading on the textbook market through publishing the *Mengxue keben* 蒙學課本, one of the earliest and most influential textbooks, originally written by members of the Sandeng Modern School (Sandeng xuetang 三等學堂), including Yu Zhonghuan 俞中環, who had already written a textbook as early as 1898, the *Mengxue duben* 蒙學讀本 (Primary reader). In addition he was even more successful in writing the series *Kexue quanshu* 科學全書 for primary and elementary levels, because they were the products of various extensive research projects into the educational systems abroad, and based on the publisher's own teaching experience (Jiang Weiqiao 1987, pp. 55–6; Wang Jianjun 王建軍. 1996. *Zhongguo jindai jiaokeshu fazhan yanjiu* 中國近代教科書發展研究 (Study on the development of modern textbooks in China). Guangdong: Guangdong jiaoyu chubanshe, pp. 128–9).

for the lower elementary level. Among them, 54 (52,9%) were pub-
lished by the Shanghai Commercial Press and 30 textbooks by the
Wenming Publishing House (29,4%).[17] However, the ethics textbooks
of both publishing houses, the *Elementary Ethics* and the *Ethics
Primer*, were first on the list of primary textbooks authorized by the
Ministry of Education in 1906.[18]

The *Ethics Primer* can be considered a modern textbook, since it
was designed for the prescribed two hours of moral education each
week. It was more in accord with the first draft of school regulations
in 1902, which was based on a three year primary level (*xunchang
xiaoxue* 尋常小學) as opposed to the five year primary (*chudeng
xiaoxue* 初等小學) level which was introduced later.[19] Though the
Commercial Press' textbooks became the most widely read, it is
intriguing to look at the different concepts and materials of these two
major Late Qing publishing houses for designing modern-style moral
textbooks in general, and how they introduced the new Western political virtues in particular. Moreover, the success of the Commercial
Press' textbook series shows that their framework for textbooks was
more popular, which can be considered one reason for the declining
influence of the Wenming Publishing House.

3. COMPILATION AND CONTENTS OF THE ELEMENTARY ETHICS

The *Elementary Ethics* of the "New Textbook" series were edited
solely by Cai Yuanpei 蔡元培 (1868–1940), Gao Fengqian 高鳳謙
(1869–1936) and Zhang Yuanji 張元濟 (1866–1959)—apart from two
Japanese advisors, the education official Ōtani Shigeru 大谷重 (dates
unknown) and the professor Nagao Otarō 長尾槙太郎 (dates
unknown), who helped with the first edition. All three were well-
known figures in the public educational debate at that time. Cai Yuanpei was a member of the prestigious Hanlin Academy, who together

---

[17] Wang Jianjun 1996, p. 129; Wang Zhen 王震 and He Yueming 賀越明 . 1991.
Zhongguo shi da chubanjia 中國十大出版家 (Ten great publishers in China). Taiyuan: Shanxi chubanshe, p. 27. Wang Jianjun refers to elementary textbooks in general. According to Peake, the Commercial Press produced about 60% of modern textbooks on the market in Late Qing (Peake 1970, p. 98). He further states that by 1905
it had published 60 different textbooks in Chinese and 50 other books on education
(Peake 1970, p. 52).
[18] "Shending shumu" 審定書目 (Index to authorized books), *Xuebu guanbao* 3,
October 28, 1906, p. 3.

with a group of educators, including the aforementioned Jiang Weiqiao 蔣維喬 (1873–1958), founded the Chinese Educational Association (*Zhongguo jiaoyuhui* 中國教育會) in Shanghai in 1902. He
taught at the Nanyang College and the Patriotic School for Girls
(*Aiguo nüxuexiao* 愛國女學校) in Shanghai, which he founded with
Zhang Binglin 張炳麟 (1869–1936) and others in 1902. He was
briefly involved with the Shanghai Commercial Press until 1903. Cai
was translator of Japanese works on ethics and was later well-known
as the president of the Beijing University.[20] Gao Fengqian had
received a traditional education and had teaching experience as chief
instructor at the University of Zhejiang. He had been a supervisor of
Chinese students in Japan. His research into the reasons for Japan's
prosperity drew his attention to the role of education, in particular at
the primary school level. Thus he became interested in textbooks for
that level. After his return from Japan he was appointed director of the

---

[19] It is difficult to assess whether the Ethics Primer follows the regulations of
1902 or 1904. Even though it was published after the second set of regulations had
been issued, the textbook reflects a mixture of both regulations. In the regulations
from 1902, the school was divided into *mengxue* 蒙學 (primary level) for 4 years
starting at the age of 6, *xunchang xiaoxue* 尋常小學 (normal primary level) for 3
years and *gaodeng xiaoxue* 高等小學 (higher primary level) for another 3 years.
("Zouding xiaoxuetang zhangcheng 1902" 奏定小學堂章程 1902 (Regulations for
primary modern schools 1902), in: Shu Xincheng 1985, vol. 2, pp. 400–11; 400).
Whereas in the regulations of 1904 the school is divided into *chudeng xiaoxue* 初等小
學 (lower primary level) for 5 years starting at the age of 7 ("Zouding chudeng xiaoxuetang zhangcheng 1903" 奏定初等小學堂章程 1903, p. 412) and *gaodeng xiaoxue*
高等小學 (higher primary level) for 4 years ("Zouding gaodeng xiaoxuetang
zhangcheng 1903" 奏定高等小學堂章程 1903 (Regulations for the higher primary
modern schools 1903), in: Shu Xincheng. 1985, vol. 2, pp. 427–39, p. 429.). The term
mengxue in the title seems to suggest that it adheres to the first set of regulations, but
the book's three year time span is more in accord with *xunchang-* or *gaodeng-*
schools. On the other hand, the introduction and the subtitle "Chudeng xiaoxuetang
xuesheng yongshu" 初等小學堂學生用書 (Textbook for lower primary level stu-
dents) indicate clearly that the book is meant for the lower primary level, as stated in
the second set of regulations, which was then planned for a period of 5 years. It can be
presumed that this book, which was meant for the modern school system, was
planned in advance, shortly after the 1902 regulations were issued. Wang Yangzong
王揚宗 has voiced an equal presumption. However, the *Ethics Primer* was authorized
as a lower primary school book by the Ministry of Education in 1906 (see note 18).

[20] See further Bailey 1990, p. 72; 1997; *Zhongguo jindai xueren xiangzhuan* 中國
近代學人像傳 (Illustrated biographies of Chinese modern scholars). 1992 Yangzhou:
Jiangsu guangling gujie keyinshe, p. 302; *Zhonghua liuxue mingren cidian* 中華留學
名人辭典 (Dictionary of famous Chinese overseas-students). 1992. Changchun:
Dongbei shifan daxue chubanshe, p. 714.

section for national studies at the Shanghai Commercial Press. He is also known as a regular contributor to *Jiaoyu zazhi* 教育雜誌 (The Educational Review) as well as a translator of many Japanese articles on education for the *Jiaoyu shijie* 教育世界 (Educational World).[21] Zhang Yuanji, also member of the Hanlin Academy, established a modern school in 1896, the Tongyi Xuetang 通藝學堂, in Beijing and asked Yan Fu 嚴復 (1835–1921) to participate. Zhang was a teacher of English and mathematics. At that time he had been in contact with the revolutionary Kang Youwei 康有為 (1858–1927).[22] After the closure of the school he worked at the Nanyang College, in the department for translation. In 1902 he became director in the department for translation and compilation at the Commercial Press, and in 1904 he also became chief editor of the journal *Dongfang zazhi* 東方雜誌 (Eastern Miscellany).[23] To sum up, all three authors had teaching experience, had an insight into the requirements of educational institutions as well as educational thought, and they had been in direct or indirect contact with Japan.

The Japanese influence on the compilation of *Elementary Ethics* by the Shanghai Commercial Press was threefold: not only indirectly through the official regulations, which did not differ in the slightest from the principles of the Japanese educational system,[24] but also through the intellectual experience of its authors. Moreover, the Shanghai Commercial Press had had direct connections with Japan since 1903, when it had formed a joint venture agreement with the important publisher Kinkōdō 金港堂 in Tokyo, which also published textbooks. Indeed, the Commercial Press grew from a minor printing house to an influential publishing house through Kinkōdō's financial support.[25] Apart from financial support, there seems to have been a temporary arrangement for the employment of provisional staff from

---

[21] *Zhongguo jindai xueren xiangzhuan*, p. 154.

[22] According to Zhou Wu Zhang had been influenced by the socio-political concepts of Liang Qichao, especially the concept of community (Zhou Wu 周武. 1999. *Zhang Yuanji. Shujuan rensheng* 張元濟。書卷人生. (Zhang Yuanji. A life of books and scrolls). Shanghai: Shanghai jiaoyu chubanshe, pp. 95–6).

[23] Bailey 1990, p. 67 and the biography by Zhou Wu. 1999, pp. 54–63; *Zhongguo jindai xueren xiangzhuan*, p. 212.

[24] Reynolds cites the concurring opinions of a few scholars. such as those by Wolfgang Franke and Abe Hiroshi 阿部洋 (Reynolds 1993, pp. 139–40).

[25] According to Zhou Wu the Shanghai Commercial Press was able to quadruple its capital from 50,000 yuan in 1901 to 200,000 yuan in 1903, and this grew further

Japan. Nagao Ameyama 長尾雨山 (dates unknown), a Japanese professor, was appointed to the new compilation and translation division of the Shanghai Commercial Press.[26] Another source mentions Ōtani Shigeru and Nagao Otarō, who were involved in the compilation of *Elementary Ethics*, and a certain Katō Komaji 加藤駒二 (dates unknown), invited by Zhang Yuanji as advisors to the Commercial Press.[27]

Cai Yuanpei, who remained only until 1903, laid the foundation for the textbooks. Zhang Yuanji, who took over Cai's position, was the main driving force. He laid out his guiding principles for education in "Letter in answer to a friend's question on the matter of schools" (*Da youren wen xuetangshi shu* 答友人問學堂事書), principles that are clearly reflected in the *Elementary Ethics*. Zhang states his preference for mass education over the education of few specialists in order to build up a strong country. He does not agree with the division of Western and traditional studies between different schools, but wants a combination of both:

> I say that when establishing learning today, it has to embrace this meaning, that one has to study in order to become a Chinese instead of becoming a foreigner. However, this does not mean one should adapt Eastern learning as substance, Western learning for application. Our scholars speak of cultivation of the individual self, the establishment of one's family, governing the nation, and unification of the world. On the

---

[25] (*cont.*) to 1,000,000 yuan in 1905. The volume of business grew accordingly from 300,000 yuan in 1903 to 870,000 yuan in 1905 (Zhou Wu 1999, p. 90). Douglas R. Reynolds states that there had been a connection even before 1903. In 1897 the Japanese publishing house Kinkōdō assisted the Commercial Press in the acquisition of printing equipment, and in 1900 with the purchase of the entire stock of a well-equipped Japanese print shop in Shanghai (Reynolds 1993, pp. 121–3; citing also the research of Sanetō Keishū 實藤惠秀 . 1940. "Shoki no Shōmu Inshokan" 初期の商務印書館 (The early years of the Commercial Press), in: Sanetō Keishū 實藤惠秀 . *Nihon bunka no Shina e no eikyō* 日本文化の支那への影響 (Japanese cultural influences on China). Tokyo: Keisetsu shoin, pp. 241–8).

[26] A fact that is not mentioned in the annals of the Commercial Press in 1931, which point to some kind of temporary arrangement with Kinkōdō, including the employment of technical experts and one or two others. Nothing seems to be known about Nagao Ameyama (Reynolds 1993, p. 122). It is also not quite clear whether it is the same Nagao—with a different first name perhaps—who assisted in compiling the *Elementary Ethics*, but it seems probable, since there were not that many Japanese employees. It is also not clear as to what position Nagao Ameyama held. Reynolds states (see above, ibid.) that Nagao was appointed as chief to that division, which contradicts the fact that Zhang Yuanji held the same position.

[27] Zhou Wu. 1999, p. 80.

other hand, is it not that Western scholars talk about *physics and philosophy*? Is it not that the substance is great, I do not dare to say so. My intention is to take all kinds of Western of learning and arrange them in accordance with the characteristics of the people, the customs, the religion and the governmental system of our nation. Getting rid of the stale sayings of narrow-minded scholars in order to renew the spirit of the people of our nation.[28]

Though he renounces the widely circulated idea of *ti-yong* 體用 as "Chinese learning for basic principle, Western learning for practical use" (*zhongxue wei ti, xixue wei yong* 中學為體, 西學為用, it seems very similar. Unfortunately he does not specify any further. In his letter Zhang repeatedly emphasizes China's self-reliance in matters of education. The lessons in school were to be conducted in Chinese by Chinese educators. He advises the compilation of textbooks by Chinese rather than the adoption of foreign books. On the other hand, he warns against an excessive use of the Four Books and the Five Classics, especially for the elementary level, since they are too difficult to understand. Though he concedes that the sayings of Confucius and Mencius might be employed for the high school level, he finds that memorising their contents wastes the intellectual capabilities of young children.[29]

The *Elementary Ethics* consists of ten volumes with 20 lessons, each designed for two hours of moral education a week at the five year primary level.[30] The first of the 11th editions varied very little in content.[31] In the preface, tribute was made to the benefit of a moral education (*deyu* 德育). In contrast to intellectual and physical education (*zhiyu* 智育 / *tiyu* 體育), it is considered as the "root of every-

---

[28] Zhang Yuanji 張元濟. 1903. Da youren wen xuetangshi shu 答友人問學堂事書 (Letter in answer to a friend s question on the matter of schools), in: *Xinxue Dacongshu*, vol. 81, pp. 1a—3a, 1B. See also Chen Jingpan 陳景磐 and Chen Xuexun 陳學恂 (ed.). 1997. *Qingdai houqi jiaoyu lunzhu xuan* 清代後期教育論著選 (Selection of works on education in Late Qing). Beijing: Renmin jiaoyu chubanshe, vol. 3, pp. 413—6, 414.

[29] Ibid.

[30] "*Zouding chudeng xiaoxuetang zhangcheng 1903*". pp. 417–20.

[31] For instance, the heading of the last two lessons in the eighth volume was changed from 'Zeal for Public Welfare' (*jigong* 急公) in lesson 19 to 'Citizen(ship)' (*guomin* 國民), and the 'Duty of the Citizen' (*guomin zhi yiwu* 國民之義務) abbreviated to 'Citizen(ship)' in lesson 20. The changes were made from the first to the second edition.

thing".[32] This was well in accord with the opinions of other contemporaries, such as Yan Fu, and official opinion regarding the importance of moral training.[33] It appears that here also terminologically the Western influenced educational framework of moral education is combined with the content of the traditional concept of *xiushen*, literally the cultivation of oneself. The *Elementary Ethics* can be considered an amalgam of traditional and new western-oriented virtues, in particular political virtues which arose out of a changing international environment and were due to a transformation in the understanding of the notion of nation-state.

Each lesson deals with a different kind of virtue or behaviour. This is then combined with a story about the "wise sayings or brave deeds of the ancient"[34] as well as an illustrative picture. The texts are usu-

---

[32] There are different divisions of education. The encyclopaedic compilation on Western knowledge by Yuan Zonglian 袁宗謙 *Xixue santong* 西學三通 published in 1902 divides education first into *tiyu* 體育 and *xinyu* 心育, education of the body and the mind, which is further divided into *zhiyu* 知育 and *deyu* 德育, intellectual and moral education, (Yuan Zonglian 袁宗謙 and Yan Zhiqing 宴志清 (ed.). 1902. *Xixue santong* 西學三通 (Three investigations in Western learning). Cuixin shuju, vol. 10, p. 4a). In the case of Sparta it refers to the three-fold division of *tiyu - zhiyu - deyu* 體育 - 知育- 德育 (ibid. vol. 22, p. 1a). This seems to be in contrast to Bailey's observation in an article in the journal *Jiaoyu shijie* 教育世界 no. 77 in 1904 (Bailey 1990, p. 76), that Luo Zhenyu introduced the division of education into the three branches based on his understanding of Aristotle. Liang Qichao made a distinction between intellectual and moral education in his *Deyu jian* 德育鑒 (Mirror for moral education) in 1905 (Hao Chang 1971. *Liang Ch'i-ch'ao and the Intellectual Transition in China 1890–1907*. Cambridge, Mass.: Harvard University Press, p. 283).

[33] In his article on elementary textbooks Yan Fu considers moral education more important than intellectual education, which he again regarded as more important than physical education. He identifies the knowledge of physical matters (*qi* 器) as the basis of intellectual education, and the wisdom of the metaphysical basis of *dao* as fundamental to moral education. Yan Fu writes that since "fire-machines" can also be used by morally inferior persons to kill others, but that (morally defined) human relations and the heavenly principle, are the real bases of society. Here he also refers to the Neo-Confucian school of the Song. His article was published by the Commercial Press in the same year 1906 as *Elementary Ethics*, in the *Zhongwai ribao* 中外日報 (Universal Gazette) (Yan Fu 嚴復 1997 [1906]. "Lun jiaoyu yu guojia zhi guanxi" 論教育與國家之關係 (On the relation of education and the state), in: Chen Jingpan and Chen Xuexun 1997, pp. 235–9; 236–7). Contrary to this opinion, in 1904 (see note 29), Luo Zhenyu took a more radical stance that all three branches of education were of equal importance. In another article he states the same opinion. Especially physical education, which had not always received attention, should be promoted, since in times of war a physically weak people will bring great losses upon the state (Luo Zhenyu 1903, p. 17a).

[34] *Elementary Ethics*, vol. 1 (8th ed.), 1a.

ally taken directly from traditional sources,[35] which are mainly historical works such as the *Songshi* 宋史 , the *Shiji* 史記 , the *Zuozhuan* 左傳 or *Lienüzhuan* 列女傳 . Occasionally stories from *Han Feizi* 韓非子 , *Mengzi* 孟子 or from the *Lunyu* 論語 are introduced, as well as traditional moral tales from the *Shishuo xinyu* 世説新語 , *Yanshi jiaxun* 顏氏家訓 or *Kongzi jiayu* 孔子家語 , which formerly served as the basis for general education.

In *Elementary Ethics*, the individual is placed into four different situational contexts: the individual by himself, the individual in connection with the family and familial friends, within society, and in relation to the state. The individual was, for example, urged to be orderly, hygienic and diligent. In the familial sphere one was expected to practice filial piety, worship one's ancestors, or to demonstrate reliability towards one's friends. Within society, social welfare, helping the poor in difficult times, incorruptibility or benevolence to one's subordinates was praised as exemplary conduct. Towards the nation, the duties of the citizen were enumerated, as well as the duty of patriotic behaviour.

In the preface, the authors emphasize that in contrast to tradition, their selected texts and sayings were not meant for memorising and recitation, which they considered to be the best method for allowing texts to sink into oblivion. Instead, the teacher was suppose to explain the meaning of the story and to impress it upon the students by explaining the illustrations and asking comprehensive questions. This method accorded well with the official statement on teaching methods. Another difference when compared to traditional primers, such as the *Thousand Character Essay*, was that the lessons were systematically constructed to gradually build on the knowledge of the student, proceeding from easy parallel sentences to two-page texts by the end of the primary level. The first volume contained only pictures for dis-

---

[35] Only sometimes, for example in the case of the *Zuozhuan* 左傳 or *Zhanguo ce* 戰國策 , were abbreviations made. There is an exception to the traditional Chinese sources in the first volume, which contains only pictures. A reference is made to the Western fables of Aesop's the hare and the turtle (chap. 18) as well as of the egret and the fox (chap. 13). A possible Japanese influence can be inferred, since the fable of the hare and the turtle was given as an example in explaining the method of moral training in an article translated from the Japanese and published in the Makise Goichirō 牧瀬五一郎 et al. (ed.). 1901. *Mengxue congshu erji* 蒙學叢書二集 (Encyclopaedia of pedagogy). Translated by Wang Guowei et al. Shanghai: Jiaoyu jieshe, vol. 3, chap. 4, sec. 3, p. 8a.

cussion, since the students at that level were not yet able to read and write. The first three lectures taught basics, such as how to behave during the lesson and the break, and how to enter and leave the school.

But not only students were prompted to exemplary conduct, the teachers were also required to adopt conducts different from the traditional roles of the stern, dreaded personage. As stated in the teacher's manual, "The teacher's faces should be composed and their voices mild in order not to frighten the students."[36] Since many teachers were not accustomed to the new ways of teaching, the textbooks were each accompanied by a teacher's manual, *Zuixin chudeng xiaoxue xiushen jiaokeshu jiaoshoufa* 最新初等小學修身教科書教授法 (*The Methods for Teaching Elementary Ethics*). Each lesson was explained in four steps: the aim of the lesson (*benke yaozhi* 本科要旨); the text of the lesson as given to the students (*jiaokeshu benwen* 教科書本文); the proceedings for conducting the lesson (*jiaoshou cixu* 教授次序)— usually by summarising the text, providing the historical context of the story, or in some cases the two stories, and matching them with the kind of conduct or virtue introduced in that lesson; at the end, the teacher was to ask the students comprehensive questions for exercise (*xiwen* 習問). These did not refer exclusively to a particular story, but rather to universal truths and practical lessons which could be derived from the text. Sometimes attention was drawn to one last point of significance (*zhuyi* 注意). The procedure was very similar to what the Ministry of Education advised for the reading of the classics in the regulations for elementary education: the guiding principle of the lesson was to be provided, the meaning explained, and the content transferred into the context of practical life.[37]

This arrangement is similar to many Japanese elementary textbooks of ethics.[38] There are also textbooks that are accompanied by a handbook for the teacher which mentions similar points to assist the instructor, such as the aim of the lesson, comprehensive questions, and points of attention. The Kinkōdō publishing house compiled ethics textbooks such as the *Jinjō shōgaku jissen shūshin kyōkasho nyū-*

---

[36] *The Methods for Teaching Elementary Ethics*, vol. 1, 2a.

[37] "Zouding chudeng xiaoxuetang zhangcheng (1903)", pp. 414–5.

[38] I am especially grateful to Shen Guowei 沈國威 and Uchida Keiichi 內田慶一 for giving me access to the library of the Kansai University, where I found the following six different Japanese ethics textbooks: 1) Higashikuze Michitomi 東久世通

mon 尋常小學實踐修身教科書入門 (A practical introductory ethics textbook for primary schools), first published in 1892, and the *Jinjō shūshin kyōkasho nyūmon* 尋常修身教科書入門 (an introductory ethics textbook for primary schools), published from around 1901 in various editions. Similar to the *Elementary Ethics*, the first thirty lessons of the *Introductory Ethics Textbook for Primary Schools* are exclusively comprised of pictures. It also contains Aesop's story of the turtle and the hare in the second volume. But it is interesting to note that the *Elementary Ethics* lacks any reference to everyday life, apart from the few school scenes found in the first chapters. By contrast, in various Japanese ethics textbooks one finds not only traditional stories, but also a variety of stories on everyday life,[39] sometimes of the life of modern Japanese soldiers,[40] the encounter with Westerners[41] or even stories about famous Western persons.[42]

---

[38] (*cont.*) (ed.). 1893 [1892[1]]. *Jinjō shōgaku shūshinsho* 尋常小學修身書 (Ethics textbook for primary schools). Revised by Soejima Taneomi 副島種臣. Tokyo: Kokukōsha, vol. 1; 2) *Shūshinkei. Jinjōka. Kyōshi yō* 修身經. 尋常課. 教師用 (Ethics classic. Primary level. For the teacher's use) 1900. Tokyo: Toyamabō, vol. 9; 3) Monbushō 文部省. 1907. *Jinjō shōgaku shūshinsho. Daiichi gakunen, kyōshi yō*. 尋常小學修身書第一學年. 教師用 (Ethics textbook for first year primary schools. For the teacher's use) 1905 repr. [1872]. Tokyo: Ōzorasha, vol. 1; 4) *Jinjō shōgaku shūshinsho. Kyōshi yō* 尋常小學修身書. 教師用 (Ethics textbook for primary schools. For the teacher's use). 1893 rev. [1892]. Tokyo: Shinshōin, vols. 2, 4; 4a) *Jinjō shōgaku shūshinsho. Seito yō* 尋常小學修身書. 生徒用 (Ethics textbook for primary school. For the student's use) 1893 rev. [1892]. Tokyo: Shinshōin, vol. 7; 5) Higuchi Kanjiro 樋口勘次郎 and Noda Tatsusaburō 野田龍三郎. 1901. *Jinjō shūshin kyōkasho nyūmon* 尋常修身教科書入門 (Introductory ethics textbook for primary schools). Tokyo: Kinkōdō, vols. 1–3 (for the student's use); 6) Takada Yoshitarō 高田芳太郎. 1893 [1892]. *Jinjō shōgaku jissen shūshinsho nyūmon. Kyōshi yō*. 尋常小學實踐修身書入門. 教師用 (Practical introductory ethics textbook for primary schools. For the teacher's use). Revised by Maruo Nishiki 丸尾錦. Tokyo: Kinkōdō, vols. 1–2. Since the collection is not complete, the textbooks cannot be taken as representative. The following merely serves as an overview of the possibilities and alternatives in writing ethics textbooks in Japan that might have served as a basis for Chinese textbooks. However, none of the Japanese textbooks mentioned here served as a model for the *Ethics Primer*.

[39] See ibid. 1), 3), 4a), 5)

[40] See ibid. 1)

[41] See ibid. 4a) and 3).

[42] For instance, Bach or Columbus. See ibid. 3).

4. COMPILATION AND CONTENT OF THE ETHICS PRIMER

The *Ethics Primer* was written by Li Jiagu 李嘉鼓, of whom little is known. Its compilation is related to the Jiangsu Wuxi Sandeng Modern School (*Jiangsu Wuxi Sandeng xuetang* 江蘇無錫三等學堂), at which the founders of the Wenming Publishing House Yu Zhonghuan 俞中環 (dates unknown), Lian Nanhu 廉南湖 (1868–1932) and Ding Yi-xuan 丁藝軒 (1865/1866–1935/1936) among others were instructors. The Sandeng Modern School was a school that experimented with new educational models, especially at the elementary level. This was partly the reason for the success of the earlier *Mengxue keben* 蒙學課本 (primary textbook, 1902), written by Yu Zhonghuan, Ding Yixuan and others.[43]

The author of the *Ethics Primer* seems to have had a more modern notion of moral training. Apart from the universal content of the lessons, the author places moral training in a scientific framework, describing it in the introduction as a most profound and extensive science. In lesson 51, under the heading of freedom, moral training is defined as self-government (*zizhi* 自治). It is considered to be basis of freedom, since it gives the subject autonomy.[44] In lesson 117 the result of education itself is explained as the progress of civilization, into which the East and the West are equally included.

With 38 double-pages, it is far shorter than the *Elementary Ethics* even though it was created for a mere three year lower elementary level. In the preface, this feature is further explained. The lessons are composed of texts for reading and are kept short, since it was important to maintain the interest of the students, who at this age had not been exposed to a wide knowledge of the written word. It was decided that long-winded stories would have bored them.

The *Ethics Primer* contains 120 lessons. One lesson is meant for each week. The textbook is divided into four large chapters which are in turn subdivided into sections comprised of usually two to five lessons, but sometimes even 12 lessons, as in the case of hygiene. The first chapter is the largest, entitled 'Cultivating one's personality' (*xiuji* 修己), and contains 51 lessons divided into sections such as

---

[43] Wang Jianjun 1996, p. 128.
[44] This is very similar to Liang Qichao's notion of citizenship. He explains it as Western individual freedom, exemplifying self-mastery or character discipline (Hao Chang. 1971, pp. 218–9).

'Courage' (*yonggan* 勇敢), 'Knowledge of Shame' (*zhichi* 知恥), or 'Virtue' (*daode* 道德). It also groups four lessons under the heading of 'Study' (*qiuxue* 求學). In the last lesson the author reasons quite rationally with the children and admonishes them to study hard, since their parents have to pay for their tuition (lesson 8). The second chapter 'Taking Care of Oneself' (*baoshen* 保身) is comprised of 22 lessons, in which the majority are devoted to mental and bodily hygiene. The attitude towards others (*dairen* 待人) is the topic of the following 23 lessons of chapter 3, and deals both generally and in greater detail with different aspects of human relationships. The last chapter on 'Being in the World' (*chushi* 處世) steps out of the familiar and intimate realm into the political environment and explains such subjects as 'Abiding by the Law' (*shoufa* 守法), 'Property' (*caichan* 財產) or 'Paying Taxes' (*nashui* 納稅).

The lessons are easier to read than the long texts of the *Elementary Ethics* taken from the classics, since each text consists of one-and-a-half to two-and-a-half lines of text. Contrary to the *Elementary Ethics* they do not tell any stories, let alone Chinese traditional stories. They contain no pictures to illustrate the virtue explained. There are no connections drawn to Chinese history, neither to historical persons, nor to heroes. Even traditional connotations to virtues like piety, which does not form a heading itself but is treated in three different lessons (73–75) under the neutral heading of 'parents' (*fumu* 父母), is not placed in a traditional Confucian context. Instead, the author tries to reason with the children why, for example, the duty to love one's parents is obvious—the parents give birth to the children and educate them; and how it can be fulfilled—for example, through making a name. The texts can rather be considered as abstract imperatives of what one has to do or how one should behave, which is in each case explained by way of common sense. They consist mostly of short sentences in which a part is underlined in order to emphasize its meaning. At times they already refer to the answers of the questions asked. Since the texts were written especially for the ethics textbook, the virtue discussed in a particular section is often repeated in the text of the first lesson under that heading, in contrast to the texts under the headings of the *Elementary Ethics*. Due to the brevity of the texts, new terms of Western influence are not always very well explained. For example, lesson 115 of the last chapter merely states that there is no nation without politics; or lesson 108 talks about law as the basis of the state, and the necessity of establishing a state, with a constitution, the last a rather complicated Western term for that time that cannot be considered to have been common knowledge.

The *Ethics Primer* also lacks an additional book instructing the teacher in the modern methods of education. At the end of each text, the book gives one sentence of explanation on the guiding principle of the lesson and two questions which the teacher was suppose to ask the students. As explained in the introduction, the aim of the questions is twofold: to exercise the Chinese words through written answers and to inspire the process of thinking through oral examination. The task of answering the questions, however, does not seem very challenging, since they only require reproducing the sentences in the text and are therefore not comprehensive questions. Hence, although teachers are required to make the content of the lessons more accessible to the students by analysing meanings, drawing analogies to or giving examples taken from everyday life, these books do not give as much assistance as the Commercial Press' textbook.

The *Ethics Primer* takes a more universal point of view, since the texts are mostly abstract formulas with an explanation and an imperative which can be applied universally—and, in the case of education, the West is explicitly included. At times there seems to be an amalgam of Western and traditional Chinese ideas. So for example the traditional Chinese term *li* 理 (principle) can be found, e.g. to describe a government that is not in accord with the 'universal principle' (*gongli* 公理), as in lesson 118, or to argue with others according to the principle, as in lesson 26. But on the whole, the book takes a modern outlook and seems to have been in accord with the intellectual currents of the time: The *Ethics Primer* contains two lessons on the notion of public virtue (*gongde* 公德), lessons 20 and 21; it is more concerned with everyday problems than the *Elementary Ethics*, e.g. it treats the problems of alcoholism (lesson 43) and the smoking of opium (lesson 44/45); it admonishes students not to spit or to throw up as one pleases (lesson 62) and gives practical advice, such as to get up early (lesson 60) or to take part in physical exercise (lesson 59).

5. PATRIOTISM AS A NEW POLITICAL VIRTUE

In the *Elementary Ethics*, patriotism was particularly stressed. Patriotic behaviour was treated in four lessons, once as early as volume four (4.20), after two years of schooling, twice in volume 7 in successive lessons (7.19 / 7.20), and again in volume 10 (10.1). In the *Ethics Primer* just the last two chapters are devoted to patriotism.

In the *Elementary Ethics* all virtues, including patriotism, are placed within the familiar realm of Chinese thought and ways of understanding. In the first two cases encountered patriotism is indirectly connected to traditional well-known virtuous conduct. In the first example, in volume 4, the story taken from the *Zuozhuan* is told about Shen Baoxu 申包胥 , who comes to Qin 秦 to ask for assistance after Wu 吳 has invaded his country Chu 楚 .[45] When Qin invites him to stay with his family while they decide upon a plan, Shen starts to cry and refuses the offer. He does not eat and sleep for several days since he cannot bear to live in comfort knowing that his prince has to live uncomfortably in exile. Thereupon the ruler of Qin is deeply moved and sends out his troops to immediately drive Wu out of Chu. The story in itself seems to deal exclusively with the loyalty of a subject to his prince, rather than the exemplary behaviour of a citizen towards his country, as implied in the guiding principles of the teacher's manual.

In the second example (7.19), patriotism is also connotated with the traditional value of filial piety. It tells the story of Confucius, taken from *Kongzi jiayu*,[46] and Mozi, taken from the *Mozi*,[47] who are deeply disturbed when they hear that their countries are under siege by another state. Confucius sends out his disciple and Mozi personally tries to offset the invasions with intellectual wit and reasoning. In the teacher's manual, it is stressed that their love for their parents drives Confucius and Mozi to such 'patriotic behaviour', considered here to be the first duty of a citizen.

In the following lesson (7.20), the individual is bound more firmly to the state, in the story of Lord Jing Guo 靖郭 , taken from the *Zhanguo ce*. A Lord wants to separate his fief Xue 薛 from the state Qi 齊 ,which had granted him the fief by building a wall around it. The Lord is reminded by a simple man that the well-being of his small fief is directly connected to Qi.[48] The second story, taken from the *Shiji*, is similar. It tells of a nobleman of Wei 魏 staying in Zhao 趙

---

[45] *Chunqiu zuozhuan zhengyi* 春秋左傳正義 , *Ding gong* 4.
[46] *Kongzi jiayu* 孔子家語 , *juan* 8.
[47] *Mozi* 墨子 , *bian* 50.
[48] *Zhanguo ce* 戰國策 , *juan* 8, 1b–2a.

who refuses to come to the rescue of his country when it is attacked
by Qin 秦 . Two other noblemen explain to him that his personal fate
is connected with that of own his country Wei, and that he will be
without personal or family support when the temples of his ancestors
are destroyed by Qin. Thereupon he sets out to defend his country.[49]
Hence, the patriotism in the lesson is presented twofold: on a practical
level the behaviour of the subject, a simple man, is praised for demonstrating his courage to speak up against a superior; and the two noblemen are praised for their insight. Moreover, here is characterised as
the proper patriotic attitude of a subject towards his state. Whereas in
the previous lesson the love for one's country is instilled through the
love of one's parents, now it is the result of considering one's personal fate and well-being as directly tied to the well-being of the state.
The teacher's manual stresses in particular that the duty and love to
one's country is to be placed first, or is, rather, a natural condition for
personal and family gain.

Once the relation between the individual and the state has been
established, in the guidelines of the first lesson to volume 10, the
authors proceed to emphasize patriotism as the responsibility of each
individual and each class towards the state, including peasants and
noblemen. The story from the *Zuozhuan* depicts a businessman from
Zheng 鄭 , who on the spur of the moment cunningly deceives Qin on
his way to invade Zheng. He pretends that his superior has sent him to
receive the troops of Qin and offer them presents. Thus the ruler of
Qin, fearing that Zheng has already made preparations against the
invasion, refrains from attacking it.[50] In the second section the hermit
scholar Wang Shu 王蜀 , who had retired from politics due to a disa-
greement with his ruler, refuses to become a general for a usurper
such as Yan 燕 who has just invaded his country. In the end he com-
mits suicide rather than cooperate with Yan and destroy his country.[51]

In the *Ethics Primer* the last two lessons are devoted to patriotism.
The first text states the interdependence of the state and its people:

> The state is established through its people and the people exist because
> of the state. I am born in China. I should consider it my duty to love
> China. If making concerted efforts, placing the public before the indi-

---

[49] *Shiji* 史記 , *juan* 44.
[50] *Chunqiu zuozhuan zhengyi, Xi gong*, 33.
[51] *Shiji, juan* 82.

vidual [interest], the state will be prosperous and strong and it can be established and upheld.[52]

Only with unified spirit and joint force can the prosperity of one's own country be achieved. The aim of lesson 119 is stated as the explanation of patriotism. The guiding principle is similar to that of lesson 7.20 in the *Elementary Ethics*; however, the difference in the ways of introduction are striking. In the *Elementary Ethics* patriotism is introduced through the individual stories of Lord Jin Guo or the nobleman of Zhao, and explained by way of the personal and familiar experiences of these individuals. By contrast the *Ethics Primer* presents only the bare universal truth, employing abstract terms such as the people and the state. It thus lays greater emphasis on the autonomy of the individual.

Lesson 120 in the *Ethics Primer* shows how to preserve one's country. Again, it shows the interdependence between the abstract political entity of the state and the individual. It states that in peaceful times the state seeks to protect all matters and business of the general public. It prevents the taking of their rights and privileges through force by outsiders. It continues that in times of difficulty, the individual has to relinquish his own gains and be willing to make a sacrifice to rescue the country from great peril and decline. The text closes with the statement that if everybody were to take that attitude the state would exist forever. Again, the simplicity of the text in contrast to the story of the noble Wang Shu is remarkable.

The universality of the two lessons in the *Ethics Primer*, where the homeland, China, is not mentioned, is striking. It does not mention the presence of a Chinese Emperor, who might represent the government, or the duty of loyalty to an imperial court. The Chinese political identity of the individual seems to be solely related to the political entity of China, which has to be protected in order to survive as an individual. The individual has to subordinate his or her own interest for the benefit of the common interest, since s/he exists in the political entity of the state that protects him/her rights and guarantees prosperity.

The idea of patriotism in the West after the French Revolution is a combination of three elements that seem to be almost absent in the stories and explanations of the lessons of the *Elementary Ethics*.[53] First, it is connected with the idea of nationalism, by which an indi-

---

[52] *Ethics Primer*, 38a.

vidual identifies himself with a political entity such as the state or a group. The stories told in the *Elementary Ethics* take place in ancient times and although they deal with the affiliation of an individual to a state, apart from a few remarks in the teacher's manual, there is almost no reference drawn to the West, which posed a threat to China at that time. The nation might be defined as the country of one's parents and ancestors, but it remains somewhat remote from the conditions of the new international environment, and cannot yet be seen as a political entity. On the other hand, the *Ethics Primer* outlines the interdependence of state and individual through universal definitions, without further delving into the particular circumstances of China. Especially in the context of the second text it does not explain who the responsible persons in the state are, for example, the Chinese Emperor and his administration, who protect the rights and privileges of the public.

Secondly, in Western thought patriotism is defined as a political virtue, since the individual will always try to act for the common good of the political entity. In the first story of the *Elementary Ethics*, it is merely a case of loyalty to the prince. The other stories seem to give a pragmatic view, according to which the individual acts 'patriotically' because he feels his personal fate is firmly tied to the state; he does not act out of some selfless devotion for an abstract common good to the political entity he belongs. However, the lessons in the *Ethics Primer* come closer to this aspect of patriotism. Especially in the first text, the individual acts for the general interest and the prosperity of the state.

This leads to a third point, namely heroism, by which the individual is supposed to sacrifice himself, even to the extent of giving his life for the common good of the political entity. Apart from the retired scholar official who gives his life in order to prevent the invasion of his country, the other patriotic individuals in the stories of the *Elementary Ethics* do not risk their lives, but instead employ personal wit and strategy to attain their aims. In spite of the suicide of Wang Shu, his sacrifice might be classified as a noble rather than a heroic deed, since he lived as a hermit no longer taking part in or belonging to the

---

[53] 'Patriotismus' as defined in: *Historisches Wörterbuch der Philosophie*. 1989. Basel, Stuttgart: Schwabe, 1989, vol. 7, pp. 207–17 and *Wörterbuch der Philosophischen Begriffe*. 1998. Hamburg: Meiner, p. 486.

political entity. What is surprising is that the authors did not choose other more suitable stories of heroism. By contrast, the *Ethics Primer* in the second text clearly calls for a personal sacrifice to the state.

CONCLUSION

On the whole, apart from the first story, the individuals in the stories in the *Elementary Ethics* are portrayed as acting independently and responsibly. This reflected the attitudes of the intellectuals at that time, especially modern educators such as Zhang Jian, Luo Zhenyu or Liang Qichao. In the *Ethics Primer* the independence and sense of responsibility of politically mature citizens is stressed even further. This was in opposition to the Qing court, which wanted to maintain a monopoly over political responsibility and for which the independent individual posed a threat. Concerned primarily with maintaining its sovereignty, the Qing court tied the notion of patriotism strictly to the notion of loyalty to the sovereign.

In this period, the reception of Western ideas is no longer a question of understanding or misunderstanding: the definitions and introduction of some Western ethical ideas into China, especially political virtues, should be considered a political issue. The selection of the stories for the *Elementary Ethics* shows a deliberate attempt to connotate some Western ideas, such as patriotism, with a slightly different meaning in order to serve the political purpose of educational reformers, while simultaneously keeping them within tolerable bounds, given the Qing court's intentions and wishes.[54] In addition, the employment of traditional stories for the introduction of virtuous behaviour reflects Zhang Yuanji's emphasis on the folk spirit in conjunction with Western inspired ideas. This conformed to his idea of using Western notions, e.g. patriotism, in combination with traditional stories, with the effect that Western virtues become part of China's own tradition.

---

[54] In a Japanese text translated into Chinese, moral science had also a clear political implication and was seen as the basis for the education on citizenship, as well as for virtuous behaviour in general (Makise Goichirō 1901, vol. 3, chap. 4, sec. 1, p. 7a).

REFERENCES

Bailey, Paul. 1990. *Reform the People. Changing Attitudes towards Popular Education in Early Twentieth-Century China*. Edinburgh: Edinburgh University Press.

Bastid, Marianne. 1971. *Aspects de la Réforme de l'Enseignement en Chine au Début du 20e Siècle. D'après les Ecrits de Zhang Jian*. Paris: Mouton.

Monbushō 文部省. 1907. *Jinjō shōgaku shūshinsho. Daiichi gakunen, kyōshi yō* 尋常小學修身書第一學年. 教師用 (Ethics textbook for first year primary school. For the teacher's use) 1905 repr. [1872]. Tokyo: Ōzorasha, vol. 1.

Chen Jingpan 陳景磐 and Chen Xuexun 陳學恂 (ed.). 1997. *Qingdai houqi jiaoyu lunzhu xuan* 清代後期教育論著選 (Selection of works on education in Late Qing). 3 vols. Beijing: Renmin jiaoyu chubanshe.

Chen Xuexun 陳學恂 (ed.). 1986. *Zhongguo jindai jiaoyushi jiaoxue cankao ziliao* 中國近代教育史教學參考資料 (Reference material on pedagogy and the history of education in China). 3 vols. Beijing: Renmin chubanshe.

Chunqiu zuozhuan zhengyi 春秋左傳正義, in: 1966–1975 [1935]. *Sibu beiyao* 四部備要 ed.

Hao Chang. 1971. *Liang Ch'i-ch'ao and the Intellectual Transition in China 1890–1907*. Cambridge, Mass.: Harvard University Press.

Higashikuze Michitomi 東久世通禧 (ed.). 1893 [1892¹]. *Jinjō shōgaku shūshinsho* 尋常小學修身書 (Ethics textbook for primary schools). Revised by Soejima Taneomi 副島種臣. Tokyo: Kokukōsha.

Higuchi Kanjiro 樋口勘次郎 and Noda Tatsusaburō 野田龍三郎. 1901. *Jinjō shūshin kyōkasho nyūmon* 尋常修身教科書入門 (Introductory ethics textbook for primary schools). 3 vols. Tokyo: Kinkōdō.

Historisches Wörterbuch der Philosophie. 1989. Basel, Stuttgart: Schwabe, vol. 1.

Jiang Weiqiao 蔣維喬. 1987 [1935]. "Bianji xiaoxue jiaokeshu de huiyi (1897–1905 nian)" 編輯小學教科書的回憶 (1897–1905年) (Recollections of the compilation of primary textbooks (1897–1905)), in: *Shangwu yinshuguan jiushi nian. Wo he Shangwu yinshuguan* 商務印書館九十年. 我和商務印書館 (Ninety years of the Commercial Press. The Commercial Press and I). Beijing: Shangwu yinshuguan, pp. 54–61.

Jinjō shōgaku shūshinsho. Kyōshi yō 尋常小學修身書. 教師用 (Ethics textbook for primary schools. For the teacher's use). 1893 rev. [1892]. Tokyo: Shinshōin, vols. 2, 4.

Jinjō shōgaku shūshinsho. Seito yō 尋常小學修身書. 生徒用 (Ethics textbook for primary school. For the student's use) 1893 rev. [1892]. Tokyo: Shinshōin, vol. 7.

Kongzi jiayu 孔子家語, in: 1966—1975[1935]. *Sibu beiyao* 四部備要 ed

Lee, Thomas H. C. 2000. *Education in Traditional China. A History*. Leiden: Brill. (Handbook of Oriental Studies, IV China, 13).

Li Jiagu 利嘉鼓 (ed.). 1905. *Mengxue xiushen jiaokeshu* 蒙學修身教科書 (Ethics Primer). Shanghai: Wenming shuju.

Luo Zhenyu 羅振玉. 1903. "Riben jiaoyu dazhi" 日本教育大旨 (Principles of education in Japan), in: *Xinxue dacongshu* 新學大叢書 (Great compendium to new knowledge). Shanghai: Jishan qiaoji shuju, vol. 81, pp. 14b–17b; 16b–17a.

Makise Goichirō 牧瀬五一郎 et al. (ed.). 1901. *Mengxue congshu erji* 蒙學叢書二集 (Encyclopaedia of pedagogy). Translated by Wang Guowei et al. Shanghai: Jiaoyu jieshe.

Mozi 墨子, in: 1966—1975[1935]. *Sibu beiyao* 四部備要 ed.

Peake, Cyrus H. 1970. *Nationalism and Education in Modern China*. New York: Howard.

Reynolds, Douglas R. 1993. *China, 1898–1912. The Xinzheng Revolution and Japan*. Cambridge, Mass.: Harvard University Press.

Sanetō Keishū 實藤惠秀. 1940. "Shoki no Shōmu Inshokan" 初期の商務印書館 (The early years of the Commercial Press), in: Sanetō Keishū 實藤惠秀. *Nippon bunka no Shina e no eikyō* 日本文化の支那への影響 (Japanese cultural influences on China). Tokyo: Keisetsu shoin.

Shangwu yinshuguan jiushi nian. Wo he Shangwu yinshuguan 商務印書館九十年. 我和商務印書館 (Ninety years of the Commercial Press. The Commercial Press and I). 1987. Beijing: Shangwu yinshuguan.

"Shending shumu" 審定書目 (Index to authorized books), *Xuebu guanbao* 3, October 28, 1906, p. 3.–

Shiji 史記, in: 1966—1975[1935]. *Sibu beiyao* 四部備要 ed.

Shu Xincheng 舒新城 (ed.). 1985. *Zhongguo jindai jiaoyu ziliao* 中國近代教育資料 (Source material on the history of Chinese education). 3 vols. Beijing: Renmin chubanshe.

Shūshinkei. Jinjōka. Kyōshi yō 修身經. 尋常課. 教師用 (Ethics classic. Primary level. For the teacher's use). 1900. Tokyo: Toyamabō, vol. 9.

Taga Shūgorō 多賀秋五郎 (ed.). 1972–1976. *Kindai Chūgoku kyōiku shi shiryō. Shimmatsu hen*. 近代中國教育史資料. 清末編 (Source material on the history of education in China. Late Qing). 3 vols. Tokyo: Nihon gaku jitsu shinkōkai.

Takada Yoshitarō 高田芳太郎. 1893 [1892]. *Jinjō shōgaku jissen shūshinsho nyūmon. Kyōshi yō*. 尋常小學實踐修身書入門. 教師用 (Practical introductory ethics textbook for primary schools. For the teacher's use). Revised by Maruo Nishiki 丸尾錦. Tokyo: Kinkōdō. vols. 1–2.

Wang Jianjun 王建軍 1996. *Zhongguo jindai jiaokeshu fazhan yanjiu* 中國近代教科書發展研究 (Study on the development of modern textbooks in China). Guangdong: Guangdong jiaoyu chubanshe.

Wang Zhen 王震 and He Yueming 賀越明. 1991. *Zhongguo shi da chubanjia* 中國十大出版家 (Ten great publishers in China). Taiyuan: Shanxi chubanshe.

Wörterbuch der philosophischen Begriffe. 1998. Hamburg: Meiner.

Xinxue Dacongshu 新學大叢書 (Great compendium to new knowledge). Shanghai: Jishan qiaoji shuju.

Xixue dongjian yu wan Qing shehui 西學東漸與晚清社會 (The dissemination of Western learning and the Late Qing society). Shanghai: Shangwu yinshuguan.

Yan Fu 嚴復. 1997 [1906]. "Lun jiaoyu yu guojia zhi guanxi" 論教育與國家之關係 (On the relation of education and the state), in: Chen Jingpan 陳景磐 and Chen Xuexun 陳學恂 (ed.). 1997. *Qingdai houqi jiaoyu lunzhu xuan* 清代後期教育論著選 (Selection of works on education in Late Qing). Beijing: Renmin jiaoyu chubanshe. vol. 3. pp. 235–9.

Yuan Zonglian 袁宗謙 and Yan Zhiqing 宴志清 (ed.). 1902. *Xixue santong* 西學三通 (Three investigations in Western learning). Cuixin shuju.

Zhang Yuanji 張元濟. 1903. Da youren wen xuetangshi shu 答友人問學堂事書 (Letter in answer to a friend s question on the matter of schools), in: *Xinxue Dacongshu*, vol. 81, pp. 1a—3a.

—— et al. 1906a. *Zuixin chudeng xiaoxue xiushen jiaokeshu* 最新初等小學修身教科書 (*Elementary Ethics*). 10 vols. Shanghai: Shangwu yinshuguan.

—— et al. 1906b. *Zuixin chudeng xiaoxue xiushen jiaokeshu jiaoshoufa* 最新初等小學修身教科書教授法 (*The Methods for Teaching Elementary Ethics*). 10 vols. Shanghai: Shangwu yinshuguan.

Zhanguo ce 戰國策 , in: 1966–1975 [1935]. *Sibu beiyao* 四部備要 ed.

Zhonghua liuxue mingren cidian 中華留學名人辭典 (Dictionary of famous Chinese overseas-students). 1992. Changchun: Dongbei shifan daxue chubanshe.

Zhongguo jindai xueren xiangzhuan 中國近代學人像傳 (Illustrated biographies of Chinese modern scholars). 1992. Yangzhou: Jiangsu guangling gujie keyinshe.

Zhou Wu 周武 . 1999. *Zhang Yuanji. Shujuan rensheng* 張元濟 . 書卷人生 (Zhang Yuanji. A life of books and scrolls). Shanghai: Shanghai jiaoyu chubanshe.

Zhuang Yu 莊俞 . 1987. "Tantan wo guan bianji jiaokeshu de bianqian" 談談我館編輯教科書的變遷 (Talking about the evolution in the compilation of textbooks in my publishing house), in: *Shangwu yinshuguan jiushi nian. Wo he Shangwu yinshuguan* 商務印書館九十年 . 我和商務印書館 (Ninety years of the Commercial Press. The Commercial Press and I). 1987. Beijing: Shangwu yinshuguan. pp. 62–72.

"Zouding chudeng xiaoxuetang zhangcheng 1903" 奏定初等小學堂章程 1903 (Regulations for lower primary modern schools 1903), in: Shu Xincheng 舒新城(ed.). 1985. *Zhongguo jindai jiaoyu ziliao* 中國近代教育資料 (Source material on the history of Chinese education). Beijing: Renmin chubanshe, vol. 2. pp. 411–27.

"Zouding gaodeng xiaoxuetang zhangcheng 1903" 奏定高等小學堂章程 1903 (Regulations for the higher primary modern schools 1903), in: Shu Xincheng 舒新城 (ed.). 1985. *Zhongguo jindai jiaoyu ziliao* 中國近代教育資料 (Source material on the history of Chinese education). Beijing: Renmin chubanshe, vol. 2, pp. 427–39.

"Zouding xiaoxuetang zhangcheng 1902" 奏定小學堂章程 1902 (Regulations for primary modern schools 1902), in: Shu Xincheng 舒新城 (ed.). 1985. *Zhongguo jindai jiaoyu ziliao* 中國近代教育資料 (Source material on the history of Chinese education). Beijing: Renmin chubanshe, vol. 2, pp. 400–11.

"'Zouding xuetang zhangcheng' guanyu xiaoxuetang xueji bianzhi he jiaoshou fangfa de guiding" ' 奏定學堂章程 ' 關於小學堂學級編制和教授方法的規定 13.1. 1904 (The 'regulations for modern schools' in reference to the rules for the organization of class levels and teaching methods), in: Chen Xuexun 陳學恂 (ed.). 1986. *Zhongguo jindai jiaoyushi jiaoxue cankao ziliao* 中國近代教育史教學參考資料 (Reference material on pedagogy and the history of education in China). Beijing: Renmin chubanshe, vol. 1, pp. 665–6.

INDEX

SINICA LEIDENSIA

45. Pohl, K.H. *Chinese Thought in a Global Context*. A Dialogue Between Chinese and Western Philosophical Approaches. 1999. ISBN 90 04 11426 2
46. De Meyer, J.A.M. and P.M. Engelfriet (eds.). *Linked Faiths*. Essays on Chinese Religions and Traditional Culture in Honour of Kristofer Schipper. 2000. ISBN 90 04 11540 4
47. Ven, H. van de. *Warfare in Chinese History*. 2000. ISBN 90 04 11774 1
48. Wright, D. *Translating Science*. The Transmission of Western Chemistry into Late Imperial China,1840-1900. 2000. ISBN 90 04 11776 8
49. Schottenhammer A. (ed.). *The Emporium of the World*. Maritime Quanzhou, 1000-1400. 2000. ISBN 90 04 11773 3
50. Jami, C.P. Engelfriet & G. Blue (eds.). *Statecraft and Intellectual Renewal in Late Ming China*. The Cross-cultural Synthesis of Xu Guangqi (1562-1633). 2001. ISBN 90 04 12058 0
51. Tapp, N. *The Hmong of China*. Context, Agency and the Imaginary. 2001. ISBN 90 04 12127 7
52. Lackner M.I. Amelung & J. Kurtz (eds.). *New Terms for New Ideas.Western Knowledge and Lexical Change in Late Imperial China*. 2001. ISBN 90 04 12046 7
53. Jing, A. *The Water God's Temple of the Guangsheng Monastery*. Cosmic Function of Art, Ritual,and Theater. 2001. ISBN 90 04 11925 6
54. Zhou Mi's Record of Clouds and Mist Passing Before One's Eyes. An Annotated Translation by A. Weitz. 2002. ISBN 90 04 12605 8
55. B.S. McDougall & A. Hansson (eds.). *Chinese Concepts of Privacy*. 2002. ISBN 90 04 12766 6
56. K.-H. Pohl & A.W. Müller (eds.). *Chinese Ethics in a Global Context*. Moral Bases of Contemporary Societies. 2002. ISBN 90 04 12812 3
57. Gulik, R.H. *Sexual Life in Ancient China*. A Preliminary Survey of Chinese Sex and Society from ca. 1500 B.C. till 1644 A.D. 2003. ISBN 90 04 12601 5
58. Sato, M. *The Confucian Quest for Order*. The Origin and Formation of the Political Thought of XunZiy. 2003. ISBN 90 04 12965 0
59. Blussé, L. & Chen Menghong (eds.). *The Archives of the Kong Koan of Batavia*. 2003. ISBN 90 04 13157 4
60. Santangelo, P. *Sentimental Education in Chinese History*. An Interdisciplinary Textual Research on Ming and Qing Sources. 2003. ISBN 90 04 12360 1
61. Mather, R.B. *The Age of Eternal Brilliance*. Three Lyric Poets of the Yung-ming Era (483-493). 2003. ISBN 90 04 12059 9 (set)
62. Van Gulik, R.H. *Erotic Colour Prints of the Ming Period*. With an Essay on Chinese Sex Life from the Han to the Ch'ing Dynasty, B.C. 206-A.D. 1644. 2004. ISBN 90 04 13664 9 (volume one). ISBN 90 04 13665 7 (volume two). ISBN 90 04 13160 4 (set)
63. Eifring, H. *Love and Emotions in Traditional Chinese Literature*. 2004. ISBN 90 04 13710 8
64. Lackner, M. & N. Vittinghoff (eds.). *Mapping Meanings*. The Field of New Learning in Late Qing China. 2004. ISBN 90 04 13919 2